The C. S. Lewis

Readers'
Encyclopedia

The C.S. Lewis

Readers' Encyclopedia

Foreword by Christopher Mitchell

Edited by Jeffrey D. Schultz and John G. West Jr.

Assistant Editor: Mike Perry

Advisory Board Members:

Bruce L. Edwards, Kathryn Lindskoog,

Christopher Mitchell, George Sayer

ZondervanPublishingHouse

Grand Rapids, Michigan

A Division of HarperCollinsPublishers

To my son Sasha with whom I will revisit Narnia many times—JDS

To my sister Joanne who first introduced me to Narnia—JGW

The C. S. Lewis Readers' Encyclopedia
Copyright © 1998 by Jeffrey D. Schultz & Co.

Requests for information should be addressed to:

ZondervanPublishingHouse
Grand Rapids, Michigan 49530

Library of Congress Cataloging-in-Publication Data

The C. S. Lewis readers' encyclopedia / edited by Jeffrey D. Schultz and John G. West, Jr.
    p. cm.
    Includes bibliographical references.
    ISBN: 0-310-21538-2
    1. Lewis, C. S. (Clive Staples), 1889–1963—Encyclopedias. 2. Authors, English—20th century—biography—Encyclopedias. 3. Church of England—England—Biography—Encyclopedias. 4. Christian literature, English—Encyclopedias. 5. Christian biography—England—Encyclopedias. 6. Fantastic fiction, English—Encyclopedias. I. Schultz, Jeffrey D. II. West, John G.
    PR6023.E926Z459 1998
    823'.912—dc21 [B]   98-5459
                                          CIP

This edition printed on acid-free paper and meets the American National Standards Institute Z39.48 standard.

All photos of people and book covers are courtesy of the Marion E. Wade Center and Sarah Hadley Photography. Used by permission.

Excerpts from *Surprised by Joy: The Shape of My Early Life* by C. S. Lewis, copyright © 1956 by C. S. Lewis PTE Ltd. and renewed 1984 by Arthur Owen Barfield, reprinted by permission of Harcourt Brace & Company. Excerpts from *Letters of C. S. Lewis*, copyright © 1966 by W. H. Lewis and the Executors of C. S. Lewis and renewed 1994 by C. S. Lewis PTE Ltd., reprinted by permission of Harcourt Brace & Company. Excerpts from *Narrative Poems* by C. S. Lewis, copyright © 1969 by C. S. Lewis PTE Ltd., reprinted by permission of Harcourt Brace & Company. Excerpts from *Poems* by C. S. Lewis, copyright © 1964 by the Executors of the Estate of C. S. Lewis and renewed 1992 by C. S. Lewis PTE Ltd., and Walter Hooper, reprinted by permission of Harcourt Brace & Company.

Every effort has been made to contact all the copyright holders of the quoted material. If anyone holding a legitimate copyright feels they have been neglected, we would kindly ask them to write the editors of this volume care of Zondervan Publishing House so that proper credit can be given and fees, where appropriate, paid.

Interior design by Sherri L. Hoffman
Zondervan project editor: Bob Hudson

Printed in the United States of America

---

98 99 00 01 02 03 04 /❖ DC/ 10 9 8 7 6 5 4 3 2 1

Contents

FOREWORD

Thirty-five years after his death, C. S. Lewis remains one of the most enduring and often-quoted writers in England and America, and one of the very few writers of his time who has never gone out of print. Lewis was already a best-selling author by 1942 and in 1947 was heralded as "one of the most influential spokesmen for Christianity in the English-speaking world" by *Time* magazine, which featured his picture on the front cover. In 1963, the year of Lewis's death, distinguished poet and teacher Chad Walsh measured the impact of Lewis on American religious thinking as something rarely, if ever, "equaled by any other modern writer." Perhaps even more telling was the whimsical proposal offered by Catholic editor Joseph Fessio to a meeting of leaders from Orthodox, Roman Catholic, and Protestant traditions who in 1995 gathered in South Carolina to re-examine the theological differences that separated them: "What if we all agreed to accept," Fessio proposed, "sacred Scripture, the early creeds, the first four ecumenical councils, and the writings of C. S. Lewis?"

But continued interest in Lewis has not been built solely on Lewis's religious writings. While less pronounced than his influence as a representative of traditional Christianity, Lewis's writings as a scholar of Medieval and Renaissance literature and his popularity as a writer of fiction evince a similar enduring quality. A striking example of the sustained popularity of Lewis's fiction is reflected in the sale of over a million copies, in little more than a year, of the HarperCollins 1994 reissue of the *Chronicles of Narnia* (which had never been out of print). Lewis's reputation in literary history and criticism is rather more difficult to assess. Yet, even here, his work in these fields continues to garner respect.

There are those who are baffled, possibly even dismayed, by the enduring popularity of Lewis's work. Certainly he has attracted his share of debunkers. There is as well a persistent claim that an enormous amount of hagiography has grown up around Lewis, especially with regard to his person. While an over-idealized Lewis may be found at times in the vast corpus of writing on him, the great majority of it simply cannot be characterized as hagiography. In fact, it may well be that in recent years there is a growing tendency to over-exaggerate Lewis's character flaws in an attempt to "humanize" him.

On balance, it is not Lewis the man, however, but rather Lewis the theological and philosophical writer, the literary scholar and teller of stories that accounts for his longevity. Writing to Lewis in 1941 in response to her reading of *Out of the Silent Planet* and *The Problem of Pain*, Evelyn Underhill described Lewis's "remarkable" ability for making ideas come alive as his "capacity for giving imaginative body to the fundamental doctrines of Christianity." Lewis had a gift for illuminating a subject, and in an age of often fuzzy thinking, his ability to bring clarity to ideas and to touch both mind and heart with the force of those ideas continues to be compelling for many.

FOREWORD

While books by C. S. Lewis continue to sell briskly, books about Lewis (and there are many) sell comparatively sluggishly. The public is far more interested in reading Lewis than in reading books about Lewis. So what commends this present volume in light of the flurry of new books about him marking the one hundredth anniversary of his birth? To begin with, the *C. S. Lewis Readers' Encyclopedia* (*CSLRE*) is designed chiefly to help the reader get more out of his reading of Lewis—to gain a deeper and richer understanding of Lewis's own work and thinking. Further, the serious reader of Lewis is often drawn into the larger world of people and ideas that fill the pages of his books, essays, and letters, and often sent off to explore any number of other literary, theological and philosophical points addressed by him. I have met numerous people who have received a first-rate education by reading the seemingly endless number of books referred to in the Lewis corpus. The *CSLRE* helps facilitate this wider investigation by offering entries on hundreds of related and interconnecting facets of Lewis's intellectual and literary interests along with bibliographies directed toward further study.

There is, understandably, a certain amount of overlap between this reference work and previous ones, such as Paul F. Ford's *Companion to Narnia*, Colin Duriez's *The C. S. Lewis Handbook*, and the more recent *C. S. Lewis: A Companion and Guide* by Walter Hooper. The *CSLRE*, however, offers a more comprehensive approach than others with its more than 800 entries alphabetically arranged, many which are not found in previous works. For example, there are entries describing the sixty-three letters to editors Lewis wrote during his lifetime, the vast majority of which have never been collected and published elsewhere. Likewise, there are entries for the many poems Lewis wrote that are not available in any of the collections yet printed. Another distinctive and strength of this reference work is the diversity brought to the project by its forty-three contributors who, when possible, wrote in the areas of their expertise. Like all reference works of this nature, a certain amount of unevenness with respect to particular entries is unavoidable and to be expected. Yet, as an encyclopedia, the wider range of opinion represented by the contributors is one of the strengths of the book.

I would like to commend Jeffrey D. Schultz for bringing this monumental project together. It is my hope that those who use this volume will not only enrich their reading of Lewis but allow themselves to be drawn into the larger world of ideas it offers.

Christopher W. Mitchell
The Marion E. Wade Center
Wheaton College

CLIVE STAPLES LEWIS
1898–1963
A Brief Biography by John Bremer

To convey the sheer brilliance of Lewis's natural talents is not easy.[1] He combined an intelligence of the highest order with a prodigious memory and a creative imagination, and his energy was such that everything he did had an intensity, and sometimes exclusivity, that heightened the impact of his impressive talents. He had a way of using all that he read and experienced to transform the way he lived. There was no such thing as purely academic knowledge for him, and what he understood (and misunderstood) affected how he lived. He struggled to unify intelligence, imagination, and morality and ultimately saw that, while reason gives access to the truth, imagination gives access to reality—which is what truth is about. Thus, imagination was for Lewis a higher power or faculty than reason.

---

1. This brief biography attempts to outline the structure or pattern of the life of C. S. Lewis. Chronology is not always strictly followed; nor are people, places, events, and publications given full treatment; they are treated, not as important in themselves, but only insofar as they illuminate the life of Lewis. For a fuller account of them, the reader is invited to consult their entries elsewhere in this volume.

This account is deeply indebted to the publications, letters, and diaries of C. S. Lewis himself, of his brother, Warren H. Lewis, and of his friends, and to the biographical work of George Sayer and Roger Lancelyn Green.

Lewis's moral character was also intense and unrelenting; his loyalty to his friends or to those to whom he had made a commitment, for example, was legendary. On the other hand, it was only late in life that he achieved what the Greeks called *sophrosyne*— a moderation, or temperance, a gentleness. His physical appetites were comparable in their excessiveness. He enjoyed food, eating quickly and with great gusto, although the fare was usually plain. He drank strong tea and strong liquor (mostly beer and whiskey), smoked both cigarettes and a pipe, and had a potent sexual animality that he fought to control most of his life. He was clumsy with his hands, partly because his thumbs, like those of his father and his brother, lacked the joint furthest from the tip, and he never could learn how to drive a car. Yet he could, notably in his younger years, draw fine illustrations.

The sheer power of his nature often made him appear coarse and brutal, especially in the first half of his life, but he treated others no more harshly than he treated himself. Later in life he showed, both in his writings and in his relations with students, a gentleness and sensitivity that were in strong contrast to the ruthless and contentious wrangler and bully of earlier years.

The story of his life is the story of a man whose remarkable talents were gentled, civilized, made creative of good, and Christianized. His life was a struggle with and within himself—a struggle that in the end was won. In Platonic terms, his soul became well-ordered, true to its own nature. The way in which he understood this struggle and its outcome is told in *Surprised by Joy*, which is the closest thing to a formal autobiography that we have. But it must be remembered that, given his commitment to relate what he knew to how he lived, all of the writings of Lewis are, in a sense, autobiographical.

Lewis himself saw his development in broadest terms as a passage from atheism to Christianity, followed by a living of the Christian life that he saw was required of him. His devotion, even in its more public aspects, was remarkable, and the replacement of his besetting sin of pride by a deep and genuine humility before God is a testament to his honesty. He said his prayers, usually more than once a day, and received communion weekly; he also gave (anonymously) two-thirds of his royalties to charity, to people in need, and to institutions.

An account of the life of Lewis by an agnostic or atheist could easily turn into a derisive exercise—how naïve he was to imagine *that*—and one by a Christian into an exultation of God's mercy and goodness—how he was saved effortlessly (although this was, in another sense, true). The former supposes that "we know better, don't we?" the latter that "we can—or need—do nothing to help ourselves." But, however they are to be understood and related to each other, the life of Lewis has both faith and works.

A biography of Lewis requires us to consider the question "If such a man saw his life in that way, and re-made it, how can we disagree?" It invites us to accept the responsibility for deciding whether or not Lewis was and is right; in that sense, the life of Lewis is, itself, an education in Christianity for us all. His life confronts us, gently but decisively, and we must discover how to view it. If we are guided by reason, we may be content with a conventional chronological history, but if by imagination, we will require it to be nothing less than theological, moved, as it was, by grace.

1898–1908

Until the death of his mother, Lewis was raised in a comfortable middle-class home, where intellectual pursuits were taken for granted. Books were plentiful and were read. While the topics of conversation were restricted, they provided the only material—the social reality—on which imagination could work. Fortunately there was also another kind of reality, nature, which provided the prime source of beauty and joy.

Clive Staples Lewis was born on November 29, 1898, in a suburb of Belfast. Both parents were Irish, but their families had roots abroad.

His father, Albert James Lewis, was descended from an 18th-century Welsh farmer, Richard Lewis, whose son Joseph was Albert Lewis's grandfather. Joseph was a religious enthusiast and father of eight children. He became a Methodist minister and had a reputation as a fine, moving speaker. His son Richard migrated to Ireland, worked as a boilermaker and engineer, and wrote many evangelical pamphlets, although he returned to the Anglican Church. Albert, the youngest of his six children, was born August 23, 1863, in Cork, but the family soon moved, first to Dublin, then to Belfast.

In 1877 Albert was sent to Lurgan College in County Armagh. He got on well with the headmaster, W. T. Kirkpatrick (1848–1921), who helped him establish a legal career, which began in a solicitor's office in 1879. Albert was highly regarded and was soon fully qualified. He became

Clive Staples Lewis in 1899 or 1900.

a junior partner in a law firm, but only for a short time. He established his own office in Belfast in 1885, often acting as a prosecutor in the Belfast police court, which in later years became his full-time occupation.

Albert had the qualities needed for success. He was intelligent and had an exceptional memory. He was also able to penetrate to the central issue or principle of a legal case and to present a simple, clear account of often highly complex affairs—gifts shared by both his sons. Albert was very adept at verbal give-and-take, both in daily life and in the courtroom. He had a sharp wit, could engage in persiflage, and was remorseless in his close, severe, but fair cross-examination. He worked hard and soon achieved a high professional standing. Yet, although competent professionally and well-organized intellectually, he did not understand how to manage his own finances, was inept at dealing with his investments, and had a pathological fear of bankruptcy.

Albert had a strict moral code, derived in part, no doubt, from his staunchly Protestant background, but he was not unkind. He had a somewhat narrow religious perspective, though certainly not as narrow as that of many of his contemporaries. He was, moreover, a compassionate and generous man, with considerable integrity. He was also very emotional, and his sons came to distrust and fear his passionate outbursts.

Privately, Albert wrote poems and short stories, although few were published. He also had political ambitions, and he might well have been a successful politician if it had not been for his lack of social status and wealth.

Clive's mother, Florence Augusta Hamilton, better known as Flora, was the daughter of Thomas Hamilton, the vicar of St. Mark's in Dundela, the Belfast suburb where Albert Lewis and Flora lived. The paternal Hamiltons were of aristocratic Scottish ancestry and had owned land in Ireland since the time of James I (1603–25). Flora's mother, Mary Warren Hamilton, could claim descent from Robert Warrene, a Norman knight who had come over with William the Conqueror in 1066 and fought at Hastings. The maternal side of Flora's family had been landowners in Ireland since the reign of Henry II (1154–1189).

Thomas Hamilton was a highly emotional preacher who embarrassed his family— and especially his grandsons—by often weeping, even in the pulpit, and he never tired of expatiating on the evils of Roman Catholicism. Mary Hamilton, who was more intelligent than her husband, was dedicated to feminism and achieving Irish Home Rule and discussed politics endlessly and with great ardor.

Flora, born the third of four children in 1862, was a slender girl with fair hair and light blue eyes. She had considerable mathematical ability, none of which was inherited by her son Clive, and she was an avid reader. Although it was very uncommon at that time for a young woman to attend university, she studied mathematics and logic at Queen's University, Belfast, and between 1880 and 1885 took First Class Honors in logic and Second Class in mathematics. She was awarded a B.A. in 1886 but made no public use of her education and obvious talent. She remained at home until she married Albert Lewis in 1894.

Flora was cool towards Albert. She would rather have had him as a friend than as a suitor, but after keeping Albert waiting for seven years, she felt that in all justice she either had to accept Albert as a husband or to reject him. She did not want to let him go, and so, rather tentatively, in 1893 they entered into a yearlong, secret engagement. Flora was full of anxieties. She did not know how to manage a household and could not cook. Her health was often bad; she suffered from asthma and frequent headaches. Moreover, she felt keenly the fact that she was two years older than Albert. Above all, she wanted to give Albert something in return for his devotion yet felt that she had nothing, not even strong feelings, to offer him.

The wedding took place on August 29, 1894, in St. Mark's Church. After a honeymoon in North Wales, Albert and Flora moved into Dundela Villas, a rented, semidetached house nearby. There, two sons were born: Warren Hamilton Lewis on June 16, 1895, and Clive Staples Lewis on November 29, 1898.

The two boys considered their ancestors on their mother's side to be superior to those on their father's side. In terms of pedigree they were undoubtedly correct. Aristocratic attitudes and values—not always desirable—had been part of the life of their mother's family for a thousand years. How they were passed on may be elusive, but passed on they were, and it may only be because of her early death that they were not apparent in her sons. The boys had not learned to regard themselves as superior to others, as inheritors of the earth. They were by no means sure of their place in the world and lacked that aristocratic self-confidence that serenely assumes, and is utterly sure of, one's centrality in the universal scheme of things. But they knew of tradition and its defining character.

Warren, while dedicated to his brother and his brother's superlative abilities, found no further purpose in the world and used his own talents, which were not insignificant, very sparingly. Being two-and-a-half years older than his brother, he may have absorbed more of the aristocratic assumption that gracing the world with his presence was all that could or should be expected of him. The world should be pleased to support him.

Circa 1900. Front row: Flora, Warnie, grandfather, cousin Irene, Aunt Agnes and Jacks. Back row: Albert, grandmother.

When Clive was one month old, Flora engaged a nursemaid named Lizzie Endicott from County Down, "in whom even the exacting memory of childhood can discover no flaw—nothing but kindness, gaiety, and good sense." Rather surprisingly, Flora limited the attention she herself gave her two sons and did not read to them nor help them learn the well-known nursery rhymes. This was done by the staunchly Protestant Lizzie Endicott, who undoubtedly added the Celtic myths and legends of her own childhood to the approved canon, especially as bedtime stories.

By the time Clive was four he had become a hearty eater (which he remained for most of his life). About this time, and for no known reason, he suddenly and emphatically announced that his name was Jacksie and that he would answer to no other. The name got shortened to Jacks, then to Jack, the name by which his family and friends knew him for the rest of his life (although Albert and Warren often still called him Jacks).

The boys had a governess every morning, but in the afternoons they were left to their own devices and since they got on well together, it was a happy time for them. They became fast friends, and throughout their lives they would continue to think of themselves as best friends. Because they did not go to school they had little chance to meet any other boys of their own age.

In the summer Flora and the servants would take the boys to a rented house at Castlerock in County Derry. The boys loved the seaside and the train journey that took them there. Both made a lasting impression; the sea and trains delighted them throughout their lives. Albert did not accompany them, preferring the routine and security of his office.

Belfast was known for its shipyards. The *Titanic* was built there between 1909 and 1912, while Jack and Warren were growing up. Albert sometimes took the boys to visit the docks, where all three would draw nautical pictures. Albert also encouraged his sons' writing, and before Jack learned to write Albert would record the stories Jack made up.

Albert wanted to share in whatever his sons did, to the extent that he found it impossible to let the boys be by themselves. He would insist on being with them whenever he was available, never realizing that by doing so he inhibited and offended them. When he and Flora had visitors, Albert, on the ground of politeness, required the boys to be present, silently listening to conversations and declamations about politics and religion that they did not understand. Almost inevitably these topics became the substance of their own stories.

Albert was flourishing professionally, and in April 1905 Flora persuaded him to move to a new house. It was quite a triumph for Flora, who thought that their social position required a more stately kind of home, a consideration Albert would not have found totally convincing.

The house was called Little Lea and was built for them about two miles from Dundela Villas on the outskirts of Belfast, close to open farmland. It was a large, three-story brick house and provided ample accommodation for the parents, the two boys, and the servants, as well as for Albert's father, who came to live with them in a room on the second floor. Warren later recalled, as an example of Albert's lack of business acumen, that the builder swindled him by providing inadequate foundations.

It was around this time that the two boys began to refer to Albert as the "Pudaita," or the "Pudaita-bird," or simply "P." It is hard to imagine that these nicknames were affectionate or even respectful. They arose from the way in which their father, with his broad Irish accent, pronounced the word "potato." But how had the two boys come to despise and make fun of this accent? Who did they know who spoke differently, in some preferred way? Their mother?

Little Lea was ideally suited to the brothers. It was large, with room for many books and a gramophone complete with large horn, so that the boys soon began to collect recordings. Above all, there was an attic, and through its passages they would crawl and hide from each other, though more often from the servants. They found the "secret dark hole upstairs," the "Little End Room" where housemaids would not—and could not—find them. Here, in the little, low rooms below the ridge tiles they had "glorious privacy." The attic soon became their special home-within-a-home. Here, high up and remote from the rest of the house, Jack and Warren drew pictures, wrote stories, and created an imaginary world they called Boxen. Jack later wrote: "I am a product of long corridors, empty sunlit rooms, upstairs indoor silences, attics explored in solitude, distant noises of gurgling cisterns and pipes, and the noise of wind under the tiles."

From the age of six onward, Jack experienced a recurring vague sense of longing as he looked through his nursery windows at the seemingly remote "Green Hills." Warren later wrote: "We would gaze out of our nursery window at the slanting rain and the grey skies, and there, beyond a mile or so of sodden meadow, we would see the dim high line of the Castlereagh Hills—our world's limit, a distant land, strange and unattainable."

Flora protected the boys and even coddled them. Bad weather (that is, ordinary rain) kept them indoors a great deal of the time. But they had bicycles and in fine weather would explore the adjacent countryside.

One month after moving into Little Lea, ten-year-old Warren was sent to England to attend Wynyard School in Watford, one of the worst schools imaginable. Albert was committed to giving his sons the social and educational advantages that came, he thought, from an English boarding-school education followed by entry into a public school (in the English sense of a private school for fee-paying pupils) and possibly into a university.

When the time came to send Warren to school, Albert inquired of his old head-master, W. T. Kirkpatrick, who thought that a well-established school in Rhyl, Wales, would be suitable. But the fees were £90 a year and Albert, haunted by the fear of going bankrupt, thought this was too expensive for him. Instead he chose Wynyard, sight unseen, in large part because the annual fee was only £70 pounds.

Warren sent uncomplaining letters home (he thought it would do no good to complain), but he kept a close tally of the number of days to the end of term, when he could escape back to Belfast and Boxen. He wrote to Jack, mostly about the "Animal-Land" stories they had written and illustrated together and the new ones that Jack had recently written. Jack, aged about eight, replied to one letter:

> At present Boxen is SLIGHTLY CONVULSED. The news has just reached her that King Bunny is a prisoner. The colonists (who are of course the war party) are in a bad way: they dare scarcely leave their houses because of the mobs. In Tararo the Prussians and Boxonians are at fearful odds against each other and the natives. General Quicksteppe is making plans for the rescue of King Bunny.

The influence of the overheard conversations of Albert and his guests is evident, as is the way in which it restricted the boys' imaginations. It was only late in life that Jack felt that his imagination had been freed.

Jack was also writing a play, began a history of Mouse-Land, and involved himself in other projects, including a diary. History led to geography, with Warren providing a map of "India" (spelled "indai"). He was, incidentally, of the opinion that he wrote so much because his jointless thumbs prevented him from making things.

With Warren away at school, Jack spent more time with his mother. In the morning he had lessons in French, Latin, and mathematics, and in the afternoons they would occasionally go out for a walk together. But mostly he was by himself during the afternoons and free to do as he liked—which meant spending time with books.

Albert and Flora shared only one leisure activity: voracious reading. Their regular practice was to sit down after dinner and read until bedtime. Later in life, Jack would do the same. The books they read were good books, many of them well-established classics, and they were kept on open shelves. Jack explored his parents' library and devoured all the books about animals, including *Black Beauty*, and delighted in the *Strand* magazine, especially the magical stories of Edith Nesbit. He was introduced to romance and chivalry through Mark Twain's *A Connecticut Yankee at King Arthur's Court* and Conan Doyle's *Sir Nigel*, which was serialized from December 1905 to December 1906. And in a diary entry for March 5, 1908, Jack wrote, "I am carpentring a sword. I read Paradise Lost, reflections thereon."

Reading was not just a delight to Jack, it was also a powerful and moving experience. Yet the most moving experiences transcended books. They were experiences of what Jack came to call "Joy."

The longing for the "Green Hills" that were visible from his nursery window was real but puzzling. What is a longing? What was the longing for? Beauty, perhaps, since he characterized his childhood at home as lacking beauty. He did not know. His later introduction to the northern myths increased this longing, this dissatisfaction. This was

15

how Joy began, and Jack reported in *Surprised by Joy* that there were three very distinct occasions on which he had a powerful experience of Joy.

The first was when, standing before a flowering currant bush on a summer day at Little Lea, the memory came to him of his brother bringing from the old house, Dundela Villas, his miniature toy garden, which had given Jack his first experience of beauty. Warren later reported that he was also affected by the currant bush:

> The flowering currant is now out in several places, and this is always one of the highlights of my year. Enjoyment of it and the wallflower are the earliest aesthetic experiences of my life—dating back to long before we left Dundela Villas. I can still remember the thrill of joy with which I used to greet the arrival of both, a thrill which one never experiences once childhood is past; and which is perhaps the purest one ever receives. Is it I wonder wholly fanciful to think that this thrill is a dim recollection of having just come from a better world?

The second experience of Joy came from Beatrix Potter's book *Squirrel Nutkin*. Jack loved all the Potter books, but this one administered a shock that he describes as "a trouble"—the "Idea of Autumn." This experience, too, had the same sense of surprise and of immeasurable importance.

The third glimpse of Joy came from Longfellow's "Saga of King Olaf." Idly turning the pages, Jack came upon the unrhymed translation of Tegner's "Drapa" (1825):

> I heard a voice that cried,
> "Balder the beautiful
> Is dead, is dead!"
> And through the misty air
> Passed like the mournful cry
> Of sunward sailing cranes.

Jack knew nothing of Balder, but he was "instantly uplifted into the huge regions of northern sky" and then immediately transported back again.

Of these three experiences Jack wrote,

> The reader who finds these three episodes of no interest need read this book no further, for in a sense the central story of my life is about nothing else. For those who are still disposed to proceed I will only underline the quality common to the three experiences; it is that of an unsatisfied desire which is itself more desirable than any other satisfaction. I call it Joy, which is here a technical term and must be sharply distinguished from Happiness and from Pleasure. Joy (in my sense) has indeed one characteristic, and one only, in common with them; the fact that anyone who has experienced it will want it again.

It seems that it was Joy that gave Jack the motive for his lifelong interest in myths, for myths often gave form or shape to the longing that he felt. And it must have been Joy that prompted him to write fantasies, descriptions of "other worlds," of supernatural or spiritual habitations. The content of Boxen was matter-of-fact, derived from Albert's political conversations, but Joy gave free rein to the imagination.

Reason, dependent on the overheard conversations of Albert and his friends, told Jack that human life was about politics and war, and so he wrote stories accordingly. The Boxen stories included elements of fantasy—King Bunny and General Quicksteppe are rather nice—but their actions did not come from his imagination. Only in the second half of his life did Jack come to see that we are dominated by homelessness. We all know what home means, even though we cannot express it. Joy is what we long for; it is a foretaste of heaven, of what our world was meant to be. "Joy," he wrote, "is the serious business of Heaven." But such words came much later. In the meantime, Joy gave Jack something to imagine, to create out of and for himself.

1908—1914

After the death of his mother, Jack went to school. This should have been the occasion for the development of both his intellectual and imaginative powers, but the formal requirements of school were virtually useless as far as his intellectual development was concerned. Only in his private, inner world did imagination have any free play, and then only prompted by accident. His life was split. Because of his youth, he was not confident that his imaginative life had any sanity or validity. When he finally left school for private tutoring, his intellectual training really began, but his imagination was still not integrated. And his only friend was his brother. God seemed either nonexistent, a mere superstition, or else malignant. Jack called himself an atheist.

In early 1908, Flora's health deteriorated. Her chronic symptoms—tiredness, headaches, and lack of appetite—all worsened. It was decided that she suffered from abdominal cancer and an operation was performed at home, as was then customary, on February 15 by three doctors and two nurses. For a short time Flora improved, and she took Jack to the seaside in May, but in June she relapsed. She died at 6:30 A.M. on August 23, 1908, Albert's birthday.

Albert was devastated. "As good a woman, wife and mother as God has ever given to man," he wrote. His grief was heightened by the fact that his father had died earlier in the year and then, only ten days later, his brother Joseph also. What was Albert to do? More particularly, what was he to do with Jack? Warren was about to return to Wynyard School in September 1908, and Albert decided to send nine-year-old Jack with him.

What Jack had to suffer! First, the loss of Warren who had departed for school, compensated for by a new closeness to his mother. Then her illness and the operation in his own home. Then her death and his father's inconsolable grief. And

Jack and Warren, circa 1908.

Warren, Jack, Albert, and neighbor, 1910.

finally his own banishment to a foreign country and an alien school, a banishment mitigated only by the company of his brother, Warnie.

Wynyard was about as bad as a school could be. In the 1950s Jack referred to it as "the concentration camp" or just "Belsen." The headmaster at Wynyard, the Reverend Robert Capron, nicknamed Oldie, was a sixty-year-old Anglican clergyman, powerfully built, intimidating, brutal, and close to insanity. He was assisted by his son, known as Wee-Wee. No educational work went on, as witnessed by the report of Warren that, to fulfill the daily requirement of doing a certain number of arithmetic problems, he simply copied the same four problems every day onto his slate.

Both Warren and Jack pleaded to be removed from Wynyard, even if it meant going to Belfast's Campbell College, the local independent school less than two miles from Little Lea. But Albert wanted his sons to become "gentlemen," which involved, among other things, losing the speech and manners of Irish boys. So he made arrangements for Warren to attend School House, one of ten boarding houses at Malvern College in Worcestershire, England.

Warren entered Malvern in September 1909, but Jack remained at Wynyard for another school year. Even with Warren gone there were some bright spots. The physical education program consisted of dispatching the boys on unsupervised walks, and they talked, of course, about every subject imaginable. Jack enjoyed the walks, since they required no special skill, and the talks because he was good at them and interested. He recollected much later that his first philosophical argument had been about time and the nature of the future. Is it like a long, straight line that you cannot see, or is it more like a line not yet drawn?

He also extended his reading: historical novels of the ancient world, like *Quo Vadis?* and *Ben Hur*, Rider Haggard, the science fiction of H. G. Wells, space travel adventures, and much more. He was fascinated by the scenes of cruelty in the stories from the ancient world—slave beatings, gladiatorial combats, and the like. He later recognized that the feelings these scenes aroused were sexual, and throughout his adolescent years he was tormented with sadistic fantasies that he created for himself.

Wynyard required attendance at two services in St. John's Anglo-Catholic church in Watford every Sunday, and there, for the first time, Jack heard sermons that dealt with Christianity and its teachings. He had, of course, gone to church on Sundays with his family, but those services were meaningless to him. The sermons preached by his grandfather Hamilton were mostly bigoted anti-Catholic diatribes, and he had never learned how to pray. Hating formulaic prayers, he set himself to be serious about his prayers, and he also began to read the Bible, which he discussed with other boys. It was here, and not in supposed Puritanical Ulster, that he learned about hell and began to fear for his soul. He also came to recognize the reality of sin. Of course, his narrow Irish Protestant upbringing made it impossible to approve of the candles and incense, and he castigated St. John's as an "abominable place of Romish hypocrites . . ."

In later years Jack claimed that some good had come of his Wynyard experience. "It taught all of us at least one good thing . . . to stick together, to support each other in resistance to tyranny."

Soon Wynyard was down to only five boarders and it mercifully closed at the end of the 1909–10 school year. Oldie was appointed vicar of a nearby parish, but he caned the choirboys and within two years was declared legally insane.

Jack now was sent to Campbell College, as he had requested. Being a boarder (except for Sundays, when he was permitted to go home), his privacy was very limited and he complained about the noise: it was "very like living permanently in a large railway station." He only spent a half term there, but in that short time he had one powerful experience—he heard his English master, nicknamed Octie, read, in a deep dramatic voice, Matthew Arnold's epic *Sohrab and Rustum.* Jack was deeply impressed by the almost Homeric poem.

In the poem, Sohrab and Rustum are the champions of their respective armies. Sohrab, a young man, challenges the older Rustum to single combat, neither being aware that they are father and son. They fight, with tragic consequences, for they learn of their relationship only after Sohrab has been mortally wounded. This must have affected Jack's feelings and imaginings about his father. Albert was no Rustum, but was he, like Sohrab, a filial competitor? And who was to be slain?

In November, Jack became sick with a bad cough and was removed from Campbell. Albert, concerned about Jack's health, made arrangements to send him to Cherbourg, a prep school in Malvern, a town well-known for its fine air and pure water. There the surroundings would be healthful and he would be near Warren. After two months of reading at home, Jack went to Cherbourg in January 1911.

Jack liked Malvern—"one of the nicest English towns I have seen yet. The hills are beautiful but of course not so nice as ours"—and the education he received at Cherbourg was quite good. But his association with Warren, then aged a sophisticated fifteen, was not all for the good. Among other things, the two boys, traveling together, would delay their arrival in Malvern to the last possible moment and spend their time in the Lime Street Hotel in Liverpool, smoking cigarettes. It was at the ripe age of twelve that Jack developed the habit of smoking that lasted all his life.

Jack appears to have been mischievous and rebellious, and his diary reports "hundreds of impots" (impositions: homework or copying exercises assigned as punishment for breaking school rules). Yet his scholastic achievement was impressive. In only two years he was able to take and pass the Malvern College entrance examination, in spite of the handicap of having learned little or nothing at Wynyard.

Jack developed intellectually during his two-and-a-half years at Cherbourg. He got a good grounding in both Latin and English, studied the classical authors, particularly Virgil, and began writing stories and essays on a wide variety of subjects, ranging from "Party Government" to "Richard Wagner" to "Are Athletes Better than Scholars?" He thought a performance of Handel's *Messiah* "simply lovely" and enjoyed productions of Shakespearean plays. His horizons were widening while he himself was changing—emotionally, spiritually, and sexually.

The matron at Cherbourg, a Miss Cowie, mothered Jack and supported his complaint about the school censoring his letters to his father. This led to her dismissal. Jack once again lost a comforter, and his sense of justice was outraged.

Jack's sexuality became very powerful in him and showed itself in seemingly contradictory ways. He was prudish and thought his school-prize book, *Charicles: or Illustrations of the Private Life of the Ancient Greeks* by Wilhelm Becker (1796–1846), to be pornographic and blamed it for corrupting him. No doubt some, though very few, of the descriptions were lurid, but then, so were certain aspects of Greek life.

But he also began to masturbate—"a violent and wholly successful assault of sexual temptation"—which caused him both pain and guilt, made all the more intense by repeated resolves to give it up and repeated failures to do so. It was the source of great misery.

His failure to free himself either from the act or from the associated guilt affected his religious convictions. He prayed, but it appeared that his prayers were in vain: God did not help him nor did he enable Jack to free himself. He rejected Christianity, a process made somewhat easier by conversations he had had with the motherly Miss Cowie, who seems to have held a (possibly confused) belief in some esoteric, oriental religion, which was either not clearly formulated or not clearly communicated. Any belief that Jack had in Christianity was further diminished.

The classical authors he was studying, especially Virgil, focused on religious ideas, but they were treated as "sheer illusion. No one ever attempted to show in what sense Christianity fulfilled Paganism or Paganism prefigured Christianity." Nor did Jack hear any grounds for believing Christianity to be true.

When Miss Cowie left, probably in July 1912, an assistant master who had been a good if not strong influence also left and was replaced by a young master nicknamed "Pogo," straight from university. Pogo obviously fancied himself a wit, a man-about-town, and a "bit of a lad," full of all the superficial frippery of fashionable life. Most of the boys at Cherbourg worshipped him, not least Jack, who said later, "I began to labour very hard to make myself into a fop, a cad and a snob." A new element had entered his life: vulgarity.

At home during the school holidays, Jack continued to write, but it was mostly in the infantile style from his pre-school days. During the Easter holiday of 1912 he wrote *Boxen, or Scenes from Boxonian City Life,* profusely illustrated in color, in two school exercise books. It was an escape to an earlier innocence, perhaps, and is hard to reconcile with other aspects of his life at that time. His imagination had not grown.

Not liking the atmosphere at home, Jack and Warren spent as little time as possible there during holidays. It is clear that they both despised their father, the "Pudaita-bird," for what they regarded as his lack of culture. Jack and Warren were, as always, close friends, but Warren was not a particularly good influence on Jack and contributed to his "vulgarity." Warren was happy at Malvern, but he was failing academically. He did so badly that he was transferred from arts to science—a real degradation in those days, but he referred to as "a non-stop Fun Fair." He was lazy and his conduct was bad. After being caught smoking once too often he was asked to leave Malvern at the end of the spring term in 1913 at the age of eighteen.

Albert was mortified and once again sought the advice of Kirkpatrick, who proposed an army career on the grounds that neither brains nor industry was required. This judgment was unfair, at least in the case of Warren, who did not lack brains, but he was placed under the tutelage of Kirkpatrick, now retired and living in England at Great Bookham, Surrey. Kirkpatrick successfully prepared Warren for the entrance examination to the Royal Military College at Sandhurst, the British equivalent of West Point.

Jack remained at Cherbourg for another year (1912–13), at the end of which he took the entrance scholarship examination to Malvern College. Unfortunately, he was sick in bed at the time of the exams but nevertheless did well enough to achieve a second-rank, or junior, scholarship. His English essay was the best of all those submitted, he did fairly well in Greek and Latin, and was decidedly poor in mathematics.

During his time at Cherbourg Jack discovered Wagner, the real romantic passion of his life. This began, as did so much for Jack, with a visual experience. In 1911 Jack, by chance, came across a review of Margaret Armour's recently published translation of *Siegfried and the Twilight of the Gods*, which included one of Arthur Rackham's illustrations: Siegfried gazing in wonder at the sleeping and bare-breasted Brunhild. This brought him a sense of Joy akin to that of "Balder the beautiful is dead, is dead . . . ," which lifted him again "into huge regions of northern sky," with "the sunward sailing cranes" into a world that was "cold, spacious, severe, pale, and remote."

During the next school holiday Jack and Warren discovered in a gramophone magazine a synopsis of Wagner's *Ring* cycle. Jack immediately started a heroic poem based on it, in the style of Pope's version of Homer. The next holiday they acquired a recording of *The Ride of the Valkyrie*. Listening to *The Ring* inflamed him, and it became "a conflict of sensations without name." The passion was intensified when Jack found at a cousin's house an actual limited-edition copy of Armour's *Siegfried and the Twilight of the Gods*, complete with all the Rackham illustrations. He was able, with Warren's help, to buy a cheaper edition, and for weeks on end he lived in the world of Richard Wagner. Going beyond Wagner he read everything on Norse mythology he could find. Jack's love of "northernness" grew, and later in life he said that he liked Greek mythology, liked Irish mythology better, and liked Nordic mythology best of all.

This immersion and total absorption was characteristic of Jack. He could enter completely into the imaginative world of a great creator, of a Spenser or a Wagner. He usually delighted in the world of the imagination, but he felt that he could not control it, and sometimes he was afraid that he was going mad. His imaginative life was an isolated world, secret, except in part from Warren, because he had no friend who might understand it and share it, and no older person who could be a model for him. His vulnerability to ridicule and the potential accusation of madness forced him to create a persona that hid his rare talent and extreme sensitivity, his longing and desire for Joy. He acted like an insolently intelligent, overtly blasphemous, foul-mouthed, and sex-obsessed schoolboy. And with the absolute logic of adolescence, since he had ceased to be a Christian, he must be an atheist. And so he saw and declared himself.

Jack entered Malvern College in September 1913. His account of Malvern in *Surprised by Joy,* where he calls it Wyvern, occupies two chapters, and much exception has been taken to his terrible descriptions. Warren, in later years, was at great pains to "correct" the unfavorable impression that Jack's words had made.

The truth of the matter would seem to be that bad things certainly went on at Malvern, but not only bad things, and that Jack's emotional and spiritual condition required him to notice and to anguish over those bad things. He himself, in *Surprised by Joy*, warns the reader of the duality of his life. "Reading through what I have just written about Wyvern, I find myself exclaiming, 'Lies, lies! This was really a period of ecstasy. . . .'" But as he explains, he is really telling the story of two lives, and if the eye is fixed on either one of the two, that one will claim to be the whole truth to the exclusion of the other.

According to Jack's recollection, Malvern was "riddled" with homosexuality, it had a system of fagging in which younger boys were at the command of older boys, and it had a prefect system that encouraged bullying.

> Spiritually speaking, the deadly thing was that school life was a life almost entirely dominated by the social struggle—and from it, at school as in the world, all sorts of meanness flow.

Disappointed in his expectation of an intellectual life and freedom for his imagination, all that happened at Malvern, according to Jack's own account, was that he became a prig, an intellectual snob, feeling greatly superior to the other boys around him.

> When I went there nothing was further from my mind than the idea that my private taste for fairly good books, for Wagner . . . gave me any sort of superiority to those who read nothing but magazines and listened to nothing but the (then fashionable) Ragtime.

This statement is open to doubt. He was already becoming, perhaps without realizing it, an intellectual snob even before entry into Malvern College.

There were two good things—"blessings that wore no disguise"—at Malvern. One was the school library, called the Grundy. It was a veritable sanctuary, for once one was inside it one was "unfaggable." It had a better, wider collection of books than any library Jack had ever seen, and in it he discovered Yeats, "an author exactly after my own heart." The Grundy also had the two-volume *Corpus Poeticum Boreale,* which not only made Norse poetry available to him but also provided the inspiration for his opera libretto, *Loki Bound,* which, while based on Norse mythology, was classical in form. It was perhaps to be expected that he would model his thought and plot on the story of Prometheus, the savior of mankind, and his struggle with the tyrannical Zeus, with Jack taking the part of the oppressed.

The other undisguised blessing was Smugy (pronounced and spelled by Lewis as Smewgy)—Harry Wakelyn Smith, Jack's form master, who taught him English and

Latin for fourteen hours a week. His form had as its motto *Virtus Tentamine Gaudet,* "Excellence Rejoices in Competition."

Smugy was a great teacher for Jack:

> Even had he taught us nothing else, to be in Smewgy's form was to be in a measure ennobled. Amidst all the banal ambition and flashy splendors of school life he stood as a permanent reminder of things more gracious, more humane, larger and cooler. But his teaching, in the narrower sense, was equally good. He could enchant but he could also analyze. An idiom or a textual crux, once expounded by Smewgy, became clear as day. He made us feel that the scholar's demand for accuracy was not merely pedantic, still less an arbitrary moral discipline, but rather a niceness, a delicacy, to lack which argued "a gross and swinish disposition." I began to see that the reader who misses syntactical points in a poem is missing aesthetic points as well.

Jack later said that his own style of reading poetry was based on what he had heard from Smugy, although there were differences. Jack's voice was more suited to heroic and other "grand style" poetry, whereas Smugy had a musical voice and was an enchanting reader of romantic, lyrical poetry.

Scholastically, Jack was usually placed in the lower half of his class, with little signs of special ability in Greek and Latin. In mathematics he was, as always, weak. But he had a certain kinship with Smugy, with whom he shared an understanding and appreciation of poetry that separated Jack from the other boys.

After only one year at Malvern, Jack was very unhappy and physically exhausted— "cab-horse tired" he called it—but it was only when he threatened to shoot himself that Albert took his complaints seriously. Warren could not understand how his brother could not be contented at the school that he himself had enjoyed, but he made the useful suggestion that Jack should be sent to study with Kirkpatrick, as Warren himself had done. Albert approved, Jack agreed, and the next two-and-a-half years were spent at Great Bookham with Kirkpatrick.

Warren later wrote:

> The fact is that he should never have been sent to a public school at all. Already at fourteen, his intelligence was such that he would have fitted in better among undergraduates than among schoolboys; and by his temperament he was bound to be a misfit, a heretic, an object of suspicion within the collective-minded and standardized Public School system. He was, indeed, lucky to leave Malvern before the power of this system had done him any lasting damage.

Given the overall inadequacy of his formal education and the various diversions from his studies, Jack's intellect could not be expected to have achieved the kind of discipline that its innate power required if it was not to be self-destructive. From September 1914 to March 1917 Jack studied under Kirkpatrick, a teacher whose strengths were exactly what Jack required and whose limitations were unimportant at that time. These were the most calm and peaceful years of his life. They gave him the opportunity to discover something about himself without the excessive pressure and expectations of an institution and of peers.

William T. Kirkpatrick (1848-1921), who rejoiced in the nickname "the Great Knock," was a somewhat eccentric man, once a Presbyterian but by 1914 an outspoken atheist, with no use for frivolous conversation. An inveterate pipe smoker, he cultivated his vegetable garden assiduously, and his clothes and hands usually bore witness to it. He thought himself to be a severe logician, an old-fashioned rationalist, and even the most casual remark could be taken as a "summons to disputation." Warren once remarked, "You could not say something about the weather without being pounced on." But Jack reveled in such arguments, being well able to hold his own, and it became part of his intellectual stock-in-trade.

Jack improved his Greek with Kirkpatrick to the point of being able to think in it. His Latin similarly improved, even though he did not enjoy Virgil. He also learned French with Mrs. Kirkpatrick, and later also Italian and German. Of these, he mastered German least, but he became fluent in the other languages.

With the discipline and structure provided by the Great Knock, Jack had both the ability and the desire to teach himself. He developed habits of study that lasted all his life. Kirkpatrick guided Jack, but, more importantly, he allowed him to develop into what he really was. There is, for example, no evidence that Kirkpatrick had any liking for poetry, and he certainly did not have Jack's poetic sensibility, but he recognized it in Jack and respected it:

> I do not think there can be much doubt as to the genuine and lasting quality of Clive's [Jack's] individual abilities. He was born with the literary temperament, and we have to face that fact with all it implies.... [I]t is the maturity and originality of his literary judgements which is so unusual and surprising.

Jack still led a double life. On the one hand he mastered and employed the logical, rationalistic methods of Kirkpatrick in his studies, but he was at the same time intensely romantic and imaginative. The problem he faced was how to integrate these two sides of himself, a problem that was not solved in principle until 1931. As he wrote:

> The two hemispheres of my mind were in the sharpest contrast. On the one side a many-islanded sea of poetry and myth; on the other a glib and shallow "rationalism." Nearly all that I loved I believed to be imaginary; nearly all that I believed to be real I thought grim and meaningless.

1914–1918

Imagination and intellect began to move closer together through Jack's friendship with Arthur Greeves. In an academic setting, Jack was well able to master complex issues and problems, but he had never been able to apply his intellect to the problems of his own life: the incredible power of his imagination, his experience of Joy, and his intense sexuality. These could now be shared with Arthur, either face-to-face or in letters.

In 1914, before leaving home for his last term at Malvern, Jack found a new friend, Arthur Greeves (1895–1966), who lived across the road from Little Lea. They discovered by accident their common delight in Grueber's *Myths of the Norsemen*, which began,

> Northern mythology is grand and tragical. Its principal theme is the perpetual struggle of the beneficial forces of nature against the injurious, and hence it is not graceful and idyllic in character, like the religions of the sunny south....

This appealed to both Arthur and Jack. They discussed the book and discovered that they both liked the same thing "and even the same parts of it and in the same way." The book was enhanced by many pages of fine illustrations, with extensive quotations from the *Eddas* and *Sagas,* the *Lays,* and the Nordic works of English poets.

Through Arthur, who was three years older, Jack encountered William Morris for the first time and also became reacquainted with Matthew Arnold. He was impressed very deeply by Carlyle's statement, quoted by Grueber,

> To know the old Faith brings us into closer and clearer relation with the Past—with our own possessions in the Past. For the whole Past is the possession of the Present; the Past had always something true, and is a precious possession.

And from William Morris: "This is the great story of the North which should be to all our race what the Tale of Troy was to the Greeks. . . ."

Arthur Greeves, with blond hair and blue eyes, had a Nordic beauty about him, and this undoubtedly made him attractive to Jack, who throughout his life responded to beauty in all its forms. But to find in Greeves a fellow enthusiast about the North as well was almost too good to be true. They became close friends and confidants, sharing not only books but also ideas and their sometimes turbulent emotional lives.

They became secure enough in their relationship to be able to share the most personal matters, including their sexual fantasies. Jack related his sadistic tendencies and included an account of his habit of masturbation, called IT and THAT in his letters. Arthur was probably homosexual.

Later, in 1933, Jack called Arthur Greeves, "after my brother, my oldest and most intimate friend." Both were very aware of the importance of loyalty, and their disagreements never affected their friendship. Yet their loyalty to each other is in some ways surprising. Arthur did not have the same intellectual capacity as Jack and, it seems, did not enjoy poetry. Moreover, he was childish and bad-mannered. And yet they remained friends for fifty years. They influenced each other in a variety of ways and shared often conflicting opinions. They recommended books (and bindings) to each other and usually read whatever was recommended, although Jack never got Arthur to like poetry. But he did applaud Arthur's composing as well as his painting and encouraged him to enroll in the Slade School of Fine Art in London in 1921. They were both romantics but approached nature and experience from different points of view: Jack would extrapolate fantasies, while Arthur was engrossed in the immediate, in whatever was concrete and before him.

Because of Arthur, Jack read many of the classical English writers he found in his father's library, such as the Waverley volumes of Sir Walter Scott and the novels of Jane Austen and the Brontës.

After Jack went to Great Bookham to study under Kirkpatrick, he and Arthur wrote long, intimate, and intellectual letters to each other. Jack wrote, for example, that he had discovered more of the poems and Celtic plays of W. B. Yeats, that Malory, while not a great author, had the gift of lively narrative, and so forth. Jack also told Arthur how, in March 1916, he found *Phantastes* by George MacDonald (1824–1905) on the bookstall in the railway station at Leatherhead and that reading it was "a great literary experience." Appreciating the beauty of MacDonald's writing, Jack was mostly influenced, unconsciously perhaps, by the symbolism and the way in which MacDonald sees divinity in ordinary things. Jack later called this "holiness." The only other work of Mac-Donald's that he read at Bookham was *The Golden Key,* an entrancing children's story.

Jack encouraged Arthur to develop his interests in painting, composing, and writing, and he suggested that Arthur should compose the music for the opera libretto he had written, *Loki Bound*, and perhaps also provide illustrations. About this time, Jack wrote the major part of a Medieval romance in which a young knight, Bleheris, sets out on his quest for manhood. In interpreting it for Arthur, who was a Christian, Jack claims that he was not attacking Christianity itself but rather "Christianity as taught by a formal old priest like Ulfin, and accepted by a rather priggish young man like Bleheris." The story is strangely Christian in many ways, although it is clearly opposed to organized or institutionalized religion.

Jack wrote to Arthur about "the sensuality of cruelty," by which he seems to have meant the pleasure derived from self-indulgent cruelty, especially centered on the whip and the rod. By February 1917 he is quite explicit (although Arthur seems not to have shared his taste) and even signs himself J. Philom.—an abbreviated form of *philomastix*, the Greek for "lover of the whip." He tells Arthur of his pleasure in reading the flagellation section in Rousseau's *Confessions*: "His taste is altogether for suffering rather than inflicting: which I can feel too, but it is a feeling more proper to the other sex."

He seems to have had powerful sexual feelings, not understood, not controlled, not controllable, but confused. While admitting that he could appreciate being the "sufferer," he felt that this was more appropriate for women, and it was his role to inflict pain (as he wanted to do at Oxford in June 1917 when he got drunk for the first time in his life and pleaded with other men to let him whip them at a shilling a lash).

What is even more perplexing is that beautiful women are the predominant partners in Jack's flagellation scenes. Although a confused sadomasochist, writing to Arthur must have helped him because it enabled him to acknowledge to another his "sensuality of cruelty" and to make clear the extent of his feelings. He wrote candidly to Arthur, feeling neither shame nor guilt, but playfully chastising Arthur, calling him on one occasion a prude, and addressing him for a time as Galahad, that is, the innocent and pure one.

In their correspondence, Arthur asked Jack about his religious views. Jack, who had read Frazer's *Golden Bough* and Lang's *Myth, Ritual, and Religion* and was well-trained by Kirkpatrick, replied that there was no ground for believing in any religion; proof was entirely lacking. And, following his authorities, he declared that all gods were derived from natural forces and were, properly speaking, mythologies, human inventions. He was careful to add that this does not undermine morality, since our very humanity requires us to be "honest, chaste, truthful, etc." But the universe is a mystery, and Jack made it clear that until he understood the matter he would not go "back to the bondage of believing in any old . . . superstition." He saw the Christian God as "a spirit more cruel and barbarous than any man." He admitted to Arthur that he had gone to Belfast to be confirmed on December 6, 1914, merely to please his father and to avoid endless argument. Jack wrote, "As to the immortality of the soul, though it is a fascinating theme for day-dreaming, I neither believe nor disbelieve: I simply don't know anything at all, there is no evidence either way." Immortality was always a problem for Jack, and later he was glad that he had found God before believing in it.

These conventional rationalist views are in strong contrast to the imaginative and romantic world of Jack's literary preferences. He was, in fact, still divided, but the rationalism of Kirkpatrick helped to keep his talents and interests under some measure of control.

Kirkpatrick also helped Jack gain the discipline required if he was to obtain an Oxford scholarship in classics. This was the goal that had emerged in his work with Kirkpatrick. But there was a problem:

> The fact is that a critical and original faculty, whatever may be its promise for the future, is as much a hindrance as a help in the drudgery of early classical training. [Jack] has ideas of his own, and is not at all the sort of boy to be made a mere receptive machine.

In May 1916 the Great Knock wrote that Jack was "the most brilliant translator of Greek plays I have ever met" and that he would probably gain an award in classics in any of the Oxford colleges, although he "knows nothing of science and loathes it and all its works."

Jack took the entrance examination for a scholarship at Oxford on December 4, 1916. He was not happy with his performance, but fifteen days later he received a letter from University College, awarding him the second of three scholarships in classics.

It was (and is) necessary to be accepted first by an Oxford College. Acceptance by a college suggests that acceptance by the University, via an examination, will be a mere formality. But Jack was not prepared for the university examination, called Responsions, not least because it included mathematics, at which Jack was hopeless and in which Kirkpatrick could be of little help, although Jack studied with him another term to acquire the necessary amount of "the low cunning of algebra."

Jack took Responsions on March 20 and 21 and then returned to Belfast for a month. There he dedicated his time and energy to a collection of poems, provisionally titled *Metrical Meditations of a Cod,* that he had begun writing at least as early as Easter 1915. He copied out the finished poems and added "no fewer than ten pieces." He also worked on a prose piece, *Dymer*, that was eventually rewritten and published as a long narrative poem, and on *The Childhood of Medea*.

Not altogether surprisingly, Jack failed the mathematics portion of Responsions. He was nevertheless allowed to go into residence at his college, provided that he took the exam again and passed in all subjects. It is possible, though not certain, that he took it again in June and failed again. This might have been the end of his academic career if it had not been for the war. Jack fought in France, and after the war the examination was waived for those who had served in the armed forces.

Jack's notebook entry for April 28 reads: "Matriculated. College Library. Entered name in Coll. books." He also joined the Officer's Training Corps, with the expectation that when he joined the army he would be commissioned. Being Irish, he was not liable for war service, but he chose to follow Warren, who had a commission in the regular British army and had been in France since 1914.

Jack arrived at University College on April 26, 1917, keenly anticipating the start of his university career, but in this he was disappointed. His college would not provide him with a program of studies because he would shortly be in the Officer's Training Corps and have no time for scholastic work. But he did get a sorely needed mathematics coach.

Jack began to enjoy the beautiful, natural setting of Oxford, which included swimming at Parson's Pleasure "without the tiresome convention of bathing things." He also joined the Union, the debating society and social club, which had a useful library, and found friends to talk with, often late into the night. One friend, named Edwards, particularly interested him because he had been an atheist and was then "engaged in becoming a Catholic."

Letters to Albert give the impression that Jack was leading a good Christian life, including Sunday attendance at church or college chapel. But this was not true, as letters to Arthur make clear, and thus began the deception of his father that continued until Albert's death.

After only eight weeks at University College, the OTC program transferred Jack to a "carpetless little cell" in Keble College, Oxford, and put him in a cadet battalion for training. Jack wrote condescendingly and mostly disparagingly about the other members of his battalion. He also mentioned his roommate, assigned by the alphabetical order of names, first as "a little too childish for real companionship" but later as "a very decent sort of man."

This was Edward Francis Courtenay Moore (1898–1918), known as Paddy and born in the same year as Jack. In a letter written to Albert a few days later, Jack mentioned Paddy's mother, "an Irish lady," who was in Oxford, accompanying her son to the last possible moment before he was shipped off to the carnage of the western front. Her daughter, Maureen, then eleven years old, was with her. In the same letter Jack invited Albert to visit him in Oxford during a short period of leave, but the invitation was declined.

Mrs. Janie King Askins Moore (1872–1951) did not get on all that well with Paddy but obviously felt that she ought to be with him whenever possible. She was also, as Jack later reported, very hospitable and entertained her son's roommate and several other cadets in the furnished rooms she had taken in Oxford.

This was the beginning of Jack's relation with Janie Moore, a relationship that lasted until her death in 1951. They lived under the same roof for about thirty years, and although the pattern of their relationship no doubt changed through time, it persisted.

It is not hard to explain the initial attraction. Janie Moore was Irish, and Jack was homesick. She was the mother of his contemporary, Paddy, and Jack had been motherless for nine years. She offered hospitality, and Jack was without a real home anywhere. Finally, she was attractive, and Jack was always susceptible to beauty. All this apparently more than outweighed the fact that Janie Moore was twenty-six years older than Jack.

At the end of his OTC course on September 25, 1918, Jack first went to stay with the Moores in Bristol, which offended Albert, who only got to see his son on October 12. It is highly probable that the relationship between Jack and Janie Moore became sexual at this time and that Albert had greater cause for jealousy than he knew. About a month after returning to his regiment, on November 15, Jack sent a telegram to Albert saying that he had to report to Southampton and had been granted forty-eight hours leave. This meant that Jack was going to France. Albert—possibly not understanding that—refused to travel to see him.

Second Lieutenant C. S. Lewis arrived in France with his regiment, the Somerset Light Infantry, on November 17. Within twelve days, on his nineteenth birthday, he was in the front lines (a fact he did not mention to Albert). In February 1918 Jack was in the hospital with pyrexia or "trench fever" and stayed there for twenty-seven days. He returned to active duty on February 28, and from March 21 on he seems to have been in the front lines again. At one point he captured sixty German soldiers—although he always insisted that they only surrendered to him. In early April he reported that he was having "a fairly rough time" and nine days later, that he was in the Liverpool Merchants' Mobile Hospital in Etaples with a wound "to his left arm," received in the Battle of Arras on April 15, 1918.

As soon as Warren heard what had happened, he borrowed a bicycle and rode to the Etaples hospital, a distance of fifty miles. He was delighted to find Jack sitting up in bed, "only slightly wounded and in great form, expecting to be sent home. Thank God he is out of it for a bit." Jack and Warren had been distant ever since Jack's condemnation and rejection of Malvern College, but at this point their friendship was renewed and it remained close for the rest of their lives.

Jack's wounds, caused by shrapnel from a British shell that fell short, were more serious than Warren thought. In fact, he was wounded in three places: the back of the left hand, the left leg just above the knee, and the left side of his chest, under the arm. The latter turned out not to be, as Warren had understood, a minor injury. It was decided to leave the shrapnel where it was since it was close to the heart and difficult to remove. (It was finally removed twenty-six years later, in 1944.)

By May 25 Jack was back in England. He was taken to London to the Endsleigh Palace Hotel, which had been converted into a hospital. From there he sent a telegram to his father, imploring him to visit. Albert replied that he was unable to travel because of bronchitis; he was, however, at his office every day.

Within a few days of Jack's arrival in London, Janie Moore was also there, staying with her sister. Jack wrote, "We have seen a good deal of each other. . . . [S]he has certainly been a very, very good friend to me." The implication was that Albert had not. Paddy Moore had been posted as missing in March, and in September it was confirmed that he had been killed in action.

In June, towards the end of his hospital stay, Jack was able to go out and visited the Kirkpatricks at Great Bookham. He wrote a long letter to his father, reporting his visit but also pleading with him to visit him in London. He confessed that his conduct towards his father had not always been proper, "but please God, I shall do better in the future. Come and see me. I am homesick, that is the long and short of it." But still Albert did not come.

After his hospital stay Jack was sent to a convalescent home. Because none was available in Ireland, where, as he told Albert, he would have preferred to go, he chose to be sent to Ashton Court, near Bristol and the home of Janie Moore, arriving there on June 25. The expectation was that he would have two months in which to recuperate, after which he might well be sent back to France. From Bristol he wrote again to his father, asking him to visit, but Albert did not budge. Jack's recovery was slower than expected, and the convalescent home was quarantined with an outbreak of an infectious disease. On October 3 he wrote again to his father: "It is four months now since I returned from France, and my friends laughingly suggest that 'my father in Ireland' of whom they hear is a mythical creation. . . ." But still Albert did not visit. The relationship between father and son was strained almost to the breaking point, although they continued to write to each other. Albert was stubborn and mortified; Jack was repentant and lonely.

Janie Moore and Jack wrote to each other every day, and when Jack was later moved from Bristol to Eastbourne to Andover, she followed him with the now twelve-year-old Maureen. They were joined by friendship, companionship, Irishness, the reading of books, the surrogate mother-son relationship, and Paddy's death. There was also a physical, sexual bond between them.

Jack had told Arthur in at least three letters in late 1917 and early 1918 that he was in love with Janie Moore. Although the disparity in age and experience between them is not usual between lovers, there is no reason to disbelieve him.

Janie Askins, born on March 28, 1872, in Pomeroy, County Tyrone, was married on August 1, 1897, to Courtenay Edward Moore, a Dublin civil engineer. They had two children, Paddy and Maureen, but the marriage was unsuccessful, and Janie Moore separated from her husband without being divorced. One of her brothers, Dr. Robert Askins (1880–1935), was a government medical officer in Bristol, and she moved there and enrolled Paddy in nearby Clifton College in May 1908. Her intention was to give Paddy the advantages of a public school education, as Albert had wanted to give Warren and Jack.

Janie Moore herself had not attended college or university. As the oldest member of her family she had been fully occupied looking after her younger brothers and sisters after their parents' death. She liked reading books and would discuss what she had read with Jack; they often lent each other books and shared their thoughts on them.

She called Jack "Boysie" and he called her either "Mother" or "Minto." Later, when they were living in Oxford, she always referred to Jack and Warren as "the boys." Warren reports that it was sometimes difficult to explain to guests who had been introduced to Janie Moore as "Mother" what the actual (and reportable) relationship was. Minto, incidentally, was the name of her favorite confection, Nuttall's Peppermint Candy or Mintos. In Jack's diary she is also referred to by the capital of the Greek letter delta, probably hiding the name of Diotima, the priestess in Plato's *Symposium* who introduced Socrates to the meaning of love.

Jack's ever-present sexuality is underlined by his strange confession to Arthur Greeves in three separate letters (May 23 and 29, and June 3, 1918). He found it significant to record that his views were getting "almost monastic about all the lusts of the flesh." The lessening of lust seems to be unexpected, and it strongly suggests that usually sexuality was noticeably present. The diminution was not due to any change in Jack, in all probability, but to the "bromides," or sexual suppressants, that were routinely added to the daily fare, usually in the tea, of "other ranks" and also of those confined in hospital.

While convalescing, Jack had been depressed but not idle. He wrote to Arthur on July 17, 1918, that he had been preparing his earlier poems for publication, revising them, rejecting some, having them typed out, but not actively writing any new ones.

The "cycle of lyrics" was offered first to Macmillan, who rejected it, and then to Heinemann, who accepted it, with some revisions, in the first week of September 1918.

A week after telling Arthur, Jack told Albert.

Originally the title had been *Spirits in Prison*, a reference to Peter's First Epistle, which reports that Christ "went and preached unto the spirits in prison." There can be no doubt that this was Jack at his arrogant and immodest worst, casting himself in the role of Christ, preaching to the misguided and ignorant souls who were confined by their adherence to "a phantom" of the good, to the established religion. Whether Albert saw it this way is not known, but he did object to the title for a more mundane reason: there was already a novel with the title *A Spirit in Prison*, by Robert Hichens. He recommended a change, and so it became *Spirits in Bondage: A Cycle of Lyrics*.

Jack's tenacity and perversity are equally well illustrated by the new title, however, for it came from Milton's *Paradise Lost*, from the speech of Satan to his army, swearing eternal rebellion:

> For this Infernal Pit shall never hold
> Cœlestial Spirits in Bondage, nor th'Abysse
> Long under darkness cover. But these thoughts
> Full Counsel must mature: Peace is despaird,
> For who can think Submission! Warre then, Warre
> Open or understood must be resolv'd.

Jack's initial usurpation of the role of Christ and then settling for that of Satan is borne out by his description of the poems. Writing to Arthur Greeves on September 12, Jack said that the book was

> mainly strung around the idea that I mentioned to you before—that nature is wholly diabolical and malevolent and that God, if he exists, is outside of and in opposition to the cosmic arrangements. . . .

Later, Warren found this idea anathema and wrote to Albert that

> it would have been better if it had never been published. . . . Jack's Atheism is I am sure purely academic, but even so, no useful purpose is served by endeavouring to advertise oneself as an Atheist.

But Jack was—or imagined himself to be—an Atheist.

Spirits in Bondage was published on March 20, 1919, under the pseudonym Clive Hamilton, since Jack expected to remain for some time in the army, where poetry and poets were not necessarily appreciated. In truth, the poems are not very good and one wonders why Heinemann wanted to publish them except for the fact that "soldier-poets" were in vogue. Albert Lewis wrote "for a first book—and of poetry—written by a boy not yet twenty it is an achievement. Of course we must not expect too much from it." The reviewers praised it, but it did not sell very well, and Jack gave up the idea of being a lyric poet.

Between the acceptance of the cycle and its publication the war had come to an end on November 11, 1918. Jack was still not properly healed and, somewhat to his surprise, was discharged from the army because of his wound. He arrived back in Belfast unannounced on December 27, 1918. To his delight, Warren was there, who had arrived on Christmas leave four days earlier.

Warren, Jack, and Albert were reunited, and Warren records that he drank champagne—"the first time I have ever had champagne at home." After the festivities, Warren returned to his army post and Jack prepared to return to Oxford.

But the effects of the Great War lingered. Warren, in his diary entry for November 11, 1918, wrote, "Thank God Jacks has come through it safely, and the nightmare is now lifted from my mind." It was typical of Warren to be more concerned for Jack than for himself. While Jack was in France, Warren would frequently be awakened by anxiety in the middle of the night. Was Jack still alive? Warren's nightmare was all too real. Jack too was troubled for years with nightmares, "or rather the same nightmare over and over again." He wrote little or nothing about the Great War.

1919–1925

Going to Oxford did not cut him off from Arthur, but he made new friends—especially Owen Barfield and Nevill Coghill, who allowed his vision of the imagination at least to have some validity. If the war gave him new insights into cruelty and meaningless destruction, Janie Moore contained his sexuality. She also gave him a home.

In late January 1919, Jack returned to University College, Oxford, for the eight-week Lent Term. "It was a great return and something to be very thankful for," he wrote to Albert on January 27. Janie Moore was in Eastbourne.

He was now admitted to the university, since his war service excused him from taking Responsions again. He could have proceeded directly to a degree in Greats, the popular name for the Honours School of *Literae Humaniores*, a course devoted to the classics, philosophy, and ancient history. But he thought he wanted a scholarly career, and for him that meant obtaining a fellowship at Oxford. He had confided this ambition to his tutor, A. B. Poynton, who had recommended that instead of proceeding directly to Greats he should begin with the Honour Moderations course in Greek and Latin, taking its final examination in March 1920, and then proceed to Greats, taking finals in June 1922. This would give him a firmer grounding in the field of classics and a better chance to show his worth.

In the spring vacation of 1919 Jack helped Janie Moore move from Eastbourne to Bristol, and at the beginning of the summer vacation he helped her move again from Bristol to 28 Warneford Road, Headington, on the outskirts of Oxford.

Jack's daily routine was to spend all morning either attending lectures or doing research in the college library, to have lunch with Janie Moore in Headington and spend the afternoon with her, to return to college for dinner in Hall, and then to work in his rooms in the evenings. He still wrote when he had time and still

C.S. Lewis, 1919.

thought of himself as a poet, albeit not a lyric poet, and even envisaged the possibility of a literary circle of some kind because his own romantic poetry was out of fashion, the current taste running more to "modernism, vers libre, and that sort of thing."

For five terms, starting in January 1919, Jack studied for Honour Mods. He was able to report to his father on April 4, 1920, that he had passed his examinations and had passed them quite well: "I did get a First after all." (Basically, Oxford and Cambridge undergraduates were classified as achieving First, Second, or Third Class degrees; the number of Firsts awarded was extremely small.)

In 1921 he competed for the Chancellor's English Essay Prize, writing on the assigned subject of "Optimism." Although he declined to admit the existence of God in the essay, it won the Prize. While writing, it almost possessed him: "I have almost lived with my pen to the paper. It has been one of those rare periods . . . when everything becomes clear and we see the way before us."

His religious beliefs at the time are reflected in a letter to a friend:

> The trouble about God is that he is like a person who never acknowledges your letters and so, in time, you come to the conclusion either that he does not exist or that you have got his address wrong.

He also met W. B. Yeats in Oxford at this time and was considerably impressed.

Two years later, in June 1922, Jack sat for the Greats examinations, and on August 4, 1922, it was announced that he had been awarded First Class Honours; the following day he took his B.A.

Jack had been thinking about his future and the possibility of staying at Oxford in some capacity. The alternative was to take a job, probably as a schoolmaster somewhere. The future of classics and philosophy was uncertain, and Jack was counseled to stay at Oxford one more year and take a degree in English Literature, which was a newly instituted degree subject and normally a two-year course.

At that time, the Oxford Honours School of English Language and Literature was deeply committed to language study, and Anglo-Saxon (Old English) was a requirement. (Jack had had "a dream of learning Anglo-Saxon" since his Bookham days.) This included not only grammar but also a detailed analysis of *Beowulf*. Next, Middle English was studied and then the development of the language into modern English. The reading list included most of Chaucer, selections from Gower and Langland, and all of *Gawain and the Green Knight;* of later writers, Milton, Spenser, and Shakespeare are dominant.

In this period of intense academic work, from January 1919 to July 1923, Jack met many people and made a few good friends:

> The first lifelong friend I made at Oxford was A. K. Hamilton Jenkin, since known for his books on Cornwall. . . . My next was Owen Barfield. There is a sense in which Arthur and Barfield are the types of every man's First Friend and Second Friend. The First is the alter ego, the man who reveals to you that you are not alone in the world by turning out (beyond hope) to share all your most secret delights. . . . But the Second Friend is the man who disagrees with you about everything. He is not so much the alter ego as the antiself. Of course he shares your interests; otherwise he would not become your friend at all. But he has approached them all at a different angle. . . . Closely linked with Barfield of Wadham was his friend (and soon

mine) A. C. Harwood of the House, later a pillar of Michael Hall, the Steinerite school at Kidbrooke. He was different from either of us; a wholly imperturbable man.

In 1923 Jack met Nevill Coghill, who read a paper on realism in one of his classes. Coghill was from Castle Townshend in County Cork, Ireland. He, like Jack, had been advised to complete an English degree and, again like Jack, to take one year instead of the customary two in which to do it. He had already noticed Jack because of a paper he had read on *The Faerie Queene,* in which Jack, with infectious enthusiasm for the text, had championed Spenser's ethical values. They had the same tutor, F. P. Wilson, and their studies ran on parallel tracks, so that they were able to share views on the common required readings, often on long country walks. They became friends for life. Jack "soon had the shock of discovering that he—clearly the most intelligent man in that class— was a Christian and a thorough-going supernaturalist."

Jack took his finals in June 1923. His oral examination or "viva" (for *viva voce*) on July 10 was perfunctory and, in spite of all his gloomy forebodings, he was awarded another First Class Honours degree.

The pressure of academic work, heightened by Jack's ambition to achieve a fellowship at Oxford, caused great strain, sufficient in itself to destroy a lesser man. But in addition to the academic program, Jack had to deal with his relationships with his father, his brother, and with Janie Moore and Maureen.

Jack had virtually no money of his own. Albert provided a yearly allowance of £85, and he was generous enough to provide this through the completion of Greats, then through the English degree, and finally until Jack was elected to a fellowship at Magdalen College in May 1925.

Jack, Maureen, and Mrs. Moore, 1927.

Although this sum would have been sufficient for a normal, single student, Jack helped to support Janie Moore and her daughter. Had Albert known this, he would almost certainly have cut off the allowance, but Jack never told him of his domestic arrangements and repeatedly lied about his affairs and actions.

University regulations allowed Jack to live outside college from the beginning of his second year. He did so by moving into the same house as Janie Moore in Headington. From then on, Jack made his home with Janie, with scrupulous attention to the external decorum required by the university. For the next eleven years they lived in rented houses— at least ten of them—before they eventually were able to purchase their own home, the Kilns, in 1930.

Jack was secretive in many ways, a habit that was reinforced by the fact that Albert had never respected the privacy of his sons and had always expected to see every letter they received. He would often search their rooms and read anything he came across. Shortly after Jack's arrival in Belfast in August 1920, for example, Albert asked him how much money he had in the bank. Jack replied that it was about £15, and Albert then produced a letter, found in Jack's room, in which the bank drew attention to the fact that his account was overdrawn.

They had a fairly loud and violent quarrel. Jack, according to Warren's diary, "instead of defending himself, . . . weighed in with a few home truths about P [Pudaita]." That August was one of the unhappiest months of Albert's life, for he could not understand how Jack could have lied and then said "terrible, insulting and despising things."

There were numerous reasons why Jack would have been secretive about his relationship with Janie Moore. He did not want to cause anxiety and recriminations in his own family, he needed to seem respectable in the eyes of the university, and Janie Moore did not want her husband to discover the arrangement—which had all the appearances of adultery, whatever it actually was—for then she could be the respondent in the divorce courts, which would deprive her of any financial support.

Janie Moore was a woman with a strong and demanding nature. She would order Jack around, send him on sometimes fruitless errands, and give him many and frequent menial tasks to do, in spite of his academic workload. She said that having Jack around was good as having another maid. After her death Jack wrote:

> I have lived most of [my private life] in a house which was hardly ever at peace for 24 hours, amid senseless wranglings, lyings, backbitings, follies and scares. I never went home without a feeling of terror as to what appalling situation might have developed in my absence. Only now that it is over do I begin to realize quite how bad it was.

If it was bad, why did Jack not terminate the relationship? The answer is probably that he owed Janie Moore too much—he says several times that she taught him to be generous and hospitable—but she also quieted the destructive sexual impulses he undoubtedly had and initiated him into one whole dimension of himself. Since there was no formal arrangement—no marriage, no contract—what was to be dissolved? It would be hard to say, and the absence of formality would make it more difficult. And then there is the strong sense of loyalty that Jack always had. He had made an unspoken commitment to Janie Moore, and nothing could dissolve it, even if it was unpleasant, hard to define, and had been entered into gradually and blindly. In 1930, Jack wrote to Warren,

> I have definitely chosen and I don't regret the choice. Whether I was right or wrong, wise or foolish, to have done so originally, is now only an historical question: once having created expectations, one naturally fulfills them.

Would he have been better off had he left? Certainly, he would have had more energies available for the many aspects of his university work, and he would have had better relations with Albert and Warren, but his was a strong nature and it needed a strong yoke. Perhaps he would not have been the good man he ultimately became without being domestically dominated, for the domination of another showed him that the forces within him could be mastered. He learned how to control them in himself, to control his feelings and his actions.

Warren never liked or approved of Janie Moore, but those who met her casually or socially at one of her teas found her to be a charming and gracious hostess, even if it was disconcerting to discover that she was not Jack's mother.

In *Surprised by Joy* Jack says that "one huge and complex episode will be omitted." It is obvious that this refers to his relationship with Janie Moore, whose name does not appear in the book. It was certainly huge, lasting some thirty-four years, from 1917 to 1951, but it was also complex. This complexity forbids the making of any simple generalization about their relationship.

It is possible that Jack himself could not say what it was that bound them together. It had many components and changed over time, and to try to describe it to anyone else—or to answer the questions of others—would have been difficult, even apart from the intimate things. They chose to be together in the way that they were, and perhaps we should simply accept that. Clearly, Albert and Warren could not.

Nevill Coghill, describing Jack in 1922–23, reports that, unlike most men of his age, he "seemed to have no sexual problems or preoccupations, or need to talk about them if he had." This intense and powerful aspect of him was obviously satisfied or fulfilled or, at least, brought under control, in the relationship with Janie Moore.

The reason Jack gave in *Surprised by Joy* for omitting his life with Janie Moore altogether is that he doubted "if it has much to do with the subject of [the book]," that is to say, with the story of his conversion. It is almost as if his life with Janie Moore and Maureen was sealed off from his "real" life, like a play that has begun and must be played out to its conclusion but is curiously irrelevant to reality. His loyalty, quite apart from any other possibilities, required him to see the performance through, to see the curtain come down, as it finally did in January 1951.

Janie Moore contributed nothing to Jack's intellectual development. There is very little in his published diary, written at her request or behest, about the books he was reading or the writing he was doing, and there is no mention of the ongoing argument over supernaturalism (the "Great War") he conducted with his friend Owen Barfield through the 1920s.

Although Janie Moore was the mother-mistress of Jack's passion and was the center of his home, she was never a friend in the sense that Warren, Arthur Greeves, Owen Barfield, Nevill Coghill, or Charles Williams were, nor in the sense that Joy Davidman Gresham was to be later.

Jack had put on weight since leaving the army. He was, according to Nevill Coghill's description,

> a largish unathletic-looking man, heavy but not tall, with a roundish, florid face that perspired easily ... [he] had a dark flop of hair and rather heavily pouched eyes; these gave life to the face, they were large and brown and unusually expressive.... [There] was a sense of simple masculinity, of a virility absorbed into intellectual life.

Jack learned that he was nicknamed "Heavy" by other members of his college, although this may have originated in the seriousness of his interests and the profundity of his arguments rather than in his bodily weight.

W. T. Kirkpatrick, the Great Knock, died in March 1921, and Jack wrote,

> I owe him in the intellectual sphere as much as one human being can owe another. That he enabled me to win a scholarship is the least he did for me. It was an atmosphere of unrelenting clearness and rigid honesty of thought that one breathed from living with him.

Jack was a brilliant student. He was also ambitious. But he had to face the practical necessity of earning a living. His tutors thought that a university position would surely become available, but in the meantime, in spite of his First Class Honours degree in English Language and Literature, he was still without employment.

In the spring of 1923, Jack and Janie Moore moved to yet another rented house, their tenth since 1919, called Hillsborough. The house was in a very bad state of disrepair, which was remedied, in part, by Jack and Maureen. Janie Moore was of little help in the renovation process, since she was ill with indigestion, varicose veins, and injuries suffered when a wardrobe fell on her during the move.

To add to the stress, Janie's brother, John Askins (known as Doc), had moved to Iffley near Oxford in 1922, and visited nearly every day. Deeply troubled, he and Jack had long conversations that always ended on the topic of immortality. Doc began to suffer from serious mental illness, possibly the result of syphilis contracted as a young man, and required attention through the long hours of the night. He stayed with Jack and Janie for more than a month, struggling with delusions and nightmares, "awful mental tortures ... maniacal fits." Eventually he was sent to a hospital in Richmond, where he died on April 23, 1923, of a heart attack. Jack took this frightening experience as a warning of what excessive occultism and supernaturalism could do, and he reacted by burying himself in the ordinary things of life.

Jack was depressed, a condition he suffered from even when things seemed to be going well. In order to save money he gave up smoking, and the household managed without a maid, although the latter increased the burden on Jack. His health was not good, and he suffered from headaches, indigestion, insomnia—all symptoms of what today we would call stress. His frustration about his career and about money was exacerbated by a sense that his best and most creative years were being wasted, slipping away without the production of the great poem or prose work he believed he could write.

To supplement his meager income, Jack graded school examination papers and tutored a student at University College. Then, in May 1924, almost a year after he had completed his English degree, he was offered a one-year appointment to replace University College's philosophy tutor, E. F. Carritt, who was going on leave. It entailed giving lectures as well as conducting tutorials, all for £200 a year. Jack accepted. His lectures, given twice a week, were on a topic of his own choice: "The Moral Good— its place among the values."

During the 1924–25 academic year, Jack slept at Hillsborough on weekends and during vacations; in term time he stayed at University College. He would give tutorials in the morning, go to Hillsborough for lunch, do odd jobs or take a walk, and return to college in the late afternoon for more tutorials. He dined formally in college, enjoyed the conversation of the Senior Common Room, and then retired to his rooms where breakfast would be brought in in the morning.

He gave up philosophy for English, but with few regrets:

> I have come to think that if I had the mind, I have not the brain and nerves for a life of pure philosophy. A continued search among the abstract roots of things, a perpetual questioning of all the things that plain men take for granted, a chewing the cud for fifty years over inevitable ignorance and a constant frontier watch on the little tidy lighted conventional world of science and daily life—is this the best life for temperaments such as ours? Is it the way of health or even of sanity?

He continued to apply for positions at Oxford. These were for the most part positions such as a lecturer in philosophy or English that would provide a salary but little security or status. He also applied for Oxford fellowships, which would make him part of the college corporation—very different from being a "hired hand." His last application was for a fellowship in English Language and Literature at Magdalen College. He did not expect to be successful but thought he should at least try. It turned out that, since he could teach both English and philosophy, he was the preferred candidate and was elected.

1925–1931

Jack's election to a fellowship at Magdalen College gave his intellectual powers the opportunity they required. It also gave him new friends and colleagues—especially J. R. R. Tolkien and Hugo Dyson—whose views on myth and imagination greatly affected him. He grappled intellectually with religion, particularly with Christianity, but found that reason could only take him to a belief in God, to theism. It was the imagination and the function of myth that took him beyond theism to Christianity.

On May 20, 1925, Jack sent a telegram to Albert: "Elected fellow Magdalen. Jack." Albert wrote in his diary: "I went to his room and burst into tears of joy. I knelt down and thanked God with a full heart. My prayers have been heard and answered."

Soon after, Jack wrote to Albert and expressed his deep appreciation for the financial and other support that he had provided since 1919. This included the assistance for his second degree in English, and he underscored this by pointing out that his success was largely due to the combination of English and philosophy that he could offer. It must be kept in mind that English was at that time a new subject at Oxford and that there was some uncertainty as to whether students would want to study it.

His income would be quite good—£500 a year—and in addition he would be given rooms in college, a pension, and an allowance for dining. The days of poverty were over, but Jack never lived lavishly. He never owned a watch (at lectures he usually borrowed one from a student) or a decent fountain pen, and in the years that followed he gave away thousands of pounds to people in need. His only self-indulgent luxuries were beer and tobacco—almost indispensable—and, less frequently, whiskey.

Jack spent the next thirty years of his life at Magdalen College. It is certainly one of the most lovely colleges in either Oxford or Cambridge, and he described it as "beautiful beyond compare." The buildings were part Medieval and part 18th century; Jack's rooms were in the latter, in New Buildings, erected in 1733.

As a tutor Jack was at first too demanding of his students. Some of them found him exacting, harsh, and contentious. But it did not take Jack long to become more gentle, more realistic in his demands, and more sympathetic, and to treat his students with good humor and courtesy. One of them wrote:

> He was personally interested in his pupils and permanently concerned about those who became his friends. Though he was a most courteous and considerate person his frankness could, when he wanted, cut through the ordinary fabric of reticences with a shock of sudden warmth or sudden devastation, indeed of both at once. No one knew better how to nourish a pupil with encouragement and how to press just criticism when it was needed, without causing resentment.

His wide learning and the extent of his reading were universally acknowledged. He had a prodigious memory, quoting authors at length, and reciting or declaiming poetry with special attention to the meter and with infectious excitement.

In the early days of his fellowship he completed his long narrative poem *Dymer*. He had worked on it for almost ten years. The first prose version was written in 1916 with the title *The Redemption of Ask*. It was written again in verse, the first four cantos in 1922 (with incredible spontaneity, it seems) and the last five cantos in 1924 and 1925.

Dymer reveals some of Jack's innermost and deepest feelings. He tells us that it is based on a myth he had known since he was about seventeen, although he did not read the myth anywhere, nor dream it, nor invent it. He just found it in his mind. It is the "story of a man who, on some mysterious beast, begets a monster, which monster, as soon as it has killed its father, becomes a god."

Jack had long been troubled about the intensity of his imagination (often fearing insanity) and about his retreat into self-inflating fantasies of love, lust, cruelty, and heroism. He knew that he withdrew from life in these fantasies and condemned them and himself as self-indulgent. The writing of *Dymer* was undoubtedly therapeutic as Jack worked out, in both his reason and his imagination, the connection between fantasy and reality.

Heinemann, as publishers of *Spirits in Bondage*, had the right of first refusal, and refuse it they did, but J. M. Dent and Sons accepted it. It was published, like *Spirits in Bondage*, under the pseudonym Clive Hamilton, on September 20, 1926, and received quite favorable reviews. The public did not share the reviewers' good opinions, and very few copies were sold.

As the original title, *The Redemption of Ask*, attests, Jack was concerned with redemption even when still an avowed atheist in 1926. The publication of *Dymer* seems to mark the acceptance of a belief in a power outside himself. It was not a formed belief, not defined, perhaps not even definable, and the power itself was vague and nebulous, but it was evidently there.

The Christmas of 1926 was the last one that Jack, Warren, and their father spent together. In April 1927 Warren was posted to China and did not return for three years. The next two Christmas holidays Jack and Albert spent alone.

It may be easy for an observer to look back on Jack's early life and see hints and intimations of his final conversion to Christianity, but it was a long and tortuous process. Warren wrote that Jack's conversion "was no sudden plunge into a new life but rather a slow steady convalescence from a deep-seated spiritual illness of long standing."

The years from 1925 to 1931 were a period of remarkable progress. Election to the Magdalen fellowship gave him financial security. The nature of his teaching and research satisfied his rational and professional needs. His friends, colleagues, and the beauty of Oxford gave him congenial surroundings. But Jack did not settle down comfortably into a secure and pleasant life. He was still restless, his energies were not unified, and he still experienced glimpses of Joy from time to time and remembered its origin in his sense of longing. Longing, but for what?

Church worship had never been very meaningful for either Jack or Warren. As children they had regularly attended St. Mark's Church in Dundela and listened to the rabid preachings of their grandfather, but they were offered only "the dry husks of Christianity." They both hated church services and had in general a low opinion of Christianity. At school Jack had attended services because they were compulsory, but at Great Bookham, with Kirkpatrick, he seems not to have gone to church at all. Compulsory church parades (a frequent and unpopular affair for those in the British armed forces) did not make Christianity more attractive, and the experiences in the war only confirmed Jack in his atheism, or at least in his belief in a malign god.

Nor were Jack's intellectual activities able to provide satisfaction for his longing. He could never regard them as purely academic, that is, as taking place in isolation and remote from his everyday life. They had, in some way, to make a difference in how he lived. Ideas were never simply thought, they were also felt. But the prevailing and fashionable schools of philosophy did not permit any such fusion of thought and feeling. The best they could offer was some form of Hegelian subjective idealism, irreconcilable with and distant from daily living. Most tutors, by their attitude, encouraged their students to be skeptics. Jack, however, began to meditate on the Hegelian Absolute, a thing held to be impossible to do, and on the supreme Spirit, of which, according to idealists, everything else is a mere expression. He later wrote that this was "more religious than many experiences that have been called Christian."

In 1924 he was influenced by Samuel Alexander's *Space, Time and Deity*, especially by the distinction it made between enjoyment (the experience of something) and contemplation (the thinking about it). Jack related this to his idea of Joy:

> I saw that all my waitings and watchings for Joy, all my vain hopes to find some mental content on which I could . . . lay my finger and say, "This is it," had been a futile attempt to contemplate the enjoyed.

And this was impossible. He came to think that Joy must be the desiring of something outside the self. But what was it?

He was perplexed and wrote in his diary on January 18, 1927, that he was

> thinking about imagination and intellect and the unholy muddle I am in about them at present; undigested scraps of anthroposophy and psychoanalysis jostling with orthodox idealism over a background of good old Kirkian rationalism. Lord, what a mess! And all the time (with me) there's the danger of falling back into most childish superstitions, or of running into dogmatic materialism to escape them.

He mentions anthroposophy because two of his closest friends, Owen Barfield and A. C. Harwood, had joined Rudolf Steiner's movement in 1922, causing him to write, "I was hideously shocked. . . . For here . . . were all the abominations . . . gods, spirits, after-life and pre-existence, initiates, occult knowledge, meditation."

It was at this point that Jack began his long-running argument with Barfield, their "Great War" as they called it. It lasted a long time and, if not violent, was scarcely gentle, at least on Jack's part. But through their arguments and conversations Jack gave up realism—the idea that our sensible world is self-explanatory and is all there is—and moved closer to what he had always disparagingly referred to as "supernaturalism."

While Jack had studied Freud, he disliked and distrusted psychology and considered analysis in terms of the "latest perversions" simply morbid. He also had no regard for occultism and introspection and was frightened by what had happened to Janie's brother, Doc, in 1923. He did not know it at the time, but he would only have been satisfied by a religion with an objective, traditional morality.

By 1926 he had been intellectually driven to becoming a practicing theist, a believer in God. But this God had nothing to do with Christianity, which, he said, "was very sensible apart from its Christianity." He did not want to have his life disturbed, he was fearful, but his longing continued.

A 1926 conversation with T. D. Weldon, an atheistic and uncongenial colleague, gave Jack serious pause. Weldon remarked that there was substantial evidence to support the Gospels as history, and so Jack began to study them very carefully. Weldon referred to J. G. Frazer's discussion of the "dying God" and remarked, "It almost looks as if it really happened once." Much to his surprise, Jack found that the available evidence in the Gospels themselves was highly supportive of the Christian story. He also began to attend church or college chapel regularly because, he said, he wanted to show that he was a theist. His honesty required this of him, but at the same time, it must be added, he was making a provocative statement, being well aware of the atheism of some of the fellows of Magdalen.

But it was not easy. He later described part of the process:

> You must picture me alone in that room in Magdalen, night after night, feeling, whenever my mind lifted even for a second from my work, the steady, unrelenting approach of Him I so earnestly desired not to meet. That which I had greatly feared had at last come upon me. In the Trinity Term of 1929 I gave in, and admitted that God was God, and knelt and prayed; perhaps, that night, the most dejected and reluctant convert in all England. I did not then see what is now the most obvious and shining thing; the Divine humility which will accept a convert even on such terms.

To admit that God was God was one thing—it made Jack a theist. But to admit that Christ was the Son of God was something else—it would have made him a Christian, and he could not do it.

41

One stumbling block for Jack was the preservation of his freedom. He reports that going up Headington Hill on the upper deck of a bus he was suddenly aware of being offered a completely free choice. He could either reject God or accept him. In such a situation, when it is quite clear what one ought to do, Jack realized that freedom and necessity almost came to the same thing. He later wrote:

> The Prodigal Son at least walked home on his own feet. But who can duly adore that Love which will open the high gates to a prodigal who is brought in kicking, struggling, resentful, and darting his eyes in every direction for a chance to escape? The words *compelle intrare*, compel them to come in, have been so abused by wicked men that we shudder at them; but, properly understood, they plumb the depth of the Divine mercy. The hardness of God is kinder than the softness of men, and His compulsion is our liberation.

Yet his conversion was to theism, not to Christianity.

Warren was still in the army, posted to Shanghai. Albert had retired from practicing law in May 1928 and was lonely. In August 1929 he was seriously ill. Jack visited him for a month and, being assured after an operation that he would live, left for Oxford, only to be immediately called back to Belfast. He returned, but Albert had died the previous afternoon, on September 24, 1929. He wired Warren.

Jack felt a great deal of shame at how he had treated his father. He had lied to him, misled him, and denigrated him. He made a conscious effort to change himself and to understand and deal with his lack of paternal respect. This was made easier by a strong feeling that Albert was somehow still alive, helping him—a feeling that also strengthened his still vague and unfounded belief in a personal immortality. In January 1930, Jack wrote to Arthur Greeves that he was alarmed at the discovery that his besetting sin was pride, "the mother of *all* Sin, and the original sin of Lucifer."

And in March 1930, Jack wrote to a friend that his outlook was changing:

> It is not precisely Christianity, though it may turn out that way in the end. I can't express the change better than by saying that whereas once I would have said "Shall I adopt Christianity?" I now wait to see whether it will adopt me: i.e., I now know there is another Party in the affair—that I'm playing poker, not Patience, as I once supposed.

Warren finally returned from Shanghai, arriving in England in April 1930. To Jack's astonishment he reported that he had been thinking of becoming a Christian and had been attending church regularly. The brothers realized that they might both be able to change their lives—Warren could, perhaps, give up his laziness and alcoholism, while Jack would have a more integrated foundation for his work as a scholar-teacher. But there were many things about Christianity that bothered them both.

On September 19, 1931, Jack invited J. R. R. Tolkien and Hugo Dyson to dine with him at Magdalen. After dinner they went outside, into Addison's Walk, and the conversation turned to myths. Jack could not suppose them to be true, although he admitted his love of reading them and thinking about them. Tolkien differed. In his view, myths, like everything else, originated with God, and they preserved, sometimes in a disguised or distorted form, something of God's truth. If this is so, Tolkien continued, then writing myths, telling or retelling myths, might well be a way of doing God's work.

As Tolkien talked, there was such a sudden rush of wind in an otherwise still evening that all three of them felt a kind of ecstasy. Jack felt it to be a message from God, although his reason cautioned him not to get carried away. Tolkien told Jack that in order to find out the importance of the Christian story for his own life he would have to accept it. Tolkien left at 3:00 A.M. and Dyson continued the conversation, maintaining that Christianity works for the believer, bringing peace and the possibility of changing into a new person.

The final act of Jack's conversion took place nine days later, on September 28, 1931. Jack was being taken to Whipsnade, a pioneer open-air zoo, in the sidecar of Warren's motorcycle: "When we set out I did not believe that Jesus Christ is the Son of God, and when we reached the zoo I did." There was no emotional or intellectual activity, it just happened. "It was more like when a man, after long sleep, still lying motionless in bed, becomes aware that he is now awake."

Soon after, on October 1, Jack wrote to Arthur Greeves: "I have just passed on from believing in God to definitely believing in Christ. . . . My long night talk with Dyson and Tolkien had a great deal to do with it."

Jack had not received communion since his boyhood, probably not since 1914, but on Christmas Day 1931 he attended Headington Church and took communion. In a quite remarkable coincidence, Warren, who was then back in Shanghai, also received communion, after many years, on the same day. Initially, Jack received communion only at the great festivals, like Christmas and Easter, but soon after he wrote to Warren that he was receiving communion once a month, and from about 1948 on he received communion once a week.

1931–1940

Christianity gave Jack a new foundation for his life and with his searing honesty changed the meaning of all that he did. He began writing Christian books of an apologetic nature, and his home life changed, especially when Warren, now a Christian, returned to England to live with him and Janie Moore at the Kilns. His scholarly work continued, the Inklings were founded, and then, in 1939, World War II broke out.

Conversion gave Jack a new stability and a point of view from which he could see things differently and more clearly. When he became a theist he had begun a prose account of the change, but he gave it up, almost certainly because he saw that he was still changing. In 1932 he attempted to describe his conversion to Christianity in verse but gave that up as well. He finally finished a prose account, a book called *The Pilgrim's Regress*. It took two weeks to write during a holiday in Ireland in August 1932 and was accepted by J. M. Dent in December 1932. Jack drew maps for the endpapers and the book was published in May 1933 to mostly favorable reviews.

The book was an allegorical account of Jack's return to "Mother Kirk" after all the experiences, temptations, and false philosophies he had met during his life. It tells of his search for Joy, for what is spiritually highest, for God, and of the temptations of all the false joys he met on his journey. It was published with the subtitle *An Allegorical Apology for Christianity, Reason, and Romanticism*. For Jack, "Romanticism" meant, in part, the desire for Joy, the longing for what is spiritual.

Warren remained in England for almost two years, from April 1930 to December 1931. Soon after his arrival he and Jack visited Little Lea, selecting some items of furniture to keep and arranging for the disposal of the rest. Albert had kept most of the family papers, including much of the correspondence with Warren and Jack. Warren proposed that he should edit these papers, type them, and produce a family history that covered the years from 1850 to 1930. Jack agreed, and eventually there would be eleven thick volumes constituting The Lewis Family Papers.

After considerable discussion, it was decided that Warren, who expected to retire in 1932, would live with Jack and Janie Moore in a house financed by the sale of Little Lea. The money realized was less than expected, and so additional money was provided through Janie Moore from the Askins trust fund. They bought the Kilns in Headington Quarry, about three miles from the center of Oxford. The property of eight acres was in Janie Moore's name, but to safeguard their interest she made a will leaving the house to Jack and Warren for their lifetimes. After the death of both brothers, the house would become Maureen's property. They moved in during the second week of October 1930.

Jack, Mrs. Moore, Warren, 1930.

Considerable improvements were made, including the addition of two ground-floor rooms to serve as studies for Jack and for Warren. Until 1939 they had servants—a gardener, Fred Paxford (who actually remained until Lewis's death), and one or two maids—and a variety of dogs and cats. Paxford's knowledge of gardening was extensive, and under his direction and with his help the property was improved. Trees were planted, an orchard established, ditches cleaned or filled, fences erected, the pond cleared, and brambles cut away.

Warren was back in Shanghai by early 1932. Alcoholism was still his besetting vice, but Jack took a very lenient and loving view of it, because, "while his idea of the good is so much lower than mine, he is in so many ways better than I am. I keep on crawling up to the heights and slipping back to the depths, he seems to do neither."

Beginning in 1931 the brothers took holidays together for several years, enjoying the scenery and each other. On their last joint holiday, in 1939, they visited Malvern. It was during one of these holidays, this one also with Janie Moore and Maureen, that Jack first conceived of a book that appeared ten years later as *The Great Divorce*.

In 1925, his tutor, F. P. Wilson, had suggested that Jack write a book on certain aspects of Medieval thought. This was the origin of *The Allegory of Love*, begun in 1927 and worked on intensively between 1933 and 1935. As a work of literary criticism and history it was a masterpiece, equaled only by Jack's volume in the Oxford History of English Literature series. He sent the manuscript to the Clarendon Press on September 18, 1935, and heard on October 29 that the press had accepted it. By Christmas the book was in proof, and it was published on May 21 the following year.

Originally called *The Allegorical Love Poem*, Jack wrote of it:

> The book as a whole has two themes: 1. The birth of allegory and its growth from what it is in Prudentius to what it is in Spenser, 2. The birth of the romantic conception of love and the long struggle between its earlier form (the romance of adultery) and its later form (the romance of marriage.)

The reviewers were without exception enthusiastic, and the book became a source of excitement and intellectual ferment. Hitherto little-known Medieval literature became significant. The book is characterized by Jack's moral approach to literary criticism, which is particularly appropriate in dealing with authors who were, at bottom, moralists themselves.

During the 1930s, one of Jack's delights was the regular Thursday evening meeting of a group of friends who assembled in his rooms to read aloud their own writings and those of others, and then to discuss, criticize, encourage, and laugh, all lubricated by hot tea—or wine or beer. The meetings had no formal agenda, there were no by-laws and no officers. Jack called them the Inklings, and one joined by invitation.

The first "member" was J. R. R. Tolkien, who later, in 1935, was elected Bosworth Professor of Anglo-Saxon. He was a champion of the study of Anglo-Saxon and Middle English and also of the Icelandic *Eddas* and *Sagas*. He had formed a group of dons, known as the Coalbiters, to read and translate the latter. In 1929 Jack was invited, with Nevill Coghill, to attend the Coalbiters' meetings, and he soon learned that he shared with Tolkien a love of "northernness" and a delight in the Norse mythology. Tolkien and Jack began to have regular meetings that grew into the Inklings.

Some of the other members were Warren, then Hugo Dyson and Robert E. Havard (who was Jack and Warren's personal physician and was known as Humphrey), Adam Fox, Nevill Coghill, Charles Wrenn, Owen Barfield, Charles Williams, and later John Wain. The meetings were often small, with perhaps only three or four members present. Invariably, after Warren had made tea, Jack would ask, "Well, has nobody got anything to read us?"

The same people also met, as they were available, during the week, first on Tuesdays but later, when Jack was at Cambridge, on Mondays. They met before lunch at the pub the Eagle and Child, commonly known as the Bird and Baby. They would drink beer for an hour or so and talk. In 1962, when the pub was remodeled, the meetings moved to the Lamb and Flag.

The evening meetings of the Inklings effectively ended after fifteen years when, on a demoralizing night in October 1949, nobody turned up. The Inklings helped a number of writers and thinkers, but above all, perhaps, gave Jack a circle of congenial friends who supported him by their very presence. This did much to alleviate the isolation he felt at the beginning of his career and the opposition to his views by the dominant "inner circle" at Magdalen, which was intensely political, and by the "moderns" in the Oxford English School, who wanted to subvert the established curriculum for which Tolkien and Lewis had argued.

In the late 1930s Jack and Tolkien, who was a staunch Roman Catholic, agreed that what we would now call science fiction needed to be written from a Christian point of view, and so it was decided that Tolkien would write a "time-journey" and Jack a "space-journey." Tolkien produced the first part of a story called *The Lost Road*, which was rejected by his publisher. Jack wrote *Out of the Silent Planet*.

After being refused by two publishers, *Out of the Silent Planet* was accepted by the Bodley Head and appeared in the autumn of 1938. It had about sixty reviews, which was quite remarkable. Most thought the book to be an H. G. Wells imitation and felt that Wells was the superior writer. Only two reviewers recognized the underlying Christian theology.

Reflecting on the response of the reviewers, Jack suddenly had the idea that gradually became a more conscious principle in him:

> If there was only someone with a richer talent and more leisure I think that this great ignorance might be a help to the evangelisation of England; any amount of theology can now be smuggled into people's minds under the cover of romance without their knowing it.

This intent was not often explicit, but he slowly realized that he had the power to evangelize through popular books in which Christianity was only implicit.

The Allegory of Love had been very successful, and this prompted Jack to send two more academic works to Oxford University Press in 1939, *Rehabilitations* and *The Personal Heresy: A Controversy*. The former consisted of essays on literary or linguistic subjects, with some interesting reflections on the curriculum of the Oxford English School that stimulated discussion among Oxford dons.

The Personal Heresy consisted of six essays that were exchanges between Jack and E. M. W. Tillyard. Jack believed that "all criticism should be of books not of authors."

This was a direct challenge to Tillyard, who had said in his book on Milton that the real subject of *Paradise Lost* is "the state of Milton's mind when he wrote it." Reviewers deplored the biographical approach to literature and literary criticism but were quick to add that it could be pleasurable. This joint-authored book did not sell well but was influential in the teaching of literature.

A few months later, in September 1939, World War II broke out.

Jack had no doubt about the rightness of going to war against Nazi Germany. His understanding of Christianity did not require him to be a pacifist, and he thought that England should meet its treaty obligations to Poland. There was no alternative, and he did everything he could to help the war effort.

Warren, of course, as a retired regular army officer, was in the reserve. He had been called up several weeks before hostilities began and sent to France. Warren's departure was a cause for sorrow, not least because Jack was troubled about Warren's heavy drinking when under stress. Few details are known of what Warren did in the eleven months he served, but he was evacuated from Dunkirk, sent to a hospital in Wales, and discharged in August 1940.

Jack wanted to be active and so volunteered to be an instructor of cadets, but his offer was refused. The recruiting office suggested that he should join the Ministry of Information, but Jack would not tell lies and create propaganda, so he declined. Instead, he joined the Oxford City Home Guard Battalion, a volunteer force of part-time soldiers.

Another way to help the war effort was to take in "evacuees," children who had been removed from the wartime dangers of city living. The Kilns provided shelter for a number of girls. Their presence taught Jack something. He had always been shy around children and did not understand them. He now learned how to relate to them and to have affection for them. Without this experience, the Chronicles of Narnia might never have been written or not written so well.

When Jack was invited to give talks to those serving in the Royal Air Force in the early months of 1941 he agreed, although he was doubtful about his effectiveness. All through the summer vacation of 1942 he dedicated every weekend to travel and talks and then, by request, continued throughout the rest of the war.

The Problem of Pain was written during the first six months of the war at the invitation of Geoffrey Bles of the Centenary Press. It was part of a series of books on popular theology and was published in October 1940. The reviews were very favorable and the book became an immediate best-seller with nine printings in the first three years. Jack did not think that what he wrote was original. Rather, he "believed himself to be re-stating ancient and orthodox doctrines," without any sectarian or denominational content. Written in plain ordinary language, the book was simply Christian. Jack wrote: "Any fool can write *learned* language. The vernacular is the real test. If you can't turn your faith into it, then either you don't understand it, or you don't believe it."

1940–1951

Janie Moore, who was hostile to Christianity, became less significant, if more tiresome, until her death in 1951. Jack's wide vision of reason and imagination working together produced remarkable results, in both scholarly books and religious writings. After The

Screwtape Letters *appeared he gave his famous radio talks, later to appear as* Mere Christianity. *The Socratic Club was founded, he wrote science fiction, and met Charles Williams. He also began the Chronicles of Narnia.*

In July 1940 Jack described in a letter to Warren an idea for a book called *As One Devil to Another.* The book consists of thirty-one letters written by a senior devil, Screwtape, to Wormwood, a younger devil whose job it is to steer people away from God, "The Enemy." The manuscript was completed by February 1941 and sent to the *Guardian,* a Church of England weekly paper, primarily because its editor had already agreed to publish Jack's paper "Dangers of National Repentance."

The letters were serialized in the *Guardian*, starting in the beginning of May 1941. Jack had his fee, a mere £62, paid to a charity. *The Screwtape Letters*, as they came to be called, were immediately successful and Geoffrey Bles bought the book rights.

The book appeared in February 1942, and Jack was deluged with mostly appreciative comments. To handle the correspondence, Warren took on the task of dealing with routine letters and became a close assistant to his brother. *Screwtape* was so successful that the first edition of 2,000 copies was sold out before publication, and it was reprinted eight times by the end of the year. It was published in the United States the following year. Suddenly, Jack was famous and money was flowing in from royalties. Owen Barfield set up the Agape Fund, a charitable trust into which two-thirds of all royalties were paid to help the poor.

Charles Williams wrote his review of *Screwtape* in the form of a letter that began "My dearest Scorpuscle" and signed it "Snigsozzle." He added a postscript: "You will send someone to see after Lewis?—some very clever fiend?"

But Jack felt corrupted by writing *Screwtape*. Almost twenty years later, in the preface to the 1961 edition, he wrote:

> The strain produced a sort of spiritual cramp. The world into which I had to project myself while I spoke through *Screwtape* was all dust, grit, thirst, and itch. Every trace of beauty, freshness and geniality had to be excluded. It almost smothered me before it was done.

Being successful with *Screwtape* while imitating a devil made him conscious of his need for spiritual support and comfort, and in October 1940 Jack asked the Cowley Fathers (Church of England priests of the Society of Saint John the Evangelist) to appoint a spiritual director who would hear his confession and give him advice.

Jack hated radio as much as he later hated television, but when in 1941 his help was sought by the religious broadcasting division of the BBC, Jack agreed to give four radio talks of fifteen minutes each, on Wednesday evenings in August. He realized that he could reach at least a million people through radio, most of whom would never read anything he wrote.

Jack knew that the original readers of the New Testament brought with them certain assumptions. For example, they took it for granted that they lived under natural law, an objective and independently existing right and wrong. When they violated that law they felt guilty because they knew what they had done. But the "modern reader" had different assumptions. The belief in natural law had largely disappeared and a sense of guilt was unfashionably "Victorian." Jack wanted to help his audience to recover that implicit background to the Christian Scriptures. The live broadcasts were billed as "Right and Wrong: A Clue to the Meaning of the Universe?" Jack's voice, down-to-earth yet educated, commanded attention, and people listened. The broadcasts were a great success.

Immediately after the first talks Jack was flooded, directly and via the BBC, with letters. It was proposed that he should give another talk to discuss listeners' objections and to answer their questions. This, instead of satisfying his correspondents, only produced another flood of letters, including "many from serious inquirers whom it was a duty to answer fully." The latter he answered in longhand, using an old-fashioned pen with detachable nib and a bottle of ink, while Warren gave invaluable help by typing formulaic letters to the others.

As might be expected, the BBC asked Jack to give another series of talks. In this series, titled "What Christians Believe," he tried to set forth, rationally and understandably, what all Christians, regardless of denomination or sect, believe, without involving the controversies between various "kinds" of Christianity.

The two series of radio talks were published in one volume under the title *Broadcast Talks* in July 1942 and immediately became a best-seller. Two months later Jack began a third series of talks, "Christian Behaviour," in which he devoted most of his time to the Christian virtues of faith, hope, charity, and forgiveness, and very little time to sin. Avoiding the negative and critical, he gave positive, practical advice, grounded in his own life experience.

His final series of seven talks for the BBC, delivered in early 1944, was called "Beyond Personality: The Christian View of God." This series was published as *Beyond Personality*, and also sold extremely well. Finally, in 1952, all the talks were combined into a single volume and published as *Mere Christianity,* a title borrowed from the Puritan theologian Richard Baxter (1615–91).

The popularity of the talks was such that it was inevitable that Jack would be asked to give more. He refused on the grounds that he had said all that he could usefully say and besides, the amount of correspondence was already overwhelming,

While the public response to the talks and to their printed versions was entirely favorable, the critics were mixed in their reactions. The positive ones stressed Jack's clarity, his ability to make theology attractive and exciting, the simplicity of his expression; the negative ones accused him of being vague, pantheistic, puritanical, and of oversimplifying. The talks, however, made a definite contribution to Britain's morale at a critical time of the war.

A number of Oxford students, often wavering between belief and unbelief, made it known that they needed some way of discussing their religious questions. They wanted to hear an exposition and defense of Christianity but also a serious presentation of agnostic and atheistic views. This led to the formation of the Oxford Socratic Club in January 1942. After a preliminary meeting at which churches and organized religion came under severe attack, it was decided that Oxford needed an "open forum for the discussion of the intellectual difficulties connected with religion and with Christianity in particular." The Oxford Socratic Club was to be that open forum.

Jack, because it was known that he had been an atheist, was invited to be president and, as a senior member of the university, to effectively sponsor the club. He believed

49

that the club was "long overdue" and accepted the position enthusiastically, helping to devise a policy and a program. But he insisted that it should not have an exclusively Christian agenda. Rather, that it should give candid consideration to "the pros and cons of the Christian religion." Its aim was the Socratic examined life, not propaganda.

The Club soon became the second-largest society in the university and attracted famous and gifted speakers. At the meetings, someone would read a paper that espoused either a Christian or a non-Christian viewpoint. This was followed by an opposing speaker, after which the meeting was opened for discussion, although Jack usually began with an attack on the unbeliever's statement.

Jack's energy was great, but the Club depended too much on him, and when he left Oxford in 1954, membership declined. It finally disbanded in 1972.

His wholehearted commitment to Christianity did not always increase Jack's popularity and status. It had become a convention in Oxford that one's religion was a private matter, personal, and properly unobtrusive. Jack's enthusiasm and energy and his desire to bear witness to his belief and to be honest violated this convention. Many dons, though not all, gave the appearance of complete indifference to Christianity and in their supposed superior wisdom deemed a discussion of it to be in bad taste and also pointless—"These things are really undecidable, don't you think?" Jack was quite prepared to talk about Christianity, but more than that, he would discuss any and every subject from a Christian point of view, not only at the Socratic Club but also at dinner and in the Senior Common Room afterwards. This made some members of the university uncomfortable and made others downright hostile. Proselytizing, radio broadcasting (on a subject "not his field"), his popular success as a speaker and a writer, and his fiction—all this was not acceptable Oxford behavior.

Jack came to feel increasingly isolated in Magdalen, and he came to hate the destructive and totally uncharitable machinations of his politically minded colleagues and of "the inner circle." His distaste is clearly reflected in *That Hideous Strength*.

Given Jack's energy and combative nature, it is not, perhaps, surprising that his output of Christian apologetics did not diminish. In the years from 1942 to 1946 he wrote, in addition to other minor writings, *Beyond Personality*, *Perelandra*, *That Hideous Strength*, *The Abolition of Man*, *The Great Divorce*, and a draft of *Miracles*. His more scholarly work continued as well—writing and the teaching and supervision of students. In 1943 he also published *A Preface to Paradise Lost*, dedicated to Charles Williams.

Charles Williams was an editor at the London office of Oxford University Press. He and Jack had had occasional meetings after Jack had written Williams to praise his novel *The Place of the Lion*. When the war caused the evacuation of the press to Oxford they met regularly from September 1939 to May 1945, usually twice a week with other Inklings, and at the Bird and Baby.

Williams was a member of the Church of England and wrote novels—spiritual thrillers—and, more important to him, Arthurian poems. Jack rated the latter very highly (although most people found them obscure) and worked on a study of them. *Arthurian Torso*, he wrote, was among "the two or three most valuable books of verse produced in this century." He prized the poems for "the soaring and gorgeous novelty of their technique and for their profound wisdom."

Jack was captivated by Williams' talk. He was excited and enthralled by his imaginative speculation and by his wide-ranging and encompassing ideas in Romantic theology, such as the Way of Affirmation, which transformed earthly delights into a Christian vision, and his theory of substitution by which one person's suffering could be offered for the benefit of another. They also shared a passion for the poetry of Milton and Wordsworth. Jack called him "my friend of friends."

A book of essays to be presented to Charles Williams was initiated, but it became a memorial, for Williams died unexpectedly in May 1945 and was buried in St. Cross Churchyard, Oxford. His own words, "Under the mercy," were his epitaph. Jack was deeply grieved, but the loss strengthened his faith, and for a few days afterwards he was acutely aware of Williams' presence; these feelings slowly faded but they recurred from time to time. He wrote: "The odd thing is that his death has made my faith stronger than it was a week ago. And I find all that talk about 'feeling that he is closer to us than before' isn't just talk. It's just what it does feel like."

Essays Presented to Charles Williams was published by Oxford University Press in 1947, with contributions by Dorothy Sayers, Tolkien, Barfield, Gervase Mathew, and Warren Lewis, as well as Jack. In his preface, Jack wrote: "His face we thought ugly . . . but the moment he spoke it became like the face of an angel. . . . No man whom I have known was at the same time less affected and more flamboyant in his manners: and also more playful."

Jack liked the space travel story *Perelandra* (1943) the best of all his own novels. The story is that of Genesis, and also, of course, of *Paradise Lost.* The original and proper condition of humans is a state of dependence upon God, their wills and whole natures joyfully submitting to their Creator. But disobedience lurks. An unfallen woman, the Green Lady, is subtly tempted and Ransom, the hero of *Out of the Silent Planet,* has to help and protect her.

In the main, *Perelandra* was well received. Some reviewers found the book too theological—one suggested that Jack "should read more Verne and less Aquinas." But another claimed that the book was the outcome of "the poetic imagination at full blast."

A Preface to Paradise Lost, on the other hand, was greeted with much hostility from fellow academics. Since the 1930s Lewis had been developing an original approach to *Paradise Lost* that involved both an exposition of its theology and an explication of the style and form of the epic poem: without understanding these, it is impossible to appreciate *Paradise Lost.* The aversion resulted from the not mistaken perception that Jack was concerned with morals—his own and his readers'. In spite of the hostile critics, the book had a powerful impact and radically changed the interpretation of Milton.

In 1942 Jack made a careful and searching study of the ethics of religions other than Christianity. He also investigated the secular ethics of various philosophical systems. His students made him aware that school textbooks assumed and took for granted the subjective nature of all literary and moral values. He was so appalled that he devoted three Memorial Lectures at Durham University to assert the objectivity of values and the natural law, which together he referred to as the Tao. The lectures were published in 1943 but were not well received. A second edition appeared in England in 1946 and a U.S. edition was issued in 1947, but it took a long time for reviewers and readers to realize the importance of *The Abolition of Man.*

The mythological counterpart to the philosophical *Abolition of Man* was the last of his space-travel novels, *That Hideous Strength*. It reflects Jack's conviction that if scientists ever were to succeed in their purpose to dominate nature, man would indeed be abolished. *That Hideous Strength* depicts a world in which the men of science, who are tinged with black magic, are opposed by a small group of creative nonconformists under the leadership of Ransom. Above and beyond them are supernatural powers, including those of a reawakened Merlin.

The critics did not like the book. They objected to its construction, the moralizing, the mixing of imaginative worlds, and the presence of the supernatural. It was called "intellectually overstuffed." The public differed, and *That Hideous Strength* has been the most popular of Jack's novels. A shortened version was published in the U.S. under the title of *The Tortured Planet*.

While writing *That Hideous Strength* Jack had begun another book, *The Great Divorce*. It was originally published in fourteen weekly installments in the *Guardian*, from November 10, 1944, to April 13, 1945. A number of residents of hell go on holiday to heaven, with George MacDonald as their guide. If they prefer heaven over hell—which a number of them don't—they are free to remain, but on the condition that they give up some vice that hinders them from experiencing real Joy.

> There are only two kinds of people in the end: those who say to God, "Thy will be done," and those to whom God says, "Thy will be done." Without that self-choice there can be no Hell. No soul that seriously and constantly desires joy will ever miss it.

It is between these two groups and their habitations, heaven and hell, that the great divorce exists.

Jack had begun yet another book in the summer of 1943, *Miracles: A Preliminary Study*, which was finally published in 1947. It dealt with the fact that many people reject the Gospels because they cannot accept the miracles in them. Jack's argument depended on the distinction between naturalism and supernaturalism. Within naturalism, reason cannot explain itself and therefore requires for its existence a supernatural reality. This was elaborated in the third chapter and constituted the basis for a proof of the existence of God.

But the philosophy in fashion at Oxford in 1948 was different from that of the 1920s, when Jack had been a student. Hegel and Hegelianism had virtually vanished and logical positivism and linguistic analysis reigned supreme. Jack had not really kept up with these developments in philosophy, and as far as he could see they precluded what he considered to be philosophical thinking. At a meeting of the Oxford Socratic Club on February 2, 1948, G. E. M. Anscombe, a Roman Catholic and later professor of philosophy at Cambridge, read a paper criticizing Jack's argument that naturalism is self-refuting. Jack replied and a tremendous debate followed. Opinions differed about who won, but Jack felt defeated and thought that his proof for the existence of God had been destroyed. He revised the third chapter of *Miracles* before it was reissued as a paperback in 1960.

This was the last of Jack's theological books, partly because modern philosophy, in his opinion, made any discussion of morals impossible. He did not wish to participate in the negativism of logical positivism and, indeed, was scarcely trained to do so. Also, the debate with Anscombe had humbled him, a fact that he fully recognized and accepted, although it caused him much pain. But as he had told Arthur, pride was his besetting sin.

The war had taken its toll. Janie Moore was exhausted and, in fact, spent most of 1947 in bed because her varicose veins had almost deprived her of the use of her legs. She became more autocratic and more demanding, causing Jack more work and more frequent interruptions. Warren's alcoholism was getting worse; his drinking bouts became more frequent and he was often admitted to the hospital.

Whenever Warren was in the hospital, Jack suffered because he was without his secretary and administrative assistant. In the summer of 1949 Jack himself went to the hospital with what was called "a severe infection." Their doctor, Havard, told Warren that Jack was exhausted and needed a long holiday away from the Kilns. Arrangements were made for Jack to go to Ireland ("I'm coming home," as he wrote Arthur), but Warren immediately started drinking heavily again and the trip was canceled. There was no holiday, and Jack was sick again that fall. Warren recovered enough to spend a month in Ireland, but without Jack.

Janie Moore's ancient dog, Bruce, died in January 1950. His walks had become an obsession with his mistress, and Jack was continually being required to take him out. Warren wrote, ". . . the penultimate gate of poor Jack's prison is down at last."

The ultimate gate soon opened as well. In April 1950 Janie Moore, now seventy-eight years old, was taken to Restholme, a nursing home in north Oxford. Jack visited her nearly every day, but she was scarcely coherent and could be very grumpy and blasphemous. All Jack could do was suffer and pray.

On January 12, 1951, Janie Moore died of influenza. Warren reacted by getting so drunk that he could not attend the funeral. Some months later her husband, "The Beast," died in County Wicklow, Ireland.

Jack described the following year as the happiest of his life, even though it began with his failure to be elected Professor of Poetry at Oxford. He planned a holiday in Ireland with Arthur at Crawfordsburn, about ten miles from Belfast, near home. "I now know how a bottle of champagne feels when the wire has at last been taken off the cork and it's allowed to go POP!"

In spite of the events in both his personal and professional life, Jack's academic work continued. In 1944 he had been commissioned to write a volume in the Oxford History of English Literature series (which had the unfortunate acronym OHEL, causing Jack to refer to it as the "O Hell"). This volume, *English Literature in the Sixteenth Century*, occupied much of his time. His honesty prevented him from giving an opinion on a book he had not read, and so his reading, much of it in the Duke Humphrey room of the Bodleian Library, was immense. The first draft was completed in 1952, revisions, bibliography, and chronological tables took another year, and the volume appeared in the fall of 1954.

It was—and is—a remarkable work. He refused to subscribe to accepted opinions, to conventional orthodoxy, to hypocrisy, and to literary fashions, and set out his own opinions in a fearless and forthright manner. What is remarkable is that they were all *his* opinions—there was nothing secondhand about his sometimes startling views. For example, in a summary of the first chapter, "New Learning and New Ignorance," he writes:

> I think I have succeeded in demonstrating that the Renaissance, as generally understood, never existed.... There was nothing whatever humane about humanism. The humanists were intolerant and Philistine. There is not a humanist philosopher of any importance.... I have given only five pages to Donne. His place is that of a minor poet.

After putting the humanists in their place, Jack interprets the Puritans anew, asserting that they were not morose killjoys, terrified at the prospect of hellfire; on the contrary, they were full of joy, feeling blessed by their belief in salvation by grace. The teaching of Calvin "was the creed of progressives, even of revolutionaries.... The fierce young don, the learned lady, the courtier with his intellectual leanings were likely to be Calvinists. He was a dazzling figure, a man born to be the idol of revolutionary intellectuals."

With such unconventional and independent judgments, the book could not be expected to receive only favorable reviews, and it didn't. Jack was somewhat disappointed. Reviews in newspapers and magazines were mostly good, while the reviewers in the academic journals usually objected to Jack's radical approach and his reassessment of humanism, of which, it must be said, they considered themselves heirs.

The book was exciting and stimulating if, in the opinion of Oxford tutors, dangerous. Its popularity has increased rather than diminished, and it seems to be the best-selling volume in the series.

In this same period of turmoil at the Kilns and of profound academic writing, Jack was also engaged in writing the Narnia stories. *The Lion, the Witch and the Wardrobe* was published in the fall of 1950, and a new Narnia book was published every following year until 1956. *The Voyage of the "Dawn Treader"* was written in two months, January and February; *The Horse and His Boy* was finished by the end of July, and *The Silver Chair* was begun in the Christmas vacation of 1950 and finished by the beginning of March 1951. The remaining two volumes, *The Magician's Nephew* and *The Last Battle*, were written more slowly and were finished in 1953.

As each volume of the Chronicles of Narnia appeared, the reviews became more uniformly approving and the response of children overwhelming. The frightening incidents in the books are not so frightening that children cannot enjoy them, and Jack was such an excellent storyteller that they take the moralizing in their stride.

Jack wrote, "All my seven Narnian books, and my three science fiction books, began with seeing pictures in my head," pictures of a wide variety of human, animal, and mythological creatures. His imaginative world was both natural and supernatural, with continuing interaction between the two. Together they constitute one world, a world filled with diversity celebrating with joy its own diversity.

The Chronicles accept without question what Jack called the Tao, the traditional moral code, although they do not preach it but simply exemplify it. They also freed children's minds from what adults call "realism," for it had been fashionable to insist that children's stories should be grounded in the social and economic circumstances of their readers. This was the political correctness of socialistic times, when energies were supposed to be harnessed to an agenda for social reform and not dissipated in fancy and fantasy.

Underlying them all is Jack's own theological position, his Christianity. Bede Griffiths wrote:

> The figure of Aslan tells us more of how Lewis understood the nature of God than anything else he wrote. It has all his hidden power and majesty and awesomeness which Lewis associated with God, but also all his glory and the tenderness and even the humor which he believed belonged to him, so that children could run up to him and throw their arms around him and kiss him. There is nothing of "dark imagination" or fear of devils and hell in this. It is "mere Christianity."

1951–1963

The living of a Christian life was a full-time occupation for Jack. His personal devotions, although little publicized, were remarkable for their extent and intensity. He completed his volume in the Oxford History of English Literature, continued Narnia, wrote Surprised by Joy, *and became professor at Cambridge, and he met Joy Davidman Gresham. They shared intelligence and humor as well as a deep sense of Christian commitment, and they fell in love and were married. That Jack could share, marry, and fall in love is a testament to his Christian maturity. His life was fulfilled and he knew it. Joy's death, after a period of intense grief, only confirmed his spirituality, and his own death was softened by the love that he and his brother had for each other.*

In 1955, *Surprised by Joy: The Shape of My Early Life* appeared. Jack had been working on it since at least 1948. It had taken so long to write simply because the pattern of his life became clearer only as Jack reflected on it over time. As an autobiography in the sense of a recital of all of the events and influences in a life it is less than satisfactory, but that is not what it pretended to be. Jack told the story of his conversion, and for that story his earlier years are more important than his later life. He was ruthlessly selective, and the book confines itself "strictly to business and omit[s] everything else (however important by ordinary biographical standards) which seems, at that stage, irrelevant."

The initial public reaction was less than positive. The reviewers were disappointed—some because there was no salacious detail, some because it was not an autobiography, some because it did not try to convert anyone, nor even tell them how to convert themselves. Jack had not given them a lot to go on. Janie Moore did not get mentioned, his childhood writings are slighted, and there is little about his own sexual-sadistic obsessions. As Humphrey Havard said, the book should have been called *Suppressed by Jack.*

It is, however, a fascinating story and constituted a milestone in Jack's life. He wrote it partly to get free "from the past as past by apprehending it as structure." It tells, with incredible honesty and clarity, how Jack was surprised by Joy—and by God.

After the death of Janie Moore in 1951, Jack's freedom increased. Professionally, he was no longer tied to Oxford, since he could move, and he could associate more closely with women, such as poet Ruth Pitter, if he chose to do so.

In January 1950 Jack had received the first of many letters from an American woman, Joy Davidman Gresham, who in 1952 arrived in England with the purpose of seeing him. Joy Davidman was born of a Jewish family in 1915 and educated at Hunter College and

Columbia University in New York City. She became a Communist in 1938, and her book of free verse, *Letter to a Comrade*, won the Yale Poetry Award that same year. Although she had taken up teaching English in a high school, she decided to try to make her living as a writer and resigned. In 1940 she published a novel, *Anya*. Attending a Communist party meeting in 1942, Joy met a fellow Communist, William Lindsay Gresham. He was charming but unstable; six years older than Joy, he was divorced, an atheist, and an alcoholic. But they were married shortly thereafter and had two sons, David (born 1944) and Douglas (born 1945). The idealism that attracted them both to the Communist party was eroded by internal politics and blatant dishonesty, and they soon left the party.

They lived on their farm in New York State, near Staatsburg, with Bill working as a magazine editor in New York City. One day he phoned Joy to say that he thought he was going mad. He could no longer put up with his office and yet was not able to return home to Staatsburg. Where was he to go? He hung up and then simply disappeared.

Joy was beside herself, unable to find her husband anywhere. "All my defenses—the walls of arrogance and cocksureness and self-love behind which I had hid from God—went down momentarily. And God came in." She became aware that God loved her and found herself kneeling in prayer. She was a Christian.

Bill reappeared in due course and was deeply moved by Joy's experience, so much so that they began to study theology. In 1948 Bill attended the local Presbyterian church with Joy, and he prayed for release from his alcoholism. For three years he was a teetotaler.

Joy had been deeply impressed with the writings of C. S. Lewis and, after making inquiries of Father Victor White and Chad Walsh (whose *C. S. Lewis: Apostle to the Skeptics* had appeared in 1949), decided to write to him in an attempt to settle some of her religious doubts.

Joy wanted to visit Jack in England but could not leave her family. In 1952 Joy's cousin, Renee Pierce, suddenly arrived on their doorstep. She was five years younger than Joy and had been living in Florida with her two children and an alcoholic husband from whom she was now trying to escape. Staatsburg became her secret refuge. After a time, she offered to take care of Bill, David, and Douglas while Joy went to London.

Joy needed to talk with someone she trusted and had decided that Jack was that person. She was concerned about her marriage as well as the general shape of her life, and she needed advice about the book she was writing on the Ten Commandments. She arrived in London in August 1952.

She wrote to him from London, inviting him to lunch with her and Phyllis Williams, her London friend, at the Eastgate Hotel in Oxford in early September. Jack agreed and later invited them to lunch in his rooms at Magdalen. Warren was invited but backed out, and, since Jack was shy around women, George Sayer was asked to make up the fourth. After their Magdalen lunch and a tour of the College, Jack decided he liked Joy and after more lunches invited her to be a guest at the Kilns for two weeks. She accompanied Jack and Warren on walks, drinking beer and eating bread and cheese in pubs.

Joy stayed on in London, but she did not see Jack again until December 6, 1952. Jack gave her a copy of *A Preface to Paradise Lost*, in which Joy wrote a poem:

> I read it over fish and chips
> And now I read it with my beer—

Of wandering Trojans and their ships
And lightless hell aflame with fear;
As Housman said there's power in malt
And likely it's not Milton's fault—
But Jack can do more than Milton can
To justify God's ways to man!

That Christmas, Joy spent two weeks at the Kilns with Jack and Warren, cooking their turkey dinner and enjoying long walks and pub crawls. They read each others' unpublished writings, and Jack wrote a preface to Joy's latest book, *Smoke on the Mountain: An Interpretation of the Ten Commandments*.

Towards the end of her stay, a letter arrived from Bill Gresham, saying that he and Renee, her cousin, were in love and asking Joy for a divorce.

Joy shared the letter with Jack. He said that she should divorce Bill, but Joy was initially opposed to this on religious grounds. She later changed her mind, went back to the United States in January 1953, arranged a divorce (which was not final until August 1954), and returned to England in April 1953 with her two sons. She lived in Belsize Park, London, and the boys were enrolled in Dane Court, a well-established prep school, for which Jack paid the fees through his charitable trust.

The next December, Joy and the two boys were invited to spend four days at the Kilns. Jack enjoyed it but found the boys exhausting. Before they left, he gave the boys the typescript of *The Horse and His Boy* and promised that he would dedicate it to them when it was published—which he did.

Between that visit and August 1955 Jack did not see much of Joy. Once or twice he was in London, and she was invited to Oxford on a few occasions, to lunch and to meet some of his friends. She was not liked by most of them. With all her intelligence, she was considered too outspoken, vulgar, and abrasive. Her virtues—her kindness, generosity, humor, and affection—were hidden by her brusque New York manner. Many of Jack's friends knew little or nothing about his friendship with Joy, and even those who did know had little understanding of the kind of person Joy was. They were also, almost on principle, protective of Jack.

A group of Jack's admirers at Cambridge persuaded the English Faculty there to create a professorship of Medieval and Renaissance studies for him. He was deeply affected by the kindness and respect this showed, but he was not sure about leaving Oxford, which he had entered as a student thirty-seven years before. He loved Oxford, and he could not sell the Kilns in order to buy a house in Cambridge, since he and Warren only had a life interest in it. Furthermore, there was no reason for Warren to move. And if Jack left, would Warren collapse?

Cambridge offered a solution. He would live in Cambridge from Monday afternoon through Friday but could spend his weekends and all vacations in Oxford or anywhere he wanted. To this Jack agreed and he moved to Cambridge in January 1955.

His Cambridge inaugural lecture (published as *De Descriptione Temporum*) was delivered on November 29, 1954, to an audience so large that a party of his Oxford friends had to be seated on the platform behind him—the hall was full to overflowing. Unbeknownst to Jack, Joy Gresham was among those present. She wrote that the occasion had "as much fuss . . . as a coronation." The theme of the inaugural was Jack's belief that the great divide in culture and civilization had occurred between the time of Jane Austen and the present day. It was the machine that had altered "man's place in nature" and provided the modern myth that new is better. Not without some irony, Jack described himself as a dinosaur, one of the Old Western Men, which caught the imagination of many in the audience.

Jack had rooms at Magdalene College, Cambridge, but they were paneled in dark wood and sparsely furnished. They needed attention, in spite of Jack's ascetic leanings, and he obviously had to vacate his rooms at Magdalen, Oxford. In all of this Joy was a tremendous encouragement, and she came to help him with the actual move.

Jack found Cambridge quieter and smaller than Oxford. He felt more relaxed in Magdalene and was treated with both courtesy and friendliness. He had plenty of time to write, but to his utter dismay he could not find an idea to write about. No pictures presented themselves to his mind. Jack had nothing to say.

Joy, when she found out that Jack "couldn't get a really good idea for a book," affectionately tried to help him. They sat down and talked or, as she put it, "kicked a few ideas around until one came to life. Then we had another whiskey each and bounced it back and forth between us." It did not take long for this to produce results, and by the end of the following evening Jack had written the first chapter of a book that was well on the way to completion by month's end. It was published as *Till We Have Faces*.

Joy later admitted in a letter that she could not "write one tenth as well as Jack" but "I can tell him how to write more like himself! He is now about three-quarters of the way through his new book . . . and says he finds my advice indispensable."

In August 1955, Joy, the two boys, and Sambo the cat, moved from London to 10 Old High Street, Headington. Jack insisted on paying the rent.

The next month, Jack was on holiday in Ireland and discussed with Arthur Greeves his relationship with Joy. He was considering marrying her in a registry office, that is, in a civil ceremony, so that she and the boys could stay in England. It would not be a "real" marriage: "The 'reality' would be, from my point of view, adultery and therefore mustn't happen. (An easy resolution when one doesn't in the least want it!)"

The following April, Jack told George Sayer that he had decided to go through a civil marriage ceremony with Joy. It would be simply a legality, a pure formality, and should be kept secret lest people misunderstood. Somewhat unrealistically, perhaps, Jack insisted that this civil marriage would not alter the relationship with Joy. He admitted that he liked and admired her, but he denied that he was in love with her. The marriage took place on April 23, 1956. Even Warren did not know about it.

In June 1956 Joy was suddenly and unexpectedly taken ill. She was diagnosed with fibrositis. Then, at the end of October, Joy suffered a fall. She was taken to the hospital, where it was discovered that she was suffering from cancer. The left femur was weakened and had been broken in her fall, she had a malignant tumor in her left breast as well as secondary sites in her shoulder and right leg. During the next month she had three operations to remove the cancer.

Joy's illness and suffering made Jack aware of his love for her. Writing to Arthur, Jack said,

> If she gets over this bout and emerges from hospital she will no longer be able
> to live alone so she must come and live here. That means (in order to avoid scan-

dal) that our marriage must shortly be published. W[arren] has written to Janie and the Ewarts to tell them I am getting married, and I didn't want the news to take you by surprise.

On December 24, 1956, the London *Times* carried a notice:

> A marriage has taken place between Professor C. S. Lewis of Magdalene College, Cambridge, and Mrs. Joy Gresham, now a patient in the Churchill Hospital, Oxford. It is requested that no letters be sent.

Jack and Joy both wanted an ecclesiastical ceremony, but although Jack may have come to believe that Joy's marriage to Bill Gresham was invalid, since Bill's first wife was still alive, and that she was therefore free to marry, the Bishop of Oxford said that the official Church of England's position was otherwise and refused to give permission for any of the priests in his diocese to marry them.

To comfort Joy in her pain, Jack asked one of his former students, the Reverend Peter Bide, who had a reputation as a healer, to come and lay hands on her and pray for her. He was from another diocese, and during his visit they discussed the impediments to an ecclesiastical marriage ceremony. Bide agreed with Jack that it would be right to conduct a religious ceremony and promised to perform it the day after he had prayed for her recovery.

And so, on March 21, 1957, as Warren records in his diary,

> At 11 A.M., we all gathered in Joy's room at the Wingfield—Bide, J., sister, and myself, communicated, and the marriage was celebrated. I found it heartrending, and especially J.'s eagerness for the pitiable consolation of dying under the same roof as J.; though to feel pity for anyone so magnificently brave as Joy is almost an insult. She is to be moved here [the Kilns] next week and will sleep in the common room, with a resident hospital nurse. . . . There seems little left to hope but that there may be no pain at the end.

Joy returned to the Kilns, and what seemed to be a miraculous transformation took place. Within a month, by the end of April 1957, Joy could move about the house. But by midsummer Jack himself was suffering great pain due to osteoporosis. Jack wrote:

> The intriguing thing was that while I (for no discernible reason) was losing the calcium from my bones, Joy, who needed it much more, was gaining it in hers. One dreams of a Charles Williams substitution! Well, never was gift more gladly given; but one must not be fanciful.

Jack, his weakened spine protected by a surgical brace, continued in pain and at times could scarcely walk.

As Joy continued to improve she became more active, doing secretarial work and helping Warren with his writings about 17th-century France, a subject in which, to his surprise and delight, she was both interested and knowledgeable. Warren had made a careful study of France under Louis XIV and in 1953 had published *The Splendid Century*, followed by *The Sunset of the Splendid Century* (1955). He later published five more contributions to the field of French history.

Joy was well for all of 1958, walking, with a limp, for distances of up to a mile. She investigated the estate and had flower beds dug and planted. She also improved the

Kilns—the exterior was painted, the interior redecorated, and the radiators reconnected to a functioning boiler. Jack, who had always lived economically and, like his father, was afraid of bankruptcy, was not comfortable spending a large amount of money on such things as curtains, carpets, and furniture, so there was a limit to the improvements Joy could make.

By April 1958 Jack's osteoporosis was much better, and he asked his doctor if a man of his age and health could have sexual intercourse, to which the answer was, yes, "if you are careful and sensible." The marriage of Jack and Joy was consummated at this time, and Joy told a correspondent that Jack was a "wonderful lover." And Jack told Nevill Coghill in the summer of 1958, "I never expected to have, in my sixties, the happiness that passed me by in my twenties."

That summer they went to Ireland by plane. It was Jack's first flight, and he prayed throughout takeoff but was enchanted by being in and above the clouds. They were driven to Crawfordsburn and later to Donegal by Arthur Greeves.

Jack gave George and Moira Sayer the impression of a very happily married man, in love with someone he could respect and admire; he said, in fact, "intellectually I often feel her inferior." Jack and Joy seemed to accept their equality quite naturally and had no need to pretend to be what they were not.

Jack's friends were not as confident about his marriage as he himself was. In the opinion of Tolkien, "a strange marriage" to a "sick and domineering woman," together with Warren's alcoholism, was too much for Jack.

In June and July of the following year (1959) they vacationed again in Ireland. Joy seemed very well, but a routine checkup at the hospital after their return showed that the cancer was back. Even with drugs and radiation therapy the outlook was not good:

> The doctors say there is some hope of her being able to live without pain for a year or two. Well, we've enjoyed the fruits of a miracle. I am not sure it would be right to ask for another. Nor do I think it would be given if I did. They tell me that there is no example on record of anyone who was granted the same miracle twice.

So wrote Jack in November. Joy herself was under no illusions. With her usual sense of humor, grim though it was, she wrote, "I've got so many cancers at work on me that I expect them to start organizing a union."

In spite of pain and unpleasant medical side effects, Joy followed the usual pattern of their lives with both cheerfulness and courage. She had always wanted to go to Greece, and so, in April 1960, she and Jack went on an eleven-day trip with Roger and June Lancelyn Green. They saw all the famous sites and went to a Greek Orthodox cathedral for a service—but nearly "lapsed into paganism in Attica." At Delphi "it was hard not to pray to Apollo the Healer." Both Jack and Joy had read about Greece and its heritage for a very long time, and they were delighted at being able to see it. The trip was a huge success.

But Joy was not doing well and after their return had to go the hospital frequently. She had breast surgery, with better results than expected, and was home on May 2, although confined to a wheelchair. On June 20 she was taken ill again and went to the Acland Nursing Home—for the last time, Warren feared. But he was wrong. Joy returned to the Kilns on June 27 and went out to dinner with Jack on July 3. She died on July 13. Jack wrote:

At quarter past six on Wednesday morning, my brother, who slept over her, was awakened by her screaming and ran down to her. I got the doctor who fortunately was at home, and he arrived before seven and gave her a heavy shot. At half past one I took her into the hospital in an ambulance. She was conscious for the short remainder of her life, and in very little pain, thanks to drugs; and died peacefully about 10:15 the same night.

In *A Grief Observed*, Jack wrote, "She said not to me but to the chaplain, 'I am at peace with God.' She smiled but not at me. Poi si torno all' eterna fontana." But she had already said to Jack, "You have made me happy." (The quotation is from the *Divina Commedia;* Beatrice, seeing Dante for the last time, looked down on him and smiled, "then turned back to the Eternal Fountain." And so Joy turned from Jack toward God.)

His marriage to Joy taught Jack that Coventry Patmore was right: "Heaven becomes very intelligible and attractive when it is discerned to be—Woman." It was a Christian marriage, and Jack felt that through it he had matured and achieved manhood.

After Joy's death, Jack prayed that God would take away the lifelong powerful sexual drive that had plagued him, and he later told Dom Bede Griffiths that he had indeed been freed of it.

The three books Jack wrote during his marriage to Joy all owe something to her and to their relationship.

The first is *Till We Have Faces*, a novel published both in England (1956) and the United States (1957). It is Jack's final attempt to retell the classical Greek myth of Cupid and Psyche, with which he had struggled on at least three occasions as an undergraduate. Jack introduced a new character as the narrator of the story, Orual, queen of Glome, the ugly sister of Psyche. Although she is passionate and longs to love and to be loved, her jealousy and possessiveness preclude it. The plot tells how she is redeemed.

The title, which is not the one that Jack originally proposed, comes from Orual's speech almost at the end of the book:

Often when he was teaching me to write in Greek the Fox would say, "Child, to say the very thing you really mean, the whole of it, nothing more or less or other than what you really mean; that's the whole art and joy of words." A glib saying. When the time comes to you at which you will be forced at last to utter the speech which has lain at the center of your soul for years, which you have, all that time, idiot-like, been saying over and over, you'll not talk about joy of words. I saw well why the gods do not speak to us openly, nor let us answer. Till that word can be dug out of us, why should they hear the babble that we think we mean? How can they meet us face to face, till we have faces?

After discussing the book with Jack as it was being written, Joy had edited and typed it. Its reception, however, was disappointing. Reviewers praised it—"a masterwork," "love is . . . given wings again"—but the public did not buy it. Later it became much more popular, and Jack was in two minds about which novel was his best—*Till We Have Faces* or *Perelandra*.

The second book, *Reflections on the Psalms,* appeared in the fall of 1958. It was written at the suggestion of Jack's friend, the theologian Austin Farrer, and was strongly supported by Joy, who again offered to edit and type the manuscript. Much of its content was deeply discussed with both of them during the summer vacation of 1957.

Prepublication orders ran high, but the reviews were lukewarm, mostly because it was not a work of scholarship—which it explicitly said it wasn't. In the preface, which he suspected the reviewers had not read, Jack says that he is writing "as one amateur to another."

The third book was *The Four Loves*. It originated in a request for some tape recordings by an American Christian organization. After discussions with Joy he agreed and chose the subject that was occupying his thoughts and that would "bring in nearly the whole of Christian ethics." It was contained in the four Greek words *storge, philia, eros,* and *agape*, translated as Affection, Friendship, Eros, and Charity. After the talks had been recorded, it was objected that Jack had brought sex into them, at which he laughed and said, "How can anyone talk about Eros without bringing it in?"

Jack had retained the right to turn the talks into a book, which he did by midsummer 1959, and it was published in March 1960. The book was agreeably reviewed, although some reviewers did not realize that it was a work of Christian apologetics and seemed oblivious of the fact that, for Christians, God is love.

Shortly after this, Jack was invited to join a committee to revise the translation of the Psalms as they appeared in the *Book of Common Prayer*. Later his opinions were sought on specific points of translation in the New Testament of the New English Bible, which appeared in 1961.

After the three books written while Joy was alive, Jack's next book was *A Grief Observed*. The grief was his own and only he had fully observed it. He had lost Joy, and with her all of his creativity; he was unable even to think or to write or to pray. He had no words of his own but could only repeat the conventional and often childish prayers that everybody knew—something he had never done before. This was clearly an impediment to his spirituality, something that Joy herself would not have wanted, and so he began a close analytic study of his grief, what it was like and how it worked in him. The intense search for understanding helped him control his grief.

He discovered that Joy was more real to him now than in life—her death was "not the interruption of the dance, but the next figure"—and that he did not need to remember her how she was, but to see her, mystically, as she is. One night Jack had an experience of Joy that was "just the impression of her mind momentarily facing my own," and he says, banishing all sentimentality, "there was an extreme and cheerful intimacy." In his typical, robust way Jack said, "I know the two great commandments and I'd better get on with them." And he felt close to God again.

A Grief Observed was published by Faber and Faber in 1961 under the pseudonym N. W. Clerk. Jack had published poems in *Punch* and elsewhere with the initials N. W., which stood for Nat Whilk, Anglo-Saxon for "I know not who," that is, anonymous. The only person besides Lewis's agent who was told of the book's existence was Roger Green. It did not sell very well until it was reissued posthumously under Jack's own name in 1964. Then it found its public, the public for whom Jack had written the book: the bereaved.

Jack was back in Cambridge in October 1960, three months after Joy's death. He continued to follow his usual routine, traveling to the Kilns on weekends and meeting friends every Monday morning. The changes in his life were not obvious, although he depended on his friends more; he sometimes took the slow train—the "Cantab Crawler"—to Cambridge, but he was more often driven there.

He continued to write. In the study of literature, Jack was opposed to the reading of commentaries and criticism before, and even instead of, the works themselves, and his next academic book was *An Experiment in Criticism*, published by Cambridge University Press in 1961. It was not as polemical as most of his critical books, but it is probably the most influential, although it was not very well received. He argues for looking at books from the point of view of the reader:

> Literature enlarges our being by admitting us to experiences not our own. . . . in reading great literature I become a thousand men and yet remain myself. . . . Here, as in worship, in love, in moral action, and in knowing, I transcend myself: and am never more myself than when I do.

Within five years *An Experiment in Criticism* was referred to as "a now classic broadside."

In June 1961 Jack became ill, and after belatedly consulting his doctor he was diagnosed with a seriously enlarged prostate. Surgery was scheduled, but it turned out that Jack's health was not good enough to withstand an operation. A strict regimen was prescribed, and he agreed to all but one item.

> If I [gave up smoking], I know that I should be unbearably bad-tempered. What an infliction on my friends. Better to die cheerfully with the aid of a little tobacco, than to live disagreeably and remorseful without.

But he was forbidden to return to Cambridge in the fall of 1961.

During that fall and the ensuing winter Jack rested and read voraciously, but he needed blood transfusions ("For the first time I feel some sympathy for Dracula. He must have led a miserable life"). While his humor remained, he found consolation in religious experiences and being close to Joy. He also took satisfaction in putting his papers and lectures in order, and out of this activity he produced what was later published as *The Discarded Image* (1964).

He gradually improved and in April 1962 returned to Cambridge, but he knew inwardly that his health would not improve enough to undergo the vital surgery. He continued to write and sent the manuscript of *Letters to Malcolm: Chiefly on Prayer* to Geoffrey Bles, his publisher. As it turned out, it would be published posthumously.

Late in June Jack was feeling very weak and needed long periods of rest. He was suffering from renal failure—his kidneys were permanently damaged—and, after admission to the Acland Nursing Home, he had a heart attack on July 16. It seemed that he was dying, and the next day, while in a coma, was given the sacrament of extreme unction. Strangely, immediately after the anointing he woke up, opened his eyes, and asked for a cup of tea, as if everything was normal. His condition improved, his heart became steady, and it seemed that he was out of immediate danger.

Warren knew nothing of all this. He had gone on holiday to Ireland and, getting drunk again, was in the hospital of Our Lady of Lourdes at Drogheda. As Jack suspected, he had not opened a single letter with an Oxford postmark.

Jack returned to the Kilns with a nurse, Alec Ross, in early August. A thirty-one-year-old American teacher, Walter Hooper, who attended a summer school at Exeter College from July 1 to August 9, 1963, volunteered to help with correspondence, and Jack spent the mornings writing letters. Lunch (supposedly, but not actually, low protein) was followed by a nap until tea time, about four o'clock. Then he read or wrote until dinner and went to bed about ten o'clock. In spite of the doctor's orders he still smoked and drank his strong tea.

He did not expect to live long and wrote a letter of resignation to Cambridge in early August 1963. Hooper left his lodgings in Oxford before the end of August to go back to the United States, and Jack was without secretarial help (as he says in a letter dated August 30) until the final return of Warren from Ireland.

Before the end of September Warren arrived, and although he found it hard to face his brother's impending death, he settled down and enjoyed with Jack the companionship they had known in earlier days. Warren wrote that they talked of the past,

> cheerfully reminiscent, but not such as will bear repetition for it was only of long-forgotten incidents in our shared past. When such were recalled the old Jack, whimsical, witty, laughter-loving, would for a minute or two come back to life again and we would be almost gay together. In fact these were more often than not pleasant days, for as the end drew nearer, more and more did we recapture our old schoolboy technique of extracting the utmost from the last dregs of our holidays. It was only when I went to bed that the horrible fear recurred each night—shall I find him alive in the morning?

"Don't think I am not happy," Jack wrote in a letter. "I am re-reading the Iliad and enjoying it more than I have ever done." And in another letter, written to Jane Douglas in October 1963, he said, "Yes, autumn is really the best of the seasons: and I'm not sure that old age isn't the best part of life. But, of course, like autumn it doesn't *last*."

He did very little, occasionally going out for a drive with a friend. On Monday, November 18, he was well enough to visit the regular meeting at the Lamb and Flag. But over the next few days Jack found it difficult to keep awake (apparently the effect of uremia). On November 22, Warren reported,

> After lunch [Jack] fell asleep in his chair: I suggested that he would be more comfortable in bed, and he went there. At four I took in his tea and found him drowsy but comfortable. Our few words then were the last: at five-thirty I heard a crash and ran in to find him lying unconscious at the foot of his bed. He ceased to breathe some three or four minutes later.

He would have been sixty-five the following week.

Jack's funeral at Headington Quarry church was attended by a few close personal friends, including George Sayer, Owen Barfield, A. C. Harwood, the Tolkiens, father and son, Austin Farrer, Colin Hardie, Humphrey Havard, John Lawlor, Peter Bayley, J. H. Dundas-Grant, Maureen and her husband Leonard Blake, Peter Bide, Douglas Gresham, Leonard and Maude Miller (who had been housekeepers at the Kilns), and Fred Paxford. Magdalen College and Oxford University were also represented. Warren was not there; he could not bear the anguish and had drunk himself into a stupor.

Jack's estate was not large—about £38,000—because he had given away or put into the Agape Fund most of his literary earnings, which were, of course, considerable. His will named Barfield and Harwood as executors and trustees of the estate. After a few legacies, the remaining assets were left in trust for the completion of the education of David and Douglas Gresham, then in trust to Warren for life, and then to David and Douglas.

Epilogue

Around 1930, Jack had written a short poem:

Set on the soul's acropolis the reason stands
A virgin, arm'd, commercing with celestial light,
And he who sins against her has defiled his own
Virginity: no cleansing makes his garment white;
So clear is reason. But how dark, imagining,
Warm, dark, obscure and infinite, daughter of Night:
Dark is her brow, the beauty of her eyes with sleep
Is loaded, and her pains are long, and her delight.
Tempt not Athene. Wound not in her fertile pains
Demeter, nor rebel against her mother-right.
Oh who will reconcile in me both maid and mother,
Who make in me a concord of the depth and height?
Who make imagination's dim exploring touch
Ever report the same as intellectual sight?
Then could I truly say, and not deceive,
Then wholly say, that I BELIEVE.

This search for concord, this longing for reconciliation, is at the heart of the story of Jack's life. The poem was written when he understood what he longed for—reconciliation—but before it had been achieved.

In his early years, while his reason was developing, his honesty tried to keep it pure. His imagining was dark, however, and became inhabited by ghoulish fantasies. Fearful, he rebelled against imagination's "mother-right," trying to deny its power and validity. And yet, there was always Joy to remind him, to save him from abandoning Demeter altogether.

By 1926, Athene had brought him to theism—which was as far as she could take him—but the 1931 conversations with Tolkien and Dyson about myth were needed to complete the understanding of imagination toward which he had been moving. Imagination was the only valid way to reality, and reality was embodied in imagination's works, especially in myths.

From then on there grew in him "a concord of the depth and height," signaled finally by his understanding in *Surprised by Joy* and by his love for and marriage to Joy Davidman Gresham. Faith and love had finally reconciled reason and imagination. He could "wholly say, that I BELIEVE."

A

"Abecedarium Philosophicum"

The Oxford Magazine. 52 (November 30, 1933): 298 (with Owen Barfield). An earlier version of this poem appears in the Lewis Family Papers, IX: 164–65.

This bit of silliness is a *tour de force* in which Lewis and **Owen Barfield** collaborated to write a poem with lines dedicated to each letter of the alphabet. Famous philosophers or philosophical ideas serve as the jokes of each sentence.

Don W. King
Montreat College

The Abolition of Man

Riddell Memorial Lectures, Fifteenth Series. London: Oxford University Press, 1943.

The Abolition of Man is perhaps the best defense of **natural law** to be published in the 20th century. The book is outstanding not because its ideas are original but because it presents so clearly the common sense of the subject, brilliantly encapsulating the Western natural-law tradition in all its Greco-Roman and Judeo-Christian glory. Interestingly, Lewis's defense of objective morality here resonates not only with ideas from the giants of Western thought (including **Plato, Aristotle, Augustine,** and **Aquinas**), but also draws on the wisdom of the East, including Confucius and the sages of Hinduism.

The book originated during World War II when Lewis was asked by the University of Durham to present the Riddell Memorial Lectures. Lewis traveled to the city of Durham (and then further north to the village of Newcastle-upon-Tyne, where the lectures were actually delivered) with his brother **Warren Lewis** in February 1943. Warren recalled the journey with gratitude in his diary, noting that the trip was "a little oasis in the dreariness, and the first holiday we have shared since our last walk." The years since the start of the war had been bleak ones, and the brothers found welcome relief in what

Warren called their "jaunt together." Lewis's three lectures were delivered on the evenings of February 24, 25, and 26. They were published in book form the same year by Oxford University Press.

The Abolition of Man is divided into three essays. Essay one, "Men without Chests," indicts the modern attempt to debunk objective **virtues** and sentiments. According to Lewis, traditional moral theorists once believed that virtues such as courage and honor were true regardless of **culture**; these theorists also maintained that the purpose of **education** was to inculcate virtues in people by linking them to the proper emotions. This process of reinforcing virtue with emotion produced "sentiments" in people, supplying them with "chests" that safeguarded them from savagery. By debunking all sentiments as merely subjective, however, modern critics have generated "men without chests"— human beings who are unable to resist their basest appetites because they have been deprived of the very means of resistance. This situation makes civilization unsustainable according to Lewis. "We make men without chests and expect of them virtue and enterprise," he observed. "We castrate and bid the geldings be fruitful."

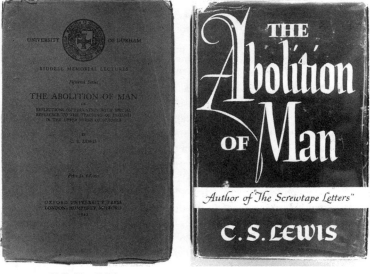

U.K. First Edition

Lewis's critique in this first essay focuses largely on the moral relativism implicit in two English textbooks, neither of which Lewis referred to by name in order to spare the authors the embarrassment of being pilloried by him in print. The first text, which Lewis calls "The Green Book" by "Gaius and Titius," is in reality *The Control of Language* (1940) by Alex King and Martin Ketley. Lewis probably called this volume "The Green Book" because its cover is green; the reason he referred to its authors by the names of Gaius and Titius is more obscure. There are several figures from antiquity with those names, but it seems likely that Lewis chose the names because they were used in ancient literature for illustrative purposes, much like "Smith and Jones" are employed in English today. The second English text Lewis attacked in this chapter is cited as being authored by "Orbilius." The real title and author of this second work is *The Reading and Writing of English* (1936) by E. G. Biaggini. Lewis's identification of Biaggini as "Orbilius" is likely a reference to Orbilius Pupillus, an infamous grammarian known for inflicting beatings on the Roman poet Horace while teaching him Homer's *Odyssey*.

Lewis concluded his first essay in *The Abolition of Man* by launching his argument for the existence of an objective moral code that transcends time and culture. Lewis claimed that an honest study of different cultures, far from showing ethical confusion, indicates the existence of a universal moral code, which Lewis (drawing on ancient Chinese philosophy) called **"The Tao."** Lewis backed up his case for the Tao by supplying appendices that catalogue common moral maxims from civilizations around the world.

Lewis defended the existence of the Tao more fully in essay two of *The Abolition of Man* ("The Way"). His main point in this second essay is that those who deny the validity of moral judgments are usually self-contradictory because they cannot escape making moral judgments themselves. The only way for relativists to escape self-contradiction is to deny the existence of objective truth altogether and to claim that we create our own meaning by a sheer act of willpower. This was the solution offered by philosopher **Friedrich Nietzsche**, but it is a cure that may be worse than the disease, as Lewis points out in his third and final essay of the book.

That essay—"The Abolition of Man"—discusses the potential for tyranny in a world where the elites no longer believe in any sort of objective **truth**. If everything is simply reduced to a struggle for power, then there is no constraint on what societal elites might do to reshape society in their own image. The fundamental question in society becomes not "Which policy is more just?" but "Which group has the most power to impose its will on society?" Lewis sees this mentality as the wellspring of tyranny.

The main ideas in *The Abolition of Man* can be found throughout Lewis's other writings and lectures, especially those that date from the 1940s. In fact, Lewis's first talk on the BBC ("The Law of Human Nature," broadcast August 1941) dealt with natural law. The talk was published in 1942 in the collection titled **Broadcast Talks**, and it ultimately became the first chapter of **Mere Christianity**. Some time later, Lewis apparently worked on a speech covering much the same ground as the Riddell lectures, but for another audience; his text was published after his death as the essay **"On Ethics."** And on February 8, 1943 (only a couple of weeks before the Riddell lectures), Lewis presented a talk at the **Oxford Socratic Club** titled "If We Have Christ's Ethics, Does the Rest of the Christian Faith Matter?" which previewed part of the Riddell lectures by showing how Christianity's ethical teachings share considerable common ground with the moral teachings of other religious and philosophical traditions. During the summer of 1943, Lewis published **"The Poison of Subjectivism,"** an essay that is largely a synopsis of *The Abolition of Man*.

However, perhaps Lewis's most intriguing treatment of the ideas expressed in *The Abolition of Man* came in the novel *That Hideous Strength*. There Lewis depicted in fictional form the dire social consequences that follow from a Nietzschean **science** allied with the tools of government bureaucrats. In many respects, *That Hideous Strength* and *The Abolition of Man* are parallel books that ought to be read together. Written during the same period in Lewis's life, both books present the same critique of subjectivism, and Lewis himself advised readers of *That Hideous Strength* that they could find the message of that novel presented in nonfiction form in *The Abolition of Man*.

Lewis's interest in natural law continued to the end of his life. After World War II, his classic study on *English Literature in the Sixteenth Century* (1954) examined natural law and its relevance to **politics**. In chapter 7 of *The Discarded Image* (1964), Lewis discusses the conception of **reason** in the Medieval world, which includes the capacity of humans to rationally apprehend the first principles of morality. In *Studies on Words*

(1960, rev. ed. in 1967), Lewis explores themes relating to natural law in his essays on the words "Nature" and "Conscience and Conscious." Natural-law themes can also be found in the **Chronicles of Narnia**.

The Abolition of Man remains one of Lewis's most prophetic works, for the moral subjectivism that he predicted in the 1940s has come to pass with a vengeance, not only in Europe but in **America**. Such subjectivism was uncritically adopted by much of the social sciences, and it still undergirds much of modern economics, political science, **psychology**, and sociology. The denial of the old moral absolutes has paralleled a dramatic increase in the authority of government to plan people's lives down to the last detail. It has also led to a moral vacuum in many disciplines, opening the door to the postmodern claim (springing ultimately from Nietzsche) that people are free to create their own **reality** through a sheer act of the will.

John G. West, Jr.

Also See: Ethics and Morality, Good and Evil, Modernity

Bibliography

Aeschliman, Michael D. *The Restitution of Man: C. S. Lewis and the Case Against Scientism.* Grand Rapids, MI: Eerdmans, 1983.

Bentley, Eric. *The Cult of the Superman.* Gloucester, MA: Peter Smith, 1969.

Hooper, Walter. *C. S. Lewis: A Companion and Guide.* San Francisco: HarperSanFrancisco, 1996.

Lewis, Warren. *Brothers and Friends: The Diaries of Major Warren Hamilton Lewis.* Clyde S. Kilby and Marjorie Lamp Mead (eds). San Francisco: Harper and Row, 1982.

West, John G., Jr. "Finding the Permanent in the Political: C. S. Lewis as a Political Thinker." *Permanent Things.* Andrew Tadie and Michael Macdonald (eds). Grand Rapids, MI: Eerdmans, 1996.

_____. "C. S. Lewis and the Materialist Menace," lecture published by Discovery Institute, Seattle, 1996.

Wolfe, Gregory. "The Abolition of Man Revisited: College Textbooks in the Social Sciences." *The University Bookman.* Summer 1982: 75–94.

Above the Smoke and Stir (Letter)

The Times Literary Supplement. (14 July 1945): 331.

Lewis attempted to reconcile the spirit's seemingly contradictory origins in **Milton**'s *Comus* as being both from the "broad fields of the sky" and the gardens of Hesperus. Lewis pointed out the general consensus that *Comus* bears a relationship to the Platonic theology of Milton's day. He also found some assistance in understanding this matter in Henry More's *Immortality of the Soul.*

Marjorie L. Mead
The Marion E. Wade Center

Above the Smoke and Stir (Letter)

The Times Literary Supplement. (29 September 1945): 463.

B. A. Wright disputed (*TLS,* 4 August 1945, 367) that Henry More would have been a source of instruction for **Milton** in writing *Comus* (see previous letter), and offered other more obvious classical sources such as **Plato** and Plutarch. Lewis's reply corrected the erroneous impression that he believed More's work to be a source for *Comus,* since it was not published until twenty-two years later. He also agrees that Mr. Wright's suggestion of Plato's *Phaedo* as a possible source for the mythological machinery of the poem is worth considering. Lewis said, however, that he is less concerned with the source of Milton's machinery than he is with how seriously Milton viewed it given his Christian faith. B. A. Wright responded once again (*TLS,* 27 October 1945, 511), this time disagreeing with Lewis that the *Phaedo* is inconsistent with Christian theology and further maintaining that *Comus* is a genuinely Platonic poem derived from Milton's own understanding of Plato and not based on contemporary Neoplatonism.

Marjorie L. Mead
The Marion E. Wade Center

Bernard Acworth (1885–1963)

A decorated World War I submariner and a pioneer in the development of sonar, Bernard Acworth founded Britain's Evolution Protest Movement (1935) and published books criticizing **evolution**. It is not known when Acworth and C. S. Lewis first met, but the earliest of the ten surviving letters from Lewis to Acworth show that a warm **friendship** already existed in 1944, with Acworth sometimes staying with Lewis when he was in **Oxford**. In their earliest correspondence, Lewis stated his willingness to accept any theory that does not contradict the fact that "Man has fallen from the state of innocence in which he was created." By 1951, however, he had begun to believe that Acworth might be right, that evolution was "the central and radical lie in the whole web of falsehood that now governs our lives." But that same year he politely declined to write a preface for one of Acworth's books, pointing out that a "popular Apologist" had to be careful because so many people were looking for "things that might discredit him."

Mike Perry

Bibliography

Acworth, Bernard. *The Progress: The Tragedy of Evolution.* London: Rich & Cowan, 1934.

Ferngren, Mary, and Ronald Numbers. "C. S. Lewis on Creation and Evolution: The Acworth Letters, 1944–1960." *Perspectives on Science and the Christian Faith.* 48 (March 1996): 28–33.

Numbers, Ronald L. *The Creationists.* New York: Knopf, 1992: 145–47, 153.

"Adam at Night"

Punch. 216 (May 11, 1949): 510 (under the pseudonym Nat Whilk). Revised and retitled "The Adam at Night" and reprinted in *Poems* and *Collected Poems.*

This poem considers how Adam had never slept before **Eve** was formed from him. Free from **sin**, Adam could lie awake at night and commune directly with the earth and the stars above him.

Don W. King
Montreat College

"The Adam Unparadised"

See entry on "A Footnote to Pre-History"

"Addison"

Essays on the Eighteenth Century Presented to David Nichol Smith. Oxford: Clarendon Press, 1945: 1–14. Reprinted in *Selected Literary Essays.*

Lewis's essay on 18th-century writer Joseph Addison (1672–1719) is found in *Selected Literary Essays.* Addison is primarily noted for his literary and sociopolitical essays in the journals *The Tatler* and *The Spectator,* coedited with Richard Steele.

In the essay, Lewis contrasted Addison's personality traits with those of Swift and Pope. Addison, according to Lewis, was ever cheerful and serious; Swift and Pope were more extreme in each direction, being mirthful and melancholy. Lewis found Addison a pious writer, living at a time when **theology** was becoming less important than being a good person; while Addison may not take us to the heights, Lewis noted, he does provide a foundation for decency and good common sense.

The essay contains splendid instances of subtle humor for those conversant with British literature, as when Lewis remarked about the Tories that they had trouble forgiving, even if it be "only a Shakespearian editor found guilty of some real English scholarship." The reference, as scholars would recognize, is to Pope's anger at Theobald, evinced in *The Dunciad.*

As is ever the case with Lewis, while reading an article on one subject we learn about many others—liter-ary, historical, and theological—in a pleasant and quiet way.

Marvin D. Hinten
Bowling Green State University

Also See: Addison's Walk, Literary Theory

Addison's Walk

Eighteenth-century essayist Joseph Addison (1672–1719) attended Oxford's **Magdalen College**, the same college where Lewis taught, in the late 1600s. Because he liked walking a forested path beside a stream behind Magdalen, the path has become known as Addison's Walk.

It was here that Lewis engaged in the conversation with **Hugo Dyson** and **J. R. R. Tolkien** that led almost directly to Lewis's conversion from theism (belief in God) to **Christianity**. On September 19, 1931, the three of them were strolling along Addison's Walk and discussing **myths**, particularly Lewis's reaction to stories of dying gods and to the sacrifice of **Christ**. They reminded him how moved and impressed he was when reading of dying gods in other belief systems, as with Balder in Norse mythology. Dyson and Tolkien encouraged Lewis to think of Christ's sacrifice with the same sense of awe, accentuated by the fact that it actually happened. Nine days later, on September 28, Lewis committed himself to Christianity while riding in a motorcycle sidecar on the way to a zoo.

Marvin D. Hinten
Bowling Green State University

Aesthetics

Depending on their point of view, people have two different attitudes toward C. S. Lewis's aesthetics. To most people, Lewis seemed highly cultured; he adored high brow literature and liked classical music, art, and foreign languages. To an art-for-art's-sake advocate such as **Matthew Arnold**, however, Lewis seemed a low brow and a Philistine. He always maintained that his love of the classics was not a particularly praiseworthy characteristic; he just happened to have a personality that enjoyed those things. One of his most scholarly works, his volume of the *Oxford History of English Literature*, is unusual for a scholarly work in its casual, almost chatty tone. It gives no sense of literary works as sacred *objets d'art* that should be handled with care. The book reads more like a tour through a garden, with a knowledgeable caretaker pointing out some of the prettiest flowers, identifying their types, and telling how they grow. In addition, some highbrows might consider

Lewis plebeian for enjoying not only the "high points" of **culture**, but also what they would consider more common pleasures—children's novels and **science fiction**, for instance.

Lewis believed the Horatian dictum that the purpose of literature was to delight and instruct, or as his literary predecessor **Samuel Johnson** would have put it, to teach by pleasing. If it is set up as an idol, Lewis believed, literature and the arts in general would be pernicious; but if used as tools to support morality, they could be not only innocent but useful. This did not mean that Lewis felt the moral part of literature had to be put foremost. He did not consider "didactic" a negative term but felt it was perfectly acceptable for a writer to simply write what interested him; and if that writer were a moral person, morality would flow through the book naturally. In describing in various essays how he came to write the **Chronicles of Narnia**, Lewis always insisted that he did not decide to write an overtly Christian or even overtly moral piece of work and then come up with a story; actually, he had pictures in his mind that he formed into a story, and the **Christianity** found its way in because of who he was as a person.

Even as a child, Lewis had always been interested in aesthetics. In his autobiography, *Surprised by Joy*, he recounted how he had longings for **beauty** from seeing a miniature garden. Unlike most children, who read stories for the plot, Lewis usually seemed more captured by the atmosphere. He loved the sense of "Northerness" in Norse mythology. Even as an adult, Lewis had some difficulty in accepting Christianity because the aesthetic, or "mythic," aspects of it did not appeal to him.

Perhaps Lewis's strongest and clearest comments on aesthetics can be found in a letter of April 16, 1940, to **Dom Bede Griffiths**. In it, Lewis asserts that art (by which he meant cultural things in general) is healthy only when it is either merely recreational or deliberately the supporter of moral **truth**; art for art's sake, Lewis says, is "balderdash," and he considers the excessive elevation of it to be dangerous.

Marvin D. Hinten
Bowling Green State University

Also See: Ethics and Morality, Human Nature, Literary Theory, Myth

Bibliography

Carter, Margaret L. "Sub-Creation and Lewis's Theory of Literature." *The Taste of the Pineapple*. Ed. Bruce L. Edwards. Bowling Green, OH: Bowling Green State University Press, 1988: 129–37.

Edwards, Bruce. *A Rhetoric of Reading: C. S. Lewis's Defense of Western Literacy*. Provo, UT: Brigham Young University, 1986.

Lewis, C. S. *An Experiment in Criticism*; *They Asked for a Paper.*

Lindskoog, Kathryn. *C. S. Lewis, Mere Christian*. Downers Grove, IL: InterVarsity, 1981.

Neuleib, Janice W. "The Creative Act: Lewis on God and Art." *The Longing for a Form*. Ed. Peter J. Schakel. Kent, OH: Kent State University Press, 1977: 40–47.

"After Aristotle"

The Oxford Magazine. 74 (February 23, 1956): 296 (under the pseudonym Nat Whilk). Reprinted in *Poems* and *Collected Poems*.

The Greek subtitle of this poem, *Areta polmocqe* ("Won After Much Toil"), is an apt epigram since the subject of the piece is **virtue**. After describing the unsurpassing value of virtue, Lewis claimed that **Aristotle**, because of his lifelong devotion to virtue, was her best champion and receives praise for this from the Muses and Zeus himself.

Don W. King
Montreat College

"After Kirby's *Kalevala*"

The Oxford Magazine. 55 (May 13, 1937): 595. (under the pseudonym Nat Whilk).

This poem focuses upon the suicide of Coolruff as described in the *Kalevala* ("Land of Heroes"), the national epic poem of Finland. One of Lewis's favorites, he attempted imperfectly to translate the Kalevala meter: unrhymed octosyllabic trochees and dactyls.

Don W. King
Montreat College

"After Prayers, Lie Cold"

See entry on "Arise, my Body"

"After Priggery—What?"

The Spectator. CLXXV (7 December 1945): 536. Reprinted in *Present Concerns*.

This 1945 essay appeared in *The Spectator*, a weekly journal for an intellectual readership. It is this intelligentsia that Lewis often saw as at high risk for corruption. Lewis's focus was on a kind of inverted priggery that can be seen in people who are smug about their open-mindedness. He wrote in mocking tone about a society of individuals, like the readers of the journal perhaps, who are too smart and too modern to espouse traditional **values**. These are unshockable sophisticates who pride themselves on their broad-minded tolerance and despise as priggish the "self-righteousness" of those who uphold traditional moral standards. Unlike Lewis, such people do not believe they are in danger of corruption. It is not acceptable, Lewis claimed, to fraternize with people whose morals are inferior because immorality does corrupt. He used as a specific example a journalist whose work is abominable; its poison affects the minds of those who read it. Lewis said that not only should people shun this journalist's presence and refuse to read what he writes but they should also boycott the paper that publishes him. Public opinion rather than legal censorship should dictate common decency; people should actively reject pernicious distortions of the **truth**.

Susan Henthorne
White Pines College

Bibliography

Lewis, C. S. "High Brow and Low Brow."

After Ten Years (Fragment)

The Dark Tower and Other Stories. Walter Hooper (ed). New York: Harcourt Brace Jovanovich, 1977.

The narrative fragment "After Ten Years" was Lewis's last attempt at fiction. After his wife's death in 1960, Lewis abandoned it. However the fragments we have left suggest what a powerful novel it might have been. It is the story of Helen of Troy and her husband, Menelaus, after the Trojan War.

It opens with a vivid scene of Menelaus inside the Trojan Horse waiting for the signal to emerge from the Horse and take Troy. As we follow Menelaus's thoughts we get a picture of his marriage to Helen and his feelings toward her at the moment of the taking of Troy. In his thoughts he calls her "The Wicked Woman," and Lewis gives a fascinating picture of his emotions of longing and resentment and his conflicting thoughts on how to treat her after her rescue from the Trojans.

When the Greeks are released from the Horse there are some good scenes of the fighting when the Greeks took Troy. When Helen is discovered, the ten years that have passed since the beginning of the Trojan War have taken away her beauty—she is no longer the beautiful Helen whom Menelaus has longed for and been jealous of. There is then a scene with Agamemnon, who reveals that economics and politics were the real motives for the Trojan War: Helen was only an excuse. Agamemnon is pictured very much as Homer paints him, as somewhat of a braggart and a bully. Menelaus, who is called "Yel-

lowhead" in the story, is based on Homer, but is a far more complex character than in Homer. He is not, in the fragments we have, an especially sympathetic character. One of the problems that Lewis talked about with his friend Alastair Fowler was "to tell the story of a cuckold in such a way to bring out the meaninglessness of his life. In the eyes of others, Menelaus might seem to have lost almost all that was honorable and heroic, but in his own he had all that mattered: **love**."

The last scene shows Menelaus confronted with an image of a beautiful Helen who never went to Troy nor was unfaithful to him; an image or "Eidolon" of Helen as he wanted her to be. As Lewis told another friend, **Roger Lancelyn Green**, "Menelaus had dreamed of Helen, longed for Helen, built up an image of Helen and worshipped it as a false idol; in Egypt is offered that idol, the Eidolon. I don't think that he was to know which was the true Helen. . . . But I think that he was to discover in the end that the middle-aged, faded Helen he had brought from Troy was the real love, or its possibility; the Eidolon would have been a *belle dame sans merci*."

I think that a novel by Lewis based on these ideas might have been one of Lewis's best novels, even surpassing *Till We Have Faces,* which I regard as his best work. I have myself tried to tell the story Lewis set out to tell in one of my books (Richard Purtill, *The Mirror of Helen,* New York: DAW Books, 1983), and I hope that in some respects Lewis would have liked the book, since I used many of his themes.

Richard Purtill
Western Washington University

"Ajax and Others"

See entry on *On Aristotle and Greek Tragedy* (Book Review)

Alcohol/Tobacco

C. S. Lewis drank alcoholic beverages with relish every day and considered this a normal part of life. (In his culture it was.) He believed in moderate use of alcohol; and he had no patience with the cause of Christian teetotalism, although his brother's alcoholism plagued their lives. (At the end of his grueling adventures in *Out of the Silent Planet*, the hero Ransom automatically ordered a pint of bitter.)

In contrast, Lewis deeply regretted his addiction to tobacco, although that was also common in his culture. He started smoking at thirteen and became an extremely heavy smoker of cigarettes and pipes. He tried to quit and failed, complaining that for him not smoking was a full-time job. Lewis advised nonsmokers never to start. (In *Out of the Silent Planet*, the villain Devine tried to teach Martians to smoke cigarettes.)

Kathryn Lindskoog

Also See: Warren Lewis

Elia Estelle "Stella" Aldwinckle (1907–1990)

A member of the **Oxford** pastorate and founder of the **Oxford University Socratic Club**, Aldwinckle was born of English parents on December 16, 1907, in Johannesburg, South Africa. After receiving her early education in England she returned with her father to South Africa in 1926. Three years later, at the age of twenty-one, feeling called to "help people find God," she returned to England to pursue the training necessary for a lifetime of ministry. She entered St. Anne's College, Oxford, in 1932 where she read theology. During this period she came under the influence of **Austin Farrer** who significantly shaped her theological and philosophical development. Following Oxford she taught Divinity at Yorkshire and then at St. Christopher's College in Blackheath. In 1941 she joined the Oxford pastorate, a team of pastoral workers who provided spiritual counseling to University undergraduates. For the next twenty-five years she labored to remove the hindrances and misunderstandings that prevented people from becoming Christians. This aspect of her ministry found its most profound expression in the Oxford University Socratic Club, which she founded near the end of 1941. The Club's phenomenal success had much to do with her choice of C. S. Lewis as the Club's first president. In addition to leading the Club she also edited five volumes of the *Socratic Digests*. Her metaphysical poem *Christ's Shadow in Plato's Cave: A Meditation on the Substance of Love* was published in 1990, the year of her death.

Christopher W. Mitchell

The Marion E. Wade Center

Bibliography

Aldwinckle, Stella. "Stella Aldwinckle Papers" (Archive), the Marion E. Wade Center, Wheaton College, Wheaton, IL.

_____. "Socrates was a Realist," *Socratic Digest*. 1 (June 1943): 6–8.

_____. "Concerning the Question: 'Jesus, Prophet or Son of God,'" *Socratic Digest*. 2 (June 1944): 31–33.

_____. *Christ's Shadow in Plato's Cave*. Oxford: The Amate Press, 1990.

Leachman, Richard. "Biographical Postscript." *Christ's Shadow in Plato's Cave*. Oxford: The Amate Press, 1990.

Murdoch, Iris. "Foreword." *Christ's Shadow in Plato's Cave*. Oxford: The Amate Press, 1990.

Waterfield, Robin. "A Note on the Socratic Club." *Christ's Shadow in Plato's Cave*. Oxford: The Amate Press, 1990.

Samuel Alexander (1859–1938)

Samuel Alexander was a philosopher who was born in Australia and taught for many years at the Lincoln, Oriel, and Worcester Colleges, **Oxford**, and at the University of Manchester. In 1916–18 Alexander delivered the Gifford Lectures at Glasgow which were published in 1920 as *Space, Time and Deity*. This work had a profound influence on Lewis, and caused him to change his ideas about "**joy**" and introspection. In *Surprised by Joy*, Lewis wrote that after reading Alexander, he made a discovery that "flashed a new light back on my whole life." He came to realize that his lifelong search for the desire or longing he had called "joy" was an "imprint" or "mental track" of something greater. As Lewis continued his journey toward salvation, he began to understand that this was the "Absolute" or **God**. From then on he began to distrust introspection and to concentrate on what was outside the self: "I should never have to bother again about these images or sensations."

Perry C. Bramlett

C. S. Lewis for the Local Church

Also See: Books of Influence

Bibliography

Alexander, Samuel. *Space, Time and Deity*. New York: The Humanities Press, 1950.

Brettschneider, Bertram D. "The Philosophy of Samuel Alexander: Idealism." *Space, Time and Deity*. New York: The Humanities Press, 1964.

Allegory

C. S. Lewis wrote one allegorical prose work, *The Pilgrim's Regress*, which traced the various influences on his thought. In the story, John, a kind of Everyman, searches for the Landlord (**God**). He goes through Eschropolis, a city of filth and excrement, encounters the Clevers, and meets Sigismund (**Freud**), the son of Mr. Enlightenment. He later sees Mother Kirk (the **Church**). She calls herself the Landlord's daughter-in-law (the Bride of **Christ**), but John calls her "an old creature clearly insane." He then encounters Mr. Sensible, a scatterbrain who hides his ignorance behind seemingly erudite quotations. He meets Neo-Angular (**T. S. Eliot**), Classical (Irving Babbitt, who opposed **Romanticism**), and Humanist (an atheist, George Santayana). John moves to theism and thence to **Christianity**.

Lewis recognized that allegory is not a popular form in the 20th century. His friend **J. R. R. Tolkien** regarded allegory as artificial and manipulative and took pains to deny that there are allegorical elements in *The Lord of the Rings* trilogy. Lewis was not so dogmatic and genuinely appreciated an allegory done well. In **"The Vision of John Bunyan,"** he praised the great English allegory *Pilgrim's Progress* for its "enthralling narrative" and "dramatic dialogue," and he suggested that allegory was the perfect vehicle for the story Bunyan had to tell. Nevertheless, Lewis—like Tolkien—was more apt to use **symbolism** in his writings than allegory. In *The Great Divorce*, for example, the red lizard is a symbol of whispering lust and the lifeless Grey Town is of course symbolic of **hell**. The outskirts of **heaven**, meanwhile, are a verdant forest where the travelers from hell arrive and which is made available to them if only they decide to stay. Strangely, only one can stay—the man with the red lizard—is able to accept the offer.

Corbin Scott Carnell
University of Florida

Bibliography

Piehler, Paul. "Visions and Reuisians: C. S. Lewis's Contributions to the Theory of Allegory." *The Taste of the Pineapple*. Bruce Edwards (ed). Bowling Green, OH: Bowling Green State University Press, 1988.

The Allegory of the "Faerie Queen" (Book Review)

The Cambridge Review. LXXXI (11 June 1960): 643–45.

This brief review praised Parker's book as sane and well written. The author covers the images of **good and evil** very well, but Lewis wished for a more complete discussion of "the iconography of pageant and emblem." Lewis also distinguished between the logical and imaginative argument in principle and in specific instances. He also praised the author for "the almost Johnsonism finality" of her statements.

Anne Gardner

Bibliography

Parker, M. Pauline. *The Allegory of the "Faerie Queen."*

The Allegory of Love: A Study in Medieval Tradition

Oxford: Clarendon Press, 1936. First US edition, New York: Oxford University Press, 1960 (paperback).

At the beginning of his most famous and influential scholarly work, C. S. Lewis frankly confessed, "The allegorical love **poetry** of the Middle Ages is apt to repel the modern reader both by its form and its matter," and then he proceeded by his winsome style and prodigious knowledge of his subject matter to engage the attentive reader, against all odds making interesting and clear what is almost by definition dense, obscure, and elusive. *The Allegory of Love* thus may be read as an ingenious detective story in which Lewis, clue by clue, explicated the nature of allegorical form and its relationship to the paradoxical Medieval **love** tradition—or as Lewis described its main themes when he submitted the manuscript for publication in 1935, "the birth of **allegory** and its growth from what it is in Prudentius to what it is in **Spenser**" and "the birth of the romantic conception of love and the long struggle between its earlier form (the romance of adultery) and its later form (the romance of marriage)."

Chapter 1 of *The Allegory of Love* surveys the phenomenon of "courtly love," which depicts the love between a man and a woman in terms of the kind of fealty relationship a feudal vassal owes his lord. He must obey his Lady implicitly, promise feats of great courage in her honor, and lavish her with inordinate praise; most importantly, his beloved must not be his wife, for arranged marriages made personal attraction between spouses unlikely and unwarranted. The **Medieval world**, Lewis generalized, finds room for "innocent sexuality" but not "passion"; pleasure in **sex** even for one's spouse is a **sin**, akin to adultery and just as damning as any lust. As a result, the tradition of courtly love succeeds in inventing (and exulting in) "romantic love," volitional, dynamic love between a man and woman, something rare or unknown in the literature of classical or biblical times, or even the early Medieval age, but universal in our modern era.

In chapter 2 Lewis suggested that allegory is less a literary form than a state of mind, for "it is the very nature of thought and language to represent what is immaterial in picturable terms"; but his question was then all the more poignant: how does something "latent" in human speech suddenly become explicit in the structure of poems and predominant as a genre in the Middle Ages? To answer his question, Lewis exhaustively surveyed the development of allegory from classical times forward. In reaching the Middle Ages, Lewis called allegory "the subjectivism of an objective age," by which he means its poets frequently used allegory to present inner conflict or spiritual reality in picture form. Allegory in one way or another involves an equivalence of the material and immaterial; medievals started with immaterial fact—a passion or a sin—and sought a visible item to represent it; moderns, by contrast, prefer **symbols**, which work in the other direction, directing the reader away from the "copy" to a world that is "more real." Thus, the allegorist takes the given and invents something, a fiction, that is less real, to convey its meaning; the symbolist employs the given as a means to point to and discover what is transcendent beyond the local and time-bound. It is Lewis's contention that to understand the Middle Ages aright, we must attune ourselves to the fact that its poets are allegorists, not symbolists, at work.

Lewis follows with five chapters of rigorous, direct application, beginning with *The Romance of the Rose*, and then on to **Chaucer**, Gower, and Thomas Usk, saving his greatest exposition for **Spenser**'s *Faerie Queene*. By the time allegory has reached Spenser's era, it is dominant, and a monotonous sameness pervades it, unnoticed by the age in which it has evolved. In Spenser, however, both allegory and courtly love are transformed, the intertwining of the form and the sentiment yielding "the final defeat of courtly love and its displacement by the romantic conception of marriage." Ultimately, Spenser's work is to be seen as having had enormous influence on "all our love literature from **Shakespeare** to Meredith," and Spenser himself as the "great mediator between the Middle Ages and the modern poets, the man who saved us from the catastrophe of too thorough a renaissance."

The Allegory of Love is warmly dedicated to **Owen Barfield**, whom Lewis called "the wisest and best of my unofficial teachers," and unabashedly exemplifies one of the key lessons that Lewis attributes to Barfield: "not to patronize the past ... and to see the present as itself a 'period,'" thus rejecting what Lewis labeled "**chronological snobbery**" in *Surprised by Joy*. Hence, *Allegory* is designed to be "an effort of the historical imagination," a reconstruction of "that long-lost state of mind for which the allegorical love poem was a natural mode of expression."

Such a mode of—and motive for—scholarship was a lightning bolt to the community of literary historians Lewis had now joined, energizing what had been a moribund discussion, settled in its familiar judgments about Medieval literature in general and allegory in particular. Lewis's tactics in *Allegory* formed, in fact, his signature approach to literary scholarship in his field of expertise, Medieval and **Renaissance** literature. For in numerous

papers and articles throughout his early career, and in such later major works as *English Literature in the Sixteenth Century* and *The Discarded Image*, Lewis delighted in sketching for readers what critic Helen Gardner has called an "imaginative map of the past." Simply put, Lewis had few rivals as a scholar who could skillfully extrapolate from its texts the operating worldview of a civilization or period, thereby creating in his readers the sensation of truly abandoning one's own age and inhabiting another.

Originally submitted to **Oxford**'s Clarendon Press under the title, *The Allegorical Love Poem*, the work was given for review to none other than **Charles Williams**, who would shortly become a close associate of Lewis's and, indeed, an "**Inkling**" with a profound effect on Lewis's **theology** and writing. Williams suggested that the title be changed to *The Allegory of Love* and wrote Lewis an ebullient letter of praise to him, calling the book "practically the only one that I have ever come across since **Dante**, that shows the slightest understanding of what this very peculiar identity of love and **religion** means." When the book was published in May 1936, reviewers were as adulatory as Williams, extraordinarily impressed with its original thesis and its sweeping command of such a vast array of texts and historical eras. Lewis, who had been little known outside academic circles in Oxford before its publication, found himself now established as a premier scholar with uncommon scope and depth.

The Allegory of Love well illustrates several recurring features and strengths of Lewis's critical practice. First and foremost, *Allegory* is filled with Lewis's characteristically provocative generalizations, which categorize, summarize, and evaluate whole genres and eras with such intuitive force that one finds them difficult to counter. Secondly, *Allegory* demonstrates Lewis's supreme command of language and literature across time, genre, culture, and thus his uncanny ability to multiply relevant and convincing example after example in service of his main thesis. Any critic attempting to refute Lewis is obliged to commandeer as much or more terrain in fashioning a response of any merit. Finally, Lewis is seen in *Allegory* performing his most distinctive mode of **literary criticism**, that of "rehabilitation," defending and/or reconceptualizing a period (the Middle Ages), a genre (allegory), or an author (Spenser) for which appreciation or critical understanding had been lacking. *The Allegory of Love* continues to be regarded as one of the seminal works on the tradition of Medieval love poetry, the role of allegory in the Middle Ages, and, certainly, Spenser's *Faerie Queene*. As Spenser and Lewis scholar Margaret Hannay has observed, "Lewis is still frequently cited—not to settle critical arguments, but to start them. Nothing would have delighted him more."

Bruce L. Edwards
Bowling Green State University

Bibliography

Green, Roger Lancelyn, and Walter Hooper. *C. S. Lewis: A Biography.* San Diego: Harper, 1974.

Hannay, Margaret. *C. S. Lewis.* New York: Ungar, 1981.

_____. "Provocative Generalizations: *The Allegory of Love* in Retrospect." *The Taste of the Pineapple: Essays on C. S. Lewis as Reader, Critic, and Imaginative Writer.* Bruce L. Edwards (ed). Bowling Green, OH: Popular Press, 1988.

Piehler, Paul. "Visions and Revisions: C. S. Lewis's Contributions to the Theory of Allegory." *The Taste of the Pineapple: Essays on C. S. Lewis as Reader, Critic, and Imaginative Writer.* Bruce L. Edwards (ed). Bowling Green, OH: Popular Press, 1988.

Sayer, George. *Jack: A Life of C. S. Lewis.* Wheaton, IL: Crossway, 1988.

"The Alliterative Metre"

See entry on "A Metrical Suggestion"

All My Road Before Me: The Diary of C. S. Lewis 1922–1927

Hooper, Walter (ed). London: HarperCollins, 1991. First US edition, San Diego: Harcourt Brace Jovanovich, 1991.

At the suggestion of **Janie Moore**, Lewis began keeping a diary. Written down originally in several notebooks, this handwritten diary for the period 1922–27 was typed out by **Warren Lewis** during his preparation of the eleven volumes of **The Lewis Family Papers**, and annotated by both brothers. The original diaries were supposed to have been destroyed in 1936, and The Lewis Family Papers were given by Warren to the **Wade Center** where they are now on deposit.

Lewis's diary began on April 1, 1922, and went through March 1, 1925, and then, after a break, resumed on August 16, 1925, and terminated on March 2, 1927. It was open to Janie Moore who either read it or had Jack read it to her (as he reported in the

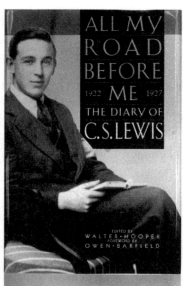

diary itself), and this must have restricted what it could contain. The reported view of Lewis towards his diary changed over time. On June 20, 1923, he wrote: "Decided at whatever cost of labour to start my diary rigorously again, wh. has been dropped during Schools [examinations], as I think the day to day continuity helps one to see the larger movement and pay less attention to each damned day in itself. . . ." But in 1955 he had a different view: "If Theism had done nothing else for me, I should still be thankful that it cured me of the time-wasting and foolish practice of keeping a diary. (Even for autobiographical purposes a diary is nothing like so useful as I had hoped. You put down each day what you think important; but of course you cannot each day see what will prove to have been important in the long run.)"

In the first period covered by the diary, April 1, 1922, to March 1, 1925, there are 1,097 calendar days, and Lewis wrote entries for 583 of them; in the second period, August 16, 1925, to March 2, 1927, there are 700 calendar days, with 153 entries. Thus, in the first period Lewis wrote, on the average, almost every other day, but in the second period only once every four or five days. For whatever reason, he wrote considerably less after March and after his election to a Magdalen Fellowship in May 1925. One circumstantial factor is that during term time thereafter Lewis lived in college and saw less of Janie Moore; he was involved in fewer domestic chores, a recurring topic in the earlier period of the diary, and more involved in college affairs, which are partially recorded but can have been of only limited interest to Janie Moore.

The diary, as transcribed, has been edited by **Walter Hooper**. In this editing process the amount of text has been reduced, it is claimed, by about a third. The published, edited version has about 170,000 words, and the original must have had about 250,000 words. The editor states that, in reducing the length of the diary, he has "tried to do this in such a way that none of Lewis' main interests— friends, books, domestic life—would be lost. There was a great deal of repetition in the complete diary. I have mainly cut out some of the many details of domestic chores."

The content, as edited, has few surprises. In April 1922, for example, there are brief reports of walks, weather, visits, Doc **John Askins** and **immortality**, plays, cooking, writing more of *Dymer*, bridge, reading aloud, letters, study, housing, news from Ireland, sickness, shopping, a marriage, brief opinions of books read, trying to write, a drink at the White Horse, dreams, College, **church**, **Plato**'s *Republic*, a civil service career, domestic jobs, wasted time, builders, Herodotus, Greek history, examinations, **Maureen Moore** and her music. Later on, there is much anguish over the difficulty of finding employment.

These throw some light on that part of Lewis's inner life that he is willing to put on paper and share with Janie Moore. But overall, what is more significant is what is *not* talked about.

In his Foreword, **Owen Barfield** expresses his surprise that there is no mention of the "**Great War**" between himself and Lewis. This was a long, running argument, through the 1920s, about the existence of what Lewis called the **supernatural**, that is, a world over and beyond the world of **nature**; it included all aspects of **theology**, especially immortality. Barfield also expresses surprise at the amount of domestic work, household chores, that occupied so much of Lewis's time and so many words in his diary. He claims that he was "given no hint of all that household background." It is hard to avoid the impression that he was given hints but was blind to their meaning. Leaving on one side Warren, **Arthur Greeves** was Lewis's first friend and Barfield his second, but Barfield saw only one aspect of Lewis, partly because of his own myopia and partly because of Lewis's secrecy and capacity for keeping the various parts of his life in separate compartments.

In the Introduction, the editor finally admits, after years of denial, that "the notion of sexual intimacy between" Lewis and Janie Moore "must be regarded as likely." There is nothing in the diary that relates to this matter however. The editor also claims that Maureen, daughter of Janie Moore, had told him "some years ago" that she remembered Lewis and her brother, **Paddy Moore** (who was killed in 1918), promising that if only one survived he would look after the other's parent. This is unlikely and was invented, presumably, to excuse the fact that Lewis and Janie Moore lived together. Otherwise, the Introduction gives a simple background to the relationship between Janie Moore and the diary.

Throughout the diary, Janie Moore is usually referred to as D. In the original, Lewis used the Greek letter Delta, but since Warren did not have any Greek characters on his typewriter, he transcribed the Delta as D. The probable origin of this is that it stands for Diotima, the Greek priestess who introduced Socrates to the meaning of **Love**, a service that Janie Moore had performed (in a very different sense) for Lewis. As mentioned above, the original notebooks were supposed to have been destroyed in 1936. But in the introduction to *All My Road Before Me*, Walter Hooper states that one of Lewis's original notebooks (containing diary entries from April 1926 to March 1927) survived and that it includes a few additional entries that were never transcribed by Warren Lewis.

The last English words in the diary transcribed by Warren are "—oh curse it all! Is there never to be any peace or comfort?" However, in the surviving notebook there are further entries for January 19–22 and June 2–3, 1928, written in Old English and a single entry for June 4, 1928, in Latin. The use of Old English in the final entries precluded Warren from transcribing them (not being reproducible on his typewriter), although he could have typed out the Latin entry but did not. Janie Moore would not have known the content of these entries without a translation by Jack, and this may well have been his intention. None of these added entries are included in the published volume.

The published edition of the diary concludes with two appendices, one of biographies of people mentioned and another of portraits of colleagues at **Magdalen College, Oxford**. It is claimed that (with two exceptions) they are reproduced from the notebook mentioned above. Some of these portraits may not be wholly by C. S. Lewis, as a complete analysis of them by A. Q. Morten in 1992 indicated that the portraits were not the work of one author.

The title of the published diary, *All My Road Before Me*, is a quotation from *Dymer*, Lewis's narrative poem, published under the pseudonym of Clive Hamilton in 1926. It appears in the first stanza of the first Canto, line four. It was selected by the editor.

John Bremer

America

Lewis had a rather ambiguous relationship with America. He never particularly desired to visit the country except perhaps for the rural parts of it. His biographer and one-time pupil, **George Sayer**, reports that he held an anti-American prejudice. Nevertheless, his books enjoyed tremendous success there, and as a result he received parcels of rare foodstuffs at a time when food was being rationed in Britain in the wake of World

War II. Less welcome to Lewis was the stream of correspondence that resulted from his post-war literary fame. He regarded it his Christian duty to answer this mail, a task that took up much of his valuable time and that he did not relish. Ironically, because he took the trouble to answer every letter, in 1950 he met through the mail an American woman whose background could not have been more different than his own. She was a Jewish, ex-Atheist, ex-Communist convert to **Christianity** with two small sons and a **marriage** breaking up. This was not typical of the sort of people Lewis sought out. Nevertheless he struck up a **friendship** with **Joy Davidman (Lewis)** in 1953 that led eventually to his marriage to her in early 1957. He also knew and respected many Americans such as **Clyde Kilby**, **Chad Walsh**, and Davy and **Sheldon Vanauken**, so whatever dislikes he may have had, they did not interfere with his ability to befriend individual Americans.

Probably Lewis's most direct statement on an aspect of American **culture** was his last essay, **"We Have No 'Right to Happiness,'"** first published in the December 1963 issue of the *Saturday Evening Post* and republished in *God in the Dock*. In the essay Lewis attacked the peculiarly American habit of creating imaginary rights where none existed, especially a man's "right" to abandon his spouse and commit adultery on the grounds that it led to his greatest **happiness**. Lewis looked upon that as nothing less than a failure of good faith and honor for a dubious principle. He predicted that a culture that embraced such an ethic was doomed and perhaps deservedly so.

James Prothero

Also See: Communism and Fascism, Democracy, Education, Ethics and Morality

Bibliography

Lewis, C. S. *God in the Dock*; *Letters of C. S. Lewis.*
Sayer, George. *Jack: C. S. Lewis and His Times.* New York: Harper, 1988.
Schofield, Stephen. "Lewis and (North) Americans." *Canadian C. S. Lewis Journal.* 22 (October 1980): 7.
Walsh, Chad. "Impact on America." *Light on C. S. Lewis.* New York: Harcourt Brace Jovanovich, 1965.

Analogy

An analogy is a way of illuminating something unfamiliar by comparing it to something familiar. A brief example would be explaining to someone unversed in the metric system that a flat object three millimeters by five millimeters is about the size of a small postage stamp.

Philosophers are generally trained in forming analogies to communicate their ideas, and Lewis's first degree was in **philosophy**, so he was active in using analogies in his writing. In fact, Lewis is perhaps the most analogical writer on **theology** in the 20th century.

Lewis was at his most analogical when writing nonfiction for a general audience, and a clear example of that can be seen in the opening chapter of the **"Christian Behaviour"** section in *Mere Christianity*. To explain three forms of morality, Lewis compared human beings to a fleet of ships. We must avoid ramming each other (external morality) and must be individually seaworthy (internal morality). Lewis noted that the two moralities affect each other—ships that ram one another will go wrong internally, and ships with faulty steering mechanisms will ram one another. In addition, Lewis observed that even if the ships are running properly and in formation, they still must head in the right direction, which he compared to humans going in the direction our Creator wants.

One of the distinctive features of Lewis's prose style is that he often presented a second analogy to further clarify the point. In this case, he said humans are like band members; our instruments must be tuned, we must come in at the right time, and we must play the right song.

To some extent, it could be said that even much of Lewis's fiction writing involves extended analogies. *Perelandra* is a way of presenting **the Fall** of humanity (in this case, avoided) before our eyes so we can understand the issues involved more easily. And the **Chronicles of Narnia** are, as Lewis himself observed, in some ways parallel to the situation on our own planet, where a Creator became a Redeemer. Lewis's own conversion was helped along by his recognition that some parts of Greek and Norse mythology were analogous to **Christianity**.

Marvin D. Hinten
Bowling Green State University

Also See: Allegory, Ethics and Morality, Metaphor, Myth, Symbolism

And Less Greek (Letter)

Church Times. CXLV (20 July 1962): 12.

Responding in part to a comment in "Short Notices" (*Church Times*, 13 July 1962, 6) that declared the transliteration of Greek words in a particular commentary to be a "silly practise," Lewis maintained when he encountered a transliterated word (in his particular case in Hebrew, and not in Greek, which he knew), it allowed him to remember the word and later use it as he would a new English word. This would not be possible if he were forced to remember the Hebrew characters. Thus, Lewis saw value in transliteration for those who don't know the original language, just as he questioned why such a practice should be an irritant to those who do know the original.

Marjorie L. Mead
The Marion E. Wade Center

Angels

Lewis stated some of his beliefs about angels in his 1962 preface to *The Screwtape Letters*: Angels are created, rational beings. Above humans in the natural order, some fell and became devils. They either are wholly spiritual or have "bodies of a sort we cannot experience." They lack human sense organs; but by words like "supersense" and "trans-sexuality" Lewis asserted that they have a "mode of consciousness" not subhuman but *beyond* our power to imagine. Lewis added that art requires symbols to present angels: human form betokens **reason**, wings "the swiftness of unimpeded intellectual energy." **Dante** and Fra Angelico successfully conveyed their peace, authority, and awesomeness; later cultural expressions are "degenerated" (Raphael's fluffy cherubs, the Victorians' "soft, slim, girlish" angels) and "pernicious," overstressing their "consolatory" function. Even as guardians (in *The Screwtape Letters,* the dying protagonist with eyes "clear[ed]" recognizes the life-long protectors whose existence he had "even doubted") Lewis's angels, unlike today's popular image, protect against spiritual dangers, not physical.

In angelological traditions Lewis distinguished two strains: Scholasticism considered angels immaterial, assuming visible or illusory form when required; Neoplatonism held that angels have bodies finer than flesh and that they move, change size and shape, receive needed nourishment, suffer wounds and heal, have sensations, and make love.

Lewis made imaginative and speculative use of many traditional ideas about angels, including their role as God's servants; their hierarchical arrangement in nine "orders"; their ignorance regarding certain divine mysteries; their brightness and numinousness; terminology identifying angels as lesser "gods"; the idea that humanity is destined finally for angelic status; and the conflation of scriptural angels with the planetary intelligences of ancient Greek thought. In Narnia, star-angels sing at Creation and vanish at the end, and the *Dawn Treader* voyagers meet two, Coriakin and Ramandu, temporarily reassigned for discipline and rejuvenation respec-

tively. The Ransom trilogy presents two orders of angelic beings, ordinary eldils (or *eldila*) and higher-ranking ones, oyarses (or *oyéresu;* sing. *oyarsa*), who rule the planets, but hints at more—calling oyarses "Powers" with "many degrees . . . of created beings" above them. The trilogy described "rank behind rank . . . rank above rank" and speculatively labels earth's angels a "special military caste." Eldils are "transcorporeal intelligences," virtually innumerable, "of extreme simplicity," "more permanent" than man, "dispos[ing] of more energy," higher in intellect. They do not eat, breathe, or reproduce. Oyarses differ individually in ways resembling but transcending biological gender.

Their abode is "Deep Space"; some ride the whirling planets. They move at light-speed (or nearly). Their bodies ("photosomes") seem "faint rod[s] . . . of light" but have a supersolidity to which walls and rocks are no barrier. They assume other appearances at will, perhaps by "directly manipulating" our brains. They have "silvery" voices but also communicate telepathically. Their powers—extending to transporting spacecraft, annihilating matter, and shaping a planet—are derived from, and used in the service of, Maleldil, whom the oyarses obey, commanding in turn the lesser eldils.

On Mars, Oyarsa commands *hnau* (sentient corporeal beings) also, but on earth and Venus Maleldil commands directly, leaving to angels roles of messengers, guides, and protectors, but never overriding human free will. In *The Great Divorce* angelic power awaits assent before liberating a man; an angel-waterfall warns and instructs; angels escort and venerate a saintly human. In *Perelandra* Tor and Tinidril receive dominion over their planet and anticipate physical transformation to become more angel-like—much like the Heaven-dwellers in *The Great Divorce* and resurrection bodies in Ransom's speculations.

Charles A. Huttar
Hope College

Bibliography

Downing, David C. *Planets in Peril: A Critical Study of C. S. Lewis's Ransom Trilogy.* Amherst: University of Massachusetts Press, 1992: Ch. 2.

Huttar, Charles A. "Angels in the Thought of C. S. Lewis." *Perspectives* 9 no. 2 (February 1994): 12–15.

Purtill, Richard. *Lord of the Elves and Eldils: Fantasy and Philosophy in C. S. Lewis and J. R. R. Tolkien.* Grand Rapids, MI: Zondervan, 1974.

Willis, John Randolph. *Pleasures Forevermore: The Theology of C. S. Lewis.* Chicago: Loyola University Press, 1983: Ch. 3.

Anglicanism

Lewis emphasized the importance of being a "mere Christian," one not committed to a denomination as much as one committed to the historic Christian **faith**. In fact, he stated in the beginning of *Mere Christianity*, "I offer no help to anyone who is hesitating between two Christian denominations." However, when asked about his own church commitment, he described himself as "a very ordinary layman of the Church of England, not especially 'high,' and not especially 'low.'" Lewis was baptized in the Church of Ireland in 1899 and later, after his conversion, joined the Church of England, both of them Anglican.

The Anglican communion refers to a worldwide fellowship of churches in communion with the Church of England and the archbishop of Canterbury. With about 385 dioceses throughout the world, the total membership of the churches, including the Episcopal Church in the United States, is estimated to be approximately 73 million.

Anglicans historically have accepted the **Bible** as the sole criterion in matters of dogma. Stephen Neill states the typical Anglican attitude this way: "Show us that there is anything clearly set forth in Holy Scripture that we do not teach and we will teach it. Show us that anything in our teaching or practice is clearly contrary to Holy Scripture, and we will abandon it." The Apostles' Creed and the Nicene Creed are the accepted statements of faith. Anglicans hold the sacraments, including baptism and communion, in high esteem, believing them to be "outward and visible signs of inward and spiritual grace, given by **Christ** as sure and certain means by which we receive that grace." The church also believes in apostolic succession, that the ministry of the church is derived from the apostles through a continuous succession of bishops.

Churches in the Anglican communion use the revised *Book of Common Prayer* as their guide for worship. It includes the order for services in the church, prayers, the Psalter, the lectionary, and certain historical documents of the church including the Articles of Religion and the catechism. The *Book of Common Prayer* was first completed by Thomas Cranmer and Nicholas Ridley during the reign of Henry VIII. The prayer book has been revised numerous times; Lewis grew up with the 1662 prayer book, and it was the version used by his parish church. He used the Coverdale version of the Psalms, found in the *Book of Common Prayer*, in writing his book *Reflections on the Psalms*.

Despite his faithful attachment to Anglicanism, Lewis was not afraid to voice disagreements with his church on occasion. Anglicans are spoofed in the character of Mr. Angular in *Pilgrim's Regress*, and Lewis said that the Tableland in that book "represents all high and dry states of mind, of which High Anglicanism then seemed to me to be one." He noted somewhat ruefully that "it would be idle to pretend that we Anglicans are a striking example of the gusto expressed in the **Psalms**." Lewis was also critical of the drift toward theological liberalism in Anglicanism—criticizing, for example, a proposal for women priests.

Lewis further expressed dislike for the Anglican worship services in *Surprised by Joy*: "The fussy, time-wasting botheration of it all! the bells, the crowds, the umbrellas, the notices, the bustle, the perpetual arranging. . . ." He added, "Clergymen, though I liked, as I liked bears, I had as little wish to be in the Church as in the zoo." Despite this natural resistance, he went to church faithfully, asserting frankly: "**Christianity** is not a solitary religion. We must go to church."

The church where he chose to go was Holy Trinity Church, an Anglican parish at Headington Quarry. Surely one of the attractions of this church was the regular structure of the liturgy, as laid out in the *Book of Common Prayer*: "My whole liturgiological position really boils down to an entreaty for permanence and uniformity. I can make do with almost any kind of service whatever, if only it will stay put." He was also fond of "formal, ready-made prayers," written and read, claiming they kept him from falling into selfishness and connected him with the timeless "voice of the great saints."

Lewis was also drawn to weekly worship because of the sacramental nature of communion, "the only rite which we know to have been instituted by Our Lord Himself (and therefore cannot be altered)." Lewis admitted that his understanding of Holy Communion "would probably be called 'magical' by a good many modern theologians." He believed in the real presence of Christ when Christians partake of the elements of The Lord's Table. He did not attempt to explain how this occurs. But his commitment to this sacrament was such that when his health failed toward the end of his life and church attendance was no longer possible, he made arrangements to have communion brought to him at his home twice each week.

Lewis's commitment to Anglicanism notwithstanding, it must be emphasized that Lewis was, as **Douglas Gresham** has observed, "A Christian not given to 'isms.'" He viewed sectarianism as one of the Devil's keenest weapons. Only the church united, he said, can be what it is called to be, "spread out through all time and space and rooted in eternity, terrible as an army with banners."

Diana Pavlac Glyer
Asuza Pacific University

Also See: Roman Catholicism

Bibliography

Christenson, Michael. *C. S. Lewis on Scripture*. Nashville, TN: Abingdon Press, 1989.

Kilby, Clyde S. *The Christian World of C. S. Lewis*. Grand Rapids, MI: Eerdmans, 1995.

Neill, Stephen. *Anglicanism*. New York: Oxford University Press, 1958.

Payne, Leanne. *Real Presence: The Holy Spirit in the Works of C. S. Lewis*. Wheaton, IL: Crossway, 1979.

Walsh, Chad. *Knock and Enter*. Harrisburg, PA: Morehouse Publishing, 1953.

Webber, Robert E. *Evangelicals on the Canterbury Trail: Why Evangelicals Are Attracted to the Liturgical Church*. Harrisburg, PA: Morehouse Publishing, 1989.

G[ertrude] E[lizabeth] M[argaret] Anscombe (1919–)

Philosophers know Professor G. E. M. Anscombe as a scholar, an author, and the English translator of Ludwig Wittgenstein and René Descartes. C. S. Lewis's contemporaries, however, remember her as the speaker who reduced Lewis to silence at an **Oxford Socratic Club** debate in which she challenged his claim that naturalism was self-refuting. Many have concluded that her challenge (and, by some accounts, victory) prompted him to move away from philosophical **apologetics** and to focus his work on fiction.

The first edition of *Miracles* (1947) devoted Chapter III, "The Self-Contradiction of the Rationalist," to a discussion of human **rationality**, which Lewis claimed was not human in origin at all, but sparked by irresistible forces outside the brain. Thus, one believes certain things, such as the existence of **God**, not out of choice but because it is the only possibility. Elizabeth Anscombe, then a research fellow at Somerville College, **Oxford**, took exception to this theory, in part because Lewis treated rationality not as a subject worthy of intensive study, but as a superficial point used to prove a larger thesis. On February 2, 1948, the two scholars met at the Socratic Club to debate the topic in public. Lewis arrived prepared to argue his theory from a theological standpoint, only to find that Professor Anscombe—an expert in the fields of intention and causality—considered it a purely philosophical issue. She took the floor first and proceeded to dissect his argu-

ment point by point, not stating directly that he had made errors but noting overstatements and generalities. Lewis gamely responded and, to all accounts, provided solid arguments for his own position; even so, he considered himself the loser of the debate.

Hugo Dyson and **George Sayer** have claimed that Lewis was humiliated by his public defeat and resentful of his opponent; Professor Anscombe has disagreed, noting that she and he dined together with **Humphrey Havard** only a few weeks later. It is true, however, that Lewis wrote no further apologetics for ten years. Instead, he turned his energies to fiction, an act that gained him a wider audience and recognition as an author as well as a scholar. He may have used the Socratic Club experience to his advantage in one book. In *C. S. Lewis: A Biography* (1990), A. N. Wilson suggests that the scene in *The Silver Chair* in which the Queen of Underland attempts to persuade the children that there is no above-ground world "is a nursery nightmare version of Lewis's debate with Miss Anscombe." Twelve years after the event, Lewis revised and greatly expanded Chapter III of *Miracles*, which he retitled "The Cardinal Difficulty of the Naturalist." The new version takes into account the conscious choice of the individual; Professor Anscombe read and approved of the changes, noting that the book was now "much less slick and . . . much more of a serious investigation."

In the years since the Socratic Club debate, G. E. M. Anscombe has established herself as the definitive interpreter of Wittgenstein and as an expert translator. She has written many collections of original philosophical essays, some in collaboration with her husband, Peter Geach.

Katherine Harper

Bibliography

Anscombe, G. E. M. "A Reply to Mr. C. S. Lewis's Argument That 'Naturalism' is Self-Refuting." *Socratic Digest* 4 (1948). Reprinted in *Collected Philosophical Papers*, Vol. 2. Cambridge: Cambridge University Press, 1981.

Diamond, Cora, and Jenny Teichman, eds. *Intention and Intentionality: Essays in Honour of G. E. M. Anscombe*. Ithaca: Cornell University Press, 1979.

Purtill, Richard L. "Did C. S. Lewis Lose His Faith?" *A Christian for All Christians: Essays in Honor of C. S. Lewis*. Andrew Walker and James Patrick (eds). Washington, DC: Regnery Gateway, 1992: 27–62.

"Answers to Questions on Christianity"

Hayes, Middlesex: Electric and Musical Industries Christian Fellowship, 1944. Reprinted in *God in the Dock, Undeceptions,* and *Timeless at Heart.*

This is a series of seventeen questions and answers, posed and answered at a "One Man Brains Trust" held on April 18, 1944, at the Head Office of the EMI. A typescript was made from shorthand notes and revised by Lewis prior to publication.

In his introductory statement, Lewis said that "**Christianity** does *not* replace the technical." He also said that modern industry is, in his opinion, a "radically hopeless system." The questions that were directed at Lewis ranged from general advice on "finding **God**" to the church's position on the prevention and treatment of venereal diseases. Lewis was characteristically direct and honest, and occasionally played a little with the question-master (in his response to Question 4, for example). He spoke from his own experience and did not claim to speak for any institution. When asked what **religion** gave its followers the greatest **happiness**, Lewis answered that "the religion of worshipping oneself is best" while it lasts. However, he looks for **truth**, not apparent happiness. He reminded his audience that the Christian cannot be told from his exterior—there are no telltale signs of a Christian because the material with which God works can be radically different. The cantankerous Christian would be so much more cantankerous were he not found by God, and the gentle man who is not a Christian would be so much more kind were he Christian. Ultimately, what is important is that God finds us, and that, even if we are unaware of it, we can then find him.

Anne Gardner

Also See: Modernity, Science, Technology

"The Anthropological Approach"

English and Medieval Studies Presented to J. R. R. Tolkien on the Occasion of His Seventieth Birthday. Norman Davis and C. L. Wrenn (eds). London: Allen and Unwin, 1962: 219–30. Reprinted in *Selected Literary Essays*.

"The Anthropological Approach," originally published in a Festschrift for **J. R. R. Tolkien** in 1962, discusses whether a person needs to know unintended anthropological parallels in order to fully appreciate a work of literature. For instance, does a person's familiarity with the Celtic cornucopia maximize his enjoyment of a Holy Grail legend?

Characteristically, Lewis denied this. He argued that literary characters and activities often seem more real than the anthropological parallel that is supposed to make them real to us. According to Lewis, most of the readers of his generation could readily enter into

Medieval works of **fantasy** before they recognized what items the fantasy objects were intended to parallel; thus, even though the anthropological facts might be interesting, they cannot increase the enjoyment of the work. To use the terms of another Lewis essay, **"Meditation in a Toolshed,"** readers of his day could "look along" fantasy works rather than being limited to simply "looking at" them.

If we have been in **love**, we can more fully appreciate a love poem; that type of aid is intrinsic to the poem. The other type is extrinsic to the poem, such as an easy chair. Lewis placed knowing about parallels from other cultures into the second category. This essay, written toward the end of his academic life, resonates with the critical practice that informed Lewis's work throughout his career and is explored explicitly in *An Experiment in Criticism*: the defense of the reader seeking primary experience of a text over against the professional critic who wittingly or unwittingly substitutes a secondary experience of elements extrinsic to the text and offered as superior to the original text itself.

Marvin D. Hinten and Bruce L. Edwards
Bowling Green State University

Also See: Literary Criticism

Bibliography

Edwards, Bruce L. *A Rhetoric of Reading: C. S. Lewis's Defense of Western Literacy.* Provo, UT: Brigham Young University Press, 1985.
Lewis, C. S. "De Audiendis Poetes"; "What Chaucer Really Did to *Il Filostrato.*"

Anthroposophy

Anthroposophy (like Christian Science) was an early branch of what is now called New-Age thought. It is an arts-and-crafts-oriented belief system developed in 1912 by Rudolf Steiner (1861–1925), who served previously as the first leader of the German Theosophic Association. Steiner taught that human consciousness is evolving and that his methods (rather than mere reason, tradition, or science) provide a valid way to know reality. He called his movement "spiritual science" and revealed new details about spiritual hierarchies. His exposition of Anthroposophy was titled "Occult Science."

Anthroposophy concerned C. S. Lewis because his two friends **Owen Barfield** and **Cecil Harwood** fervently embraced it. Lewis's nightmare experience with his friend **John Askins** recorded in his diary in 1923 (the year Harwood and Barfield committed themselves to Anthroposophy) no doubt intensified his aversion to anything occult. In 1932 Lewis placed Anthroposophy in the shire of the occult in *Pilgrim's Regress* and portrayed "Rudolph" consorting with magicians.

Disagreement about occultism was central to the long, friendly debate between Lewis and Barfield called "The Great War." In an undated letter that Lewis wrote to Barfield from **Magdalen College** at some point between 1923 and 1927, he tried to show the danger of occultism. He headed the letter "The Real Issue between Us" and drew a couple of pen sketches with explanations attached. In the sketches an ambitious little man tied to the post of his own personality uses occult tools to chip away at the mirror before him that gives him the normally restricted human view of reality. He seems not to notice the loving hands of ultimate reality stretched out from the clouds behind him. Once the mirror is all chipped away, an evil spirit comes through the empty frame and grabs him. Ahead are an ambulance, an asylum, and a cemetery, all clearly sketched. These sketches and Lewis's commentary are reproduced in two books: Douglas Gilbert and **Clyde S. Kilby**, *C. S. Lewis, Images of His World* and John Warwick Montgomery, *Principalities and Powers: The World of the Occult.*

Seventy years after Lewis's unsuccessful letter, Barfield spoke about Rudolph Steiner and Anthroposophy with Astrid Diener. Barfield told Diener that he first became acquainted with Steiner's writing in 1922 and gradually realized that Steiner's teaching confirmed his own independent convictions. Unfortunately, he said, he had just married a member of the High Anglican church, and his wife's intense disapproval of Anthroposophy (she especially detested the doctrine that there were "two Jesus boys") somewhat "spoiled" their marriage.

Barfield also expressed continuing regret over Lewis's rejection of Anthroposophy. "His reaction to Anthroposophy was a tragedy, in a way." Barfield attributed Lewis's disapproval to the fact that some Theosophists had been involved in occultism in the bad sense, and to Lewis's conviction that all occultism is dangerous.

For Lewis disagreements did not destroy friendships. When Cecil Harwood's extremely handsome son was a pupil of Lewis's, Lewis joshed Harwood about his faith in Steiner's dramatic theory of evolution: "It gives me a queer feeling when I suddenly look up and see your old phiz looking out at me through his handsome features. It almost makes a chap believe in evolution." Ironically, when Barfield prepared Lewis's will, he appointed Harwood to the post of co-trustee; thus it was that for some years after Lewis's death two of England's

leading Anthroposophists administered his literary estate.

Kathryn Lindskoog

Bibliography

Adey, Lionel. "C. S. Lewis's 'Great War' with Owen Barfield." *English Literary Studies Series, No. 14.* Victoria, British Columbia: University of Victoria, 1978.

Diener, Astrid. "An Interview with Owen Barfield." *Mythlore* 78 (winter 1995): 14–19.

Gilbert, Douglas and Clyde S. Kilby, *C. S. Lewis, Images of His World* Grand Rapids, MI: Eerdmans, 1973.

Harwood, S. C. "About Anthroposophy" *C. S. Lewis at the Breakfast Table.* James Como (ed). New York: Macmillan, 1979.

Montgomery, John Warwick. *Principalities and Powers: The World of the Occult.* Minneapolis: Bethany House, 1973.

Apologetics

Apologetics is the explanation and defense of the beliefs of a religion, so what is needed in apologetics is the ability to teach and argue well. C. S. Lewis was an outstanding teacher and one of the greatest prose stylists of this era. His ability to use **metaphor** and **analogy** served his purpose of making **Christianity** clear to the ordinary listener or reader. He thus was one of the outstanding apologists of this century. Many of his apologetic works grew out of talks given originally to audiences at Royal Air Force bases in World War II and radio broadcasts carried by the British Broadcasting Company in 1941 and 1942.

In the essay **"Christian Apologetics"** (originally a talk given to a Church of England conference of priests and youth leaders) Lewis supplied clues to his own success as an apologist. First he asked what the Christian apologist must defend. His answer was Christianity itself—the faith preached by the apostles, attested by the martyrs, embodied in the creeds, and expounded by the fathers of the church. He contrasted this with our individual opinions on **God** and humanity. Each of us, he said, have many opinions that we think are consistent with this faith as well as being true and important. But it is not our business as apologists to defend these. He thought that this gives the apologist a great tactical advantage, emphasizing that he is defending Christianity because it is true, not just because it agrees with our own opinions.

In the chapter "Time and Beyond Time" in Book IV of *Mere Christianity* Lewis gave an explanation of the Boethian view that God is "outside" of time. But he then emphasized that although this idea has helped him a great deal it is not in the **Bible** nor in any of the Creeds.

He said that you can be a perfectly good Christian without accepting it.

Lewis next argued that this care to distinguish one's own ideas and reactions from the Christian faith is excellent for apologists themselves. It forces them to face up to those elements in Christianity which they find obscure or repulsive. For example, in talking about the doctrine of **hell** in *The Problem of Pain*, Lewis said that there is no doctrine he would rather remove from Christianity, but that the evidence of the Bible and tradition (especially some of the words of Christ) seems to leave us no alternative to such a belief. From this Lewis argued that instead of reading only the latest writing on religion the apologist should read as many old books as new ones because these older works contain precisely the truths of which our own age is neglectful. On the other hand, in the sciences one should keep abreast with current developments but be wary of using them for apologetic purposes since just as we put the finishing touches on such appeals to what "**science** has proved" science has changed its mind and withdrawn the theory we had been using.

An interesting idea at this point in the essay is what one might call "indirect apologetics." Instead of writing directly apologetic works, said Lewis, Christians should write short works on other subjects with their Christianity *latent*: for it is not the books written in defense of **materialism** that make an impression on people but the materialist assumptions in many scientific works.

Lewis then turned to the apologetic situation in England in the 1940s. He found that the average listener to his **RAF talks** at the air bases had a number of obstacles to apologetics. First, his audiences were total skeptics about history, though they had a faith in "prehistory," which they regarded as "science." Second, they had a distrust of ancient texts. Third, they had almost no sense of **sin**, and finally, they spoke a different language than that of the educated apologist.

For each of these difficulties, Lewis suggested partial solutions. With regard to skepticism about history and ancient documents he found that modern listeners found assurance in the science of textual criticism. With regard to a sense of sin, Lewis knew that many no longer regarded fornication as wrong, so it was no use trying to arouse a sense of sin in generalities. Rather he found that if modern listeners started with the sins that had been their own chief problems recently, they better understood the concept.

With regard to the "different languages" problem, Lewis gave a glossary of commonly misunderstood terms. He argued that there is no use at all laying out *a priori* what ordinary people do or do not understand: you must find out by experience. He said that ability to put your theological ideas into ordinary language is a test of your own understanding of them.

He now turned to actual cases. He stated that perhaps the ideal team of apologists would include one person who took an intellectual approach and another who took an emotional approach to defending Christianity. In this essay, Lewis said he would talk only of the intellectual approach. Lewis thought that intellectual defenses of the faith are apt to be more effective than some might think because the ordinary person is not put off by argument: in fact, the sheer novelty of this approach often engages them.

In talking about the Incarnation, Lewis recommended using some of the "either God or a bad man" argument (based on his own claims, **Christ** could either be God or an impostor; but he couldn't simply be a "good moral teacher"). With regard to the historicity of the Gospels, Lewis said he was able to use his own expertise as a literary critic to emphasize that the Gospels were certainly not legends. Other apologists with different backgrounds may also be able to apply it to this and similar questions.

At several points in this essay, Lewis emphasized that an important thing to get across to the apologists is that apologetics is a matter of finding the truth about religion. If apologists allow their audience to direct the question to what good Christianity does, the discussion will be bogged down with questions of the behavior of specific groups of Christians. As Lewis said, it is a question of truth: Christianity if false is of no importance; if true is of infinite importance; what it cannot be is moderately important.

Lewis went on to make the distinction between "Thick and Clear" religions. Hinduism is the only religion that rivals Christianity in the combination of "Thick" religion, with its ecstasies and mysteries and local attachments, and "Clear" religion, with its "philosophical, ethical and universalizing" tendencies. But Hinduism satisfies these two needs imperfectly: the Clear religion of the Brahmin hermit goes on *side* by *side* with the Thick religion of the village temple. But in Christianity these two tendencies are united.

Finally Lewis observed that nothing is more dangerous to one's own faith than the work of an apologist (a thought echoed in poetic form in his poem "An Apologists Evening Prayer"). Lewis said that when he has successfully defended an article of the faith it seemed for the moment to depend on his arguments. For this reason apologists should fall back continually from the web of their own arguments to the experienced reality of Christ himself. And for this reason apologists should certainly pray for each other.

Richard Purtill
Western Washington University

Also See: Books of Influence, G. K. Chesterton, Evolution, Materialism, Miracles

Thomas Aquinas (1224?–1274)

The greatest theologian of the Middle Ages (and one of the greatest theologians of all time), Thomas Aquinas was born near the city of Aquino located between Rome and Naples in Italy. He is called the *Angelic Doctor* and ranks with **Augustine** in importance as a Christian philosopher and teacher. He was a member of the Dominican monastic order. Early on his fellow friars dubbed him the "dumb ox," a reference to both his corpulence and personal reserve. Aquinas loved books; when he was asked for what he thanked **God** most, he answered: "I have understood every page I ever read."

Aquinas' method of solving the "problem" of **culture** (human achievement in the sphere of art, **politics**, **philosophy**, **psychology**, etc.) has become the standard model for many Christians, particularly Roman Catholics. In Saint Thomas' synthesis, all institutions like the above are organically related to each other. Therefore, the study of the humblest fact can lead to the study of the highest **truth**.

Aquinas, therefore, contended that there is no conflict between **faith** and **reason**. It is the very essence of the Thomist teaching that reason and common sense can be trusted. Much truth can be reached by a rational process, if only the process is rational enough. Aquinas, enormously influenced by **Aristotle**, concluded that philosophy is based on reason, and theology is based on the revealed Word of God. For him, faith rests on a rational foundation, and philosophy does not conflict with historic **Christianity**.

In his famous *Summa Theologica*, Aquinas summarized and synthesized human knowledge derived from both reason and **revelation**, using Aristotle's logic to deal with apparent contradictions. His system, called *Thomism*, was made the official view of the Roman Catholic Church in 1879 and is highly respected throughout the Christian world.

Lewis had considerable respect for Aquinas and Roman Catholic tradition. His own synthesis of faith and reason (presented in *Mere Christianity* and elsewhere) owed much to Thomism, as did his defense of **natural law** in *The Abolition of Man*. Lewis also always included **Roman Catholicism** in his definition of orthodox Christianity. At one point in *The Great Divorce* he indicated that perhaps both the Roman Catholic and Protestants positions were right.

Michael H. Macdonald
Seattle Pacific University

Also See: Anglicanism, Hierarchy, Medieval World, Rationalism

Bibliography

Aquinas, *Summa Theologica*.

Chesterton, G. K. *Saint Thomas Aquinas*. New York: Doubleday, 1974.

"Are Athletes Better than Scholars"

Cherbourg School Magazine. 2 (1913). Reproduced in The Lewis Family Papers. III: 318–19.

An extract (transcribed in **The Lewis Family Papers** by **Warren Lewis**) from an article in the *Cherbourg School Magazine* dated 1913. It raises questions about the meaning of "better"; points out difficulties in the assumptions of the title; and asserts that although the **scholar** "benefits and glorifies his fellow beings," yet success of England's cricket team in Australia would be of more interest than success of England in a "dangerous and even unequal **war**." Lewis concluded that popular opinion should not blind us to the fact that "athletic success is transitory," and "one cannot lose sight of the mistakes and wrong ideas arising from an exaggerated estimate of [athletics'] value." ("Mistakes" is itself probably a typographical mistake for "mistaken.")

An impressive essay by a fourteen-year-old Lewis, more noted for its vocabulary and ideas than for its **logic**. Lewis hated athletics.

John Bremer

Also See: Cherbourg School

"Arise my Body"

Fear No More: A Book of Poems for the Present Time by Living English Poets. Cambridge: Cambridge University Press, 1940: 89. Revised and retitled as "After Prayers, Lie Cold" in *Poems* and *Collected Poems*.

This poem was originally published anonymously. However, six copies of *Fear No More* contained an additional leaf identifying the authors. One of these copies is in the **Bodleian Library**, Oxford. This meditation concerns experiencing forgiveness and how when one is spent with weary struggling with **God** and life, the best course is to rest, patiently enduring all that is sent one's way; such passivity may be cold comfort, but it is superior to the coming of certain **pain**.

Don W. King
Montreat College

Aristotle (384–322 B.C.)

Aristotle was one of the greatest philosophers who ever lived. His influence is felt in numerous philosophical areas, including **metaphysics, ethics, politics,** and **aesthetics**. Lewis often spoke in general terms of "great pagans" like **Plato** and Aristotle.

Lewis was well aware that we in the Western world are "heirs to centuries of logical analysis." We are "sons to Aristotle" (*Miracles*). Lewis understood that when Aristotle's name is made into an adjective, it is usually attached to the word "logic." It seems that there are certain "laws of thought" that pertain to all things that exist, i.e., that pertain to all Being. This insight that logical principles express the most general nature of things was first clearly expressed by Aristotle. If this is true, it would appear that the study of logic is the study of the most general or most pervasive characteristics of both whatever is and whatever may be. With reference to the idea of **truth**, for example, Lewis accepted a definition of truth that consists in a correspondence between the mind and **reality**. There are no degrees of truth. Either a statement is true or not. Lewis applied logic frequently in his work. For example, in *The Screwtape Letters* Lewis noted: "Of course, there is no conceivable way of getting by reason from the proposition 'I am losing interest in this' to the proposition 'This is false.'"

Lewis was also very familiar with Aristotle's ethics and aesthetics. Many of Lewis's key concepts were influenced by Aristotle, although Lewis modified them substantially. Important examples include: the good, right action, a good and wise man, **happiness**, pleasure and **pain**, **friendship**, the moral **virtues** (including prudence), and freedom. Aristotle's *Poetics* has probably been the single most influential work in all **literary criticism**. It expresses the view that **poetry** is something more philosophical and of greater importance than history, since it deals with universals, whereas history treats only the particulars of what has happened.

Michael H. Macdonald
Seattle Pacific University

Also See: Good and Evil, Natural Law, Paganism

Bibliography

Aristotle. *Metaphysics; Nicomachean Ethics; Poetics.*
Lewis, C. S. *The Abolition of Man*; *Christian Reflections*; *Miracles* (particularly "Miracles of the New Creation"); *Oxford History of English Literature; The Screwtape Letters.*

Matthew Arnold (1822–1888)

Matthew Arnold was an influential 19th-century writer and literary critic who brought liberal ideas about **education** and **culture** from France and Germany to the English-speaking world.

In *An Experiment in Criticism,* C. S. Lewis spoke favorably of Arnold's **literary criticism** with its curiosity-driven desire to see something as "it really is." Lewis was much more negative about Arnold's attempt to replace historic **Christianity** with culture. In **"Christianity and Culture"** Lewis blamed the "present inordinate esteem of culture" on Arnold. In **"Unreal Estates"** he spoke of Arnold's "horrible prophecy that literature would increasingly replace **religion**" with the resulting "bitter persecution, great intolerance, and traffic in relics." Unfortunately, Lewis did not go on to challenge the academic dogma equating religion with intolerance. Far better is his argument in **"A Reply to Professor Haldane"** that those whose ideas "lead to **Hell**" will adopt whatever ideas are powerful at a given time. In a religious age, they will appear religious. In an age where culture and **science** are worshipped, they will cloak themselves in culture and scientific planning.

Mike Perry

Bibliography

Arnold, Matthew. *Culture and Anarch* (1869).
_____. *God and the Bible* (1875).
_____. "The Study of Poetry" in *Essays in Criticism* (1888).

"Arrangement of Pindar"

Mandrake. 1 no. 6 (1949): 43–45. Revised and retitled as "Pindar Sang" and reprinted in *Poems* and *Collected Poems.*

Pindar (518?–438? B.C.), the greatest lyric poet of ancient Greece, the master of *epinicia* (odes), is the subject of this piece. Pindar is pictured with his chorus dancing while he somberly speaks of the demands on an artist. Pindar argues an artist is born, not made; hard work is also necessary, but if the gods do not give genius and blessing, the best effort will achieve but silence. Hymnlike, the poem follows loosely the epinicia pattern: praise of the gods, reference to myth, and aphoristic moralizing.

Don W. King
Montreat College

King Arthur

This quasi-historical king of 6th-century Britain has inspired some of England's finest writers, including Sir Thomas Malory, **Edmund Spenser**, and Alfred, Lord Tennyson. Lewis particularly admired Malory's *Le Morte D'Arthur*, the 15th-century prose romance featuring King Arthur, Queen Guinevere, Merlin the Magician, and the Knights of the Round Table. At the heart of the Arthurian **myth** lies the Quest for the Holy Grail, the vessel allegedly used by **Christ** and his disciples at the Last Supper.

Although Lewis told a former pupil that he knew "very little" about the legend of the Grail, he nonetheless incorporated elements of the Arthurian cycle into both his fiction and **literary criticism**. His narrative poem "Launcelot," written in the 1930s and published posthumously, is an account of the knight's adventures in his quest for the Grail. In *That Hideous Strength*, the final novel of Lewis's space trilogy, a small remnant of Logres, Arthur's mythical kingdom, survives in modern Britain. One of its members, Dr. Dimble, notes that "something we may call Britain is always haunted by something we may call Logres. Haven't you noticed that we are two countries? After every Arthur, a Mordred; behind every Milton, a Cromwell." Under attack by an evil bureaucracy, the remnant of Logres relies upon the re-awakened Merlin and his magical powers for their very survival. Critics have suggested that the novel reflects the influence of his friend and fellow author, **Charles Williams**, who wrote two narrative poems based upon Arthurian myth, *Taliessin through Logres* and *The Region of the Summer Stars*. Following Williams' death, Lewis edited his friend's unfinished prose history, *The Figure of Arthur*, and wrote a commentary on Williams' Arthurian cycle, both of which were included in *Arthurian Torso*, published in 1948. For Lewis, the kingdom of Logres represents the idealistic quest for virtue essential to those who live in "merry middle earth," between the perfection of Galahad and the depravity of Mordred. "If the round table is abolished," he warned, "for every one who rises to the level of Galahad, a hundred will drop plumb down to that of Mordred.... Galahad must not make common cause with Mordred, for it is always Mordred who gains, and he who loses, by such alliance." As he does so often, Lewis discovered an essential **truth** within the realm of the mythopoetic.

Lynn Summer
Georgia State University

Also See: Imagination, Paganism

Bibliography

Fitzgerald, Dorothy H. "Arthurian Torso: Lewis's Commentary of Williams' Arthuriad." *CSL: The Bulletin of the New York C. S. Lewis Society.* 15 (September 1984): 1–11.

Lewis, C. S. *Letters of C. S. Lewis*; *Narrative Poems*; *A Preface to Paradise Lost*; *That Hideous Strength.*

Malory, Thomas. *Le Morte D'Arthur.* R. M. Lumiansky (ed). New York: Charles Scribner's Sons, 1982.

Williams, Charles. *Arthurian Torso.* London: Oxford University Press, 1948.

_____. *The Arthurian Poems of Charles Williams: Taliessin through Logres* and *The Region of the Summer Stars.* Cambridge: D. S. Brewer, 1938, 1944.

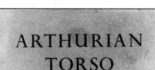

ARTHURIAN TORSO

CONTAINING THE POSTHUMOUS FRAGMENT OF *THE FIGURE OF ARTHUR* BY CHARLES WILLIAMS AND A COMMENTARY ON THE ARTHURIAN POEMS OF CHARLES WILLIAMS BY C. S. LEWIS

OXFORD UNIVERSITY PRESS

U.K. First Edition

Arthurian Torso (Commentary)

London: Oxford University Press, 1948.
US title: *Taliessin Through Logres.* Grand Rapids, MI: Eerdmans, 1974.

When **Charles Williams** died in 1945 his great work on the Arthurian legend remained incomplete. Some **poetry** had been published as *Taliessin Through Logres* (1938) and *The Region of the Summer Stars* (1944), but the poems were difficult for many readers to understand. In addition, his prose history of the Arthurian legend, "The Figure of Arthur," was unfinished.

C. S. Lewis had discussed the poetry with Williams and understood much of what Williams was saying. He agreed to write a commentary on the poetry ("Williams and the Arthuriad") to be published with the incomplete text of the history. The two were published together in 1948 as *Arthurian Torso*. In 1974 the two books of poetry and Arthurian Torso were published in one volume.

Mike Perry

Also See: King Arthur, Epic, Heroes, Magic, Medieval World, Myth

Bibliography

Fitzgerald, Dorothy. "Arthurian Torso." *CSL: The Bulletin of the New York C. S. Lewis Society*. 15 (September 1984): 1–10.

"Arthuriana"

See entry on *Arthurian Literature in the Middle Ages: A Collaborative Study* (Book Review)

Arthurian Literature in the Middle Ages: A Collaborative Study (Book Review)

"Arthuriana." *The Cambridge Review*. LXXXI (13 February 1960): 355, 357.

This book is characterized by Lewis as an encyclopedia of Arthuriana. The articles span a wide range of subject matter and purpose. Lewis singled out Faffier's entry on Chrétien de Troyes as an example of superlative work. Other articles he found "entirely taken up with close reasoning to conclusions about matter of fact." He pronounced the book "civilized," a crowning achievement.

Anne Gardner

Bibliography

Loomis, R. S. (ed). *Arthurian Literature in the Middle Ages: A Collaborative Study*.

The Art of Courtly Love (Book Review)

The Review of English Studies. XIX (January 1943): 77–79.

According to Lewis, this lucid translation is made more accessible to a general audience through notes and an introduction that combines "a good deal of information about the circumstances in which medieval love **poetry** arose and the suggestions offered by scholars as to its origins." Lewis said this useful book should be included in college libraries.

Anne Gardner

Bibliography

Capellanus, Andreas. *The Art of Courtly Love* (with introduction, translation, and notes by John Jay Parry).

John Hawkins Askins (1877–1923)

John Askins was the younger brother of **Janie Moore**. Always known as "Doc," he attended Trinity College, Dublin, taking a medical degree in 1904. Joining the Royal Army Medical Corps, he was wounded in January 1917. He married and lived in Clevedon, where a daughter Peony was born. The war had profoundly disturbed him, and, perhaps to help himself, he studied psychoanalysis; in 1922 he and his family moved to Iffley,

near **Oxford**, so he could be near his sister, Janie Moore, whom he visited nearly every day. He and Jack had long conversations, always coming round to **immortality**.

It seems that as a young man he had contracted syphilis, and Doc thought that, after a dormant period, it was affecting his brain. It is unclear whether this was so. His symptoms were terrible dreams and hallucinations accompanied by wild ravings and the wildest struggles— the final ones in the house of C. S. Lewis and Janie Moore, where he lived in February and March 1923. He was taken to a hospital, where he died of a heart attack on 23 April 1923. Lewis regarded the Doc as an object lesson for a time, fearing that his fate had to do with emotionalism, psychoanalysis, and the occult; Lewis, who had feared for his own sanity, wanted to avoid them. Lewis's experiences with Dr. Askins may be reflected in his unfinished novel known as **The Easley Fragment**.

John Bremer

"As One Oldster to Another"

Punch. 218 (March 15, 1950): 294–95 (under the pseudonym Nat Whilk). Revised and reprinted in *Poems* and *Collected Poems*.

The physical hardship of growing old is symbolized by a train moving through various stations. The struggle and **pain** of the journey, however, are muted by **joy** that catches one unawares, breathing moments of unspeakable delight and beautiful desire.

Don W. King
Montreat College

Atheism

C. S. Lewis was an atheist for much of his youth and young manhood, a background that enabled him to understand unbelief from the inside. As a result, his arguments against atheism are particularly compelling. He was able to use logic and **reason**, the atheist's favorite tools, to show that atheism is neither logical nor reasonable.

Raised a nominal Christian, Lewis became angry with **God** when his prayers did not save his mother from an early and painful death. A lack of real religious guidance set him spiritually adrift in his adolescence. While he experienced fleeting intimations of transcendence, which he called "**Joy**" (and which he compartmentalized as an "aesthetic" experience), he rejected God in the characteristic contradiction of the young atheist: "I maintained that God did not exist. I was also very angry with God for not existing. I was equally angry with Him for creating a world."

Working from this immature atheism to the views of more sophisticated atheist philosophers, Lewis did feel the relief that most atheists feel for a time—a sensation of being set free from any cosmic overseer, of being finally "let alone." But his rigorous training in **philosophy** soon denied him that comfort. He came to realize that if matter is random and all value is subjective—if nothing in the world has any real meaning beyond what the philosopher gives it, if all the universe is merely atoms spinning aimlessly—then the philosopher's brain is merely atoms too. Thus, all his philosophy is as meaningless and subjective as everything he pronounces that judgment upon. "If the whole universe has no meaning," Lewis observed in *Mere Christianity*, "we should never have found out it has no meaning."

In his autobiography, ***Surprised by Joy***, Lewis admitted a certain respect for unbelievers who claim to expect nothing from the universe. His resolutely atheist **tutor William Kirkpatrick** was a sturdy practitioner of this philosophy, "a rationalist of the old high and dry nineteenth century type." But later Lewis would argue that all "rational" philosophies are really parasites upon **religion**, for their ideas of **justice** and rationality cannot be built on the shifting sand of a random universe. In his **allegory** *Pilgrim's Regress,* Lewis portrayed various representatives of "humanism" coming out at night to picnic upon the food provided by Christian **ethics**. They eat heartily but ignore the question of who laid the picnic in the first place.

Most of Lewis's arguments against unbelief confront such illogical attitudes. With a mock sigh, he laments that 20th-century atheism has lost its dignity and devolved into a sort of popular-science **paganism**. In **"The Funeral of a Great Myth,"** Lewis dissected the tenets of modern "scientific" unbelief and found that worldview remarkably similar to ancient Norse myths, with elements of **fairy tales** and various literary archetypes thrown in for good measure. The "Great Myth" of Creative **Evolution** begins with a formless universe, wherein by chance the tiny underdog life bubbles up one-celled from the void. The tiny "life force" forges on, growing in complexity and intelligence against all odds. Finally, like biblical David or Jack the Giant Killer, it begins to conquer the monsters in its environment, to rise from serf to noble despite the hostile world. Next, the life force becomes king of nature, both organic and human. Finally, the once-one-celled peasant becomes a demigod, crowned with eugenics, rational socialism, and a scientifically adjusted psyche. But as in Norse mythology or Elizabethan tragedy, this hero is fated to fall swiftly as nature asserts herself. Suns cool, the universe runs down, and the demigods must fade, like their heroic Norse antecedents, into the final twilight of the gods. Lewis enjoyed the **myth**, but said he would keep it with Balder and Helen and the Argonauts where it belongs. In what one suspects is further dry humor, Lewis ascribed unquestioned acceptance of the atheist myth to the same human shortcomings that atheists attribute the embrace of religion: wish fulfillment, subconscious urges and complexes, sociopolitical strivings, and the like.

In other writings Lewis aimed for something more important than skillful argument or turning smug modern thinking on its head. The serious and very real problem with rejecting God, as Lewis illustrated so vividly in his novels, is that nature abhors a vacuum. When finally "set free" from God, the atheist too often finds himself inexplicably drawn to darker yearnings—to "dabbling in dirt" of quasi-spiritual philosophies that rationalize self-centeredness as a **virtue**, that promote raw power, cruelty, and finally loss of the coveted self.

Lewis himself, after solemnly rejecting the Christian God and becoming a scientific atheist, was fascinated by theosophy, **magic**, and other occult manifestations, and felt that if he had not accepted Christ, he might have ended up a **Satan** worshipper or insane. But for all his rejection of the vacuum that leads to the occult, Lewis did not deny the existence of Satan, the real director of human strivings for occult power. According to Lewis, to disbelieve in the Devil, to reject him on the grounds that silly popular anthropomorphic imagery disproves him, is as dangerous and wrongheaded as rejecting God on the same grounds. As senior devil Screwtape tells junior tempter Wormwood in *The Screwtape Letters*, the first step to enslaving a human is getting him to disbelieve in Satan; the second step is fostering disbelief in God. Characters in Lewis's **space trilogy** embody the downward spiral of those who deny God. Weston begins as a scientific atheist who rejects all notions of anything beyond experimental proof. He next becomes a creative evolutionist, then a believer in a formless **supernatural** "force," and by the end of *Perelandra* he degenerates into a kind of horrible protoplasmic hand puppet for Satan himself. In ***That Hideous Strength***, Devine, who rejects all but the material, who has not even Weston's spark of Creative Evolutionary altruism, becomes yet another pawn of evil. And a variety of other clever modern types in *Strength*—the logical positivist, the scientist with a fetish for "objectivity"—all who choose to turn from the light are sucked from the "freedom" of unbelief in a loving God into the clutches of a more brutal master than they ever imagined the Christian God could be.

As Lewis learned from **George MacDonald,** "The one principle of **Hell** is, 'I am my own.'" Hell's inhabitants in *The Great Divorce* seem to be in less trouble than in the trilogy or in Screwtape's scenario, but they are no less doomed for their voluntary rejection of God. Lewis once again postulated that we are not free to "just be left alone"; if we do not serve God, we serve the Devil, or, almost as terrible, we serve our corrupted selves, choosing an eternity of self-deception to the **free will** offer of Paradise.

Whatever atheism's denouement, for Lewis the philosophy of "unfaith" is neither smart nor scientific, neither rational nor harmless. It is, given our fallen **human nature,** a foolish business at best and an extremely dangerous attitude at worst. Put in modern evolutionary terms, one must either evolve from selfishness to God-consciousness or devolve into anonymous cannon fodder for Satan's rebellion against God.

Richard A. Hill
Taylor University

Also See: Aesthetics, Apologetics, Materialism, Non-Christian Religions, Paganism, Spirituality

Bibliography

Lewis, C. S. *The Great Divorce*; "The Funeral of a Great Myth"; *Mere Christianity; Miracles; The Pilgrim's Regress; The Screwtape Letters; Out of the Silent Planet; Perelandra; That Hideous Strength; Surprised by Joy.*

W[ystan] H[ugh] Auden (1907–1973)

W. H. Auden and the fellows of his circle in the 1930s aroused Lewis's ire at modern English **poetry**. In *The Pilgrim's Regress* are parodies of modern poets; most of them appear in III.i–iii; but Gus Halfways' "machine on wheels," with its mechanism that looks like "a nest of hedgehogs and serpents" (II.viii), may refer to Auden's early verse. For example, Auden wrote in "1929": "Yet sometimes men look and say good / At strict beauty of locomotive. . . ."

It is also likely that Lewis had in mind Auden's early poetry when he denounced the privatism of modern poets who published poems that could only be understood by their select friends. Lewis, however, was more polite when he directly mentioned Auden's name in print, as in his comment about John Skelton as an amateur poet and the use of Skelton's works by better modern poets: "Mr. [Robert] Graves, Mr. Auden, and others

receive from Skelton principally what they give and in their life, if not alone, yet eminently, does Skelton live."

Auden's own attitude toward Lewis was mixed. He did not mention him often, but he was influenced by Lewis's religious writings. His citations of Lewis in the notes to the first edition of "New Year Letter" (in *The Double Man* [1941]) were scholarly; his review of *The Great Divorce* (1945) was ambivalent; his review of *English Literature in the Sixteenth Century*, in a book-club magazine, was appreciative. But more significantly, in a poem written near the end of his life, he mentioned Lewis along with Kierkegaard and **Charles Williams** as bringing him back to **Christianity**: "A Thanksgiving" (probably written in May 1973; published in 1974), Auden included these lines: "Finally, hair-raising things / that Hitler and Stalin were doing / forced me to think about God. / Why was I sure they were wrong? / Wild Kierkegaard, Williams and Lewis/guided me back to belief."

According to **Nevill Coghill**, who had been Auden's **tutor** at **Oxford**, Lewis and Auden eventually met; and "I believe that when they met, they liked each other."

Joe R. Christopher

Bibliography

Coghill, Nevill. "The Approach to English." *Light on C. S. Lewis.* Jocelyn Gibb (ed). London: Geoffrey Bles, 1965: 51–66.

Augustine (354–430)

Augustine of Hippo was one of the greatest leaders of the early Christian **church**. When Lewis refers to the great "Christian teachers," he is thinking of theologians such as Saint Augustine.

As a young man, Augustine pursued worldly pleasures and success. His early life and spiritual struggles are described in his *Confessions*, one of the first great autobiographies. In contrast to Greek philosophers, Augustine insisted that to know the **truth** is not necessarily to do the truth, for the essential nature of humankind is not **reason** but will. His magnum opus was *The City of God*, in which Augustine noted that history from beginning to end is divided by two alternative loves—the earthly love of self, and the heavenly love of **God**. These two invisible cities, the *Civitas Dei* ("the City of God") and the *Civitas Mundi* ("the Earthly City"), with their members interspersed in all institutions, are reminders that in the end our minds and hearts (i.e., our wills) are either focused on the earthly city by the love of self or the heavenly city by the love of God. Similarly, Lewis stressed that in the final analysis the choice will be **Heaven** (when we say to God: "Thy will be done") or **Hell** (when God says to us: "Thy will be done"). (Compare Lewis's *The Great Divorce*.)

In numerous key places (for example, his conclusions on **pride**, **pain**, glory, Heaven, infinite **happiness**, and **Joy**) Lewis was mindful of Augustine. Both Lewis and Augustine were convinced that humans are eternally restless until they find their rest in God.

Michael H. Macdonald
Seattle Pacific University

Also See: Free Will, Philosophy, Reality, Sex, Spirituality

Bibliography

Augustine. *Confessions*; *City of God*.

Brown, Peter. *Augustine of Hippo*. New York: Dorset Press, 1987.

Lewis, C. S. *The Great Divorce; Mere Christianity*; *The Problem of Pain*.

Jane Austen (1775–1817)

C. S. Lewis, in the sympathetic essay **"A Note on Jane Austen,"** observed that as a writer, she was the daughter of **Samuel Johnson**, in her style, morality, and common sense. It is consistently the case in her novels that her heroines are overtaken by self-deception—often the result of self-hatred or contempt. The pivotal moments in her stories come as a kind of awakening, or what Lewis termed "undeception." Once corrected of this self-deception, the heroines become observers of this deception in others. Austen was, for Lewis, a guide in the "grammar of conduct" and an expositor of "cheerful moderation."

Jerry Root
Wheaton College

"The Author of *Flowering Rifle*"

See entry on "To Mr. Roy Campbell"

"Awake, My Lute"

The Atlantic Monthly. 172 (November 1943): 113, 115. Reprinted in *Collected Poems*.

The key to understanding this concoction of incoherent revelries concerning boring lecturers, shipmates on the Ark, and insufficient answers on **Oxford** examinations is they are the disconnected fragments of a **dream**.

Don W. King
Montreat College

B

Leo Kingley Baker (1898–1986)

After a distinguished career as an aviator in the Royal Flying Corps during World War I, Leo Baker returned to Wadham College, **Oxford,** in 1919 to study history. Baker and Lewis met during 1919, and while Baker was a student of Modern History, he shared with Lewis a love of **poetry**. They worked together on an anthology of poetry, which was never published. Baker was a close friend and often visited Lewis and **Janie Moore**. Additionally, Baker introduced Lewis to **Owen Barfield** who was also a student at Wadham.

Jeffrey D. Schultz

Bibliography

Baker, Leo. "Near the Beginning." *C. S. Lewis at the Breakfast Table*. James T. Como (ed). New York: Macmillan, 3–10.

Lewis, C. S. *All My Road Before Me*.

Arthur James Balfour (1848–1930)

Arthur James Balfour, first Earl of Balfour, philosopher and statesman, delivered the 1914 Gifford Lectures, *Theism and Humanism*, mentioned by Lewis as one of the ten most important **books of influence** on him. However, there is only one reference in Lewis's published writings to this book and its author: Lewis cited Balfour in his 1944 Socratic Society paper, **"Is Theology Poetry?"** where he called *Theism and Humanism* "a book too little read." It would appear that Lewis read Balfour no earlier than the late spring of 1944; otherwise the considerable influence of *Theism and Humanism* upon the writing of the book *Miracles* would show up in Lewis's earlier apologetic works, *The Problem of Pain, Broadcast Talks, The Abolition of Man*, **"The Funeral of a Great Myth,"** and the sermon

"Transposition." Any one of these might have prompted a reader or listener to suggest to Lewis that he read Balfour; but this is speculation. What can be said with certainty is that the thesis and even the language of Balfour's first Gifford lectures permeates the first five chapters of *Miracles*. It was from Balfour that Lewis derived the self-refutability of naturalism. And Balfour's "plain man's point of view, the creed of common sense" greatly appealed to Lewis.

Paul F. Ford
St. John's Seminary

Also See: Apologetics, Atheism, Miracles, Materialism

Bibliography

Balfour, Arthur James. *Theism and Humanism: The Gifford Lectures for 1914*. New York: George H. Doran, 1915.

"Ballade of Dead Gentlemen"

Punch. 220 (March 28, 1951): 386 (under the pseudonym Nat Whilk). Reprinted in *Poems* and *Collected Poems*.

A lighthearted poem asking the question: "Where have all the gentlemen husbands gone?" Lewis referred to numerous literary husbands whose wives outshine them, leaving the men only as curious memories.

Don W. King
Montreat College

Arthur Owen Barfield (1898–1997)

Author and philosopher Owen Barfield was born just two weeks before C. S. Lewis, on November 9, 1898. The men met as undergraduates at **Oxford** and became lifelong friends. This **friendship** flourished despite— or perhaps as a result of—significant differences between them, differences expressed in a series of letters (1925–27) that they called **"The Great War."** In *Surprised by Joy*, Lewis described Barfield as the kind of friend who "disagrees with you about everything. He is not so much the alter ego as the anti-self.... When you set out to correct his heresies, you find he forsooth has decided to correct yours! And then you go at it hammer and tongs, far into the night, night after night.... Out of this perpetual dogfight a community of mind and a deep affection emerge."

Barfield began writing at an early age. He published his first poem "Air-Castles" in *Punch* in 1917, at the age of nineteen, and continued to write and publish poetry throughout his life. His first book was a fairy tale entitled *The Silver Trumpet* (1925). It was followed by *History in English Words* (1926), and then the publication

of his B.Litt. thesis, *Poetic Diction* (1928), a book that had a profound influence on C. S. Lewis, and even more on **J. R. R. Tolkien**.

Barfield's philosophical ideas were wide-ranging, concerned primarily with the relationships of **language**, myth, and perception. Among his key beliefs was the evolution of consciousness, his conviction that the way people perceive the world changes significantly over time. Barfield believed that language change is the best evidence of the evolution of consciousness, an idea he develops at some length in *History in English Words*. He was strongly influenced by his commitment to **Anthroposophy**, a religious school of thought developed by Rudolph Steiner.

While Lewis completely rejected Anthroposophy, evidence of Barfield's thought and references to him are found throughout Lewis's nonfiction, perhaps most directly in chapter 10 of *Miracles* and in *Studies In Words* (1960). Furthermore, some have speculated that Ramandu, the retired star in *The Voyage of the "Dawn Treader,"* is an affectionate portrait of Barfield. That book was dedicated to Geoffrey Barfield, Owen Barfield's son, and the first book in the series, *The Lion, the Witch and the Wardrobe*, was dedicated to his daughter, Lewis's godchild, Lucy.

Lewis described Barfield as "the wisest and best of my unofficial teachers." He wrote that perhaps his greatest debt to Barfield was to be freed from **chronological snobbery**, which he defined as "the uncritical acceptance of the intellectual climate common to our own age and the assumption that whatever has gone out of date is on that account discredited." Lewis learned from Barfield that his own age is also a "period" and, as such, is subject to many flawed assumptions. This realization was foundational to much of Lewis's thought, both literary and theological, and served as the philosophical basis of *The Discarded Image* (1964).

After seven years as a freelance writer and editor, Barfield moved from Oxford to London and trained as a solicitor, joining his father's law firm in 1929. In the 1940s, when Lewis decided to channel his royalties into a charitable trust he called his "Agapargyry," he asked Barfield to establish and maintain it. This event was fictionalized in *This Ever-Diverse Pair*, where Lewis appears as a character named Ramsden. Lewis also appears as a character named Jak in Barfield's "Night Operations."

Many of Barfield's most important books were published when retirement from law in 1959 allowed him to devote himself to full-time scholarship. He also traveled extensively as a lecturer and visiting scholar, making a number of trips to the United States. His most recently published book is *Orpheus: A Poetic Drama* (1983). He made his home in Kent, England, before his death, at age ninety-nine, on December 14, 1997.

Diana Pavlac Glyer
Azusa Pacific University

Bibliography

Adey, Lionel. *C. S. Lewis's Great War with Owen Barfield.*
_____. "The Barfield–Lewis 'Great War.'" *CSL: The Bulletin of the New York C. S. Lewis Society.* 6 (August 1973): 10–14.
_____. "A Response to Dr. Thorsen." *CSL: The Bulletin of the New York C. S. Lewis Society.* 15 (March 1984): 6–10.
Barfield, Owen. *The Silver Trumpet* (1925). Grand Rapids, MI: Eerdmans, 1968.
_____. *History in English Words.* London: Faber and Faber, 1926.
_____. *Poetic Diction: A Study in Meaning* (1928). New York: McGraw Hill, 1964.
_____. *Romanticism Comes of Age* (1944). Middletown, CT: Harcourt, Brace, Jovanovich, 1957.
_____. *This Ever-Diverse Pair.* London: Gallancz, 1950.
_____. *Saving the Appearances: A Study in Idolatry.* New York: Harcourt, Brace, Jovanovich, 1957.
_____. *Worlds Apart: A Dialogue of the Sixties* (1963). Middletown, CT: Wesleyan University Press, 1977.
_____. *Unancestral Voice.* Middletown, CT: Wesleyan University Press, 1965.
_____. *Speaker's Meaning.* London: Rudolf Steiner Press, 1967.
_____. *What Coleridge Thought.* Middletown, CT: Wesleyan University Press, 1971.
_____. *The Rediscovery of Meaning and Other Essays.* Middletown, CT: Wesleyan University Press, 1977.
_____. *History, Guilt and Habit.* Middletown, CT: Wesleyan University Press, 1979.
_____. *Orpheus: A Poetic Drama.* E. John C. Ulreich Jr. West Stockbridge, MA: Lindisfarne Press, 1983.
Thorsen, Stephen. "Knowing and Being in C. S. Lewis's 'Great War' with Owen Barfield." *CSL: The Bulletin of the New York C. S. Lewis Society.* 15 (November 1983): 1–8.
_____. "A Reply." *CSL: The Bulletin of the New York C. S. Lewis Society.* 15 (March 1984): 1–11.

Basic Fears (Letter)

The Times Literary Supplement. (2 December 1944): 583.

An article, "On Basic English: A Challenge to Innovators" by Arthur Quiller-Couch (*TLS*, 30 September 1944, 474 and 478), precipitated a variety of responses including this letter from Lewis in which he asserted the importance of the accuracy of translation over against the less essential aspect of style when evaluating a particular translation of the New Testament, in this case the Basic English Version.

Marjorie L. Mead
The Marion E. Wade Center

Basic Fears (Letter)

The Times Literary Supplement. (3 February 1945): 55.

S. H. Hooke (*TLS*, 27 January 1945, 43) responded angrily to Lewis's initial letter (see previous letter) by discussing the rationale for his translation of Colossians 1:15. In this letter, Lewis answered that unfortunately he understands no better even after reading Hooke's explanation. Hooke tried once again to make his point but ends with his continuing displeasure at Lewis's criticism of his Basic English Version translation (*TLS*, 10 February 1945, 67).

Marjorie L. Mead
The Marion E. Wade Center

Pauline Baynes (1922–)

Pauline Baynes was born in England in 1922, and her imagination was enriched by her early childhood in India. After attending art school, she drew charts for the Admiralty during the World War II. In 1949 **J. R. R. Tolkien** was pleased with her illustrations for *Farmer Giles of Ham*, and C. S. Lewis promptly selected her to illustrate his **Chronicles of Narnia**. Ironically, she did those famous line drawings as modestly paid work for hire. (Years later, she said that even minimal royalties would have "supported" her for life.)

Pauline Baynes has illustrated over a hundred books of many kinds and enjoyed an immensely successful career. In 1968 she won Britain's coveted Kate Greenaway Medal for her work in Grant Uden's *Dictionary of Chivalry*. In 1975 Penguin Books published *Puffin Annual, Number 2*, featuring a two-page autobiographical painting of her life. Her art is distinguished by its immensely energetic linear quality, profusion of fine detail, lyrical colors, and wit.

In the 1990s HarperCollins released three new Narnia books featuring color illustrations by Pauline Baynes: *The Land of Narnia*, **The Lion, the Witch and the Wardrobe**, and *A Book of Narnians*.

Kathryn Lindskoog

Bibliography

Patterson, Nancy-Lou. "An Appreciation of Pauline Baynes." *Mythlore.* 7 (Autumn 1980): 3–5.

Beauty

Lewis was both romantic and rational about beauty. For him it was closely associated with **nature**, but not strictly so. In fact, though he felt that earth's beauty hinted at a future healing of the breech between Spirit and Nature, he also cautioned that beauty was the sign and not the signifier and that to make it a "first thing" was to crush and lose it. He saw beauty as something coming down to us from the transcendent Beauty himself, **God**. Like **George MacDonald**, and **William Wordsworth** before him, Lewis found that beauty often and unexpectedly brought **joy**. This joy was a hint of what one could expect in **Heaven**. Lewis referred to such moments as "patches of Godlight," evoking the image of patches of sunlight in a wood. The pursuit of rare and unexpected beauty and moments of joy was a mark of Lewis's younger years and fueled his **romanticism** through many years of atheistic pessimism. In *Surprised by Joy* he relates how his full understanding of the nature of beauty developed and how the search eventually led him to **Christ**.

In **"The Weight of Glory"** Lewis cautioned against locating beauty in any one place. We are to recognize that beauty comes *through* our remembered moments or books or music, and does not exist intrinsically in them. Lewis's most complete statement on the balance of the rational and the romantic in the quest for beauty is succinctly put in the poem "No Beauty We Could Desire," in which he speaks of the search for beauty as a hunt for a hart through a wood where the hounds are perplexed by the shifting scents and clues. In the third stanza, the speaker turns from the hunt and leaves the forests behind for the "appointed place where you pursue." There the speaker finds his quarry, "Not in Nature, not even in Man, but in one / Particular Man, with a date, so tall, weighing / So much, talking Aramaic, . . ." and in " . . . this wine, this bread . . . no beauty we could desire."

James Prothero

Also See: Aesthetics, Atheism, Christianity, Imagery, Rationalism

"Before We Can Communicate"

Breakthrough. 8 (October 1961): 2. Reprinted in *God in the Dock, Undeceptions,* and *First and Second Things.*

Lewis wrote this article as a response to the problem of "communication under modern conditions between Christians and the outer world." Lewis said that his ideas were "purely empirical" and provided two anecdotes to illustrate his experience. The first dealt with the **prayer** in the old Prayer Book that asked "that the magistrates might 'truly and indifferently administer **justice**.'" The word *indifferently* was read by many as meaning "without concern," and so it was changed to *impartially*, which resulted in some people misunderstanding it and to others it was meaningless. The second anecdote dealt with a conversation between Lewis and a man who claimed to believe in a devil, but "not a personal Devil." The debate continued until Lewis realized he meant *corporeal* by the word *personal*. The difficulty in both these cases rests on the idea that the meanings of words are consistent among believers (and nonbelievers), which they clearly are not. Lewis suggested that, just as an ordination exam includes a paper on translation, there should be a compulsory translation of theological works into plain vernacular English. The result would be, according to Lewis, a respect for the value of learned language and an understanding of the degree to which you have understood the language. Lewis said that "[a]gain and again [he] has been most usefully humiliated in this way." If you cannot explain what you have to say "to any sensible person whatever (provided he will listen), then you don't really understand it yourself." Lewis warned that we must beware lest "our private language . . . delude[s] ourselves as well as mystifying others."

Anne Gardner

Also See: Language/Rhetoric, Satan

"Behind the Scenes"

Time and Tide. XXXVII (December 1, 1956): 1450–51. Reprinted in *God in the Dock, Undeceptions,* and *Christian Reunion.*

"Behind the Scenes" presents one of C. S. Lewis's most engaging critiques of the reductionism spawned by modern **materialism**. Likening life to a stage play, Lewis pointed out that in one sense nothing in a play is real. It is all imaginary. It is not really set in the countryside, and the people onstage are not really who they pretend to be. The only "realities" are the physical sets and props and costumes. The play is mere "appearance" and the sets are "**reality**." Despite this fact, few people would maintain that the sets and props used to stage a play are more important than the play itself. To the contrary, the sets and props exist only for the sake of the play, and they would be worthless without it. Similarly, human beings may be made up of material components, but that fact does not mean that these components are the most important parts of human life. Just as sets and costumes do not negate the meaning of a play, the physical processes of the human body do not negate the higher purposes of human life. Lewis here hearkened back to **Aristotle** and his teleological approach to understanding **human nature**.

John G. West, Jr.

Bibliography

West, John G., Jr. *C. S. Lewis and the Materialist Menace.* Seattle: The Discovery Institute, 1996.

Belfast

C. S. Lewis was born in 1898 in Dundela Villas on the outskirts of Belfast. In 1905 his family moved to "**Little Lea,**" a house on Holywood Road. In *Surprised by Joy* he described the beauty of the Irish countryside and the boyish delight of living in a port filled with ships from around the world. The well-known Titanic was built in Belfast shipyards while Lewis was in his early teens.

Since 1920, Belfast has been the capital of Northern Ireland, and after Ireland won independence, it remained politically united to Britain. The city is troubled by tensions between a population roughly two-thirds Protestant and one-third Catholic. Lewis described the religious climate of his youth in "**Christian Reunion.**" Hints that the conflict is more ethnic than religious appear when he noted that both Protestant and Catholic mothers would rather their son be an atheist than a member of the rival faith. While not downplaying doctrinal differences, Lewis discovered more "heavenly unity" with devout Catholics than with the "lukewarm" among his own Anglicans.

Mike Perry

Also See: Anglicanism, Campbell College, Dundela Villas, Little Lea, Roman Catholicism, St. Marks

Bibliography

Lewis, C. S. "Christian Reunion"; *Surprised by Joy.*

J(ack) A(rthur) W(alter) Bennett (1911–1981)

J. A. W. Bennett was a pupil, close friend, and colleague of Lewis at **Magdalen College, Oxford,** and also studied with Lewis's friends **J. R. R. Tolkien** and Charles L. Wrenn. Upon Lewis's retirement, Bennett succeeded him as Professor of Medieval and Renaissance Literature at **Cambridge** (1964–1978). A devout Roman Catholic and **Inkling**, Bennett started attending meetings sometime after 1945. Like Lewis, he was a Medieval scholar, and he produced several volumes on **Chaucer,** including *Chaucer's Book of Fame* and *Chaucer at Oxford and Cambridge*. His inaugural lec-

ture at Cambridge, called *The Humane Medievalist* (1965), was dedicated to Lewis. Bennett wrote two essays in honor of Lewis, "Grete Clerk," in *Light on C. S. Lewis*, and "Gower's 'Honest Love,'" in *Patterns of Love and Courtesy: Essays in Memory of C. S. Lewis*. In "Grete Clerk" (taken from *The Humane Medievalist*), he pays tribute to Lewis as a teacher and to his ability to make the Medieval culture attractive and accessible to students.

Perry C. Bramlett
C. S. Lewis for the Local Church

Also See: Cambridge, Inklings, Roman Catholicism, Tutor

Bibliography

Bennett, J. A. W. *The Human Medievalist.* Cambridge: Cambridge University Press, 1965.

Gibb, Jocelyn (ed). *Light on C. S. Lewis.* New York: Harcourt Brace, 1965.

Lawlor, John (ed). *Patterns of Love and Courtesy: Essays in Memory of C. S. Lewis.* :1966.

John Betjeman (1906–1984)

Betjeman was Lewis's pupil at **Magdalen College, Oxford**. While the two shared a love of **poetry** and literature, their early relationship was not very friendly. Lewis did not think much of Betjeman as a student— mostly because of Betjeman's unwillingness to apply himself. In fact, Betjeman failed the divinity examination and after spending another term at Oxford chose to leave without a degree. He blamed Lewis for his failure and made Lewis the target of ridicule in several poems. Later in life, the two men were cordial to one another. Betjeman, a very successful poet, was knighted in 1969 and two years later was chosen as Poet Laureate.

Jeffrey D. Schultz

Bibliography

Betjeman, John. *Chastly Good Taste* (1933); *Continual Dew* (1937); *Old Lights for New Chancels* (1940); *New Bats in Old Belfries* (1945); *A Few Late Chrysanthemums* (1954); *Collected Poems* (1958).

Lewis, C. S. *All My Road Before Me.*

Beyond the Bright Blur

New York: Harcourt, Brace & World, 1963.

A limited edition of selections (chapters 15–17) from *Letters to Malcolm: Chiefly on Prayer*.

Beyond Personality: The Christian Idea of God

London: Geoffrey Bles, The Centenary Press, 1944. First US edition, New York: Macmillan, 1945.

95

Beyond Personality contains talks C. S. Lewis gave over the Home Service network of the British Broadcasting Corporation (BBC) in the spring of 1944. In 1952, with the title *Beyond Personality: Or First Steps in the Doctrine of the Trinity*, it was combined with **Broadcast Talks** (in America, *The Case for Christianity*), and **Christian Behaviour** to make **Mere Christianity**. Lewis wrote the scripts for the talks in December of 1943, and they were pre-recorded, in ten- to fifteen-minute segments, from 22 February to 4 April 1944. Three additional chapters ("Time and Beyond Time," "Two Notes," and "Nice People or New Men") were added before publication and "The New Men" segment was substantially edited as well. The series was initially

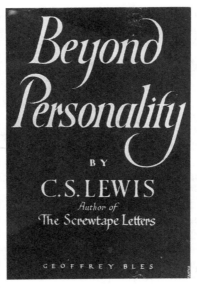

published under the title "What Christians Believe about the Nature of God" in weekly installments in *The Listener*, a BBC weekly journal. The original titles of the essays were "**The Map and the Ocean**," "**God in Three Persons**," "**The Whole Purpose of the Christian**," "**The Obstinate Tin Soldiers**," "**Let Us Pretend**," "**Is Christianity Hard or Easy?**" and "**The New Men**."

In the preface to *Beyond Personality*, Lewis wrote that the talks were "an attempt to put into simple modern language the account of **God** which the vast majority of Christian churches have agreed in giving for a great many centuries," and that he was not trying to "prove anything" but rather describe what the Christian belief in God was. He had been asked by the BBC to give a series of final talks that would explain difficult theological doctrines, and in this work Lewis explained the **theology** of the **Trinity** and exhorted his audience to try to understand this and to accept the new personhood that God gives a believer, which is "beyond personality."

In chapter 1, "Making and Begetting," Lewis maintained that all Christians need to know about theology, which he called "the science of God" and a "map" that will lead one to correct doctrines about God and correct wrong ("bad, muddled, out-of-date") ideas. Correct theology for Lewis was grounded in the great creeds of the **faith**, and its center was the fact that because of **Christ**, humans ("statues or pictures" of God) have the potential to attain true spiritual life: "The world is like a great sculptor's shop. We are the statues and there is a rumour

going round the shop that some of us some day are going to come to life."

"The Three-Personal God" is primarily about the Trinity, and in it Lewis stated that although God is personal, he is "beyond personality," or has three dimensions by which he can be known. Lewis illustrated this by saying that in **prayer** we pray to God, are prompted to pray by the God inside us, and the God beside us is helping us to pray and even praying for us. The initiative in knowing God comes from God (not us), and if he doesn't show himself, "nothing you can do will enable you to find Him." The most adequate instrument for learning about God is the church ("the whole Christian community") waiting on God together as one.

In the third chapter, "Time and Beyond Time," Lewis continued his thoughts about prayer and the Trinity by discussing the idea of God and time, and how God is not limited to human ideas about time. He was attempting to answer a question that many had in his day: how could God be personal (in prayer) while millions of people all over the world were addressing him at the same moment? Lewis went on to say that God's life does not consist of "moments following one another" and illustrated this by saying that God has "all eternity in which to listen to the split second of prayer put up by a pilot as his plane crashes into flames." Lewis also declared that God, because he is "outside and above the Time-line," sees us doing things (yesterday, now, and tomorrow) because he is "already in" all states of our time.

Lewis's fourth chapter, "Good Infection," deals with the role of the **Holy Spirit** in the life of the **church**. He cautioned his hearers that their idea of the Spirit might be "rather vaguer or more shadowy" than God or Jesus. The reason for this is that the Spirit acts through a person, rather than standing "out there" (the Father God) or standing at our sides (the Son Jesus). For Lewis, the Christian life was a dance, or drama, of **love**, and the Spirit is that part of the Trinity that allows and helps a person to share in the life of Christ.

In "The Obstinate Toy Soldiers," Lewis stated his belief in the Incarnation and God's plan of salvation by saying that "the son of God became a man to enable men to become sons of God." He asked his hearers to imagine themselves as a slug or crab to understand what

Jesus went through (as God, "the Eternal Being") in becoming human and emphasized his humanness in enduring physical and emotional hardships that led to death. Near the end of his talk, Lewis mentioned several theories of the atonement and then said they were all true and that one should "get on with the formula" that appealed most. The next chapter, "Two Notes," was an addition to "The Obstinate Toy Soldiers" and answered objections and questions (from letters to *The Listener*) about the process of becoming a Christian and the worth of the individual Christian in God's eyes.

In "Let's Pretend," Lewis used illustrations from *The Beauty and the Beast* and the Lord's Prayer to show his hearers what it means to "dress up as Christ" and to know that Christ is at their sides. He cautioned that the Christian is not to base his or her Christian actions on feelings but is to "behave as if you were a nice person." The Christian should not worry about feeling like a child of God, but know on faith that this is true, then act accordingly.

Discipleship and sanctification are the primary themes of the next two chapters, "Is Christianity Hard or Easy?" and "Counting the Cost." Christianity is "hard" according to Lewis because Christ demands the whole person in obedience. It is "easy" because Christ himself helps make authentic Christian living a delight and the best way to live, despite the toughness of his demands. Lewis also discussed Jesus' command that his followers "be perfect" and compared Jesus with the dentist (!) who takes all "if you give him an inch." Jesus' followers will suffer, perhaps even to the point of death, but his almost impossible demands can be met because, according to Lewis, "he is going to make good his words ... and he meant what he said."

In chapter 10, "Nice People or New Men," Lewis answered the question, "If Christianity is true, why are not all the world's Christians obviously nicer than non-Christians?" Lewis believed that some people are on the way to becoming Christians; others who call themselves Christians are "slowly ceasing" to be Christian; and others "belong to Christ without knowing it." Some Christians are not as nice as non-Christians, not because Christianity does not work but because the person has not yielded their will to God. Lewis ended the chapter by reminding his hearers not to speculate on the "stupid and unsatisfactory" Christians they know but rather on their own lives, which stand before God alone.

The final chapter in this book is "The New Men," and here Lewis focused on Jesus' resurrection and what it means to the Christian. He used the evolutionary idea of the "Next Step" in a Christian sense to mean the change that God's creatures undergo to become part of the family of God. The more a person "dies to self" and gives himself or herself to God, the more that person will become a "little Christ" and start to have what God intended, a "real personality" that is grounded in his love. Lewis's last words in this chapter expressed the hope he had for all who heard and read his words: "But look for Christ and you will find Him, and with Him everything else thrown in."

The reviews of *Beyond Personality* were mixed, though most were favorable. One reviewer thought it "not wholly orthodox," some believed Lewis's ideas about the church, the sacraments, and the atonement were too limited, and one critic wrote that the volume was vague and "not arresting in thought." But many others were enthusiastic, calling the work "the best of the Lewis books," an "admirably simple explanation of the essential facts of the Christian Revelation," and Lewis's explanation of "basic" theology as "an attractive, exciting and ... uproarious quest." Perhaps the most perceptive view of the book came from a military officer who wrote to Lewis's friend and later biographer **George Sayer**: "It was a time of strain and difficulty for all of us. The war, the whole of life, everything tended to seem pointless. We needed ... a key to the meaning of the universe. Lewis provided just that ... he gave us back our old, traditional Christian faith so that we could accept it in confidence...."

Perry C. Bramlett
C. S. Lewis for the Local Church

Bibliography

Christopher, Joe R., and Joan K. Ostling. *C. S. Lewis: An Annotated Checklist of Writings about Him and his Works*. Kent, OH: The Kent State University Press, 1974.

_____. *C. S. Lewis*. Boston: G. K. Hall, 1987.

Cunningham, Richard B. *C. S. Lewis: Defender of the Faith*. Philadelphia: Westminster, 1967.

Hannay, Margaret Patterson. *C. S. Lewis*. New York: Ungar, 1981.

Hooper, Walter with Theodore Baehr. *Mere Christianity by C. S. Lewis: Study Guide*. Atlanta: The Episcopal Radio-TV Foundation, 1982.

Keefe, Carolyn (ed). *C. S. Lewis: Speaker and Teacher*. Grand Rapids, MI: Zondervan, 1971.

McLaughlin, Sara Park. "A Legacy of Truth: The Influence of George MacDonald's Unspoken Sermons on C. S. Lewis's *Mere Christianity*." *CSL: The Bulletin of the New York C. S. Lewis Society*. 24 no. 4 (February 1993): 1–6.

Walsh, Chad. *C. S. Lewis: Apostle to the Skeptics*. New York: Macmillan, 1949.

_____. *The Literary Legacy of C. S. Lewis*. New York: Harcourt Brace, 1979.

The Bible

Despite the almost universal admiration for the life, works, and influence of C. S. Lewis since the 1940s, surprisingly little has been written about his approach to the Bible. Only four of the more than one hundred books (not including the nine biographies) written about Lewis to this date have any substantial discussion of his views and use of the Scriptures. A few more works have briefly mentioned various aspects of his literary approach to the Bible. It is clear that Lewis cannot be held to any one theological position concerning Holy Scripture. He was not a systematic or lay theologian as some have claimed, nor was he an evangelical, as is often written today. But Lewis often wrote about various aspects of the Bible and biblical scholarship. In books, letters, essays, and private conversation he discussed the Bible as literature, individual books of the Bible, biblical **inspiration** and **revelation**, types and ways of biblical translation, Bible scholars and criticism, the historicity of the Bible, and the study of the Bible. He also wrote about many of the themes of the Bible from both testaments, such as **heaven**, **hell**, **miracles**, **Satan**, **God**, the atonement, the resurrection and second coming of **Christ**, baptism, **Holy Communion, sin**, salvation, the nature of God. Lewis once wrote that "It is Christ himself, not the Bible, who is the true word of God. The Bible, read in the right spirit and with the guidance of good teachers, will bring us to Him" (***Letters of C. S. Lewis***, November 8, 1952). The Bible was Lewis's vehicle to Christ, and his approach to and devotional use of Holy Scripture are well worth remembering for that reason.

Lewis's approach to the Bible—An important discussion of what Lewis thought about the Bible is contained in a chapter titled "Scripture" in his ***Reflections on the Psalms***. Lewis believed that the Bible contained the holy, inspired oracles of God. In his view, the final canonical form of Scripture has God's "stamp" of inspiration and authority, and its various literary genres, such as **myth**, chronicle, **allegory**, **poetry**, romance, stories, prophecy, and statements of **faith** are all to be used in the service of God. The Bible, according to Lewis, "carries" God's word. The actual written words of the Bible are the literary packages—the vehicle, the expression, the medium—that carries God's divine message of salvation. The Bible may contain some human errors, contradictions, or distortions, but when the Bible is received in faith, it teaches no error, particularly in matters of faith and **redemption**.

Lewis also maintained in this chapter that the **truth** revealed in God's written Word is not systematic. Not only do we not have enough "divine data" to build a sys-

tem, but God's truth is complicated. Thus we should not use the Bible as an encyclopedia of divine truth, but we should, rather, live by "steeping ourselves in its tone or temper, and so learn its overall message." For Lewis, the Bible was not a theological textbook or doctrinal primer; nor was it to be used as a rule book to settle denominational squabbles. Lewis encouraged us not to abstract or systematize the Bible, for when we do, we lose its center, which is Christ.

Lewis thought that the main tools for interpreting the Bible were the abilities and gifts that God has given us, such as our intelligence, learning, attention to tradition, and wise interpreters. We may receive God's Word to us when using these gifts and abilities with an acceptance of God's grace. A more specific tool of interpretation for Lewis was literary analysis, which enables one to understand better the forms of literature in Scripture, thus helping to comprehend God's word. For instance, the literary style of the Gospels demanded for Lewis that they be taken as history, while the style of Job and Jonah pointed him in another direction. Lewis never specifically ruled out the tools of **science**, historical research, and archeology, but warned that these are changing disciplines that must be "updated" from time to time. He also implied in his writings that knowledge in these fields of study is often based on modern naturalistic assumptions and should be used with caution.

Lewis's devotional use of the Bible—After Lewis became a Christian, he read the Bible devotionally virtually every day, except when he was very ill. It is well known that he always reread the books that he enjoyed, and the Bible was the book he reread the most. He enjoyed the **Psalms** very much and would also read from the Gospels, particularly the gospel of Mark, and from Paul's writings. While traveling by train, he often enjoyed reading from the Greek New Testament and the *Book of Common Prayer*. In one of his letters (*Letters of C. S. Lewis*, July 18, 1957) he mentioned that he read the New Testament in the Latin *Vulgate*. His favorite modern translation was by James Moffatt, which he mentions as "particularly good" (**"Modern Translations of the Bible"**), and he also recommended Ronald Knox's translation (*Letters of C. S. Lewis*, March 26, 1940). Lewis's close friend and biographer **George Sayer** has noted that Lewis would read from any translation available, and Lewis's stepson **Douglas Gresham** has written that he would read from the Authorized Version (the older King James) and from J. B. Phillips' translation of the New Testament (letter to this author, April 26, 1995). It is interesting that Lewis apparently did not use the New English Bible; its New Testament translation was published in 1961. He wrote that he did know enough about its Greek to make a criticism of it (*Letters of C. S. Lewis*, May 25, 1962).

Lewis read his Bible devotionally for a variety of reasons. He wrote often that he read it (particularly the Psalms) for its literary and imaginative **beauty**. In *Mere Christianity* he implied that reading the New Testament would give a "pretty clear hint" as to what a fully Christian society would be like. He wrote that the combination of **prayer** and Bible reading was the best way to start to understand the doctrines of one's faith (see *Letters of C. S. Lewis*, June 13, 1951). And in a paper originally read to the **Oxford Socratic Club** on May 20, 1946, he wrote that the Bible, along with ritual and miracle, was an "avenue for knowing God" (**"Religion Without Dogma?"**). Lewis's core belief that the Bible was holy and inspired by God led him to a persistent and faithful devotional reading of the Scriptures, one that he maintained for his entire Christian life. He read the Bible for its beauty, its guidance for faith and Christian living, and primarily because it pointed him to God as revealed in Jesus Christ. His life is a wonderful and abiding testimony that he did indeed read the Bible in the right spirit.

Perry C. Bramlett
C. S. Lewis for the Local Church

Also See: Christianity, Literary Theory, Literary Criticism, Reason

Bibliography

Bramlett, Perry C. *C. S. Lewis: Life at the Center*. Macon, GA: Smyth and Helwys, 1996.
Christensen, Michael J. *C. S. Lewis on Scripture*. Nashville: Abingdon, 1979.
Cunningham, Richard. *C. S. Lewis: Defender of the Faith*. Philadelphia: Westminster, 1967.
Freshwater, Mark E. *C. S. Lewis and the Truth of Myth*. Lanham, MD: University Press of America, 1988.
Kilby, Clyde S. *The Christian World of C. S. Lewis*. Grand Rapids, MI: Eerdmans, 1964.
Lewis, C. S. "Letter from C. S. Lewis to Janet Wise" (May 10, 1955). *The Canadian C. S. Lewis Journal*. 68 (Autumn 1989): 1.
Patterson, Nancy-Lou. "Trained Habit: The Spirituality of C. S. Lewis." *The Canadian C. S. Lewis Journal*. 87 (Spring 1995): 37–53.
Schofield, Stephen (ed.). *In Search of C. S. Lewis*. South Plainfield, NJ: Bridge Publishing, 1983.
Williams, Terri. "CSL, Scripture, and Inerrancy." *The Chronicle of the Portland C. S. Lewis Society*. VII no. 1 (January-March 1978): 3–12.

Peter William Bide (1912–)

When **Joy Davidman Lewis** became ill in 1956, C. S. Lewis wanted to have an ecclesiastical wedding ceremony. The Bishop of Oxford, however, would not give permission for the wedding because Joy's first husband, **William Gresham**, was still alive. Lewis turned to a former student, Bide, who had a reputation as a healer. Bide arrived and "laid his hands on her and prayed." In addition Bide agreed to perform an ecclesiastical wedding ceremony the following day on March 21, 1957.

Jeffrey D. Schultz

Bibliography

Lewis, C. S. "The Efficacy of Prayer."
Sayer, George. *Jack: C. S. Lewis and His Times*. Wheaton, IL: Crossway, 1988.

Biographies, Review of

There is no definitive biography of C. S. Lewis. There are four biographies and one photo biography, the different qualities of which are discussed below. In addition, there are the letters and diaries of Lewis himself, his brother **Warren Lewis**, his friend **Arthur Greeves**, personal recollections (such as are contained in *C. S. Lewis at the Breakfast Table*, for example), and books dealing with a single aspect of Lewis (such as *The Inklings* by Humphrey Carpenter or *And God Stepped In* by Lyle W. Dorsett).

The most satisfactory and useful biography is *Jack: C. S. Lewis and His Times* by **George Sayer**, 1988. Sayer, a Roman Catholic, was a student of Lewis at **Oxford**, later a friend of both Lewis and his brother, and English master at **Malvern College** (which the brothers had attended thirty years earlier). Sayer and Lewis were friends for twenty-nine years and visited each other often.

Sayer gives a very full account, is sympathetic to Lewis's devout **Christianity**, and speaks from personal knowledge. The broad outlines of Lewis's life are sound, there are many details and explanations that are available nowhere else, and the errors are few and minor. Perhaps the account could have been edited down, especially in the early chapters, but it reads well and presents an affectionate portrait without, however, omitting Lewis's faults and vices.

The pictorial biography, *C. S. Lewis: Images of His World* by Douglas Gilbert and Clyde S. Kilby, 1973, is well worth looking at; it does not pretend to be a full biography but the pictures give concrete embodiment to the words of the biographies (some of which have a few black-and-white illustrations).

Clive Staples Lewis: A Dramatic Life by William Griffin, 1986, is more noted for its drama than its life. The quotations are frequent and accurate, but no over-all picture of Lewis in the period 1927–63 emerges, partly because every reported incident is given equal importance. It is often hard to know whether the comments, vignettes, and interpretations are founded on any kind of evidence or are just fanciful products of Griffin's imagination. But in short doses it can be entertaining.

C. S. Lewis: A Biography by **Roger Lancelyn Green** and **Walter Hooper**, 1974, revised 1989, is certainly readable but suffers from the imbalance of authority and credibility between the two authors. Green knew Lewis, first as a student, from the late 1930s until his death in 1963, visited and took holidays with him, and was asked by Lewis to be his biographer. The American Hooper did not meet Lewis until June 1963, only saw him on a few occasions, volunteered to write letters for him when Lewis was sick and Warren was away in August 1963, and departed at the end of the month. Moreover, Hooper's inflation of his brief relationship with Lewis intrudes on whatever he says or writes. This makes him untrustworthy and often wrong.

Originally, it was planned that Green would write chapters 1, 2, 3, 6, 7, and 10. These chapters were completed by him in 1971, but Hooper failed to complete the remaining chapters until late 1973. The apparent reason for this unexplained delay related to the fact that it had been agreed that the chapters would be reviewed by Warren Lewis. It was only after Warren's death in April 1973 that the book was completed. Although the preface states that Warren had read and approved all but the last chapter, he had earlier denied some of the claims that Hooper made.

There is much that is good in this biography, but the book paints a much kinder and more reverential picture of Lewis than the facts warrant.

C. S. Lewis: A Biography by A. N. Wilson appeared in 1990, but rather than a life of Lewis it is more a display of the author's ingenuity and callowness. It is undoubtedly a clever and crafty book, but when compared to the intelligence and honesty of its subject, it is easy to see how it fails. With little or no respect for Lewis's own words and interpretations (or his religion), Wilson, a journalist and novelist, offers a simplistic psychoanalytic interpretation of certain parts of Lewis's life—maintaining that he was a "deeply-troubled" man.

He uses the biography as an opportunity to impress upon the reader his own brittle brilliance and superficial scholarship. The text is easy enough to read, in spite of its tone, but it is riddled with errors of the most elementary kind. For example, Wilson states that Malcolm Muggeridge's typewriter is at **The Wade Center,** which it is not. Wilson also asserts that *Perelandra* was "an artistic failure," though critics have not thought so. As a final example, Wilson writes that Lewis's marriage to Joy was announced "the next day" (March 22) when it was not publicly announced until December 24. One might just as well have asked Oedipus to write the history of Laius.

John Bremer

"The Birth of Language"

Punch. 210 (January 9, 1946): 32 (under the pseudonym Nat Whilk). Revised and reprinted in *Poems* and *Collected Poems.*

One of Lewis's best poems, "The Birth of Language" is imaginative speculation on how human language came to man. Lewis wrote that the Sun showered fiery flakes on the surface of the planet Mercury where the flakes shaped themselves into figures similar to the gods' messenger, Mercury, and then flew through space to earth where they miraculously became words.

Don W. King
Montreat College

David Geoffrey Bles (1886–1957)

Geoffrey Bles, who founded the publishing house bearing his name in 1924, was Lewis's main religious-books publisher in England for many years. Their association started in 1940 with the publication of *The Problem of Pain*. Thereafter Bles and Lewis joined on numerous projects: *The Screwtape Letters*; the three slender volumes (*Broadcast Talks*, *Christian Behaviour*, and *Beyond Personality*) that later became *Mere Christianity*; *The Great Divorce*; and the first five **Chronicles of Narnia**, among many other books. When Bles retired in 1954, Lewis continued publishing with the new manager of the firm, **Jocelyn (Jock) Gibb**.

Bles and Lewis corresponded frequently about the books and became friends through their mutual interest in good writing. One way Bles was able to improve Lewis's style was in coming up with effective titles, an area Lewis never entirely mastered. For instance, for the fifth Chronicle of Narnia, Lewis suggested several titles to Bles, among which was the pedestrian *The Horse and* the Boy. Bles altered it to **The Horse and His Boy**, making a solid improvement through a single word change.

Marvin D. Hinten
Bowling Green State University

Also See: Friendship

Bibliography

Green, Roger Lancelyn, and Walter Hooper. *C. S. Lewis: A Biography*. Rev. ed. New York: Harcourt Brace, 1994.

"Blimpophobia"

Time and Tide. XXV (9 September 1944): 785. Reprinted in *Present Concerns*.

Colonel Blimp was a famous cartoon character—a "muddle-headed type of complacent reactionary," a retired army type, used to authority (his own mostly), and, like a blimp, full of hot air. In this essay, Lewis said that the only thing that made infection of the whole English population by Blimpophobia possible was that seventy percent of those emerging from World War I hated the regular army more than they hated the Germans. Lewis was one of the former, although he had been wrong. He now draws attention not to **justice** but to the danger of Blimpophobia. Those who have taken power during the **war** may claim that the continuance of their power is necessary for national security, "But I say that the disappearance of all these Masters at an early date is just what security demands." If they do not relinquish power they will become hated, and, when swept away later, will take with them the real requirements of national security.

John Bremer

Also See: Democracy, Politics

"Bluspels and Flalansferes"

Originally published in *Rehabilitations*. Reprinted in *Selected Literary Essays*.

This essay, delivered as an address at Manchester University during the 1930s and originally published in *Rehabilitations* (1939), differs from most of the other pieces in *Selected Literary Essays* in being about linguistics and meaning rather than about literature itself. Here Lewis offered commentary and critique on a dispute C. K. Ogden and I. A. Richards had with his good friend **Owen Barfield** over whether language is always metaphorical or whether one can speak in a more rigorously nonfigurative, objective manner. Ogden and Richards had strenuously argued in their work *The Meaning of Meaning* that a nonmetaphorical, "scientific language" was both possible and, indeed, necessary in order to serve the cause of objective investigation and expression of **truth**. Lewis naturally took the Barfieldian view that language is "incurably" metaphorical and that **science** cannot escape this fact.

The title of the essay comes from Lewis's conflation of two phrases. He discussed **Kant**'s idea that "whatever I see next will be blue because I am wearing blue spectacles" and imagined the idea eventually becoming referred to as "bluspels." Then he took the idea of the "Flatlanders' sphere" (from Edwin Abbott's *Flatland*, a book that significantly influenced Lewis) and contracted it into "Flalansfere." According to Lewis, even after people had forgotten the origins of these words the original **metaphors** would still be operating in their minds, particularly if the speakers had rather limited knowledge about what they were discussing. Thus Lewis considered poets to speak more meaningfully than philosophers, who cannot really understand the metaphysical things they are discussing.

Lewis's conclusion is that while one may regard **reason** as the "natural organ of truth," **imagination**, which produces new metaphors, is the "organ of meaning," and, though not the "cause of truth," it is, in fact, its "condition."

Marvin D. Hinten and Bruce L. Edwards
Bowling Green State University

Also See: The Great War

Bibliography

Barfield, Owen. *Poetic Diction* (1928).
_____. *Saving the Appearances* (1957).
Hart, Dabney. *Through the Open Door*. Tuscaloosa, AL: University of Alabama Press, 1984.
Lewis, C. S. *Studies in Words*.
Myers, Doris T. *C. S. Lewis in Context*. Kent, OH: Kent State University Press, 1994.
Ogden, C. K., and I. A. Richards. *The Meaning of Meaning* (1923).
Schakel, Peter J., and Charles A. Huttar (eds). *Word and Story in C. S. Lewis*. Columbia, MO: University of Missouri Press, 1991.

Bodleian Library

The Bodleian is the library of the University of **Oxford** and the repository of one of the finest collections of C. S. Lewis manuscripts anywhere. The oldest portion of the library is the Duke Humphrey's Library, named after Humphrey, the Duke of Gloucester (son of Henry IV) who secured its existence in 1410 by endowing the library with money and hundreds of manuscripts. The library declined in importance over the next century, however, and in 1550 the decision was made to disperse the remaining books. It was restored by Sir Thomas Bodley and reopened in 1602. Since 1610 the Bodleian has been entitled to receive a free copy of all books printed in England, and today the library contains well over 5 million volumes and thousands of manuscripts.

The Bodleian collection of C. S. Lewis manuscripts began in 1967 with fifty-six letters from Lewis deposited by **Sister Penelope**. The following year, **Walter Hooper** began collecting additional Lewis manuscripts and papers on behalf of the Library. Due mainly to his efforts the Bodleian today shares with the **Marion E. Wade Center** of Wheaton College the distinction of being the largest collection of Lewis manuscripts in existence. Both collections have benefited from a reciprocal photocopying agreement between the two libraries that allows much of their manuscript holdings to be accessible in both places. The Bodleian collection contains over 2,300 letters from Lewis (not all originals) and the entire manuscripts of many of Lewis's books, fragments of others, and the originals of many of his essays and shorter works. In addition, the Library holds a microfilm of the **Lewis Family Papers** and hundreds of foreign translations of Lewis's books. For information write to: Department of Western Manuscripts, Bodleian Library, Broad Street, Oxford OX1 3BG.

Christopher W. Mitchell
The Marion E. Wade Center

Ancius Boethius (c. 480–524)

Boethius, a Roman and Christian, was an advisor to the Ostrogothic King, Theodoric. Falling under suspicion, he was imprisoned, tortured, and executed. While in prison, he wrote *The Consolation of Philosophy,* which became the most translated book of the Middle Ages and second only to the **Bible** in its influence on that period. The book held great importance for C. S. Lewis, as a medievalist. Its themes of true **happiness**, suffering, and Divine Providence influenced every later treatment of the problem of freedom including Lewis's *The Problem of Pain*.

Jerry Root
Wheaton College

Also See: Medieval World, Pain

Bibliography

Lewis, C. S. *Allegory of Love*; *The Discarded Image*.

Boethius: Some Aspects of His Times and Work (Book Review)

Medium Aevum. X (February 1941): 29–41.

Lewis noted that this book by Helen M. Barrett is accessible to the "ordinary student." All Latin is translated, and it includes a short sketch of Theodoric, a biography of **Boethius**, an account of his fall, and three chapters on the *De Consolatione*. Barrett's work upholds tradition, and Lewis found the philosophic part of her work good.

Ann Gardner

Bibliography

Barrett, Helen M. *Boethius: Some Aspects of His Times and Work.*

Book Dedicatees

The chart on the following page lists all those people to whom C. S. Lewis dedicated his various books.

See entries for the individual dedicatees as listed in the chart.

Books for Children (Letter)

The Times Literary Supplement. (28 November 1958): 689.

Lewis wrote to correct a statement made in a review of **Roger Lancelyn Green**'s **fantasy**, *The Land of the Lord High Tiger* ("The Light Fantastic," *TLS, Children's Books Section*, 21 November 1958, x) that suggested that Lewis's Narnia books influenced Green's story. Lewis made it clear that this perceived influence was chronologically impossible. Accordingly, Lewis used this example to caution critics (including himself) that other literary criticisms may only seem valid because those who know the facts are already dead and unable to correct misconceptions.

Marjorie L. Mead
The Marion E. Wade Center

Books of Influence

A comprehensive list of the books that influenced C. S. Lewis and of the reasons why he chose them and often reread them would be beyond the scope of this book. One list stands out, however, to which several other titles that appear on nearly every other list could be added.

The June 6, 1962, issue of *The Christian Century* published C. S. Lewis's answer to its question to famous authors, "What books did most to shape your vocational attitude and your **philosophy** of life?":

(1) *Phantastes* by **George MacDonald**
(2) *The Everlasting Man* by **G. K. Chesterton**

BOOK DEDICATEES

Book	Dedicatee	Who's Who
The Allegory of Love	Owen Barfield	See entry.
Arthurian Torso	Michal Williams	Wife of Charles Williams
The Discarded Image: An introduction to Medieval and Renaissance Literature	Roger Lancelyn Green	See entry.
Dymer	None in the 1926 edition. 1950 edition to Marjorie Milne	A fan of Lewis's introduced to him by Owen Barfield
The Four Loves	Chad Walsh	See entry.
George MacDonald: An Anthology	Mary Neylan	A student and friend of Lewis
The Great Divorce	Barbara Wall	Sister-in-law of Collin Harding who typed several manuscrips for Lewis
The Horse and His Boy	David and Douglas Gresham	See entries.
The Lion, the Witch, and the Wardrobe	Lucy Barfield	Adopted daughter of Owen Barfield and Lewis's god-daughter
The Magician's Nephew	The Kilmer Family	Correspondents with Lewis out of which grew several of his post-humously published *Letters to Children*
Miracles	Cecil and Daphne Harwood	See entry of Cecil Harwood.
Out of a Silent Planet	Warren H. Lewis	See entry.
Perelandra	Some Ladies at Wantage	See entry on Sister Penelope and the other nuns at The Community of St. Mary the Virgin in Wantage, Berkshire
The Pilgrim's Regress	Arthur Greeves	See entry.
A Preface to "Paradise Lost"	Charles Williams	See entry.
Prince Caspian	Mary Clare Havard	Daughter of R. E. Humphrey Havard
The Problem of Pain	The Inklings	See entry.
Reflections of the Psalms	Austin and Katherine Farrer	See entries.
Rehabilitations and other Esseys	Hugo Dyson	See entry.
The Screwtape Letters	J. R. R. Tolkien	See entry.
The Silver Chair	Nicholas Hardie	Eldest son of Colin Hardie
Studies in Words	Stanley and Joan Bennet	Long-time friends
Surprised by Joy	Dom Bede Griffiths, OSB	See entry.
Till We Have Faces: A Myth Retold	Joy Davidman	See entry.
The Voyage of the "Dawn Treader"	Geoffrey Corbett	Foster son of Own Barfield

(3) *The Aeneid* by Virgil

(4) *The Temple* by **George Herbert**

(5) *The Prelude* by **William Wordsworth**

(6) *The Idea of the Holy* by Rudolf Otto

(7) *The Consolation of Philosophy* by **Boethius**

(8) *Life of Samuel Johnson* by James Boswell

(9) *Descent into Hell* by **Charles Williams**

(10) *Theism and Humanism* by **Arthur James Balfour**

Other than the **Bible**, especially the **Psalms** and the New Testament, the following books not already listed above are the most frequently mentioned as influential and recommended: *Centuries of Meditations* by Thomas Traherne, *Confessions* by **Augustine**, the fantastic novels and *He Came Down from Heaven* by **Charles Williams**, *The Imitation of Christ* by Thomas à Kempis, *Introduction to the Devout Life* by Francis de Sales, *The Man Born to be King* by **Dorothy Sayers**, *Pilgrim's Progress* by John Bunyan, *The Sermon on the Mount* and *Philosophy of the Good Life* by Charles Gore, *A Serious Call to a Devout and Holy Life* and *An Appeal* by William Law, *Smoke on the Mountain* by **Joy Davidman**, *Symbolism and Belief* by Edwyn Bevan, and *Theologia Germanica*. Lewis's favorite authors to read when ill were **Jane Austen**, Scott, and Trollope.

Lewis's last mention of influential books was in his May 1963 interview with Sherwood Wirt retitled **"Cross-Examination"** and reprinted in *God in the Dock*. In answer to Wirt's question, "What Christian writers have helped you?" Lewis said, "The contemporary book that has helped me the most is Chesterton's *The Everlasting Man*. Others are Edwyn Bevan's book, *Symbolism and Belief*, and Rudolf Otto's *The Idea of the Holy*, and the plays of Dorothy Sayers."

Paul F. Ford

St. John's Seminary

Bibliography

The Christian Century. 79 no. 23 (June 6, 1962): 719.

"Boswell's Bugbear"

See entry on *The Life of Samuel Johnson* (Book Review)

Boxen: The Imaginary World of the Young C. S. Lewis

Hooper, Walter (ed). London: Collins, 1985. First US edition, San Diego: Harcourt Brace Jovanovich, 1985.

As Lewis related in ***Surprised by Joy***, when he was a young boy, he wrote stories about Animal-Land. His brother, **Warren H. Lewis**, had an imaginary realm based on India. When they combined the two (making India into an island near the island of Animal-Land), they called the combined nation Boxen. Lewis warned his readers in a note that the relationship between Animal-Land and Narnia was not what they might imagine: "The best way of putting this would be to say that Animal-Land had nothing whatever in common with Narnia except the anthropomorphic beasts. Animal-Land, by its whole quality, excluded the least hint of wonder."

The Boxonian materials are also far duller than the **Chronicles of Narnia** for the same reason. In 1985, **Walter Hooper** edited a collection of Lewis's early stories, histories, and drawings under the title: *Boxen: The Imaginary World of the Young C. S. Lewis*. This volume is incomplete, as Hooper indicated in his introduction, lacking three Boxonian items; it also is edited for the general public, not reproducing all of Lewis's juvenile problems with language and format, as can be seen by comparing the reproduced Dramatis Personae to "The King's Ring" with Hooper's printed version. For example, Lewis wrote "Boscen" in one of his titles, which Hooper has turned into "Boxen"; Hooper also moved some illustrations around. Some of the drawings were colored in the original, as can be seen in the two drawings on the dust jacket, but they are reproduced in monotone photographs in the book. (One additional color plate, in addition to the two

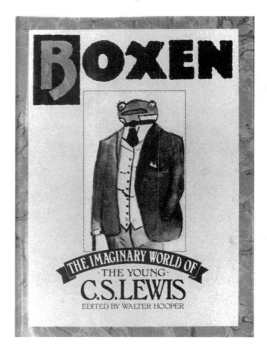

on the dust jacket, appears in Douglas Gilbert and **Clyde S. Kilby**'s *C. S. Lewis: Images of His World*.) Another scholarly problem will be discussed below in connection with "Encyclopedia Boxoniana."

Hooper has arranged the materials into three sections: "Animal-Land" (23–57), "Boxen" (59–194), and "Encyclopedia Boxoniana" (195–206). Seven works appear in the first section: "The King's Ring" (A Comedy) (25–34), "Manx Against Manx" (35–36), "The Relief of Murry" (37–38), "History of Mouse-Land from Stone-Age to Bublish I" (Old History) (39–41), "History of Animal-Land (New History)" (43–49), "The Chess Monograph" (50–53) and "The Geography of Animal-Land" (55–57). Also included in this section are seventeen drawings, two reproductions of manuscripts, and one map.

"The King's Ring" is a play in three acts, each act divided into three scenes. The year is 1327, in the seventeenth year of the rule of King Bunny I. The main action is the theft of King Bunny's ring by Archibald Hit (a mouse, who is acting as a bartender in the first scene of Act I); the ring is disguised and sold to an innocent person but recovered. The one literary allusion—a typical technique of the later Lewis—is to Edward Lear's "The Owl and the Pussycat," which is followed by two puns, a touch of (very early) Lewisian humor:

> Mr. Icthus-oress: . . . this is the way I sing. (sings)
>   the owl and the pussycat went to sea.
> Dorimie: To see what?
> Mr. Icthus-oress: To the sea.
> Dorimie: O, was it the see of, what Bishop? (31)

The next two items are reversed in chronology, but probably Hooper was putting them in the order of composition, as well as he could discover it. "Manx Against Manx" (the title is not explained) is a story about Sir Peter Mouse, whose tail is cut off, whose whiskers are trimmed, and whose left ear is cut off on consecutive nights, while he sleeps. Since he is a detective, he finds tracks in the snow outside his house; he later apprehends the culprit (whose motives are not explained). "The Relief of Murry" is another story about Sir Peter Mouse, this time with a Medieval setting and with Sir Peter having Medieval locutions in his speech. Sir Peter attacks (at night) and defeats the cats who are besieging Murry, a castle. (At least in later times, Murry is the capital of Animal-Land.) In "History of Animal-Land," a father (47) and son (48–49)—both named Sir Peter Mouse—are mentioned: probably the first is that of "The Relief of Murry" (even though he is killed by the cats in the

"History" before they besiege Murry) and the second is that of "Manx Against Manx."

The two histories can be considered together. The "History of Mouse-Land" is an episodic and short (nine-paragraph) account running from 55 B.C. to A.D. 1216 or so (1307 is mentioned in the first paragraph). Evidently, the first contact between W. H. Lewis's Indians and C. S. Lewis's Mice occurred in 1216. The "History of Animal-Land" is divided into two books, of four and two chapters; unlike the previous history, this one has few dates. The first paragraph begins before the first history but also comes up to the first contact with Indians. (It mentions that the Indians and the Mice can intermarry and—it is indicated in the second paragraph—interbreed. But Lewis's animals are drawn like humans with animal heads, so their socialization is not too odd.) The second chapter describes the rule of King Bublish I (whose rule, with some differences in the events before it, was prepared for, but not described, in the first history).

In the third chapter, Benjamin ("the Bunny") comes to the throne. He is the same as King Bunny of "The King's Ring"; in this history Jas. Hit, not Archibald Hit, steals the Crown Jewels, not just a ring. In the fourth chapter, King Mouse the Good is ruling; but in Book II, the monarchical rule gives way to a republic. In the first chapter, Lord Big (described in *Surprised by Joy*, Ch. 5) is mentioned; in chapter 2, the Chessaries are introduced, and a place named Tararo is mentioned (the latter name is the title Walter Hooper has given to an unpublished fragment). It is not clear from these histories the relation of Mouse-Land to Animal-Land, but in "The Geography" Mouse-Land is one province of Animal-Land; it is also not clear when the various provinces were united into one country, but in the "Encyclopedia Boxoniana" the union takes place in 1331 (204).

"The Chess Monograph" (in two parts) seems to capture something of Lewis's youthful views of the Jews, for it says that in the 12th through the 14th centuries, the Chessmen in Animal-Land were treated as the Jews "in England at the same time." The parallel of "the Chess" and Jews is made even clearer later, in "The Locked Door," when Lord Big declares that "Chessmen are aliens, nothing more" (98), and asks rhetorically, "Who are these Chess? They are a nation without a country" (100). Four Chessmen left Animal-Land and sailed to Clarendon (evidently another island), where they established the first Chessary (ante 1380 [205]). Chessaries seem to be like forts, with living quarters. The account indicates that later Chessaries were constructed in various cities, including "the Royal Chessary" in Murry. Certainly a suggestion of the separateness of the Jews as a religio-ethnic group is suggested in the development of Chessmen, not Animals, for this account. On the other hand, the Chessaries certainly suggest greater strength than ghettos gave the Jews. Perhaps the youthful Lewis was suggesting, indirectly, what he thought the Jews should do: arm themselves and live in forts. On the other hand, in "The Locked Door," the Boxonian forces seem well on their way to subduing the Chessmen on Tracity Island, despite the latter's weapons, in a trade war, before the peace is declared.

"The Geography of Animal-Land" describes the island, giving the thirteen provinces and their capitals and other information. The Mourme Mountains in the north were probably suggested by Ireland's Mourne Mountains, and this suggests that Animal-Land is parallel, in a general way, to Ireland.

In the second section, "Boxen," four works appear: "Boxen: or Scenes from Boxonian city life" (61–88), "The Locked Door: Sequel to 'Boxen'" (91–144), "Than-Kyu: A Sketch" (145–51), and "The Sailor: A Study" (153–94). A number of the same characters appear in most of these works—Lord Big, the Little-master (a frog); James Bar, a sailor (a brown bear); Viscount Puddiphat, the owner of a number of music halls and an elegant dresser (an owl), for example. This section has thirty-three drawings, six maps or diagrams, six reproductions of (fictional) notes or tickets, and one reproduction of Lewis's manuscript.

In general, the material is much better written in this section. The content can be suggested briefly. "Boxen" (in fourteen sections) is primarily a political story about the election of a new Clique (evidently referring to a Boxonian cabinet). The early 20th-century date is indicated in the next story with its combination of automobiles ("the powerful purr of motors") and horse-drawn carriages ("the music of horses' hoofs"). "The Locked Door" (in twenty-two chapters), laid three months after the previous story, involves political bribery and the start of a trade war between Boxen and Tracity Island; almost incidental is a stage parody of the kings of Animal-Land and India and of the Little-Master. (The locked door of the title is not mentioned or explained.) "Than-Kyu" (in four sections) is an episode early in the life of Lord Big, when he had been ill and was sent by his father for a brief rest in the state of Than-Kyu, between Turkey and Pongee, inhabited by Islamites; Big overstays his legal visit by one day and is tossed into the bay. (The punning title and name of the country—"Thank You"—seems to be ironic.) "The Sailor" (in two volumes with four-

teen continuously numbered chapters) is a story of a Persian cat named Alexander Cottle who has recently graduated from the naval college and been named junior marine officer on His Majesty's Ship Greyhound; in volume one, he tries to reform the lax performances of the sailors and his fellow officers, and in volume two, he has been corrupted by James Bar and others and joins in their lifestyle. Lewis's background in **Belfast** is shown in details of ships throughout these stories.

The third section consists solely of "Encyclopedia Boxoniana"; this consists of a plan, a list of the documents and where they were to be found (a number are mentioned that no longer seem to exist), a chronology of the Boxonian world, and a brief note on the geography. One page (written on both sides) is missing. One drawing prefaces this material.

Lewis mentioned his plan to draw up an "Encyclopedia Boxoniana" in a letter to his brother of October 5, 1927 (printed in the revised edition of *Letters of C. S. Lewis*, not in the original edition). However, Kathryn Lindskoog has argued from the style that "Encyclopedia Boxoniana" (as published) is a forged addition to the Lewis canon; she quotes three sentences and one phrase as examples of passages that by 1927 Lewis would not have written. Certainly she has found very poor sentences; and, while style by itself (as judged by an individual sensibility) is not a certain criterion, she has at least raised a legitimate question. Her whole discussion of the Boxonian materials, "Stealing The King's Ring," is broader than just questions of style.

Joe R. Christopher

Also See: Fantasy, Fairy Tales, Magic, Non-Christian Religions, Politics

Bibliography

Christopher, Joe R. "Publishing Boxen." *The Lamp-Post of the Southern California C. S. Lewis Society* 11 no. 4 (November 1988): 8–10.
Gilbert, Douglas, and Clyde S. Kilby. *C. S. Lewis: Images of His World*. Grand Rapids, MI: Eerdmans, 1973.
Lindskoog, Kathryn. "Appendix One: Stealing The King's Ring." *Light in the Shadowlands: Protecting the Real C. S. Lewis*. Sisters, OR: Multnomah, 1994: 279–94.

"Break, Sun, My Crusted Earth"

Fear No More: A Book of Poems for the Present Time by Living English Poets. Cambridge: Cambridge University Press, 1940: 72. Revised and retitled as "A Pageant Played in Vain" and reprinted in *Poems* and *Collected Poems*.

This poem was originally published anonymously. However, six copies of *Fear No More* contained an additional leaf identifying the authors. One of these copies is in the **Bodleian Library**, Oxford. Using a mining **metaphor**, Lewis invited light to pierce his unconscious self just as shafts of sun penetrated and exposed the hidden depths of caves.

Don W. King
Montreat College

Also See: Light and Darkness

The Bride of Christ (Book Review)

See entry on *Passion and Society* and *The Bride of Christ* (Book Review)

Broadcast Talks

London: Geoffrey Bles, The Centenary Press, 1942. First US edition titled *The Case for Christianity*. New York: Macmillan, 1943. Reprinted as Books I and II of *Mere Christianity*.

Broadcast Talks was the title under which, in 1942, C. S. Lewis's first two series of British Broadcasting Corporation talks, originally given in 1941, were published in England. (The American title was *The Case for Christianity,* published in the U.S. by Macmillan in 1943.) Most contemporary readers know them as the first two books of one of Lewis's most popular books *Mere Christianity* (New York, the Macmillan Company, 1952), where they were lightly revised as Lewis explained in the preface. A third series of twelve talks was published under the title *Christian Behaviour* (reprinted as Book III of *Mere Christianity*) and a fourth series was published under the title *Beyond Personality* (reprinted as Book IV of *Mere Christianity*).

In the first series of talks, "Right and Wrong as a Clue to the Meaning of the Universe," Lewis had two major objectives: to convince his audience of the existence of a moral law and to show that by the standards of this moral law we are in trouble. In Lewis's words, **Christianity** tells people to repent and promises them forgiveness, but first we must be convinced that we need repentance and forgiveness.

Lewis's argument for the existence of the moral law has two aspects: an appeal to our common moral experience and a defense of the moral law against certain

attempts to explain it away. In our everyday moral experience he showed that we appeal to some standard of behavior and that other people accept these appeals. Even if people break the rules themselves, they appeal to them against others: often no one is more indignant than a cheater who has been cheated.

There are various common explanations of why we have this recognition of a moral law. One is a "herd instinct," which directs us to preserve our species (today an explanation might be given in terms of our genetic makeup, the "selfish gene" theory). But Lewis pointed out that often we have to choose between this "herd instinct" and self-preservation, and it is the moral law we appeal to judge this issue: thus, the moral law itself is not an instinct but rather directs our choice between instincts.

Another explanation of our recognition of the moral law is that it is learned behavior; our society "socializes" such behavior in us. But Lewis pointed out that some learned behavior is objectively valid: rules of arithmetic, for example. The fact that we *learn* our moral behavior does not settle the question of whether or not it is objectively valid.

In fact the general agreement across cultures that certain things are right and wrong points in the direction of an objective **natural law**. (The material in the appendix of *The Abolition of Man* reinforces this point.) As Lewis said, "Men have differed as regards what people you ought to be unselfish to.... But they have always

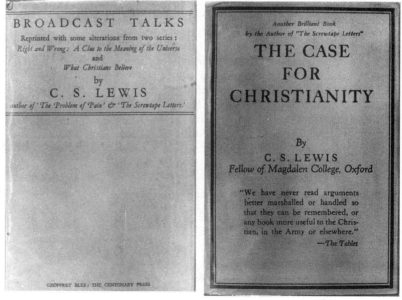

U.K. First Edition   U.S. Edition

agreed that you ought not to put yourself first. Selfishness has never been admired. Men have differed about whether you should have one wife or four. But they have always agreed that you must not simply have any woman you liked."

Once Lewis defended the view that there is a "law of human nature" he went on to point out that none of us really keeps the law; by standards we ourselves endorse we fail to be as moral as we feel we ought to be. And then he goes on to argue that there are two possible explanations of the law of **human nature**. On a materialist view, we are simply the result of accidental forces, and any moral law we think we know is similarly an accidental result. *Or* we may be the result of a plan by a conscious person. And if, as is most likely, we are the result of design, then the person behind the moral law "must hate most of what we do."

Having called our attention to this predicament, Lewis then outlined what is now the second book of *Mere Christianity,* "What Christians Believe." He started off with some rival conceptions of **God**. Among people who believe in God, as most of the human race does, we can see him as bound up in the universe, the "soul," so to speak, of the physical universe. Or we can see him as transcending the physical universe. If God is the "soul" of the universe then it is hard to see God as opposed to the evil in the universe: God must embody both **good and evil** aspects, or be "beyond good and evil." But if God is separate from the universe, its Creator, then it is possible that "a great many things have gone wrong in the world that God made, and God insists and insists very loudly, on our putting them right again."

Atheism, the view that God does not exist, does not explain our indignation at the injustice of the universe according to Lewis. Our idea of **justice**, which gives rise to the argument from evil against the existence of God, cannot be accounted for by atheism. Another view of God is that there are two Gods, one being good and one evil, but again by calling one God good and the other evil we presume some higher standard by which we can judge this.

If God then is opposed to the evil in the universe, what has God done about it? Since God has created

human beings with **free will** he cannot simply abolish evil without abolishing free will. So God has become incarnate, said Lewis, and given us an example of a "perfect penitent" in **Christ**.

"We need God's help to do something which God, in His own nature never does at all—to surrender, to suffer, to submit, to die. . . . But supposing God became a man—supposing our human nature which can suffer and die was amalgamated with God's nature in one person, then that person could help us. You and I can go through the process only if God does it in us. . . . That is the sense in which he pays our debts and suffers what He Himself need not suffer at all." (The further consequences of this are explored in "Beyond Personality," the last book of *Mere Christianity.*)

In the last chapter, "The Practical Conclusion," Lewis pointed out that there are three things that bring the Christ life to us—baptism, **faith**, and Holy Communion. We may not see how these things bring the Christ life to us, but this is clearly what Christ taught. As Lewis said, "When Christians say that the Christ life is in them, they do not simply mean something mental or moral. When they speak of Christ being 'in them' this is not simply a way of saying that they are thinking of Christ or copying Him, they mean that Christ is operating through them: that the whole mass of Christians are the physical organism through which Christ acts."

So, "The Practical Conclusion" is by baptism, faith, and Holy Communion to become part of this body of Christ and help God overcome the evil in the world.

Richard Purtill
Western Washington University

Also See: Apologetics, Theology

"'Bulverism' or The Foundation of 20th Century Thought"

See entry on Notes on the Way (29 March 1941)

The Business of Heaven: Daily Readings from C. S. Lewis

Walter Hooper (ed). London: Collins, 1984. First US edition, New York: Harcourt Brace Jovanovich, 1984.

A collection of 365 readings.

C

C. S. Lewis: Letters to Children

Dorsett, Lyle W., and Marjorie Lamp Mead (eds.). New York: Macmillan, 1985. First UK edition, London: Collins, 1985.

Among the most significant of C. S. Lewis's writings are those that he never envisioned would be published: his personal letters to correspondents from many different countries. Some of these letters were typed by his brother, **Warren Lewis**, but the rest were handwritten reflecting Lewis's willingness to spend time on those who asked for his counsel. Indeed, the pastoral nature of many of Lewis's letters is both touching and edifying as he thoughtfully responded to the issues raised by his generally unknown correspondents. Lewis's letters to children are no exception to this pattern; he replied to the inquiries of his youngest readers with the same courtesy and respect he afforded his adult correspondents.

Gathered together, *C. S. Lewis: Letters to Children* prints a sampling of Lewis's letters to his young correspondents. The selected letters illustrate the deep connection Lewis had with young people despite his many years as a bachelor. As quoted in the introduction to the volume, Lewis described his approach to writing for children thus: "The child as reader is neither to be patronised nor idolised: we talk to him as man to man.... We must of course try to do [children] no harm: we may, under the Omnipotence, sometimes dare to hope that we may do them good. But only such good as involves treating them with respect."

The range of topics covered by these letters is instructive: writing, **nature**, work, animals, school, books, **poetry**, languages, spiritual matters, and, of course, numerous questions relating to Narnia. In brief, most of these subjects were concerns that filled Lewis's days as well as those of his young correspondents. Thus, Lewis's adult world easily touched the world of these children and found there "common, universally human, ground."

Other patterns can be discerned by reading these letters in sequence. One can observe, for example, how young children who first wrote simply to thank a favorite author soon began to form a "pen pal" **friendship** with Lewis. In the same way, one can see how some children's early love for the Narnia books developed upon occasion into an appreciation for the space trilogy and *Till We Have Faces*. This chronological reading of the letters also allows one to observe how the natural maturation process of the child inevitably influenced the subject matter of the letters. In particular, it was in the letters from older children that Lewis, the teacher, became most evident as he generously read their stories, essays, and poems—and then, carefully offered advice and guidance to the hopeful authors. A few children sent photographs, while many enclosed their own artwork, most often of Narnia; but all of them somehow wanted to reach out to this man who made a difference in their young lives. It is clear from his replies that Lewis understood this and responded in kind.

Some of these responses were simple messages of gratitude and greetings, but many contained thoughtful passages that are of value to readers of all ages. The letter to his god-daughter Sarah on the occasion of her confirmation and first communion is one of these. Writing on April 3, 1949, Lewis sent regrets that he could not be present and then went on to caution Sarah that appropriate feelings are not necessary to a meaningful communion. He advised her that when taking communion "real things" are happening to you whether or not you feel as you wish to feel. Drawing on his own experience, he explained that it was only in recent years that his emotions at such moments joined with his actions. Often in the past, he had found his feelings to be "dull" or that his attention wandered at the most significant times in the liturgy. But now, at long last, he has begun to find that his feelings fit with the sacramental act. Thus, he concluded, right actions often beget proper responses, and we must trust to the Lord in this regard.

Another such letter is one of May 6, 1955, to a young man named Laurence

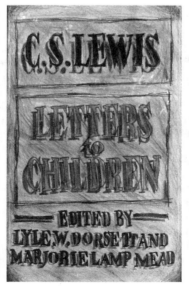

who feared he loved Aslan more than Jesus. Lewis responded contritely (writing first of all to Laurence's mother), asking forgiveness for the "trouble" he has caused and gently reassuring the nine-year-old American boy that **God** knows what little boys' imaginations are like because he created them that way. Thus, God understands that the body of a lion holds more appeal than the ordinary figure of a man, but that this attraction would fade with time as Laurence grew older. Further, Lewis explained that when Laurence loved Aslan for doing certain things, he was only responding to the things that Jesus really did. Therefore, when Laurence thought he was loving Aslan, he was really loving Jesus. Just a year later, Laurence would write and ask Lewis why the children in *The Last Battle* were uncertain what would happen to them if they died, wondering if they didn't know the Apostles' Creed, especially where it stated: "I believe in ... the resurrection of the body, and the life everlasting"? Clearly, Lewis's original reassurance was founded in good stead as Laurence was maturing into a young Christian with a firm understanding of his **faith**.

There are significant letters on other topics as well. Writing to a class of fifth-grade students on May 29, 1954, Lewis carefully explained why he did not intend the Narnia books to be read allegorically but rather "suppositionally," a distinction often missed by even adult readers. To Joan, a frequent correspondent with an interest in writing, Lewis offered a very succinct and yet powerful lesson in how to write well; this letter of June 26, 1956, contains advice worth noting by writers of any age. In several letters, Lewis recommended some of his favorite books to eager young readers, while in others, he advises students who are beginning to learn Latin. Of course, Lewis also answers many questions about the Narnia books including such issues as the correct order for reading the seven stories (April 23, 1957) and Susan's fate (January 22, 1957). In all of these instances and more, Lewis respects the age and interest of his young correspondents, yet with a teacher's deft touch, challenges them to reach a bit higher than they might on their own.

Among the most poignant of the letters in this volume are those in which Lewis touched on his own personal life. In the letter dated April 23, 1957, mentioned above, he also wrote of his wife's illness and then said: "I am sure Aslan knows best and whether He leaves her with me or takes her to His own country, He will do what is right. But of course it makes me very sad." Six years later, on October 26, 1963, nearing the end of his own life, Lewis wrote to a young girl named Ruth: "If you continue to love Jesus, nothing much can go wrong

with you, and I hope you may always do so." This simple, yet profound hope can serve as a benediction for each one of the letters in this collection, expressing as it does Lewis's underlying desire for all of his young correspondents.

This volume includes a foreword by Lewis's stepson, **Douglas H. Gresham**, the editors' introduction, a biographical piece on Lewis's childhood, and an annotated children's bibliography to C. S. Lewis.

Marjorie Lamp Mead
The Marion E. Wade Center

Bibliography

Ford, Paul. *Companion to Narnia*. San Francisco: Harper & Row, 1980.
Gibran, Jean. "Review of *C. S. Lewis: Letters to Children.*" *Harvard Educational Review*. 55 no. 4 (November 1985): 476.
Hooper, Walter. *Past Watchful Dragons*. New York: Macmillan, 1979.
Lindskoog, Kathryn. "From the Child in Him to the Child in Us All" *Books & Religion*. 13 no. 4–5 (May-June, 1985): 12.
Schakel, Peter J. *Reading with the Heart: The Way into Narnia*. Grand Rapids, MI: Eerdmans, 1979.

C. S. Lewis: Readings for Reflection and Meditation

Walter Hooper (ed). London: HarperCollins, 1995.

See entry on *Daily Readings with C. S. Lewis*

Giovanni Calabria (1873–1954)

After reading an Italian translation of *The Screwtape Letters*, Don Giovanni, founder of an order known as the Poor Servants of Divine Providence, began a correspondence with Lewis that has since been collected into a volume entitled *Letters of C. S. Lewis and Don Giovanni Calabria*. The letters were written in Latin as Calabria could not read or write in English. The letters contain a broad discussion that included **church** unity, distinctions between **Roman Catholicism** and **Anglicanism**, as well as much on **prayer**.

Jeffrey D. Schultz

Bibliography

Foffano, Ottorino. *Il Servo di Dio Don Giovanni Calabria*. Verona, 1959.
Lewis, C. S. *Letters: C. S. Lewis and Don Giovanni Calabria; The Screwtape Letters*.

Campbell College

In 1910 C. S. Lewis was sent to Campbell College, which was located about a mile from his home, **Little**

Lea. Lewis was a boarding student. He disliked the common rooms and complained about the lack of privacy, writing that it was "like living in a large railway station." It was, however, a definite improvement over his previous school, **Wynyard**. Jack spent little time at Campbell as he fell ill in November 1910. Still, it was at Campbell that he heard his English master read **Matthew Arnold**'s heroic poem "Sohrab and Rustum." The experience left a deep impression on him.

Jeffrey D. Schultz

Bibliography

Lewis, C. S. *Surprised by Joy.*
Sayer, George. *Jack: C. S. Lewis and His Times.* Wheaton, IL: Crossway, 1988.

Canonization (Letter)

Church Times. CXXXV (24 October 1952): 763. Reprinted in *God in the Dock, Undeceptions,* and *Timeless at Heart.*

Eric Pitt's letter of October 17, 1952 (*Church Times*, 743), raised the issue of the desirability of an appropriate means for canonization of saints within the Anglican communion. Lewis stated that before such a system is even discussed, it is essential that certain points be clarified. Within **Roman Catholicism**, Lewis understood canonization to assert that saints are those who are dead and "worthy of God's special **love**"; further, these saints, once they are canonized, are deserving of *dulia* (honor and reverence). Accordingly, Lewis questioned how the church can determine exact knowledge of the status of departed souls and whether such knowledge will contribute to the salvation of those now living. If not, he believed such a decision carries a "frightful risk" of schism, with no redeeming value.

Marjorie L. Mead
The Marion E. Wade Center

Capital Punishment: Grounds for Abolition (Letter)

Church Times. CXLIV (1 December 1961): 7. Reprinted in *God in the Dock, Undeceptions,* and *Timeless at Heart.*

This controversy over capital punishment apparently began with an unsigned obituary for Bishop H. H. Williams, entitled "In Memoriam" (*Church Times*, 6 October 1961), the final paragraph of which declared Williams' view that "the 'deterrent' view of punishment was wholly immoral." For the next few weeks, the letters to the editor section of *Church Times* dealt with this issue. Lewis's first contribution to the discussion stated that he does not know whether capital punishment

should be abolished or not but that it would be valuable to learn from prison chaplains as to whether a death sentence or a long imprisonment is more likely to result in repentance on the part of the convicted criminal. He also cautioned against the dangers of punishment intended as either deterrent or as a means of reforming the criminal.

Marjorie L. Mead
The Marion E. Wade Center

Robert Capron (1851–1911)

Robert Capron was the headmaster of **Wynyard School**, which both **Warren Lewis** and C. S. Lewis attended. Capron was noted for his cruelty, and the Lewis boys implored their father, **Albert Lewis**, to remove them from the school. Nicknamed "Oldie," Capron was a powerfully built man who was intimidating and brutal. After the school closed in 1910 because of a lack of enrollment, Capron spent a short time at another school before being hospitalized and dying in an asylum.

Jeffrey D. Schultz

Bibliography

Lewis, C. S. "My First School"; *Surprised by Joy.*
Sayer, George. *Jack: C. S. Lewis and His Times.* Wheaton, IL: Crossway, 1988.

The Case for Christianity

See entry on *Broadcast Talks*

"Caught"

See entry on "You rest upon me all my days"

David Cecil (1902–1986)

After a number of years as a fellow at Wadham College where he taught modern history and English literature, David Cecil (Lord Edward Christian David Gascoyne) was elected a fellow of English at New College, **Oxford**. A popular lecturer, Cecil became an **Inkling**, though other commitments prevented him from attending the meetings often.

Bibliography

Cecil, David. *The Stricken Deer* (1929). Indianapolis: Bobbs-Merrill, 1930.
_____. *Sir Walter Scot.* London: Constable, 1933.
_____. *Jane Austen.* Cambridge: The University Press, 1935.
_____. *Early Victorian Novelists* (1934). London: Constable, 1935.
_____. *The Young Melbourne.* Indianapolis: Bobbs-Merrill, 1939.
_____. *Two Quiet Lives.* Indianapolis: Bobbs-Merrill, 1948.

_____. *Poets and Story-Tellers*. Indianapolis: Bobbs-Merrill, 1949.

_____. *Lord Melbourne* . Indianapolis: Bobbs-Merrill, 1954.

_____. *Max* (1964). Boston: Houghton Mifflin, 1965.

_____. *Visionary and Dreamer: Two Poetic Painters—Samuel Palmer and Edward Burne-Jones* (1969). Princeton, NJ: Princeton University Press, 1970.

_____. *The Cecils of Hatfield House*. Boston: Houghton Mifflin, 1973.

_____. *A Portrait of Jane Austen*. New York: Hill and Wang, 1978.

_____. *A Portrait of Charles Lamb*. New York: Scribners, 1983.

Cranborne, Hannah (ed). *David Cecil: A Portrait by His Friends*. Stanbridge UK: Dovecote Press, 1991.

Robson, W. W. *Essays and Poems Presented to Lord David Cecil*. London: Constable, 1970.

Celtic Origin (Letter)

Walsh, Chad. *C. S. Lewis: Apostle to the Skeptics*. New York: Macmillan, 1949: 2–3.

A brief quotation from a letter for which no citation is given, though it is possible that this letter was sent in response to an inquiry from Macmillan, Lewis's American publisher. In the portion quoted, Lewis commented that his Celtic origins did not seem to influence his **imagination**, which he believed to be thoroughly Germanic. He also declared his love for Norse mythology.

Marjorie L. Mead
The Marion E. Wade Center

Also See: Myths

"Chanson D'Aventure"

The Oxford Magazine 56 (May 19, 1938): 638 (under the pseudonym Nat Whilk). Revised and retitled as "What the Bird Said Early in the Year" and reprinted in *Poems* and *Collected Poems*.

While strolling **Addison's Walk** at **Magdalen College**, Lewis heard a bird's song promising that this particular summer would not fade, that autumn would never come. Though he might have wished for this, he knew the bird's song in itself could not make it happen.

Don W. King
Montreat College

"Charles Walter Stansby Williams (1886–1945)"

The Oxford Magazine. LXIII (24 May 1945): 165 (obituary).

Lewis was always loyal to his friends and favorably reviewed their books, or wrote introductions or appreciations of them that could be lavish. This obituary notice of his close friend **Charles Williams** was no

exception and contains some remarkable judgments. For example, Lewis observed that Williams might "in the end stand as the great English poet of this age. At least, if the difficulty of his work prevents this, we shall have lost the only poetic experience in English which can, in any profound sense, be called Pindaric." Overall, Lewis paints a dignified and loving portrait of a most gifted man who must have been an enigma to many at **Oxford**. He was a novelist, a poet, and a critic, whose **Christianity** and scholarship were original and powerful.

John Bremer

Geoffrey Chaucer (c. 1340–1400)

Chaucer, the son of a prominent London wine merchant, had a broad and varied career as a soldier, government official, international diplomat, justice of the peace, Member of Parliament, translator, and poet. C. S. Lewis observed that the literature of the 14th century is merely background to Chaucer. Lewis described him as having few rivals and no masters, claiming that Chaucer is to **poetry** what Mozart is to music. Chaucer was the poet of Courtly Love—a theme often discussed by Lewis. While it remains to future scholarship to reveal the degree of Lewis's debt to Chaucer, it is readily apparent that the debt is significant.

Jerry Root
Wheaton College

Bibliography

Lewis, C. S. *The Allegory of Love*; *The Discarded Image*; "What Chaucer Really Did to *Il Filostrato*."

Cherbourg School

Called "Chartres" in his autobiography, ***Surprised by Joy***, Lewis was sent to Cherbourg School in January 1911 because his father, **Albert Lewis**, believed that the air and water of Malvern would aid in his son's recovery from the illness that forced him to leave **Campbell College** in November 1910. In addition to being a good school scholastically, Cherbourg was located a short distance from **Malvern College** where **Warren Lewis** was in attendance. At Cherbourg, C. S. Lewis studied both Latin and English and began writing stories and essays including **"Are Athletes Better than Scholars."** It is at Cherbourg that he rejected **Christianity** because he felt his prayers were not being heard. His rejection of Christianity was aided by Miss Cowie, a motherly matron, who believed in some esoteric oriental religion.

In July 1912 the school hired a new assistant master who was nicknamed "Pogo." The students, including Jack, worshipped him and tried to emulate him. In the process, Lewis "began to labor very hard to make [himself] into a fop, a cad, and a snob." Lewis left Cherbourg in July 1913 having successfully passed the Malvern College entrance exam.

Jeffrey D. Schultz

Bibliography

Lewis, C. S. *Surprised by Joy.*
Sayer, George. *Jack: C. S. Lewis and His Times.* Wheaton, IL: Crossway, 1988.

G[ilbert] K[ieth] Chesterton (1874–1936)

Chesterton—a Roman Catholic convert and social critic—was much admired by and had great influence on C. S. Lewis. Excluding matched sets of such authors as Tolstoy, Lewis owned more books by Chesterton in his personal library than any other author except his other great mentor, **George MacDonald**. And here there is an interesting connection as well. Chesterton was asked by George MacDonald's son Greville MacDonald to write the introduction for Greville's wonderful book on his parents: *George MacDonald and his Wife* (London: George Allen and Unwin, 1924).

Lewis thought Chesterton "a great Roman Catholic, a great writer and a great man" (**"Donne and Love Poetry"**), and he referred to Chesterton in many letters and in over thirteen of his published books. By Lewis's own admission, Chesterton's extraordinary work *The Everlasting Man* (1922) played an important part in his conversion to **Christianity**. In that book, said Lewis, he "saw the whole Christian outline of history set out in a form that seemed to me to make sense" (*Surprised by Joy*). In a letter to the late **Sheldon Vanauken**, Lewis referred to *The Everlasting Man* as "the best popular apologetic" he knew, and the year before he died, he listed it as one of the ten books that were the greatest influence in shaping his "philosophy of life."

Lewis's essay **"Willing Slaves of the Welfare State"** bears the mark of Chesterton's critique of intrusive government, the welfare state, and "the world-wide paternalism of **technology**." Both writers agreed that "planned societies" threaten freedom by depriving ordinary citizens of the right to make decisions about the ordering of their lives. Both writers also saw the coming attacks on the family and religion, believing that families and communities of free people had much to fear from the "new ethics" in such areas as public **education**, health care, and criminal justice.

Lewis's essays, his short book *The Abolition of Man,* and his fiction all discuss the importance of a proper understanding of tradition and the development

and transmission of moral teaching—what Lewis called "the freeborn mind." In *That Hideous Strength*, for example, the scientists as "social experts" have a plan for society that is cut off from a coherent moral vision. In the novel they have, quite literally, separated the head from the heart. Lewis would no doubt have agreed with Chesterton's statement in his masterpiece, *Orthodoxy*, that "every man who will not have softening of the heart must at last have softening of the brain."

Many of Lewis's best apologetic arguments appear, often in strikingly parallel ways, in earlier works by Chesterton. Thus, the famous "lord, lunatic or liar" argument in Lewis's *Mere Christianity* is to be found in Chesterton's earlier book *Orthodoxy*. Many other parallels of theme, **metaphor**, or example abound.

The more one reads of these two great 20th-century apologists the more one comes to appreciate that, in a sense, they form complementary halves of one extraordinary being—and, in terms of **apologetics**, much is to be gained by reading them together. In some ways it may be more apt to speak of a Chesterlewis than it was for George Bernard Shaw to have spoken of the Chesterbelloc. But the influences of Chesterton were, generally, philosophical and theological rather than literary per se. As Lewis said himself in a letter, Chesterton's influence was more in the realm of thought than on **imagination**, but there can be no doubt that his influence on Lewis was significant, long-lasting, and beneficial.

Iain Benson

Also See: Science

Bibliography

The Chesterton Review. XVII (November 1991). This is a special issue that focuses on Lewis.
Mackey, Aidan. "The Christian Influence of G. K. Chesterton on C. S. Lewis." *A Christian for All Christians.* A. Walker and J. Patrick (eds). London: Hodder and Stoughton, 1990: 68–82.

Christ

Traditionalist that he was, Lewis always took the standard, orthodox, "mere Christian" position regarding the nature of Christ. He viewed Christ as fully **God** and fully man, Lord and Savior. He accepted the Virgin Birth and other **miracles** and believed that the New Testament provides an absolutely accurate account of who Christ is and what he said. He saw God the Son as perpetually emanating from God the Father, a continual self-expression that in *Mere Christianity* Lewis compared to light from a lamp or thoughts from a mind.

Lewis's clearest and most famous statement about who Christ is comes in the third chapter of "What Christians Believe" in *Mere Christianity*, the well-known "liar, lunatic, or Lord" trichotomy. In this section, Lewis indicated that the attempt of many people to accept Jesus as a good moral teacher is ill-founded. In claiming to be God, either Jesus really believed it but was wrong (which would make him a lunatic), or he didn't believe it (which would make him a liar), or he believed it and was right (which would make him Lord). Since Jesus seemed otherwise sane and righteous throughout the rest of his life, the only logical conclusion left, according to Lewis, is that Jesus was indeed God.

Although Lewis accepted orthodox views, he did seem to have trouble with the idea of Christ's atonement. This had been an initial stumbling block in the way of his accepting Christianity, cleared up somewhat by a talk with **Hugo Dyson** and **J. R. R. Tolkien**. But even after conversion, Lewis had difficulty believing Christ's sacrifice purified Christians completely. In *Mere Christianity*, he referred to the atonement as a "fresh start"—rather weak language. And his inclinations toward belief in **purgatory** were caused by his belief that Christians did not enter heaven morally pure, but dragging their stains of sin with them. Lewis declared our entry into **heaven** the moral equivalent of a person entering a classy establishment wearing dirty rags and having bad breath. Christ's death, in his view, appears to enable Christians to undergo purification rather than actually purifying them.

Perhaps the best place to find Lewis's understanding of the characteristics of Christ is the **Chronicles of Narnia**. Just as in our world Christ became a man, the creator and sustainer of that world became, like its inhabitants, an animal—a lion. Much of Lewis's presentation of Christ in the Chronicles comes directly from Scripture, such as with the animal imagery. Throughout the Chronicles, Aslan is a lion, as in the Lion of Judah, and in *The Voyage of the "Dawn Treader,"* Aslan appears as a lamb (the Lamb of God). In Narnia, Aslan is the Son of the Emperor-over-the-Sea, a clear picture of the Father-Son relationship. He is both the Creator of Narnia (*The Magician's Nephew*) and its final Judge (*The Last Battle*).

When the Pevensie children enter Narnia in *The Lion, the Witch and the Wardrobe*, they are told about Aslan and wonder whether he is safe. The Beavers tell them Aslan is not safe, but good—a key motif in Lewis's views of Christ that runs throughout the Chronicles. A common saying there about Aslan is that he isn't a "tame lion"; and indeed, he comes and goes as he pleases. Aside from one odd section in *The Voyage of the "Dawn Treader"* where Aslan says he has to "obey the rules," he is clearly in charge of events. Characters have **free will**, but Aslan certainly intervenes and interacts with them freely and frequently.

Lewis perceived Jesus as a person who had to struggle to overcome his reluctance at Gethsemane and fulfill his mission. This, according to Lewis, is of great benefit for us; if Jesus had been a person naturally courageous, his example of obeying God under difficult circumstances would have less value for us.

In some ways, one is tempted to wonder how comfortable Lewis felt with Jesus and the whole idea of God's humanity. Lewis never wrote a book centering on the person of Jesus and, in fact, sometimes seems to have gone out of his way to avoid using the name of Jesus. When Lewis speaks of God the Son, it is most often as "Our Lord," sometimes as "Christ," and occasionally in cumbersome honorifics such as "the holiest of all petitioners." Perhaps this was simply Lewis's attempt to avoid overfamiliarity, but he actually did seem to be more comfortable with the concept of God as a judge rather than a friend.

Marvin D. Hinten
Bowling Green State University

"Christian Apologetics"

First published posthumously in *God in the Dock* and *Undeceptions*.

"Christian Apologetics" was originally read to an assembly of Anglican priests and youth leaders at the Carmarthen Conference for Youth Leaders and Junior Clergy at Carmarthen during Easter 1945.

Lewis began his discussion by saying that it is not his place to teach the priests and leaders of the church, but for them to teach him. As for the youth, he says that although he was young once, he spent his youth avoiding "being organized."

Lewis said that one of the first things that we must do is clarify what we defend in Christian **apologetics**. For his purposes, and for the purposes of his audience, it is **Christianity** as understood by the Church of Wales. The questions that Lewis invited his audience to consider have to do with the fact that they "serve One who said '**Heaven** and Earth shall move with the times, but my words shall not move with the times.'" The business of everyone—the priests, the youth leaders, the audience—is to present "that which is timeless." In the process of presenting a world where **sin** is possible, it is necessary that the language be clear. What is meant by "**Church**" will vary, and generally it is accepted as a building or the clergy rather than "the company of all faithful people." The same holds true for much of the lexicon that Christians and non-Christians share. It is also true that Christians do not necessarily use the language of the church in a manner consonant with the meanings of the church. Lewis provided a dictionary of terms which cause concern.

Lewis also addressed the danger of **apologetics** to "one's own **faith**." Successful defense sometimes results in an apparent weakness. The strength is not in the argument, in Christian apologetics, but in **Christ** himself.

Anne Gardner

Christian Behaviour

London: Geoffrey Bles, 1943. First US edition, New York: Macmillan, 1944. Reprinted as Book III of *Mere Christianity*.

Christian Behaviour is a survey of traditional Christian moral teachings. Lewis began with the **analogy** of a fleet of ships; one regulation necessary for it to be an effective fleet is that each ship will not collide with the others or get in each other's way. The second regulation is that each ship must be seaworthy and have its engines in good order, and the last regulation is that the ships of the fleet must all be going to the right place. Similarly in morality we first must have rules that keep us from injuring others—rules that make for fair play and harmony between individuals. Second, we must have rules that help us tidy up or harmonize things within ourselves, and finally, we must have rules that point out the purposes of human life.

Lewis observed that many modern people think morality is only about fairness and harmony, without seeing that we cannot be just to others without controlling our own greed, cowardice, ill temper, and self-conceit. Further, the eternal **destiny** of human beings makes an important difference to how we shall act. "There are a good many things which would not be worth bothering about if I were going to live only seventy years, but which I had better bother about very seriously if I am going to live forever."

In a section added to the talks after they were broadcast, Lewis made the same point in terms of the traditional

cardinal **virtues**. What he added to the points already made is a very Aristotelian insistence on virtues as good habits that are strengthened by repetition and weakened by failure. A person who perseveres in doing the right thing gets in the end a certain quality of character, and it is this quality that ultimately counts. "The point is not that **God** will refuse you admission to His eternal world if you have not got certain qualities of character: the point is that if people have not got at least the beginning of those qualities inside them, then no possible external conditions could make a **heaven** for them."

There is next a chapter on "Social Morality," in which one of Lewis's major points is that **Christianity** does not in itself lay down any program for a just social order: it is the job of Christian laypeople to work within their own fields of expertise to bring about such a social order. There is next a chapter on "Morality and Psychoanalysis" where Lewis pointed out that psychoanalysis if successful can only clear away obstacles to moral choice—it cannot make people choose well. If psychoanalysis clears away neurotic or psychotic fears then one person may decide to act morally, another may decide to act badly.

The following two chapters focus on "Sexual Morality" and "Christian **Marriage**," and here Lewis taught the lessons (unpalatable to moderns) that we must control our sexual passions and that Christian marriage demands fidelity. It is not the way we feel by which we are judged, but the way in which we act. But Lewis also pointed out that sexual morality is not central to Christian morality. "If anyone thinks that Christians regard unchastity as the supreme vice, he is quite wrong. The sins of the flesh are bad, but they are the least bad of all sins. All the worst [sinful] pleasures are purely spiritual. . . . That is why a cold, self-righteous prig who goes regularly to church may be far nearer to **hell** than a prostitute. But, of course it is better to be neither."

The next chapter is on "Forgiveness," and here Lewis highlighted the fact that according to **Christ** unless we forgive the sins of others against us we shall not be forgiven ourselves. Forgiving others does not mean excusing them. We may hate the **sin** but love the sinner. Lewis pointed out that we love ourselves in this way: we like ourselves but are often appalled or disappointed in what we do. The best way to forgive a sinner is to *act* as if we forgive them—God will give us the *feeling* of forgiveness if we need it.

The following chapter, "The Great Sin," points out that **pride** is the worst sin by Christian standards, indeed "as long as you are proud you cannot know God." This brings up the question of "how . . . people who are quite obviously eaten up with Pride can say they believe in God and appear to themselves very religious. . . . I am afraid it means they are worshipping an imaginary God. . . . They pay a pennyworth of imaginary humility to Him and get out of it a pounds' worth of Pride toward their fellow-men."

The last four chapters in the book are on charity, **hope**, and two chapters on **faith**. Charity is not necessarily liking other people, but wishing for their best interests. But Lewis called to our attention the fact that if we act for the best interests of others we often come to like them. Similarly, "The more cruel you are the more you will hate. . . . Good and evil both increase at compound interest. That is why the little decisions you and I make everyday are of such infinite importance."

In the chapter on "hope" Lewis pointed out the fact that the experiences we expect to make us happy in this world are all ultimately unsatisfying. He sketched three ways of dealing with this: (1) The Fools Way, in which we try to gain satisfaction by discarding old commitments, always hoping that the next marriage, the next journey will bring us the **happiness** we long for. (2) The Way of the Disillusioned "Sensible Man," in which we give up hopes of happiness. (3) The Christian Way, in which we enjoy the experiences that bring us partial happiness, but hope for ultimate satisfaction in God. As **Augustine** said, "Thou hast made us for thyself, Lord, and our hearts are restless until they rest in Thee."

In the two chapters on "faith" Lewis explained that faith is a **virtue** because we can always choose *not* to believe: our emotions and temptations lead us to reject things we know to be true: "It is not **reason** that is taking away my faith: on the contrary, my faith is based on reason. It is my **imagination** and emotions."

There are many excellent and outstanding things in *Christian Behaviour* that I could only hint at in this brief description. Lewis's account of *Christian Behaviour* and the whole of *Mere Christianity* repay rereading more than any of Lewis's nonfictional works. The attempt to summarize it for this *Encyclopedia* was a spiritual experience; if nothing else, it taught me humility—how

much worse I am at trying to express what Lewis had to say than Lewis was.

Richard Purtill
Western Washington University

Also See: Aristotle, Ethics and Morality, Sigmund Freud, Good and Evil, Sex

"Christian Hope—Its Meaning for Today"

Religion in Life. XXI (Winter 1952–53): 20–32. Retitled "The World's Last Night" and reprinted in *The World's Last Night* and *Fern-Seed and Elephant.*

Lewis was an expert on the Christian **virtue** of "hope," which along with **faith** and charity is one of the three "theological virtues." In the "hope" chapter of *Mere Christianity* Lewis defined this virtue as that real longing for **Heaven** that is present in each one of us. We all, if we were really to look into our hearts, would recognize that we want, acutely, something that this world does not offer. The longings we have when we fall in **love**, when we think of some foreign country, when we think of some subject, book, film, or artifact—these are desires that none of these things are able to satisfy. In **reality**, even the most positive examples within these categories leave us unsatisfied.

According to Lewis, there are two wrong ways to deal with this unsatisfied longing deep within us. We can be a fool, putting the blame of the things themselves, thinking that if only we would try something else, then we would catch the mysterious something we are all after. We might also become disillusioned and "sensible" and settle down and learn not to expect too much of life and repress that part of ourselves that used to "cry for the moon."

Then there is the Christian solution, the one right way. Lewis's view is that humans are not born with desires unless these desires can be satisfied. To paraphrase Lewis: If we find in ourselves a Desire that no experience in this world can satisfy, that does not prove that the universe is a fraud. Probably earthly pleasures were never meant to satisfy it, but only to arouse it, to suggest the real thing—**Christ**, the **Joy** of Man's Desiring. For Lewis, as well as for Plato and many others (compare **Plato**'s theme of the "Great Banquet" in the *Phaedrus*), the food we are seeking to satisfy our hunger is the triumph of good over evil, the conquest of death, the resurrection, and infinite **happiness**, all this and more is the ultimate hope of the Christian.

Michael H. Macdonald
Seattle Pacific University

Also See: Christianity, Destiny, Good and Evil, Hell, Immortality, Materialism, Redemption, Sin, Spirituality

Bibliography

Lewis, C. S. *Mere Christianity*; *Miracles*; *The Problem of Pain*.

Kreeft, Peter. *For Heaven's Sake*. New York: Thomas Nelson.

Pieper, Josef. *The Four Cardinal Virtues*. South Bend, IN: University of Notre Dame Press, 1966.

Plato. *The Phaedrus* (section 247a-e).

The Christian in Danger

See entry on "None Other Gods: Culture in War Time"

Christian Reflections

Walter Hooper (ed.). London: Geoffrey Bles, 1967. First US edition, Grand Rapids, MI: Eerdmans, 1967.

See separate essay entries on the following:

"Christianity and Culture"
"Christianity and Literature"
"*De Futilitate*"
"The Funeral of a Great Myth"
"Historicism"
"The Language of Religion"
"Modern Theology and Biblical Criticism"
"On Church Music"
"On Ethics"
"Petitionary Prayer: A Problem Without an Answer"
"The Psalms"
"The Poison of Subjectivism"
"Religion: Reality or Substitute?"
"The Seeing Eye"

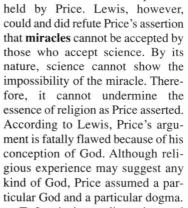

"A Christian Reply to Professor Price"

The Phoenix Quarterly. I no. 1 (Autumn 1946): 31–44. The original lecture was published as "Religion Without Dogma?" *The Socratic Digest.* 4 (1948): 82–94. Reprinted in *God in the Dock, Undeceptions,* and *Timeless at Heart.*

Lewis originally presented this piece to the **Oxford Socratic Club** on May 20, 1946. Lewis began the article by summarizing Professor Price's position: (1) that the essence of **religion** is belief in **God** and **immortality**; (2) that in most actual religions the essence is found in connection with "accretions of dogma and mythology" that have been rendered incredible by the progress of **science**;

(3) that it would be very desirable, if it were possible, to retain the essence purged of the accretions; but (4) that science has rendered the essence almost as hard to believe as the accretions.

Lewis then addressed these positions one at a time, beginning with a lengthy discussion of the nature of religion. He disagreed with Professor Price as to the nature and essence of religion, and said that immortality is most emphatically not present as an essence in many religions, and were it to comprise the essence of any religion, that religion would be doomed from the outset.

Because of this fundamental difference with Professor Price, Lewis could not discuss the second position held by Price. Lewis, however, could and did refute Price's assertion that **miracles** cannot be accepted by those who accept science. By its nature, science cannot show the impossibility of the miracle. Therefore, it cannot undermine the essence of religion as Price asserted. According to Lewis, Price's argument is fatally flawed because of his conception of God. Although religious experience may suggest any kind of God, Price assumed a particular God and a particular dogma.

To Lewis, in our discussion, and in our lives, we are not entitled to extract the ethical element and make of it a religion. Rather we are to participate "in that tradition which is at once more completely ethical and most transcends ethics."

Anne Gardner

Also See: Christianity, Ethics and Morality

"Christian Reunion"

First published in *Christian Reunion.*

In his writings, Lewis stressed the "mere **Christianity**" that united believers rather than the beliefs that divided them. As a result, this essay has been called his "only sustained piece of writing" on differences between Catholics and Protestants. It was not published during his lifetime nor does it appear to have been shown to anyone else. It first reached the public in 1990 in a book also entitled *Christian Reunion.*

Perhaps the most moving portion of the essay is the contrast Lewis made between the religious bitterness of his north Irish childhood and the "mutual edification" he later found "between really devout persons of differing creeds." He stressed, however, that this bond did not mean that doctrines were not important, just that **God** was able to work in our lives in spite of them.

Controversy exists as to whether the entire essay was written by Lewis. An analysis of the text by A. Q. Morton, a forensic expert specializing in questions of authorship, found that the first two and last four paragraphs were genuine, but that paragraphs three to six of the ten-paragraph essay were not by Lewis. Interestingly, the essay retains its coherence when read without the middle paragraphs.

Mike Perry

Also See: Anglicanism, Church, Roman Catholicism

Bibliography

Lewis, C. S. *Mere Christianity.*
Lindskoog, Kathryn. *Light in the Shadowlands.* Sisters, OR: Multnomah, 1994.
Morton, A. Q. "Ascertaining Authorship Today: The Disunion of Christian Reunion." *The Lamp-Post.* March 1993.

Christian Reunion and Other Essays

Walter Hooper (ed). London: Collins, 1990.

See separate entries on the following:

"Behind the Scenes"
"Christian Reunion"
"Cross-Examination"
"Dangers of National Repentance"
"Delinquents in the Snow"
"Evil and God"
"Lilies That Fester"
"Meditation on the Third Commandment"
"Miserable Offenders"
"Scraps"
"Two Ways with the Self"
"What Christmas Means to Me"

Christianity

From his reconversion to Christianity in 1931, C. S. Lewis was (by his own description) a "very ordinary layman of the Church of England." However, he also became well known for defending a "mere Christianity" common to all traditional forms of Christianity, and he is just as popular with traditional Catholic, Orthodox, and Evangelical believers, as he is in his own church. By "mere Christianity" Lewis meant the historic doctrines held in common by Christians throughout history; as he put it on one occasion, "the **faith** preached by the Apos-

tles, attested by the martyrs, embodied in the creeds, expounded by the Fathers." In this article I will use the Nicene Creed as a guide to explaining what this faith is in Lewis's view.

The Creed begins, "I believe in **God** the Father almighty, creator of **heaven** and Earth, and of all things visible and invisible." Lewis believed in and defended the doctrine of a Being who is (1) personal, (2) the creator, and (3) in a relation to us which can best be described by the word "Father." As opposed to those who say, "I believe in a God, but not in a personal god," Lewis defended the idea that God is a person—that is that God has knowledge and choice. Anything less than this, anything without knowledge of Himself and the world, or anything without freedom of choice would be impersonal, and God must be more than that. That God is even *more* than personal is an idea Lewis also defended (see the entry on **"God in three Persons"**). The idea of God as a "Life Force" without knowledge of us as human beings or instructors for us was recognized by Lewis as one of the greatest achievements of wishful thinking the world has yet seen. God is personal, and we must have personal relations with him.

That God is the Creator of the world, distinct from it, and existing before the world, is also part of the faith Lewis defended. That God created spiritual creatures, "things ... invisible," was likewise something that Lewis defended in various ways: for example his pictures of "eldils" in the space trilogy is one of the best literary portraits of angels, and his devils in *The Screwtape Letters* is also chillingly accurate.

That God is our Father for whom we must have the greatest respect is another doctrine Lewis defended. In an introduction to a selection of readings from **George MacDonald** he said that one of the best preparations for appreciating this doctrine is to have a really good earthly father.

The next lines of the Nicene Creed are "And in one Lord, Jesus **Christ**, the only begotten son of God, born of the Father before all ages, God of God, light of light, true God of true God, consubstantial with the Father, by whom all things were made." In the section of *Mere Christianity* entitled **"Beyond Personality,"** the first chapter is called, "Making and Begetting," and in it Lewis explained these lines of the Creed. "What God begets is God," wrote Lewis, so although we too are children of God, we are not children of God in the same sense as Christ is. The scene in *The Magicians Nephew* where Aslan (representing Christ) creates Narnia provides a literary commentary on these lines of the Creed.

The Creed goes on, "who, for us men and for our salvation, came down from heaven and was incarnate by the **Holy Spirit** of the Virgin Mary, and was made man." In all of Lewis's apologetic work the Incarnation is at the center, but especially in chapters two and three of the "What Christians Believe" book of *Mere Christianity*. For Lewis the Incarnation is the central fact of Christianity, as it is the central fact of history.

The next lines of the Creed are, "He was crucified for us, suffered under Pontius Pilate and was buried. The third day he rose again, according to the scriptures and ascended into heaven where he sits at the right hand of God." Lewis described some of these events in an allegorical form in the **Chronicles of Narnia**, but they were always in the background of his **apologetics**, for Lewis's teaching was always Christ-centered. Lewis plainly believed that the events recorded in the New Testament actually happened and that the New Testament is a reliable guide to them.

The Creed's next lines, "He shall come again to judge the living and the dead, and his kingdom will have no end," are also central to Lewis' defense of Christianity: as he put it in *Perelandra* these events, which we are used to thinking of as "the Last Things," are really "only the wiping out of a false start, in order that the world may *then* begin." Or, as Lewis put it in *The Last Battle*, our motto for those days must be "further up and further in," for in Christopher Fry's fine phrase, "Our enterprise is exploration into God."

The next lines of the Creed are "And in the Holy Spirit, the Lord and giver of life, who together with the Father and the Son is adored and glorified; who spoke by the prophets." In *Mere Christianity*, Lewis counseled Christians not to worry if they found the Holy Spirit "rather vague or more shadowy" than the other two persons of the **Trinity**. "In the Christian life you are not usually looking *at* Him: He is always acting through you ... this spirit of **love** is, from all eternity, a love going on between the Father and Son."

The final part of the Nicene Creed is, "and in one holy catholic and apostolic church. I confess one Baptism, for the remission of sins. And I await the resurrection of the dead and the life of the world to come." That Lewis believed that God intended the church to be a visible sign, not an invisible unity, and that baptism was the rite of entrance to that church is clear. But he regarded controversy as to which church or churches can claim to be founded by Christ as not part of his apologetic task. As he said in the preface to *Mere Chris-*

tianity: "I offer no help to anyone who is hesitating between two Christian 'denominations.' ... Ever since I became a Christian I have thought that the best, perhaps the only, service I could do for my unbelieving neighbors was to explain and defend the belief that has been common to nearly all Christians at all times." Lewis went on to say that "mere Christianity" is "like a hall out of which doors open into several rooms.... When you have reached your own room be kind to those who have chosen different doors and to those who are still in the hall. If they are wrong they need your prayers all the more; if they are your enemies you are under orders to pray for them. That is one of the rules common to the whole house."

Richard Purtill
Western Washington University

Also See: Allegory, Anglicanism, Church, Non-Christian Religions, Roman Catholicism, Religion, Theology.

"Christianity and Culture"

Theology. XL (March 1940): 166–79. Reprinted as Part I of "Christianity and Culture" in *Christian Reflections*.

The essay "Christianity and Culture" was first published in *Theology* (March 1940). A reply by S. L. Bethell and E. F. Carritt was published in the May 1940 issue. Lewis's replies, as well as the original article, are published in *Christian Reflections*.

The debate about the relationship between **Christianity** and **culture** is many sided and ongoing. **Aquinas** (and **Roman Catholicism**) sought a synthesis between Christ and culture by combining, yet also keeping separate, **philosophy** and **theology**, state and church, the natural and the divine. Luther, in contrast, tended to see the conflict between Christianity and culture (or the world), while Calvinists and the "reformed tradition" tended to be more hopeful and to seek a transformation of culture in this world.

Lewis noted in "Christianity and Culture" that the New Testament teaches that whatever is highly valued on the natural level must be abandoned "without mercy" the moment it conflicts with service to **God**. Even though Lewis found some passages more favorable to culture, he concluded that the New Testament is, if not hostile, yet definitely cold to culture. Still Lewis applauded the conclusions of the Roman Catholic John Henry Newman in his lectures on University Education, for Newman seemed to be aware of both sides of the question. No one had spoken so eloquently as Newman "on the **beauty** of culture for its own sake, and no one ever so sternly resisted the temptation to confuse it with things spiritual."

Lewis concluded by pointing to familiar passages of Scripture like "Whether you eat or drink or whatsoever you do, do all to the glory of God." He stressed that all of our natural activities will be accepted, if they are offered to God, and all of them, even the noblest, will be sinful if they are not. As Lewis stated later in the essay **"Learning in War-Time,"** the work of a charwoman and the work of a Beethoven become spiritual on precisely this same condition.

Michael H. Macdonald
Seattle Pacific University

Also See: Human Nature, Nature, Sin, Spirituality

Bibliography

Lewis, C. S. *Christian Reflections*; "Learning in War-time"; *Surprised by Joy.*
Niebuhr, Richard H. *Christ and Culture.* New York: Harper Torchbook, 1951.

Christianity and Culture (A Letter)

Theology. XL (June 1940): 475–77. Reprinted as Part II of "Christianity and Culture" in *Christian Reflections.*

This was Lewis's second contribution to a 1940 debate in *Theology.* The first, **"Christianity and Culture,"** appeared in March. In May, "Christianity and Culture: Replies to Mr. Lewis" by S. L. Bethell and E. F. Carritt came out. Lewis wrote this June letter in preparation for a longer reply. In September the magazine published "In Defence of Criticism" by George Every. Lewis responded in December with **"Peace Proposals for Brother Every and Mr. Bethell."** Lewis's articles are reprinted in *Christian Reflections.*

In his first article, Lewis criticized a belief that cultural activities could "in themselves improve our spiritual condition." Mr. Bethell claimed this "logically implies" total depravity. Lewis denied any logical connection. Mr. Carritt criticized Lewis's use of **theology.** Lewis responded that in an Anglican magazine he was free to appeal to "the **truth** of the creeds."

Lewis went on to say that, at best, **culture** records man's striving after ends that have "some degree of similarity" to the true end of man in **God.** This similarity makes cultural activities "less evil" than physical pleasure or money. But it also makes "the danger of resting in them greater and more subtle."

Mike Perry

Also See: Aesthetics, Literary Criticism

Bibliography

Lewis, C. S. "Lilies That Fester."

"Christianity and Literature"

First published in *Rehabilitations.* Reprinted in *Christian Reflections.*

In this essay, delivered at the invitation of a religious society in **Oxford** and published first in *Rehabilitations* (1939), Lewis considered whether there is a distinctively "Christian" form of literature and whether there is any particular relationship between piety and literary artistry. Taking the terms at face value, Lewis's answer to both questions is no; except in the most trivial sense, "Christian Literature . . . could succeed or fail only by the same excellences and the same faults as all literature."

Nevertheless, according to Lewis, even if there is no more a "Christian literature" than there is a "Christian cookery," there still are crucial questions to be raised about Christian principles of **literary criticism** and **literary theory**—how one recognizes and values literary achievement. There is a decided difference, Lewis posited, between modern criticism's obsession with creativity, spontaneity, and freedom—juxtaposed positively with the more pejorative terms, derivation, convention, and rule-keeping—and the Christian who takes seriously the model of **Christ**, whose incarnation teaches us not to despise but to honor imitation, order, and reflected glory.

The New Testament, Lewis pointed out, is not interested in genius, but goodness, and the epitome of the Christian critic is not his or her preoccupation with originality or novelty, but with that which is eternal; such a critic will never "make literature a self-existent thing to be valued for its own sake," but rather will see this as an idolatry that must give way to the recognition that "the salvation of a single soul is more important than the production or preservation of all the epics and tragedies in the world."

Bruce L. Edwards
Bowling Green State University

Also See: Matthew Arnold, Culture, Epic

Bibliography

Carter, Margaret L. "Sub-Creation and Lewis's Theory of Literature." *The Taste of the Pineapple.* Bruce L. Edwards (ed). Bowling Green, OH: Popular Press, 1988: 129–37.

Edwards, Bruce L. *A Rhetoric of Reading: C. S. Lewis's Defense of Western Literacy*. Provo, UT: Brigham Young University Press, 1985.

Hannay, Margaret. *C. S. Lewis*. New York: Ungar, 1981.

Lewis, C. S. "Christianity and Culture"; "Good Work and Good Works"; "High and Low Brows."

The Chronicles of Narnia

The Chronicles of Narnia are the seven children's books, begun by Lewis in 1948 and finished in 1954, which probably will cause Lewis to be read for centuries to come. In order of publication, the books are ***The Lion, the Witch and the Wardrobe*** (1950), ***Prince Caspian*** (1951), ***The Voyage of "The Dawn Treader"*** (1952), ***The Silver Chair*** (1953), ***The Horse and His Boy*** (1954), ***The Magician's Nephew*** (1955), and ***The Last Battle*** (1956). It is significant that Lewis wrote the Chronicles, particularly *The Lion, the Witch and the Wardrobe* and *Magician's Nephew*, at the same time he was writing his autobiography, ***Surprised by Joy***. Just as Lewis's first chronicle tells how Aslan brings spring to the land of Narnia after a seemingly endless winter, *Surprised by Joy* describes how **God** restored Lewis's feelings and **faith**, both of which had been frozen after the death of his mother **Florence Lewis**.

In "On Fairy Stories" **J. R. R. Tolkien** reminded us that "spell means both a story told and a formula of power over men," and in **"The Weight of Glory"** Lewis declared: "Spells are used for breaking enchantments as well as for inducing them. And you and I have need of the strongest spell that can be found to wake us from the evil enchantment of worldliness which has been laid upon us for nearly a hundred years." The Chronicles of Narnia can be seen as Lewis's seven-volume Magician's Book written to disenchant children of all ages of all the things that Lewis found illusory and to re-enchant, by way of a baptism of the **imagination**, all the things that really matter.

Lewis claimed that all the stories began with pictures, often provided by his **dreams**. He was adamant that the tales were not **allegories** and therefore should not be decoded. He preferred to think of them as "supposals," as he explained to many correspondents: "[Aslan] is an invention giving an imaginary answer to the question: 'What might Christ have become like, if there really were a world like Narnia and He chose to be incarnate and die and rise again in that world as He has actually done in ours?' ... Allegory and such supposals mix the real and the unreal in different ways.... The Incarnation of Christ in another world is mere supposal; but granted that supposition, He would really have been a physical object in that world as He was in Palestine, and His death on the Stone Table would have been a physical event no less than his death on Calvary" (***Letters of C. S. Lewis*** and ***C. S. Lewis Letters to Children***).

An essential thing to understand about the Chronicles of Narnia is what Lewis wrote an American eleven-year-old, Laurence Krieg: "The series was not planned beforehand.... When I wrote *The Lion* I did not know I was going to write any more. Then I wrote *P. Caspian* as a sequel and still didn't think there would be any more, and when I had done *The Voyage* I felt quite sure it would be the last. But I found I was wrong." Lewis seemed to have written what Marion Lockhead has called his "Narniad" in four bursts of creativity. The first burst produced *The Lion, the Witch and the Wardrobe* and a rough draft of *The Magician's Nephew*; the second resulted in *Prince Caspian*, the third in *The Voyage of "the Dawn Treader,"* and the fourth in the last four tales. The first five books were written between summer of 1948 and spring of 1951, flowing freely from his pen, one (*Voyage of the "Dawn Treader"*) in less than three months. The major effort of the Narniad was in producing *The Magician's Nephew*, which took eighteen months and was actually finished after *The Last Battle*.

There has arisen a question for scholars and readers as to the order in which the Chronicles are to be read. Although Lewis is supposed to have said he preferred the order of their internal chronology, he was aware of the internal inconsistencies in the books. Two days before his death, Lewis met with Kaye Webb, editor of the Puffin books edition of the Chronicles, and he promised her to "re-edit the books (connect the things that didn't tie up)." It appears that Lewis prepared an "Outline of Narnian history so far as it is known" in anticipation of this revision.

If this revision had been carried out, reading the Chronicles in the order of their internal chronology might be advised; but would that impose a too rational scheme on a much more magnanimous project? Peter Schakel, Doris Myers, and Colin Manlove argue to retain the original order of publication. In her essential essay which looks at the literary structure of the Narniad as a unified attempt to describe the "emotional climate of Christian commitment at various age levels, from very young childhood to old age and death," Myers reasons that rearranging the Narniad chronologically "lessens the impact of individual stories" and "obscures the literary structure as a whole." Schakel explains: "The only reason to read *The Magician's Nephew* first ... is for the chronological order of events, and that, as every storyteller knows, is quite unimportant as a reason. Often the early events in a sequence have a greater impact or effect as a flashback, told after later events which provide background and establish perspective. So it is ... with the Chronicles. The artistry, the archetypes, and the pattern of Christian thought all make it preferable to read the books in the order of their publication."

Manlove sees in the Narniad "a Christian pattern to the Chronicles, a pattern that for Lewis is precisely Christian in not being quite the pattern that we know, for here, in the sense of the order in which the books were written, the Passion, **Redemption**, and Resurrection take place 'before' the creation of the world." That pattern is Jewish as well: some **Bible** scholars tell us that the oldest written parts of the Old Testament are about the rescue from slavery in Egypt and that the creation stories came to be written much later. In order to allow the first-time reader to experience the way in which they emerged shining new from Lewis's heart and imagination, it is perhaps best to read the Chronicles in the order in which Lewis finished the first five, namely, *The Lion, the Witch and the Wardrobe*, *Prince Caspian*, *The Voyage of "the Dawn Treader,"* *The Horse and His Boy*, *The Silver Chair*, *The Magician's Nephew* and *The Last Battle*. At the same time he was penning his autobiography, Lewis began writing the Chronicles of Narnia. After writing Narnia's and Edmund's redemption story, Lewis tried to write the Narnian creation story. He was unable to complete it because he had not lived long enough in the world and with the characters he had created. It was only after Lewis had involved himself in the transformation stories of several of these characters, especially Shasta's in *The Horse and His Boy*, that he was able to tell the story not only of Narnia's beginnings but also of its consummation. Reading the stories in the order just given enables the reader to experience the primordial necessity of passing first through redemption, then into a reinterpretation of one's own story, and finally allowing one's future to take its provident course.

Paul F. Ford
St. John's Seminary

Order the Stories were written

The Lion, the Witch and the Wardrobe	(1950)
Prince Caspian	(1951)
The Voyage of the "Dawn Treader"	(1952)
The Silver Chair	(1953)
The Horse and His Boy	(1954)
The Magician's Nephew	(1955)
The Last Battle	(1956)

Chronology of the Plots

The Magician's Nephew
The Lion, the Witch and the Wardrobe
The Horse and His Boy
Prince Caspian
The Voyage of the "Dawn Treader"
The Silver Chair
The Last Battle

See the separate entries on the individual stories: *The Lion, the Witch and the Wardrobe; Prince Caspian; The Voyage of the "Dawn Treader" ; The Silver Chair; The Magician's Nephew; The Horse and His Boy; The Last Battle*. Also See: Film, Drama, and Music, which provides charts of all film and stage-play versions of the Chronicles of Narnia.

Bibliography

Ford, Paul F. *Companion to Narnia*. San Francisco: HarperSanFrancisco, 1994.

Hooper, Walter. *C. S. Lewis: A Companion and Guide*. San Francisco: HarperSanFrancisco, 1996.

____. *Past Watchful Dragons: The Narnian Chronicles of C. S. Lewis*. New York: Macmillan, 1979.

Huttar, Charles. "C. S. Lewis's Narnia and the 'Grand Design.'" *The Longing for a Form: Essays on the Fiction of C. S. Lewis*. Peter Schakel (ed). Kent , OH: Kent State University Press, 1977.

Lewis, C. S. "It All Began with a Picture"; "On Three Ways of Writing for Children"; "Sometimes Fairy Stories May Say Best What's to be Said"

Lindskoog, Katherine. *The Lion of Judah in Never-Never Land: God, Man and Nature in C. S. Lewis's Narnia Tales*. Grand Rapids, MI: Eerdmans, 1973.

Lochhead, Marion. *The Renaissance of Wonder in Children's Literature*. Edinburgh: Canongate, 1977.

Manlove, Colin N. *The Chronicles of Narnia: The Patterning of a Fantastic World*. New York: Twayne Publishers, 1993.

Myers, Doris. "The Compleat Anglican: Spiritual Style in the Chronicles of Narnia." *Anglican Theological Review* LXVI no. 2 (April 1984): 148–60.

Schakel, Peter. *Reading with the Heart: The Way into Narnia*. Grand Rapids, MI: Eerdmans, 1979.

Sibley, Brian. *The Land of Narnia: Brian Sibley Explores the World of C. S. Lewis*. New York: Harper & Row Junior Books, 1989.

Tolkien, J. R. R. "On Fairy Stories." *Essays Presented to Charles Williams*. C. S. Lewis (ed). Grand Rapids, MI: Eerdmans, 1966.

Yandell, Steven. "The Trans-cosmic Journeys in the Chronicles of Narnia." *Mythlore*. 12 no. 1 (August 1985): 9–23.

Chronological Snobbery

Chronological snobbery is, according to Lewis, the mistaken belief that newer things and ideas ought to be preferred to older or traditional ones. Lewis credited **Owen Barfield** with developing the term in the dedication to *Allegory of Love*. Lewis defined chronological snobbery in chapter 13 of *Surprised by Joy*.

Also See: Modern, Tradition

Church

Publicly, C. S. Lewis was a very nonsectarian, nondenominational communicator. Before publishing *Mere Christianity*, he submitted the manuscript to clergymen from four different denominations: **Anglicanism**, **Roman Catholicism**, Methodism, and Presbyterianism. Even within his own group, Anglicanism, Lewis claimed to be an ordinary believer, neither very low nor very high.

Privately, Lewis (like all believers) consistently adhered to some theological **traditions** far more than others. In this case, "traditions" is a particularly apt word, since he most admired and respected the theologians who wrote before 1700. And his **theology** was virtually always defined by those who wrote within the Anglican/Catholic tradition. Lewis humbled himself before Athanasius, **Augustine**, **Aquinas**, and Hooker; he appeared virtually uninfluenced by writers outside the Anglican/Catholic point of view, for instance, revivalists and provocateurs such as John Wesley, George Fox, Alexander Campbell, and Menno Simons. Religiously, his was a somewhat Medieval mindset; he regarded with suspicion any thinker who did not conform in most ways to the ancient "auctores."

Within his own group, Lewis was a conservative. Living in a time when most Anglican priests had become more liberal than their congregations, Lewis challenged them to stop serving "**Christianity** and water" and return to the undiluted spiritual wine taught by **Christ** and the apostles.

Any close examination of Lewis's views of the church runs repeatedly into what first seem like contradictions, but turn out to have an eminently logical basis. He disliked going to church, for instance, saying that he much preferred private **prayer** and meditation. Yet Lewis attended multiple church services each week. The reason is a bow to humility; Lewis felt he needed to engage in time-honored acts of worship whether he found them very meaningful or not, and he wanted to encourage others who engaged in them. Lewis could not really conceive of Christianity apart from gathering with others; upon his return to **God**, one of his first acts was to return to the church. He and his brother **Warren**

Lewis both saw their first communion upon coming back as an act of spiritual significance and commitment.

Forbearance, Lewis felt, should be the guiding light of the worshiper. Those who liked gospel songs should give reverent attention to trained choirs; those with sophisticated musical backgrounds should not look down upon churches and worshipers who sing "low-brow" music. In *The Screwtape Letters*, Lewis noted the tendency most of us have to hallow the concept of "church"; we glorify Christ's earthly body in our minds, thinking his followers should be the local equivalent of **angels**. Then, when we see the local angels come to church services dressed inappropriately or hear them sing off-key, we may tend to look down upon these people as not measuring up to our churchly ideal. Lewis noted that the person who looks or sounds "wrong" may be, spiritually, far beyond our own level.

His own major point of difficulty with church attendance was hymns, which he described as "fifth-rate poems set to sixth-rate music." When asked, late in life, to serve on a committee to select songs for an Anglican hymnal, Lewis politely declined. Yet, despite his view of hymn-singing as a sort of convivial, lusty braying, Lewis never actively crusaded to reduce congregational singing.

Lewis favored liturgy. He recognized that the biblical admonition was not against repetitions but against vain repetitions, and he felt it was easier to worship by joining in traditional prayer recitations than by listening to people make up prayers as they went along—provided the liturgy did not regularly change, for then he felt the Christian worshiper had to use prayer time for evaluation (of theological accuracy) rather than worship.

In conclusion, it is probably useful to point out that John's journey back to the truth in Lewis's autobiographical *The Pilgrim's Regress* is made possible by his trust in Mother Kirk, or the church, whose counsel originally he disdained but which he later finds to be essential in finding his way home and discovering the true identity of the Landlord he has so long and earnestly sought.

Marvin D. Hinten and Bruce L. Edwards
Bowling Green State University

Bibliography

Lewis, C. S. "Christian Reunion"; "Modern Theology and Biblical Criticism"; "On Church Music."

The Church's Liturgy (Letter)

Church Times. CXXXII (20 May 1949): 319. Reprinted in *God in the Dock, Undeceptions,* and *Timeless at Heart.*

Writing in response to Eric L. Mascall's article, "Quadringentesimo Anno," on possible revisions of the Anglican liturgy (*Church Times*, May 6, 1949, 282), Lewis drew attention to two concerns. First, he asked for uniformity in the time of the service, as a parishioner is often bound by an inflexible schedule and thus subject to anxiety and distraction over lengthened services. Second, Lewis reminded those making the revisions that alterations in the liturgy will be primarily viewed by the congregation in terms of how the liturgy reflects orthodox doctrine rather than simply as matters of liturgical variation.

Marjorie L. Mead
The Marion E. Wade Center

The Church's Liturgy (Letter)

Church Times. CXXXII (1 July 1949): 427. Reprinted in *God in the Dock*, *Undeceptions,* and *Timeless at Heart.*

W. D. F. Hughes ("The Church's Liturgy," *Church Times*, 24 June 1949, 409) responded to Lewis's second point (see previous letter) by maintaining that liturgy and belief are inextricably bound up together and, thus, Lewis's distinction is without significant difference. Lewis, in turn, agreed that the connection between belief and liturgy is "close" but added that he doubted whether it is "inextricable." He also cautioned that there is danger in assuming that alterations in the liturgy necessarily reflect the orthodox doctrines of the church and that individual priests should not be forced to be the primary judges of such critical issues.

Marjorie L. Mead
The Marion E. Wade Center

Arthur C. Clarke (1917–)

Arthur C. Clarke has won an array of awards for both science and **science fiction**, and has sold over 20 million books. Although Clarke and C. S. Lewis disagreed about both space **technology** and **theology**, Lewis recommended Clarke's *Childhood's End*, and Clarke recommended Lewis's *Out of the Silent Planet* and *Perelandra*. "I only met Lewis once, but," recalls Clarke, "I had an extensive correspondence with him, which is now in the **Bodleian Library**. And I used to see Joy Gresham almost every week." On January 26, 1995, Clarke was awarded an honorary doctorate at the University of Liverpool because fifty years earlier he originated the idea of communications satellites. In his acceptance address, he entered the **controversy** over the authenticity of certain manuscripts purported to be by Lewis by stating that he "and millions of others—would like to know if there is indeed a 'Lewisgate' scandal."

Kathryn Lindskoog

Also See: Walter Hooper, Joy Gresham Lewis

Bibliography

Clarke, Arthur C. *2001: A Space Odyssey.*
_____. *Childhood Encyclopedia.* New York: Harcourt, Brace & World, 1953.
_____. *The Deep Range.* New York: Harcourt, Brace & World, 1957.
_____. *The Exploration of Space.* New York: Harper, 1951.
_____. *Voices across the Sea.* New York: Harper, 1958.
Lindskoog, Kathryn. *Light in the Shadowlands.* Sisters, OR: Multnomah, 1992.

"A Cliché Came Out of its Cage"

Nine: A Magazine of Poetry and Criticism. 2 (May 1950): 114. Revised (a second stanza is added) and reprinted in *Poems* and *Collected Poems.*

In this poem Lewis attacked those moderns (he mentioned F. R. Leavis, with whom he so sharply disagreed regarding **literary criticism**, and Bertrand Russell, whose ideas on society and related issues he directly opposed) who believe they are heralds for a return to the "golden age" of **paganism**. In fact, Lewis suggested they know little about classical paganism, mistaking their pale, insipid, godless modern version for the healthy, robust, theistic paganism of old.

Don W. King
Montreat College

Nevill Henry Kendall Aylmer Coghill (1899–1980)

Coghill was the Merton Professor of English Literature at **Oxford** from 1957 until his retirement in 1966. He and Lewis first met as students in George Gordon's Discussion Class in 1923. Coghill had read a paper on "realism" and Lewis thought of him as "sensible rather than brilliant." Having the same **tutor**, F. P. Wilson, the two young men were kept together in their studies. They would often discuss the required readings on long country walks. Coghill was a lifelong friend who was an active member of the **Inklings**.

Jeffrey D. Schultz

Bibliography

Lewis, C. S. *Surprised by Joy.*
Sayer, George. *Jack: C. S. Lewis and His Times.* Wheaton, IL: Crossway, 1988.

The Collected Poems of C. S. Lewis

Hooper, Walter (ed). London: HarperCollins, 1994.

This collection is not the complete poems of Lewis. Instead, **Walter Hooper** has collected *Spirits in Bondage*

(1919), **Poems** (1964), and "A Miscellany of Additional Poems," a supplement of seventeen other short poems (eleven previously unpublished). With one exception, the previously unpublished poems date from the time Lewis was seventeen to nineteen years old; all appear in the Lewis Family Papers, the eleven-volume typed manuscript of the Lewis family (1850–1930) compiled by **Warren Lewis** (available at the **Marion E. Wade Center** at Wheaton College, Wheaton, Illinois). In addition, Hooper publishes for the first time an introductory letter purportedly written by Lewis, though this is disputed by Kathryn Lindskoog. Since both *Spirits in Bondage* and *Poems* are discussed elsewhere, the focus here will be upon the miscellany.

The poems in the miscellany (* denotes previously unpublished) are: "The Hills of Down,"* "Against Potpourri,"* "A Prelude,"* "Ballade of a Winter's Morning,"* *Laus Mortis,*"* "Sonnet—To Sir Philip Sydney,"* "Of Ships,"* "Couplets,"* "Circe—A Fragment,"* "Exercise,"* "Joy," "Leaving Forever the Home of One's Youth,"* "Awake My Lute!" "Essence," "Consolation," **"Finchley Avenue,"** and "Epitaph for Helen Joy Davidman." Especially interesting are the unpublished poems because all except "Leaving Forever the Home of One's Youth" were a part of the lost "Metrical Meditations of a Cod" and bear special notice.

In "The Hills of Down," dated by Warren Lewis as Easter 1915, Lewis anticipated some of the poetry in *Spirits in Bondage* since the poem indicates both a longing for the "faery town" and a love for the immediate **beauty** of **nature**. While the former also frightens him ("I dare not go / To dreaming Avalon"), the latter powerfully draws him:

Were I not there
   To roam the hills I love.
For I alone
   Have loved their loneliness;
None else hath known
   Nor seen the goodliness
Of the green hills of Down.
The soft low hills of Down.

In a similar vein, the persona in "Death in Battle" from *Spirits in Bondage* notes his own heightened, when solitary, love of Nature: "Ah, to be ever alone, / In flowery valleys among the mountains and silent wastes untrod, / In the dewy upland places, in the garden of God, / This would atone!" Characteristic of Lewis's youthful **poetry** is the tension between the physical and mental ugliness of his present **reality** and the beauty and

wonder of Nature and the faery world. Since much of his early poetry was written under the shadow of World War I, either in anticipation of serving or during his time at the front, this tension is not surprising. His search for **joy** could have often been realized through the beauty he found in Nature or the faery world.

"Against Potpourri" (summer 1915) is a mild invective against those who believe that they can capture the essence of flower's summer beauty through a potpourri: "Folly! Though they shed / Some fragrance yet, there is no man shall find / Delight and beauty here among the dead." Such futility is underscored in the poem's dark conclusion: "For but one flower shall outlive them all— / The eternal poppy, deathless weed of death."

"A Prelude" (summer 1915) chronicles how thoughts before bed can charm away the winter's chill and night's phantoms.

"Ballade of a Winter's Morning" (Christmas 1915) celebrates a **friendship** (probably with **Arthur Greeves**) whose essential link is love of books: "Old tomes full oft re-read with care, / Where hoary rhymes and legends blend / With noble pictures rich and rare / To make us merry friend by friend."

Laus Mortis (Easter 1916) is an almost clinical description of "the wone of old horse-mastering Hades," inspired no doubt by Lewis's readings of **Dante**'s *Divine Comedy* and Virgil's *Aeneid*: "Time this people knoweth not, nor treason / Of his guile that steals swift joys away, / Nor this garish pomp of changing season / And the interflow of night and day."

Lewis's love of literature continues, particularly for Sydney's "Arcadia," in his "Sonnet—To Sir Philip Sydney" (autumn 1916) where he praises the poet, "stainless knight of God," for his "silver chimes of old romance." In "Of Ships" (Christmas 1916), written upon one of his returns to **Little Lea** from his studies with **William T. Kirkpatrick** at Bookham, Lewis muses on "the soul of a ship" and notes no matter the type "the man of honest heart shall love them all": "'Argo' or 'Golden Hind' or 'Mary Lee,' / From every country where man's foot has trod, / Sure they're all ships to brave the winds of God / And have their business in His glorious sea." A second Christmas poem from this year, "Couplets," celebrates spring and connects its annual rebirth with "fairy men who nightly habit there" and "the earthy gods / [Who] have left their cloven print in the dewy sods."

"Circe—A Fragment" (April 1917) is primarily a descriptive two-stanza piece, inspired no doubt by Lewis's reading of the *Odyssey*: "Her couch was of the mighty sea beast's tusk/With gold and Tyrian scarlet overlaid / Set in a chamber where the wafted musk /

With scent of pines a wanton medly made / Through the wide pillared arches of her hall."

"Exercise" (April 1917) is an *ubi sunt* poem with Lewis asking a series of rhetorical questions about where the glory and romance of faery have gone: "Where are the magic swords / That elves of long ago / Smithied beneath the snow / For heroes' rich rewards?" In the tradition of *The Wanderer,* his rhetorical questions have a melancholy reply: "The loves, the wisdoms high, / The sorrows, where are they? / They are nothing at all today, / They are less than you and I."

"Leaving Forever the Home of One's Youth" (1930) is a bittersweet remembrance of **Little Lea** for the delights he and Warren had there with each other in childhood combined with the blank reality of the present: "The past you mourn for, when it was in flight, / Lived, like the present, in continual death."

The miscellany is notable both for what it tells us about Lewis's life and for what it shows us about Lewis's development as a poet. Here we see many of the themes he develops later in *Spirits in Bondage* and *Dymer,* including love of the faery world, **nature**, and art as well as a kind of overshadowing melancholy so common among adolescents. The poems as a whole are well-written, finger exercises for his later, more mature efforts. In addition, our knowledge of them enhances our understanding of the vital role poetry played in Lewis's aesthetic maturation.

One curious thing in closing. While the title page says *The Collected Poems of C. S. Lewis*, the cover of the book says *Poems*. In a letter Hooper explained this error: "After deciding to re-print the earlier *Poems* (1964), the publishers rushed to get the cover ready. However, I saw this as an opportunity to include many poems which were either out of print, such as *Spirits in Bondage*, or had never been published. In the end, the publishers used the cover they had already printed, and so the cover gives one title and the title-page another" (letter of 24 March 1996).

Don W. King
Montreat College

Also See: Aesthetics, Fairy Tales, Poetry

Bibliography

Lindskoog, Kathryn. "Here We Go Again: Two New Lewis Forgeries." *The Lewis Legacy* no. 64 (Spring 1995): 1. The entire *The Lewis Legacy* no. 65 (Summer 1995), especially pp. 1–8, 12; she raises numerous questions about the poem "Finchley Avenue" (252).

Walsh, Chad. *The Literary Legacy of C. S. Lewis*. New York: Harcourt Brace Jovanovich, 1979.

William "Billy" Collins (1900–1976)

Collins was the publisher of many of Lewis's books. He headed his family's firm, William Collins, Sons & Co., Ltd., the leading Scottish publisher. With the help of Ronald Politzer, he focused his publishing activities on religious writings. In 1953 his firm acquired the publishing house of **Geoffrey Bles** and with it the rights to the works of Lewis.

Jeffrey D. Schultz

Collins (Book Review)

The Oxford Magazine. XLVIII (16 May 1929): 633.

According to Lewis, this book, edited by H. W. Garrod, is a thorough and scholarly discussion of the poetry of William Collins (1721–1759), with ode by ode and often line by line examination in the search for meaning. This rigorous (and all too rare) search for meaning uncovers confusions. Although the methods and findings of the book's editor may be disputed, Lewis considered this an appropriate and necessary challenge that contributes to "the abundant interest of this book."

Anne Gardner

Bibliography

Garrod, H. W. *Collins*.

Communism and Fascism

Unlike many intellectuals of his era who attacked totalitarianism only when it was engaged in by their political enemies, C. S. Lewis was a consistent critic of totalitarianism on both the right and the left. Indeed, in his **allegory *The Pilgrim's Regress*** (1933), Lewis depicted Marxists and Fascists as common vassals to a warrior named Savage, a Nietzschean superman who worshipped power and preached violence (Book VI, chapter 6). In other words, Lewis believed that both communism and fascism were products of the same poisonous philosophy. Lewis emphasized this same point in a poem he published in 1939 in response to "Flowering Rifle," a five-thousand-line epic by Roy Campbell that glorified the Nazi-backed forces of Francisco Franco during the Spanish Civil War. In **"To Mr. Roy Campbell,"** Lewis declared that the activities of the fascists and communists in Spain were identical: "Your shrill covin-politics and theirs / Are two peas in a single pod." Near the end of his life in the early 1960s, Lewis restated this point yet again in the essay **"Screwtape Proposes a Toast,"** where he had elder devil Screwtape declare that "both the Nazi and the Communist state" were contrived by the forces of **Hell**, who built on the work of the philosophers Rousseau and Hegel. In Lewis's view, both communism and fascism were tyrannical systems that led to the subjugation of innocent people, and so both were to be regarded with equal contempt.

Lewis's most direct rebuke against fascism came in *The Pilgrim's Regress,* although brief references to Hitler and Nazi Germany are also scattered among his later essays and letters. Perhaps the most notable of these references is a letter Lewis wrote in November 1933 to close friend **Arthur Greeves**. Greeves had apparently written previously that he thought the Allies from the last war were partly to blame for what was then happening in Germany. Lewis responded that while the Allies might be partly responsible, nothing could justify "Hitler's persecution of the Jews." Lewis then blasted Hitler's nonsensical claims that the Jews had not contributed to **culture** and that he was doing the "will of the Lord" by destroying them. Pointing out that the "idea of the 'Will of the Lord' is precisely what the world owes to the Jews, the blaspheming tyrant has just fixed his absurdity for all to see in a single sentence and shown that he is as contemptible for his stupidity as he is detestable for his cruelty." Given the anti-Semitism prevalent among British intellectuals of the time, including Christians such as **T. S. Eliot**, Lewis's defense of the Jews in 1933 was admirable.

The Pilgrim's Regress also contains Lewis's most direct attack on communism, although here again other references are scattered throughout his letters, essays, and poems (including his pre-Christian poem *Dymer*). In addition to his rejection of the tyranny of communism, Lewis also made a point of critiquing its reductionism. In the essay **"Bulverism,"** for example, Lewis observed that the Marxist claim that all other ideas can be rejected because they are merely the by-products of economic self-interest is ultimately self-defeating. If all ideas are merely the products of economic interests, then that includes the **philosophy** of Marxism itself—hence, there is no reason according to Marxism to suppose that Marxism is itself true.

An opponent of tyranny in all its forms, Lewis spent the later years of his life reminding people that the end of fascism and containment of communism did not mean the end of tyranny. He warned those in the democratic West that the same currents in modern thought that produced fascism and communism elsewhere were also cultivating tyranny in their own backyards. In the essay **"Is Progress Possible? Willing Slaves of the Welfare State,"** Lewis decried the decreasing sphere of personal sovereignty in the modern state and the increasing efforts by bureaucrats to treat citizens as guinea pigs.

In an era when communism seems to have been vanquished just as fascism was, Lewis's warning is a useful reminder about the potential for tyranny that will always lurk within the human heart.

John G. West, Jr.

Also See: Democracy, Materialism, Friedrich Nietzsche, Politics

Bibliography

Aeschliman, Michael D. *C. S. Lewis and the Case Against Scientism.* Grand Rapids, MI: Eerdmans, 1983.
Johnson, Paul. *Modern Times: The World from the Twenties to the Eighties.* San Francisco: Harper and Row, 1983.

"The Condemned"

See entry on "Under Sentence"

The Conditions for a Just War (Letter)

Theology. XXXVIII (May 1939): 373–74. Reprinted in *God in the Dock, Undeceptions,* and *Timeless at Heart.*

E. L. Mascall's six conditions for a just **war** (*Theology,* January 1939) caused Lewis to reflect that the final determination of the **justice** of a given war is a complex decision requiring expertise and knowledge that must as a result be delegated to government officials versed in international affairs. Thus, a Christian witness may not lie so much in the determination of a just war as in the exercise of individual conscience when faced with specific military situations (e.g., the bombing of civilians). Mr. Mascall responded (*Theology,* June 1939, 457–58).

Marjorie L. Mead
The Marion E. Wade Center

"A Confession"

See entry on *"Spartan Nactus"*

The Conflict in Anglican Theology (Letter)

Theology. XLI (November 1940): 304. Reprinted in *God in the Dock, Undeceptions,* and *Timeless at Heart.*

A brief response to Canon Quick's statement in the October 1940 issue that "moderns hate Liberalism." Lewis went one step further and comments that moderns of all kinds are characteristically negative, or in other words, "moderns" simply "hate."

Marjorie L. Mead
The Marion E. Wade Center

Conservatism

C. S. Lewis was naturally conservative—so much so that he once joked to his brother **Warren Lewis** that he wished someone would start a "Stagnation Party" that he could support at election time. When a Society for the Prevention of Progress actually offered him a membership, Lewis responded that he felt he was "born a member" of the group.

Lewis was conservative culturally, morally, and politically. Culturally, he regarded himself as one of the few remaining "Old Western men" who could talk about the Western intellectual **tradition** from the inside, rather than trying to study it from the vantage point of **modernity**. Morally, Lewis was a champion of the maxims of traditional morality, which he explained in *Mere Christianity* and defended in *The Abolition of Man*. Politically, Lewis was also conservative, though not rigidly so. He worried about the effects of the welfare state on individual liberty, and he defended a system of retributive **justice** for criminals. Yet he harbored doubts about the consequences of unbridled capitalism, some of which he aired in *Mere Christianity*. And for all of his reservations about the welfare state, he supported the British system of socialized health care.

John G. West, Jr.

Also See: Culture, Ethics and Morality, Politics

Bibliography
Lewis, C. S. *The Abolition of Man*; *"De Descriptione Temporum"*; *Mere Christianity*.

Controversy

Despite his incredible popularity, C. S. Lewis has been the subject of considerable controversy over the years. During his own lifetime, he was criticized by some for his perceived **conservatism**. Lewis was so concerned about this charge that when Prime Minister Winston Churchill offered him the title Commander of the British Empire in 1951, he refused to accept it because he thought the award would give credibility to those who believed that his writings were "covert anti-Leftist propaganda." Lewis was also controversial during his lifetime because of his defense of orthodox **Christianity**. He was likely voted down for a professorship by his secular colleagues at **Oxford** because of his championing of the Christian **faith**, and his **apologetics** were attacked as simple-minded and vulgar by such contemporaries as Alistair Cooke and W. Norman Pittenger.

After Lewis's death, the controversies continued. Fundamentalists questioned Lewis's views on the **Bible** and his literary use of **magic**. Feminists claimed wrongly that Lewis was anti-**women**. And philosopher John Beversluis resurrected the charge that Lewis's case for Christianity is untenable. In his book *C. S. Lewis and the Search for Rational Religion*, Beversluis chided

Lewis for supposed lapses in logic and claimed that Lewis had a penchant for attacking straw men. However, Beversluis himself attacked a straw Lewis, refuting Lewis's arguments only by seriously misstating them.

Perhaps the most significant recent controversy involving Lewis has centered on works that he may not have written. Kathryn Lindskoog and others have raised doubts about the authenticity of several posthumously published manuscripts supposed to have been penned by Lewis (including *The Dark Tower*, *The Man Born Blind*, "Christian Reunion," "Encyclopedia Boxoniana," and *Forms of Things Unknown*). Lindskoog has also raised questions about alterations made to Lewis's **poetry** after his death.

John G. West, Jr.

Also See: Walter Hooper

Bibliography
Beversluis, John. *C. S. Lewis and the Search for Rational Religion*. Grand Rapids, MI: Eerdmans, 1985.
Cooke, Alistair. "Mr. Anthony at Oxford." *The New Republic*. (April 24, 1944): 578–80.
Henthorne, Susan. "The Image of Woman in Fiction of C. S. Lewis." Ph.D. dissertation, State University of New York at Buffalo. 1985.
Lindskoog, Kathryn. *Light in the Shadowlands: Protecting the Real C. S. Lewis*. Sisters, OR: Multnomah, 1994.
Pittenger, W. Norman. "Apologist Versus Apologist." *Christian Century*. (October 1, 1958): 1104–7.

"Conversation Piece: The Magician and the Dryad"

Punch. 217 (July 20, 1949): 71 (under the pseudonym Nat Whilk). Revised and retitled "The Magician and the Dryad" and reprinted in *Poems* and *Collected Poems*.

A dialogue between an ambitious magician who proves his power by calling forth from a tree the dryad that inhabits it. Exalting in his success, he imagines the dryad will thank him for releasing her from prison; instead, she laments that he has destroyed her peace and unity, resulting in the death of the tree.

Don W. King
Montreat College

"Coronation March"

The Oxford Magazine. 55 (May 6, 1937): 565 (under the pseudonym Nat Whilk). Reprinted in *Poems* and *Collected Poems*.

The coronation of George VI (May 12, 1937) is the subject of this slightly irreverent commentary. Lewis suggested the glory and heraldry associated with this event is all that is left of England's once proud stance on the international stage.

Don W. King
Montreat College

Correspondence with an Anglican who Dislikes Hymns (Letters)

The Presbyter. VI no. 2 (1948): 15–20. A series of four letters (two by Erik Routley and two by C. S. Lewis, which were printed under the initials "A. B."). Reprinted in *God in the Dock, Undeceptions,* and *Timeless at Heart.*

The correspondence began with a letter from Routley to Lewis (July 13, 1946) asking him to join a panel assessing the merits of new hymns for the Hymn Society of Great Britain and Ireland. Lewis responded briefly (July 16, 1946) indicating that he would be a poor choice for such a position as he did not have a personal appreciation for the values of hymns in the worship service. This comment drew a long and thoughtful response from Routley (September 18, 1946) asking Lewis to reconsider his opinion of the significance of hymns. Routley maintained that hymns, particularly within the Reformed tradition, are the congregation's primary means of responding in *unity* to the gospel message. Routley felt it necessary to discuss the use of hymns in worship further with Lewis because of Lewis's position of influence among British Christians. Accordingly, Routley feared that Lewis's negative view on the value of hymns could have a detrimental impact on others. Lewis's final letter (September 21, 1946) suggested that Routley publish the foregoing letter (i.e., the letter in which Routley gives his "defense" of hymns) while omitting Lewis's name (hence the use of the initials "A.B."), and agreed that if hymns hold significance for others in the congregation then he out of charity must submit to their practice; Lewis also assures Routley that he has never spoken *publicly* against the use of hymns.

Marjorie L. Mead
The Marion E. Wade Center

Corruption of Nature

C. S. Lewis was all his life a lover of **nature** and a connoisseur of woodland and skyscapes. Yet he also saw nature as a being that, like man, was corrupted by **the Fall**. Discounting the theory of Creative **Evolution** (that all of nature is evolving toward perfection) Lewis viewed nature as almost synonymous with **human nature**: both wonderful and terrible, capable of great **beauty** and great cruelty, but bound to corruption rather than improvement.

Parasitism, survival of the fittest, the "air of a good thing spoiled"—these are nature's own manifestations of the sins humans became subject to when they rejected **God**. Lewis never called upon readers to reject nature; in his mind, the scientists in *That Hideous Strength* who do are infinitely worse than pagan nature worshippers. But we should see her not as a "Mother" (such a relationship would be "terrifying and even abominable"), but as a quarrelsome but interesting sister with whom we share a common Creator. In *Miracles*, Lewis explored this idea of nature as an ambiguous fallen personality: an "ogress, hoyden, incorrigible fairy . . . ," an "enemy, friend, playfellow" who will share in the **redemption** of **Christ**.

Lewis's novels offer vivid scenarios of Nature without the Fall. In *Out of the Silent Planet* the inhabitants of Mars and its natural world coexist in harmony. In *Perelandra*, just as the inhabitants of unfallen Venus are sentient but without **sin**, so too is the natural world of that planet uncorrupted by decay, death, or even inclement weather. Ransom, the visitor/redeemer from earth, realizes that all corruption—even in human **reason** and perception—came with the "unhappy division between soul and body which resulted from the Fall." Inclement weather does go along with the Fall on other worlds: Narnia of *The Lion, the Witch and The Wardrobe* is shackled in winter by the White Witch, and spring comes when Aslan is killed and resurrected. In *The Last Battle* the best of Narnia pales before the redeemed, springlike Narnia Aslan reveals after the destruction of the original.

Lewis believed that the very distinction between Nature and Man is characteristic of the Fall; in an unfallen world, "where spirit's power over the organism was complete and unresisted," death would have no place. But whether we perceive nature as beautiful or terrible, it is but a shadow of the **reality** that awaits us in the World beyond "natural" corruption.

Richard A. Hill
Taylor University

Also See: Good and Evil, Heaven, Hell, Paganism, Science

Bibliography

Christopher, Joe R. "Transformed Nature: 'Where Is It Now, The Glory and the Dream?'" *CSL: The Bulletin of the New York C. S. Lewis Society.* 7 (September 1976): 1–7.

Lewis, C. S. *The Last Battle; the Lion, the Witch and the Wardrobe; Mere Christianity; Miracles;* "On Living in an Atomic Age"; *Out of the Silent Planet; Perelandra.*

Lindskoog, Kathryn. *The Lion of Judah in Never-Never Land: God, Man and Nature in C. S. Lewis's Narnia.* Grand Rapids, MI: Eerdmans, 1973.

Walsh, Chad. *C. S. Lewis: Apostle to the Skeptics*. New York: Macmillan, 1949.

The Cosmic Trilogy

Special collected work of Lewis's space trilogy published in 1990. See entries on *Out of the Silent Planet, Perelandra,* and *That Hideous Strength*

Cosmology

Cosmology refers to the study of the cosmos (or universe) in two senses: as a branch of astronomy that explores the origins and **evolution** of the universe as an orderly system of heavenly bodies; and also as the philosophical inquiry into the **nature**, purpose, and destiny of the universe that speculates about the effects of planets, stars, skies, and space on human consciousness and significance. Lewis was precociously interested in cosmology in both senses from a young age (his telescope was a prized possession in his adolescent years), and this interest continued into his adulthood with his work as a literary critic.

In works such as *The Discarded Image* and **"Imagination and Thought in the Middle Ages,"** Lewis sought to provide readers a "map" of the universe as seen by our Western ancestors. The Medieval man or woman, Lewis wrote, did not look up into the sky and see a universe dark, silent, or empty in the way moderns tend to, but rather "melodious, sunlit, and splendidly inhabited," for "the whole universe was an answer, not a question." The skies were filled with Planetary Intelligences, levels upon levels of angelic beings, and the sanctuary of **God** himself—all in appropriate order and relation to each other. The Heavens were *Deo Plenum*: full of God. Moreover, the medievals' belief that the earth was the center of the universe led them to believe not that they were more significant than they were—a typically erroneous modernist jab—but, rather, that they were in their proper habitation—a much more secure and confident perspective, bereft of **pride** or foolish self-exaltation.

Lewis freely admitted his affection and preference for this "model" of the universe, and it made its way into his space trilogy in a quite pronounced way in both *Out of the Silent Planet* and *Perelandra*. When Ransom is kidnapped and taken to Malacandra his journey causes him to repent of his ignorance of space—ignorance of its **beauty** and bright contours, and of its prestigious population of wonderfully distinct and august beings—fed by years of reading bad **science fiction** on a "quarantined planet." Ransom's encounter with Eldila and Oyarsa there and on Perelandra further challenge both his limited cosmology and his inadequate **theology**, confirming Lewis's

own determination that the motions of the universe are best conceived "not as a machine ... or army" but as "a dance, a festival, a symphony, a ritual, a carnival, or these all in one."

Bruce L. Edwards
Bowling Green State University

Bibliography

Brewer, Derek. "The Tutor: A Portrait." *C. S. Lewis at the Breakfast Table*. James T. Como (ed). New York: Macmillan, 1994.

Downing, David. *Planets in Peril*. Amherst, MA: University of Massachusetts Press, 1992.

"The Country of the Blind"

Punch. 221 (September 12, 1951): 303 (under the pseudonym Nat Whilk). Reprinted in *Poems* and *Collected Poems*.

Philosophically, "The Country of the Blind" is one of Lewis's most profound poems. In it he lamented the modern penchant to abuse words until meaning is lost. He pictured a race of people blind to what words really say; no objective **truth** can be conveyed through words, only feelings. As a result, what remains is marketed jargon (see *Studies in Words*).

Don W. King
Montreat College

"Cradle-Song Based on a Theme from Nicolas of Cusa"

The Times Literary Supplement. (June 11, 1954): 375. Revised and retitled "Science-Fiction Cradlesong" and reprinted in *Poems* and *Collected Poems*.

The title of this poem refers to the German cardinal and philosopher, Nicolas of Cusa (1401–1464) and probably his *De docta ignorantia* ("On Learned Ignorance") where he describes the learned man as one who is aware of his own ignorance. It argues that outer space is not so much a place as it is a concept, and we are more likely to find the stuff of life on earth, not there.

Don W. King
Montreat College

Creation

Creation is a prominent motif in Lewis's adult and children's fiction. In the early 1930s Lewis became distressed by the increasing prominence of Evolutionism as it was being popularized by writers such as Olaff Stapledon and J. B. S. Haldane. Soon after, Lewis embarked on his **science fiction** trilogy in the interest of debunking this **philosophy** and offering a Christian vision of man's relationship to the universe. The second book of the trilogy, ***Perelandra***, tells the story of a newly created world endangered by the introduction of evil. The novel expresses both the utterly satisfying experience of this Edenic setting and the peril facing the race as the Green Lady acquires the knowledge of **good and evil**.

The Narnian creation story is depicted in ***The Magician's Nephew***. Beginning in absolute nothingness the principal characters of the novel, Polly, Digory, the cabby, Uncle Andrew, and Queen Jadis, witness the formation of the celestial and planetary realm of Narnia. Creation is sung into existence by Aslan the lion, the son of the Emperor-beyond-the-Sea, in an ordered fashion reminiscent of Genesis 1 and 2. It strongly parallels the biblical account that states that creation was spoken into being by the Word, or the second person of the Godhead, Jesus the Son of **God**. Aslan's representation of **Christ** as the Son and the Redeemer in ***The Lion, the Witch and the Wardrobe*** is expanded as the active Logos, creating the new world in *The Magician's Nephew*.

Lewis's theological views regarding **cosmology**, creation, and **nature** are woven throughout his **apologetics**, notably in ***Miracles***, ***The Case for Christianity***, and ***The Problem of Pain***. His view of creation greatly impacted his approach to literature, particularly **fantasy**. Lewis held that as an image-bearer of the Creator man is a possessor of creativity. Unlike **God**, however, man's creativity is limited. As Lewis expressed in a letter to **Arthur Greeves**, man cannot imagine with true originality, but can only rearrange that which God has created. Lewis was influenced by **J. R. R. Tolkien**'s concept of sub-creation, the act of creating imaginative worlds so consistent that they elicit a secondary belief in the reader. Tolkien contended that within a well-constructed fantasy there exists a **joy** that "has the very taste of primary **truth**." The sub-creations of Tolkien and Lewis in Middle Earth, Narnia, and Perelandra exemplify such believable secondary worlds.

Alice H. Cook

Also See: Bernard Acworth, Evolution, Imagery, Imagination

Bibliography

Druiz, Colin. *The C. S. Lewis Handbook*. Grand Rapids, MI: Baker, 1990.

Glover, Donald E. *C. S. Lewis: The Art of Enchantment*. Athens: Ohio University Press, 1981.

Lewis, C. S. *The Magician's Nephew; Mere Christianity*.

"Critical Forum"

Essays in Criticism. VI (April 1956): 247.

This short essay responds to a review of Lewis's inaugural lecture at **Cambridge University**, *"De*

Descriptione Temporum.*"* On one point, according to Lewis, the "kind review" seems to have misunderstood him. He had not meant that reading the 16th-century scholar Joannes Rainoldus for a whole morning was "a natural entertainment for any educated reader," but that, in order to understand something of Rainoldus's style, we need to begin by "reading a good many pages of him." Interestingly, Rainoldus is not ever mentioned in the published text of Lewis's lecture.

John Bremer

"Cross Examination"

See entries on "Heaven, Earth and Outerspace" and "I Was Decided Upon"

The Cult of the Superman (Appreciation)

Bentley, Eric. *The Cult of the Superman: A Study of the Idea of Heroism in Carlyle and Nietzsche, with Notes on Other Hero-Worshippers of Modern Times*. London: Geoffrey Bles, 1947.

During 1940, as Europe plunged into war, Eric Bentley wrote a book on "heroic vitalism" in the writings of Thomas Carlyle, **Friedrich Nietzsche**, **Richard Wagner**, George Bernard Shaw, Stefan George, and **D. H. Lawrence**. It came out in the United States as *A Century of Hero Worship* (1944) and in Britain as *The Cult of the Superman* (1947).

C. S. Lewis provided a long paragraph of appreciation for the book, praising the "freshness and pungency" of Bentley's style and the importance of his topic, "the source from which most of the great antidemocratic movements of our day proceed." Lewis noted that the author, although critical of the literary champions of the superman, still displayed more sympathy for them than Lewis himself felt.

Eric Russell Bentley was born in England in 1916. He came to the United States to study in 1939 and stayed, becoming a citizen in 1948. He has had a long and successful career as a teacher, theater critic, and playwright. Politically, Bentley is on the left and once described his religion as "a matter of definition." Lewis may have appreciated his distaste for modern drama and the fairness with which the book treats **Christianity**.

Mike Perry

Also See: Culture, Communism and Fascism, Hero, Literary Criticism, Politics, Utopia, War

Bibliography

Contemporary Authors, Vol. 6 (new revision): 53–57.

Uiereck, Peter. *Metaphysics: The Roots of the Nazi Mind*. New York: Capricorn, 1965.

Culture

Lewis categorically rejected the view (which he attributed to **Matthew Arnold**) that culture was an end in itself and gave meaning to human existence like a **religion**. He also rejected I. A. Richards' atheistic view that good culture or art was a way to achieve psychological adjustment and bad culture or art was psychologically harmful. Lewis, as a Christian and as a student of the Middle Ages, could never agree to give culture—the search for knowledge and **beauty** through the arts and literature—such a primary place. And yet he was faced with the contradiction that his own career as a writer, critic, **tutor**, and reviewer meant that he was making a living supplying the demand for culture.

If Lewis rejected the view that made culture humanity's highest end, he also failed to embrace the idea that culture should be used by Christians primarily as a tool of evangelism. Taking money for producing art and supplying sermons and **apologetics** instead was "stealing" (**"Christianity and Culture"**). Lewis felt it was the duty of the Christian artist to do his or her best work to provide quality art with the Christian element subtly interfused, not to attempt to transform thinly disguised sermons into bad art.

Lewis did believe that culture in itself was neither intrinsically good or bad, and that if for the Christian it was justified, it was justified on the same basis as any work: on the grounds that it was done for the glory of **God**, especially if art was a Christian's calling. "The work of a Beethoven and the work of a charwoman become spiritual on precisely the same condition, that of being offered to God, of being done humbly 'as to the Lord'" (**"Learning in Wartime"**). Finally, Lewis also recognized that as knowledge and learning might be for some a road out of **faith**, for others it might be a road in. Art and literature might possibly contain the best of "sub-Christian **values**," those values are part of the **natural law**.

James Prothero

Also See: Aesthetics, Atheism, Christianity, Good and Evil, Medieval World, Psychology

Bibliography

Arnold, Matthew. *Culture and Anarchy.* Cambridge: Cambridge University Press, 1932.

Richards, I. A. *Poetries and Sciences.* New York: Norton, 1972.

Cupid and Psyche

This well-known **myth** haunted Lewis through much of his life. Its earliest known version is by the Latin author Apuleius, 150 years after Christ; thereafter, it appears in the work of many writers and artists. Psyche, the youngest daughter of a king and queen, was so beautiful that people worshipped her as a goddess and neglected the worship of Venus. The oracle of Apollo told her father that she was to be exposed on a mountain, where a serpent would take her as his bride. Venus sent Cupid to cause her to fall in love with the most deformed and ugly man he could find. But Cupid fell in love with her himself and had her carried from the mountain to his magnificent palace. He came to her at night and made her his bride but forbade her to see his face.

After some time, Psyche begged for a visit from her two sisters, and Cupid reluctantly consented. When the sisters saw Psyche's wealth and the magnificence of her palace, they grew jealous of her and set out to destroy her happiness. They convinced her to disobey Cupid by lighting a lamp and looking at him as he slept. He awoke and was furious at her disobedience. As a result Psyche was abandoned, left homeless, and assigned (by the jealous and spiteful Venus) a series of impossible tasks, which she fulfilled with assistance, and eventually was reconciled with Cupid and gave birth to their child, who was named "Pleasure."

Lewis, from the first time he heard the story, was frustrated because Apuleius, and later accounts that allegorized the tale as the soul's search for **love**, failed to recognize its mythical potential, the sense of divine mystery or awe latent in it. This was evinced particularly by the fact that the sisters could *see* the god's palace. From his first reading of the story, Lewis thought that could not have been the way it was. He therefore attempted several times to retell the story. Fragments of two attempts to write it as a poem survive. In his twenties he thought of turning it into a masque or a play. Three decades later he returned to the myth and used it as the source for what he considered his best work of fiction, ***Till We Have Faces: A Myth Retold***.

Peter J. Schakel
Hope College

Bibliography

Donaldson, Mara E. *Holy Places Are Dark Places: C. S. Lewis and Paul Ricoeur on Narrative Transformation.* Lanham, MD: University Press of America, 1988.

Schakel, Peter J. *Reason and Imagination in C. S. Lewis: A Study of Till We Have Faces.* Grand Rapids, MI: Eerdmans, 1984.

Van Der Weele, Steve J. "From Mt. Olympus to Glome: C. S. Lewis's Dislocation of Apuleius's 'Cupid and Psyche' in *Till We Have Faces.*" *The Longing for a Form: Essays on the Fiction of C. S. Lewis.* Peter J. Schakel (ed). Kent, OH: Kent State University Press, 1977: 182–92.

D

Daily Readings with C. S. Lewis

Walter Hooper (ed). London: HarperCollins, 1992. Retitled and reprinted as *C. S. Lewis: Readings for Reflection and Meditation* (1995).

"Dangerous Oversight"

Punch. 212 (May 21, 1947): 434 (under the pseudonym Nat Whilk). Revised and retitled as "Young King Cole" and reprinted in *Poems* and *Collected Poems*.

A curious poem about an overconfident and reckless king who denies his kingdom is being taken from him piece by piece until he is murdered by his enemies. Yet, from his flesh springs a tree that grows up amid his enemies, appears to offer cooling shade, but then poisons them. Both the king and his enemies are guilty of a dangerous oversight.

Don W. King
Montreat College

"Dangers of National Repentance"

The Guardian. (15 March 1940): 127. Reprinted in *God in the Dock*, *Undeceptions,* and *Christian Reunion*.

In this article, Lewis remarked on the number of young Christians who were turning to the idea of national repentance and who were perfectly prepared to accept responsibility for the decisions of England and her leaders, which may have lead to **war**. These young Christians, many of whom were barely born when these decisions were made, may be repenting "what they have in no sense done." Lewis said that if this is true, it might be supposed harmless. However, "repentance presupposes condemnation," and so these young Christians are in fact attributing to their fellow Englishmen, their leaders, their neighbors, "every abominable motive that **Satan** can suggest to our fancy." In repenting for others, the young Christian supposes what he should not and displays moral cowardice. While he may appear to atone for a sinning England, he is in no way repenting for himself. In the vastness of the supposed **sin**, his own are apparently minor. Given the propensity of young Christians for assuming and presuming to adopt a policy of national repentance, should the church encourage it? Yes, said Lewis, but this "office—like many others—can be profitably dis-

charged only by those who discharge it with reluctance."

Anne Gardner

Dante Alighieri (1265–1321)

Dante's *Divine Comedy* was a strong influence on Lewis. This great poem is an allegorical account of the narrator's spiritual journey from earth through the *Inferno*, *Purgatorio*, and *Paradiso*, and back to earth. It manifests Medieval concepts such as the music of the spheres and the celestial hierarchies (echoed in Lewis's poem **"The Planets"**). Dante's apparent grasp of gravity and the spherical earth were advanced by Lewis as evidence that these theories were known earlier than is commonly reported. His images of **Satan**, beating his batlike wings to freeze **hell**, and of the eternal light of Empyrean were praised by Lewis for their vision. In ***The Allegory of Love***, Lewis proposed that "Dante remains a strong candidate for the supreme poetical honours of the world," and in **"Shelley, Dryden, and Mr. Eliot,"** he agreed with **T. S. Eliot** that "the last canto of the *Paradiso* [is] 'the highest point that **poetry** has ever reached.'"

Kristine Ottaway

Also See: Allegory, Hierarchy, Imagery, Light and Dark, Spirituality

Bibliography

Butler, Arthur J. *Dante: His Times and His Work*. North Stratford, NH: Ayer, 1977.
Dante. *Divine Comedy*.
Luke, Helen M. *Dark Wood to White Rose*. Pecos, NM: Dove Publications, 1975.

"Dante's Similes"

Nottingham Mediaeval Studies. IX (1965): 32–41. Reprinted in *Studies in Medieval and Renaissance Literature*.

This essay studied how **Dante**'s similes may differ from those of other writers. Lewis astutely noted that *The Divine Comedy* performs a variety of functions; it is a travel book, a work of **philosophy**, a religious **allegory**, and an epic poem all at the same time. Like other Medieval works, it can be simultaneously high brow and low brow. Thus Dante's similes operate in diverse ways. Sometimes they are "Virgilian" similes, drawing comparisons to nature; sometimes they are tour-guide similes thrown in for realism; sometimes they are more aesthetic, comparing emotions; and sometimes they are philosophical, showing multiple levels of relationships.

The last type of simile interested Lewis most. Lewis gave the example of Dante gazing at the sun. According to the poem the sun is like a pilgrim longing to return home. But Dante himself is also a pilgrim, longing for his heavenly home—so the simile uses multiple levels of comparison simultaneously.

This essay is more readable than Lewis's other articles on Dante, primarily because the subject is more generalized, but as its original audience was Oxford's Dante Society, contemporary readers will need some familiarity with *The Divine Comedy* to appreciate this essay.

Marvin D. Hinten
Bowling Green State University

Also See: Aesthetics, Poetry, Reality

"Dante's Statius"

Medium Aevum. XXV no. 3 (1957): 133–39. Reprinted in *Studies in Medieval and Renaissance Literature.*

People wondering "Who is Statius?" will find little or nothing here to interest them. The essay, from *Studies in Medieval and Renaissance Literature*, was written for scholars. In one sentence alone, Lewis casually referred to Bernardus Silvestris, Alanus ab Insulis, Jean de Meung, and **Plato**'s *Timaeus*, and the numerous Latin and Italian lines cited were left untranslated. Statius, a character in canto XXI of **Dante**'s *Purgatorio*, was a Latin poet most famous for the *Thebaid*. The question Lewis attempted to answer was why Dante allowed Statius into **purgatory**, implying eventual entry into **heaven**, whereas Virgil was left in limbo.

Lewis first showed that Dante was steeped in the *Thebaid*, showing numerous parallels between events in it and in *The Divine Comedy*. This would have led Dante, at least emotionally, to want to look for Christian evidence in Statius's work. He would have found, according to Lewis, support for the fallenness of humanity, indications of "diabolical agents," and a presentation of Jupiter as a transcendent Creator, upright yet merciful. Thus Lewis believed it would have been logical for Dante to accept Virgil as the greater poet but Statius as the poet with greater insight into ultimate things.

Marvin D. Hinten
Bowling Green State University

Also See: Christianity, The Fall, Poetry, Redemption

The Dark Tower

London: Collins, 1977. First US edition, New York: Harcourt Brace Jovanovich, 1977.

First published in 1977, *The Dark Tower* stands at the center of a **controversy** over several manuscripts published after C. S. Lewis's death under his name. Many scholars question whether *The Dark Tower* is actually by Lewis. (Other disputed items include **"Christian Reunion,"** *The Man Born Blind*, *Forms of Things Unknown*, and from **Boxen**, "Encyclopedia Boxoniana.")

Walter Hooper has stated that he acquired the manuscript of *The Dark Tower* (as well as sundry other manuscripts) from Lewis's gardener **Fred Paxford**, who saved the manuscripts from a bonfire ordered by **Warren Lewis**. When asked about the bonfire during the 1970s, however, Paxford could not recall it. In 1988, independent scholar Kathryn Lindskoog questioned the authenticity of *The Dark Tower* in her book, *The C. S. Lewis Hoax*, later revised and expanded as *Light in the Shadowlands*.

Those who doubt the authenticity of *The Dark Tower* first point to the problems with its provenance (or origins). The story was first mentioned in the preface to a Lewis anthology *Of Other Worlds* in 1966, but inquiries made of Warren Lewis and **Clyde S. Kilby** revealed that they had no knowledge of such a work. Lewis himself made no mention of it in his letters, and there is no authenticated mention of it by Lewis's friends. The only unauthenticated mention is alleged to have been made by Gervase Mathew who was reported to have said that he had heard the first four chapters read at an **Inklings** meeting in 1939 or 1940. Unfortunately, when this was made public, Mathew was dead and could not confirm it; moreover, there is no record that Mathew attended an Inklings meeting before 1946.

Although it has been asserted that Warren Lewis, **Owen Barfield**, and **Roger Green** saw the manuscript in 1964, neither Warren nor Green were able to confirm the veracity of this claim, which was not made until after Warren's death in 1973. Green, in his co-authored biography (1974), reported that the novel was only a fragment, although up to that point it had been implicitly presented as a complete work. He later thought the fragment spurious.

Furthermore, two independent computer tests of *The Dark Tower* have been carried out, analyzing the story in terms of two different parameters (letter and letter-pair frequencies, and statistical ratios of key sentence elements), and both indicate that the primary author of this fragment was not the author of Lewis's space trilogy. Interestingly, the second of these tests—by forensic expert A. Q. Morton—shows that the first part of chapter 7 of *The Dark Tower* could be by Lewis.

If the provenance of *The Dark Tower* raises doubts, the story itself is no more encouraging. The story is ostensibly told by Lewis himself, as a companion to Ransom, whose name links the story with Lewis's authentic science fiction trilogy. Supposedly, this work falls chronologically between *Out of the Silent Planet* and *Perelandra,* but it is impossible to see why the completeness of the trilogy should be interrupted by what appears to be such an anachronistic, lifeless, and inconsistent piece of indifferent writing. The work has a few passages that are acceptable, but there is no overarching theological or moral view (surely a Lewis hallmark), and its main **symbolism** is overtly sexual and obscene.

Ransom, Lewis, Orfieu, Scudamour, and MacPhee (curiously counted as four in the second sentence of the fragment) meet in Cambridge and look into a "chronoscope," which displays what is happening in some other time. They look into a dark tower (a replica of the Cambridge University Library, but still being built) where a sinister man, with a red oversized thorn growing out of his forehead, waits to transform seminaked human beings into automata by plunging the thorn into their spines. While watching, Scudamour's double appears, growing a sting in his forehead. Then, Camilla, Scudamour's fiancée also appears, and just as she is about to be stung, Scudamour breaks the chronoscope in anger and changes place with his double. The rest of the fragment deals with his doings in Othertime, until it breaks off in midsentence. The last ten pages are an account of Othertime science, concentrating on the nature of time.

The story gives the impression of having been written by an undergraduate fascinated with homosexuality and using science fiction as a vehicle for indulging his fantasies but incorporating into the story some fragments of a more mature and serious author. The writer also seems to have been influenced by Madeleine L'Engle's *A Wrinkle in Time,* which appeared in 1962.

Defenders of *The Dark Tower*'s authenticity have included David Downing, Jared Lobdell, and M. J. Logsdon, the last of whom engaged in an extensive debate on the subject with Kathryn Lindskoog in the newsletter of the Salinas Valley C. S. Lewis Society. Paper chemist Julius Grant (who helped expose the Hitler diaries as a forgery) also apparently thought the manuscript of *The Dark Tower* was genuine. The elderly Grant looked at (but did not test) the manuscript at the **Bodleian Library** in **Oxford** in 1990, but he died before he issued a formal report. Also in 1990 Lewis scholar Richard Purtill tried to suggest how Lewis might have continued the story in a lecture at a conference in Seattle.

The controversy over *The Dark Tower* is not likely to dissipate either easily or soon. There are too many questions that remain to be answered, and interest in the dispute has continued to grow. In 1992 more than eighty distinguished scholars and writers signed a petition asking for a full public airing of the questions raised about *The Dark Tower* and several other pieces published posthumously under Lewis's name. (Signers of the petition included noted science fiction author **Arthur C. Clarke**, former Poet Laureate of the United States Richard Wilbur, and former director of the **Wade Center,** Lyle Dorsett.)

John Bremer

Bibliography

Downing, David. *Planets in Peril*. Amherst, MA: University of Massachusetts Press, 1992.

Jones, Carla Faust. "The Literary Detective Computer Analysis of Stylistic Differences Between The Dark Tower and C. S. Lewis' Deep Space Trilogy." *Mythlore* (Spring 1989): 11–15.

Lindskoog, Kathryn. *Light in the Shadowlands*. Sisters, OR: Multnomah, 1994.

Lobdell, Jared C. "C. S. Lewis's Ransom Stories and Their Eighteenth-Century Ancestry." *Word and Story in C. S. Lewis*. Peter J. Schakel and Charles A. Huttar (eds). Columbia, MO: University Press of Missouri, 1991: 213–31.

Rateliffe, John. "The Kathryn Lindskoog Hoax: Screwtape Redux." *Mythlore*. (Summer 1989).

Salinas Valley Lewisian.

The Dark Tower and Other Stories

Walter Hooper (ed). London: Collins, 1977. First US edition, New York: Harcourt Brace Jovanovich, 1977.

See separate entries on the following:

After Ten Years (fragment)
The Dark Tower
Forms of Things Unknown
The Man Born Blind
Ministering Angels
The Shoddy Lands

"The Day with the White Mark"

Punch. 217 (August 17, 1949): 170 (under the pseudonym Nat Whilk). Revised and reprinted in *Poems* and *Collected Poems.*

Despite that present **reality** for the speaker is really rather bleak and grim, **joy** sweeps through every insignificant action of his day. Although he wonders if the source of his **happiness** could be an elf, bird, or **angel**, he ends by noting joy is never predictable and always a surprise.

Don W. King
Montreat College

"De Audiendis Poetis"

First published posthumously in *Studies in Medieval and Renaissance Literature.*

"De Audiendis Poetis" was begun as an introductory chapter to an unpublished work Lewis began several years before his retirement from Cambridge. It focuses on a theme that occurs throughout his critical oeuvre and most notably in his book ***The Discarded Image***: in order to appreciate and understand "the old books" one must deliberately place oneself within its linguistic and cultural context and refuse merely to translate it grossly into one's own modern era.

Lewis's essay begins as a reply to a critic who found "discouraging" the notion "that before the modern reader can properly appreciate a Medieval poem he must first have somehow put himself back" into the age when it was composed, and along the way it addresses the classic dilemma posed by 20th-century **New Criticism**: When does context inhibit experience of the "poem itself"? Lewis's answer here is that anything that would take readers "outside" a work and strand them there would be "regrettable." However, effective criticism, Lewis averred, must sometimes take one first outside the poem "in order that we may presently come inside it again, better equipped."

In the body of the essay Lewis amply demonstrated that **literary criticism** is not an either/or but rather a both/and proposition; it is strategic, particularly when confronted with a noncontemporary text, to consider temporarily certain factors external to the text which have become important because they formed the context for both the original conception and the original audience.

Employing his favorite **metaphor** (vision) to convey his conviction, Lewis declared: "What a poem may 'mean' to moderns and to them only, however delightful, is from this point of view merely a stain on the lens. We must clean the lens and remove the stain so that the real past can be seen better." To do otherwise would be to lose the poem doubly, both in its antiquity and in its presence.

Bruce L. Edwards
Bowling Green State University

Bibliography

Edwards, Bruce L. *A Rhetoric of Reading: C. S. Lewis's Defense of Western Literacy.* Provo, UT: Brigham Young University, 1985.

Edwards, Bruce L. (ed). *The Taste of the Pineapple: Essays on C. S. Lewis as Reader, Critic, and Imaginative Writer.* Bowling Green, OH: The Popular Press, 1988.

Hannay, Margaret. *C. S. Lewis.* New York: Ungar, 1989.

Lewis, C. S. "The Anthropological Approach"; "What Chaucer Really Did to *Il Filostrato.*"

"De Descriptione Temporum"

Cambridge: Cambridge University Press, 1955. Reprinted in *Selected Literary Essays.*

"De Descriptione Temporum" (Latin for "a description of the times") is the inaugural lecture Lewis delivered as newly appointed Professor of Medieval and Renaissance English Literature at Cambridge University in 1954. Lewis had accepted the post at **Oxford**'s rival campus only because his colleagues there had, for political reasons, denied him a professorship for which he was eminently well-qualified.

Lewis used this auspicious occasion to air his cherished conviction that the barrier between the **Medieval world** and the **Renaissance** had been greatly exaggerated, adamant that "the Great Divide" be put instead between the present day and the age of Jane Austen and Sir Walter Scott. The modern West, Lewis argued, has broken from both its pagan and Christian past, embracing an aesthetic that exalts ambiguity and ambivalence, thus succumbing to a political order that preferred "magnetism" to character and surrendering man's place in **nature** to the machine.

The effect of this abdication, Lewis averred, is a society that would "shock and bewilder" our Western ancestors. In a dramatic climax, boasting that he was an "Old Western man" who read "as a native" texts for which coming generations will need a translator, he exhorted his audience "to use your specimens while you can. There are not going to be many more dinosaurs." *"De Descriptione Temporum"* is a pivotal statement of Lewis's principles as a literary historian and critic, and a prophetic lament for the disintegration of Western **culture** as he witnessed it at mid-century.

Bruce L. Edwards
Bowling Green State University

Also See: Literary Criticism, Literary Theory, Modernity

Bibliography

Edwards, Bruce L. *A Rhetoric of Reading: C. S. Lewis's Defense of Western Literacy.* Provo, UT: Brigham Young University Press, 1985.

Myers, Doris T. *C. S. Lewis in Context.* Kent, OH: Kent State University Press, 1994.

"De Futilitate"

First published posthumously in *Christian Reflections.*

This essay, originally delivered during World War II, was an address at **Magdalen College, Oxford,** at the invitation of Sir Henry Tizard, president of Magdalen. In the essay, Lewis, admitting the superficial plausibility of the notion that the universe may be meaningless, pointed out its fallacy. He proposed that there are only three responses that address a futile universe—Stoicism, Idealism, and simple denial. Denial refuses the problem, treating it as a disillusioned response to the discovery that human thought does not reflect the real universe. If that proposition were true, however, it would be a paradox. Unless logical thought corresponds to **reality**, we can have no reason to believe in the real universe. This rules out any simply materialistic account of thinking.

Stoicism accuses the universe of futility. For that accusation to be valid, however, one must tacitly accept a standard of comparison that enables one to distinguish between futility and meaning, thus admitting that at least one thing produced by the universe—the standard—is meaningful and good. This shows that what happens to the proposition that logic is invalid happens as well to the proposition that morals bear no relation to reality. As long as we try to attach any importance to our own reasoning, we cannot reject the objective validity of **reason**; and as long as we attach any importance to our own values, we cannot reject the validity of a standard of value external to ourselves. In Lewis's view, both results implicitly support the third alternative, Idealism.

Lyle Smith
Biola University

Also See: Destiny, Materialism, Plato

"Death in Battle"

Reveille. 3 (February 1919): 508 (under the pseudonym Clive Hamilton). Reprinted in *Spirits in Bondage* and *Collected Poems.*

This poem expresses the thematic tension found in many poems later published in *Spirits in Bondage*: the brutal reality of WWI battlefield horror versus the longing for the worlds of **beauty**, desire, and **dreams**. Death,

as the possible entrée to these worlds, is not to be avoided.

Don W. King
Montreat College

The Death of Tragedy (Book Review)

"Tragic Ends." *Encounter.* XVIII (February 1962): 97–101.

This book attempted to account for "the decay of tragic drama." In Lewis's view, there was some confusion as to what was meant by "tragedy." Steiner said we know "not exactly, but well enough" what it means, but Lewis suggested that we do not. According to Lewis, tragedy varies its meaning not only over time but also between works. Lewis included a discussion of melodrama as a pejorative term for "near-tragedy."

Anne Gardner

Bibliography

Steiner, George. *The Death of Tragedy.*

"The Death of Words"

The Spectator. CLXXIII (22 September 1944): 261. Reprinted in *Of This and Other Worlds* and *On Stories.*

Beginning from a statement of Rose Macaulay's that "dictionaries are always telling us of words 'now used only in a bad sense'; seldom or never of words 'now used only in a good sense,'" Lewis expanded the observation to include as well words that once had a definable sense but are now used only as a vague compliment. According to Lewis, words die when, instead of being used to describe facts, they are used to express indefinite likes and dislikes. The words "villain" and "gentleman," for instance, were once used to denote legal social standing. Now it has become "merely eulogistic." A word is likewise in trouble when it begins to be modified by "real" or "true."

Lewis concluded the essay by warning that the word **"Christianity"** is losing denotative meaning. Today it is often used as a synonym for "civilized," "modern," "democratic," or "enlightened," all themselves "ruined words." Lewis pointed out that it is the friends of the concepts denoted by words who can be their greatest threat; admiring the concept, they seek to deepen the word's connotation at the expense of its denotation, with the unfortunate effect of blotting out of people's minds the idea the "word originally stood for."

Lyle Smith
Biola University

Also See: Language/Rhetoric, Modernity

Death Penalty (Letter)

Church Times. CXLIV (15 December 1961): 12. Reprinted in *God in the Dock, Undeceptions,* and *Timeless at Heart.*

Claude Davis responded the following week (*Church Times,* 8 December 1961, 14) to Lewis's letter (see **Capital Punishment: Grounds for Abolition**) by objecting to Lewis's statement that it was archaic and erroneous to believe that "murder is primarily an offence not against society but against individuals." Using an example from Demosthenes, Lewis reiterated why he believed that murder cannot simply be viewed as an offense against one family rather than against society as a whole. Lewis concluded by restating that while he is on neither side in this controversy, he was disappointed with how the abolitionists were conducting their case. He challenged his fellow Christians to consider the tone and logic of their arguments with a view toward how their lack of civility and charity might appear to unbelievers.

Marjorie L. Mead
The Marion E. Wade Center

"The Decline of Religion"

The Cherwell. XXVI (29 November 1946): 8–10. Reprinted in *God in the Dock, Undeceptions* and *First and Second Things.*

Lewis began this essay by saying that there is evidence for both "a decline" and "a revival" of what may be called **religion** among the current undergraduate body at **Oxford**. The emptiness of the chapels is seen as proving "decline," but the "decline" was not gradual. It occurred when chapel was no longer compulsory.

According to Lewis, this apparent decline is true everywhere. The "visible practice of **Christianity**" has decreased. Lewis argued, however, that the decline was not of Christianity but of "a vague Theism with a strong and virile ethical code." The "decline," seen in this way, is good, because it makes the choice between the World and Christianity inescapable.

As for a revival, Lewis remarked that the growing intellectual interest in Christianity is very different from conversion to it. The interest is fashion, and fashion does not last. Revival is only useful when it helps real conversion. Lewis noted that what appears to harm may not, but that what also appears to help may not.

Anne Gardner

"Delinquents in the Snow"

Time and Tide. XXXVIII (December 7, 1957): 1521–22. Reprinted in *God in the Dock, Undeceptions,* and *Christian Reunion.*

Lewis's experience with neighborhood juvenile delinquents provided the impetus for this essay. Lewis was upset with local youth who vandalized his property even while his wife, Joy, suffered at home from cancer. The police actually caught one group of delinquents who stole some of Lewis's property, but the judge who sentenced the criminals let them off with a "small fine" and an ineffectual scolding. Lewis wrote that the easy treatment of these youthful offenders was merely a symptom how the **justice** system increasingly protected criminals at the expense of their victims. Lewis pointed out that according to classical liberal political theory, the people surrender their own right to deal with criminals on the understanding that the state will do the job for them. But if the state fails to uphold its part of the bargain, the people can be expected to take the law back into their own hands. Lewis did not favor this result, because he believed that vigilante groups "would soon be ... filled by the same sort of hooligans who provoked" them. But he thought that the middle class could put up with only so much. The way to avoid such vigilante efforts was to maintain a justice system that took crime and punishment seriously again.

John G. West, Jr.

Also See: Joy Davidman Lewis

Bibliography
Lewis, C. S. "On the Humanitarian Theory of Punishment."

Democracy

Winston Churchill once said that "democracy is the worst form of Government except all those other forms that have been tried." C. S. Lewis likely would have agreed. Unlike some thinkers who extolled democracy because they thought human beings were capable of perfecting themselves in society, Lewis was a democrat because he thought the intractability of **sin** made any other type of system untenable. "I am a democrat because I believe in **the Fall** of Man," he declared in an essay on **"Equality"** published in 1943. "Mankind is so fallen that no man can be trusted with unchecked power over his fellows." By emphasizing human imperfection as the foundation for democracy, Lewis placed himself within a long line of democratic realists, ranging from British thinkers such as Edmund Burke to American Founders such as James Madison and Alexander Hamilton. Because in Lewis's view democracy is based on sin, it is not the ideal form of government. Indeed, in a perfect world Lewis's preferred mode of government would likely be **monarchy** rather than democracy. Thus, in the

Chronicles of Narnia, the divinely appointed rulers of Narnia are kings and queens; and in Lewis's space trilogy, each planet is governed by a single powerful angel.

Although Lewis supported democracy in **politics** and economics, he feared its spread to other spheres of human life. Political democracy and economic democracy are premised on the idea that all citizens are equal; as a consequence, every citizen is guaranteed the equal protection of the laws and an equal right to vote. While Lewis thought such equality was necessary for politics and economics, he believed it would be lethal if applied anywhere else. Much like Alexis de Tocqueville in *Democracy in America*, Lewis worried that an unrestrained democratic impulse could destroy society by leading to the denial of every kind of human superiority. In an essay on **"Democratic Education,"** Lewis warned about the spread of democracy to the arts and sciences for precisely this reason. In Lewis's view, democracy has no place in the realm of the mind, because **beauty**, virtue, and **truth** are not matters to be decided by majority vote. All art is not equally beautiful. All people are not equally virtuous. And all truth claims are not equally valid. Societies that pretend otherwise are suicidal. Hence, the purpose of **education** in a political democracy should not be to equalize everyone in their abilities; it should be to foster the intellectual and moral excellence required for society to survive.

If Lewis believed that unrestrained democracy could be intellectually and morally subversive, he also thought it could be spiritually toxic. In **"Screwtape Proposes a Toast,"** he argued that the democratic impulse could place people on the road to **hell** by instilling in them the lie that they are "just as good" as everyone else. In traditional ethics, Lewis pointed out, this false craving to be "just as good" as others was known as envy. By spreading envy (as well as **pride**), the democratic impulse makes it harder for people to recognize the **virtues** of humility and obedience. It also blinds them to the real nature of the universe, which operates on the principle of **hierarchy** rather than equality.

John G. West, Jr.

Bibliography

John G. West, Jr., "Finding the Permanent in the Political: C. S. Lewis as a Political Thinker." *Permanent Things*. Andrew Tadie and Michael Macdonald (eds). Grand Rapids, MI: Eerdmans, 1996.

_____. "Politics from the Shadowlands: C. S. Lewis on Earthly Government." *Policy Review*. (Sprint 1994): 68–70.

"Democratic Education"

See entry on "Notes on the Way" (29 April 1944)

Demons

Demon (a word Lewis rarely used) derives from Greek *daimon,* a being intermediate between divine and human—ontologically, spatially (populating the air), materially (its body attenuated to invisibility), and functionally (a bridge for divine-human communication). Morally demons vary. They can be good, bad, or neutral. This concept survived into the late Middle Ages and returned in Renaissance humanism. Lewis played with it in shaping the figure of Merlin and Jane's encounter with the terrestrial Venus (*That Hideous Strength*).

However, New Testament *daimonia* are the evil sort, associated nearly always with harmful possession, and since **Aquinas** demon has generally meant *devil*—one of **Satan**'s lesser followers.

Lewis acknowledged one could be a Christian without believing in devils, but his **theology** traced **pain** and evil back to the rebellion of a "Dark Power" "created ... good" but gone wrong and now ruling our world at the head of an army of demons—fallen **angels** who fill the air. Distrusting any "pseudo-science of Demonology" born of "morbid inquisitiveness," Lewis largely avoided further speculation except in fiction.

Demons (without the *a*) are spirits, hence undying, but without hope of **happiness**. **God**'s presence, to which as creatures they owe continuing existence, produces for them only "anguish." In intelligence and knowledge they surpass humans but have fallen below angels, ignorant of **joy** and **love** and subject to crucial gaps in knowledge. Such failure of intellect is an aspect of moral decay resulting from total egocentrism. They feed on other spirits, "sucking ... out ... weaker sel[ves]" as Screwtape hopes to dine on the imp Wormwood and his human charge.

They have more than earthly power but cannot create. Instead, they typically pervert, destroy, annoy. Since laying waste to the Martian highlands (*Out of the Silent Planet*) they have been prevented from direct physical destruction but must work on and through humans.

The most common way they do this is temptation. *Perelandra, That Hideous Strength,* and **The Screwtape Letters** provide explicitly demonic examples, including attacks on **rationality** and violent emotional assaults. Another is by a Mephistophelean illusion of servitude, letting the sorcerer believe he is in command. The "macrobes" who run Belbury in *That Hideous Strength* let Filostrato and Straik credit their **science**. But the full initiates, Frost and Wither, know themselves mere servants; willing submission to demonic control erodes their own intellectual powers and selfhood. Wither is perhaps already demon-possessed—like Weston certainly was in *Perelandra*, after "call[ing] that Force into" himself: his body invaded, his personality submerged and tormented but not eradicated, his physical functions mechanized ("the Un-man") but not enhanced, his mind commandeered. Such radical possession seems beyond exorcism.

Demonic activity in Lewis's writings also included manipulation and would-be domination of institutions and systems. Screwtape takes credit for totalitarianism and the whirligig of intellectual fashions. But Lewis mainly focused on the individuals who make such demonic triumphs possible, whether knowingly or not—for even those who side with good are vulnerable.

Charles A. Huttar
Hope College

Also See: Angels, Cosmology, Hierarchy, Magic, John Milton

Bibliography

Filmer, Kath. *The Fiction of C. S. Lewis: Mask and Mirror.* Basingstoke and London: Macmillan; New York: St. Martin's, 1993.

Huttar, Charles A. "C. S. Lewis and the Demonic." *Perspectives* 3/3 (March 1988): 6–10.

Smith, Robert Houston. *Patches of Godlight: The Pattern of Thought of C. S. Lewis.* Athens: University of Georgia Press, 1981.

Destiny

Lewis stressed destiny far more than most Christian writers. In **"The Weight of Glory"** he wrote: "We walk every day on the razor edge between these two incredible possibilities." At any moment we may find ourselves thrust into the presence of **God** only to be banished forever—"I never knew you. Depart from me." Or we may be welcomed by the very One for whom we have always longed. This destiny, unique to humanity, has a special significance. "There are no ordinary people," Lewis wrote. "You have never talked to a mere mortal. Nations, cultures, arts, civilisations—these are mortal, and their life is to ours as the life of a gnat. But it is immortals whom we joke with, work with, marry, snub and exploit—immortal horrors or everlasting splendors."

For Lewis, our eternal destiny as either a horror or a splendor is being forged in the choices we make every day. "Each of us at each moment," he wrote in *Mere Christianity*, "is progressing to one state or the other." We are becoming either a "heavenly creature" or a "hellish" one. He cautioned that we cannot judge just what

sort of person each is becoming. "Nice things" about us may be little more than "good digestion." "Nasty things" about others may result from bad health. Only in eternity will we see people as they are. "There will be surprises," he noted.

Lewis explored the destiny of the lost in *The Problem of Pain*. He suggested that "the doors of **hell** are locked on the inside" and those within "enjoy forever the horrible freedom they have demanded." Earlier in the book he warned that there is only one alternative to sharing in God's goodness and that is misery: "If we cannot learn to eat the only food the universe grows—then we must starve eternally."

In *Miracles* Lewis turned to the destiny of **Nature**, comparing it to a house being rebuilt. He rejected the idea that the world-to-be would be "tamed" or "sterilised." We will still recognize it and "that will be a merry meeting."

Mike Perry

Also See: Corruption of Nature, The Fall, Free Will, Good and Evil, Hell, Immortality

"The Dethronement of Power"

See entry on *The Two Towers* and *The Return of the King* (Book Review)

A Difference of Outlook (Letter)

The Guardian (27 June 1947): 283.

In an article (May 30, 1947) entitled "Adult Colleges," an unnamed correspondent quotes a passage from C. S. Lewis's *A Preface to Paradise Lost*. Lewis wrote to clarify what he considered to be an unintentional misrepresentation of his thought. Lewis distinguished the meaning of his maxim "Death is bitter" from the correspondent's paraphrase, "War is horrible," as well as the maxim "Virtue is lovely" from the revision, "Honesty is the best policy." He did not write to debate the merits of the various statements but simply to point out that the maxims are fundamentally different.

Marjorie L. Mead
The Marion E. Wade Center

"Different Tastes in Literature"

See entry for "Notes on the Way" (25 May 1946)

"Difficulties in Presenting the Christian Faith to Modern Unbelievers"

Lumen Vitae. III (September 1948): 421–26. Retitled as "God in the Dock" and reprinted in *God in the Dock* and *Undeceptions*.

Lewis said he wrote this essay in response to a request to write "about the difficulties which a man must face in

trying to present the Christian Faith to modern unbelievers." Lewis drew upon his own experience of speaking to members of the Royal Air Force and university students in order to answer the question. Lewis remarked that the RAF is composed of what he referred to as the "Intelligentsia of the Proletariat." He initially had considered **materialism** to be the biggest single obstacle, but instead he encountered many non-Christian creeds. At **Oxford** Lewis noted the theological vagueness apparent in the students with whom he spoke. The members of the RAF and the students lacked historical perspective which in turn made language a constant problem. The meanings of words which had a strict meaning to Lewis meant something altogether different to these groups. Most distressing to Lewis was the "almost total absence from the minds of [his] audience of any sense of **sin**." Early Christians were assured that their audience felt guilt. "We have to convince our hearers of the unwelcome diagnosis before we can expect them to welcome the news of the remedy." Lewis concluded, "I must add that my own work has suffered very much from the incurable intellectualism of my approach." Lewis concluded that "the simple, emotional appeal ... is still often successful. But those who, like myself, lack the gift for making it, had better not attempt it."

Anne Gardner

Also See: Christianity, Language/Rhetoric, Morality, RAF Talks, Religion

The Discarded Image: An Introduction to Medieval and Renaissance Literature

Cambridge: Cambridge University Press, 1968.

The reader of Medieval and **Renaissance** literature (or of any literature) finds that some of the words are familiar and some are not. It is easy to imagine that we can take the former for granted and look the latter up in some reference work. But as Lewis pointed out, in *Studies in Words* (1960), a word may look familiar but its meaning to us may be markedly different from its meaning to the writer and to the audience for which he wrote.

In *The Discarded Image,* Lewis found a key to the meaning of words in Medieval and Renaissance literature in the "Model of the Universe," the imagined universe that is presupposed by the writers of the period. Unless we have some understanding of the Medieval Model, we will not be able to appreciate the full weight of a word, simply because it is connected with a number of other words that show, by the connections themselves, some of the unstated yet powerful associations that contribute to the meaning. A seemingly simple example that will strike the modern ear is the way in which a Medieval doctor might have attributed a malady that defied all other diagnosis to "an influence in the air," or, if he were Italian, "questa influenza." But the Model lying behind this usage is very different from that of the modern physician who diagnoses "Influenza."

The Medieval Model did not spring up suddenly. It had roots in the classical world. Nor did it die suddenly but continued, among most writers, until the end of the 17th century, so that it is shared by **Edmund Spenser**, **John Donne**, and **John Milton**. It should be noted that this view implicitly denies the conventional distinction between the Middle Ages and the Renaissance; this denial was explicit in Lewis's earlier work *English Literature in the Sixteenth Century, Excluding Drama*.

Lewis did not hide the fact that the Medieval Model delighted him, as, he believes, it delighted our ancestors. "Few constructions of the **imagination** seem to me to have combined splendour, sobriety, and coherence in the same degree. It is possible that some readers have long been itching to remind me that it had a serious defect: it was not true." Lewis agreed that it is not true but points out that the meaning of "true" now means something different from what it did in the past. "It would therefore be subtly misleading to say 'The medievals thought the universe to be like that, but we know it to be like this.' Part of what we now know is that we cannot, in the old sense, 'know what the

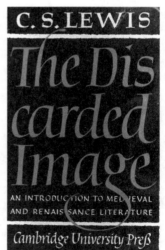

universe is like' and that no model we can build will be, in that old sense, 'like' it."

Lewis was not recommending a return to the Medieval Model but only suggesting that a consideration of that Model will enable us to look at all Models in an appropriate way, "respecting each and idolising none," not even our own.

While it is true that our minds are affected by the current, accepted Model, it is equally true that the Model is affected by "the prevailing temper of mind." There is a two-way traffic. "No Model is a catalogue of ultimate realities, and none is a mere fantasy. Each is a serious attempt to get in all the phenomena known at a given period, and each succeeds in getting in a great many. But also, no less surely, each reflects the prevalent **psychology** of an age almost as much as it reflects the state of that age's knowledge. Hardly any battery of new facts could have persuaded a Greek that the universe had an attribute as repugnant to him as infinity; hardly any such battery could persuade a modern that it is hierarchical."

Our own model will change when far-reaching changes in mental temper demand that it should. "The new Model will not be set up without evidence, but the evidence will turn up when the inner need for it becomes sufficiently great. It will be true evidence. But nature gives most of her evidence in answer to the questions we ask her." But even the new Model will not account for everything.

John Bremer

Also See: Allegory, Cosmology, Literary Theory, Medieval World, Modernity

Bibliography

Musaccio, George. "Foreign Words in The Discarded Image." *CSL: The Bulletin of the New York C. S. Lewis Society.* 14 (July 1983): 5–7.

Sammons, Martha C. "Further in the Onion Skin: Lewis' Multi-Leveled Models." *Lamp-Post.* 11 no. 1 (March 1987): 3–15.

"Dogma and Science"

See entry on "Dogma and the Universe"

"Dogma and the Universe"

The Guardian. (19 March 1943): 96 and (26 March 1943): 104, 107. The second installment was originally titled "Dogma and Science." Reprinted in *God in the Dock* and *Undeceptions.*

Lewis began by saying that "[i]t is a common reproach against **Christianity** that its dogmas are unchanging, while human knowledge is in continual growth." He argued that "wherever there is real progress in knowledge, there is some knowledge which is not superseded." We should not, we must not, use the vastness of space and the smallness of ourselves to disprove **God.** We would then be like doctors, performing an autopsy and determining that the subject had been poisoned without the knowledge of how a subject would look if he hadn't been poisoned. We know something is or has happened because of what is different. How then can we look at the universe and see it as disproving God's existence when we do not know how we could expect it would look without him? "The doctrines that God is **love** and that He delights in men, are positive doctrines, not limiting doctrines." Whatever else God may be, whatever else he made, this is true, but it does not place any boundary on him, his actions, his creations. Lewis asked that we do not deceive ourselves, that we realize "no possible complexity which we can give to our picture of the universe can hide us from God."

Anne Gardner

"Donkey's Delight"

Punch. 213 (November 5, 1947): 442 (under the pseudonym Nat Whilk). Revised and reprinted in *Poems* and *Collected Poems.*

Three times the speaker had sought wisdom—first how to **love** best, second how to write best, third how to think best—but each time his effort was shown to be foolish. Finally he realizes how arrogant his search has been and sees himself good-humoredly as Balaam's ass; indeed, the poem concludes with him braying *Gloria* with **joy.**

Don W. King
Montreat College

John Donne (1572–1631)

A scholar, courtier, clergyman, and poet, John Donne is recognized as the founder of **poetry**'s metaphysical school. Donne's metaphysical form employed colloquial language, various rhythms, and complex **metaphors** (known as "conceits"). His *Songs and Sonnets* are primarily amorous poems. It is the vindication of the body exhibited in these love poems that Jane Studdock intends to examine as her thesis in *That Hideous Strength*. However, the *Divine Poems* that conclude the *Songs and Sonnets* treat religious themes. Donne's allusions in his poems to the ideas of the celestial **hierarchy**, the spheres, and other Medieval cosmic beliefs are evidence that the Medieval mind continued to influence the **Renaissance** period. In *Surprised by Joy*, Lewis says he was "intoxicated (for a time) by Donne." *Holy Sonnet XIII* provides the title and question for Lewis's essay **"The World's Last Night."** Lewis also appears to have been very interested in Donne's portrayal of **angels** in "Aire and Angels."

Kristine Ottaway

Also See: Cosmology, Demons, Language/Rhetoric, Medieval World, Metaphysics, Religion

Bibliography

Bald, Robert C. *John Donne: A Life*. Clarendon: Oxford University Press, 1986.

Lewis, C. S. *The Allegory of Love*; *The Discarded Image*.

"Donne and Love Poetry in the Seventeenth Century"

Seventeenth-Century Studies Presented to Sir Herbert Grierson. Oxford: Clarendon Press, 1938: 64–84. Reprinted in *Selected Literary Essays*.

This essay was first published in 1938 as part of the collection *Seventeenth-Century Studies Presented to Sir Herbert Grierson*; it is also part of Lewis's *Selected Literary Essays*. Lewis began the essay by noting the blending in **John Donne** of elements from Thomas Wyatt and **Edmund Spenser**; with his usual pithy insight, he called Wyatt "a Donne with most of the genius left out." Lewis's generalized dislike of Donne comes through in various ways; in typically Lewisian fashion, he described Donne's **poetry** as "froth," "simple," and "parasitic," but said disingenuously these are not pejorative terms. The best parts of the essay occurred when Lewis moved from Donne to brief discussions of other authors and of metrics.

Some weaknesses of the essay can be seen by reading it with its companion piece, Joan Bennett's "The Love Poetry of John Donne." The two articles appeared together in the Grierson collection, and they can also be found together in the first Norton Critical Edition of *John Donne's Poetry*. Bennett indicated Lewis's real problem with Donne's poetry may be that it is unlike the love poetry of Spenser and other poets he admired deeply. She responded to several specific points and corrected Lewis's reading of "Aire and Angels."

Marvin D. Hinten
Bowling Green State University

Sir Arthur Conan Doyle (1859–1930)

The second paragraph of *The Magician's Nephew* notes that it begins in the time when "Mr. Sherlock Holmes was still living in Baker Street." Thus Lewis quietly paid tribute to one of the early influences on his writing career, the detective stories of Sir Arthur Conan Doyle.

The Lewis **family** received *Strand* magazine, in which the Sherlock Holmes stories began appearing about six years before Lewis's birth. After a lapse of years, during which Doyle wanted the series to end permanently, he started producing them again during Lewis's youth. One interesting incident, which may reveal the influence of Doyle, occurs in *Prince Caspian* when Lucy recognizes that the Pevensie children are indeed back in Cair Paravel by noting that the number of steps where they are exploring equals the number of steps to their old treasure chamber. This may be an allusion to the very first Sherlock Holmes story, in which Holmes tells Watson that knowing the number of steps up to their apartment is a sign of observational powers.

Marvin D. Hinten
Bowling Green State University

Also See: Rationality, Reason

Bibliography

Lewis, C. S. *The Magician's Nephew*.

"A Dream"

The Spectator. CLXXIII (28 July 1944): 77. Reprinted in *Present Concerns*.

This essay is a whimsical piece that details four (fictional) absurdities in real **war**time life, followed by an account of the dream that (fictionally) ensued. Lewis was pointing out the danger that those who are given or seize authority in an emergency will transform the purpose of their inferiors after the emergency is over, rather than surrender their authority. A funny piece on a serious theme.

John Bremer

Dreams

Like many children, C. S. Lewis as a child suffered from nightmares; his were often about giant insects. Like many creative writers, Lewis continued to have an active dreamlife and took an interest in it. He said he consciously pruned and polished creative ideas that came from his unconscious much as he evaluated dream material when he was awake. Some elements from his dreams found their way into his fiction; he had a series of dreams about lions just before he wrote *The Lion, the Witch and the Wardrobe*.

In 1939 he stated in *The Personal Heresy* that everything that is real is a real something, although it may not be what it pretends to be. "What pretends to be a crocodile may be a (real) dream; what pretends at the breakfast-table to be a dream may be a (real) lie."

Like many other authors through the centuries, Lewis set some of his fiction in dreams. He did this first in his earliest prose book, ***The Pilgrim's Regress***, in which he pretended to dream the semi-autobiographical adventures of a protagonist named John. (When John dreamed in the story, Lewis was describing a fictional dream within a fictional dream.) Twelve years later he published ***The Great Divorce***, in which readers aren't told until the very end that the story was all a dream. Dreams of characters played important parts in his space trilogy, his Narnian Chronicles, and his favorite of his books, ***Till We Have Faces***. Lewis believed even bad dreams could do good.

Lewis once remarked about dream amnesia that by the time a man is sufficiently awake for a clear description, the thing he wants to describe is gone; but he often recalled his dreams. He recorded some in his diary. (See ***All My Road Before Me: The Diary of C. S. Lewis 1922–1927***.) For example on February 1, 1923, he had a nightmare that turned out to be precognitive about an event that later triggered his unfinished novel called ***The Easley Fragment***.

Lewis took an interest in dreams of his friends and relatives, and he told them about some of his own. Most of his surviving dream accounts can be found in his letters. For example, he described dreams about being chased by Germans and by a corpse, finding an acquaintance's head in one of his kitchen cupboards, and missing his train because he was absorbed in a new story by **Edith Nesbit**. In a dream about his deceased father, the two agreed that his father's body was only an appearance, then went on chatting cheerily.

Lewis was well aware of Freudian dream interpretation, but after a strong initial interest in **Sigmund Freud** in his early adulthood, he discounted much psychoanalytic theory. In his essay **"Psycho-Analysis and Literary Criticism,"** he refutes the idea that wish fulfillment and infantile sexuality account for so much as contemporary Freudians claim.

In the last book he ever wrote, ***Letters to Malcolm***, he said, "A dream ceases to be an illusion as soon as we wake. It is a real dream, and it may also be instructive."

Kathryn Lindskoog

Also See: Carl Jung

John Dryden (1631–1700)

John Dryden was the foremost British poet of the Restoration Period (1660–1700), a prolific playwright and "the father of English criticism." His religious life moved from skeptic to fideist, deist, Anglican, then Catholic—changes chronicled in his poems. One might expect Lewis to praise him highly for this reason alone. Lewis would allow that Dryden was a "genius" but called him a "great, flawed poet." He did well with **satire**, but failed to execute his own designs in most other kinds of poems. His faults included a failure to exert his strength of intellect and invention, breaches in tone, and weakness in design and conception. Though Dryden, like others in his period and most in the following century, praised the classical writers and consciously attempted to wear their mantle, Lewis maintained that they are very unclassical, failing at forms like tragedy and **epic**, and embracing unclassical elements like satire, wit, and the couplet form.

Lewis's only sustained treatment of Dryden is in his essay **"Shelley, Dryden, and Mr. Eliot."**

Wayne Martindale
Wheaton College

Also See: Anglicanism, Poetry, Roman Catholicism

Dundela Villas

After **Albert Lewis** and **Florence Lewis** were married on August 29, 1894, they moved into one of a pair of semi-detached houses in **Belfast** known as Dundela. The home was owned by Albert's brother-in-law at the time. Both **Warren Lewis** and C. S. Lewis were born in the home. In April 1905 the family moved to a larger home called **Little Lea**.

Jeffrey D. Schultz

Bibliography

Sayer, George. *Jack: C. S. Lewis and His Times*. Wheaton, IL: Crossway, 1988.

Dymer

Originally published under the pseudonym Clive Hamilton. London: J. M. Dent, 1926. First US edition, New York: E. P. Dutton, 1926. Reprinted as by C. S. Lewis. London: J. M. Dent, 1950. US edition, New York: Macmillan, 1950.

Dymer is Lewis's most important poem, both because of the effort he put into writing it and because of its ambitious narrative. Though even he judged it harshly, it deserves a careful reading; it is his supreme effort at writing narrative **poetry**, that kind of poetry by which he hoped to achieve poetic acclaim. Seeing himself in the tradition of Homer, Malory, **Spenser**, the Pearl Poet, **Milton**, Shelley, **Wordsworth**, and Tennyson, Lewis longed to write a significant, sustained piece of narrative poetry.

We know from his diary that he worked on various prose versions of *Dymer* as early as 1916 when he was just seventeen and living with his tutor, **William T. Kirkpatrick**; this version has not survived but was entitled *The Redemption of Ask*. The version that we have was begun in 1922 and completed in 1925. Published in 1926, seven years after *Spirits in Bondage*, *Dymer* continues on with several themes of *Spirits in Bondage*, though it attempts to break new ground as well.

Critics have for the most part avoided *Dymer*; some who have worked on the poem offer momentary insights but often fail to provide an intelligible or objective reading of the poem. For instance, Richard Hodgens admits to disliking narrative poetry, so we are not surprised to find him saying, "Modern as I am, I cannot adopt a fighting attitude on behalf of Lewis's narrative poems in particular. I must admit that I have not enjoyed reading the poems as much as I have enjoyed reading almost all of his fiction or, in fact, almost all of his prose." **Chad Walsh** is more helpful in identifying three themes: that totalitarian **utopia** and lawless anarchy are equally undesirable; the renunciation of wishful thinking; and the perils of the occult. However, he sees no coherence: "All in all, the various themes twisting through *Dymer* are loosely connected indeed." Michael Slack offers a potentially fruitful reading by noting the connection between the search for **joy** (Sehnsucht) in *Dymer* and Platonic Eros, but his essay is not comprehensive nor systematic; we are left with a peculiarly fragmented view of the poem. Still another critical reading worthy of note is the essay by Patrick Murphy. While not as helpful as some because he is too wedded to reader-response theory, Murphy is to be commended for urging readers to give *Dymer* a fair reading "as a poem, separate unto itself, and not as a comparative adjunct to whatever else one finds most dear written by Lewis."

By far the best piece of writing on *Dymer* is **George Sayer**'s essay "C. S. Lewis's *Dymer*." Sayer offers the most comprehensive analysis of the poem to date, and he presents helpful background information. For example, he notes the philosophical influences working on Lewis when he was writing the poem. Crucial, however, is his unified reading. According to Sayer, "the main subject of *Dymer* . . . is without doubt the temptation of fantasies—fantasies of **love**, lust, and power." Unlike other critics, Sayer then attempts a thoughtful analysis of the entire poem, rather than focusing upon some obscure idea or theme. His essay is must reading for anyone interested in a helpful interpretation of *Dymer*.

Two other insights on *Dymer* are noteworthy, both found in the prefaces of *Narrative Poems*. **Walter Hooper**'s "Preface" offers little commentary on *Dymer*, but it does offer some bibliographical background and attempts to put the poem in the context of the other poems printed in the book. More important is Lewis's own "Preface by the Author to the 1950 Edition." Although we must be careful to accept an author's discussion of his own work, readers are well advised to read this piece carefully, particularly since Lewis, by 1950 a seasoned Christian, felt compelled to permit this poetic child of his pagan youth to be reissued. Moreover, in the preface he provides a summary of the important ideas influencing him when he was composing the poem.

Summary of Dymer

Canto I

Dymer, a nineteen-year-old student living in a repressed, constrained, totalitarian state, stimulated by Nature's fecundity, rebels against his situation, murders his teacher in class, and escapes to **Nature**. There, he strips off his clothes and wanders about in a mad desire for desire. In a forest clearing he discovers and enters a castle.

Canto II

Inside he finds great **beauty**, further exciting his desire. After admiring his naked reflection in a great mirror, he dresses himself in rich clothing he finds nearby. Haughty and yet guilty at the same time, he eats and drinks at a rich banquet table; the result is that he is further stimulated to fulfill his lust for desire. Passing through a low curtain, he enters a dark room where an unidentified girl slips into his arms and fulfills his sexual desires.

Canto III

The morning after, still never having seen her face, he gets up and goes outside to enjoy the morning. When he decides to return to his beloved, all ways into the castle are blocked by a hideously ugly old hag. He tries to **reason** with the hag, threatens her, boasts of his might, and finally throws himself against her in an effort to pass. He is struck senseless and stumbles away, broken, humbled, crushed.

Canto IV

Dymer wanders about during an awful tempest, distraught over his loss. He hears someone groaning and discovers a man whose hands and feet have been cut off; from this man Dymer learns that his personal rebellion had led to a social rebellion in his city headed by someone named Bran. Following Dymer's example, Bran led the rebels against the city's loyalists and a savage battle took place. Before he dies, the mutilated man curses Dymer.

Canto V

Dymer runs away in horror and falls into a nightmarish sleep; when he awakens, he cries out in his loneliness, feeling even more guilt for his past. He curses his fate, defends his actions, and tries to shift the blame to someone other than himself. He contemplates death but changes his mind after seeing a sunrise and continues his wanderings. Descending into a wild ravine with luscious undergrowth, he tumbles down in exhaustion; he dreams again, hears a bird singing, and awakens encouraged.

Canto VI

Reconciled with himself, he hears a lark and searches for food. In a house he meets a magician; while they eat, Dymer tells his story. The magician offers to help Dymer control his **dreams**; though Dymer refuses, the magician tells him the only way to rediscover his beloved is through dreams. Dymer believes his only hope of seeing her is through repentance; the magician belittles him for such morality and convinces Dymer to drink from his cup of dreams.

Canto VII

The magician joins Dymer in drinking. While Dymer's dreams are somewhat unsettling, the magician's dreams are fantastic and take him to the verge of madness. Dymer awakens and relates a dream of meeting his beloved; although he was initially enchanted by her in the dream, he came to see that the beloved of his dream was actually himself. He was in love with his own lust. The magician, descending into total madness, pulls out a gun and gives Dymer a terrible wound as he flees from the magician's house.

Canto VIII

When he becomes conscious, Dymer feels sharp pain in his side from his wound. Turning, he sees what he thinks is his beloved. She will not give her name but does say she understands his **pain.** In their conversation he learns that she is simply his desire for desire; she became what he wanted. He laments his lost love, longing for human affection. His soul dialogues with his body momentarily before he drags himself to a tower in a graveyard.

Canto IX

A great wind begins to blow and he meets an angelic guardian. Dymer offers to join the guardian but is rebuffed since he is mortal. The guardian tells him of a fabulous monster and his parentage. As he listens to the story, Dymer realizes that the monster is the offspring of his sexual encounter with the unidentified girl. Confronting his own son in battle, Dymer is killed. After his death, Nature appears to be reborn and his son becomes a god.

Don W. King
Montreat College

Also See: Allegory, Sex

Bibliography

Hodgens, Richard. "Notes on *Narrative Poems*." *CSL: The Bulletin of the New York C. S. Lewis Society.* 7 no. 78 (April 1976): 1–14.

Murphy, Patrick. "C. S. Lewis's *Dymer*: Once More with Hesitation." *CSL: The Bulletin of the New York C. S. Lewis Society.* 17 no. 200 (June 1986): 1–8. Republished in *The Poetic Fantastic: Studies in an Evolving Genre.* Patrick Murphy and Vernon Hyles (eds). Westport, CT: Greenwood Press, 1989.

Sayer, George. "C. S. Lewis's *Dymer*." *VII: An Anglo-American Literary Review.* 11 (1980).

Slack, Michael. "Sehnsucht and the Platonic Eros in *Dymer*." *CSL: The Bulletin of the New York C. S. Lewis Society.* 11 no. 130 (August 1980): 3–7.

Walsh, Chad. *The Literary Legacy of C. S. Lewis.* New York: Harcourt Brace Jovanovich, 1979.

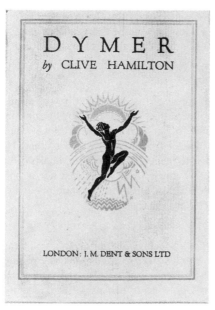

U.K. First Edition

Henry Victor "Hugo" Dyson (1896–1975)

Hugo Dyson, an **Inkling**, considered by Lewis to be one of "the immediate human causes of my conversion" (**Letters of C. S. Lewis**) was lecturer and tutor at the University of Reading (1921–45) and a fellow and tutor of Merton College, **Oxford** (1945–63). Originally introduced to Lewis by **Nevill Coghill**, Lewis described him to **Arthur Greeves** as one of his friends of the second class, on a level with his **friendship** with **J. R. R. Tolkien** (*They Stand Together*). Lewis expressed his appreciation for Dyson's help in the preface of *The Allegory of Love* and dedicated *Rehabilitations* to him.

Richard James
Burkesville Christian Church

Bibliography

Bratman, David. "Hugo Dyson: Inkling, Teacher, Bon Vivant." *Mythlore*. 21 no. 4 (Winter 1997): 19–34.

Dyson, H. V. D., and John Butt. *Augustans and Romantics, 1689–1830*. Introductions to English Literature: Volume 3. London: Cresset Press, 1940.

_____. "'The Old Cumberland Beggar' and the Wordsworthian Unities." *Essays on the Eighteenth Century, Presented to David Nichol Smith in Honour of His Seventieth Birthday*. London: Oxford University Press, 1945: 238–51.

_____. "The Emergence of Shakespeare's Tragedy." *Proceedings of the British Academy* 36 (1952): 69–93.

Havard, Robert E. "Philia: Jack at Ease." *C. S. Lewis at the Breakfast Table*. James T. Como (ed). New York: Harcourt Brace Jovanovich, 1992: 218–20.

Hooper, Walter. *C. S. Lewis: A Companion & Guide*. San Francisco: HarperCollins, 1996.

E

Eagle and Child

Affectionately known as the "Bird and Babe" or the "Bird and Baby," the Eagle and Child was the Oxford pub where the **Inklings** met beginning in 1939. The Inklings met in a little back room (the Rabbit Room) on Tuesday mornings until 1962 when the Rabbit Room was made part of the main bar. The group then moved to the Lamb and Flag.

Jeffrey D. Schultz

Bibliography

Sayer, George. *Jack: C. S. Lewis and His Times*. Wheaton, IL: Crossway, 1988.

The Easley Fragment or The Most Substantial People

In 1927 C. S. Lewis began his first novel, and well over 5,000 words have survived in Volume 9 (pages 291–300) of the eleven-volume Lewis Family Papers at the **Marion E. Wade Center**. This intriguing fragment combines Lewis's masterful style and readability with his usual focus on **truth**, character, and **ethics**. It is proof that by 1927 Lewis was a master of description and dialog and was passionately concerned about the cure of souls, his own and others'. Although he knew practically nothing about medicine, Lewis portrayed himself as Dr. Easley, an earnest young medical doctor from Bristol who needed to separate illusions from reality. The story is about two kinds of pathology: ethical and religious.

Chapter 1 satirically traces the neglect and exploitation Easley and his widowed mother have suffered at the hands of their supposedly poor relatives in **Belfast**. Now his cousin Scrabo Easley has summoned him to meet the family and help with Aunt Mary, and he makes the overnight crossing on the Liverpool ferry. On the way, Hughie McClinnichan, a worldly businessman, cheats him. McClinnichan knows Easley's relatives and reveals that they are "very substantial" and live among "the most substantial people." The story revolves around the substantiality or insubstantiality of people, their claims, and their beliefs. (Later this became the theme of *The Great Divorce*, in which the unredeemed are as ghostly as in **Dante**'s *Inferno* and the redeemed are "solid people.") Thus the ideal title for the Easley fragment is "The Most Substantial People."

In the second part of the story Dr. Easley is trapped in Belfast, arguing about spiritual evil and **hell** with sinister Reverend Bonner, who is killing Aunt Mary with a psychotic terror of hell. But who is more deluded and endangered, Lewis asks: those blithely indifferent to eternal damnation or those obsessed by it? (Lewis actually considered writing a thesis on the **metaphysics** of modern **psychology**.)

This plot was inspired by Lewis's nightmare experience with Dr. **John Askins** and Dr. Robert Askins in February and March of 1923. A full account is in the Lewis Family Papers, and part is in *All My Road Before Me: The Diary of C. S. Lewis 1922–1927*. For Lewis's philosophical and metaphysical view of reality in 1927, see letters to **Owen Barfield** in the Wade Center, *The Pilgrim's Regress*, and *Surprised by Joy*.

Until managers of C. S. Lewis's literary estate allow publication or photocopying of "The Easley Fragment," it must be read in the Wade Center, the **Bodleian Library**, or **Walter Hooper**'s alma mater, the University of North Carolina at Chapel Hill. A close rendition of the story, preceded and followed by analysis, is available in Chapter 5 of *Light in the Shadowlands: Protecting the Real C. S. Lewis*.

Kathryn Lindskoog

Also See: Ethics and Morality, Good and Evil, Immorality

"Edmund Spenser"

Fifteen Poets. London: Oxford University Press, 1941: 40–43. Retitled "On Reading *The Faerie Queene*" and reprinted in *Studies in Medieval and Renaissance Literature*.

Written in 1941, this essay advises that the best way to meet **Edmund Spenser** is in a very large, preferably illustrated, edition of *The Faerie Queene*, on a wet day, between the ages of twelve and sixteen. Failing that, it offers some suggestions and expectations. First, start with *The Faerie Queene*, the great poetic romance, and think of it as a book for "devout, prolonged, and leisurely perusal." The illustrations (real or imagined) will be of two kinds—**Renaissance**, gorgeous, florid ones or those of "homespun." Expect the latter, but enjoy the "cloth of gold" when it comes. The poem is not really Medieval, and yet those who enjoy it regard it as "the very consummation" of the **Medieval world**. This is the paradox of Spenser—the last of the Medieval poets and the first of the romantic medievalists—for he denies "in his own person, the breach between the Middle Ages and the Renaissance." If the characters seem vaguely familiar, it is because of the moral **allegory**, the embodiment in potent forms of "moral and psychological realities of the utmost simplicity and profundity."

John Bremer

Also See: Literary Theory, Poetry

"Edmund Spenser 1552–99"

Major British Writers, Vol. I. G. B. Harrison (ed). New York: Harcourt, Brace & Co., 1954: 91–103. Reprinted in *Studies in Medieval and Renaissance Literature*.

This introduction (of about 10,000 words) to **Edmund Spenser** was written by Lewis in 1953 for the first volume of *Major British Writers*. It provides a sketch of Spenser's education and his resistance to the two fashionable intellectual movements of his day—Puritanism and humanism (although these terms did not mean in his day what they mean to us). According to Lewis, Spenser devoted his "whole poetical career to a revival, or prolongation, of those medieval motifs which humanism wished to abolish." Spenser spent many years on government service in Ireland and came to love the countryside; his absence from England precluded him from spending his energies on the fashions and intrigues of the Court, and his "exile" gave him time. *The Faerie Queene* should perhaps be regarded as "the work of one who is turning into an Irishman."

Lewis thought that English **poetry** was "in a deplorable condition," when Spenser and Sidney began writing. They had to struggle out of the "horrible swamp of dull verbiage, ruthlessly over-emphatic meter, and screaming rhetoric." This can be seen in Spenser's minor poems. Lewis regarded Spenser's major work, *The Faerie Queene*, as his continuation of the Medieval tradition of chivalrous romance. As a scholar, Spenser knew little about Medieval literature according to Lewis, but he was acutely aware of the elements of the Middle Ages that were still living around him—in tournaments, heraldry, pageants, and symbolical pictures. He also knew the **epic** through Boiardo, Ariosto, and Tasso, and by studying them he turned his back on the humanists (who would have preferred Virgil as a model). Spenser, believing that the poet ought to be a moral teacher, wanted his national epic to be "a continued **allegory**." For his work, he invented a new stanza—nine lines, with a concluding alexandrine. Lewis discussed, in turn, the polyphonic narrative technique, the double allegory of "moral" and "historical," and the texture of the language. He concluded with an appraisal of the Christian and Platonic elements in Spenser's long but unfinished poem.

John Bremer

Also See: Medieval World, Plato

Bibliography

Lewis, C. S. *The Discarded Image*; "Neoplatonism in the Poetry of Spenser"; "Spenser's Cruel Cupid"; *Spenser's Images of Life*.

Education

One might imagine modern education is like a huge kettle of vegetable soup tended by multiple chefs. Each chef adds special ingredients designed to meet educational dietary needs or please student palates or promote market interests. The recipe is constantly in flux. C. S. Lewis, facing the educational squabbles of his day, remembered when only the seven liberal arts went into the brew. He disliked the new cookery and said so.

Of primary importance to Lewis was the question, "What **values** should be taught to students?" His answer was unequivocal: the objective values that differentiate between right and wrong and thus provide the true way to assess attitudes and behavior. These values, which historically had undergirded education, were being eroded through textbook espousal of subjective values based on feelings. Lewis contended that this approach doomed its advocates because it stripped them of their rational and spiritual motives and left only impulse strength as the grounds for preferring one response over another. Gone was any reliable authority for making value judgments.

To avoid the societal disintegration from subjectivism, each generation must pass on the laws and duties that span the centuries and cultures—the **Tao**. This transmission should occur through a propagation process as uncontrived as the way old birds teach young birds to fly. But, Lewis cautioned, teachers cannot pass on what they do not possess.

In alarming contrast to propagation stood the conditioning methodology of subjectivists. By using scientific techniques and following governmental directives, educators had the power to program student attitudes. Because the conditioners had rejected the Tao, they could not be governed by it. Therefore, only their impulses, including irrational ones, could serve as justifications for molding student minds. With prophetic eyes, Lewis saw modern education adopting this approach.

As secondary schools began adapting to student needs and abilities, the question, "Should the educational system provide vocational training?" became important. Lewis took a dim view of vocational courses because they were narrowly directed at skill acquisition rather than the overall mental and spiritual growth of the individual. Lewis was a thoroughgoing classicist who viewed the pursuit of knowledge as a distinctly humanizing endeavor. Through it—assuming the Tao was foundational—came the development of alert, interesting people of good taste and sensibility, those who served the community and used leisure well. These

he saw as free human beings. Vocational courses, on the other hand, only prepared students for work, to be slaves, he said. No society could long survive the dehumanizing effects of vocationalization.

Decisions about the curriculum and teaching methods were at stake in a third question: "How can academic rigor be maintained?" During the 1940s, when Lewis wrote much on education, he argued against some proposals for change and others that already had been implemented. A recurring point is that the changes would lower academic standards: increasing the number of courses would mean less depth of instruction; offering electives would encourage students to take subjects they like and that would reward them for meager attainment; stressing literary appreciation over close textual study would give readers no real knowledge, only a deceptive feeling of culture and accomplishment; authorizing English to be taught by those who were not specialists would drop the educational quality to that of the popular press. Rigor can only be spelled as diligence.

Unfortunately many of the predictions have materialized. If Lewis were a professor today, he would find the academic soup even more distasteful than before.

Carolyn Keefe
West Chester University

Bibliography

Lewis, C. S. *The Abolition of Man*; *"De Descriptione Temporum"*; "Democratic Education"; "Equality"; "Is English Doomed?"; "Learning in War-Time"; "Lilies that Fester"; "On the Transmission of Christianity"; "Our English Syllabus"; "The Parthenon and the Optative"; "The Poison of Subjectivism"; "Screwtape Proposes a Toast."

"The Efficacy of Prayer"

The Atlantic Monthly. CCIII (January 1959): 59–61. Reprinted in *The World's Last Night* and *Fern-Seed and Elephants*.

After relating personal experiences (one trivial, one more dramatic) involving the seeming power of **prayer**, Lewis addresses the question of whether any evidence can prove prayer's efficacy. **Natural laws**, like gravitation, are proven by their unbroken uniformity. Prayer, however, is a request; therefore, says Lewis, the "success" of the prayer cannot be contingent on whether it is always answered. Neither is prayer provable by experiment—as in having a prayer team pray for one set of patients and not another—because the motive for prayer would be compromised in such a trial. Thus empirical proof is unobtainable; furthermore, as with our requests to fellow humans, we can never know whether the thing prayed for would not have come about in any case, with or without the request. As in personal human relations, however, we do not question granted requests—acceptances of **marriage** proposals and the like. Believers who know **God** gain assurance that God hears and sometimes grants prayers, and they obtain that assurance without benefit of experiment or tabulation. As in his article **"On Obstinacy in Belief,"** Lewis here drove home the point that God is not an ineffable "force," not a disinterested First Cause, but rather a Someone with whom the believer has a personal relationship.

Richard A. Hill
Taylor University

Also See: Materialism, Miracles, Prayer, Science, Spirituality, Supernatural

Bibliography

Lewis, C. S. "On Obstinacy in Belief."

T[homas] S[tearns] Eliot (1888–1965)

T. S. Eliot was a Nobel Prize-winning poet, critic, playwright, editor, and publisher. Associated with the Modernist movement, Eliot's poetry includes such works as *The Waste Land* (1922), *Ash Wednesday* (1930), and *The Four Quartets* (1935–1942). Like Lewis, Eliot converted to **Christianity** as an adult and subsequently joined the Church of England. Their shared interests, however, did not lead to professional collegiality, for Lewis detested the Modernist innovations apparent in Eliot's **poetry**. According to Lewis's friend and biographer **George Sayer**, "He tended to regard the new poetry with its formlessness and lack of poetic diction as a revolutionary movement deliberately directed against the traditions of English poetry." Although Lewis admired Eliot's play, *Murder in the Cathedral* (1935), he attacked much of Eliot's poetry and **literary criticism**, frequently citing *The Love Song of J. Alfred Prufrock* (1917) in which Eliot likens evening to "a patient etherised upon a table." Lewis found Eliot's **imagery** so distasteful that he later wrote his own poetic response (*A Confession*). In *A Preface to Paradise Lost*, published in 1942, Lewis argued that the role of poetry is to teach its readers proper reactions ("stock responses") to universal themes such as **love**, death, and virtue. He maintained that modern poets including Eliot have abandoned their responsibility to elicit "that elementary rectitude of human response," much to the detriment of contemporary society. Hoping to expose what he termed the "Eliotic" style, Lewis and several friends submitted nonsensical poems to *The Cri-*

terion, the influential journal Eliot edited, but their poems were never accepted for publication. Not until 1958, when the Archbishop of Canterbury invited both men to serve on the Commission to Revise the Psalter, did they become friends. Indeed, Lewis developed a genuine liking for the man whose poetry he had so long reviled. Ironically, perhaps, Lewis's most personal work, *A Grief Observed*, was submitted for publication to Faber and Faber in 1961, the publishing house where Eliot served as director. Although Lewis never fully appreciated Eliot's poetry, he recognized that their shared faith ultimately transcended their differences, observing, "I agree with him about matters of such moment that all literary questions are, in comparison, trivial."

Lynn Summer
Georgia State University

Bibliography

Eliot, T. S. *Collected Poems: 1909–1962*. New York: Harcourt Brace & Company, 1963.

_____. *Murder in the Cathedral*. New York: Harcourt, Brace & World, Inc., 1935.

Gordon, Lyndall. *Eliot's Early Years*. Oxford: Oxford University Press, 1977.

_____. *Eliot's New Life*. New York: Farrar Straus Giroux, 1988.

Lewis, C. S. *A Preface to Paradise Lost*.

Sayer, George. *Jack: A Life of C. S. Lewis*. 2nd ed. Wheaton, IL: Crossway, 1994.

Tetreault, James. "C. S. Lewis and T. S. Eliot." *CSL: The Bulletin of the New York C. S. Lewis Society*. 8 (December 1976): 1–5.

_____. "Parallel Lines: C. S. Lewis and T. S. Eliot." *Renascence: Essays on Value in Literature*. 38 (Summer 1986): 256–69.

"The Empty Universe"

See entry on *The Hierarchy of Heaven and Earth* (Preface)

Encounter with Light

See entry on Letters to a Member of the Church of the Covenant (Letters)

"The End of the Wine"

Punch. 213 (December 3, 1947): 538 (under the pseudonym Nat Whilk). Revised and retitled as "The Last of the Wine" and reprinted in *Poems* and *Collected Poems*.

A group of wine bibbers sigh as they finish the last drop of a fine vintage and defend themselves against a pedant who wants to chide them for their indulgence.

They tell a story suggesting the life-sustaining effects of wine, particularly its penchant to recall the glories of civilized life in the midst of primitive society.

Don W. King
Montreat College

English Literary Criticism: The Medieval Phase (Book Review)

The Oxford Magazine. LXII (30 February 1944): 158.

This brief review credited Atkins with having undertaken the task of sorting through copious and often unilluminating writings to find what he admits is "very small beer." Apparently "the history of criticism is at first merely the history of rhetoric."

Anne Gardner

Also See: Language/Rhetoric, Literary Criticism

Bibliography

Atkins, J. W. H. *English Literary Criticism: The Medieval Phase.*

English Literature in the Sixteenth Century, Excluding Drama

Oxford: Clarendon Press, 1954. Retitled *Poetry and Prose in the Sixteenth Century.*

English Literature in the Sixteenth Century, Excluding Drama is C. S. Lewis's volume in The Oxford History of English Literature. (In 1990, Oxford University Press abandoned its plans for a half volume on Anglo-Saxon literature in the series and retitled and renumbered the volumes: Lewis's book, originally Vol. III, is now Vol. IV and is titled *Poetry and Prose in the Sixteenth Century.*) Lewis was asked to write the volume in June 1935; it was finally published in 1954.

Lewis's purpose was simply to write a literary history of the 16th century. In *An Experiment in Criticism* (1961), Lewis discusses the value of the literary historians, who told him "what works exist" and put the works "in their setting[,] thus showing [him] what demands they were meant to satisfy"; he continues: "They have headed me off from false approaches, taught me what to look for, enabled me in some degree to

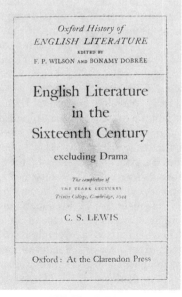

Oxford History of
ENGLISH LITERATURE
EDITED BY
F. P. WILSON AND BONAMY DOBRÉE

English Literature
in the
Sixteenth Century

excluding Drama

The completion of
THE CLARK LECTURES
Trinity College, Cambridge, 1944

C. S. LEWIS

Oxford : At the Clarendon Press

U.K. First Edition

put myself into the frame of mind of those to whom they were addressed. This has happened because such historians on the whole have taken **[Matthew] Arnold**'s advice by getting themselves out of the way. They are concerned far more with describing books than with judging them."

In Lewis's book, he can be said to give his readers the social setting of his period in his "Introduction: New Learning and New Ignorance"; he then describes the literature that is there in three books and an epilogue. Of course, it is not quite that simple. Lewis's introduction is polemical, and he certainly evaluates the literature as well as describes it.

This introduction begins with a brief description of the three divisions of the literature that will follow in the succeeding chapters: Late Medieval, "Drab," and "Golden." Lewis then denied that the Renaissance, as he defined it ("the recovery of Greek and the substitution of Augustan for medieval Latin"), had much effect on the good literature at the end of the century. His survey of the major ideas of the century takes up these topics: Copernican astronomy, **magic** vs. astrology, Platonism, **science**, concepts of man (2–14); the New World and related discoveries, the Natural Man (14–17); humanism and Puritanism, the Divine Right of Kings, **Natural Law,** Machiavellianism (17–52); Stoicism, Cynicism, Magnanimity, the word *Renaissance* (52–56). The rest of the introduction deals with social, political, and economic conditions; but this catalogue of ideas illustrates well enough the complaints against Lewis's survey. The critics reacted to two topics, primarily—his refusal to use the word *Renaissance* for the period (Lewis held it had been used for too many topics to be useful) and his attack on the humanists. Lewis may have been led by his religious beliefs into both of these positions, refusing to say there was a glorious "rebirth" after the Medieval period, as if the Christian culture of the Middle Ages needed to be overcome; and refusing to see the extreme humanists (whom Lewis took as typical), who tried to revive classical Latin and ignore Medieval Latin, as valuable. For example, Helen Gardner, in her obituary of Lewis, writes of the latter: "The introduction is devoted to proving by skilfully selected quotations and a complete refusal of imaginative sympathy that Humanism was inhumane.... It is never suggested that reforms in education, and the Humanist insistence on the aesthetic merits of ancient literature, could have any connexion with the appearance of our 'Golden Age.'"

On the other hand, one finds a comment like this from **J. A. W. Bennett**: "In the ten years since [Lewis's volume], ... specialist works ... have demonstrated ... the validity of Lewis's charges against the arch-humanists."

Book I, "Late Medieval," discusses the literature in the first of the century in England and Scotland. These have excited few quarrels. That on Scottish literature covers such good poets as Gavin Douglas, William Dunbar, and David Lyndsay; that on English, such poets (all poor except Skelton) as Stephen Hawes, Alexander Barclay, John Skelton, and John Heywood. Perhaps it is worth noting that the epigraph to and the title of Lewis's *That Hideous Strength* came from Lyndsay's *Monarche*.

Book II, "'Drab,'" has three sections: Religious Controversy and Translation, Drab Age Verse, and Drab and Transitional Prose. Yvor Winters voices a common complaint about this and the next section: "Lewis sees the sixteenth century in terms of two schools: the Drab and the Golden. He says that these two terms have no evaluative connotations; but of course they have such connotations, as everyone who has read the book has remarked. He would have done better to employ the terms of the age, to refer to the plain style and to the sugared or eloquent style: he would thus have come closer to seeing things as they were seen at the time and perhaps as they really were."

The other major complaint about Book II has been that Lewis biased his coverage toward the Anglicans. Peter Milward suggests the controversy between Sir Thomas More and William Tyndale is loaded in Lewis's handling by his incidental comments. Milward points out that Lewis covered John Foxe's *Book of Martyrs* (a book about the inquisition in England under Queen Mary), but even gets the first name wrong of Thomas Harding who answered Foxe and does not mention Robert Persons who refuted (says Milward) Foxe on contemporary evidence. Milward also points to a contemporary statement that John Jewel (Anglican) and Thomas Harding (Catholic) were like Demosthenes and Aeschines—Lewis discussed the writings of the first but not the second in their controversy. Milward sums up: this book "is throughout both personal and partial, reflecting more clearly than any other of [Lewis's] books the author's own religious leanings." Milward's position may be overstated—Lewis disliked religious controversy and so may have avoided some full treatments of topics, and Lewis wrote in his book, "I have at least intended to be impartial"—but some unconscious bias seems to remain.

In Book II, the other religious writers and topics covered are Dean Colet, John Fisher, Hugh Latimer, Thomas Cranmer, John Knox, various biblical translators, and *The Book of Common Prayer*. The poets and poetic works discussed are Sir Thomas Wyatt; Henry Howard, Earl of Surrey; the *Mirror for Magistrates*; various translators; minor poets; and George Gascoigne. The prose writers (in addition to Foxe and Jewel) are Sir Thomas Elyot, Edward Hall, Roger Ascham, John Cheke, Raphael Holinshed's *Chronicles,* John Lyly, and a number of minor figures—writers of dialogues, histories, travel literature, translated fiction, and the like.

Book III, "Golden," consists of three sections: Sir Philip Sidney and **Edmund Spenser**, Prose in the "Golden" Period, and Verse in the "Golden" Period. The debate about the titular term has been mentioned, but few critics (except Yvor Winters, who preferred poetry in the plain style) have complained of the other content of this book. The section on prose writers covers a number of minor pamphleteers, Robert Green, the writers of the Martin Marprelate controversy, Thomas Nashe, various minor fiction writers, a few poetic theorists, two writers on witchcraft, Richard Hakluyt's *Principal Navigations,* a number of religious controversialists, and Richard Hooker. The discussion of poets is multitudinous, but the major topics are the discussions of satire, lyrics, mythological-erotic epyllions, sonnet sequences, some translations, didactic poetry, heroic epistles, and historical epics; the major poets (beyond Sidney and Spenser, who got their own section) are Christopher Marlowe, William Shakespeare, George Chapman, Samuel Daniel, and Michael Drayton. (Marlowe and Shakespeare are not considered as dramatists, as the title of Lewis's book indicates.)

The "Epilogue: New Tendencies" has a brief discussion of three developments in literature at the end of the century: prose, with mention of the early work of Francis Bacon; the Metaphysical poetry, in Guillaume de Salluste du Bartas, Robert Southwell, and John Donne; and a type of counterpointed poetry, in the lyrics of Thomas Campion. (It seems odd that Lewis does not mention Southwell's most famous lyric, "The Burning Babe," but sometimes Lewis may be seeking fresh works to discuss.)

This survey has omitted the wit and intelligence of Lewis in order to mention the controversial aspects; but the sheer outlining of the scope of Lewis's book implies how successful it is in offering the literary history that Lewis agreed to write.

Joe R. Christopher
Tarleton State College

Also See: Literary Criticism, Literary Theory

Bibliography

Milward, Peter, S. J. *A Challenge to C. S. Lewis.* Madison and Teaneck: Fairleigh Dickinson University Press, 1995.
Watson, George, ed. Critical Thought Series: 1: Critical Essays on C. S. Lewis. Aldershot, England: Scolar Press, 1992.

"The English Prose *Morte*"

Essays on Malory. J. A. W. Bennett (ed). Oxford: Clarendon Press, 1963: 7–28.

Written in 1962, this reviewed the work of Eugene Vinaver on Sir Thomas Malory, author of the 15th-century English romance about **King Arthur**, *Morte D'Arthur*. Lewis pointed out that the discoveries of the previous fifty years about Malory and his text printed by Caxton in 1485 had "thrown up" five paradoxes: 1. While the work is a mirror of virtue, the author appears little better than a criminal. 2. The work is full of marvels, but Malory seems to have labored to eliminate them. 3. The work uses a polyphonic technique, which Malory detested. 4. While the Grail story sounds religious, Malory ignored or severed its connection with the final tragedy. 5. To many, Malory made a unity out of eight disparate stories, but it appears he never intended them to be taken together. It is paradoxical that a man, Malory, should have succeeded by his failure to realize every single intention he had when he wrote. Lewis discussed each paradox in turn, although "the net result is that Malory eludes me." Perhaps he can be found in his style, but unfortunately he has several styles. Our difficulty has to do with our assumptions about "the-author-and-his-book," which is different from the composite works of the Middle Ages.

John Bremer

Bibliography

Lewis, C. S. "The Morte D'Arthur."
Vinaver, Eugene. *The Works of Sir Thomas Malory.* Oxford: Clarendon Press, 1947.

Enlightenment

The Enlightenment is primarily a philosophical movement of the 18th century. Its roots are in France, but its branches are just about everywhere, especially in the West. Enlightenment thinkers, following Descartes, begin with skepticism about everything except their own ability to think. They typically assume that **truth** exists and attempt to ground all knowledge in the rational and logical, and rely heavily on the scientific method. Enlightenment thinkers tend to be skeptical about **religion** and institutional beliefs and customs, and typically pen their hope for human progress in political policy and control. While many enlightenment figures were atheists (like Voltaire in France), many were deists (believing in **God**, but not **Christ**—like Jefferson and Franklin in America).

While a teenager preparing to enter **Oxford University**, Lewis was thoroughly tutored in enlightenment thinking (rationalist, atheist, and materialist) by **W. T. Kirkpatrick**, who had also been his father's tutor. Lewis's rigorous training in logic, which would in time help to lead him to **Christianity** (see *Surprised by Joy*), contributed greatly to his effectiveness as a Christian apologist (defender). For over fifteen years, Lewis argued for the **faith** in regular debates of **Oxford's Socratic Club**, which was founded for the purpose of wrestling intellectually with the best atheistic and agnostic thinkers of the day. He also fought enlightenment thinking on its own grounds in sermons and lectures across England and even on BBC radio.

More importantly, his logic (as well as his **imagination**) was employed in books showing Christianity to be not only intellectually defensible, but superior to **materialism** and naturalism in explaining reality. Such books include *The Abolition of Man*, *Mere Christianity*, *The Problem of Pain*, and *Miracles*. In *Miracles* Lewis argued more extensively than anywhere else in his work that reason and mind are themselves **supernatural** or spiritual and evidences for God.

Wayne Martindale
Wheaton College

"Epanorthosis (for the end of Goethe's *Faust*)"

The Cambridge Review. 77 (May 26, 1956): 610 (under the pseudonym Nat Whilk). Revised and retitled as "Epigrams and Epitaphs, No. 15" and reprinted in *Poems* and *Collected Poems*.

The title of this poem refers to the idea of something being set right again. At the end of Goethe's drama, Faust escapes from Mephistopheles while he is trying to seduce **angels** who come to redeem Faust. Lewis's poem contrasted the vain futility of Mephistopheles' attempt with Faust's experience with the solidity of **heaven**, an idea seen elsewhere in Lewis, especially *The Great Divorce*.

Don W. King
Montreat College

Epic

Written on a grand scale, epics are noble in tone and reach sublime heights at times. The oldest epics are Homer's *Iliad* and *Odyssey*, but there are epic qualities in **Alighieri Dante**'s *Divine Comedy, The Nibelungenlied,* and *The Song of Roland* as well as **John Milton**'s *Paradise Lost*. Lewis was well acquainted with such works, and references to them are scattered throughout his writings. Epic qualities can also be seen in many of Lewis's own works, including the **Chronicles of Narnia**, *The Pilgrim's Regress*, *The Great Divorce*, and *Till We Have Faces*. One finds in them the same sublime moments and noble tone that one sees in the classical epics of Homer.

Ransom, the hero of Lewis's space trilogy, is a character of epic proportions. He has traveled to Malacandra (Mars) and Perelandra (Venus) and stood against the satanic Weston. In the struggle with the Un-Man, Ransom defeats Weston in an archetypal underground struggle. Ransom is the spiritual leader of the St. Anne's company in *That Hideous Strength,* and the members of that little community look to him for guidance and instruction. He discusses the subject of **marriage** with Jane Studdock, whose own marriage is troubled, and gets her to see marriage in a new light and to recognize the importance of co-inherence in the marriage relationship.

Aslan in the Narnia stories is of epic proportions as well. He is wise, noble, magnanimous, kind, and good—in fact, he represents **Christ**. He energizes his followers to do good and gives them strength and courage.

Orual in *Till We Have Faces* also has epic qualities. She is an astute queen, ruling wisely and well. But unfortunately she devours people, using her chief guard, Bardia, Redival her half-sister, Psyche (on whom she dotes), and the Fox, her old tutor. She gives him his freedom but does not let him feel free to return to Greece.

Corbin Scott Carnell
University of Florida

Also See: King Arthur, Heroes

"Epigrams and Epitaphs, No. 11"

See entry on "Epitaph" (June 6, 1942)

"Epigrams and Epitaphs, No. 12"

See entry on "On Receiving Bad News"

"Epigrams and Epitaphs, No. 14"

See entry on "Epitaph" (July 30, 1948)

"Epigrams and Epitaphs, No. 15"

See entry on "Epanorthosis (for the end of Goethe's *Faust*)"

"Epigrams and Epitaphs, No. 16"

See entry on "Epitaph in a Village Churchyard"

"Epigrams and Epitaphs, No. 17"

See entry on "Epitaph" (July 1949)

"Epitaph"

The Spectator. 181 (July 30, 1948): 142. Revised and retitled "Epigrams and Epitaphs, No. 14" and reprinted in *Poems* and *Collected Poems*.

An attack on the notion of **democracy**, Lewis suggested its greatest weakness is the incessant noise that endless discussions and debates cause. Using the constant drone of a wireless (radio) that cannot be turned off as a **symbol** for democracy's excessive clamoring, the speaker here would prefer one quiet spot in **hell** for a **heaven** filled with music.

Don W. King
Montreat College

"Epitaph"

The Month. 2 (July 1949): 8. Retitled "Epigrams and Epitaphs, No. 17" and reprinted in *Poems* and *Collected Poems*.

This epitaph finds the dead person both a microcosm of the universe and a promise of future life in Lenten lands. Lewis later reworked this epitaph at **Joy Davidman Lewis**'s request and used the revision as the epitaph marking her memorial at the Oxford Crematorium (see **"Epitaph for his Wife: Remember Helen Joy Davidman"**).

Don W. King
Montreat College

"Epitaph"

Time and Tide. 23 (June 6, 1942): 460. Retitled "Epigrams and Epitaphs, No. 11" and reprinted in *Poems* and *Collected Poems*.

Similar in style to a haiku, this brief World War II poem compares the delicate **beauty** of a woman with that of a bomb, ironically the very one that took her life.

Don W. King
Montreat College

Also See: War, Women

"Epitaph for his Wife: Remember Helen Joy Davidman"

Gilbert, Douglas, and Clyde S. Kilby. *C. S. Lewis: Images of His World*. Grand Rapids, MI: Eerdmans, 1973: 65 (holograph). This is a revision of "Epitaph" (July 1949) and serves as the epitaph marking her memorial at the Oxford Crematorium. Reprinted in *Collected Poems*.

This version of the epitaph is superior because of its simple directness. It makes a thoughtful and poignant connection between Joy's ashes and the promise of her renewal as she is reborn in **heaven**.

Don W. King
Montreat College

"Epitaph in a Village Churchyard"

Time and Tide. 30 (March 19, 1949): 272. Retitled "Epigrams and Epitaphs, No. 16" in *Poems* and *Collected Poems*.

The poem chronicles the lament by one who is ashamed that his grave marker reminds those who knew him of his true character. The speaker invites the onlooker to consider how painful that moment of self-revelation was to the dead man.

Don W. King
Montreat College

"Equality"

The Spectator. CLXXI (27 August 1943): 192. Reprinted in *Present Concerns*.

In this essay Lewis claimed that he was a democrat because he believed in the **Fall** of Man, whereas most people are democrats for the opposite reason. They believe that men are so wise and good they should govern themselves. Lewis replied that he didn't deserve "a share in governing a hen-roost, much less a nation," but that mankind is so fallen that no man can be trusted with unchecked power over his fellows. Equality is not good in itself—it offers no spiritual sustenance—but is like medicine, which is good when we are ill. "Legal and economic equality are absolutely necessary remedies for the Fall, and protection against cruelty." When equality becomes an ideal it stunts the mind and makes it envious, hating all superiority.

Under the outer covering of legal equality, our "deep and joyously accepted spiritual inequalities should be alive." In **marriage**, the laws should be equal, but "at some level consent to inequality, nay, delight in inequality, is an *erotic* necessity." But men have horribly abused their power over women in the past, and so equality is seen by wives as an ideal. The error has been to assimilate all forms of affection to **friendship**. "Friends look in the same direction. Lovers look at each other; that is, in opposite directions."

In Britain, legal equality has been reached without losing ceremonial **monarchy**. "Every intrusion of the spirit that says 'I'm as good as you' into our personal and spiritual lives is to be resisted just as jealously as every intrusion of bureaucracy or privilege into our **politics**."

John Bremer

Also See: Democracy

Bibliography

Williams, Terri. "C. S. Lewis on Equality." *Chronicle of the Portland C. S. Lewis Society*. 7 no. 3 (July-September 1978): 5–10.

"Eros on the Loose"

See entry on *The Erotic in Literature* (Book Review)

The Erotic in Literature (Book Review)

"Eros on the Loose." *The Observer*, (Weekend Review). 8905 (4 March 1962): 30.

Lewis noted that Loth does not seem to differentiate between copulation and pornography. Regarding this book as merely a "romp," Lewis suggested that the busy reader confine himself to the last three chapters and the appendix. It is here that the author is useful, because he gives an account of the law's attempts to define and control pornography.

Anne Gardner

Bibliography

Loth, David. *The Erotic in Literature*.

Essays Presented to Charles Williams (Preface)

London: Oxford University Press, 1947.

Lewis began his eulogy of **Charles Williams** by noting the breadth of Williams' friendships. He described Williams as a "romantic theologian," one who considers the theological implications of romance. Williams' outlook was generously expressed in his **poetry**, his criticism, and in his novels. Lewis described his first meeting with Williams and their **friendship** between 1939 and 1945. He saw his friend's character as complex, combining the skeptic and pessimist with the believer and optimist.

Lyle Smith
Biola University

"Essence"

Fear No More: A Book of Poems for the Present Time by Living English Poets. Cambridge: Cambridge University Press, 1940: 4. Reprinted in *Collected Poems*.

This poem was originally published anonymously. However, six copies of *Fear No More* contained an additional leaf giving the names of the authors of the poems; one of these is in the **Bodleian Library, Oxford**. Lewis's poem is an internal musing on thought and will and their relationship to the essence of self. Rejecting bifurcation, Lewis sought an integration of thought and will.

Don W. King
Montreat College

The Essential C. S. Lewis

Lyle W. Dorsett (ed). New York: Macmillan, 1988.

A collection of Lewis's writings.

"'The establishment must die and rot'"

"C. S. Lewis Discusses Science Fiction with Kingsley Amis," *SF Horizons*. 1 (Spring 1964): 5–12. Retitled "Unreal Estates" and reprinted in *Of Other Worlds, Of This and Other Worlds,* and *On Stories*.

This informal conversation between Lewis, Kingsley Amis, and Brian Aldiss was recorded on tape in Lewis's rooms in **Magdalene College, Cambridge**, on December 4, 1962. The "establishment" that must die and rot is what Lewis calls the "whole present dynasty" of "highbrow critics" that refuses to take **science fiction** seriously as a literary genre.

According to the discussants, science fiction allows the author to take readers to unknown places—what Aldiss calls "unreal estates." Worlds in space allow incorporation of characteristics that tell the story without dragging in a mass of realistic detail. Creating such imaginary places is the initial motive for writing; once they exist, something must happen in them. Lewis explained that *Perelandra* began as a mental picture of floating islands; once he built up the sort of world in which they could exist, something had to happen in it. Lewis did not begin the story with didactic intent.

Science fiction can deal broadly with issues of human destiny according to Lewis, Amis, and Aldiss. Religious themes are thus well-accommodated to the genre. However, the present dynasty of highbrow critics will have to die before criticism can change its emphases. Lewis said that he did not expect to outlive it, though he hoped Amis and Aldiss might.

Lyle Smith
Biola University

Also See: Fantasy, Literary Criticism, Literary Theory, Science, Space Travel

Bibliography

Sammons, Martha C. *"A Better Country" : The Worlds of Religious Fantasy and Science Fiction*. New York: Greenwood Press, 1988.

Ethics and Morality

Discussions of ethical theory, of norms for human action, and of the relation between religion and morality are scattered throughout Lewis's writings, including much of his fiction. Ethical theory is most explicitly treated in *The Abolition of Man*, Book I of *Mere Christianity*, chapter 5 of *Miracles*, and the essays **"On Ethics"** and **"The Poison of Subjectivism."** Norms for human action are most explicitly treated in *The Four Loves*, Book III of *Mere Christianity*, and short essays such as some of those in *The Weight of Glory* or *God in the Dock.* There are fewer explicit discussions of the relation between **religion** and morality, although the first chapter of *The Problem of Pain* takes up the issue succinctly.

Perhaps the most significant of Lewis's treatments of ethical theory is the deceptively slight treatise on moral education titled *The Abolition of Man*. In it Lewis discussed both how we come to know moral truth and how, if at all, such knowledge may be justified. The viewpoint he develops may roughly be termed Aristotelian. In his view, the basic imperatives of morality—what Lewis called The **Tao**—have been known to all developed human societies. Principles of The Tao include (1) general beneficence (i.e., that we try to avoid harming others and seek to help them); (2) special beneficence (particular concern for those who have claims of kinship upon us); (3) duties to parents, elders, and ancestors; (4) duties to children and posterity; (5) **justice**; (6) good faith and truthfulness; (7) **mercy**; and (8) magnanimity (i.e., willingness to give oneself in service of what is good).

What justification can be offered for the claim that these principles should govern our behavior? Lewis argued, in effect, that no justification can be offered. We can argue *from* the principles of The Tao but not to them. They are the premises, not the conclusions, of moral argument. What then is their status? They are part of **reason** itself, grounded in the structure of **reality**, but this reality is not the modern concept of a **"nature"** denuded of moral value. It is the classical concept of a "nature" in which the good is already embedded. (Thus, on this issue Lewis is closer to **Aristotle** than to **Kant**.) Hence, to ask for a justification of such first principles is to misunderstand their status.

How may we come to know these first principles? In *Mere Christianity* Lewis suggested that the maxims of The Tao—or what he there calls simply the "Law of Nature"—are known by almost everyone and do not need teaching. They are "obvious" to all. Such a view, however, is not consistent with the better and more careful claim of *The Abolition of Man*—that the maxims of the Tao are "self-evident." Such self-evident principles may still need to be taught, and they are not necessarily "obvious." To term them self-evident is only to say that they cannot be justified by reference to any more fundamental principles; rather, they are themselves the starting point of all moral argument. How do we know them? That may be hard to specify, although Lewis sometimes uses the language of "intuition" in a sense not unlike that of W. D. Ross's theory of "prima facie duties." But there is, for Lewis at any rate, nothing mysterious about how we become able to know them. That requires moral **education**, the central theme of the Aristotelian approach set forth in *The Abolition of Man*.

An emphasis on the necessity of exemplars, of moral education that inculcates in the young a love for what is good, is the strongest and most permanent theme of Lewis's ethical theory and one of the purposes of his fiction (especially of the **Chronicles of Narnia**). This emphasis on moral education is crucial in several respects. It keeps Lewis's understanding of morality from being overly "intellectualistic." More important, it takes account of what Lewis, as a Christian thinker, could not ignore: the effects of sin on human reason. Coming to acquire moral knowledge is neither easy nor assured. Genuine moral education requires a disciplining of human passion and an attack upon the unruly ego. Without this emphasis on moral education it would be difficult to reconcile Lewis's (Aristotelian) ethical theory with his (Augustinian) understanding of the destructive effects of **sin**.

The abstract question of how one may justify claims to moral knowledge is, however, separate from the question of how one ought to live. In Lewis's case it is not entirely separate, because he invoked the principles of the Tao in order to set forth his claim that moral goodness is embedded in the structure of reality. But the moral life is far more than a few principles. In *Mere Christianity* Lewis suggested that we can understand the several aspects of morality if we think of human beings as a fleet of ships sailing in formation. Their successful voyage requires three things: (1) that the ships do not collide; (2) that each ship is seaworthy, with its engines

working properly; and (3) that the fleet is actually headed toward the proper destination. Put in the language of ethics we might say that morality requires (1) an understanding of what is right and wrong (behavior identified at least in part by the Tao); (2) the development of virtuous habits of behavior; and (3) an understanding of what is good.

The first and third of these aspects of morality—the right and the good—may sometimes seem to clash. That is, achieving good results—or the best results—may seem to require that we do what is wrong. If and when this happens, the direction of Lewis's thought is clear: he turned against utilitarianism (which defines the right act simply as that which leads to the best consequences on the whole) and defends what moralists often call a "deontological" ethic. The rightness of an action is not a function of its consequences alone. Good results should, of course, be pursued, but only within moral limits (set down by principles such as those of the Tao). Another way to put the point would be to say that general beneficence is only one of the principles of the Tao, and it does not always have priority over its fellow principles. A standard problem for the sort of theory Lewis adopted, and a problem for which Lewis himself offers no solution, is that it offers little guidance when several equally fundamental principles seem to conflict. In such circumstances Lewis probably would direct us to the second aspect of morality noted above—the development of virtuous character. We may look to the virtuous man or woman—as to Lucy, Reepicheep, or Trumpkin—to discern what ought to be done when confronted with conflicting duties.

Whatever the precise relation of religion and morality, Lewis did not think the moral law can be grounded in a theory of divine command. If we obey God's commands because we fear punishment, we actually disobey because we do not act disinterestedly. If we obey not because we fear punishment but because our own reason agrees with God's command, we seem to make God unnecessary. Although Lewis did not want to ground the moral law in God's command, neither did he want to make it greater than God—as if God himself were compelled to obey the law. In "The Poison of Subjectivism" Lewis suggested that we must content ourselves with a double negation: that God neither creates nor obeys the moral law.

Morality is important for religion in a different way. The very fact that we have a sense of duty—that we often experience an obligation to do what we do not want to do—suggests that we are not yet whole. It suggests that morality itself must be transcended, that we must be reborn—as demonstrated, for example, in the way Lewis depicts the natural loves becoming "modes of charity." Hence, Jesus is best thought of not as a moral teacher but as one who calls for repentance and offers forgiveness and a new birth.

Gilbert Meilaender

Also See: Aquinas, Augustine, Friendship, Good and Evil, Love, Plato, Natural Law, Pride, Values

Bibliography

Carnell, Corbin Scott. *Bright Shadow of Reality: C. S. Lewis and the Feeling Intellect.* Grand Rapids, MI: Eerdmans, 1974.

Holmer, Paul L. *C. S. Lewis: The Shape of His Faith and Thought.* New York: Harper & Row, 1976.

Lindskoog, Kathryn. *The Lion of Judah in Never-Never Land: God, Man & Nature in C. S. Lewis's Narnia Tales.* Grand Rapids, MI: Eerdmans, 1973.

Meilaender, Gilbert. *The Taste for the Other: The Social and Ethical Thought of C. S. Lewis.* Grand Rapids, MI: Eerdmans, 1978.

Ross, W. D. *The Right and the Good.* Oxford: Clarendon Press, 1930.

Schakel, Peter J. *Reading With the Heart: The Way Into Narnia.* Grand Rapids, MI: Eerdmans, 1979.

Eve

The name Eve occurs in the **Chronicles of Narnia** in reference to human females, denoting their race and often emphasizing their fallen spiritual condition. More significantly in the second novel in Lewis's **science fiction** trilogy, *Perelandra,* the plot involves the planet's first woman, known as the Green Lady or the Queen. She, like Eve, is tempted by evil personified. Weston, a visitor from earth, invites evil to take control of his being and thus becomes the Un-Man. His wicked intention is to undermine her allegiance to Maleldil, the Creator of the universe, with a continuous stream of lies and twisted arguments. His most persuasive appeal suggests that Maleldil desires her to exercise her autonomy. As Ransom, another earthman, observes her vulnerability he recognizes that it is his duty to foil the Un-Man's temptation. Ransom's battle and defeat of the Un-Man results in the Queen and the King gaining the knowledge of **good and evil** without suffering **the Fall**. The Eve of Perelandra enters into her role as Queen and mother of the race in perfect relationship with Maleldil, her Creator, and with her husband the King.

Alice H. Cook

Also See: Marriage, Women

Bibliography

Downing, David C. *Planets in Peril: A Critical Study of C. S. Lewis's Ransom Trilogy.* Amherst: University of Massachusetts Press, 1992.

Kilby, Clyde. *Images of Salvation: In the Fiction of C. S. Lewis.* Wheaton: Shaw, 1978.

Lewis, C. S. *Perelandra.*

"Evil and God"

The Spectator. CLXVI (7 February 1941): 141. Reprinted in *God in the Dock, Undeceptions,* and *Christian Reunion.*

"Evil and God" is a response to Dr. Joad's article "Evil and God," that appeared in *The Spectator* on January 31, 1941. In his article, Dr. Joad rejected "mechanism" and "emergent **evolution**," and said that we must choose between monotheistic **philosophy** (like **Christianity**) or dualism (like Zoroastrianism). Lewis extended this argument by saying that the view that two equal but opposite forces (that is, **good and evil**) exist is necessarily flawed. Evil must have a parasitic existence. It is secondary to good, and it is by good that it is judged. In this way, evil (as **Satan**) does not have the power of good (as **God**) but is necessarily subordinate to it. Bad is not bad in the same way that good is good. The two are not opposite, but different in both type and kind. The good is reality, the original and single standard.

Anne Gardner

Evolution

Throughout his life, C. S. Lewis remained reticent about speaking publicly on evolution. His three great apologetic works from the 1940s dealt with human origins only briefly and where absolutely necessary. Lewis believed he would do little good taking on a controversial subject in which he was not an expert.

It is clear, however, from letters and essays that remained unpublished during his lifetime that Lewis did much reading and thinking in private about evolution. Until the 1950s, he tried to find a middle ground, accepting the "biological theorem" while rejecting its "metaphysical statements." In the 1950s he grew more skeptical. Between 1944 and 1960, he corresponded privately with **Bernard Acworth** (1885–1963), one of Britain's leading anti-evolutionists. In a 1951 letter, he noted that his doubts about evolution were being stimulated by the "fanatical and twisted attitudes of its defenders." In 1957 he made his only public attack on the theory. In a poem entitled "Evolutionary Hymn" he mocked evolution's pretensions to be a **religion** leading us, "Up the future's endless stair."

After his death, two essays from the 1940s, **"A Reply to Professor Haldane"** and **"The Funeral of a Great Myth"** were published which contain his views on **science** and evolution.

Mike Perry

Bibliography

Ferngren, Gary and Numbers, Ronald. "C. S. Lewis on Creation and Evolution: The Acworth Letters, 1944–1960." *Perspectives on Science and the Christian Faith* 48 (March 1996): 28–33.

Lewis, C. S. "Evolutionary Hymn"; "The Funeral of a Great Myth"; "The Pain of Animals"; "A Reply to Professor Haldane."

Wrong, Charles. "Christianity and Progress." *CSL: The Bulletin of the New C. S. Lewis Society* 6 (August 1975): 19–24.

"Evolutionary Hymn"

The Cambridge Review. 79 (November 30, 1957): 227 (under the pseudonym Nat Whilk). Reprinted in *Poems* and *Collected Poems.*

Tongue in cheek, this hymn of praise (some suggest **Joy Davidman Lewis** assisted Lewis in composing this poem and that it can be sung to the tune of *Joyful, Joyful We Adore Thee*) blithely assumes a Darwinian view of the world and assumes the inevitability of human progress. Old static norms of **good and evil** are to be rejected since new ways and ideas are inherently superior (elsewhere Lewis called this attitude **chronological snobbery**).

Don W. King
Montreat College

"Expedition to Holly Bush Hill"

Cherbourg School Magazine. (November 1912). Reproduced in The Lewis Family Papers. III: 310–11.

Reproduced in the **Lewis Family Papers** from the magazine, **Warren Lewis** descried it as the "first appearance in print" of his brother. Dated November 1912, it describes a day's outing (arranged by the headmaster) to celebrate the academic success of two students. The style is somewhat stilted but the vocabulary is extensive; it is highly conventional and shows little **imagination**, although it accurately describes the holiday.

John Bremer

Also See: Cherbourg School

"Expedition to Holly Bush Hill"

Cherbourg School Magazine. (July 1913). Reproduced in *The Lewis Family Papers.* IV: 51.

This article records a second outing to Holly Bush Hill (see **"Expedition to Holly Bush Hill,"** 1912). Lewis does not report that the occasion was another academic success—of Lewis himself this time (he had won a scholarship to **Malvern College**)—but **Warren Lewis** provides this information in a footnote in *The Lewis Family Papers.* The article is followed by Lewis's first published poem, a version of **"Quam Bene Saturno"** by Tibullus.

John Bremer

Also See: Cherbourg School

"Experiment"

The Spectator. 161 (December 9, 1938): 998. A slightly different version entitled "Metrical Experiment" is printed in *Augury: An Oxford Miscellany of Verse and Prose.* A. M. Hardie and K. C. Douglas (eds). Oxford: Blackwell, 1940: 28. Revised and retitled as "Pattern" and reprinted in *Poems* and *Collected Poems.*

A speculation that trees do not sleep in the winter; instead, they are most active when the sharp cold awakens them. Indeed, the summer seduces them and leaves them drowsy. Frost stimulates their wakeful souls.

Don W. King
Montreat College

An Experiment in Criticism

Cambridge: Cambridge University Press, 1961.

C. S. Lewis anticipated by several decades contemporary **literary theory**'s inquiry into the role of the reader in interpretation, a category of **literary criticism** ("Reader-response theory") commonly associated with such writers as Stanley Fish, Wolfgang Iser, and Louise Rosenblatt. In his last major critical work, *An Experiment in Criticism* (1961), Lewis explored the act of criticism and the significance of reading in a systematic way, elucidating notions that were often implicit or explored only in passing in his earlier works. Indeed, *An Experiment* offers a kind of *summa* of Lewis's mature critical views: a survey of principles that inform responsible criticism, an inquiry into the nature of aesthetic experience of all kinds, an eloquent summary of his views on **Myth**, **Fantasy**, and Realism, and, most importantly, an impassioned defense of the ordinary reader as an active participant in "meaning-making."

The "experiment" signified in Lewis's title consists of reversing the normal procedures of evaluative criticism—criticism whose main purpose is to judge the "quality" of works by their compliance with a series of age-bound abstractions ordained by professional critics. Instead of judging "men's literary taste by the things they read," Lewis proposed that we judge "literature by the way men read it." In other words, let us define what constitutes "good reading" rather than what criteria make for "good books." Lewis thus began his experiment with a clever depiction of two kinds of readers: the "Literary" and the "Unliterary," the "Few" and the "Many."

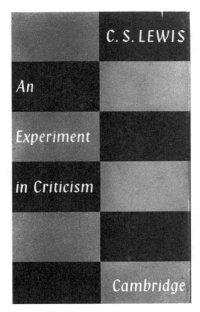

The literary, because they are schooled in literary technique and appreciative of aesthetic achievement, reread "the great works" throughout their lives, feel impoverished when denied the "leisure and silence" that sanctifies their reading experience, find first readings so momentous they can only be compared to **love**, **religion**, or bereavement, and talk to each other about books "often and at length." The unliterary, by contrast, rarely reread a work, use reading only for "odd moments of enforced solitude" or pure diversion, finish a work without perceptible change to their worldview, and rarely think or talk about their reading with others. Identifying himself with the literary, Lewis concluded: "We treat as a main ingredient in our well-being something which to them is marginal."

Lewis's aim was to inspire a legion of impassioned and informed readers, yet not at the cost of valorizing the "literary," who in their sophistication and inordinate concern for "taste" can surreptitiously grant literature a cultic status that displaces true piety. Indeed some critics, whom Lewis labeled "the Vigilants," have tried single-handedly to fulfill the prophecy of Victorian critic, **Matthew Arnold**, that "**poetry** would replace **religion**" in the popular mind. The literary, Lewis pointed out, tend to "confuse art with life," something the unliterary rarely do, and thereby make of literature a solemn creed that will reinforce a "tragic 'view' or 'sense' or 'philosophy' of life."

Having described what one might call the motives of reading, Lewis then articulated a tool for distinguishing "good" reading from "bad": "A work of (whatever) art

can be either 'received' or 'used.' When we 'receive' it we exert our senses and imagination and various others according to a pattern invented by the artist." "Receptive reading" invites in the reader the reflective awareness of difference, of something new, challenging, or ineffable and thus the possibility of change or "enlargement of being." By contrast, readers who "use" a text treat it as an appliance to reinforce their preexisting set of **values** or to push them along in familiar and established ways of thinking and behaving. This latter experience is thus a closed and privatizing one—the product of what Lewis earlier in the work calls "egoistic castle-building."

While works of art may invite both "use" and "reception," Lewis ultimately concluded that a work whose readers only *use* and never *receive* it may be judged inconsequential, or worse. An otherwise complex work featuring pockets of eroticism may be read spuriously by adolescent readers only for its pornographic effects—"users" who pursue their prurient interests by finding the proverbial "good parts"; but such a work that produced *only* such readings, and that from a variety or majority of readers, absent of other redeeming features, is clearly a forgettable and inferior work. The converse is also true: a despised or neglected work may yet entice a handful of loyal and dedicated readers "who had read and reread it, who would notice, and object, if a single word were changed," and whose reading had represented to them a "lifelong delight." Such a work, Lewis averred, deserves reconsideration and begrudging respect: "We must, therefore, say that what damns a book is not the existence of bad readings but the absence of good ones." (One is reminded here of Lewis's own affection for and defense of "genre" writers such as **H. Rider Haggard** and John Buchan, and the general critical disdain they engendered.)

It was Lewis's point that both literary and unliterary readers may be "users" rather than "receivers" of art, and that, in fact, literary readers can be the worst offenders. The latter may inculcate in their comrades and pupils a process of reading that devalues primary experience of a work and elevates a stylized "critical reading" that demands evaluation of the work before it is fully "received." For Lewis, the "necessary condition of all good reading is 'to get ourselves out of the way,'" and thus to encounter fully what an author has provided, untethered to the motive of evaluation. The works of great writers—Lewis mentions **Jane Austen** and Anthony Trollope—resist "use" and demand "reception," and thus stand the test of time. By contrast, modern critics have succeeded not only in discouraging "primary experience" in readers, inadvertently they have inspired a new brand of poetry that "involves the unmaking of your mind, the abandonment of all the logical and narrative connections which you use in reading prose in conversation." In short, modern readers are doubly disadvantaged by such critics who, on the one hand, condition readers to become mere "users" of texts, and, on the other, create a market for literature that demands such "use." Lewis had in mind here modernist poetry and fiction that exalt obscurity and ambiguity, solicit idiosyncratic or pluralistic readings, and deliberately frustrate the "common" reader's quest for accessible meaning.

The last two chapters offer Lewis's grand climax and resolution of the "experiment." First, Lewis challenged the popular slogan, "poems should not *mean* but *be*," a rallying cry of the formalist critics he opposed who posited that true literature is nonpropositional and exists as art and has meaning as art only in its "form." Not so, Lewis countered, for a literary work both *means* and *is*: it is both "Logos" (something said) and "Poiema" (something made). The pleasure of an aesthetic experience cannot be reduced to its form or Poiema, and the content of a text or Logos cannot be divorced from its experienced beauty. Readers respond to both, and both are crucial to primary experience of a text. A mark of the *receptive* reading Lewis was at pains to articulate is that "we need not believe or approve the Logos" of a text in order to enjoy it. Likewise, we may find compelling the message of or deeper myth behind a text whose form is significantly flawed or negligible.

In the end good reading actualizes what is typically only a potential aesthetic experience: the reader is enabled to inhabit another's selfhood in a foreign landscape, yet remaining oneself—a marriage of vicarious experience and objective reflection on that experience. Concluding in a crescendo of praise for this endangered "immediacy" in reading, Lewis exulted, "in reading great literature I become a thousand men and yet remain myself.... Here, as in worship, in love, in moral action, and in knowing, I transcend myself; and am never more myself than when I do."

An Experiment is at once a winsome apology for Lewis's own reading habits and preferences, and a cogent critique of all forms of critical snobbery that rob readers of literary pleasure in the dubious name of "Good Taste"; it is among his very best scholarly works and instructive for all who would understanding his own motivations for writing.

Bruce L. Edwards
Bowling Green State University

Bibliography

Edwards, Bruce L. *A Rhetoric of Reading: C. S. Lewis's Defense of Western Literacy*. Provo, UT: Brigham Young University Press, 1985.
_____. (ed). *The Taste of the Pineapple: Essays on C. S. Lewis as Reader, Critic, and Imaginative Writer*. Bowling Green, OH: Popular Press, 1988.
Hannay, Margaret. *C. S. Lewis*. New York: Ungar, 1981.
Lewis, C. S. *The Personal Heresy*.

"An Expostulation (against too many writers of science fiction)"

The Magazine of Fantasy and Science Fiction 16, no. 6 (June 1959): 47. Reprinted in *Poems* and *Collected Poems*.

A gentle rebuke of **science fiction** writers who take us to other worlds only to tell the same tired old stories we have on earth: criminals on the run, conspirators and their schemes, or lovers' triangles. Instead, what Lewis wanted were stories that focused on the "otherness" of these worlds. He wrote about this theme in his essays **"On Stories"** and **"On Science Fiction."**

Don W. King
Montreat College

F

Fairy Tales

Lewis loved **fantasy** stories, including fairy tales, from a young age. Some of his earliest favorite reading included the stories of **Beatrix Potter**, especially *Squirrel Nutkin*, and the novels of **Edith Nesbit**, such as *Five Children and It*. His greatest love for traditional fairy tales, however, came at a somewhat older age; around twelve, as he said in *Surprised by Joy*, "I fell deeply under the spell of Dwarfs."

Unlike many adults, however, he did not lose his love for "childish" literature as he grew older; if anything, he grew to love fairy tales more because he was able to "bring more to them," as he put it.

A significant portion of Lewis's commentary on fairy tales as a genre is found in three essays from *On Stories*: **"On Stories," "On Three Ways of Writing for Children,"** and **"Sometimes Fairy Stories May Say Best What's to Be Said."** In the first of these, Lewis begins by speaking of stories in general, but the second half moves to tales of the marvelous. According to Lewis, one of the advantages of writing stories about animals (and he uses **Kenneth Grahame**'s *The Wind in the Willows* as an example) is that one can mix the attributes of adults and children. The animals are like children in that they have no jobs or responsibilities; they are like adults in that they can go and do as they like. Lewis's fairy-story animals share these characteristics, and his children do as well; significantly, though adults appear in the **Chronicles of Narnia**, none of them are the parents of child characters.

In "On Three Ways of Writing for Children," Lewis wrote about his love for fairy stories as an adult and indicated that this is praiseworthy rather than ridiculous, noting that in most areas of life, people who retain old tastes while adding new ones are considered richer for it. He also argued that children need to have examples of moral **virtues** placed before them and that the traditional fairy tale, with its emphasis on chivalry and courage, often supplies that. He concluded by saying that adults and children often have more in common than is generally recognized and that in fairy stories he tried to write to children as equals.

In the final essay of the group, Lewis wrote specifically of his own compositions, pointing out that rather than deciding initially to write a fairy tale, he first had

a story he wanted to tell, then realized that casting it in fairy-tale form was the ideal method for telling it. He then repeated his position of the previous essay, saying that one should not use a patronizing tone in writing for children, but should consider them equals. If a story is good enough for children, Lewis said in essence, it's good enough for adults.

Lewis subtitled *That Hideous Strength* "A Modern Fairy-Tale for Grown-Ups," and one can see why he may have felt it fit into that genre. It portrays a struggle between **good and evil**, won by good with the combination of personal valor and **magic**. The evil side seems initially stronger and is filled with menacing ogres, but in the end evil is destroyed and good lives happily ever after.

To some extent, most of Lewis's fiction writing bears affinities with fairy stories. *Out of the Silent Planet* involves meetings with various strange creatures; *Perelandra* is a moral and physical fight in which good defeats evil; and *Till We Have Faces* is based on an episode from Greek mythology. But of course the fairy tales with which Lewis is most readily identified are the Chronicles of Narnia. This influence can clearly be seen in *The Lion, the Witch and the Wardrobe*, where (1) the main characters are children; (2) they meet odd creatures; (3) they fight against a witch; (4) evil initially seems to be winning; (5) the children forge forward through a combination of personal goodness and magic; and (6) in the end evil is destroyed, or at least seems to be, and good reigns.

The fairy-tale influence can be seen in the other books of the series as well. Throughout the Chronicles, children are the main characters, they meet mythical creatures, and they have to use a combination of magic and goodness to overcome evil. Allusions to fairy tales and mythology (which one can think of as "adult" fairy tales) can be found in many places in the Chronicles: Bacchus, Pomona, and Silenus, for example, are all characters from Greek mythology.

Lewis retained his interest in and love for fairy stories to the end of his life. During his last summer, Lewis lapsed into a coma; while recovering, he sometimes had difficulty recognizing people. One day **Maureen Moore**, **Janie Moore**'s daughter, came to visit. She had been warned of Lewis's memory difficulties; that very day, in fact, he had failed to recognize his longtime friend **J. R. R. Tolkien**. She identified herself to him as "Maureen." To her surprise, he replied, "No, it is Lady Dunbar of Hempriggs." Maureen was taken aback; that was indeed her name now, since she had recently inherited a title, but, as she asked him, "How could you remember that?"

"On the contrary," he replied, "how could I forget a fairy tale?"

Marvin D. Hinten
Bowling Green State University

Also See: Allegory, Ethics and Morality, Imagery, Andrew Lang, George MacDonald, Myth, Science Fiction

Bibliography

Filmer, Kath. "Speaking in Parables." *Mythlore* 11 (Autumn 1984): 15–20.
Grahame, Kenneth. *The Wind in the Willows*. New York: Scribner's, 1913.
Lewis, C. S. *Surprised by Joy*.
Nesbit, Edith. *Five Children and It*. London: E. Benn, 1957.
Potter, Beatrix. *Squirrel Nutkin*. New York: F. Warne, 1987.

Faith

Modern arguments against Christian faith usually go something like this: "Christians of old used to believe all sorts of silliness that Christians today know isn't true. The sun doesn't revolve around the earth. The powdered bones of saints don't cure disease. For the honest and educated person to have faith in primitive superstitions despite scientific evidence to the contrary is illogical, if not downright childish." In his role as Christian apologist, C. S. Lewis liked to point out that such arguments do not invalidate **Christianity**, and in the process of doing so, he gave much assistance to educated Christians struggling to explain their faith.

Lewis's own journey to Christian faith was circuitous; he renounced **God** as an adolescent, dabbled in various quasi-occult philosophies, and then came by turns to pantheism, deism, and at last to **Christ**. For him faith was not primarily an emotional proposition; rather, it was a matter of logic and honesty. While not a biblical literalist, Lewis believed in Christ's virgin birth and saw the resurrection as central to the Christian faith. He also had no difficulty in allowing the possibility of other biblical **miracles**, for if one believes in an all-powerful God, then acts that go against the "laws of nature" are, by definition, not impossible for that God. Maintaining that the dead cannot be resurrected because the laws of nature forbid it is like arguing that, because the rules of billiards preclude moving billiard balls without cue sticks, it is impossible for the owner of the table to pick up a ball with his hands.

In *Mere Christianity* Lewis discusses two levels of Christian faith, the first one synonymous with "belief." A stumbling block in arguments both for and against faith is that they confuse belief with knowledge. But no one "believes" the multiplication table, and no one "has faith" that putting a hand on a hot stove will be painful; most of us know by experience or observation that two times two is four and that a hot stove will burn. But as Lewis explained, faith is a different proposition, more in the line of belief in the face of seeming evidence to the contrary. In the hot stove example, faith means believing that a hot stove will burn, even when someone else has apparently gotten away with putting a hand on that stove.

Lewis says that Christians must recognize, even if atheists do not, that not all contrary evidence is based on **reason**. Often faith is attacked by false evidence, or by emotion, wishes, desires, or moods. The fear of an animal caught in a trap may intensify when it sees a hand reaching to release it, but no one will think the animal stupid if he refrains from biting the hand. A drowning lawyer will not be blamed for waiving his usual insistence upon expert testimony if he trusts someone swimming out to save him. In these instances, faith must precede a fortunate conclusion, even though faith may not be apparently logical. As a committed atheist will strive to hold onto his unbelief in a mood where Christianity seems probable (Lewis says he faced this test of unfaith in his own years as an atheist), so a Christian will hold onto his acceptance of Christianity even when "reason" seems to rise up against it. Those who argue against faith do so without absolute knowledge that faith is unfounded; therefore, they should not demand, on logical grounds, that Christians forgo their faith with "every fluctuation of the apparent evidence."

This second sort of faith is faith through which Christ's saving **grace** can work. This grace can only come with *lack* of faith in oneself—with the conviction, based upon trial and error, that one cannot become a good person by unaided will. "A serious moral effort [with repeated failures] is the only thing that will bring you to the point where you throw up the sponge. Faith in Christ is the only thing to save you from despair at that point, and out of that Faith in Him good actions must inevitably come." For Lewis, the classic theological dispute over the ascendancy of faith or works was a sideline issue, like arguing that one side of the scissors is more important than the other.

The Christian's faith is an outgrowth of **love**, for Jesus is a personal God who has not only revealed himself to the consciousness of the believer, but has made certain promises as well. Of course, not all promises made in life are trustworthy, but the relationship with Christ is a loving trust rather than a business deal. "No man," said Lewis, "is our friend who will believe good intentions only when they are proved. No man is our friend who will not be very slow to accept evidence against them." Whether or not God exists, or whether or not Christ is what he said he was, is an open question to non-Christians. But once one is convinced that Christ is who he said he was, the issue is no longer theoretical. It becomes then a matter of trust in a particular loved one, in "this God, the increasingly knowable Lord."

Richard A. Hill
Taylor University

Also See: Atheism, the Bible, Natural Law, Paganism, Pride, Rationalism, Revelation, Science, Theology

Bibliography

Holmer, Paul. *C. S. Lewis: The Shape of His Faith and Thought.* New York: Harper and Row, 1977.

Lewis, C. S. *Mere Christianity*; *Miracles;* "On Obstinacy in Belief"; "Religion: Reality or Substitute?"; *Surprised by Joy.*

A Faith of Our Own (Preface)

Farrer, Austin Marseden. *A Faith of Our Own.* Cleveland: World Publishing Company, 1960.

Dr. **Austin Marseden Farrer** was a well-known Anglican theologian and writer, the chaplain of Trinity College, **Oxford**, from 1935 to 1960, and the Warden of Keble College, Oxford until his death in 1968. He was present at the secret 1956 civil ceremony where Lewis married **Joy Davidman** and conducted Joy's funeral service in July 1960. That same year Farrer published a collection of essays on the Christian life entitled *A Faith of Our Own.* Lewis wrote the book's preface and praised the quietness, simplicity, and discipline with which the book was written.

Mike Perry

Also See: Christianity, Faith, Friendship, Inklings

Bibliography

Farrer, Austin. "In His Image," *C. S. Lewis at the Breakfast Table.* ed. James T. Como, New York: 1979: 242–44.

The Fall

The Fall is a theological term based on the story of Adam and **Eve** that describes the tendency toward **sin** in humanity that requires **God**'s **redemption** as a remedy. C. S. Lewis referred to the Fall and fallen **human nature** many times in his writings and letters, including *Mere Christianity*, *God in the Dock*, *The Weight of Glory* ("**Membership**"), *Miracles* ("**The Grand Miracle**"), *The World's Last Night* ("**Religion and Rocketry**"), *Christian Reflections* ("**The Poison of Subjectivism**" and "**The Seeing Eye**").

Lewis's longest essay on this doctrine is a chapter titled "The Fall of Man" in *The Problem of Pain*. Here Lewis elaborated on **Augustine**'s "classical" view of original sin, which, simply put, links Adam's choice to sin (as a result of **pride**) with the perpetual sinfulness of the human race. Lewis's ideas about fallen human nature and the nature of sin and evil are often shown in his imaginative stories and in his **science fiction**. In *Perelandra* an "unfallen" (sinless) world is tempted, but unlike this world, evil is resisted. The Green Lady, her husband, and the Un-man are perhaps archetypal of Genesis' Adam, Eve, and **Satan**. In the Narnia stories (especially *The Magician's Nephew* and *The Last Battle*) Lewis introduces evil, tests of obedience, and characters who cannot resist temptation into a delightful and innocent world.

Lewis's views about the Fall are basic to much of today's theological thinking. In *The Problem of Pain* he wrote that the only proper function of the Fall as a doctrine was to show that human beings are a "horror to God" and to themselves because they have abused God's **free will**. Furthermore, he maintained that the doctrine of the Fall is important because it is a corrective to any theory that asserts that God created an evil nature in humans, or that he allowed an independent power to create, and thus be responsible for, humanity's tendency toward sin (dualism).

Perry C. Bramlett
C. S. Lewis for the Local Church

Also See: Anglicanism, Corruption of Nature, Creation, Eve, Evolution, Free Will, Good and Evil, Pain, Roman Catholicism

Bibliography

Kilby, Clyde S. *Images of Salvation in the Fiction of C. S. Lewis.* Wheaton, IL: Shaw, 1978.

Lindskoog, Kathryn. *C. S. Lewis—Mere Christian.* Wheaton, IL: Shaw, 1987.

White, William Luther. *The Image of Man in C. S. Lewis.* Nashville: Abingdon, 1969.

Family

After the age of nine, Lewis never had what could be termed a normal, traditional family life. Shortly after the obvious emotional trauma of his mother's death, he had to leave at a young age for boarding school, a commonplace of upper-class British life at the time, but a practice that seems odd and dangerous to most contemporary Americans. He and his brother were close, but for much of his life he felt somewhat estranged from his father, and the home he eventually set up, with a partner old enough to be his mother, was certainly unconventional. Near the end of his life, his **marriage** to a dying wife and his sudden parental role over two stepchildren again provided a somewhat unusual situation.

Despite Lewis's own untraditional family life, his views about children, parenthood, and marriage were very traditional. He believed children need to learn obedience at an early age and that parents should apply corporal punishment as needed to ensure that obedience. In nautical terms, Lewis saw the father/husband as the captain of the family ship, the mother/wife as the first mate, and the children as deckhands. Structure and **hierarchy** should be maintained; affection could develop properly only if this order were adhered to and understood by all.

Of course, we must see Lewis's "family values" in terms of the era in which he lived. **Oxford** dons were traditionally connected at least as closely with their colleges as with their families, which Lewis, during his single years, seemed to feel right and proper. He appeared never to ask the other **Inklings** about their families or care about the fact that Thursday night meetings might cut into "family time." Upon his own **marriage**, on the other hand, Lewis wanted **Joy** included in everything.

A place where one can clearly see Lewis's views on what might go wrong with a family is *The Voyage of the "Dawn Treader,"* in which we learn that Eustace Scrubb, a lad poorly brought up, is unused to corporal punishment and calls his parents by their first names. Those factors, Lewis seems to imply, have contributed to Eustace's failings.

Marvin D. Hinten
Bowling Green State University

Also See: David Gresham, Douglas Gresham, Albert Lewis, Florence Hamilton Lewis, Joy Davidman Lewis, Warren Hamilton Lewis, Tradition

Bibliography

Dorsett, Lyle. *And God Came In*. New York: Ballantine, 1983.
Lewis, C. S. *The Abolition of Man; The Voyage of the "Dawn Treader."*

Fantasy

Lewis loved fantasy literature his entire life; in fact, he felt that **fairy tales** and fantasy stories that weren't enjoyed by people in their fifties probably weren't very enjoyable to children. As a preschooler, Lewis's primary source of oral fantasy was his Irish nurse, Lizzie Endicott, who used to tell stories of leprechauns and other fantastic creatures. His first experiences with written fantasies came through the writings of **Beatrix Potter**, particularly *Squirrel Nutkin*. It was here that Lewis became enthralled with anthropomorphism, giving animals human characteristics such as speech. This interest led to his creation of Animal-Land, a world in which, as he commented in his autobiography, mice and rabbits donned suits of armor to fight cats. Lewis's brother Warnie, perhaps more interested in history than fantasy, had a favorite land of his own, India. The fact that one country was real and the other invented did not stop the Lewis brothers from combining them into one geographical area, **Boxen**, about which the brothers, especially Jack, created many stories and historical episodes.

The other major fantasy author in Lewis's youth was **Edith Nesbit**, especially with such works as *The Amulet* and *Five Children and It*. If Beatrix Potter contributed thinking animals to Narnia, Nesbit contributed youthful main characters. The Bastable children of Nesbit, like the Pevensie children of Lewis's Narnia, are ordinary elementary-aged children who keep having unusual things happen to them. In *Five Children and It*, for instance, the Bastable come across a "psammead," a sand-dwelling creature of colorful personality with the power to grant wishes. As one might expect, the wishes come true with unforeseen and uncomfortable side effects. If the language of the Pevensie children in the **Chronicles of Narnia** occasionally seems stilted and old-fashioned, as some critics have charged, perhaps part of the blame may be laid on Nesbit's influence; her children are notable for saying "Crikey!" and similar interjections.

As an adult, Lewis continued to love fantasy literature and fairy tales. The movies he went to see, for instance, tended to be from this genre: *King Kong* and *Snow White* are two notable examples from the 1930s. Although Lewis had, by his adult years, expanded his horizons into science fiction and adult fantasy, he still was pleased to find works of children's fantasy which he had never read; one example of this is **Kenneth Grahame**'s *The Wind in the Willows*, which Lewis claimed lost no enjoyment for him simply because he had first discovered it as an adult.

All of the novel-length fiction Lewis ever wrote was more or less fantasy literature. Even the works usually placed into another category, such as *Pilgrim's Regress* (allegory), clearly have strong fantastic elements built in. Lewis appreciated the growth during his lifetime of **science fiction** ("scientifiction," he called it), but as the years went by he became disappointed that much of it began leaning more toward science and less toward fantasy. To Lewis, the best science fiction had just enough science necessary to create an opening element of plausibility; after that, the revelation of a new world was the real reason for the book's existence. In his writing, we can clearly see a progression, where *Out of the Silent Planet*, the first book in his "space trilogy," is clearly more science-based than the two books (*Perelandra* and *That Hideous Strength*) that follow it. In *Planet*, Lewis has a rocket take the lead character, Ransom, to Mars; in *Perelandra* an angel-like being from another planet provides transportation to Venus. And in *Strength*, the resurrection and magical abilities of Merlin show a clear departure from *Planet*'s effort to use only realism on our home world.

Lewis's next fiction series, the Chronicles of Narnia, moves outside our solar system altogether; it is thus more oriented toward fantasy and less toward science fiction than the space trilogy. By the time his final major novel, *Till We Have Faces*, Lewis has moved into a world of mythology disassociated from contemporary times altogether.

One of the main purposes of literary fantasy, as opposed to the fairy tale proper, is that literary fantasy intends to make a thematic point. Most often its purpose is to describe something wrong with our world that can more safely or effectively be described in terms of another society. In the 18th century, *Gulliver's Travels* is a clear example of this; as Gulliver becomes acquainted with the societies of Lilliput and Brobdingnag, Swift enables readers by contrast to see British society more clearly. And in our own era, such works as Kurt Vonnegut's "Harrison Bergeron" and television's *Star Trek* are clearly intended as contemporary morality plays, set far enough into the future to avoid the need for absolute realism, but showing clearly the disastrous results possible if current trends are not curbed or reversed.

Most of Lewis's fantasy fits this tendency to make a thematic point. There is no question that *Out of the Silent Planet* and *That Hideous Strength* express, to some extent, his concerns about scientism and bureaucracy. And the Narnian tales obviously reveal, through the agency of Aslan's interactions with beings in that world, Lewis's views (in a modified form) on **Christ's** interactions with us in this world. Literary fantasy allowed Lewis to delight and instruct at the same time.

Marvin D. Hinten
Bowling Green State University

Also See: Imagery, Warren Lewis, Paganism, Symbolism

Austin M. Farrer (1904–1968)

Austin Farrer was a close friend of C. S. Lewis and a renowned Anglican theologian, philosopher, and **preacher**. He was chaplain at St. Edmund Hall and Trinity College, **Oxford**, and finished his career as warden of Keble College. A prolific author, Farrer published several hundred articles, reviews, books, and sermons during his lifetime. His books fall under the categories of philosophical **theology**, Bible commentary, sermons and devotional works, and general studies of **religion**. Perhaps his most famous work is *A Faith of Our Own* (1960; *Said or Sung,* in Britain), a collection of sermons and addresses, for which Lewis wrote the preface to the American edition. Other well-known works include *Finite and Infinite* (1943), *The Glass of Vision* (1948), *Saving Belief* (1964), and *A Celebration of Faith* (1970).

Farrer met and became friends with Lewis in the forties and was an active participant in the **Oxford Socratic Club**, which Lewis helped found for discussing **Christianity**, **philosophy**, and **culture**. From 1942–54 he contributed twelve addresses to the Socratic Club, and sometimes his and Lewis's interests overlapped. Lewis's essay **"Myth Became Fact?"** appeared in a journal a few months before Farrer's address "Can Myth Become Fact" was delivered to the Socratic Club (1945). Lewis dedicated *Reflections on the Psalms* to Farrer and his wife, **Katherine D. Farrer**, and his respect for his friend is evident in the **Preface to A Faith of Our Own**. Farrer wrote an appreciative but critical essay about Lewis called "The Christian Apologist" for the collection *Light on C. S. Lewis* (1965), and his memorial to Lewis, "In His Image," was published in *C. S. Lewis at the Breakfast Table* (1979). He also referred to Lewis and his works several times in his sermons.

Farrer and Katherine were present at Lewis's first (civil) **marriage** to **Joy Davidman Lewis** and were among the few of his friends to befriend her. Farrer was present when she died on April 11, 1960, and officiated at her cremation service on July 18, under great emotional strain, as **Warren Lewis** has noted in his diaries. He also read the Scripture lesson and helped conduct the funeral service of Lewis, who died on November 22, 1963.

Perry C. Bramlett
C. S. Lewis for the Local Church

Also See: Anglicanism, Apologetics, Friendship

Bibliography

Conti, Charles C. (ed). *Austin Farrer: Reflective Faith—Essays in Philosophical Theology.* Grand Rapids, MI: Eerdmans, 1972 (contains a complete bibliography of Farrer's published works).

Curtis, Philip. *A Hawk Among Sparrows: A Biography of Austin Farrer.* London: SPCK, 1985.

Hefling, Charles C., Jr. *Jacob's Ladder: Theology and Spirituality in the Thought of Austin Farrer.* Cambridge, MA: Cowley, 1979.

Katherine D. Farrer (1911–1972)

Katherine Farrer was the wife of the famed Anglican theologian and preacher **Austin Farrer**, a close friend of C. S. Lewis, and an active member of the **Oxford Socratic Club**. A novelist and translator, she was best known for her detective stories, which include *The Missing Link* (1952), and *Gownsman's Gallows* (1957). Her **friendship** with Lewis included mutual **literary criticism**; he discussed his novel *Till We Have Faces* several times with her before it went into publication. He also read and commented briefly about *The Missing Link* (unpublished letter dated June 1952), telling Mrs. Farrer he was an "inexperienced reader of whodunits" but that the mystery was "well constructed and it thoroughly excited me." He read an unpublished manuscript of hers (probably *Gownsman's Gallows*) and made several corrective comments about it in an unpublished letter dated August 1955.

Mrs. Farrer was one of Lewis's friends who was also a good friend of his wife **Joy Davidman Lewis**. She was one of the first of his close friends to be introduced to Joy, and she was one of the few who knew about the civil ceremony at which Lewis and Joy were married. They became such good friends that Joy typed the manuscript for *Gownsman's Gallows* in 1956, and she often confided in Mrs. Farrer when she was lonely and needed a friend to talk to. On October 18, 1956, Mrs. Farrer had a premonition that something was not right with Joy. At the very moment she (not Lewis, as the film *Shadowlands* portrays) was dialing Joy's number, Joy tripped over the telephone wire and broke a bone in her leg. Mrs. Farrer and her husband Austin took Joy to the hospital, where she was discovered to have cancer. After Joy's death on July 13, 1960, Lewis wrote (unpublished letter dated July 22, 1960) to the Farrers and told them that Joy "loved you both very much." Austin and Katherine Farrer had been the only friends of Lewis to attend Joy's cremation service on July 18, 1960. Later,

Lewis dedicated **Reflections on the Psalms** to them. Katherine Farrer is buried next to her husband in the St. Cross churchyard cemetery in Oxford, as are several of Lewis's other close friends.

Perry C. Bramlett
C. S. Lewis for the Local Church

Also See: Anglicanism

Bibliography

Dorsett, Lyle W. *And God Came In.* New York: Macmillan, 1983.

Griffin, William. *Clive Staples Lewis: A Dramatic Life.* San Francisco: Harper & Row, 1986.

Kilby, Clyde S., and Marjorie Lamp Mead (eds.). *Brothers and Friends: The Diaries of Major Warren Hamilton Lewis.* San Francisco: Harper & Row, 1982.

The Fellowship of the Ring (Book Review)

"The Gods Return to Earth." *Time and Tide.* XXXV (14 August 1954): 1082–83. Reprinted with *The Two Towers* (Book Review) as "Tolkien's *The Lord of the Rings*" in *Of This and Other Worlds* and *On Stories.*

This review praised the first volume of *The Lord of the Rings* cycle. Lewis delighted in **Tolkien**'s acts of "sub-creation," including his invention of names for characters and places. Lewis marveled at how Tolkien imbued his tale with its own history, languages, **myths**, theology, and geography. "[The book] is the cool middle point between illusion and disillusionment."

Anne Gardner

Bibliography

Tolkien, J. R. R. *The Fellowship of the Ring.*

"Fern-Seed and Elephants"

See entry on "Modern Theology and Biblical Criticism"

Fern-Seed and Elephants: and Other Essays on Christianity

Walter Hooper (ed). London: Collins, 1975.

See separate essay entries on the following:

"The Efficacy of Prayer"
"Fern-Seed and Elephants"
"Historicism"
"Learning in War-Time"
"Membership"
"On Forgiveness"
"Religion and Rocketry"
"The World's Last Night"

"The Fifteenth-Century Heroic Line"

Essays and Studies by Members of the English Association.
XXIV (1939): 28–41. Reprinted in *Selected Literary Essays.*

This essay displays Lewis at his scholarly finest, using well-reasoned imagination to solve a literary mystery—like an academic Sherlock Holmes. In the article Lewis argued that 15th-century poetic meter is not as flawed as had been traditionally supposed; the real difficulty is in modern critics' erroneous presuppositions regarding what the early poets were trying to accomplish. Lewis noted that contrary to literary practice from 1550–1900—where writers of lengthy poems preferred to use the same number of beats in virtually every line—earlier English writers sometimes mixed three different beat patterns together; i.e., a half-line could have two beats, three beats, or two beats with a lightly stressed third (which Lewis calls a half-accent).

Lewis wisely presented extended bits of Medieval poetry to make his points, noting that meter comes from poems, not individual lines. One may occasionally quibble with his reading of individual lines, but overall the case is solidly reasoned and sheds light on the probable intentions of Hawes, Barclay, Elyot, and other poets of the 15th century. Readers who cannot "feel" the difference between iambs and dactyls or tetrameters and pentameters will find nothing here; readers interested in metrics will find this fascinating.

Marvin D. Hinten
Bowling Green State University

Also See: Literary Criticism, New Criticism, Poetry

Film, Drama, and Music

A: Plays and Films about C. S. Lewis
See Chart below

B: Film Versions of the Chronicles of Narnia
See Chart on page 166.

C: Stage and Play Adaptations of the Chronicles of Narnia
See Chart on page 167.

Also See: *Shadowlands* (the Play and Film Versions as Art), *Shadowlands* (the Play and Film Versions as Biography)

PLAYS AND FILMS ABOUT C. S. LEWIS

Title	Key People	Additional Information
Shadowlands (original BBC film)	Written by William Nicholson Directed by Norman Stone Produced by Samuel French	Aired on BBC December 22, 1985 Starred Joss Acland as Lewis and Claire Bloom as Joy
Shadowlands (script)	Written by William Nicholson Published by Samuel French	London 1989 and revised 1992
Shadowlands (stage play)	Written by William Nicholson Directed by Elijah Moshinsky Produced by Brian Eastman	Premiered October 5, 1989 at the Theatre Royal in Plymouth
Shadowlands (Hollywood version)	Directed by Richard Attenborough Produced by Richard Attenborough and Brian Eastman	Starred Anthony Hopkins as Lewis and Debra Winger as Joy
Through Joy and Beyond (Three Part Documentary of Lewis. Parts I and II are of Lewis's Life. Part III "Jack Remembered" is interviews of Friends and Associates)	Written by Walter Hooper and Anthony Marchington Directed by Bob O'Donnell Produced by Lord & King Associated	One-hour condensed version of Parts I and II: Bridgestone Management Group Entire Film: Bob O'Donnell

FILM VERSIONS OF THE CHRONICLES OF NARNIA

Title	Key Players	Additional Information
The Lion, the Witch, and the Wardrobe (Live Action TV)	ABC Television Network Production Adapted by Trevor Preston Produced by Pamela Lonsdale	Aired on TV (UK) in 9 20-minute episodes from July 9 to September 3,1967. Bernard Kay starred as Aslan, Jack Woogar as the Professor, Paul Woller as Peter, Zueika Robson as Susan, Edward McMurray as Edmund, and Elizabeth Crowther as Lucy.
The Lion, the Witch, and the Wardrobe (Animated TV)	The Episcopal Radio-TV Foundation and The Children's Television Workshop Animated by Steve and Bill Melendez	Aired on CBS in 2 one-hour episodes on April 1 and 2, 1976. First aired in UK on ATV Easter, April 6, 1980 in a redubbed version with Stephen Thorne as Aslan, Sheila Hancock as the White Witch, Arthug Lowe as Mr. Beaver, June Whitfield as Mrs. Beaver and Leo McKern as the Professor.
The Lion, the Witch, and the Wardrobe (Live Action and Animation)	Adapted by Alan Seymour Directed by Marilyn Fox Produced by Paul Stone Music by Geoffrey Burgon	Aired on BBC in 6 half-hour episodes from November 13 to December 18, 1988. Starred Ailsa Berk and William Todd-Jones as Aslan, Barbara Kellerman as the White Witch, Richard Dempsey as Peter, Jonathon R. Scott as Edmund, Sophie Cook as Susan and Sophie Wilcox as Lucy.
Prince Caspian (Live Action and Animation)	Directed by Alex Kirby Produced by Paul Stone	Aired on BBC in 2 half-hour episodes on November 19 and 26, 1989. Starred Jean-Marc Perret as Prince Caspian, Warwick Davis as Reepicheep, Robert Land as King Miraz, Big Mick as Trumpkin and the Pevensie children were the same as from LWW.
The Silver Chair (Live Action and Animation)	Directed by Alex Kirby Produced by Paul Stone	Aired on BBC in 6 half-hour episodes from November 18 to December 23, 1990. Starred David Thwiltes as Eustace, Camila Power as Jill Pole, Tom Baker as Puddleglum, Richard Henders as Prince Rilian and the Black Knight, Barbara Kellerman as the Green Lady, Stephen Reynolds as the Giant King, Lesley Nicol as the Giant Queen and Warwick Davis as Glimfeather.
The Voyage of the "Dawn Treader" (Live Action and Animation)	Directed by Alex Kirby Produced by Paul Stone	Aired on BBC in 4 half-hour episodes from November 26 to December 24, 1989. Starred Ailsa Berk, William Todd-Jones and Time Rose as Aslan, Samuel West as King Caspian, John Hallam as Captain Drinian, the Pevensie children were the same as those from LWW and Ronald Pickup provided Aslan's voice.

STAGE AND PLAY ADAPTATIONS OF THE CHRONICLES OF NARNIA

Title	Key Players	Additional Information
The Horse and His Boy (stage play)	Adapted by Glyn Robbins Directed by Richard Williams Produced by Vanessa Ford Productions	Premiered September 25, 1990 at the Charter Theatre, Preston.
The Lion, the Witch, and the Wardrobe (musical)	Music, book, and lyrics by Irita Kutchmy. Published by Joseph Weinberger Ltd.	
The Lion, the Witch, and the Wardrobe (play)	Adapted by Joseph Robinette Published by The Dramatic Publishing Company	
The Lion, the Witch, and the Wardrobe (stage play)	Adapted by Glyn Robbins Directed by Richard Williams Produced by Aldersgate, Westminster and Vanessa Ford Productions	Premiered November 19, 1984 at the Westminster Theatre, London.
The Magician's Nephew (stage play)	Adapted by Aurand Harris Published by The Dramatic Publishing Company	
The Magician's Nephew (play)	Adapted by Glyn Robbins Directed by Richard Williams Produced by Vanessa Ford Productions and Alderstage Productions	Premiered September 20, 1988 at the Ashcroft Theatre in Croydon.
Narnia (musical)	Written by Jules Tasca Lyrics by Ted Drachman Music by Thomas Tierney Published by The Dramatic Publishing Company	
The Voyage of the "Dawn Treader" (stage play)	Adapted by Glyn Robbins Directed by Richard Williams Produced by Aldersgate Productions Ltd.	Premiered September 9, 1986 at the Theatre Royal, Bath.

"Finchley Avenue"

Occasional Poets: An Anthology. Richard Adams (ed). Harmondsworth, Middlesex: Penguin Books, 1986: 102–4. Reprinted in *Collected Poems*.

A pedestrian poem so unlike Lewis (except in part) that its authorship has been called into question by Kathryn Lindskoog; see the entire *The Lewis Legacy* 65 (Summer 1995), especially pages 1–8 and 12 where she raises numerous questions about "Finchley Avenue."

Don W. King
Montreat College

"First and Second Things"

See entry on Notes on the Way (27 June 1942)

First and Second Things: Essays on Theology and Ethics

Walter Hooper (ed). London: Collins, 1985.

See separate entries on the following:

"Before We Can Communicate"
"Bulverism"
"The Decline of Religion"
"First and Second Things"
"Horrid Red Things"
"The Humanitarian Theory of Punishment"
"Meditation in a Toolshed"
"Modern Translations of the Bible"
"On the Reading of Old Books"

"On the Transmission of Christianity"
"Revival or Decay?"
"Some Thoughts"
"The Sermon and the Lunch"
"Two Lectures"
"Vivisection"
"Work and Prayer"
"Xmas and Christmas"

"A Footnote to Pre-History"

Punch 217 (September 14, 1949): 304 (under the pseudonym Nat Whilk). Revised and retitled "The Adam Unparadised" and reprinted in *Poems* and *Collected Poems*.

Picking up where **John Milton**'s Book XII of *Paradise Lost* ends, Lewis pictured Adam and **Eve** leaving Eden and discovering other creatures: dwarves, monopods, giants, and other mythical beings. The fears they might have felt as a result have been transmitted down the ages to all mankind who share the fears when they come into contact with such beings.

Don W. King
Montreat College

Form and Style in Poetry (Book Review)

The Oxford Magazine. XLVII (6 December 1928): 283–84.

This collection of *opuscula* is composed primarily of lectures reconstructed from verbatim reports and notes. According to Lewis, a unity of theme is derived from the "doctrine of the pure Forms—the abstract pattern of the **epic**, the abstract tone of a stanza." Although other topics are covered, including chapters on "Poetical Logic" and "The Simile," Lewis praised the central theme and its author, a man who approached the "critical ideal of being 'like God—easy to please and hard to satisfy.'"

Anne Gardner

Bibliography

Ker, W. P. *Form and Style in Poetry*. R. W. Chambers (ed).

Forms of Things Unknown

First published posthumously in *Of Other Worlds*. Reprinted in *The Dark Tower*. An abridgment of the story appears in *Fifty-Two: A Journal of Books & Authors*. 18 (August 1966): 3–9.

In this short story, six British astronauts have been mysteriously lost on missions to the Moon. Lieutenant John Jenkins has volunteered to go on the next trip alone.

Confessing to a friend that he has been emotionally petrified since the end of a love affair, he adds that he is intrigued by the three brief radio messages from the Moon. The last two suggest that whatever interrupted the speakers came from behind them. Jenkins suggests the presence of non-carbon-based life-forms; his friend dismisses the idea of "animated stones" as impossible. Jernkins replies that trips to the Moon were once considered the stuff of mythology.

The stress of the Moon voyage cures Jenkins' emotional anaesthesis; he is indeed "flesh, not stone." Thirty-five minutes after landing, he finds three perfectly rendered stone images of space-suited astronauts, each posed as though having turned to look behind him.

Elated, taking these artifacts as evidence of life on the Moon, he returns to his ship, sets up the radio on the Moon's surface and begins transmission to earth, his back turned to the dazzling sun so that he can see. Noiselessly emerging from behind his own dark shadow is another shadow, that of a human head surmounted by thick, writhing hairs. Shocked, and realizing that there is no wind on the moon to make the hairs move about like that, he turns. The last words of the story are enigmatic: "His eyes met hers."

Forms of Things Unknown is prefaced by an epigraph from **Perelandra**, "that what was myth in one world might always be fact in some other," which may provide a clue to its ultimate meaning. A difference of opinion exists over the literary quality of the story, with some praising it and others arguing that both the style and content are inferior to Lewis's usual standards. The story itself is part of the **controversy** over posthumously published Lewis manuscripts that also includes *The Dark Tower*. Some think that *Forms of Things Unknown* may not be by Lewis.

Lyle Smith
Biola University

Also See: Myths, Space Travel

Bibliography

Fitzpatrick, John. "The Short Stories: A Critical Introduction." *CSL: The Bulletin of the New York C. S. Lewis Society*. 14 (July 1983): 1–5.

"Founding of the Oxford Socratic Club"

See entry on *Socratic Digest* (Preface)

"Four-Letter Words"

The Critical Quarterly. III (Summer 1961): 118–22. Reprinted in *Selected Literary Essays*.

In this essay, Lewis explored the function of obscenities, or "four-letter words," examining how they reflect or affect the behavioral climate of a particular age. Lewis's inquiry was prompted by a remark attributed to British novelist **D. H. Lawrence**, who suggested that modern **culture**, putatively more sophisticated and evolved well beyond the taboos of Medieval times, was mature enough to respond to obscenity in literature for erotic provocation (for instance, his own notorious and controversial pornographic novel, *Lady Chatterly's Lover*). According to Lawrence, medievals in their primitivism could be inflamed to indecorous behavior by the mere appearance of such words, hence their inhibitions.

Lewis relied on his prodigious knowledge of ancient and Medieval literature to refute this gratuitous attack on Medieval culture. Proceeding to catalogue the word histories of numerous "four-letter words" across Medieval and classical culture, Lewis concluded that human beings never employed obscenities with the motive of seduction or eroticism: "Four-letter words were condemned not on the ground that they are aphrodisiacs but precisely on the ground that they are not."

In other words, the modern sensibility that courts obscenity as a liberating experience misread or imposed upon earlier cultures a mind-set that did not exist. The pagan and Christian authors of pre-modern literature understood the use of "four-letter words" as serviceable for "farce or vituperation" but never eroticism; they would not stoop so low. Lawrence's wishful thinking, Lewis concluded, is a "rebellion against language," not a "return to nature from some local or recent inhibition."

Bruce L. Edwards
Bowling Green State University

Bibliography
Lewis, C. S. "Prudery and Philology."

The Four Loves

London: Geoffrey Bles, 1960. First US edition, New York: Harcourt, Brace & World, 1960.

First published in 1960, *The Four Loves* treats themes that had been at the heart of Lewis's professional work from the very beginning, when he published the book that established his scholarly reputation, *The Allegory of Love*. Some of the book's themes had also been present in his earlier Christian writings—as, for example, in many of the vignettes in *The Great Divorce*. Nevertheless, *The Four Loves* may be regarded as Lewis's definitive treatment of the nature of **love**, the several kinds of love, and the relation between **nature** and **grace**. Although some of the book's discussion of particular loves is dated and reflects its time and place, it

is nevertheless a profound treatment of the relation of "natural" and "supernatural" love and deserves the status of a minor classic in Christian ethics.

Lewis's discussion of the several loves draws heavily upon not only his wide reading but also his personal experience. The discussion of affection and some of the ways in which it may go wrong may have been influenced by Lewis's many years of domestic life with Mrs. **Janie Moore**. There can be little doubt that the chapter on **friendship** reflects strongly the experience of the **Inklings**. And it is unlikely that Lewis would have written the chapter on *eros* as he did had not his marriage with **Joy Davidman** occurred. Their civil marriage took place in 1956 and their ecclesiastical marriage in 1957. Lewis had known Joy for a few years before their marriage and had first corresponded with her in 1950. She died in 1960, the year that *The Four Loves* was published.

Lewis's searing discussion of the possible rivalry between charity and our natural loves, although present through the entire body of his writing, is strongest in several works clearly influenced by Joy Davidman— *Till We Have Faces* (which is dedicated to Joy and in the writing of which she was instrumental), *A Grief Observed* (occasioned, of course, by her death), and *The Four Loves*.

Lewis begins with a distinction between "gift-love" and "need-love" (not unlike the distinction between *agape* and *eros* that has become a staple of Christian **ethics**, especially since the work of Anders Nygren in this century). In Lewis's hands, however, this is not a distinction between divine and human love. There are natural, created forms of both gift-love and need-love (just as there are grace-given forms of each). God, however, is pure gift-love and in relation to God our being is "one vast need." Whether as gift-love or need-love, however, every natural love left to itself is inadequate. That is the fundamental theme of Lewis's treatment. Left to itself, any natural love—*storge, philia,* or *eros*— cannot be what it naturally seeks to be.

After a preliminary discussion of love of nature and love of country, Lewis launches into his treatment of affection. For it, as for friendship and erotic love, the discussion follows a general pattern. Lewis first characterizes at length the natural love, exhibiting features of it that offer at least a mirror of divine love. He then notes the dangers inherent in the natural love's insufficiency (dangers that usually manifest themselves when the love is at its best) and suggests that something more is needed for the love truly to be itself. Affection mirrors divine love especially in its undiscriminating character. Given familiarity over time, almost anyone can become an object of affection. Hence, this love manifests a kind of implicit openness to the worth of every human being, even though it is not, of course, directed to everyone.

What are its dangers? As need-love affection seems so natural, so "built into" human life, that we may come to assume it as a right, as if we are entitled to be loved. Then too, so accustomed is affection to familiar ways that it may have difficulty dealing with change—especially with the presence of another loved one. In such circumstances, affection can be marked by fierce jealousy. As gift-love affection may be unstinting in

its care and concern, but it can never by nature be free of the "need to be needed." In affection we desire the good we can give, and our love cannot work toward "its own abdication." It needs to be supplemented with **reason**, **justice**, and humility, but these are not always naturally within its power.

Of the natural loves, friendship is, according to Lewis, the least grounded in biological need. Emphasizing our individuality and our free choice of other individuals, *philia* always has about it something of the character of a "withdrawal"—a subversive or even world-renouncing quality. Precisely because it is so "spiritual" a love, it can powerfully mirror divine love. This is seen especially in friendship's freedom from jealousy. Although it is a discriminating love, although we are friends only with certain people whom we have chosen for particular reasons, our circle of friends will be open to anyone who shares the interest that binds us together. In this sense it might even be said to be implicitly universal.

In the very grandeur and spirituality of friendship lies its danger. Rightly excluding those who do not share our interests, we may quickly come to value exclusivity for its own sake. Priding ourselves in the special qualities of our group of friends, we may easily become a mutual admiration society. The psychological and moral complexities here are considerable. As Lewis notes, friends are quite right to admire each other. Indeed, it is hard to imagine a close friendship without such admiration. Only the smallest of steps—but a morally crucial step—

separates that appropriate mutual admiration from the sinful corporate **pride** of a circle that values exclusivity for its own sake. Left to itself, friendship is likely to go wrong in this way. Therefore, it should not be left to itself. It too needs to be supplemented—by what Lewis simply calls "goodness"—if we are to learn to see the beauty not only in our friends but also in others.

Friends stand side by side, absorbed in their shared interest. Erotic lovers stand face-to-face, absorbed in each other. In its selfless devotion *eros* (which is something quite different from sexual appetite, called "Venus" by Lewis) mirrors divine love; for it plants "the interests of another in the centre of our being." If affection is jealous but not discriminating, and friendship is discriminating but not jealous, *eros* is both discriminating and jealous. That is simply its natural, created condition and should not be deplored. But it may easily go wrong. So godlike is its claim upon us when we are in its grip that we may make an idol of *eros* itself, and in its name we may do great injustice to others. Left to itself, it cannot keep its own promise to be faithful. It must therefore be supplemented by the whole of the Christian life in which fidelity is given pride of place.

We know how to describe charity in part because each of the natural loves mirrors some aspect of it. Charity is (like affection) undiscriminating, loving even those who do not seem lovable. It is (like friendship) free of jealousy, ready to receive the outsider. It is (like *eros*) selfless, devoted to the good of the beloved. When the natural loves are taken up into charity, when they become incarnate as "modes of charity," they are gradually transformed and perfected. Nevertheless, Lewis's concluding chapter on charity is haunting because it recognizes that this transformation is often likely to be painful. We say the natural loves are transformed and perfected. But it may seem that they must be put to death so that a new life marked by charity can arise. Wise and insightful as the chapters on the natural loves are, *The Four Loves* will be especially read for the power of its concluding discussion of charity, for its recognition of how painful is the perfection of our nature by God's grace.

Gilbert Meilaender

Bibliography

Burnaby, John. *Amor Dei: A Study of the Religion of St. Augustine.* London: Hodder & Stoughton, 1938.

Carpenter, Humphrey. *The Inklings: C. S. Lewis, J. R. R. Tolkien, Charles Williams, and Their Friends.* Boston: Houghton Mifflin Company, 1979.

Meilaender, Gilbert. *Friendship: A Study in Theological Ethics.* Notre Dame and London: University of Notre Dame Press, 1981.

_____. *The Taste for the Other: The Social and Ethical Thought of C. S. Lewis.* Grand Rapids, MI: Eerdmans, 1978.

Nygren, Anders. *Agape and Eros.* Tr. Philip S. Watson. New York: Harper & Row, 1969.

Pieper, Josef. *About Love.* Tr. Richard and Clara Winston. Chicago: Franciscan Herald Press, 1974.

Adam Fox (1883–1977)

The Rev. Adam Fox was a fellow and dean of Divinity at **Magdalen College**, **Oxford**, from 1929 to 1941. His essay "At the Breakfast Table" tells some anecdotes of Lewis in the common room at breakfast with Paul Benecke, J. A. Smith, and Fox himself. (According to Lewis's letter to his brother of November 22, 1931, John Traill Christie was part of these breakfasts.) But Fox's two main importances to a student of Lewis are as Professor of Poetry (1938–43) at Oxford and as an **Inkling**. The first occurred because he exclaimed over the nomination of E. K. Chambers, "This is simply shocking; they might as well make me Professor of Poetry." Lewis replied, "Well, we will" ("At the Breakfast Table"). According to Fox, Chambers and another candidate (Lord David Cecil) split the vote of "the learned," and he was elected with the vote of the rest, after a campaign by Lewis and **J. R. R. Tolkien**. That same year Lewis's pastiche **"From Johnson's *Life of Fox*"** appeared in *The Oxford Magazine* (never reprinted). Fox commented that his lectures as Professor of Poetry were not very successful: he should have been more outrageous.

In 1951, Lewis was nominated to be the Professor of Poetry; he lost by nineteen votes to C. Day Lewis—and one of the reasons he lost was the election of Fox, a very minor poet, years earlier. The basic information about Fox's membership in the Inklings comes from a letter written by Lewis to his brother **Warren Lewis** on March 3, 1950: "Fox read us his latest 'Paradisal' on Blenheim Park in winter. The only line I can quote (wh. seems to me very good) is 'Beeches have figures; oaks, anatomies.' It was in the Troilus stanza and full of his own 'cool, mellow flavour' as the tobacconists say. He

has really in some respects a considerable similarity to Miss Sackville West."

Probably the reason Adam Fox was writing "Paradisals" is that he had a twin sister named Eve. While there is no record that his shorter poems were ever collected, he had published a narrative poem, "Old King Coel" (1937). Probably as an acknowledgment of Fox's published poem, Lewis wrote a lyric "Young King Cole" (as **"Dangerous Oversight,"** 1947) and planned to use it as a title poem for a collection *"Young King Cole" and Other Pieces.*

Joe R. Christopher

Bibliography

Christopher, Joe R. "Who Were the Inklings?" *Tolkien Journal.* 15 (Summer 1972): 5–13.

Fox, Adam. "At the Breakfast Table." *C. S. Lewis at the Breakfast Table.* James T. Como (ed). New York: Macmillan, 1979: 89–95.

Sayer, George. *Jack: C. S. Lewis and His Times.* San Francisco: Harper and Row, 1988.

Sir James George Frazer (1854–1941)

Sir James George Frazer was a Scottish classical scholar and anthropologist, best known for his twelve-volume study *The Golden Bough: A Study in Comparative Religion* (1890–1915). The work originated in Frazer's interest in the rite at Lake Nemi, near Rome, in which the priest-king of Diana of the Wood was succeeded by whoever could slay him. This scene was depicted in J. M. W. Turner's famous picture in the National Gallery, London. *The Golden Bough* itself was the mistletoe, with magical properties (including the power to kill Balder). The abridged edition (1922) of *The Golden Bough* was subtitled *A Study in Magic and Religion.* The work collected an enormous amount of anthropological material from around the world, all shedding light on the Dying and Reviving God, whose story is that of Adonis, Attis, Osiris, Balder, Dionysus, and many others, including **Christ**. Lewis read Frazer and initially took the prevalence of the Dying God story as a disproof of the truth of **Christianity**, but the conversation with Weldon in 1926 began to change this view to what is expressed in **"Myth Became Fact"** (1944).

John Bremer

Also See: Myth

Free Will

The term *free will* is probably misleading because, strictly speaking, the faculty of will itself is neither free nor unfree; it is rather the *person* who does the willing—

or the choosing, or the acting—who is either free or unfree. And a person does something freely only if it is also within the person's power, at the time of acting, to refrain from doing it.

Now perhaps the most important philosophical question concerning the nature of *moral* freedom is whether such freedom is compatible with determinism. In a fully deterministic universe, every event would have a sufficient cause and every *present* event, including every human choice, would also be the product of causes that already existed even before the dawn of human civilization. So every choice would be the product of causes that are totally beyond the chooser's control. Those who argue, as many do, that moral freedom could exist in such a universe are commonly called *compatibilists*; and those who deny this, as Lewis did, are commonly called *incompatibilists*. In **Miracles**, Lewis expressed his incompatibilism, without using the term, this way: "Free will would mean that human beings have the power of independent action, the power of doing something more or other than what was involved [or caused] by the total series of events." It also means, he suggested, the "power of originating events"; that is, of causing events to occur, even though nothing beyond one's control determines one to cause just these events to occur. This means that human beings are, within their own sphere of free actions, a kind of uncaused (or self-determining) cause, even as **God** was the uncaused cause of the universe as a whole.

Moral freedom of the incompatibilist kind plays an important role, of course, in Lewis's understanding of moral evil. If moral virtue requires moral freedom and moral freedom is incompatible with determinism, then any created person with a potential for moral virtue will also have a potential for moral evil; and it is therefore quite possible that God simply could not have created a universe in which great moral virtues are realized and yet no moral evil exists. It is even possible that God could not have achieved his loving purposes for *all* of his children without permitting as much suffering over the short run and as much temporary tragedy as in fact exists.

But is it also possible that a person should freely reject the true God, not merely for a season, but forever? Lewis thought it is; he believed that "the damned are, in one sense, successful rebels to the end" and therefore do in fact defeat God's loving purpose for them. But here his account seems less plausible. We can imagine, easily enough, someone in bondage to ignorance, illusion, and self-deception rejecting a caricature of God, as even Saint Paul did at one time in his life. It is much more difficult, however, to imagine someone making a free and *fully informed* decision to reject the true God. If God is the ultimate source of human **happiness**, as Lewis insisted; if his aim is to satisfy our deepest yearnings in the end; and if separation from God can produce only more and more misery in our lives, then no motive would seem to exist for a *fully informed* decision to reject God. Does not God have the power, therefore, to shatter every illusion over time, even as he shattered Paul's illusions on the road to Damascus, and to undermine over time every possible motive we might have for rejecting him?

Thomas Talbott
Willamette University

Also See: Ethics and Morality, Materialism

Bibliography

Purtill, Richard, *Philosophically Speaking*. Englewood Cliffs: Prentice-Hall, 1975: chapter 3.

Taylor, Richard, *Metaphysics*, 4th ed. Englewood Cliffs: Prentice-Hall, 1992: chapter 5.

Jill Flewett Freud (1927–)

Jill Flewett, a wartime evacuee from London, entered the Lewis household when she was sixteen, in 1943, and was shocked when she eventually realized that her kind host "Jack" Lewis was the famous author C. S. Lewis. She was cherished at the **Kilns** because of her cordial, peaceful personality and her eagerness to help. She stayed until she entered the Royal Academy of Dramatic Art on January 3, 1945.

In his diary, partially published as *Brothers and Friends: An Intimate Portrait of C. S. Lewis,* Warren Lewis recorded his pain about her departure, and on September 4, 1950, he wrote about attending her London wedding. (C. S. Lewis was not well enough to go.) Jill married **Sigmund Freud**'s grandson Clement Freud, who became a Member of Parliament. The Freuds visited at the Kilns two or three times, and Jill was going there for dinner when Lewis died. (She called on the telephone a half hour after Lewis's death and got the news from **Warren Lewis**.) In 1968 and 1969 Warren made use of her cottage at the seashore.

Stephen Schofield interviewed Jill Freud and obtained a detailed account of Lewis's kindness and her life in the Kilns. "Lewis was the first person who made me believe I was an intelligent human being and the whole time I was there he built up my confidence in myself and in my ability to think and understand."

Lewis always called her June. He inscribed a copy of *The Screwtape Letters* for her: "**Beauty** and brains and virtue never dwell / Together in one place, the critics say. / Yet we have known a case / You must not ask her name / But seek it 'twixt July and May."

Jill Freud reared five children but never lost interest in her acting career. Almost fifty years after she left the Kilns for drama school, she played the part of Madame Trochau in "Maigret and the Night Club Dancer," a television mystery that aired on Public Television in the United States in 1994.

Kathryn Lindskoog

Bibliography

Freud, Jill. "Pam B: With Girls at Home." *The Search for C. S. Lewis.* Stephen Schofield (ed). South Plainfield, NJ: Bridge, 1983: 55–59.

Sigmund Freud (1856–1939)

Sigmund Freud was a brilliant Vienna physician whose explanations of mental illness have had an enormous impact on modern attitudes toward sexuality and human nature. His influence on society has even been reckoned by some to be as significant as that of Copernicus and Darwin. During his lifetime, however, some of those he trained to carry on his ideas (Alfred Adler and **Carl Jung**) rejected his teachings. Since his death, his theories have been increasingly seen as personal interpretations placed on the mental problems of a small number of people from a narrow segment of turn-of-the-century Vienna.

Though Freud was middle-aged when Lewis was born, Lewis's career as a writer roughly paralleled the period when Freud's ideas were having their greatest influence. This is perhaps one reason why Lewis's disdain for Freudian psychiatry was so deep and abiding. Lewis devoted nine chapters of *Pilgrim's Regress* to Freudianism. Placed in prison by Sigismund Enlightenment, John (the chief character) finds himself under the gaze of a giant called Spirit of the Age. The giant's eyes have a chilling property, "whatever they looked on became transparent." John and those in prison about him have their inner organs and even cancerous tumors exposed for all to see. Shocked, John falls on his face, crying out "I am in **hell** for ever." In the end, John escapes, aided by his common sense and a woman knight named Reason.

In a chapter of *Mere Christianity* entitled "Morality and Psychoanalysis," Lewis expressed a more restrained view of Freud. He had no problem when Freud spoke as a specialist on treating mental illness. But he objected when Freud gave a "general philosophical view of the world," because that was a field in which the famous psychiatrist remained a mere "amateur." Lewis went on to draw a sharp distinction between mental problems and moral issues. Psychiatry could deal with the former, it had no special insight into the latter.

In **"Psycho-Analysis and Literary Criticism"** (first published in 1942), Lewis spoke from his own literary expertise. He dealt with Freud's theory that "all art" could be traced to fantasies about "honour, power, riches, fame or the love of women." He also dealt with the **symbolism** that Freud saw in **dreams** and literature. In both cases, he agreed that Freud was sometimes right about hidden meanings, but went on to insist that literature meant much more than the often sex-saturated interpretations offered by Freud and his followers.

Freud's most lasting impact lies in a common impression that has been taken from his ideas. In the fourth chapter of *The Problem of Pain* Lewis explained that psychoanalysis had left most people thinking that "the sense of Shame is a dangerous and mischievous thing." In the past, people concealed their moral failings. Now they were told to be open about many sins because "we need not be ashamed of them." As a result, **Christianity** has to convince modern people of the diagnosis, human wickedness, before it can offer the proper diagnosis, the good news of salvation.

Mike Perry

Also See: Guilt, Human Nature, Literary Criticism, Myth, Psychology, Symbolism

Bibliography

Kirkpatrick, Hope. "Some Preliminary Thoughts on Lewis and Freud." *CSL: The Bulletin of the New York C. S. Lewis Society.* 3 (September 1972): 2–4.

_____. "Lewis contra Freud." *CSL: The Bulletin of the New York C. S. Lewis Society.* 5 (February 1973): 2–6.

_____. "A Reply to Dr. Plank." *CSL: The Bulletin of the New York C. S. Lewis Society.* 4 (April 1973): 8–9.

Lewis, C. S. *Mere Christianity*; *Pilgrim's Regress*; *The Problem of Pain*; "Psycho-Analysis and Literary Criticism."

Plank, Robert. "Can Lewis and Freud Be Reconciled?" *CSL: The Bulletin of the New York C. S. Lewis Society.* 4 (March 1973): 5–7.

Friendship

Of all the loves, friendship should be the one most particularly identified with Lewis, because of the strong emphasis he placed upon it and the extensive ways he explored it.

Friendship, or *philia*, is the second of the four loves discussed by Lewis in *The Four Loves*. As Lewis defined friendship, it is not just companionship, not just having lots of friends whose company one enjoys. *Philia* is a deep, lasting relationship based on a common insight, interest, or taste between two or more people, which others do not share. Although the ancient world regarded friendship as the highest of the loves, Lewis complained that the modern world discounts it. Part of his effort, in *The Four Loves* and elsewhere, was to rehabilitate it.

Lewis explained that friendship declined for two reasons: because it is not an instinctive or organic love, like affection or *eros*, so that many people never experience it; and because of the widespread tendency to regard a close friendship as a homosexual relationship. Lewis in his discussion of friendship developed a lengthy explanation of the ways friendship and erotic love are different, though one can have both for the same person. That led into the question of whether friendship can exist between the sexes. Lewis concluded that it is indeed possible and it does occur, but he regarded it as fairly rare because men and women tended not to share the same type of **education** and lacked the common interests that are the basis of *philia*. Lewis also pointed out as a danger in friendship the sense of **pride** and indifference to outside opinion that can arise out of excluding others from what is by definition an exclusive relationship and the dangers inherent in forming what he elsewhere called an "inner ring" (**"The Inner Ring"**), the willingness to compromise oneself to obtain membership in a group and the cruelty practiced against those who are kept outside.

Male friendships formed a very important part of Lewis's own life, in his words the "greatest of worldly goods" (*They Stand Together*), and "by far the chief source of my happiness" (*Surprised by Joy*). In *Surprised by Joy* he called **Arthur Greeves** his First Friend—defined as someone who shares one's interests and agrees with one's ideas about them—and **Owen Barfield** his Second Friend, someone who shares one's interests but disagrees with one's approaches and ideas. Other close friends included **A. C. Harwood, J. R. R. Tolkien, Charles Williams**, and others in the group called the **Inklings. Warren Lewis**, in addition to being his brother, was among his closest friends throughout his life. It was male friendship that he chiefly delighted in, and that could be achieved most fully only if **women** were excluded. Thus, fewer examples of friendships of Lewis with women are evident, though **Sister Penelope** and **Ruth Pitter** deserve mention. Lewis also said that

his love for **Joy Davidman Gresham** began as friendship, and continued as friendship even after it grew into erotic love.

Of his friendships, perhaps the most notable was that with Barfield. Barfield was elected to a scholarship at Wadham College, **Oxford**, the same year Lewis entered University College. Common interests drew them together, particularly their love of **poetry**—both wrote poetry that was not in the mode of **T. S. Eliot** and other proponents of modern verse. They engaged in furious arguments regarding their differences in things that mattered most to them. They often took holidays together and began in 1927 **walking tours** with a couple of other friends almost every spring. In the late 1920s to early 1930s, they carried on a correspondence they called **"The Great War,"** whose central subject was the **imagination**, with Barfield contending that poetry initially conveyed knowledge and therefore imagination disseminated **truth**, and Lewis holding that imagination conveyed meaning, not truth. In 1928 Barfield dedicated his first book, *Poetic Diction*, to Lewis, using an aphorism from Blake, "Opposition is true friendship." Lewis in 1936 dedicated *The Allegory of Love* "to Owen Barfield, wisest and best of my unofficial teachers."

Lewis wove friendship into several of his stories, as important thematic motifs. Ransom forms deep friendships with Hyoi and Whin, two *hrossa* in *Out of the Silent Planet*. The narrator ("Lewis") in chapters 1 and 2 of *Perelandra* is a close friend of Ransom. The difficulties Mark Studdock encounters in *That Hideous Strength* are to some extent a result of his lack of friendships and his desire to be a part of an influential inner circle of power.

Friendship is most important, however, in *Till We Have Faces*, which could be called a development in fiction of the central themes spelled out a few years later in *The Four Loves*. The thesis of *The Four Loves* is that the natural loves (affection, friendship, and *eros*) can remain loves only if they are infused with, or transformed by, divine love (*agape*). The self-absorbed Orual perverts each of the natural loves through need and possessiveness into a kind of unlove, even hatred: the motherly affection, or *storge*, she has for Psyche; the friendship, or *philia* she shares with the Fox; and the well-hidden sexual desire, or *eros*, she felt toward Bardia.

Orual's love for the Fox begins as, and always remains partly, *storge*, but it is also to a considerable extent *philia*, for they are drawn together by their mutual interests, especially the hunger for knowledge. Because she has few friends, Orual comes to depend on the Fox and clutches at him possessively, subtly pressuring him to remain with her in Glome, despite his deep desire to return to Greece. After persuading him to stay, she begins to neglect him, since her life is full of activity as Queen and she no longer has time for him as she did before. Similarly, her relationship with Bardia begins as *philia*, as Bardia teaches her to use a sword and serves as her closest advisor when she becomes queen. However, she steadily becomes more and more greedy and devouring, craving his presence and the sound of his voice, fantasizing that someday he would come to her, begging her to become his wife. The story of Orual moves toward her recognition that genuine love is selfless and giving, while her love, which she thought had been selfless and giving, was in fact the opposite. Only as she begins to think of others instead of self and opens herself to *agape* can perverted friendship be transformed into genuine love and can she find salvation through love for and the love of a loving **God**.

Peter J. Schakel
Hope College

Bibliography

Armstrong, Robert L. "Friendship." *The Journal of Value Inquiry*. 19 (1985): 211–16.

Carpenter, Humphrey. *The Inklings: C. S. Lewis, J. R. R. Tolkien, Charles Williams, and Their Friends*. Boston: Houghton Mifflin, 1979.

Meilaender, Gilbert. *The Taste for the Other: The Social and Ethical Thought of C. S. Lewis*. Grand Rapids, MI: Eerdmans, 1978.

Nakao, Setsuko. "Friendship." *Canadian C. S. Lewis Journal*. 50 (Spring 1985): 1–13.

Schakel, Peter J. *Reason and Imagination in C. S. Lewis: A Study of Till We Have Faces*. Grand Rapids, MI: Eerdmans, 1984.

"From Johnson's *Life of Fox*"

The Oxford Magazine. LVI (9 June 1938): 737–38.

"From Johnson's *Life of Fox*" was originally published anonymously in *The Oxford Magazine* on June 9, 1938. The essay was occasioned by **Adam Fox**'s (1883–1977) election to the **Oxford University** Chair of Poetry, achieved largely with the support of Lewis and **J. R. R. Tolkien**. Fox was a member of the **Inklings** and dean of Divinity at **Magdalen College**, Oxford, where Lewis was also a fellow (faculty member). When the scholarly but dry E. K. Chambers was nominated, Fox had said offhandedly at breakfast that they may as well elect him. Lewis said, "We will." Since Fox had

only published one long poem called "Old King Coel" in 1937, many of the Oxford fellows with M.A.s (the voting group) were upset, whereupon they nominated an additional candidate. The vote was split and Fox won the five-year term as Professor of Poetry. Many never forgave Lewis, and it may have been a factor in his never being elected to a professorship at Oxford. Lewis said in later years that he had made a mistake in supporting Fox.

The essay itself imitates the style of **Samuel Johnson**'s 18th-century *Lives of the English Poets*, which is richly allusive, has a varied vocabulary and a sophisticated syntax with many clauses and parallel structures. Lewis especially echoed the well-known passage from Johnson's *Life of Pope* comparing Pope and **John Dryden**. Lewis used the essay to defend the selection of Fox, slam the pedantic and obscurantist **poetry** of **T. S. Eliot** and Ezra Pound, and praise Fox's poetry as "simple and unadorned," with "the regularity of **nature** and the sobriety of **reason**."

Wayne Martindale
Wheaton College

"From the Latin of Milton's *De Idea Platonica Quemadmodum Aristoteles Intellexit*"

English. 5 no. 30 (1945): 195.

This poem is Lewis's translation of **John Milton**'s "On the Platonic Idea as Understood by Aristotle" (probably a school exercise dated between 1628–30). It asks the Muses to answer the Platonic riddle: "Who was the first being who served as the archetype for the creation of mankind?" In a headnote, Lewis said he hoped his translation, poor as it is, would send others off to explore Milton's "exquisite grotesque."

Don W. King
Montreat College

"Funeral of a Great Myth"

First published posthumously in *Christian Reflections*.

In this essay, Lewis gently satirized the **myth** of inevitable human progress (called by Lewis "Developmentalism" or "Evolutionism"), demonstrating its mythical character from literary, internal, and scientific evidences. As described by Lewis, the myth of inevitable progress (a theme also developed in **"Is Theology Poetry?"**) is dramatic in nature, beginning in the lifeless void, then introducing life, which struggles to produce man, whose destiny is godhead. In the tragic denouement, **nature** cools the sun, extinguishing all life in endless darkness.

According to Lewis, the myth is based on logical fallacies. Whereas **science** treats reason as an absolute, the myth treats **reason** as the by-product of irrational forces, undercutting the rational basis of the myth required for credibility. The central fallacy of the myth—development from simplicity to complexity—is supported by observation of such development in organic life and in mechanical inventions. However, in both cases, the simple beginning is the product of something already more complex: the oak produces the acorn; the first locomotive is the product of a human mind.

Lewis noted that the myth's ambivalence encourages ethical relativism, while producing a scenario in which to play out Oedipal resentments; it enables salesmen to appeal to the human desire for the latest thing; and modern **politics** would be impossible without the myth, for

it obscures the fact that change is less likely to produce progress than regress.

Lyle Smith
Biola University

Also See: Bernard Acworth, Evolution, H. G. Wells.

"The Future of Forestry"

The Oxford Magazine. 56 (February 10, 1938): 383 (under the pseudonym Nat Whilk). Reprinted in *Poems* and *Collected Poems.*

One of several poems written by Lewis which questions the encroachment of the modern world upon the traditional English countryside. In particular, Lewis wondered when all the trees were gone—victims of roads and shops—who would tell the children what trees were?

Don W. King
Montreat College

G

"The Genesis of a Medieval Book"

First published posthumously in *Studies in Medieval and Renaissance Literature.*

This essay, drafted as the first chapter of a book never completed, dates to and has much in common with two other works Lewis wrote toward the end of his professional career: *The Discarded Image* (1961) and *An Experiment in Criticism* (1961). Lewis intended the work to elucidate the conventions of authorship and readership in the Middle Ages, and this essay reflects in miniature those mature critical principles and historical perspectives characteristic of Lewis's canon of **literary criticism**.

The essay compares in some detail two dissimilar 13th-century Anglo-Saxon works, the *Brut* and *Sawles Warde.* Despite their differences, the two works share one crucial element according to Lewis: a process of composition "wholly foreign to modern literature but normal in the literature of the Middle Ages."

That process involves a concept of "shared authorship" that bespeaks the collaborative mind-set of Medieval authors. Such authors, Lewis said, are at once "the most unoriginal or the most original of men": in some ways they care little for their own innovation and

seem "enslaved" to their sources; but in other ways they "cavalierly" supplement the now evolving text from their own knowledge and **imagination**. Thus, they produce works more like "cathedrals" constructed from disparate styles than books resembling an organic whole.

For critics of Medieval literature, this means that "all criticism should be of books, not authors," since the conception of authorship as a single mind that brings into being some wholly new work or genre is inconceivable to the Middle Ages. These works must be allowed to "work on us in [their] own way" and judged on their own merits.

Bruce L. Edwards
Bowling Green State University

Also See: Medieval World

Bibliography

Edwards, Bruce L. *A Rhetoric of Reading: C. S. Lewis's Defense of Western Literacy.* Provo, UT: Brigham Young University Press, 1985.

_____ (ed). *The Taste of the Pineapple; Essays on C. S. Lewis as Reader, Critic, and Imaginative Writer.* Bowling Green, OH: Popular Press, 1988.

Hannay, Margaret. *C. S. Lewis.* New York: Ungar, 1981.

"Genius and Genius"

The Review of English Studies. XII no. 46 (1936): 189–94. Reprinted in *Studies in Medieval and Renaissance Literature*.

This short essay is a rather narrowly focused, technical discussion by Lewis intended to resolve the confusion introduced by the double role of "Genius" in **Edmund Spenser**'s allegorical poem *The Faerie Queene*, a favorite of Lewis's, and one that he explores in great depth in *The Allegory of Love*.

Lewis traced the literary history of Genius by noting that he begins as a character who represents a higher, "second self" and then becomes associated with reproduction. The character of Genius thus evolved dually— as a "spiritual double" who may be good or evil, and as "the god of generation." Under **Christianity**'s influence this literary image develops into a "guardian **angel**" and, later, in modern uses, "the poetic self," or what many think of as one's "genius" or creativity.

The critical question revolved around Spenser's paradoxical use of Genius as god and Genius as demonic self within a few lines of each other in the poem. Lewis's speculative solution was to suggest that Spenser's intention—obscured by modern punctuation of the poem— was to draw attention to these contrasting characters, not to equate the two—hence, providing a warning to the reader that it is the evil Genius under view.

Non-Spenserian scholars may be most interested in this essay because of Lewis's explication of the term *Oyarses*, identified in some Medieval literature with Genius. Lewis employed the term in his space trilogy as the interplanetary intelligences through whom Maleldil rules the cosmos.

Bruce L. Edwards
Bowling Green State University

Bibliography

Lewis, C. S. *Out of the Silent Planet; Perelandra; Spenser's Images of Life; That Hideous Strength*.

The Genuine Text (Letter)

The Times Literary Supplement. (2 May 1935): 288.

Raised in response to J. Dover Wilson's *Manuscript of Hamlet*, the question of what is the genuine text of **Shakespeare**'s *Hamlet*. Lewis suggested that since Shakespeare wrote with theatrical performance in mind any textual alterations made as a result of the collaboration of the playwright with the actors (i.e., the "prompt book") should in fact be viewed as the genuine text and not as "contamination."

Marjorie L. Mead
The Marion E. Wade Center

The Genuine Text (Letter)

The Times Literary Supplement. (23 May 1935): 331.

In a follow-up response of May 16, 1935 (*TLS*, 313), to Lewis's initial letter of May 2 (see previous letter), Wilson suggested that a comparison of the two texts— the full *Hamlet*, and the "maimed" prompt-book version—"in action" (i.e., as staged) is the only way to determine which in fact is the genuine text as **Shakespeare** intended it to be. Lewis, in turn, cautioned that "best text does not [always] equal genuine text." Wilson continued the discussion in two additional letters (*TLS*, 30 May 1935, 348; *TLS*, 13 June 1935, 380).

Marjorie L. Mead
The Marion E. Wade Center

George MacDonald: An Anthology (Preface)

MacDonald, George. *George MacDonald: An Anthology*. London: Geoffrey Bles, 1946.

In 1947, C. S. Lewis edited a book with 365 brief quotations gleaned from the religious writings of **George MacDonald** (1824–1905). In the preface Lewis explained that he had done so to discharge "a debt of **justice**." Though he had never concealed the debt that he owed to MacDonald, he felt that many of his readers failed to "take even now sufficient notice of that affiliation." *George MacDonald: An Anthology* was intended to make that debt clear to all. MacDonald was a Congregational minister as well as a Scottish novelist and poet who is best remembered for his children's **fairy tales**. In the preface Lewis noted that MacDonald's "writing as a whole is undistinguished, at time fumbling." But he also pointed out that there are "passages, many of them in this collection, where the wisdom and (I would dare call it) the holiness that are in him triumph over and burn away the baser elements of his style." He went on to praise MacDonald as "better than any man" at the art of "**fantasy** that hovers between the allegorical and the mythopoeic."

Mike Perry

Bibliography

Edwards, Bruce L., Jr. "Towards a Rhetoric of Fantasy Criticism: C. S. Lewis's Reading of MacDonald and Morris" 3 *Literature and Belief*: 63–67.
Horsman, Gail. "C. S. Lewis and George MacDonald: A Comparison of Styles" *CSL: The Bulletin of the New York C. S. Lewis Society* 13 (December 1981): 1–5.

"George Orwell"

Time and Tide. XXXVI (8 January 1955): 43–44. Reprinted in *Of This and Other Worlds* and *On Stories*.

This review of George Orwell's *Animal Farm* contrasted that work with Orwell's more popular *1984*. Though both novels deal with Orwell's postwar disillusionment with Soviet Communism, Lewis questioned the popularity of the latter work, arguing that as a work of art, *Animal Farm* is the better of the two.

Lewis pointed out that *Animal Farm* is shorter than *1984* and does all the longer work does and more. In Lewis's view, the "dead wood" in *1984*—the attention given State anti-sexual propaganda—probably reflected Orwell's acquaintance with the "anti-Puritanism" of the 1920s, inspired by the novels of **D. H. Lawrence**. *Animal Farm*, on the other hand, unburdened of Orwell's personal likes and dislikes, is distanced, allowed to become a **myth** and to speak for itself. Wit and humor are liberated, the satire more effective. Making his characters animals, Orwell actually makes them more human; the tyranny of the pigs is all the more detestable because of the nobility and idealism of the other animals whom they exploit; the death of Boxer the horse moves us more deeply than all the cruelties of *1984*. By contrast, the cruelty of the State rulers in *1984* is odious but not tragic, because the novel's hero and heroine lack nobility.

Lyle Smith
Biola University

Also See: Communism and Fascism, Democracy, Monarchy, Politics

Bibliography

Filmer, Kath. "That Hideous 1984: The Influence of C. S. Lewis' *That Hideous Strength* on Orwell's *Nineteen Eighty-Four*." *Extrapolation*. 26 no. 2 (Summer 1985): 160–69.

Jocelyn Easton "Jock" Gibb (1907–1979)

Gibb worked for two book publishers, Methuen and Geoffrey Bles, and in 1954, when **Geoffrey Bles** retired, Jock became the managing director. His relationship, first with C. S. Lewis until 1963, and then with **Warren Lewis** until 1973, and with **Walter Hooper** and other estate trustees until 1974, played an important, but behind-the-scenes role in the total production, promotion, distribution, and sale of millions of Lewis's books.

In 1965 he edited, with a preface, a book of essays, *Light on C. S. Lewis*, about Lewis as viewed by his friends. Gibbs hoped that it would be "something of a prologue to *The Letters of C. S. Lewis*." In 1971 he contributed an article on C. S. Lewis to the *Encyclopaedia Britannica*, calling Lewis "a bold and doughty conversationalist, . . . a varied man of letters whose real intellectual brilliance might well take years of study to appreciate fully."

Richard James
Burkesville Christian Church

Bibliography

Gibb, Jocelyn (ed). *Light on C. S. Lewis*. New York: Harcourt Brace Jovanovich, 1965.
_____. "Lewis, C. S." *Encyclopaedia Britannica. Vol. 13.* Chicago: Encyclopaedia Britannica, 1971: 1007–8.
Gilbert, Douglas, and Clyde S. Kilby. *C. S. Lewis: Images of His World*. Grand Rapids, MI: Eerdmans, 1973.
Green, Roger Lancelyn, and Walter Hooper. *C. S. Lewis: A Biography*. New York: Harcourt Brace Jovanovich, 1974.
Hooper, Walter. *C. S. Lewis: A Companion & Guide*. San Francisco: HarperCollins, 1996: 659–61.
Lewis, Warren Hamilton. *Brothers and Friends: The Diaries of Major Warren Hamilton Lewis*. Clyde S. Kilby and Marjorie Lamp Mead (eds). San Francisco: Harper & Row, 1982.
Lindskoog, Kathryn. *Light in the Shadowlands*. Sisters, OR: Multnomah, 1994.

God

Lewis thought that many modern people have a grossly inadequate concept of God. Even otherwise intelligent and well-educated people have an idea of God that is either so primitive or so abstract—or is such a curious mixture of both—that it gives them no help at all in thinking about God.

By a primitive idea of God, I mean first of all an anthropomorphic one: the picture of an old man with a white beard enthroned on a cloud somewhere in the sky. But aside from anthropomorphism in that physical sense, many people seem to think of God as having human characteristics and human limitations. No doubt this is sometimes due to misunderstood or half-remembered biblical imagery, and many who believe this probably realize this primitive idea of God is not held by the Christians they know. But even so, the image has its effect. As the senior devil Screwtape says to the junior devil Wormwood in *The Screwtape Letters*, "Suggest to [the person you are tempting] a picture of something in red tights and persuade him that since he cannot believe in that . . . he therefore can't believe in you." This is a ploy for persuading moderns not to believe in devils, and a similar ploy seems to have its effect on belief in God: "Suggest to them a picture of an old man enthroned on a cloud and persuade them that since they can't believe in that they can't believe in God."

At the opposite extreme is a picture so abstract and remote as to kill interest: God as a "force" or "power" somehow "behind" or "before" the universe. About this Lewis said, "Never … let us think that while anthropomorphic images are a concession to our weakness the abstractions are the literal **truth**. Both are equally concessions; each singly misleading and the two together mutually corrective. Unless you sit to it very lightly … the abstraction is fatal. It will make the life of lives inanimate and the love of loves impersonal" (**Letters to Malcolm**).

Lewis himself always emphasized the intense *personality* of God: not only is God a person, he is the only *real* person; our personhood is a pale and remote shadow of God's. Since for some people "being a person" seems to mean "having a body," it may be worthwhile to explain what Lewis meant (and what traditional theologians and philosophers meant) by being a person. A person is a being capable of *knowing* and *choosing*. (A baby may not *yet* be making choices, a person in a coma may not *now* be making choices, but both are *capable* of knowing and choosing.) God has both knowledge and choice in the highest degree, always aware of everything capable of being known, and able to choose perfectly. God's choices are always morally perfect but otherwise completely unimpeded: God can choose anything but evil, and his choices determine what occurs in reality.

Perfect knowledge, or *omniscience*; unimpeded choice, or *omnipotence*; and morally perfect choice, or *perfection*—these are the defining characteristics of God in traditional **theology** and **philosophy**. And these are the characteristics that Lewis emphasized in his writings. If God were not aware, if he were unable to choose, then God would be *sub*personal: less than we are. But, in fact, Lewis wrote, God is *super*personal: all that we are, and far more. The primitive idea of God takes away God's superpersonality to substitute a human personality; the abstract idea of God takes away personality altogether.

The modern person sometimes asks, "Why should I care about God?" The first step in answering is to point out that if the traditional idea of God is true, we would cease to exist if God did not think of us and will to keep us in existence. God is interested in us; that in itself is a reason. Think of some person you admire intensely; imagine that person wanted you to get to know him or her better: would you not respond? (If you admire no one you are in a bad way; but if you think, "I'd rather get to know N than God," recall that God *invented* N.) Lewis's vivid sense of the "personalness" of God is due partly to his poetic, insightful side, but it is founded on his logical, analytic side.

Richard Purtill
Western Washington University

Also See: Apologetics, Christianity, Free Will, Good and Evil, Imagination, RAF Talks, Reason

"God in the Dock"

See entry on "Difficulties in Presenting the Christian Faith to Modern Unbelievers"

God in the Dock: Essays on Theology

Walter Hooper (ed). London: Collins, 1979.

See separate essay entries on the following:

"Dogma and the Universe"
"God in the Dock"
"The Grand Miracle"
"The Laws of Nature"
"Man or Rabbit?"
"Miracles"
"Must Our Image of God Go?"
"Myth Became Fact"
"Priestesses in the Church?"
"Religion and Science"
"The Trouble with 'X' …"
"What are We to Make of Jesus Christ?"
"We Have No 'Right to Happiness'"

God in the Dock: Essays on Theology and Ethics

Walter Hooper (ed). Grand Rapids, MI: Eerdmans, 1970. First UK edition titled *Undeceptions*. London: Geoffrey Bles, 1971.

See separate essay and letter entries on the following:

"Answers to Questions on Christianity"
"Before We Communicate"
"Behind the Scenes"
"'Bulverism' or The Foundation of 20th-Century Thought"
Canonization (Letter)
Capital Punishment (Letter)
"Christian Apologetics"
The Church's Liturgy (Letter)
Conditions of a Just War (Letter)
Conflict in Anglican Theology (Letter)
Correspondence with an Anglican Who Dislikes Hymns (Letters)
"Cross-Examination"
"Dangers of National Repentance"
Death Penalty (Letter)
"The Decline of Religion"
"Delinquents in the Snow"
"Dogma and the Universe"
"Evil and God"
"First and Second Things"

"God in Three Persons"

The Listener. XXXI (2 March 1944): 224. Retitled "The Three-Personal God" and reprinted in *Beyond Personality* and *Mere Christianity*

"God in Three Persons" was the title of the second article in the fourth, or "Beyond Personality," series of articles as published by the BBC's magazine, *The Listener*. The typescript title of the radio talk given two days earlier was "The Three-Personal God," the same as that in **Beyond Personality** and **Mere Christianity.** In the article Lewis pointed out that when some people say that **God** is not a person, they can hardly mean that God is less than a person. To avoid having creatures (ourselves) greater than their Creator, we must say that God is more than a person. But what it means to say that God is more than a person is not explained by any **religion** other than **Christianity**: "If you are looking for something super-personal there is not a question of choosing between the Christian idea and the other ones. The Christian idea is the only one on the market."

The "Christian idea" that God is three persons in one nature gives us an idea of what a "super-personal" being might be like. To say that they have the same nature is to say that each of the three persons has the same knowledge, the same power, and the same will. To say that each is a distinct person from the others is to say that they have different relationships to each other.

Richard Purtill
Western Washington University

"The Gods Return to Earth"

See entry on *The Fellowship of the Ring* (Book Review)

"Going into Europe: A Symposium"

Encounter. XIX (December 1962): 57.

This article was a brief contribution to a symposium on "Going into Europe." Lewis was one of thirty-two listed contributors—and one of the briefest. He seems to have supposed that the Common Market was inevitable and wanted "a super-national state built out of units far smaller than the existing nations . . . units so small, and real, would then safely develop the greatest local diversity of language, culture, and custom."

John Bremer

Also See: Culture, Politics

Good and Evil

Two possible views of good and evil are: (1) that each of them has independent **reality**; or (2) that evil is dependent on goodness and is a mere lack or misdirection of good. C. S. Lewis defended the second view and examined the arguments for and against this view on a number of occasions. In essence, this view says that no substance is by nature evil and that all moral evil is due to choice. Certain things that we regard as "natural evils" such as disease, insanity, and suffering of all kinds are not by nature evil but can be regarded as punishments for evil or opportunities to do good.

That this is the biblical view is clear. In the Creation story in *Genesis*, everything that **God** created is said to be good. Human evil is attributed to the **sins** of the first humans, tempted by **Satan**. (Satan and devils are fallen **angels** who have fallen by their own choice.) According to the **Bible**, if there were no sin, there would be no suffering, and acceptance of suffering is the way to get rid of sin.

One literary manifestation of this view in Lewis is *Out of the Silent Planet* where the only word that Ransom can find for "bad" in the language of the unfallen race of hrossa on Mars is "bent." This idea that evil is simply a "bending" of good and not an entity in itself is powerfully expressed by this word. In other respects too, Lewis showed that with unfallen races, such as the races of Mars, what we regard as natural evils—death, natural dangers, and so on—can be seen as part of living and accepted as such.

A more explicit consideration of good and evil occurs in the chapter "The Invasion" in *Mere Christianity*. There Lewis considered the idea that there are two Gods—a good and an evil god—as a solution to the problem of evil. This view is called Dualism, and Lewis pointed out two major difficulties with it. First, if we can call one God "good" and the other evil "we are putting into the universe some third thing, a standard or rule of good which one of the powers conforms to and the other fails to conform to, but since the two powers are judged by it this standard, or the Being which made this standard is higher up than either of them, and it will be the real God."

The second difficulty with Dualism is that although we can choose goodness for its own sake, we cannot choose badness for its own sake: "pleasure, money, power, and safety are all, in so far as they go, good things. The badness consists in pursuing them by the wrong method or in the wrong way, or too much ... wickedness when you examine it, turns out to be the pursuit of some good in the wrong way. You can be good for the mere sake of goodness, you cannot be bad for the mere sake of badness."

At its core, Lewis's view of goodness was premised on Saint John the Evangelist's teaching that "God is **love**." As Lewis pointed out in the chapter "Good Infection" in *Mere Christianity* the doctrine of the **Trinity** gives content to Saint John's affirmation, because "Love is something that one person has for another person. If God was a single person then before the world was made He was not love." As a matter of fact God contains three persons, and the love between "Father and Son is such a live concrete thing that this union is itself a person." So "God is not a static thing ... but a dynamic pulsating activity." This activity of God is "a great fountain of energy and beauty spurting up at the very centre of reality," and we must be involved with this activity if we are to be united with God and enter fully into Love.

This being so, we can see how evil is simply not participating in this activity, not loving God as he deserves to be loved, not loving our neighbors as God loves them. All moral evil—wars, tortures, abuses, and exploitations—arise from this lack of love.

The doctrine developed by the ancient and Medieval philosophers that all desire is the desire for some good ties into this view. When we choose evil we are really choosing some limited good—power, sexual pleasure, freedom. Even the picture of **Satan** as given in **Milton**'s *Paradise Lost*, with his slogan "evil be thou my good," is an illustration of this. Those who have idealized Satan have emphasized his desire for freedom: what God commands is just what Satan does not want, simply because God wants it, and Satan's "freedom" is shown by doing the opposite of what God wants. (Much teenage rebellion against parents is based on the same principle.)

In his book *Preface to Paradise Lost* Lewis denied that Milton does, even unconsciously, idealize Satan in this way and showed how Satan's desire for this kind of freedom destroys his being. "He begins by fighting for liberty, however misconceived: but almost at once sinks to fighting for 'Honour, Dominion, glorie, and renoune.' Defeated in this he sinks to that great decision which makes the main subject of the poem—the design of ruining two creatures who had never done him any harm ... to annoy the Enemy whom he cannot directly attack." As Lewis pointed out, "To admire Satan is to give one's vote not only for a world of misery, but also for a world of lies and propaganda, of wishful thinking and incessant autobiography. Yet the choice is possible. Hardly a day passes without some slight movement toward it in each of us." Here as always, Lewis's treatment of good and evil is not only an intellectual examination, but a moral examination, urging us to choose good rather than evil in our own lives.

Richard Purtill
Western Washington University

Also See: Corruption of Nature, Ethics and Morality, The Fall, Free Will, Philosophy

"Good Work and Good Works"

Good Work. XXIII (Christmas 1959): 3–10. Reprinted in *The World's Last Night* and *Screwtape Proposes a Toast.*

Good works, Lewis wrote in this delightful essay, are the charitable deeds we do for others. Good work, on the other hand, means doing a job properly. Jesus **Christ**'s first miracle at the Cana wedding in John 2 illustrates both. Good works saved a poor bridal couple from embarrassment, while good work provided an excellent wine when only mediocre was expected.

Lewis saw good work in decline. Modern society encourages built-in obsolescence, mass production isolates workers from customers, and advertising persuades people to buy things they do not need. Lewis believed that all too many people must work simply to earn money and not because they believe that what they are doing is necessary. Even the artist no longer does the good work of delighting or instructing. Instead, he demands "recognition." Lewis said that such "haughty indifference" to the artist's public "is not genius nor integrity; it is laziness and incompetence."

Lewis closed with a plea for great works of art and good works of charity to also be good work. The essay first appeared in *Good Work* in 1959 and was republished with other essays in *The World's Last Night* and *Screwtape Proposes a Toast.*

Mike Perry

Also See: Aesthetics, Beauty, Culture, Miracles, Pride, Technology

Bibliography

Lewis, C. S. "What Christmas Means to Me."

Grace

Once the human race set off on the path of **sin**, it became harder for each individual to resist sin. That is an essential part of the doctrine of Original Sin: we inherit from our sinful ancestors a **human nature** more inclined to sin than human nature was when **God** made it. Lewis did not share the idea held by some Christians that human nature is so "totally depraved" by Original Sin that our natural powers are no use at all for leading us to God. But he did hold, along with the majority of traditional Christians, that we need special help from God to be worthy of the wonderful destiny of sharing God's life. The technical term for this help is "grace" or "sanctifying grace." As Lewis said in a letter, he avoided the *term* "Grace," but the thing itself he dealt with in at least "a rough and ready way."

Christians have argued whether our salvation and reformation is due entirely to God's help, or grace, or whether our own efforts play some essential part. Lewis pointed out that Scripture often seems to give both answers: "Work out your [own] salvation in fear and trembling" seems to put it all on our own efforts; but the next verse, "for it is God who works in you," emphasizes God's part (Phil. 2:12–13). Lewis pictured the situation as one in which God is continually battering on our defenses, asking us to open our hearts. But God will not enter without our consent; we have the power to say "no." Once we do say "yes," we can say that what happens after that is due to God; but until we say "yes" he respects our freedom and will not—we might even say cannot—save us.

This raises the issue of what will happen if we *never* give our consent, keep God out of our hearts throughout our whole existence. The traditional answer, which Lewis accepted sorrowfully, is **hell**: a state of final and total separation from God.

Some great Christian teachers have held the universalist doctrine that all human beings will eventually be saved. One of these was **George MacDonald**, of whom Lewis said, "I have always regarded him as my master." Other Christians have speculated that those who finally refuse obedience to God will eventually be destroyed, rather than remain in some state of endless **pain.** The chief image used in Scripture for hell, that of fire, may suggest this, for the normal action of fire is to eventually consume what it burns. Those who have held this destructionist position have even pointed out that Christ's most definite words about the duration of hell, "where 'their worm dies not and the fire is not quenched'" (Mark 9:48), seem to refer to the eternal quality of the means of punishment rather than of the duration of time souls are punished.

However, neither destructionism nor universalism has been widely accepted by Christians, and Lewis thought it only honest to give the best defense he could of the majority doctrine. Once it is seen that the suffering of those who go to hell would be due not to some arbitrary command of God but rather to their own stubborn refusal to accept life and **love**, a good many objections are answered.

Richard Purtill
Western Washington University

Also See: Free Will, Redemption

Kenneth Grahame (1859–1932)

Although they were born forty years apart and in different countries, Kenneth Grahame's early life closely paralleled that of C. S. Lewis, and the Scottish author's *The Golden Age* (1895) and *The Wind in the Willows* (1908) would strongly influence Lewis's fiction. Grahame, like Lewis, was the son of scholarly parents. When his mother died, nine-year-old Kenneth and his older brother were sent away to a terrifying boarding school in England. Unlike Lewis, Grahame never attended university, though he was equally passionate about the classics; instead, he went into the Bank of England and by age thirty-five was its national Secretary.

While Jack and Warnie Lewis devised **Boxen** and its "dressed animals" as a game, Grahame created *The Wind in the Willows'* Mole, Rat, Toad, Otter, and Badger in bedtime stories for his son Alastair; the characters' adventures in the English countryside have delighted generations of children. Like Lewis, Grahame makes use of pagan imagery that nevertheless has a Christian element. When Mole and Rat discover a lost baby safe at the feet of Pan, they react as Narnians later would to Aslan: "'Afraid?' murmured the Rat, his eyes shining with unutterable love. 'Afraid! Of Him? O, never, never! And yet—and yet—O, Mole, I am afraid!' Then the two animals, crouching to the earth, bowed their heads and did worship."

Lewis makes no secret of the inspiration he found in Grahame: Mr. and Mrs. Beaver's house in *The Lion, the Witch and the Wardrobe*, with its "bunks, like on board ship, built into the wall," is a near-duplicate of Mole's cozy hole, and Mr. Tumnus' cave of Old Badger's. In *Out of the Silent Planet*, Ransom's first glimpse of the rodent-like Malacandran Hyoi—a twinkling eye that gradually emerges as a face—echoes Mole's introduction to Rat. Lewis's affectionate tributes to favorite authors are a treat for readers who know the earlier books.

Katherine Harper

Bibliography

Green, Peter. *Beyond the Wild Wood: The World of Kenneth Grahame*. New York: Facts on File, 1982.
Kuznets, Lois R. *Kenneth Grahame*. Boston: Twayne, 1987.
Prince, Alison. *Kenneth Grahame: An Innocent in the Wild Wood*. London: Allison and Busby, 1994.

Wullschlager, Jackie. *Inventing Wonderland: The Lives and Fantasies of Lewis Carroll, Edward Lear, J. M. Barrie, Kenneth Grahame and A. A. Milne*. New York: The Free Press, 1995.

"The Grand Miracle"

The Guardian. (27 April 1945): 161, 165. Reprinted in *God in the Dock* and *Undeceptions*.

"The Grand Miracle" was originally delivered as a sermon in St. Jude on the Hill Church, London. In the sermon, Lewis began his discussion of "The Grand Miracle" by pointing out that people often ask whether or not **Christianity** could be stripped of its miraculous elements and remain Christianity. He suggested that Christianity is perhaps the only **religion** that cannot remain intact, because **miracles**, and more specifically the Grand Miracle, are integral to Christianity. Christianity "is precisely one great miracle."

To consider the probability or improbability of the Grand Miracle is fruitless, since it happened exactly once and only once. The most sensible way to consider the Grand Miracle is like a piece of text that may (or may not) belong in the center of a work of literature. If the inserted section of text gives new meaning or new clarification to our understanding, it is most likely authentic. If the new section of text fails to help you notice what was there before, it is most likely invalid. The Grand Miracle is the missing text, "the chapter on which the whole plot turns."

Anne Gardner

The Great Divorce

Originally published in installments in *The Guardian* as "Who Goes Home? or The Grand Divorce" from November 10, 1944, to April 13, 1945. First published in book form, London: Geoffrey Bles, 1946. First US edition, New York: Macmillan, 1946.

Conversation is the essence of this novel, which features nearly a dozen encounters between ghosts released from **Hell** for a *refrigerium*—an excursion to **Heaven**—and redeemed spirits who try to talk them into staying. In each conversation, Lewis presented a common human passion, dramatizing how the determination to have one's way regardless keeps a person out of heaven. Nearly every passion presents itself to the ghost it rules as a lofty principle—dedication to art, practicality, intellectual independence, philosophical sophistication, a demand for **justice**, modesty, even **love**. These are in reality thin disguises for less attractive motives: Achilles' wrath, Coriolanus's grandeur, revenge, injured merit, self-respect, tragic greatness, and **pride**.

The story, which is revealed on the last page as being a **dream** vision, begins with the first-person narrator finding himself alone at dusk and in the rain, in what appears the shabby commercial-industrial district of a modern city in which no one seems to live. He therefore joins a bus queue, the only company he is able to find. The people are touchy, quarrelsome, and often cruel to one another. The narrator is astonished when one of them casually mentions his own death in the past tense. Through conversations he discovers that all the buildings in the Grey Town are merely the products of wishes and can't keep the rain out. Because the inhabitants quarrel, they keep moving apart from one another. In consequence of their alienation from **God**, the belligerent and deluded ghosts are also alienated from **reality** and from one another.

The contrast is striking between the Grey Town, which will fully become Hell when night finally falls, and the Country (Heaven), where sunrise seems only a minute or two away. The fresh morning air, the song of the invisible lark, the sense of being in a bigger kind of "outside," combine to portray a perfected, qualitatively transcendent **Nature**. The River of Life and the Tree of Life are the Country's most prominent features. Fauna include lions and unicorns, beasts of heraldry that, found together, unite nature and **myth** in a combination transcending both. "Solid People"—souls of the redeemed—appear to welcome the ghosts on the bus, who discover to their own dismay that they are insubstantial, in

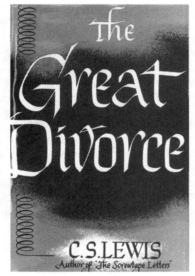

U.K. First Edition

fact dimly transparent; that the Solid People are more real than they, that the entire Country is in fact so solid in comparison to themselves that they can barely walk on the grass, which does not bend underfoot because they have no substance with which to bear it down. This imagery brilliantly reverses the popular modern belief that only the tangible and material are real, and that spirituality is evanescent and unreal. Only the ghosts from the Grey Town are "ethereal" in a land where even a flying insect could be as dangerous to them as a bullet.

The narrator reluctantly witnesses a number of meetings between ghosts and Solid People, some of which surprisingly reverse conventional conceptions of merit and demerit. For instance, a self-respecting working man is met by a former workmate who murdered a fellow laborer. Giving up on himself, the murderer began a new life. His old foreman, however, insists on regarding himself as the better man, one who had "done his best" all his life and now expects just recompense for his efforts. The gospel of **grace** is repellent to him, and he rejects it. An Episcopalian bishop who prides himself for his "fearless" intellectual honesty is told that he was neither intellectually rigorous nor honest, but a time-server. A hardworking entrepreneur's toilsome effort to take some real "commodity" back to the Grey Town ironically stems from his blindness to real value. A cynic's "realism" is dramatically revealed as a device allowing him to evade responsibility and choice. The shame of an embarrassed woman, seeking only to hide her insubstantiality from the Solid People, is ironically indistinguishable from pride of appearance, or vanity.

Halfway through the story, the narrator meets a familiar Solid Person who turns out to be **George MacDonald**, the Victorian Scottish mythopoetic novelist whose *Phantastes* "baptized" Lewis's **imagination** when he was sixteen. Lewis has introduced himself into the novel, counting himself among the souls enjoying this *refrigerium* from the place that, for those who choose to stay in the Country, will only have been **Purgatory**. Until he meets MacDonald, he doesn't seem sure he wants to stay and is spiritually in much the same condition as the other passengers from Grey Town—a good way to avoid being read as "holier-than-thou." Yet, with MacDonald as his guide, he moves toward understanding the implications of the conversations he overhears between his fellow passengers and the Solid People who attempt to persuade them to stay in the Country and to go with them, further up and further in, to the distant Mountains.

MacDonald offers the key to the mystery of why nearly none of the ghosts decide to stay, though they are free to do so. They would have to give up too much. There is in every case some attitude they insist on keeping. Respectability, tolerance, modesty, and mother-love are innocent things in themselves, but in every case the soul has prioritized a single virtue and willingly sacrifices other goods to it. As Lewis pointed out in *Mere Christianity*, and as the MacDonald character reiterates in *The Great Divorce*, any natural impulse, no matter how virtuous, becomes destructive if regarded as the sole Absolute. What keeps the damned soul from surrendering its chosen Absolute is pride, the most deadly of the sins because it locks the sinner into an attitude of refusal of the joys of heaven. Even mother-love, patriotism, and art can become false religions.

The patient arguments of the Solid People are psychologically as well as theologically interesting; in fact, **psychology**, **theology**, and **philosophy** blend together as the narrative continues. The narrative's second half deals extensively with the issue of **free will**: Can a person presented immediately with hell, then heaven, and asked to choose between them, especially by a loving friend or relative, really reject heaven? Given the universality of human fallenness, there are few of the ghosts whose point of view will not arouse at least some sympathy in the reader. Who has not enjoyed feeling morally superior to another person? Who has not enjoyed the sense of temporary power conferred by refusing another's entreaty? Who at some time has not taken revenge for disillusionment by retreating into passive aggression, as does the Hard-Bitten man the narrator encounters on the bank of the River of Life? Who would not sympathize with Pam, the mother whose chief object in going to heaven at all was to find her dead son? Who has not known someone who resembles to some degree one of the type-characters presented in the story? And who has not become at least fleetingly aware at some point in life of the blind power of their own defenses against God?

Given the great difficulty of choosing rightly, Lewis asks MacDonald whether the happiness of the Solid People would not be marred if they did not pity the damned enough to go, if necessary, into Hell themselves to rescue them. MacDonald replies that Hell is too small—nothing of Heaven is small enough to get in. The spirit of negation that is the essence of Hell is reductive, reducing all reality to "nothing but" the individual's personal obsessions and allowing room for nothing else. Lewis then asks MacDonald about MacDonald's Universalism—the belief that all men would be saved. MacDonald replies that from any point of view within time, choice and its consequences are certain. Both Predestination and Universalism try to describe eternity from outside of time, and both in consequence destroy human freedom by depriving choice of real significance.

Consequently, any answer MacDonald could give to the question would be meaningless to one who still lives in time. The conversation is cut short as the light of dawn brightens to full sunrise, hammering the dreamer with unbearable light, and he awakes from his dream to find that, falling asleep at his table, he has slipped out of his chair, pulling his books down on his head.

Lyle Smith
Biola University

Also See: Allegory, Destiny, Good and Evil, Immortality, Redemption

Bibliography

Kilby, Clyde. *The Christian World of CSL*. Grand Rapids, MI: Eerdmans, 1964.

Manlove, C. N. *C. S. Lewis: His Literary Achievement*. New York: St. Martin's Press, 1987.

Walsh, Chad. *The Literary Legacy of C. S. Lewis*. New York: Harcourt Brace Jovanovich, 1979.

"The Great War"

"The Great War" was what C. S. Lewis called the running "battle of ideas" between him and his lifelong friend **Owen Barfield**, after Barfield was converted to the **anthroposophy** of Rudolf Steiner in 1923, soon after his graduation from Wadham College, **Oxford**. In *Surprised by Joy*, Lewis wrote, "It was an almost incessant disputation, sometimes by letter and sometimes face to face, which lasted for years." Barfield has written that "this intense interchange of philosophical opinions" was finished by the time of Lewis's conversion to **Christianity**, around 1931.

At first, Lewis was disturbed by Barfield's enthusiasm for Steiner's teachings, with their use of words like "occult knowledge" and their belief in reincarnation and "spirits." But he soon discovered that anthroposophy had a "reassuring Germanic dullness which would soon deter those who were looking for thrills" and that it did not seem to affect the character of those embracing it. One thing that may have helped Lewis was that Steiner's teachings did not specifically deny the **truth** of Christianity (while adding to it), and many anthroposophists (like Barfield) regarded themselves as practicing Christians.

In "The Great War" Lewis tried to discredit anthroposophy and to persuade Barfield (and their mutual friend **A. C. Harwood**) to cease their reliance upon it. Barfield maintained that **imagination** conveys truth, while Lewis believed that imagination merely showed the "difference a given statement might make if true"; the truth or falsehood of a statement depended on rational judgment. The other primary disagreement between them was on the nature of **metaphor** in religious language. Barfield believed metaphor was dependent on intuition, while Lewis said metaphor was a "concrete mental picture."

The "Great War" was more beneficial to Lewis than to Barfield. Although Lewis never accepted all of Barfield's ideas, especially those on the occult and some on the nature and teachings of Jesus **Christ**, he did come to reject **"chronological snobbery"** (the belief that newer things are always to be preferred) and to see that imagination was a gift from **God**, enabling him to accept the **supernatural**, thus being able to more fully understand the truth of Christianity. Lewis called Barfield "the wisest and best of my unofficial teachers" and in *Surprised by Joy* wrote that "I think he changed me a great deal more than I him."

Perry C. Bramlett
C. S. Lewis for the Local Church

Bibliography

Adey, Lionel. *C. S. Lewis's "Great War" with Owen Barfield.* Victoria, BC: University of Victoria, 1978.
_____. "The Barfield-Lewis Great War." *CSL: The Bulletin of the New York C. S. Lewis Society.* 6 no. 10 (August 1975): 10–13.
Barfield, Owen. *Owen Barfield on C. S. Lewis.* G. B. Tennyson (ed). Middletown, CT: Wesleyan University Press, 1989.
Carpenter, Humphrey. *The Inklings.* Boston: Houghton Mifflin, 1979.

Roger Lancelyn Green (1918–1987)

Roger Lancelyn Green is best known in Lewis circles for his 1974 biography of Lewis, *C. S. Lewis: A Biography,* cowritten with **Walter Hooper**. Green met Lewis at **Oxford** in the 1930s, when as an undergraduate he attended Lewis's lectures. The two became friends, and during the 1950s Lewis came to assume Green would one day write his biography. Perhaps their longest period of close contact came in 1960, when Roger and June Green accompanied Jack and **Joy Davidman Lewis** on a ten-day trip to Greece.

Green and Lewis shared similar reading tastes, including interests in Arthurian legend, mythology, Greek drama, **Edith Nesbit**, and **Rider Haggard**. As this list indicates, both men's literary tastes were an eclectic mix of children's and adult reading; in the introduction to his first book, *Tellers of Tales*, Green notes that for a period of time he alternated his reading between Tarzan novels and **Shakespeare**'s plays. *Tellers of Tales*, first published in 1946, presents introductions to British writers of children's fiction from 1800 through World War II. The orig-

inal work covered only dead authors, but for a 1953 revision his publishers requested living authors be included as well, and Green took the opportunity to add sections on **J. R. R. Tolkien** and Lewis.

Lewis and Green shared an interest in **fairy tales**; in fact, Green's undergraduate thesis at Oxford dealt with fairy tales and **Andrew Lang**. The don and former student began reading their own stories aloud to each other in the 1940s; when Green first heard the opening chapters of *The Lion, the Witch and the Wardrobe* (which Tolkien had roundly criticized), he praised the work highly and encouraged Lewis to finish it. The Narnian series made a solid impression on Green from the beginning; it is interesting to note in *Tellers of Tales* that he covers the seven novels not in publication order or in chronological order, but in the order they were written (and thus the order in which he first read them), with *The Horse and His Boy* being discussed before *The Silver Chair*. Roger Green died in 1987.

Marvin Hinten
Bowling Green State University

Bibliography

Green, Roger L. *Tellers of Tales.* Rev. ed. New York: F. Watts, 1965.
_____. "In The Evening." *C. S. Lewis at the Breakfast Table.* New York: Macmillan, 1979.

Joseph Arthur Greeves (1895–1966)

Joseph Arthur Greeves was a lifelong friend of C. S. Lewis, to whom Lewis wrote more letters in his voluminous correspondence than to anyone else. Lewis characterized his close friend as the youngest son of a mother, Mary Margretta Gribbon (1861–1949), who doted upon him, and a father, Joseph Malcolmson Greeves (1858–1925), who treated all their five children harshly. Arthur Greeves was diagnosed with a weak heart while still a child, and he lived the rest of his life as a person of delicate health.

The Greeves and Lewis households shared a **Belfast** neighborhood. C. S. Lewis recalled that Arthur made several unrequited overtures of **friendship**. Then, on an April day in 1914, while confined at home by illness, Greeves invited Lewis to visit. Within minutes the two youths discovered that they shared the same tastes in literature, the same interest in Norse mythology, and the same sense of wonder at all things northern. Lewis later made this experience a cornerstone in his understanding of **friendship**, in his chapter on "Friendship" in *The Four Loves*. By June of 1914, the two friends began their long correspondence, which continued to within a few months of Lewis's death in 1963. Lewis's letters to Greeves are collected in *They Stand Together*.

Arthur Greeves' **education** at **Campbell College**, Belfast (1906–12), had concluded before he gained Lewis's friendship. As a young man he spent a few years, between recurrent illnesses, as an employee of his brother Thomas Greeves, a linen merchandiser. From 1921 to 1923 he studied at the distinguished London art school, the Slade School of Fine Art, earning a Certificate. He later studied briefly in Paris, and by 1936 he was exhibiting with the Royal Hibernian Academy in Dublin.

In the expression of meaning through landscape, the two friends shared a common language. Greeves created visual landscapes of sufficient quality to please the artistic academy; Lewis sent him occasional pen sketches in an attempt to communicate with him in visual form. In his letters to Greeves, which reveal his growth from a voluble boy to a man of literary genius, Lewis repeatedly wrote in passages of surpassing **beauty**, about landscape in all its moods. Greeves thus spoke with his brush, while Lewis painted with his pen.

Their friendship included additional reciprocities. As adolescents they confided to one another their most intimate secrets. As an adult, Lewis wrote that Greeves taught him to be charitable, while he had failed totally to teach Arthur to be arrogant. During Lewis's early career, Greeves accurately criticized *The Pilgrim's Regress* for containing too many quotations and too little simplicity, mistakes that Lewis never made again. More than twenty years later their friendship remained so strong that Lewis could ask Arthur to proofread *Till We Have Faces*.

Though reared in the Plymouth Brethren tradition, Arthur Greeves tested a variety of religions. He ended his life as a Quaker, the **faith** of his father's ancestors. In his last years, Greeves' heart continued to deteriorate, and on August 29, 1966, he died quietly in his sleep.

Nancy-Lou Patterson

Also See: Fantasy, Myths, Religion

Bibliography

Lewis, C. S. *The Four Loves*; *The Pilgrim's Regress*; *They Stand Together*; *Till We Have Faces*.

David Lindsay Gresham (1944–)

C. S. Lewis's elder stepson, David Lindsay Gresham, was born on March 27, 1944, in New York City to **William Lindsay Gresham** and his wife **Joy Davidman**, both writers. A brother, **Douglas Howard Gresham**, was born a year and a half later in November 1945. The family moved to upper New York state in 1946, eventually purchasing a large house and grounds in Staatsburg with the proceeds from the film rights to Bill Gresham's first novel, *Nightmare Alley*. When marital difficulties culminated in the breakup of the Greshams' marriage, Joy left with her two sons for England in November 1953. Bill remained behind, and after receiving a divorce in 1954, he married Joy's cousin, Renée Pierce. Settling in London, Joy took her sons to meet C. S. Lewis during a four-day visit to Oxford. The meeting was a success and Lewis indicated his intention to dedicate his fifth Narnia book, *The Horse and His Boy*, to the Gresham brothers. However, in spite of positive moments such as this, from the very first David missed America and strongly disliked his new home in England.

Along with his younger brother, David began his formal English education at Dane Court, a preparatory school in Surrey where he remained until September 1957 when he became a day-boy at Magdalen College School, **Oxford**. During this interval, however, David had seen many changes in his home life as well. In August 1955, Joy moved with her sons to a house in Headington, a suburb of Oxford, and roughly a mile from the home C. S. Lewis shared with his brother, **Warren Lewis**. Her **friendship** with Lewis continued to deepen and on April 23, 1956, they married in a registry office in order to allow Joy legal status to remain in England. When Joy was diagnosed with cancer in October 1956, her sons went to live with the Lewis brothers at the **Kilns**. Then on March 21, 1957, convinced of their love for each other, Lewis and Joy were married in an ecclesiastical ceremony while Joy remained seriously ill as a patient in the hospital.

After his mother's death in July 1960, David continued to live with his stepfather at the Kilns while attending Magdalen College School. He also began to seriously study Judaism at this time (his mother was of Jewish ancestry), as well as undertaking private lessons in Hebrew and later in Yiddish. In April 1962, he enrolled as a student at the North West London Talmudical College. After his year there, David returned to the United States for further study under Rabbi Isaac Hutner. In 1967, he traveled to Israel and studied at both the Hebron Yeshiva and the Hebrew University. Then, in 1969, he returned to England where he enrolled at **Magdalene College, Cambridge**, and read Oriental Studies; he graduated in 1972.

Since then, David has lived at various times in Spain, France, Switzerland, and India while pursuing the study of Hebrew, Latin, and modern languages. In 1985, he moved to Dublin, Ireland. David married Miss Padmavati Hariharan at the Magen Aboth Synagogue in Alibag, Maharashtra, India, on November 1, 1992. They have a son, Joseph Isaac, born May 17, 1994. His main pursuits today are the study of the Hebrew Bible and the Talmud, as well as efforts to further Jewish education in general.

Marjorie Lamp Mead
The Marion E. Wade Center

Bibliography

Dorsett, Lyle W. *And God Came In*. Wheaton, IL: Crossway, 1991.

Gresham, Douglas. *Lenten Lands*. San Francisco: HarperCollins, 1994.

Hooper, Walter. *C. S. Lewis: A Companion & Guide*. San Francisco: HarperSanFrancisco, 1996.

Sayer, George. *Jack*. Wheaton, IL: Crossway, 1994.

Douglas Howard Gresham (1945–)

C. S. Lewis's younger stepson, Douglas Howard Gresham, was born on November 10, 1945, to the writers, **William Lindsay Gresham**, and his wife, **Joy Davidman**. His elder brother, **David Lindsay Gresham**, was born twenty months earlier in March 1944. Douglas's earliest memories are of his family home in Staatsburg, New York, where he reveled in the beauty of the rural estate. His early years were happy ones, but as his parents' marriage became increasingly troubled, his secure world began to crumble. By the time of his parents' separation, he understood only too well the tension and unhappiness that had come between them. Taking her two young sons with her to England in November 1953, Joy left behind a husband who wanted a divorce in order to marry her cousin Renée Pierce. In spite of the painful circumstances, however, Douglas had grown to love his soon-to-be stepmother, Renée, as well as her children, Bob and his younger sister, Rosemary. They were to remain important family ties in his life.

Once in England, Douglas found himself in his new home, a small, underheated flat in "grey" London. However, a bright spot occurred in December 1953 when his mother brought Douglas and David to meet her friend C. S. Lewis. Though surprised at the actual man (who bore no resemblance to the knight in shining armor he had anticipated), Douglas still enjoyed meeting the author of his beloved Narnia tales and was thoroughly delighted with his Oxford visit. One month later, Douglas entered boarding school at Dane Court in Surrey. It was a difficult transition for Douglas, due in part to his all-too-obvious American accent. He quickly learned to adapt in order to "fit in" with the other boys, but this did nothing to ease the homesickness of a young eight-year-old away from his mother.

In August 1955, Joy moved with her sons to a home in Headington, Oxford, about a mile from the **Kilns** where Lewis lived with his brother, **Warren Lewis**. Joy's friendship with Lewis continued to deepen, and they were married in a registry office in April 1956. Soon afterwards, Joy was diagnosed with cancer, and the Gresham boys went to live at the Kilns. In March 1957, Lewis and Joy were married in an ecclesiastical ceremony while Joy lay ill in the hospital. She recovered to return home, and there were several good years before her death in July 1960. During this time, Douglas learned to love his stepfather and step-uncle, but the loss of his mother was, nonetheless, devastating. Still, through it all, he was able to be of help to his stepfather in their shared grief. This experience would later be dramatically recreated through the film, *Shadowlands*, which Douglas described as "emotionally authentic" if not historically exact.

Following his mother's death, Douglas attended various schools, eventually receiving agricultural training in preparation for farming. He met and fell in love with Meredith (Merrie) Conan-Davies, and they were married in Westminster Cathedral on February 20, 1967. Soon after, they left for Tasmania where they were engaged in various pursuits including farming, restaurant work, and broadcasting. Their first four children were born in Australia: three sons, James (1968), Timothy (1969), Dominick (1971), and their daughter, Lucinda (1976). Their fifth child, daughter Melody, was adopted in 1990 from Korea when she was five years old.

Committed Christians, Douglas and Merrie moved to County Carlow, Ireland, in 1993 in order to be able to pursue various ministry opportunities, including opening their home as a center for the Institute for Pregnancy Loss and Child Abuse Research and Recovery. Together they also direct Rathvinden Ministries, offering evangelism, counseling, and Christian hospitality to those in their immediate community as well as to many visitors from around the world. In addition, Douglas is heavily involved as a consultant with the C. S. Lewis literary estate and is frequently invited as a guest lecturer throughout the world. Douglas is also the author of the book *Lenten Lands*, several short stories, and various articles.

Marjorie Lamp Mead
The Marion E. Wade Center

Bibliography

Dorsett, Lyle W. *And God Came In*. Wheaton, IL: Crossway, 1991.

Gresham, Douglas. *Lenten Lands*. San Francisco: Harper-Collins, 1994.

_____. Various devotionals in *Gentle Darkness*. ed. Rowland Croucher. Claremont, CA: Albatross Books, 1994.

_____. Oral history interview with Douglas Gresham, conducted by Lyle W. Dorsett for the Marion E. Wade Center, June 4, 1982.

Hooper, Walter. *C. S. Lewis: A Companion & Guide*. San Francisco: HarperSanFrancisco, 1996.

Sayer, George. *Jack*. Wheaton, IL.: Crossway, 1994.

William Lindsay Gresham (1909–1962)

Author and first husband of **Joy Davidman Lewis**, William Lindsay Gresham was born August 20, 1909, in Baltimore, Maryland. When he was eight, he moved with his family to New York. Always his own person, Bill Gresham supported himself with a variety of jobs after high school—including singing folk music in Greenwich Village nightclubs. About 1935, he married and began a career as a writer. Success, however, did not come quickly, and a restless Bill Gresham, now a member of the Communist Party, volunteered to serve as a freedom fighter in the Spanish Civil War. Returning home ill after fifteen months in Spain, Bill suffered from alcoholism and mild tuberculosis, and, close to a nervous breakdown, he also faced a ruined marriage. After a failed attempt at suicide, Bill sought relief in Freudian analysis from the psychological damage he believed he had suffered as a child. He had outward scars as well resulting from a case of severe acne, and in an effort to overcome this perceived physical limitation, Bill intentionally and successfully cultivated a charming personality. However, philosophically he still struggled, seeking answers in his Marxist beliefs but finding little help in his quest for "personal moral guidance."

It was this troubled yet compelling man who met and fell in love with fellow Communist Party member Joy Davidman in the spring of 1942. Having divorced his first wife, Bill Gresham married Joy on August 2 that same year. Both were working as writers but making only meager salaries and living in a tiny apartment in Queens. Despite financial pressures, there were happy moments as the Gresham's first son, David, was born on March 27, 1944, followed twenty months later by their second son, Douglas, on November 10, 1945. Using money from the sale of film rights to Bill's first novel, *Nightmare Alley* (1946), the Greshams purchased a large home and grounds in Staatsburg in upper New York state. Unfortunately, this move did not solve Bill's deepest problems, and before long, his continuing alcoholism and an extramarital affair had etched a troubled path through the Gresham household. Worried that Bill was on the verge of a nervous breakdown and perhaps suicidal, a desperate and broken Joy turned to **God**. As a result of this momentous occurrence in Joy's life, Bill joined his wife in examining the claims of various faiths. During this search, the writings of C. S. Lewis were influential in their eventual acceptance of **Christianity**.

Even as Joy's faith deepened, however, Bill continued to drift, abandoning Christianity first for Scientology and later Buddhism. Other problems remained as well, and not even the success of Bill's second novel, *Limbo Tower* (1949), could alleviate their mounting financial pressures. Their marriage also continued deteriorating and while Joy was in England in 1952 visiting friends, including Lewis, she learned that Bill had fallen in love with her cousin Renée Pierce. Agreeing to Bill's request for a divorce, Joy came home to gather her two sons and returned to England in November 1953 to start a new life. Bill married Renée, becoming stepfather to her two children, Bob and Rosemary, from her first marriage.

After Joy's death in July 1960, Bill traveled to England to visit his sons, but allowed them to remain with their stepfather, C. S. Lewis, rather than seeking to bring them back to America. Two years later, threatened with the loss of his eyesight due to cataracts and diagnosed with cancer, Bill Gresham checked into a New York hotel room and took his own life with an overdose of sleeping pills on September 14, 1962. He was fifty-three.

Marjorie Lamp Mead
The Marion E. Wade Center

Also See: David Lindsay Gresham, Douglas Howard Gresham

Bibliography

Anon., "Gresham, A Writer is Found Dead Here," *The New York Times*, September 16, 1962, p. 85.

Dorsett, Lyle W. *And God Came In*. Wheaton, IL: Crossway, 1991.

Gresham, Douglas. *Lenten Lands*. San Francisco: Harper-Collins, 1994.

Gresham, William Lindsay. *The Book of Strength: Body Building the Safe, Correct Way*. New York: John Day Co., 1961.

_____. *Houdini: The Man who Walked Through Walls*. New York: Holt, 1959.

_____. *Limbo Tower*. New York: Rinehart and Co., 1949.

_____. *Monster Midway*. New York: Rinehart and Co., 1953.

_____. *Nightmare Alley*. New York: Rinehart and Co., 1946.

_____. "From Communist to Christian," in *These Found the Way*, edited by David Wesley Soper, Philadelphia: Westminster Press, 1951.

_____. "Preface" to Charles Williams, *The Greater Trumps*. New York: Pellegrini & Cudahy, 1950.

Hooper, Walter. *C. S. Lewis: A Companion & Guide*. San Francisco: HarperCollins, 1996.

Morehead, Albert H. "Bridge: Death of Gresham, Writer, Loss to Bridge World, Too," *The New York Times*, September 25, 1962, p. 34.

A Grief Observed

Originally printed under the pseudonym N. W. Clerk. London: Faber & Faber, 1961. First US edition, Greenwich, CT: Seabury Press, 1963. Reprinted as by C. S. Lewis. London: Faber & Faber, 1964. First US edition, Greenwich, CT: Seabury Press, 1964.

Few would deny that the death of a loved one, particularly a spouse or a child, is one of the most shattering experiences that humans are required to endure, and psychologists have described several stages in the typical grieving process: shock and numbness at the beginning, an intermediate period of intense mourning and great anger, and finally a sense of healing and restoration. As his highly personal journal, *A Grief Observed*, illustrates, C. S. Lewis passed through similar stages after his beloved wife, **Joy Davidman Lewis**, died from cancer. But the journal is not so much an *account* of Lewis's grief as it is a *manifestation* of it, a record of his immediate thoughts and feelings as he searches, seemingly in vain at first, for some consolation in the death of his wife and the separation it entailed.

The thoughts and feelings recorded here revealed, perhaps better than anything else Lewis wrote, his solidarity with the rest of humanity. He wanted desperately for his earthly life with Joy Davidman to continue in the form he had come to know it. Had she been transported magically to a wondrous life in another galaxy, he would have been no less grieved by the separation. He thus wrote: "You tell me 'she goes on'. But my heart and body are crying out, come back, come back." It is

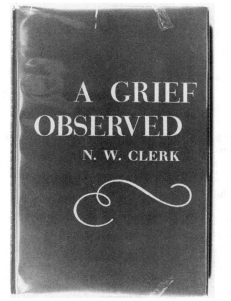

not her past *suffering*, in other words, but his own need—his attachment to the life he had known—that here occupied his attention: "I know that the thing I want is exactly the thing I can never get. The old life, the jokes, the drinks, the arguments, the love-making, the tiny, heartbreaking commonplace." But even in the depth of his despair, Lewis seemed incapable of deluding himself. "I never even raised the question," he confessed a little later, "whether such a return, if it were possible, would be good for her. I want her back as an ingredient in the restoration of *my* past." And once he began to recover some from his grief and anger, he emphatically declared in his final paragraph: "How wicked it would be, if we could, to call the dead back!"

In his darkest hours, however, Lewis still had to confront the depth of his despair, and his journal records a fascinating dialectic between his intense feelings on the one hand and his theological reasonings on the other. Toward the end of Part II, for example, a distraught Lewis in effect blamed **God** for having choked "every prayer and every hope" with "false diagnoses," "strange remissions," and the like. "Time after time," Lewis lamented, "when He seemed most gracious He was preparing the next torture." But Lewis then reprimanded himself almost immediately: "I wrote that last night. It was a yell rather than a thought. Let me try it over again. Is it rational to believe in a bad God? ... The Cosmic Sadist, the spiteful imbecile?" To this his intellect answered: No, this is not rational. A Cosmic Sadist could never "create or govern anything" and could never have thought of "**love**, or laughter, or daffodils, or a frosty sunset." But the war within continued; and after rejecting the view that God's standards of goodness are radically different from ours, Lewis again plunged into despair: "Why do I make room in my mind for such filth and nonsense? Do I hope that if feeling disguises itself as thought I shall feel less?" Still later, when his despair subsided again, he countered: "All that stuff about the Cosmic Sadist was not so much an expression of thought as of hatred. I was getting from it the only pleasure a man in anguish can get; the pleasure of hitting back."

Then, Lewis was fully conscious of the internal war raging between his intellect and his feelings. At the beginning of Part III, he thus exclaimed: "Feelings, and feelings, and feelings. Let me try thinking instead. From the rational point of view, what new factor has [my wife's] death introduced into the problem of the universe?" The obvious answer: None whatsoever. "I knew already that these things, and worse, happened daily. . . . We were even promised sufferings. They were part of the programme." Indeed, Lewis himself had known tragedy before and had experienced the death of loved ones before. So why, he asked, did this particular death precipitate such a crisis for him? Never one to spare himself, he concluded that his faith had been "a house of cards"—not in the sense that his beliefs were false, but in the sense that he had not been as secure in them as he should have been. "If I really cared, as I thought I did, about the sorrows of the world, I should not have been so overwhelmed when my own sorrow came."

Some admirers of Lewis have found the honesty in *A Grief Observed* disturbing; others, such as George Musacchio, have found it impossible to believe that their hero, C. S. Lewis—this "rational and insightful Christian writer"—should have been "so shattered by his wife's death" or "plunged so near to despair." They have therefore invented the fiction that *A Grief Observed* is itself a work of fiction. But it is simply naive to suppose that Lewis could not have experienced his own "mad midnight moments" or even, in response to great trauma and sleep deprivation, have experienced an emotional breakdown of sorts. You might as well suppose that a "rational and insightful Christian writer" could never develop a brain tumor or Alzheimer's disease. And besides, why should Lewis have been any different from the prophet Habakkuk, whose complaints against God were every bit as heartfelt as Lewis's own?

Others, especially Lewis's critics have gone to the opposite extreme and have supposed that Lewis spoke most wisely when overcome by grief and plagued by doubts. But as usual, Lewis was wiser than his critics. "You can't see anything properly," he observed, "when your eyes are blurred with tears." And only a week after recording some of his blackest thoughts, he asked: "Why should the thoughts I had a week ago be any more trustworthy than the better thoughts I have now? I am surely, in general, a saner man than I was then."

The remarkable thing about Lewis's blackest thoughts, moreover, is how consistent they are with the **theology** he expressed elsewhere. In *The Problem of Pain*, for example, he spoke of God's "loving us, in the deepest, most tragic, most inexorable sense," and he calls this an "intolerable compliment" because, in his view, the sufferings we endure in the present are a means by which God eventually perfects us and secures our blessedness in the future. So did Lewis simply forget this point during his own period of testing and trial? Not at all. Throughout *A Grief Observed*, he consistently expressed exactly the same point. But with this difference: he now wrote from the perspective of a *sufferer*—of someone who has, so to speak, *received* this "intolerable compliment." So now it is from a troubled heart that he asked: "What do people mean when they say, 'I am not afraid of God because I know He is good?' Have they never been to a dentist?" Likening God to "a surgeon whose intentions are wholly good," Lewis also pointed out that the "kinder and more conscientious" a surgeon is, "the more inexorably he will go on cutting. If . . . he stopped before the operation was complete, all the **pain** up to that point would have been useless." And that is why, given our normal human weaknesses, "a perfectly good God" who seeks our perfection may indeed seem no "less formidable than a Cosmic Sadist."

But in time Lewis's heavy heart began to lighten and mourning gave way, gradually, to a sense of restoration and peace. He then discovered that, even as he began to accept his wife's departure, his sense of her continued reality and presence increased—as did his sense that "all manner of things shall be well" in the end.

Thomas Talbott
Willamette University

Bibliography

Dorsett, Lyle W. *And God Came In*. New York: Macmillan Publishing Co., 1983: chapter 4.

Kübler-Ross, Elizabeth. *On Death and Dying*. New York: Macmillan Publishing Co., 1969: chapter 9.

Lindskoog, Kathryn. *Light in the Shadowlands*. Sisters, OR: Multnomah, 1994: chapter 6.

MacDonald, George. "The Consuming Fire." *Creation in Christ*. Rolland Hein (ed). Grand Rapids, MI: Eerdmans, 1976: 157–166.

Meilaender, Gilbert. *The Taste for the Other*. Grand Rapids, MI: Eerdmans, 1978: chapter 3.

Musacchio, George. "Fiction in *A Grief Observed*." *VII: An Anglo-American Literary Review*. 8 (1987): 73–83.

Vanauken, Sheldon. *A Severe Mercy*. San Francisco: Harper and Rowe, 1977: chapters 8 and 9.

Dom Bede Griffiths (1906–1993)

Alan Richard Griffiths was an idealistic young student of C. S. Lewis's in the 1920s and a friend of Lewis's from then on. Both were unbelievers from

Anglican backgrounds when they met; and both became believing Christians in 1931. By 1932 Griffiths had joined the Roman Catholic Church, and a few months later he took the name Bede when he entered the Benedictine Order.

As a monk, Griffiths became interested in Hindu thought and spent the rest of his life trying to reconcile its teachings with those of **Roman Catholicism**. Although he tried, he was never successful in his attempts to get Lewis to accept his blend of Catholicism and Hinduism. In spite of their differences, the two enjoyed a lifelong correspondence, and in 1955 Lewis dedicated *Surprised by Joy* to him. That is the year when Griffiths moved to India and began an interfaith ministry that made him famous as the saffron-robed leader of a Roman Catholic and Hindu ashram. In 1970 Griffiths told **Clyde Kilby** that he had most of Lewis's books in the library he was building at Shantivanam, South India. He contributed his rich collection of revealing Lewis letters to Kilby's collection at the **Marion E. Wade Center**.

On June 30, 1987, Griffiths wrote to Kathryn Lindskoog, "You may remember that [Lewis] once wrote to me that we had once agreed that Hinduism & Christianity were the only religions that could claim to present the final truth. As I have gone on studying Hinduism I have felt more & more how close it is in its deepest insights to Christian truth. But it means also that I see Christian truth in a new perspective. I am engaged on a book at present on Western Science, Eastern Mysticism, & Christian Faith [*A New Vision of Reality*], in which I have tried to work out this understanding. It is very different from Lewis's view, but I would like to know what his reaction would be."

Lewis made his objections to Griffiths' attempt to blend Christianity and Hinduism clear in a number of letters. In 1949 Lewis noted that the kind of union with God that Hinduism sought was "precisely the opposite to that which He really intends for us." In another he told Griffiths, "that refined, philosophical eastern pantheism is far further from the true Faith than the semi-barbarous pagan religions."

Kathryn Lindskoog

Also See: Anglicanism, Atheism, Non-Christian Religions, Paganism

Bibliography

Griffiths, Dom Bede. "The Adventure of Faith." *C. S. Lewis at the Breakfast Table.* James T. Como (ed.) New York: Macmillan, 1979: 11–24.

_____. *Christian in India* (1966); *Vedanta and Christian Faith* (1973); *Return to the Centre* (1976); *The Marriage of East and West* (1982); *The Cosmic Revelation* (1983); *A New Vision of Reality* (1989); *Universal Wisdom: A Journey through the Sacred Wisdom* (1994); *Psalms for Christian Prayer* (1995); *Pathways to the Supreme* (1996).

Palisade Home Video. *A Human Search* (biography), *History & Interpretation of the Bible* (lectures in Australia), and *Discovering the Feminine* (end-of-life insights in India).

Guilt

"The recovery of the old sense of **sin**," Lewis wrote in *The Problem of Pain*, "is essential to **Christianity**." For without a sense of guilt we lack the "first condition" for understanding the gospel. Those who feel no guilt, he warned, feel no need for forgiveness. On this matter Lewis spoke from experience, having noted in *Surprised by Joy* that as a youth he rarely experienced any guilt feelings, that it took him almost as long to acquire inhibitions as it takes others to lose them.

Lewis saw two causes for the modern loss of guilt feelings. One began in the mid-19th century with an exaggerated emphasis on kindness to the exclusion of all other virtues. Kindness is easy to feel, he noted. But as long as we do not expect our kindness to lead to any personal sacrifices, it only means that we are feeling happy rather than annoyed. It is much harder to deceive ourselves about our temperance, chastity, or humility.

The other cause Lewis traced to what the general public believed psychoanalysis taught about repressions and inhibitions. Shame, an idea closely tied to guilt, was now regarded as harmful, while being open and unashamed of one's sins was regarded as good and healthy. In *Letters to Malcolm*, Lewis was even more specific about where modern psychologists went wrong. He had no problem when they condemned as unhealthy a "vague feeling of guilt." His disagreement arose when they went on to treat "all guilt-feelings" as pathological, even when those feelings were tied to a specific unkind deed or insincerity. Lewis called "nonsense" the idea that everyone felt more guilty than necessary. Some needed to feel much more guilt than they did.

Lewis's experience speaking at RAF bases during World War II gave him insight into what modern Englishmen believed. Near the end of the war he condensed what he had learned into a speech to Anglican leaders (later published as **"Christian Apologetics"**). Today, he said, the sense of sin is "almost totally lacking." People have been taught to blame the faults of the world on someone else—capitalists, governments, Nazism, military leaders, or the like. As a result, **God** shares the blame for creating such a terrible world, and everyone else is the innocent victim of a bad system. In dealing with such people, Lewis felt it was useless to try to recreate a sense of sin by focusing on either sins your audience did not commit or sins they do but do not regard as sins. Instead, he offered from his own experience a suggestion to begin with "the sin that has been one's own chief problem during the past week." At any rate, he said, we must draw attention away from public affairs and highly visible crimes and focus on "the whole network of spite, greed, envy, unfairness and conceit in the lives of 'ordinary decent people' like themselves (and ourselves)." In doing so, we are stimulating the very feelings that, as Lewis pointed out in *The Problem of Pain*, cause everyone to "stand condemned not by alien codes of ethics, but by their own."

Lewis commented on guilt in an "upside down" way in ***The Screwtape Letters***. There Screwtape offers revealing advice about how a sense of sin affects the spiritual life. Wormwood is told that a vague and uneasy feeling of not doing well is fine because it "increases the patient's reluctance to think about the Enemy [God]." On the other hand, that sense should not be allowed to become too great or to focus on specific sins lest it "flower into real repentance." Ironically, it is God who does not want a man to dwell overmuch on his sins but to repent and turn his attention outward.

The same sort of distinction between good and bad guilt exists for believers as for unbelievers. Guilt is good when it brings repentance for concrete sins and leads to a changed life, restitution for those who have suffered, and assistance for those in need. It is bad when it keeps believers from the rejoicing that should characterize the Christian life. In **"Man or Rabbit?"** Lewis even made the bold claim that God was as interested in ridding us of the "worried, conscientious, ethical rabbit," as he was of the "cowardly and sensual" one.

Lewis dealt with guilt most extensively in *The Problem of Pain*. He wrote that it was "mad work" to get rid of guilt by lowering moral standards. He pointed out that an awareness of our own guilt transforms the "wrath of God" from a "barbarous doctrine" into a "mere corollary from God's goodness." He criticized those who use the problems of the social system and "corporate guilt" to evade "those hum-drum, old-fashioned guilts of your own." He also noted that those who condone the sin of others share in their sin. Most important of all, he attacked the "strange illusion" that the mere passage of time will cancel out sin. Guilt, he stressed, is "washed out not by time but by repentance and the blood of **Christ**."

Mike Perry

Also See: Ethics and Morality, The Fall, Good and Evil, Happiness, Mercy, Psychology

---

H

Sir H[enry] Rider Haggard (1856–1925)

An English civil servant, lawyer, and prolific writer, H. Rider Haggard spent six years in the colonial service in South Africa. Many of his stories combine detailed African landscapes with adventure and fantasy elements. Haggard loved crumbling ruins, ancient customs, and extinct civilizations. He was also drawn to the pseudo-science of spiritism.

Haggard wrote fifteen books that featured Allan Quartermain. His fourth book, *King Solomon's Mines* (1885), brought him significant fame, and *She* (1887) enjoyed even greater success. He worked with **Rudyard Kipling** on *Allan and the Ice Gods* (1927) and *When the Earth Shook* (1919). He also collaborated with **Andrew Lang** on *The World's Desire* (1890), a sequel to Homer's *Odyssey*. Haggard's tales have influenced many **science fiction** writers, notably Edgar Rice Burroughs and Philip Jose Farmer.

Lewis enjoyed Haggard very much, labeling his work "low-brow but certainly very good." He called Haggard's *The People of the Mist* "a tip-top yarn." He further described Haggard as one who writes "a boy's book:—distant lands, strange adventures, mysteries not of the American but of the Egyptian kind." Though not a fan of movies, Lewis went to the theater to see *King Kong* simply because "it sounded the sort of Rider Haggardish thing that has always exercised a spell over me."

Despite this unabashed enthusiasm for Haggard's work, Lewis was very critical of Haggard's writing ability, condemning him for abusing clichés and inserting long philosophical digressions. Lewis wrote to **Arthur Greeves**, "I recently re-read ... both *She* and the sequel *Ayesha* and found the story good in both; what troubles one is the v. silly talk put into She's mouth, which is meant to be profound" (March 29, 1931). For Lewis, Haggard's saving grace is his power as a **myth**-maker, one who uses archetypes and evocative imagery to explore issues of lasting importance to the human condition.

Diana Pavlac Glyer
Azusa Pacific University

Also See: Myth

Bibliography

Lewis, C. S. "Haggard Rides Again."

"Haggard Rides Again"

Time and Tide. XLI (3 September 1960): 1044–45. Retitled as "The Mythopoeic Gift of Rider Haggard" and reprinted in *Of This and Other Worlds* and *On Stories.*

Lewis began this article as if it were a review of *Rider Haggard: His Life and Works* by Morton Cohen. It quickly becomes evident, however, that his real purpose is not to write a book review but to address the following dilemma: even though H. Rider Haggard was a poor writer, his fiction (notably *King Solomon's Mines* and *She*) had lasting value. How is this possible?

Lewis commenced by asserting in no uncertain terms that Haggard "can't write." His prose is frothy and littered with clichés. Even worse, his stories are filled with "an eclectic outfit of vaguely Christian, theosophical and spiritualistic notions." By way of example, Lewis cited the long-winded speeches that pour forth from Ayesha, one of Haggard's characters, observing, "If she was really Wisdom's daughter, she did not take after her parent."

What keeps us reading Haggard despite these near fatal flaws? The mythic quality of his stories. Haggard possessed the mythopoeic gift, the gift of a mythmaker. "This gift, when it exists in full measure, is irresistible. ... It triumphs over all obstacles and makes us tolerate all faults." **Myths** are important because myths work to "externalise" our deepest psychological needs. Therefore, says Lewis, "A great myth is relevant as long as the predicament of humanity lasts; as long as humanity lasts." The lasting importance of myth, for Lewis, explains Haggard's lasting greatness.

Diana Pavlac Glyer
Azusa Pacific University

Bibliography

Lewis, C. S. "Myth Became Fact"

"Hamlet: The Prince or the Poem?"

The Proceedings of the British Academy, XXVIII. London: Oxford University Press, 1942. Reprinted in *They Asked for a Paper* and *Selected Literary Essays*

This is perhaps the quintessential Lewis academic speech. He began the lecture by saying he is no scholar in the field of **Shakespeare**, but more like a child; the "child" immediately began analyzing the positions of seventeen Shakespearean scholars over the past two hundred years. Lewis was rigorously logical and illuminatingly analogical in dissecting problems with the various views of *Hamlet.* Taking a minority position, Lewis declared that what makes the play fascinating is not the character of Hamlet but the situation that this very ordinary character is placed in. He asserted that in general, plays are not character-centered but situation-centered, and illustrated this point at some length from *Merchant of Venice,* which he said is not about men but metals.

Hamlet, in Lewis's view, is about dying. He provided numerous references from the play to death and the afterlife to support his interpretation. Death is the fate of everyone, and thus, to Lewis, Hamlet is a sort of Everyman (unlike such notable characters as Beatrice or Falstaff) whose musings represent the thoughts of us all. If someone were to ask what C. S. Lewis was like as a literary critic, this would be the article to cite.

Marvin D. Hinten
Bowling Green State University

Also See: Literary Criticism, Literary Theory

Bibliography

Colman, E. A. M. "Hamlet: The Poem or the Play?" *Sydney Studies in English* 1 (1975): 3–12.

Happiness

Lewis believed that the human emotion called "happiness" was a "second" not "first thing"—that is, a secondary effect and not a primary aim in life—and that a great deal of what most people regarded as unhappiness was disappointment caused by the false expectation that happiness could be expected as the rule, not the exception. Lewis went on to point out that **God** dared not give us the happiness we think we desire, for it might teach us to find our happiness in this world, and any worldly happiness would be short-lived and shallow at best. Lewis pointed out that God can only give us the kind of happiness that exists, not the happiness we imagine; and that happiness is only found in relationship with him and is merely the by-product of having God himself:

"God intends to give us what we need, not what we now think we want" (*Problem of Pain*). Once we have discovered this principle, we can understand that all our suffering and trials are given us in order to make us the sort of people that can experience the "deep, strong, unshakable kind of happiness" of being beloved of God (*Mere Christianity*).

As a corollary to this idea, Lewis cautioned that placing any sort of **faith** in happiness in this life was almost the surest guarantee to make one unhappy. Conversely, to expect nothing of worldly happiness, to see the world as a kind of training ground for the **reality** beyond this world—in short, to do one's duty, happy or not—is to risk finding great and unexpected pleasure in the world. The fictional picture of this is in Lewis's novel *Perelandra*, where the **hero**, Ransom, senses that life is best if one accepts pleasures as they come and does not try to grab for more.

Lewis also warned against thinking that the natural by-product of **Christianity** was constant and reliable happiness. The crown, he said, is accompanied by the cross. **Christ** suffered, and we are bound to share in his sufferings. What's more, Lewis recognized that it was more important that we be people who can behave in a moral way than it is that we be happy. Only through sanctification can we become the kind of creature who can *possibly* be happy and ultimately experience **heaven**. Without our becoming holy, we are ultimately incapable of any sort of real happiness. We would not recognize this inability, and we do not recognize it, unless we have grown from the inside out into the sort of people that can be happy.

Lewis illustrated this in the ending of *The Last Battle*, where a group of skeptical dwarves enter the door into Aslan's Country and are privileged to have Aslan lay a feast before them. But they are unable to appreciate the feast, perceiving it to be scraps of food in the straw and dung of the stable they falsely imagine themselves to be inside. Nor can they see nor hear Aslan or the **beauty** of the country all about them. Thus Lewis warned that the sort of skepticism that is common in the 20th century "scientific" mind-set does not bring clarity but rather causes the skeptic to be entirely blind and deaf to ultimate **reality**.

Another fictional picture Lewis drew of the incapacity for fallen man to appreciate happiness, even when it is placed before him, is the inability of the ghosts in *The Great Divorce* to appreciate the **beauty** around them as they tour the perimeters of heaven. With one exception, each ghost is too obsessed with some **sin** that

he falsely believes will lead to his happiness, but which in fact condemns him to **hell** and eternal self-imposed misery. This picture of the "The gates of Hell being locked from the inside" comes from Lewis's maxim that everyone gets what they want in the end—but many won't like it. Happiness is only found in God, and the distractions of this life that we allow to get between him and ourselves only impede our ability to ever be happy.

Of his own happiness in life, Lewis admitted to having very little as he grew up. He said he was far more eager to escape **pain** than to achieve happiness. Probably his first solidly happy time in his life was the years he lived with his tutor, **W. T. Kirkpatrick**, reading for entry into **Oxford University** and taking long walks through the Surrey countryside. Following his experience in World War I, Lewis settled down to a sort of domestic happiness with his adopted **family** and later his brother **Warren Lewis** in their home, **the Kilns**. But he was surprised by the depth and the nature of the happiness that he found in his **marriage** to **Joy Davidman Lewis**, telling a friend that he was finding the happiness in his sixties that he would have expected to experience in his twenties. After Joy's death in 1960, Lewis realized that sort of happiness would never return, but knew enough not to expect it to. He lived by his own principle of not minding happiness, but attending to one's duty and taking the pleasures that God sends until his own death three years later.

James Prothero

Also See: Destiny, Joy, Redemption, Science

Bibliography

Lewis, C. S. "Answers to Questions on Christianity"; "Is Progress Possible?"; *Mere Christianity*; *The Problem of Pain*; *Surprised by Joy*; "We Have No 'Right to Happiness'"; "The Weight of Glory."

Colin Hardie (1906–)

In 1936 after several years as a fellow at Balliol and as director of the British School in Rome, Colin Hardie was elected a fellow and classical **tutor** at **Magdalen College, Oxford**. Hardie became a regular member of the **Inklings**.

Bibliography

Hardie, Colin. *Vitae Vergilianae Antiquae* (1954).

Alfred Cecil Harwood (1898–1975)

A. C. Harwood was a boyhood friend of **Owen Barfield**, and C. S. Lewis described him as a wholly imperturbable man. As **Oxford** students the three shared a strong interest in poetry. Lewis was shocked and disturbed when Harwood and Barfield became Anthroposophists, but the friendships continued unabated. In 1936, when Lewis first read a copy of **Charles Williams'** *The Place of the Lion*, he promptly sent it to Harwood and urged him to read it, then to pass it on to Barfield. In 1937 Harwood became Chairman of the Anthroposophical Society in Great Britain, and in 1947 Lewis dedicated *Miracles* to him and his first wife, Daphne.

For his last thirty years Harwood lived in Forest Row, Essex, where London's Steinerite school relocated after World War II. As a lifelong leader of the Anthroposophical Society, he frequently stayed at the Rudolph Steiner House in London. Upon Lewis's death, Harwood became co-executor of his estate along with Owen Barfield, and their titles eventually changed to co-trustees.

Kathryn Lindskoog

Also See: Anthroposophy

Bibliography

Harwood, A. C. "About Anthroposophy" and "A Toast to his Memory." *C. S. Lewis at the Breakfast Table.* ed. James Como. New York: Macmillan, 1976: 25–30, 237–41.

Robert Emlyn "Humphrey" Havard (1901–1985)

Havard, an **Inkling**, served as an official witness to Lewis's civil **marriage** to **Joy Davidman Gresham.** Havard first met Lewis while making a house call at the **Kilns**. In his essay, "Philia: Jack at Ease," he described this visit and a typical Inklings' meeting, along with a boating holiday he took with Jack and **Hugo Dyson**. Although he thought of himself "as the only nonliterary and nonteaching member of the Inklings," Lewis asked him to write an appendix to *The Problem of Pain*. Havard was also the first speaker to the **Oxford University Socratic Club** and played an important background role in the debate Lewis had with G. E. N. Anscombe on the "self-refutation of naturalism."

Dr. Havard had several nicknames, "Humphrey" (a name used in error by Dyson, but then continued and also used by Lewis in referring to him in *Perelandra*), "the Red Admiral" (due to his reddish beard), and the "U.Q." ("Useless Quack," dubbed such by **Warren Lewis** in a situation unrelated to medicine). Havard's medical role did play an important part in his relationship to Lewis's household. Lewis referred to him as "my Doctor friend," and in the biography *Jack* by **George Sayer**, we learn about Havard's medical advice to Lewis concerning the consummation of his marriage. However, after Joy's cancer was discovered, and later, after Lewis's own medical problems began, some associates began to doubt Humphrey's diagnostic abilities.

Richard James
Burkesville Christian Church

Bibliography

Anonymous. "Report of the 248th and 249th Meetings." *CSL* 21, No. 10 (August 1990): 5–7.
Anscombe, G. E. M. *The Collected Philosophical Papers of G. E. M. Anscombe, Vol. II: Metaphysics and the Philosophy of the Mind.* Minneapolis: University of Minnesota, 1981.
Carpenter, Humphrey. *The Inklings: C. S. Lewis, J. R. R. Tolkien, Charles Williams and Their Friends*. Boston: Houghton Mifflin, 1979.
Griffin, William. *Clive Staples Lewis: A Dramatic Life*. San Francisco: Harper & Row, 1986.
Havard, Robert E. "Observed Effects of Pain."
_____. "Philia: Jack at Ease." *C. S. Lewis at the Breakfast Table*. James T. Como (ed). New York: Harvest/HBJ Book, 1992.
_____. "Professor J. R. R. Tolkien: A Personal Memoir." *Mythlore* 17, No. 2 (Winter 1990): 61.
Hooper, Walter. *C. S. Lewis: A Companion & Guide*. San Francisco: HarperCollins, 1996.
Lewis, C. S. *The Problem of Pain*. New York: Macmillan, 1962.
Lewis, Warren Hamilton. *Brothers and Friends: The Diaries of Major Warren Hamilton Lewis*. Clyde S. Kilby and Marjorie Lamp Mead (eds). San Francisco: Harper & Row, 1982.
Sayer, George. *Jack: A Life of C. S. Lewis*. Wheaton, IL: Crossway, 1988. rev. 1994.

Ronald Edwin Head (1919–1991)

The Rev. Head served as both curate from 1952 until 1956 and Vicar from 1956 until 1990 of the Church of the Holy Trinity in Headington Quarry, Oxford—the parish which Lewis and **Warren Lewis** attended.

Heaven

Lewis's imaginative realizations of heaven are the best and most convincing to appear in English literature since **John Milton**'s *Paradise Lost*. Unlike **Dante** and Milton, Lewis does not attempt to show his readers heaven. Rather, as does the 14th-century poet of *Pearl* or **J. R. R. Tolkien** in his short story *Leaf by Niggle*, he introduces the outlying regions of a blessed eternity that suggest the full reality without detailed speculation. Additionally, Lewis's accounts of various earthly paradises—unfallen worlds such as Malacandra, Perelandra, and Narnia at the moment of **creation**—in which the primitive harmony between **God**, humanity, and **nature** is intact, provide a bridge for the reader's **imagination** between the blisses suggested by the natural creation and those to come in the heavenly. Finally, Lewis's apologetic presents a cogent argument why the hope for heaven is not only reasonable but consistent as well with humanity's deepest desires.

The reader gathers components of Lewis's conception of heaven from various sources, no two of which are exactly alike, though all bear a family resemblance. The heaven of *The Great Divorce* is a beautiful countryside, in which the River of Life and the Tree of Life are prominent features, and sunrise (Sonrise) is only minutes away, heralded by the glow at the tops of the mountains on the eastern horizon that are the true goal of all the redeemed—mountains being a symbol of deep heaven shared with Tolkien's *Leaf by Niggle*. It is also more solidly real than any earthly **reality**, a reversal of the popular modern notion of the vague insubstantiality of spirituality. The outskirts of heaven are encountered in *Voyage of the "Dawn Treader"* as the edge of Aslan's country, visible only as distant mountains ringing but not actually in the land of Narnia. They are approached through a calm, silent sea of lilies bathed in brilliant light, filling the traveler with a sense of well-being and a longing to follow the valiant talking mouse Reepicheep as he mounts the last, never-falling wave in his coracle. Aslan's country is revealed a bit more in the first and last chapters of *The Silver Chair* as wooded, silent except for the music of birdsong, and containing a stream of revivifying water; the resemblance between Aslan's woods and the transformed woods of *Pearl* is especially noticeable. Aslan's country also reminds us of the Earthly Paradise of Dante and the Eden of *Paradise Lost* in that all three are atop an unimaginably high mountain. The heaven of *The Last Battle* is the most fully developed picture, a Platonic realization of familiar places—Narnia and England—in their Ideal form, at the center of which lies the enclosed Garden (the *hortus conclusus* of Medieval romance) containing the Tree of Life, again atop a high mountain. Idealized nature—countryside, rivers, trees, songbirds, mountains, and sunlight—figures prominently in all these visions, joining Platonic Idealism and biblical imagery to anticipate the Scriptures' promise of a New Heaven and New Earth.

The modern reader receives from Lewis's earthly paradises a lively impression of the contrast between the fallen world and the perfect creation God intended. The unfallen worlds of Malacandra and Perelandra, as well as Narnia at its birth, are characterized by harmonious relations among the creatures as well as between nature and rational beings; and communication between rational beings (hnau), God the Son (Maleldil), and **angels** (eldila and Oyéresu) is uninhibited. This is Eden, or Paradise—a conception heavenly enough compared with postlapsarian human experience. To live there vicariously for even a short time is enough to awaken the universal human desire for the lost Garden, man's original home.

Ransom's sojourn among the hrossa and seroni of Malacandra reveals beings whose instinctive conceptions of spirituality, economics, **politics**, race (species), sexuality, and death are consistent only with humanity's highest—and virtually unpracticed—ideals. Hnau and eldila communicate routinely, and both unite in worship of Maleldil. Planetary economics are based on distribution according to need and mutual division of labor among the three rational species—hrossa, seroni, and pfifiltriggi. Politically, Oyarsa rules, and no species desires dominance over another. The three species find one another endlessly amusing as well as mutually useful, but antagonism is unknown. Sexually, the species are monogamous, and abstinent before and after breeding. Death is anticipated as the best of all experiences, for it brings the hnau into the immediate presence of Maleldil. Conditions on Perelandra are different owing to the fact that the planet has only two rational inhabitants, and communication between them and Maleldil is direct, unmediated by angels. There is no need for agriculture and crafts in a world where nature itself feeds and shelters. Malacandra is a utopia, Perelandra an Eden—conceptions older than **Plato**'s *Republic* or the book of Genesis.

On both planets, Ransom discovers realities corresponding with earthly myth. Space itself makes him think of "the Heavens," replete as it is with images of chariots, a reminiscence of Dana, and Apollonian vitality. On Malacandra's sacred isle of Meldilorn he discovers a stone-carved schematization of the solar system generally consistent with the universe of Plato's *Timeaus* as modified in the *Cosmographia* of the Medieval scholar Bernardus Sylvestris. In *Perelandra*, Ransom lives among mythic entities—dragons, and trees bearing golden fruit, both from the Garden of the Hesperides (Hesper being an ancient name for Venus); the abundant food, warm climate, and friendly beasts of a Golden Age; an **Eve**, who is later joined by an Adam; and a tempter, personified in Weston, who becomes the Un-man. Ransom's ultimate confrontation with this Satan-possessed being virtually reenacts **Christ**'s death, burial, resurrection, and ascension. His heel is wounded by the adversary whose head he crushes; he descends under the earth; and, after a three-day recuperation upon emerging from underground, he ascends to the highest and holiest place in Perelandra, where he encounters the Oyéresu of Malacandra and Perelandra in their manifestations as the archetypes of mythology's Mars and Venus. There, for the first time, he meets Tor, the Adam of this world, whose face he instantly recognizes as the image of Christ in his earthly ministry.

Though Perelandra is not heaven, the distinctions between heaven and earth, time and eternity break down in the antiphonal hymn of the Great Dance in the novel's last chapter. The Great Dance itself is an exemplary notion of planetary relations borrowed from the **Renaissance**, treated explicitly and at length in Sir John Davies' Orchestra, and in our time helpfully discussed by E. M. W. Tillyard in *The Elizabethan World Picture*. In this chapter, Ransom approaches a vision of God reminiscent of Dante's in the last canto of the *Paradiso*, reminiscent also of **T. S. Eliot**'s description of God as being "the still point of the turning world."

In **"The Weight of Glory"** and in the chapter entitled "Hope" in *Mere Christianity*, C. S. Lewis argues directly, and elsewhere indirectly, that natural desires have real objects, that our longing for heaven is a natural desire, and that therefore our longing for heaven is a longing for a real object. This longing, or *Sehnsucht*, which Lewis calls **Joy** in *Surprised by Joy*, was the driving motive of his conversion and was triggered in his childhood by such catalysts as nature, myth, **poetry,** and music. These objects must be called catalysts because none of them could satisfy the instant of longing, triggered and fading in the same moment, which itself became in turn an object of unattainable desire. In *The Pilgrim's Regress*, John is told by the Hermit History that God has, throughout history, sent to pagan and post-pagan humanity a series of pictures—archetypes—arousing longing for that which is not to be found in the world. These pointers all lead us off the map of the visible universe. Philosopher Peter Kreeft has called Lewis's treatment of this longing the "Argument from Desire."

Lyle Smith
Biola University

Bibliography

Kreeft, Peter J. "C. S. Lewis's Argument from Desire." *G. K. Chesterton and C. S. Lewis: The Riddle of Joy*. Michael H. Macdonald and Andrew A. Tadie (eds). Grand Rapids, MI: Eerdmans, 1989.

"Heaven, Earth and Outer Space"

Decision. II (December 1963): 4.

See entry on "I Was Decided Upon"

"Hedonics"

Time and Tide. XXVI (16 June 1945): 494–95. Reprinted in *Present Concerns*.

The conclusion of this essay is that "we have had enough, once and for all, of Hedonism—the gloomy **philosophy** which says that Pleasure is the only good. But we have hardly yet begun what may be called *Hedonics*, the science or philosophy of Pleasure." The essay is not presented as philosophy, however, but through the pleasures Lewis experiences in a mundane journey by tube—the London Underground—from Paddington to Harrow. The report is of concrete details, but they are, as it were, on two levels: there are the outside things—the train itself, the people, the stations—and there are the inside things—the charm of other peoples' domesticities, the change from being underground to being in a gully to being fully in the evening sunlight. The latter are just there, offering, inviting **happiness**, and Lewis was free to accept or not. He accepted—and described his state as one of **joy**. The two elements of our lives run side by side, but the joy is often forbidden by the Jailer, who claims to represent reality. And yet the "distant blue hills" fifteen miles away (Lewis must have had the Castlereagh Hills in mind) really appear blue. "It is a mere brute fact that patches of . . . boyhood, remembered in one's forties at the bidding of some sudden smell or sound, give one (in the forties) an almost unbearable pleasure. The one is as good a fact as the other." The Jailer, who has dominated our minds for thirty years or so, especially in literature, is a sham realist who claims that myth, **fantasy**, and romance are wishful thinking. But they are just as real as the events in a biography or newspaper.

John Bremer

Hell

Writer William F. Buckley was once asked why he spelled Hell with a capital H. "Because," he said, "it's a real place, like Scarsdale [an affluent New York suburb]." C. S. Lewis also spelled Hell with a capital H and definitely thought it a real place, but although he was a religious conservative, he did not see Hell as necessarily a domain of fire and brimstone. Nonetheless, his visions of grim, rainy towns full of relentless malcontents and modern bureaucracies full of smiling cannibals are in many ways more horrifying than the traditional

imagery of Hell, and his summation of the fate of the damned is at least as chilling.

Lewis saw the essence of Hell as separation from **God**, arrived at voluntarily by a process of self-deception and self-centeredness. Taking a cue from **Milton**'s **Satan**, the denizens of Hell believe it is better to reign in Hell than serve in Heaven. But for everyone but Satan himself, this choice means to hold on to self-deceptions, growing ever more "shrunk up into oneself" at the cost of eternal **joy**. One cannot be sent or taken to Hell: "You can only get there on your own steam." The doors to Hell may or may not be locked from the outside, but they are certainly locked from the inside.

Lewis offered two extended visions of Hell in his writing: the Grey Town in *The Great Divorce* and the modern corporate office of *The Screwtape Letters*. In the former, Hell seems almost too easy—at first. Houses appear just by thinking of them, and no tormentors are in view. But the eternally quarrelsome must live with each other, which they are of course unable to do, and so the Grey Town spreads out for millions of miles as the inhabitants try to escape one another's company. And of course the houses, being only imaginary, don't keep out the rain, or the relentless frustration and unpleasantness, or the fear of darkness coming.

In *The Screwtape Letters*, Hell is streamlined, well-lighted, and meticulously managed. It is the nightmare of bureaucracy, of which the worst police state, or even the N.I.C.E. abomination of *That Hideous Strength*, is but a pale shadow. From "Our Father Below" on up, Screwtape's Hell is a hive of resentful and envious backstabbers, a Byzantine "lowerarchy" of treachery and deceit. It is a dog-eat-dog concern, both figuratively and literally, for **devils** who do not stay ahead of the game are absorbed—eaten—by the ravenous devils they plotted to absorb themselves. Human souls are the cattle upon which devils feed as they plot to devour one another.

In *Screwtape* the young man is killed on earth, but saved from Hell when he repents at his death. In *The Great Divorce,* lost souls are given a chance to repent even after they have been in Hell. If they do decide to repent, Hell has then been **Purgatory** for them. The free choice of whether or not to repent must exist, however—there must be a Hell for those who absolutely want to be separate from joy. Of the final disposition of those who "only want to be left alone" by God, Lewis said, "Alas, I am afraid that is what He does."

Richard A. Hill
Taylor University

Bibliography
Lewis, C. S. *The Dark Tower*; *Miracles*; *Preface to Paradise Lost*; *The Problem of Pain*; "The Trouble with 'X.'"
Lindskoog, Kathryn Ann. *C. S. Lewis: Mere Christian*. Glendale, CA: Regal, 1973.

George Herbert (1593–1633)

Herbert was arguably C. S. Lewis's favorite Lyric poet; and of the Metaphysical poets, Lewis preferred Herbert to **John Donne**. While Lewis was often critical of the subtle and ebullient style of the Metaphysicals, there are elements of Herbert's honesty and self-effacing manner that prefigure a similar quality in Lewis's own work. Lewis's appreciation for Herbert was clear when he compared him to his literary mentor **George MacDonald**, calling them both, "Delicious, earthy, homespun." Lewis explained that Herbert described life as it is really lived—managing to minimize pretense in both his own life and writings.

Jerry Root
Wheaton College

Also See: Poetry

Bibliography
Lewis, C. S. *English Literature in the Sixteenth Century, Excluding Drama*; *Surprised by Joy*.

"Hermione in the House of Paulina"

Augury: An Oxford Miscellany of Verse and Poetry. A. M. Hardie and K. C. Douglas (eds). Oxford: Blackwell, 1940: 28. Revised and reprinted in *Poems* and *Collected Poems*.

Shakespeare's *The Winter's Tale* is the subject of this poem, particularly Hermione, spurned wife of the insanely jealous Leontes, King of Sicilia. Falsely accused of infidelity, Hermione was brutally treated by Leontes and thought to have died of a broken heart. Actually she was secretly cared for by her lady-in-waiting, Paulina, for sixteen years in an isolated chapel before she is dramatically reunited with Leontes and her family. This lovely poem captures the still, quiet **beauty** of her years in the chapel; whatever bitterness she may have initially had has been replaced by contented peace, in part because of the dedicated love of Paulina.

Don W. King
Montreat College

"Hero and Leander"

The Proceedings of the British Academy, XXXVIII. London: Oxford University Press, 1952. Reprinted in *Selected Literary Essays*.

This masterful article from *Selected Literary Essays* lucidly sets forth how the authorial switch in the middle of *Hero and Leander* caused it to be a greater poem than it would have been otherwise. The first two books of the poem are written by Marlowe; the next four, after Marlowe's death, by Chapman. Lewis began by saying the two parts are "very seldom" read together; if that is hardly true today, perhaps Lewis's argument here is one reason. Lewis compared the Marlovian portion with **Shakespeare**'s *Venus and Adonis*, to Marlowe's advantage. Marlowe's hyperbolic, heavenly style presents erotic **poetry** better than Shakespeare's earthy mode.

Then Chapman, a graver poet, takes over just as a graver voice is needed—to tell how Hero and Leander's illicit love led to their downfall and to point out the moral lessons to be learned. In a brilliant observation, Lewis noted the morality here is based neither on pagan nor Christian grounds, but on "ceremony"—what writers a century later would have called "decorum." Lewis concluded by noting insightfully that the change from Marlowe to Chapman is virtually a parable of the change in love poetry from the 16th to 17th centuries. This essay is a genuine learning experience.

Marvin D. Hinten
Bowling Green State University

Also See: Ethics and Morality, Poetry

Heroes

Heroism was a subject that interested Lewis throughout his life—from his childhood enchantment with the heroic tales of Norse mythology (and the exalted music of **Richard Wagner**) to his adult appreciation of the works of such authors as **John Milton**, Thomas Malory, and his own close friend, **J. R. R. Tolkien**. Lewis's insights into heroism were displayed in both his fiction and his scholarly writings.

In Lewis's fiction, one can easily see the heroic ideal at work in his earliest published novels—*Out of the Silent Planet*, *Perelandra*, and *That Hideous Strength*. The champion of these stories is named Ransom, an appellation which signifies the character's role in saving entire planets from demonic domination. Throughout the **science fiction** trilogy, Ransom displays great valor in battling evil powers both human and spiritual. His eventual destiny is revealed in the third book of the series as the Pendragon of Logres, a successor to the mythical hero **King Arthur**.

Lewis's appreciation for heroism also permeates his **Chronicles of Narnia**. The four children in *The Lion, the Witch and the Wardrobe*, like the heroes of roman-

tic literature, courageously defeat the cruel villain under whom many suffer. The testing of their character, honor, and valor prove them worthy to become rulers of Narnia. The heroic tradition is evident throughout the rest of the series as well, particularly in the princes Caspian, Rilian, and Shasta, and the valiant talking mouse, Reepicheep. Their adventures include the recovery of lost identity, the engagement in a quest, the overthrow of evil, and the restoration of rightful rulership. True to the archetype, the origin of these heroes is often either mysterious or unusual; and their tale comes to an end as they enter **marriage** (signifying their attainment of maturity), or assume their place of authority, or complete their Narnian lives.

In his nonfiction work, Lewis made perceptive comments about the "Heroic Age" in literature in chapter 5 of *A Preface to Paradise Lost*, and he wrote the contemporary application of the heroic ideal of chivalry in **"The Necessity of Chivalry."**

Alice H. Cook

Also See: Fantasy, Good and Evil, Myth

Bibliography

Folkenflik, Robert (ed). *The English Hero, 1660–1800*. Newark, DE: University of Delaware Press, 1982.

Hanay, Margaret P. *C. S. Lewis*. New York: Ungar, 1981.

Lindskoog, Kathryn. *The Lion of Judah in Never-Never Land*. Grand Rapids, MI: Eerdmans, 1973.

Schakel, Peter J. *Reading with the Heart: The Way into Narnia*. Grand Rapids, MI: Eerdmans, 1979.

Hierarchy

Lewis rejected the hierarchical principle in practical politics and economics, but thought it a necessary condition of healthy moral and spiritual life. The primary hierarchy is that of Creator and creation. In a perfect world, there would be no equality, but neither would the higher abuse and exploit the lower. This conception is expressed most fully in the "Great Dance" portion of *Perelandra*'s concluding chapter. Hierarchy, far from being a rigid and static gradation of rank, is for Lewis a living and dynamic circle—with Maleldil and, in their turn, all created things at the center of concatenating patterns of relation.

Nevertheless, Lewis applauded resistance to the abuse of political authority in practical life, claiming that the cynicism of the ordinary man in the street limits governmental control of public opinion. He was hostile to any idea of a managed society, as shown in *The Abolition of Man* and the novel *That Hideous Strength*. Yet that same novel also reveals a willing, unforced submission of natural inferiors to natural superiors in the community at St. Anne's. Such a relation comes naturally to human beings who, currently deprived of traditional objects of respect, at present acclaim professional entertainers and athletes.

Lyle Smith
Biola University

Also See: Politics

Bibliography

Lewis, C. S. *The Abolition of Man;* "Equality"; "Kipling's World"; *Perelandra;* "Private Bates"; *That Hideous Strength;* "Transposition."

Hierarchy of Heaven and Earth (Preface)

Harding, D. E. *The Hierarchy of Heaven and Earth: A New Diagram of Man in the Universe.* London: Faber & Faber, 1952. Retitled "The Empty Universe" and reprinted in *Present Concerns.*

Douglas Edison Harding was born in English Sussex in 1909. As a young man, he rejected his parents' **Christianity.** While working as an architect in Britain and India, he developed his own blend of Zen Buddhism and Hindu Jnana Yoga that stressed a practical awareness of one's identity.

In his preface, C. S. Lewis called D. E. Harding's *Hierarchy of Heaven and Earth* the "first attempt to reverse a movement of thought that has been going on since the beginning of philosophy." That progression, he said, emptied the universe of vividness and reduced everything to mere human sensations. Eventually humanity itself became empty as philosophers claimed we had no souls, selves, or minds. Lewis noted that governments intent on killing people find such an idea "very congenial," but ordinary people find it unpleasant and unlivable.

Lewis felt Harding's book offered an opportunity to reverse that trend. But his skepticism about whether it would work proved correct. The author's unique way of looking at man and the universe has not caught on. With great politeness, Lewis also hinted that he found the author stimulating in the same way he found value in other great writers whose basic beliefs he rejected.

Mike Perry

Also See: Cosmology, The Fall, Metaphysics, Materialism, Non-Christian Religions, Tao

Bibliography

Contemporary Authors, 1986, Vol. 116: 192.
Kreeft, Peter. "C. S. Lewis and the Future of the World." *CSL: The Bulletin of the New York C. S. Lewis Society.* 15, no. 7 (May 1984): 1–13.

"High and Low Brows"

First published in *Rehabilitations.* Reprinted in *Selected Literary Essays.*

In this essay, originally an address to the English Society at **Oxford** in the 1930s, and published first in *Rehabilitations* (1939), Lewis began by noting that books are generally divided into literary and ordinary, or, as he settled on calling them, high brow and low brow. He told of a discussion with one of his students in which he asked whether her literary theories would apply to *The Tale of Peter Rabbit;* after a pause, she informed him that, since the book was trivial, it was not germane to a literary discussion. Lewis spent most of the essay exploring this question: What makes a book "literature"?

He considered and discarded a variety of possibilities: quality, weight, style, unpopularity, elevation, and (half-facetiously) difficulty. Lewis showed in every case that there are books both "highbrow" and "lowbrow"— with the specified qualities (the low brow books including those by derided authors Lewis himself loved such as **H. Rider Haggard** and John Buchan). Lewis then predicted (and we have seen his prophecy come to pass) that in the future fewer people would read great books because of their greatness; instead, great books would be kept alive by their academic prestige. Throughout the essay, Lewis quietly but forcefully indicted the work of then influential critical theorist I. A. Richards, who championed, in Lewis's view, a schizophrenic professionalism that robbed readers of the enjoyment of reading in the name of a dubious and artificial standard of "good taste."

The incipient themes of this essay are developed at length in Lewis's 1961 work, *An Experiment in Criticism,* where Lewis delineated the different modes and motives of readers, and the necessity of judging books "by the way in which they are read," rather than merely by who reads them or by their subject matter.

Bruce L. Edwards and Marvin D. Hinten
Bowling Green State University

Bibliography

Edwards, Bruce L. *A Rhetoric of Reading: C. S. Lewis's Defense of Western Literacy.* Provo, UT: Brigham Young University Press, 1985.
Lewis, C. S. "Bluspels and Flalansferes"; "Christianity and Culture"; "Christianity and Literature"; "On Church Music."
Myers, Doris T. *C. S. Lewis in Context.* Kent, OH: Kent State University Press, 1994.

"The Hills of Down"

Wilson, A. N. *C. S. Lewis: A Biography*. London: Collins, 1990: 48. Reprinted in full in *Collected Poems*.

In this 1915 poem Lewis anticipated some of the **poetry** in *Spirits in Bondage*. The poem indicates both a longing for the "faery town" and a love for the immediate **beauty** of **nature**. While the former frightens him, the latter powerfully draws him. (Note: Wilson incorrectly prints "fast" for "past" in line twelve.)

Don W. King
Montreat College

"Historicism"

The Month. IV (October 1950): 230–43. Reprinted in *Christian Reflections* and *Fern-Seed and Elephants*.

This essay distinguished between historians (whose conclusions are themselves historical) and Historicists (who claim, by the use of their natural powers, to discover an inner meaning in the historical process). The latter claim conclusions that are more than historical—"conclusions metaphysical or theological or (to coin a word) atheo-logical." Lewis argued that Historicism is an illusion and that Historicists are, at the very best, wasting their time. Historicism has a Pantheistic ancestor in Hegel and a materialistic progeny in the Marxists, and these have been stronger than the Christian Historicists who claim that all calamities are "judgments." It is true that "all things happen by the divine will or at least by divine permission, and it follows that the total content of time must in its own nature be a **revelation** of **God**'s wisdom, **justice**, and **mercy**." But we do not have that text, nor the capacity to read it, even if we had it. The natural **reason** cannot do that. If the reading of such a text is done by someone claiming to be inspired, that is another matter, and it must be evaluated in another way. But Historicists do not claim to be prophets, to be inspired; they use only their natural reason.

Lewis distinguished six senses of history, and he said that those who claim that history is a revelation, or has meaning, must state the sense they have in mind. To say that the important parts of history (in whatever sense) survive begs the question, simply because "standards of historical importance are themselves embedded in history.... Why should Gengis Khan be more important than the patience or despair of some one among his victims?" We all, however, have a "certain limited, but direct, access to" the revelation of God in history. "We are allowed, indeed compelled, to read it sentence by

sentence, and every sentence is labelled *Now*.... The real or primary history which meets each of us moment by moment in his own experience. It is very limited, but it is the pure, unedited, unexpurgated text, straight from the Author's hand."

John Bremer

Also See: Communism and Fascism, Materialism

Bibliography

Kreeft, Peter. "Western Civilization at the Crossroads." *Christian History*. 4 no. 3 (1985): 25–26.

"The Hobbit"

See entry on *The Hobbit: or There and Back Again* (Book Review)

The Hobbit: or There and Back Again (Book Review)

"A World for Children." *The Times Literary Supplement*. (2 October 1937): 714 (unsigned). Reprinted as "The Hobbit" in *Of This and Other Worlds* and *On Stories*.

"'The Hobbit' may well prove a classic," predicted Lewis in this glowing review. The story begins as a matter-of-fact tale, and grows "saga-like." Lewis thought the book would be read and reread with great appreciation for Tolkien's "scholarship and profound reflection."

Anne Gardner

Also See: J. R. R. Tolkien

Bibliography

Tolkien, J. R. R. *The Hobbit: or There and Back Again*.

The Hobbit: or There and Back Again (Book Review II)

"Professor Tolkien's Hobbit." *The Times*. (8 October 1937): 20 (unsigned).

This short review invited "[a]ll who love that kind of children's book which can be read and re-read by adults" to read **J. R. R. Tolkien**'s book. According to Lewis, *The Hobbit* combined "humor, an understanding of children, and a happy fusion of the scholar's with the poet's grasp of mythology." The maps were pronounced excellent, as was Tolkien's firsthand study of trolls, dragons, and the like.

Anne Gardner

Also See: Fantasy, Myths

Bibliography

Tolkien, J. R. R. *The Hobbit: or There and Back Again*.

The Holy Name (Letter)

Church Times. CXXXIV (10 August 1951): 541. Reprinted in *God in the Dock*, *Undeceptions,* and *Timeless at Heart.*

Writing in response to Leslie E. T. Bradbury's letter (*Church Times,* 3 August 1951, 525) on the use of reverential prefixes before various holy names (e.g., the Blessed Virgin Mary), Lewis disagreed that the absence of such prefixes necessarily implies a lack of respect. Rather Lewis believed this difference in forms of address reflects a contrast in style not **faith** and, further, that such differences should not be allowed to cause division within the **church**.

Marjorie L. Mead
The Marion E. Wade Center

Also See: Anglicanism

The Holy Spirit

C. S. Lewis followed traditional theological thinking of his time in presuming the Holy Spirit was the third person of the **Trinity**. He said people should not be worried or surprised if their notion of the Spirit was vague or "shadowy" but should think of the Spirit as inside or behind them. He wrote one correspondent that it would be erroneous to think that the Spirit spoke *only* within a person, and that in reality the Spirit also spoke "through Scripture, the **Church**, Christian friends, books, etc. . . ." For Lewis, the Spirit was "most operative" when a person could feel it least; a person may not always *sense* the presence of the Spirit.

In his sermon **"Transposition"** (May 28, 1944), Lewis explored the validity of speaking in tongues as a manifestation of the Holy Spirit. He admitted this was a problem for many Christians (including himself) but defended its use in the book of Acts. The most notable allusions to the Spirit in the Narnian stories are in *The Horse and His Boy* ("the Thing") and *The Lion, the Witch and the Wardrobe* (Father Christmas). The activity of the Spirit, meanwhile, is symbolized by Aslan's breath.

Perry C. Bramlett
C. S. Lewis for the Local Church

Bibliography

Lewis, C. S. *Mere Christianity* (see chapter titled "Good Infection").

Lindskoog, Kathryn. "C. S. Lewis and the Holy Spirit." *The Canadian C. S. Lewis Journal.* 86 (Autumn 1994): 9–11.

Payne, Leanne. *Real Presence: The Christian Worldview of C. S. Lewis as Incarnational Reality.* Wheaton, IL: Crossway, 1988.

Mrs. Hooker

In early 1952 a hotel keeper's wife in Ramsgate called C. S. Lewis and asked when he was going to pay Mrs. Hooker's bill, which was overdue. He asked who Mrs. Hooker was and why he should pay her bill, and his caller said, "But she's your wife!" In fact, Mrs. Hooker was a confidence artist with twenty-one previous convictions, who had been borrowing money and running up bills by posing as Lewis's wife.

Lewis had to go to Ramsgate police court twice to testify against Mrs. Hooker; he pitied her but was glad she was exposed and sent to Holloway Prison. In a May 17, 1952, letter to **Dom Bede Griffiths** (in the **Marion E. Wade Center**) he said he found the unmalicious spirit of her victims an occasion of **joy**.

Kathryn Lindskoog

Walter Hooper (1931–)

For over three decades, Walter Hooper has been one of the most important and controversial figures in Lewis affairs. From his close association with the Lewis literary estate, he has made a career of editing Lewis's works and being a Lewis scholar. Most recently, he completed the landmark volume *C. S. Lewis: A Companion and Guide* (1996). Nearly every publication of Lewis's works since Lewis's death in 1963 has been edited or re-edited by Hooper's hand: **Poems** (1964); *Studies in Medieval and Renaissance Literature* (1966); *Of Other Worlds* (1966); *Christian Reflections* (1967); *Narrative Poems* (1969); *Selected Literary Essays* (1969); *God in the Dock* (1970); *Undeceptions* (1971); *Fern-Seed and Elephants* (1975); *The Dark Tower* (1977); *God in the Dock* (1979); *Of This and Other Worlds* (1982); *On Stories* (1982); *The Business of Heaven* (1984); **Boxen** (1985); *First and Second Things* (1985); *Present Concerns* (1986); *Timeless at Heart* (1987); **Letters of C. S. Lewis**, revised and enlarged (1988); *Christian Reunion* (1990); **All My Road Before Me** (1993); *Daily Readings with C. S. Lewis* (1992); **The Collected Poems of C. S. Lewis** (1994); and *C. S. Lewis: Readings for Reflection and Meditation* (1995), among others. An engaging and seemingly humble speaker, conference attendees and Lewis society members enjoy his presentations on Lewis. Perhaps no other individual—with the possible exception of **Douglas Gresham** (Lewis's stepson)—has had as much control or influence as Hooper over the Lewis literary estate (now managed by Curtis Brown, Ltd.).

Hooper has been a controversial figure because of his influence in affairs of the estate and for other reasons.

Early on, Hooper allowed the intimacy he shared with C. S. Lewis to be exaggerated. Furthermore, he did not correct assertions that he had lived for a year at **the Kilns** with Jack and **Warren Lewis**. Warren spoke out against the assertions which were chronologically impossible. In the biography of Lewis that he co-authored with **Roger L. Green**, Hooper claimed Lewis told Mollie Miller, the housekeeper, that Hooper "was the son he never had." Mollie Miller later said that the statement was never made. While his exaggerations are easily dismissed, more disturbing have been the questions raised over Hooper's editing of works as well as the authenticity of several manuscripts he published after Lewis's death. Chief among the disputed manuscripts is *The Dark Tower*, which Hooper has said **Fred Paxford** saved from a bonfire of Lewis's writings ordered by Warren Lewis. Another disputed item is the essay **"Christian Reunion,"** first published in 1991. According to A. Q. Morton's cusum (statistical) analysis of the essay, the central forty percent of that essay matches the invisible sentence pattern of Walter Hooper rather than that of C. S. Lewis.

Hooper's legacy will be a mixed one. He has undoubtedly contributed extensively to Lewis scholarship. He will likely continue that service and others on behalf of the Lewis estate. But the serious allegations about tampering with the Lewis canon are not likely to go away quickly or quietly. Despite repeated calls from scholars, Hooper and the estate have been relatively mute.

Born on March 27, 1931, Walter McGehee Hooper (known as Coot as a child and young adult) grew up in Reidsville, North Carolina, a tobacco and textile town of about 11,000 residents. He was the third child of five born to Arch Boyd Hooper, a self-employed plumber, and Madge Kemp Hooper. Hooper attended the University of North Carolina at Chapel Hill, earning bachelor's and master's degrees in education. He taught elementary school in Chapel Hill during the academic year 1956–57. In 1957 he entered the Virginia Episcopal Seminary and was admitted as a candidate for holy orders on March 16, 1959. However, Hooper dropped himself from candidacy on September 8, 1959, because he did not approve of the seminary's practice of psychological evaluations and counseling. After leaving the seminary, Hooper taught at a boys boarding school, Christ School, in Arden, North Carolina, from 1959 until 1961.

In 1961 he left Christ School and moved to Lexington, Kentucky, and lived with a family of a recent student. There, Hooper decided to pursue a course of study in literature at the University of Kentucky. He discussed with Robert O. Evans, a professor at the university, the possibility of studying and writing a dissertation on Lewis. According to university records, Hooper never enrolled at Kentucky, although he did attend Evans' class on modern British authors in the spring of 1963.

After having exchanged several short letters with Lewis between 1954 and 1962, Hooper first met Lewis on June 7, 1963. This was undoubtedly a watershed event in Hooper's life. Hooper (also known as Hoot) was in England attending a summer course at Exeter College, Oxford, from July 1 to August 9. During Lewis's August convalescence from a heart attack, Hooper assisted Lewis with correspondence and other duties as Warren was away. He returned to Kentucky in late August 1963, planning to visit Lewis during the 1964 vacation. However, Lewis's death in November altered that plan. Instead, he moved to England in January 1964 to help **Owen Barfield** manage the Lewis literary estate, and that became his lifetime career. His first task was editing Lewis's poems for a 1964 book. Even this first edited book has had some scholars raising concerns about inexplicable and deleterious changes made in many of the poems that Lewis published in periodicals during his lifetime.

In addition to his work with the literary estate, Hooper was ordained a deacon on September 27, 1964, by the Bishop of Oxford acting on behalf of the Bishop of Lexington, Kentucky. He served as deacon at Headington Quarry—the church where Lewis had worshipped before his death—from September 27, 1964, until June 27, 1965. He remained a part-time cleric for more than two decades, but then in 1988 he renounced the Episcopal and Anglican priesthood and joined the Roman Catholic Church as a layman.

In 1980 he either sold or donated his collection of correspondence from Lewis associates to the library of the University of North Carolina at Chapel Hill. However, in 1995 researchers' access to that collection (#4236) was restricted.

Jeffrey D. Schultz

Bibliography

"Dialogue." *Christianity & Literature.* 28 (Fall 1978): 9–11.

Dart, John. "Questions Raised on C. S. Lewis Heir." *Los Angeles Times.* (March 24, 1979): 1:30–36.

Green, Roger, and Walter Hooper. *C. S. Lewis: A Biography.* 1974.

Lindskoog, Kathryn. *Light in the Shadowlands.* Sisters, OR: Multnomah, 1994.

"Horrid Red Things"

Church of England Newspaper. LI (6 October 1944): 1–2.
Reprinted in *God in the Dock, Undeceptions,* and *First and Second Things.*

In this essay, Lewis wrote that although many theologians and some scientists say that the conflict between **science** and **religion** is over, the ordinary man is still very much aware of the conflict. The parallels the ordinary man draws are the result of considering **God** as a god, or as imagining the Son coming down from **Heaven** like a parachutist. These imaginings may be simply explained as merely allegorical or spiritual, the ordinary man thinks. Lewis said that there are two things that the ordinary man must understand. The first is that, once all the explaining is done, what is left will be "unambiguously **supernatural**, miraculous, and shocking." Without **Christianity**, there would be no explanation for what is. The second thing that must be understood is the difference between thinking and imagining. There is also the distinction that must be made between thought and the images that the thinker erroneously believes to be true. Lewis recounted the story of the little girl who equated "horrid red things" with poison, but who was told by her mother that aspirin, taken in large doses, was poisonous. Although the aspirin was not the right color, she still had some basic knowledge of poison and what it could do, and so her knowledge was amended but not essentially changed. What she imagines to be true is, in part, true. The difficulty for her, and for us, is to separate the imagined from the real. Christianity is "either fact, or legend, or lie." Ultimately, we, the ordinary men, must learn the distinction.

Anne Gardner

The Horse and His Boy

London: Geoffrey Bles, 1954. First US edition, New York: Macmillan, 1954.

The Horse and His Boy is the fourth Chronicle of Narnia Lewis completed. Pausing after writing **Prince Caspian** and **The Voyage of the "Dawn Treader,"** Lewis seems to have gone back to his Narnian canvas so as to fill in the background by telling the story of Calormen, a land briefly introduced in *"Dawn Treader"* as the main market for slaves from the Cane Islands. Lewis wrote *The Horse and His Boy* almost as effortlessly as he did *"Dawn Treader"*—slightly more than three months compared to slightly less than three. In writing this Chronicle Lewis appears to have been captivated by the

characters he created, especially Shasta, whose encounter with Aslan is among the most moving in the entire **Chronicles of Narnia**. Indeed, this chapter 11, "The Unwelcome Fellow Traveller," can be seen as the link between the more mythopoeic first three Chronicles and the more didactic last three; Lewis showed in a new way the power of the story line he created.

The Horse and His Boy is the first Chronicle that features a strong heroine (Aravis) who is distinguished by her independence and strength. Similarly vibrant heroines also appear in the three remaining Chronicles written by Lewis (Polly in **The Magician's Nephew** and Jill in **The Silver Chair** and **The Last Battle**). Those who argue that Lewis was anti-**women** should read these books. It is possible that Lewis's increased facility in depicting women reflected the influence of Joy Davidman, the gifted poet and novelist who eventually became his wife. Davidman started writing Lewis just months before he began *The Horse and His Boy*, and he dedicated the book to her two sons, **David Gresham** and **Douglas Gresham**.

As far as the story's meaning is concerned, Lewis wrote that *The Horse and His Boy* is about "the calling and conversion of a heathen" (Letter to Anne, March 5, 1961). This heathen, Shasta, is an anticipation of Emeth, the good Calormene soldier in *The Last Battle*. At the feeling level, the book explores the spiritual tasks of young adults and the whys of self-discipline, especially under the classical **metaphor** of equestrianship, the management of the irascible and the concupisible (the two plots of *Prince Caspian* and an underlying theme of all the Chronicles) and the relationship between humankind and **nature**. The very title, humorous though it is, gives a clue that the relationship between the horses and the boy and girl needs realignment; the boy and her horse will learn courage; the girl and his horse will learn humility. All will learn the meaning of providence.

The story opens in Shasta's tightly circumscribed world as the "son" of a rude fisherman. Overhearing the negotiations for his sale to a Calormene warlord, Shasta is relieved to learn that he is a foundling whose people are northerners. The warlord's proud horse Bree reveals to the boy that he too is a northerner, and they conspire to escape home together, speaking of a freedom it will take them a long time to understand. Bree teaches Shasta the rudiments of riding but dispenses with instructions as to the reins and the whip, critical lacks that will hamper their journey. Bree and Shasta throw in their lots together with the haughty aristocratic girl Aravis and her mare, Hwin, also fleeing to the north, from a forced **marriage**, and the four plan a journey in disguise through Tashbaan, Calormen's capitol, a rendezvous at the tombs outside on the city's other side, and then a trek north across the desert. In Tashbaan, however, Shasta gets separated from the others and falls in with Narnians and Archenlanders, who mistake him for the missing Prince Corin. Shasta learns from them of a secret route north but also of the northerners' need to escape themselves to prevent an arranged marriage for Queen Susan. Corin returns in time to release Shasta to go to the tombs; his fear of what lies behind and in front of him is relieved by a "stray" cat. Aravis meets her friend Lasaraleen, and they send the horses on to the tombs. Together the young women overhear of the north's danger from an invasion led by the jilted crown prince, Rabadash. Aravis rejoins her companions for the hot ride across the desert and a desperate search for the narrow valley and the river that will take them into Archenland. Finding water, they rest too long, so they need to be pursued by a lion to go top speed. They take refuge with a hermit just as the lion claws Aravis's back, and Shasta stands up to the lion who bounds away. But instead of the refreshment he has earned, Shasta receives the commission to run to meet King Lune of Archenland with the warning about Rabadash's impending assault. Shasta catches up with the King who is temporarily distracted by the boy's resemblance to his son. After delivering his message, Shasta is given an ordinary horse to ride as all repair to the castle of Anvard. Knowing nothing of reins and whip, however, Shasta cannot get the horse to keep up. So he is left alone, exhausted, hungry, and in the foggy darkness when he is alarmed by deep breathing and heavy footfalls at his side.

Here occurs one of the most powerful passages of the book. Finding out that his unwelcome fellow traveler is not a giant or a ghost, Shasta recounts his story as asked. The voice objects to Shasta's calling himself unfortunate and reveals that he was the provident lion who not only accompanied every step of the boy's way from southern Calormen but guided the boat ashore in which the infant Shasta lay so that he could be raised by the fisherman. The lion refuses to explain why he clawed Aravis, explaining that he tells no one's story but his own. Asked who he really is, the lion reveals his Trinitarian identity in a threefold "myself," the first earth-shakingly deep and low, the second a glad, young adult's, and the third an all-encompassing, leaf-stirring whisper. Aslan the lion is then disclosed to Shasta in all his glory, and Shasta has a numinous experience redolent of Jane Studdock's at the corner of the gooseberry patch in *That Hideous Strength*. He falls adoringly at the feet of the lion who disappears "into a swirling glory."

Shasta meets friendly animals and dwarfs who minister to him until the arrival of the Narnian army on their way to help King Lune. With them is Corin whom everyone can see is Shasta's double. The boys conspire to get Shasta into the battle that takes place at Anvard. Rabadash's forces are routed and Rubadash himself is captured. King Lune subsequently introduces Shasta as his long-ago kidnapped son Cor. The scene switches to the hermitage where Bree, Hwin, Aravis, and the hermit have seen the battle in the mirror of the hermit's pool. Bree has been feeling so ashamed at running from the lion instead of fighting like Shasta that he hesitates to finish his journey into Narnia. Aslan himself bounds into their conversation, greets Hwin as a beloved friend, humbles Bree (along the lines of Jesus and Doubting Thomas), and explains to Aravis his chastening of her before leaving. The new Prince Cor then visits them and tells them his story. Leaving the hermit, all four attend the victory celebration and the judgment of Rabadash. So unrepentant is he that Aslan intervenes, turning him into a braying donkey, whose punishment will consist in

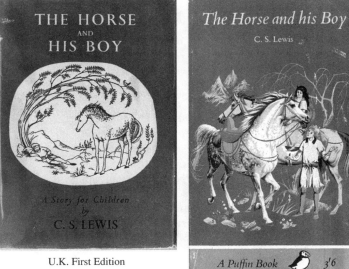

U.K. First Edition

A Puffin Book 3'6

returning thus to Tashbaan where he will be restored to human shape as long as he stays within ten miles of Tash's temple. The story ends with both the revelation that Cor is Lune's heir and also a glimpse into the future where Cor and Aravis marry each other and become good rulers.

Doris Myers observes that the issues of *The Horse and His Boy* and *The Silver Chair* are those of young adults: "In both, the protagonists learn about God's providence and the need for self-discipline" ("The Compleat Anglican"). *The Horse and His Boy*, in particular, "focuses ... on social maturity. The four protagonists all have to find out who they really are and how they fit into the structure of their world." Yes, and as Lewis completed *The Horse and His Boy*, he must have been deeply satisfied with his restoration of meaning— through his appeal to the **imagination**—of profound human and Christian truths.

Paul F. Ford
St. John's Seminary

Bibliography

Ford, Paul F. *Companion to Narnia*. San Francisco: HarperSanFrancisco, 1994.

Myers, Doris. "The Compleat Anglican: Spiritual Style in the Chronicles of Narnia." *Anglican Theological Review*. LXVI (April 1984): 148–60.

Schakel, Peter. *Reading with the Heart: The Way into Narnia*. Grand Rapids, MI: Eerdmans, 1979.

Yandell, Steven. "The Trans-cosmic Journeys in the Chronicles of Narnia." *Mythlore* 43 (August 1985): 9–23.

How Heathen is Britain? (Preface)

Sandhurst, B. G. *How Heathen is Britain?* London: Collins, 1946. Retitled "On the Transmission of Christianity" and reprinted in *God in the Dock, Undeceptions,* and *First and Second Things*.

How Heathen is Britain? by B. G. Sandhurst examined the attitudes of British youth toward **Christianity**. According to Lewis, Sandhurst's most hopeful finding was that the chief obstacle to the acceptance of Christianity among British youth was not hostility but ignorance. This meant that the younger generation could still be won for **Christ**. Lewis cautioned, however, that it was unrealistic to expect government-run schools in Britain to do the job. Lewis thought that a better method of evangelization would be to rely on voluntary efforts by committed Christians.

John G. West, Jr.

Human Nature

Lewis took a balanced view of human nature in several ways. On the one hand, he rejected the modern view that **sin** could be explained away with **psychology**, and he rejected any form of subjectivism by which individuals could become their own judge and excuse themselves by saying nonsense such as, "all things are relative." Though he thought that because of **the Fall** human nature "must be corrected and the evil within it must be mortified." On the other hand, Lewis believed that the essence of human nature (as created by **God**) was still good (**"Some Thoughts"**). Thus, following **George MacDonald**, he rejected the Puritan, Calvinistic view of depraved mankind incapable of any **good**. In *Letters to Malcolm: Chiefly on Prayer*, he quoted a Puritan author who describes the Puritan vision of **hell** as being one of "the Filth of a Dungeon, where I discerned Millions of crawling living things in the midst of that Sink and liquid Corruption" (Letter XVIII). Lewis wrote that he did not believe this vision to be "merely pathological," so acknowledging that sin was and is a horrific reality. But he objected to the Puritan view that one must keep one's darkest side constantly before the mind's eye: "Can [the puritan writer] be right? It sounds so very unlike the New Testament fruits of the Spirit—**love, joy,** peace. And very unlike the Pauline programme: 'forgetting those things which are behind and reaching forth unto those things that are before.' And very unlike St. Francis de Sales' green, dewy chapter on *la douceur* towards one's self. Anyway, what's the use of laying down a programme of permanent emotions? They can be permanent only by being factitious. What do you think? I know that a spiritual emetic at the right moment may be needed. But not a regular diet of emetics!"

Lewis also discussed human nature with the so-called "Law of Nature" in the opening of his book *Mere Christianity*. There he called the belief in an objective right and wrong that humans constantly appeal to, the "Law of Human Nature" and the "**Natural Law,**" and he associated human nature with **supernatural** and objective morality. Lewis disputed the Naturalistic notion that human consciousness was a mere product of accidental **evolution**, for then **reason** would be impossible, as the process of reasoning itself would be a mere accident and not capable of objective **truth**. (See the opening chapters of *Miracles* for a more detailed presentation of this argument.)

In sum, Lewis held that human nature was "amphibious"—God's mixing of spirit and flesh (*Screwtape*

Letters). We can see representations of Lewis's thought here in his lighter fiction. The strength of *The Screwtape Letters* is its inverted look at human nature as Lewis supposed it might look to the minions of **Satan**. In it, through the unsympathetic eyes of a senior tempter named Screwtape, we see human nature and all its frailty and yet its ability to grasp the little lifelines that God drops to us in the confusion of everyday life in the world. Of the examples provided for us in *The Screwtape Letters*, the most repeated theme is what Screwtape calls "the Law of Undulation." Through Screwtape, Lewis held that the very nature of human experience is to have emotional highs followed inevitably by emotional lows. The very essence of the Christian walk and sanctification is the process of clinging to faith in spite of this emotional undulation.

Lewis's other great fictional picture of human nature is *The Great Divorce*, where he punctured the all too frequent image of **Heaven** as being somehow unjustly exclusionary. Here we are treated to an unflattering picture of human nature as grasping after destructive emotions and false idols. With one exception, the ghosts that come for a day visit to the edges of Heaven are so wrapped up in some form of sinful self-absorption that they cannot and will not enter the joy of Heaven. The one exception, a ghost given to coddling his lusts, shows however once again that Lewis rejected the Puritan view. For the lustful ghost, upon giving up his lusts, turns into a brilliant, joyful being, and his crushed lusts turn into a magnificent horse that he rides to joyful union with God. This is the final picture Lewis has for us of what the glorified human nature can become, what God intends for us if we will but let him change us.

Lewis speculated that the **miracles** of **Christ**, such as walking on water and the ascent into Heaven, are previews and foretastes of what the glorified, post-resurrection human nature might be like. As our reason is, when at its best, not subject to **nature**, but having power over it, so Lewis speculated that our physical bodies too will be not subject to nature but have power over it. Thus the supernatural power implied by the Lord's walking on water, the dream of control over nature of which humankind dreamed of in inventions like the airplane, may turn out to have been true dreams after all. Yet in creating the image of the ghost in *The Great Divorce* who became a bright spirit when he surrendered totally to God, Lewis reminded us that the glorified human nature is a gift to those who have surrendered all.

James Prothero

"The Humanitarian Theory of Punishment"

20th Century: An Australian Quarterly Review. III no. 3 (1949): 5–12. Reprinted in *Res Judicate.* VI (June 1953): 224–30. Also reprinted in *God in the Dock, Undeceptions,* and *First and Second Things.*

In light of the controversy surrounding capital punishment, Lewis addressed the so-called humanitarian theory of punishment, which he regarded as a dangerous illusion. He suggested a return to retributive theory "not solely, not even primarily, in the interests of society, but in the interests of the criminal." According to Lewis, the humanitarian theory says that punishment because the criminal deserves it is revenge, and therefore, immoral. The only legitimate motives for punishment are as a deterrent and as a means to rehabilitate the criminal. According to the theory, punishment becomes therapeutic. This theory, argued Lewis, means that at the moment we break the law we are deprived of the rights of a human being because punishment is designed to be a deterrent not a form of **justice**.

Anne Gardner

Also See: The Fall, Human Nature, Psychology

Bibliography

Cole, G. A. "Justice: Retributive or Reformative?" *The Reformed Theological Review.* 45 no. 1 (January-April, 1986): 5–12.

Kirkpatrick, Hope. "Was Lewis Consistent on Punishment and Purgatory?" *CSL: The Bulletin of the New York C. S. Lewis Society.* 11 (December 1979): 9–10.

Richards, Jerald. "C. S. Lewis, Retributive Punishment, and the Worth of Persons." *Christian Scholar's Review.* 14 (1985): 347–59.

Wennberg, Robert. "Legal Punishment and Its Justification." *Christian Scholar's Review.* 3 (1973): 99–112.

David Hume (1711–1776)

The leading skeptical philosopher of the early modern period, Hume managed to formulate a system that was constructive and yet incorporated elements of skepticism that his predecessors (Descartes, Bayle, and Berkeley) had grappled with in their attempts to prove the existence of the external world.

His best-known works are *A Treatise of Human Nature, Essays, An Enquiry Concerning Human Understanding, An Enquiry Concerning the Principles of Morals,* and *The Natural History of Religion.* In Hume's view, **philosophy** "cannot go beyond experience; and any hypothesis, that pretends to discover the ultimate original qualities of **human nature**, ought at first to be rejected as presumptuous and chimerical."

Hume was regularly read at **Oxford**, and Lewis read him not only as a student but also as a **tutor** and found his views (and style) quite compatible with his own skepticism and **atheism** in the 1920s. But he was not satisfied, writing on June 18, 1922: "Read Hume's *Of Morals*. This contains nearly all my own fallacies in ethics—which look more fallacious in another person's language."

Hume attacked **miracles** and maintained that the popular view of them as violations of the law of **nature** is incoherent. Lewis argued against this view in his chapter on probability in *Miracles*. Hume's discussion of the **imagination** in *A Treatise of Human Nature* must have challenged Lewis for it both outlined the dangers of fantastically combining ideas and, at the same time, acknowledged its vital function in knowledge.

John Bremer

Also See: Ethics and Morality, Materialism

Aldous Huxley (1894–1963)

There are two primary connections between the lives of C. S. Lewis and Aldous Huxley. The first is that they were both writing **science fiction** in England in the 1930s. Lewis published *Out of the Silent Planet* during that decade; Huxley, of course, published *Brave New World*, a "dystopia," or a picture of the world gone wrong (a reverse utopia). Lewis briefly referred to Huxley's work twice in the essay **"On Stories."**

The more famous connection is that they both died, along with John F. Kennedy, on November 22, 1963. Philosophy professor Peter Kreeft wrote a rather ingenious book based on this coincidence, *Between Heaven and Hell*, in which he hypothesizes a conversation among the three authors while they are in a sort of holding area awaiting their final destination. Kreeft has Lewis represent the traditional Christian point of view, Huxley the Eastern Pantheistic, and Kennedy modern Western humanism. In effect, the conversation is a last opportunity for Kennedy and Huxley to understand and accept **Christianity**. Both the dialogue and the insightful ideas make interesting reading.

Marvin D. Hinten
Bowling Green State University

Bibliography

Kreeft, Peter. *Between Heaven and Hell*. Downers Grove, IL: InterVarsity Press, 1982.

I

"I Was Decided Upon"

Decision. II (December 1963): 3. Reprinted with "Heaven, Earth and Outer Space" as "Cross-Examination" in *God in the Dock, Undeceptions,* and *Christian Reunion.*

This essay is the text of an interview by Mr. Sherwood E. Wirt of the Billy Graham Association of Lewis at **Magdalene College**. Wirt's first questions dealt with the subject of Christian writing. Lewis said that **Christianity** must be learned as any craft but that writing is an impulse that must strongly move. The manner in which a writer addresses his topic is largely one of temperament, and so it is not profitable to speak of a correct way to write about sacred topics. Lewis mentioned **Chesterton**, Edwyn Bevan, Rudolf Otto, and **Dorothy Sayers** as Christian writers who have helped him. When questioned about *Surprised by Joy*, he said that "I would

say that the most deeply compelled action is also the freest action," and that is how he felt about his conversion. Lewis talked about his writing in general; noting that the only displeasure he felt about his writing occurred while writing *The Screwtape Letters*, which he found "fatiguing." He discussed briefly his thoughts about Billy Graham. Wirt then asked Lewis for his predictions for the next few years of history. Lewis replied that he had no way of knowing. Finally, he was asked if he thought "there will be wide-spread travel in space." He said that he anticipates this with horror, as we transport our **sin** beyond the boundaries of our planet. Lewis concluded that we should first "get right with **God**," so that we would be able to take good things with us.

Anne Gardner

Also See: Good and Evil, Space Travel

"The Idea of an 'English School'"

First published in *Rehabilitations*.

This essay is one of nine published in Lewis's 1939 volume, *Rehabilitations*, a collection whose title indicates its theme: the defense of poets and poems, genres and traditions—in short, ways of educating—that had in varying degrees been dismissed in Lewis's time. In this address, and in a companion essay, **"Our English Syllabus,"** Lewis defended the place of Anglo-Saxon and Middle English literature in **Oxford**'s curriculum.

Originally read to a joint meeting of the Classical and English Associations at Oxford, Lewis began by carefully distinguishing the curriculum of an "English school" from mere "philology," taken in its most negative sense as dry or irrelevant grammatical or lexical history. Oxford undergraduates are reading real texts, not merely studying word origins—texts that reveal the essential Englishness of works from *Beowulf* forward. One must not, Lewis argued, displace the reading of authentically English works like *Pearl* or authors like Chaucer with the texts of antiquity on the grounds that in knowing their influences, one somehow knows them. There is a unique canon of works that deserve to be studied by contemporary undergraduates.

In his conclusion, Lewis proposed not that the Greek and Roman classics be ignored, but that they be learned either before or after. In essence, Lewis's essay presented the case for pursuing what he and colleagues like **J. R. R. Tolkien** most loved and best taught: the genres, texts, authors, idioms, and vocabulary of premodern English literature.

Bruce L. Edwards
Bowling Green State University

Bibliography

Como, James T. (ed). *C. S. Lewis at the Breakfast Table*. New York: Macmillan, 1992.
Myers, Doris T. *C. S. Lewis in Context*. Kent, OH: Kent State University Press, 1994.

Imagery

C. S. Lewis was such an effective writer in part because he was a powerful and memorable image-creator. Who can forget the red lizard of lust that is transformed into the magnificent stallion (desire transfigured) in chapter 11 of *The Great Divorce*. And even in his nonfiction he was able to come up with the image that will illustrate and fix in the mind a particular concept.

Lewis never spoke down to his readers. He treated them as mature, intelligent human beings, capable of thinking for themselves and reaching proper conclusions. ***Out of the Silent Planet*** and ***Perelandra*** are filled with memorable images as Lewis described the setting and the characters. The colors are always beautiful and unusual. The Green Lady, Tinidril, in *Perelandra* is an appealing and interesting character. She is unfallen, living on an unfallen planet, and when she learns something she says that she is made older. She has no concept of sin and when Weston, who becomes the Un-Man, tries to persuade her to stay overnight on the Fixed Land (something that is forbidden by Maleldil), she resists with Ransom's help.

And who can forget the strange bus that transports the inhabitants of the Grey Town (**hell**) to the outskirts of **heaven** in *The Great Divorce*. Each character is given some trait (unusual height, tousled hair, a winning manner) that sets him or her apart.

In ***That Hideous Strength***, the several biblical parallels function as imagery, adding color to the narrative. There is a parallel to Pentecost in the descent of the gods on St. Anne's (especially on Merlin and Ransom), and there is ecstatic speaking (glossolalia). There is an event similar to the confusion of language at the Tower of Babel found in Genesis in the confused speech at the N.I.C.E. banquet. There is an echo at the last battle of Armegeddon in the attack on the N.I.C.E. by the animals they have been experimenting on. There is a parallel to **Christ**'s ascension to Heaven in Ransom's ascension to Perelandra at the end of *That Hideous Strength*. He goes to Perelandra to be healed of his till-then incurable wound in the heel.

Corbin Scott Carnell
University of Florida

Also See: Allegory, Analogy, Beauty, Fantasy, Myth, Symbolism

"Imagery in the Last Eleven Cantos of Dante's *Comedy*"

First published posthumously in *Studies in Medieval and Renaissance Literature*.

Lewis noted that this essay, originally a speech to the Oxford **Dante** Society, is in some ways a more focused extension of his previous speech given eight years earlier to the society, **"Dante's Similes."** Since this article is so specifically focused, it requires more of the reader than the one on similes; here, considerable familiarity with *Paradiso* is taken for granted.

Lewis noted the influence of Caroline Spurgeon, Shakespearean imagery scholar, on his thinking, and classified Dante's imagery according to the subject matter from which the figures of speech are drawn; from least to most frequent, they are images relating to smell, the sea, student life, landscapes, psychology, childhood, history, *eros*, weight, astronomy, the military, clothing, enclosure, travel, physiology, emission, eating and drinking, zoology, meteorology, social life, heat and light, agriculture, and technology. As anyone who has done this sort of analysis knows, images can make nearly any point the speaker wants, depending on how the classification is skewed, but in this case Lewis seemed less interested in statistical analysis than in simply using the types as a springboard for talking about Dante's mind.

Marvin D. Hinten
Bowling Green State University

Also See: Imagery

Bibliography

Cobb, Lawrence. "The Beginning of the Real Story: Images of Heaven in C. S. Lewis and Dante." *CSL: The Bulletin of the New York C. S. Lewis Society* 7 (December 1975): 1–5.

Daigle, Marsha Ann. "Dante's *Divine Comedy* and C. S. Lewis's Narnia Chronicles." *Christianity and Literature.* 34 no. 4 (Summer 1985): 41–58.

Lewis, C. S. *The Discarded Image.*

Imagination

It could be urged that the theme of imagination constitutes the taproot of Lewis's entire work (excepting the Christian **faith** itself). There is scarcely a line in any work of his—theological treatise, **literary criticism**, topical essay, fiction, or **poetry**—that does not bespeak some vast assumptions on Lewis's part as to the inevitable and crucial place that imagination must be given among us mortals in all of our discourse.

Lewis was a sacramentalist. Hence the notion that **Reality** tends toward the concrete seemed axiomatic to him. From its superficial place in ordinary **metaphors** ("He's making heavy weather of things," or "A bird in the hand is worth two in the bush"), which evinces our human inclination to reach for the concrete to assist us with the abstract—from that level in the presence of all of more weighty assumptions we must make in the presence of all art (let us agree that John Geilgud is Hamlet; let us grant that these smears of grease and pigment on this square of canvas *are* "**Aristotle** Contemplating the Bust of Homer"; let us hear the profoundest depths of penitentiality in the Allegri *Miserere*, or of the Divine Love in Tomas Luis Victoria's "reproaches" for Good Friday)—it is entirely clear that we are a species whose

attempts to approach and grip Reality are very far from being exhausted by logical, the discursive, or the propositional.

In this sense, Lewis, for all of his rigorous and remorselessly logical manner of pursuing an argument, was at bottom a "catholic." That is, he was always primarily aware that the Ineffable has made itself known to us, not merely in a book (although God has done that, but it is a book full of narrative, and not of syllogisms), but rather that from the beginning Reality—this Ineffable, which is to say **God**—has disclosed himself in a Garden (or at least the language of "garden"), and in the bloody pelts of animals slain to cover our nakedness, and in stone altars and burned fat and incense and a golden throne overshadowed with golden cherubim. But, far, more sharply and finally, his self-disclosure took the form of a conceiving, a pregnancy, a birth, a life, a violently physical oblation of a male body, and then Resurrection and Ascension, when our mortal flesh, in the person of the Incarnate God was raised and enthroned in the midst of the Holy and Undivided **Trinity**.

All of this, of course, is by way of pointing out that we are creatures such that our grasp of **truth** is scarcely a merely propositional matter. We call for an image. We want a picture, a **symbol**, a **metaphor**, a sacrament, and ultimately an Incarnation. Sheer proposition will not do the trick. The **angels** may regard Reality directly: for us mortals it must be mediated by the concrete.

Hence imagination, which is the image-making faculty in us. The most gaunt mathematicians and philosophers know that they do not proceed one inch without the assistance of metaphor, which is a form of image in which A (three apples) is put to work to help us come to terms with B (the "number" three).

For Lewis, orthodox Christian that he was, all of this is rooted in Reality itself. It is not mere gimmickry, or infantile show-and-tell. The sacraments are the great sign and pledge of this, for here we find water (on Lewis's "catholic" view—not shared by all Christians) not only "standing for" our cleansing from Original Sin, but actually pressed into service by the Holy Ghost to wash away that **sin**. And we find bread and wine (again, Lewis was catholic) raised far above a mere symbol to jog our memory of an ancient event: it actually bears and vouchsafes that of which it speaks, namely the Savior in his saving work. It is our imagination—our image-making faculty—which is addressed here, as well as our **faith**. Or put it this way: that which faith grasps is characteristically mediated to us via solid images, most notably the Incarnation.

It is, of course, in Lewis's fiction that we see the matter of imagination at work most sumptuously. Those familiar with his tales can conjure a thousand instances. The White Witch with her petrifying wand; the Stone Table that cracks at the moment of Aslan's "resurrection," Eustace Clarence Scrubb metamorphosed into a dragon (the stark truth, veiled from us here in our own dim world but disclosed in the pellucid air of Narnia, is that he *is* a dragon: what do dragons do but sit brooding on piles of gold? What is Edmund but a wholly selfish little boy?).

Lewis is justly praised for the fruitfulness of his own imagination, which presumably was a talent native to his own make-up, but which was nourished by his whole understanding of things, namely that Reality itself tends toward solidity. The obverse of this is that **hell** is a vacuity; or that the natural tendency of evil is always, always, to leech away the good solidity that marks all that God creates, and to leave only the detritus behind. We see this most horrifyingly in the figure of Wither in *That Hideous Strength*. Wither, the academic who has never in his life used language for any purpose other than to dilute, or be-fog, the truth, has himself become a wraith. His own choice of tergiversation rather than language-in-the-service-of-truth has leeched away all that was human in him. The Wither that existed in God's mind (the final locale of all true substantiality) is no more. With his dreamy, unfocused eyes, his loose mouth, his humming, his interminably frayed syntax, and the difficulty of our saying just where he *is* at any given moment: here Lewis unfurled a picture of the damned soul more vivid than anything we might encounter in propositions about damnation.

On the other hand, Lewis is capable of regaling us with images of glory that we commonly suppose to be abstractions. In the two figures of Malacandra and Perelandra who appear at the end of *Perelandra*, we have perhaps the most remorselessly convincing images in all of literature of precisely what Masculinity and Femininity are. Forty years before gender became a war zone, Lewis offered images that tower above whole shelves of books that labor away at the topic from political, sociological, or sexual angles.

Or again, in the Descent of the Gods on St. Anne's in *That Hideous Strength*, Lewis hailed us with the mystery of language in the arrival of Mercury, and of kingship in the arrival of Glund, and of **love** in both its erotic and its hearthside aspects in the arrival of Venus.

The theological, or we might even say ontological, backdrop to all of this for Lewis lay in the biblical assumption that Word tends toward substance. Both the Genesis 1 account of Creation, and Saint John's great panegyric to the Word in the preface to his Gospel, link Word and Creation (solidity; substance; image) indissolubly. Lewis's fiction as well as his **theology**, depends almost wholly on assumptions to be drawn from that linkage.

Corbin Scott Carnell
University of Florida

Also See: Allegory, Analogy, Imagery

Bibliography

Kilby, Clyde S. "Into the Land of the Imagination." *Christianity Century* 4 no. 3 (1985): 16–18.
Schakel, Peter J. *Reason and Imagination—C. S. Lewis A Study of Till We Have Faces*. Grand Rapids, MI: Eerdmans, 1984.
_____. *Reading with the Heart: The Way into Narnia*. Grand Rapids, MI: Eerdmans, 1979.

"Imagination and Thought in the Middle Ages"

First published posthumously in *Studies in Medieval and Renaissance Literature*.

This essay was originally delivered as two lectures to a group of Cambridge Zoologists in July, 1956. It captures in very condensed form the views Lewis articulated more fully in his lecture series, "Prolegomena to Medieval Literature" and "Prolegomena to **Renaissance** Literature," which were later collected in book form as *The Discarded Image* (1961).

As a professional literary historian, Lewis was thoroughly familiar with and delighted in the **Medieval world**, that is, how men and women of the Middle Ages understood what they saw in the night sky and how they incorporated this understanding into their **theology** and their daily existence. This Medieval worldview informed everything Lewis said about Medieval literature, and it greatly affected his own fictional landscapes, particularly the **space trilogy.**

In this essay, Lewis intended to provide his audience a "map" for encountering Medieval **cosmology** for the first time. According to the Medieval mind, the earth was the center of the universe and the stars, planets, and constellations were arrayed in a radically significant hierarchy of being and beings—a Ptolemaic universe whose regions bespoke order, relationship, harmony, and coherence, however mysterious and vast it was. Lewis's breathtakingly lucid explanation of this "great chain of being" demonstrated his unmatched prowess as both a prose stylist and a chronicler of ancient wisdom and practice.

Lewis was concerned here not only to illuminate Medieval cosmology but also to defend medievals from the charge that they were "ignorant savages"; they were, he suggested, despite their illiteracy, a peculiarly "bookish" people, i.e., what they believed stemmed from their acquaintance with a learned tradition, not mere legend or superstition. Medievals were above all organizers, codifiers, syncretists—in short, they were earnest systematizers who discerned and preferred **hierarchy** and order over against radical individualism and chaos, thus echoing Lewis's own predilections.

Bruce L. Edwards
Bowling Green State University

Bibliography

Brewer, Derek. "The Tutor: A Portrait." *C. S. Lewis at the Breakfast Table*. James T. Como (ed). New York: Macmillan, 1994.

Downing, David. *Planets in Peril*. Amherst, MA: University of Massachusetts Press, 1992.

Immorality

Lewis viewed immorality as neither daring nor "naughty fun," but simply as a failure to live well and practice one's full humanity. He never uses the term to mean just sexual immorality, but rather the failure to practice any part of the moral law. As Lewis firmly believed in **natural law**, he assumed that all people innately sensed basic right and wrong, and therefore immorality and morality are both possible for every human being. Yet, though he saw immorality as nothing "zestful" or "lively," as is the common misperception, neither did he see morality as an end in itself. In *The Problem of Pain* he warned that "morality unconnected with a Law-giver yields 'the cold, sad self-righteousness of sheer moralism.'" Morality was no end, but a means; **Love** himself (God in Christ) is the goal. The true practice of love fulfills all the law.

Put another way, immorality is the failure to love, and the failure to be fully human. Lewis saw morality as concerned with three things: "Firstly, with fair play and harmony between individuals. Secondly, with what might be called tidying up or harmonising the things inside each individual. Thirdly, with the general purpose of human life as a whole" (*Mere Christianity*). Lewis recognized that most persons would agree to the first principle of morality, of doing no harm to one's neighbor. The second principle, conversion of one's inner nature, would meet more resistance, and the third principle, of the need to act according to divine plan, would meet even more fierce resistance. But he believed all three were necessary, interlocked, and indispensable. To do away with the third principle would eventually undercut even the first principle to which most men agree.

Thus, immorality is the three principles in reverse: the disregard of one's fellow man; the disregard of one's own need to become Christlike and therefore, fully human; and the disregard of following the divine plan for one's life and acts, thus perverting one's gifts. As Lewis pointed out in *Mere Christianity*, the technical name for existing in this sort of state for eternity would be **Hell**.

James Prothero

Also See: Ethics and Morality, Good and Evil, Sin, Values

Immortality

Both his **reason** and his experience of "**joy**," a stab of desire for something unsatisfied on earth, demanded Lewis's belief in the immortality of persons, a belief fundamental to his thinking about **religion**, **politics**, **ethics**, and persons.

Nations and civilizations, even the physical creation, are temporary. The days of life on earth are numbered by the fuel supply of the sun; and long before that moth and rust, and the waxing and waning of civilizations and governments places limits on the work of mortal hands. But when the sun is cold, when the parade of civilizations ends, the person lives on in eternity. As Lewis said many times, it would make little difference how we lived our lives on earth if that were the end of it. But it makes a very great deal of difference if we live forever and if the implications of mortal life reach into eternity.

In religion and worldview, the fundamental arena of concern, the fact of our immortality is paramount. Jesus **Christ** taught on one hand the certainty of judgment for **sin** in this life and on the other the availability of **mercy** through Jesus' death for those sins. Lewis's teaching of "mere **Christianity**" was essentially this: a holy **God** demands **justice**; a merciful God offers salvation. This salvation comes by belief in the atoning death and resurrection of Jesus and acceptance of the **supernatural** gift of salvation or new birth. This, Lewis taught, was the means of attaining immortality in **heaven**. The failure to accept this mean guarantees one an immortality in **hell**.

The political implications of this are that individuals are more important than nations because nations come and go; and **democracy** is a more desirable form of government than socialism because it values that which endures:

the person. In ethics, Lewis saw that our behavior toward others is crucial, since we are each moment helping each other toward an immortal glory or immortal horror. Lewis's view of persons is likewise affected by his belief in immortality. Persons, though physically dwarfed by the cosmos, are supremely more important than stars and galaxies, whose days are numbered: and not merely because of their immortality, but because persons bear the image of God (however we have marred it by sin). Our relationships are, therefore, not of passing importance, but of eternal consequence. It is with immortals that we laugh and cry, play and work (**"The Weight of Glory"**).

Except for his belief in the Jesus of the **Bible** and his relationship to him, Lewis's belief in the immortality of persons explained more than anything else the direction of his life and writing from his conversion to Christianity at age thirty-two to his death at almost sixty-five. This is why Lewis the author of ten titles of **literary criticism** could say that the salvation of a single soul is more important than all of the books of literary criticism in the world; why he wrote books for the common person and the spiritual seeker in the teeth of intense contrary pressure from the academic community of **Oxford**; why this "stay at home man" logged hundreds of miles to speak evangelistically; why the man whose perfect day included no visit from the postman, carrying letters that needed answers, spent one to two hours a day in what he felt, under God, to be his duty to those who sought his counsel.

Though a constant in Lewis's work, the single best statement of Lewis's view of immortality comes in the closing paragraphs of his greatest sermon, "The Weight of Glory." For a fuller treatment of these issues, also see *Surprised by Joy*, *Mere Christianity*, *The Problem of Pain* (especially the chapters on heaven and hell), and *The Great Divorce* (a fictional journey from hell to heaven).

Wayne Martindale
Wheaton College

"Impenitence"

Punch. 225 (July 15, 1953): 91 (under the pseudonym Nat Whilk). Reprinted in *Poems* and *Collected Poems*.

This poem is a lighthearted defiance of those who are too sophisticated to find in the animal stories of literature (including clear reference to Homer, **E. Nesbit**, and **Kenneth Grahame**) both delightful entertainment and fables of human foibles (see **"On Three Ways of Writing for Children"**).

Don W. King
Montreat College

"Importance of an Ideal"

See entry on "Notes on the Way" (17 August 1940)

The Incarnation of the Word of God: Being the Treatise of St. Athanasius' "De Incarnatione Verbi Dei" (Introduction)

Athanasius. *The Incarnation of the Word of God: Being the Treatise of St. Athanasius' "De Incarnatione Verbi Dei."* London: Geoffrey Bles, 1944. Retitled "On the Reading of Old Books" and reprinted in *God in the Dock*, *Undeceptions*, and *First and Second Things*.

Saint Athanasius was the Greek patriarch of Alexandria who lived from 293–373. In this preface to a translation of Saint Athanasius by his friend **Sister Penelope**, C. S. Lewis advocated the reading of old books in order to gain a deeper perspective on the central truths of **Christianity**. Every age is blind to certain insights and questions, wrote Lewis, and reading old books will help us recognize the particular blindnesses of our own age.

John G. West, Jr.

Inklings

From the mid1930s through the end of the 1940s, a group of writers met in Lewis's rooms at **Magdalen College** each Thursday evening to read and discuss their writings. They described themselves as "practising poets," but they called themselves the Inklings, a name **J. R. R. Tolkien** described as "a pleasantly ingenious pun in its way, suggesting people with vague or half-formed intimations and ideas plus those who dabble in ink."

About a dozen men participated, including Lewis, Tolkien, **Hugo Dyson**, **Lord David Cecil**, **Nevill Coghill**, Commander Jim Dundas-Grant, **Adam Fox**, **Colin Hardie**, R. B. McCallum, C. E. "Tom" Stevens, **Charles Wrenn**, **R. E. Havard**, **Gervase Mathews**, **J. A. W. Bennett**, and **John Wain**. Lewis's brother **Warren Lewis** attended nearly all of the meetings, and his accounts are among the most useful sources of information about the group.

With the start of World War II, **Charles Williams** was transferred from London to safer quarters in Oxford, and he became an important member. **Owen Barfield**, a writer and solicitor who lived in London, was not able to attend meetings frequently, but was considered a full-fledged member due to his important work on **language**, **myth**, and perception, and his long and influential **friendship** with C. S. Lewis. In later years, Tolkien's son Christopher also attended.

Some of the Inklings gathered regularly on Tuesday mornings for beer and conversation at the **Eagle and**

Child Pub, but, according to Warren Lewis, the Thursday meetings were more focused and structured: "When half a dozen or so had arrived, tea would be produced, and then when pipes were well alight Jack would say, 'Well, has nobody got anything to read us?' Out would come a manuscript, and we would settle down to sit in judgment upon it." Lewis read *Perelandra*, *That Hideous Strength*, *The Great Divorce*, *The Problem of Pain*, *Miracles*, and other works to the group, chapter by chapter as they were written. He also read *The Screwtape Letters*, and, according to Havard, "they were greeted hilariously." Tolkien generally read a chapter from *The Lord of the Rings*, referred to at the time as "The New Hobbit." Charles Williams read each chapter from *All Hallows' Eve*, as well as his Taliessin poems and an occasional play. Nevill Coghill might have some light verse, Adam Fox read his poetry, and R. E. "Humphrey" Havard shared a few articles related to his medical practice.

During the years that they met, Warren Lewis began to write and publish historical studies concerned with the court of Louis XIV, most notably *The Splendid Century*. Warren Lewis's work is highly praised in letters of the time; apparently he provided some of the best and most thought-provoking material that was read aloud to the Inklings. Tolkien, for example, reported of one meeting, "The best entertainment proved to be the chapter of Major [Warren] Lewis' projected book—on a subject that does not interest me: the court of Louis XIV; but it was most wittily written (as well as learned)."

The Inklings also worked on a number of books together. One is Lewis's *The Problem of Pain*, which contains an appendix written by R. Havard, M.D. Another is *Arthurian Torso*. This edition of Williams' essays and Lewis's commentary was first published by Oxford University Press in 1948; Lewis and Williams are listed as co-authors. The largest work entered into jointly by the Inklings is *Essays Presented to Charles Williams*. The book contains six essays, five by Inklings J. R. R. Tolkien, C. S. Lewis, Owen Barfield, Gervase Mathews, and Warren Lewis, and a sixth by **Dorothy Sayers**.

When the Inklings met together, reading of the manuscripts was followed by extensive discussion. R. E. Havard remembers, "Criticism was frank but friendly. Coming from a highly literate audience, it was often profuse and detailed." According to Warren Lewis, "We were no mutual admiration society: praise for good work was unstinted, but censure for bad work—or even not-so-good work—was often brutally frank. To read to the Inklings was a formidable ordeal."

Criticism may have been frank, but clearly it was also fruitful. The Inklings came to rely on this feedback as they revised their work and planned new projects. It is also clear that the group provided one another with a great deal of support and encouragement. In September of 1954, Tolkien emphasized the part Lewis played in seeing *The Lord of the Rings* to completion: "Only by his support and friendship did I ever struggle to the end of the labor." In a similar spirit, Lewis wrote of the Inklings, "What I owe to them all is incalculable." So great was their gratitude that Lewis dedicated *The Problem of Pain* to the Inklings; Williams dedicated *The Forgiveness of Sins* to the Inklings; Tolkien dedicated the first edition of *The Lord of the Rings* to the Inklings. Throughout the acknowledgment pages of their books, the Inklings honor and thank the group and emphasize the importance of its members. Even John Wain, who was known to be somewhat cynical about the nature and purpose of the group, said of the meetings, "The best of them were as good as anything I shall live to see."

Diana Pavlac Glyer
Azusa Pacific University

Bibliography

Carpenter, Humphrey. *The Inklings*. Boston: Houghton Mifflin, 1978.

Christopher, Joseph R. "Who Were the Inklings?" *Tolkien Journal*. 15 (Summer 1972): 5, 7–10, 12–13.

GoodKnight, Glen. "The Social History of the Inklings, J. R. R. Tolkien, C. S. Lewis, Charles Williams, 1939–1945." *Mythlore*. 2 (Winter 1970): 7–9.

Hillegas, Mark (ed). *Shadows of Imagination: The Fantasies of C. S. Lewis, J. R. R. Tolkien, and Charles Williams*. Carbondale, IL: Southern Illinois University Press, 1969.

Kilby, Clyde S. "Tolkien, Lewis, and Williams." *Mythcon I Proceedings*. Glen GoodKnight (ed). Los Angeles: The Mythopoeic Society, 1971: 3–4.

Knight, Gareth. *The Magical World of the Inklings*. Longmead, UK: Element Books, 1990.

Moorman, Charles. *The Precincts of Felicity: The Augustinian City of the Oxford Christians*. Gainsville, FL: University of Florida Press, 1966.

Reilly, R. J. *Romantic Religion: A Study of Barfield, Lewis, Williams and Tolkien*. Athens, GA: University of Georgia Press, 1971.

Tolkien, J. R. R. *Sauron Defeated*. Christopher Tolkien (ed). London: HarperCollins, 1992.

"The Inner Ring"

First published in *Transposition* and *The Weight of Glory*. Reprinted in *Screwtape Proposes a Toast*.

This is one of Lewis's most powerful essays; it was originally delivered as a "Commemoration Oration" at

King's College, University of London, on December 14, 1944. The title phrase describes the existence of unspoken cliques among any organization or group of people. There are two different hierarchies in any organization, observed Lewis. One is on paper and consists of the formal relationships of who reports to whom; the other consists of informal groupings where the real power may lie. Lewis said that while the existence of inner rings is inevitable, the desire to get inside them is dangerous. The unceasing ambition to join the "in" group can lead to the mistreatment of others; and once inside an inner ring, the insular mentality of the clique is a breeding ground for **pride** and the breaking of the ordinary rules of morality. A fictional exposition of the ideas in this essay can be found in Lewis's novel *That Hideous Strength*. There Mark Studdock desperately seeks to get into inner ring after inner ring, only to find emptiness and horror at the heart of the innermost ring.

Not all informal groups of individuals are inner rings according to Lewis. Those groups that form between people who share common loves, talents, or **virtues** are based on **friendship** rather than a craving for power over others.

John G. West, Jr.

Also See: Ethics and Morality, Rudyard Kipling

Inspiration

C. S. Lewis had a broad and what might be called "general" view of biblical inspiration. In *Reflections on the Psalms* he wrote of the "Divine pressure" that **God** placed over all phases and persons connected with the writing of the **Bible**, including the Christians who preserved and canonized the writings, and the redactors and editors who had modified them. In a letter to Professor Clyde S. Kilby, Lewis maintained that Bible reading also requires inspiration. For Lewis, not all of Scripture was inspired in the same way or for the same purpose, nor did he believe that every sentence of the Bible contained scientific or historical **truth**. In *Reflections on the Psalms* he wrote that "the total result is not 'the Word of God' in the sense that every passage, in itself, gives impeccable **science** or history." He was aware of the various literary genres and of the seeming errors, contradictions, and non-Christian ideas contained in Scripture, although these in his eyes did not contradict God's plan of salvation through Jesus **Christ**. He understood the story of Adam and **Eve** mythically, and he questioned whether the books of Job, Jonah, and Ruth were historical. Lewis was much troubled by the "curs-

ing" **Psalms**, and he wrote that he struggled to hear God's word through the pessimism of Ecclesiastes.

Nevertheless, Lewis believed that the Bible was reliable, inspired ("God-breathed"), and holy; and using Paul's language from his Roman letter, he thought the Bible contained the "oracles of God." The different literary genres such as **allegory**, parable, romance, lyric **poetry**, etc., were in his view just as inspired as the chronicles or historical stories—the writers of these were guided, either knowingly or unknowingly, by God, but they were not free from human error. This led Lewis to state that Scripture "carries" the word of God along with human impurities and imperfections. He also believed that the inconsistencies of some biblical passages, particularly the gospel genealogies and the two different accounts of Judas' death (Matthew 27 and Acts 1), ruled out the view that every statement in the Bible must be "historical" truth. Along with this, Lewis saw Bible books such as Jonah and Esther as "moral romances," stories that entertained with ethical overtones. But in **"Modern Theology and Biblical Criticism,"** Lewis defended the basic historicity of the Gospels and attacked modern theologians who treat the Gospel narratives as **myth**. He accused modern theologians of letting their conclusions be dictated by their naturalistic assumptions rather than textual evidence.

Lewis's position on inspiration traveled a middle road between extreme theological liberalism, which often denied the miraculous, and fundamentalism, which stressed total inerrancy and a lack of factual, scientific, and historical errors in the Bible. Perhaps his unique contribution to the "inspiration debates" of today is to help his readers view the Bible as human literature that is divinely inspired—a human vehicle carrying a holy cargo. His writings also remind the modern reader that the divine message of God is not confined to the medium of Scripture alone. According to Lewis, God has used many means of reconciling the world to himself, including the great myths and literature of history, human consciousness and religious experience, and primarily Jesus Christ, who came to the human race as the "sacred fish" demanding loving faith of the whole person.

Perry C. Bramlett
C. S. Lewis for the Local Church

Also See: Christianity, Ethics and Morality, Religion, Revelation

Bibliography

Bramlett, Perry C. *C. S. Lewis: Life at the Center*. Macon, GA: Smyth & Helwys, 1996.

Christensen, Michael J. *C. S. Lewis on Scripture*. Waco, TX: Word, 1979.

Cunningham, Richard B. *C. S. Lewis: Defender of the Faith*. Philadelphia: Westminster, 1967.

Friesen, Garry L. "Scripture in the Writings of C. S. Lewis." *Evangelical Journal*. 1 no. 1 (1980): 17–27.

Lewis, C. S. "Fern-Seeds and Elephants"; *Reflections on the Psalms*.

Williams, Terri. "CSL, Scripture, and Inerrancy." *The Chronicle of the Portland C. S. Lewis Society*. 7 no. 1 (January-March 1978): 3–12.

Inspirational Writings of C. S. Lewis

New York: Inspirational Press, 1994.

A collection of Lewis writings.

"Interim Report"

The Cambridge Review. (21 April 1956): 468–71. Reprinted in *Present Concerns*.

Written in 1956, this article compared the two ancient universities of **Oxford** and **Cambridge**. Lewis had been **tutor** and university lecturer at Oxford for nineteen years, and had been Professor of Medieval and Renaissance English Literature, which entailed only lecturing, at Cambridge for two years. The difference in status and duties affected his perceptions. Cambridge was still a country town, while Oxford was industrialized; Oxford had the Philosopher, while Cambridge had the Literary Critic; there seemed to be more Christian dons and undergraduates at Cambridge, but the unbeliever at Oxford was less militant, less organized—he was more of a relaxed skeptic. The two universities—Oxbridge—shared "the fine flower of humane studies." Male Cambridge dons were more likely to meet their female counterparts than Oxford dons. There were two similarities—neither desirable. First, both universities had a share of real malcontents—they were rude on principle "in the cause of 'integrity' or some other equally detestable virtue." This suggests that the method of intake was wrong, and, in the future, they could do great harm. The second evil was "the incubus of 'Research'"—in which the different needs of the humanities and the sciences were not recognized.

John Bremer

Also See: Magdalen College

Invocation (Letter)

Church Times. CXXXII (15 July 1949): 463–64. Reprinted in *God in the Dock, Undeceptions,* and *Timeless at Heart*.

Edward Every continued the discussion (see **Church's Liturgy [Letter]**) in his letter, "Doctrine and Liturgy," (*Church Times*, 8 July 1949, 445–46) by asking if Lewis had not blunted a useful distinction between *devotion to* and *invocation of* the saints, and that reinstituting a past liturgical expression in this regard did not have to imply the reformers erred when originally removing it. Lewis agreed that such a distinction is appropriate and even finer than he first believed. However, he went on to say that this simply reinforces his point that great care must be exercised in any liturgical changes since the implications for meaning can be great as well. He reasserted that the laypeople within the **church** simply want to believe as the church believes, and they need assurance that changes in the liturgy are made under the teaching and authority of the church.

Marjorie L. Mead
The Marion E. Wade Center

Invocation of Saints (Letter)

Church Times. CXXXII (5 August 1949): 513. Reprinted in *God in the Dock, Undeceptions,* and *Timeless at Heart*.

Edward Every (*Church Times*, 22 July 1949, 481–82) issued a final challenge in this ongoing discussion (see previous letter) believing that Lewis's definition of "devotion," as regards the saints, was too restrictive. Lewis replied that he agreed with Mr. Every that he wished the controversy within the Anglican Church over devotion to the saints would cease. However, he was concerned lest this controversy be settled simply by changing "custom" (e.g., revisions to the liturgy) rather than by the **church** actively and authoritatively deciding such matters. Such unconscious and gradual erosion of the orthodox doctrines of the church was Lewis's central concern, not the specific issue of devotion to the saints.

Marjorie L. Mead
The Marion E. Wade Center

Also See: Anglicanism

"Is Christianity Hard or Easy"

The Listener. XXXI (30 March 1944): 356. Reprinted in *Beyond Personality* and *Mere Christianity*.

This is the title of the sixth essay in the series "Beyond Personality," originally published in the BBC's magazine *The Listener*. The essay is taken from the radio broadcast of the same title delivered on March 28, 1944. In **"Let Us Pretend"** Lewis discussed the idea of imitating **Christ**. In this essay, Lewis pointed out that this is what **Christianity** is all about. He said that our ordinary ideas of morality assume that the Christian life is something *added onto* our ordinary life. Then morality adds on to this version claims which *interfere* with our ordinary life, making us do things that we do not want to do but that morality demands.

Christianity, on the other hand, asks for a total commitment: it asks for our whole natural self to be handed over to **God** and reformed by God. Once we decide to do this and try our best to do it, then God will help us and reform us into God's own image. Once this decision is made then we are not merely trying to add Christianity onto our ordinary lives, we are living in Christ and with Christ. And this is what Christianity is all about.

Richard Purtill
Western Washington University

Also See: Ethics and Morality

"Is English Doomed?"

The Spectator. CLXXII (11 February 1944): 121. Reprinted in *Present Concerns.*

This essay was Lewis's response to a government report "Curriculum and Examinations in Secondary Schools" (known as the Norwood report after its chairman Sir Cyril Norwood), which recommended that any teacher can teach "English" and that "premature external examination" is undesirable, with the consequence that universities should devise "a general honours degree involving English and . . . some other subject."

Lewis saw these proposals as the death knell of the study of English at the universities and the demise of English as an academic discipline—for without examinations, there would be no scholarships and no funding. Without a demand for teachers trained specifically in English, there would be no professional career for English graduates. Nevertheless, Lewis thought that if the proposals killed English, they would do so inadvertently. The authors of the Norwood report believed that English would be safeguarded because teachers could instruct their pupils in good grammar in the course of teaching their own subjects. But this view missed the point, according to Lewis. The true reason for teaching English is neither good grammar nor simply literary "appreciation." Rather "the true aim of literary studies is to lift the student out of his provincialism by making him 'the spectator,' if not of all, yet of much, 'time and existence.'"

This essay can only be fully understood in the context of English educational practice, politics, and governmental policy-making in the 1940s and before.

Lewis's concerns about the Norwood report were understandable because such government reports overtly affected government policy in England.

John Bremer

Also See: Education

Bibliography

Lewis, C. S. *The Abolition of Man*; "The Parthenon and the Optative"

"Is History Bunk?"

The Cambridge Review. LXXVIII (1 June 1957): 647, 649. Reprinted in *Present Concerns.*

This article was a response to a review by H. A. Mason of *The Poetical Works of Charles Churchill*, edited by Douglas Grant. In that review Mason said that the history of literature "is the study of what is valuable; study of minor figures is only justified if it contributes to the understanding of what is meant by *major*." According to Lewis, this can only be agreed to if the discipline of literary history "is, or can be, or ought to be, merely ancillary to the art of **literary criticism**." But, Lewis claimed, this is not so. Literary history is not a department of criticism, but of history. Literary history and criticism often overlap, and this creates a danger of confusion, but each has a right to exist. The whole question invites further discussion. In Lewis's view, only a Fordist (a reference to inventor/manufacturer Henry Ford who said "History is more or less bunk.") would maintain that any historical study must be "useful" or "practical." In this essay and elsewhere (see *The Screwtape Letters*: "Great scholars are now as little nourished by the past as the most ignorant mechanic who holds that 'history is bunk.'") Lewis argued that the study of history was possible and valuable for its own sake.

John Bremer

Bibliography

Barfield, Owen. "C. S. Lewis and Historicism." *CSL: The Bulletin of the New York C. S. Lewis Society.* 6 (August 1975): 3–9.

Kreeft, Peter. "Western Civilization at the Crossroads." *Christian History.* 4 no. 3: 25–26, 1985.

_____. "C. S. Lewis and the History of the World." *CSL: The Bulletin of the New York C. S. Lewis Society.* 15 (May 1984): 1–13.

"Is Progress Possible?: Willing Slaves of the Welfare State"

See entry on "Willing Slaves of the Welfare State"

"Is Theism Important?"

See entry on "Is Theism Important? A Reply"

"Is Theism Important? A Reply"

The Socratic Digest. 5 (1952): 48–51. Retitled as "Is Theism Important?" and reprinted in *God in the Dock, Undeceptions,* and *Timeless at Heart.*

This article is a reply to a paper delivered by Professor Price and later published under the title "Is Theism Important?" in *The Socratic Digest.* Price apparently expressed the fear "that England is relapsing into **Paganism**." This pleased Lewis, for "a Pagan, as history shows, is a man eminently convertible to **Christianity**." Lewis continued his examination of Price's contentions by drawing a distinction between the two senses of the word **faith**. In one sense, it means "a settled intellectual assent" or "belief." In the other, faith means "a trust, or confidence, in the **God** whose existence is thus assented to." The first faith is acquired through philosophic argument and thought, and the second faith is "a gift." The one does not lead naturally from the other. The second meaning—the one to which Lewis subscribed—asserts that the gift of faith does not come from argument or from experience, moral or otherwise, or from history. Rather, it comes directly and purely from God. "The operation of Faith is to retain, so far as the will and intellect are concerned, what is irresistible and obvious during the moments of special **grace**."

Anne Gardner

"Is Theology Poetry?"

The Socratic Digest. 3 (1945): 25–35. Reprinted in *They Asked for a Paper* and *Screwtape Proposes a Toast.*

Speakers are not generally at their best when assigned a topic, and this speech is no exception. Lewis pointed out in the first sentence that the topic was assigned and spent some time defining terms. He then argued that, from purely dramatic terms, **Christianity** is not one of the world's most appealing belief systems. Norse mythology he found more intrinsically appealing because the gods lose in the end, giving it an element of tragedy that Christianity lacks. Lewis added that Christianity, like most belief systems, sometimes resorts to **metaphor** to get points across, and in fact ultimate things must virtually always be brought to our minds in terms of metaphor. Finally, Lewis argued at some length against **evolution** and concluded by saying that Christianity enabled him to make sense of the world.

The essay seems somewhat disjointed. While the first half focuses on poetic aspects of **theology**, the second moves from topic to topic in a way that does not fit very well with the announced subject. Lewis's antievolutionary views will strike readers as conservative; his anti-inerrancy views, in which he indicated that he did not find certain biblical episodes to be historical, will seem to most readers liberal. Individual paragraphs are interesting, but the whole does not work well.

Marvin D. Hinten
Bowling Green State University

Also See: the Bible, Conservatism, Creation, Myths, Poetry, Reality

Bibliography
Lewis, C. S. "Funeral of a Great Myth."

"It All Began with a Picture"

Radio Times. CXLVIII (15 July 1960). Reprinted in *Of Other Worlds, Of This and Other Worlds,* and *On Stories.*

In this article, Lewis briefly told how he came to write ***The Lion, the Witch and the Wardrobe***, but first he warned readers that it is difficult for authors to give an accurate account of how they came to write their books. The creative process is so exciting that the writer is often too busy to think about how he is writing a certain story. With that disclaimer given, Lewis shared that all seven of his Narnian books (as well as his adult **science fiction** novels) "began with seeing pictures in my head." In the case of the Narnian stories, the first picture that came to Lewis (at about age sixteen) was "a Faun carrying an umbrella and parcels in a snowy wood." Around age forty, he tried to turn the picture into a story. At about that same time, he was having dreams about lions. Suddenly he had the character of Aslan, and Aslan "pulled the whole story together."

John G. West, Jr.

Also See: Chronicles of Narnia

Bibliography
Sayer, George. *Jack: A Life of C. S. Lewis.* Wheaton, IL: Crossway, 1988.

J

Alfred Kenneth Hamilton Jenkin (1900–1980)

Jenkin attended University College, **Oxford**, where in 1919 he became a friend of C. S. Lewis. Both were members of the **Martlets** Literary Society. They often met for tea, then talked or went for walks or bicycle rides. Lewis's diary mentions Jenkin about fifty times during the school terms of 1922–24 (*All My Road Before Me*).

Lewis wrote that Jenkin was the "first lifelong friend" that he had met at Oxford. He showed Lewis how to "enjoy everything; even ugliness," by making "a total surrender to whatever atmosphere was offering itself at the moment," rubbing one's nose in the "very quiddity of each thing" (*Surprised by Joy*). This enjoyment of the essence of all things possibly led to Lewis seeing the "patches of Godlight" mentioned in *Letters to Malcolm,* plus sharpened his critical and imaginative talents.

Richard James
Burkesville Christian Church

Bibliography

Carpenter, Humphrey. *The Inklings*. Boston: Houghton Mifflin, 1979.

Glover, Donald E. *C. S. Lewis: The Art of Enchantment*. Athens, OH: Ohio University Press, 1981.

Green, Roger Lancelyn, and Walter Hooper. *C. S. Lewis: A Biography*. New York: Harcourt Brace Jovanovich, 1974.

Griffin, William. *Clive Staples Lewis: A Dramatic Life*. San Francisco: Harper & Row, 1986.

Hooper, Walter. *C. S. Lewis: A Companion & Guide*. San Francisco: HarperCollins, 1996.

Jenkin, A. K. Hamilton. *The Cornish miner: an account of his life above and underground from early times, 1927*. Pomfret, VT: David & Charles, 1972.

_____. *Cornwall and its people: being a new impression of the composite work including Cornish seafarers, 1932, Cornwall and the Cornish, 1933, Cornish homes and customs, 1934*. North Pomfret, VT: David & Charles, 1988.

Lindskoog, Kathryn. *Creative Writing: For People Who Can't Write*. Grand Rapids, MI: Zondervan, 1989.

Samuel Johnson (1709–1784)

In 1963, during their brief time together, **Walter Hooper** asked Lewis if he ever took an afternoon nap. Lewis replied, "No, but sometimes a nap takes me!" Upon reading this remark, we are inclined to admire Lewis's quick wit and originality, but in this case the wit and originality belong to Dr. Samuel Johnson, for it was he who first uttered that reply; Lewis was simply quoting him.

It is little wonder Lewis admired and quoted Johnson frequently, for in many ways Dr. Johnson, as he was generally known, was the 18th-century equivalent of Lewis. Among their similarities: both were poets, novelists, literary critics, and thoroughgoing Christians. Both men were witty conservatives with an inclination toward pessimism; both were married, but spent most of their adult lives single, always seeking conversational companionship.

Lewis wrote to **Arthur Greeves** in 1930 that at one point in his life he "used to read a *Rambler* [a Johnsonian essay] every evening." The most noticeable similarities between the writing styles of Lewis and Johnson are their moral tone, persuasive nature, and use of **analogy** to make a point clearer. **Christianity** permeated their **literary criticism** as well as their lives. Perhaps the chief difference between the two is that, where Lewis was a blend of **Rationalism** and **Romanticism**, Johnson was almost entirely oriented toward rational thought. Thus it was that Lewis described Johnson's criticism to Greeves as "always sensible and nearly always wrong." Lewis felt Johnson was impervious to the **magic** of **poetry**, the "call of faerie."

Until about the age of thirty, Lewis frequently kept a diary, and he later claimed that the main, and virtually only, value he had gained from this experience was a greater appreciation for the accomplishment of Boswell. Lewis read Boswell's biography of Johnson repeatedly, and one of his speeches to the **Martlets** society as a don (when he had the luxury of selecting congenial topics) was on Boswell.

Marvin D. Hinten
Bowling Green State University

Also See: Conservatism, Marriage

Bibliography

Boswell, James. *Life of Johnson*. Clarendon: Oxford University Press, 1980.

Johnson, Samuel. *The Rambler*. New Haven, CT: Yale University Press, 1969.

Lewis, C. S. *They Stand Together*.

Wain, John. *Samuel Johnson*. New York: Viking, 1975.

"Joy"

The Beacon. 3 no. 31 (May 1924): 444–45 (under the pseudonym Clive Hamilton). Reprinted in *Collected Poems*.

This poem is one of Lewis's earliest and most successful attempts to capture the essence of **joy**; here he chronicled a sleeper's awakening to unexpected joy and **beauty**. Yet even in this breath of joy comes the melancholic realization it cannot last. Joy, full of aching beauty, is fleeting.

Don W. King
Montreat College

Joy

Lewis experienced early the type of Romantic longing that is called, in German, *Sehnsucht*. As the *Oxford English Dictionary II* indicates, this term (quoted from German or used as English since 1847) can mean a type of wistful longing, such as adolescents may feel for each other; but Lewis used it in a stronger sense, with **imagery** from German **Romanticism**, when recounting his childhood experience: "Every day there were what we [his brother and he] called 'the Green Hills'; that is, the low line of the Castlereagh Hills which we saw from the nursery windows. They were not very far off but they were, to children, quite unattainable. They taught me longing—*Sehnsucht*; made me for good or ill, and before I was six years old, a votary of the Blue Flower" (*Surprised by Joy*).

Three topics need to be developed in connection with *Sehnsucht:* (1) the varying terms Lewis used for this longing, which will also provide a survey of its meaning for him; (2) the various images to which it was applied by him (the mountains are already a given); and (3) his use of it in his works. The first point will receive the fullest discussion.

First, the terms Lewis used for *Sehnsucht*. In *The Pilgrim's Regress* (1933), his early semi-autobiographical **allegory**, Lewis referred to *Sehnsucht* by the term Romanticism, as he used it in his subtitle: *An Allegorical Apology for Christianity, Reason and Romanticism*. In his preface to the third edition (1943), Lewis discussed this "Desire" (with a capital, eight times, and "Sweet Desire" twice), explaining what he meant by Romanticism: "The experience is one of intense longing ... though the sense of want is acute and even painful, yet the mere wanting is felt to be somehow a delight. ... even when there is no hope of possible satisfaction, [this desire] continues to be prized, and even to be preferred to anything else in the world, by those who have once felt it."

But, Lewis added, "there is a peculiar mystery about the object of this Desire." Lewis went on to list some of the things that people have thought to be the object: distant hills, one's past, imaginative settings (through literature), a loved person, magic and the occult, historical or scientific knowledge. He suggested he had, to some degree, tried all of these, and none of them is the true object of Desire. His statement that the Desire ultimately leads one to the presence of **God** was obscured with much jargon. Perhaps the reason for this way of expressing the idea was that Lewis did not want to give away one of the main points of his book in his introduction.

In his later memoir, *Surprised by Joy*, Lewis used the term Joy predominantly; it is his best-known term for *Sehnsucht*, and, as such, it has been used for this article's listing. In his first chapter, Lewis gave three examples of objects from which this Joy arose for him, in addition to the Castlereagh Hills: from "a flowering currant bush on a summer day," with a memory of a toy garden his brother had made earlier; from the presentation of autumn in **Beatrix Potter**'s *Squirrel Nutkin*; and from a translation by Longfellow of a poem mentioning a Norse **myth**. Later in the book, Lewis told of seeking the works related to Norse myths because of this connection and of his increasing love of **nature** for the same reason. After the experience had led him to **faith**, he recorded, in his penultimate paragraph, that he still felt this Joy: "I cannot, indeed, complain, like **Wordsworth**, that the visionary gleam has passed away. I believe (if the thing were at all worth recording) that the old stab, the old bitter-sweet, has come to me as often and as sharply since my conversion as at any time of my life whatever." Besides the use of Wordsworth's term (from "Ode: Intimations of Immortality from Recollections of Early Childhood"), Lewis added to his own terms or paraphrases "the stab" and "the bitter-sweet," which complement such descriptions as Sweet Desire and Joy.

Three more directly religious discussions of *Sehnsucht* may be added to these. In "Hope" (Ch. 10 of **Christian Behaviour** [1943], later collected in *Mere Christianity* [1952]), Lewis discussed the Christian hope for **Heaven**. He does not mention the term *Sehnsucht*, but his point is based on it: "Most people, if they had really learned to look into their own hearts, would know that they do want, and want acutely, something that cannot be had in this world."

He mentioned two foolish ways to deal with immortal longings—the constant seeking of new examples of the stimuli of the feeling, and the settling down into disillusioned common sense that denies the existence of

Sehnsucht except as an adolescent mood—and a Christian way, in which the Christian decides: "If none of my earthly pleasures satisfy it [my longing], that does not prove that the universe is a Fraud. Probably earthly pleasures were never meant to satisfy it, but only to arouse it, to suggest the real thing."

The other religious discussions, which can only be mentioned here, are in a 1941 sermon **"The Weight of Glory"** and in "Heaven," the last chapter of *The Problem of Pain* (1940). Here again the emphasis is on *Sehnsucht* as desire for Heaven—specifically, in the sermon, for the glory of salvation. In a footnote to the sermon, Lewis used the phrase "immortal longings" for *Sehnsucht*.

In addition to employing various terms for *Sehnsucht*, Lewis utilized a variety of images in his works to depict the stimuli of *Sehnsucht*. According to Corvin Scott Carnell's basic study of Lewis and *Sehnsucht*, four: (1) distant hills, (2) an exotic garden, (3) an island of the "Utter East" or the "Utter West," although sometimes just an island, and (4) sweet music. These, of course, are **symbols** that Lewis thought would speak to many readers; they are not (or not usually, in Lewis) the false images that are mistaken for the goals of *Sehnsucht*.

Finally, we should discuss Lewis's literary uses of *Sehnsucht*. The following list is extensive but not complete. In Lewis's early non-Christian *Spirits in Bondage* (1919), "Song of the Pilgrims" describes the search for a garden beyond the Northern snows, "The Roads" describes a desire to journey the earth to the distant valley of the gods, and "Death in Battle" suggests "the garden of God" beyond life; these are the images, but Lewis may not yet have been analytic about their meaning. In *Dymer* (1926), Dymer at one point hears music above his head (I.23–25), which guides him, it seems, to a large house. In "The Queen of Drum" (written c. 1933–34), the Queen escapes to faerie, running to the far hills (Canto V); since this poem clearly sets up the contrast of faerie and God, Lewis was not yet saying that *Sehnsucht* leads to Heaven. In *The Pilgrim's Regress*, John hears a musical tone and a voice saying "Come," sees a wood full of primroses, remembers a childhood experience of picking primroses, and imagines he sees a far island (I.2). In *Out of the Silent Planet* (1938), Ransom has to journey on Malacandra to an island with a hill on it (Ch. 17, 3d para.). In *The Screwtape Letters* (1942), at the moment of the patient's death, "that central music in every pure experience which had always just evaded memory was now at last recovered" (Ch. 31). In *Perelandra* (1943), the second fixed island has a mountain on it, the twin peaks of which are covered with red flow-

ers (Ch. 15, 4th–2d para. from the end). In *That Hideous Strength* (1945), Jane Studdock's conversion—her experience of God—takes place in a garden (Ch. 14, 6th para.). In *The Great Divorce* (1945), the souls wavering between salvation and damnation are invited to make the journey to far mountains (Heaven). In *The Voyage of the "Dawn Treader"* (1952), the land in the utter east is Aslan's land, preceded by white water "lilies"; the land itself extends outside of the world of Narnia with tall mountains beyond the rising sun (Ch. 16). In *Till We Have Faces* (1956), Psyche confesses to Orual that looking at the Gray Mountain in the distance has set her "longing, always longing. . . . Everything seemed to be saying, Psyche come!" (Ch. 7).

Joe R. Christopher

Also See: Dreams, Fairy Tales

Bibliography

Carnell, Corbin Scott. *Bright Shadow of Reality: C. S. Lewis and the Feeling Intellect*. Grand Rapids, MI: Eerdmans, 1974.

Fernandez, Irene. "C. S. Lewis on Joy." *International Catholic Review: Communito*. (Fall 1982): 247–57.

Lindskoog, Kathryn. "C. S. Lewis's Search for Joy." *Radly*. 10 no. 6 (May-June 1979): 6–11.

The Joyful Christian: 127 Readings from C. S. Lewis

Henry William Griffin (ed). New York: Macmillan, 1977.

Carl Jung (1879–1961)

The Swiss-born Carl Jung was a colleague of **Sigmund Freud** and was at one time assumed to be Freud's successor. In 1912, however, he broke with Freud to found analytical **psychology**—in part due to his disagreement with Freud's attempt to connect neurosis with **sex**. Lewis mentions that break when he discussed "Morality and Psychoanalysis" in *Mere Christianity*.

Jung's most widely accepted idea was the distinction he drew between extroverted and introverted personalities. His most controversial ideas concerned archetypes and the collective unconscious. An archetype is an inborn pattern in the human mind that is expressed in **dreams** and **religion**. The collective unconscious is the part of the mind that holds images common to all humanity.

Lewis commented on Jung's collective unconscious in **"Psycho-Analysis and Literary Criticism."** He expressed skepticism despite the idea's attractions: "I perceive at once that even if it turns out to be bad science it is excellent **poetry**." He may have also alluded to the seductive appeal of Jung's scientific mythology in the seventh chapter of *Screwtape Letters*.

Mike Perry

Also See: Human Nature, Literary Criticism, Myth, Psychology, Symbolism, Sin

Justice

In *Mere Christianity*, Lewis proposed that the human notion of justice is inextricably connected to the concept of moral law. When he was an atheist, Lewis rejected **God** because the universe seemed cruel and unjust. However, the very idea of justice—which compares this flawed universe to an outside standard—ties justice to a **supernatural** being. Lewis was "forced to assume that one part of **reality**—namely my idea of justice—was full of sense," and if this was full of sense, there was room for God.

Lewis argued that "Justice means much more than the sort of thing that goes on in law courts. It is the old name for everything we should now call 'fairness'; it includes honesty, give and take, truthfulness, keeping promises, and all that side of life." Another requirement for justice is "the recognition of guilt and ill-desert in the recipient," for "as there are plants which will flourish only in mountain soil, so it appears that Mercy will flower only when it grows in the crannies of the rock of Justice." Social justice is focused on the commandment "Do as you would be done by."

But Lewis was quick to distinguish divine justice from a form of bargaining where one works for forgiveness: "Any idea that we could perform our side of the contract and thus put God in our debts so that it was up to Him, in mere justice, to perform His side—that has to be wiped out." To our good fortune, our just God is also a merciful God, who redeems us despite our sinful nature. This undeserved **mercy** seems foreign to our human notion of justice, leading Lewis to say he would "sooner pray for God's mercy than for His justice on my friends, my enemies, and myself" (*Letters to an American Lady*).

Kristine Ottaway

Also See: Democracy, Good and Evil, Grace, Guilt

K

Immanuel Kant (1724–1804)

Immanuel Kant was an exceedingly important German philosopher whose primary achievements lay in the areas of **metaphysics**, ethics, and **aesthetics**. Lewis appreciated Kant's emphasis on **God**, freedom, and **immortality** as chief problems for metaphysicians. Many subsequent philosophers became interested only in the problems of this world.

Kant attempted to reconcile the world of **science** with the world of morality and religious consciousness. In his ethics he concluded that besides our knowledge of objects, there is also moral knowledge. We can be said to know, for example, that we ought in all situations to tell the **truth**, keep our promises, honor our parents, etc. Kant concluded further that a person who acts for the sake of duty is a good person. His main concern was to bring out the difference between acting for the sake of duty and acting to satisfy one's natural desires and inclinations. His main point was that a moral person will perform his duty when his duty is contrary to his inclinations. While Lewis appreciated some of Kant's conclusions, he did trace to Kant the fallacious view that to desire our own good and to hope to enjoy it is a bad thing (**"Weight of Glory"**). In contrast, Lewis stressed frequently that we should rejoice in our talents and in all pleasure in its healthy and normal forms. After all, bemoans Screwtape, he (**God**) made the pleasures, and "all our research so far has not enabled us to produce one" (*Screwtape Letters*).

In the end, Kant postulated his Categorical Imperative that we should so act as to treat humanity always at the same time as an end and never merely as a means. It is in freedom that Kant found the condition for the possibility of this categorical imperative. For obligation and oughtness implies the freedom to obey or disobey the law. Lewis saw Kant as "perfectly right on that point, at least the imperative is categorical." For Lewis, "unless the ethical is assumed from the outset, no argument will bring you to it" (**"On Ethics"**).

Michael H. Macdonald
Seattle Pacific University

Also See: Ethics and Morality, Good and Evil, Religion

Bibliography

Kant, Immanuel. *The Critique of Pure Reason; The Critique of Practical Reason; The Critique of Judgment.*

John Keats (1795–1821)

One of the great Romantic poets, Keats is recognized for his concrete sensory description, his presentation of irreconcilable opposites, and his focus on the problems of evil, suffering, and **pain**. His early death at age twenty-six is often mourned as a tragic loss of literary potential. *The Eve of St. Agnes* and *La Belle Dame sans Merci* are the most representative of Keats' sensuous descriptions, but their sensuality was not enjoyed by Lewis, who found the swooning and fainting **love** of Porphyro particularly lacking. However, Lewis lauded Keats' attempt to write an **epic**, saying that "what mythological scenes in ancient literature can compare for a moment with Keats' *Hyperion*?" Discussing the historical treatment of Darwinism, Lewis referred to this work of Keats as an expression of the developmental or progressive idea, quoting the lines "tis the eternal law / That first in **beauty** should be first in might."

Kristine Ottaway

Also See: Evolution, Good and Evil, Myth, Poetry

Bibliography

Bate, W. Jackson. *John Keats.* Cambridge, MA: Belknap Press, 1979.
Lewis, C. S. "The Weight of Glory," and "The World's Last Night," *The World's Last Night and Other Essays.*

Clyde S. Kilby (1902–1986)

The founder of the **Marion E. Wade Center** and an early Lewis scholar, Clyde S. Kilby was born September 26, 1902, in Johnson City, Tennessee, the youngest of eight children. In 1930, he married Martha A. Harris, whose sense of warm Southern hospitality graced their home throughout their long married life together. He came to Wheaton College, Illinois, in 1935 as Assistant Professor of English, the first step in a distinguished career in the world of literature. As chairman of Wheaton's English Department, he began in 1956 the college's Annual Writers' Conference, which continues

today. He was also instrumental in the creation of the Conference on Christianity and Literature and served as its first president. However, he is best known for his significant contribution to C. S. Lewis studies. His excellent volume *The Christian World of C. S. Lewis* remains one of the best introductions to Lewis's works, even thirty years after it was first published in 1964. As founder and first curator of the Wade Center, Kilby diligently worked to build a comprehensive collection of books, manuscripts, and related materials by and about the seven Wade authors including Lewis. He was also one of the founders of *SEVEN: An Anglo-American Literary Review*, now in its fourteenth year of publication. At his death in 1986, he left behind a rich legacy of those who had been challenged by his love for excellence in literature and the life of the imagination.

Marjorie Lamp Mead
The Marion E. Wade Center

Bibliography

Bechtel, Paul M. "Clyde S. Kilby: A Sketch." In *Imagination and the Spirit*, ed. Charles Huttar. Grand Rapids, MI: Eerdmans, 1971.
Hooper, Walter. *C. S. Lewis: A Companion & Guide.* San Francisco: HarperSanFrancisco, 1996.
Kilby, Clyde S. *The Christian World of C. S. Lewis.* Grand Rapids, MI: Eerdmans, 1964.
_____. *Images of Salvation in the Fiction of C. S. Lewis.* Wheaton, IL: Harold Shaw Publishers, 1978.
_____. *Letters to an American Lady.* Grand Rapids, MI: Eerdmans, 1967, and London: Hodder and Stoughton, 1969.
_____. *A Mind Awake: An Anthology of C. S. Lewis.* London: Geoffrey Bles, and New York: Harcourt Brace and World, 1969.
_____. *Tolkien and the Silmarillion.* Wheaton, IL: Harold Shaw Publishers, 1976.
_____, and Douglas Gilbert. *C. S. Lewis: Images of His World.* Grand Rapids, MI: Eerdmans, and London: Hodder and Stoughton, 1973.
_____, and Marjorie Lamp Mead. *Brothers and Friends: The Diaries of Major Warren Hamilton Lewis.* San Francisco: Harper & Row, 1982.
Mead, Marjorie Lamp. "A Kilby Legacy," *Wheaton Alumni*, 58, no. 3 (June-July 1991): 15.

The Kilns

The Kilns was C. S. Lewis's home in the Oxford suburb of Headington Quarry, in the southeast section of the city. It is located on (now) Lewis Close, just off Kiln Lane, about three miles from the Oxford city center. The house was built in 1922 on nine acres, and the property had a garden, tennis court, large pond, greenhouse, and the remains of a brick kiln. Lewis, his brother **Warren**

Lewis, and Mrs. **Janie Moore** bought the Kilns for £3,300, and the three, along with Mrs. Moore's daughter **Maureen Moore**, moved into the house in October of 1930. The gardener **Fred Paxford** came to the Kilns in late 1930 and stayed until Lewis's death in 1963. Mrs. Moore lived at the Kilns until early 1950, and through the years the rest of the household was composed of one or two maids and assorted dogs and cats, with Mrs. Molly Miller coming as permanent housemaid in 1952.

The Kilns originally had four bedrooms, a kitchen, two reception rooms, a scullery, and a small maid's bedroom; two rooms were added in 1932 for Warren on his return from military service in China. Under Paxford's guidance, the Lewis brothers and Mrs. Moore made many improvements to the property, including planting an orchard, adding fish to the pond, and building fences and walking paths. Lewis found the Kilns a delightful and idyllic place to live. He loved walking in the woods, especially during seasonal changes, and during the years he often invited close friends, students, and colleagues to visit.

When **Joy Davidman Lewis** and her sons **Douglas Gresham** and **David Gresham** moved into the Kilns early in 1958 after her diagnosis of cancer, she made many improvements to the Kilns, including painting, redecorating, and reconnecting the radiators. After his brother's death in 1963, Warren Lewis moved away from the Kilns for three years, then returned to live at the home until his death on April 9, 1973. In 1969, part of the surrounding property was purchased by an Oxford Trust and made into a nature preserve, and in 1984 the Kilns itself was acquired by investors intent on preserving it in honor of C. S. Lewis. The project was eventually taken over by the C. S. Lewis Foundation of Redlands, California, which has been spearheading a full-blown restoration of the Kilns and the creation of a Lewis study center there.

Perry C. Bramlett
C. S. Lewis for the Local Church

Bibliography

Kilby, Clyde S., and Marjorie Lamp Mead (eds.). *Brothers and Friends: The Diaries of Major Warren Hamilton Lewis.* San Francisco: Harper & Row, 1982.

Paxford, F. W. "Observations of His Gardener—He Should Have Been a Parson." *The Canadian C. S. Lewis Journal.* 55 (Summer 1986): 8–13.

Sayer, George. *Jack: C. S. Lewis and His Times.* San Francisco: Harper & Row, 1988.

The Kingis Quair (Letter)

The Times Literary Supplement. (18 April 1929): 315.

Lewis endeavored to illustrate the significant connection between the introductory and autobiographical stanzas of the Scottish poem, "The Kingis Quair," and the subsequent stanzas of the poem which deal with the imprisonment of James I, King of Scotland, by the English in 1405 and his love affair with Joan Beaufort.

Marjorie L. Mead
The Marion E. Wade Center

Rudyard Kipling (1865–1936)

The talented writer of many poems, short stories, and novels, Rudyard Kipling was the first British citizen to receive the Nobel Prize for Literature (1907). After the First World War, his popularity declined as the British, traumatized by war, lost interest in stories of soldiers and empires.

Lewis and Kipling shared similar childhoods. Both were born outside England (Kipling in Bombay, India) and both were tormented and unhappy in English boarding schools. Perhaps partly because of those experiences, both were able to write children stories that have become classics.

Lewis had mixed feelings about Kipling's adult stories. In a 1948 essay on **"Kipling's World"** he explained why he could find the author delightful one moment and in the next become "sick to death" with him. Kipling, he said, was a "slave of the Inner Ring." His glorification of shared camaraderie was "morally neutral," and thus justified evil schemes as well as good. Even the tolerance that Kipling displayed toward **Christianity** was the "weary and skeptical" attitude of "reverent Pagan agnosticism about all ultimates."

Mike Perry

Bibliography

Chesterton, G. K. *Heretics* North Stratford, NH: Ayer, 1977.

"Kipling's World"

Literature and Life: Addresses to the English Association, I. London: Harrap and Co., 1948: 57–73. Reprinted in *They Asked for a Paper* and *Selected Literary Essays.*

"Kipling's World"—originally an address to the English Association in the 1940s, and later published in *Literature and Life*—begins with a focus on the extremes of appreciation and denunciation engendered by the work of **Rudyard Kipling**. Lewis confessed he himself had a love/hate relationship with Kipling, and this essay quickly becomes Lewis's personal exploration of the causes for this paradox.

One reason for his ambivalence, Lewis said, is attributable to an excess, not a defect of Kipling's art: according to Lewis, Kipling's work is overwrought—too consciously revised, too concise, too condensed. The other, and, for Lewis, more serious problem, involved Kipling's attention to the world of work. Kipling was one of the few fiction writers who steadily focused on work, said Lewis; but what Kipling really valued in the work experience was being "in the know," part of an **inner ring**, a phrase used by Lewis in the title of another essay and repeatedly brought forth here.

Kipling's emphasis on vocational snobbery eventually put us off, Lewis claimed, and for his chauvinism alone, Kipling becomes unbearable. By the end of the essay, Lewis has complimented Kipling for the "great merit" of demonstrating the power of this "inner ring" to produce "obedient servants of valour and public spirit," but, he wryly averred, captive to it as he himself is, Kipling failed to notice, or was ultimately indifferent to, the inner ring's more inhumane consequences: "cruelty, extortion, oppression, and dishonesty."

Lewis deplored such snobbery in all its forms—and depicted its deadly apotheosis among the N.I.C.E. of Bracton Wood in *That Hideous Strength*. There is no better portrayal in Lewis's work of a seduction by an "inner ring" than what befalls its protagonist, Mark Studdock.

Marvin D. Hinten and Bruce L. Edwards
Bowling Green State University

Bibliography
Lewis, C. S. "Inner Ring."
Lindskoog, Kay. *C. S. Lewis: Mere Christian*. Chicago: Cornerstone Books, 1997.

William T. Kirkpatrick (1848–1921)

William T. Kirkpatrick, a retired headmaster of Lurgan College, Northern Ireland, served as Lewis's tutor during the years 1914–17. A friend of Lewis's father, **Albert Lewis**, who had himself been tutored by Kirkpatrick (1877–79), Kirkpatrick had previously consulted him regarding both Jack and Warnie's schooling. When boarding school did not work out well for Jack, father and friend agreed that perhaps individualized instruction was what their precocious teenager needed, and Jack went to live with Kirkpatrick.

Kirkpatrick's teaching method, vividly and reverently depicted in Lewis's *Surprised by Joy*, could be described only a bit of exaggeration as Socratic bullying. If Jack would look outdoors and comment that it was a nice day, Kirkpatrick would vigorously call out "Stop!" and require Jack to define a nice day and explain his reasons for labeling this particular day a nice one.

The method would probably have driven many a student into rebellion or silence. Jack, however, blossomed under Kirkpatrick's rigorous attention to detail and **logic**, and he eventually began to dispute with Kirkpatrick on near-equal terms. Lewis described Kirkpatrick as one who came closer to being a "purely logical entity" than anyone he had ever met. (Like all human beings, Kirkpatrick was not unfailingly logical; a lapsed Presbyterian, he wore nicer clothes for Sunday gardening than for weekday gardening.)

Kirkpatrick's form of language instruction also succeeded with Lewis, where again it would have failed with a pupil of lesser intellect. During Jack's time with his tutor, they studied French, German, Italian, Greek, and Latin, and their method always remained the same. Kirkpatrick would give his charge some basic grammar rules as a starter, then would hand him a dictionary and a major work in the new language, and Jack would take it from there. Obviously, this meant that while Jack was learning Greek he was also learning *Medea*; as he studied Italian, he also studied **Dante**'s *Divina Commedia*. The young man thus entered **Oxford** with a greater command of both languages and great works in those languages than the average student.

Despite his thoroughgoing **rationalism** and fierce **atheism**, Kirkpatrick became one of Jack's most formative influences and remained so for life, commemorated in Lewis's autobiography and elsewhere as "The Great Knock." Among the several places his character surfaces in Lewis's fiction include the **Chronicles of Narnia**, where Professor Kirke's (note the name) attention to logic and his disappointment in "what the schools are teaching" is an amalgam of feelings shared by Lewis and Kirkpatrick; and in *That Hideous Strength*, in the skeptical, rationalistic MacPhee.

Marvin D. Hinten and Bruce L. Edwards
Bowling Green State University

Kolbitar

The Kolbitar was a literary society founded by **J. R. R. Tolkien** at **Oxford University** in 1926. The purpose of the group whose name means "men who lounge so close to the fire in winter that they bit the coal" was to read in the original Icelandic **myths**. Lewis became a member in 1927. Lewis struggled with the translation but was enthralled to be tackling Norse mythology in the original.

Bibliography
Lewis, C. S. *All My Road Before Me*.

L

Richard William Ladborough (1908–1972)

Ladborough was a fellow and director of studies at **Magdalene College, Cambridge,** as well as dean and Pepys librarian when Lewis was elected a fellow there. Ladborough and Lewis became friends. He wrote of their relationship in his essay "In Cambridge," which appears in *C. S. Lewis at the Breakfast Table*.

"The Landing"

Punch. 215 (September 15, 1948): 237 (under the pseudonym Nat Whilk). Revised and reprinted in *Poems* and *Collected Poems*.

This poem recalls Heracles' labor to retrieve one of the golden apples of the garden of Hesperides. Heracles is not its subject, however. Instead the poem concerns a speaker who is delighted finally to be landing at the garden of Hesperides, a place he had only seen from afar (at the Helicon) until this moment. Rather than finding golden apples, he looks through a golden telescope pointed to the West and sees "true" Hesperides. Inspired, he and his companions journey forth to satisfy this final longing. The poem has obvious connections to Lewis's lifelong pursuit of **joy** and also recalls the conclusion of *The Last Battle*.

Don W. King
Montreat College

Andrew Lang (1844–1912)

Andrew Lang was a Scottish scholar and author who inspired Lewis's interest in **fairy tales**, **myths**, and **epic** literature. Lang wrote **poetry** and collaborated on a prose translation of Homer's *Odyssey*. Lewis never lost his delight in the multiple epithets and heroic language in Butcher and Lang's *Odyssey*. Lewis read Lang's *History of English Literature* in school at Bookham. Lewis also knew Lang's *Myth, Ritual, and Religion*; its discussion of dying gods and fertility rites fueled his early **atheism**. When Lewis discussed with **Roger Green** possible titles for the **Chronicles of Narnia**, Green suggested the name on the **analogy** of Lang's *Chronicles of Pantouflia*. In a letter, Lewis proclaimed his interest in "the land where I shall never be; / the love that I shall never see." Lewis used the couplet on the title page of *Spirits in Bondage*, writing that, "Andrew Lang quotes it somewhere, but I have never been able to discover the author. Whoever it be, he deserves immortality for these two lines alone." The slightly misquoted lines are from a poem by Lang that was itself a misquote from Baudelaire's "The Moon's Minion."

Jonathan L. Thorndike
Lakeland College

Bibliography

Green, Roger. *Andrew Lang: A Critical Biography*. Leicester: Ward, 1946.

———. "C. S. Lewis and Andrew Lang." *Notes and Queries*. 22 (May 1975): 208–9.

Lang, Andrew.

"The Language of Religion"

First published posthumously in *Christian Reflections*.

In this essay, Lewis wrote that the true language of religion is **language** people use in ordinary conversation and **poetry** ("something that ranges between the Ordinary and the Poetical"). He then distinguished between ordinary, scientific, and poetic language, and pointed out that the language of religion and that of poetry are more alike than either is like the language of science. For Lewis, poetic language is remarkable (and becomes religious) because it reveals to us "the quality of experiences which we have not had," and it points us toward something outside our own experience, like a road map. Ordinary language is one of the best ways to describe emotional experiences, and when it is used to express religious beliefs and other religious experiences, it becomes theological language when combined with the poetic. Lewis thought that more of our religious experience is communicable through ordinary or poetic language than it is through scientific language, but scientific language is more verifiable. According to Lewis, this is a disadvantage to the Christian apologist, who has to "prove God" in definable terms.

Perry C. Bramlett
C. S. Lewis for the Local Church

Also See: Apologetics, Imagination, RAF Talks

Bibliography

Schakel, Peter J., and Charles A. Huttar (eds). *Word and Story in C. S. Lewis*. Columbia, MO: University of Missouri Press, 1991.

Language/Rhetoric

Lewis saw language as a gift bequeathed to humans by a Creator-**God** whose own defining attributes include an ability to speak and create through speech. Through language the human creature is both sentient and social, aware of self and other selves, and thereby capable of maintaining fellowship not only with fellow creatures but also with a Transcendent, Infinite Being who is yet also a Person. According to Lewis, humans are never more like God than when they are "doing things with words." We live, thus, in a "wordly world." In his essay **"Christianity and Literature,"** Lewis offered one of his most endearing tributes to the person of **Christ** by portraying him as the Eternal Word (echoing the Gospel of John) who is an apprentice wordsmith to his Father in **Heaven**. A Son "who does only what He sees His Father doing," Christ is a wordsmith as much as a carpenter, crafting words of life, healing, and **redemption** to a fallen world desperate for good news.

Language plays a key role in the plot and characterization of much of Lewis's fiction. For instance, Ransom, Lewis's philologist protagonist in the space trilogy, discovers what it means to be human—and, by contrast, inhuman—by explaining the language and contrasting roles and means of communication among sorns, hrossa, and pfifltriggi on Malacandra. While on Perelandra, Ransom discovers to his horror the limitations of words and the end of mere **reason** when he reluctantly obeys the command to kill the Unman with an act of physical courage. Finally, in the climactic scene on Earth in *That Hideous Strength*, the braintrust of the N.I.C.E. disintegrates into a Babel of violence, as language ceases to "mean," and evil is conquered in a reversal of Pentecost.

In his literary scholarship and **apologetics**, Lewis was himself an accomplished philologist and linguist, an astute chronicler of words, **images**, ideas, and meanings, and their impact on texts and **culture** over time. Scattered throughout his writings are countless reflections on language and its role in equipping reason for objective inquiry into the nature of things and fueling the **imagination** for the apprehension of **truth**. In his essay, **"The Language of Religion,"** Lewis delineated the then conventional academic wisdom that there are three kinds of language—the ordinary, the scientific, and the poetic, and that the scientific is the superior of the three because of its supposed precision and literalness. Lewis then proceeded to problematize this easy categorization by demonstrating that each "language" really entails or conceals a particular motive for expression or a specific set of skills, and that, while each is

capable of doing something better than the others, all are necessary components of human communication. Lewis made these points in the service of defending the meaningfulness of religious propositions—and of indirectly establishing that reason, experience, and imagination are all viable—and complementary—means of coming to true knowledge.

As a cultural critic, in particular, Lewis was acutely aware of the necessity of defending language as an adequate tool to allow human beings to see and not just "see through" the world. In *The Abolition of Man* (1943) Lewis took great pains to analyze and refute the pseudo-positivism and incipient deconstructionism of "the Green Book," an elementary composition textbook that implicitly denied that humans could utter predicates of value. Lewis was a lifelong anti-positivist, opposing the notion that there could be a neutral, "scientific" way of speaking that avoided **metaphor** or "poetic diction." He saw this positivism as a stalking horse for an anti-supernaturalism and a God-denying subjectivism that robbed human beings of access to that which lies beyond **nature** and, indeed, beyond words. Here, as elsewhere, Lewis is an indefatigable champion of "objective value" and the role language plays in the articulation and transmittal of enduring human aspirations and civilizing institutions.

Studies in Words (1960) probably represents Lewis's most sustained, scholarly treatment of language, albeit from a metaphysical point of view, offering elaborated histories of such epoch-making words as "nature," "free" and "world." The truth is, Lewis was always pointing his readers to a conception of language that upheld its heuristic and epistemic functions, that is, its utter suitability for enabling mere human beings to observe, discover, and express both mundane and profound truth in accurate and reliable ways. Under the influence of his friend and linguistic mentor, **Owen Barfield**, Lewis saw language as "incurably" metaphorical and analogical—both referring hearers/readers to items, persons, and relations and thus "making meaning" on one plane of existence; and pointing them backwards and forwards to ever deeper layers of meaning that lay beyond any single lifetime or civilization.

In his scholarly career and his imaginative writing, Lewis understood "rhetoric" in its traditional, classical sense—a compendium of tools that equipped an artist or essayist with strategies to communicate truth more memorably, to express difficult ideas more accessibly, to appeal to the imagination with greater aplomb and delight, and, certainly, to make confrontation with the deeper facthood of transcendent reality less avoidable. His canon of compelling texts are an enduring legacy that point to his own mastery of these venerable strategies of persuasion, instruction, and engagement.

Bruce L. Edwards
Bowling Green State University

Bibliography

Edwards, Bruce L. *A Rhetoric of Reading: C. S. Lewis's Defense of Western Literacy*. Provo, UT: Brigham Young University Press, 1985.

Keefe, Carolyn. *C. S. Lewis: Speaker and Teacher*. Grand Rapids, MI: Zondervan, 1967.

Myers, Doris T. *C. S. Lewis in Context*. Kent, OH: Kent State University Press, 1994.

Schakel, Peter J., and Charles A. Huttar (eds). *Word and Story in C. S. Lewis*. Columbia, MO: University of Missouri Press, 1991.

The Last Battle

London: Geoffrey Bles, 1956. First US edition, New York: Macmillan, 1956.

The Last Battle is the sixth in the **Chronicles of Narnia** Lewis completed and the second in the fourth and final burst of creative energy that produced the Narniad. In a letter to Anne of March 5, 1961, Lewis said that *The Last Battle* is about "the coming of the Antichrist (the Ape). The end of the world and the Last Judgement." In that sense, *The Last Battle* can be seen as a more developed version of *Prince Caspian* because both books ask the questions: "Is the Christian story real now or only something that may have happened long ago?" and "What does the effect of the passage of time have on the reality and experience of **faith**?" In *The Last Battle* there are also echoes of another major theme in both *Prince Caspian* and *The Magician's Nephew*, the uses and misuse of **nature** and people.

The Last Battle in addition further develops the main theme of *The Horse and His Boy*, "the calling and conversion of a heathen." The heathen of *The Horse and His Boy*, Shasta, is an anticipation of Emeth, the good Calormene soldier in *The Last Battle*. Lewis had long contemplated the eternal fate of the virtuous unbeliever, linking it to his reflections on Matthew 25:31–46 (*Letters of C. S. Lewis* of April 5, 1939;

December 9, 1941; January 31, 1952; November 8, 1952; August 3, 1953, and February 18, 1954; the November 8, 1952 letter is especially significant because it was written just as Lewis was writing *The Last Battle*). Lewis contrasted Emeth's salvation with the damnation of the dwarfs and the hopefully temporary lapse of Susan, whose indifference to matters Narnian is attributed to her overeagerness to appear adult (prepared on the first pages of *The Lion, the Witch and the Wardrobe* and explained in *C. S. Lewis Letters to Children*, February 22, 1955, and January 22, 1957, and in *Letters to an American Lady*, August 1, 1953). It is critical to note in this connection that Lewis was not a universalist (he made that clear in *George MacDonald: An Anthology*); his concern was to point out Aslan's prior election of Emeth in terms of endearment redolent of "Love bade me welcome" by **George Herbert**.

The first six words of *The Last Battle* announce to the readers that this is the story of Narnian endings. Called friends but in reality master and slave, Shift the crafty Ape and Puzzle the naive Donkey see something floating in Cauldron Pool. Shift manipulates Puzzle into risking his life to fetch what they both learn is a lion's skin. Shift makes the skin into a costume for Puzzle who expresses several times his dread of aping Aslan, even if he is only Shift's spokesman. Shift's calling the discovery of the skin a providential opportunity to improve Narnia provokes a warning earthquake, which Shift twists into a confirming message. The lie that "Aslan"

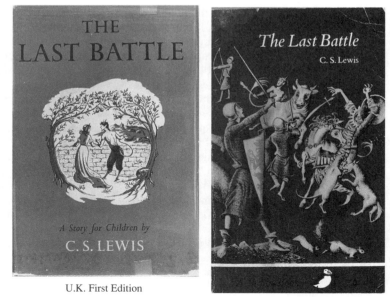

U.K. First Edition

has returned reaches the real friends King Tirian and unicorn Jewel but the centaur Roonwit pronounces that the truth-telling Narnian heavens speak of impending disaster. Jewel and Tirian remember that the old tales say that Aslan is not a tame lion and wonder if that means he does not have to obey the laws he has set for the stars and planets (this argument is akin to the age-old question about the priority of God or the moral law, which Lewis answers in **"The Poison of Subjectivism"**). A dying tree-spirit interrupts their colloquy and they set off rather rashly to avenge her death.

On their way they discover that "Aslan" has ordered the pillaging of Narnia's forests and the enslavement of talking beasts by Calormen. Tirian and Jewel rashly kill two Calormenes and then surrender to "Aslan's" forces. At Stable Hill where "Aslan" is supposed to reside, Tirian witnesses Shift claiming that Aslan and Tash are one and cruel—Tashlan and Ginger the cat and Rishda the Calormene insinuating that they are one and don't exist. Tirian would endorse the Narnian belief that only Aslan is and is good, but he is struck in the mouth. In the night he remembers how Aslan sent children in the times of Narnia's need so he calls out for help. He first sees a vision of people at dinner and then Eustace and Jill are untying him. The three go off to talk and to disguise themselves as Calormenes. They then return to rescue Jewel, and Jill rescues Puzzle. They meet dwarfs on forced march, show them Puzzle, and kill their Calormene guards; but the dwarfs, far from being grateful and having been taken in by a lie, refuse to be taken in by the truth and go off to their own pursuits—all except Poggin. Doffing their disguises, the tiny band seeks to meet Roonwit's reinforcements. After the terrifying vision of the demon Tash on its way to Shift, who invoked him, hearts lift, but only temporarily because soon they receive the news that Cair Paravel has fallen to invasion and that Roonwit is dead.

What remains to them is to return to Stable Hill, proclaim the truth about Aslan, and take the adventure he sends them. They hear Shift's distortions and his announcement that any animals who wish may enter the stable door to see Tashlan. Ginger coolly enters and flies out mad, reduced to a dumb beast. A Calormene soldier steps forward, Emeth by name and heart (the Hebrew word for "truth"), desirous of seeing Tash. After he enters, what appears to be his body is thrown out. Tirian steps into the light and the Last Battle begins. The ape is tossed to Tash. Only the dogs come to Tirian's side. The dwarfs kill the horses and Calormene reinforcements arrive. Eustace is then thrown into the stable, followed by the dwarfs and Jill. Finally Tirian and Rishda go in the sta-

ble and face radically different fates: Rishda is taken away by the evil god Tash, but Tirian finds himself in a beautiful paradise in the presence of the children who visited Narnia in the other books of the series. They are all dressed as Kings and Queens. The weather is early summer's but the fruits are autumn's; every pleasure feels allowed. Lucy tells the story from inside the stable and leads all to the dwarfs who are convinced they are in a filthy stable. Not even Aslan, coming on the scene, can do anything to make the dwarfs happy. Aslan steps to the door and calls an end to Narnia. All creatures are forced through the door and to look at Aslan's face, either to cease to be talking beasts and disappear into his shadow or to love him with reverent fear. Most animals set off "further up and further in," but some stay to see Peter lock the door on Narnia. Aslan runs ahead. The rest meet Emeth—who tells the story of his reconciling encounter with Aslan—and all the good characters from the Narniad. As they now run off to the west, they realize that not only the real Narnia is inside the stable but also all real worlds, including earth. Aslan bounds down to greet them, telling them that they have died and that now is the time for the holidays that will have no end.

Paul F. Ford
St. John's Seminary

Bibliography

Ford, Paul F. *Companion to Narnia*. San Francisco: Harper-SanFrancisco, 1994.

Myers, Doris. "The Compleat Anglican: Spiritual Style in the Chronicles of Narnia." *Anglican Theological Review.* LXVI (April 1984): 148–60.

Schakel, Peter. *Reading with the Heart: The Way into Narnia.* Grand Rapids, MI: Eerdmans, 1979.

Yandell, Steven. "The Trans-cosmic Journeys in the Chronicles of Narnia." *Mythlore* 43 (August 1985): 9–23.

"The Last of the Wine"

See entry on "The End of the Wine"

"The Late Passenger"

See entry on "The Sailing of the Ark"

"The Laws of Nature"

The Coventry Evening Telegraph. (4 April 1945): 4. Reprinted in *God in the Dock* and *Undeceptions.*

"The Laws of Nature" revisits the argument in **"Religion and Science."** It begins with a comment from a friend who expresses a condescending and abstract sadness that a woman believes her son survived Arnheim because she prayed for him. The friend explains that his survival was simply due to the laws of **nature**. As the person considers the remarks of his friend, he decides that the events are derived from two sources. First, there are the acts of human will, and second, there are the acts derived from the laws of physical nature. In thinking about this, he comes to realize that he has been thinking of the bullet's flight as caused by the laws of nature. In fact, the flight is not caused by the laws, but by things that obey laws. The law doesn't set the bullet in motion, but the bullet moves in accordance with the laws of nature. He concludes that "in the whole history of the universe the laws of Nature have never produced a single event." In other words, "The laws of Nature explain everything except the source of events." The issue then becomes one of identifying the source of events. The source is **God**. "It is His act alone that gives the laws any events to apply to."

Anne Gardner

Also See: Natural Law

D[avid] H[erbert] Lawrence (1885–1930)

Lawrence was a poet of controversy and rebellion. Lawrence's objections to the First World War, combined with his wife's German origins, led to trouble with English authorities. His novel *The Rainbow* (1915) was banned in England. His stories rebel against class-feelings, **tradition,** and habit while examining **nature**'s war with the artificial and mechanical and the distortion of **love**. Intuition, instinct, and intellect are highly favored in his novels. He creates a rhythm of meanings through psychological precision and intense poetic **symbolism**. Lewis generally disliked Lawrence's writings. In *Experiment in Criticism*, however, he indicated that readers can, to a certain degree, "enjoy" reading even the controversial **sex** scene of Lawrence's *Sons and Lovers*, recognizing it as a "good expression of what, in general, we think bad." Lewis later explained that, since we seek an enlargement of ourselves, "We therefore delight to enter into other men's beliefs (those, say, of Lucretius or Lawrence) even though we think them untrue."

Kristine Ottaway

Also See: Modernity, Poetry, Psychology, Reason, Romanticism, Truth

Bibliography

Draper, Ronald P. *D. H. Lawrence*. New York: Twayne, 1964.

"Le Roi S'Amuse"

Punch. 213 (October 1, 1947): 324 (under the pseudonym Nat Whilk). Revised and reprinted in *Poems* and *Collected Poems*.

Lewis imagined Jove creating the universe, the natural world, Aphrodite, Athena, and eventually man.

When Jove saw it all, he smiled though he knew he no longer could control all he had created.

Don W. King
Montreat College

Edward Tangye Lean (1911–1974)

Lean founded a literary group at **University College, Oxford,** for both dons and undergraduates called "The **Inklings**" in 1929. Both C. S. Lewis and **J. R. R. Tolkien** were members of this group. The meetings consisted of readings from unpublished manuscripts followed by comments and criticisms. While Lean's group soon died, the name "Inklings" was transferred to the informal group of Lewis's friends.

Bibliography

Lean, Edward. *Of Unsound Mind* (1932); *Storm in Oxford* (1933); *The Napoleonists* (1970)

"Learning in War-Time"

See entry on "None Other Gods: Culture in War Time"

"Leaving For Ever the Home of One's Youth"

Occasional Poets: An Anthology. Richard Adams (ed). Harmondsworth, Middlesex: Penguin Books, 1986: 101. Reprinted in *Collected Poems*.

This poem is a bittersweet remembrance of **Little Lea** and the delights Lewis and his brother **Warren Lewis** had there with each other in childhood combined with the blank reality of the present.

Don W. King
Montreat College

A Lectionary of Christian Prose from the Second Century to the Twentieth Century (Book Review)

Theology. XXXIX (December 1939): 467–68.

This anthology was designed to provide lessons for reading aloud at services where specific scriptural lessons are not dictated by the church. It included both Christian and pagan writers, forty of whom belong to the 19th century, nearly three times that of any other. Lewis lamented the exclusion of some at the expense of others but said that "to disagree is one of the pleasures of using an anthology." Bouquet and Lewis both suggested continued revision for a second edition.

Anne Gardner

Also See: Paganism

Bibliography

Bouquet, A. C. (ed). *A Lectionary of Christian Prose from the Second Century to the Twentieth Century.*

"Legion"

The Month. 13 (April 1955): 210. Revised and reprinted in *Poems* and *Collected Poems.*

This poem is a **prayer** begging **God** to see the real person praying as the one who turns to him at this present moment, not the myriad of other selves that in only a few minutes will feign to be real. While the speaker knows God will not override his **free will**, he implores him to see his real will in this moment.

Don W. King
Montreat College

"Let Us Pretend"

The Listener. XXXI (23 March 1944): 328. Retitled "Let's Pretend" and reprinted in *Beyond Personality* and *Mere Christianity.*

"Let Us Pretend" was the fifth installment of the "Beyond Personality" series in the BBC's *The Listener* magazine. The essay was first delivered on the radio March 21, 1944, by Lewis. In this essay, Lewis took the traditional idea of the "imitation of **Christ**" and put it into terms which are perhaps more understandable to moderns. When we say the words "Our Father" in the Lord's Prayer, Lewis said we are "dressing up as Christ," pretending to be Christ. Once we put on Christ's persona in this way it gives a new standard for judging our actions. There are many things that most of us do which, while our conscience does not definitely condemn, would not be appropriate if we are really trying to be sons and daughters of **God**. As Lewis said, "You will find several things going on in your mind that would not be going on if you were really a son of God. Well, stop them. Or you may realize that instead of saying your prayers you ought to be downstairs writing a letter or helping your wife with the dishes. Well go do it." Lewis pointed out that Christ is at our side helping turn our pretense into a **reality**. We are no longer thinking only in terms of morality, we are trying to catch the good infection from a Person. And this is in one way far easier than keeping rules.

Richard Purtill
Western Washington University

Also See: Ethics and Morality

Letter to Charles Moorman (Letter)

Moorman, Charles. *Arthurian Triptych: Mystic Materials in Charles Williams, C. S. Lewis, and T. S. Eliot.* Berkeley and Los Angeles: University of California Press, 1960: 161.

Excerpt from a letter in which Lewis explained his use of various mythological figures in ***That Hideous Strength*** (i.e., the Seven Bears of Logres and the Atlantean Circle) were "pure invention" and intended to serve as a means of providing appropriate background for the story. He also clarified that *Numinor*, or True West, is his misspelling of **J. R. R. Tolkien**'s *Numenor.*

Marjorie L. Mead
The Marion E. Wade Center

Letter to Don Luigi Pedrollo (Letter)

L'Amico die Buoni Fanciulli (Verona). I (1955): 75. Reprinted in *Letters: C. S. Lewis–Don Giovanni Calabria.*

A letter of condolence to Don Pedrollo (December 16, 1954) on the death of their mutual friend and Lewis's correspondent, **Don Giovanni Calabria**. Writing in Latin, Lewis expressed his grief and thanks Don Pedrollo for a photograph of Don Calabria that he had enclosed in his letter to Lewis. Don Pedrollo was a member of the Congregation at Verona, the Poor Servants of Divine Providence, which Don Calabria had founded in 1932. Lewis's letters to both Don Calabria and Don Pedrollo can be found in the published volume, ***Letters: C. S. Lewis–Don Giovanni Calabria***, edited and translated by **Martin Moynihan**.

Marjorie L. Mead
The Marion E. Wade Center

Letter to Dorothy L. Sayers (Letter)

Sayers, Dorothy L. "Ignorance and Dissatisfaction." *Latin Teaching.* XXVIII no. 3 (October 1952): 91.

Excerpt from Lewis's letter in which he gave suggestions for selections from secular Medieval Latin texts that contain, as **Dorothy L. Sayers** requested, "exciting, moving and memorable bits," useful in the teaching of Latin.

Marjorie L. Mead
The Marion E. Wade Center

Letter to J. B. Phillips (Letter)

Fifty-Two: A Journal of Books and Authors. I (Autumn 1957): 9.

Excerpt from a letter (August 3, 1943) that Lewis wrote to Phillips enthusiastically thanking him for his paraphrase of Colossians and encouraging him to continue on with his plan of paraphrasing all of the epistles.

Marjorie L. Mead
The Marion E. Wade Center

Letter to Mahmoud Manzalaoui (Letter)

Manzalaoui, M. "Lydgate and English Prosody." *Cairo Studies in English.* (1960): 94.

Lewis's response after reading a draft of this essay shows appreciation for the author's refinement of terminology but still disagreed with the author's conclusion. He believed that ultimately they are disagreeing over a matter of taste, and he encourages the author to publish the essay.

Marjorie L. Mead
The Marion E. Wade Center

Letter to Roger Lancelyn Green (Letter)

Green, Roger Lancelyn. *C. S. Lewis.* London: The Bodley Head, and New York: Henry Z. Walck, 1963: 26. The letter was originally dated December 28, 1938.

Lewis listed Olaf Stapledon's *Last and First Men* and an essay in J. B. S. Haldane's *Possible Worlds* as the initial impetus for his first volume in the space trilogy, *Out of the Silent Planet* (1938). Taking a mythological approach to interplanetary struggles, Lewis explained that he intentionally sought to bring his Christian **faith** to bear on the concepts of **space travel** and colonization.

Marjorie L. Mead
The Marion E. Wade Center

Letter to the Editor (Letter)

Delta: The Cambridge Literary Magazine. 23 (February 1961): 4–7.

In the March 9, 1960, issue of the Cambridge *Broadsheet* (VIII no. 17: [1]), C. S. Lewis offered a brief four-point critique of contemporary undergraduate **literary criticism** (see **"Undergraduate Criticism"**). In response to this critique, an anonymous article entitled "Professor C. S. Lewis and the English Faculty" (*Delta*, 22 [October 1960]: 6–17) took great offense at Lewis's assessment. Lewis, in turn, issued a ten-point response to the various accusations. He carefully distinguished between a "quarrel" and a "disputation," and disavows the charge that he has shown contempt for undergraduates. Lewis cautioned the author against ignoring his own bias, reminding him that he has thirty-six years of experience in observing undergraduate criticism that gave him a valid basis for judgment.

Marjorie L. Mead
The Marion E. Wade Center

Letter to the Editor (Letter)

English. XIV (Summer 1962): 75.

Lewis corrected the erroneous, though widespread, belief that his book *Experiment in Criticism* was intended to be a "veiled attack" on Dr. F. R. Leavis. Rather than targeting an individual, Lewis explained that he was responding to a "climate of critical opinion" that he found prevalent in his day.

Marjorie L. Mead
The Marion E. Wade Center

Letter to the Milton Society of America (Letter)

A Milton Evening in Honor of Douglas Bush and C. S. Lewis. Modern Language Association (28 December 1954): 14–15.

Honored for his contribution to Milton Studies, Lewis wrote this letter of appreciation to the Society as he could not be present at this occasion. In response to the Society's request for a list of his books as well as a comment about them, Lewis drew a common thread from amongst the diversity of his work. In this significant summary of his own literary expression, Lewis stated that "the imaginative man in me is older, more continuously operative, and in that sense more basic than either the religious writer or the critic."

Marjorie L. Mead
The Marion E. Wade Center

Also See: John Milton

Letter to the publisher on dust jacket of A Religious of C.S.M.V. [R. P. Lawson], *The Coming of the Lord: A Study in the Creed* (Letter)

London: A. R. Mowbray, 1953.

A wholehearted and warm recommendation of this work, Lewis indicated his genuine delight with *The Coming of the Lord,* declaring it to be the best book the author has done so far, as well as the best theological volume he has read for some time.

Marjorie L. Mead
The Marion E. Wade Center

Also See: Sister Penelope

Letter to the publisher on dust jacket of Arthur C. Clarke, *Childhood's End* (Letter)

London: Sidgwick and Jackson, 1954.

Excerpt (with minor editorial revisions) of a letter to Joy Davidman (December 22, 1953). In it, Lewis commended **Arthur C. Clarke** for rising above other **science fiction** writers with a powerful work of "grandeur," which exhibits an understanding that there may be "things that have a higher claim on humanity that its own 'survival.'"

Marjorie L. Mead
The Marion E. Wade Center

Letter to the publisher on dust jacket of C. S. Lewis, *Perelandra* (Letter)

Perelandra. New York: Macmillan, 1944.

Biographical details briefly describing his early childhood, wartime service, and conversion to **Christianity**. Lewis also comments on his love for conversation with close friends over beer, tea, and tobacco, as well as his delight in **walking tours**.

Marjorie L. Mead
The Marion E. Wade Center

Letter to the publisher on dust jacket of David Bolt, *Adam* (Letter)

London: J. M. Dent, 1960.

Warmly praising this story on the life of Adam, Lewis rejoiced in the author's delicate yet robust **imagination**, which retells this familiar narrative with a richness that does not overwhelm. He called the story "splendid" and without a single misstep.

Marjorie L. Mead
The Marion E. Wade Center

Letter to the publisher on dust jacket of E. R. Eddison, *The Menzentian Gate* (Letter)

London: Curwen Press, 1958. Retitled "A Tribute to E. R. Eddison" and reprinted in *Of This and Other Worlds* and *On Stories*.

E. R. Eddison's novels—*The Worm Ouroboros* (1922), *Styrbion the Strong* (1926), *Mistress of Mistresses* (1935), *A Fish Dinner in Memison* (1941), and *The Mezentian Gate* (1958)—became great favorites of Lewis. Lewis wrote that Eddison's novels gave him a new kind of imaginative experience. "Nowhere else," he concluded, "shall we meet this precise blend of hardness and luxury, of lawless speculation and sharply realised detail, of the cynical and the magnanimous."

Lewis's appreciation of Eddison led him to write a letter to Eddison's publisher that appeared as a tribute on the dust cover of *The Mezentian Gate*.

Lyle Smith
Biola University

Letter to the publisher on dust jacket of *Essays Presented to Charles Williams* (Letter)

London: Oxford University Press, 1947.

A listing of the contributors to this Festschrift volume, indicating first their professions, and second their religious affiliations. Lewis commented that the diversity represented here is but a token of the actual breadth of variety as represented by Williams' friends. This brief paragraph is a slight adaptation of the first few sentences of Lewis's Preface to this volume.

Marjorie L. Mead
The Marion E. Wade Center

Letter to the publisher on dust jacket of J. R. R. Tolkien, *The Fellowship of the Ring* (Letter)

London: George Allen and Unwin, 1954.

Favorably comparing this volume with Ariosto, Lewis enthusiastically applauded the multifaceted and complex imaginary world created by **J. R. R. Tolkien**. This world, Lewis marveled, is at once both comic and homely, and also **epic** and diabolic.

Marjorie L. Mead
The Marion E. Wade Center

Also See: Fantasy

Letter to the publisher on dust jacket of Mervyn Peake, *Titus Alone* (Letter)

London: Eyre and Spottiswoode, 1959.

Lewis pointed the reader towards the disquieting nightmarish world of Peake where "escape" and "home" have no settled meaning. Lewis commended both the delicacy and the force of Peake's prose and said this is a work that the reader will not easily forget.

Marjorie L. Mead
The Marion E. Wade Center

Letters, C. S. Lewis-Don Giovanni Calabria: A Study in Friendship

Moynihan, Martin (trans. and ed.). London: Collins, 1989. First US edition, Ann Arbor, MI: Servant Books, 1988.

This volume publishes thirty-five letters written in Latin (with English translations) between C. S. Lewis and **Don Giovanni Calabria**, a priest in Italy, and after his death in 1954, to Don Luigi Pedrollo, a priest in Calabria's church, the Poor Servants of Divine Providence Congregation in Verona. The letters span the years 1947–61, with no letters included from the years 1955–58. Seven of the letters are from Calabria to Lewis, twenty-one from Lewis to Calabria, and seven from Lewis to Pedrollo, with one (December 5, 1954) to Calabria from Lewis the day after Calabria's death. Of the twenty-eight letters from Lewis in the book, twenty-two were written from **Magdalen College**, **Oxford**, and the last five to Pedrollo were written from **Magdalene College**, **Cambridge**.

The correspondence began in 1947 after Calabria had read Lewis's ***The Screwtape Letters*** (Le Lettere di Berlicche) and was so attracted by it that he immediately wrote Lewis (September 1); Lewis's first letter to Calabria was sent about a week later. When this work was published, the existence of the letters had been known already for a long while. Two Italian articles about Calabria in the 1950s mentioned his correspondence with Lewis, and one was reprinted in the London journal *The Month* and titled "God's Care-Taker." In **Walter Hooper**'s bibliography of the writings of Lewis (in *Light on C. S. Lewis*, 1965, and *C. S. Lewis at the Breakfast Table*, 1979; revised 1991) there is listed an "Open Letter to Fr. Berlicche" (1955), which is Lewis's first letter to Pedrollo.

The letters were edited and translated by Lewis's friend and former student Martin Moynihan, who learned about their existence at the **Marion E. Wade Center** (Wheaton College), from Dr. Barbara Reynolds, the distinguished scholar of **Dorothy L. Sayers**. Moynihan first wrote about the existence of the letters and his inspiration to translate them in the 1985 issue of *VII: An Anglo-American Literary Review*, an annual journal devoted to the writings and influence of Lewis, **George MacDonald**, **J. R. R. Tolkien**, **G. K. Chesterton**, Dorothy L. Sayers, **Charles Williams**, and **Owen Barfield**. This article was later published in 1987 as *The Latin Letters of C. S. Lewis* and contains a valuable afterword by Lyle W. Dorsett.

This collection of letters enhances Lewis's already deserved reputation as a loyal friend, a Christian of strong **faith** and integrity, and a man who was willing to listen, encourage, and sometimes disagree with those whom he cared about. Lyle W. Dorsett wrote that the letters also "remind us of how eclectic Lewis was in his learning and reading." Lewis not only corresponded with Calabria and Pedrollo in Latin, a "dead language," but the letters also show his wide interests in **theology**, **philosophy**, history, and especially literature. There are quotes and references to Virgil (*The Aeneid*), Thomas à Kempis (*The Imitation of Christ*), **Dante** (*Inferno*), Charles Williams, Bernard of Morlaix (c. 1140, a French monk, poet, and hymn writer), Horace, and the Latin Vulgate.

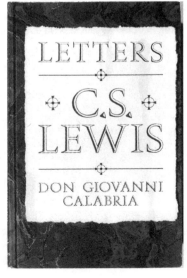

An interesting element of the letters is Lewis's more direct reliance on the **Bible** than was usual in his books. There are over thirty direct or partial quotes, references, allusions, and "echoes" (Moynihan, notes) to the Holy Scripture in this collection. Among others, Lewis mentioned Jesus' warnings about "wars and rumours of wars," Uzziah's touching the ark of the covenant without authority, and Saint Paul's classic statement about love "bearing and believing all things." In Letter 17 to Calabria (December 25, 1951), Lewis wrote that he had, after a long time, finally believed in the forgiveness of sins with his "whole heart"; he later adds that Scripture (Philippians 4:4) has "bidden us to rejoice and always rejoice." In Letter 32 to Pedrollo (December 15, 1959), Lewis told of the return of the fatal cancer that was to kill his wife, **Joy Davidman Lewis,** a few months later and then added that even in his grief he and his wife experienced the truth and joy of the beatitude in Matthew 5: "For has he not promised comfort to those who mourn?"

Lewis mentioned his own books several times in his letters to Calabria, including one of his space novels, ***Out of the Silent Planet***. He had evidently sent Calabria ("Father John") a copy of the story ("my tale recently translated into Italian"), and in Letter 16 (December 13, 1951) he wrote rather surprisingly, "I do not know whether you will like this kind of trifle. But if you do not, perhaps some boy or girl will like it from among your 'good children'." In Letter 31 (March 28, 1959), Lewis mentioned his work ***The Four Loves*** to Pedrollo and asked for prayers that "God grant me to say things helpful to salvation, or at least not harmful."

Prayer and spiritual matters were what Lewis and Calabria wrote about most, and it is well known that prayer and its problems was a major concern for Lewis his entire Christian life. In Letter 20 (January 5, 1953) Lewis wrote to Calabria and mentioned the problems he was having in writing "a book about private prayers for the use of the laity" (later ***Letters to Malcolm***), and asked for prayer for himself because "I find many difficulties nor do I definitely know whether God wishes me to complete this task or not." By Letter 23 (January 5 or June 1953), Lewis was still having difficulty with the project, and expressed his concerns to Calabria about the nature of petitionary prayer: "Two models of prayer seem to be put before us in the New Testament which are not easily reconcilable with each other." Lewis later brought his questions about this type of prayer to a minister's society in Oxford with an address titled "**Petitionary Prayer: A Problem Without An Answer**" (December 9, 1953, later reprinted in *Christian Reflections*).

While Lewis did not agree with "Father John" about all Roman Catholic doctrines and teachings, the two men were in agreement about the prejudices of both Protestants and Catholics toward each other, and shared a common interest and love for Holy Communion, liturgy, and the liturgical calendar. Calabria's primary concern was in seeking unity among all Christians, and both he and Lewis saw sin as the cause of this schism. From their letters one can see Lewis's emphasis on evangelism ("bravely and sweetly bring[ing the] brethren to the Gospel of Christ"), and both were intensely concerned about compassionate charity and service ("this unity of love and action") to people of all races, creeds, and social backgrounds. In Letter 10 (January 14, 1949), Lewis referred to his "aged mother" as his "daily care" and asked Calabria to pray that he have peace in learning to care for her. This was undoubtedly a reference to Mrs. **Janie King Moore**, the lady whom Lewis took into his household after her son was killed in World War I.

Lewis's letters to Pedrollo were briefer and less personal than the ones to Calabria, except for the references to his wife Joy. He expressed great grief and concern over Calabria's death (Letter 29, December 16, 1954), and thanked Pedrollo for the photograph of Calabria that he had sent. In Letter 30 (January 19, 1959), Lewis thanked Pedrollo for a biography of Calabria, and in his last letter (April 8, 1961), he shared his grief over the death of Joy: "I know that you pour forth your prayers both for my most dearly-longed-for wife and also for me who—now bereaved and as it were halved—journey on, through this Vale of Tears, alone."

Perry C. Bramlett
C. S. Lewis for the Local Church

Also See: Roman Catholicism

Bibliography

Hooper, Walter. *C. S. Lewis: A Companion and Guide.* San Francisco: HarperCollins, 1996.

Reynolds, Barbara. "Review of Don Calabria, C. S. Lewis: Una giota insolita. Lettere tra un Prete Cattolico e un Laico Anglicano, edited by Luciano Squizzato, translated by Patriza Morelli, with a Preface by Walter Hooper." *VII: An Anglo-American Literary Review.* 13 (1996): 104–6.

Sarrocco, Clara. "The Latin Letters, Recalled." *CSL: The Bulletin of the New York C. S. Lewis Society.* 20 no. 8 (June 1989): 1–4.

Letters of C. S. Lewis (1966)

Edited with a memoir by W. H. Lewis. London: Geoffrey Bles, 1966. First US edition, New York: Harcourt Brace & World, 1966. Revised and expanded by Walter Hooper. London: Font Paperbacks, 1988. US edition, San Diego: Harcourt Brace & Company, 1993.

Letters of C. S. Lewis is not a random sampling of important Lewis letters, but a deliberate selection of letters and diary entries originally prepared by Lewis's brother, **Warren H. Lewis**. When C. S. Lewis died in 1963, **Jocelyn "Jock" Gibb** approached Warren and asked him to write a biography of his brother. Warren agreed. He used *The Lewis Family Papers: Memoirs of the Lewis Family 1850–1930* as his basis, an eleven-volume collection of letters, diary entries, and family papers he had assembled some thirty years earlier, at the time their father died. In order to prepare the new biography, he retyped letters and diary entries, interspersed them with explanatory notes and commentaries, and added a lengthy memoir, all running nearly a thousand pages.

Warren Lewis did his work with a clear purpose in mind: "In making this selection from my brother's correspondence, I have kept in mind not only those interested in the literary and religious aspects of his mind, but also—and perhaps more urgently—those who want to know what manner of man he was, and who may derive from these letters some idea of the liveliness, the colour and wit displayed throughout his life by this best of brothers and friends."

Warren Lewis titled his book *C. S. Lewis: A Biography* and turned it over to Gibb, who assigned Christopher Derrick as editor of the work. Gibb and Derrick changed Warren Lewis's book substantially. First, they revisioned the biography as a collection of letters. Second, they cut the contents, including the memoir, in half. Finally, they added an assortment of letters from others.

When Warren Lewis saw an advanced copy of the revised book, he was outraged. He felt cheated that such radical changes had been made without his input. He regretted that so much material had been cut and, in particular, regretted the loss of the earliest letters, those of Lewis's childhood. His biggest complaint, recorded in his diary (April 16, 1966) was the addition of letters that are "philosophical, or in other words unintelligible to the ordinary reader." In adding these letters, Warren Lewis felt that his purpose of designing a book of interest to the general reader had been seriously violated.

Despite this somewhat unhappy history, *Letters of C. S. Lewis* is enormously valuable and richly interesting. The memoir by Warren Lewis is clear, compact, and extremely well written. It is largely descriptive rather than interpretive: "My own contribution to the world's understanding of my brother must be limited: I do not propose in this memoir to give a full account of his work and still less any evaluation of it. I offer only my own memories of Jack, as man, friend, and brother." Warren describes his relationship with his brother as an intimate friendship that offered him "the greatest happiness" of his life.

In discussing their childhood together, Warren credits the wet Irish weather for the blossoming of his brother's creativity. Forced to play indoors much of the time, they "turned to pencils, paper, chalk and paintboxes." Together they created the imaginary world of **Boxen**, and out of this grew Lewis's first novel, written while he was twelve years old.

Their childhood was shaken by two significant events: the death of their mother in 1908 and, subsequently, their being sent off to boarding school. Of their mother's death, Lewis wrote, "With my mother's death all settled happiness, all that was tranquil and reliable, disappeared from my life.... It was sea and islands now; the great continent had sunk like Atlantis."

Of his brother's antipathy to school, Warren notes, "The fact is that he should never have been sent to a public school at all. Already, at fourteen, his intelligence was such that he would have fitted in better among undergraduates than among schoolboys; and by his temperament he was bound to be a misfit, a heretic, an object of suspicion within the collective-minded and standardising Public School system."

Despite honest consideration of these and other hardships, Warren's memoir emphasizes the exuberance that was so great a part of his brother's nature. In speaking of his work as a **tutor** and **scholar**, he writes, "Jack was one of those rare and fortunate people whose idea of recreation overlaps and even coincides with their necessary work." And in speaking of the quality of his life,

Warren notes, "He was a man with an outstanding gift for pastime with good company, for laughter and the love of friends—a gift which found full-scope in any number of holidays and **walking tours**, the joyous character of his response to these being well-conveyed in his letters."

The letters themselves fall rather clearly into two sections. The first half (1916–32) is comprised of family letters, addressed to **Albert Lewis** or Warren Lewis, and some few to Lewis's childhood friend **Arthur Greeves**. These letters show Lewis the student, the soldier, and the atheist. The last half (1933–63) contains letters addressed to students, friends, and readers, including fellow **Inklings Owen Barfield** and John Wain, and authors **T. S. Eliot** and **Dorothy L. Sayers**. The topics are as varied as the people to whom they are addressed.

From the start, Lewis writes about the books he is reading. The very first letter mentions his astonishment at discovering **George MacDonald**'s *Phantastes*. Lewis seems to read absolutely everybody. He mentioned (among others) **Aristotle**, Austen, Balzac, Boswell, Blake, the Brontës, Bunyan, Burroughs, **Chaucer**, Coleridge, **Dante**, Descartes, Dickens, Dostoevsky, **Kipling**, **Milton**, Trollope, **Yeats**, Virgil, and **Wells**. Letters to his family have a surprisingly literary quality and often contain extensive descriptions of which edition he bought, where he purchased it, and how much he paid for it.

From these early letters we also learn a great deal about Lewis's experience during World War I, a part of his life often overlooked or underplayed by his biographers. Lewis joined the army on June 8, 1917, was gazetted into the Third Somerset Light Infantry, and arrived on the front trenches in France on his nineteenth birthday. Although these wartime experiences were of lasting importance, it was clear to Lewis that soldiering would not be his calling in life: "I make every effort to cling to the old life of books, hoping that I may save my soul alive and not become a great, empty headed, conceited military prig" (38).

During this early period, there is relatively little mention of spiritual things. In one particularly telling section, Lewis observed that **God** seems absent: "The trouble about God is that he is like a person who never acknowledges one's letters and so, in time, one comes to the conclusion either that he does not exist or that you have got the address wrong." Lewis converted to theism in 1929 and to **Christianity** in 1931. It was a long struggle for him, and in his autobiography he explains that when he knelt for the first time to confess that God was God, he felt "the most dejected and reluctant convert in all England."

From this point, the letters clearly demonstrate Lewis's growing faith in God. He answered questions and concerns of others, and constantly reflects upon the meaning of the Christian life. This growing presence of spiritual concerns may be the only thing these later letters have in common: the proliferation of topics is testimony to the breadth of Lewis's interests and the fertility of his mind.

In 1993, Harcourt Brace brought out a "revised and enlarged" version of *Letters of C. S. Lewis*. It contains a lengthy introduction by **Walter Hooper**, who has made hundreds of minor changes in punctuation, capitalization, and wording. Many letters are slightly lengthened as well, perhaps to undo some of the editing that Warren's original biography received. Hooper has also added eighty-nine letters, supplied missing dates, identified some formerly anonymous recipients, and provided a number of explanatory annotations. Perhaps the most useful of all are the two new indexes.

Plans are under way for a complete letter collection to be published as *Collected Letters*. It is expected to be a six-volume set.

Diana Pavlac Glyer
Azusa Pacific University

Also See: Atheism, Spirituality

Bibliography

Kilby, Clyde S., and Marjorie Lamp Mead. *Brothers and Friends: The Diaries of Major Warren Hamilton Lewis.* San Francisco: Harper & Row, 1982.

Lewis, C. S. *They Stand Together: The Letters of C. S. Lewis to Arthur Greeves (1914–1963); C. S. Lewis: Letters to Children; Letters to an American Lady; The Latin Letters of C. S. Lewis*

Letters to a Member of the Church of the Covenant (Letters)

Encounter with Light. Lynchburg, VA: Church of the Covenant, June 1961: 11–16, 20. The three letters from C. S. Lewis (dated December 14, 1950; December 23, 1950, and

April 17, 1951) were later published anonymously in an article, "Encounter with Light." *His.* (December 1968) and for the first time under the name Sheldon Vanauken in pamphlet form by the Marion E. Wade Center, Wheaton College, IL (1976).

These letters are a key part of **Sheldon Vanauken**'s spiritual journey from **atheism** to **Christianity**. An American studying in **Oxford**, Vanauken first wrote to Lewis while he was still considering whether to believe in **God**, Vanauken sought Lewis's counsel because Lewis had earlier made a "similar leap" from unbelief to **faith**. Lewis replied that their journeys differed in that Vanauken *wanted* to believe Christianity is true, but he had hoped it was *not*. In his second letter, Vanauken explained his dilemma: he couldn't believe without faith, but he couldn't have faith unless he believed. Then he asked, "Why does God expect so much of us?" In his second letter, Lewis compared the dilemma Vanauken raised to the act of swimming (you can't swim without supporting yourself in the water, and you can't support yourself in the water unless you can swim). But in spite of this contradiction, Lewis said, we *do* swim. He continued that while there is no demonstrative proof of Christianity, there are indicators that show that aspects of our nature are more than simply material and temporal. A bit frightened by Lewis's final paragraph that warned that the **Holy Spirit** was in pursuit of him, Vanauken took several months of careful consideration before he was ready to write to Lewis on March 29: "I choose to believe . . . in **Christ**, my Lord and my God." Lewis replied, "My prayers are answered." He offered a few words of encouragement on Vanauken's continuing struggle to find demonstrative certainty, and then, "Be busy learning to pray. . . . Blessings on you and a hundred welcomes. Make use of me in any way you please: and let us pray for each other always."

Marjorie L. Mead
The Marion E. Wade Center

Letters to an American Lady

Kilby, Clyde S. (ed). Grand Rapids, MI: Eerdmans, 1967. First UK edition, London: Hodder and Stoughton, 1969.

In October of 1950, Lewis answered a letter from an American lady—Mary Willis Shelburne of Washington, D.C.—and began a regular correspondence lasting thirteen years. This book is a collection of 138 letters to Shelburne: 132 from Lewis, one from **Joy Davidman Lewis**, three from **Warren Lewis**, and two from **Walter Hooper**. Shelburne was a widow three years older than Lewis. She was a journalist, a poet, and a critic, whose published works include a review of *Surprised by Joy*. She and Lewis never met.

As **Clyde Kilby** points out in his thoughtful preface, these are not literary letters, but casual, personal, even pastoral ones. Shelburne was somewhat fretful and expressed constant concern about her health, her work, and her job. In return, Lewis offered her a regular stream of encouragement. They demonstrate a very sincere, very personal **faith**, and are full of telling details of Lewis's day-to-day life.

Lewis wrote the first of these letters when he was fifty-one years old, and they are the letters of his older years. At one point, he referred to himself as "an old fogey," and, in another place, "a tired traveler, near the journey's end." He suffered from rheumatism, sinus headaches, muscle spasms in his back, anemia, kidney problems, and osteoporosis. He further observed, "I'm afraid as we grow older life consists more and more in either giving up things or waiting for them to be taken from us." And yet these letters are not cheerless; in fact, the greater part of them consist in cheering and encouraging Shelburne. Even the most dire topic is given the most positive point of view including death.

Despite his bouts with failing health, Lewis continued to write and publish at an astonishing rate: *English Literature in the Sixteenth Century; Surprised by Joy; Till We Have Faces; Reflections on the Psalms; The Four Loves; Studies in Words; An Experiment in Criticism ; A Grief Observed; The Discarded Image; Letters to Malcolm*. The last four books in the Chronicles of Narnia were written during this period, as were several collections of essays. Yet these letters are more likely to contain musing about cats or the weather or holiday plans rather than even scant mention of the books he is writing. Although he neglected to mention his own literary efforts, Lewis took time to make frequent, thoughtful critique of the poetry and reviews that Shelburne submitted to him.

During this time, Lewis left **Magdalen College, Oxford,** to take the newly formed Chair of Medieval and Renaissance English at **Magdalene College, Cambridge**. Lewis wrote to Shelburne that the move would result in more pay for less work. He also noted that he

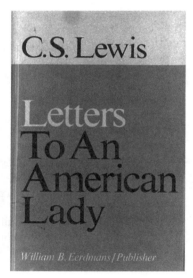

expected to like Magdalene better than Magdalen because it was smaller, and his colleagues were "so old-fashioned, and pious, and gentle and conservative—unlike this leftist, atheistic, cynical, hard-boiled, huge Magdalen."

These are also the years during which he met and married and lost **Joy Davidman Lewis**. The first hint about their relationship appears in a letter of October 20, 1956, when he wrote about Joy's "sudden illness," which caused him much distress. One month later he wrote again: "I may soon be, in rapid succession, a bridegroom and a widower. There may, in fact, be a deathbed marriage. I can hardly describe the state of mind I live in at present—except that all emotion, with me, is periodically drowned in sheer tiredness, deep lakes of stupor."

The tide turned, however, and Joy gathered strength as the cancer went into remission. On June 6, 1958, she wrote to Shelburne in Lewis's stead, as he was busy with examinations at Cambridge. However, Joy's cancer returned about a year later. Lewis told Shelburne, "Apparently the wonderful recovery Joy made in 1957 was only a reprieve, not a pardon. The last X-ray check reveals cancerous spots returning in many of her bones." Joy died on July 13, 1960.

What we learn about Lewis from these letters is not startling, but it is significant. He wrote of his fears: "[P]overty frightens me more than anything else except large spiders and the tops of cliffs." He wrote about grief: "If you must weep, weep: a good, honest howl! I suspect we—and especially, my sex—don't cry enough now-a-days." He wrote of his own limitations: "I am intensely stupid about everything that might be called business." But on the whole, these letters were very personal, filled with comments on the weather, reflections on the state of his health, observations about his cats, assurances that she is in his prayers, requests that she might be so kind as to remember him when she prayed.

In the end, the existence of these letters in the first place may be the most remarkable thing about them. Lewis loathed letter writing: in *Surprised by Joy* he defined the good life as one in which no letters come, and in a letter to **Arthur Greeves** he grumbled, "The daily letter writing without [my brother Warren] to help me is appalling—an hour and a half or two hours every morning before I can get to my own work." Kilby rightly described Lewis as a man who "could have found a whole bag of reasons to justify pitching his mail into the wastepaper basket." And yet Lewis faithfully wrote hundreds of letters to people he did not know and had little or no chance of ever meeting. Why? Lewis wrote, again to Arthur Greeves, "My correspondence involves a great number of theological letters already which *can't* be neglected because they are answers to people in great need of help & often in great misery." In his commitment to Mary Willis Shelburne, Lewis demonstrated more than anything else the charity that he saw as inextricable from his commitment to **Christ**.

Diana Pavlac Glyer
Azusa Pacific University

Bibliography

Lewis, C. S. *Letters of C. S. Lewis; They Stand Together: The Letters of C. S. Lewis to Arthur Greeves (1914–1963); C. S. Lewis: Letters to Children; The Latin Letters of C. S. Lewis*

Letters to Malcolm: Chiefly on Prayer

London: Geoffrey Bles, 1964. First US edition, New York: Harcourt, Brace & World, 1964.

This is the last book Lewis wrote; written in April and May of 1963, it was published in 1964, several months after his death. He began a book on **prayer** in 1952 and worked at it in 1953, but he gave it up early in 1954. A decade later he thought of constructing the book as a series of letters to an imaginary correspondent. Once he found the right form, the book came easily and successfully—indeed, many readers regard it as the best of his theological works.

To make the correspondence effective required developing a clear and fairly rounded character for Malcolm. In this Lewis was so successful that many readers find it hard to believe that there was no actual Malcolm or that the "I" of the letters, referred to below for convenience as "Lewis," is a persona, not the real-life Lewis. Malcolm is imagined as a longtime friend, since their undergraduate years, with whom Lewis had corresponded on previous occasions. He is

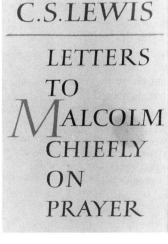

a layman, probably a teacher, a scientist, middle-aged, Anglican, less High-Church than Lewis and less flexible and accepting of new approaches. He is married to Betty; they have a son named George. Despite many of his differences with the real-life Lewis, the persona does express ideas and positions held by the real Lewis, and many—though not all—of his biographical details fit Lewis in 1963.

The fiction is sustained by giving the relationship between "Lewis" and "Malcolm" a history—Lewis mentions places they were together (a pub, the Forest of Dean, Edinburgh) and a friend named Bill who once asked them for a loan—and by suggesting that Malcolm is receiving and replying to Lewis's letters: Lewis quotes from Malcolm's replies, sometimes disagrees with Malcolm, answers his questions, makes an appointment for dinner, and arranges a weekend visit to Malcolm and Betty's home.

Lewis's choice of form makes the book very enjoyable to read. But it also affects the expression of ideas. It serves to remove Lewis from a position of claiming authority. He does not have to come across as an expert on prayer, as someone qualified to write a book on the subject (he says, tongue in cheek, in the twelfth letter, he would never try that). These are "just letters" (not even a "correspondence"), in which he can share experiences, raise questions, and suggest possible answers, without the need for a fully developed treatment of the entire subject.

The form also allows him to give dramatic immediacy to what in a different kind of book on prayer might remain just abstract issues. After a discussion in the seventh letter of the relation between petitionary prayer and determinism, Lewis creates a situation in which George is ill, perhaps seriously ill; the diagnosis awaits the results of medical tests. The eighth letter opens with a comment on the difference this situation makes, as one asks not whether **God** hears petitionary prayers, but will he grant prayers in a particular concrete instance. Lewis brings out the feelings of anxiety, anguish, and abandonment such a situation creates and comments that they are to be expected and are not evidences of defective **faith**.

The use of an imaginary correspondence is a traditional form, one Lewis had used before in *The Screwtape Letters* and in the letter at the end of *Out of the Silent Planet*. Lewis expected readers to recognize and accept the correspondence for what it is, a literary convention, and to enter the form imaginatively, accepting the pretense that Malcolm, Betty, and George and their problems and anxieties are real. Such imaginative involvement takes the reader outside the self to share imaginatively the experience of others. The book's ideas about prayer and the Christian life are not conveyed as concepts but embedded in the events and activities of personal life stories.

Some highlights of the book can be noted. The opening letters discuss practical matters regarding prayer. Letter 1 discusses liturgy, explaining the value of a common, stable liturgy and expressing Lewis's dislike of change and novelty in worship. In Letter 2 Lewis says that the staple of his devotions is prayer in his own words, though ready-made prayers also are important for sound doctrine, looking beyond oneself and providing an element of ceremony. Best of all, however, is wordless prayer, when one is in top form and can achieve it. Letter 3 discusses when to pray (don't wait until bedtime, when one is too tired to concentrate) and where (any place will do—on a train or walking in a park—though a place that permits kneeling is preferable).

The fourth letter, addressing the question of why we should make our requests known to God when he already knows our needs, develops Lewis's idea of prayer as unveiling (see also Letters 15 and 21, and compare with Orual's veil in *Till We Have Faces* and the reference to the nakedness of the soul in prayer in the fourth of *The Screwtape Letters*). Letter 5 offers Lewis's "festoonings," or glosses, on the phrases in the Lord's Prayer, the private elaborations that clarify and enrich words that can become overly familiar.

A group of letters deals with petitionary prayer, which, Lewis emphasizes, is recommended by precept and example in the New Testament. Letter 7 replies to the arguments often advanced against petitionary prayers. Letter 8 moves from abstract petitions to the concrete instance of George's illness, discussed above. And Letter 9 confronts the problem of time (it appears also in Letter 20): God and his acts are not in time and that prayer, so all relations between God and man, requires a way of thinking different from our usual causal thinking. Letter 10 suggests that for prayers to be heard, to be "taken into account," is more important than for them to be granted. And Letter 11 discusses the discordance between promises that whatever is requested in prayer will be granted and the fact that requests (even

Christ's) sometimes are not granted.

Letter 20 deals with praying for the dead (which seems natural, even inevitable, to Lewis) and with **Purgatory**. Lewis says he believes in Purgatory—not the 16th-century idea of a place of torturous punishment for sins committed and thus a place to be escaped as soon as possible, but the Purgatory of **Dante** and Cardinal Newman, a place of cleansing, of purification, which prepares one for entering Paradise and which involves suffering but not punishment, so that one would not wish it to be shorter than it needs to be.

Other letters discuss the importance of seeing **Christianity** as different from **religion** (6), the contrast between the undeveloped type of prayer many Christians settle for and the nearly unattainable level of the mystics (12), the implications of the fact that although we pray to God, it is also God who gives us the words to pray (13–14), the process by which Lewis prepares himself to enter the presence of God in prayer (15), the use of images in prayer (16), the prayer of worship or adoration (17), penitential prayers (18), Holy Communion (19), and the irksomeness of prayer, which is a result of our imperfections—if we were perfected, prayer would be a delight, not just a duty (21).

The book closes with a letter disagreeing with "liberal" Christianity and its rejection of the supernatural elements. Lewis's acceptance of the supernatural leads into a discussion of the resurrection of the body, which Lewis explains as a resurrection not of the material components of the body but of the senses, through which matter enters our experience and becomes soul. But these thoughts, like much else in this book, Lewis says he offers as guesses, not authoritative doctrine; if they are not true, something better will be.

Peter J. Schakel
Hope College

Bibliography

Houston, James M. "The Prayer Life of C. S. Lewis." *Crux.* 24 no. 1 (March 1988): 2–10.

Meilaender, Gilbert. *The Taste for the Other: The Social and Ethical Thought of C. S. Lewis.* Grand Rapids, MI: Eerdmans, 1978.

Schakel, Peter J. *Reason and Imagination in C. S. Lewis: A Study of Till We Have Faces.* Grand Rapids, MI: Eerdmans, 1984.

Smith, Robert Houston. *Patches of Godlight: The Pattern of Thought of C. S. Lewis.* Athens: University of Georgia Press, 1981.

Letters to the publisher on the dust jacket (a

portion of one letter on the inside front flap and the portion of another on the back dust jacket) of C. S. Lewis, *Till We Have Faces: A Myth Retold* **(Letter)**

London: Geoffrey Bles, 1956.

Lewis explained that this story had lived in his **imagination** for almost forty years until recently when the right literary form became evident to him. In his second letter, he discussed his reinterpretation of Apuleius's first telling of the **Cupid and Psyche** myth in the Latin novel *Metamorphoses* and stated that this story was simply a "source" rather than an "influence" on his own version.

Marjorie L. Mead
The Marion E. Wade Center

Letters to Young Churches: A Translation of the New Testament Epistles (Preface)

Phillips, J. B. *Letters to Young Churches: A Translation of the New Testament Epistles.* London: Geoffrey Bles, 1947. Retitled "Modern Translations of the Bible" and reprinted in *God in the Dock, Undeceptions,* and *First and Second Things.*

In this preface to a translation of the New Testament epistles into modern English by J. B. Phillips, C. S. Lewis defended Saint Paul's writings from attacks by liberal theologians and chided traditionalists who believe that the King James Version is the only legitimate translation of the **Bible**. According to Lewis, the primary duty of a good translation is to be clear, and the antiquated language of the "Authorized Version" often obscures the real meaning of the text; thus, new translations such as this one are both useful and appropriate.

John G. West, Jr.

Bibliography

Lewis, C. S. "The Literary Impact of the Authorised Version"

Albert James Lewis (1863–1929)

The father of C. S. Lewis, Albert James Lewis was born in 1863 in Cork, Ireland. He was the youngest of four sons of Richard Lewis, a partner in a Belfast shipping firm. His sensitive nature caused his father to send him to a boarding school where he was fortunate in befriending the headmaster, **W. T. Kirkpatrick**, who later in life would tutor his sons. After his **education** was complete, Albert apprenticed to a solicitor in Belfast and was soon practicing law successfully on his own. He was a verbally gifted man with a deep sense of integrity, equally respected on the prosecution or the defense. The story was told that when faced in his office with a prospective client that he felt was probably guilty,

he would reply: "In fact, then, you want me to use my legal knowledge to help you to commit a swindle. Get out of this office." He could be both generous and stingy with his money and his talents, and he lived in constant fear of bankruptcy. He was a voracious reader and even had an interest in writing that he did not pursue. His two sons inherited a great many of his characteristics.

For seven years Albert courted Flora Hamilton, daughter of the rector of the local Anglican church. She felt **friendship** for Albert but did not feel any romantic ardor and freely told him so. Albert did not give up and they were finally married on August 29, 1894, by her father in the parish church at Dundela. Their eldest son, **Warren Hamilton Lewis,** was born on June 16, 1895, and their youngest son, Clive Staples Lewis, on November 29, 1898.

Albert's life and relationship to his sons was forever altered for the worse when **Flora Hamilton Lewis** died of cancer in August 1908, an event that caused him great grief and left him unable to communicate with his sons. The local Irish accent by which Albert pronounced the word "potato" caused the boys to irreverently label him "the Pudaita-bird"—and eventually simply "P." C. S. Lewis said of his father during this period of their life, "His intense desire for my total confidence co-existed with an inability to listen (in any strict sense) to what I said." Albert, longing to communicate better with his sons, tried hard. But he forced their confidences so roughly, all the while reading into their words something other than what they said, that he destroyed all communication with them.

When C. S. Lewis returned wounded from the trenches of World War I, he begged Albert to visit him. Albert, disliking any break from his routine, did not—further dividing father from son. Yet Albert unstintingly supported his youngest son through extra years at **Oxford** that allowed Jack to secure a fellowship at **Magdalen College**. C. S. Lewis was grateful for this, but the fact did not stop him from using the money that Albert sent for his use alone to support his adopted family of Mrs. **Janie Moore** and her daughter. Later in life C. S. Lewis considered it one of his greatest failings to properly relate to his father. Albert died from cancer in the summer of 1929 at his home in Belfast.

James Prothero

Also See: Dundela Villas, Little Lea, Love, Malvern, Maureen Moore, Pain

Bibliography

Green, Roger L., and Walter Hooper. *C. S. Lewis: A Biography*. San Diego: Harcourt, 1974.

Lewis, C. S. *Surprised by Joy*.

Sayer, George. *Jack: C. S. Lewis and His Times*. San Francisco: Harper, 1988.

"A Gallery of Thumbnail Sketches of Close and Influential Family and Friends of C. S. Lewis." *Christian History*. 4 no. 3 (1985): 12–15.

C. S. Lewis: The Man

C. S. Lewis was quite unlike the person described in some recent biographies and hardly to be recognized as the man depicted in *Shadowlands* and other films. During the years of our **friendship,** which lasted from the summer of 1934, when I first became his pupil, to the autumn of 1961, he was rarely unhappy or depressed. He was usually great fun, witty and amusing, often boisterously so. And in spite of a workload that would have weighed down most men, his days were organized so that he lived a balanced life. While he worked for most, sometimes the whole of each morning, he liked, after a midday meal that consisted of bread, cheese, and a glass of beer, to take some exercise in the open air. This usually took the form of brisk walking, but he might also chop wood or saw logs on the grounds of his house, **the Kilns**. At about four o'clock he liked to have a cup or two of strong tea. Then more work, tutorial, or literary or spiritual reading until it was time to prepare for dinner in Hall, the dining room of **Magdalen College**. Here he ate very fast, even voraciously, talked and argued, and drank more beer. The evening might be spent talking with friends or writing. During the course of the evening he liked to be refreshed once or twice by more strong tea. I think he normally went to bed fairly early, perhaps by eleven and usually went to sleep at once.

When did he pray? I don't know what he did at **Oxford**, but when staying with me in Malvern it was for about an hour from six to seven every evening. He explained that he did not like to leave it until he was too tired to do it properly. He also prayed early in the morning, but not, I think, for so long. He asked to have in his bedroom "a **Bible** in any translation."

Some biographers give the impression that he drank too much and was not always sober. They do not quote any evidence. This is not true in my experience or in that of **Martin Moynihan** and John Lawlor, friends of his with whom I have discussed it. He often refused an extra glass. I remember his saying: "No more, George, or I shall be drunk, and that must never be." Americans and others who are shocked that he should have drunk alcohol at all should be reminded that it was part of the culture in which he was brought up. The Belfast water supply was of doubtful quality, so many people drank beer. Jugs of beer, from which boys could help themselves, were on the tables at **Malvern College**, and it was customary for undergraduates at Magdalen to drink beer or cider at dinner in Hall. Some people are surprised at the amount of time he spent in pubs. He used a local pub as a sort of man's club where he could talk, argue, and discuss literary, theological, and philosophical questions without domestic interruptions.

He was a fairly heavy smoker, a habit that became established long before its serious damage to health was understood. I remember a conversation in the 1950s in which his doctor, **Humphrey Havard,** spoke of the link between smoking and cancer and other diseases. "Do you think I should give it up?" Lewis asked Havard. "Yes, Jack," replied Havard, "if you can without excessive strain and difficulty." Lewis tried several times, especially during Lent, but never succeeded. He found that not smoking made him uncontrollably bad-tempered; so for the sake of his mental and even moral balance he continued.

Much of his conversation was about the books he had read or was rereading. He was immensely enthusiastic about a wide range of books and **poetry**. He spoke with often striking freshness about the great classics such as Homer, Pindar, **Plato**, Virgil, **Dante**, **Spenser**, **Wordsworth,** and **Keats**, but also even more excitedly about writers who were unfashionable or about whom I had never heard, such as Coventry Patmore and **Charles Williams**.

The film *Shadowlands* conveys an altogether misleading impression of his teaching. Most of it was done through tutorials. At these the pupil would turn up once or twice a week by himself or with one other pupil, sit in an armchair and read an essay he had written on a subject set the week before. Lewis would listen, apparently attentively, and perhaps make a few notes. At the end he would criticize the essay in considerable detail. He might want to know what the pupil had read before writing it, ask for his views on aspects of the work, and so on. Certainly it was exacting. Lewis could be severe especially on anyone who had done very little work or was guilty of the "personal heresy" of writing about the author instead of what he had written. Yet I have met only one man who did not enjoy these tutorials. They often had the quality of Lewis's conversation. The tutorial would end with a short discussion of the work the pupil was to do during the following week. There was usually a great deal of reading and always an essay to be written. This, the classical Oxford tutorial system, was the way he taught English literature. He did not deliver many lectures, and he did not often recommend the lectures given by his colleagues. At their best, his tutorials turned into discussions between enthusiasts.

Sometimes, especially when revising set books for schools, he taught in small classes of perhaps four or five. These also tended to be discussions and certainly humor was never far away. The atmosphere remained informal; we sat in armchairs or on sofas. There would be a jug of beer and a box of Oxford Memory cigarettes on the table. Of course the idea was to help us feel at home and certainly not to encourage us to smoke or drink more than we wanted to.

Literary enthusiasms are infectious. I owe to Lewis's enthusiasm a love for Edmund Spenser, **George Herbert,** and William Wordsworth that has permanently enriched my life.

In my book *Jack*, I quote his friend **Owen Barfield**'s view that the likelihood of Lewis being Mrs. **Janie Moore**'s lover was "fifty-fifty." One of the very few people to know the truth was Mrs. Moore's daughter, **Maureen Moore** (Lady Dunbar), who died February 1997. In one of the conversations my wife and I had with her not long before her death, she made it clear that Jack and her mother had been for a time lovers. They would have married if Mr. Moore ("the Beast") had consented. True they did not share a bedroom at the Kilns, but Jack occupied a room that, until an outside staircase for the fire escape was built, could only be entered by going through Mrs. Moore's room. Their sexual relationship continued until his entry into the Church of England in the autumn of 1931. I think that he was celibate from this time until after his marriage to Joy.

Though often lighthearted, he was a serious moralist and above all one who practiced what he preached. Though often bothered by a fear of going bankrupt—a fear he seems to have inherited from his father—he gave away most of his large literary earnings. After the death of his father, he was certainly not a poor man, but he believed in living in a state of great simplicity and spent a minimum on himself and on the house in which he lived. Thus he never wore a wristwatch, rarely carried a fountain pen, and was more shabbily dressed than Anthony Hopkins in *Shadowlands*. The house was extremely shabby. The walls had been stripped of their rotting wallpaper and showed heavy staining. There was no central heating and little hot water. On one of the very few occasions he spoke to me about Mrs. Moore, he said: "She had the great virtue of hospitality, of giving generously to those in need. Her example, living with her, taught me to be hospitable too." He rarely spoke about his charitable giving, yet he said enough to make me think that he tried to follow the gospel direction by giving to all who asked.

G. S. B. Sayer

Florence Augusta Hamilton "Flora" Lewis (1862–1908)

The mother of C. S. Lewis, Florence Augusta Hamilton was born in 1862 and called "Flora" by those who knew her. She was the third of four children of Thomas Hamilton, rector of **St. Mark's Church** in Dundela, Northern Ireland. On her father's side she was descended from a Scotch family transplanted to Ireland in the reign of King James I; on her mother, Mary Hamilton's side she was descended from the Warren family and a Norman knight who fought for William the Conqueror. C. S. Lewis remembered his mother's family as "a cooler race [that] ... had the talent for happiness in a high degree" (*Surprised by Joy*). Yet the Rev. Thomas Hamilton was given to emotional outbursts in the pulpit and Flora's mother was an indifferent housekeeper at best. Both parents favored the older children and neglected Flora and her younger brother.

Flora was quite intelligent and despite her parents managed to earn a B.A. in mathematics and logic from Queen's University. Beginning in 1886 she was courted by **Albert Lewis**, a neighbor and young solicitor. Though she liked him, she had no feeling for him and freely told him so. As he persisted, she cooled his ardor but never risked outright rejection and the loss of his **friendship**. Finally, in 1893, fearing that she could not keep him and turn him down forever, she agreed to marry Albert but confessed: "I wonder do I **love** you? I am not quite sure. I know that at least I am very fond of you, and that I should never think of loving anyone else." They were married the following year, and Flora bore Albert two sons: **Warren Hamilton Lewis** was born on June 16, 1895, and their youngest son, Clive Staples Lewis (known as "Jack") on November 29, 1898.

Flora was always plagued with headaches and her health began to fail in early 1908. She was diagnosed as having cancer, and she died in August. C. S. Lewis later wrote that "with my mother's death all settled happiness, all that was tranquil and reliable, disappeared from my life."

James Prothero

Also See: Belfast, Dundela Villas, Little Lea, Marriage

Bibliography

Green, Roger L., and Walter Hooper. *C. S. Lewis: A Biography.* San Diego: Harcourt, 1974.

Lewis, C. S. *Surprised by Joy.*

Sayer, George. *Jack: C. S. Lewis and His Times.* San Francisco: Harper, 1988.

(Helen) Joy Davidman Gresham Lewis (1915–1960)

Joy Davidman was born on April 18, 1915, in New York and raised in the Bronx. Her parents, Jewish immigrants, saw to it that Joy and her brother Howard "sucked in atheism with [their] canned milk." Enormously intelligent, Joy started reading at age two. At eight, she read **H. G. Wells'** *Outline of History* and declared that she was an atheist, delighting her father. She completed high school at age fourteen, college at nineteen, and a master's degree three semesters later.

Joy taught high school for two years but did not enjoy it, so she turned to writing. *Letter to a Comrade* (1938) won her the Yale Series of Younger Poets Award. She shared the 1939 Russell Loines Memorial Fund Award with poet Robert Frost. Her novel *Anya* (1940) also brought critical acclaim. On the strength of these publications, MGM invited her to participate in their young scriptwriter's program. She moved to Hollywood, but her scripts were not well received, and she left somewhat bitter about the experience.

Returning to New York, she devoted her talent as a writer, editor, and critic to the communist publication *New Masses.* She had become a communist several years before: "I entered the Party with a burst of emotion, without making the slightest effort to study Marxist theory. All I knew was that capitalism wasn't working very well, war was imminent—and socialism promised to change all that."

Attending a Communist Party function, Joy met **William "Bill" Lindsay Gresham,** a freelance writer and a veteran of the Spanish Civil War. They married in 1942. Their son **David Gresham** was born on March 27, 1944, and **Douglas Gresham** on November 10, 1945. With marriage and motherhood, Joy lost interest in communism. "My little son was a real thing and so was my obligation to him; by comparison, my duty to that imaginary entity the working class seemed the most doubtful of abstractions."

The marriage was quite strained. Bill Gresham was an alcoholic who became violent when drunk; he was also compulsively unfaithful. Financial problems added to the stress. In 1946, Bill Gresham suffered a mental collapse. Joy later wrote that for "the first time" in her life she "felt helpless."

Joy felt her defenses fall away: "And **God** came in. How can one describe the direct perception of God? It is infinite, unique; there are no words, there are no comparisons. Can one scoop up the sea in a teacup? . . . There was a Person with me in that room, directly present to my consciousness—a Person so real that all my precious life was by comparison a mere shadow play. And I myself was more alive than I had ever been; it was like waking from sleep." Joy found herself on her knees, praying. "I think I must have been the world's most astonished atheist."

Gresham returned several days later. Joy was remarkably serene; she told her husband about her experience of God. He expressed interest in **Christianity,** and they joined a local Presbyterian church. Joy read voraciously, trying to make sense of her experience. "When I read the New Testament, I recognised Him. He was Jesus."

Things improved: Gresham sold a novel entitled *Nightmare Alley,* then sold the film rights as well. Financial pressures eased, they bought a fourteen-room mansion in the country. But while Joy pursued Christianity more seriously, Bill grew interested in tarot cards, the I Ching, and Dianetics. However, as Lyle Dorsett observes, "The most devastating blow to the marriage came with Bill's continuing infidelity. . . . Bill never tried to hide these indiscretions, and he could not understand why Joy was hurt by them."

Joy began to read the works of C. S. Lewis. She also met **Chad Walsh,** an expert on C. S. Lewis who encouraged Joy to write to the author. Lewis was struck by her amusing and well-written letters, and soon they had become "penfriends."

In August of 1952, Joy visited England and invited Lewis to lunch at the Eastgate Hotel. Several days later, Lewis introduced her to **Warren Lewis,** who described her as "medium height, good figure, horn-rimmed specs, quite extraordinarily uninhibited." The three of them got along famously for, as Douglas Gresham observed, "she had the rare ability to converse, walk, drink and behave sufficiently as an equal and a colleague to put Warnie completely at his ease." Joy remained in England for about five months, completing work on a new book, *Smoke on the Mountain.*

Just before Joy headed home, she received a letter from Bill: "I don't want to cloud your holiday with things that would upset you, but Renee and I are in love." Joy returned to New York on January 3, 1953. Her marriage proved irretrievable. She decided to move to London with her two sons to try to rebuild her life. When the divorce was finalized, Bill and Renee were married.

Unhappy with a cramped London flat, Joy, David, and Douglas moved from London to Headington, about a mile from **the Kilns**. Lewis visited them daily. Douglas Gresham said of this period, "As time went by, the relationship between Mother and Jack was surely and swiftly changing in its nature. I don't believe it took Jack long to develop love rather than friendship for Mother, but it may have taken considerably longer for him to come to a conscious identification of his feelings, and then even longer to a conscious admission of them even to himself. As early as 1955, I, a mere child, could see how he brightened in her presence, and how she positively revelled in his proximity."

Joy and the boys thrived in their new home, but then Joy had trouble renewing her visa, possibly due to her earlier involvement with the Communist Party. Lewis offered to extend his British citizenship to her through **marriage**, and on April 23, 1956, they were married in a civil ceremony. Joy kept her name and her Headington home. That October, however, things suddenly changed. Joy was taken to Wingfield-Morris Hospital. She had cancer.

Joy's prognosis was grim. Warren noted in his diary, "Sentence of death has been passed on Joy, and the end is only a matter of time . . . though to feel pity for anyone so magnificently brave as Joy is almost an insult." Lewis wanted to take her home to the Kilns, but first sought to be married by the church. The Bishop of Oxford, Harry Carpenter, refused to permit it since Joy was divorced. Lewis approached a former pupil of his, and on March 21, 1957, the Reverend **Peter Bide** presided at the bedside ceremony.

Bide also prayed for her healing. Much to the astonishment of her doctors, Joy regained her strength. In April 1957, she moved to the Kilns, and in June 1958, the cancer was in complete remission.

The Lewises enjoyed a belated honeymoon in Ireland. But in October of 1959, Joy's cancer returned. Despite her serious condition, the Lewises went to Greece, a vacation both had long desired. Lewis noted, "Joy knew she was dying. I knew she was dying. . . . But when we heard the shepherds playing their flutes in the hills it seemed to make no difference."

When they returned to Oxford, Joy's strength was spent. Nevertheless, Lewis noted, "It is incredible how much happiness, even how much gaiety, we sometimes had together after all hope was gone." Joy Lewis died on July 13, 1960. They had been married four years.

In *A Grief Observed*, Lewis described Joy as "my trusty comrade, friend, shipmate, fellow-soldier. My mistress, but at the same time all that any man friend (and I have had good ones) had ever been to me." Friends who knew them testify to the unusually strong bond between them, and the obvious enjoyment each felt in the presence of the other. Lewis said simply, "We feasted on love, every mode of it—solemn and merry, romantic and realistic, sometimes as dramatic as a thunderstorm, sometimes as comfortable and unemphatic as putting on your soft slippers." Joy's ashes were scattered at the Oxford Crematorium. A plaque on the garden wall bears a poem written by Lewis.

Diana Pavlac Glyer
Azusa Pacific University

Bibliography

Davidman, Joy. *Anya* (1940); *Weeping Bay* (1950); *Smoke on the Mountain* (1953); *Letters to a Comrade* (1938); *War Poems of the United States* (1944)

Dorsett, Lyle. *And God Came In: The Extraordinary Story of Joy Davidman, Her Life and Marriage to C. S. Lewis*. New York: Macmillan, 1983.

Gresham, Douglas. *Lenten Lands: My Childhood with Joy Davidman and C. S. Lewis*. New York: Macmillan, 1989.

Sibley, Brian. *Shadowlands: The Story of C. S. Lewis and Joy Davidman*. New York: Macmillan, 1985.

Soper, David Wesley (ed). *These Found the Way*. Philadelphia: The Westminster Press, 1951.

Warren Hamilton "Warnie" Lewis (1895–1973)

The first child of **Albert James Lewis** and **Florence (Flora) Hamilton Lewis**, Warren Lewis was born on June 16, 1895, in **Dundela Villas** on the outskirts of **Belfast**. His brother C. S. "Jack" Lewis was born in 1898, and the two became lifelong companions. As children, they amused themselves by writing and illustrating stories. Warren called his invented country India and Jack called his Animal-Land; they combined them into one country they called **Boxen**. Many of the characters in these stories were inspired by toys they owned.

The family moved to **Little Lea** in 1905, and shortly thereafter Warren was sent to **Wynard School**, Watford, Hertfordshire, England. His mother died of cancer three years later, in August of 1908, after which both Warren Lewis and his brother Jack were sent to Wynard, a school they both hated. Their antipathy appears to be with good cause: the brutal headmaster was later certified insane. Warren went from there to **Malvern Col-**

lege, where he decided on the Royal Army Service Corps (RASC) as a career.

Warren spent four months studying with his father's tutor, **William T. Kirkpatrick**, in preparation for entrance to the Royal Military Academy at Sandhurst. He placed twenty-first out of 201 candidates in his entrance exams and was awarded a prize cadetship. He entered the Royal Military Academy in February of 1914, and just five months later, Britain declared war on Germany. As a result, his officer's training was accelerated, and in November he was sent to France as a second lieutenant. Throughout his career, promotions came quickly. Warren's posts included service in Sierra Leone, West Africa (1921–22), and Shanghai, China (1927–30 and 1931–32).

During his first assignment in China, Warren Lewis's Christian faith was renewed. About a year later, on May 13, 1931, he wrote, "I have started to say my prayers again after having discontinued doing so for more years than I care to remember: this was no sudden impulse but the result of a conviction of the truth of Christianity which has been growing on me for a considerable time. . . . The wheel has now made the full revolution—indifference, skepticism, atheism, agnosticism, and back again to Christianity."

Some five months later, his brother Jack also returned to belief in **God**—while riding in the sidecar of Warren's motorcycle on the way to the Whipsnade Zoo. On January 19, 1932, Warren recorded that he had received a letter from Jack "containing the news that he too had once more started to go to Communion, at which I am delighted."

On December 21, 1932, Warren retired from the RASC. He then moved into **the Kilns** with his brother, Jack, and **Janie Moore** and **Maureen Moore**. The Lewis brothers enjoyed annual **walking tours**, each one covering forty to fifty miles or more. Warren had a twenty-five-foot motorboat built, which he dubbed the *Bosphorus*. He enjoyed classical music, especially Beethoven, Brahms, and Chopin, and went often to the symphony. And like his brother, he was a voracious reader, observing, "A book, a good chair, my pipe and a good bed to go to when night falls, and I'm about as happy as one can be in this very trying world."

The Inklings began to meet during this time, and Warren was an integral member of this writing group. In the early meetings, it appears that Warren Lewis's key involvement was helping his brother play host by preparing the tea. Warren had a sunny disposition and a genuine gift for hospitality; **John Wain** describes him as "a man who stays in my memory as the most courte-

ous I have ever met—not with mere politeness, but with genial, self-forgetful considerateness that was as instinctive to him as breathing." But it is **J. R. R. Tolkien** who noticed that the group had a powerful influence on Warren Lewis, suggesting that he wrote more and more as a result of their interaction: "It's catching!" cried Tolkien after Warren Lewis read his first section of French history aloud at a Thursday meeting.

In all, Warren Lewis wrote and published six books covering various aspects of 17th-century France. Humphrey Carpenter has observed that these were books "whose readability, wit and good sense almost equaled his brother's work." Edwin Morgan reviewed *The Sunset of the Splendid Century,* saying, "This book not only has scholarship; it has wit and a warm insight into human nature—endowments which are not always found in an historian." In his review of the same book, Geoffrey Bruun has written, "there is no shadow of sunset in Mr. Lewis's crystalline prose. He manipulates his new material with even greater deftness than formerly and wields his diamond-pointed pen with a lighter touch."

Warren also completed the formidable task of editing the **Lewis Family Papers**. He began to collect and arrange them while on leave in December of 1930. They included numerous diaries, letters, photographs, and miscellaneous documents that had been kept by their father, Albert Lewis, and brought from Little Lea to the Kilns following Albert's death. After his retirement, Warren arranged and typed the material, adding extensive notes. When he finished, he preserved his diary but (with his brother's permission) destroyed all of the other original material.

Warren's retirement did not last indefinitely. On September 4, 1939, he was recalled to active service for World War II, and posted to Catterick, Yorkshire. On January 27, 1940, he was granted the temporary rank of Major. After short stints in France and Wales, Warren was transferred to the Reserve of Officers and finally sent home to Oxford for good. He devoted himself to his writing and also served as his brother's secretary, helping to handle the growing influx of letters from Jack's readers and fans.

After his brother's death in 1963, Warren Lewis was asked to write a biography. He produced *C. S. Lewis: A Biography*, a long, insightful work running nearly a thousand pages. This was extensively shortened and edited, and finally published under the title ***Letters of C. S. Lewis***.

As Lewis grew older, his struggle with alcoholism increased. As **Douglas Gresham** has noted, "His years in the Army had also left him with a dark legacy of alcoholism, a disease which he fought with astonishing valiance for year after year, achieving some successes and suffering some cataclysmic failures."

In 1970, Warren Lewis developed circulation problems, and in 1972 had a pacemaker installed. Problems persisted: he complained of dizziness and developed gangrene in both feet, requiring surgery. On April 9, 1973, Warren Lewis died peacefully at home in the Kilns while reading a book. He and his brother are buried in the same grave at Holy Trinity Church, Headington Quarry.

Diana Pavlac Glyer
Azusa Pacific University

Bibliography

Kilby, Clyde S., and Marjorie L. Mead (eds.). *Brothers and Friends*. Wheaton, IL: Crossway, 1982.

Lewis, Warren. *The Splendid Century: Life in the France of Louis* (1953); *Assault on Olympus: The Rise of the House of Gramont Between 1604 and 1678* (1958); *Louis XVI: An Informal Portrait* (1959); *The Scandalous Regent: A Life of Phillipe, Duc d' Orleans 1674–1723 and of His Family* (1961); *Levantine Adventurer: The Travels and Missions of the Chevalier d' Arvieux, 1653–1697* (1962); *The Sunset of the Splendid Century* (1963); *Memoirs of the Duc de Saint-Simon* (1964).

The Lewis Family Papers

In December of 1930, **Warren H. Lewis** began to arrange the Lewis Family Papers while home at the **Kilns** on leave from the Royal Army Service Corps. These papers consisted of numerous diaries, letters, photographs, and miscellaneous documents that had been gathered by the Lewis brothers from the family home in **Belfast** after their father **Albert Lewis**'s death in 1929. After Warren's retirement in January 1933, he returned to this task, arranging, excerpting, and typing the materials he selected to illustrate the recent history of his family. Once the papers had been entered into the typed volumes, the original manuscripts were destroyed—with the exception of Warren's diaries. On June 1, 1933, the first volume of these papers was returned from the binders, now with the official title, *Memoirs of the Lewis Family: 1850–1930, Volume One: From October 17th., 1850 to September 23rd., 1881*. The final and eleventh volume was completed in 1935. The original typescript of the Lewis Family Papers were willed to the **Marion E. Wade Center** by Warren Lewis at his death in 1973.

Marjorie Lamp Mead
The Marion E. Wade Center

Bibliography

Kilby, Clyde S., and Marjorie Lamp Mead. *Brothers and Friends: The Diaries of Major Warren Hamilton Lewis.* San Francisco: Harper & Row, 1982.

The Lewis Library

C. S. Lewis's love for not only the substance but also the physical **beauty** of a well-bound book was apparent from his early years. In letters to his friend **Arthur Greeves,** Lewis often wrote of his book purchases, noting both their price and binding as well as discussing with great delight the content of the volumes. These initial acquisitions eventually grew into a significant personal collection, for in spite of Lewis's extensive use of the **Bodleian Library,** he valued having certain titles close at hand. At Lewis's death, he left his library to his brother, **Warren Lewis,** with the stipulation that his Trustees, **Owen Barfield** and **Cecil Harwood,** be allowed to make a selection from those books that Warren did not want. Other friends, including **George Sayer** and **J. A. W. Bennett,** were invited to choose some books as well.

The balance of Lewis's library was then sold to Blackwell Booksellers, Oxford. Of these, approximately 200 were purchased by **Walter Hooper** while the remaining 2,710 books were bought by Wroxton College in Banbury (the British branch of Fairleigh Dickinson University, New Jersey) for use as an undergraduate library. In 1985, when the library was acquired from Wroxton College by the **Marion E. Wade Center** at Wheaton College, it consisted of only 2,363 books; this diminished number was due to a security problem at Wroxton that had resulted in the theft of many volumes. Of the books purchased by Walter Hooper, some were donated to the Bodleian Library and 176 volumes were given to the Southern Historical Collection of the University of North Carolina at Chapel Hill.

Many of the books from Lewis's library were inscribed and annotated by him, some heavily, while others have only brief underlining and marginalia. In this regard, see also Lewis's letter of February 1932 to Greeves in which he described his practice of marking books as he read them.

Marjorie Lamp Mead
The Marion E. Wade Center

Bibliography

Hooper, Walter. *C. S. Lewis: A Companion & Guide.* San Francisco: HarperSanFrancisco, 1996.

Rogers, Margaret Anne. *C. S. Lewis: A Living Library.* M.A. thesis. Wroxton College, 1969.

Clive Staples Lewis (1898–1963)

See Preface to this volume: "Clive Staples Lewis (1898–1963): A Brief Biography"

The Life of Samuel Johnson (Book Review)

"Boswell's Bugbear." *Sunday Telegraph*. 61 (1 April 1962): 8.

Lewis thought that the editing of Davis detracted from this publication of Sir John Hawkins' *Life of Samuel Johnson*. Davis "processes" Hawkins, which Lewis regrets. Hawkins, while he is often displeased by Johnson, has a character all his own, one that mixes unintentional humor and a style reminiscent of the 17th century. Hawkins' information is useful and his style pleasurable, and he does not improve upon "processing."

Anne Gardner

Bibliography

Hawkins, Sir John. *The Life of Samuel Johnson*. B. H. Davis (ed).

"Life Partners"

See entry on *This Ever Diverse Pair* (Book Review)

Light and Darkness

Images of light and darkness in the fiction of C. S. Lewis denote the spiritual merit of an individual, entity, locality, or event. In his stories, traditional theological associations of light with deity, **redemption**, godliness, **truth**, and **heaven** are transferred to their fictive counterparts. Regarding evil, Lewis's writing attests to his Augustinian view, not that evil is the opposite of good, but that it is the utter absence of it. Darkness symbolizes the absence of **God** and godliness and depicts **hell**, **Satan**, disobedience, evil, and **sin**.

Images of light and darkness provide critical clues to the spiritual landscape of his stories. Lewis's allegorical *Pilgrim's Regress* contains many references to light and darkness. Light accompanies significant moments in the protagonist's spiritual journey. As he moves toward conversion he travels in a sphere of light. Light and noise open the scenes immediately following his conversion and preceding his crossing the brook (meeting his death). In *The Great Divorce* the landscape and population of heaven are bright and radiant. The story's last scene, the apocalyptic dawn following the end of Time, is drenched in the light of the Morning.

The **creation** of Narnia is marked by blazing stars, a brilliant sun, and Aslan so bright Digory could not take his eyes from him. Aslan is described as shining at his resurrection. He emits a shining whiteness when he reveals himself to Shasta in *The Horse and His Boy*. In Lewis's **science fiction** trilogy the spiritual beings who act as **angels** and assist Ransom are described in terms of light and movement.

The polarity of the participants in Lewis's science fiction is quite clear. The perpetrators of the spread of darkness on Mars, Venus, and earth threaten the planets' natural and spiritual life. Those who are of the light—Ransom, the eldila, Jane, Merlin, the congregation at St. Anne's—bring an end to the evil exploitation of creation for selfish gain. In *Perelandra*, Weston, once referred to as "the Prince of Darkness" by Ransom, says he is down in the bottom of a big black hole. The phrase, "the black hole," also appears in *Pilgrim's Regress* referring to a boundaried region of evil, or hell, reserved for lives spent in resistance to the Landlord. Lewis's stories typically close with the defeat of evil and images of light evoking renewal and impending glory.

Alice H. Cook

Also See: Allegory, Good and Evil, Imagery, Revelation

Bibliography

Dockery, Carl Dee. "The Myth of the Shadow in the Fantasies of Williams, Lewis and Tolkien." Ph.D. dissertation, Auburn University, 1975.
Downing, David C. *Planets in Peril*. Amherst: University of Massachusetts Press, 1992.
Filmer, Kath. *The Fiction of C. S. Lewis: Mask and Mirror*. New York: St. Martin's, 1993.
Lewis, C. S. *The Magician's Nephew; Pilgrim's Regress*
Lindskoog, Kathryn. *Finding the Landlord: A Guidebook to C. S. Lewis's Pilgrim's Regress*. Chicago: Cornerstone, 1995.
Sammons, Martha C. "*The Man Born Blind*: Light in C. S. Lewis." *CSL: The Bulletin of the New York C. S. Lewis Society*. 9 (December 1977): 1–7.
Westerlund, Lois. "Excerpts from *The Great Divorce*: Life After Death in Metaphor." *CSL: The Bulletin of the New York C. S. Lewis Society*. 2 (October 1975): 1–2.

"Lilies That Fester"

Twentieth Century. CLVII (April 1955): 330–41. Reprinted in *The World's Last Night, They Asked for a Paper,* and *Christian Reunion*.

In this rebuttal to a 1955 *Twentieth Century* article, Lewis explained why modern manifestations of intellectualism and **culture** are avoided by intelligent people. Drawing parallels with Pharisees who spoil their **religion** by practicing it for selfish motives, Lewis first pointed out that seeking "culture" for self-improvement rather than enjoyment not only negates its own aim but also ruins the aesthetic experience itself. In a discussion of whether the modern notion of culture makes one a better person, Lewis examined the sensibilities of those who claimed to be "sensitive" and found that they have no lack of snobbishness, resentment, and egotism; their **"faith in culture"** is but another manifestation of the in-group scrabbling he explored in **"The Inner Ring."** Lewis also discussed why people instinctively shun ersatz culture, but the real purpose of the essay was to decry the growing tendency of self-appointed elites to stamp their tastes on others by making those tastes a prerequisite to academic success, social standing, and career advancement. "Cultured" rulers with high pretensions are "meddlesome and impertinent" in their rule, just as "lilies that fester smell far worse than weeds." Lewis called on all real lovers of art to enjoy culture without talking about it too much and to fight the hypocrisy of "faith in culture."

Richard A. Hill
Taylor University

Also See: Aesthetics, Beauty, Modernity, Pride

Bibliography

Lewis, C. S. "The Inner Ring"; "On Church Music"; and Christianity and Culture (A Letter)

The Lion, the Witch and the Wardrobe

London: Geoffrey Bles, 1950. First US edition, New York: Macmillan, 1950.

The first book in the **Chronicles of Narnia**, *The Lion, The Witch and the Wardrobe* is about what **pride** and betrayal feel like and what the dying and rising of **Christ** does about **sin** and death. Lewis began the book in 1939, perhaps as a consequence of having to entertain schoolgirls billeted at the **Kilns** in order to escape the London air raids. *The Lion, the Witch and the Wardrobe* is the only Chronicle to have this wartime feel and setting, both of which are gone at the beginning of *Prince Caspian* and *The Voyage of the "Dawn Treader."*

According to Lewis in **"It All Began with a Picture,"** this first Narnian book (like all of the Chronicles) began with him seeing pictures in his head. In this case, he saw "a picture of a faun carrying an umbrella and parcels in a snowy wood. This picture had been in my mind since I was about sixteen. Then one day, when I was forty, I said to myself, 'Let's try to make a story about it.'" It wasn't until a decade later, however, that the character of Aslan the lion came to Lewis, allowing him to complete the story. (Lewis recalled that he had been having many dreams about lions at that time.) The plot that Lewis ultimately developed about a witch and a wardrobe likely showed the unconscious influence of **Edith Nesbit's** short story, "The Aunt and Amabel," which Lewis probably read as a child.

The book begins with the evacuation of four siblings, two boys, Peter and Edmund (ages thirteen and ten), and two girls, Susan and Lucy (ages twelve and eight), from London at the beginning of World War II. The children are sent to the country home of a bachelor professor. Playing hide-and-seek, Lucy finds a way through a wardrobe into a snowbound country ("Narnia") where talking animals and mythological creatures are real. But she is unable to convince her siblings of the truth of her experience. During a second game, Edmund follows Lucy into the wardrobe and discovers Narnia is real. Unfortunately while there, he falls under the influence of the White Witch due to his pride, greed, and gluttony.

All four children are then chased into Narnia and are met by Mr. and Mrs. Beaver, who tell them of the evil enchantment by the Witch that makes it "always winter and never Christmas" in Narnia. The Beavers also tell the children about Aslan, their lion liberator who is "on the move." The very sound of Aslan's name causes a numinous experience in all but Edmund, who sneaks out to rendezvous with the Witch. The Beavers advise the children to seek Aslan's help with Edmund, whom the Witch has enslaved for her purposes. On their way to see Aslan they see that the Witch's spell is breaking and spring is coming again to Narnia, and they receive gifts for battle from Father Christmas. Seeing the splendor of Aslan surrounded by all the good Narnians is another numinous experience for the children. Peter slays the wolf sent by the Witch, and Aslan's emissaries rescue Edmund, who asks for and receives forgiveness from Aslan and his brother and sisters. The Witch then demands an audience to remind Aslan of the Deep **Magic**, the law of the talon, in this case treachery as a capital offense. (Paul Clasper compares the Deep Magic to the law of sowing and reaping, a way of speaking about the universe as moral). Aslan and the Witch confer privately, and he announces that the Witch has renounced her claim on Edmund's blood. She departs to prepare for the slaying of Aslan instead, and Aslan repositions his forces under the captainship of Peter.

After night falls, Aslan sorrowfully walks back to the Stone Table. He is accompanied by Susan and Lucy, who try in vain to comfort the great lion. The scene is reminiscent of Christ's sufferings in the Garden of Gethsemane as recounted by the Gospels (see Matthew 26:36–46; Mark 14:32–42; Luke 22:40–46). Lewis took profound comfort from the knowledge that Christ could understand our struggles and doubts because he himself struggled at Gethsemene (see **Letters of C. S. Lewis**, May 8, 1939, July 17, 1953, and April 29, 1959); hence it is fitting that Aslan's Gethsemene should be one of the most moving sequences in the first Chronicle. Upon reaching the Stone Table, Susan and Lucy watch in horror as Aslan is demeaned and executed by the White Witch and her followers. Her armies then depart to fight with Peter's troops, while Susan and Lucy stand watch with Aslan's body. At dawn the girls hear the tremendous crack of the Table as it is split in two by the resurrection of Aslan. He explains that there is a magic deeper than the Deep Magic which comes from the willingness of an innocent victim to be slain in a traitor's place. Aslan roars and carries the girls to the Witch's castle where he liberates those whom she has turned to stone. All the liberated creatures join in the fight with Peter's forces against the Witch's army. Aslan slays her and her army is trounced. Lucy uses her Christmas present of the healing cordial to mend the wounded and all go off to celebrate the coronation of the children as the rightful kings and queens of Narnia. Peter, Susan, Edmund, and Lucy spend sixteen years in Narnia. Then, while hunting, they stumble back through the wardrobe into the professor's house where they discover that they have not aged one minute of earth time but have matured greatly spiritually.

Sometimes mistaken for an **allegory**, *The Lion, the Witch and the Wardrobe* is instead what Lewis called a "supposal." That is, it seeks to describe how God might appear were he to intervene in an entirely different world. Writing to a young girl named Patricia, Lewis said his first Narnian story tried to answer the question: "Suppose there were a world like Narnia and it needed rescuing and the Son of God ... went to redeem it, as He came to redeem ours, what might it, in that world, all have been like?" (**C. S. Lewis: Letters to Children**, June 8, 1960; also see, *Letters of C. S. Lewis*, December 29, 1958). Thus, the character of Aslan in the Chronicles is not intended to represent **Christ**; he is supposed to be Christ. Similarly, the "Emperor-Beyond-the-Sea" is supposed to be God the

Father; and Father Christmas (the giver of gifts) is likely supposed to be the **Holy Spirit**.

Part of Lewis's purpose in his supposal was to help people whose religious feelings had been frozen by false conceptions of duty and reverence. As Lewis explained in the essay, **"Sometimes Fairy Stories May Say Best What's to Be Said,"** he thought by importing Christ's suffering "into an imaginary world, stripping them of their stained-glass and Sunday school associations, one could make them for the first time appear in their real potency."

The Lion, the Witch and the Wardrobe shows Lewis at his most mythopoeic and his least didactic. He allowed his readers to feel again—or perhaps for the first time—the meaning of the crucifixion and the resurrection, as facts born again as **myth** (see **"Myth Become Fact"** and **"Meditation in a Toolshed"**). As Lewis said in his seminal essay **"Bluspels and Flalaspheres,"** "[R]eason is the natural organ of truth; but imagination is the organ of meaning." The central truths of **Christianity** take on new meaning in *The Lion, the Witch and the Wardrobe*.

Paul F. Ford
St. John's Seminary

Bibliography

Ford, Paul F. *Companion to Narnia*. San Francisco: HarperSanFrancisco, 1994.

Leyland, Margaret M. "Lewis and the Schoolgirls." *The Lamppost*. 1, no. 3 (July 1977): 1–2, 8.

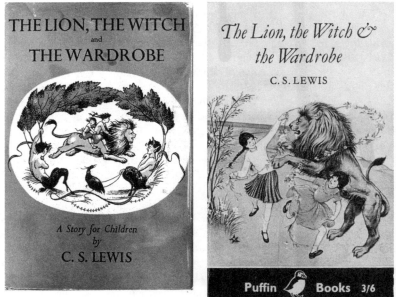

U.K. First Edition

Myers, Doris. "The Compleat Anglican: Spiritual Style in the Chronicles of Narnia." *Anglican Theological Review.* LXVI (April 1984): 148–60.

Nesbit, E. "The Aunt and Amabel." *The Magic City.* London: Macmillan, 1912.

Schakel, Peter. *Reading with the Heart: The Way into Narnia.* Grand Rapids, MI: Eerdmans, 1979.

Yandell, Steven. "The Trans-cosmic Journeys in the Chronicles of Narnia." *Mythlore* 43 (August 1985): 9–23.

Literary Criticism

Literary criticism traditionally concerns the task of interpreting a literary work, usually as an inquiry into its unique genre, rhetorical, and philological features and within the context of its national, cultural, and historical origins and pertinent biographical information about its author. Western literary critics throughout most of the last two hundred years have thus concerned themselves with three basic questions: (1) what does this work "mean," in whole or in part? (2) how and why does the author attempt to convey this meaning? (3) what place does this work have within the tradition or genre it represents?

One of the challenges literary criticism has always faced is that inordinate attention to any one of these questions can yield an imbalance in critical method that, in effect, "loses the poem itself." The biographical critic strives to illuminate the author's experience and **psychology**; the historical critic probes the socio-economic conditions of the era in which the work is produced and read; the philological critic patiently traces the history of a single word from this text to another; the source critic labors to uncover the influences and origins of particular themes or characters in the work; and so on— where in all of this *data* is the "meaning" or the import of the reader's experience of the text itself?

Lewis solved this dilemma in his own critical practice by refusing to locate "meaning" exclusively in the text itself, choosing to reckon the text as the essential "meeting place" for the encounter between author and reader, but defining the "meaning" of a work as "the series of emotions, reflections, and attitudes produced by reading it." Such a move establishes a creative tension among the roles of author, reader, and text in interpretation that conscientious critics cannot ignore and insures that the product of criticism is not merely an arbitrary evaluation of one or more isolated components of the text. As he explained it in his most sustained theoretical work on the practice of criticism, *An Experiment in Criticism* (1961), the goal of a reader should be to "receive," rather than "use" a literary work, which

means "exerting our senses and imagination and various others according to a pattern invented by the artist." Therefore, the most helpful critic is one who assists in this crucial reception of the work by explicating any and all aspects of the author's craft, the work's original form and context, and both its first and the present reader's likely expectations.

This prohibitively reader-centered notion of the critical task is foundational to all of Lewis's critical oeuvre; his consistent aim was to invite readers to consider "the poem the author really wrote" instead of one of their own making, and to avoid the equally egregious error of slavishly identifying the author's biography with his or her work. To do otherwise would merely aggrandize the self at the expense of the author, the obverse of true reading, which for Lewis was always to lift the reader "out of his provincialism by making him 'the spectator' if not of all, yet of much, 'time and existence' . . . and into a more public world." Such a "public world" allows a text to speak out of its own time or culture into the present and make possible valuable perspective on one's own age as a "period" that may elicit needed correction as it is compared with the past or the future.

In Lewis's estimation, the critic should not be too intrusive in directing the reader and should as much as possible allow the text work its own magic on a modern. Lewis's observation that one needs **Chaucer** to enjoy the critics and not vice-versa, is telling. Still, especially in reading ancient texts, Lewis believed that one may need "a tolerable map" of the work's original milieu to make this distant encounter possible, and thus a critic may be justified in temporarily guiding a reader outside a work "in order that we may presently come inside it again, better equipped." This indeed is one of Lewis's greatest strengths as a literary critic, his ability to enable a reader to better understand with more immediacy the conceptual framework and commitments which undergird a particular work or, indeed, an entire period. His *The Discarded Image* (1964) is a masterful recreation of the medieval worldview, its assumptions about the cosmos, the meaning of human existence, and its readerly expectations of books.

Lewis's critical canon is replete with such influential studies; his truly magnum opus, *The Allegory of Love* (1936) radically altered critical perceptions of **Edmund Spenser**'s *The Faerie Queene* and reinvigorated discussion and debate about the role and meaning of both courtly **love** and the genre of **allegory** in the medieval tradition; his *A Preface to Paradise Lost*

(1942) nearly single-handedly rehabilitated **Milton**'s reputation in an era in which his **epic** poem was either undervalued or valued for the wrong reasons; and his massive *English Literature in the 16th Century Excluding Drama* (1954), Volume III in the Oxford History of English Literature, offered breathtaking characterizations of and provocative generalizations about scores of texts, authors, and movements with lucidity and grace. He was equally adept at shorter, succinct, and well-aimed rebuttals of critical judgments of works he felt capriciously deprived readers of pleasure and enlightenment, as such collections as *Rehabilitations* (1939), *Studies in Medieval and Renaissance Literature* (1966), and *Selected Literary Essays* (1969) well exemplify.

In reading Lewis's literary criticism, one encounters an uncommon enthusiasm for reading itself and a contagious delight in inhabiting the fictional landscapes of other authors. As in his apologetics and his fiction, Lewis exuded a generous and earnest spirit that enlists his readers in a partnership of joyful discovery, the chief benefit being the companionship of Lewis himself.

Bruce L. Edwards
Bowling Green State University

Also See: Literary Criticism, New Criticism

Bibliography

Edwards, Bruce L. *A Rhetoric of Reading: C. S. Lewis's Defense of Western Literacy*. Provo, UT: Brigham Young University, 1985.

_____ (ed). *The Taste of the Pineapple: Essays on C. S. Lewis as Reader, Critic, and Imaginative Writer*. Bowling Green, OH: Popular Press, 1988.

Hannay, Margaret. *C. S. Lewis*. New York: Ungar, .

Myers, Doris T. *C. S. Lewis in Context*. Kent, OH: Kent State University Press .

"The Literary Impact of the Authorized Version"

London: The Athlone Press, 1950. Reprinted in *They Asked for a Paper* and *Selected Literary Essays*.

"The Literary Impact of the Authorised Version," originally a 1950 speech at the University of London, is the ninth essay in *Selected Literary Essays*. Lewis began the essay by discussing the **Bible** in general, then listed five ways a book can be an influence: (1) Source, (2) Quotation, (3) Allusion, (4) Vocabulary, (5) Literary influence, subdivided into structure, rhythm, **imagery**, and style.

Like most of Lewis's work, the essay is deeply learned, with numerous obscure references, ancient and modern. It is also provocative, as in Lewis's use of "Papist" for "Catholic" and his marked preference for Tyndale's writing over More's. In his iconoclastic way, Lewis attempted to show that most influences are not real influences. Regarding vocabulary, for instance, he remarked that using the phrase "consummation devoutly to be wished" shows less influence by **Shakespeare** on our **language** than the use of the word "weird." Allusions, according to Lewis, are used because they stand out from a writer's regular style; thus, the more a writer alludes to a work, the less influence it has had on his style. Using these standards, Lewis unsurprisingly concluded that the Authorised Version (in America, the King James) has had surprisingly little influence on English literature.

Marvin D. Hinten
Bowling Green State University

Also See: Roman Catholicism

Literary Theory

Contemporary literary theory focuses on the interrelationships between writers, readers, and texts, and their triune relationship to the world at large that impinges upon them. It is to be distinguished from the term *literary criticism* in that it tends to focus less on explicating and understanding individual texts as such, the traditional province of the literary critic and historian, and more upon how and why texts "act" upon readers or reflect the cultural or gender milieu out of which they come. It may not be overstating the distinction to say that while critics consider texts, theorists consider textuality.

Consequently, much contemporary theory rejects the premises of previous scholarship, questioning whether there can be a stable text that communicates reliably out of its own time and context, whether there can be an "innocent" reader who can have the immediate experience of a text or any direct confrontation with the "meaning an author intended." Under the influence of philosophical nihilism, some radical platforms—such as that identified under the rubric of "deconstruction"—aim to locate contradictions and disunities in texts in order to demonstrate the inability of **language** to communicate **truth** faithfully. This "unraveling" of texts claims to reveal that all alphabets, sounds, words, and grammars are ultimately arbitrary or imposed. Thus, the professional discussion of literature has become somewhat preoccupied with the epistemology of reading itself. The result has sometimes meant the "death" of authorship coupled with the ascendancy of the reader as one whose activity constitutes the text, that is, usurps the role of the author and makes of the text what she or he wishes.

Lewis's own critical oeuvre reflects few book-length attempts to present a comprehensive literary theory, at least in the contemporary sense of the word. Always preferring attention to the work at hand to speculation over its origins or what lies "between the lines," Lewis was much more inclined to offer "theory" in rebuttal to theoretical wrongheadedness in another critic rather than to elaborate a self-standing model of his own. *The Personal Heresy* (1939), wherein Lewis debates E. M. W. Tillyard on the topic of whether "all **poetry** is about the poet's state of mind," is a case in point; in framing Tillyard's stance as "the personal heresy," Lewis constructed on the fly a theoretical model of the author/reader contract in order to elucidate his conception of the literary experience: "To see things as the poet sees them, the reader must share his consciousness and not attend to it." Here, as elsewhere, Lewis opposed notions of reading or theory that equate knowing an author's psychology with knowing his or her poem.

Lewis was thus aware of the growing theoretical foment within the profession of literature from the 1930s onward, and took an active part in the critical skirmishes that frequently erupted. Prescient as ever, Lewis noted that controversy most often emanated from disciplines outside literature itself, from philosophers or scientists—or critical "amateurs" appropriating **philosophy** or **science** for their own purposes. Having studied philosophy at **Oxford** first before coming to English literature, Lewis found himself often rebuking such critics and quasi-critics on their own ground for their naive handling of complex issues. In *The Abolition of Man* (1943), Lewis critiqued the theoretical subjectivism that had crept into an otherwise undistinguished composition textbook and proceeded to extrapolate a theory of objective value, indigenous to the Western **tradition**, to undergird both the teaching and the reading of texts.

One of the most influential critical theorists active during Lewis's early career was philosopher-critic I. A. Richards, whose presuppositions and critical postures Lewis often found himself standing against, since Richards and his followers, he believed, made "criticism . . . a form of social and ethical hygiene." Lewis's *A Preface to Paradise Lost* (1942), written primarily to rehabilitate the reputation of **Milton**'s great **epic**, offers a thoroughgoing though respectful challenge to Richards' "therapeutic" model of poetry.

Lewis's most sustained attempt at literary theory was his book *An Experiment in Criticism* (1961). Here Lewis offered masterful discussions of the themes that echo throughout his lifelong pursuit of responsible literary criticism and history: how and why professional or "literary" readers differ from their amateur or "non-literary" counterparts—and what their comparative advantages and disadvantages are; why "readings" and not books themselves should be judged good or bad; how **myth** and **fantasy** operate in the **imagination** of both author and reader; and why reading should be championed not primarily as a self-aggrandizing, privatizing experience but rather as a transcendental one. A work built upon Lewis's nearly sixty years of precocious and perspicacious reflection on why authors create texts, how texts evoke their fictive worlds, and how readers inhabit them, *Experiment in Criticism* reflects a mature critic's profound balance in treating the components of a sound theory of literary discourse.

Bruce L. Edwards
Bowling Green State University

Bibliography

Edwards, Bruce L. *A Rhetoric of Reading: C. S. Lewis's Defense of Western Literacy.* Provo, UT: Brigham Young University Press, 1985.

_____. (ed). *The Taste of the Pineapple.* Bowling Green, OH: Popular Press, 1988.

Myers, Doris T. *C. S. Lewis in Context.* Kent, OH: Kent State University Press, 1994.

Little Lea

Little Lea was the home that C. S. Lewis's family moved to in April 1905. Lewis's mother, **Florence Lewis**, did not think that **Dundela Villas** was appropriate for their social position and convinced **Albert Lewis** to have the home built. The large three-story brick house, located about two miles from their previous home, was on the outskirts of **Belfast** and had plenty of room for the family and servants. Lewis and his brother, **Warren Lewis**, would often play in the attic, with its tunnel-like passageways. The housemaids would not go in after them and as a result they found privacy and a place to create the imaginative world **Boxen**.

Jeffrey D. Schultz

Bibliography

Lewis, C. S. *Surprised by Joy*

Sayer, George. *Jack: C. S. Lewis and His Times.* Wheaton, IL: Crossway, 1988.

Longinus and English Criticism (Book Review)

The Oxford Magazine. LIII (6 December 1934): 264.

Henn's work showed "much skill and judgement," according to Lewis, although Lewis disagreed with him on a number of points. Henn's book is "something much more exciting, and less utilitarian" than the title might suggest, and Lewis's major regret was its shortness. After a brief discussion of the sublime (which Lewis said need not be theistic), Lewis quoted a printer's error that "commits Burke to the theory that 'excessive litters' are sublime."

Anne Gardner

Also See: Literary Criticism

Bibliography

Henn, T. R. *Longinus and English Criticism*

Love

The nature of love, both human and divine, has received considerable attention in 20th-century Christian thought. Lewis's reflections on the subject—scattered throughout works such as ***The Screwtape Letters*** and ***The Problem of Pain***—constitute a substantial contribution to this discussion. ***The Four Loves*** is a minor classic in its treatment of human and divine love, and both ***A Grief Observed*** and ***Till We Have Faces*** explore the mystery and terror of a divine love that wounds us simply by being what it is.

For Lewis the prominent image of love comes from the triune nature of **God**. From eternity the Father gives all that he is and has to the Son; from eternity the Son offers his begotten deity back to the begetting Father; from eternity Father and Son engage in this mutual bond of love through the self-giving of the Spirit who unites them. Such an image of love underlies chapter 10 of *The Problem of Pain*, and it is from this picture of God's triune life that we may derive three aspects of love, all of which play a role in Lewis's thought: (1) a steady affirmation of the good of the loved one (benevolence); (2) mutuality or reciprocity; and (3) a spirit of self-giving.

While it may sometimes be difficult to say which of these three aspects of love is the most fundamental for Lewis, we can probably say with some confidence that self-giving is more fundamental than reciprocity. Lewis, in fact, described self-giving as "a rhythm not only of all creation but of all being." It is the rhythm of all being because it is present first in the divine life when the Father gives what is his to the Son and the Son, rather than clasping this life to himself, offers it back to the Father. To describe love as self-giving is to say more than that it is unselfish. Screwtape's "Generous Conflict Illusion" (Letter XXVI) deftly illustrates the way in which unselfishness is not yet the positive affection of Christian love. Without the presence of a self-giving spirit,

mutual love can be neither elicited nor sustained. We may therefore describe reciprocal love as the fulfillment or fruition of self-giving love, but the latter will be more fundamental. If mutuality does not arise, self-giving may, in a sinful world, have to become self-sacrifice. From this perspective Lewis could even say that martyrdom is the supreme expression of the Christian spirit as suicide is the typical expression of the stoic spirit.

It is harder to know precisely how to relate self-giving love to benevolence and love. Are we set free to affirm the loved one because we are moved by a spirit of self-giving? Or does benevolent attention to the good of the loved one elicit from us a self-giving spirit? Granting priority to benevolence may seem to have the advantage of making clear that love is not mere kindness, and, indeed, that love may have to punish precisely because it is committed to the good of the loved one. Such themes are quite common in Lewis's writings—appearing, for example, in ***Mere Christianity*** and *The Problem of Pain*. The legitimate role of punishment in love is especially true of God's love for sinful humanity, according to Lewis. In actively seeking to perfect us, God may out of love inflict pains upon us for our good. Such a description of love stands in some tension with an image of love as sheer self-giving and of punishment as something chosen by the sinner rather than inflicted by God. Certainly in *The Four Loves*—as also in *A Grief Observed* and *Till We Have Faces*—sinners cannot reorient their loves toward God, cannot let their loves become "modes of charity" without suffering. For as sinners our loves are inevitably disordered and inordinate. To learn to love rightly will mean, as Orual puts it in *Till We Have Faces*, that the divine nature, simply by being what it is, must seem to wound us.

Lewis did not, however, treat love only in these theoretical ways. In many genres and from many angles he discussed most of the loves that are important in human life. Love of animals is explicitly discussed in *The Four Loves* and is depicted in ***That Hideous Strength***. Love of one's country and love of nature are perceptively treated in *The Four Loves*. Family affection is treated not only in *The Four Loves* but in ***The Great Divorce***, in an essay such as **"The Sermon and the Lunch"** and in several of Screwtape's letters. It is also given an enduring image in the home of Mr. and Mrs. Beaver in ***The Lion, the Witch and the Wardrobe***. Lewis's treatment of **friendship** in *The Four Loves*—a treatment that must be supplemented by his account of his own friendships in ***Surprised by Joy***—is one of the few serious contemporary discussions of a love that was more prominent in the ancient world. Erotic love and **marriage** are straightfor- wardly discussed in both *Mere Christianity* and *The Four Loves*, but they are also examined from different angles in *The Great Divorce*, *A Grief Observed*, and *That Hideous Strength* (one of the central themes of which is the marriage of Jane and Mark Studdock).

Lewis regularly related these natural loves to the love of charity especially enjoined by **Christ** upon his fol- lowers. He will at times describe the natural loves sim- ply as "incomplete" and in need of something more that only a grace-given charity can provide. At other times, however, his picture was more somber, and he used the language of death and rebirth to describe the means by which our natural loves can become modes of charity. The needed transformation of our natural loves "will always," Lewis wrote in *The Four Loves*, "involve a kind of death." From this angle—the angle of Orual, or of Lewis himself in the experience he recorded in *A Grief Observed*—God must appear as the great rival to all the natural loves.

From this perspective the whole of life is constituted by a great either-or. Either we are gradually becoming people all of whose loves are directed toward God, or we are liv- ing more and more within the self, becoming those who are gradually losing entirely the taste for the other. This very Augustinian theme had in **Augustine** not only a per- sonal but also a social dimension. The two loves give rise to two cities, which Augustine called the earthly city and the City of God. Those two cities are given fictional depic-

tion by Lewis in the clash between Belbury and St. Anne's in *That Hideous Strength*. Every actual community—every possible England—is in fact caught in the tension between Logres (the ideal Arthurian community) and Britain (the secular community). The empirical community of England is best described simply as a "swaying to and fro between Logres and Britain." That is the communal dimension of a world in which, ultimately, there are only two kinds of love and two kinds of people according to Lewis: those who say to God, "Thy will be done," and those to whom God must finally say, "Thy will be done."

Gilbert Meilaender

Also See: Ethics and Morality, Family, Good and Evil

Bibliography

Meilaender, Gilbert. *The Taste for the Other: The Social and Ethical Thought of C. S. Lewis*. Grand Rapids, MI: Eerd- mans, 1978.

Moorman, Charles. *The Precincts of Felicity: The Augustin- ian City of the Oxford Christians*. Gainesville: University of Florida Press, 1966.

Nygren, Anders. *Agape and Eros*. Philip S. Watson (trans.). New York: Harper & Row, 1969.

Pieper, Josef. *About Love*. Richard and Clara Winston (trans.). Chicago: Franciscan Herald Press, 1974.

Riga, Frank P. "Self-Love in Augustine and C. S. Lewis." *Cithara*. 26 no. 2 (May 1987): 20–30.

Sayers, Dorothy L. *The Mind of the Maker*. London: Methuen & Co., 1941.

M

George MacDonald (1824–1905)

George MacDonald, poet, preacher, lecturer, and novelist, was perhaps the single most important influence upon C. S. Lewis, which few readers of Lewis fully appreciate. Most note MacDonald's central place in *The Great Divorce* (as Lewis's Virgil in his very British version of *The Divine Comedy*) and most notice the many attributed citations throughout Lewis's writings. Many are aware that it was Lewis's reading in March 1916 of MacDonald's *Phantastes* that baptized Lewis's **imagination**; fewer are aware that Lewis reread this book devotionally, as well as MacDonald's *Diary of an Old Soul*. But only when full attention is paid to Lewis's preface to *George MacDonald: An Anthology*, and only when that book's 365 lovingly selected and edited citations from MacDonald are thoroughly studied—only then can the immensity of Lewis's debt to MacDonald be appreciated. As Lewis stated in the preface, "I have never concealed the fact that I regard him as my master; indeed I fancy I have never written a book in which I did not quote from him. But it has not seemed to me that those who have received my books kindly take even now sufficient notice of the affiliation."

Assembling the anthology allowed Lewis to put the best of MacDonald into the hands of the many correspondents who asked him to recommend books worth reading (the book is dedicated to Mary Neylan who sought Lewis's advice). Seventy percent of the extracts (numbers 1–257) are from MacDonald's three series of *Unspoken Sermons* (Lewis said, "My own debt to [these sermons] is almost as great as one man can owe another"). Of the rest, only two (258 and 259) are taken from *Phantastes*, two (279 and 280) from *The Golden Key* (Lewis's favorite **fairy tale**), eight (333–340) from *Diary of an Old Soul*, and the rest from the novels and children's stories.

From MacDonald Lewis learned many major themes that became central to his thinking and writing: the Fatherhood of **God** and the Sonship of **Christ**, the providence of God (especially in the face of death), the meaning of **prayer** and solutions to the problems associated with prayer, how one becomes a self, and the importance of obedience and of doing one's duty.

Questions about MacDonald's "universalism" have marred his reputation with some Christians. MacDonald believed that **hell** was not everlasting. MacDonald's most succinct explanation of his position is found in the preface he wrote to Thisted's *Letters from Hell*: "There is one growing persuasion of the present age which I hope this book may somewhat stem.... In these days, when men are so gladly hearing afresh that 'in Him is no darkness at all;' that God therefore could not have created any man if He knew that he must live in torture for all eternity; and that His hatred to evil cannot be expressed by injustice, itself the one essence of evil,— for certainly it would be nothing less than injustice to punish infinitely what was finitely committed, no sinner being capable of understanding the abstract enormity of what he does,—in these days has arisen another falsehood—less, yet very perilous: thousands of half-thinkers imagine that, since it is declared with such authority that hell is not everlasting, there is then no hell at all." Despite its finitude, hell was very real to MacDonald: it is the "consuming fire" of God's **love** smelting from the soul every trace of **sin**.

Though he heartily wished otherwise, Lewis parted company with his master on this issue, giving reasons that are detailed in chapter 8 of *The Problem of Pain*. Lewis agreed with MacDonald about the soul's inability to contemplate the enormity of its sin; but the possibility of hell comes not from the soul's rational power but from the will. This disagreement with his master is behind the following statement from the preface to *George MacDonald: An Anthology*: "I dare not say that he is never in error; but to speak plainly I know hardly any other writer who seems closer, or more continually close, to the Spirit of Jesus Himself. Hence his Christlike union of tenderness and severity. Nowhere else outside the New Testament have I found terror and comfort so intertwined."

In **G. K. Chesterton**'s introduction to Greville MacDonald's biography of his parents, *George MacDonald and His Wife*, Chesterton observed: "[W]hen [MacDonald] comes to be more carefully studied as a mystic, as I think he will be when people discover the possibility of collecting jewels scattered in a rather irregular setting, it will be found, I fancy, that he stands for a rather important turning point in the history of Christendom, as representing the particular Christian nation of the Scots. As Protestants speak of the morning stars of the Reformation, we may be allowed to note such names here and there as morning stars of the Reunion." Not only does this passage seem to foresee

Lewis's anthology as a collection of MacDonald's jewels of wisdom and holiness, but it can be made to bestow on MacDonald—and on Lewis—the high vocation of "morning stars of the reunion."

Paul F. Ford
St. John's Seminary

Bibliography

Hein, Roland. *George MacDonald: Victorian Mythmaker*. Nashville: Star Song Publishing Group, 1993.

MacDonald, George. *Unspoken Sermons* (Three Series); new editions are available from Eureka, CA: Sunrise Publishers, and Whitethorn, CA: Johannesen Printing and Publishing.

MacDonald, Greville. *George MacDonald and His Wife*, with an Introduction by G. K. Chesterton. New York: Johnson, 1981.

Raeper, William. *George MacDonald*. Batavia, IL: Lion, 1987.

Thisted, Waldemar Adolph. *Letters from Hell*, with a Preface by George MacDonald. New York and London: Funk and Wagnalls, 1885.

Magdalen College, Oxford University

Founded in the 15th century, **Magdalen** is the most impressive of the **Oxford** colleges. Its Tower is a famous landmark and on its roof a carol is sung at sunrise every May 1st. Its hall is a vast, magnificent place with a great soaring roof and walls lined with portraits of famous Magdalen worthies. Its gardens are a blaze of glory from spring to fall.

I attended Magdalen from 1935 to 1938, while C. S. Lewis was there. Accommodations were spacious but primitive. I was lodged (as was Lewis) in a building erected about 1709. Every student had a living room and bedroom to himself. Mine, on the ground floor, opened onto Deer Park, and I could feed the deer from my windows. Heat came from a coal fire, which warmed the living room only. A college servant brought a daily pitcher of water. Every bedroom was provided with a chamber pot. The lavatories were at the far end of an open colonnade. For a hot bath, you had to go to the bathhouse, across a quadrangle and through the cloisters.

Dinner was in Hall at 7:30. (You were not obligated to attend, but you were charged anyway for four dinners a week.) The students ate at long tables, crowding in wherever they found friends; the fellows (the faculty or "dons") at High Table at the far end. Magdalen, unlike some colleges, ate well. When the deer in Deer Park grew too numerous, venison, duly seasoned, would appear on the menu.

The dons had their Senior Common Room where they drank port after dinner. The students had the Junior Common Room with comfortable armchairs, a supply of magazines, and an adjoining shop. The elected president of the J.C.R. was head of the college student body.

About half the students came from "grammar" (public) schools. Most of the others were from the expensive private schools like Eton or Marlborough. The two groups did not mix well. However, college sports, especially rowing, did something to break down the barriers. American Rhodes Scholars were popular. More mature than the young British students and without class consciousness, they mixed with everybody. The Boat Club, to which I belonged, reveled in singing the songs it learned from a Rhodes Scholar from West Point.

Charles Wrong
University of South Florida (retired)

Also See: Addison's Walk, Cambridge, Oxford, Oxford Socratic Club, Tutor

Bibliography

Hunt, David. "Observations of a Magdalen Don." *In the Search for C. S. Lewis*. Stephen Schofield (ed.). South Plainfield, NJ: Bridge, 1983: 123–25.

Magdalene College, Cambridge University

In the autumn of 1954, some of Lewis's friends and admirers at Cambridge University heard that he was increasingly burdened by difficulties at **Magdalen College, Oxford University**: the time commitment that his tutorial work involved kept him from writing, and the changing nature of the Oxford English faculty that clamored for inclusion of more modern authors in the reading curriculum. Furthermore, despite his significant scholarly work, there was little hope that he would ever be offered a professorship at Oxford, perhaps because of a disapproval among some of the faculty of his Christian **apologetics**. As a result, his Cambridge friends on the English faculty there created the professorship of Medieval and **Renaissance** studies at Cambridge expressly for him.

Lewis was reluctant at first to take the position, because of his attachment to Oxford and his financial inability to sell **the Kilns**, his Oxford home, in order to be able to move to Cambridge. His Cambridge friends suggested that he live in Cambridge during the workweek and commute back to Oxford on weekends. To this arrangement Lewis agreed and he gave his inaugural lecture on November 29, 1954. Titled *"De Descriptione Temporum,"* the address caused great excitement at the time of its delivery. He moved into his new rooms at Magdalene College (with an 'e' on the end), Cambridge, the following January, and took up his duties as professor, which involved occasional lecturing and no tutorials, leaving him much more time to write and read. He continued at Cambridge through the whole of his **marriage**, until his failing health forced him to resign his chair in August of 1963.

That Lewis took delight in the different atmosphere of Cambridge was obvious, and he was particularly fond of Magdalene College. He told one correspondent that the job meant "rather less work for rather more pay." He found that he preferred Magdalene, Cambridge, to Magdalen, Oxford, for it was "tiny," "old-fashioned, and pious, and gentle and conservative—unlike this leftist, atheist, cynical, hard-boiled, huge Magdalen." Shortly before he died he learned that the fellows of Magdalene College had elected him an Honorary Fellow. He wrote back half in jest, "I shall haunt the place whence the most valued of my honours came."

James Prothero

Also See: Atheism, Communism and Fascism, Conservatism, Medieval World

Bibliography

Fryer, W. R. "Disappointed at Cambridge?" *Canadian C. S. Lewis Journal.* 20 (August 1980): 1–5.
Lewis, C .S. *Letters of C. S. Lewis*; *Letters to an American Lady.*

Magic

Lewis defined magic as an attempt to subdue **reality** to the wishes of men, to wrest control of **creation** from the Creator. In *Miracles* Lewis called magic a longing for power without paying the price. The price that is paid in seeking such power is stated in *The Abolition of Man* as the "magician's bargain: give up our soul, get power in return." In *The Magician's Nephew*, Uncle Andrew's arrogant belief that his hidden wisdom excuses him from common rules is typical of the magicians found in Lewis's fiction.

In Narnia the terms magic, deep magic, and deeper magic show the relationship between magic and the natural and **supernatural** orders in his **fantasy**. Magic has good associations only as it occurs in compliance with Aslan. More often it is employed as a device of control and exploitation by wicked persons. Deep magic, the rule by which Edmund was judged and sentenced, is the universally understood moral law ordained by the Emperor-beyond-the-Sea. But in the deeper magic the plan of **redemption** was established before time between the Emperor and Aslan, and to this eternal **truth** all aspects of **natural law**, even death, are subject.

Alice H. Cook

Also See: Fairy Tales, Fantasy, Good and Evil, Miracles, Nature

Bibliography

Ford, Paul. *Companion to Narnia.* New York: Harper, 1980.
Glover, Donald. *C. S. Lewis: The Art of Enchantment.* Athens: Ohio University Press, 1981.
Lewis, C. S. *The Abolition of Man; Miracles; That Hideous Strength.*

"The Magician and the Dryad"

See entry on "Conversation Piece: The Magician and the Dryad"

The Magician's Nephew

London: Geoffrey Bles, 1955. First US edition, New York: Macmillan, 1954.

The Magician's Nephew, the story of Narnia's beginnings, is the last Chronicle of Narnia Lewis completed and the last in the fourth and final burst of creative energy that produced the Narniad. Evan Gibson is perhaps more theologically astute than he intends in discussing *The Magician's Nephew* and *The Last Battle* as the "First and Last Things" because, at the same time he resumed writing *The Magician's Nephew*, Lewis was doing some significant thinking about eschatology that became the essay, **"Christian Hope—Its Meaning for Today"** (later titled **"The World's Last Night"**). *The Magician's Nephew* and *The Last Battle* are interrelated not only because they were composed together, but also because even *The Magician's Nephew*, ostensibly about the beginning of Narnia, vividly describes the ending of a world, Charn. In fact, the Charnian apocalypse needs to be set beside the Narnian one in order to appreciate the severe mercy of Narnia's quick demise described in the last eight chapters of *The Last Battle*.

In a letter to Anne of March 5, 1961, Lewis says that *The Magician's Nephew* is about the "the Creation and how evil entered Narnia." But for that reason should it be read first? Note the prosaic quality of *The Magician's Nephew*'s first paragraph; there is nothing of the numinous as there is in the way Narnia is discovered in *The Lion, the Witch and the Wardrobe*. The "feel" of the book is not first; along with the glory of creation, what *The Magician's Nephew* portrays are (in the words of Doris Myers) "the sins of middle age as well as its tasks and longings, the sins of lust, self-indulgence, and an overweening desire for power."

Borrowing from the psychoanalyst Erik Erikson, we can identify the crises of *The Magician's Nephew* as intimacy versus isolation and generativity versus stagnation; and the choices to be made are between **love** and lust and between care and apathy. In this book Lewis crafted a spectrum of behaviors which demonstrates the consequences of Digory's actions in terms of what the two main villains are both predisposed to and actually guilty of doing (see chart below).

It should be noted that both *The Magician's Nephew* and *The Last Battle* were written at the same time as **Surprised by Joy**, and they are further interrelated for their portrayal—the first obvious and deeply moving, the second subtle—of Lewis's imaginative resolution of the greatest crisis of his life (the death of his mother and the failure of petitionary **prayer** on her behalf) and the reconciliation with his father (Tirian with Erlian in *The Last Battle*, chapter 16).

Set in London in the first decade of the 20th century, the story of *The Magician's Nephew* opens with the introduction of Polly (age eleven and the last of the modern **women** Lewis created to tell the Narnian story) and her new neighbor, Digory (age twelve, the future professor of *The Lion, the Witch and the Wardrobe*), whose joyful life has been shattered by the mortal illness of his mother Mabel and their relocation to the home of her sister Letitia and their mad brother Andrew. Polly sweeps Digory into her life, and they explore their way into Andrew's laboratory. Andrew then tricks Polly into touching a ring, and she disappears. Andrew cruelly quiets Digory and tells him that the rings are made from otherworldly dust and maneuvers Digory into going to Polly's rescue. The boy finds himself and her in the very-much-alive Wood between the Worlds. They experiment to discover the nature of the rings and use them to find their way into a dying world, Charn. They can see Charn's moral and political devolution in the statues of its kings and queens.

Much against Polly's judgment (à la **The Abolition of Man**, her stock responses are in good order) and her will (her arm is twisted), Digory rings the bell whose music brings down the world (in contrast to Aslan's subsequent song creating Narnia) and revives Charn's empress, Jadis. She presumes that Polly and Digory have been sent to take her to their world. The children, escaping, unwittingly take her first to the Wood between the Worlds and then to London. Jadis (now also called "the witch") abandons the children for Andrew who begins to experience the consequences of all of his experimenting with **magic** and his vivisecting of animals. Overhearing that fruit from the land of youth might heal his mother moves Digory to grab hold of Jadis, returned from a stealing spree; but she, Andrew, Polly, the cabby Frank, and his horse Strawberry are all carried first to the Wood and then into a dark world. Thinking themselves dead, Frank strikes up a hymn, which is interrupted by a beautiful solo voice, joined later by other voices as stars break out in the sky. Only Jadis and Andrew are repelled by this unfolding numinous experience. The dawning of a new sun reveals a glorious lion as the singer who is singing this world into being. Andrew dreams about the commercial possibilities of this place when he sees a whole lamppost grown from the piece thrown at the lion by Jadis; but he cares nothing for Digory's quest for something here that will cure Mabel. At this point Digory goes to seek the lion's help. The lion sings the animal-making song and all the animals appear. He selects pairs of many kinds, breathes on them, and bids them speak, naming this world Narnia, as a Pentecost-like fire falls on them. They respond, with the lion's name, Aslan, in obedience, humility, and humor. The lion selects a council to confer about the evil introduced into Narnia. Digory is admitted to their deliberations, admits his responsibility, and speaks his quest (Aslan's tears indi-

Digory	Andrew	Jadis
misuses Polly	misuses guinea pigs	misuses her people
succumbs to the secret of the bell, but respects that of the garden	succumbs to the secret of the box	succumbs to the secret of the deplorable word
breaks no promises	breaks deathbed oath	breaks oath to her sister
embraces the lot of ordinary people	exempts himself from the lot of ordinary people	exempts herself from the lot of ordinary people
does not seize the apple for his own purposes	would seize Narnia for his own purposes	would seize the earth and Narnia for her own purposes

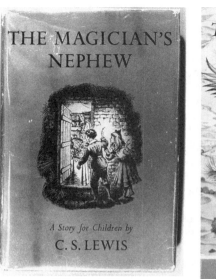

U.K. First Edition

cate that he is more sorrowful for Mabel even than Digory). Aslan sends Digory on a mission (helped by Polly who will fly with him on Strawberry-turned-Fledge) to retrieve a special apple from a mysterious western garden, while Frank and his sent-for wife, Helen, are prepared for their coronation as Narnia's Adam and Eve. Digory is received through the garden's gates but encounters Jadis and her temptation to steal the apple to save his mother. She betrays her wickedness in suggesting that he ignore his promise and abandon Polly. Digory refuses and returns to sow the apple at Aslan's direction. The lion consoles the boy with the explanation that "there might be things more terrible even than losing someone you love by death" (certainly the emotional climax of the book for Lewis). Aslan gives Digory an apple for his mother from the new tree that has sprung from his sowing and sends him, Polly, and a scarcely changed Andrew back. The apple heals Mabel, its seeds are buried with the rings, and a tree grows from whose wood the wardrobe of *The Lion, the Witch and the Wardrobe* is later made.

Paul F. Ford
St. John's Seminary

Bibliography

Ford, Paul F. *Companion to Narnia*. San Francisco: HarperSanFrancisco, 1994.
Gibson, Evan K. *C. S. Lewis: Spinner of Tales: A Guide to His Fiction*. Washington, DC: Christian College Consortium, 1980.

Myers, Doris. "The Compleat Anglican: Spiritual Style in the Chronicles of Narnia." *Anglican Theological Review*. LXVI (April 1984): 148–60.
Schakel, Peter. *Reading with the Heart: The Way into Narnia*. Grand Rapids, MI: Eerdmans, 1979.
Yandell, Steven. "The Trans-cosmic Journeys in the Chronicles of Narnia." *Mythlore* 43 (August 1985): 9–23.

Malvern

C. S. "Jack" Lewis attended Malvern College from September 1913 to July 1914. Malvern was a university preparatory school that his older brother, **Warren Lewis,** had attended. Jack disliked Malvern and found it impossible to join in the rounds of work and athletics, as he was not athletically gifted. By his own admission, he was given to being a "prig," that is, he looked down on other boys placed over him who did not share his artistic and academic interests. He wrote a lurid attack on Malvern in *Surprised by Joy*, calling it "Wyvern College," and painted a picture of a school tyrannized by brutish older boys supported by the faculty and a den of rampant homosexuality. Later in life he admitted to Warren and his biographer, **George Sayer**, that his picture of Malvern was distorted. Jack begged his father **Albert Lewis** to take him out of the school. His father finally caved in to Jack's complaints and withdrew Jack from Malvern, sending him to **W. T. Kirkpatrick**, Albert's old headmaster, to be tutored in preparation for the university.

James Prothero

Also See: Education, Sex

Bibliography

Green, Roger Lancelyn, and Walter Hooper. *C. S. Lewis: A Biography*. San Diego: Harcourt, 1974.
Lewis, C. S. *Surprised by Joy*.
Sayer, George. *Jack: C. S. Lewis and His Times*. San Francisco: Harper, 1988.

The Man Born Blind

Church Times. No. 5947 (4 February 1977): 4–5. Reprinted in *The Dark Tower*, *Of This and Other World,* and *On Stories*.

In the 1920s C. S. Lewis wrote a short story about the problems that follow a successful eye surgery for a man born blind. Lewis was probably familiar with speculations about this subject in Locke's *Essay Concerning*

Human Understanding or George Berkely's *A New Theory of Vision*.

According to the 1977 introduction to *The Dark Tower and Other Stories*, the long-lost *Man Born Blind* was rescued from a three-day bonfire at the **Kilns** in 1964. In the story, newly sighted Robin learned to read print immediately but frustrated his affectionately "stupid" wife, Mary, with questions about the nature of the light that "**Milton** was talking about." "[Robin] was searching, searching with a hunger that had already something of desperation in it." One morning he walked out into the country, saw sunlit mist "spiraling" in a quarry pit, and jumped into it to his (possibly intentional) death.

In spite of its potential, the existing story is a failure; it lacks both neurological and psychological validity and has neither allegorical nor fantastic coherence. Worse yet, it is amateurishly written, with remarkably inept dialogue (dating from the same period as Lewis's superb *The Easley Fragment* fiction).

In answer to 1988 charges that *The Man Born Blind* is not the story written by Lewis in the 1920s, in 1989 **Walter Hooper** made the bonfire manuscript available to researchers for the first time. Nicolas Barker, Deputy Keeper of Britain's National Library, promptly examined it and found that it was written in ink that did not exist before 1950.

Kathryn Lindskoog

Also See: Fred Paxford

Bibliography

Gregory, A. L. "Recovery from Early Blindness." *Concepts and Mechanisms of Perception*. London: Duckworth, 1974.
Lindskoog, Kathryn. *The C. S. Lewis Hoax*. Portland, OR: Multnomah Press, 1988.
Sacks, Oliver. "To See or Not To See." *An Anthropologist on Mars*. New York: Alfred A. Knopf, 1995.

"Man is a Lumpe Where All Beasts Kneaded Be"

See entry on "The Shortest Way Home"

"Man or Rabbit?"

Student Christian Movement, 1946 (?). Reprinted in *God in the Dock* and *Undeceptions*.

In this essay, Lewis responded to the question "Can't you lead a good life without believing in **Christianity**?" Lewis suggested that this kind of question is only asked by people who choose beliefs because they are in some sense helpful. He had difficulty sympathizing with people who search for helpfulness rather than **truth**. Christianity does not claim to be helpful but "to give an

account of *facts*." The division between the man who seeks help and the man who seeks truth is the difference between the man who will do something to increase the **happiness** of the majority and the man who will not do what is unjust, no matter what the promised outcome may be. In the end, Lewis argued that it is impossible to reach a truly good life without **Christ**. According to Lewis, the man who seeks to live a good life as an end has "missed the very point of [his] existence."

Anne Gardner

"The Map and the Ocean"

The Listener. XXXI (24 February 1944): 216. Reprinted in *Beyond Personality* and *Mere Christianity*.

This was the original title of one of Lewis's fourth series of radio talks, which were later revised and collected to make "Beyond Personality," the fourth book of *Mere Christianity*. The first printed version of the talk was published in *The Listener*—a publication of the British Broadcasting System in which some radio talks are reprinted. The talk was then revised for *Mere Christianity*, where it became the chapter titled "Making and Regretting."

Lewis began the radio talk with an anecdote. Once when Lewis spoke about **theology** to the Royal Air Force, an officer said to him, "I've no use for all that stuff, but mind you, I'm a religious man. I know there's a **God**. I've felt him out in the desert at nights." Lewis said that he did not doubt that the officer did have a real experience of God, and that when he turned from that to theology he did turn from that experience to something less real. But Lewis pointed out that a map of the Atlantic Ocean is also less real than an experience of it. Yet the map has some advantages over individual experience. First, the map is based on what hundreds and thousands of people have found out about the Atlantic; second, if one wants to get from one place to another, the map is more useful. Theology is like the map according to Lewis: it is based on many, many experiences, and if you want to get further into **Christianity,** you must use it.

Richard Purtill
Western Washington University

Also See: RAF Talks

"March for Drum, Trumpet, and Twenty-one Giants"

Punch. 225 (November 4, 1953): 553. Revised and reprinted in *Poems* and *Collected Poems*.

The crisp iambic cadence of each line in this poem creates an apt rhythm for the procession of giants Lewis imagined stomping along in their parade of pride and pomp.

Don W. King
Montreat College

Marriage

In a letter to a former pupil (April 18, 1940, *Letters of C. S. Lewis*), C. S. Lewis wrote that the four generally accepted reasons for marrying were to have children, to provide the "only innocent outlet" for one's sexuality, to be in a partnership, and because of "being in love." He went on to say that the last reason is never an adequate basis for marriage; it is "simply moonshine" and "usually transitory." Before his own marriage, Lewis followed the Anglican church in maintaining the primacy of the headship of the male in Christian marriage, while also seeing it as an expression of the nature of the union between **Christ** and the **Church**. In his address **"Membership"** (1945), Lewis said that equality in marriage was not the Divine plan, but a necessity due to **the Fall**. His late marriage to Joy Gresham was by all accounts very happy and one of equal partnership. In *A Grief Observed* he wrote that his marriage was "too perfect to last" and called Joy all and "perhaps more" that any male friend had ever been to him.

Perry C. Bramlett
C. S. Lewis for the Local Church

Also See: Anglicanism, Joy Davidman Lewis, Love, Women

The Martlets

Lewis became a member of the Martlets—a literary society founded at **University College**, **Oxford,** in 1892—in January 1919. An active member of the group, Lewis served as secretary and then as president.

Bibliography

Hooper, Walter. "To the Martlets." *C. S. Lewis: Speaker and Teacher.* Carolyn Keefe (ed). Grand Rapids, MI: Eerdmans, 1971.

Materialism

Materialism is the philosophy that all things—including human thought and morality—can be explained fully as the by-products of material forces such as brain chemistry, heredity, and environmental conditioning. Propagated in modern times by such thinkers as Charles Darwin, Karl Marx, and **Sigmund Freud**, materialism is the operating principle of modern **science**, and it depicts a universe where **God** does not exist, where ideas do not matter, and where every human behavior is reduced to nonrational causes. C. S. Lewis spent much of his life debunking the sterility of materialist thinking, beginning with his first book as a Christian, ***The Pilgrim's Regress,*** and continuing with books such as ***Miracles*** and ***The Abolition of Man*** and essays such as **"Behind the Scenes"** and **"The Poison of Subjectivism."**

In *The Pilgrim's Regress* and *Miracles*, Lewis attacked the materialist account of human thought as contradictory. Materialists dismiss human thought as the mindless product of brain chemistry or environmental conditioning; but if this critique is correct, the materialists' own **philosophy** is also merely the result of nonrational causes, and hence there is no **reason** to accept the materialist account of the universe as true. In *The Abolition of Man*, Lewis critiqued the materialist claim of moral relativism, showing that objective moral standards cannot be avoided even by those who claim to deny them. In his novel ***That Hideous Strength***, Lewis supplied a chilling portrait of the totalitarian utopianism spawned by materialism in the area of **politics** and government. According to Lewis, materialists who deny the existence of both God and an unchanging moral law may feel free to reengineer society using other citizens as their guinea pigs—which is what happened in both Nazi Germany and the Soviet Union.

At its core, Lewis's critique of materialism was positive rather than merely reactive. He attacked materialism in order to defend human dignity. He sought to rearticulate for the modern age the traditional Christian doctrine of man as an accountable being created in the image of God. In line with this purpose, Lewis called on those in the sciences to develop a new natural philosophy that could explain human beings without explaining them away.

John G. West, Jr.

Also See: Communism and Fascism, Modernity, Rationality

Bibliography

Aeschliman, Michael D. *The Restitution of Man: C. S. Lewis and the Case Against Scientism.* Grand Rapid, MI: Eerdmans, 1983.

West, John G. Jr. "C. S. Lewis and the Materialist Menace." Lecture published by Discovery Institute, Seattle, 1996.

Matthew Arnold (Book Review)

The Oxford Magazine. XLVII (15 November 1928): 177.

This scathing review began with the idea that biography is becoming the dominant form of literary endeavor. These thoughts were occasioned by Kingsmill's work on

Matthew Arnold. Kingsmill hated Arnold, the 19th century, and **poetry**, but wrote two hundred odd pages on him nonetheless.

Anne Gardner

Bibliography
Kingsmill, Hugh. *Matthew Arnold.*

Jane Agnes McNeill (1889–1959)

A lifelong friend from **Belfast**, Lewis dedicated *That Hideous Strength* to McNeill. She was the daughter of James Adams McNeill who was **Florence Lewis**'s mathematics master at Methodist College, Belfast. James McNeill, known as "Octie," served as headmaster at **Campbell College**, Belfast, from 1890 until his death in 1907. Janie was well educated and intellectually motivated but never pursued her dreams of **Oxford** or **Cambridge** because of her widowed mother. Lewis often mentioned her in his letters and diaries.

Jeffrey D. Schultz

Bibliography
Lewis, C. S. *All My Road Before Me; They Stand Together*
Rogers, Mary. "Jane McNeill and C. S. Lewis." *Chronicle of the Portland C. S. Lewis Society.* 8.1 (January-March 1979): 9–12.
Sayer, George. *Jack: C. S. Lewis and His Times.* Wheaton, IL: Crossway, 1988.

Medieval World

The Medieval world (or Middle Ages) is the period between antiquity and the Renaissance, roughly dated from the close of the 5th century A.D. to the latter half of the 15th century. Lewis was captivated early by the Medieval world, initially romanticized and filtered through writers like Longfellow, Mark Twain, **William Morris**, and **Conan Doyle**, but soon encountered firsthand. It inspired his own writing experiments as a young man, most notably a romance (*The Quest of Bleheris*) and a classical tragedy based on Norse myth (*Loki Bound*). At sixteen he acquired a copy of Malory and raced through it. This was followed by *Gawain and the Green Knight*, the *Canterbury Tales*, the French *Tristan*, and the Song of Roland. At seventeen a long letter to **Arthur Greeves** described his method for imaginatively projecting himself into the world of *Beowulf* as he read a translation of that poem; he argued the necessity for and value of such sympathetic reading. But his university studies of Medieval philology from about 1922 on convinced him that such "reconstructing" of the Medieval "state of mind" must also be historical—informed by scholarship—to escape being distorted by

the outlook one already has. Once he decided, around 1927, to specialize in Medieval studies, a major aim in his scholarly writing was guiding others to achieve such imaginative participation. Later, when he had a voice in such matters, he argued for the **Oxford** curriculum's continuing to emphasize the older periods. His object was not merely antiquarian, a more accurate reading of old classics; Lewis believed that a better understanding of the Medieval world and the "Old Western Culture" of which it is a part would yield liberation from narrow **modernity**—"the idols of our own market-place"—and thus a truer perspective on our own milieu. Lewis's scholarly work, in the judgment of **J. A. W. Bennett**, his successor in the Cambridge chair of Medieval and Renaissance Literature, "gave [Medieval studies] a new dimension."

Lewis warned against three pitfalls in Medieval studies. First, there is the tendency to draw the period too sharply and treat all of its ideas as unique. In fact, many Medieval ideas and attitudes had roots in antiquity, and many survived for a century, or even two or three, into "modern" times, as *The Discarded Image* and *"De Descriptione Temporum"* abundantly demonstrate. **Magic** and astrology are examples of phenomena not "specially typical" of the Middle Ages. Second, there is the danger of seeing as monolithic a world that embraced many centuries, much variety, and some great changes. Ballad and romance, for example, and even the "Gothic" in one popular sense, loom large in today's notions of the "Medieval" but occupy relatively small niches in the totality of Medieval culture. Finally, there is the temptation to think of the Medieval world as inferior (as the humanists' self-serving period labels sought to imply). Lewis believed that important ideals (e.g., heroism, chivalry, courtesy, and kingship) had suffered decline with the passing of the Middle Ages. Only with effort can Gower's "politeness" or Malory's "sensitivity" even be grasped today.

Given Lewis's bent to intellectual history (rather than, say, social, economic, or military), it is no surprise that the chief features of the Medieval world that he described were artistic and philosophical. According to Lewis, Medieval authors revered the past, especially bookish authority; they did not pursue originality but saw their role as transmitting, "realizing," synthesizing. The Medieval appetite for encyclopedism and the principle of unity in diversity could encourage a taste for "formlessness" and "garrulity"—but at their best could produce a Salisbury Cathedral, a *Summa*, a *Commedia*. **Allegory** developed as an expression of this principle but, in the late Middle Ages and after, declined into a more limited genre. Preeminent among these imaginative creations, the now-"discarded" "Medieval Model," or system of received cosmology and **psychology**—like all models, including our own, a provisional product of its culture—reflects that age's vision of a teeming, orderly, moral universe.

The Medieval world appears in Lewis's fiction and poetry in various ways. Its general features—e.g., castles, weapons, transportation, social structure, clashes between alien cultures—provide the setting for the **Chronicles of Narnia**. Its stories furnished Lewis with characters, like Lancelot (titular hero of a Lewis poem), Merlin, and the Pendragon, also named Fisher-King; archetypes, such as Ransom's Beowulf-like mortal combat in the depths (**Perelandra**); and the elements of faery in Narnia. Its literary forms he imitated in *The Pilgrim's Regress* (produced while he was writing *The Allegory of Love*) and poems using alliterative and other Medieval prosodic patterns. *The Great Divorce* and *Perelandra* owe something structurally to **Dante**; the *Dawn Treader* voyage, to Medieval geographers, bestiaries, and iconography. The Wood between the Worlds and the term *oyarsa* come from Bernardus Silvestris, the ending of *The Queen of Drum* (**Narrative Poems**) from Thomas the Rhymer. For Doctor Cornelius in **Prince Caspian** and Merlin in **That Hideous Strength**, stellar conjunctions deserve serious regard. Verbal echoes of Dante and other Medieval writers appear everywhere in Lewis. The challenge to presuppositions that Ransom undergoes in the trilogy (discovering, for example, the splendor of the heavens and the "plenitude" of Venus, both of which seem to vindicate the Medieval Model) parallels what Lewis hoped would happen for readers of his own scholarly writings. Beyond all this, Lewis appropriated Medieval authors' approach to inherited material. "They feel free to illuminate it … even to correct what seems to them … unedifying," he wrote in **"The English Prose Morte"**; it well describes his own procedure in *Till We Have Faces*.

Charles A. Huttar
Hope College

Bibliography

Adey, Lionel. "Medievalism in the Space Trilogy of C. S. Lewis." *Studies in Medievalism* 3 (1991): 279–89.

Bennett, J. A. W. *The Humane Medievalist.* Cambridge: Cambridge University Press, 1965.

Christopher, Joe R. *C. S. Lewis.* Boston: Twayne, 1987.

Daigle, Marsha Ann. "Dante's Divine Comedy and C. S. Lewis's Narnia Chronicles." *Christianity and Literature* 34 no. 4 (1958): 41–58.

Kerby-Fulton, Kathryn. "'Standing on Lewis's Shoulders': C. S. Lewis as a Critic of Medieval Literature." *Studies in Medievalism* 3 (1991): 257–78.

Kollmann, Judith J. "C. S. Lewis as Medievalist." *CSL: The Bulletin of the New York C. S. Lewis Society* 10 (July 1979): 1–5.

Kranz, Gisbert. "Dante in the Works of C. S. Lewis." *CSL: The Bulletin of the New York C. S. Lewis Society* 4 (December 1973): 1–8.

Lewis, C. S. *Arthurian Torso; English Literature in the Sixteenth Century Excluding Drama; Letters; Narrative Poems;* "The Necessity of Chivalry"; *Studies in Words; They Stand Together.*

Myers, Doris T. *C. S. Lewis in Context.* Kent, OH and London: Kent State University Press, 1994.

Patterson, Nancy-Lou. "Ransoming the Wasteland: Arthurian Themes in C. S. Lewis's Interplanetary Trilogy." *Lamp-Post* 8.2–3 (1984): 16–26; 8.4: 3–15.

Walsh, Chad. *The Literary Legacy of C. S. Lewis.* New York and London: Harcourt Brace Jovanovich, 1979.

"Meditation in a Toolshed"

The Coventry Evening Telegraph. (17 July 1945): 4. Reprinted in *God in the Dock, Undeceptions,* and *First and Second Things.*

The narrator of this essay is standing in a toolshed when he notices the sunbeam coming through the crack at the top of the door. Everything else was almost pitch black, but the beam was striking. As he moves, the beam falls on his eyes. Suddenly he can see the leaves of the tree outside and beyond it the sun. "Looking along the beam, and looking at the beam are very different experiences." The distinction is simple, and it applies to all our experiences. We get one experience from looking at something and another from looking along it. Which experience is "true" or "valid," and which tells you the most about the thing? "The people who look *at* things have had it all their own way; the people who look *along* things have simply been brow-beaten." It is a characteristic of modern thought that we assume that distance lends perspective and provides a picture of reality. But you cannot discount inside experiences. In order to think, you must have something to think about, and in order to identify what is being seen—what you are looking at—you must have had inside experience—you must have looked along it. "We must, on pain of idiocy, deny from the very outset the idea that looking *at* is, by its own nature, intrinsically truer or better than looking *along*. One must look both *along* and *at* everything…. [T]he period of brow-beating has got to end."

Anne Gardner

Also See: Imagination, Modernity, Reality, Truth

"Meditation on the Third Commandment"

The Guardian. (January 10, 1941): 18. Reprinted in *God in the Dock*, *Undeceptions*, and *Christian Reunion*

The Third Commandment forbids taking the Lord's name in vain, and in this essay Lewis implied that founding a Christian political party would violate this prohibition. Lewis saw two major problems with a Christian political party. First, Christians disagree widely and deeply about the nature and purposes of government, and so arriving at a common political agenda for all Christians would be next to impossible. Second, once a Christian party was created, its members would ascribe a divine authority to their agenda that it did not have. Claiming to speak for God in areas where he had not spoken, party members would be tempted to justify every action (no matter how self-interested) as sanctioned by God. Lewis had a keen appreciation of human sinfulness, and he thought that dressing up political claims with divine authority opened the door to all kinds of evil.

Despite his doubts about a Christian party, Lewis did not believe that Christians should avoid **politics**. Instead, he proposed the creation of a "Christian Voters' Society" that would produce a list of general principles and policies that its members might use when deciding whether to support a particular party. Lewis also suggested that the most practical act a Christian could do to influence politics would be to convert his neighbor.

John G. West, Jr.

Also See: Sin

Bibliography

West, John G. Jr. "Politics from the Shadowlands: C. S. Lewis on Earthly Government." *Policy Review*. (Spring 1994): 68–70.

"Membership"

Sobornost, New Series. 31 (June 1945): 4–9. Reprinted in *Transpositions*, *Weight of Glory,* and *Fern-Seed and Elephant*.

Lewis observed that **religion** is not considered in the New Testament to be merely a private activity; Christians are to join a group known as a body. The word "membership" is to us today somewhat misleading; it implies interchangeable parts, as soldiers are in an army. Lewis found a better **analogy** for membership in the concept of **family** members because these members have different roles. Both the state and the **church** need inequality to function most effectively. Our contemporary states operate as democracies because this is a fallen world, and we need checks on one another. Lewis

noted in closing that all of our structures are brief things compared to the life span of an eternal individual.

This often-overlooked essay is one of the most typically Lewisian. He repeatedly quoted literature, used analogies, and brought in authorities to make his points. Many of the ideas are traditional ones that led in another context to Lewis referring to himself as a "dinosaur": e.g., he argued that human beings do not have worth apart from God and that husbands should by the very nature of things rule over wives. Both in style and content, this is standard Lewis.

Marvin D. Hinten
Bowling Green State University

Also See: Analogy, Anglicanism, Democracy, Hierarchy, Marriage, Roman Catholicism

Bibliography

Griffiths, Alan. "The Adventure of Faith." *C. S. Lewis at the Breakfast Table*. James Como (ed). New York: Macmillan, 1979.

"Memory of Sir Walter Scott"

The Edinburgh Sir Walter Scott Club Forty-ninth Annual Report. (1956): 13–25. Retitled "Sir Walter Scott" and reprinted in *They Asked for a Paper* and *Selected Literary Essays.*

Lewis was always a fan of large, meandering novels, and few writers meander better than Scott. In this selection reprinted as "Sir Walter Scott" in *Selected Literary Essays*, first given to a Walter Scott club, Lewis discussed both the works and the writer. Scott, Lewis said, was a wise and gentle man who cared about both people and animals. He kept a journal, from which Lewis quoted regularly, showing Scott's sincerity and self-awareness. Lewis noted the weakness of Scott's polysyllabic style, then praised Scott for developing historical awareness in modern readers and for having a sense of proportion and accuracy.

This is one of Lewis's most typical nonscholarly essays. He clearly enjoyed Scott, yet was aware of flaws. The specific topic led Lewis, as was usual with him, into a discussion of past and present cultures, and as usual he found danger in leaving behind the values of the past. In this talk, Lewis argued that the modern desire for "seriousness" in art, overriding all other values, would be a loss to both life and literature if allowed to overwhelm us. In a typical oddity, Lewis spoke of cheerfulness as "masculine," but generally in this pleasant piece he comes across as a knowledgeable, genial lover of literature.

Marvin D. Hinten
Bowling Green State University

Also See: Culture, Modernity

Mercy

Lewis believed **Christianity** attached much importance to mercy. In *The Problem of Pain*, he noted that, "if one virtue must be cultivated at the expense of all the rest, none has a higher claim than mercy." He rejected as cruel those who would label it mere humanitarianism or sentimentality. But Lewis also felt that since the mid-19th century, our society had stressed that one virtue to such an extent that many people thought kindness or mercy was the only virtue and cruelty the only evil. The problem with that, he said, was that it was quite easy to confuse genuine mercy—which can be quite difficult—with a vague feeling of benevolence that simply means no one is annoying us at present. Pilate, he wrote in the twenty-ninth of Screwtape's letters, was inclined to be merciful until Jesus **Christ**'s foes pointed out the risk of protecting a possible foe of Rome. Other **virtues**—such as temperance, chastity, or humility—are not as easy to confuse with security or **happiness**.

Lewis's most sustained attack on the modern attitude toward mercy came in his controversial 1949 magazine article, **"The Humanitarian Theory of Punishment."** There he attacked the idea that punishing a man "because he deserves it" was "mere revenge" and that the only legitimate reason for punishment was to deter others or to reform the criminal. Lewis believed that such an idea, while appearing merciful, actually deprived lawbreakers of their rights as human beings. If crime no longer deserved punishment, then the link between punishment and **justice** was severed. Anything could be done to anyone, guilty or innocent, if the net effect was to deter others from a particular crime. Any degree of punishment, however harsh or lengthy, could be justified by arguing that it was necessary to ensure a reformed individual. The older view of punishment, Lewis said, was that "mercy tempered justice." In the new theory, mercy simply replaced justice and 'kindness' was imposed without considering the rights of those imposed upon. The result was that "Mercy, detached from Justice, grows unmerciful." Despite the appearance of mercy, the humanitarian theory of punishment could be quite cruel because it treated its subjects as less than human.

The same principles that are true in human society are also true in the spiritual realm. The mercy of **God** is closely tied to his justice. When he discussed **Hell** in *The Problem of Pain*, Lewis stressed the need to understand retributive punishment in order to explain how God's justice and mercy are reconciled. Taking as an example a man who lived a life totally devoted to evil yet was never troubled by guilt and who dies without remorse, Lewis asked if it makes sense that such a man, having never felt himself under the judgment of God, should receive God's mercy. To do so, God must either behave like the advocates of "humanitarian punishment" and reform such a man against his will or God must condone rather than forgive the man's sins for: "the man who admits no guilt can accept no forgiveness." True mercy can only come to those who admit that their punishment is just and well-deserved.

Mike Perry

Also See: Good and Evil, Guilt, Redemption, Sin

Bibliography

Cole, G. A. "Justice: Retributive or Reformative?" *The Reformed Theological Review* 45 no. 1 (January-April 1986): 5–12.

Lewis, C. S. "The Humanitarian Theory of Punishment"; *The Problem of Pain*

Richards, Jerald. "C. S. Lewis, Retributive Punishment, and the Worth of Persons." *Christian Scholar's Review* 14 (1985): 347–59.

Mere Christianity

"Mere Christianity" was Lewis's term for the essential Christian message as espoused historically by Catholics and Protestants alike. Thus, "Mere Christianity" is the theological core on which different Christian traditions can agree; in Lewis's words, it is the collection of "the common doctrines of **Christianity**." Rather than being a watered-down version of the real thing, "Mere Christianity" in Lewis's view was "not only positive but pungent," and it was "divided from all non-Christian beliefs by a chasm to which the worst divisions inside Christendom are not really comparable at all."

Lewis adapted the term from Protestant divine Richard Baxter (1615–1691), a prolific and persecuted author of more than 160 works who was known for articulating the "fundamentals of religion" shared by Christians from competing denominations. One Bishop said of Baxter that had he lived during the earliest years of Christianity, he would have been "one of the fathers of the **church**."

"Mere Christianity" ultimately became the title of one of Lewis's most popular books, an edited collection of essays originally published in three separate volumes as *The Case for Christianity*, *Christian Behaviour*, and *Beyond Personality*.

Lewis's articulation of "Mere Christianity" has gained increased relevance of late as many Catholics and Protestants have sought common ground for joint actions in the area of **culture**.

	Chapter Title	Other Published Sources	BBC Radio Broadcast	Comments
	BOOK 1: Right and Wrong as a Clue to the Meaning of the Universe			
BROADCAST TALKS	*Chapter 1:* "The Law of Human Nature"		"Common Decency" August 6, 1941	
	Chapter 2: "Some Objections"		"Answers to Listeners' Questions" September 6, 1941	
	Chapter 3: "The Reality of the Law"		"Scientific Law and Moral Law" August 13, 1941	
	Chapter 4: "What Lies Behind the Law"		"Materialism or Religion" August 20, 1941	
	Chapter 5: "We Have Cause to be Uneasy"		"What Can We Do About It" August 27, 1941	
	BOOK II: What Christians Believe			
U.S. Edition Titled THE CASE FOR CHRISTIANITY	*Chapter 1:* "The Rival Cenceptions of God"		First Talk January 11, 1942	
	Chapter 2: "The Invasion"		Second Talk January 18, 1942	
	Chapter 3: "The Shocking Alternative"		Third Talk February 1, 1942	
	Chapter 4: "The Perfect Penitent"		Fourth Talk February 8, 1942	
	Chapter 5: "The Practical Conclusion"		Fifth Talk February 15, 1942	
	BOOK III: Christian Behavior			
CHRISTIAN BEHAVIOR	*Chapter 1:* "The Three Parts of Morality"		First Talk September 20, 1942	
	Chapter 2: "The Cardinal Virtues"			
	Chapter 3: "Social Morality"		Second Talk September 27, 1942	
	Chapter 4: "Morality and Psychoanalysis"		Third Talk October 4, 1942	
	Chapter 5: "Sexual Morality"	"This Was a Very Frank Talk—Which We Think Everyone Should Read." *Daily Mirror.* (13 October 1942): 6-7.	Fourth Talk October 11, 1942	Lewis read a revised manuscript. The original is in the BBC Archives. The *Daily Mirror* article was an illegal publication of the talk.

Chart by Jeffrey D. Schultz and Mike W. Perry

Chart continued on page 269

	Chapter Title	Other Published Sources	BBC Radio Broadcast	Comments
BOOK III: Christian Behavior CONTINUED				
CHRISTIAN BEHAVIOR	*Chapter 6:* "Christian Marriage"			
	Chapter 7: "Forgiveness"		Fifth Talk October 18, 1942	
	Chapter 8: "The Great Sin"		Sixth Talk October 25, 1942	
	Chapter 9: "Charity"			
	Chapter 10: "Hope"			
	Chapter 11: "Faith"		Seventh Talk November 1, 1942	
	Chapter 12: "Faith"		Eighth Talk November 8, 1942	
BOOK IV: Beyond Personality				
BEYOND PERSONALITY	*Chapter 1:* "Making and Begetting"	"The Map and the Ocean" *The Listener.* February 24, 1944	"Making and Begetting" February 22, 1944	
	Chapter 2: "The Three-Personal God"	"God in Three Persons" *The Listener.* March 2, 1944	"The Three-Personal God" February 29, 1944	Recorded, but no copies survive.
	Chapter 3: "Time and Beyond"			
	Chapter 4: "Good Infection"	"The Whole Purpose of the Christian" *The Listener.* March 9, 1944	"Good Infection" March 1944	
	Chapter 5: "The Obstinate Toy Soldier"	"The Obstinate Tin Soldier" *The Listener.* March 16, 1944	"The Obstinate Tin Soldier" March 14, 1944	
	Chapter 6: "Two Notes"			
	Chapter 7: "Let's Pretend"	"Let Us Pretend" *The Listener.* March 23, 1944	"Let's Pretend" March 21, 1944	
	Chapter 8: "Is Christianity Hard or Easy?"	"Is Christianity Hard or Easy?" *The Listener* March 30, 1944	"Is Christianity Hard or Easy?" March 28, 1944	Recorded, but no copies survive.
	Chapter 9: "Counting the Cost"			
	Chapter 10: "Nice People or New Men"			Audiotape of March 21, 1944 recording is available from the Episcopal Radio-TV Foundation (See Resources for contact information).
	Chapter 11: The New Man"	"The New Man" *The Listener* April 6, 1944	"The New Man" April 4, 1944	

Also See: Anglicanism, Roman Catholicism

Bibliography

Baxter, Richard. *The Practical Works of Richard Baxter, Select Treatises.* Grand Rapids, MI: Baker Book House, 1863.

Colson, Charles and Richard John Neuhaus. *Evangelicals and Catholics Together.*

Lewis, C. S. Introduction to *St. Athanasius' The Incarnation of the Word of God.*

Mere Christians (Letter)

Church Times. CXXXV (8 February 1952): 95. Reprinted in *God in the Dock, Undeceptions,* and *Timeless at Heart.*

Spurred by R. D. Daunton-Fear's letter on "Evangelical Churchmanship" (*Church Times,*1 February 1952, 77), Lewis questioned why the Evangelical and the Anglo-Catholic do not embrace their obvious commonality as supernaturalists as opposed to the stance of the liberals or modernists within the **church**. He further asks why the Evangelicals and Anglo-Catholics do not value their essential agreement with each more highly than they count their differences. Finally, he conjectures that the problem is one of vocabulary (i.e., "low" church versus "high" church) and suggests that both groups substitute instead, "mere Christian."

Marjorie L. Mead
The Marion E. Wade Center

Also See: Anglicanism, Roman Catholicism

Metaphor

As most readers are aware, the difference between similes and metaphors is that similes use "like" or "as" to make comparisons ("he eats like a pig") while metaphors make the point directly ("what a pig he is!"). In terms of classical rhetoric, metaphors, like all figures of speech, are rhetorical devices used to light up truth; they are flashes of lightning in the metaphysical darkness, enabling readers to briefly see a glimpse of truth and move toward it. (And that lightning image is itself a metaphor.)

Lewis understood metaphors in the traditional rhetorical sense. In his essay **"Bluspels and Flalansferes,"** he says that **reason** produces **truth**, but **imagination** produces meaning; in other words, metaphors and other products of the imagination make truth understandable. In the tenth chapter of *Miracles*, Lewis remarked that people tend to underestimate the importance of metaphors; they think metaphors are linguistic tidbits thrown in by poets for decoration, whereas actually ultimate things cannot be talked about without metaphor.

Our relationship with our conscience can be used to illustrate this. None of us would think of our conscience as an actual person inside us. Yet we say we need to obey our conscience, thus linguistically giving it the qualities of a master. If we "follow" our conscience, it's a leader; if we "listen to" our conscience, it's a speaker. According to Lewis, such difficulties are inherent in the use of human language to talk about more-than-human things.

Metaphor was important to Lewis from the very beginning of his Christian experience. In his first post-conversion work, *Pilgrim's Regress*, he said in chapter 5 of Book IX: "The words of Wisdom are also myth and metaphor . . . was there any age in any land when men did not know that corn and wine were the blood and body of a dying and yet living God?"

Lewis stressed this example because it was one crucial to his becoming a Christian. During a lengthy amble with **Hugo Dyson** and **J. R. R. Tolkien** on **Addison's Walk**, a wooded pathway behind **Magdalen College** in **Oxford**, the three of them discussed at some length Lewis's difficulties regarding the death and resurrection of **Christ**. Lewis described the conversation at length in an October 11, 1931, letter to his close friend **Arthur Greeves**; significant excerpts from the letter are accessible in various places, including the collection of letters to Greeves and the Green-Hooper biography of Lewis. In essence, Lewis says that he recognized from Dyson and Tolkien that the idea of sacrifice, particularly of a god sacrificing himself to himself, he always found moving in pagan stories. (Probably Lewis was particularly thinking of the sacrifice of Odin to himself in later Norse mythology.) Lewis also appreciated and was even moved by stories of dying and resurrected gods—again, provided they were in a mythical context. In a key sentence, Lewis noted, "The reason was that in Pagan stories I was prepared to feel the **myth** as profound and suggestive of meanings beyond my grasp even tho' I could not say in cold prose 'what it meant.'" Dyson and Tolkien convinced Lewis that the death and resurrection of Christ was a real event that also reverberated with meanings beyond what he was able to grasp or express.

This concept of multiple meanings in events beyond what reason can express became a key factor not only in Lewis's conversion, but in his whole understanding and expression of **Christianity**. All language regarding non-sensory concepts, especially **metaphysics**, uses metaphors, Lewis contended. In his essay "**Horrid Red Things**," he noted that some people feel calling God a "Father" or "King" is metaphorical, so it would be better, since we do not understand His nature, to call Him a "Force." But as Lewis astutely pointed out, this simply means substituting the idea of wind or a dynamo for one of the other images.

Virtually all of Lewis's writings are flooded with brief and extended figures of speech. He comments in his 1936 work *The Allegory of Love* that "every metaphor is an **allegory** in little." (In the same way, one could note that every simile is an analogy in little.) And it is worth observing that if one were to select the key continuing literary element of Lewis's style, both fiction and nonfiction, it would be the repeated use of allegories, analogies, metaphors, and similes. His first fiction work after conversion is an allegory, *Pilgrim's Regress*; and his first nonfiction book after conversion is *The Allegory of Love*. And in those books, as well as throughout his career, Lewis used little allegories—metaphors.

Perhaps his most famous large metaphor is his use of a Christ-figure, Aslan, in the **Chronicles of Narnia**. Aslan's "task," if one may so call it, is to be a metaphor for Christ—to present elements of Christ and his work to the imagination in such a way that they move the reader and illuminate truth. Just as Balder in Norse mythology, with his dying and resurrection, could be a mythical picture of Christ, Aslan is a picture of Christ in a context not overtly Christian. Although the Chronicles were not originally intended for "evangelism" purposes, Lewis did feel that Aslan could be used as a metaphor to show the meaning of Christ's life and death.

Marvin D. Hinten
Bowling Green State University

Also See: Imagery, Language/Rhetoric, Polemics, Symbolism

Bibliography

Filmer, Kath. "The Polemic Image: The Role of Metaphor and Symbolism in the Fiction of C. S. Lewis." *Seven* 7 (1986): 61–76.

Pyles, Franklin Arthur. "The Language Theory of C. S. Lewis." *Trinity Journal*. 4 no. 2 (1983): 82–91.

Metaphysics

Metaphysics is the area of **philosophy** which deals with the question "what is most real?" Lewis was keenly interested in this and his answer to this question was one of the basic themes that unified his life and his work.

It was Lewis's view (*Mere Christianity*) that ever since humans were able to think, they have been wondering what this universe really is and how it came to be here. Lewis outlined the two opposing metaphysical views in their classical forms. The first is what Lewis and many philosophers call **materialism**. People who accept this view think that matter, motion, and empty space are most real, that they have always existed, and nobody knows why. According to this view, matter over millions of years has just happened by chance to produce creatures like us who are self-conscious and able to think and **reason**. In contrast to the materialist view is what many philosophers call "philosophical idealism." Lewis called it "the religious view." According to both philosophical idealists and religious people of all stripes, what is behind the universe is more like a mind than it is like anything else we know. It is conscious, has purposes, and prefers some things to other things.

Lewis encouraged Christians to see the common ground they shared in the area of metaphysics. He believed that the first big division of humanity is into a majority who believe in some kind of **God** or gods and a minority who do not. On this point, **Christianity** lines up with ancient Greeks and Romans, modern savages, Hindus, and Muslims.

Lewis believed, somewhat similar to **Plato**, that there are two *real* worlds, not one. There is the world of changing physical things that we apprehend by means of our senses, and there is the world of intelligible objects that we apprehend, in our natural human state, only by means of our intellects or minds.

According to Lewis, God created human beings with **free will** so that they could choose between right and wrong. A world of automata—creatures who worked like machines—would hardly be worth creating. And the moment one has a free self there is the possibility of putting oneself first, wanting to be the center, wanting to *be* God, in fact. That was the **sin** of **Satan**, and that was the sin he taught the human race.

We come now to the essence of Christianity and the center of Lewis's metaphysics. Among the Jews we find a man who talks as if he were God. He claims to be able to forgive sins. He says he has always existed, that he is coming to judge the world at the end of time. According to Lewis, we must all choose between Jesus as lunatic, Jesus as the Devil of **Hell**, and Jesus as who he says he is. Lewis did not think it is logical to say (as millions continue to say) that Jesus is a great moral teacher but not God.

Michael H. Macdonald
Seattle Pacific University

Also See: Anglicanism, Creation, Evolution, Good and Evil, Modernity, Reality, Religion, Roman Catholicism, Science

Bibliography

Aristotle. *Metaphysics*.

Plato. *Republic*; *Phaedo*.

Chesterton, G. K. *The Everlasting Man*. Greenwood, CT: Greenwood Press, 1974.

Kreeft, Peter. *Love Is Stronger than Death* and *Heaven*. New York: Harper & Row, 1979,

Lewis, C. S. *The Great Divorce; Mere Christianity; The Problem of Pain; The Screwtape Letters*

Patrick, James. *The Magdalen Metaphysicals*. Macon, GA: Mercer University Press, 1985.

"The Meteorite"

Time and Tide. 27 (December 7, 1946): 1183. Reprinted in *Poems* and *Collected Poems*.

This poem is a thoughtful reflection on the continuity of matter. The speaker considers how a meteorite weathering out in the English countryside is easily hosted by the earth.

Don W. King
Montreat College

"Metre"

A Review of English Literature. I (January 1960): 45–50. Reprinted in *Selected Literary Essays*.

In this essay Lewis bemoaned the "hair-raising barbarity" of contemporary English majors who do not understand or recognize scansion (the analysis of verse into metrical patterns). If this was true in his own place and time, it is even truer today, as any college English teacher of traditional **poetry** knows. People conversant with traditional metrics, however, will greatly appreciate this article, one of the wittiest and most emotionally involved that Lewis ever wrote in the literary vein.

He began by indicating how metricism must be determined from the "feel" of the whole poem, not inductively, line by line. An inductive method would allow irregular lines to fit the poem as alternatives rather than as exceptions. Lewis mourned how contemporary readers cannot get from **John Milton**'s "Burnt after them to the bottomless pit" the "sense of falling into a void" that a reader sensitive to metrics would find. He did not spell out why that occurs, assuming readers of this essay to be metrically sensitive and able to recognize the rapidity of the unaccented syllables caused by the enjambment of the accented ones. Lewis closed by defending traditional metrical terminology and lamenting once again the lack of sensitivity to metrics among modern students.

Marvin D. Hinten
Bowling Green State University

Also See: Education, Literary Criticism, Literary Theory, New Criticism

"Metrical Experiment"

See entry on "Experiment"

"A Metrical Suggestion"

Lysistrata. II (May 1935): 13–24. Retitled "The Alliterative Metre" and reprinted in *Rehabilitations* and *Selected Literary Essays*.

This remarkable essay is an attempt to explain the intricacies of the Anglo-Saxon/Medieval alliterative line to a modern audience. Lewis took this complex subject step by step, showing how appreciating the alliterative line's metricism requires a solid understanding of syllabic quantity as well as alliteration. The article is profusely illustrated; when he discussed the "Type D" line, for instance, with its "Lift, Lift-dip" pattern (i.e., a lengthy accented syllable, followed by another, closed with two short unaccented syllables), he provided six examples, such as "HARD HAYmaking" and "HELL'S HOUSEkeeper."

The article flowed from Lewis's long and loving lifetime of reading Anglo-Saxon **poetry**. His memory of thousands of lines enabled him to toss off minor points that escape many readers, such as that four alliterative syllables in a line is a defect rather than a virtue, and that the words flow more smoothly across line-ends than across the medial break. The essay closed in a way that separates Lewis from other scholars; he invented a poem on the planets, of well over 100 lines, to illustrate the five main Anglo-Saxon lines and their several offshoots. Like most of Lewis's literary essays, this one will be appreciated mainly by scholars.

Marvin D. Hinten
Bowling Green State University

Also See: Literary Criticism

Mgr. R. A. Knox (Letter—with others)

Church Times. CXLI (6 June 1958): 12.

Lewis along with others announced a subscription campaign to raise funds for a memorial in honor of Mgr. Ronald Knox at Trinity College, **Oxford,** where he had served as both Chaplain and Honorary Fellow until his death. The signatories invited gifts to endow a grant which will allow a member of the College to travel abroad, as well as to purchase a bust of Mgr. Knox as a visible memorial. They intended this memorial to be "inter-confessional" in order to represent Mgr. Knox's many friendships from various denominations.

Marjorie L. Mead
The Marion E. Wade Center

The Millers

Leonard and Maud Emily (Len and Molly, sometimes spelled Mollie) Miller were both born in 1901. They were a childless couple who owned a house near **the Kilns** and had a nodding acquaintance with the Lewis brothers. In 1953 Mrs. Miller felt bored and wished for some part-time employment as a pastime, just when the Lewises needed a housekeeper. She took the job, became very fond of the Lewis brothers and **Joy Davidman Lewis**, and was part of life at the Kilns for approximately twenty years. She was a peppery, talkative person; her multitalented husband Len had a keen mind and high standards.

In 1965 **Warren Lewis** asked the Millers to sell their house and move into the Kilns with him, which they did. As noted by **Roger Lancelyn Green** and **Walter Hooper** in *C. S. Lewis, A Biography*, "He was supremely fortunate in his domestic arrangements: Mr. and Mrs. Miller, who looked after him (with some help from Paxford, whose real domain was the garden) were devoted to 'Mr. Jack' and 'The Major,' and tended Lewis with the love and care of the true friends which they had become." Warren Lewis considered the pair his adopted family and mentioned them often in his diary.

When Warren Lewis died in 1973, the Millers were displaced because the Kilns automatically became the property of **Maureen Moore**. (A published claim that Len Miller stole Warren Lewis's gold cuff links off his warm corpse and then spirited away all the contents of the Kilns before it could be secured proved to be manifestly untrue. It has been retracted.) In his will Warren arranged to provide a brand-new house for the Millers to live in for the rest of their lives. In that house in Eynsham they warmly welcomed visitors from America who came to chat about the Lewis brothers. (Most of the material in this essay is from an interview recorded there on December 27, 1975.) Mrs. Miller died in 1976, and Mr. Miller died a few years later.

Kathryn Lindskoog

Bibliography

Lewis, Warren. *Brothers and Friends: An Intimate Portrait of C. S. Lewis*

Lindskoog, Kathryn. *Light in the Shadowlands*. Sisters, OR: Multnomah, 1994.

John Milton (1608–1674)

Little biographical material of importance has been added to the life of poet John Milton since the publication of Hanford's *Handbook* in 1926, nor for that matter since Dr. **Samuel Johnson's** *Lives of the English Poets* (1779–81). One substantial mystery remains: how he escaped the hangman after the Restoration, though the answer doubtless lies in his friends and supporters who had the ear of the court. Pardon was secured, and Milton, though blind, went on to his greatest achievements, *Paradise Lost*, *Paradise Regained*, and *Samson Agonistes*. Milton was born into a prosperous scrivener family in Bread Street, London. His Protestant father, also John Milton, had been disinherited by his Catholic family after converting.

We can trace the younger Milton's education from about his tenth year when he was tutored by Thomas Young, later Master of Jesus College, Cambridge. He then entered St. Paul's School, perhaps because of a proficiency in music, and at the age of about fifteen entered Christ Church, Cambridge.

Milton's lifetime ambition, early formed, seems to have been to become England's greatest poet (at least since **Shakespeare**.) In this early period he produced such exquisite lyrics as *l'Allegro* and *Il Penseroso*, the masque *Comus*, and the eulogy *Lycidas*.

His second period is marked by his appointment as Secretary of the Latin tongue to Parliament and to Oliver Cromwell. It begins with his journey to Italy, whence he returned Civil War having broken out in England. In time Milton married and brought home to London a young woman from Oxford whose family had strong royalist ties. She was seventeen and he thirty-five. His wife soon left him to return to her family with no intention of rejoining her husband. It is generally believed that this brought about Milton's famous (and then scandalous) divorce pamphlets. However, ironically, **Oxford** fell to the forces of the Protectorate, and soon his wife was back with a ruined family all living on Milton. This period in Milton's life is marked mainly by public service, although his job as Latin Secretary does not seem to have been overly demanding. At the time the royalist position with respect to church discipline was primarily supported by Bishop Joseph Hall (of Exter). Hall's works, it was said, were in every royalist household. Milton of course sided with the Protestants and actually did some pamphlets (or parts thereof) for them. Some scholars believe the high point in Milton's prose career came in a speech he gave to Parliament called *Areopagitica* in favor of what is now seen as "freedom of Press." Milton could pen an immortal line when he wished; here, "I cannot praise a fugitive and cloistered virtue."

After the Restoration and Milton's fortunate escape from the scaffold, the poet, now blind, spent most of his time on his great works, *Paradise Lost*, *Paradise*

Regained, and *Samson Agonistes*. Milton first seems to have considered English history for the subject matter of his great **epic**; several false starts still exists. But he came soon instead to turn to biblical subject matter, as we know. *Paradise Lost* first appeared in a ten-book format but was soon altered to twelve books to stay in form with the classical epics. Milton's language resembles nothing ever spoken; it is indeed an epic, literary tongue. And his subject matter has given birth to a large amount of interpretation (and argument).

C. S. Lewis first read *Paradise Lost* at the age of nine, and by the time he became a pupil of **W. T. Kirkpatrick**, he was expressing his delight with Milton in letters to his friend **Arthur Greeves**. Lewis occasionally lectured on Milton during the 1930s, but his major scholarly work on Milton came in the early 1940s when he delivered lectures that were ultimately published as the now classic study, *A Preface to Paradise Lost*. Lewis attributed that work to an apotheosis he felt hearing his friend, **Charles Williams**, lecture on *Comus* in 1940. Other references to Milton by Lewis are scattered throughout Lewis's various literary writings, including *Selected Literary Essays, The Allegory of Love, The Discarded Image, Studies in Words*, and *English Literature in the Sixteenth Century*.

Robert O. Evans

Bibliography

Uereich, John C. "Prophets, Priests, and Poets: Toward Definition of Religious Fiction." *Cithara*. 22 no. 2 (May 1983): 3–31.

Milton and His Modern Critics (Book Review)

The Cambridge Review (21 February 1941): 280.

According to Lewis, the two purposes of this book are "to flay alive the critics" and to defend **Milton**. The first purpose is accomplished, but the second is not. Smith is "at bottom (I think) quite sceptical about the possibility of truth and the majesty of moral virtue." The defense of Milton is based solely in the "'charm' and 'enchantment' of his words." The author is not, in Lewis's opinion, on Milton's side—he only thinks he is.

Anne Gardner

Bibliography

Smith, Logan Pearsall. *Milton and His Modern Critics*

A Mind Awake: An Anthology of C. S. Lewis

Clyde S. Kilby (ed). London: Geoffrey Bles, 1968. First US edition, New York: Harcourt, Brace & World, 1969.

An anthology of quotes taken from Lewis's writings.

The Mind of the Maker (Book Review)

Theology. XLIII (October 1941): 248–49.

Dorothy L. Sayers' book offered an analogy between the divine act of **creation** and the process whereby a work of art (specially of literature) is produced. Lewis praised the book, but wished more constant reminders that the "creative" artist does not summon the new, but is creative only metaphorically. He argued with Sayers when she said the difference between Creation and "creation" is one of quality and degree, not of category.

Anne Gardner

Bibliography

Sayers, Dorothy L. *The Mind of the Maker*

Ministering Angels

The Magazine of Fantasy and Science Fiction. XIII (January 1958): 5–14. Reprinted in *Of Other Worlds* and *The Dark Tower and Other Stories*.

This short story is a response to Dr. Robert S. Richardson's article "The Day after We Land on Mars" which appeared in *The Saturday Review* (28 May 1955). Lewis's story opens at a five-man scientific station on Mars crewed by a Captain, a Monk, a Botanist, and two technicians. A ship from earth arrives, carrying three crewmen and two female passengers. The thin one, an ideologue spouting sociologese, leads the first unit of the Woman's Higher Aphrodiso-Therapeutic Humane Organisation (W.H.A.T.-H.O.). The grotesquely fat one is a seventy-year-old prostitute. They have been sent by the Advisory Council to provide sexual relief for the station crew, none of whom needs such relief. The newly married Captain wants to return to his wife. The celibate Monk values his hermitage-like posting to Mars. The Botanist wants only to complete his research. One of the technicians is homosexual; the other is simply repelled by the women.

In a series of vignettes, the Thin Woman humorlessly attempts to administer hygienic "comfort" to the homosexual technician; the Fat Woman confesses to the Monk, who realizes her potential for salvation; the captains of the station and of the space craft denounce the decision of the "Fools at the Top," noting that in previous centuries, sailors and soldiers easily put up with prolonged sexual deprivation. Without warning, the earth ship blasts off, carrying two frantic crewmen and an equally desperate station technician away from the W.H.A.T.-H.O. unit. The story concludes with the bemused Monk, reflecting on this new opportunity for ministry, confessing to God that his love of isolation was self-indulgent.

Lyle Smith
Biola University

Also See: Sex, Space Travel, Women

Bibliography

Foreman, Lelia. "A Short Look at C. S. Lewis' Short Science Fiction." *Chronicle of the Portland C. S. Lewis Society.* 13 no. 1 (January-March 1984): 1–7.

Miracles

Lewis's views on miracles are examined more closely than those of most Christian writers because so much of his nonfiction work deals with **apologetics**, and miracles are an intellectual difficulty for many people, including the younger Lewis. He considered this topic of such importance that he devoted an entire book to it, the aptly named *Miracles*, published in 1947. The prompting for the work may have come from **Dorothy Sayers**, who mentioned to Lewis in 1943 that she felt someone needed to write a book on this subject. But undoubtedly the idea was already of interest to him.

In chapter 10 of *Miracles*, Lewis noted that **Christianity** differs from many of the world's major religions in that miraculous elements are essential to its very nature. Islam and Hinduism, he observed, could survive without attested miracles, but Christianity is, as he put it, "precisely the story of a great miracle."

To Lewis, that great miracle was the Incarnation. He considered that, even more than the Resurrection, the miracle upon which Christianity was based. In chapter 14 of *Miracles* Lewis said, "The central miracle asserted by Christians is the Incarnation. . . . Every other miracle prepares for this, or exhibits this, or results from this." Lewis always found it odd when people wanted to believe in Christianity but not accept the miracle of the virgin birth, thereby voluntarily digging away the foundation upon which their belief system sat. A person who refused to accept the great miracles of Christianity was, for Lewis, not a Christian at all; thus in *The Great Divorce* the bishop who began with disbelieving the Resurrection and

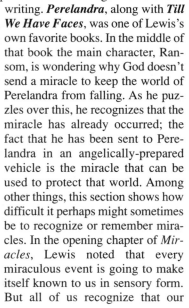

U.S. First Edition

now refuses to accept the supernatural at all winds up in **hell**. Lewis called this type of attitude "Christianity and water"—a diluted view without the potency of the real thing.

Some people might object that, since they have lived their whole lives without ever seeing a miracle, nothing beyond the natural exists. Lewis responded to that attitude in the seventeenth chapter of *Miracles*, where he remarked that miracles occur on "great occasions" in history, and that the average person is unlikely to be around at those particular moments. In his analogical way, Lewis compared our likelihood of seeing a miracle to our likelihood of being around when a dictator commits suicide or when a world-changing scientific discovery is made. By definition, he implies, unusual events are rare occurrences.

Some people considered Lewis a fundamentalist because of his belief in miracles. Lewis was willing, in private communications, to indicate that he was not. In a May 7, 1959 letter to **Clyde Kilby** of Wheaton College, Lewis noted several difficulties he had with the doctrine of inerrancy and presented specific places where the **Bible** seemed to be historically inaccurate. His reputation for being religiously conservative came because Lewis did not rule out the historicity of a passage simply on the grounds that it included a miraculous event.

One place where we can clearly see how Lewis's views on miracles pervaded his thinking is in his fiction writing. *Perelandra*, along with *Till We Have Faces*, was one of Lewis's own favorite books. In the middle of that book the main character, Ransom, is wondering why God doesn't send a miracle to keep the world of Perelandra from falling. As he puzzles over this, he recognizes that the miracle has already occurred; the fact that he has been sent to Perelandra in an angelically-prepared vehicle is the miracle that can be used to protect that world. Among other things, this section shows how difficult it perhaps might sometimes be to recognize or remember miracles. In the opening chapter of *Miracles*, Lewis noted that every miraculous event is going to make itself known to us in sensory form. But all of us recognize that our minds and senses are not infallible. Therefore, if something seemingly miraculous would happen, it can generally be explained away as a hallucination, misapprehension, or mental quirk. And naturally those who are not eyewitnesses to the phenomenon can assume human error on the part of the observers: sleepiness leading to dreams, perhaps, or a failure to examine closely.

The Chronicles of Narnia contain miracles in every book. The first book of the series (as renumbered), *The Magician's Nephew*, shows the **Christ**-figure Aslan creating Narnia out of nothing. In *The Lion, the Witch and the Wardrobe*, Aslan is killed and resurrected. Other books in the collection exhibit sick people being healed, appearances out of nowhere, and instantaneous changes in matter.

Perhaps the most interesting aspect of Lewis's belief in miracles is the effect it had on his personal life. In a May 28, 1945 letter to one of the nuns to whom *Perelandra* had been dedicated, Lewis remarked that he was "very interested" in her story of the healing of a dog and commented that he did not see any intrinsic reason miraculous events could not involve animals as well as human beings. With a commendable mixture of sensitivity and caution, Lewis did not say he believed the dog was miraculously healed; he only said he did not think such a thing impossible.

A more significant matter is the cancer remission of Lewis's wife Joy. In 1957 a priest named **Peter Bide** came to the hospital where **Joy Davidman Lewis** was dying to lay hands on her in scriptural fashion and pray for her. Lewis observed in a June 25 letter to Dorothy Sayers that Bide "has on his record what looks very like one miracle"—a cautious, interesting way to phrase the matter. When Lewis wrote of the matter to **Bede Griffiths** on September 24, he remarked that Joy "has improved, if not miraculously (but who knows?) at any rate wonderfully." This way of putting things was characteristic of Lewis and not only about miracles. Whenever new scientific discoveries or assertions were made, Lewis would caution people about saying that this "proves" Christianity, for the next discovery or assertion might show the previous one to have been in error, and then where would Christianity be?

In a November 6, 1957, letter to **Sister Penelope**, she of the healed dog, Lewis said that during that year he had been losing calcium in his bones as fast as Joy was gaining it, "a bargain (if it were one) for which I'm very thankful." Lewis was referring here to the doctrine of transference, championed by **Charles Williams**, the idea that one human being can voluntarily take on part

of the sufferings of another. Lewis had indicated in prayer his willingness, if it were lawful, to take on part of Joy's pain so she would not have to suffer so much. He felt the calcium shift may well have been an example of that happening; but again we can see, in parentheses, his reluctance to assert that fully.

As Joy's cancer went into a most remarkable remission for approximately two years, Lewis became willing to admit to friends, privately, that he considered it miraculous. Upon the cancer's return, he wrote to **Roger Green** on November 25, 1959, "Whether a second miracle will be vouchsafed us ... remains uncertain." To Peter Milward a month later he wrote of the cancer from which Joy was "as I believe, miraculously" delivered. Regarding miracles, Lewis's **theology** and his life showed an admirable consistency.

Marvin D. Hinten
Bowling Green State University

Bibliography

Lewis, C. S. *Letters of C. S. Lewis; The Lion, The Witch, and the Wardrobe; Miracles; Perelandra*

Mitchell, L. J. "Miracles, Natural Laws and Christian Theology." *Theological Evangelica*. 16 no. 3 (September 1983): 51–58.

"Miracles"

St. Jude's Gazette. 73 (October 1942): 4–7. An expanded version appeared in *The Guardian*. (2 October 1942): 316. Reprinted in *God in the Dock* and *Undeceptions*.

"Miracles" was preached in St. Jude on the Hill Church, London, on November 26, 1942. In this sermon, Lewis began with a story that demonstrated seeing is not necessarily believing. He said that "[w]hatever experiences we may have, we shall not regard them as miraculous if we already hold a **philosophy** which excludes the **supernatural**." He went on to argue that our interpretation depends on our preconceptions. To believe in **miracles**, we must believe in the stability of **nature** and in some **reality** beyond nature. The tendency of people to dismiss miracles is based on their "almost aesthetic dislike of miracles" and the confusion between the laws of nature and the laws of thought. Lewis discussed the relationship of the miracles performed by **Christ**, which are acts performed on a scale visible to men locked within the three dimensions, and the miracles performed by **God**, which are performed on a universal scale outside man's limited sensory realm. Miracles, signs, "do not take us away from reality; they recall us to it."

Anne Gardner

Miracles (Letter)

The Guardian (16 October 1942): 331. Reprinted in *God in the Dock*, *Undeceptions,* and *Timeless at Heart.*

Lewis replied to a Mr. May who had written to *The Guardian* with several questions based on a sermon which Lewis gave on "Miracles" at St. Jude's, Hampstead Garden (a summary of this address was published in *The Guardian*, 2 October 1942, 316). May had questions on the virgin birth and the turning of water into wine.

Marjorie L. Mead
The Marion E. Wade Center

Miracles: A Preliminary Study

London: Geoffrey Bles, 1947. First US edition, New York: Macmillan, 1947.

Written for a more sophisticated audience than many of his other apologetical works, *Miracles* (1947) is comprised of seventeen lucid and succinct chapters and two appendices crafted with Lewis's characteristic care for precision of definition, ample and multiple illustration of key points, and the anticipation and critique of objections from earnest readers. A self-consciously "philosophical" work that is difficult to paraphrase, *Miracles* clearly draws upon the assumptions about the primacy of **reason** and the validity of **natural law** that Lewis had employed broadly in his autobiographical **allegory**, *The Pilgrim's Regress* (1933), and explicitly in later apologetical writings including *The Problem of Pain* (1940), *Broadcast Talks* (1942) (later republished as part of *Mere Christianity* in 1952), *The Screwtape Letters* (1942), and *The Abolition of Man* (1943).

Here Lewis offered a thoroughgoing defense of supernaturalism as a rational option for 20th-century thinkers, explaining the place of **miracles** within such a belief system. Belief that miracles may occur does not obligate the believer to accept any and all claims of the miraculous as fact; it merely invites the inquiry into the nature and credibility of the claim, which must be decided on reasoned criteria. Lewis's case for the miraculous is accompanied by a vigorous refutation of naturalism as ultimately an illogical, self-defeating worldview which fails to account even for the validity of its own reasoning process; it is the quasi-religion of a "chronologically snobbish" age rather than a convincing alternative to theism. In later chapters, Lewis championed **Christianity** as a supernatural **faith** whose power depends upon the historical veracity of its miracles as depicted in the New Testament: chiefly its

"Grand Miracle," the Incarnation of **Christ**, which is, if true, "the central event in the history of the Earth—the very thing that the whole story has been about." He is the Fact which cannot be explained away, and from which all Facthood descends.

Having subtitled his work "a preliminary study," Lewis began *Miracles* with an epigraph from **Aristotle**, "Those who wish to succeed must ask the right preliminary questions," which in this case are two: "are miracles possible, and, if so, are they probable?" Lewis's specific goal was to answer these "philosophical questions" as a necessary first step in equipping his readers to go on to examine with integrity the miracles of the **Bible** on their own merits. To do so, he had to remove numerous "red herrings" the modern world places in the path of otherwise objective readers, and Lewis spent the first ten chapters in this endeavor. Those whose philosophies constrain them by definition from entertaining even the possibility of miracles are, Lewis said, "wasting their time" by looking into the New Testament texts that record the miraculous; their "question-begging" will only return them the negative answers determined before they start.

Lewis carefully defined "miracle" as "an interference with **Nature** by **supernatural** power," and quickly makes a distinction between two kinds of thinkers: the Naturalist who believes that nothing exists "except Nature," and the Supernaturalist, who believes that "besides Nature, there exists something else." The Naturalist tends to think that Nature is "everything" or "the whole show" or "whatever there is," and envisions a universe of interlocking things and events that permit no serendipity, spontaneity, or independent action—"a vast process of space and time *which is going on of its own accord.*" The "system," if well-described and understood, can account for all circumstances that exist or ever will. As an article of "faith," naturalism excludes the miraculous.

In contrast, the Supernaturalist believes in a **hierarchy** of order and being, an "open universe" which may allow for **reality** to encompass all manner of surprises, mysteries, and discontinuities—including the intervention of a Divine Being seeking to accomplish his purposes. Whereas the Naturalist believes in "One Thing," i.e., Nature and its components within a Total System, the Supernaturalist believes in One Self-existent Thing and a class of items derived from that "One Thing" that bear distinct personal relationships to it, thus making room for a Creator God, and a creation that reflects his image and is subject to his will.

In his controversial third chapter, entitled, "The Self-Contradiction of the Naturalist," Lewis boldly declares that consistent Naturalism is, in fact, self-refuting, for if it is true, "every finite thing or event must be (in principle) explicable in terms of the Total System," and thus even Reason itself is suspect, arising as it does as an artifact of inexorable, nonrational causes. Reason must be subject to the same fatalistic explanation as that of other phenomena, which therefore guarantees us no independent agency by which we can validate the theory of Naturalism itself. Naturalism, Lewis avers, represents "a proof that there are no such things as proofs—which is nonsense." His philosophical statement of this "rule" is that "no thought is valid if it can be fully explained as the result of irrational causes." As Richard Purtill explains Lewis's argument, "If mind is only a chance product of nature, how can we trust our reasoning powers, how can we expect our minds to give us the truth about anything?"

During a celebrated exchange in February 1948 at the **Oxford Socratic Club**, an undergraduate organization which Lewis helped found for the purpose of religious debates, philosopher **Elizabeth Anscombe** challenged the cogency of this particular attack on Naturalism. Anscombe, herself a Roman Catholic who later became a professor of philosophy at Cambridge, argued that at best Lewis overstated his case, and at worst seriously misunderstood the differences in philosophical argumentation between "cause and effect" and "ground and consequent." One result of Anscombe's rebuttal was Lewis's revision of chapter 3 of *Miracles* when Fontana, a British publisher, brought out a paperback version in 1960. Lewis retitled the chapter, "The Cardinal Difficulty of the Naturalist."

Having established the broad grounds for his argument, Lewis proceeded systematically to build a case for the superiority of supernaturalism, which can account for both Reason and Nature. If Nature cannot logically produce Reason, it is more probable to posit an order of being in which Reason or, theistically speaking, a Divine Mind is self-existent and each human mind "an off-shoot . . . or incursion of that Supernatural reality into Nature." Hence, God's creation of nature is a more reasonable doctrine and more probable event than the prospect that Nature by chance produced Mind. There is no logical contradiction in believing that Nature is an orderly system governed by Reason and in also believing that the God Who is Reason may intervene by his power to alter the course of natural events for his purposes: "In **science** we have been reading only the notes to a poem; in Christianity we find the poem itself."

Lewis's concluding chapters on the incarnation and the miracles of the old and new creation and offer stirring expositions of the kinds and quality of miracles presented in the New Testament and rank among Lewis's most lucid and inspiring theological reflections.

Miracles is, in essence, Lewis's last sustained work of **apologetics**, and save occasional, usually solicited, essays on specific topics, for the rest of his career Lewis turned almost exclusively to writing fiction (the **Chronicles of Narnia**, 1950–56; *Till We Have Faces*, 1956), memoir (*Surprised by Joy*, 1955), biblical exposition and **theology** (*Reflections on the Psalms*, 1958; *The Four Loves*, 1960), and devotional literature (*Letters to Malcolm*, 1964). While some biographers have argued that Lewis's 1948 debate with Elizabeth Anscombe was a watershed moment in his career, shaking his confidence in his ability to write effective apologetics, a more balanced account would suggest that he simply had entered a stage in his life in which Reason had given him all that it had to convey about Christianity, and it was now time for Lewis to trust his **Imagination** to complete his vocation.

Bruce L. Edwards
Bowling Green State University

Bibliography

Anscombe, G. E. M. *Collected Philosophical Papers.* Cambridge: Cambridge University Press, 1981.

Lindskoog, Kathryn. *C. S. Lewis: Mere Christian.* Chicago: Cornerstone Press, 1997.

Purtill, Richard. "Did C. S. Lewis Lose His Faith?" *A Christian for all Christians: Essays in Honor of C. S. Lewis.* Andrew Walker and James Patrick (eds). Washington, DC: Regnery Gateway, 1992: 27–62.

———. *C. S. Lewis's Case for the Christian Faith.* San Francisco: Harper, 1981.

The Mirror of Love: A Reinterpretation of "The Romance of the Rose" (Book Review)

Medium Aevum. XXII no. 1 (1953): 27–31.

Gunn presents his theory that the *Romance* has a fundamental (and not simply rhetorical) unity. He argues that the text has an implicit—and very modern—oneness, a claim which apparently might mean a revolution in the history of ideas as perceived in modern times. Lewis suggested a rereading of the *Romance* in light of this book.

Anne Gardner

Bibliography

Gunn, Alan M. F. *The Mirror of Love: A Reinterpretation of "The Romance of the Rose."*

"Miserable Offenders"

See entry on "Sermon"

Modernity

Between 1789 and 1914, most Western intellectuals shared the ultimately illusory but immensely potent belief in inevitable human progress. Despite the seventy-five years of spectacular disconfirmation of this belief since 1914, the faith in a benign future that **science** and **technology** will ineluctably bring about is with us still.

Relatively few 19th century intellectuals dissented from what Lewis called in 1954 this "nineteenth-century belief in spontaneous progress," but their names are worth recalling: the Roman pontiffs, John Henry Newman, Kierkegaard, Dostoevsky, the historian Jacob Burckhardt, and—intermittently—writers as different as Baudelaire, Hawthorne, and Melville. In the English-speaking world a major philosophical-cultural current of dissent from the cult of the future was developed by the conservative Romantics and their Victorian successors. These included Blake, **Wordsworth**, and Coleridge; William Cobbett and Thomas Carlyle; Dickens (especially in *Hard Times*); Newman and the Oxford Movement; and John Ruskin and **Matthew Arnold**. Recoiling from the horrors of industrialization in Britain but also from the radicalism of the French "philosophes" and their fanatical Jacobin offspring (and often drawing on Edmund Burke's critique of the latter), these writers created an anti-modernist literature of enduring power that is one of the glories of English and world civilization and was to exercise a profound influence on 20th-century critics of modernity such as **G. K. Chesterton**, **Aldous Huxley**, F. R. Leavis, **T. S. Eliot**. R. G. Collingwood, W. R. Inge, and C. S. Lewis.

The enduring power of C. S. Lewis's critique of modernity cannot be accurately understood unless he is seen in the light of this particular tradition of cultural criticism. Of course, it is also important to consider his philosophical antecedents, from **Plato** and **Aristotle** to his **Magdalen College** contemporaries C. C. J. Webb, J. A. Smith, and Collingwood, whom James Patrick has studied. Theological and literary sources as diverse as Tyndale, Hooker, Bunyan, **Samuel Johnson**, **George MacDonald**, and G. K. Chesterton helped shape Lewis's ideas and style. But for the philosophical analysis and critique of modernity that he was to develop and deploy so powerfully in *The Abolition of Man* (1943) and the third volume of the space trilogy, *That Hideous Strength* (1945), we need to be aware of and look at the influence of those Romantic and Victorian cultural critics, as well as a figure intermediate between them and Lewis, G. K. Chesterton (1874–1936).

"Wordsworth's great autobiographical poem '*The Prelude*,'" according to Lionel Trilling, "gives the classic account of the damage done to the mind of the individual, to its powers of cognition no less than to its vital force, by the scientistic conception of mind that prevailed among intellectuals at the time of the French Revolution." The Romantic and Victorian cultural critics reacted against this scientistic conception, which was really a series of reductionist definitions of person, mind, **nature**, and society, a series that reached its logical extension to absurdity in Thomas Henry Huxley's notion of the human mind as an epiphenomenon, a fully determined and accidental by-product of irrational physical forces. But the scientistic ideologies of "progressive" intellectuals have grown steadily—despite catastrophic consequences—since the late 18th century, ranging on a spectrum from "left"—Marxist "scientific socialism", Skinnerian Behavorism, and secular liberal utilitarianism—to "right"—libertarian Social Darwinism or racist/nationalist Social Darwinism.

Lewis's dissent from these belief systems came from profound philosophical learning and from meditation of their inconsistencies. His concentrated analysis benefited immensely from lifelong engagement with the great works of Western Literature, which he, like Matthew Arnold and his own colleagues Collingwood and J. A. Smith, saw as illuminating and preserving "man's painfully acquired knowledge of his own mind" (Smith). The great Romantics and Victorians insisted that the mind is not an "epiphenomenon" or a mere passive register of percepts and the slave of passions. At least potentially, the mind is active and, as the classical-Christian humanist **Jonathan Swift** put it, "rationis capax"—capable of **reason**. By the early 1920s Lewis had emerged from modernist confusions and came to believe in the *philosophia perennis,* which he shared not only with his great predecessors from Aristotle and the Bible onward but also with contemporaries such as the French Thomists and **Oxford** colleagues such as A. E. Taylor, E. L. Mascall, **Austin Farrer**, Webb, Smith, and Collingwood, and with **Aldous Huxley**, another Oxford-trained mind. Huxley's great books *Ends and Means* (1937), *The Perennial Philosophy* (1946), and the 1932 *Brave New World*, with its mordant 1946 Preface, are outstanding articulations and applications of a critique of modernity nearly identical to that of Lewis.

Like Lewis, Huxley too had come to believe that "our logic," if careful and correct, is no epiphenomenon (or mechanism), but "participation in the cosmic logos" (Lewis, *Surprised by Joy*). In an epoch of feckless neophilia—fanatical devotion to novelty as such—that oscillated between ideological fervor (Marxist or Fascist) and aesthetic decadence (in Berlin, Paris, and Bloomsbury), Huxley, Lewis, and Collingwood all subscribed to the view that the latter articulated when he said that he was "anxious above all not to pose" as a unique repository "of a new revelation," but only "to say once more, in words suited to our generation, something that" every wise person "has always known" (*Speculum Mentis*, 1924).

Lewis sometimes affected a Platonist or Christian "contemptus mundi" or disdain for the 20th-century barbarities and banalities of what his Cambridge colleague F. R. Leavis usefully called "techno-Benthamism" and what Lewis himself called "Futilitarianism." He never ceased to attack critically and rationally, and to mock satirically, the conception "lodged in popular thought that improvement is, somehow, a cosmic law" (*"De Futilitate"*), a conception that the historical period 1914–45 alone should have thoroughly—and permanently—discredited, but apparently did not. But on occasion Lewis's rhetorical pose of detachment served him ill, as it does at the end of his otherwise powerful meditation on history, *"De Descriptione Temporum,"* his 1954 inaugural lecture as Professor of Medieval and Renaissance Literature at Cambridge University. In calling himself a "dinosaur," in depicting himself as one of a dying breed of classical humanists, Lewis both disguised and diminished the relevance of his own thought to the human future. Identifying himself as an atavistic moral dinosaur, he invited being neglected as one.

Of course, Lewis's book sales are a massive testimony to the fact that his concerns, views, and insights are not only a part of the human past but of the human present and future too. Who now seriously reads the nonfiction prose of **H. G. Wells**? Or of Lenin? Who considers A. J. Ayer or B. F. Skinner to be serious moralists? Deconstructiontism does massive damage, to be sure, but Logical Positivism and Behaviorism are dead, and Lewis helped to bury them. Great poets such as Elizabeth Jennings, Richard Wilbur, Geoffrey Hill, and Czeslaw Milosz have concerns similar to Lewis's; novelists such as Piers Paul Read, George Garrett, and Frederick Buechner continue to portray the human person as a soul, not merely a body. Sound literary critics such as Christopher Ricks, Roy Battenhouse, Martin Battestin, and Edward Tayler are writing, often very much in Lewis's tradition. Sound philosophers such as Alasdair MacIntyre and Basil Mitchell—the latter a disciple of Lewis—have produced distinguished work recognizably within his tradition and affirming the same doctrines. Sociologists such as Daniel Bell, Peter Berger, David Martin, Bryan Wilson, Robert Nisbet, James D. Hunter, and the social psychologist Philip Rieff, have shown that a field that in the 1930s was virtually identical with secular radical or liberal perspectives is capable of profound, nuanced extensions of the very moral tradition that Lewis spent his adult life espousing. As for theologians, both the present Pope and Cardinal Ratzinger have explicitly expressed their admiration of Lewis, the former especially of *The Four Loves*, the latter of *The Abolition of Man*. Large numbers of Evangelical Protestants continue assiduously to read Lewis.

Yet in profound ways the state of what Lionel Trilling called "mind in the modern world" *is* as bleak as Lewis suggested it was when he wrote, in 1956: "the barbarism on which we now seem to be entering [may] prove to be the last illness, the death-bed of humanity." The worship of technology and the virtually universal propagation of scientist ideology have brought us a culture of nihilistic consumerism, pornography, and violence. Perhaps the most powerful critiques of this development are those framed by the Pope, the social psychologist Rieff, and the sociologist and theologian Jacques Ellul. But it is a revealing and gratifying fact, and one that vindicates Lewis's work as an aid to the humane future for which we should strive that he is still so widely read by so many people in so many walks of life. In their important anthology *Philosophy and Technology: Readings in the Philosophical Problems of Technology* (New York, 1972, 1983, et seq.), Carl Mitcham and Robert Mackey reprint outstanding essays on some of the most exigent problems of our time. A substantial selection from *The Abolition of Man* is among them.

M. D. Aeschliman

Also See: Communism and Fascism, Evolution, Literary Criticism, Materialism, Medieval World, Tao

Bibliography

Aeschliman, M. D. *The Restitution of Man: C. S. Lewis and the Case Against Scientism*. Grand Rapids, MI: Eerdmans, 1998.

Ellul, Jacques. *The Technological Bluff* (Eng. tr., 1990). Grand Rapids, MI: Eerdmans, 1990.

Lewis, C. S. *The Abolition of Man* (1943).

Lewis, C. S. *That Hideous Strength* (1945).

Patrick, James. *The Magdalen Metaphysicals: Idealism and Orthodoxy at Oxford, 1901–1945*. Macon, GA: Mercer University Press, 1985.

Rieff, Philip. *Fellow Teachers* (rev. ed., 1985). Chicago: University of Chicago Press, 1985.

"Modern Man and his Categories of Thought"

First published posthumously in *Present Concerns*.

In this article, Lewis addressed the difficulties of converting nonbelievers to **Christianity** in modern times. He argued that men in the time of the apostles had a fairly universal psychological and intellectual predisposition to Christian practices and beliefs. Modern man has no such predisposition. Lewis offered six reasons for this recent radical departure from traditional thought: **education** has been revolutionized so that the most educated are the most isolated, insulated from times and beliefs other than their own; the emancipation of **women** has changed the focus of intellectual institutions; Developmentalism or Historicism, or the belief that continual change is an end unto itself and "Almost nothing may be expected to turn into almost everything," is accepted as principle; Proletarianism, which is anticlerical and encourages discussion of salvation only in secular terms; practicality, or the narrow consideration of Christianity as useful rather than "objectively *true*"; and skepticism about **Reason**, or the belief that "all thought is conditioned by irrational processes," and thoughts are therefore invalid. Lewis concluded that conversion is most likely to be accomplished when there is "a preliminary intellectual barrage" followed up "with a direct attack on the heart."

According to **Walter Hooper**, this essay "was written at the request of Bishop Stephen Neill (1899–1984) for the Study Department of the World Council of Churches." Existing only in typescript, the essay is dated October 1946.

Anne Gardner

Also See: Apologetics, RAF Talks

"Modern Theology and Biblical Criticism"

Originally delivered as a lecture on May 11, 1959. First published in *Christian Reflections*. Retitled "Fern-Seed and Elephant" and republished in *Fern-Seed and Elephant*.

First delivered on May 11, 1959, at the request of the Rt. Rev. Kenneth Carey as a speech to students at Wescott House, **Cambridge**, it was posthumously published in *Christian Reflections* (1967).

Lewis offered four criticisms of modern **theology** in this essay. First, New Testament critical scholars confidently assert that elements in the Gospels are legends or myths without a clear standard of either in their own critical experience. Second, liberal theology's claim that the purpose and teaching of **Christ** has only been recovered in its full purity by modern scholarship is fatally anachronistic. Third, modern theologians interpret Scripture on the unchallenged philosophical assumption that **miracles** do not occur. Fourth, the claim of *Sitz im Leben* criticism, to accurately reconstruct the genesis of biblical texts, is suspect because Lewis found that when reviewers attempted to reconstruct the origins of books whose genesis he knew personally, their guess were always wrong.

Lewis concluded with a criticism of the underlying premise of "demythologizing" theology—that since present experiences does not allow humanity adequate expression of "the religious idea," all such expression must be symbolic. Lewis pointed out that one cannot know that everything in a representation is symbolic unless independent access to the thing presented allows comparison with the representation. He observed in parting that current fashions of skeptical theology threaten to make the future history of **Anglicanism** short.

Lyle Smith
Biola University

Also See: Apologetics, the Bible, Inspiration, Literary Criticism, Literary Theory, Modernity, Revelation

Bibliography

Lewis, C. S. "Myth Became Fact"; "Religion Without Dogma"

"Modern Translations of the Bible"

See entry on *Letters to Young Churches: A Translation of the New Testament Epistles* (Preface)

Courtenay Edward Moore (1870–1951)

Born June 26, 1870, Courtenay Edward Moore attended Haileybury College (1884–1888), and then Trinity College, Dublin, B.A. 1893. A civil engineer, he married **Janie Moore** on August 1, 1897, and they were separated (but not divorced) after the birth of their second and last child, Maureen, in 1906. Known to Janie Moore and C. S. Lewis as "The Beast," he died in County Wicklow, Ireland in June 1951.

John Bremer

Also See: Edward Francis Courtenay "Paddy" Moore, Maureen Daisy Helen Moore

Edward Francis Courtenay "Paddy" Moore (1898–1918)

Born November 17, 1898, Paddy Moore was the son of **Janie Moore** and **Courtenay Edward Moore**. He lived with his mother after his parents separated, attended

Clifton College from May 1908 until he entered the cadet battalion in 1917 at Keble College, **Oxford**, where, by accident of the alphabet, he roomed with C. S. Lewis. It was through this chance assignment that Lewis met Janie Moore. At first, Lewis thought Paddy "a little too childish for real companionship," but this was later softened (perhaps because of affection for his mother) to the opinion that he was "a very decent sort of man." He was posted as missing in France in March 1918, and was confirmed dead in September. The familial relationship was idealized, according to **Warren Lewis**, who was surprised to learn from his brother, after Janie Moore's death in 1951, that Janie and Paddy did not get on very well together.

John Bremer

Also See: Maureen Daisy Helen Moore

Janie King Askins Moore (1872–1951)

Born March 28, 1872 ,in Pomeroy, County Tyrone (Northern Ireland), Janie Moore was the eldest child, daughter of William James Askins (1842–1895) and Jane King Askins (1846–1890). Her father was a clergyman in the Church of Ireland, and she grew up in Dunany, County Louth, where her father was vicar. She had three younger brothers, William, John, and Robert, and two younger sisters, Edith and Sarah. After the early death of their mother, she acted in her place, looking after the other five children, and, after her father's death, she supervised their upbringing.

On August 1, 1897 she married **Courtenay Edward Moore** by whom she had two children, **Edward Francis Courtenay "Paddy" Moore** in 1898, and **Maureen Daisy Helen Moore** in 1906. The marriage was not happy and shortly after the birth of Maureen they separated, but were not divorced. She went to live in Bristol where her brother, Dr. Robert Askins, was a government medical officer. Paddy was enrolled at Clifton College, near Bristol, in May 1908.

In 1917, when Paddy, as a preliminary to induction into the army, was assigned to a cadet battalion at Keble College, **Oxford**, Janie Moore moved to Oxford to be near him, taking ten-year-old Maureen with her. She was used to mothering and also was hospitable by nature, so she entertained Paddy and his friends, notable among them C. S. (Jack) Lewis, his roommate. Thus began a relationship that lasted until her death in January 1951.

Paddy did not get on particularly well with his mother—and he may have resented her move to Oxford to be near him. But she obviously liked Jack, who, in turn, liked her "immensely." It was easy for Jack to like her—

she was Irish, motherly, attractive, and he was away from home, motherless, attracted by beauty, and sexual. At the end of his cadet training Jack spent the first part of his leave with the Moores in Bristol, much to his father's chagrin. It is highly probable that the relationship became overtly sexual at this time. It seems that from early on, Janie Moore and Jack exchanged letters or notes almost every day. This continued when Jack and Paddy (in different regiments) went to France in November 1917.

Paddy was reported missing in March 1918 and this must have drawn Janie and Jack closer together. Jack himself was wounded by shrapnel in three places on April 15, 1918, and was sent back to England on a stretcher in May 1918. Janie went to London to be near him, and later moved, in turn, to Bristol, Andover, Eastbourne, back to Bristol, and, finally, to Oxford after Jack had resumed his studies.

In late summer 1920, Janie Moore rented a house in Headington and Jack (who had lived in college, as he was required to do, in his first year, but visiting Headington every day) made his home with her. In the next eleven years, they lived in nine or ten different houses, with Jack contributing his paternal allowance (unbeknownst to his father) to supporting Janie and Maureen. Her husband—"The Beast"—was unreliable in his financial support.

Throughout this period, Janie Moore was referred to by Jack as "my mother," "Minto" (after her favorite candies), and the Greek letter Delta in Jack's diaries (transcribed by **Warren Lewis** in *The Lewis Family Papers* as "D"). The last almost certainly stands for Diotima, the priestess in **Plato**'s *Symposium*, who introduces Socrates to the meaning of **love** (although quite a different kind from that to which Jack was introduced). Janie called Jack "Boysie"—and later referred to him and Warren as "the boys." When she needed him to help, usually in some trivial domestic task, she would call out "Barboys."

The other side of Janie Moore's propensity for hospitality and mothering was her need to dominate and control others, making them subservient to whatever tasks, needed or not, that she chose to impose on them. She observed that having Jack was as good as having an extra maid. She seems to have had little real sense of the importance of his work and was ruthless in interrupting it—even if she was also capable of preventing others from doing so. This infuriated Warren.

She had little formal education, and took small joy in reading, except when she and Jack read something together and talked about it. Of the intellectual life she had no idea.

She was, however, a gracious hostess and the house was frequented by odd characters and the needy. It was also a haven for lost animals. Her generosity—often at Jack's expense—was far-reaching. Although Jack knew, in some measure, of the enormity of her demanding nature, and of her senseless wranglings, lyings, and follies, he had made a commitment to her, telling Warren that he had made a choice, did not regret it, and would stick by it. Only after her death did he begin to realize "quite how bad it was."

However long their sexual relationship lasted, it must have ended when Jack was converted to **Christianity** in 1931 because, according to Jack himself, outside of **marriage** celibacy was demanded. This may, in part, account for Janie Moore's hostility to Jack and Warren taking Communion—for taking part in "blood feasts," as she said. She was a decided atheist in later life— excusing this by attributing it to an effect of Paddy's death, which she blamed on **God**.

As Janie Moore got older she became even more demanding and difficult to please. She had suffered from severe varicose veins (which had confined her to her bedroom for nearly all 1947) and various other ailments—all of which were useful as controlling mechanisms. In April 1950, at the age of seventy-eight, she had to enter Restholme, a nursing home, where Jack visited her nearly every day; she was incoherent, senile, very grumpy, and given to blasphemous outbursts. All Jack could do was to pray for her. On January 12, 1951, she died of influenza.

John Bremer

Maureen Daisy Helen Moore (1906–1997)

Lady Dunbar of Hempriggs, known to C. S. "Jack" Lewis as Maureen, later to become Lady Dunbar of Hempriggs, was born in Ireland. Maureen lived with Lewis and her mother **Janie Moore** until 1940, when she married Leonard Blake. Jack's diary (*All My Road Before Me*), his correspondence with **Arthur Greeves** (*They Stand Together*), and **Warren Lewis**'s diary all give a picture of Jack's relationship to her as a provider, tutor, and caring "family member," especially concerned about her musical training and language studies. Sometimes, even before his conversion, he went to church with her. Towards the end of her mother's life Maureen would sometimes trade houses with Lewis, helping him take care of her mother, who died in 1951.

Richard James
Burkesville Christian Church

Bibliography

"Dunbar of Hempriggs." *Who's Who 1994*. New York: St. Martin's Press, 1995: 552.
"Dunbar of Hempriggs." *Burke's Peerage*. London: Burke's Peerage Limited, 1970.
Hooper, Walter. *C. S. Lewis: A Companion & Guide*. San Francisco: HarperCollins, 1996: 647–49.
Lewis, Warren H. *Brothers and Friends: The Diaries of Major Warren Hamilton Lewis*. Clyde S. Kilby and Marjorie Lamp Mead (eds). San Francisco: Harper & Row, 1982.

William Morris (1834–1896)

William Morris was a designer, a poet, a political activist, and a fantasy novelist. His first book of poems was *The Defence of Guenevere and Other Poems* (1858). In 1861, with Dante Rossetti, Edward Bourne-Jones and others, he formed an artisan firm which initiated the British Arts and Crafts Movement. His poem, *The Life and Death of Jason*, was published in 1867, followed by *The Earthly Paradise* (1868–70), the longest poem in the English language. Working with Eirikr Magnusson he then translated several Icelandic sagas. His latter years were devoted to socialist politics, the founding of the Kelmscott Press (1891), and writing the fantasy novels, *The Wood Beyond the World* (1894) and *The Well at the World's End* (1896).

C. S. Lewis took notice of Morris when he found a copy of *The Well at the World's End* in new friend **Arthur Greeves'** bookcase. He immediately bought his own copy. He wrote of Morris being "my great author" at this period (*Surprised by Joy*). In corresponding with Greeves, Lewis mentioned Morris and his works over 75 times—second only to **George MacDonald** (*They Stand Together*).

Lewis delivered two lectures on Morris for the **Martlets**. The second essay, **"William Morris,"** is reprinted in *Selected Literary Essays*. This essay attempts to restore Morris to his proper place in English literature. Lewis concluded that "there are many writers greater than Morris. You can go on from him to all sorts of subtleties, delicacies, and sublimities which he lacks. But you can hardly go behind him."

Richard James
Burkesville Christian Church

Bibliography

Hooper, Walter. "To the Martlets." *C. S. Lewis: Speaker & Teacher*. Carolyn Keefe (ed). Grand Rapids, MI: Zondervan, 1971: 47–83.
Morris, William. *The Collected Works of William Morris*. May Morris (ed). New York: Russell & Russell, 1966.

_____. *Selected Writings and Designs*. Asa Briggs (ed). Baltimore: Penguin Books, 1968.

"The Morte D'Arthur" (Book Review)

The Times Literary Supplement. (7 June 1947): 273–74. Reprinted in *Studies in Medieval and Renaissance Literature.*

For centuries British literature scholars had only known the *Morte D'Arthur* in Caxton's printed version. Then in the middle of Lewis's professional lifetime a manuscript of Thomas Malory's original (which Caxton had altered for printing) came to light. This was a momentous occasion for Medieval literature scholars— roughly the equivalent to Shakespearean scholars discovering a new version of Hamlet with an added scene. When, after thirteen years of waiting, the manuscript was released in a multivolume work, Lewis reviewed it for *The Times Literary Supplement;* the review is now part of *Studies in Medieval and Renaissance Literature.*

Lewis began by discussing Malory's life—whether a criminal could really have written such a noble piece as the *Morte,* and how culpable Malory was given his times. Lewis then turned to the work itself and pointed out that the *Morte* is a composite book, with bits of Middle English, Anglo-Norman, Malory, and Caxton all mixed together. Lewis found this fascinating, and he praised the work of the scholar who edited and commented upon Malory's manuscript. Lewis closed the essay by reminding readers that Malory requested our prayers for his soul; it's hard to imagine another scholar of the period taking that request so seriously.

Marvin D. Hinten
Bowling Green State University

Also See: King Arthur, Myth

Bibliography

Lewis, C. S. *The Discarded Image*; *English Literature in the Sixteenth Century*; "The English Prose *Morte*"
Vinaver, Eugene (ed). *The Works of Sir Thomas Malory.* Oxford: Clarendon Press, 1947.

The Most Substantial People
See the entry on *The Easley Fragment*

Mr. C. S. Lewis on Christianity (Letter)

The Listener. XXXI (9 March 1944): 273. Reprinted in *God in the Dock*, *Undeceptions,* and *Timeless at Heart.*

"**The Map and the Ocean**," which was the first of Lewis's installments in the radio series entitled, "Beyond Personality," was published in *The Listener* (24 February 1944). It provoked a letter from W. R. Childe (2 March 1944, 245). Lewis answered by agreeing that we must act on what **Christ** teaches if we call him Lord, but also taking issue with Childe's charge that he (Lewis) was ready to engage in "the usual heresy hunt" when confronted with opposing views. Lewis maintained, to the contrary, that he was passionately against religious compulsion. Childe's final response lauding Blake and Shelley as guides to understanding the "Spirit of Life" was published on March 16, 1944, 301.

Marjorie L. Mead
The Marion E. Wade Center

"Must Our Image of God Go?"

The Observer. (24 March 1963): 14. Reprinted in *The Honest to God Debate*. David L. Edwards (ed). London: SCM Press, 1963: 91. Also reprinted in *God in the Dock* and *Undeceptions.*

This article is a response to the Bishop of Woolwich, Dr. J. A. T. Robinson's article "Our Image of God Must Go," which appeared in *The Observer* (17 March 1963) as a summary of Dr. Robinson's book *Honest to God* (London, 1963). The Bishop contended that we must rid ourselves of the image of **God** in a localized **heaven**. Lewis claimed that we have done so, many years ago. Lewis argued that Christians know that God is everywhere, and if God is "'outside' or 'beyond' space-time, [it is in the same sense] 'as **Shakespeare** is outside The Tempest,' i.e. its scenes and persons do not exhaust his being." Lewis said that he did not understand why the Bishop forbade one image and chose to canonize the other. Lewis claimed our freedom to use both, or either.

The Bishop's view of Jesus **Christ** as a "window" was to Lewis orthodox. Any novelty in the doctrine is difficult to discern, partly because the author is obscure. Lewis gave his discussion of God as a person as an example. The Bishop draws a distinction between being a person and being personal. His argument could survive, said Lewis, if "'not a person' were taken to mean 'a person and more.'" According to Lewis, the Bishop's heart was in the right place; his failure was a literary one.

Anne Gardner

"My First School"
See entry on "Notes on the Way" (4 September 1943)

Myth

Popularly, "myth" refers to the ancient fictional stories with **supernatural** characters and fantastic events. These stories often embody the **values** of a **culture** and were at times accorded religious status. Such myths were Lewis's delight from his earliest days, especially

Norse mythology. In *Surprised by Joy* Lewis recounted how myth (along with other things) awakened in him a longing for other worlds and was one of the conduits for "**joy**." At first his lumping of **Christianity** with the pagan myths kept him from finding the source of the longing (**God** and **heaven**) until his early thirties.

Recounting his recent conversion to lifelong friend **Arthur Greeves**, Lewis explained that he had always found the notion of a god dying for his subjects and coming back to life very moving when he encountered it in the pagan myths, though not moving in the Gospels. The pagan myths moved him because they suggested a **reality** which he at some level must have thought or felt to be true, but to which he had given no assent. Lewis explained that an important part of his conversion was learning from his friends **J. R. R. Tolkien** and **Hugo Dyson** that Christianity was like the myths he loved, except that here it is a "true myth." The pagan myths were human myths; the Gospels are God's myth: the stories happen in actual human history (*They Stand Together*, October 18, 1931). Lewis maintained that people throughout history have intuited the necessity of God or a god dying for his people, and further that corn (bread) and wine have always been symbolic of his body and blood. Lewis says that in these myths God was sending humanity "good dreams" (*Mere Christianity*).

Some may be disturbed at Lewis's use of myth as a term applied to Christianity. Make no mistake: from 1931 to his death, Lewis was firmly committed to the historicity of Jesus and the **Bible**. He put the whole weight of his belief and hope in it. The great advantage of this concept is in allowing him to make two important points about **truth** and how we apprehend it. First, it undergirds the concept, found in books like *The Abolition of Man* and *Mere Christianity,* that the moral law and a supernatural order were always present in human thinking.

Second, it allows him to explain a phenomenon in human experience. In "**The Mythopoeic Gift of Rider Haggard**" (1960), Lewis uses "myth" to mean a story treating the "permanent and inevitable," those elements which are always a part of human experience. The greatest truths, like those about God or universal truths about humanity, are not a part of our concrete experience, so we understand them and speak of them as abstractions.

In myth, however, we experience imaginatively, in the concreteness of story, something which would be abstract if translated out. For example, we can't experience love and think reflectively on love at the same time. We either have a single experience in lived reality, or we step back from the experience to think about it; the thought we have in stepping back is abstraction. But when we read a story, like the Gospel account of the Incarnation or even a fictional story which is a shadow of it, we come closest to having an (imaginative) experience which "incarnates" the abstraction "God is love."

For elaboration of this and others of Lewis's ideas on myth, see "Is Theology Poetry?" (1944) in *The Weight of Glory and Other Addresses*; "Myth Became Fact" (1944) in *God in the Dock*; and the chapter "On Myth" in *An Experiment in Criticism* (1961).

Wayne Martindale
Wheaton College

Also See: Paganism

Bibliography

Lewis, C. S. *An Experiment in Criticism*; "Is Theology Poetry?"; "Myth Became Fact"

"Myth Became Fact"

World Dominion. XXII (September–October 1944): 267–70. Reprinted in *God in the Dock* and *Undeceptions*.

"Myth Became Fact" is a reply to "the charge that none of us are in fact Christians at all." This assertion is based on the idea that modern man cannot believe in **Christianity**, but rather has retained the lexicon and exploits the emotions generated from it while dispensing with its doctrines. Lewis asked that we "suppose that modern 'Christianity' reveals a system of names, ritual, formulae and metaphors which persists although the thoughts behind it have changed." Even if this is true, and historic Christianity is merely mythical, this **myth** is vital—both central and life-giving. The myth has outlived its proponents and opponents. What comes from the myth "is not truth but **reality** (**truth** is always *about* something, but reality is that *about which* truth is)."

Anne Gardner

"The Mythopoeic Gift of Rider Haggard"
See entry on "Haggard Rides Again"

N

Narrative Poems

Hooper, Walter (ed). London: Geoffrey Bles, 1969. First US edition, New York: Harcourt Brace Jovanovich, 1972.

In addition to *Dymer*, this volume contains three other examples of Lewis's narrative poems: "Launcelot" (Hooper dates as early 1930s), "The Nameless Isle" (August 1930), and "The Queen of Drum" (which **Walter Hooper** dates as 1933–34).

"Launcelot" is an unfinished poem set within the context of a quest for the holy grail by the knights of **King Arthur**'s court. Though Gawain is mentioned early, the poem essentially concerns Launcelot's quest, Guinevere's distress while he is gone and subsequent anger at his delay in coming to her after his return, and the story he tells her about his quest. His adventures include meeting a hermit in a dry, sterile land who tells him the land will not be renewed "until there come / The good knight who will kneel and see, yet not be dumb, / But ask, the Wasted Country shall be still accursed / And the spell upon the Fisher King unreversed, / Who now lies sick and languishing and near to death." After the hermit's unexplained death, Launcelot buries him and rides off on the quest into a rich, fertile country thinking of Guinevere. Eventually he meets the Queen of Castle Mortal who invites him into her chapel where she shows him three stone coffins where "the three best knights of earth shall lie." She reveals that she

intends to seduce Sir Lamorake, Tristram, and Launcelot and behead them: "For endless love of them I mean to make / Their sweetness mine beyond recovery and to take / That joy away from Morgan and from Guinevere / And Nimue and Isoud and Elaine." Here the poem breaks off. Almost no critical work has been done on this poem other than by Caroline Geer who finds it "an effective dramatic narrative.... The story is a dramatization of the quest as the real struggle in men's lives as they search for truth and strive to consecrate themselves to the holy journey."

"The Nameless Isle" reflects Lewis's love of Old English alliterative verse and is a fast-paced story of a shipwrecked mariner and his adventures on a **magic** isle. While there he encounters a crazed, dwarf-like man from an earlier shipwreck, a Circe-like witch, her estranged magician husband, and their daughter, turned to stone by her father to protect her from both her mother and "The murmuring, mixed, much thwarted stream / Of the flesh, flowing with confused noise, / Perishing perpetually." Though the conflict between husband and wife has effectively disrupted vital life on the island, the mariner's discovery of a magic flute and the dwarf's playing of it produces a magic that leads to a swirling conclusion where husband and wife are reconciled, the daughter is reawakened to love the mariner, and the latter two are joined by the dwarf in an idyllic voyage back to England. Lewis handles the alliterative verse well and produces one of his finest poems.

"The Queen of Drum" is Lewis's most ambitious poem after *Dymer*. Though Walter Hooper considers it "Lewis's best poem," John Masefield gets to the heart of the problem with this poem: "I have greatly enjoyed it, and feel an extraordinary **beauty** in the main theme—the escape of the Queen into Fairyland ... [but] at present, I cannot help feeling, that the design is encumbered." Indeed, while the poem contains beautifully lyrical passages, it fails as a compelling work because of its flawed design. This weakness, characteristic of almost all of Lewis's narrative **poetry**, may be stated simply: In Lewis's narrative poetry he focuses primarily upon *prosody*, at the expense of *plot*. In effect, he writes a number of powerfully evocative passages where metrical structures, rhyme, stanza forms, and so forth dazzle while at the same time narrative and plot stumble. In the end we suspect we have read something wonderful, but we are unsure as to how it all fits together. Ironically, this is a problem Lewis solves in his fiction, perhaps because with prose he has less "mechanical" restraints to confine his creative **imagination**.

The "Queen of Drum" is written in five cantos and concerns an old, pompous king whose young wife enjoys wandering at night enjoying the beauty of the evening and visions of the faery world. When the decay of the kingdom is blamed on her by the pious, bigoted Council, the Queen defies them. She calls them hypocrites because they too wander in the evening and intimates that their adventures are sexual in nature: "Five hours ago / Where were you?—and with whom?—how far away?" Embarrassed, the King sends his wife off to a tower to be counseled by the Archbishop while he and the Chancellor decide to search the dungeon for a man condemned years earlier for espousing views similar to the Queen's. The Queen rejects the Archbishop's counsel that she recant, since "I've met you / When you were also there, is that not true?" Though he cannot recall such meeting, he admits to having dreamed something like what she says, and advises her: "How can it profit us to talk / Much of that region where you say you walk. / We are not native there: we shall not die / Nor live in elfin country, you and I." Instead, he advises her to hold to orthodox belief: "Hence, if you ask me of the way / Yonder, what can I do but say . . . / Go, learn you catechism and creed." She cannot accept this counsel.

Soon the Queen and Archbishop are sent for by the fascist-like General who has murdered the King and the Chancellor. He asks the Archbishop to head a new state **religion**, "A Drummian kind of **Christianity**." When the Archbishop refuses, the General has him beaten to death. He offers to wed and bed the Queen, provided she agree to "no more night wanderings nor no talk of them." She buys time by asking for a chance to consider his proposal and escapes from her jailer while being led back to the tower. Her escape from her pursuers is chronicled with some beautiful passages describing her flight through meadows and forests, culminating in her having to choose one of three roads: to **Heaven**, to **Hell**, or to fairyland. In an obvious allusion to the Medieval *Thomas Rhymer*, she chooses "to glide out of all the world of men, / Nor will she turn to right or left her head, / But go straight on. She has tasted elven bread. / And so, the story tells, she passed away / Out of the world."

Don W. King
Montreat College

Also See: King Arthur, Epic, Fairy Tales, Medieval World, Poetry

Bibliography

Brown, Carol Ann. "Three Roads: A Comment on 'The Queen of Drum.'" *CSL: The Bulletin of the New York C. S. Lewis Society.* 7 no. 78 (April 1976): 14.

Christopher, Joe. "C. S. Lewis Dances Among the Elves: A Dull and Scholarly Survey of *Spirits in Bondage* and 'The Queen of Drum.'" *Mythlore* 9 (Spring 1982): 11–17, 47.

Geer, Richard. "Notes on *Narrative Poems*." *CSL: The Bulletin of the New York C. S. Lewis Society.* 7 no. 78 (April 1976): 1–14.

Kawano, Roland. "C. S. Lewis and 'The Nameless Isle': A Metaphor of Major Change." *CSL: The Bulletin of the New York C. S. Lewis Society.* 15 no. 173 (March 1984): 1–4.

_____. "C. S. Lewis' *The Queen of Drum*." *The Lamp-Post of the Southern California C. S. Lewis Society.* 11 (November 1987): 10–14.

Purcell, James. "*Narrative Poems*." *CSL: The Bulletin of the New York C. S. Lewis Society.* 2 no. 38 (November 1972): 2–3.

The Natural Law

Natural Law (also known as traditional morality, virtue, the Way) is a pervasive theme in the writing of C. S. Lewis. From his first book of prose (***The Pilgrim's Regress***, 1933) to his last article (**"We Have No Right to Happiness,"** 1963), Natural Law was the foundation for much of what he had to say.

Natural Law was the first topic in his popular wartime broadcasts eventually published as ***Mere Christianity***. Lewis discussed the fact that people are always referring to some standard of behavior they expect other people to know about. Although cultural interpretations and applications vary, all over the earth humans know about this law, and all over the earth they break it. People defend themselves by arguing that they do not violate the Natural Law or that they have some special excuse for violating it.

Natural Law was the topic of his Riddell Memorial Lectures at the University of Durham (1943), and he published them in ***The Abolition of Man*** (1947). There Lewis claimed that until recently everyone believed that things could merit our approval or disapproval, our reverence or our contempt. It was assumed that some emotional reactions were more appropriate than others. According to **Aristotle** the aim of education was to make a pupil like and dislike what he ought. According to **Plato**, we need to learn to feel pleasure at pleasant things, liking for likable things, disgust for disgusting things, and hatred for hateful things.

Without Natural Law's traditional precepts such as loyalty, honesty, and courage, the standard of behavior is apt to be, in the last analysis, the preservation of the person who thinks of himself as a moral innovator or the preservation of the society of his choice. But Lewis pointed out that without the Natural Law there is no logical reason to preserve anything. "The preservation of the species?—But why should the species be preserved?"

In 1971 B. F. Skinner responded to Lewis in *Beyond Freedom and Dignity*, insisting that the inner man and traditional morality should indeed be abolished now for the species to survive. But Skinner didn't try to answer Lewis's question about why such a species should survive.

According to Lewis, modern innovations in ethics are just shreds of the old Natural Law, sometimes isolated and exaggerated. There never has been and never will be a radically new value or value system. The human mind has no more power of inventing a new value than of inventing a new primary color. People who live outside Natural Law have no logical grounds for criticizing that law or anything else. A few who reject it intend to go on to the next step: they will live without any values at all, according to their whims.

Lewis's love for the Natural Law permeates his fiction, including the **Chronicles of Narnia**. It is also the overt theme of some of his poems: **"The Country of the Blind"** (*Punch*, 1951), **"On a Theme from Nicolas of Cusa"** (*Times Literary Supplement*, 1955) **"After Aristotle"** (*Oxford Magazine*, 1956), and **"Evolutionary Hymn"** (*The Cambridge Review*, 1957).

Psalm 19, Lewis's favorite, parallels his life experience by moving from praise of the beauties of nature to praise of the goodness of Natural Law, and from there to personal dedication to **God**.

Kathryn Lindskoog

Also See: Aquinas, Poetry

Bibliography

Aquinas, Thomas. *Summa Theologica* (I–II. Q 90–100).

Kreeft, Peter. "Can the Natural Law Ever Be Abolished from the Heart of Man?" *C. S. Lewis for the Third Millennium.* San Franscisco: Ignatius Press, 1994.

Lindskoog, Kathryn, and Gracia Fay Ellwood. "C. S. Lewis: The Natural Law in Literature and Life." *The Lewis Legacy.* (Autumn 1996): 12–17.

Nature

Lewis wrote about nature in several ways. First, he defined it as "all that is out there," i.e., the complete material universe, in his argument against naturalism in **Miracles**. But like **George MacDonald** before him, he resisted any attempt to view nature as a complete, self-existent system. To do so would mean that all things in existence were mere accident, including all human thought. Therefore naturalism contradicted itself, for no accident could consciously think about itself in any way that was objectively true.

But Lewis was more likely to speak of nature as the channel by which we receive hints of the beauty, glory, and majesty of **God**. Throughout his childhood Lewis was constantly enthralled by the **beauty** of nature. Even into his final years, one of his greatest pleasures was a four- or five-day ramble across the English or Irish countryside with a group of his friends. Yet Lewis came to recognize the limitations to the admiration of nature. He insisted that we must recognize that nature is, like ourselves, but a creature. Thus, he was not disturbed by the fact that nature could be at once both beautiful and cruel. Nature was not God, only a creature. And he believed that the fall of angelic beings might well account for this dual nature before the arrival of human beings. Nature fell in some sense with humanity and will be resurrected with humanity and remade. "The old field of space, time, matter and the senses is to be weeded and sown for a new crop."

Because Lewis saw nature as a mere creature like ourselves, Lewis cautioned against trying to find a complete philosophy or worse, a religion in nature. The first error that might come of looking at nature and not beyond her was that one could take almost any conclusion away from one's study of nature. The Wordsworthian nature lover might see beauty and derive goodness just as easily as another observer of nature might see cruelty and destruction and come to worship "the dark gods of the blood."

Lastly, Lewis felt that certain miracles of the Lord pointed to what the redeemed, post-resurrection nature might be like, such as the walking on water and the raising of Lazarus. He expected that all creatures in post-resurrection creation will be more themselves and more complete.

James Prothero

Also See: Human Nature, Materialism, Natural Law, Romanticism, William Wordsworth

Bibliography

Lewis, C. S. *The Four Loves*; *Miracles*

"The Necessity of Chivalry"

See entry on "Notes on the Way" (17 August 1940)

Neoplatonism in the Poetry of Spenser (Book Review)

Etudes Anglaises. XIV (April-June 1961): 107–16. Reprinted as "Neoplatonism in the Poetry of Spenser" in *Studies in Medieval and Renaissance Literature*.

Lewis began this discussion of Robert Ellrodt's book *Neoplatonism in the Poetry of Spenser* by saying "[t]he thesis of this important book is that **Spenser** knew (and cared) much less about Neoplatonism and even about **Plato** than many of his critics believe, and that numerous interpretations of his work which their belief had led them to advance are chimerical." Ellrodt distinguished three forms of Platonism, one of which he labels Neoplatonism. According to Lewis, this is "[t]he ... theosophy which men like Ficino, Pico, and Abrabanel got, or thought they were getting, out of Zoroaster, Orphism, Plato, Plotinus, Porphyry, and the Hermetica." The *Amoretti* and the *Foure Hymnes* contain some Neoplatonic elements, but they are "less, and less important, than some suppose." Spenser receded from Medieval Platonism, and owes more to the "Christian naturalism" of the Middle Ages in Lewis's view. Lewis applied and paraphrased Ellrodt's work in a relatively lengthy discussion of *The Faerie Queene*, discussing his agreement with and dissent from the book. Lewis said, "I am not certain that I am right and [Ellrodt] wrong on any of the disputed points. But I am quite certain that he has often set me right where I had been wrong; and where I was already right he has strengthened my hand." This discussion ended with praise for both the book and its author.

Anne Gardener

Bibliography

Ellrodt, Robert. *Neoplatonism in the Poetry of Spenser*. Geneve: Librairie E. Droz, 1960.

E[dith] Nesbit [Bland] (1858–1924)

Although she wrote volumes of adult love and horror stories, Fabian social commentaries, and poetry, E. Nesbit is best known for her children's books, particularly **fantasy** stories. Her Bastable Family and Five Children series were strong influences on C. S. Lewis's own juvenile fiction.

Nesbit's fantastic books thrust ordinary middle-class youngsters into extraordinary situations. In *The Magic City* (1910), which may have inspired *The Magician's Nephew*, lonely Philip and his hated new stepsister find themselves transported to a "kingdom" the boy had built from household items. They are pursued by a witch who usurps the city and populates it with evil creatures she looses from the book "walls," much as Jadis and her followers would take over Narnia. (The children are saved not by a Christ-lion, but by Julius Caesar and his legions, courtesy of Philip's Latin reader.) Lewis was particularly fond of the trilogy *Five Children and It* (1902), *The Phoenix and the Carpet* (1904), and *The Story of the Amulet* (1906), in which young Cyril, Anthea, Robert, and Jane discover the delights and terrors of supernatural

magic. "The last [book] did most for me," Lewis reported. "It first opened my eyes to antiquity, the 'dark backward and abysm of time.' I can still reread it with delight." The children from this series would reemerge, almost unchanged, as Peter, Susan, Edmund, and Lucy Pevensie. Nesbit's short story "The Aunt and Amabel" was likely another source of inspiration for Lewis, though he did not consciously remember it. The story tells how young Amabel enters another world through a wardrobe just like Lewis's children in *The Lion, the Witch and the Wardrobe*. It also includes a magical train station called "Bigwardrobeinspareroom." In chapter 2 of *The Lion, the Witch and the Wardrobe* Mr. Tumnus the Faun similarly speaks about "the far land of Spare Oom" and "the bright city of War Drobe."

Nesbit populated her works with pagan, legendary, and occult characters, a feature which appealed to Lewis. In *The Story of the Amulet*, a psammead, or sand-fairy, transports the children to ancient Egypt, Babylon, and Assyria, where they conjure up the demon-god Nisroch/Tash, who also appeared in *The Last Battle*. Other books contain ghosts, dragons, a talking phoenix, and a terrifying troop of living scarecrows. Lewis borrowed many plot devices from Nesbit, including a vagrant's being mistaken for a personage, a child being allowed to "see" distant friends, a powerful woman from another dimension being loosed on contemporary London, and a pair of Cockneys being made the rulers of an emerging kingdom. He acknowledged his debt in the opening paragraphs of *The Magician's Nephew*, which is set in the days when "the Bastables were searching for treasure in the Lewisham Road."

Katherine Harper

Also See: Kenneth Grahame, Andrew Lang, George MacDonald, Beatrix Potter, J. R. R. Tolkien, Charles Williams

Bibliography

Briggs, Julia. *A Woman of Passion: The Life of E. Nesbit, 1858–1924*. New York: New Amsterdam Books, 1987.
Lochhead, Marion. *The Renaissance of Wonder in Children's Literature*. Edinburgh: Canongate, 1977.
Streatfeild, Noel. *Magic and the Magician: E. Nesbit and Her Children's Books*. London: Ernest Benn, 1958.

New Criticism

New Criticism was the dominant critical paradigm in Anglo-American **literary criticism** from the late 1920s to the mid-60s. Born of an attempt to redress purported imbalances in existing critical practice, New Criticism sought to discredit critical practice that relied exclusively on bio-historical and philological inquiry, and to direct critical attention back to texts themselves, and away from "gossip" about origins, backgrounds, and influences. New Critics' basic mode of operation was "explication de texte," or close reading, which focused on the text as an organic unity whose diction, internal rhetoric, and symbol system revealed to readers all the information needed to experience and "understand" the work.

One of the New Critics' rallying slogans, "a poem should not mean, but be," identifies a key premise in their critical arsenal: the text is best encountered as an autonomous artifact whose "meaning" is not a paraphrase of its "message," but the total immersion of the reader in its evoked world. In search of an objective mode of inquiry, New Critics rejected "authorial intention" as trivial or artificial as a factor in interpreting texts and dismissed out of hand any consideration of the affective experience of readers as relevant to the ultimate interpretation of a text. Such formidable proponents as I. A. Richards, William Empson, Monroe Beardsley, William Wimsatt, and **T. S. Eliot** endeavored to keep criticism from "confusing the poem with its effects" and thus losing the "poem itself" in a morass of subjective responses grounded primarily outside the text.

While C. S. Lewis regarded some strains of New Criticism as salutary—for example, he found the disappearance of the "poem itself" distasteful in much biographical and psychological criticism—he posited a via media that preserved the integrity of the "work itself" while licensing the reader/critic to investigate context, intention, and readerly impact in service of "recovering the poem the author actually wrote." Short of such effort, Lewis surmised, a contemporary reader of ancient or of any transcultural works would be at the mercy of the accidental impression an image, word, or proposition would make on his or her mind.

In his major critical works and in various essays on topics related to literary criticism, Lewis articulated a stance that conceived the text as the fulcrum of the interpretative enterprise but in tension with the competing claims of both authors and readers. In the final analysis, Lewis saw "meaning" always as incarnate and participatory, a marriage of content and form, or, as he expressed it in *An Experiment in Criticism*, a composite of a reader's encounter with a text's "logos" and "poiema," always filtered through personal experience and perceived context.

Bruce L. Edwards
Bowling Green State University

Also See: Literary Theory

Bibliography

Edwards, Bruce L. *A Rhetoric of Reading: C. S. Lewis's Defense of Western Literacy*. Provo: Brigham Young University Press, 1986.

Graff, Gerald. *Poetic Statement and Critical Dogma*. Chicago: University of Chicago Press, 1980.

Hirsch, E. D. *Validity in Interpretation*. New Haven: Yale University Press, 1979.

Lentricchia, Frank. *After the New Criticism*. Chicago: University of Chicago Press, 1980.

Myers, Doris T. *C. S. Lewis in Context*. Kent, OH: Kent State University Press, 1994.

"The New Men"

The Listener. XXXI (6 April 1944): 384. Reprinted in *Beyond Personality* and *Mere Christianity*.

This essay was the concluding installment in the series "Beyond Personality" originally published in the BBC's magazine *The Listener*. The broadcast talk was first aired over the BBC on April 4, 1944. It is the only talk for which a copy of the broadcast survives and is available from The Episcopal Radio-TV Foundation.

In this final essay, Lewis listed some characteristics of the Christian who is really living in Christ, whose natural life has been replaced by the life of **Christ**. He analogized this to a new step in **evolution**, not a biological step, but a spiritual one. These "New Men" are not what we might expect, not like our idea of "religious people." Lewis said, "They do not draw attention to themselves. You tend to think that you are being kind to them when they are really being kind to you. They love you more than other men do, but they need you less." Lewis thought that these new men recognize each other and once we have recognized one of them, we will recognize the rest more easily. Lewis emphasized that being holy is rather like joining a secret society. "To put it at the very lowest, it must be great *fun*."

Probably Lewis's most successful fictional depiction of one of the "New Men" is the figure of Ransom in *That Hideous Strength*. Jane Studdock's ideas of **religion** are formed on the usual stereotypes: in Ransom, she encounters a really holy person and her stereotypes are upset.

Richard Purtill
Western Washington University

The New Miltonians (Letter)

The Times Literary Supplement (29 November 1947): 615.

An anonymous review criticizing A. J. A. Waldock's *Paradise Lost and its Critics* (*The Times Literary Supplement*, November 1, 1947) elicited a letter from

F. R. Leavis (*TLS*, November 22, 1947) defending the value of Waldock's work and castigating the reviewer for "gibbetting Mr. Waldock as pretentious, ludicrous and negligible." Lewis agreed with Leavis (if not his tone) that the book deserves to be read and considered in a thoughtful manner even though Lewis, himself, disagreed with many of Waldock's views.

Marjorie L. Mead
The Marion E. Wade Center

Friedrich Wilhelm Nietzsche (1844–1900)

In contrast to **Plato**, **Aristotle**, **Augustine**, and **Aquinas**, Nietzsche served in Lewis's writings as a negative example from the world of **philosophy**. He was a thinker of the first rank who doubted that our judgments of value are rational and objective. Nietzsche proclaimed in numerous ways the relativity of all **values** and moralities. "Nothing is true, everything is permitted," declared Nietzsche, likely paraphrasing one of Dostoevsky's characters. According to Lewis in *The Abolition of Man*, Nietzsche's "new morality" was "mere innovation."

Nietzsche is the climax of a horizontal philosophy that sees the world as ours to make, not discover, and that maintains we are the center and the lawgiver of it all. Nietzsche said that **God** is dead. If Nietzsche is right, and God is identified with **truth**, then truth must also be dead. This is another way of stating that there is no unchanging objective order that we should acknowledge as higher than ourselves. According to this view, the **supernatural** world (which Lewis defended so splendidly) is without operative power. Humans are no longer determined in the least by anything outside of themselves.

During 1940, as Europe plunged into World War II, Eric Bentley wrote a book on "heroic vitalism" in the writings of Friedrich Nietzsche, **Richard Wagner**, George Bernard Shaw, and others. Lewis provided a brief preface to the *Cult of the Superman*, noting that Bentley had identified "the source from which most of the great antidemocratic movements of our day proceed."

Several of Lewis's evil fictional characters remind (and warn) us of Nietzsche's philosophy of power. These characters emphasize, as Nietzsche did, that society is only a foundation and scaffolding by means of which a select class of beings can elevate themselves to new duties and to a higher existence. One excellent example is Weston in the interplanetary **science fiction** trilogy. When Weston and Ransom are discussing the morality appropriate for future generations, Weston states that the world leaps forward through great men and greatness always transcends morality. Lewis's fic-

tional works are comprised of characters who, in the end, either affirm self or God. In the final analysis, as Lewis's mentor **George MacDonald** says in *The Great Divorce*, God either says to you, "Thy will be done," or you say to God, "Thy will be done."

Michael H. Macdonald
Seattle Pacific University

Also See: Communism and Fascism, Democracy, Ethics and Morality, Good and Evil, Natural Law, Nature, Politics, Rationalism, Reason

Bibliography

Nietzsche, Friedrich. *Beyond Good and Evil*; *Thus Spake Zarathustra*

Non-Christian Religions

In *Mere Christianity*, C. S. Lewis observed that Christians need not believe all other religions wholly wrong, whereas atheists must deny the validity of any religious conviction. As a Christian apologist, however, he argued that **Christianity** is the one true **faith**, for no other **religion** so completely embraces the mystery and ritual of primitive or "thick" religions, along with the ethics and **philosophy** of those that are "clear." For Lewis, a "thick" religion, such as **paganism**, is "orgiastic, sacramental, and appeals to the emotions rather than the intellect or conscience." On the other hand, "clear" religions, represented by Judaism, Islam, and Hinduism among others, incorporate ethics and a rational system of belief. Lewis concluded that true religion must encompass both thickness and clearness, for "**reality** can't be one that appeals *either* only to savages *or* only to high brows. Real things aren't like that...." Only Hinduism and Christianity meet this criteria; yet, he believed, even Hinduism distinguishes between the **metaphysics** of a hermit and the ritual of suttee practiced among peasants. Ultimately, for Lewis, Christianity alone incorporates the ritual and mystery of paganism with the ethical demands and systematic **theology** of the world's great religions. Thus, Lewis concluded, "When a prig like ... me accepts Christianity he is told he must rise early on Sunday morning and participate in a prehistoric blood feast." Even as Lewis argued the case for Christianity, he maintained that all who truly seek **God** will find him. Writing to one of his correspondents, he affirmed that salvation comes to many who do not recognize **Christ**, as indicated in the Gospel account of the Last Judgment (Matthew 25:31–46). Nowhere does Lewis present this belief more eloquently than in *The Last Battle*. Emeth, the noble Calormene warrior, has loyally served the false god Tash. Following his death,

Emeth finds himself in the land of his enemy Aslan, the Christ-figure in the **Chronicles of Narnia**. When Aslan calls Emeth "Son" and bids him welcome, Emeth replies in astonishment that he has been a servant of Tash and has sought *him* all of his days. In language resonating with power and grace, Aslan answers, "Beloved,... unless thy desire had been for me thou wouldst not have sought so long and so truly. For all find what they truly seek." For Lewis, then, all those who sincerely seek God will one day be a part of his kingdom.

Lynn Summer
Georgia State University

Bibliography

Lewis, C. S. *The Last Battle*; *Letters of C. S. Lewis*; *Mere Christianity*

Vanauken, Sheldon. *A Severe Mercy*. San Francisco: Harper & Row, Publishers, 1977.

Walsh, Chad. *C. S. Lewis: Apostle to the Skeptics*. New York: Macmillan, 1949.

"None Other Gods: Culture in War Time"

Mimeographed sermon given at the Church of St. Mary the Virgin, October 22, 1939. Retitled and reprinted as *Christian in Danger*. London: Student Christian Movement, 1939. Retitled as "Learning in Wartime" and reprinted in *Transpositions*, *The Weight of Glory,* and *Fern-Seed and Elephant.*

Lewis delivered "Learning in Wartime" as a sermon on October 22, 1939, about seven weeks after World War II had started. Many **Oxford** students would naturally have wondered whether continuing their studies was appropriate under the circumstances. Lewis observed that the larger issue is not whether one can study during wartime but whether one can study **culture** at any time. If at any moment we are advancing toward **heaven** or **hell**, how can we waste time studying art and literature?

Lewis replied by noting that even on a battlefront, people still eat and converse; ordinary life never ceases entirely. Even during **war**, people will be reading and thinking, so Christians need to continue providing useful thoughts.

According to Lewis, war raises three enemies against the **scholar**: excitement, frustration, and fear. Lewis responded by showing (1) distractions always abound, something that he knew about very well from his own life, in which Mrs. **Janie Moore** repeatedly asked his help with errands and housework; (2) people can never be sure they will live to see their work completed; (3) war does not increase the frequency of death, but only

our awareness of it. And that, he concluded, is probably a good thing. This is one of Lewis's clearest, most cogent essays.

Marvin D. Hinten
Bowling Green State University

Also See: Culture, Destiny, RAF Talks

"A Note on *Comus*"

The Review of English Studies. VIII (April 1932): 170–6. Reprinted in Studies in *Medieval and Renaissance Literature.*

In this essay, Lewis examined five manuscripts of **John Milton**'s *Comus* to consider what could be determined from the types of alterations that were made. The study proceeded in Lewis's usual methodical way. For instance, he noted fifteen errors between the first and second editions and provided illuminating commentary on both cause and effect. Where Milton had "by due steps" and a copyist put "with due steps," Lewis intelligently observed that the copyist was thinking of walking-steps rather than Milton's ladder-steps.

The cumulative effect of the alterations, Lewis noted, is to make the poem less dramatic and more didactic. This makes the poem less pleasing to modern palates; it is clear that Lewis excluded himself from those less pleased.

It is interesting to see Lewis examine the poem stylistically; he later expressed his delight in the poem's content, as well, when **Charles Williams** gave a lecture on it at **Oxford** that Lewis claimed held the undergraduates spellbound. The point of the poem is the importance of chastity; **Hugo Dyson** commented about Williams' lecture, "The fellow's becoming a common chastitute." To Lewis, the solid blend of style and substance made *Comus* well worth commenting upon.

Marvin D. Hinten
Bowling Green State University

"A Note on Jane Austen"

Essays in Criticism. IV (October 1954): 43–44. Reprinted in *Selected Literary Essays.*

In this essay, Lewis examined four novels—*Emma*, *Pride and Prejudice, Sense and Sensibility*, and *Northanger Abbey*—by the 19th-century English writer **Jane Austen**. In Lewis's view, each work had a heroine who undergoes a similar process, he termed "disillusionment." Each protagonist, according to Lewis, had to experience an "undeception," recognizing and correcting an incomplete or outright mistaken worldview in order to realize her true identity and **destiny**.

These women, Lewis argued, are in stark contrast to the "solitary heroines" in two other Austen novels, *Persuasion* and *Mansfield Park*, who, because they "make no mistakes," need not experience such an "undeception" but rather must personally persevere to achieve their dreams while others come to their senses.

Lewis found much to admire in Austen's narratives and specifically commends her in this essay for her "hardness," that is, her unblushing use of "the great abstract nouns of the classical English moralists," such as "good sense," "indelicacy," "vanity," "folly," and "**reason**." But Lewis saved his greatest accolade for his conclusion, referring to Austen as "the daughter of **Samuel Johnson**," drawing attention to her emulation of his common sense, his morality, and his lucidity of style—the epitome of Lewis's own ambitions as a writer.

Bruce L. Edwards
Bowling Green State University

Bibliography

Edwards, Bruce L. (ed). *The Taste of the Pineapple: Essays on C. S. Lewis as Reader, Critic, and Imaginative Writer.* Bowling Green, OH: The Popular Press, 1988.

Hannay, Margaret. *C. S. Lewis.* New York: Ungar, 1989.

Lindskoog, Kathryn. *Finding the Landlord: A Guidebook to C. S. Lewis's Pilgrim's Regress.* Chicago: Cornerstone Press, 1996.

"Notes on the Way"

Time and Tide. XXI (17 August 1940): 841. Retitled "Importance of an Ideal" and reprinted in *Living Age.* CCCLIX (October 1940): 109–11. Retitled "The Necessity of Chivalry" and reprinted in *Present Concerns.*

This essay advocated the practice of chivalry in modern life. Lewis pointed out that we are the chivalrous ideal to the **Medieval world**, and he argued that it is best expressed by the words of Sir Ector to the dead Launcelot in Malory's *Morte D'Arthur*: "Thou wert the meekest man that ever ate in hall among ladies; and thou wert the sternest knight to thy mortal foe that ever put spear in the rest." This makes a double demand on **human nature**—not a compromise between ferocity and meekness; the chivalrous knight must be "fierce to the nth degree and meek to the nth degree." He is a paradox, but the Middle Ages saw that the combination was necessary for "any lasting **happiness** or dignity in human society."

The knightly, paradoxical character is achieved by art, not by nature. It was once the preserve of a specialized class. But in a classless democratic society, observed Lewis, people must either learn chivalry by

themselves or else choose between "brutality and softness." This is a problem that is "too seldom mentioned."

John Bremer

Also See: Democracy, Modernity

Bibliography

Kollmann, Judith J. "C. S. Lewis as a Medievalist." *CSL: The Bulletin of the New York C. S. Lewis Society.* 10 (May 1979): 1–5.

"Notes on the Way"

Time and Tide. XXII (29 March 1941): 261. Expanded and retitled "'Bulverism', or, The Foundation of 20th Century Thought" and printed in *The Socratic Digest.* 2 (June 1944): 16–20. The expanded version also reprinted in *God in the Dock, Undeceptions,* and *First and Second Things.*

Lewis began this essay with Emerson's comment that "it is a disastrous discovery ... that we exist." We exist as "bundles of complexes" and as "members of some economic class." These are two of the newer ways in which we exist. In the past, a thing that seemed obviously true to a hundred men was probably true. Now, Freudians or Marxists will tell us that the apparent **truth** is due to something quite different from **reality**. Does this mean that thoughts are necessarily tainted and that the taint invalidates them? The best that we—and they—can do is say that some are tainted and some are not. However, we must not forget that "you must show *that* a man is wrong before you start explaining *why* he is wrong." The assumption of modern arguments is that the man is wrong, a common vice Lewis called Bulverism. The results of Bulver's thinking are everywhere, and the result is that many people assume **Christianity** is wrong. "Until Bulverism is crushed, **reason** can play no effective part in human affairs." Our knowledge is inferred from our sensation, our experiences. If these are not genuine insight, we know nothing. "Either we can know nothing *or* thought has reasons only, and no causes." (*From this point on, the paper is reconstructed from notes taken by the Secretary of the Socratic Club.*) Lewis suggested that "[he is] a colony of some Thought and Will that are self-existent," and therefore derived from some **supernatural** source. According to this view, there is not making or causing, only projection. "But 'projection' is itself a form of causing, and it is more reasonable to suppose that Will is the only cause we know, and that therefore Will is the cause of **Nature**." (*The record of the questions asked after the talk are not complete, but a list of points is part of the text.*)

Anne Gardner

Also See: Sigmund Freud, Modernity

"Notes on the Way"

Time and Tide. XXVIII (27 June 1942): 519–20. Retitled "First and Second Things" and reprinted in *God in the Dock, Undeceptions* and *First and Second Things*.

In this article Lewis was delighted that the Germans selected Hagen rather than Siegfried as their national hero. He recalled the impact of *The Ring*, and of **Arthur Rackham**'s illustrations, and was happy that the Nazis "have proved unable to digest it." According to Lewis, the Nazis were attempting "to appropriate 'the Nordic' as a whole." Paradoxically, the people so bent on reviving their pre-Christian mythology were incapable of understanding it. However, Lewis warned, looks may be deceiving. Just as the Romantics first began to "take art seriously," so are the Nazis taking mythology seriously, and by doing so miss the point "by valuing too highly a real, but subordinate good," and thereby coming close to losing that good. Lewis came to suspect that this is a universal law: "On cause mieux quand on ne dit pas Causons" (One converses better when one does not say "Let us converse."). Second things don't come from being put first. The difficulty is to determine what things are first. Civilization was endangered when it became "the exclusive aim of human activity." Something must come before civilization, but what? "The only reply [Lewis] can offer here is that if we do not know, then the first and only truly practical thing is to set about finding out."

Anne Gardner

Also See: Communism and Fascism, Myth, Richard Wagner

"Notes on the Way"

Time and Tide. XXIV (4 September 1943): 717. Retitled "My First School" and reprinted in *Present Concerns*.

A cruel, deranged headmaster, a group of "beaten, cheated, scared, ill-fed" schoolboys, and a revolting latrine/storage shed—these were some features of Lewis's first school. Yet in retrospect Lewis found that from the horrific **Wynyard School** he learned three lessons. First, groups that refuse to spy on their members enjoy greater freedom and cohesiveness than those with sneaks. Lewis praised his peers for their tight lips. Second, **joy** differs markedly from pleasure. Joy has a delectable sensation that is at once sweet and sharp, exciting and scary, whereas pleasure lacks pungency. Lewis's intense longing for vacation and home helped him distinguish between the two emotions. Third, living

by hope and longing is an art. It puts present concerns in their rightful place and makes adverse conditions bearable and the future—be it good or bad—an incredible experience.

Lewis concluded that educational outcomes cannot be predicted. Although educators should provide good programs, they should not overestimate their control of results. Destiny, Lewis claims, is at work.

Had the cruel headmaster of Wynyard, **Robert Capron,** been tried for child abuse, even Lewis's three lessons would not have exonerated him. Also culpable would have been **Albert Lewis,** who failed to inspire open communication with his son. If he had, C. S. Lewis might have found that the place to inform on a bad schoolmaster is at home.

Carolyn Keefe
West Chester University

Bibliography

Davey, Mary Ellen. "My First School." *CSL: The Bulletin of the New York C. S. Lewis Society*. 19 (December 1987): 1–3.

Lewis, C. S. *Surprised by Joy*

"Notes On the Way"

Time and Tide. XXV (11 March 1944): 213. Retitled "The Parthenon and the Optative" and reprinted in *Of this and Other Worlds* and *On Stories*.

In this essay, Lewis targeted the demand for more appreciation in the literary classroom (symbolized by the Parthenon) and the parallel demand for less of grammar, dates, and prosody (symbolized by the Optative—a grammatical mood). He criticized proposals for eliminating external examinations in English focusing on facts and testing instead for the "sensitive and elusive core" of meaning rather than the "coarse fringe" of objective learning.

Lewis argued that whereas appreciation may not lead to a love of good books, it will certainly result in factual ignorance and the inability to distinguish **truth** from error. The drier factual sort of **education** may fail as well, but at least the student will know what knowledge is like, and though he doesn't care for it, he will know he hasn't got it. Ironically, appreciation is often taught by teachers who, having hard knowledge, fail to see that because appreciation is a delicate growth it is not the sort of thing that can be taught. Facile students will fake it, and shyer ones in whom genuine appreciation is beginning to bud will not bring it forth easily for the purposes of examination.

Thus, Lewis showed proposed examination reforms to be both highly subjective in nature and prone to abuses stemming from lack of an objective standard.

Lyle Smith
Biola University

Also See: Books of Influence, Literary Criticism

"Notes on the Way"

Time and Tide. XXV (29 April 1944): 369–70. Retitled "Democratic Education" and reprinted in *Present Concerns.*

Requiring Latin and mathematics is unfair and undemocratic. Only bright students can excel; the others cannot compete successfully and consequently feel inferior. Against such reasoning Lewis argued in this essay.

Lewis distinguished between liking particular studies and devising a curriculum that preserves **democracy**. He predicted the effects of abolishing compulsory (disliked) courses in favor of wide-ranging (liked) electives. The changes would enable all students, even the inept, to be "praised and petted" for whatever they enjoy. Good feelings would increase, but the learning necessary for democratic survival would drop dangerously low. "A nation of dunces," he warned, "can be safe only in a world of dunces."

Noting that nothing about the mind is democratic, Lewis mainly attributed the call for parity to envy of superiority. He advocated a "ruthlessly aristocratic" approach that does not pander to envy but furthers the interests of first-rate students and therefore the well-being of democracy.

What, then, will the slow students gain from Latin? Whittling their way along, playfully mocking authority, and keeping the brainy students in check, they will learn the lesson essential for democracy—not to take big men too seriously nor regard themselves as big.

Lewis's educational vision is both myopic and far-sighted. In classifying students he overlooked the large average group, but he saw ahead to the harmful outcomes of basing educational decisions on course likability.

Carolyn Keefe
West Chester University

Also See: Education, Hierarchy

Bibliography

Lewis, C. S. "Equality"; "Membership"; "Screwtape Proposes a Toast"

"Notes on the Way"

Time and Tide. XXVII (25 May 1946): 486. Reprinted as the first part of "Different Tastes in Literature" (the second part is "Notes on the Way" of June 1, 1946) in *Of This and Other Worlds* and *On Stories.*

Noting that the idea persists, despite the apparent lack of objective tests, that some tastes, or preferences, in art are superior to others, Lewis proposed to at least simplify the problem by arguing that people do not in fact "like bad art in . . . the same way as others like good art"—that bad art in fact "never succeeds with anyone."

By "bad" art, Lewis meant to distinguish popular music, novels, and pictures from work that is capable of producing "intense and ecstatic delight." Bad art does not do this, nor is it meant to. Rather, it serves as a pleasant background to life, and passes with a change of fashion. Bad novels are not reread; bad pictures are hung where seldom seen. They are articles of consumption. Good art is a source of **joy**, a mind-changing experience. Passing from bad art to good, one does not simply get a quantitative or qualitative increase of pleasure; one gets an entirely different thing—as if a food one enjoyed for the taste one day enabled one to understand the speech of birds.

Thus, in the absence of an objective test of taste, one still finds the empirical fact that some people care for good art in a way that no one cares for bad. Subtler critical distinction between works of admittedly good art involve criteria that are technical or moral, not only aesthetic. The experiences of bad art are not of the same kind as those of good art; one might as well suppose a world in which many people could "get drunk on water."

Lyle Smith
Biola University

Also See: Literary Criticism

Bibliography

Lewis, C. S. "Christianity and Culture"; "Good Work and Good Works"; "High and Low Brows"

"Notes on the Way"

Time and Tide. XXVII (1 June 1946): 510–11. Reprinted as the second part of "Different Tastes in Literature" (the first part is "Notes on the Way" of May 25, 1946) in *Of This and Other Worlds* and *On Stories.*

See entry for "Notes on the Way" (25 May 1946).

"Notes on the Way"

Time and Tide. XXVII (9 November 1946): 1070–71. Retitled "Period Criticism" and reprinted in *Of This and Other Worlds* and *On Stories*.

In this essay, Lewis responded to James Stephens' charge that the works of **G. K. Chesterton** are "dated" ("The 'Period Talent' of G. K. Chesterton." *The Listener*. [17 October 1946]), pointing out, first, that the same thing might be said with greater plausibility of Stephens' own novels. After a paragraph in which he generously praised much of Stephens' work, Lewis returned to the kind of criticism that "turns on dates and periods," labeling the criterion of "up to dateness" confusing because it confounds two possible senses of being "of a period."

In the negative sense, poets might be dated because they deal with current fashions of no permanent interest. An example is **George Herbert**'s shaped poems. Positively, writers might be "dated" simply because they deal with things of permanent interest in the style that is of their own time. The real question, wrote Lewis, is in which sense Chesterton was "of his period." His journalism and essays are dated in the first sense. But his imaginative works deal with ideas and personalities of enduring interest; *The Man Who Was Thursday* bears favorable comparison to the works of Kafka. Thus, a critic dismissing Chesterton's fiction as Edwardian period pieces would be as foolish as one who dismissed the fiction of Stephens as simply more of "All the old Abbey Theatre stuff."

Lyle Smith
Biola University

Also See: Literary Criticism, Literary Theory, New Criticism

"Notes on the Way"

Time and Tide. XXIX (14 August 1948): 830–1. Retitled "Priestess in the Church" and reprinted in *God in the Dock* and *Undeceptions*.

In this 1948 essay C. S. Lewis tackled the issue of whether **women** should be ordained to the Christian priesthood. Lewis focused his argument on the nature of the Christian priest as a mediator between **God** and human beings. According to Lewis, women are not able to represent God in priestly ministry because the traditional **language** of the Christian **faith** consistently casts God in masculine language. This language sets definite patterns of thought for the Christian life, and the ordination of women would result in a fundamental shift in the Christian conception of God and transform **Christianity** from a religion of **revelation** to "that old wraith Natural Religion." Lewis also objected to women's ordination on the basis that women's equality in the Church is based on complementarity, not interchangeability, with men.

While Lewis's arguments have not been persuasive in his own Anglican communion, they are echoed in recent pronouncements by the Roman Catholic Church that women may not be ordained. Both Lewis's conception of the priest as mediator and his insistence that women's equality does not entail absolute access to ordination have been strongly reiterated in recent papal arguments against women's ordination.

Mark Edward DeForrest

Also See: Anglicanism, Church, Roman Catholicism, Women

Bibliography

John Paul II. *Ordinatio Sacerdotalis* (Apostolic Letter on Reserving Priestly Ordination to Men Alone), 1994.

"The Novels of Charles Williams"

First published posthumously in *Of This and Other Worlds* and *On Stories*.

This essay was written by C. S. Lewis for the British Broadcasting Corporation, and he read it over the BBC on February 11, 1949. Lewis wrote the essay to answer certain criticisms of **Charles Williams**' novels—primarily that they mixed the realistic and the fantastic ("the probable" and "the marvelous" in Lewis's terminology). Lewis pointed out that critics often resented the pairing of ordinary people with the **supernatural** ("ghosts, magicians, and archetypical beasts"), believing that the mixing of "straight fiction" with "pure **fantasy**" caused the reader to "skip to and fro" between genres in the novel.

Lewis suggested that Williams' novels (not allegories) fit into a type that belonged neither to realism or fantasy. Williams (in *The Place of the Lion, Descent Into Hell,* and *All Hallows' Eve*) followed a formula used by such writers as **Edith Nesbit** and pictured "the everyday world as invaded by the marvelous" or "both sides of the frontier." For Lewis, Williams' novels created "good characters" (very difficult in fiction, according to Lewis), shed rich light on a supernaturally invaded world, were "good guesses" about unknowable things, and extended a sense of grandeur ("courtesy") to the world.

Perry C. Bramlett
C. S. Lewis for the Local Church

Also See: Allegory, Fairy Tales, Literary Criticism, Myths

O

"The Obstinate Toy Soldiers"

The Listener. XXXI (16 March 1944): 300. Reprinted in *Beyond Personality* and *Mere Christianity.*

"The Obstinate Toy Soldier" was the fourth essay in the "Beyond Personality" series published in the BBC's *The Listener* and then revised for inclusion into **Beyond Personality** and **Mere Christianity.** In the essay, Lewis pointed out that **God**'s plans for us are that our natural life (*Bios*) be replaced by a share in the life of God (*Zoe*). He gave an illustration in terms of a child whose toy soldiers come to life. Suppose that the soldier did not like being turned into flesh and resists it insofar as he can. Lewis compared this with our resistance to the replacement of our *Bios* with God's *Zoe*. The soldier could see that his original material was being changed and perhaps thinks that the process is killing it, rather than bringing it to a new life. Similarly we see the death of our natural life and the replacement of it with God's life as a threat, not seeing that we are coming into a fuller life.

Lewis said that in the case of the tin soldiers the process would only involve one tin soldier at a time, but in the case of human beings we are all interconnected. What has happened in the case of God becoming man is that a sort of "good infection" has started, which gradually spread from one human being to another.

Richard Purtill
Western Washington University

"*Odora Canum Vis* (A defence of certain modern biographers and critics)"

The Month. 11 (May 1954): 272. Revised and reprinted in *Poems* and *Collected Poems.*

"Odora Canum Vis" (Latin for "With Keen-Scented Hunting Dogs"—a reference to Virgil's *Aeneid* 4.132)—is a witty and pointed poem. A sarcastic defense of writers who churn out works that titillate, glorifying and headlining smut, it is an example of what it is like to fall under the wrath of Lewis's unrestrained critical faculties.

Don W. King
Montreat College

"Odysseus Sails Again"

See entry on *The Odyssey* (Book Review)

The Odyssey (Book Review)

"Odysseus Sails Again." *Sunday Telegraph.* 84 (9 September 1962): 6.

This translation attempts to make Homer sound as if he were a 20th-century American, according to Lewis. The result is that Homer sounds very much like Stephen Vincent Benét. The characters become "the guy next door." Although the poetic diction is sacrificed (rightly, it appears), there is "rhythmical vigour." Of its type of translation, Lewis found it adequate.

Anne Gardner

Bibliography

Homer. *The Odyssey.* Robert Fitzgerald (trans).

Of Other Worlds: Essays and Stories

Walter Hooper (ed). London: Geoffrey Bles, 1966. First US edition, New York: Harcourt, Brace & World, 1967.

See separate essay and story entries on the following:

After Ten Years (fragment)
Forms of Things Unknown
"It All Began with a Picture ..."
Ministering Angels
"On Criticism"
"On Juvenile Tastes"
"On Science Fiction"
"On Stories"
"On Three Ways of Writing for Children"
"A Reply to Professor Haldane"
The Shoddy Lands
"Sometimes Fairy Stories May Say Best What's to be Said"
"Unreal Estates"

Of This and Other Worlds: Essays and Stories

Walter Hooper (ed). London: Collins, 1982. First US edition titled *On Stories: And Other Essays on Literature.* New York: Harcourt Brace Jovanovich, 1982.

See separate essay and story entries on the following:

After Ten Years (fragment)
"The Death of Words"
"Different Tastes in Literature"
Forms of Things Unknown

"George Orwell"

"The Hobbit"

"It All Began with a Picture . . ."

Ministering Angels

"The Mythopoeic Gift of Rider Haggard"

"The Novels of Charles Williams"

"On Criticism"

"On Juvenile Tastes"

"On Science Fiction"

"On Stories"

"On Three Ways of Writing for Children"

"A Panegyric for Dorothy L. Sayers"

"The Parthenon and the Optative"

"Period Criticism"

"A Reply to Professor Haldane"

The Shoddy Lands

"Sometimes Fairy Stories May Say Best What's to be Said"

"Tolkien's *The Lord of the Rings*"

"A Tribute to E. R. Eddison"

"Unreal Estates"

"The Old Grey Mare"

Green, R. L. "C. S. Lewis." *Puffin Post*. 4 no. 1 (1970): 14–15.

Written when Lewis was ten or eleven, this is his earliest surviving poem. Simple and not profound, it celebrates the valor of a knight's battlefield charger.

Don W. King
Montreat College

"Oliver Elton (1861–1945)"

The Oxford Magazine. LXIII (21 June 1946): 318–19 (obituary).

In this obituary, Lewis praised Elton for holding "dogmas, without being 'dogmatic' in the popular sense of that word. His sensibility is not in the least hampered by his integrity: he can be as catholic and sensitive as the pococurantists without having paid their price." According to Lewis, Elton's work on the six-volume *Survey of English Literature* would be his monument, balancing as they do chronological appreciations with aesthetic standards; and "it is rarer praise than it should be for literary historians—he never wrote of what he had not well and truly read." (Although it was not mentioned by Lewis, he must have known that Elton had written the biography of Frederick York Powell [1850–1904], the editor and translator of *Corpus Poeticum*

Boreale, which had delighted and influenced Lewis while at **Malvern**.)

John Bremer

"On Another Theme from Nicolas of Cusa"

The Times Literary Supplement. (January 21, 1955): 43. Revised and retitled "On a Theme from Nicolas of Cusa" and reprinted in *Poems* and *Collected Poems*.

This gem-like poem inspired by Lewis's reading of Nicolas of Cusa's (1401–64) writings on plant growth cleverly contrasted the different ways body and soul are affected by food. On the one hand, the body takes in food, changes it, and uses it to produce energy. On the other hand, the soul takes in its food (good and **truth**) and instead is changed by it.

Don W. King
Montreat College

"On a Picture by Chirico"

The Spectator. 182 (May 6, 1949): 607. Revised and reprinted in *Poems* and *Collected Poems*.

A picture by the metaphysical artist Giorgio de Chirico (1888–1978) is the subject of this poem. Chirico focused upon horses in works such as *The Enigma of the Horse* and *The Apparition of the Horse* (1913) and *Horses by the Sea* (1926). In this poem two horses dominate the scene, survivors of an apocalypse; their noble features suggest to Lewis their archetypal character, called to live in peace untouched by man.

Don W. King
Montreat College

On Aristotle and Greek Tragedy (Book Review)

"Ajax and Others." *Sunday Telegraph*. 98 (16 December 1962): 6.

In his book *On Aristotle and Greek Tragedy,* John Jones maintained that there are vast differences between the modern man and the Greeks. His book is divided into two parts. The first deals with "Poetics," and here Lewis found Jones correct and profound, if not lucid. The second part is on the tragedians, and about this Lewis was more doubtful.

Anne Gardner

Bibliography

Jones, John. *On Aristotle and Greek Tragedy*

"On a Theme from Nicolas of Cusa"

See entry on "On Another Theme from Nicolas of Cusa"

"On Being Human"

Punch. 210 (May 8, 1946): 402 (under the pseudonym Nat Whilk). Revised and reprinted in *Poems* and *Collected Poems.*

One of several poems in which Lewis noted that while **angels** have some real advantages over mankind, they are also limited. Lewis pointed out that while angels have direct knowledge of spiritual and philosophical **truth** denied to mankind, they lack the faculty of sensory impressions **God** shares with mankind. Lewis concluded that in some ways, it is better to be human than angelic.

Don W. King
Montreat College

On Church Music

English Church Music. XIX (April 1949): 19–22. Reprinted in *Christian Reflections*

Lewis wrote this 1949 article for *English Church Music* openly professing his ignorance. Without a musical education, he could only speak from his experience in a small parish church. That experience was obviously bad for, as Lewis put it, what he wanted in **church** were "fewer, better, and shorter hymns, especially fewer."

Music in church, he said, should either glorify **God** or edify the people. Music that is high brow (too far above the tastes of the public) may glorify God while failing to edify. On the other hand, music that is low brow may be of no more spiritual significance than singing Auld Lang Syne on New Year's Eve. Within church, differing musical tastes can be an opportunity for **grace** as those with different tastes respect each other. It can also create **pride** and resentment.

In the end Lewis conceded that God's perspective may be different from our own. We may be frustrated, as Lewis was, that we shout and bellow rather than sing, but God may take our offerings "like the intrinsically worthless present of a child, which a father values indeed, but values only for the intention."

Mike Perry

Also See: Aesthetics, Anglicanism, Church

Bibliography

Lewis, C. S. "Correspondence with an Anglican Who Dislikes Hymns"; "High and Low Brows"

"On Criticism"

First published posthumously in *Of Other Worlds.* Reprinted in *Of This and Other Worlds* and *On Stories.*

In this unfinished essay, Lewis discussed what author-critics can learn about reviewer-critics who are tainted by interested motives; reviewers who criticize books without having read them carefully, or at all; reviewers who believe they know more than they do about the work they are reviewing; and two categories of interpretive mistake to which Lewis found critics prone. The one arises when the critic writes fiction rather than criticism; the other when the critic is honestly attempting interpretation.

Interpretation is the attempt to find out the meaning or intention of a book. Lewis tentatively defined meaning as the series or system of emotions, reflections, and attitudes produced by reading. "The ideally true . . . 'meaning' would be" one "shared . . . by the largest number of the best readers after repeated and careful readings over several generations." Where critics "most often . . . go wrong," according to Lewis, "is in the hasty assumption of an allegorical sense." They should remember that "no story can be devised" that some clever critic cannot interpret allegorically, and that the "mere fact" that one can allegorize a work "is no proof that it is an **allegory**."

Lyle Smith
Biola University

Also See: Literary Criticism

On Cross-Channel Ships (Letter)

The Times. (18 November 1938): 12.

An appeal to preserve open deck spaces on the cross-channel ships by one who values "the sight, the smell, and the airs of the sea." Based on his own frequent experience sailing to and from Ireland, Lewis advised that such open deck spaces are not only a safeguard for many travelers against seasickness, but also a welcome refuge from the heat and noise below deck.

Marjorie L. Mead
The Marion E. Wade Center

"On Ethics"

First published posthumously in *Christian Reflections.*

In this essay Lewis argued against the view "that the world must return to Christian **ethics** in order to preserve civilization." In the essay Lewis defended the view (compare also a similar defense in his later *The Abolition of Man*) that all who urge on us a moral code of any kind are already moralists. According to Lewis, there are few differences from a practical standpoint between Stoics, Aristotelians, Thomists, Kantians, and Utilitarians.

By studying diverse ethical theories we exaggerate the practical differences between them. Traditional morality "is neither Christian nor Pagan, neither Eastern nor Western, neither ancient nor modern, but general." Until modern times teachers, and almost everyone else, believed that "objects did not merely receive, but could *merit* our approval or disapproval, our reverence, or our contempt." The only alternative is the poison of subjectivism where it is believed that the world is ours to make, not discover, and where it is maintained that we are the center and the lawgiver of it all (see **Nietzsche** for one example of this subjectivist view).

It should be noted that even though Lewis concluded that Christian ethics is not a novelty, Christian **metaphysics** is. Everyone either accepts or rejects the "transcendent novelty" of the Christian faith, which has to do with the deity and resurrection of **Christ**, the Atonement, and the forgiveness of sins.

Michael H. Macdonald
Seattle Pacific University

Also See: Aristotle, Aquinas, Christianity, Kant, Paganism, Redemption, Sin, The Tao

Bibliography

Lewis, C. S. "The Poison of Subjectivism"
Purtill, Richard L. *Thinking About Ethics.* Englewood, NJ: Prentice-Hall, 1976.

"On Forgiveness"

Reprinted in *God in the Dock* and *The Weight of Glory.*

"On Forgiveness" is an essay written in 1947 for a church magazine. After some opening remarks on the importance of forgiveness, Lewis noted that what we often want, rather than forgiveness, is to be excused—to have **God** or another person recognize that we really couldn't help what we did wrong. But, as Lewis pointed out, if everything can be excused, then there is no need for forgiveness in the first place. Actually, he observed, God is already aware of extenuating circumstances, but the unexcused part left over still needs to be forgiven. While we are quick to excuse ourselves, Lewis said, we are often not quick enough to find excuses for others. He closed by reminding readers that forgiving others is necessary, according to Scripture, to be forgiven.

This is a very light essay, by Lewis standards—no literary or historical references, no foreign phrases. And it is relatively lacking in **analogy** and example, two of his staple techniques. But it does have the typically Lewisian insight into **human nature**, as in his recognition that the hardest things to forgive are not isolated instances but repeated annoyances.

Marvin D. Hinten
Bowling Green State University

Also See: Grace, Mercy

Bibliography

Morrison, John. "God Means What He Says: C. S. Lewis on Forgiveness." *CSL: The Bulletin of the New York C. S. Lewis Society.* 13 (January 1982): 1–7.

"On Juvenile Tastes"

Church Times, Children's Book Supplement. (28 November 1958): i. Reprinted in *Of this World, Of This and Other Worlds,* and *On Stories.*

In this letter, Lewis criticized the theory that children's reading tastes are very unlike those of adults on the ground that there is no one literary taste common to all children. Although it may be replied that a specifically childish taste for the adventurous and marvelous does exist, this, Lewis answered, implies that we regard as childish a taste that has generally been that of humanity as a whole; even the **fairy tale** proper was originally told and enjoyed at the court of Louis XIV.

Lewis pointed out that children read for pleasure; adults read in obedience to changing literary fashions. So-called "juvenile taste" is simply universal human taste. The literary establishment is little interested in narrative art but is rather preoccupied with technical novelties and with social or psychological themes. Writers with a story to tell must appeal to the audience that still cares for storytelling as such. Very often, that means they will write for children.

According to Lewis, the wrong sort of children's writers treat children almost as a distinct **culture** and cater to that age group from educational, moral, and commercial motives. The right sort work within a universally shared ground of interest common to both children and adults.

Lyle Smith
Biola University

Also See: Rudyard Kipling, Andrew Lang, Beatrix Potter

"On Living in an Atomic Age"

Informed Reading. VI (1948): 78–84. Reprinted in *Present Concerns.*

In this essay, Lewis wrote that we should not exaggerate the novelty of living in the atomic age. Death is a certainty, and all that the scientists have done is to add "one more chance of painful and premature death." We should pull ourselves together and let any bomb that comes find us doing sensible and human things—praying, working, teaching, reading, and so forth. If the destruction of civilization is the issue, that was known before the atomic bomb was made. The real question is whether **Nature** is the only thing in existence. If so, all the atomic bomb does is to hasten the end. There are three alternatives for us: suicide, having a good time, or defiance. As long as we are materialists, we adopt an uneasy alternation between the second and third, but ultimately, if Nature is all, our standards are as meaningless as the universe of which they are part. The naturalistic conclusion is unbelievable. We are not simply the offspring of Nature—"We must simply accept it that we are spirits, free and rational beings." Nature then is not our mother, but our sister; we have a common Creator. Nature has nothing to teach us, and we must live by our laws not hers, and it is part of our spiritual law never to put survival first. This essay should be compared with chapter 3 of the original edition of **Miracles**, Lewis's argument with **G. E. M Anscombe**, and the revised version of chapter 3.

John Bremer

Also See: Destiny, Materialism, War

"On Obstinancy in Belief"

The Sewanee Review. LXIII (Autumn 1955): 525–38. Reprinted in *The World's Last Night, They Asked for a Paper,* and *Screwtape Proposes a Toast.*

In this paper prepared for the **Oxford Socratic Club**, Lewis declared that the seeming disparity between Christian and "scientific" attitudes toward belief is not as great as the scientific camp might suppose. The word "belief" has many meanings, including hypothesis, weak opinion, and strong negative opinion. After examples of each, Lewis showed that the concept of **faith** is not exclusively religious. For instance, in order to be helped, a child with a splinter must trust someone with a sharp instrument in apparent disregard of evidence that the "help" will hurt even more. Proof is also arrived at differently by various disciplines. Scientists determine proof by experiment, historians by documents, judges by sworn testimony. While a Christian's faith in the face of seemingly contrary evidence would be shocking in a historian pursuing his discipline, everyone has faith and beliefs to which methods of proof do not apply. A drowning judge must trust that his rescuer is capable without benefit of sworn

testimony, and a scientist will believe in a friend beyond evidence. Just so does the Christian believe in **God**, "even against much evidence." So, concluded Lewis, the seeming Christian "obstinacy" in belief is not part of "the logic of speculative thought" but rather the "logic of personal relations"—by faith in God as a Person more trustworthy than any friend.

Richard A. Hill
Taylor University

Also See: Christianity, Materialism, Religion, Science, Supernatural

Bibliography
Lewis, C. S. "The Efficacy of Prayer"; "Is Theism Important?"

"On Punishment: A Reply"

Res Judicatae. VI (August 1954): 519–23. Reprinted in *God in the Dock, Undeceptions,* and *First and Second Things.*

This brief article replied to two critiques of Lewis's article **"The Humanitarian Theory of Punishment"** (1953). One critique had treated in a new way an ancient distinction between Positive Law and **Natural Law** asserting that **justice** is only applicable to the first. It claimed that this view avoided begging the question and also "dogmatic subjectivism," but Lewis disagreed.

The second critique assumed that our safeguards, lie in the courts—in their incorruptible judges, their excellent techniques, and "the controls of natural justice which the law has built up." But, for Lewis, this was precisely the question: will the tradition of natural law, based on **free will**, responsibility, and rights, survive the notion that courts should provide therapy and not "deserts"? "I wish society to be protected and I should be very glad if all punishments were also cures. All I plead for is the *prior* condition of ill desert; loss of liberty justified on retributive grounds *before* we begin considering the other factors."

John Bremer

Also See: Ethics and Morality

"On Reading *The Faerie Queene*"
See entry on "Edmund Spenser"

"On Receiving Bad News"

Time and Tide. 26 (December 29, 1945): 1093. Retitled "Epigrams and Epitaphs, No. 12" and reprinted in *Poems* and *Collected Poems.*

This poem is a somber reflection on the certainty of hard times. When the first painful experience comes to us, this poem warns us not to assume it is the worst (see

Edgar in *King Lear*); in fact, it is only the initial dose of the increasingly distasteful medicine ladled out by life.

Don W. King
Montreat College

"On Science Fiction"

First published posthumously in *Of Other Worlds*. Reprinted in *Of This and Other Worlds* and *On Stories*.

This essay, originally an address to the Cambridge University English Club in 1955, provides some details on Lewis's personal interests as a reader of **science fiction**, tries to account for the appeal of the genre to those who like it, and lays out a scheme of formal types into which the genre falls. Lewis did not care for science fiction that situated ordinary stories in an imagined future or that used stories to spell out scientific theories by which **space travel** might actually occur. He found more interesting those that described what it would be like to experience actual space travel and arrive at real places in space or that speculate about the ultimate destiny of our species.

But the only type he was really drawn to were those that satisfied the age-old love for **fantasy** and **fairy tale**, that allowed one to experience the emotions of traveling to and being in unfamiliar places (a dark forest, a far-off land, another planet) and that enlarged our conception of the range of possible experience. For this kind of fiction, the plausibility of the scientific means of travel is immaterial, and Lewis notes that the **supernatural** method of transport he used in *Perelandra* is preferable to the more realistic spaceship he used in *Out of the Silent Planet*.

Peter J. Schakel
Hope College

Bibliography

Sammons, Martha C. "'A Better Country': The Worlds of Religious Fantasy and Science Fiction." *Contributions to the Study of Science Fiction and Fantasy, no. 32.* New York: Greenwood Press, 1988.

"On Stories"

Essays Present to Charles Williams. London: Oxford University Press, 1947. Reprinted in *Of Other Words, Of This and Other Worlds,* and *On Stories*.

While many readers value plot primarily for the sake of the excitement it may provide, Lewis pointed out in this essay that there is another factor to be considered— atmosphere, country, weather, the sense of what it is like to be in a place. Readers who reread stories do so because they are interested in the quality of experience. What

Lewis valued in romances is atmosphere and the sense of a fully realized alternate world. The world of a good **fantasy**, he wrote, is built according to a consistent **logic**.

Lewis argued here for the equal importance of qualitative elements of the plot. In the **fairy tale** "Jack the Giant Killer," for instance, the plot presents not only danger but danger from giants. So in *King Solomon's Mines* or *The First Men in the Moon*, the protagonists are in danger not only of death but death of a certain kind.

For many readers, Lewis added, romances may provide access to profound, even religious, experiences they would reject if encountered in any other form. The plot of a story is a kind of net for catching something else—namely, a qualitative state of being.

Lyle Smith
Biola University

Also See: Rider Haggard

On Stories: and Other Essays on Literature
See entry on *Of This and Other Worlds*

"On the Atomic Bomb (Metrical Experiment)"

The Spectator. 175 (December 28, 1945): 619. Reprinted in *Poems* and *Collected Poems*.

This poem gently mocks those who believe living under the nuclear sword of Damocles makes the fear and certainty of death greater than ever before in history. Indeed, man when born is sentenced to death, so the threat of an atomic bomb makes this tragedy no more inevitable (see **"On Living in the Atomic Age"**).

Don W. King
Montreat College

"On the Death of Charles Williams"

Britain Today. 112 (August 1945): 14. Revised and retitled as "To Charles Williams" and reprinted in *Poems* and *Collected Poems*.

One of several poems Lewis wrote lamenting the loss of friends. This poignant piece indicated the dissonance and disorientation of Lewis's life with the unexpected death of **Charles Williams**. Ironically, Lewis noted that it would only be with Williams he could hope to talk through and make sense of this death.

Don W. King
Montreat College

"On the Reading of Old Books"

See entry on *The Incarnation of the Word of God: Being the Treatise of St. Athanasius' 'De Incarnatione Verbi Dei'* (Introduction)

"On the Transmission of Christianity"

See entry on *How Heathen is Britain?* (Preface)

"On Three Ways of Writing for Children"

Library Association Proceedings, Papers and Summaries of Discussions at the Bournemouth Conference on 29 April to 2 May 1952. London: Library Association, 1952: 22–8. Reprinted in *Of Other Worlds, Of This and Other Worlds,* and *On Stories.*

The worst way to write for children, Lewis argued, is to write for a "market," regardless of one's own tastes. The best ways are to work from extemporaneous oral storytelling or from the recognition that a children's story is the best art form for what one has to say. Certain kinds of stories appeal to all ages of readers because the fantasy allows the writer to exercise the human function of "sub-creator." The **fairy tales** liberate archetypes according to Lewis, and giants, dwarfs, and talking beasts are an "admirable hieroglyphic" for illustrating **psychology** and character types.

Lewis acknowledged that fairy tales are criticized for giving children a false impression of the world, for being escapist, and for frightening children. But he replied first that children do not expect the real world to be like fairy stories. Second, "realistic" writing invites wish-fulfillment fantasies, whereas fairy stories arouse a longing for something beyond reach and give the natural world new dimension and depth. Third, childhood phobias arise quite independently of fairy stories, and it would be escapist to try to conceal from children the fact that they live in a dangerous world in which courage and virtue matter.

Lyle Smith
Biola University

Also See: Fantasy, Beatrix Potter, Reality

"Onward, Christian Spacemen"

Show. III (February 1963): 57, 117. Retitled "The Seeing Eye" and reprinted in *Christian Reflections.*

In this article Lewis noted that he was not surprised by the report that the Russians had not found **God** in outer space. The conclusion that some wanted to draw that God did not exist, however, in no way followed according to Lewis: "To look for Him as one item within the framework which He Himself invented is nonsensical." Indeed, how can God be reached—or avoided? Lewis considered himself qualified to deal with the avoidance of God, but in the reaching for God, he thought himself "a less reliable guide," because he never looked for God—God sought him. At the time, Lewis was trying to obey his conscience, which he believed may turn out to be the closest contact one has with the mystery of life. "Space-travel

has really nothing to do with the matter. To some, God is discoverable everywhere; to others, nowhere." The real problems about **space travel** are, in increasing order of importance, the loss of the immemorial Moon, the Moon of myths and poets and lovers; the fact that we are not yet fit to visit other worlds—do we have to infect new realms?; and that people seem delighted, and others troubled, about finding innumerable rational species scattered about the universe—but even if this were so, it would not affect Christian **theology** at all.

John Bremer

Also See: Atheism, Revelation

"Open Letter to Dr. Tillyard"

See entry on *Personal Heresy: A Controversy*

Open Letter (Letter)

The Christian News-Letter. 119 (4 February 1942): 4.

Description of a course of study similar to the **Oxford** Honours School of English, which was being made available to British prisoners of **war** as a result of the efforts of C. S. Lewis and others: books were supplied to the prison camps with the assistance of the Red Cross, German authorities allowed the forwarding of exams, and Oxford faculty volunteered to be unpaid examiners for this nondegree work.

Marjorie L. Mead
The Marion E. Wade Center

George Orwell (1903–1950)

George Orwell was the pen name of Eric Blair, a British novelist, critic, essayist, and journalist whose writing protested the inequalities and injustices imposed by class differences and political ideologies. Born in India but educated in England at Crossgates, a preparatory school, Orwell had a difficult childhood complicated by comparative poverty, a prolonged experience credited with forming his bitterness toward the English class system.

After attending Eton, Orwell served in Burma as a policeman, during which time he gathered the observations that went into his novel *Burmese Days* (1934) and such celebrated essays as "Shooting an Elephant" and "A Hanging." Returning to Europe, and by now thoroughly disenchanted with the colonial system, Orwell deliberately lived for a time on the fringes of society, washing dishes in Paris and living with tramps in England. Out of these experiences came *Down and Out in Paris and London* (1933) and *The Road to Wigan Pier* (1937), careful observations of life at the bottom of the social ladder. Orwell's undoctrinaire socialism was founded on personal experience and observation and on a fierce dedication to common decency in human relationships. These traits are prominent in *Homage to Catalonia,* an autobiographical account of the Spanish Civil War as he saw it from the perspective of a volunteer fighting with the United Marxist Workers party. He returned to England in 1937 badly wounded and disillusioned with the behavior of the international Communists who had captured the workers' movement and forced it to serve their priorities.

After 1937, Orwell's central message was a warning against totalitarianisms whether of the left or the right. Rejecting **Christianity** as well as uncritical class and party loyalties, Orwell's vision for the future was a bleak and somber one, reflected in his most famous novels written near the end of his long struggle with tuberculosis, *Animal Farm* (1945) and *Nineteen Eighty-Four* (1949). Critics praise the former for the sympathetic warmth with which Orwell draws the oppressed farm animals, as well as the wit with which he parodies the history of the Russian Communist movement since the days of Lenin. The latter is widely recognized for its powerful portrayal of the inevitable destruction of human feeling even in the lives of middle-level apparatchiks of totalitarian systems. C. S. Lewis considered *Animal Farm* "a work of genius" but was puzzled by the popularity of *Nineteen Eighty-Four,* which he regarded as "merely a flawed, interesting book."

Lyle Smith
Biola University

Also See: Communism and Fascism, Utopia

Bibliography

Filmer, Kath. "That Hideous 1984: The Influence of C. S. Lewis' *That Hideous Strength* on Orwell's *Nineteen Eighty-Four.*" *Extrapolation.* 26 no. 2 (Summer 1985): 160–69.

"George Orwell." *Studies in Twentieth Century Literature,* Vol. 2: 497–514.

Legg, L. G. Wickham, and E. T. William, eds. "Eric Blair." *The Dictionary of National Biography, 1941–1950.* Oxford: Oxford University Press, 1959: 83–84.

Lewis, C. S. "George Orwell"

Othello (Letter)

The Times Literary Supplement (19 June 1948): 345.

Lewis offered several classical references to help illuminate the meaning of the line "her motion blushed at herself" from **Shakespeare's** *Othello,* I, iii, 95.

Marjorie L. Mead
The Marion E. Wade Center

The Other World, According to Descriptions in Medieval Literature (Book Review)

Medium Aevum. XX (1951): 93–94.

This book is concerned with other worlds in literature. According to Lewis, the author explores the relationship of the other world and folklore, and searches for recurrent barriers between this world and the other. Each barrier is physical as much as metaphoric; perhaps a sea, a river, a cave, and—although this is not mentioned—a wardrobe.

Anne Gardner

Bibliography

Patch, Howard Rollin. *The Other World, According to Descriptions in Medieval Literature.*

"Our English Syllabus"

First published in *Rehabilitations.*

This essay, published first in Lewis's 1939 volume, *Rehabilitations,* arises from the provocation announced in its preface: "A man is seldom moved to praise what he loves until it has been attacked." In this address to a group of **Oxford** undergraduates, Lewis defended the role of **education** in advancing civilization, the process that produces the "goodman." By this, Lewis meant the person of character and right sentiments, "the interesting and interested man," who is steeped "in the literature both sacred and profane on which the **culture** of the community is based."

Such education, Lewis observed, is threatened by a new paradigm of vocational training that takes "civilization" for granted and thereby endangers the possibility of its continuation. A generation that values learning only as a means to acquiring a trade reduces education to mere training. In an increasingly egalitarian society, education's chief value, Lewis said, is that it "actualizes the potential for leisure." According to Lewis, what separates us from the animal world is this fact: humans possess the capacity to distinguish what we do from who we are. Animals, by contrast, are always "professionals," and can make no distinction between being and doing.

Readers of Lewis's ***The Abolition of Man*** and ***That Hideous Strength*** will note here Lewis's early critique of modern education as dangerously reductionist, at its best offering narrow vocational specialization, at its worst, a "conditioning" of students to dehumanizing propaganda.

Bruce L. Edwards
Bowling Green State University

Bibliography

Como, James T. (ed). *C. S. Lewis at the Breakfast Table*. New York: Macmillan, 1992.

Myers, Doris T. *C. S. Lewis in Context*. Kent, OH: Kent State University Press, 1994.

Out of the Silent Planet

London: Bodley Head, 1938. First US edition, New York: Macmillan, 1943.

One of the questions that arises about Lewis's longer works of fiction is "What are they?' The category "novel" won't quite do, if we are thinking of the lineage from Fielding through **Jane Austen** to Henry James. But the category "space fiction" is, paradoxically, even more misleading even though in the present work and in *Perelandra* we find ourselves spirited off to Mars and Venus respectively. It is the word "space" that is the rub. At the very end of the tale we find Elwin Ransom, the hero, saying this to Lewis himself, who appears in a minor role in the narrative: "If we could even effect in one per cent of our readers a change—over from the conception of Space to the conception of **Heaven**, we should have made a beginning."

The "Heaven" in question here is not the City of God of Saint John's apocalypse. It is closer to what we call the universe. But it is not the clockwork, vacuous, and cold universe perceived by modern **imagination**, accustomed as it is to approaching the topic via radio telescopes, satellites, and other hardware. It is a blissful universe. It is a populated universe full of beings of ineffable beauty and dignity. It is a universe concerning which we find we must finally invoke the word "glory."

The conflict in this tale arises over these two points of view. Professor Edward Weston, an atheist physicist, has embarked on a program of conquest. Since he worships nothing but an inexorable Life Force he wants to invade and conquer planet after planet, annihilating their population and colonizing them with denizens of earth. He can do this because he believes that we are the most advanced species and hence have a axiomatic "right" to wipe out all lower forms of life. He and his henchman Devine are in the process of bundling a slow-witted farm boy into their spaceship, to be offered as a sacrifice to the ruler of Mars (or Malacandra), whom they suppose to have demanded such a sacrifice, when Dr. Elwin Ransom, a **Cambridge** don on his solitary walking hol-

iday, blunders into the scuffle. As a result Ransom finds himself a prisoner in the spaceship, having been substituted for the boy, and eighty-five thousand miles from earth.

Ransom manages to escape from his captors within a few minutes of landing on Malacandra. His journey through the landscape reveals to him a strange and beautiful terrain whose principal quality seems to be color. Pink, purple, rose, and soft gray tones predominate, and the blue of the water "was not merely blue in certain lights like terrestrial water, but 'really' blue."

This is a theme that is carried through in a number of ways, both in Malacandra, but infinitely more intensely in the next book in the series, *Perelandra*. There is an intensity, a clarity, a sharpness and substantiality—even a sort of inexorability—about everything in comparison with which the "reality" on our planet seems somewhat attenuated. This has also been Ransom's experience of "space" en route to Malacandra: "The light was paler than any light of comparable intensity that he had ever seen; it was not pure white but the palest of all imaginable golds.... The heat ... seemed to knead and stroke the skin like a gigantic masseur: it produced no tendency to drowsiness: rather, intense alacrity.... he felt vigilant, courageous and magnanimous...."

Readers of Lewis's other works, both fiction and nonfiction, will recognize a theme very close to the center of Lewis's entire vision; the precincts of goodness are marked by alacrity, keenness, readiness, and sheer, tingling vitality. Evil casts a soporific pall over everything, most especially man's mind and conscience. "Hell is murky," said Lady Macbeth, and her remark could be

U.K. First Edition, 1943

308

written as a superscript over virtually all of Lewis's work—with the corollary, of course, "Heaven is clarity such that it can only be hinted at in the phrase 'the weight of glory.'"

We find this theme controlling much of the narrative in Malacandra. Ransom, a good man, is initially prey to all the usual Wellsian notions that creatures from other worlds are hideous and hostile, but he finds that there may be a startling "otherness" that turns out to be wise, innocent, brave, and good. He meets the three articulate species of creatures on Malacandra: the hrossa, tall otter-like creatures with a lovely fur pelt whose great specialty is the making of song and poetry; the sorns (*seroni* is the correct plural), great pale gangling giants, spindly limbed but with large heads all out of proportion to these limbs, who turn out to be the philosophers; and the pfifltriggi, little busy creatures who wear spectacles and seem to fall somewhere between our badgers and piglets, and whose specialty is the working of gold and carving of stone inscriptions.

Ransom, because he is a good man, is not driven by any notion of lording it over the Malacandrians, much less destroying them. He is enthralled by the excellences that mark each species, and very quickly learns the hrossas' language, which is the *lingua franca* of this world. He is intrigued that no species claims sovereignty over the others but that all acknowledge fealty to Oyarsa, the tutelary intelligence (see Medieval **cosmology**) of Malacandra.

Weston, on the other hand, sullen and humorless because of the tyrannical egoism that holds him in thrall, assumes that these creatures are stupid, infantile, and to be eliminated. In the course of the action, he actually does shoot and kill three of the hrossa.

He and Devine are taken prisoner by the other hrossa and hauled before Oyarsa where they find Ransom; who has himself been summoned, although not, of course, for such a severe judgment as awaits Weston and Devine. Ransom, it seems, has been culpably slow to respond to Oyarsa's summons, although he himself would wish to plead that there had been only the faintest hints of any such summons. Readers will once again recognize a favorite Lewisian theme that appears repeatedly in the Narnia Chronicles in connection with Aslan. The will of God (of Oyarsa or of Aslan) may well present itself to us in the most unobtrusive of circumstances, but the ready servant will be alive to it. Most of us miss our cues repeatedly.

Ransom discovers, in the course of his encounter with Oyarsa, that our own planet is known as Thulcandra—the silent planet, because its Oyarsa (we would

call him Lucifer or Satan) opted out of the great cosmic Dance, in a vain attempt to seize the omnipotence of Maleldil, the ruler and maker of all worlds. Hence our deafness to the Music of the Spheres and our blindness to the glory that gilds and packs a universe but shows only a dead face to our lenses.

The scene in the court of Oyarsa is tragicomic. The good Ransom recognizes the immense solemnity of the occasion and the setting, thronged not only with the visible denizens of Malacandra but also with the scarcely visible angel-like beings, the eldila, and disposes himself fittingly. Weston, purblind to all splendor, insists on treating the assembly as a conclave of idiots or at best Cro-Magnon men, threatening them with his "puff-bang" (gun), chattering babytalk to them, dandling gewgaws in front of them for their delectation, and finally dancing in a grotesque travesty of the maladroit uncle vainly trying to divert an infant nephew or niece. It takes an embarrassingly long time for Oyarsa to flag him down and oblige him to attend.

Weston's diabolical agenda for universal conquest comes out in the testimony he gives, but we also learn of Oyarsa's ability to have annihilated him long since. The only judgment meted out to him and Devine is to be sent back to earth. Ransom, of course, accompanies them and bursts into grateful tears upon landing in an English field with rain, grass, cows, a gate, a lane, and, presently, an English pub where he orders a pint of bitter in the last line of the book.

This touch is archetypically Lewisian. There may be celestial splendors about which a good man's heart will descry and in which he will rejoice. But sheer village ordinariness is overwhelmingly the milieu in which we mortals will find our duty and our joy for as long as our mortal life lasts.

Thomas Howard

Also See: Destiny, Light and Darkness, Science Fiction, Technology, H. G. Wells

Bibliography

Lutton, Jeanette Hume. "The Feast of Reason: *Out of the Silent Planet* as the Book of Hnau." *Mythlore.* 13 (Autumn 1986): 32–41, 50.

Musacchio, George. "Elwin Ransom: The Pilgrimage Begins." *Mythlore.* 13 (Summer 1987): 15–17.

The Oxford Book of Christian Verse (Book Review)

The Review of English Studies. XVII (January 1941): 95–102.

This review tackled some of the issues raised (perhaps unwittingly) by the author in his preface. The first is the rarity of good Christian **poetry**, which Lewis dismissed as a question of statistics. The second issue is the tendency of Christian poets to insincerity or borrowed attitudes. This Lewis refuted with examples from the anthology and beyond, and a discussion of the process of overcoming the difficulties of treating such a "high" subject in verse.

Anne Gardner

Also See: Lord David Cecil

Bibliography

Cecil, Lord David (ed). *The Oxford Book of Christian Verse.*

Oxford University

Oxford in the late 1930s was very different from North American universities. It was essentially a collection of separate colleges with no university campus. There were twenty-nine colleges, none of them coeducational. One, All Souls, consisted almost entirely of fellows. Of the others, twenty-three were for men and five for women. No college had more than about four hundred students, and none was restricted to students in any particular field.

Socially, the most prestigious college was Christ Church (known as "The House"). The intellectual leader was Balliol. Among the women's colleges, the most eminent was Somerville. Significantly, **Dorothy L. Sayers** (who went to Somerville herself) sent the intellectual Lord Peter Wimsey to Balliol, but his dissolute playboy nephew to The House.

Students spent their first two years in residence in college. In their third year, they were required to move into lodgings in the town. No undergraduate was allowed to enter a pub at any time, and they had to be in college or their lodgings by midnight. "Proctors" selected dons who prowled the streets to catch violators of these rules. Evading the proctors, visiting the pubs, and climbing into college after midnight were activities that added spice to students' lives.

Apart from special occasions like lectures and club meetings, men were allowed in the women's colleges and women in the men's, only between 2:00 and 6:00 P.M. Men outnumbered women five to one, so an active social life was much easier for the latter. In fact, an attractive woman student needed to be strong-minded to get any work done at all.

Once past a tiresome preliminary examination, a student worked entirely in his or her specialized field. There was no "course" work, and only medical students were required to attend lectures. In most fields, a stu-

dent's basic responsibility was to visit his assigned **tutor** once a week and read him the essay the tutor had assigned. The tutor would then criticize it and assign the essay for the following week.

Apart from the reading required for the essays, students read assiduously in their fields using the superb University library (the **Bodleian**), the student's college library, and (if the student was a member) the library of the Oxford Union. But the three University terms only totaled twenty-four weeks, and during term time there were many more interesting things to do than read. The time for laborious study was during vacations.

At the end of the last summer term came the University examinations known as the "Schools." On the student's performance in "Schools" depended the degree. About eight percent got Firsts; most of the rest, Seconds. To get a Third was a stigma you never lived down (see *That Hideous Strength*). But below the Third came the Fourth, and the "Pass" degree; and of course one could flunk outright.

Distractions from work included the Union, an expensive private club famous for its debates (and like the Dramatic Society, all-male in membership). There were clubs for every political opinion and for every conceivable field of interest, including Arctic exploration. Sports were entirely amateur (there were no athletic scholarships), and no one paid to watch them. For Eights Week, in the summer, all the men's colleges (except All Souls) fielded several "Eights," which rowed in a series of heats all afternoon. Spectators, fortified by strawberries and ice cream, watched from the lavishly painted college "barges" on the riverbank.

Except for those grim final examinations, it was a most enjoyable life.

Charles Wrong
University of South Florida (retired)

Also See: Eagle and Child, Inklings, Magdalen College, Oxford Socratic Club

Bibliography

Fryer, W. R. "Power in Oxford." *Canadian C. S. Lewis Journal.* (Winter 1982): 7–9.

Houston, James. "Reminiscences of the Oxford Lewis." *Lamp-Post.* 7 no. 2 (August 1983): 6–12.

Schofield, Stephen. "Oxford Loses A Genius." *Canadian C. S. Lewis Journal.* (July-August 1981): 1–11.

_____. "When C. S. Lewis' *Pilgrim's Regress* Appeared in 1932 The British People Had No Daily Newspaper." *Canadian C. S. Lewis Journal.* (Winter 1982): 10–11.

Oxford University Socratic Club

The Socratic Club was founded near the end of 1941 by **Stella Aldwinckle**, a member of the **Oxford** pastorate. As the result of an encounter with a freshman student of Sommerville College, Aldwinckle perceived the need for an open forum for the discussion of the intellectual difficulties connected with religion in general and **Christianity** in particular. C. S. Lewis was appointed the Club's first president, a position he held until 1954. Basil Mitchell, Professor of Christian Religion, Oxford, assumed the presidency when in 1955 Lewis moved to **Magdalene College, Cambridge**. Mitchell remained the Club's president until it came to an end in 1972. Meetings were held every Monday evening during each of the three academic terms. The typical format consisted of two speakers, one who would read a paper and the other who would bring a reply. Following this exchange, the meeting was opened for questions and discussion from the floor.

The Club's name reflected the Socratic maxim "follow the argument wherever it led" and was to be applied to the *pros* and *cons* of the Christian religion. Miss Aldwinckle and Lewis envisioned the Socratic meeting as an arena where Christian and non-Christian could dispute the intellectual claims of Christianity, where the various intellectual prejudices arrayed against Christianity could be properly challenged, and where the integrity of the Christian's belief system could be demonstrated. Accordingly, non-Christian speakers who were specialists in their fields of study were invited to come and "propagate their creed." During the years Lewis presided as president, the Socratic hosted some of the most influential atheists of the day and entertained the weighty arguments they brought against the Christian faith. As the Socratic's point man, Lewis was relied upon to represent the Christian position and to argue its case against the opposition; his one aim was to create and maintain an atmosphere in which faith could flourish.

Christopher W. Mitchell
The Marion E. Wade Center

Bibliography

Aldwinckle, Stella. "Oral History Interview," the Marion E. Wade Center, Wheaton College, Wheaton, Illinois.
_____. *Socratic Digest*. 1 (June 1943).
Hooper, Walter. "Oxford's Bonny Fighter." *C. S. Lewis at the Breakfast Table*. James T. Como (ed). (New York: Macmillan, 1979).
Mitchell, Basil. "Reflections on C. S. Lewis, Apologetics, and the Moral Tradition: Basil Mitchell in Conversation with Andrew Walker." *A Christian For All Christians*. Andrew Walker and James Patrick (ed). London: Hodder & Stoughton, 1990.
Mitchell, Christopher W. "University Battles: C. S. Lewis and the Oxford University Socratic Club." *C. S. Lewis: Light-Bearer in the Shadowlands*. Angus J. L. Menuge (ed). Wheaton, IL: Crossway, 1997.

P

Paganism

In **"Is Theism Important?"** Lewis said he was tempted to reply "Would that she were," to those who fear society is relapsing into paganism. Taking a minority view among modern Christians, he viewed paganism not as an evil child of **Satan** but rather as a ragged and wild but essentially good uncle of **Christianity**. An earlier article **"Religion Without Dogma"** noted that the ragged and wild part involves many "obscenities and cruelties"; still, a pagan is at least "something to work on"—he is "imminently convertible" to Christianity.

Lewis always enjoyed turning secular suppositions on their head, and he was especially deft with the notion that Christianity is merely an outgrowth of primitive religion, a more advanced distillation of ancient corn god **myths** and the like. On the contrary, said Lewis in *Mere Christianity*, pagan corn gods, rebirth stories—all these were like heralds blowing trumpets before a king, all foreshadowed the actual historical event of **Christ**'s life, death, and resurrection. Paganism played a large part in Lewis's own journey to **faith**. His first stirrings of "**Joy**" (the feeling he later identified as a longing for God) were Norse myths, and he loved the majestic paganism of Wagner's *Ring* cycle. His conversion was a sort of mini-religious evolution from ancient gods, to modern agnostic evocations of Greek **rationalism**, to the deism of the Hebrews, to a final understanding of the historical Christ as God.

But conversion notwithstanding, Lewis's work reflected his lifelong interest in pagan myths, and his novels are a riot of pagan images. *Pilgrim's Regress* begins with a vision of beautiful "brown girls"—a sort of Polynesian fertility/lust image that leads at last to solid old Mother Kirk, an **allegory** of the Christian **Church**. While his space **cosmology** in *Out of the Silent Planet* contains nothing to offend Christians (for the Old One, Maleldil the Young, and the Eldila conform to God, Christ, and **angels** in Christian **theology**), Lewis delighted in incorporating as many mythical elements as he could into a Christian overview. In *Perelandra*, Ransom actually meets Venus and Mars in all their glory, and their glory is a part of Christian **truth**. In *That Hideous Strength* Venus and Mars appear on earth exuding the essence of **love** and **war**, and they are joined by Merlin and other ancient Celtic mythical figures in a Christian battle against Satan's agents.

Another vivid Christian **metaphor** among pagan images is Aslan in *The Lion, the Witch and the Wardrobe*, where he suffers the Narnian version of Christ's death and resurrection. Like Maleldil, Aslan is surrounded by an army of Greek, Celtic, ancient European pagan images come to life, and they all recognize the sovereignty of Aslan the Christlike figure. *Till We Have Faces*, Lewis's last novel, seems to condemn paganism at first, as protagonist Orual indicts the gods for their capriciousness. But again Lewis turned the notion of selfish pagan gods around, for the resolution of the story is that humans' self-delusion and dim apprehensions of God are the real problem.

The "gods" are certainly mysterious in *Faces*, but their actions suggest another favorite theme of Lewis's: that God brings humanity to understanding much as a parent brings along a child, from simple safety restrictions for toddlers to more sophisticated lessons as the youth grows older. By sublimating pagan ideas to Christianity, Lewis is able to mesh seemingly incompatible, mutually exclusive elements into a coherent Christian witness. Paganism, as Lewis saw it, was spiritual kindergarten: mankind was not meant to toddle there long, but its basic lessons were necessary to prepare for a higher spiritual matriculation.

Richard A. Hill
Taylor University

Also See: Demons, Good and Evil, Imagery, Spirituality

Bibliography

Chervin, Ronda. "Paganism and Christianity: A Commentary on C. S. Lewis' Novel *Till We Have Faces*." *Faith & Reason*. 14 (Fall 1988): 243–53.

Derrik, Christopher. *C. S. Lewis and the Church of Rome: A Study in Proto Ecumenism*. Harrison, NY: Ignatius Press, 1982.

Fisher, Robert. "Lewis's Acceptance of Paganism," *CSL: The Bulletin of the New York C. S. Lewis Society* 15 (1984).

Lewis, C. S. "Is Theism Important?"; *The Lion, the Witch and the Wardrobe; Mere Christianity; Out of the Silent Planet; Pilgrim's Regress; Perelandra;* "Religion Without Dogma"; *That Hideous Strength; Till We Have Faces*

Maclay, Peter W. "Myth as the Way We Taste Reality: An Analysis of C. S. Lewis's Theory." *Lamp-Post of the Southern California C. S. Lewis Society.* 6 no. 3 (July 1982): 1–2.

Walsh, Chad. *C. S. Lewis: Apostle to the Skeptics*. New York: Macmillan, 1949.

"A Pageant Played in Vain"

See entry on "Break, Sun, my Crusted Earth"

Pain

Once pain passes beyond a certain threshold, it is, said Lewis in *The Problem of Pain*, "unmistakable evil"; it is "impossible to ignore" and absolutely "insists upon being attended to." In that respect, Lewis contended, pain is quite different from "error and sin," because the latter two "both have this property, that the deeper they are the less their victim suspects their existence." So even when our attitudes are utterly selfish and vicious, we may yet remain blissfully unaware that something is terribly wrong. But whenever we experience intense pain, whether it be in the form of a bodily sensation or mental anguish, we know that something is indeed terribly wrong.

Now for the very reason that severe pain is so undesirable in itself, it can also be an instrumental good, serving a useful purpose. As an illustration, Lewis cited "the universal human feeling that bad men [vicious rapists and murderers, for example] ought to suffer." The justification for such a feeling is not, as some retributivists might like to believe, that a bad person's suffering somehow cancels out, or makes up for, the wrong done, thus balancing the scales of justice; the justification is that nothing else is likely, or as likely, to get the bad person's attention, which is the indispensable first step, however tiny, in the direction of **redemption**. We feel as if those who victimize others must learn a hard lesson; that if they are required to become "victims" of suffering themselves, then perhaps they will eventually learn to see things from a victim's perspective. Or, as Lewis also pointed out, "A bad man, happy, is a man without the least inkling that his actions . . . are not in accord with the laws of the universe"; we therefore think it appropriate that such a person's happiness be removed.

But even for those of us who are not rapists, murderers, and the like, pain is, according to Lewis, **God**'s "megaphone to rouse a deaf world," a means by which he shatters our illusion of self-sufficiency and prevents us from being satisfied with our moral imperfections. It is also one of the essential means by which God perfects "fortitude, patience, pity and forgiveness" in his children. And beyond all of that, one person's suffering, particularly if the person is relatively innocent or helpless, can have a dramatic impact upon the character of others, arousing compassion and encouraging acts of **mercy**. Not even the arrogant and the proud can typically remain unmoved when a loved one suffers.

Are such observations as the above "callously inappropriate," as one of Lewis's critics, John Beversluis, has charged? Not at all. It is no more inappropriate to clarify ways in which pain can be an instrumental good than it is to clarify ways in which something good in itself, such as **love**, can be an instrumental evil. Nor is there any question here of Lewis adopting a callous attitude towards some truly horrible evil, such as a child's suffering and dying from a terrible disease. There is nothing callous, after all, in the hope that a child who suffers and dies has not suffered and died in vain, or in the **hope** that the child's own suffering will somehow (and someday) contribute to the fulfillment of a loving purpose in the life of the child. And two considerations, implicit in Lewis's discussion, are perhaps relevant to such a hope.

The first concerns the happiness (or blessedness) that God wants his children to achieve. The astronomer Fred Hoyle once commented that he would not want immortality because after a few centuries he would eventually weary of his infirmities and lose interest in life itself. And Lewis would, I believe, agree with Hoyle to this extent: in our present condition, we are not yet fit for eternity. Even honest, hardworking people will find eventually that "their modest prosperity and the happiness of their children are not enough to make them blessed" or even to prevent them from becoming "wretched" in time. For true blessedness, the kind that will endure forever, costs something; it requires that we be purged of all the selfishness and arrogance and lust for power that separates us from others, that we learn to love others even as we love ourselves, and that we be brought into a community in which others love us even as we love them. In short, true blessedness requires that, as preparation for union with God, we learn the lessons of love, and this in turn requires that we live, at least for a time, in an environment in which genuine, albeit temporary, tragedy is also possible.

The second relevant consideration concerns Lewis' claim that "martyrdom always remains the supreme enacting and perfection of **Christianity**." To understand why Christianity places such a high value upon martyrdom and upon suffering for the sake of others, we must appreciate a dilemma that God himself faces in his effort to secure blessedness for his children. For even as love is a condition of true blessedness, so also can it be an instrumental evil, making one vulnerable not only to rejection but to a host of other miseries as well. If I truly love my daughter, for example, and love her even as I love myself, then I simply cannot be happy knowing that she is suffering or otherwise miserable—unless, of course, I can somehow believe that, in the end, all will be well for her. Indeed, the more one is filled with love for others, the more the unhappiness of others will inevitably jeopardize one's own happiness. Despite his omnipotence, therefore, God faces the following dilemma: In any environment in which he might create free, independent persons, the very condition essential to their ultimate blessedness, namely love, will inevitably open up additional possibilities for pain and suffering.

As an illustration, consider serial killer Ted Bundy's mother, who declared so appropriately and yet with such obvious agony her continuing love for a son who had become a monster. Had this poor woman loved her son less, she presumably would have suffered less, but a callous heart of the required kind would be neither fit for eternity nor a place where true joy could reside. So how is God to bring blessedness to such a woman, who would gladly have endured a lifetime of suffering herself in exchange for her son's eventual redemption? How is God to satisfy this dear woman's deepest yearnings if her own suffering should be his only available means for bringing reconciliation into the life of her son? And suppose, for a moment, that God confronts a countless number of similar dilemmas as he prepares his children for eternity. If so, then the following seems altogether plausible: Not even God could prepare *all* of his children for an eternity of blessedness and, at the same time, eliminate all instances of temporary suffering on the part of the weak, the innocent, and the morally upright; not even God could have improved the world as a whole by eliminating, for example, the sufferings of Christ. But God can, according to the Christian faith, bring good out of our sufferings; he can use our sufferings as a means (in the next life, if not in this one) of perfecting us and redeeming others; and he can therefore guarantee that no one—not Ted Bundy's mother, not a child dying of cancer, and certainly not **Christ** himself—suffers in vain.

The Christian religion, then, is a religion of consolation and hope, both of which rest upon the believer's confidence in the loving nature of God: the confidence that, however bewildering our present sufferings, God would not have created us in the first place unless he had the power to fulfill his loving purpose for us in the end.

Thomas Talbott
Willamette University

Bibliography

Beversluis, John. *C. S. Lewis and the Search for Rational Religion.* Grand Rapids, MI: Eerdmans, 1985: chapter 7.

Kilby, Clyde S. *The Christian World of C. S. Lewis.* Grand Rapids, MI: Eerdmans, 1964: chapter 3.

Lewis, C. S. *The Problem of Pain*

Meilaender, Gilbert. *The Taste for the Other.* Grand Rapids, MI: Eerdmans, 1978: chapter 3.

Purtill, Richard. *C. S. Lewis' Case for the Christian Faith.* New York: Harper and Row, 1981: chapter 3.

Talbott, Thomas. "C. S. Lewis and the Problem of Evil," *Christian Scholar's Review*, XVII no. 1 (1987): 36–51.

"The Pains of Animals: A Problem in Theology"

The Month. CLXXXIX (February 1950): 95–104. Reprinted in *God in the Dock, Undeceptions,* and *Timeless at Heart.*

The beginning of the articles is devoted to an inquiry by C. E. M. Joad in response to Lewis's book **The Problem of Pain**. In that book, Lewis considered "how to account for the occurrence of **pain** in a universe which is the creation of an all-good **God**, and in creatures who are not morally sinful."

Lewis asked Dr. Joad to reconsider some of his arguments based on the fact that the problem of pain in animals is explored rather than explained. Lewis directed the reader to chapter 9 of his book, which he said is composed of two parts. The first (composed of the first paragraph) states that "[t]he data which God has given us enable us in some degree to understand human pain. We lack such data about beasts." The second part (composed of the remainder of the chapter) is Lewis's guesses about the apparent divine cruelty (an appearance that must be false). Among these guesses is the suggestion that animals possess sentience but not consciousness. The fact that animals behave "as if from memory" does not prove memory in the conscious sense. Lewis theorized that tame animals may be resurrected, although wild and ill-treated animals would not be, which he used "as an illustration ... of the general principles to be observed in framing a theory of animal resurrection." In response to Dr. Joad's idea of Lewis suggesting the temptation of monkeys, Lewis said that

"[m]oral corruption is not the only kind of corruption." **Corruption of nature** and impairment, distortion, is the work of **Satan**. Monkeys were not and are not tempted (which implies will), but they may become distorted. Of the caterpillar who is consumed alive, Lewis pointed out that invertebrates can eat serenely while "their interiors are being devoured by the larvae of some ichneumon fly." For all the apparent anomalies, Lewis offered two possibilities. Either there is a Great God and a "god of this world" or else "the operations of the Great God are not what they seem to me to be."

Anne Gardner

Also See: Creation, Evolution

"A Panegyric for Dorothy L. Sayers"

Originally delivered at a memorial service as "The Panegyric, written by Professor C. S. Lewis." Retitled and reprinted in *Of This and Other Worlds* and *On Stories.* Also reprinted in part in *Twentieth Century Literary Criticism*, Vol. 15, 1985.

Dorothy L. Sayers died suddenly on December 17, 1957, but it was not until January 15, 1958, that a memorial service was held at St. Margaret, Westminster. It was attended by family and friends, clergy (including the "Red" Dean of Canterbury and six bishops), as well as people from the academic, publishing, and broadcasting worlds. BBC producer Val Gielgud and Judge Gordon Clark (who wrote mysteries as Cyril Hare), read the lessons, while C. S. Lewis was asked to give the panegyric, or eulogy. In addition to being old literary friends, both Lewis and Sayers were world-renowned as spokesmen for the Church of England.

Characteristically, Lewis wrote a loving but honest portrait of a remarkable woman. In describing Sayers as a writer whose work included enormous variety, he noted that in everything she wrote, she was always the craftsman who took pride in her trade. He confessed that he never read her mysteries but reread her *The Man Born to be King* every Lent, praised her **Dante** translations, then closed by thanking the "Author who invented her" for her loyalty, courage, and honesty, and for those feminine qualities that showed through her "gleefully ogreish" manner.

Since Lewis could not be present, Bishop George Bell of Chichester, who had started the Canterbury Festival for which Sayers had written two plays, read Lewis's words for him.

Alzina Stone Dale

Also See: Anglicanism

"Pan's Purge"

Punch. 212 (January 15, 1947): 71 (under the pseudonym Nat Whilk). Reprinted in *Poems* and *Collected Poems.*

Related to "Under Sentence," this poem is an apocalyptic vision of the revolt of **nature** against mankind. As man is about to destroy nature completely, the animals, inspired by the god Pan, surge back against man and obliterate all but a remnant. These newly instructed men are permitted a place on the liberated earth. The work recalls the end of ***That Hideous Strength*** when Mr. Bultitude and his companions overwhelm N.I.C.E.

Don W. King
Montreat College

"'Paradise Lost' in Our Time: Some Comments" (Book Review)

The Oxford Magazine. LXV (13 February 1947): 215–17.

This book is a collection of lectures in which Bush tackles some of the controversy that divides critical opinions of **Milton.** He summarizes and contributes to it in his first chapter. The second chapter is devoted to a discussion of religious and ethical principles. The third and fourth chapters are primarily literary criticism. Lewis hoped Bush would deal more fully with some of the issues raised in the book at some point in the future.

Anne Gardner

Bibliography

Bush, Douglas. '*Paradise Lost' in Our Time: Some Comments.*

"The Parthenon and the Optative"

See entry on "Notes on the Way" (11 March 1944)

"*Passion and Society* and *The Bride of Christ*" (Book Review)

Theology. XL (June 1940): 459–61.

These two works focused on themes that were of great interest to Lewis. De Rougement's book traces the historical thesis that Courtly Love is not an expression of sexual passion but an expression of and symbol for a wish for death. More importantly, it traces the moral thesis that the Christian conception of **marriage** and the modern idea that marriage must have "falling in **love**" and "**happiness**" as its causes are incompatible. The second book briefly traces the "Nuptial Idea" in **theology.**

Anne Gardner

Also See: Medieval World

Bibliography

Chavasse, Claude. *The Bride of Christ.*
de Rougemont, D. *Passion and Society.* M. Belgion (trans).

"Pattern"

See entry on "Experiment"

Fredrick William Calcutt "Fred" Paxford (1898–1979)

Fred Paxford was the gardener and handyman at the **Oxford** home of C. S. Lewis known as **the Kilns.** He was hired by Lewis in 1930 and remained there living in a small bungalow until Lewis's death in 1963. Paxford was responsible for many of the improvements to the grounds and house that took place. He and Mrs. **Janie Moore** worked extensively to improve the house and land.

Fred became an important figure after the death of Lewis because of a story told by **Walter Hooper** of a three-day bonfire of Lewis's papers ordered by Lewis's brother, **Warren Lewis.** According to Hooper, Paxford asked Warren if he could save some of the notebooks from the fire for Hooper. Paxford denied that there was a three-day bonfire and that he had set aside any documents for Hooper.

Jeffrey D. Schultz

Bibliography

Hooper, Walter. "Introduction." *The Dark Tower.* New York: Harcourt Brace Jovanovich, 1977.
Lindskoog, Kathryn. *Light in the Shadowlands.* Sisters, OR: Multnomah, 1994: 37–52.
Paxford, Fred. "He Should Have Been a Parson: Observations of his Gardener." *The Canadian C. S. Lewis Journal.* 55 (Summer 1986): 7–13.

"Peace Proposals to Brother Every and Mr. Bethell"

Theology. XLI (December 1940): 339–48. Reprinted as Part III of "Christianity and Culture" in *Christian Reflections.*

This December article was Lewis's third contribution to the 1940 *Theology* debate that began with his article on **"Christianity and Culture."** Lewis believed there was "little real disagreement" between himself and George Every or S. L. Bethell. What differences that existed centered on the role of Christian critics in explaining the underlying values of modern literature to fellow believers.

Lewis had no problem with literary critics passing judgment on the spiritual value of a book. But he wondered if Mr. Bethell was clear about the distinction between what critics were saying about literature (where they were experts) and what they were saying about spiritual matters (where they were not). Lewis feared that critics would confuse matters of taste with moral sins and felt that the two must be kept distinct.

Lewis also felt that critics might miss the real moral impact of a book for good or ill. He pointed out that adults often do this, forgetting that children typically pass over the "bad elements in Peter Pan" to enjoy the story. Lewis closed with a plea not to attach spiritual value to matters of taste.

Mike Perry

Also See: Aesthetics, Culture, Film Drama and Music, Literary Criticism

Bibliography
Lewis, C. S. "High and Low Brows"

Sister Penelope (1890–1977)

Born Ruth Penelope Lawson, Sister Penelope first began correspondence with Lewis in August 1939 when she wrote to him praising *Out of the Silent Planet*. They began a long correspondence that lasted the rest of Lewis's life. In October of 1942, Lewis asked Sister Penelope to keep secure the manuscript of *The Screwtape Letters* until the work was published. She tried to return the manuscript, but Lewis did not want it back. The manuscript was sold in order to pay for repairs to St. Michael's chapel. It is now part of the Berg Collection at the New York Public Library. Lewis also dedicated *Perelandra* to the nuns of the Community of St. Mary the Virgin of which Sister Penelope was a member. Additionally, he wrote an introduction to her translation of **Saint Athanasius's** *The Incarnation of the Word of God.*

Jeffrey D. Schultz

Perelandra

London: Bodly Head, 1943. First US edition, New York: Macmillan, 1944. A paperback version was published under the title *Voyage to Venus*. London: Pan Books, 1953.

The second of Lewis's interplanetary novels, *Perelandra* tells what happens when philologist Elwin Ransom is summoned away by divine command to the planet known to us as Venus. As matters unfold, Ransom gradually realizes to his intense discomfiture that he is to be the savior of Perelandra—or at least, he is the mortal figure chosen by Maleldil (God) to interpose himself between the innocence of this freshly created world and the

evil plotted against it by the megalomaniacal Dr. Edward Weston, the scientist who previously in *Out of the Silent Planet* shanghaied Ransom off to Malacandra (Mars) in the course of Weston's scheme to conquer the solar system, obliterate or debauch the denizens of each planet, and turn them into thralls serving his suppositious omnipotence.

In the present novel, Ransom is transported through space in a coffin-like vessel made of some undefined matter resembling alabaster or ice. During the journey and, *a fortiori,* upon landing on Perelandra, Ransom has the experience (common to many of Lewis's characters in Narnia and in his adult fiction) of "seeing life." It is a key theme in Lewis's **theology** and fiction. While it is fancy heaven or eternity as a "spiritual" realm—the word "spiritual" here suggesting something attenuated, diffused, and even etiolated, as opposed to the "real" solidity and concreteness that characterizes our own planet—it is quite the other way around for Lewis. It is *our* unhappy planet that is the **Shadowland**: raspberries and heavy cream, emeralds, sexual intercourse— according to Lewis these are the attenuated, etiolated hints and harbingers of the real solidity and concreteness that we will stumble onto at the Resurrection.

In this connection, Ransom, in trying to evoke his experience for his friends (including Lewis), bursts out, "Oh, don't you see . . . that there's a difference between a trans-sensuous life and a non-sensuous life?" The heavenly raspberries will outstrip utterly our poor specimens when it comes to redness, sweetness, juiciness,

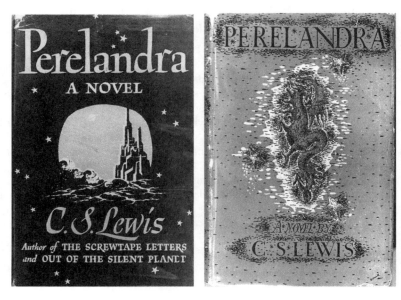

and texture. When Lewis later makes a bumbling effort to assist Ransom by volunteering that what Ransom is groping for is too vague for words, Ransom remarks, "On the contrary, it is words that are vague. The reason why the thing can't be expressed is that it's too *definite* for language."

Upon his arrival in Perelandra, Ransom discovers it to be a "fluid" world. He finds himself treading water in a warm, undulating sea, with lush green islands floating on the water. In its sumptuous fruitfulness, moistness, and warm embrace, it strongly suggests all that we imply in the word "feminine," although this is implicit rather than explicit at first. Ransom stretches language to its utmost in his effort to hint at the sheer weight of glory that suffuses this world: a "prodigious white light," a "prodigality of sweetness," and "a new kind of hunger and thirst." Presently he spies a human figure on a nearby floating island and makes contact. She is a (or *the*) Green Lady, and is to this world what Eve was to ours. She is The Mother. The great drama that gradually dawns on Ransom is that this is an as-yet *unfallen* world, and that Maleldil has summoned him to fight off—even, perhaps, to the point of shedding his blood—the assault of the Dark Archon (**Satan**) who rules the silent planet, Thulcandra (earth), who has sent his agent Weston to tempt and debauch the Lady. (We discover at the end of the narrative that her husband, Tor, the King, is off in another part of the planet, learning whatever it is that one must learn in order to be king: it is not part of this drama *yet*, and so we never learn anything about Tor's schooling.) For the Lady, the schooling entails her learning to trust Maleldil utterly and to rest in nothing but his will.

The concrete form that this lesson takes is the rule that she may step ashore on the stable island, but may never spend the night there. She must learn to rest on the undulating (read "uncertain") lands, trusting the only finally trustworthy thing there is in any world, namely the Will of Maleldil. (One thinks of **Dante**'s souls in Paradise: "In His Will is our peace.")

All too soon, Weston lands in his spaceship, and the battle is joined. He approaches the Lady by appealing to what he supposes to be feminine vanity. He gives her a mirror that introduces self-consciousness, and he murders some yellow-feathered birds in order to make a grand cloak for her, again hoping to awaken vanity in her. But his most maddening tactic is to tempt her by telling her what is technically true: that she walks spiritually holding Maleldil's hand like a little child. Weston tells her that Maleldil wants her to learn to walk by her-

self. This, of course, would be like one's growth toward a strong and mature faith in our world, but Weston's point is Satan's point: declare your independence of this God and make your own choices. All the great heroines of Thulcandra's history have done so, and therein lies their greatness.

It is Ransom's bone-wearying task to argue Weston down. In the course of their verbal battle, Weston rises to Luciferean blasphemy and is struck by a bolt of divine wrath, reduced to an appalling creature, only residually human, whom Ransom can only call the "Un-man." It is Lewis's picture of a damned soul, the ghastly detritus that is left when evil has leached away all the good solidity that is a man.

Gradually it becomes clear to Ransom that the battle is going to move beyond words; he must fight the Un-man physically. It seems nonsense, until he remembers that this is what the fight with evil comes to in our own world with whips, a crown of thorns, and nails.

The "Passion" of Ransom is drawn out to agonizing lengths, but eventually the Un-man is swallowed in to the fiery abyss. Then begins Ransom's "sabbath," in which, after long journeyings through vast caverns back to the surface (his struggle with the Un-man has entailed his "descent into hell"), he emerges into a paradisal landscape. He then witnesses the immensely solemn and blissful ceremony in which Perelandra hands over to Tor and Tinidril (the Green Lady, Tor's wife and queen) the suzerainty of the planet, which is rightfully theirs since "time turned a corner" when Maleldil became human flesh centuries ago on Thulcandra. Thenceforward human intelligences (Malacandra and Perelandra, who, in a mighty epiphany are revealed as pure masculinity and pure femininity) have only been regents of the various planets until the time comes for humanity to step into its inheritance.

Thomas Howard

Also See: Corruption of Nature, Eve, The Fall

Bibliography

Gibson, Evan K. "The Centrality of *Perelandra* in Lewis's Theology." *Chesterton and C. S. Lewis: The Riddle of Joy.* Michael Macdonald and Andrew Tadia (eds). Grand Rapids, MI: Eerdmans, 1989: 125–38.

"Period Criticism"

See entry on "Notes on the Way" (9 November 1946)

"Personal Heresy in Criticism"

See entry on *Personal Heresy: A Controversy*

The Personal Heresy: A Controversy

E. M. W. Tillyard. London: Oxford University Press, 1939. Consists of new material plus material originally published as "The Personal Heresy in Criticism." *Essays and Studies by Members of the English Association*. XIX (1934): 7–28; Tillyard, E. M. W. "The Personal Heresy in Criticism: A Rejoinder." *Essays and Studies by Members of the English Association*. XX (1935): 7–20; and "Open Letter to Dr. Tillyard." *Essays and Studies by Members of the English Association* XXI (1936): 153–68.

The Personal Heresy refers both to a concept C. S. Lewis identified early in his professional career as debilitating to effective criticism and understanding of **poetry**, and, also, the title of a 1939 publication comprised of a celebrated exchange on this concept between Lewis and then renowned **Milton** scholar, E. M. W. Tillyard.

Simply put, "the personal heresy" was Lewis's label for an idea he vigorously opposed, namely, that poetry is first and foremost the "expression of the poet's personality." What follows from such a premise, Lewis averred, is that a reader of a poem learns as much about the poet as he or she does about the poem itself and, finally, that the brand of criticism most likely to be fruitful in illuminating the poem will be prohibitively biographical or psychological. In the early 1930s, Lewis found this stance a growing menace to responsible criticism, and he saw it as epitomized in E. M. W. Tillyard's 1930 work, *Milton*. Tillyard's premise, "All poetry is about the poet's state of mind" and his other propositions derived from his Milton study—that to understand *Paradise Lost* aright one must read it as an "expression of Milton's personality" and that, therefore, "the end we are supposed to pursue in reading . . . is a certain contact with the poet's soul"—were all inimical to Lewis's own understanding of the poetic act and the proper role of critics.

In his rebuttal to such views in *The Personal Heresy*, Lewis proposed that the successful poet's achievement is to create an object that is universal not local, public not private, impersonal not personal, since thereby the poet allows the reader to see what the poet sees—and not the poet "himself" in some crude or unguarded fash-

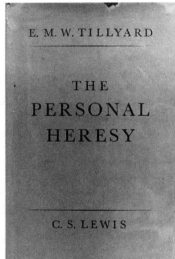

ion. Consequently, for Lewis, the critic's role is neither to reconstruct the poet's psyche between the lines of the poem nor to deconstruct the poem as concealed biography; rather, it is to help the reader see with ever greater clarity the world depicted in and through the poem that the poet has intentionally composed.

Lewis's formulation of the "personal heresy" had a long gestation, first surfacing in a presentation he made in the summer of 1924 to the **Martlets**, an undergraduate Oxford literary society. In his remarks, Lewis maintained that the biography of James Stephens, a popular Irish writer of the time, had nothing to do with understanding or appreciating the meaning of his works. Six years later, Lewis addressed the Martlets once again, this time as a don and not as a student, having fully conceptualized the malady he believed plagued contemporary criticism. This address, entitled, "The Personal Heresy in Poetics," began with Lewis's critique of an advertisement for a wartime poetry anthology that purportedly would inform readers of private feelings and traumatic events that not even soldiers' loved ones could know. The reader was compelled to infer that the soldier-poets would unwittingly "reveal" something of their psychological state through their poems. Characteristically, Lewis regarded this facile equation of the poet's mental state with the submerged subject matter of the poems more than appalling; his attack on this dubious notion would remind many readers of his critique of "The Green Book" in *The Abolition of Man* (1943), a composition text that he believed undermined "objective value" in **education**.

After this provocative introduction, Lewis proceeded to attack what he regarded as Tillyard's more insidious theorizings in his book on Milton. Because Tillyard's academic work was more intellectually respectable than a mere advertisement, Lewis believed it could convince a generation of readers and critics that Milton's own expressed intention, "to justify the ways of **God** to man," should be ignored or suppressed. And thus they would never "see what the poet saw." Lewis's verbal presentation first took published form in 1934 appearing in the journal *Essays and Studies* and was followed by a reply from Tillyard in the same journal in 1935; an exchange occurred between them in alternating years through 1937, and were eventually collected under the title, *The Personal Heresy: A Controversy* in 1939.

Tillyard's response to Lewis consists primarily of defenses of his conception of criticism against the caricature he believed Lewis had created. Tillyard contended that Lewis unfairly reduced his notion of the "poet's state of mind" merely to the trivial details of a poet's life. Tillyard countered that, in speaking of the poet's mental state, he was including the whole social and historical context out of which a poet speaks and how he reflects his own era, and that this is, indeed, the proper province of modern criticism. Collegially, Tillyard attempted to find common ground with Lewis where he could, but resisted, finally, Lewis's near total rejection of all aspects of psychobiographical modes of criticism. By the end of the exchange, Lewis expressed gratitude for the chance to sharpen his own point of view and conceded some minor points of disagreement with Tillyard on terminology. Lewis's final "refutation" of Tillyard's key operating principles as a Milton critic would eventually be offered in *A Preface to Paradise Lost* (1942).

Lewis's response to Tillyard in *The Personal Heresy* is of a piece with much of his discourse in the 1930s and 1940s, although **Owen Barfield**, Lewis's intellectual companion and mentoring friend through most of his professional career, chided Lewis for his uncharacteristic use of "pastiche" in his exchange with Tillyard, suggesting that there was too much posturing on Lewis's part—something Lewis rarely descended to in his public affairs. But in subject matter and focus, *The Personal Heresy* does exemplify what would become Lewis's consistent themes in all of his post-conversion nonfiction work, championing as it does the cogency of the doctrine of objective value, opposing the relativistic mindset ascendant in Western **culture**, and directing his readers attention to the concreteness of a real world that cannot be wished away. Lewis here and elsewhere associated the biographical and psychological criticism of his times with a resurgent gnosticism that denied the reality to which a poem pointed, and mistakenly affirmed in its place only the world of the critic's reconstructions.

Lewis's strongest contention in *The Personal Heresy* was that "when we read poetry as poetry should be read, we have before us no representation that claims to be the poet, and frequently no representation of a man, a character, or a personality at all." Lewis was interested in the reader being able to meet the poem on the landscape of an accessible and stable text provided by the

poet; for him, "poetry that is only 'about' the poet's state of mind," deprives the reader of a true text, a true world, and thus denies him or her a means of transcendence, which was for Lewis the chief value of reading. A text that is equivalent in some sense to its author's psyche—like a text which is in some sense equivalent to its reader's psyche—dissolved the crucial object/subject distinction that makes personal encounter possible, and which Lewis cherishes as a philosopher and critic.

Even when the "personal heresy" is not pushed to its logical extremes, Lewis believed it inevitably nurtures a brand of criticism that inevitably calls for "experts" and thus robs the general or "innocent" reader of the most essential feature of readerly experience, that is, a primary confrontation with a textual world offered by a real self. During the last two decades of his life, Lewis softened somewhat the stridency of the objectivism apparent in *The Personal Heresy*, finding a considerable role for the reader in constructing meaning and experiencing the text, and for the author who "discovers" the meaning of his work and the presence of his intentions by composing the work. This emerging new framework for understanding the value and purpose of reading is reflected in his last novel, *Till We have Faces* (1956), and codified in his last sustained and focused critical work, *An Experiment in Criticism* (1961).

Bruce L. Edwards
Bowling Green State University

Also See: Literary Criticism, Literary Theory, New Criticism

Bibliography

Edwards, Bruce L. *A Rhetoric of Reading: C. S. Lewis's Defense of Western Literacy*. Provo, UT: Brigham Young University Press, 1986.

_____. (ed). *The Taste of the Pineapple: Essays on C. S. Lewis as Reader, Critic, and Imaginative Writer*. Bowling Green: Popular Press, 1988.

Griffin, William. *C. S. Lewis: A Dramatic Life*. New York: Harper, 1986.

Hannay, Margaret. *C. S. Lewis*. New York: Ungar, 1981.

Schakel, Peter. *Reason and Imagination in C. S. Lewis*. Grand Rapids, MI: Eerdmans, 1984.

"Petitionary Prayer: A Problem Without An Answer"

First published posthumously in *Christian Reflections*.

C. S. Lewis read this paper to the Oxford Clerical Society on December 8, 1953. His major concern with petitionary **prayer** was that for him, the **Bible** seemed to instruct humans to pray in two different patterns that were "over and against" each other. The first was the way of **Christ** in Gethsemane ("Nevertheless, not My will but Thine"), the way of submission to **God**'s will, and this was usually Lewis's pattern of prayer. The second way was that of "sure expectation." Lewis believed that the Bible also seems to promise that if prayed for in **faith**, "the particular thing the petitioner asks will be given him." As an example, he always prayed that illnesses would be healed "if it was God's will."

Lewis said that he had taken this problem to almost every Christian he knew ("learned or simple, lay or clerical, within my own Communion or without") and had received no answer. He concluded his talk to the ministerial group with this request: "I come to you, reverend Fathers, for guidance. How am I to pray this very night?" It is not recorded if he received an answer from anyone in the group.

Perry C. Bramlett
C. S. Lewis for the Local Church

Bibliography

Bramlett, Perry C. *C. S. Lewis: Life at the Center*. Macon, GA: Smyth and Helwys, 1996.
Lewis, C. S. *Letters to Malcolm*
Lindskoog, Kathryn. *C. S. Lewis: Mere Christian*. Wheaton, IL: Shaw, 1987.

Philosophy

Lewis was not a philosopher, at least, not in the technical sense of that term. He was a student of philosophy and also, for a time, a teacher of philosophy, but he never was—and never claimed to be—a philosopher, any more than he was a theologian.

He was an extremely intelligent and widely read man whose thoughts, expressed in conversation or in writing, on any subject, always had a philosophical tincture to them. This tincture was derived from a traditional view of philosophy characterized by the free play of intelligence, by the way in which systematic inquiry was carried out, and not by a specific subject matter, as is the fashion nowadays. While priding himself on his dialectical ability (which was, undoubtedly, formidable), Lewis does not seem to have regarded philosophy simply as a method. If **logic** and dialectic provided the form of inquiry, that into which the inquiry was made—the matter—was what was important. Even when (by his own later standards), he was perversely and obstinately wrong, there is little doubt about his extreme honesty. He wanted to know the **truth** and, while not an academic philosopher, in that sense, deserved the ancient Platonic title of philosopher, as a lover of wisdom.

Between 1919 and 1922, Lewis was a student of philosophy as part of his **Oxford** course of studies, although philosophy was not a subject during his first two years (taking Mods) as it explicitly was in the last two years (taking Greats). During the preparation for Mods, Lewis read classical Greek and Latin texts, including some of **Plato** and of **Aristotle**, but they were read primarily from a classical languages point of view, although this could not and did not exclude consideration of their meaning—that is, of them as philosophy; but their truth was not in question. For Greats, however, philosophy was explicitly required and Lewis read— and not for the first time—texts of Plato (including the *Republic*, *Symposium*, *Theaetetus*, *Politicus*, *Phaedrus*, and the *Phaedo*), and of Aristotle, Spinoza, Leibniz, the triumvirate of British philosophers, (Locke, Berkeley, and **Hume**), **Kant**, the Hegelians, Bosanquet and Bradley, Bergson, and Croce. There were doubtless others, either prescribed or relevant, to which Lewis, with his voracious intellectual appetite, was drawn.

Between 1920 and 1940, the fashion of philosophy at Oxford changed and the old Hegelianism and subjective idealism of Lewis's days as a student—the school of Thomas Hill Green—gradually came to be considered outmoded. Hegel had been dominant because he provided a total system in which everything could be fitted; in fact, he had made it almost mandatory for a philosophy to be a system, if it were to deserve the title of philosophy. But Hegel's difficulty, complexity, and ultimate obscurity invited destruction of his system. This was accomplished by the rise of the two fashions of logical positivism and linguistic analysis, represented by the Vienna Circle and, later, A. J. Ayer at Oxford.

Lewis seems to have made no serious effort to keep up with these developments—which is understandable because his scholarly endeavors were not in philosophy but in literature and, later, in his Christian **apologetics**. He knew something of Bertrand Russell's opinions and read some G. E. Moore, but there is little evidence that he had ever read Whitehead and Russell, Wittgenstein, Cook, Wilson, Prichard, Ryle, Price, Austin, Carnap, Husserl, Heidegger, and many others of the new breed; nor does he seem to have studied Marx or the Existentialists, Sartre, Camus, and not even Kierkegaard. This showed itself, in the most public and humiliating manner, in 1948, at Lewis's celebrated debate at **The Oxford University Socratic Club** with **G. E. M. Anscombe**. By so limiting his study, Lewis perhaps did himself a disservice; he might have found Wittgenstein's, "There is indeed the inexpressible. This *shows* itself; it is the mystical," a congenial saying.

In the early 1920s, Lewis considered himself an atheist and opposed any thought that might lead to theism, especially idealism. His philosophy examiner told his **tutor** that "one of your men seems to think that Plato is always wrong." When Lewis learned this, it seems to have encouraged him, ironically enough, to think of becoming a professional philosopher. But he was writing *Dymer* and—contrary to Plato—wanted to be a poet instead.

While the idealism of Green was under attack by the early positivists, Lewis was undoubtedly sympathetic to the "new realism," but he was also an atheist and seems to have lived with an unreconciled radical dualism. He was more in favor of the attack upon Green than in joining the new realists, but he was considered a likely recruit. During the next few years, however, he moved closer to Bradley, Bosanquet, C. C. J. Webb, and J. A. Smith—towards the idealists, and reacted against the positivist revolution. In this, he was joined by R. G. Collingwood. He also played with occult spiritualism, but came to think it dangerous. It was during this same period that he formulated the central problem for his own thought: how can reason exist apart from participation in a cosmic logos? The counterpart of this was that naturalism is self-refuting. It was this latter proposition that was the ground of argument with Anscombe at the Socratic Club.

It is interesting to note that when Lewis was considering a research degree (D.Litt.) in 1924, he chose as his subject the 17th-century **Cambridge** Platonist Henry More, an admirer of **Spenser** and a thinker who took **Renaissance** Platonism into the center of **Anglicanism**.

Lewis's formal teaching of philosophy, in 1924–25 when he was substituting for E. F. Carritt, University College's regular philosophy tutor and as a fellow of **Magdalen** from 1925 onwards, followed the same syllabus and texts that he himself had followed only a few years earlier as a student. He chose, for his lectures in 1924–25, the philosophical topic "The Moral Good—Its Place among the Values." In Magdalen, he seems not to have lectured but only supervised philosophy students in tutorials; his main work was in English Literature, and he gave up philosophy without any regret.

The most philosophical of Lewis's works are probably *The Abolition of Man,* in which he locates a foundation for morals, and *Miracles*, in which the distinction between what Lewis called naturalism and supernatu-

ralism provides a basis for, amongst other things, a proof for the existence of **God**. *Studies in Words* and *The Discarded Image* provide material for a philosophical view of language, but Lewis never provided an overall view, contenting himself with showing his views through discussion of concrete examples.

Apart from his **literary criticism**, Lewis's extensive writings have been so influential that it is unfair to describe him only as a popularizer of the Christian philosophy of **religion**, but, in truth, he claimed to have discovered nothing new. He did claim to express what he took to be old truths in a new and vivid form, and although they persuaded many people, they did not convince many philosophers and theologians. What he certainly did was to provide a new statement of the intellectual foundations of **Christianity**. Moreover, he took to heart Barfield's reminder in 1922 that, for Plato, philosophy was not a subject but a *way*.

Perhaps the best summation is that Lewis was a philosophical writer, not a writer of philosophy.

John Bremer

Also See: Ethics and Morality, Language/Rhetoric, Metaphysics

Bibliography

Patrick, James. *The Magdalen Metaphysics: Idealism and Orthodoxy at Oxford, 1901–1945*. Macon, GA: Mercer University Press, 1985.

"Pilgrim's Problem"

The Month. 7 (May 1952): 275. Reprinted in *Poems* and *Collected Poems.*

A provocative poem challenging the notion that age brings wisdom and settled peace. A walker, late in the day, relies on his map and assumes he is nearing a restful end to his journey. He looks forward to charity, humility, contemplation, fortitude, temperance, and chastity. In fact, he realizes none of these. Thus, he wonders rhetorically whether it is he or the map that is flawed. He implies it must be the latter.

Don W. King
Montreat College

The Pilgrim's Regress

London: J. M. Dent, 1933. First US edition, New York: Sheed & Ward, 1935.

The Pilgrim's Regress was Lewis's first Christian book, his first prose book, the seedbed of many of the ideas he developed later, and his only prose **allegory**. It is the semiautobiographical story of a boy named John, who journeyed the opposite direction of the pilgrim in John Bunyan's *Pilgrim's Progress*.

The key to *Regress* is the kind of blissful, almost unendurable sense of desire called *Sensucht* Lewis first experienced as a very young child. (See the first chapter of **Surprised by Joy**.) This occasionally recurring experience of "**Joy**" was what he valued most in life, and he sought it diligently in various places, including aesthetic thrills.

Regress traces John's journey away from **Christianity**, his search for Joy, and where he found it. John was born in Puritania and terrified by his inability to follow the rules because the Landlord in the Eastern Mountains condemned rule-breakers to a black hole. He was also terrified when his uncle had to cross the brook and go to the Mountains. John caught glimpses of an Island in the West and yearned for it. After a regrettable affair with a brown girl, he headed west to find his Island. He traveled south to the city of Thrill, then north to the city called Eschropolis and the country of the Spirit of the Age. He returned to the Main Road, was blocked by the Grand Canyon, then headed north as far as the shanty of the three pale men. Next he went south to the Valley of Humiliation, and back to the Grand Canyon and a chapel in a cave.

On the way, Mr. Enlightenment convinced John there is no Landlord, and a series of encounters with other characters instructed him in other ways, many of them wrong. Some of these were Vertue, Media and Gus Halfways, **Reason**, Mr. Sensible, Mr. Broad, Wisdom, and a hermit named History. The only way to cross the Grand Canyon was to submit to help from Mother Kirk, which John resisted as long as possible. Later, at the western shore he relayed that the world is round and his Island in the West was all along the Eastern Mountains, the home of the Landlord. So he joyfully journeyed east and eventually crossed the Brook. This witty, fast-paced story is packed with allusions to a staggering array of writers, thinkers, and movements, as well as insights on **culture**, **psychology**, and **spirituality**.

As an adolescent Lewis had gladly rejected all religion, but intellectual honesty caused him to keep modifying his philosophical views.

U.K. First Edition

In 1929 he reluctantly accepted theism, and in 1931 he accepted Christianity. He realized that his experiences of *Sensucht* had all along been surges of spiritual homesickness for **heaven**.

On January 17, 1932, Lewis told his brother he was going to write an allegorical poem about the long search for Joy that had finally led him to his new faith; it would be told as an ocean voyage. In fact, he didn't get far and only three stanzas survive. (They must be read in the **Marion E. Wade Center** at Wheaton College or the **Bodleian Library** at Oxford.)

In August 1932 Lewis visited his Irish friend **Arthur Greeves** for two weeks and there wrote *Pilgrim's Regress* with prodigious speed. Greeves suggested leaving out all Greek and Latin quotations, but Lewis answered that we need more classical learning, not less. Greeves thought Lewis should use a more formal and dignified style of writing; Lewis answered that he intended to be idiomatic and racy. Greeves preferred a simpler book with less complicated meanings, but Lewis said his conversion had not been simple, so the book could not be simple.

Lewis described *Regress* to his editor at J. M. Dent, the publisher of **Dymer**. The full title was *The Pilgrim's Regress: an allegorical apology for Christianity, Reason, and Romanticism*, he said, and it was "a kind of Bunyan up to date. It is serious in intention but has a good many more comic passages than I originally intended, and also a fair controversial interest (the things chiefly ridiculed are Anglo Catholicism, **Materialism**, Sitwellianism, Psychoanalysis, and **T. S. Eliot**.)" Dent accepted the new book late in 1932. (These letters may be read in the Wade Center.)

Lewis dedicated *Regress* to Arthur Greeves and told him on February 4, 1933, "It is yours by every right—written in your house, read to you as it was written. . . ." One thousand copies were printed in May 1933, but they did not sell well. "I think it is going to be at least as big a failure as *Dymer* . . . ," Lewis reported to Greeves. However, it received a good review in the July 6, 1933, issue of the *Times Literary Supplement*.

In 1935 the book was accepted by Sheed and Ward, a Roman Catholic company that increased its sales. But Lewis was extremely unhappy with two comments on the flyleaf of the dust jacket: "Mr. Lewis's wit would probably seem to Bunyan sinful. Certainly his theology would," and "The hero, brought up in Puritania (Mr. Lewis himself was born in Ulster), cannot abide the religion he finds there." The latter was an indictment of the Anglican Protestantism of Northern Ireland. Lewis wrote in the flyleaf of the copy he gave his father, "The suggestions are put in by the unspeakable Sheed with no authority of mine & without my knowledge." (This copy may be seen in the Wade Center.)

A review in the December 8, 1935, issue of the *New York Times Book Review* referred to "A modern man's intricate journey through the worlds of thought and feeling and desire; his passionate search for **truth** . . . a picture of genuine mystical experience, rationalized by **philosophy**. . . . To many it will seem like a fresh wind blowing across arid wastes." A review in the May 1936 issue of *The Catholic World* declared: "This brilliantly written volume is a caustic, devastating critique of modern philosophy, **religion**, **politics** and art; a clear-cut, logical and effective apologia of reason and the Christian **faith**. We have rarely read a book we so thoroughly enjoyed. We are convinced that the author, too, enjoyed the writing of every line."

The widespread rumor that Lewis came to regret *Regress* is untrue. On the last day of 1939 he wrote to his brother that Mrs. Mary Neylan, an ex-pupil of his, was a gratifyingly constant re-reader of it. He hoped she might become a Christian. (She did.) In 1943 Lewis added a helpful nine-page preface and running headlines for his book's third publisher, **Geoffrey Bles**, but it was still difficult for most people to fully understand.

On January 19, 1953, Lewis wrote to Mrs. Edward Allen, a confused reader, that he wasn't surprised she had trouble with *Regress*. He explained that it was his first religious book and he did not then know how to write an easy one. Furthermore, he had not tried to make it easy because he never dreamed he would have any readers outside a small "highbrow" circle.

In 1958 Eerdmans issued *Regress* in the United States. In 1963 Lewis completed his earthly pilgrimage. In 1981 a fifth publisher, Bantam, issued *Regress* without Lewis's headlines, and Eerdmans issued a deluxe edition with illustrations by renowned illustrator Michael Hague.

Kathryn Lindskoog

Also See: Aesthetics, Anglicanism, Roman Catholicism

Bibliography

Lindskoog, Kathryn. *Finding the Landlord: A Guidebook to C. S. Lewis's Pilgrim's Regress*. Chicago: Cornerstone Press Chicago, 1995.

"Pindar Sang"

See entry on "Arrangement of Pindar"

Ruth Pitter (1898–1992)

Ruth Pitter was an accomplished poet who published her first poems when she was only thirteen years old. Her published volumes include *First Poems* (1920), *A Mad Lady's Garland* (1935), *A Trophy of Arms* (1936), *Pitter on Cats* (1947), and *Poems 1926–1966* (1968). She first encountered Lewis through his radio broadcasts of **Mere Christianity,** which she said converted her to **Anglicanism.** Her first meeting with Lewis took place on July 17, 1946. Over the years, the two met frequently and exchanged letters regularly. After **Janie Moore**'s death in 1951, Lewis was able to associate more freely with Ruth. Lewis enjoyed Ruth's company and her intellectual talents. He also had to admit that she was by far the superior poet of the two. According to Lewis's biographer, **George Sayer**, Lewis commented after a visit in 1955 that "if he were not a confirmed bachelor, Ruth Pitter would be the woman he would like to marry." Lewis did not remain a bachelor, but he married the American **Joy Davidman Lewis**. Joy and Ruth only met once on February 1, 1954. After Lewis's **marriage** to Joy, the correspondence and meetings between Lewis and Ruth became more infrequent due in part to Joy's illness. Their last meeting was on July 12, 1961, when **Owen Barfield** escorted Ruth to **the Kilns** to see Jack.

Jeffrey D. Schultz

Bibliography

Pitter, Ruth. "Poet to Poet." *Canadian C. S. Lewis Journal* 18 (June 1980): 3–7.

Russell, Arthur (ed). *Ruth Pitter: Homage to a Poet*. Chester Springs, PA: Dufour Editions,1969.

"The Planets"

Lysistrata. 2 (May 1935): 21–24 (a portion of this poem is quoted in Lewis's essay "A Metrical Suggestion"). Reprinted in *Poems* and *Collected Poems*.

Lewis toyed with Anglo-Saxon alliterative half-lines throughout this catalog celebrating the moon, Mercury, Venus, the sun, Mars, Jupiter, and Saturn.

Don W. King
Montreat College

Plato (427?–347? B.C.)

Lewis had a high regard for Plato, the great Greek philosopher. In his final Narnian Chronicle (*The Last Battle*) Lewis had the professor say: "It's all in Plato, all in Plato: bless me, what *do* they teach them at these schools!" What Lewis most admired about Plato was his **metaphysics**. Plato believed that there are two real worlds, not one. There is the world of changing physical things that we apprehend by means of our senses, and there is the world of eternally true ideas that we apprehend by means of our minds. Plato was looking for stable things in a world of change; he found this stability in Being in contrast with becoming, in forms or ideas in contrast with matter or particulars, in the invisible and eternal in contrast with the visible and temporal. Both Plato and Lewis objected to the view that matter is most real. They defended the alternative view that ultimate **reality** is more like mind or spirit than matter. Plato stressed that fire, earth, air, and water are not the cause of all that is. What is behind the universe is more like spirit or idea than anything else we know.

Lewis presented this concept of reality in *The Last Battle*, where he suggested that all our life in this world—and all our adventures in wonderful **imaginary** places like Narnia—are only shadows of something far, far greater. They are "the cover and the title page ... [of] Chapter One of the Great Story, which no one on earth has read: which goes on for ever: in which every chapter is better than the one before."

Lewis was also influenced by Plato's ethics, which is eudaemonistic in the sense that it is directed towards the attainment of man's highest good, in which our true **happiness** consists. This highest good (*summum bonum*) includes the knowledge of **God**, and it must be attained by the pursuit of virtue, that is, becoming as like God as it is possible for humans to become. In the *Laws* Plato declared that God is the measure of all things in a sense far higher than any human being can ever hope to be. It is particularly from Plato that Lewis inherited an interest in the ideals of the true, the good, and the beautiful.

Lewis in addition admired Plato's cosmology, noting in *Reflections on the Psalms* that Plato had a clear **theology** of **creation** in the Judeo-Christian sense. The whole universe—and the conditions of time and space under which it exists—is produced by the will of a perfect, timeless, and unconditioned God who is above and outside of all that he creates. One thing Lewis did not admire in Plato was the utopian political community described in Plato's *Republic*. Lewis attacked the Platonic state in his pre-Christian narrative poem *Dymer*

(1926). He later recalled that at the time he "detested the state in Plato's *Republic* as much as he had liked everything else in Plato."

Nevertheless, Lewis generally had a high regard for the achievements of the Greeks and the **culture** of "the great pagans," and he frequently listed the thought of Plato and **Aristotle** together as the peak of intellectual ascent.

Michael H. Macdonald
Seattle Pacific University

Also See: Chronicles of Narnia, Ethics and Morality, Natural Law, Paganism, Virtues

Bibliography
Plato. *Phaedo; Republic; Laws; Symposium.*

Lewis, C. S. *The Last Battle* (particularly chapters "Further Up and Further In," and "Farewell to Shadowlands"); *Reflections on the Psalms; Miracles*

"Poem for Psychoanalysis and/or Theologians"
See entry on "The World is Round"

Poems

Hooper, Walter (ed). London: Geoffrey Bles, 1964. Also reprinted in *Collected Poems.*

Poems was the first book-length collection of Lewis's **poetry** that had been published in various places over the years. The poems reprinted comment upon various issues important to Lewis at the time they were written and are not dependent upon a unified theme. Consequently, they are readily accessible and can be considered individually unlike those in *Spirits in Bondage* and *Dymer*. Problematic, however, is the fact that many of the selections in *Poems* differ from the originals published earlier in various journals and periodicals (many were published under "N W," short for the Anglo-Saxon phrase "nat whilk," or "I know not whom," Lewis's shorthand way of identifying himself as the author). While the differences are sometimes minor (alternate punctuation or capitalization), others are significant, including rearranged, deleted, or added lines, word changes, and, on occasion, extra stanzas. Most of the authors of essays about the poetry reprinted here either do not know about these variations or choose to work with the versions provided.

Compounding the textual problem is the recent publication of *The Collected Poems of C. S. Lewis* (1994), discussed elsewhere in this volume. Although recent issues of Kathryn Lindskoog's *The Lewis Legacy* discuss some of the problems associated with this new volume, they tend to comment less about the poetry of *Poems*

(1964) than about authorship. Prompted at least in part by the publication of *Collected Poems*, a series of articles in *The Lewis Legacy* questions the validity of the "Introductory Letter" purported to be by Lewis, the incompleteness of *Collected Poems*, and inexplicable revisions to poems Lewis published during his lifetime (see *The Lewis Legacy* 64 [Spring 1995]). Also targeted are specific poems and their variants, especially **"Finchley Avenue,"** first published in *Occasional Poets: An Anthology* (1986) and subsequently published in *Collected Poems* (see *The Lewis Legacy* 65 [Summer 1995]). Finally, whole-text variants of **"March for Drum, Trumpet, and Twenty-One Giants," "The Day with a White Mark,"** and "Under Sentence" (published as "The Condemned" in *Poems*) with notes and commentary are published (see *The Lewis Legacy* 66 [Autumn 1995]). These short articles are must reading.

As noted above, *Poems* lacks a unified structure such as we see in *Spirits in Bondage* and *Dymer*; however, some of Lewis's best poetry is found in this volume. **Walter Hooper** gives the book a four-part structure: Part I: The Hidden Country; Part II: The Backward Glance; Part III: A Larger World; and Part IV: Further Up & Further In. Unfortunately, he never explains this structure, nor why certain poems are placed in one section rather than another. I will use an alternate four-part structure to analyze the poems, grouping the poems thematically.

The first group of poems celebrates the ideas, traditions, and values Lewis associated with the past: honor, **truth**, chivalry, loyalty, faithfulness, honest sentiment, **nature**, and proven things. The best example of this occurs in the opening poem, "A Confession" (first published as **"Spartan Nactus."** *Punch* 227 [Dec. 1, 1954]: 685; there are significant differences between the two versions). Tongue in cheek, Lewis begins with: "I am so coarse, the things the poets see / Are obstinately invisible to me." This opening serves as his platform from which he attacked modern poetry (**T. S. Eliot** in particular) and its absurd **metaphors**: "For twenty years I've stared my level best / To see if evening—any evening— would suggest / A patient etherized upon a table; / In vain. I simply wasn't able." He ended the poem, still tongue in cheek, taking the pose of a foolish, uneducated person ("I'm like that odd man **Wordsworth** knew, to whom / A primrose was a yellow primrose") who can only appreciate stock responses, those emotional reactions to ideas, objects, and notions intrinsically connected with the past (including "Athens," Troy," and "Jerusalem"). It should be noted that Lewis's affection for the past permeates all his work from his Narnian stories through his **literary criticism**. Other poems in this group include **"Pan's Purge"** (5), **"The Late Passenger"** (47), **"The Future of Forestry"** (61), "Eden's Courtesy" (98), "The Phoenix" (121), "Noon's Intensity" (114), and "Sweet Desire" (114).

The second group of poems is related to the first, because its poems lament the shallowness of **modernity**, including the popular press, technological progress, reliance on the scientific method, the destruction of the environment, and what Lewis called elsewhere "chronological snobbery," the idea that simply because something is new, it is by nature better than something old. For instance, Lewis turned his rapier pen upon the muckrakers in "*Odora Canum Vis*: A Defence of Certain Biographers and Critics" (first published in *The Month* 272 [May 1954]: 272):

Come now, don't be too eager to condemn
Our little smut-hounds if they wag their tails
(Or shake like jellies as the tails wag them)
The moment the least whiff of sex assails
Their quivering snouts. Such conduct after all,
Though comic, is in them quite natural. (59)

Such disdain, a distinctive characteristic throughout this volume, appears again in **"Evolutionary Hymn"** [first published in *The Cambridge Review* 79 (30 November 1957): 227]. Other poems in this group include **"The Country of the Blind"** (33), **"As One Oldster to Another"** (56), **"An Expostulation"** (58), **"The Condemned"** (63), and **"Deception"** (90).

The third group consists of poems focusing on the spiritual life, including topics such as religious doubt, **angels**, God's reality and presence in the world, man's pilgrimage, and the role of the Christian apologist. In **"Caught"** (first published in *The Pilgrim's Regress* [1933]), we find a persona who is struggling to come to grips with a fierce omnipotence, much as a dog would strain at the leash of an unyielding master. The poem begins with the persona noting that he feels like a person trapped in a burning desert bathed by unrelenting, suffocating light and heat. **God**, like the sun, is the "inevitable Eye" that confines a desert traveler in smothering tents and "hammers the rocks with light." He is an unyielding, unrelenting, uncompromising force.

These lines suggest a powerful longing for freedom from the "heat" of God's eye; he is ready to retreat from the demands of an unyielding God toward the comfortable fastness of his pagan days. Such an option, however, is denied him: "But you have seized all in your rage / Of Oneness. Round about / Beating my wings, all ways, within your cage, / I flutter, but not out" (116). Here God is pictured as possessive, angry, and intent on his unanimity. At the same time the persona pictures himself as a bird trapped in a cage, straining earnestly to wing his way out, but to no avail. This poem leaves us with two distinct impressions. The first, of course, is of a "convert" who yearns for his preconversion days where, rightly or wrongly, he believes life held more freedom, more satisfaction. The second is that God is an all-encompassing, smothering, demanding entity, uncompromising in his jealous possession of a follower.

At the other end of the spectrum is "Love's as Warm as Tears," where we find a persona reflecting on the measureless love of God. Early stanzas show love as warm as tears, as fierce as fire, as fresh as spring; in all, love connects to the human experience. However, in the last stanza, love transcends the human:

> Love's as hard as nails,
>   Love is nails:
> Blunt, thick, hammered through
> The medial nerves of One
> Who, having made us, knew
> The thing He had done,
> Seeing (with all that is)
> Our cross, and His. (124)

Characteristic of *Poems* because the collection includes poems spanning Lewis's life, these two poems illustrate the spiritual maturation Lewis experienced. Other poems in this group are **"The Salamander"** (72), "Wormwood" (87), "Deadly Sins" (91), "Nearly They Stood" (102), "Relapse" (103), "Angel's Song" (107), "Forbidden Pleasure" (115), **"Legion"** (119), **"Pilgrim's Problem"** (119), **"Sonnet"** (120), "The Nativity" (122), "Prayer" (122), "No Beauty We Could Desire" (124), "Stephan to Lazarus" (125), "Evensong" (128), "The

Apologist's Evening Prayer" (129), "Footnote to All Prayers" (129), and **"After Prayers, Lie Cold"** (130).

The final group of poems deals with personal loss involving **friendships**, romantic love, and physical pleasures. At least several of the poems in this group almost certainly concern **Joy Davidman**. In "As the Ruin Falls," the persona rebukes himself with bitter honesty: "All this is flashy rhetoric about loving you. / I never had a selfless thought since I was born. / I am mercenary and self-seeking through and through: / I want God, you, all friends, merely to serve my turn" (109). His self-confession about his egocentricity continues as he admits that he "cannot crawl one inch outside my proper skin"; he talks of love, he says, but he recognizes that his has not been a giving love: "self-imprisoned, always end where I begin."

However, the other person, the beloved, has taught the persona by example both what loving means (giving) and how miserable his ability to love has been: "Only that now you have taught me (but how late) my lack" (110). But there is an added dimension because the beloved appears to be leaving him: "I see the chasm. And everything you are was making / My heart into a bridge by which I might get back / From exile, and grow man. And now the bridge is breaking." To the beloved he credits his own faltering steps toward a love that is giving; indeed, the beloved has given him the capacity to be less selfish (she has made his heart a bridge) and less isolated (she has helped to end his "exile, and grow man"). His comment that the bridge is now breaking almost certainly refers to his anticipated loss of her. And so he blesses her: "For this I bless you as the ruin falls. The pains / You give me are more precious than all other gains." Other poems in this group include "Lines Written in a Copy of Milton's Work" (83), **"To a Friend"** (104), **"To Charles Williams"** (105), "After Vain Pretence" (106), "Joys That Sting" (108), "Old Poets Remembered" (109), and "Scanzons" (118).

Don W. King
Montreat College

Bibliography

Christopher, Joe. "An Analysis of 'Old Poets Remembered.'" *The Lamp-Post of the Southern California C. S. Lewis Society.* 19 (Fall 1995): 16–18.

———. "An Analysis of 'The Apologist's Evening Prayer.'" *CSL: The Bulletin of the New York C. S. Lewis Society.* 5 (October 1974): 2–4.

———. "A Serious Limerick." *The Chronicle of the Portland C. S. Lewis Society.* 1 no. 8 (September 8, 1972): 4–5.

———. "A Theological Triolet." *CSL: The Bulletin of the New York C. S. Lewis Society.* 2 (September 1971): 4–5.

_____. "C. S. Lewis' Lingusitic [sic] Myth." *Mythlore*. 21 (Summer 1995): 41–50.

_____. "C. S. Lewis, Love Poet." *Studies in the Literary Imagination*. 22 (Fall 1989): 161–173.

_____. "No Fish for the Phoenix." *CSL: The Bulletin of the New York C. S. Lewis Society*. 23 (July 1992): 1–7.

Howard, Thomas. "*Poems*: A Review." *Christianity Today*. 9 (June 18, 1965): 30.

King, Don. "The Distant Voice in C. S. Lewis's *Poems*." *Studies in the Literary Imagination*. 22 (Fall 1989): 175–184.

Lindskoog, Kathryn. "C. S. Lewis on Christmas." *Christianity Today*. 27 (16 December 1983): 24–26.

_____. *Finding the Landlord: A Guidebook to C. S. Lewis's Pilgrim's Regress*. Chicago: Cornerstone Press, 1995.

_____. "Getting It Together: Lewis and the Two Hemispheres of Knowing." *Journal of Psychology and Theology* 3 (Fall 1975): 290–93. Reprinted in *Mythlore* 6 (Winter 1979): 43–45.

Pitter, Ruth. "Poet to Poet." *Canadian C. S. Lewis Journal*. 18 (June 1980): 3–7.

Prothero, James. "Lewis's Poetry: A Preliminary Exploration." *CSL: The Bulletin of the New York C. S. Lewis Society*. 25 (March-April 1994): 1–6.

Poetic Licence (Letter)

The Sunday Times. (11 August 1946): 6.

Lewis discussed the "poetic licence" granted to writers when working with a rhyme scheme utilizing foreign names. He offered that it is not necessary for an English poet to attempt to retain the ancient pronunciation of a Greek name such as Aphrodite and that the assimilation of such pronunciations into the English vernacular is a sign of the healthy state of the language. Lewis was responding in this letter to several other letters initially criticizing the freedom of rhyme in the poem, "Thoughts of England" by John Gwynne-Hughes (*The Sunday Times*, 23 June 1946, 4). One of these letters (H. Lang Jones, 7 July 1946) complained of other poets' rhyming Aphrodite with white, hence Lewis's letter.

Marjorie L. Mead
The Marion E. Wade Center

Poetry

C. S. Lewis was ten when he began writing poems, and until his early thirties, his highest ambition was to be a poet. In 1919, at the age of twenty, he published under the pseudonym Clive Hamilton a slim volume entitled *Spirits in Bondage*, and in 1922 he began work on *Dymer* (published 1926), a long narrative poem of over two thousand lines of rime royal stanzas about a rebellious youth who escapes a rationalist utopia and enjoys a brief love affair with **Nature**, only to discover that his anarchic deed inspired the destruction of civi-

lization and engendered a monster, which kills him when he fights it, and then becomes a god.

Though *Dymer* received good reviews, it was Lewis's last attempt at publishing narrative verse. Lewis continued to write, however, completing *Launcelot* and *The Nameless Isle* in the early 1930's, and *The Queen of Drum* probably about 1935. Though the latter poem received qualified praise from poet-laureate John Masefield, Lewis never published it. All four poems are now available in the collection entitled *Narrative Poems* (1969).

Relinquishing his poetic ambitions, Lewis nevertheless continued to publish short poems, which were collected after his death and republished as *Poems* (1964). This volume provides a feast of Lewis—his loves, antipathies, his literary learning, and his expert command of both modern and classical poetic forms. The first poem of the collection, **"A Confession,"** comments ironically on his lack of sympathy with the modernist poetic sensibility.

Other poems celebrate Lewis's love of nature, his life-long fascination with **myth**, and his appreciation of both Classical and the older forms of English poetry. **"Pindar Sang,"** for instance, is a formal tour de force, rendering a Pindaric ode in English dactylic hexameters. Another brief poem praises Andrew Marvell; a longer poem, **"The Turn of the Tide,"** reworks themes from **Milton**'s "Nativity Ode." Other poems speculate on subjects ranging from the nature of angelic consciousness to the possible consequences of the secularization of contemporary thought and culture. The bulk of Lewis's poetry is not confessional or autobiographical but relatively public in character. Of the more personal exceptions, the "Five Sonnets," written during or after his wife's last illness, exemplify great power and **beauty**.

The recent **controversy** over revisions made to Lewis's poetry after his death is discussed in the entries for *Poems*, *Complete Poems* and *Narrative Poems*.

Lyle Smith
Biola University

Bibliography

Walsh, Chad. *The Literary Legacy of C. S. Lewis*. New York: Harcourt Brace Jovanovich, :35–58.

The Poetry of Search and the Poetry of Statement (Book Review)

"Rhyme and Reason." *Sunday Telegraph*. 148 (1 December 1963): 18.

This is a series of twelve papers read by **Dorothy Sayers** between 1946 and 1957. Although the interpretations and re-interpretations "seem to work," Lewis doubted that "this distinction has really much to do with the reality of a poem as a poem." His tribute to the work and the author was that "the book everywhere exhibits the style and temper for which the author was both loved and hated. The essays are full of cheerful energy."

Anne Gardner

Bibliography

Sayers, Dorothy L. *The Poetry of Search and the Poetry of Statement.*

"Poetry and Exegesis"

See entry on *The Visionary Company: A Reading of English Romantic Poetry* (Book Review)

Poetry and Prose in the Sixteenth Century

See entry on *English Literature in the Sixteenth Century, Excluding Drama*

"The Poison of Subjectivism"

Religion in Life. XII (Summer 1943): 356–65. Reprinted in *Christian Reflections.*

Lewis argued in this essay that the theoretical error of subjectivism removes the ordinary checks to evil and has given the power philosophies of mid-20th-century totalitarian states "their golden opportunity." Historically, humanity has assumed the validity of **reason** and studied all else by means of it. When reason becomes the object of study, however, it appears to modern man as simply an epiphenomenon accompanying brain activity. Hasty conclusions based on this premise produce the view that value judgments are simply social constructions and that values are arbitrary ideologies. This removes any independent standard against which values can be measured, and if the Axis Powers define justice as that which suits their own national interests, they cannot be validly criticized for so doing.

Lewis showed why modern attempts at rejecting traditional values and substituting new value schemes are doomed to failure, and he rebutted the counterarguments that traditional morality differs as between times and places, that to tie ourselves to a rigid moral code puts a stop to progress and invites "stagnation." In conclusion, he criticized the theological dilemma—"Are these things right because **God** commands them or does God command them because they are right?"—on the ground that it fails to take into account the special character of the trinitarian personhood of God.

Lyle Smith
Biola University

Also See: Communism and Fascism, Education, Ethics and Morality, Rationalism, Tao, Tradition, Trinity

Bibliography

Lewis, C. S. *The Abolition of Man*

Nuttall, A. D. "Jack the Giant-Killer." *Seven.* 5 (1984): 84–100.

Thorson, Stephen. "'Knowledge' in C. S. Lewis's Post-Convention Thought: This Epistemological Method." *Seven.* 9 (1988): 91–116.

Polemics

A skilled disputationist, Lewis was a demanding **tutor** and, in the **Oxford Socratic Club**, a formidable antagonist for opponents of **Christianity**. His sophisticated yet broadly accessible apologetic writings are comprehensive, soundly argued, logically tight, and provide indispensable models of the work of challenging intellectual opposition to the gospel.

Lewis's style is as much a part of his argument as is his Aristotelian logic; his examples, illustrations, analogies, and *argumentes ad hominem* are immensely entertaining as well as logically impeccable. (For example, arguing the improbability of real moral relativism in *Mere Christianity*: "Think of a country . . . where a man felt proud of doublecrossing all the people who had been kindest to him.") Repeatedly, Lewis will demonstrate the illogic of a position he opposes by rendering it analogically or even imagistically; conversely, he will demonstrate the logical soundness of the position he advocates with a rising crescendo of consequences flowing from the **truth** of it. While logically rigorous, Lewis's style of argument is imaginatively appealing.

Argument is implicit not only in his **apologetics** but in his criticism and his imaginative works as well. *The Personal Heresy* (a critical debate with E. M. W. Tillyard) and *A Preface to Paradise Lost* are both courteously and firmly argumentative in tone—a complex and wide-ranging tone capable of conveying humor, solemnity, contempt, exasperation. Lewis's stylistic versatility enabled him to convey much more than is denoted by even his enormously persuasive logic. For that reason nobody, as **Austin Farrer** said, could put Lewis down (though philosopher **G. E. M. Anscombe** gave him a pretty rough time in a 1948 debate).

Lewis's imaginative works carried on the apologetic campaign of counterargument in a less direct way, making a direct appeal to desire. As he said in **"The Weight of Glory,"** he was trying to weave a spell—one to be used for breaking the evil enchantment of worldliness that has been laid upon the West for nearly a hundred years. He did so by the sort of appeal to desire that thousands of readers have reported experiencing in the **Chronicles of Narnia**, in one or more of the novels of the interplanetary trilogy, in *Till We Have Faces*, and in Lewis's **poetry**.

Lyle Smith
Biola University

Also See: Language/Rhetoric

Bibliography

Barfield, Owen. "Introduction." *Light on C. S. Lewis.* Jocelyn Gibb (ed). New York: Harcourt, Brace & World, 1965: ix–xxi.

Carpenter, Humphrey. *The Inklings: C. S. Lewis, J. R. R. Tolkien, Charles Williams, and their friends.* New York: Ballantine, 1978.

Farrer, Austin. "The Christian Apologist." *Light on C. S. Lewis.* Jocelyn Gibb (ed). New York: Harcourt, Brace & World, 1965: 23–43.

Griffiths, Alan Bede. "The Adventure of Faith." *C. S. Lewis at the Breakfast Table.* James T. Como (ed). New York: Macmillan, 1979: 11–24.

Hooper, Walter. "Oxford's Bonny Fighter." *C. S. Lewis at the Breakfast Table.* James T. Como (ed). New York: Macmillan, 1979: 137–85.

Lawlor, John. "The Tutor and the Scholar." *Light on C. S. Lewis.* Jocelyn Gibb (ed). New York: Harcourt, Brace & World, 1965: 67–85.

Wain, John. "A Great Clerke." *C. S. Lewis at the Breakfast Table.* James T. Como (ed). New York: Macmillan, 1979: 68–76.

Politics

According to his stepson **David Gresham**, C. S. Lewis was skeptical of politicians and not interested in current events. Lewis likewise avoided making partisan commitments. During the 1930s, he told a student that he refrained from donating money "to anything that had a directly political implication." Despite his seeming indifference to political life, Lewis in fact wrote about a great variety of political topics, including crime, **war**, censorship, capital punishment, conscription, socialism, vivisection, the welfare state, and the atomic bomb.

When Lewis discussed these matters, however, his primary concern was not public policy. Political problems of the day interested him only insofar as they involved matters that endured. Looked at in this light, Lewis's habit of writing about politics and his simultaneous detachment from the political arena are perfectly understandable. Uninterested in the partisan passions of the moment, he always tried to find the permanent in the political.

Lewis's political observations are scattered throughout his writings, but the most extended expressions of his political philosophy occur in *The Abolition of Man* and *That Hideous Strength*. A variety of essays on social and political themes can also be found in the posthumously published collections *God in the Dock* and *Present Concerns*.

Lewis's political thought was dominated by three overarching themes: **natural law**, prudence, and limited government. Each found articulation in a variety of his writings.

Natural Law. Unlike some Protestants, Lewis did not believe that civic morality ultimately had to be grounded in the Bible to be legitimate. Nor did he believe that arguments about social morality were fundamentally arguments about religion. Instead, Lewis championed the time-honored belief that the fundamental maxims of civic morality are accessible to all human beings by virtue of their **reason**. This natural law cannot be escaped, said Lewis; it is the source from which all moral judgments spring. Its cardinal **virtues—justice**, honesty, good faith, magnanimity, beneficence, **mercy**—are known to be true independently of experience. According to Lewis, these basic precepts form a moral common ground that undergirds all civilized societies, a point he illustrated in his book *The Abolition of Man* by cataloguing similar ethical injunctions from some of the world's major civilizations.

Prudence. Natural law provides a moral common ground for all citizens to enter politics as equals, but Lewis did not think that it supplied easy solutions to specific political problems. Translating moral principles into public policy also requires the virtue of prudence, which Lewis aptly defined in *Mere Christianity* as "practical common sense, taking the trouble to think out what you are doing and what is likely to come of it." In Lewis's view, consequences matter, and one of the problems with idealists in politics is that they often don't comprehend this fact. They crusade for perfect health, universal employment, or everlasting peace, but they don't bother to pay any attention to the disastrous effects their policies, if enacted, would likely bring about.

Fundamental to Lewis's conception of prudence was an unflinching realism about the human condition. Human beings are both limited and sinful according to Lewis. They are limited in their knowledge about the world around them. They are limited in their ability to do anything about the knowledge they have. And in those cases where they should know what to do (and be able to do it), their judgment is often derailed by their selfishness. As a result, earthly perfection is unobtainable. Political utopians who think otherwise deceive themselves.

Another facet of Lewis's prudent realism was his emphasis on political humility. Echoing **Aristotle** in the *Ethics*, Lewis more than once explained that specific applications of moral principles "do not admit of mathematical certainty." The more specific the application of a moral principle, the greater the possibility of error—especially when fallible humans are involved. Hence, political partisans should be wary of being too dogmatic. Those who proclaim their political program with absolute certainty are flirting with despotism. This was one reason Lewis opposed the creation of an explicitly Christian political party. Such a group, he feared, would raise the political stakes too high. "The danger of mistaking our merely natural, though perhaps legitimate, enthusiasms for holy zeal, is always great," he wrote, but a Christian party would make the temptation well nigh irresistible.

Limited Government. A final political theme in Lewis's writings is the moral necessity of limited government. An unrepentant critic of what he termed the "omnicompetent" state, Lewis believed that civil society's chief task was the defense of individual liberties so that citizens could live their lives in their own way. No doubt part of Lewis's support for limited government sprang from his prudent assessment of human nature. "Aristotle said that some people were only fit to be slaves . . . ," he remarked in *The Spectator*. "I reject slavery because I see no men fit to be masters."

However, Lewis also had a positive reason for defending limited government. Good societies depend upon virtuous individuals, and he knew that individual virtue could never be produced by government decree. Government can make people behave, but ultimately it cannot make them good. That is because virtue presupposes free choice. The society where all acts are compelled is a society where no act can be virtuous. Lewis acknowledged in *Mere Christianity* that the freedom required for virtue to flourish also "makes evil possible." But this is the price that must be paid for "any love or goodness or joy worth having."

According to Lewis, the problem with the modern welfare state is that it operates on premises antithetical to human freedom and the private institutions that help secure it. Lewis summarized why in an essay he wrote for *The Observer* in 1958: "The modern State exists not to protect our rights, but to do us good or make us good—anyway, to do something to us or to make us something. Hence the new name 'leaders' for those who

were once 'rulers.' We are less their subjects than their wards, pupils, or domestic animals. There is nothing left of which we can say to them, 'Mind your own business.' Our whole lives are their business."

Lewis said he understood the lure of the omnicompetent state. Confronted by the sheer volume and extent of human misery, people naturally look for an earthly savior; and many do not care what they will have to give up to get one. The problem is that an earthly savior can never really meet our expectations. Only God can do that, which was Lewis's point.

Though he lived in an era different from our own, Lewis's observations about political life remain acutely pertinent. His defense of natural law speaks to a generation yearning for a stable basis for public morality. His advocacy of prudence is a warning to ideologues from both the right and the left to lower their extravagant political claims. And his critique of the welfare state supplies the moral context of the renewed debate in America and elsewhere over the nature and extent of government. By focusing on the permanent in the political, Lewis's writings on politics continue to resonate with prophetic power for our own generation.

John G. West, Jr.

Also See: Communism and Fascism, Democracy, Sin

Bibliography

Aeschliman, Michael D. *The Restitution of Man: C. S. Lewis and the Case Against Scientism.* Grand Rapids, MI: Eerdmans, 1983.

Belloc, Hilaire. *The Servile State.* With an introduction by Robert Nisbet. Indianapolis: LibertyClassics, 1977.

Burton, John David. "G. K. Chesterton and C. S. Lewis: The Men and Their Times." *G. K. Chesterton and C. S. Lewis: The Riddle of Joy.* Michael H. Macdonald and Andrew A. Tadie (eds). Grand Rapids, MI: Eerdmans, 1989: 160–72.

Lewis, C. S. *God in the Dock: Essays on Theology and Ethics*; *Present Concerns*

Meilaender, Gilbert. *The Taste for the Other: The Social and Ethical Thought of C. S. Lewis.* Grand Rapids, MI: Eerdmans, 1978.

West, John G., Jr. "Finding the Permanent in the Political: C. S. Lewis as a Political Thinker." *Permanent Things.* Andrew Tadie and Michael Macdonald (eds). Grand Rapids, MI: Eerdmans, 1996.

_____. "Politics from the Shadowlands: C. S. Lewis on Earthly Government." *Policy Review.* (Spring 1994): 68–70.

Portrait of W. B. Yeats (Letter)

The Listener. LIV (15 September 1955): 427.

Based on his two meetings with **W. B. Yeats**, Lewis recounted his appreciation for Yeats's distinctly Irish ability to combine a sincere belief in **magic** with a sense of mischief. Declaring Yeats one of the "funniest *raconteurs*" he had ever heard, Lewis was writing in response to Mr. St. John Ervine's statement (*The Listener*, 1 September 1955) that Yeats had no sense of humor.

Marjorie L. Mead
The Marion E. Wade Center

Beatrix Potter (1866–1943)

Beatrix Potter was the eldest child of Helen and Rupert Potter, whose families had acquired their wealth running Manchester textile mills. The Potters lived in London, spending the summer months on holiday in the south of Scotland and in the English Lake District. The attitude of the Potters toward their two children was indifferent at best. Beatrix Potter spent her childhood and a considerable portion of young adulthood in near isolation; rather than sending her out to school, her parents brought teachers in. Fortunately, she learned as a child to keep herself busy by observing and sketching flora and fauna during the extended summer holidays and perfecting her drawing and painting skills the rest of the year.

In her late twenties, Potter began the Peter Rabbit stories as a series of short narratives, accompanied by drawings, for the sick child of her former governess. These were followed by others, including the beginnings of what later became *Benjamin Bunny, Squirrel Nutkin,* and *Jeremy Fisher*. Several years later she looked without success for a publisher and finally decided to publish *Peter Rabbit* herself with watercolor illustrations. This effort was successful enough to attract the attention of Frederick Warne and Company, which published Potter's books the next ten years. Before her death in 1943 Potter published thirty-one children's stories, and another six books were published posthumously.

Potter's treatment of her animal characters is affectionate but unsentimental. Her rabbits can be both timid and improvident, her squirrels chattery and impulsive, her badgers and foxes unambiguously carnivorous. The realism of her presentation of the relations between animals, and between animals and humans, give her books credibility for the juvenile audience. Her texts employ "fine words" occasionally because she felt children enjoyed some grown-up language and could gather the meaning of unfamiliar words from context. The books are full of understated humor, and various levels of meaning keep the stories interesting for older readers.

C. S. Lewis described the effect upon his early childhood **imagination** of the third Potter book, *Squirrel Nutkin* (1903), in the first chapter of his autobiography, *Surprised by Joy*. It "troubled" him with what he describes as "the Idea of Autumn," experienced as an intense though ungratified desire quite different from ordinary pleasure. He returned repeatedly to the book to reawaken that desire.

Lyle Smith
Biola University

Also See: Fairy Tales, Fantasy, Joy

Bibliography

Lewis, C. S. *Surprised by Joy*
MacDonald, Ruth K. *Beatrix Potter*. Boston: Twayne Publishers, 1986.

Prayer

It is quite possible that C. S. Lewis wrote more about prayer than any other subject. In his writings, he sought to share his understandings of prayer with his readers and to respond to their questions about and difficulties with prayer. Lewis was most interested in the nature of petitionary prayer (prayer for others) and the effectiveness ("efficacy") of prayer (how prayer actually works). In many of his writings about prayer, Lewis wrote about his own struggles, doubts, questions, and affirmations concerning these features of prayer.

Lewis's views, ideas, and advice about prayer are found in *Letters to Malcolm: Chiefly on Prayer,* in four essays later published in collections, and in his letters and poems. *Miracles, The Screwtape Letters,* and several volumes of his Narnian stories contain significant essays and references to prayer, and Lewis mentioned it in most of his other religious works, including the first two space novels (*Out of the Silent Planet, Perelandra*), where Ransom says his daily prayers and prays over meals.

Letter 4 of *The Screwtape Letters* contains a warning from Screwtape to Wormwood to "keep the patient from the serious intention of praying altogether." Screwtape instructs Wormwood about the nature and purposes of prayer, and gives advice on how to distract "the patient" from authentic prayer, including placing undue emphasis on feelings rather than God. In Letter 8, Wormwood is told that God is pleased most with prayer in "dry" periods, and in Letter 27, Screwtape orders him to lure the young couple into the "false spirituality" of always substituting "praise and communion with God" for "commonplace" petitionary prayers. Wormwood is also to remind them that all prayers for others are not answered immediately; the ones that are answered are evidence of the laws of nature ("physical causes") and "would have been answered anyway."

"On Special Providences" in *Miracles,* is an essay dealing with the providence of God and how prayer does or does not influence his loving guidance and care. Here, Lewis asked his reader to believe that all prayers are heard by God and that all are answered, whether "grantings or refusals." When an event prayed for occurs, a person's prayers contributed to it; when it does not occur, the prayers have been "considered and refused" for the good of the person and for the whole universe.

The **Chronicles of Narnia** contain several references to prayer, both explicit and implicit. In *The Voyage of the "Dawn Treader"* Lucy's prayer for deliverance from the darkness "in the land where nightmares come true" is answered by Aslan's coming in the form of an albatross to lead the ship to safety. In *The Silver Chair* Eustace Scrubb and Jill Pole call on Aslan (using simple and obedient words, two of Lewis's requirements for authentic prayer), to help them journey into Narnia. And in *The Magician's Nephew* Digory prays for his seriously ill mother to be healed, much like Lewis did for his own mother.

Poems (1964) contains several short poems that deal with prayer: **"Prayer"**; **"The Apologist's Evening Prayer"**; **"Footnote to All Prayers"** (originally in *The Pilgrim's Regress,* 1933); and **"After Prayers, Lie Cold."** The latter was probably written after and in response to **Joy Gresham Lewis**'s death.

All of Lewis's collections of letters contain references to petitionary prayer, his own personal prayer life, and advice and thoughts about prayer. These are *Letters of C. S. Lewis* (1966, revised and enlarged edition 1993); *Letters to an American Lady* (1967); *They Stand Together* (1979); *Letters to Children* (1985); and *Letters: C. S. Lewis and Don Giovanni Calabria* (1985). **Sheldon Vanauken**'s *A Severe Mercy* (1977), contains eighteen short letters by Lewis, several that mention his prayerful concern for the salvation of two young American students at Oxford in the 1950s.

God in the Dock (1970) contains two essays by Lewis with significant sections on prayer. In **"Work and Prayer"** and **"Scraps,"** Lewis discussed the differences between prayer as communion with God and as "asking for things to happen" and "praying for particular things." **"Petitionary Prayer: A Problem Without an Answer"** was a paper Lewis read to an Oxford ministers' society in 1953, later reprinted in *Christian Reflections* (1967). Here Lewis wrestled with the fact that for him, the **Bible** seemed to instruct us to pray in

two contradictory ways: the way of total submission to God's will (the way Lewis usually prayed), and the way of "sure expectation"—God grants prayers prayed for in faith. In **"The Efficacy of Prayer"** Lewis wrote about his own questions about the effectiveness of prayer, and emphasized the primacy of one's relationship to God in prayer.

In *Letters to Malcolm* Lewis pretended to be comparing notes and ideas with a friend, largely about the nature, practice, and problems of prayer. In this work, Lewis shared several of his personal attitudes about prayer, including praying for the dead, praying without words, confessional prayer, posture in prayer, how prayer is often tedious and "unwelcome," the best times for prayer, and others. He also discussed corporate and liturgical prayer, the Lord's Prayer, Holy Communion, Purgatory, mysticism, and reserved many discussions for petitionary prayer. Lewis showed his sense of humor and balanced approach to the Christian life when he wrote about combining petitionary prayer with real action on the behalf of others: "I am often, I believe, praying for others when I should be doing things for them. It's so much easier to pray for a bore than it is to go and see him."

Lewis's own prayer life was ordered and followed a basic routine. During term, he would pray early in the morning before breakfast, attend matins (a time of daily prayer) at his college chapel, and most afternoons would reserve time for prayer and meditation as he walked the college grounds and gardens. He would pray on a train while traveling, or walk and pray behind the train station while waiting. During his private devotional times Lewis would often pray the Lord's Prayer in combination with his own words and specific requests to God, which he called "festoons." Festoons were his private "grace notes" that he "liked to hang on the basic petitions" of the prayer of our Lord. It has also been well documented that Lewis adopted the attitude of "praying without ceasing," or "having an attitude of prayer." Not only would he pray as a daily routine at specific times of the day, he would often be found by his friends in prayer at any time of the day or night. For his petitionary prayers Lewis kept a list with specific names and requests and prayed for these regularly.

In *Letters to Malcolm* Lewis advised his readers not to pray at bedtime because sleepiness would make concentration too difficult and cautioned against praying in church because of distractions. He also advised that prayer was first an attitude of reverence and worship toward God that was grounded in confession: "By confessing our sins and 'making known' our requests, we assume the high rank of persons before Him. And He ... becomes a Person to us." For Lewis, petitions were only a part of prayer; confession, penitence, adoration, and the enjoyment of God were its "bread and wine."

Lewis wrote often that complete dependence on and honesty with God was essential in prayer. A person should not worry about feelings or that their prayers are "appropriate." He wrote that "I fancy that we may sometimes be deterred from small prayers by a sense of our own dignity rather than God's." Another important element of Lewis's advice about prayer was his emphasis on balance in petitionary prayer. Just as he prayed regularly for others, he often asked his friends to pray for him because he knew the difficulties of a disciplined prayer life. In a letter to Sister Penelope Lawson he wrote, "I specially need your prayers because I am (like the pilgrim in Bunyan) traveling across 'a plain called Ease'. Everything without and many things within are marvelously well at present."

Perry C. Bramlett
C. S. Lewis for the Local Church

Bibliography

Arlton, Beverly. "Lewis on Prayer." *CSL: The Bulletin of the New York C. S. Lewis Society.* 10 no. 6 (April 1979): 1–6.

Bramlett, Perry C. *C. S. Lewis: Life at the Center.* Macon, GA: Smyth and Helwys, 1996.

Glaspey, Terry W. *Not a Tame Lion: The Spiritual Legacy of C. S. Lewis.* Elkton, MD: Highland Books, 1996.

Harries, Richard. *C. S. Lewis: The Man and his God.* Wilton, CT: Morehouse, 1987.

LeFevre, Perry. *Understandings of Prayer.* Philadelphia: Westminster, 1981.

Lindskoog, Kathryn. *C. S. Lewis: Mere Christian* (4th ed.). Chicago: Cornerstone, 1997.

Macdonald, Michael H. and Andrew A. Tadie. (eds.). *G. K. Chesterton and C. S. Lewis: The Riddle of Joy.* Grand Rapids, MI: Eerdmans, 1989.

Patterson, Nancy-Lou. "Trained Habit: The Spirituality of C. S. Lewis." *The Canadian C. S. Lewis Journal.* 87 (Spring 1995): 37–53.

Sayer, George. *Jack: A Life of C. S. Lewis.* Wheaton, IL: Crossway, 1994.

White, William Luther. *The Image of Man in C. S. Lewis.* Nashville: Abingdon, 1969.

Preacher

C. S. Lewis was often in demand as a preacher after he became a household name in England in the 1940s with the publication of *The Screwtape Letters* and other popular religious works. He usually preached in the university churches and chapels of **Oxford** and **Cam-**bridge, occasionally in London and other cities, and during World War II preached to the troops on weekends while attached to the Chaplain's Department of the Royal Air Force. The theologian and hymnologist Eric Routley praised Lewis's personal attentiveness and serious concentration on his listeners, and his friend and fellow **Inkling Gervase Mathew** said that Lewis "forged a personal link with those that heard him." Others noted Lewis's use of vivid **imagery**, timely **metaphors**, and his ability to speak clearly in patterns of ordinary conversation, while identifying himself with those who heard him. It has been written that Lewis, B. L. Manning, and William Temple were the only preachers who could consistently "fill the pews to overflowing" when they preached in Oxford in the middle of this century.

Seven of Lewis's sermons in worship settings are in print. *The Weight of Glory and Other Addresses* (revised and expanded edition 1980, first published as *Transposition and Other Addresses*) contains four of his Oxford/Cambridge sermons. The sermons in this book are **"Learning in War-Time"** (1939), **"The Weight of Glory"** (1941), **"Transposition"** (1944), and **"A Slip of the Tongue"** (1956). Three of his sermons were preached to churches at London and Northampton and published in *Undeceptions* (1971), later *God in the Dock* (1971). These sermons are **"Miracles"** (1942), **"The Grand Miracle"** (1945), and **"Miserable Offenders"** (1946).

"The Weight of Glory" is Lewis's most famous sermon and has been widely read and anthologized. Its beauty, friendly scholarship, and effortless delivery made it memorable for many who heard it, according to witnesses. And although Lewis's other sermons were not popular preaching, their theological insights, unparalleled brilliance of rhetoric and imagery, and pastoral concern make them excellent models for today's preachers who want to go "farther up and farther in" with their sermons.

Perry C. Bramlett
C. S. Lewis for the Local Church

Also See: Apologetics, Language/Rhetoric, RAF Talks, Religion, Theology

Bibliography

Bramlett, Perry C. "The Weight of Glory: C. S. Lewis as Preacher." *Preaching.* 10 no. 2 (September-October 1994): 45–48.

Davies, Horton. *Varieties of English Preaching 1900–1960.* Englewood Cliffs, NJ: Prentice-Hall, 1963.

Keefe, Carolyn (ed). *C. S. Lewis: Speaker & Teacher.* Grand Rapids, MI: Zondervan, 1971.

A Preface to Paradise Lost

London: Oxford University Press, 1942.

C. S. Lewis dedicated this set of essays not to his Welsh hosts at the University of North Wales, who provided him the opportunity to reconsider **John Milton** in three lectures delivered there, but to his friend and mentor, **Charles Williams**, who in 1940 contributed a short preface to the World Classics edition of the *Poetical Works of Milton*. Williams caused Lewis to rethink and reread *Paradise Lost* and indeed change some of his earlier, perhaps hasty opinions. Williams also recommended the recovery of a "true critical tradition" after "more than a hundred years of laborious misunderstanding."

Paradise Lost is an **epic** poem in a venerated tradition and as such must be examined and understood. However, the taste for this sort of **poetry** has largely departed from English consciousness and perhaps had by Milton's time. Thus, Lewis began with an examination of forms, but first he took another swipe at **T. S. Eliot** for proclaiming that poets are the only true judges of poetry. As this is mostly a digression, we may safely set it aside and return to Lewis's main argument, which is to distinguish between primary and secondary epics. The first sort belongs to the heroic age and was mainly composed for oral presentation. Lewis may have been looking beyond his own time (he often did), but a lot of scholarship has been done since he died in 1963. He might have approached matters differently had he known, for example, Albin Lesky's monumental *History of Greek Literature*.

After several short chapters on epic technique and subject matter, necessary to bring the secondary epic into proper perspective, Lewis turned to Virgil, who in Lewis's view described the shift of civilization from east to west. "With Virgil European poetry grows up," wrote Lewis. And also the reader: "No man who has once read it (*The Aeneid*) with full perception remains an adolescent." Moreover, the explicit religious subject of any future epic poetry has been "dictated by Virgil" according to Lewis. There follow chapters on style and on the defense of style.

The title of chapter 9 is "The Doctrine of the Unchanging Human Heart." This is a tenet, Lewis said, in which he once believed but has now abandoned. The general idea is not especially complicated; that is, if we strip away from a work of art all that is superficial and timely, then we can discover its permanent value to the history of civilization. If we apply this idea to Milton,

we can see where it will take us. Lewis started with Professor Saurat's invitation to "Study what there is of lasting originality in Milton's thought and especially to disentangle from theological rubbish the permanent and human interest." Lewis saw through this nonsense immediately. "Milton's thought," he said, "when purged of its **theology** does not exist." Lewis was surely right; but the purpose of this chapter was not to prove his conclusion but rather to explain what Milton's theology really was. The following chapter (10) continues by pointing out that Milton's theology was basically that of Saint **Augustine** as seen in *The City of God*. That is: (1) **God** created all things good. (2) What we call bad arises from good things perverted. (3) It follows that God can exist without evil, as in Milton's Paradise, but evil cannot exist without good. (4) Though God made all creatures good, he foreknows that some will become bad. (This remains to this day a major crux.) (5) Had there been no **Fall**, the human race after reaching the appropriate numbers would have been promoted to **angels**. (6) **Satan** attacked **Eve** because in the scheme of things (the doctrine of degree; Lewis called it **hierarchy**) she was less intelligent and more credulous than Adam. (No modern women would agree. There are ways to get around this problem, but Milton did not need to consider them.) At this point in the chapter, Lewis continued his analysis by looking at specific characters.

Lewis pointed out that according to both Augustine and Milton, Adam was never deceived by Eve; he never believed what she told him. The Fall consisted of disobedience. The point of God's forbidding the apple had no special significance. It was at last necessary to instill obedience into rational man, and perhaps God picked Eve because Adam was a harder nut to crack and Eve was easier. But the Fall arose not from Eve's innate weakness but from her **pride** (as had Satan's fall). It was punished by man's loss of authority over his inferiors. Man became enslaved to his passions and to his body. Augustine had already pointed out that sexuality is not under direct control of the will; hence it is good logic for Milton to follow the Fall immediately with a scene of sexual indulgence. This is logical, but Lewis believed Milton may have made a mistake here; the passage is blurred by making persons too voluptuous and the passage too poetical.

In the following chapter (11), Lewis described his doctrine of hierarchy (or we might call it the Great Chain of Being). The conception removed from *Paradise Lost* seems easy enough, though plenty of critics seem to have forgotten it according to Lewis. Even

Samuel Johnson thought that Milton made men "only for rebellion and women only for obedience." The idea is clearer in **Shakespeare**, Lewis thought; not only in the speech of Ulysses in *Troilus and Cressida*, but in *Taming of the Shrew* and *Macbeth*.

In chapter 12, also on Milton's theology, Lewis began anew with Professor Saurat, dividing Milton's doctrines into four categories: (1) Doctrines that occur in *Paradise Lost* and are commonplaces of Christian theology; (2) those that are heretical but do not occur in Milton; (3) those that are heretical and occur in Milton's *De Doctrina* but not in *Paradise Lost*; (4) those that are possibly heretical and occur in *Paradise Lost*. The main problem here arises with respect to **sex**. No doubt, Lewis wrote, Milton thought that of sexual **love** as an **analogy** for Divine Love. Of those doctrines that are heretical and found in *De Doctrina* but not in *Paradise Lost*, Lewis found only one: Arianism. Milton did not accept (at least in *De Doctrina*) the doctrine of the **Trinity**. Chapters 10–12 are among Lewis's longest and most technical, but they are also necessary. Only after them could Lewis turn with confidence to the poem itself.

He began his direct analysis of the poem in chapter 13 with Satan. Adopting a fairly typical Christian interpretation, Lewis passed over **Dryden**'s remark that Satan was Milton's hero without further comment. The standard version presented here is that Satan is a liar (indisputable) and in the long run "an ass"—from hero to politician to voyeur to toad to snake—and his followers (covered in chapter 14) are no better. This is the easy interpretation to accept, but there have been a host of critics in disagreement. Some of the most important came after Lewis. Empson's *Milton's God*, for example, had not been written when Lewis died. It therefore would be a mistake to accord Lewis the final word on this point; in criticism there is no final word. Still, Lewis's *Preface* remains the best introduction available.

In chapter 15 ("The Mistake About Milton's Angels") Lewis needed to challenge Johnson's view that the corporeality of Milton's angels was a "poetic fiction." He traced this view back to **Thomas Aquinas** who believed that the angels were purely immaterial. "This is the view Milton goes out of his way to controvert." When the Archangel dined with Adam, he did not simply seem to eat; he ate. Lewis traced this opinion to Platonic theology. In Milton's angelology this becomes more important than just food. It stands with Milton's view of sexuality. The concept is difficult, and probably we shall never know just exactly what Milton thought. He stands on the crux of desire for total union,

like **Donne**'s true lovers. But angels do not die; hence they have no need to breed. Moreover the angels are all traditionally masculine. This leads to further problems that Lewis could not solve but also invited him to turn to Adam and Eve.

Lewis noted in chapter 16 that there seemed to have been an erroneous opinion that Adam and Eve were immature children in the garden. Milton's Adam and Eve do not fit the stereotype. In Milton, Adam was the wisest, smartest man on earth (if the only one). Indeed, Adam was a genuine intellectual. So was Eve, though slightly less endowed; after all she did come second. Milton's imaginative solution is never quite satisfactory, but Lewis thought that Milton appropriately grasped the challenge of portraying the majesty of Adam and Eve in their unfallen state. (Lewis himself would try his hand at portraying unfallen majesty in his novel **Perelandra**, published a year after this book.)

Chapter 17, titled "Unfallen Sexuality," discusses sex in Paradise, a subject Milton might have well omitted and probably should have. Lewis could not decide whether Milton was wise to include it or not. This chapter is preliminary to the next one on "The Fall" itself and perhaps prepares for it. In that chapter, Lewis observed that Milton's Adam "fell by uxoriousness." But, Lewis added, "If conjugal love were the highest value in Adam's world, then . . . his resolve would have been the correct one." Lewis did love to speculate: What if Adam had scolded Eve for her disobedience and begged God to forgive her? But that is not what happened. Instead he compliments Eve on her palate. This is the point where Adam and Eve become human. Sex enters in with its tang of evil. Eve becomes a sex object, a thing, worse, "all her dreams of Godhead have come to that."

We return where we began in Lewis's Conclusion. Essentially it is that one must love *Paradise Lost* for what it is, or one despises it. What Lewis did is show us more clearly than anyone before him (and perhaps after) what the poem is. For example, some critics are disposed to consider that Milton's God destroys *Paradise Lost* as a religious poem. But is it that at all? Surely not in the same sense that **Dante**'s *Divine Comedy* is. It is a poem that depicts "the objective pattern of things, the attempted destruction of that matter by rebellious self love, and the triumphant absorption of that rebellion into a yet more complex pattern." It is a "cosmic story—the ultimate plot in which all other stories are episodes." Lewis could be more specific: "Dr. [F. R.] Leavis does not differ from me about the properties of Milton's epic verse." These divergent critics differ "not about the nature of Milton's poetry, but about the nature of man." At this point we suspect Lewis skirted a little too closely to an intentional fallacy (or perhaps Christian bias). The offshoot of all this is a complex and charming volume, both delightful and extremely well written. *Paradise Lost* is another matter. It has attracted too much attention from too many critics to be in any danger. So long as the language lasts and the great tradition of European literature, *Paradise Lost* will too.

It was once a schoolboy contention that after Milton the epic had to die. Milton had had the final word. Who would ever do it again? I have a suspicion Lewis might have subscribed to this view. *The Preface* shows us what the poem really is better than anyone else had done— with a few mistakes perhaps and even a few untested judgments. How different it is from Professor Broadbent's Introduction to the Cambridge edition of *Paradise Lost* (1972), which is more or less a handbook for beginning graduate students. It has all the apparatus a student could ever need, and Lewis is only barely mentioned in the bibliographical section. How can one read *Paradise Lost* without Lewis? I wonder.

Robert O. Evans

Bibliography

Hannay, Margaret P. "Rehabilitations: C. S. Lewis' Contribution to the Understanding of Spenser and Milton." *DAI.* 37 (1977).

Present Concerns

Hooper, Walter (ed). London: Collins, 1986. First US edition, San Diego: Harcourt Brace Jovanovich, 1987.

See separate entries on the following:

"After Priggery—What?"
"Blimpophobia"
"Democratic Education"
"A Dream"
"The Empty Universe"
"Equality"
"Hedonics"
"Interim Report"
"Is English Doomed?"
"Is History Bunk?"
"Modern Man and his Categories of Thought"
"My First School"
"The Necessity of Chivalry"
"On Living in an Atomic Age"
"Private Bates"
"Prudery and Philology"
"Sex in Literature"
"Talking about Bicycles"
"Three Kinds of Men"

Pride

Pride is the all-consuming desire to consider oneself as better than others, and C. S. Lewis followed traditional Christian **theology** in counting it as the most damning of all sins. In *Mere Christianity*, he wrote that "Pride leads to every other vice: it is the complete anti-God state of mind." According to Lewis, pride is closely connected with power because "there is nothing that makes a man feel so superior to others as being able to move them about like toy soldiers." Pride poisons every virtue and feeds every vice. It prevents **friendship** with other human beings because the proud person loves only himself. Above all, pride prevents fellowship with **God**, for "as long as you are looking down, you cannot see something that is above you."

Pride surfaces as a theme in several of Lewis's non-fiction essays, perhaps most significantly in **"The Inner Ring,"** which describes man's natural craving for the power and prestige of the "in" group. Pride also appears time and again in Lewis's fiction. In *The Screwtape Letters*, Uncle Screwtape reminds his nephew Wormwood that "Spiritual Pride" is "the strongest and most beautiful of the vices." In *Till We Have Faces*, Queen Orual's prideful possessiveness brings disaster upon her sister Psyche. In *Out of the Silent Planet*, Weston and Devine display their prideful contempt for the creatures of the planet Malacandra, finding it impossible to believe that intelligent creatures exist other than human beings. In *That Hideous Strength*, Jane Studdock bristles at Ransom's old-fashioned idea that she is subject to the headship of her husband Mark. Her husband, meanwhile, is consumed by his quest for the "inner ring." In all three of his space novels, Lewis drew a connection between pride and modern **science**. Lewis viewed modern social science as largely a quest for power over man; hence, it is little surprise that the most arrogant characters in these novels (like Dr. Weston) are those who wish to play God and use the tools of science to remake society in their own image.

Pride likewise appears in Lewis's stories for children. In *The Lion, the Witch and the Wardrobe*, Edmund turns traitor because of his desire to be more important than his brother and sisters. In *The Voyage of the "Dawn Treader,"* Eustace makes everyone else miserable because all he can think about is himself. Later in the story, the Dufflepuds persist in their foolishness because they refuse to humbly obey the instructions given by the Magician for their own good. In *The Magician's Nephew*, Uncle Andrew and Queen Jadis both operate on the principle that they are exempt from the rules that apply to ordinary people.

The eternal consequences of pride are brought out in Lewis's writings on **heaven**. In *The Great Divorce*, he described how a busload of residents from **hell** are allowed to visit Heaven for a day. But the visitors do not want to stay, because they must forget about themselves to do so. Lewis's ultimate point about pride was that only the humble could be saved by God, a message that lies at the heart of the gospel.

John G. West, Jr.

Also See: Good and Evil, Virtue

Bibliography
Lewis, C. S. "The Inner Ring"; *Mere Christianity*

"Priestesses in the Church"

See entry on "Notes on the Way" (14 August 1948)

Prince Caspian: The Return to Narnia

London: Geoffrey Bles, 1951. First US edition, New York: Macmillan, 1951.

Prince Caspian is the second **Chronicle of Narnia** Lewis completed. The book introduces the great Narnian characters, Trumpkin, Caspian, and Reepicheep. Its subtitle, "The Return to Narnia," provides the most important clue as to Lewis's intended meanings for the work (no other Chronicle has a subtitle). In a letter to a girl named Anne on March 5, 1961, Lewis wrote that *Prince Caspian* is about the "restoration of the true **religion** after corruption." In some sense the book is a rough draft of *The Last Battle* for both books ask the questions: "Is the Christian story real now or only something that may have happened long ago?" and "What does the effect of the passage of time have on the reality and experience of **faith**?" Prince Caspian also echoes a major theme in both *The Last Battle* and *The Magician's Nephew*: the uses and misuse of **nature** and people. The way *Prince Caspian* handles this theme is akin to **J. R. R. Tolkien**'s

chapter "The Scouring of the Shire" in Book Six of *The Lord of the Rings*.

After writing **The Lion, the Witch and the Wardrobe**, Lewis both started and abandoned writing the story of Narnia's beginnings (now preserved in "The Lefay Fragment" published in *Past Watchful Dragons*) and also seems to have "seen" many of the mental pictures that inspired what Evan Gibson called the "The Caspian Triad" of *Prince Caspian*, **The Voyage of the "Dawn Treader"** and **The Silver Chair**: There is a record of Lewis's plot points for the triad which include human tyranny in Narnia, its history told by a dwarf, a voyage by ship to "[v]arious islands (of Odyssey and Saint Brendan)," children captured by enemies, a magic picture, and one of the Narnians admitted into our world. Once Lewis sorted these ideas out, he was able to complete *Prince Caspian* in something over six months.

The story of *Prince Caspian* takes place a year of earth-time after the events of *The Lion, the Witch and the Wardrobe*; Peter, Susan, Edmund, and Lucy (ages fourteen, thirteen, eleven, and nine, respectively), on their way to school after the summer holidays, find themselves called back to Narnia's capitol of Cair Paravel, now unrecognizable after the passage of one thousand Narnian years. The children rediscover the treasure room of the castle and retrieve their gifts from Father Christmas (all but Susan's magic horn, "lost" on their last day in *The Lion, the Witch and the Wardrobe*— Edmund had no gift because he had been a traitor in the

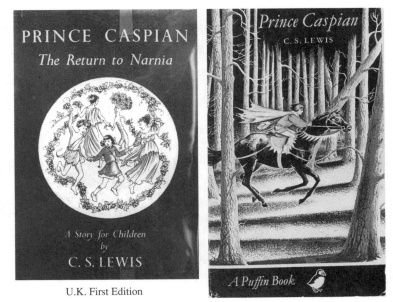

U.K. First Edition

first book). The children then rescue the dwarf Trumpkin who wished to kill him and the dwarf embarks on a three-chapter-long story-within-a-story, which brings the children up-to-date with respect to the long stretch of Narnian history since they left. Trumpkin tells how the thirteen-year-old Prince Caspian, deprived of his right to Narnia by his wicked uncle Miraz, escaped assassination and discovered that he came from a race of invaders who have usurped from Aslan and Old Narnia. The children, learning that they have been summoned by the white magic of Susan's horn (blown by Caspian on behalf of the besieged Narnians), set out to join the fight. On their way Lucy experiences mystical foreshadowings of a reliberated, dancing Narnia; but when she sees Aslan and wants to follow, the other children (except for Edmund) refuse to believe her and insist on going another route. As a result, they ran into a near ambush and must make a full retreat. Lucy then encounters Aslan who empowers her to summon the others to follow him; and the other children each see him successively according to their faith. Since Narnia needs healing along the lines of **Plato**'s distinction between the irascible and the concupiscible, the plot here divides into two strands: Aslan sends the boys and Trumpkin to war alongside Caspian while he and the girls liberate Narnia through the ecstatic. The warriors arrive just as the besieged Narnians are arguing between two courses of action: waiting upon Aslan and his help (the white **magic** of **faith**) or calling up the help of evil powers (the black magic of the practical). In the ensuing struggle the servants of the powers of darkness are slain. King Peter takes command and engages the usurper Miraz in single combat. Meanwhile, Aslan and the girls take part in the Dionysian romps that destroy the bridge imprisoning the river, set teachers and students free from schools, and heal Caspian's old nurse. The two groups meet for the conferral of the kingship on the humble Caspian, the healing of Reepicheep's tail (and **pride**), a victory celebration, and the final resolution of the Telmarine question. Aslan makes a door in the air through which the Telmarines who wished can return to the earth. The children return to England through the same door. Edmund and Lucy are to come back to Narnia again (Lewis has already resolved to write what becomes *The Voyage of the "Dawn Treader"*) but Peter and Susan learn that this will be their last visit to the temporal Narnia. In *The Last Battle*, Peter comes to the eternal Narnia, but whether Susan ever gets there is left unresolved by Lewis.

Prince Caspian allowed Lewis to explain to his adult and child readers some of the psychological problems involved in believing, themes he addressed in works as diverse as *The Screwtape Letters* and the essays, **"Religion: Reality or Substitute?"** and **"Obstinacy in Belief."** Through Aslan's relationship with Lucy, Lewis also revealed some of the fruits of his own spirituality and several of these principles are worth highlighting. First, in contrast to physical growth in which the things we experienced as children look smaller to us as adults, God is bigger (more transcendent) the older we grow. Second, there is no **reality** in the might-have-been, so we should not give it a second thought. Third, obedience and doing one's duty are paramount (here Lewis showed the influence of **George MacDonald**). Fourth, by concentrating on God we forget both ourselves and the injuries others give us. Fifth, in Aslan's presence one can enjoy rather than be terrified by the ecstatic (as Lewis said in *The Four Loves*, "When God arrives and only then the half-gods can remain"). Finally, the deepest communion between humans and God is not only possible, it is delightful and empowering (Aslan calls Lucy by name and rolls over on his side in order to allow her to repose between his front legs, and Lucy is given courage by the fragrance of his mane).

As Doris Myers points out, *Prince Caspian* portrays the mood and tone of the spiritual stage of the confirmation-age child (early adolescence): "There is a definite impression that the age level is different from that of Wardrobe, largely due to the emphasis on independent action. When the children enter Narnia in the first book, someone—Mr. Tumnus, the White Witch, the beavers—takes charge of them. Edmund's naughtiness involves going off on his own. But in *Caspian* the children come into Narnia alone. Their first task is to survive, and when Trumpkin appears, he is a companion rather than a caretaker. And Lucy's virtue involves following Aslan on her own."

Paul F. Ford
St. John's Seminary

Bibliography

Ford, Paul F. *Companion to Narnia*. San Francisco: HarperSanFrancisco, 1994.

Gibson, Evan K. *C. S. Lewis: Spinner of Tales: A Guide to His Fiction*. Washington, DC: Christian College Consortium, 1980.

Green, Roger Lancelyn, and Walter Hooper. *C. S. Lewis: A Biography*. London: Collins, and New York: Macmillan, 1974.

Hooper, Walter. *C. S. Lewis: A Companion and Guide*. San Francisco: HarperSanFrancisco, 1996.

_____. *Past Watchful Dragons: The Narnian Chronicles of C. S. Lewis.* New York: Macmillan, 1979.

Lewis, C. S. *C. S. Lewis: Letters to Children*; "It All Began with a Picture"; "On Three Ways of Writing for Children"; "Sometimes Fairy Stories May Say Best What's to be Said."

Myers, Doris. "The Compleat Anglican: Spiritual Style in the Chronicles of Narnia." *Anglican Theological Review.* LXVI no. 2 (April 1984): 148–60.

Schakel, Peter. *Reading with the Heart: The Way into Narnia.* Grand Rapids, MI: Eerdmans, 1979.

Yandell, Steven. "The Trans-cosmic Journeys in the Chronicles of Narnia." *Mythlore* 12 no. 1 (August 1985): 9–23.

Principles and Problems of Biblical Translation (Book Review)

Medium Aevum. XXVI no. 2 (1957): 115–17.

This book addresses the difficulties of reconciling two schools of thought about Bible translation. Represented by Erasmus and Luther, they are the "philological" and the "inspirational" principles. Lewis thought that although the book contained examples of strange and imperfect English, it was still useful. The index apparently needed revision, however.

Anne Gardner

Bibliography

Lewis, C. S. "Modern Translations of the Bible"
Schwartz, W. *Principles and Problems of Biblical Translation.*

"Private Bates"

The Spectator. CLXXIII (29 December 1944): 596. Reprinted in *Present Concerns.*

This remarkable essay is set on the scene in **Shakespeare**'s *Henry V*, just before Agincourt, when the King, disguised, talks with Bates, Williams, and Court. It is remarkable because it reflects the firsthand knowledge that Lewis had of soldiering in France. It is authentic. His conclusion is that the morale of soldiers is much as it has always been; what is new is that "the more educated (and credulous) classes" now "see close up what the great mass of the people in this country are, and always have been, like." The British soldiers of World War II dismissed all the stories of atrocities as "propaganda" and took it for granted that their leaders, in lying, were doing what was expected of them. But they were not indignant—which is disheartening. The masses are not being led. Rather "the only people who are really the dupes of their favorite newspapers are the *intelligentsia*. It is they who read leading articles: the poor read the sporting news, which is mostly true. Whether

you like this situation or not depends on your views. It is certainly hard if you are a Planner." It is the millions like Private Bates who make "it most improbable that anything either very bad or very good will ever happen in this island (England)."

John Bremer

Also See: Good and Evil, Human Nature, War

The Problem of Pain

London: The Centenary Press, 1940. First US edition, New York: Macmillan, 1943.

Though published in 1940, *The Problem of Pain* anticipates much recent work in the philosophy of religion and may be Lewis's most successful apologetic work. It anticipates, for example, John Hick's "soul making" theodicy as well as several important moves in Alvin Plantinga's *Free Will Defense*. But perhaps because it is aimed at a lay audience, few Christian philosophers—**Austin Farrer** and Richard Purtill being notable exceptions—have bothered to comment upon it, or even to credit Lewis where such credit is due.

This is unfortunate, because the book is an excellent example of "faith seeking understanding." In it, Lewis articulated, with care and exceptional lucidity, his reply to the most important and most forceful anti-theistic argument of all, the argument that the quantity and variety of suffering in the world is inconsistent with, or at least is evidence against, an omnipotent and perfectly loving **God**.

In an introductory chapter, Lewis tried to place his reply in a proper context. He pointed out, first of all, that **religion** does not have its "origin" in a philosophical "inference from the course of events in this world to the goodness and wisdom of its creator"; he even conceded that such an inference would be "preposterous." Instead, religion has its origin, he claimed, in certain revelatory experiences: the sense of uncanny awe or the *Numinous*, as Rudolph Otto called it, and the sense of moral obligation and moral failure. As for **Christianity** in particular, its origin lies in a specific historical event: the life, crucifixion, and resurrection of a man who claimed to be "one with" God. So as Lewis saw it, the apologist's task is not to treat Christianity as if it were "the conclusion of a philosophical debate on the origin of the universe"; it is merely to reconcile "the awkward fact of pain" with the "awkward facts" of **revelation** and, in that way, to defend against an objection.

Now the heart of Lewis's reply lies in chapter 2, where he took up the topic of divine omnipotence, and in a way, everything else in the book is ancillary. In subsequent chapters, Lewis had illuminating things to say about divine goodness, human wickedness, **the Fall**, human pain, **hell**, animal pain, and **heaven**, but it is all ancillary in this sense: even if his arguments in these subsequent chapters were substantially mistaken, his basic reply to the argument he set out to refute, the reply developed in chapter 2, would stand. We may think of that reply as consisting of three steps.

The first is to clarify the concept of omnipotence. According to Lewis, not even an omnipotent being can do the "intrinsically impossible," as he called it, or the logically impossible, as some philosophers would call it. Not even an omnipotent being, in other words, can create square circles, or make two plus two equal five, or causally determine that Saint Paul *freely* repents of his **sin**. As Lewis himself put it, "You may attribute **miracles** to Him, but not nonsense," and the power to make contradictions true is, quite literally, nonsense.

The second step is to point out the extent to which we are ignorant of what is and is not logically possible. That Smith should be a married bachelor is clearly *not* possible. But what about someone traveling backwards in time or an effect preceding its cause in time? Are these genuine possibilities? Whereas a few philosophers believe they are, many others disagree; so at least one side of this dispute is mistaken. "We may thus come to think things possible," said Lewis, "which are really impossible, and *vice versa*." And if that is true, then we are especially likely to make such mistakes when we contemplate the great mystery surrounding us.

The third step is to spell out a plausible "specimen" of what the necessities and impossibilities facing God might have been. We must come to see that the creation of persons and their perfection as children of God is no "easy task" even for an omnipotent being. Is it possible that God should have brought "a society of free souls" into being outside the context of "a relatively independent and 'inexorable Nature'?" Lewis thought not. We have "no reason to suppose that self-consciousness, the recognition of a creature by itself as a 'self,' can exist

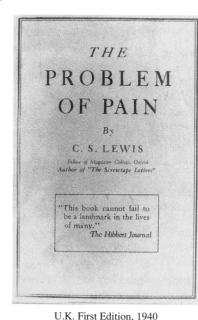

U.K. First Edition, 1940

except in contrast with an 'other,' a something which is not the self." Only in an environment of some kind, then, and "preferably a social environment, an environment of other selves," will "the awareness of Myself" emerge. Nor is it so much as possible, Lewis suggested, that an emerging consciousness should choose freely or act intelligently in a chaotic environment, governed by chance or subject to perpetual divine interference: an "environment" in which no laws of nature enable one to foresee the probable consequences of choosing this way rather than that. Nor is it so much as possible that one's actions should have genuine moral significance, or that the highest moral virtues should be cultivated, or that the conditions of supreme happiness should finally be met, except in an environment in which one can choose *freely* (and without divine interference) either to help or to harm another (at least over the short run). According to Lewis, therefore, the *kind* of environment in which we in fact live may be the only possible kind in which God could, first, love his children into existence, and second, accomplish a loving purpose for them over the long run.

Now I believe that Lewis's understanding of the relevant impossibilities facing God (or "the intrinsic necessities of a world") is essentially correct, though it would, of course, require considerable more space to argue this in full. It is important to stress, however, that Lewis himself nowhere claimed to have gotten it all right; instead, he offered his account of the relevant impossibilities and necessities "merely as a specimen of what they might be," and he went on to observe that whatever "they really are, . . . they are not likely to be *less* complicated than I have suggested." So even if the details of Lewis's account were mistaken, he would be right about this: since we cannot be certain what is and is not logically possible in the matter of creating individual centers of consciousness and in meeting the conditions of their ultimate happiness, neither can we be certain what God's options were in this matter. And for that reason alone, we are in no position to formulate a successful anti-theistic argument from suffering.

Observe finally that Lewis's reply to the anti-theistic argument from suffering, as sketched above, in no way requires the assumption that God's "goodness is wholly other than ours" or is "an utterly unknown quality," and in chapter 3 Lewis explicitly rejected this assumption. So John Beversluis, who contends that Lewis ended up revising our ordinary ethical concepts, is simply mistaken. If Lewis revised anything, it is a popular conception of *omnipotence*, not the ordinary conception of **love**. That is the whole point of his stressing the impossibilities facing God and interpreting them broadly. The basic idea is that God's options may have been very different from what some would think and that, for all we know, God prevents as much suffering as he can without making matters worse over the long run (see also the entry on **pain**). Like **George MacDonald**, then, Lewis recognized that the essence of God is love, not raw power; Lewis also understood that, on balance, those who err in the direction of limiting God's love dishonor him far more than do those who err in the direction of limiting his power.

Thomas Talbott
Willamette University

Also See: Atheism, Good and Evil, Rationality

Bibliography

Beversluis, John, *C. S. Lewis and the Search for Rational Religion*. Grand Rapids: Eerdmans, 1985: chapter 7.

Farrer, Austin. "The Christian Apologist." *Light on C. S. Lewis.* Jocelyn Gibb (ed). New York: Harcourt Brace Jovanovich, 1965: 23–43.

Hartshorne, Charles. "Philosophy and Orthodoxy: Reflections on C. S. Lewis' *The Problem of Pain* and *The Case for Christianity*." *Ethics*. LIV (July 1944): 295–98.

Hick, John. *Evil and the God of Love*. 2nd ed. New York: Harper and Row, 1997.

MacDonald, George. "Creation in Christ." *Creation in Christ*. Rolland Hein (ed). Grand Rapids, MI: Eerdmans, 1976: 15–22.

Otto, Rudolph. *The Idea of the Holy*. New York: Oxford University Press, 1958.

Plantinga, Alvin. *God, Freedom, and Evil*. Grand Rapids: Eerdmans, 1977.

Talbott, Thomas. "C. S. Lewis and the Problem of Evil." *Christian Scholar's Review*. XVII no. 1 (1987): 36–51.

"The Prodigality of Firdausi"

Punch. 215 (December 1, 1948): 510 (under the pseudonym Nat Whilk). Revised and reprinted in *Poems* and *Collected Poems*.

In this poem, Lewis retold a tradition about Firdausi (née Abul Kasim Mansur, 940?–1020?), the poet of the Persian national epic, *Shah Nameh* ("Book of Kings"). Expecting a handsome reward from the Sultan for his efforts, Firdausi received a pittance brought to him at a public bathhouse. Rather than accept, Firdausi coolly distributed the money to a bath attendant and a seller of beer. Perhaps Lewis saw this story as a parable of his own critical valuation as a poet.

Don W. King
Montreat College

"Professor Tolkien's Hobbit"

See entry on *The Hobbit: or There and Back* (Book Review II)

"The Prudent Jailer"

See entry on "The Romantics"

"Prudery and Philology"

The Spectator. CXCIV (21 January 1955): 43–44. Reprinted in *Present Concerns*.

First published in *The Spectator*, a weekly journal for an intellectual readership, this 1955 essay addressed what was an occasional concern for Lewis: society's acceptance of the encroachment of increasingly more sexually explicit material into literature. Lewis noted that while nude drawing has generally been acceptable within the realms of decency, because, he assumed, pictures are neutral, it would not be decent to describe that same nude in words, since there are no everyday, neutral words to describe "those parts of the body which are not usually mentioned." Clearly in the 1990s such words do now exist and are considered ordinary and decent for the increasing number of occasions when reference to genitalia is within the bounds of good taste. Lewis continued that references to genitalia and body functions should be confined to comic writing and jokes and did not seem to find these indecent. If explicit material was accepted into serious literature, he thought, we will no longer enjoy the humor inherent in these topics.

Susan Henthorne
White Pines College

Also See: Sex

Bibliography

Lewis, C. S. "Christianity and Culture"

The Psalms

After his conversion, C. S. Lewis began regular attendance at **Magdalen College** Chapel on weekdays, and his parish church (Holy Trinity) on Sundays. At most services in both places, *The Book of Common*

Prayer was read, which includes prayers, passages from both the Old and New Testaments, orders of service for special days of the church year, and passages from the Psalms. Lewis became an avid admirer of these poems and read them devotionally for the rest of his life. **Walter Hooper** has written that Lewis "came to know the Psalms almost by heart ... it was through the continuous reading and praying of Morning and Evening Prayer (at chapel and church services) that he came to know the **Bible** and the Psalms so well."

Most of what Lewis wrote about the Psalms is contained in *Reflections on the Psalms* (1958), and the essay **"The Psalms,"** published in *Christian Reflections* (1967). He mentioned specific psalms in a paper read to the **Oxford Socratic Club** on May 20, 1946 (later published in *God in the Dock* as **"Religion Without Dogma?"**) and commented on penitence in Psalms in *Letters to Malcolm*. He wrote favorably about the **poetry** of the Psalms in a letter to his friend **Dom Bede Griffiths**, and in *Surprised By Joy*, Lewis acknowledged his debt to the philosopher Henri Bergson for helping him to appreciate the "more exultant" psalms.

Lewis's essay "The Psalms" is an introduction to his *Reflections on the Psalms*. In it, he discussed antiquity in the Psalms, how the ethic of certain Psalms anticipates the Gospel ethic of **Christ**, how the Hebrews pictured in the Psalms have "something" in them (their knowledge that they are chosen) that allows them at times to reach a "Christian level of spirituality," and how Psalm 109 is a "hymn of hate" that may be an archetype of every person that has been mistreated. Later, Lewis discussed how bad people today have "gone away" from the Hebrew mindset and no longer "thirst for justice," and he included a long section on the Day of Judgment.

Perry C. Bramlett,
C. S. Lewis for the Local Church

Also See: Anglicanism, Church, Ethics and Morality, Revelation, Spirituality

Bibliography

Brown, Carol Ann. "Mirrors of Ourselves: Reflections from the Psalms." *CSL: The Bulletin of the New York Lewis Society.* 10 (June 1979): 1–5.
Hooper, Walter. *C. S. Lewis: A Companion and Guide.* San Francisco: Harper, 1996
Lewis, C. S. *Reflections on the Psalms.*

"The Psalms"

First published posthumously in *Christian Reflections*.

Through reading and worship, Lewis's mind became "steeped" in the **Psalms**. A 1940 letter mentions his recent "greatly increased enjoyment" of them. Soon he was imitating their themes and rhythms in his fiction. The litany of praise in *Perelandra*, chapter 17, is psalm-like in its use of parallelism and the refrain and in some of its imagery. Chapters 11 and 13 of *The Great Divorce* contain adaptations of Psalms 110 and 91, and the description of the **angel** in chapter 11 echoes Psalm 19.

As a literary historian Lewis studied the 16th-century prose psalm translations. "Sternhold and Hopkins" in meter drew mingled appreciation censure, but the period's intentionally literary metrical versions, such as Wyatt's and the Sidneys', he ignored.

Two posthumously published essays, together labeled "The Psalms," apparently are early sketches for *Reflections on the Psalms*. Unpolished, ending abruptly, they enable us to observe the writer at work—rewording, rearranging, expanding, omitting. They deal chiefly with the "problem" of the imprecatory psalms and the theme of judgment. A paragraph on the significance of **Christ**'s mother, author of the Magnificat ("unmistakably a psalm"), and the final section, dealing with the recurrent "Dark Night of the Flesh" theme (complaints of one suffering persecution), did not make it into the book.

Charles A. Huttar
Hope College

Bibliography

Warren, Eugene. "The Angel of the Law in The Great Divorce." *CSL: The Bulletin of the New York C. S. Lewis Society.* 8 (1977).

Pseudonyms of C. S. Lewis

Pseudonym: Clive Hamilton
Used In: *Spirits in Bondage, Joy, Dymer*
Derivation: Combination of his own first name and his mother's maiden name

Pseudonym: Nat Whilk also N.W.
Used In: *The Shortest Way Home*
Derivation: Anglo-Saxon for "I know not whom"

Pseudonym: N.W. Clerk
Used In: *A Grief Observed*
Derivation: Originally Lewis used the pseudonym "Dimidius" when submitted to Faber and Faber. T. S. Eliot read the manuscript and suggested a more English sounding pseudonym. Lewis kept the N. W. (see above) and added Clerk (believing that by "medieval standards" that was what he was)

"Psycho-Analysis and Literary Criticism"

Essays and Studies by Members of the English Association. XXVII (1942): 7–21. Reprinted in *They Asked for a Paper* and *Selected Literary Essays.*

This essay, originally an address to a literary society at Westfield, represents one of Lewis's most incisive critiques of the 20th century's preoccupation with the use of psychoanalysis to probe the supposed pathologies of literary artists. While he was always skeptical of Freudian **literary criticism**, he would have been more so if he had lived to see how Freudians have interpreted his *The Lion, the Witch and the Wardrobe*—witness the wardrobe offered as "the birth canal" and Narnia as the cold world outside "the mother's body" by some expositors' critical reckoning.

Lewis here took issue with the premise that all literary works may be reduced to wish-fulfillment. He admits the possibility that subconscious desires may play a part in writing; but he argued that **Sigmund Freud** was wrong in stating that "once upon a time there were a king and queen" means simply "once upon a time there was a father and mother." If the latent meaning were all we were really enjoying, why would we employ the **symbols**? But this is not the case. Even if gardens subconsciously stand for the female body, at least part of our pleasure in literary gardens comes from a pleasure in gardens.

Lewis closed the essay by drawing attention to the "more civil and humane" interpretation of **myth** and **imagery** to be found in the work of rival psychologist **Carl Jung**. Lewis offered admiration for his theory of archetypes but noted that Jung's work left unanswered the questions of why, beyond the fact of their antiquity, archetypes have any impact on us. Lewis concluded wryly that the mystery of primordial images is perhaps only made deeper and less accessible by the attention paid to them.

Bruce L. Edwards and Marvin D. Hinten
Bowling Green State University

Also See: Psychology

Psychology

In *Surprised by Joy* Lewis recounted a disturbing youthful experience in which he spent two weeks "in close contact with a man who was going mad." Later he suspected a more physical cause, but at that time he ascribed the man's insane ravings to a flirtation with odd ideas from Theosophy and Yoga to Psychoanalysis. The experience left an enduring impression on his mind and helped inspire his unfinished novel, *The Easley Fragment*.

Lewis had mixed feelings about psychology. He recognized that our mental makeup was not totally our own doing. In a chapter of *Mere Christianity* entitled "Morality and Psychoanalysis" he stressed the danger of judging people by their behavior. We only see what people make out of "raw material" that included their "psychological outfit" and upbringing. Only **God** understands what people are really making of what they have been given.

Lewis had no problem when trained experts tried to improve the basic raw material of the human mind by eliminating abnormal feelings. He even said that their techniques were something "every parson" should learn. His objections arose when psychologists tried to speak as authorities on morality and **religion**. He was particularly bothered when they went beyond warning people not to trust vague feelings of **guilt** and treated all guilt feelings as unhealthy, even those resulting from specific deeds.

In *The Four Loves* Lewis expressed his displeasure with those who would widen the categories of mental illness and turn the normal difficulties of "Being a Fallen Man" into neuroses subject to medical treatment. Spiritual direction, he said, would help such people far more than medicine. He went on to point out that the only man in history who was not warped by sin was someone who clearly did not fit the "psychologist's picture" of mental health. You cannot be considered "well-adjusted," he noted, when the world says that you have a devil and nails you to a cross.

In *Surprised by Joy* Lewis admitted that during his student years at **Oxford** he fell under the influence of a "new Psychology" and for a time believed that his childhood spiritual longing for joy was merely concealed eroticism or worse. He later dismissed that idea and dealt with it in his 1933 *The Pilgrim's Regress* and in a 1941 essay entitled **"Religion: Reality or Substitute."** In both he pointed out that it is not that easy to tell the original from a copy. Our sensual longings could just as easily be misplaced spiritual longing as the opposite. Psychologists, he stressed in *Letters to Malcolm*, often misjudge the depth of the human psyche and see far too much as merely disguised **sex**.

Lewis explained one reason for his skeptical attitude toward psychology in a 1946 paper given to the **Oxford Socratic Club** and later published as "Religion Without

Dogma." If we think about religion in general, Lewis said, then we find that mathematicians, astronomers, and physicists are often religious. Biologists, he believed, were less so, while economists and psychologists were "very seldom" religious. The principle he drew from this was that, "as their subject matter comes nearer to man himself . . . their anti-religious bias hardens."

Mike Perry

Also See: Ethics and Morality; The Fall, Sigmund Freud, Immorality; Carl Jung; Sin

Bibliography

Lewis, C. S. *The Four Loves*; *Mere Christianity*; *Pilgrim's Regress*; "Religion Without Dogma"; "Religion: Reality or Substitute?"; *Surprised by Joy*

Public Schools (Letter)

Church Times. CXXX (3 October 1947): 583.

Lewis questioned an article entitled, "Old Ties for All" (*Church Times*, September 26, 1947, 574), in which the author described the excellence of the religious training provided in Public Schools (the British term for what Americans would call private schools). Lewis referred the reader to the contrasting position presented in B. J. Sandhurst's *How Heathen is Britain?* (London: Collins, 1946, with preface by C. S. Lewis), and wondered how to reconcile these two conflicting views of religious education in the British schools. He invited further discussion on this important matter and went so far as to hope for a follow-up article.

Marjorie L. Mead
The Marion E. Wade Center

Purgatory

In *Letters to Malcolm*, C. S. Lewis avowed a belief in purgatory but demurred on the Catholic Church's official description of it. Lewis's "right view" traded complicated theological approaches for a simple (though not easy) spiritual process, beginning with the saved soul requesting to be "cleansed" before entering paradise. At the threshold of **heaven**, the soul is told that such cleansing "may hurt." For Lewis, the proper answer was "Even so."

Lewis offered another simple view of purgatory in *The Great Divorce*, when **George MacDonald** tells the narrator that **hell** can become purgatory if the damned soul is willing to repent and leave hell. **Good and evil** are retrospective in the end; earth itself will have been part of heaven or part of hell, depending on each soul's choice. Reminded that Catholics believe that souls in purgatory are already saved and Protestants believe once in hell, always in hell, MacDonald answered, "They're both right, maybe. Do not fash yourself with such questions."

Theology aside, the practical aspect of purgatory appealed to Lewis's practical mind. If we are "none of us righteous, no not one," then some cleansing certainly seems to be in order.

Richard Hill
Taylor University

Also See: Roman Catholicism

Bibliography

Derrik, Christopher. *C. S. Lewis and the Church of Rome: a Study in Proto-Ecumenism*. San Francisco: Ignatius Press, 1981.

Q

"Quam Bene Saturno"

Cherbourg School Magazine (July 1913). Reprinted in *The Lewis Family Papers*. IV: 51–52. There it is dated July 29, 1913.

"*Quam Bene Saturno*" (Latin for "How Well They Lived When Saturn Was King"—a reference to Tibullus 1.3.35) is Lewis's first published poem. It celebrates the benevolent rule of Saturn in the days of the Titans before the successful rebellion of Jove. Since that time peace has been replaced with strife and contention. Written in simple iambic tetrameter and rhyme scheme, it is almost certainly a response to a school exercise.

Don W. King
Montreat College

Quotable Lewis

Wayne Martindale and Jerry Root (eds). Wheaton, IL: Tyndale House, 1989.

An anthology of Lewis quotations.

R

Arthur Rackham (1867–1939)

Arthur Rackham was an English artist famous for his illustrations, in Art Nouveau style, for **fairy tales** such as *Peter Pan* (1906) and *Hans Andersen* (1932). Before becoming a full-time illustrator in 1893, Rackham worked as a statistician in an insurance company. Among his earlier major works were ninety-five black-and-white illustrations for *Grimm's Fairy Tales* (1900), some later redone as watercolors, the fifty-one illustrations for *Rip van Winkle* (1905), illustrations for **Shakespeare**'s *A Midsummer-Night's Dream* (1908), and for *Undine* (1909).

In 1909 Rackham produced sixty-four watercolors to illustrate a translation by Margaret Armour of the text of **Richard Wagner**'s *Ring* cycle, which was published in two volumes, *The Rhinegold & The Valkyrie* (1910) and *Siegfried & The Twilight of the Gods* (1911). Unlike his earlier work, these illustrations were not for children. Nevertheless, they were the ones that influenced C. S. Lewis as a child. Lewis was first drawn to Wagner in 1911–12 by Rackham's depiction of Siegfried reaching Brunhild as she sleeps surrounded by Wotan's fire. Lewis recorded that Rackham's pictures "seemed to me then to be the very music made visible."

Rackham's style was marked by a strong technique, with fine line and subdued color washes; his interpretation of otherworldly creatures and landscapes and his portrayal of children were notable characteristics.

John Bremer

Bibliography
Wagner, Richard. *Ring*. New York: Dover Publications, 1979.

RAF Talks, or Talks to the Royal Air Force

Lewis was asked, before his BBC radio broadcasts of August 1941, if he would give talks to servicemen and women at RAF stations near Oxford. His first presentations seem to have been to a small group of twelve men at RAF Abingdon in April 1941. He was not sanguine about the talks' success: "As far as I can judge, they were a complete failure."

Nevertheless, the success of Lewis's subsequent radio talks on "Right and Wrong" (later incorporated into *Mere Christianity*) was such that the chaplain-in-chief of the Royal Air Force invited Lewis to speak at RAF stations around the country, and Lewis, who wanted to aid the war effort, agreed. RAF stations were usually isolated and morale was always a problem. A high-ranking officer recalled: "The **war**, the whole of life, everything tended to seem pointless. We needed, many of us, a key to the meaning of the universe. Lewis provided just that. Better still, he gave us back our old, traditional Christian **faith** so that we could accept it with new confidence . . . ."

All through the summer of 1942, Lewis traveled to far and remote places (sometimes accompanied by his brother, **Warren Lewis**), away from home for two or three days at a time. This took a toll on his health, but being asked to continue, he felt it his duty to do so, which he did until the end of the war. There is no record of the number of RAF stations he visited nor of any success he might have had. Others thought that he made a valuable contribution, but he himself doubted it, taking comfort "in remembering that **God** used an *ass* to convert the prophet."

John Bremer

Also See: Apologetics

Bibliography

Gilmore, Charles. "To the RAF." *C. S. Lewis at the Breakfast Table*. James Como (ed). New York: Macmillan, 1984.

Lewis, C. S. "Christian Apologetics"; "Learning in War-Time"

Arthur Michael Ramsey (1904–1988)

Arthur Ramsey was a graduate of **Magdalene College**, **Cambridge**, a noted Anglican theologian, and Archbishop of Canterbury from 1961 to 1974. His writings include *The Glory of God and the Transfiguration of Christ* (1949), *Sacred and Secular* (1965), and *God, Christ and the World* (1969). His most famous work, *The Resurrection of Christ*, was published by Centenary Press (Geoffrey Bles) in the 1940s as part of the "Christian Challenge Series" along with C. S. Lewis's *The Problem of Pain* and **Charles Williams'** *The Forgiveness of Sins*. Ramsey read the works of Lewis and was Professor of Divinity at Durham University when Lewis gave the lectures later titled *The Abolition of Man* (1943). It has been reported that he said "Who is Malcolm?" (referring to *Letters to Malcolm*), when he met Lewis's biographer **Walter Hooper** in 1964. In 1972 he gave the memorial address for Richard Ladborough, Lewis's close friend from Magdalene College, Cambridge. In that address he compared Ladborough's piety with Saint Paul's and lauded his faith and loyalty to the church.

Perry C. Bramlett
C. S. Lewis for the Local Church

Also See: Anglicanism

Bibliography

Cross, F. L., and E. A. Livingstone (eds). *The Oxford Dictionary of the Christian Church*. Oxford: Oxford University Press, 1985.

Green, Roger Lancelyn, and Walter Hooper. *C. S. Lewis: A Biography*. New York: Harcourt Brace, 1974.

Rationalism

It can be argued that C. S. Lewis's greatest achievement in both British literature and Western thought was healing the breach between the high Rationalism of the 18th century and the **Romanticism** of **William Wordsworth**. Beyond the comprehensibility of his **apologetics** to the common man, and the depth and beauty of his fiction, this fusion of Rationalism and Romanticism can be considered his subtlest, yet most far-reaching accomplishment. Still, it is yet little recognized by the academic world. Lewis takes the best elements of **reason** and the Romantic **imagination**, and rejected the atheistic elements of both, placing them in dependent relationship to one another.

In his essay **"Bluspels and Flalansferes"** he explained the inevitable role of **metaphor** in even the simplest speech, and then he writes: "For me, reason is the natural organ of **truth**; but imagination is the organ of meaning. Imagination, producing new metaphors or revivifying old, is not the cause of truth, but its condition." Lewis went on to agree that a metaphor may be false but said that it is the role of reason to discern truth and falsehood, just as the role of the imagination is to acquire understanding. Thus reason and imagination are mutually dependent. Lewis cautioned us to both recognize the limitations of reason and never to doubt the possibility of objective, rational thought.

Regarding the limits of reason, Lewis in **"Christianity and Literature"** quoted Thomas à Kempis to warn against the atheistic tendency to consider reason as "the true Eternal Light." According to Lewis, humanity is not to overreach itself by trying to pull itself up by its own bootstrap solely through reason. In this, Lewis parted company with much of the humanistic thought of the 18th and 19th centuries. Reason is also not to be used in Lewis's view as an excuse for what he called "Universal Evolutionism"—the belief that humankind armed with **science** is evolving into an ever better and masterful sort of being. Lewis heavily satirized this sort of arrogance masquerading as reason in the character of Dr. Weston from his space trilogy. Employing rhetoric reminiscent of agnostic writers like **H. G. Wells**, Dr. Weston uses his "reason" to justify humankind's rape of Mars in *Out of the Silent Planet*. Lewis recognized that reason could be twisted in many other ways and that sinful humans used it to inflict greater pain on people and animals than would be possible for an irrational creature (see *The Problem of Pain*).

Lewis also mocked various popular 20th-century forms of so-called Rationalism in the characters who live north of the road in *The Pilgrim's Regress*. In each case the reason of the characters is twisted because their reason rests on false assumptions. As elsewhere in his writings, Lewis was pointing out that reason alone is inadequate as a presumed **philosophy** of life because reason always must begin from a premise that is usually a product of the imagination. Thus **materialism** as a basis for argument against the possibility of **miracles** fails, because materialism is an assumed premise, not a rationally proved fact. One must make the "leap of faith" that only the material world exists before one can logically rule out the **supernatural**, and that "leap of faith" in itself does not constitute reason.

Reason is further limited in that it can clear away impediments to understanding **God**, but only faith is capable of truly understanding him. Indeed, Lewis felt that reason would be inevitably overcome without faith: "Our faith in **Christ** wavers not so much when real arguments come against it as when it looks improbable— when the whole world takes on that desolate look which really tells us much more about the state of our passions and even our digestion than about reality. . . . [T]hough reason is divine, human reasoners are not" (**"Religion: Reality or Substitute?"**).

Despite these qualifications, Lewis nevertheless called himself a rationalist. He recognized that unless one started from the premise of an objective reality, reason itself was not possible. He warned about the dangers of subjectivism and the moral relativism that spawned it. He concluded that naturalism, the belief that the natural universe is self-existent and without supernatural origin, contradicted itself. For if the universe is the product of a series of accidents, then the very thought that the universe is an accident is itself an accident and not reliable. Lewis argued that to doubt the existence of a Creator and to doubt objective reality is to know nothing and destroy even the possibility of rational human communication. In an accidental universe, we are all programmed by our environment to utter what nonsense we utter before we are extinguished.

Following this line of thought, Lewis asserted that human reason must be supernatural and a miracle. He disbelieved that reason could somehow "evolve" and become self-aware. Also, he recognized the futility of arguing against God. "God is the source of all your reasoning, he wrote in *Mere Christianity*. "When you argue against Him you are arguing against the very power that makes you able to argue at all."

Lewis's spiritual autobiography, *Surprised by Joy,* details how, along with his romantic imagination, he retained in his early years a 19th-century sort of rationalism, which was nurtured in part by his tutor, **W. T. Kirkpatrick**. In time his rationalism was slowly eroded in what he metaphorically describes as a chess game with God. He adopted for some time the philosophy of Hegel and believed in the Absolute as a "reasonable" sort of compromise with Platonic Idealism. Yet he could not maintain this philosophy in the face of experiences that caused him to commune with "the Absolute" and realized that there was little distinction between that and **prayer**. In time he rationally came to Theism and remained there until a conversation with his friends **J. R. R. Tolkien** and **Hugo Dyson** gave him the imaginative context to accept **Christianity**. With this experience he was able to fuse the search of his reason with the imaginative experience and the romantic quest for what he called *Sensucht,* or **joy**.

During World War II Lewis gave a series of BBC **broadcast talks** that eventually became the book *Mere Christianity*. In these talks he began his lifelong battle with subjectivism, in the defense of a reasonable, objective reality. This theme was also prominently explored in his book *Miracles* and other essays, making Lewis rather a prophet in the wilderness for the existence of objective rationalism in 20th-century thought. It might be argued that his foretelling of the nihilistic result of subjectivism and the abandonment of a belief in objective reality predicted Post-Modern trends of thought such as Deconstructionism.

James Prothero

Bibliography

Schakel, Peter J. *Reason and Imagination in C. S. Lewis.* Grand Rapids, MI: Eerdmans, 1984.

"Re-Adjustment"

Fifty-Two: A Journal of Books and Authors. 14 (Autumn 1964): 4. Reprinted in *Poems* and *Collected Poems*.

"Re-Adjustment" is a poem lamenting the way language was being abused. Lewis began by confessing he had thought there would be comfort in his being the last of a breed (what he terms Old Western Man in his Cambridge inaugural address, *"De Descriptione Temporum"*) since the next generation would look on the cultural accomplishment of his with kindness and thanks. Sadly, Lewis concluded that this would not be the case because language and meaning were under attack—reducing all of life to the momentary present.

Don W. King
Montreat College

Reality

"What is most real?" is perhaps the most basic philosophical question, and Lewis's life and work can be considered an answer to this question which only humans ask, so far as we know. Lewis's answer? Ultimate reality is more like a mind than it is like anything else we know. It is conscious and prefers some things to other things. It should be stressed that Lewis did not denigrate this present world in any significant way. Lewis's reality contains numerous very real entities, including humans, animals, and all the myriad of things that make up the natural world. Nevertheless, for Lewis the "realities which we can't touch and see" (such as **God**) are more real (*The Screwtape Letters*).

According to Lewis, God created, among other things, human beings with **free will**—that is, creatures that can choose between right and wrong. And the moment you have a free self there is the possibility of putting yourself first, wanting to be the center, wanting to *be* God. That was, in fact, the **sin** of **Satan**, and that was the sin he taught the human race.

We come now to both the essence of **Christianity** and the center of Lewis's view of reality. We encounter a man, among the Jews, who talks as if he was God. He claims to be able to forgive sins. He says he has always existed, that he is coming to judge the world at the end of time. According to Lewis, we must all choose between this Jesus as either lunatic, the Devil of **hell**, or as the one who is who he says he is.

Lewis stressed that reality is not simple. This is one of the reasons Lewis was a Christian. Christianity has the ring of **truth** to it because it is not something you could have guessed. For example, you would think that in the Jewish Temple you saw the real sacrifice being offered, with real flesh and blood animals being used in the ritual. Yet Christians maintain that in some very mysterious sense, it is the other way around. Holy Communion is "the real sacrifice" and "all the slaughtering, incense, music, and shouting in the temple" is only a "shadow" (**"Religion: Reality or Substitute?"**).

After **Christ**'s death, the Scriptures represent Christ as passing neither into a purely "spiritual" mode of existence nor into a "natural" life such as we now know it. The Scriptures represent him as withdrawing into a new kind of "natural" life presently unknown to us. Lewis noted that Christ said that he went "to prepare a place for us," and that this "presumably means that he is about to create that whole new **Nature** that will provide the environment or conditions for his glorified humanity and, in him for ours" ("Miracles of the New Creation").

Our ultimate and final end is to close the gap between us and reality (**"The Weight of Glory"**). It is, in fact, our heart's desire and our deepest longing. To be in glory is to be accepted by God and welcomed into the heart of things. Yet the life and work of Lewis did not point only to **heaven** and the world to come; Lewis also emphasized our responsibility in this present world. All day long, in our loves, play, and **politics**, we are by our actions helping each other to one (heaven) or other (hell) of these final destinations, for it is ultimately immortals with whom we joke, work, marry, snub, and exploit.

Michael H. Macdonald
Seattle Pacific University

Also See: Augustine, Ethics and Morality, Good and Evil, Immanuel Kant, Metaphysics, Philosophy, Plato

Reason

One of the interesting paradoxes about Lewis was that, although he was in many respects deeply romantic, reason was of utmost importance throughout his life. In *Surprised by Joy* he mentioned, as a redeeming quality of **Wynyard**, the wretched boarding school he attended 1908–10, that the master, Oldie, "forced us to reason, and I have been the better for those geometry lessons all my life." Later, under the tutelage of **W. T. Kirkpatrick**, Lewis's reason was honed and became razor sharp. By encountering and engaging with Kirkpatrick's ruthless dialectic, Lewis came in some ways to resemble him (though he differed sharply from Kirkpatrick in his romantic longings, his love of **myth** and **imagination**, and eventually his acceptance of Christian **faith**). James T. Como notes that his logic books, used while studying under Kirkpatrick or more likely at **Oxford**, are very heavily annotated.

Reason and logic exerted a strong influence on all aspects of Lewis's life. His conversation tended to be argumentative, unless he was sharing anecdotes and repartee with friends. Lewis and his close friend **Owen Barfield** engaged in furious arguments whenever they were together, and his brother, **Warren Lewis,** describes him as always "talking for victory." He employed the same approach in tutorials and proved intimidating to many of his pupils. Reason and logic contributed to his conversion (or reconversion) to **Christianity** in the late 1920s. The first series of **Broadcast Talks** on BBC radio in the early 1940s (reprinted in *Mere Christianity*) lays out a path Lewis himself followed, as it describes series of logical arguments leading the reader toward acknowledgment of the existence of **natural law** and of a personal lawgiver behind that law.

In the late 1920s to early 1930s, Lewis and Barfield engaged in an extended correspondence, which they called **The Great War**. Its method was tightly reasoned, philosophical argumentation. Its central subject was the imagination, with Barfield contending that **poetry** initially conveyed knowledge and therefore imagination disseminated **truth**, and Lewis holding that imagination conveyed meaning, not truth. As Lewis wrote it in the essay, **"Bluspels and Flalansferes,"** first published in 1939 but read earlier as a paper at Manchester University, "I am a rationalist. For me, reason is the natural organ of truth; but imagination is the organ of meaning." Definite as that statement sounds, it is clear that reason and imagination made conflicting claims throughout Lewis's life, as described in *Surprised by Joy* and as expressed succinctly in an undated poem entitled **"Reason"** (in *Poems*).

In his early writings, both **apologetics** and fiction, Lewis's emphasis was on reason, with imaginative techniques as important but subsidiary vehicles for conveying effectively the truths he sought to impart. His first fictional work, *The Pilgrim's Regress: An Allegorical Apology for Christianity, Reason and Romanticism*, employs **allegory**, which of all the imaginative literary forms, has the greatest tendency to rely on the intellect for completion of its meaning and effect. Its narrative deals with the importance of romantic longing in drawing its main character, John, to salvation, and with intellectual barriers that had hindered his faith. Like the author, John progressed first to Theism and then to Christianity, as the logic of the truth became convincing and unavoidable to him. At a key point, imprisoned by modern intellectualism, he is rescued by Reason, depicted allegorically as a woman, a virgin, a knightly figure, a giant-killer, who teaches John to think through the circular arguments of Freud and the Enlightenment that had confused him.

Later works such as the space trilogy make more integral use of their imaginative forms, but the emphasis on grounding the fiction in reasoned truths continues. *Out of the Silent Planet* tells a good story, but Lewis himself referred to the story as a vehicle for smuggling **theology** into people's minds, and the book's Christian theme is spelled out in conceptual, not imaginative, terms. The imaginative, even mythical, qualities of *Perelandra* are of the highest quality, but at the center of the book is an extended philosophical-theological discussion relying on the reason, not the imagination. And the exposure of evil and instruction in the good that suffuse *That Hideous Strength* are achieved largely through mini-essays, developing in a few sentences reasoned arguments that in some cases Lewis developed into full-length essays.

Because reason contributed significantly in drawing Lewis to Christianity, it is not surprising that his early efforts in writing about his faith were reasoned efforts to demonstrate the truth of what he believed. *The Problem of Pain* uses reason and argument to meet and deal with a problem that long had haunted him—why, if **God** is good, he allows so much suffering in the world. Central to *Miracles*, with its reasoned argument for the possibility of **miracles**, is a defense of reason itself. Lewis develops a position he expressed in a number of other places (**"De Futilitate," "The Funeral of a Great Myth," "Bulverism," "Religion Without Dogma,"** and **"Is Theology Poetry,"** for example), that any particular reasoned thought, and reason generally, are valueless if they are the result of irrational causes. Lewis concluded that the position of the Naturalist, who makes the human mind a result of irrational causes, is self-contradictory. We must then, Lewis concluded, believe in the validity of reason and accept that reason exists absolutely on its own.

If reason has an independent, absolute validity, so too do the platitudes of practical reason, which we must accept as such, Lewis said, if we are to have **values** at all. That position, expressed briefly in **"The Poison of Subjectivism,"** is developed most fully in what is widely regarded as Lewis's most important book, *The Abolition of Man*. In it Lewis upholds the doctrine of objective value, or natural law, or the **Tao**: "The belief that certain things are really true, and others really false, to the kind of thing the universe is and the kind of things we are." The Tao provides a context within which we can judge our emotions and sentiments as reasonable or unreasonable, as they conform to reason or fail to conform. Lewis's book focused on **education** and urges that education be conducted within the framework of the Tao, making pupils aware of the platitudes of natural law and training them in appropriate responses to situations they encounter. Only such absolute values can provide a bulwark against the power of scientific planners and "conditioners" who reduce people to mere nature and thus abolish the moral dimension unique to humanity.

Although Lewis's thought always upheld the need for reason, a shift of emphasis is evident in the last decade and a half of his life. His later writings on Christianity are less argumentative and assertive than the earlier ones; they rely more on experience and imagination and permit the reader more freedom of response. The shift may have been caused in part by an attack by a well-known Catholic philosopher, **G. E. M. Anscombe**, on the pivotal third chapter of *Miracles*, which may have shaken Lewis's confidence in the use of logical proofs in apologetics. But it may equally derive from a sense that he had accomplished what he wanted to in reasoned apologetics and was ready to experiment with other modes of writing. His fiction from the late 1940s on (the **Chronicles of Narnia**, *Till We Have Faces*) becomes more imaginative and mythical. *Till We Have Faces*, indeed, develops the struggle between reason and imagination as one of its themes. And the very titles of his later books on Christianity (***Reflections on the Psalms***, ***Letters to Malcolm***) indicate a change in emphasis, from reasoned argument to the greater tentativeness and subjectivity that "reflections" and "letters" imply.

Peter J. Schakel
Hope College

Bibliography

Beversluis, John. *C. S. Lewis and the Search for Rational Religion*. Grand Rapids, MI: Eerdmans, 1985.

Como, James T. (ed). *C. S. Lewis at the Breakfast Table*. New York: Macmillan, 1979.

Holyer, Robert. "C. S. Lewis—The Rationalist?" *Christian Scholar's Review*. 18 (1988): 148–67.

Meilaender, Gilbert. *The Taste for the Other: The Social and Ethical Thought of C. S. Lewis*. Grand Rapids, MI: Eerdmans, 1978.

Patrick, James. "Reason in Chesterton and Lewis." *The Chesterton Review*. 17 (1991): 349–55.

Schakel, Peter J. *Reason and Imagination in C. S. Lewis: A Study of Till We Have Faces*. Grand Rapids, MI: Eerdmans, 1984.

Redemption

As a defender of orthodox **Christianity**, Lewis saw the need for human redemption and accepted as well as taught the ancient Christian doctrines of **sin**, forgiveness, and repentance. But Lewis also saw his own calling as primarily that of a "translator" and sought to give his 20th-century readers a better understanding of redemption. He realized that his task was to convince his reading audience of their need of redemption when they were most likely people who doubted the very existence of sin. He realized his readership especially doubted the existence of their own sins and were likely to be confident of their own admission into **heaven** just as they were.

First in *The Problem of Pain*, then in *Mere Christianity* and lastly in an essay, **"The Trouble with X . . . ,"** Lewis stressed that "The point is not that God will refuse you admission to His eternal world if you have not got certain qualities of character: the point is that if people have not got at least the beginnings of those qualities inside them, then no possible external conditions could make a 'Heaven' for them—that is, could make them happy with the deep, strong, unshakable kind of happiness God intends for us" (*Mere Christianity*).

In *The Problem of Pain* Lewis argued that though **Christ** spoke of **hell** as a place of positive retributive punishment, Christ himself said that "the judgement itself consists in the very fact that men prefer darkness to light, and that not He, but His 'word,' judges men." Therefore, Lewis concluded, the condemnation of the unredeemed to hell is not so much a matter of a sentence as rather it is a matter of the unredeemed refusing to let go of their egotism and self-will that causes them to want to control and consume other people around them. Of such a man, Lewis wrote, "He has his wish—to live wholly in the self and to make the best of what he finds there. And what he finds there is Hell." Thus, "the doors of Hell are locked on the inside. . . . But they [the unredeemed] certainly do not will even the first preliminary stages of that self-abandonment through which alone the soul can reach any good."

In "The Trouble with X," a telling essay that leads the reader to focus on one's own sins and not everyone else's, Lewis ended by warning, "Be sure there is something inside you which, unless it is altered, will put it out of God's power to prevent your being eternally miserable. While that something remains there can be no Heaven for you, just as there can be no sweet smells for a man with a cold in the nose, and no music for a man who is deaf. It is not a question of God 'sending' us to Hell. In each of us there is something growing up which will for itself be Hell unless it is nipped in the bud."

Lewis's fictional picture of the unredeemed in hell is in his fiction, *The Great Divorce*. Here hell is not a lake of fire wherein wallow the damned in torment, but rather a flat, gray expanse of urban nothingness, where no one can stand to be with anyone else because of their intense need to control and be "little gods" of their own insignificant corner of hell. Each wallows in self-created, subhuman misery. So redemption for Lewis is primarily the becoming of the man or woman God created us to be, the "New Man" of Paul's letters. Only this redeemed New Man is capable of looking on the Face of God and enjoying heaven, for short of becoming this New Man we degenerate into a self-deluded, subhuman creature that cannot be anywhere but in the eternally miserable hell of its own making.

Elsewhere, Lewis noted that Christ redeemed sinners, not valuable souls. For the soul's value, outside of its relationship to God, is zero (**"Membership"**). The very nature of the redemption itself, Lewis also noted, was anticipated by paganism. Redemption would only be accomplished by the shedding of blood. Indeed, in *The Problem of Pain* Lewis pointed out that this idea is not limited to Christianity even today.

One area of redemption Lewis was reluctant to discuss. That was the area of atonement. Lewis, like **George MacDonald**, was unable to accept the Calvinistic formula of God's needing to punish someone for the sins of humanity and Christ taking the punishment meted out by God the Father's righteous wrath. Though he does not deny this interpretation of the atonement and redemption, he was loath to give it support. In *Mere Christianity* he warned that we know that Christ was killed for us, and that that is Christianity. Any theories as to how this works are just theories, to be abandoned if they do not help us. Christ's debt paid for our lapsed human nature; just how this was accomplished, according to Lewis, is no more than speculation and ought not to be treated like doctrine.

Lewis also toyed with the question as to whether there are other species in the universe and, if so, whether they also need to be redeemed (**"Religion and Rocketry"**). Humanity may well be the only fallen species in the universe, and the light-years of isolation that separate us from other inhabitable bodies may well be the quarantine that confines our sickness to one planet. He explored this notion in the first novel of his space trilogy, *Out of the Silent Planet*, where the protagonist Ransom meets with three unfallen species on Malacandra (Mars). Lewis hoped that if we ever do encounter other species on other planets, that we do not try to "convert" them, assuming that they are a fallen species like our own. To Lewis this was yet another form of the sort of merciless imperialism that he expected the human race to practice against the innocent species on other planets if the human species ever got to other planets. He called on his readers to resist this evil, though he expected that such resistance would ultimately fail.

Furthermore, in *Miracles* Lewis speculated that redeemed humanity would be somehow something more than unfallen humanity might have been, and that this would result in the redemption of **nature** herself. God who makes good come forth from evil will someday make **the Fall** to have been an ultimate blessing. Lastly, though Lewis recognized that he was only speculating on the matter, he felt that the redemption of humanity

would lead to redemption of the rest of **creation**. To this end he suspected that we would find animals in heaven. To be sure, he did not believe that all animals would reach heaven, but rather he suspected that those animals on whom the redeemed had invested their love would come to somehow be part of the eternal **joy** of heaven. For, he reasoned, how could God let any good thing ultimately perish? This view, though Lewis recognized it as controversial, is part of his larger sense that the goodness of God reaches through redeemed humanity to creation itself. Thus humanity mediates the divine splendor to the animal kingdom, and redemption spreads from creature to creature like divine fire.

James Prothero

Also See: Destiny, Grace

Reflections on the Psalms

London: Geoffrey Bles, 1958. First US edition, New York: Harcourt Brace & World, 1958.

Reflections on the Psalms was written by C. S. Lewis soon after his Narnia stories (1950–55) and *Till We Have Faces* (1957), and was his first religious work since *Miracles* (1947). He was encouraged to write a book about the **Psalms** by his close friend **Austin Farrer** and by his wife **Joy Davidman Lewis**, who proofread and typed the manuscript for the book. These and other friends reinforced his belief that there was a need for a nontechnical work that would answer the questions and the doubts that ordinary people have when they read the Psalms. *Reflections on the Psalms* is Lewis's only book about a specific part of Holy Scripture, and at the end it gives his core beliefs about the **Bible**. The book was criticized by some scholars for "not being a work of scholarship," yet Lewis wrote in the introduction that it was intended for "the unlearned" (laity) like himself, or "as one amateur to another." *Reflections on the Psalms* is not a work of **apologetics**, although near the end Lewis asks the reader to make a choice about whom Jesus **Christ** was (see J. R. Christopher, *C. S. Lewis*); neither was the book intended to arouse denominational controversy. Instead, Lewis wanted his readers to enjoy the Psalms as great **poetry** (for Lewis, Psalms 18 and 19 are "perfect" poetry) and as words glorifying and praising **God** that were meant to be sung. Lewis noted that the Psalms made use of parallelism (or saying the same thing twice using different words), and he thought this could enhance a reader's enjoyment for the Psalms as poetry and help him or her understand their meaning. Finally, Lewis wrote this book (as he did so many of his works) to help others by sharing his own experiences, questions, and even doubts. For its "**beauty** in poetry" Lewis used the old Coverdale version in the Anglican *Book of Common Prayer* for his specific Scripture quotes, and he used the Moffatt version for "corrections."

Following an introductory chapter, chapters 2 through 4, "Judgement in the Psalms," "The Cursings," and "Death in the Psalms," deal with aspects of the Psalms that repelled some people, including Lewis. For him, parts of certain psalms seem to welcome a day of judgment as punishment, such as Psalm 67:4, "O let the nations rejoice and be glad, for thou shalt judge the folk righteously." Lewis cautioned the reader of the judgment Psalms to remember that God's judgment is tempered with **mercy** over and against the **justice** that we deserve.

In the third and fourth chapters Lewis deals with the frequent cursings in some of the Psalms (with their delight in the slaughter of the enemies of Israel) and their lack of belief in a life after death. **Clyde Kilby** has written that the "Hebrews seem (in the cursing Psalms) to be even more vitriolic than their Pagan neighbors." Lewis is indignant at such attitudes by the psalmist and deplores and calls "devilish" a psalm that asks God to kill enemies or give a blessing on anyone who will smash an enemy's baby against the rocks. He suggests that one way to deal with such Psalms is to ignore them, but a better way (for the Christian reader) is to learn from them. Through the cursing Psalms God shows us our own true **human**

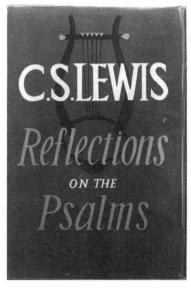

nature, which leans toward doing ill-will to others. He also reminds his readers that they cannot excuse the Hebrews because they were not "Christian." For him, the abiding ethic of the Old Testament is one of love, not hate and retaliation, toward God's created beings.

When Lewis wrote about the lack of discussion of an afterlife in the Psalms, he mentioned that many of the nations near Israel were often preoccupied with it, and how much of the Old Testament does not deal with it. In his opinion, God delayed until New Testament times his **revelation** of **heaven** and **hell** in order to teach humans **faith** and absolute dependence on him. Lewis cites his own life as a possible parallel. He had been a Christian for about a year and struggled to obey God

before any belief in a future life was given him. This insight by Lewis into the nature of God (as revealed in the Psalms) is one of his most perceptive, and many readers have profited from this idea.

The next five chapters are titled "The Fair Beauty of the Lord," "Sweeter Than Honey," "Connivance" (the Psalter's protests against **sins** of the tongue), "Nature," and "A Word About Praising." In these chapters Lewis gives many personal descriptions of the pleasure he received from reading the Psalms. He writes that "the most valuable things the Psalms do for me is to express the same delight in God which made David dance." Lewis writes about the pleasure one receives in using the Psalms in worship, the way they are often prayers for us when we cannot say the words we want to say, and their obvious "gusto" for God. He mentions the beauty of God's law and the way in which the Psalms revel in it, and he loves the way the Psalms rejoice in nature and in all of God's creation, which is good. It is interesting that in the chapter on **nature**, Lewis maintains that the doctrine of creation "empties nature of divinity," that is, that God is separate from nature. This is contrary to Martin Buber (whose work was much admired by Lewis), who wrote that **creation** (nature) has an "aliveness" to it through God's "connectedness" with everything he created (see M. Buber, *I and Thou*, Scribners, 1937).

Lewis finishes *Reflections on the Psalms* with three chapters—"Second Meanings," "Scripture," and "Second Meanings in the Psalms"—in which he talks about the interpretation of the Psalms and of the Bible. "Second meanings" are allegorical interpretations that are concerned with salvation and the meaning of Christ for the world. He cites **Plato**'s *Republic* and pagan mythologies as containing prophetic knowledge about Christ and **redemption**. Lewis then asks the reader to not view these examples as accidents but as vehicles for God's **revelation**. His chapter on Scripture discusses (in a very illuminating way), the inspiration of the Bible, his own views as contrasted to fundamentalism, the mythic elements of the Old Testament, and his idea of the "big picture" of the Bible, which is Christ, "the sacred fish." Lewis concludes by explaining the various connections between the Psalms and their place in the church calendar, and by a discussion of meter, structure, and form.

Reflections on the Psalms is a short but important book and it has remained a steady seller through the years, though it has not been quite as popular as some of Lewis's other religious works, such as **Mere Christianity** and **The Screwtape Letters**. The book has its shortcomings. Lewis could have included more discussion about the literary genres of the Psalms and explained more about their historical context, particularly their roots in Judaism. But *Reflections on the Psalms* is full of interesting, provocative, and convincing observations as well as the genuine piety that enriches Lewis's religious works. Lewis not only shows the reader how to enjoy, appreciate, and learn from the Psalms but also uncovers much of their poetic richness, theological depth, and practical implications for worship. In this book, Lewis has succeeded in doing his part to keep both the Bible and the Psalter in the minds and hearts of individual Christians and the churches where they worship.

Perry C. Bramlett
C. S. Lewis for the Local Church

Bibliography

Bramlett, Perry C. *C. S. Lewis: Life at the Center*. Macon, GA: Smyth & Helwys, 1996.

Christopher, Joe R. *C. S. Lewis*. Boston: Twayne, 1987.

Hannay, Margaret P. *C. S. Lewis*. New York: Ungar, 1981.

Kilby, Clyde S. *The Christian World of C. S. Lewis*. Grand Rapids, Michigan: Eerdmans, 1964.

Merchant, Robert. "Reflections on the Psalms." *CSL: The Bulletin of the New York C. S. Lewis Society*, 5 no. 3 (January 1974): 1–5.

Ramshaw, Walter. "Reflections on Reflections on the Psalms." *CSL: The Bulletin of the New York C. S. Lewis Society*. 11 no. 11 (September 1980): 1–7.

Walsh, Chad. *The Literary Legacy of C. S. Lewis*. New York: Harcourt Brace, 1979.

Rehabilitations and Other Essays

London: Oxford University Press, 1939.

See separate essay entries on the following:

"The Alliterative Metre"
"Bluspels and Flalansferes"
"Christianity and Literature"
"High and Low Brows"
"The Idea of an 'English School'"
"Our English Syllabus"
"Shelley, Dryden and Mr. Eliot"
"Variation in Shakespeare and Others"
"William Morris"

"Rejoinder to Dr. Pittenger"

The Christian Century. LXXV (26 November 1958): 1359–61. Reprinted in *God in the Dock*, *Undeceptions*, and *Timeless at Heart*.

This article is a reply to Norman Pittenger's "A Critique of C. S. Lewis" (*The Christian Century*. LXXV [1 October 1958]: 1104–07). Pittenger made several charges against Lewis's book *Miracles*. To the charge of "using the word 'literally' where [he] did not mean it," Lewis plead guilty. Lewis also assumed some guilt in an implication of "a shockingly crude conception of the Incarnation." However, Lewis did not seem to think that either admission would satisfy Dr. Pittenger. He claimed not to fully understand statements made in the critique but says that if Dr. Pittenger means that Jesus **Christ** is the Son of **God** by whom others become sons of God, then Lewis was in agreement.

As for Dr. Pittenger's statements about the book *Miracles*, Lewis said he is mistaken. He asked, "How many times does a man need to say something before he is safe from the accusation of having said exactly the opposite?" Apart from factually incorrect statements, Dr. Pittenger was guilty of misunderstanding Lewis's position on the Fourth Gospel and other matters of **faith**. He was critical of Lewis's lack of theological terms, which Lewis refuted by saying that he has no use for terminology that would obscure his meaning. His main purpose was "simply that of a translator" and had he adopted the style "more rich in fruitful ambiguities—in fact, a style more like Dr. Pittenger's own—[it] would have been worse than useless."

Anne Gardner

"Religion and Rocketry"

See entry on "Will We Lose God in Outer Space?"

"Religion and Science"

The Coventry Evening Telegraph. (3 January 1945): 4. Reprinted in *God in the Dock* and *Undeceptions*.

"Religion and Science" takes the form of a dialogue between a persona and his friend. The friend sneers at the idea of **miracles** on the grounds that

U.K. First Edition, 1939

"we know that **Nature** is governed by fixed laws." The friend then suggests that the Virgin Birth is impossible because we now know that there has to be a spermatozoon. The persona says that Joseph must have know that, otherwise he would not have changed his mind about **marriage**. He must have realized later that the only explanation was **supernatural**. The laws of nature say how a thing will be, provided there is no interference. If the thing is not the way the laws of nature suggest, then the interference is supernatural. The problem as it has been stated is how to reconcile what we know about the universe and traditional **religion**. That is not the real problem. The enormity of the universe relative to the insignificance of the earth has been recognized for centuries, but only recently has it been seen to have any bearing on religion. So why has it become an issue now? The conversation ends with the question, "Don't you think that all you atheists are strangely unsuspicious people?"

Anne Gardner

Also See: Atheism, Natural Law

"Religion: Reality or Substitute?"

World Dominion. XIX (September-October 1941): 277–81. Reprinted in *Christian Reflections.*

This essay by C. S. Lewis originally appeared in *World Dominion*; it was later reprinted, with some changes, in *Christian Reflections* (1967). In this important essay, Lewis dealt with the question of religious doubt and the fact that, in his time, faith was thought of by some as a substitute for the true well-being that many people have not achieved. Remembering his own experiences, Lewis wrote that often his own **religion** had "tasted thin" when compared to the "natural" life. He came to the conclusion that introspection was of no use in deciding if religion was real or a substitute; knowledge depended on authority ("of many wise men in many different times"), **reason**, and experience. But these three, according to Lewis, must also be combined with **faith**, a faith that "continues to believe what we honestly thought to be true until cogent reasons for honestly changing our minds are brought before us." Lewis also warned his readers about feelings ("the fifth column of the soul") and the conviction of real religion. For him, only the practice of faith that resulted in the habit of faith could end the hold that feelings have on human beings.

Perry C. Bramlett
C. S. Lewis for the Local Church

Also See: Reality

Bibliography

Bruce, Lenora. "Thoughts of Two Lewis Essays." *Chronicle of the Portland C. S. Lewis Society.* 3 no. 1 (February 1, 1974): 3–7.

"Religion Without Dogma?"

See entry on "A Christian Reply to Professor Price"

Renaissance

Lewis was one of the few scholars of the Medieval and Renaissance periods who was skeptical that the Renaissance constituted a separate period in history. In his volume of the *Oxford History of English Literature: English Literature in the sixteenth Century Excluding Drama*, he wrote for fifty-four pages before he even mentioned the word. He explained his reticence by writing that if the term only meant the recovery of classical Greek and Latin learning, then he would have no problem. But the term also was applied by the humanists of the period to describe what they perceived as their own achievement. The term remained because the humanist tradition persisted in scholarship, and the humanist scholarship of Lewis's time tended to laud the period because it was the birth of humanism. Lewis felt this was a biased view and not objective enough to be scholarly.

Furthermore, one of the hallmarks of this humanist version of literary and social history was the lauding of the significance and achievement of the physical sciences. This trend of thought led to what Lewis elsewhere dubbed "Scientism," that is, the treatment of physical sciences as if they were a religious **faith**. Taken far enough, the combination of these two attitudes resulted in a **philosophy** that Lewis called "universal evolutionism." This philosophy, drawing from Darwin's theory of biological **evolution**, held that man wallowed for centuries in ignorance and religious superstition until the Renaissance, at which time man's eyes were gradually opened by **science**. Man thereafter casts aside the superstition of religious faith and walks into the future growing in wisdom and power until mankind becomes a race of gods and masters of all natural forces.

Lewis found this philosophy to be an example of human self-delusion and classical *hubris* (overweening **pride**). It is noteworthy that he rarely mentioned the term "the Renaissance" in any of his writings, except for in his pre-conversion *Allegory of Love.*

James Prothero

Also See: Human Nature, Literary Criticism, Medieval World, Rationalism, Reason, Religion, Revelation

Reply to a critic (Letter)

Newsletter of the Conference on Christianity and Literature II. VII/VIII (December 1961): 6.

Harvie M. Conn in the *Westminster Theological Journal* ("Literature and Criticism." 23 [November 1960]: 16–23) criticized Lewis for failing to integrate **Christianity** into his aesthetic theory, believing he settled instead for simple humanism. **Clyde S. Kilby** wrote to Lewis seeking his response to the Conn article. Lewis replied to Kilby on January 11, 1961; in this letter, Lewis explained that he had refrained from dealing with certain questions in *Abolition of Man* because he intended to write ethics, not **theology**. Thus, though he did not say that **God** "made" the **Tao**, it was because he was attempting to avoid the perception that it was simply an arbitrary **creation**—not because he did not believe God was the Creator. Rather, Lewis believed that the Tao was a necessary expression of God's own righteous nature. Lewis gave Kilby permission to submit this letter to the *Westminster* journal, but they declined to publish it.

Marjorie L. Mead
The Marion E. Wade Center

Also See: Ethics and Morality

"A Reply to Prof. Haldane"

Hooper, Walter (ed). *Of Other Worlds*. London: Geoffrey Bles, 1966. First US edition, New York: Harcourt, Brace & World, 1967. Reprinted in *Of This and Other Worlds* and *On Stories*.

In this previously unpublished response to J. B. S. Haldane's "Auld Hornie, F.R.S.," Lewis replied to Haldane's charges that in Lewis's interplanetary trilogy his **science** was wrong; that Lewis unfairly misrepresented scientists; and that he equated scientific planning with the road to **hell**.

To the first charge, Lewis admitted that he made no attempt to portray accurate science in his novels. To the second, he replied that Haldane concentrated on the wrong novel, *That Hideous Strength*. According to Lewis, Haldane should have focused instead on *Out of the Silent Planet*, where Lewis was indeed satirizing not scientists but "scientism." Lewis said Haldane misunderstood *That Hideous Strength*, for it attacked the modern view about **values** Lewis treated in *The Abolition of Man* and the **psychology** of "the inner ring." As for Haldane's third charge about "scientific planning" in *That Hideous Strength*, Lewis explained that he was not condemning "scientific planning" per se, but rather

tyranny, which had already appeared under the guise of "scientific planning" in Nazi Germany.

Lyle Smith
Biola University

Also See: Bernard Acworth, Communism and Fascism, Education, Science Fiction

Bibliography

Hodgens, Richard M. "J. B. S. Haldane, Jailor." *CSL: The Bulletin of the New York C. S. Lewis Society*. 3 (July 1972): 6–7.

The Return of the King (Book Review)

See entry on *The Two Towers* and *The Return of the King* (Book Review)

Revelation

C. S. Lewis explained **God**'s revelation to man in a variety of ways. In the introduction to *The Problem of Pain*, he discussed two ways God shows himself to everyone. First, there is the almost universal experience of "numinous awe" that serves no biological purpose and seems to be "a direct experience of the really supernatural, to which the name Revelation may properly be given." Second is the equally universal awareness of a "moral law at once approved and disobeyed." Again this is either an "inexplicable illusion or else revelation."

Lewis pointed out that the human race has never shown much inclination to combine these revelations. Nonmoral religions and nonreligious moralities have always existed. While scattered individuals have united them, only one people, the Jews, "took the new step with perfect decision." With them, the Presence haunting the mountains and the troubling demands for righteousness were joined. With them, God began revealing himself openly with words that have become our **Bible**. In similar fashion, Lewis's *The Pilgrim's Regress* contrasts the mythical "pictures" that God sent Pagus (pagans) with the written Law given to the Shepherd People (Jews). The breach between the two could not be healed until the Landlord's Son (Jesus) came to earth.

While general revelation comes to all men and special revelation through the Jews, God also reveals himself to individuals. In *The Problem of Pain* Lewis described how God keeps us from resting "contentedly in our sins and our stupidities." "God whispers to us in our pleasures," he said, "speaks in our conscience, but shouts in our pains."

In *Surprised by Joy*, Lewis described the "steady, unrelenting approach of Him who I so earnestly desired

not to meet" and wrote of "the horror of such a revelation." But Lewis believed that God also hid himself. He
has Screwtape explain why "the Enemy does not make
more use of His power to be sensibly present to human
souls." God, it seems, wants sons who obey of their own
free will rather than servants who must be continually
prompted.

Lewis also believed that God limited his revelation
to the practical. In both *The Problem of Pain* and
"Dogma and the Universe" he stressed that God's revelation was for the present needs of Fallen Man, not to
gratify our "liberal curiosity." While the universe might
inspire in us a sense of awe, we had no way of knowing
that was why God created it.

Lewis did not accept modern ideas about revelation.
In **"Priestesses in the Church,"** he emphatically
rejected the idea that God would reveal himself in ways
that unbelievers consider rational and enlightened. The
church, he stressed, was a "bearer of a revelation" to the
world and not vice versa. In **"Historicism"** he expressed
similar skepticism about those who claim to have discovered an "inner meaning" in history or, to a lesser
extent, in **science**. Finally in **"Modern Theology and
Biblical Criticism"** he expressed skepticism about how
liberal **theology** treated biblical revelation. Screwtape
noted that the pursuit of a constantly changing "historical Jesus" could be used to keep people from discovering the "real presence" of God through **prayer**.

Mike Perry

Also See: Inspiration, Non-Christian Religions,
Paganism, Rationality

Bibliography

Lewis, C. S. "Dogma and the Universe"; "Historicism"; "Modern Theology and Biblical Criticism"; *The Pilgrim's
Regress* (bk. 8, ch. 8); "Priestesses in the Church"; *The
Problem of Pain* (esp. ch. 1, 6, 8); *The Screwtape Letters*
(ch. 8, 13); *Surprised by Joy* (ch. 14)

"Revival or Decay?"

Punch. CCXXXV (9 July 1958): 36–38. Reprinted in *God in
the Dock, Undeceptions,* and *First and Second Things.*

This article begins with a question asked by the
Headmaster of a school. He asks if his audience would
deny "that there is, here in the West, a great, even growing, interest in **religion**." The narrator of the essay
regards this question as a statistical one, and he surmises
that the Headmaster must mean something more than
that. The narrator noted that religion is a word used by
observers to denote the practice of worship. However,

once converted, a man has no interest in religion
because he is too busy. The Headmaster asks whether
his audience would deny the respect for **Christianity**
shown by intellectuals is increasing. "Of course," says
the narrator, "the converted Intellectual is a characteristic figure of our times." However, he would feel happier if it did not coincide with a period in which the
intellectual is losing touch with and influence over
"nearly the whole human race." The Headmaster continues to ask if there is not a greater defense of standards
that are part of "our spiritual heritage." The narrator is
reminded of a **prayer** in which a young chaplain asks
God to teach him "to **love** *the things [He] standest for.*"
Like the young chaplain, the Headmaster has missed the
point. "Once," says the narrator, "after I had said something on the air about **Natural Law**, an old Colonel . . .
wrote to say that this had interested him very much and
could I just tell him of 'some handy little *brochure*
which dealt with the subject fully.' That is ignorance,
striking only in degree." In the end, the question
remains: revival or decay?

Anne Gardner

"Rhyme and Reason"

See entry on *The Poetry of Search and the Poetry of
Statement* (Book Review)

Robinson Crusoe as a Myth (Letter)

Essays in Criticism. I (July 1951): 313.

Lewis's letter in response to Ian Watt's article,
"*Robinson Crusoe* as a Myth" (*Essays in Criticism,*
April 1951, 95–119), questioned Watt's statement that
"the **myths** of Midas and the Rheingold are inspired by
the prospect of never having to work again." Lewis disagreed that these myths were based on such an economic significance. Watt replied (July 1951, 313) that he
agreed with Lewis on the primary meaning of the myths,
and that he was simply using this economic aspect to
illustrate the contrasting ideology of *Robinson Crusoe.*

Marjorie L. Mead
The Marion E. Wade Center

Roman Catholicism

Lewis was reticent about addressing the subject of
Catholicism. The reason he gave most frequently for this
reticence is that to comment on divisions between Christians would emphasize differences and endanger charity. Various people wrote to him asking his views on
specific Catholic doctrines. His responses to these letters, a few comments in various of his works, a few published or anecdotal reminiscences, and one recently

published essay are all we have to go on to try and form a view of Lewis's attitude.

It is clear from his writings that Lewis thought schism amongst Christians was a scandal and a "source of grief and a matter for prayers, being a most serious stumbling block to those coming in." In this, he followed his "master" **George MacDonald** who, in an introduction to one of his lesser known works, called schism "the great Sabbath breaker" (*England's Antiphon*). Lewis looked for the day that all Christians would be one and said, "'That they all may be one' is a petition which in my prayers I never omit. While the wished-for unity of doctrine and order is missing, all the more eagerly let us try to keep the bond of charity."

In saying this, therefore, he did not necessarily subscribe to the view that "mere" **Christianity** made up of a variety of denominational expressions provided a satisfactory account of what the church (as distinct from specific teachings about aspects of the Christian **faith**) ought to be. This is clear from his statement about his own approach in *Mere Christianity* to the effect that "if I have not directly helped the cause of reunion, I have perhaps made it clear why we ought to be reunited."

Lewis was aware that there were differences between Catholicism and Protestantism and was aware of problems with both. He believed that when Catholicism became decadent it was in the direction of superstition and when Protestantism became decadent it tended towards becoming "a vague mist of ethical platitudes."

Catholic writers (such as Christopher Derrick and John Randolph Willis S.J.) have criticized Lewis's failure to deal with the claims of Catholicism. Derrick, for example, a pupil and later a close friend of Lewis, has noted that Lewis implicitly treated Catholicism as a denomination and that such a categorization (notably in *Mere Christianity*) is not ecumenical at all insofar as its starting assumption is that Catholic claims about the uniqueness of the Catholic church are simply wrong.

It is fair to note that by ignoring the claim to uniqueness that the Catholic Church holds and by treating it as something it does not claim to be (a denomination—one option amongst many), Lewis is inconsistent with his own statements in *Mere Christianity* about how **truth** claims ought to be dealt with. Lewis, after all, dismissed any attempts to say that Jesus **Christ** was simply a great moral teacher, but not what he claimed to be (the Son of God) because of the nature of the claims. But Lewis does not apply this logic to the claims of the Catholic Church.

J. R. R. Tolkien, his close friend and himself a Catholic, has been quoted as saying that Lewis did not become a Catholic due to "Ulsterior motives." Christopher Derrick has also said that Lewis's Northern Irish roots played a large part in his unwillingness to engage Catholic truth claims. Those interested in this aspect of Lewis should, in addition to Derrick's book, consult John Randolph Willis's study of Lewis's **theology**.

Whatever the reason for Lewis's approach, it is clear that he viewed Catholics as fellow brothers and sisters in Christ and in this respect he is in agreement with Catholic teaching about Protestants who are brothers and sisters in Christ by virtue of their baptisms irrespective of what denomination they belong to. In addition to this, Lewis's many friendships with Catholics (such as Tolkien, **Bede Griffiths,** and Christopher Derrick) and frequent reference to Catholic writers (not the least of which was **G. K. Chesterton**) as well as the fact that the **Oxford Socratic Club** frequently involved Catholics as speakers (such as the philosopher **G. E .M. Anscombe,** and Fr. Martin D'Arcy), shows his practical ecumenism. Given developments in **Anglicanism** in recent years and his strongly expressed views in opposition to the ordination of **women** (now an accepted aspect of Anglicanism), it is not clear where Lewis would have stood in relation to Catholicism had he lived longer.

What is clear is that Lewis's own life and works were dedicated to a form of ecumenism that sought to build bridges between all Christians and then from that coalition to the surrounding culture. He would, no doubt, have endorsed recent developments in the direction of strategic alliances between Protestants and Catholics in regard to many cultural issues. We are left to wonder what Lewis would make of the "papal claims" today given his statement to another pupil, Dom Bede Griffiths (who was a Catholic convert and became a priest), that "[n]othing would give such strong support to the Papal claims as the spectacle of a Pope actually functioning as the head of Christendom."

In a recently published article (not, therefore, covered in the books referred to above) on the subject of **"Christian Reunion,"** Lewis recognized that the central difficulty in the way of reunion amongst Christians is "disagreement about the seat and nature of doctrinal authority." In this essay, Lewis stated that "the real reason" why he could not become a Roman Catholic was not his "disagreement with this or that Roman doctrine," but the fact he would have "to accept in advance any doctrine . . . [the Roman Catholic] Church hereafter produces. It is like being asked to agree not only to what a man has said but to what he's going to say."

While Lewis saw disunity as "a tragic and sinful division" his focus and gifts lay in leading people to general truths about the faith. Insofar as he saw division as "sinful" however, Lewis did not endorse the view shared by so many, that the current divisions are normal or acceptable or that the church should be seen as merely an "invisible" reality.

There is an unresolved tension in Lewis's thought on this point, therefore, between an invisible church (which he rejected since he believed that the church was "torn and divided" and should be "reunited") and his reference to "my own Church" (referring to Anglicanism, as in his essay on **"Membership"**). If there are churches rather than "the Church," then how is unity other than invisible, and if invisible, then how is the church divided (if it is invisible, after all, one could not "see" division)? Whatever one's views, however, most would agree with what he said in one of his Latin letters to an Italian priest, "All who profess themselves Christians are bound to offer prayers for the reunion of the church now, alas, torn and divided."

Iain T. Benson
Centre for Renewal in Public Policy

Also See: Don Giovanni Calabria

Bibliography

Derrick, Christopher. *C. S. Lewis and the Church of Rome.* San Francisco: Ignatius, 1981.
Willis, John Randolph. *Pleasures Forevermore: The Theology of C. S. Lewis.* Chicago: Loyola, 1983.

Romanticism

Literary scholars routinely remind us that Romanticism is such a complex subject that it would be better to speak instead of romanticisms, in the plural. The sort of romanticism most relevant to Lewis is often referred to as "Wordsworthian," an adumbration of spiritual transcendence frequently mediated to persons through **nature**, **poetry**, art, and music, but distinctly different from aesthetic experience *per se*. In his autobiography ***Surprised by Joy***, Lewis described moments of intense longing experienced from his earliest years—responses to **beauty**, but referring his feelings to something unnamable, beyond the immediate object. Standing beside a flowering currant bush on a summer day in early childhood he remembered a toy garden his brother had once brought into the nursery. He recounted the sense of sur-

prise and of vast importance aroused by the mysteriously troubling "Idea of Autumn" communicated by **Beatrix Potter**'s *Squirrel Nutkin* and the haunting intensity of the sensation that came when he first read the words "Balder the beautiful / Is dead, is dead" in Longfellow's translation of *Tegner's Drapa*. The universal human experience of longing, *Sehnsucht*—what Lewis calls **joy**—motivated Lewis's spiritual pilgrimage toward conversion. That motive became one of the most memorable elements in Lewis's **apologetics**. In ***Mere Christianity*** Lewis identifies it as the natural longing for **heaven**. Taking the cue, Peter Kreeft has called Lewis's treatment of this motive the "Argument from Desire."

The links between Lewis's joy and romanticism are literary, psychological, and spiritual. The title of *Surprised by Joy* is taken from the first line of a sonnet by the father of English romanticism, **William Wordsworth**. Appropriately, the emotions celebrated in the sonnet are grief, joy, and then grief as the poet remembers that his young daughter, with whom he thought to share his feeling, is dead. Similarly, Lewis described the moment of longing, which is joy, as fading away even as we seek to grasp it. We, like Wordsworth, must come to terms with the realization that what we desire is, in any earthly sense, unattainable. It is a desire that implies the reality, as well as the absence, of its object. Joy shares with happiness and pleasure the fact that anyone who has felt it will want it again. Paradoxically, it might equally be called a kind of unhappiness, or grief—but it is a kind we want. Although as an adolescent Lewis was overwhelmed by the operatic mythology of **Richard Wagner**, the illustrations of Arthur Rackham and the fantasies of **William Morris** and **George MacDonald**—all late Romantic in provenance—he was drawn to them as a result of his earlier awareness and not *vice versa*.

The same story is told symbolically in ***The Pilgrim's Regress***, whose protagonist, John, one day feels a pang when, looking through a window in a stone wall alongside the road, he sees a green wood full of primroses and remembers another wood where, so long ago that the memory itself seemed out of reach, he had pulled primroses. "All the furniture of his mind was taken away. A moment later he found that he was sobbing." He thinks he remembers seeing an island through the mist, and it is his desire to find that island that first sends him on his travels. Even before setting out, he confuses his longing with adolescent eroticism, represented by a Brown Girl, and in his travels he meets her again in the form of Media Halfways, the daughter of old Mr. Halfways, who embodies the quasi-religious character of an erotically aestheticized late-Victorian romanticism.

John later finds another meaning for these early passions spending a night in the cave of the Hermit History, who tells him of messages the Landlord periodically sent the inhabitants of Pagus (in the **allegory**, the Gentile world) to fill them with desire for something that cannot be had in this life. Romanticism was the latest of these pictures, and it aroused in the hearts of its viewers a longing for "the heart's desire—as it were hiding, yet not quite hidden, like something ever more about to be" (this last another Wordsworthian echo). It did this by showing people the countryside, something they had all about them already, and still they desired. Therefore the landscape could not itself be the thing desired. John finds that the island for which he has long searched is one such picture, and it can never be reached from his world. He must reverse his steps and finally cross over the brook to the Eastern Mountains beyond—the abode of the Landlord (in the allegory, **God**) in which he has already recognized the form of the true island for which he sought at the wrong end of the world.

All his life, Lewis loved romance as a literary genre, and romance not simply as adventure, but as evoking such qualities of lived experience as local atmosphere, spirit of place, and otherworldly hopes and fears. Writers as diverse as **H. G. Wells**, **G. K. Chesterton**, **Rider Haggard**, and **Edmund Spenser** fed his imagination. **Alan Bede Griffiths** calls *Dymer*, a narrative poem Lewis published while in his twenties, a poem of "unashamed romanticism." And, in **"Bluspels and Flalansferes: a Semantic Nightmare,"** an address delivered at Manchester University in the late 1930s, Lewis wrote that whereas **reason** is the "organ of truth," **imagination**—a key concept in Wordsworthian transcendence—is the "organ of meaning."

It would be a mistake, however, to regard the mature Lewis's criticism, his apologetic, his **theology,** or his sensibility as being especially romantic. **Nevill Coghill** has compared Lewis to **Samuel Johnson**, the eminently common-sensical "Great Cham" of English literature in its most rational 18th-century phase. It is true that Lewis was capable of speaking of someone as being a romantic theologian, but it was to **Charles Williams**, not himself, that he applied the sobriquet—adding that it meant, not a person who is romantic about theology, but one who is theological about romance. The same neat turn of emphasis appeared some years earlier, in the first chapter of *Beyond Personality*, as Lewis described his response to an RAF officer's account of "religious experience" in nature. Lewis agreed that the man had experienced something real but went on to point out that there is very little to do with such an experience and offered an **analogy**. It is true that a walk on the beach provides a much more real experience of the ocean than does study of a map. But the map, made up from the "ocean-experiences" of many people over a long period of time, is much more useful if you want to sail to **America**.

Lewis distrusted romanticism because it is vague and can as easily lead one wrong as right. In the fourth Screwtape letter, Screwtape quotes the romantic poet and critic Samuel Taylor Coleridge, whose vague notion of **prayer** suits the tempter's tactics; and in the thirteenth letter Screwtape alludes to the work of Goethe and Byron as being useful for damning one's "patient" by a surfeit of *sturm und drang* romantic emotionalism. In the 1940 essay **"Christianity and Culture,"** Lewis implied that his "early experiences of romantic *Sehnsucht*" led him to eroticism and occultism. On the other hand, he attributed this to his abuse of these experiences, since they also contained much that was good and that led to his conversion.

Lyle Smith
Biola University

Bibliography

Coghill, Nevill. "The Approach to English." *Light on C. S. Lewis*. Jocelyn Gibb (ed). New York: Harcourt Brace & World, 1965: 51–66.

Griffiths, Alan Bede. "The Adventure of Faith." *C. S. Lewis at the Breakfast Table*. James T. Como (ed). New York: Macmillan, 1979, 11–24.

_____. The Golden String. New York: P.J. Kenedy and Sons, 1954.

Kreeft, Peter J. "C. S. Lewis's Argument from Desire.' *The Riddle of Joy*. Michael H. Macdonald and Andrew A. Tadie (eds). Grand Rapids, MI: Eerdmans, 1989: 249–272.

Lewis, C. S. "Beyond Personality"; "Bluspels and Flalansferes: A Semantic Nightmare"; "Christianity and Culture"; "Preface" to *Essays Presented to Charles Williams*; *Pilgrim's Regress*; *Surprised by Joy*.

Paffard, Michael. *Inglorious Wordsworths: A Study of Some Transcendental Experiences in Childhood and Adolescence*. London: Hodder and Stoughton, 1973.

Romanticism Comes of Age (Book Review)

"'Who gaf me Drink?'" *The Spectator*. CLXXIV (9 March 1945): 224.

According to Lewis, **Owen Barfield** argues that **Romanticism** need not have "shipwrecked." On the contrary, its wreck occurs as a tragic consequence of "the failure of the hero to ask the crucial question at the crucial moment," just as in the tragedy of Parsifal. The tragedy of Romanticism is that Coleridge omits the full account of **Imagination** as the organ of **truth** from *Biographia,* which is the *raison d' être* of the book. The claims for Imagination were never withdrawn or supported, as they should have been to keep Romanticism on course.

Anne Gardner

Bibliography
Barfield, Owen. *Romanticism Comes of Age.*

"The Romantics"

The New English Weekly. 30 (January 16, 1947): 130. Revised and retitled as "The Prudent Jailer" and reprinted in *Poems* and *Collected Poems.*

Prisoners, remembering freedom, long for the good old days before they were chained and bound. Their warders try to keep them from such thoughts (for obvious reasons) and mock their memories of a better place.

Lewis clearly invited us to apply the prisoners' sentiments to the human predicament.

Don W. King
Montreat College

Rossetti: His Life and Works (Book Review)

The Oxford Magazine. XLVII (25 October 1928): 66, 69 (unsigned).

Lewis pronounced this book "interesting, if not perfectly successful." In it, Evelyn Waugh resisted the temptation to create a "period" biography and instead wondered about "matters on which the prevalent modes of thought do not encourage him to wonder." Lewis commended the result as a worthwhile attempt and praised Waugh's portrayal of "minor characters," particularly Ruskin, which "confirm[s] our confidence in the author's good sense and insight."

Anne Gardner

Bibliography
Waugh, Evelyn. *Rossetti: His Life and Works.*

S

"A Sacred Poem"
See entry on *Taliessin Through Logres* (Book Review)

"The Sagas and Modern Life: Morris, Mr. Yeats, and the Originals"
See entry *The Works of Morris and of Yeats in Relation to Early Saga Literature* (Book Review)

"The Sailing of the Ark"
Punch. 215 (August 11, 1948): 124 (under the pseudonym Nat Whilk). Revised and retitled "The Late Passenger" and reprinted in *Poems* and *Collected Poems.*

Lewis imagined the sons of Noah denying entry to one last animal as the rains begin. Awakening to the pounding on the ark's door, Noah is horrified to discover the forsaken animal is the unicorn. The lively musical rhythm of the lines (frequent use of anapestic meter) makes this a very enjoyable poem to read aloud in public settings.

Don W. King
Montreat College

"The Salamander"
The Spectator. 174 (June 8, 1945): 521. See erratum: "Poet and Printer," ibid. (June 15, 1945): 550. Reprinted in *Poems* and *Collected Poems.*

This somber poem suggests insular self-righteousness and stubborn refusal to admit to **reality** beyond what one can see. In the poem, the speaker imagines a fiery salamander crawls out of the burning coals and pronounces judgment against the cold, hollow world outside his own.

Don W. King
Montreat College

Satan
In a new preface to *The Screwtape Letters* written in 1960, Lewis defined Satan ("the Devil") as "the leader or dictator of devils" and the opposite not of **God** (which would be dualism), but of the angel Michael. In Lewis's view, the existence of Satan was an explanation for much of the evil in the world, and he wrote that his opinion about Satan "agreed with the plain sense of Scripture,

the tradition of Christendom, and the beliefs of most men at most times." However, Lewis did not altogether agree with the depictions of Satan in Western art and literature. He objected especially to the image of Satan fostered by Goethe's "humorous, civilised [and] sensible" Mephistopheles—an image Lewis thought had "helped to strengthen the illusion that evil is liberating."

Lewis in *Mere Christianity* followed most of the traditional **theology** of his day in believing that Satan had rebelled against God because of **pride** and "wanting to be the center," thus going his own way and choosing not to be subject to the control of God. Lewis's ideas about Satan were greatly influenced by **John Milton**'s *Paradise Lost* (and thus by **Augustine**), especially with its emphasis on **free will** and pride. In *A Preface to Paradise Lost* Lewis wrote that Satan had no capacity "to understand anything," and his foolish and arrogant attitude was in complete ignorance of God's authority. In Lewis's thinking, Satan's abuse and misunderstanding of the free will God gave to him, along with his prideful arrogance, caused him to be the enemy of God.

Lewis believed that Satan, who represents all fallen **angels**, is the power behind death, disease, and **sin**. In *Miracles*, he wrote that God uses certain of Satan's own weapons, such as death, to defeat Satan himself; in *The Problem of Pain* he asserted that "I by no means reject the view that disease may be caused by a created being other than man," referring to Satan. And in a letter (November 1, 1954), he referred to Luke 13:16 as one scriptural basis for Satan as the originator of disease. Lewis often referred to Satan as the originator of sin in humans and that the world is "enemy occupied territory." In *Christian Reflections* (**"Christianity and Culture"**) he wrote that "There is no neutral ground in the universe: every square inch, every split second, is claimed by God and counterclaimed by Satan." This idea was brought out forcefully in his space novels, where Lewis maintained that our world is the "silent" and "tortured" planet that has been isolated by God because of the fact that Satan now, at least temporarily, rules it.

Lewis used the idea of "**chronological snobbery**" (defined in *Surprised by Joy*) to explain the frustrating fact that so many in his time believed in God but not in Satan. In *The Problem of Pain* he wrote that "the doctrine of Satan's existence and fall is not among the things we know to be untrue: it contradicts not the facts discovered by scientists but the mere, vague 'climate of opinion' that we happen to be living in." Lewis believed that Satan and his devils had infected the universe, but his certain hope was that this fallen angel would and

could not "frustrate the good that God intended when he created the world."

Perry C. Bramlett
C. S. Lewis for the Local Church

Also See: Good and Evil, Morality

Bibliography

Cunningham, Richard. *C. S. Lewis: Defender of the Faith.* Philadelphia: Westminster, 1967.

Glaspey, Terry W. *Not a Tame Lion: The Spiritual Legacy of C. S. Lewis.* Elkton, MD: Highland Books, 1996.

Houtman, Marciak. "The Bent One: C. S. Lewis' Vision of the Devil." *Lamp-Post.* 6 no. 4 (October 1982): 9–13.

Huttar, Charles A. "C. S. Lewis and the Demonic." *Perspectives.* 3 no. 3 (March 1988): 6–10.

Satire

Satire forms an important ingredient in many of Lewis's prose works and poems, particularly in works that put emphasis on intellect and **reason** rather than on **imagination** and **myth**. Lewis wrote nothing that could be called "a satire," as a form, but he often employed a satiric mode, using humor, wit, and irony to hold up vices, follies, and abuses to ridicule and contempt. (See his distinction between *satire* and *the satiric* in *English Literature in the Sixteenth Century, Excluding Drama*).

His satire generally targets facets of behavior and thought that he found objectionable: modern lifestyles and 19th- and 20th-century rationalism, for example, in *The Pilgrim's Regress*; autocratic regimes and the pseudoscientific "expertise" that has come to be used to support them, in *That Hideous Strength*; human blindness and lack of self-recognition, and various personal follies that disturbed Lewis throughout his life, in *The Great Divorce*.

Some of Lewis's best satire appears in *Out of the Silent Planet*, as he employs techniques borrowed from **Jonathan Swift**'s *Gulliver's Travels* to achieve an outsider's critique of things in our world, satirizing the competitiveness, greed, **pride**, and selfishness of humankind. *The Screwtape Letters* rests on the ironic inversion of having a senior devil writing letters of advice to his junior-level nephew. Growing out of that inversion are numerous instances of satire, mostly light, humorous ridicule of the human tendency to allow trivialities and externals to dominate over crucial internal issues.

Satire appears less frequently in Lewis's more deeply mythopoeic works, which invoke an imaginative or emotional response from the reader, rather than intellectual interaction: satire is absent from *Perelandra* and *Till We*

Have Faces, and is rare in the **Chronicles of Narnia** (though there is satire on modern parents, modern education, and the idea of "progress" in *The Voyage of the "Dawn Treader,"* on modern schools and demythological thought in *The Silver Chair*, and on totalitarian methods and religious liberalism in *The Last Battle*).

Satire also appears in Lewis's **poetry** throughout his life (for notable examples, see **"Evolutionary Hymn,"** *"Odora Canum Vis,"* and **"Science-Fiction Cradlesong"**).

Peter J. Schakel
Hope College

Also See: Education, Modernity, Science

Bibliography

Lindvall, Terry. *Surprised by Laughter*. Nashville, TN.: Thomas Nelson, 1996.

Schakel, Peter J. "The Satiric Imagination of C. S. Lewis." *Studies in the Literary Imagination*. 22 (Fall 1989): 129–48.

George Sydney Benedict Sayer (1914–)

George Sayer, born in Berkshire, England, entered **Magdalen College, Oxford,** in 1933 and was a student of C. S. Lewis. In 1936 he began his own search for **God**, becoming, in due course, a Roman Catholic, only later to learn of Lewis's own conversion to Christianity. He took his B.A. in 1938 and his M.A. in 1947. He married, was a writer, served in the army during the war, and then became English master at **Malvern College**, which **Warren Lewis** and Jack had attended many years earlier. He became a close friend of Lewis and through him of his brother, Warren, **Janie Moore**, **Maureen Moore**, **Joy Gresham Lewis** and her two sons, and others. He also was an **Inkling**. Jack Lewis was a frequent guest at the Sayers' home in Malvern and they, in turn visited **the Kilns**. George Sayer last saw Jack about two weeks before he died in November 1963, but he had known him for almost thirty years and this gives an authority to his biography of Lewis, *Jack: A Life of C. S. Lewis* (1988), which is unsurpassed. He also has contributed other reminiscences of Lewis in the *Inklings-Jahrbuch* (1988) and *In Search of C. S. Lewis*, edited by Stephen Schofield (1983). After Jack's death, Warren became a closer friend of the Sayers and often stayed with them in Malvern.

John Bremer

Also See: David Gresham, Douglas Gresham, Roman Catholicism

Bibliography

Sayer, George. "Two Guests." *Canadian C. S. Lewis Journal*. 33–34 (September-October 1981): 1–6.

———. "Jack on Holiday." *C. S. Lewis at the Breakfast Table*. James T. Como (ed). New York: Macmillan, 1992: 202–9.

———. *Jack: A Life of C. S. Lewis*. Wheaton, IL: Crossway, 1994.

Dorothy L. Sayers (1893–1957)

Dorothy Leigh Sayers was five years Lewis's senior; they first became acquainted when she wrote him a fan letter about *The Screwtape Letters* (1942). At some point, perhaps then, she sent Lewis an imitation letter, written as by a demon named Sluckdrib. In 1943, Sayers wrote Lewis, asking him why no one was writing books on **miracles** any more and suggesting he do one; he started writing *Miracles* (1947) a few weeks later. Also in 1943, Sayers' *The Man Born to be King* was published (the plays had been broadcast earlier); Lewis later said of this play cycle, that he had "re-read it every Holy Week since it first appeared, and never re-read it without being deeply moved." (See **"A Panegyric for Dorothy Sayers."**)

A few popular books have said Sayers was a member of the **Inklings**, the group around Lewis and **J. R. R. Tolkien** in **Oxford**, from 1937 (or before) until 1949, but this is not true; the closest she came was that her letters on **Dante** to **Charles Williams** were shared by him with Lewis and then read to the Inklings in 1944. After Williams' death, Lewis wrote her, asking her to contribute to a memorial *Festschrift*, *Essays Presented to Charles Williams* (1947), which she did. In a letter to **Owen Barfield**, Lewis called Sayers' essay "a trifle vulgar," which may have meant it was lively and nonacademic; at any rate, he gave it the lead in the volume. In 1948, Lewis wrote to her, asking her to write an essay against the ordination of **women** to the priesthood in the Church of England; Sayers replied that she thought they should not be ordained, since it would separate the church from "the rest of Catholic Christendom," but that she could see no theological reason why women should not be, since they also are made in the image of **God**. (Lewis subsequently wrote the essay he wanted by himself, **"Priestesses in the Church?"**) On June 3, 1954, Sayers delivered a paper, "Poetry, Language and Ambiguity," to the **Oxford University Socratic Club**, a religious debating society of which Lewis was president from 1942 until that year (when he became a professor at **Cambridge**).

Lewis kept up with her later translations: in a letter, Lewis praised her version of *Dante's Inferno* (1949), while raising some objections; in his "Panegyric," he speaks of how her *Purgatorio* (1955) was raised in style; and in his final exchange of letters with her, he discussed her translation of *Song of Roland* (1957). During Lewis's brief, late **marriage** (or possibly before it), Sayers and **Joy Davidman Lewis** met, discussing (no doubt among other things) Sayers' reason for giving up writing mystery fiction ("Panegyric"); Lewis himself did not care for mystery fiction (**"On Science Fiction"**) and presumably was not interested in Sayers' mysteries. Probably Lewis's most famous comment to (and on) Sayers is from a letter of December 10, 1945 (*Letters of C. S. Lewis*): "Although you have so little time to write letters you are one of the great English letter writers. (Awful vision for you—'It is often forgotten that Miss Sayers was known in her own day as an Author. We who have been familiar from childhood with the Letters can hardly realise!')."

Christopher gives a list of their published letters up until Reynolds's *Dorothy L. Sayers*; Lewis reviewed Sayers' *The Mind of the Maker* (1941) and *The Poetry of Search and the Poetry of Statement* (1963); she reviewed his *Surprised by Joy* (1955).

Joe R. Christopher

Bibliography

Cobb, Lawrence. "A Gift From the Sky: The Creative Process in Lewis and Sayers." *CSL: The Bulletin of the New York C. S. Lewis Society.* 16 (February 1985): 1–5.

Christopher, Joe R. "The C. S. Lewis-Dorothy L. Sayers Correspondence." *The Lewis Legacy.* 58 (Autumn 1993): 6–7.

Green, Roger Lancelyn, and Walter Hooper. *C. S. Lewis: A Biography.* New York: Harcourt Brace Jovanovich, 1974.

Martin, John. "Voices of Fire: Eliot, Lewis, Sayers, Chesterton." *CSL: The Bulletin of the New York C. S. Lewis Society.* 13 (May 1982): 1–16.

Reynolds, Barbara. *Dorothy L. Sayers: Her Life and Soul.* New York: St. Martin's Press, 1993.

———. *The Passionate Intellect: Dorothy L. Sayers' Encounter with Dante.* Kent, OH: The Kent State University Press, 1989.

Scholar

In modern usage *scholar* has a range of meanings from simply a pupil to a learned person to one who through long systematic study has acquired mastery of an academic discipline. Webster has given all teachers the perfect right to call their students scholars, although today few do, except in jest or out of courtliness. C. S. Lewis's usage of the term spanned the definitional scale.

In *Reflections on the Psalms* (1958) Lewis set the highest standard of *scholar* for himself and, by implica-

tion, for others. He denied that he was a scholar on the subject at hand. The basis of this assessment is that he was not a Hebraist, a higher critic, an ancient historian, or an archeologist. Giving no recognition to his fame as a Christian apologist and expositor, he labeled himself an amateur on the **Psalms**. While he was bending over backwards to establish common ground with his readers, he furthered the positive notion of biblical scholar as one with a thorough knowledge of the original languages, the texts themselves, the critical studies, and the relevant times, events, and cultures. By these criteria he excelled as a scholar in his professional field of **Medieval** and **Renaissance** English, but he did not pull rank on his readers even in his own area of expertise.

Almost two decades earlier, during the first days of World War II, Lewis had drawn a broader view of *scholar*. In **"Learning in War-Time,"** a sermon delivered in **Oxford**, he targeted university students who wondered why they should engage in serious study when international conflicts were exploding around them. As he answered their doubts, Lewis made several references to students as scholars, almost by virtue of their university enrollment. But he also pointed to the developmental process of **education** through which they could become scholars or philosophers, scientists, critics, or historians. The depiction here does not make a sharp demarcation between an expert and everyone else, but shows the life of learning as a continuum.

Even though Lewis by his own definition was not a biblical scholar, he showed no hesitation in taking on the experts who (as the bishop in *The Great Divorce*) undermined historic Christian beliefs. Making full use of his mastery of logic, **philosophy**, and literature, as well as his experience as author and critic, he argued against their methodology and conclusions. From these challenges—and those to literary critics who have much in common with biblical critics—we can extract several requisites for credible scholars. They should have a wide and deep grasp of literature and literary forms, thoroughly understand the texts under scrutiny, and avoid making unsubstantiated claims sound like facts.

Lewis's concern for scholars included more than their cognitive processes. Character is also crucial. This clearly emerged in the aforementioned sermon. Lewis warned against the ever-present danger of adoring one's own knowledge, talent, and reputation. He advocated working humbly "as to the Lord," realizing that **God** does not attribute any special status to scholars.

For Lewis who knew and wrote about every sense of *scholar*, being one was a sacred duty traversing time and circumstances. In discharging this duty, he had developed from a student-scholar to a learned person to a master-scholar whose prodigious output defied the distractions of **war**, professional and domestic pressures, grief, and illness. Mindful of the trap of **pride**, Lewis never hinted that he could serve as an exemplar of *scholar*, but the title is apt.

Carolyn Keefe
West Chester University

Also See: Apologetics, Literary Criticism

Bibliography

Lewis, C. S. "A Reply to Professor Haldane." and "On Criticism." *Of Other Worlds: Essays & Stories*; "Learning in War-Time." *The Weight of Glory and Other Addresses*; "Modern Theology and Biblical Criticism." *Christian Reflections*; *Reflections on the Psalms*; *The Great Divorce*.

"Scholar's Melancholy"

The Oxford Magazine. 52 (May 24, 1934): 734 (under the pseudonym of Nat Whilk). Reprinted in *Poems* and *Collected Poems*.

This sonnet wonders what might have been as a scholar comes across his old notes of a once important project. Nostalgia for this past passion flickers briefly but is subsumed by a commitment to the pressing concerns of the present.

Don W. King
Montreat College

Science

In *The Abolition of Man*, C. S. Lewis noted that nothing he could say would keep some people from saying that he was anti-science, a charge he was nevertheless eager to refute. In fact, he has received the kind of philosophical education at **Oxford** that enabled him to resist the two opposed temptations of "science deified" and "science defied."

"Science deified" is scientism, radical empiricism, **materialism**, or naturalism—an implicit or explicit rejection of all nonquantifiable realities or truths, including the truths of **reason**. Its logical terminus is determinism or "epiphenomenalism," T. H. Huxley's notion that the brain and mind are fully determined by-products of irrational physical processes. As the German materialist Karl Vogt put it, "thoughts come out of the brain as gall from the liver, or urine from the kidneys." Thoughts are thus determined and irrational; but Vogt and other materialists implicitly claim accuracy, truth, and validity for their own thoughts and assertions; thus

they contradict their own assertions about the irrational and determined nature of all thoughts and assertions. This is a classic argument that Lewis repeatedly made against scientism (see, for example, **"Miracles"** in *God in the Dock*; *Miracles*, chapter 13).

The deification of science first became explicit in the writings of the atheistic French *philosophes* La Mettrie, D'Holbach, and Diderot. Thoughtful 20th-century commentators such as Lester G. Crocker (*Nature and Culture: Ethical Thought in the French Enlightenment*, 1963), and **Aldous Huxley** (*Ends and Means*, 1938) have seen its reductionism leading straight to the moral nihilism of the Marquis de Sade, and later to Social Darwinism and the Nietzschean transvaluation of values in the interest of amoral strength and force. Lewis's *Abolition of Man* is an extended treatise against the deification of science.

Yet there is an opposite temptation that Lewis also identified and criticized—the temptation to *defy* science, from the standpoint of either romantic pantheistic gnosticism or theological fideism. The first was familiar to him from the theosophy of his close friends **Owen Barfield** and **A. C. Harwood** and from the whole history of **Romanticism**, culminating in the work and world of **W. B. Yeats**, whom Lewis admired and visited in 1921. (Yeats was probably the model for the magician in Lewis's *Dymer* and for Merlin in *That Hideous Strength*.) The appeal of pantheistic gnosticism was something that Lewis understood and withstood; it lies at the heart of occult "New Age" spirituality, "Deep Ecology," and a good deal of "Eco-feminism" today (see, for example, Theodore Roszak, "The Monster and the Titan: Science, Knowledge, and Gnosis," *Daedalus*, 103 [Summer 1974]; and the recent works of Susan Griffin, such as *The Death of Nature*).

Romantic self-absorption and sensuality and pantheistic gnosticism are targets of Lewis's satire in *The Pilgrim's Regress*, where they are identified with the South. Much as he disbelieved and criticized radical empiricism and its sterile, truncated, contradictory rationalism, he was himself too much of a rationalist in the classic, Aristotelian sense to countenance esoteric mysticism and the depreciation of reason. He would not defy science on romantic or Gnostic grounds.

Lewis knew that science was one of the great products and capacities of the human mind, but he insisted that it was a subset of reason and not simply equivalent to it. Scientific reason, if accurate, was valid, but it was not the only valid kind of reasoning; noncontradiction, validity, **truth**, value, meaning, purpose, obligation were necessary presuppositions of the scientific method but not themselves scientific phenomena. Like Alfred North Whitehead, Lewis thought that, as Whitehead put it, scientists who were contradictorily "animated by the purpose of proving that they are purposeless constitute an interesting subject for study." He satirically depicted such scientists in *That Hideous Strength*, especially in the figure of Frost. Of all sensationalists or radical empiricists, from La Mettrie and Hume to A. J. Ayer, who would undermine the authority of reason and its procedures, Lewis tirelessly pointed out this thoroughly discrediting contradiction. He believed in the old adage that "the only way to avoid **metaphysics** is to say nothing" because in some important sense **language** and thought themselves are nonnatural, supernatural, transcendent, and metaphysical. "In order to think," he wrote in 1942, "we must claim for our reasoning a validity which is not credible if our own thought is merely a function of our brain, and our brains a by-product of irrational physical processes."

Lewis's love of the Middle Ages and the **Renaissance** was largely due to his loyalty to an epistemology that he thought had been caricatured, misunderstood, and mutilated by Bacon, Descartes, and the French Encyclopedistes of the 18th century (see entry on **Modernity**). As a careful student of the history of philosophy and ideas, he knew that the great flowering of scientific thought in the 17th century had not only Greek roots, but Medieval ones. Whitehead pointed out long ago, in *Science and the Modern World*, that the habits of **Medieval rationalism** prepared the way for the scientific discoveries of the 17th century, an insight given far more depth and scope in the writings of the historian and philosopher of science Stanley L. Jaki in our time. Long before Bacon, Jaki has written, Christian **philosophy** had steadily inculcated "the conviction ... that since the world was rational it could not be comprehended by the human mind, but as the product of the Creator it could not be derived from the mind of man, a creature." The "metaphysical realism" of **Saint Thomas Aquinas** (and of Richard Hooker in England) avoided the extremes of empiricism and idealism and thus paved the way for Newton.

Jaki's work—among the most important bodies of scholarly work in the late 20th century—has confirmed some of Lewis's insights about the origin and development of Western science, and particularly its indebtedness to the doctrine of creation *ex nihilo* to escape from mistaken Aristotelian ideas about time and matter. The importance for science of the Medieval thinkers Buridan and Oresme had been rediscovered by the great 20th-century French physicist Pierre Duhem, whose own work Jaki has done so much to restore to the prominence it deserves. The active intellectual discrimination against Duhem, and subsequently against Jaki—despite their enormous erudition and unquestionable distinction—would not have surprised the man who wrote "**The Inner Ring**," "**Bulverism**," *The Abolition of Man*, and *That Hideous Strength*.

For among historians of science it is most prominently Duhem and Jaki who have provided the documentation and illumination of the importance of theism and "metaphysical realism"—not only for the origin and development of modern science but for the possibility of its coherent continuation and moral direction. Duhem and Jaki may be said to have made immensely plausible Lewis's insight that "men became scientific because they believed in a Legislator. In most modern scientists this belief has died: it will be interesting to see how long their confidence in uniformity survives it. Two significant developments have already appeared—the hypothesis of a lawless subnature, and the surrender of the claim that science is true. We may be living nearer than we suppose to the end of the Scientific Age" (*Miracles*, ch. 13).

And as a believer in the essential sanity and continuity of Western civilization, Lewis would surely have concurred with Jaki's characterization of the Middle Ages: "In Western philosophy that was the first and thus far the last major epoch in which broadly shared respect was paid to the fundamental difference between ends and means .... If we do not wish to help turn this most scientific age of ours into the most barbaric of all ages, we had better stop using the term 'medieval' as synonymous with obscurantist. In doing so, we may make our mental eyes more sensitive to that light which comes from the Middle Ages."

M. D. Aeschliman

Also See: Friedrich Nietzsche, Technology, H. G. Wells.

Bibliography

Aeschliman, M. D. "De Sade and His Progeny." *Crisis*. (September 1993): 54ff.

_____. *The Restitution of Man: C. S. Lewis and the Case Against Scientism*. Grand Rapids, MI: Eerdmans, 1998.

Jaki, Stanley. *"Patterns or Principles" and Other Essays*. Wilmington, DE: Intercollegiate Studies Institute Press, 1997.

Olson, Richard. *Science Deified and Science Defied*. 2 vols. (1982–1990). Berkeley: University of California Press, 1995.

Whitehead, Alfred North. *The Function of Reason*. Princeton, NJ: Princeton University Press, 1929.

Science Fiction

"Science fiction" is a literary portmanteau. It includes all sorts of tales, from those which occupy themselves almost wholly with bizarre and futuristic **technology** and intergalactic travel to those which veer towards alchemy, gothic horror, and the apocalyptic.

It is common to find the fiction of C. S. Lewis classified, especially in airport book racks, as science fiction. There is only the slenderest sense in which such a classification can be urged, namely that his narratives do, in fact, cross and re-cross the frontier that lies between our quotidian ordinariness and the Whatever-it-is that lies on the farther side of that frontier.

It is the word "**science**" that fails to describe Lewis's writings. If by science we mean the whole methodology of analysis and induction that has come into its own since Francis Bacon (as opposed to the jumble of scrolls and retorts and pentagrams to be found in Faust's study), then Lewis's fiction is excluded. There is virtually no technology in any of his tales. There is a spaceship, scarcely described, in *Out of the Silent Planet*, and a sort of alabaster coffin for the hero's space trip in *Perelandra*, and a tangle of tubes and spigots to keep the Head alive in *That Hideous Strength*. Otherwise there is very little sense in which we may apply the category "science" to Lewis's major fiction.

The question reaches further that a mere matter of literary genre. Lewis believed that science, as the modern world knows it, is merely *a* technique, legitimate as far as it goes. But it doesn't go very far when we are talking about **reality**. The whole vocabulary of light years and trillions and quarks and red dwarfs and black holes and DNA is thunderously impressive, and Lewis never patronizes science as such. But (see *The Discarded Image*), he has keenly aware of the limitations of the "model" of the universe suggested by that vocabulary of quantity and size and distance. His discussions of the topic never lapse into the frivolity that starts looking for elves under great oaks in the forest or fiddling with Tarot cards and seances. Nevertheless, his is an "open" not a closed universe. That is, for Lewis there really *are* seraphim and spiritual wickedness in high places which will never show up in any cloud chamber nor cause any oscilloscope to waggle.

Lewis would be extremely reluctant to say the literary genre of myth belongs only to the childhood of the race. The notion of a universe thickly populated with intelligent beings, both wicked and pure, of deities who call us to responsibility, and of eternal consequences following upon our moral choices—all of which, of course, is the stuff of **myth**—is a notion that Lewis took seriously. Myth may be, as he points out in *Perelandra*, "gleams of celestial strength and beauty falling on a jungle of filth and imbecility." Nevertheless, that celestial light is best not extinguished, even in fiction.

Thomas Howard

Also See: Fantasy, Myths, Nature

Bibliography

Collins, Michael R. "Beyond Deep Heaven: Generic Structure and Christian Message in C. S. Lewis's Ransom Novels." *Lamp-Post* 10 nos. 2–4 (1986): 17–22, 33.

Sammons, Martha C. *A Better Country: The Worlds of Religious Fantasy and Science Fiction*. New York: Greenwood Press, 1988.

"Science-Fiction Cradlesong"

See entry on "Cradle-Song Based on a Theme from Nicolas of Cusa"

"Scraps"

St. James' Magazine (St. James' Church, Birkdale, Southport). (December 1945): 4–5. Reprinted in *God in the Dock*, *Undeceptions*, and *Christian Reunion*.

This essay is composed of four "scraps," each a short conversation. Scrap 1 is a conversation between the narrator and his friend. The friend says that there will be books in **heaven**, but only those that you gave away or lend. The narrator expresses the hope that there will be no dirty thumb-marks on the pages. The friend says that there will be, "[b]ut just as the wounds of the martyrs will have turned into beauties, so you will find that the thumb-marks have turned into beautiful illuminated capitals or exquisite marginal woodcuts."

Scrap 2 is a statement made by an unidentified man that the **angels** have no senses. Because "their experience is purely intellectual and spiritual" the parts of **God**'s **love** and **joy** that are communicated through sensuous experience are not understood by angels, while other created beings (like man) enjoy them.

Scrap 3 is a heated discussion between the persona and his Body. The persona blames the Body for dragging him down, which the Body hotly contests by saying that he taught the Body to like things that were not good. The Body tries to remind him of the harm he does, but is ignored. The body blames the imagination and says, "That's Soul all over; you give me orders and then blame me for carrying them out."

Scrap 4 is a discussion about praying for specific things. Using an analogy, the narrator argues that while we know that God knows best, we still take an umbrella when it is raining. Even though God knows whether it is best for us to be wet or dry, we have choice. Although we may wonder why he lets us influence anything, it is clear that he does. Since he lets us in one way, "I don't see why He shouldn't let us do it in the other."

Anne Gardner

Also See: Books of Influence, Ethics and Morality, The Fall, Good and Evil, Human Nature, Prayer

The Screwtape Letters

Originally published in *The Guardian* from May 2, 1941, to November 28, 1941. London: Geoffrey Bles, 1942. First US edition, New York: Macmillan, 1943.

One of the most popular of C. S. Lewis's works of fiction, *The Screwtape Letters* purports to be a collection of letters to Wormwood, an inexperienced devil who has been assigned as a tempter on earth, from his uncle Screwtape, an Undersecretary for the Infernal Lowerarchy and Wormwood's supervisor. Lewis conceived the idea for the book after attending an Anglican liturgy in the summer of 1940. His purpose in writing the book, as he afterward explained to his brother, **Warren Lewis**, was "to give all the **psychology** of temptation from the other point of view."

This "other point of view" is crucial to understanding the content of the letters. In reading the letters, it is crucial to realize that they are written from a demonic perspective. Thus, a certain amount of reversal is necessary in order to grasp what Lewis is saying in the book. "The Enemy" in the story is not the real enemy at all: it is **God.** "Our Father's House" is not **heaven**, but **hell**. Those who have been rescued from the clutches of the "Enemy" are not the saved but the damned, and they are reclaimed to spend eternity in torment. While there are hierarchies of **angels**, there is a "lowerarchy" of **demons**. Thus, to really understand the book, it is necessary to keep in mind that what Screwtape sees as good is really negative, and what are setbacks for him are actually victories in the struggle against evil.

Lewis's tale revolves around the **faith** journey of an unnamed young man in England at the beginning of the

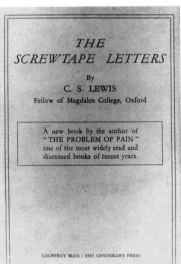

THE
SCREWTAPE LETTERS
By
C. S. LEWIS
Fellow of Magdalen College, Oxford

A new book by the author of
"THE PROBLEM OF PAIN"
one of the most widely read and
discussed books of recent years.

GEOFFREY BLES : THE CENTENARY PRESS

U.K. First Edition

Second World War. The conflict over his soul is manifested in the temporal world but is fought in the spiritual realm. Interestingly enough, Lewis's main character is an ordinary believer. He does not undergo amazing adventures or trials. He does not demonstrate heroic **virtue** or saintliness. The story of the young man is a story of a regular Christian who attempts to live out his **faith** in his daily existence. It is the story of a simple life of faith, concerned with the commonplace difficulties of being a disciple of Jesus **Christ** in a world filled with small but spiritually deadly dangers. This story of an ordinary Christian is set against the backdrop of a war, which feeds the anxiety in the spirit of man and eventually provides for the young man's liberation into the company of the host of heaven.

The story begins with Screwtape's advice to Wormwood regarding the young man. Wormwood has been assigned to be the young man's tempter. The young man has not yet embraced Christ when Wormwood is first assigned to him, but soon afterwards converts to Christianity. The man lives with his mother, and the difficulties in the relationship between the mother and the young man are seen by Screwtape as a fertile field in which to sow the seeds of dissension into the young man's newly found faith.

The young man's spiritual journey becomes more difficult with the advent of World War II. He undergoes a great deal of anxiety because he is uncertain as to whether he will be drafted into the military. He also goes through something of a "dark night of the soul," where God seems to be absent. While this is initially seen by Wormwood as a hopeful sign that the young man's faith was weakening, Screwtape, the experienced tempter, quickly attacks this idea in his nephew's mind, arguing that the emotional ups and downs of human existence make such a falling away unlikely. In fact, the young man avoids backsliding when he has a renewed faith experience, and he rededicates himself to God.

The man falls in **love** with a young woman and begins to associate with her and her **family**. The woman is a solid Christian, and his engagement with her increases the difficulty of Wormwood's task. As the war intensifies, however, the anguish that the young man suffers increases as well. Due to the war, the young man becomes an air-raid warden. In this position he experiences a great deal of fear during the bombings, fear for which he later chastises himself. Screwtape rightly perceives that in spite of his fear, the young man has done his duty, and the experience has not weakened his faith nor driven him into **sin**. During a second bombing raid, the young man is killed, leading Screwtape to give an anguished description of the death of the young man, a death that was the young man's gateway into new life.

While the young man's faith journey is the basis of the story, the main subplot in the book is the relationship between Screwtape and Wormwood. Both devils are struggling to consume each other. Screwtape blames Wormwood for every problem that befalls their attempts to corrupt the faith of the young man. Wormwood, for his part, blames his difficulties on the bad advice he has received from his uncle, and even goes so far as to report Screwtape to hell's secret police. The animosity between the two devils is dictated by the bureaucratic arithmetic of hell: one can advance only at the expense of another. Everything is a zero-sum game. This helps to explain why Screwtape, and all the other demons in hell for that matter, simply cannot comprehend that God's relationship to his creatures is one of selfless love, for they do not love, they hunger. Love is not the functioning principle of hell, and love is not what unites Screwtape and Wormwood. What unites them is their common appetite both for the soul of the young man and for each other. This appetite becomes clear at the end of the correspondence when Screwtape reveals his desire to lock Wormwood in a ravenous embrace.

Despite all the setbacks Wormwood encounters, Screwtape remains constant in his belief that hell will eventually triumph over heaven. Screwtape, grounded in a realism that denies the power of love and God's **mercy**, is continually confounded by what the real motives of the Enemy must be. Screwtape is filled with a hatred for humankind and is repulsed by the idea that God actually intends to "fill the universe with loathsome little replicas of Himself." However, Screwtape is also perplexed by the failure of hell to discover God's "true" purpose. This failure, of course, is grounded in the inability of the demonic bureaucrats to understand that love is indeed possible. If hell's **philosophy** is true—all beings are in competition with each other and all notions of love and virtue are mere facades to hide ambition and appetite—then God's actions are absolutely unfathomable. He must have some other purpose besides love. Screwtape and the forces of evil have been

unable to detect any other motive God has, but they are sure that love cannot be it. Despite his lack of knowledge, however, Screwtape never waivers in his "realistic" view that hell will emerge victorious.

In writing *The Screwtape Letters*, C. S. Lewis left an invaluable guide to the temptations that plague Christian life. Lewis emphasized that the great spiritual challenges believers face are not, in most instances, obviously important. Rather, the Christian life (and the temptations that assail those who seek to live it) is lived out in the day-to-day world. It is the little sins, born of **pride** and false humility, that in the end are the most damning. People are led into self-delusion, thinking themselves to be humble and pious, when in fact they are drowning in sin. Through such spiritual arrogance human beings are led to hell. By appealing to intellectual pride and curiosity, Screwtape proposes to divert the attention of Christians from the solid core of the faith to the ancillary points that divide Christians from each other. Christians are attacked psychologically, filled with self-doubt and suspicion on the role of **prayer** and God's loving care for them. However, hell's agenda is not simply focused on the individual Christian. It also works to corrupt whole societies, devoting the efforts of an entire philological department solely to the corruption of **language**. For if a given **culture** is corrupt, it will be easier to tempt into evil those who are a part of that culture.

Yet, despite the impressive array of tactics used by the forces of darkness, Lewis' book also bespeaks of the optimism of faith. The young man weathers his temptations and, at the end of his life, enters into glory, much to the consternation of Screwtape and Wormwood. Despite the snares of **Satan**, the young man's faith in **Christ** triumphed over the forces of evil and, in this triumph, serves as an example of the ordinary Christian running an extraordinary race of faith.

Mark Edward DeForrest

Bibliography

Gibson, Evan K. *C. S. Lewis Spinner of Tales: A Guide to His Fiction*. Washington, DC: Christian University Press, 1980.
Walsh, Chad. *The Literary Legacy of C. S. Lewis*. New York: Harcourt Brace Jovanovich, 1979.

"Screwtape Proposes a Toast"

The Saturday Evening Post. CCXXXII (19 December 1959): 36, 88–89. Reprinted in *World's Last Night* and *Screwtape Proposes a Toast*.

The setting for this 1959 story by Lewis is the annual dinner at the Tempters' Training College for young devils. Lewis's character Screwtape proposes a toast to the dignitaries assembled for the dinner in which he purports to encourage in their infernal work the young devils who have just graduated from the college.

Like *The Screwtape Letters*, this essay is written from the perspective of **hell**. It is therefore necessary for the reader to realize that he or she is reading a "backwards" story, where the Enemy is **God**, and causing suffering and damnation is perceived as a benefit.

The toast itself is a relentless attack on the errors of public **education** in the United States. Although Lewis's critiques are directed toward English education, his real target, as he revealed in the preface to the toast, was the "public schools of **America**." Lewis targeted public education's failure to instill passion and **virtue** in people. Lewis also attacked extreme egalitarianism in education and **democracy**, pointing out that such egalitarianism leads not to excellence but mediocrity.

A companion to this toast is Lewis's other work on education, *The Abolition of Man*. Both works, when taken together, present Lewis's view of the profound dangers in modern education's methods and goals.

Mark Edward DeForrest

Also See: Angels, Demons, Education, Ethics and Morality, Good and Evil, Heaven, Modernity, Pain, Redemption, Satan

Screwtape Proposes a Toast and Other Pieces

J. E. Gibb (ed). London: Collins, 1965.

See separate entries on the following:

"Good Work and Good Works"
"The Inner Ring"
"Is Theology Poetry?"
"On Obstinacy in Belief"
"Screwtape Proposes a Toast"
"A Slip of the Tongue"
"Transposition"
"The Weight of Glory"

"The Seeing Eye"
See entry on "Onward, Christian Spacemen"

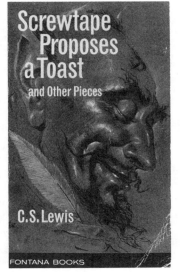

U.K. First Edition, 1965

Seeing Eye and Other Selected Essays from Christian Reflections

Hooper, Walter (ed). New York: Ballantine/Epiphany, 1980.

See separate entries on the following essays:

"Christianity and Culture"
"Christianity and Literature"
"De Futilitate"
"The Funeral of a Great Myth"
"Historicism"
"The Language of Religion"
"Modern Theology and Biblical Criticism"
"On Ethics"
"Petitionary Prayer: A Problem Without an Answer"
"The Poison of Subjectivism"
"The Psalms"
"Religion: Reality or Substitute?"
"The Seeing Eye"

Selections from Layamon's Brut (Introduction)

Brooks, G. L. *Selections from Layamon's Brut*. Oxford: Clarendon Press, 1963.

Building on earlier tales, a priest named Layamon wrote an Arthurian epic entitled *Brut* shortly before 1207. In 1963 G. L. Brooks published an untranslated portion of that work under the title *Selections from Layamon's Brut*. C. S. Lewis wrote a nine-page introduction, noting that the Arthuriad selection chosen from the longer tale was on the whole the best part of the *Brut* and describing Layamon's literary style as "sterner, more **epic**, more serious" than his source.

Mike Perry

Also See: King Arthur, Heroes, Magic, Medieval World, Myth, Poetry

Selected Literary Essays

Hooper, Walter (ed). Cambridge: Cambridge University Press, 1969.

See separate essay entries on the following:

"Addison"
"The Alliterative Metre"
"The Anthropological Approach"
"Bluspels and Flalansferes"
"De Descriptione Temporum"

"Donne and Love Poetry in the Seventeenth Century"

"The Fifteenth-Century Heroic Line"

"Four-Letter Words"

"Hamlet: The Prince or the Poem?"

"Hero and Leander"

"High and Low Brows"

"Kipling's World"

"The Literary Impact of the Authorized Version"

"Metre"

"A Note on Jane Austen"

"Psycho-Analysis and Literary Criticism"

"Shelley, Dryden, and Mr. Eliot"

"Sir Walter Scott"

"Variation in Shakespeare and Others"

"The Vision of John Bunyan"

"What Chaucer Really Did to *Il Filostrato*"

"William Morris"

"The Sermon and the Lunch"

Church of England Newspaper. 2692 (21 September 1945): 1–2. Reprinted in *God in the Dock, Undeceptions,* and *First and Second Things.*

This essay begins with the words from a sermon in which the preacher claims that "the home is the foundation of our national life." Lewis—who had been to lunch in the preacher's household—knew it was not "a retreat from the noise and stress and temptation and dissipation of daily life." Lewis, however, was not worried by the fact that "the Vicar's practice differs from his precept," but that the Vicar is not telling his congregation the truth: "home life is difficult and has, like every form of life, its own proper temptations and corruptions." Lewis suggested five fundamental principles for realistic teaching: first, that there is no natural tendency to "go right"; second, that the "sanctification of family life . . . [must be] more than the preservation of '**love**' in the sense of natural affection"; third, that at home we appear as we really are; fourth, that there is nowhere this side of **heaven** where we can "be ourselves"; and finally, that a home must be a place of rules, not the tyranny of the most selfish member.

Anne Gardner

Also See: Good and Evil, Immorality, Preacher, Sin, Virtue

"Sermon"

Five Sermons by Laymen. Northampton: St. Matthew's Church, April-May 1946: 1–6. Slightly altered and retitled as

"'Miserable Offenders': An Interpretation of Prayer Book Language" and reprinted in *Advent Paper No. 12.* Boston: Church of the Advent, [no date]. Also reprinted in *God in the Dock, Undeceptions,* and *Christian Reunion.*

This piece was originally delivered as a sermon at St. Matthew's Church, Northhampton, on April 7, 1946. It deals with three phrases in particular. The first is from the Lenten Collect in which "we ask **God** to give us contrite hearts." When we repeat the language before us, do we really mean to ask that our heart be crushed or pulverized? That is what we ask.

The second phrase it considers is from the General Confession at the Holy Communion, we repeat that "the burden [of our sins] is intolerable." Lewis believed that the Prayer Book is not primarily talking about feelings. We may not feel the burden intolerable, but ultimately it is.

Finally, the same is true of the confession that we are "miserable offenders" (from the General Confession at Morning and Evening Prayer). By miserable, we should not mean depressed, but rather deserving of pity. Seen as we are from a great height and a great distance we are a piteous spectacle. In view of this, our sins are unbearable not because they appear to be bad, but because we cannot bear them up and ultimately must break under their weight.

For all of us, there is a weight that can break us, some fatal flaw that will destroy. For many people, it is impossible to identify this fatal flaw, and even when we are told we cannot hear. It is for every Christian to make an earnest attempt to find and correct, to make our hearts contrite, ours souls no longer miserable and intolerable.

The Collect for Ash Wednesday, the General Confession, which is said at both Morning and Evening Prayer, and the General Confession, which is made at Holy Communion, appear as appendices after Lewis's sermon.

Anne Gardner

Also See: Forgiveness, Prayer, Sin

Sex

C. S. Lewis indicated that he entered adulthood as a sexually active "pagan"; but after living that way for perhaps a decade, he turned into a "middle-aged moralist." His early letters written to **Arthur Greeves** in confidence spoke of his adolescent tendency toward sadomasochism; but his mature writings were free of that and of prurience and prudery. (The only exception was *The Dark Tower*, which is of questionable origin.)

By the time he became a Christian, Lewis's recorded attitudes about sex were matter-of-fact and healthy-minded.

In 1941 Lewis delivered his lecture **"Psycho-Analysis and Literary Criticism"** at Westfield College. He said he was sometimes tempted to wonder if Freudianism is not a great school of prudery and hypocrisy. Neither he nor anyone he knew was psychologically shocked and horrified by the mere presence of sexual phenomena in their own lives, as that theory seems to insist. (Distress about one's ethical or spiritual failure is another matter.)

In 1957 Lewis recorded his radio series *The Four Loves* for an American audience, and it was published as a book in 1960. Chapter 5 is about *eros*. There he claimed that the solemnization of sex in our day is ludicrous. We should not be totally serious about sex, just as we should not be totally serious about food, because that leads to a kind of foolish idolatry. Men should remember they are akin to **angels** on one side and to tomcats on the other. (Lewis liked cats.)

In 1963 Lewis wrote his last essay, **"We Have No Right to Happiness,"** for the *Saturday Evening Post*. It is an attack on the popular idea that the right to sexual happiness with a beloved partner supersedes all the ordinary rules of civilized behavior. Every unkindness and breach of faith seems to be condoned if it is committed because of the towering promises made by sexual desire.

Lewis rarely addressed specific sexual questions; but for Christians he considered chaste celibacy the only proper alternative to conjugal sex, and he tried to live and teach accordingly. For divorced Christians he believed that remarriage was not an option so long as the previous spouse was alive; but he reasoned away **Joy Davidman Lewis**'s first marriage in order to marry her. (Lewis's first partner was not even divorced from her husband, but in his youth he had no interest in Christian living or in **marriage**.) He disapproved of contraception for mythic, symbolic reasons. He was opposed to officious government discrimination against homosexuals, and he was also opposed to the discrimination that behind-the-scenes homosexual coteries sometimes practice against innocent outsiders.

Kathryn Lindskoog

Also See: Sigmund Freud, Psychology, Women

Bibliography

Lewis, C. S. "Psycho-Analysis and Literary Criticism"; "Eros" in *The Four Loves*; "We Have No Right to Happiness"

Lloyd, Joan. "Transcendent Sexuality as C. S. Lewis Saw It." *Christianity Today.* 18 (November 9, 1973): 7–10.
Wright, John L. "C. S. Lewis on Sexuality." *Canadian C. S. Lewis Journal.* 40 (Autumn 1982): 16–20.

"Sex in Literature"

Sunday Telegraph. No. 87 (30 September 1962): 8. Reprinted in *Present Concerns*.

Commissioned by the London *Sunday Telegraph* in 1962, this essay was a response to what was perceived as a lowering of moral standards validated by sexual material in literature. The issue had been brought particularly to the public focus by the acquittal of Penguin Books after the obscenity trial that followed the publication of **D. H. Lawrence**'s *Lady Chatterley's Lover*. In his essay, Lewis distanced himself from the liberal **values** of "the modern intelligentsia," even while he argued for the abandonment of legal censorship as counterproductive. He objected to the argument left to stand in the aftermath of the trial that the status of "literature" implies that a book cannot corrupt its audience and, moreover, that "art" is outside the moral arena, exempt from ordinary moral judgment. Lewis thought that certain books might corrupt, though he was not optimistic about predicting which ones would. Lewis closed by suggesting that abandoning censorship was the lesser of evils and hoping that the newly accepted vogue for four-letter words in literature would soon decline.

Susan Henthorne
White Pines College

Also See: Ethics and Morality, Sex

Bibliography

Lawrence, D. H. *Lady Chatterley's Lover.* Harmondsworth: Penguin Books, 1960.
Lewis, C. S. "Good Work and Good Works"
Lloyd, Joan. "Transcendent Sexuality as C. S. Lewis Saw It." *Christianity Today* 18 (November 9, 1973): 7–10.

Shadowlands (the Play and Film Versions as Art)

C. S. Lewis has become a movie star. On the heels of impressive runs on television and in the theater, the most important Christian writer of the 20th century has made the leap to Hollywood. The first step of this improbable second career took place in 1985 when William Nicholson transformed Brian Sibley's literary biography *Through the Shadowlands* into a BBC teleplay starring Joss Ackland as Lewis and Claire Bloom as Joy. Two years later, encouraged by favorable response, Nicholson adapted his script for the theater.

The result was *Shadowlands*, a drama with Nigel Hawthorne as Lewis and Jane Lapotaire as Joy described by one critic as a "heart-breaking, sensitive sketching of one of Britain's most esteemed literary heroes." After running consecutively in London's West End for nearly three years, *Shadowlands* made the leap to Broadway. When the accolades continued in the U.S., Nicholson once again adapted his script, this time for the big screen. In the fall of 1993, *Shadowlands* was released as a major motion picture starring Anthony Hopkins as Lewis and Debra Winger as Joy, and Lewis's career as a movie star officially began.

In order to understand the appeal of C. S. Lewis as a theatrical character, it is necessary to recognize the conflict driving the three dramatic depictions of his life. Central to each is an issue Lewis tackled in his **apologetics** and faced in his personal relationships: "the problem of **pain**." Despite their many similarities, each drama handles this core theological dilemma differently. In the following discussion, I illustrate how seemingly minor stylistic changes as the text traverses mediums significantly alter the overall characterization of Lewis as a suffering Christian.

Of the three versions, the teleplay is least like its followers. The fact that Nicholson's first attempt closely echoes Sibley's biography may account for the dramas plodding and somewhat uninventive theatrical structure. By far the most distinguishing and, for that matter, redeeming feature of the work comes from Lewis's own writings. Nearly from beginning to end, the teleplay overflows with allusions to such texts as *The Problem of Pain* and *Surprised by Joy*, as well as Lewis's radio addresses and personal letters. With skill and grace, Nicholson artfully lifts several lines verbatim from Lewis's *A Grief Observed* as a means of bringing to life his **hero's** painful struggles; after all, few writers articulate loss better than Lewis. Although the drama as a whole suffers from a cluttered and sketchy quality, the presence of Lewis's own writing helps to create a very moving and uplifting theatrical portrait.

In many ways, the versions that seem most similar, the play and the film, conceal the greatest range of difference and, therefore, offer the most intriguing comparison. From the opening moments of the stage version, Lewis's Christian belief influences the dramatic action. Unlike the teleplay, the stage play begins with a direct, almost Brechtian address from Lewis. The lights come up to reveal the writer directly addressing the audience with: "Good evening. The subject of my talk tonight is **love**, pain and suffering." Lewis then tells a story of the senseless death of twenty-three school boys in a bus accident. After which, he asks, "Now where was He? Why didn't He stop it? What possible point can there be to such a tragedy? Isn't **God** supposed to love us?" Lewis then attempts to answer this ageless query. Drawing careful distinctions between romantic love, simple kindness, and God's unconditional love, he proposes that "God doesn't necessarily want us to be happy. He wants us to be lovable. Worthy of love. Able to be loved by him. We don't start off being all that lovable, if we're honest. What makes people hard to love? Isn't it what is commonly called selfishness? Selfish people are hard to love because so little love comes out of them." Continuing the address, Lewis introduces the idea that God battles human selfishness with a "mechanism called suffering." He describes suffering, or pain, as "God's megaphone to rouse a deaf world." Lewis eloquently concludes his address by connecting suffering with the eternal. He states: "We're like blocks of stone, out of which the sculptor carves the forms of men. The blows of his chisel, which hurt us so much, are what makes us perfect.... For believe me, this world that seems to us so substantial, is no more than shadowlands. Real life has not yet begun." This lucid intertext, loosely derived from *The Problem of Pain,* establishes a working theory that is poignantly and tragically called into practice later in the play.

Indeed, as subtext, the opening address is fresh in the minds of the audience as we witness Lewis's comical first encounters with **Joy Davidman Gresham**. The memory of the address lurks in the shadows as Lewis struggles to repress his unexpected romantic feelings. It underscores his **marriage** proposal to Joy as she lies dying of cancer. It cannot fully be forgotten as they marry and experience the euphoric, intense, and sensitive love of two people making up for lost time. Finally, the address is there, in the bleakness, haunting Lewis as he grapples with the pain, loss, and doubt that accompany Joy's relapse and eventual death. In fierce dichotomy, intellectual theory does battle with emotional **reality**.

After dramatizing the painful repercussions of Joy's death, the play concludes much as it begins. Addressing the audience in broken sentences, Lewis repeats the words that earlier slid so effortlessly from his lips: "We are like blocks of stone, out of which the sculptor carves the forms of men. The blows of his chisel, which hurt us so much, are what make us perfect." But now, interspersed in his narrative, reside faint utterances of doubt and anger, as he continues: "No shadow's here. Only darkness, and silence, and the pain that cries like a child." The inclusion of this decidedly bleak vision evokes comparisons with *A Grief Observed*. In this poignant record of his grieving process, Lewis states: "Go to Him when your need is desperate, when all other help is vain, and what do you find? A door slammed in your face, and a sound of bolting and double bolting on the inside. After that, silence. You may as well turn away."

Ultimately, the last lines of the drama may best be viewed as a compromise between intellect and suffering. Alone on stage, Lewis ponders: "So you can say if you like that Jack Lewis has no answer to the question after all, except this: I have been given the choice twice in life. The boy chose safety. The man chooses suffering ... I find I can live with the pain after all. The pain, now, is part of the **happiness**, then. That's the deal. Only shadows, Joy."

Admittedly, for audience members familiar with the entirety of *A Grief Observed*, the use of this somewhat ambiguous closing statement may seem incomplete. After all, by the time his diary runs its painful course, Lewis realizes, "We cannot understand. The best is perhaps what we understand the least." For reasons that are unclear, Nicholson chooses not to follow the precedent of his teleplay and incorporate this passage into the closing moments of his drama.

However, it would be unfair to judge the ending of *Shadowlands* as an indictment against Lewis's theories on suffering, or Christianity in general, simply because the drama's ending does not fully capture the writer's eventual belief in and surrender to the unattainable wisdom of God. The second to last line in the play: "So you can say if you like that Jack Lewis has no answer to the question after all," is not contradictory to the humble admission of powerlessness made by Lewis at the end of *A Grief Observed*. Likewise, depending on the inflection of the actor, the final line, "The pain, now, is part of the happiness, then," may easily produce a double meaning. The "then" may function as a memory of the unexpected happiness Lewis achieved during his marriage with Joy; it may also suggest a movement from past memories of Joy into a time in the near future when Lewis's suffering will dissolve into eternal joy. Based on this later reading, the final tag, "Only shadows, Joy" acts not only as a symbol of Lewis's earthly despair, but also as a reaffirming statement emphasizing his belief that "real life has not begun."

Similar to the play, the film version of *Shadowlands* contains a scene in which Lewis gives a lecture on the problem of pain. But unlike the play, Lewis's speech does not occur at the beginning of the drama; instead, it is sandwiched ten minutes into the film. Moreover, the dynamics surrounding the address are noticeably different. Rather than a direct appeal to the audience, the camera avoids Lewis and pans outward to reveal the slightly bored but well-meaning faces of an auxiliary guild of elderly ladies. This shift in focus is highlighted by the fact that, aside from the clear and concise, "The subject of my talk tonight is love, pain and suffering," the rest of Lewis's address is barely audible; indeed, the somewhat comical expressions on the faces of the elderly women demote the address to background noise. Also, the address is much shorter than its stage equivalent. Left out completely are the references to different kinds of love and allusions to human selfishness.

In the absence of a clear description of Lewis's theory, the struggle of its practical limitations cannot be fully explored or appreciated. There is no portent in the air when Lewis first encounters Joy. The unfolding of their unlikely love, although elegantly portrayed, is no longer overlaid with Lewis's intellectual and spiritual solutions to pain and suffering. For these reasons, Joy's cancer loses its tragic element and rings instead of *pathos*, an unfortunate and random coincidence. Likewise, Lewis's proposal to Joy, their short marriage, and the repercussions of her death are similarly chiseled. *Newsweek*'s David Ansen is certainly correct when he writes of the film, "You'd have to be a statue not to be moved by Winger's death scene." And yet, without the full impact of Lewis's philosophy on human suffering clearly presented, the drama lacks the spiritual/intellectual duality to operate on two levels. Rather than speaking universally about the problem of pain, the story simply becomes a film about a spouse dying.

Acknowledging the seemingly minor but ultimately major changes made to Lewis's opening address invites the recognition of several other amendments between stage and screen. Among these changes, the complete removal of **Douglas Gresham**'s visits to Narnia, the inclusion of more romantic scenes between Lewis and Joy, and the replacement of erudite Oxford professors with rebellious Oxford students may be the most telling. Noticing these differences, I cannot help but imagine a pitchman, à la Robert Altman's *The Player*, snuggling up to a Hollywood movie producer and saying, "It's C. S. Lewis meets *The Bridges of Madison County* meets *Dead Poet's Society*."

For many reasons, the stage and screen versions of *Shadowlands* appear to be kindred tales: under the same name they tell an analogous story using similar language.

However, the apparent sameness is an illusion. On the stage, audiences witness a drama of crisp intelligence, pressing **theology,** and complex tragedy—a theatrical wallop that ambitiously explores issues of faith and the problem of pain. On the screen, audiences view a secularization of the former—a drama of abridged intellectual content, coping theology, and *pathos*. Both versions depict Lewis by artfully blending fragments of his writings into the text at hand. But, in the film, something of the spirit, if not the language, of Lewis's ideas is lost. Picturesque camera shots and first-rate acting do not hide this fact. Or, as Richard Alleva keenly notes in his review of the film, "This is C. S. Lewis biopic for secular humanists in search of a good cry."

Robert J. Hubbard
Calvin College

Shadowlands (the Play and Film Versions as Biography)

Whatever their merits as art, the three productions of *Shadowlands* (for British television, for stage, and for the screen) should not be taken as biography. Despite their claim to be fact-based (the film version, for example, opens with the declaration that "this is a true story"), the productions present anything but an accurate portrait of C. S. Lewis.

Some of the inaccuracies are admittedly minor. After all, it doesn't really matter that **Joy Davidman Lewis** had two sons instead of one (though it might matter if you were the son who was left out; the television version, at least, showed both children). Nor does it really matter that the **marriage** between Joy and Jack Lewis went on a lot longer than the film and television versions of Shadowlands indicate (more than three years in reality; here the stage version got things right). Such alterations certainly fall within the domain of legitimate dramatic license.

More disconcerting from the standpoint of accuracy are the two major errors on which the whole story line seems to hinge. The first of these errors is the portrayal of Lewis's life before he met Joy. To varying degrees, all three productions of *Shadowlands* depict Lewis as leading a cloistered existence in which he avoided **women,** children, and—above all—commitments to any relationship or situation that offered him the potential for risk or **pain**. This depiction of Lewis is a convenient way to set him up for the drama's subsequent love story. But the portrayal invents a C. S. Lewis who never was.

Contrary to his dramatized life, Lewis led an existence that was anything but cloistered or free from pain or commitment. During World War I, the supposedly cloistered Lewis served in the trenches in France, where he was wounded in action. After the war, the supposedly sexless Lewis apparently became infatuated with **Mrs. Janie King Moore**, a widow old enough to be his mother. When the affair ended and Lewis became a Christian, Lewis the uncommitted somehow felt obliged to support Mrs. Moore for the rest of her life, and she lived with Lewis and his brother until she had to be moved to a rest home (where he visited her nearly every day). Meanwhile, the Lewis who did not associate with children had three children come and stay with him during World War II (they had been sent out of London because of the air raids—just like Peter, Edmund, Susan, and Lucy in *The Lion, the Witch and the Wardrobe*). Similarly, the Lewis who supposedly avoided women also developed a close friendship with English poetess **Ruth Pitter**; he even told a friend that were he the kind of man to get married, he would marry her. And the Lewis who walked through life without painful experiences had to deal with his rejection by **Oxford**'s academic community, which never saw fit to select this brilliant scholar for a professorship (Cambridge finally did in the 1950s).

The second major error of *Shadowlands* is the suggestion that Lewis's **faith** in **God** was shattered by his wife's death. While this implication comes out most clearly in the film version, all three productions tend to suggest that Lewis's faith was like a stack of cards ready to collapse at the first real suffering. At the end of each production, the status of Lewis's faith is tentative at best. In reality, Lewis's faith in **Christianity** remained vigorous until his death in 1963, a fact attested to in the many letters, interviews, and articles by Lewis during the last part of his life.

John G. West, Jr.

Also See: David Gresham, Douglas Gresham, Warren Lewis, Shadowlands (As Art)

Bibliography

Como, James T. "Land of Shadows." *National Review* (February 7, 1994): 72–4.

Shadowlands (the Term as Concept)

The term "Shadowlands," originally coined by Lewis in hyphenated form as "Shadow-Lands," occurs in *The Last Battle* as part of its last chapter title, "Farewell to Shadow-Lands." The word also appears in the last full page of text in the Narnian series; Aslan explains to the Pevensie children that "all of you are—as you used to call it in the Shadow-Lands—dead." They are now permanently members of Aslan's country.

"Shadowlands" is a word also strongly associated with Lewis because a book, television production, stage play, and movie, all depicting Lewis's courtship and marriage with **Joy Davidman Lewis** have borne that title. The book, known in the U.S. as *Through the Shadowlands,* was published by Brian Sibley (1985); the original drama (airing on the BBC, December 1995) and stage adaptation (first produced in London in October 1989) were scripted by William Nicholson; the Hollywood movie was brought into being primarily by renowned actor and director Sir Richard Attenborough in 1993.

Lewis employed "Shadow-Lands" to communicate how insubstantial our temporary world is compared to the solid reality of **heaven**. (He used a similar technique in *The Great Divorce*, where people who do not belong to heaven are simply "ghosts.") As the good characters of Narnia wander around Aslan's country, they keep seeing reminders of their former worlds, but they finally realize that their old worlds were simply "shadows" of the real worlds within Aslan's country; thus, when they find the heavenly equivalent of England, they refer to it as "real England."

The idea is derived in large measure from Lewis's beloved philosopher, **Plato**. In Book 7 of *The Republic*, Plato presented the famous **allegory** of the cave, in which human beings are kept as immobile prisoners chained in a cave, able to see objects and people only as shadows on a wall, made by a distant fire. Since all that these people have known in their lives is the shadows, they mistake them for **reality**. As Plato noted, if these people were released into the sunlight, the glare would make earthly objects appear fuzzy and less real. Plato's point, and Lewis's, is that our sight has been adjusted to life on earth; although heavenly forms are more substantial, it is hard with our limited vision to see them that way.

There may also be more than a hint of reference in the term to the **Bible**'s book of Hebrews (8:5; 10:1), wherein the sanctuary of the Levitical priesthood and the Law of Moses are contrasted as "copy" and "shadow" both with the true throne of **grace** found in heaven and with the substance of the New Covenant order achieved through the substitutionary death, victorious resurrection, and celestial coronation of **Christ**.

Marvin D. Hinten and Bruce L. Edwards
Bowling Green State University

Bibliography

Dorsett, Lyle. *And God Came in: Joy and C. S. Lewis.* Wheaton, IL: Crossway, 1994.

Kreeft, Peter. *Everything You Always Wanted to Know About Heaven But Never Dreamed of Asking.* San Francisco: Ignatius, 1990.

Gresham, Doug. *Lenten Lands.* San Francisco: Harper, 1988.

Lindskoog, Kathryn. *Light in the Shadowlands.* Sisters, OR: Multnomah, 1994.

Sayer, George. *Jack: A Biography.* Wheaton, IL: Crossway, 1994.

Sibley, Brian. *Through the Shadowlands.* New York: Revell, 1985.

William Shakespeare (1564–1616)

Lewis grew up surrounded by the influence of Shakespeare, and would have been reading Shakespeare during his early elementary years. On the day his mother died, his father tore off and stored the page from their wall calendar. It was a Shakespearean calendar with the apt saying for that day, August 23, coming from *King Lear*: "Men must endure their going hence." The quotation was later chosen for the inscription on Lewis's gravestone by his brother, **Warren Lewis**.

Even though one of Lewis's fields was British **Renaissance** literature, he did not write as much about Shakespeare's plays as one might expect, since his specialty was **poetry** rather than drama. Lewis did, of course, cover the sonnets and the longer poems in his volume of the *Oxford History of English Literature*, but he does not seem to find the pleasure in them one might expect. He enjoys Marlowe and Chapman's *Hero and Leander*, for instance, much more than Shakespeare's "Venus and Adonis": Venus in that poem made him think of a sweaty, obese aunt asking for some hugs and kisses at a **family** reunion.

Nevertheless, many of Lewis's jokes and allusions have a Shakespearean base. After viewing an all-female production of *A Midsummer Night's Dream*, Lewis later repeatedly joked to friends that it was his first time to see a female Bottom. His books, even the ones for children, include numerous sentences and concepts with a Shakespearean flavor. In chapter 8 of *Prince Caspian*, for instance, Lewis has Trumpkin say to Edmund about some teasing, "No more of that, your Majesty, if you love me." Except for slight modernization, this virtually quotes Falstaff's plea when being teased by Prince Hal in the famous "buckram" episode of *Henry IV, Part 1* (2.4.283): "No more of that, Hal, an thou lovest me." In *The Voyage of the "Dawn Treader,"* Lewis in some ways parallels Coriakin the magician's island with Prospero the magician's island from *The Tempest*, and he referred overtly to *A Midsummer Night's Dream* by saying one spell told "how to give a man an ass's head (as they did to poor Bottom)."

Marvin D. Hinten
Bowling Green State University

Also See: Heroes, Imagery, Literary Criticism, Magic, Poetry, Theme and Form

Bibliography

Adey, Lionel. "C. S. Lewis's Annotations to His Shakespeare Volumes." *CSL: The Bulletin of the New York C. S. Lewis Society* 8 (May 1977): 1–8.

Lewis, C. S. *English Literature in the Sixteenth Century, Excluding Drama;* "Private Bates;" *Selected Literary Essays*

Shakespeare, William. *The Riverside Shakespeare.* Ed. G. Blakemore Evans. Boston: Houghton Mifflin, 1974.

Shakespeare and the Rose of Love (Book Review)

The Listener. LXIV (7 July 1960): 30.

According to Lewis, Vyvyan expounds rather than proves his thesis that the work of **Shakespeare** is allegorical. This attempt to show Shakespeare's debt to *Romance of the Rose*, and in general to the Medieval conception of **love**, is similarly unsupported.

Anne Gardner

Also See: Allegory

Bibliography

Vyvyan, John. *Shakespeare and the Rose of Love.*

Shall We Lose God in Outer Space?

See entry on "Will We Lose God in Outer Space?"

The Sheepheard's Slumber (Letter)

The Times Literary Supplement. (9 May 1952): 313.

A letter giving a point of information on the authorship (unknown) and the publication data on the poem, "The Sheepheard's Slumber" (*A pleasaunte Laborinth called Churchyardes Chance & c.* London: Ihon Kyngston, 1580).

Marjorie L. Mead
The Marion E. Wade Center

Percy Bysshe Shelley (1792–1822)

Percy Shelley was one of the six major poets of the British Romantic Period (1789–1832) and the most radical in virtually every area of thought. In light of this, especially his life-long **atheism** (he was kicked out of **Oxford University** before his first full year for co-authoring a pamphlet on "The Necessity of Atheism"),

it may surprise many to learn of Lewis's unusually high praise for Shelley's **poetry**.

Shelley got high marks from Lewis for the suitability of form to content, "unity of spirit," musicality, and for having written the "greatest long poem" of the 19th century: *Prometheus Unbound*, whose conclusion Lewis called an "intoxication." Lewis noted particularly Shelley's understanding of human depravity, which he said was nearer to the Christian doctrine of original **sin** than that found in any other "heathen writer." Shelley saw in *Prometheus* the great cost of **redemption**, the need for **love**.

But Lewis also gave a warning: Shelley was "not a *safe* poet." To look into the depravity of the human soul and not to submit what is found there to the **supernatural** regeneration of **God** in **Christ** is to open ones self to becoming considerably more evil.

Lewis's only sustained treatment of Shelley is in his essay **"Shelley, Dryden, and Mr. Eliot."**

Wayne Martindale
Wheaton College

Also See: Good and Evil

Bibliography

Reimann, Donald H. *Percy Bysshe Shelley.* New York: Twayne, 1969.

"Shelley, Dryden, and Mr. Eliot"

First published in *Rehabilitations*. Reprinted in *Selected Literary Essays*.

Most of us are not at our best when our children are attacked, and Lewis felt almost fatherly toward the Romantic poets. Since the attack came from **T. S. Eliot**, who Lewis felt was doing much to ruin literature through his **poetry** and criticism, this article sounds more shrill than most of Lewis's academic articles. Lewis disputed Eliot's belief that **John Dryden** is more "classical" than **Percy Shelley**, showing various ways Dryden fails to adhere to classical modes. Some examples are well-chosen, as that of the drunken Alexander in *Alexander's Feast*; others are odd, as when Lewis felt repelled by Dryden's description of England's enemies as "Vast bulks which little souls but ill supply."

Much of the discussion of Shelley's poetry will mean little to contemporary readers, since the works discussed (*Epipsychidion, The Witch of Atlas, The Revolt of Islam, Peter Bell the Third*) are not among Shelley's most familiar works. Lewis did provide an extended treatment of *Prometheus Unbound* and, in an interesting image, calls Dante a blend of Shelley's ethereal fire and Milton's massive sublimity. The second half of the article comes across calmer and more reflective than the first.

Marvin D. Hinten
Bowling Green State University

Also See: Literary Criticism, Literary Theory, New Criticism

The Shoddy Lands

The Magazine of Fantasy and Science Fiction. X (February 1956): 68–74. Reprinted in *Of Other Worlds* and *The Dark Tower*.

In this short story, an Oxford don receives a former pupil, Durward, and his fiancée, Peggy. The conversation is superficial from the beginning, since the don and Durward cannot talk about the things they have in common without leaving Peggy out of the conversation.

Bored, the don half-consciously stares at Peggy, suddenly finding himself in an indistinct landscape of nondescript sky, imitation trees, bladeless grass, and vague flowers. He walks toward a distant light, finding a town whose people are as poorly defined as the landscape, though women's attire and flirtatious male faces stand out clearly. The shops and window displays of women's jewelry and clothing are perfectly realized. The don then sees a gigantic, idealized figure of Peggy, sunbathing in a two-piece swimsuit. The scene shifts to a bedroom in which the idealized Peggy undresses completely and admires herself in the mirror. The don hears a faint knocking, accompanied by Durward's voice saying "Peggy, Peggy, let me in." Another knocking, soft but massive, is also accompanied by a voice, saying, "Child, child, child, let me in before the night comes."

At that moment the don finds himself back in his rooms. He surmises that he has just been drawn into Peggy's mind, where the things that stood out clearly are the things she really cares about. At the center is an oversized and idealized image of herself. He pities Durward, but then suddenly wonders what another would see if his own mind were similarly explored.

Lyle Smith
Biola University

Also See: Materialism, Pride, Women

Bibliography

Fitzpatrick, John. "The Short Stories: A Critical Introduction." *CSL: The Bulletin of the New York C. S. Lewis Society.* 14 (June 1983): 1–4.

"The Shortest Way Home"

The Oxford Magazine. 52 (May 10, 1934): 665 (under the pseudonym Nat Whilk). Revised and retitled as "Man is a Lumpe Where All Beasts Kneaded Be" and reprinted in *Poems* and *Collected Poems*.

A poem about the relationship between animals and man; there is the promise that whatever conflicts exists between the two now, eventually reconciliation will occur.

Don W. King
Montreat College

The Silver Chair

London: Geoffrey Bles, 1953. First US edition, New York: Macmillan, 1953.

The Silver Chair is the fifth Chronicle of Narnia Lewis completed and the first in the fourth and final burst of creative energy that produced the Narniad. The book introduces the reader to Puddleglum, one of the most beloved Narnians (and modeled on Lewis's gardener, **Fred Paxford**), and to Jill, the second of the modern **women** Lewis creates in the more didactic phase of his writing of the **Chronicles of Narnia**. In a letter to Anne of March 5, 1961, Lewis said that *The Silver Chair* is about "the continuing war with the powers of darkness," a rather colorless description of the true significance of the book. Although Evan Gibson is correct in seeing *The Silver Chair* as the completion of "The Caspian Triad," in the record of Lewis's plot points and mental pictures for the triad (discussed in the entries for **Prince Caspian** and **The Voyage of the "Dawn Treader"**) only one image is pertinent to *The Silver Chair*: one of the Narnians (Caspian) is admitted into our world. This is because the writing of **The Horse and His Boy** intervened and Lewis crossed a threshold in his appreciation of the didactic power of the series he was creating.

Even though the heroes of *The Silver Chair*, Eustace and Jill, are nine years old, Doris Myers observes that the issues of *The Horse and His Boy* and *The Silver Chair* are those of young *adults*: "In both, the protagonists learn about God's providence and the need for self-discipline. *The Silver Chair* depicts the young adult's task of discerning **truth** in the midst of confusing appearances and embracing it despite the blandishments of positivism." Indeed many commentators (for instance, Cox, Hauerwas, Myers) see this work as the most philosophically significant of the Chronicles because in *The Silver Chair* Lewis critiqued reductionism's effect on **faith**, an indictment previously expressed by Lewis in ***The Pilgrim's Regress*** and developed in many essays—especially **"Religion: Reality or Substitute?" "Bulverism,"** and **"Transposition."** The fruit of Lewis's imaginative handling of these themes in *The Silver Chair*, especially in the critical encounter between Puddleglum and the Green Witch, can be detected in his address to the **Oxford Socratic Club** on April 30, 1953, under the title "Faith and Evidence," which became the essay, **"On Obstinacy in Belief."** He had two intentions: to explain the rigorously rational way in which Christians should come to the assent of faith and to defend the so-to-speak "trans-rational" (rather than "irrational") way in which they adhere to their belief after their assent has been given. Only the latter can be called obstinacy or, better, perseverance.

The story begins with a much-improved Eustace befriending a wary Jill, who is being bullied by other children in their progressive coeducational school. Eustace invites Jill to trust him, explaining that he has changed because he has been to Narnia and hopes that they might escape school into there. When Jill suggests that they try **magic**, Eustace says that the only way there is to call on Aslan. As they do so, they are chased by the bullies to a door in the wall that opens onto Aslan's Country, high above Narnia. Eustace bravely interposes himself between her and the cliff's edge even though he has acrophobia (later we will learn that Jill has claustrophobia). A lion steps out to blow a falling Eustace safely away.

Afraid of the lion, a thirsty Jill would avoid the lion but she cannot. The lion probes her motivations and explains that, rather than they calling him, he had been calling them for a mission to save the lost prince Rilian. Similar to Deuteronomy 6:4–9, he requests that she memorize the four signs by which they will know they are on the right track. The lion then blows Jill into Narnia to Eustace's side where immediately they muff the first sign: Greet an old friend at once. The friend is Caspian, now elderly, just embarking on a journey to search for Aslan's help in locating Rilian. Glimfeather the owl introduces himself to the children and them to the near-deaf Trumpkin who is regent in the king's absence and charged with preventing any more searches for Rilian. The owl facilitates

their escape from Trumpkin's protection; and the parliament of owls sends them to Puddleglum who might assist their trek north to the ruined city of the ancient giants. Exhibiting his habit of putting the worst face on everything, Puddleglum guides a Eustace and a Jill whose enthusiasm for adventure and memory of the signs wane with every miserable late-fall/early-winter day.

They soon meet a beautiful lady in green accompanied by a silent knight in black. The lady says that they will be welcome at the autumn feast of the gentle giants of Hartang. Discounting Puddleglum's suspicions, Eustace and Jill hasten to the feast, only to discover in the nick of time that they are to be the main course. Almost by chance ("But for a Christian, there are, strictly speaking, no chances" [***The Four Loves***]), they fulfill the third sign by falling into a tunnel below the ruined city. There they are taken captive by doleful gnomes. Conveyed by boat across a subterranean sea they begin to wonder if anything about their previous lives had been real. They are released into the custody of the black knight who explains to them that he is indebted to the Queen of Underland who rescues him daily from enchantment and is preparing to conquer Overland for him. He bids them stay with him as he suffers his daily struggle, and they witness his being strapped into the silver chair. Writhing in pain he begs them in Aslan's name to set him free (the fourth sign), and in great anguish they cut him free. He destroys the chair and introduces himself as Rilian. The queen enters,

U.K. First Edition

throws a magic powder upon the fire, and seizes her mandolin, trilling a spell of positivism by reducing their experience of Narnia, Overworld, the earth, the sun, and Aslan to psychological projections of the only real world there is: hers in Underland. Puddleglum clears the air by stomping out her fire with his foot and making his profession of faith. Turning into a green serpent (which killed Rilian's mother, the star's daughter of *The Voyage of the "Dawn Treader"*), she attacks them; but they kill her. Bidding farewell to everyday hopes and fears and trusting Aslan alone, they find their way to the place where the gnomes (now celebrating their freedom to return to the true depths) had been digging to the surface. As Underland fills with water, they work their way out, Jill first, into Narnia's annual snow dance! The others are unearthed by the eager hands of the revelers. Jill and Eustace recover overnight and ride centaurs to Cair Paravel. (Rilian had already gone to greet his father Caspian returning from his voyage.) They look on as the weakened and aged king dies after seeing his son. Heartbreaking funeral music begins as Aslan appears and blows the two children back to his country. In a deeply moving scene that gives the reader the feeling of heaven's perspective of funerals, the lion weeps as all look into the stream to see the dead Caspian. Aslan instructs Eustace to drive a thorn into his paw and his blood flows into the stream over the king who is restored to his young man's life. Caspian receives his long-held wish to visit earth: Aslan, Caspian, Eustace, and Jill return to the school and punish the bullies. All then go their separate ways; Jill and Eustace, now friends, are prepared, though they know it not, for *The Last Battle*.

Paul F. Ford
St. John's Seminary

Bibliography

Cox, John D. "Epistemological Release in *The Silver Chair*." *The Longing for a Form: Essays on the Fiction of C. S. Lewis*. Peter Schakel (ed). Kent, OH: Kent State University Press, 1977.

Ford, Paul F. *Companion to Narnia*. San Francisco: HarperSanFrancisco, 1994.

Hauerwas, Stanley. "Aslan and the New Morality." *Vision and Virtue: Essays in Christian Ethical Reflection*. Notre Dame, IN: Fides, 1974.

Hooper, Walter. "Oxford's Bonny Fighter." *C. S. Lewis at the Breakfast Table*. James T. Como (ed). New York: Macmillan, 1979.

Myers, Doris. "The Compleat Anglican: Spiritual Style in the Chronicles of Narnia." *Anglican Theological Review*. LXVI (April 1984): 148–60.

Schakel, Peter. *Reading with the Heart: The Way into Narnia*. Grand Rapids, MI: Eerdmans, 1979.

Yandell, Steven. "The Trans-cosmic Journeys in the Chronicles of Narnia." *Mythlore* 43 (August 1985): 9–23.

Sin

Every sin, Lewis wrote in *Letters to Malcolm*, is a distortion of the life that **God** has breathed into us. When we sin we "murder the melody He would play" and we "caricature the self-portrait He would paint." Thus (as Lewis said elsewhere) all sin is born of the greatest of all sins—the **pride** of a creature raising itself above its Creator. Taken this way, the size of a sin becomes less important than the mark that it makes on our lives. A great sin genuinely confessed and corrected (as much as humanly possible) marks us far less than a much smaller sin that we continue to condone and excuse. It also means that the evil in many deeds lies in their context. We want to paint some pleasure into our lives at a place different from that which God has chosen.

The close tie that Lewis saw between sin and pride also means that today's readers may need to adapt some of what he said to changing tastes in sin. For roughly two decades after World War II, the sins of the world, a desire for success, power, and wealth, did outweigh those of the flesh as Lewis often noted. In 1950s **Oxford**, adultery was generally furtive and unpleasant while homosexuality was the subject of malicious gossip. Today, however, pride has shifted its focus from the world to the flesh, a fact that would not have escaped Lewis's notice. People now boast of promiscuous lifestyles and sexual conquests. Deeply rooted in pride for many, the sins of the flesh have become more deadly than those of the world.

Lewis was a keen observer of what we do to avoid dealing with our sins. We evade responsibility by transforming them into psychological ills. We confuse our sinfulness with our finiteness. We console ourselves with the fact that our "heart is in the right place." We assume that time will cancel what only repentance and the blood of **Christ** will remove. We trivialize our sins while magnifying those of others. Even the sins of others can be an occasion for yet more sin as we either condemn too harshly or condone by silence. The list seems endless.

In dealing with sin, Lewis stressed its roots in the seemingly small choices that we make every day, choices that eventually become habits and weaken our conscience to still greater sins. In a 1946 sermon republished as **"Miserable Offenders,"** he suggested that believers "make a list" of their sins and do "a serious act of penance" for each. Above all, Lewis stressed that rooting sin out of our lives can be painful.

In *The Screwtape Letters* Lewis played the "devil's advocate" to illustrate how sin can be used to separate people from God. **Satan**'s tactics, it turns out, often involve extremes. Sin can be trivialized to the point that people no longer feel a need for repentance, or it can be magnified so much that people forget God can forgive. In either case, what matters is the wedge that sin drives between someone and God. "Murder is no better than cards," Screwtape tells Wormwood, "if cards can do the trick."

Mike W. Perry

Also See: Good and Evil, Guilt, Human Nature, Mercy, Pride, Redemption, Sex

Bibliography

Carter, Margaret L. "A Note on Moral Concepts in Lewis' Fiction." *Mythlore*. 5 (May 1978): 35.
Lewis, C. S. *Letters to Malcolm* (ch. 13); *Mere Christianity* (Bk. 3); "Miserable Offenders"; *The Problem of Pain* (ch. 4, 5, 7)

Sir Thomas Wyatt and Some Collected Studies (Book Review)

Medium Aevum. III (October 1934): 237–40.

One of the essays in Chambers' book deals with Sir Thomas Malory, and Lewis spent most of his review commenting on it. Lewis said "it is possible for our reading of an author to become . . . 'source ridden', so that we no longer see his book as it is in itself, but only as it contrasts with its sources." Chambers was apparently guilty of this. Lewis gave his own brief but useful reading of Malory as an antidote.

Anne Gardner

Bibliography

Chambers, E. K. *Sir Thomas Wyatt and Some Collected Studies*

"Sir Walter Scott"

See entry on "Memory of Sir Walter Scott"

"A Slip of the Tongue"

See entry on "Some Thoughts of a Cambridge Don"

Smoke on the Mountain (Foreword)

Davidman, Joy. *Smoke on the Mountain: An Interpretation of the Ten Commandments in Terms of Today.* London: Hodder & Stoughton, 1955.

In 1955, when C. S. Lewis wrote a foreword for Joy Davidman's 1953 *Smoke on the Mountain*, the two were simply friends who shared the fact that both had come to the **faith** as adults. Later they would marry in a bittersweet romance that would end in her death from cancer.

In the foreword, Lewis pointed out that Davidman came from a "second generation of unbelief." But he went on to note that, as a Jewish Christian, she was the best of all people to expound the central topic of her book, the Ten Commandments. Lewis even contrasted the "clinging fog" of his own northern European literary heritage with the stark unambiguity of her people's "desert landscape." The foreword provides useful insights into how Lewis viewed the relationship of Judaism and **Christianity**.

Davidman's talent as a poet had been recognized as early as 1938. Lewis described her style as a quiet, feminine fierceness, much like a cat's paw clothed in velvet. He noted that the book was written for Americans and thus dealt best with American sins, including some that the British were "hardly in a position to commit."

Mike W. Perry

Also See: the Bible, Good and Evil, Joy Davidman Lewis, Marriage, Non-Christian Religions

The Socratic Digest (Preface)

1 (1942–43): 3–5. Retitled as "The Founding of the Oxford Socratic Club" and reprinted in *God in the Dock, Undeceptions,* and *Timeless at Heart.*

Lewis failed to mention that he was the **Oxford Socratic Society**'s president from its first meeting until 1954, when he went to Cambridge. The society was formed "to follow the argument wherever it lead them." In this case, that meant "the *pros* and *cons* of the Christian Religion." The result was debate but also a realization that "the weight of skeptical attack did not always come where we expected it" and that Lewis's opponents had to correct "their almost bottomless ignorance of the **Faith** they supposed themselves to be rejecting." Lewis explained that the search for intelligent atheists lead to a thorough scouring of *Who's Who.* Lewis argued that public debate and intellectual discussion can neither build **Christianity** nor destroy it. To him, Christianity "tells of God descending into the coarse publicity of history and there enacting what can—and must—be talked about."

Anne Gardner

Also See: Atheism, Religion

Socratic Wisdom (Letter)

The Oxford Magazine. LXIV (13 June 1946): 359.

An interesting letter which precedes by several years Lewis's debate with **G. E. M. Anscombe** (February 2,

1948). It is possible that this letter refers to an earlier occasion at the **Oxford University Socratic Club** at which Lewis stated that "thoroughgoing" Naturalism is a self-contradiction. Lewis also pointed the reader to J. B. S. Haldane's *Possible Worlds* as another source for this argument.

Marjorie L. Mead
The Marion E. Wade Center

"Solomon"

Punch 211 (August 14, 1946): 136 (under the pseudonym Nat Whilk). Revised and reprinted in *Poems* and *Collected Poems*.

The grandeur and splendor of Solomon's court is the poem's focus—its rich tapestries and furniture, cedar columns, abundance of jewels and gold, magical power, and beautiful women. Ironically, however, these are the source of both Solomon's renown and his downfall.

Don W. King
Montreat College

"Some Thoughts"

The First Decade: Ten Years' Work of the Medical Missionaries of Mary. Dublin: At the Sign of the Three Candles, 1948: 91–94. Reprinted in *God in the Dock, Undeceptions,* and *First and Second Things.*

Lewis began this article by stating that there was no more self-explanatory building than the Christian hospital, except perhaps the Christian church. He went on to recognize that some people think that the Christian community is so firmly fixed on the rewards to come that prolonging life is somehow contradictory to the business of being Christian. However, the duality of the Christian **faith** seeks to preserve and—to the extent possible—improve **God**'s creation, while not fearing—and perhaps welcoming—death.

According to Lewis, death is not to be feared because it is natural; however, it is to be disliked because it is in a sense *unnatural.* It is the wage of **sin. Christ** wept with shame over the grave of Lazarus. Lewis concluded that Christians are "not so much afraid of death, as ashamed of it."

Anne Gardner

Also See: Immortality

"Sometimes Fairy Stories May Say Best What's to Be Said"

The New York Times Book Review, Children's Book Section (November 18, 1956): 3. Reprinted in *Of Other Worlds, Of This and Other Worlds,* and *On Stories.*

In this essay, published originally in *The New York Times Book Review* in 1956, Lewis suggested that writing begins with an idea or image an author wants to develop. To become a book or other work, the idea or image must find the proper form, whether verse, novel, **fantasy**, or whatever. Lewis then applies this theory to his **Chronicles of Narnia**. They began with mental images, of a faun, a queen, and a lion (**"It All Began with a Picture . . ."**). As the images began to develop into a narrative, the form they sought was that of the fairy story. The Chronicles, thus, did not grow out of a desire to convey Christian truths to children, with **fairy tales** selected as the most effective vehicle, or even start out as Christian. Lewis as author began to love the fairy tale form, and Lewis the man began to see that retelling biblical stories in an imaginary world could restore their emotional power, could enable readers to *feel* what they ought to feel about **God**. Nor are the readers of the Chronicles necessarily children. The taste for fairy story, fantasy, and myth is one that some children and some adults possess, while other children and adults do not.

Peter J. Schakel
Hope College

Bibliography

Hooper, Walter. *Past Watchful Dragons: The Narnian Chronicles of C. S. Lewis.* London: Collier Macmillan, 1979.
Manlove, Colin. *The Chronicles of Narnia: The Patterning of a Fantastic World.* New York: Twayne, 1993.

"Sonnet"

The Oxford Magazine. 54 (May 14, 1936): 575 (under the pseudonym Nat Whilk). Reprinted in *Poems* and *Collected Poems.*

This poem is Lewis's take on the defeat of the cruel Assyrian conqueror, Sennacherib, recorded in 2 Kings 19 and by the historian Herodotus. Lewis's English sonnet melded the two accounts suggesting the defeat occurred when **angels** worked through mice: the divine enfeebling itself to work through the weak, thus lending it dignity.

Don W. King
Montreat College

Space Travel

Space Travel is our modern term for a venture that has teased mortals since mythic antiquity. Daedalus and Icarus were early venturers, and their effort came to grief. For centuries, long before the actual development of airships and rocket propulsion, men labored over elaborate designs for craft that might punch through the Earth's atmosphere and take us to other worlds. The topic continues as a major theme for fiction, cinema, and TV series in our own epoch.

The attraction is obvious, incorporating elements of courage, thrill, the unknown—especially the vastly, or even the infinitely, unknown, curiosity, and of course that desire for conquest so characteristic of our species. But perhaps the most significant element is our desire to fly in the face of our finitude.

That is were Lewis's treatment of the theme enters. He was not even marginally interested in the **technology** that is the staple of modern space travel. What interested Lewis was the mystery of **good and evil**, and the particular relief into which the good and evil at work in a given man is thrown by finding itself confronted with the newness and strangeness at the far end of the journey. Actually, it is often the journey itself (see *Perelandra* especially) that begins to open up the theme. Is our traveler a man capable of being enraptured by that which is rapturous? Does he know when he has come into the precincts of the holy? Does he hesitate with an appropriate humility and reverence before the wholly other that hails him on this turf? If so, he is a man who exhibits *aidos*—that Greek virtue the essence of which is one's capacity to render the apt response in the presence of things—awe in the presence of awesome, horror in the presence of the horrible, worship in the presence of the deity.

Lewis loved the theme of human encounter with other intelligent species, most of whom in his books (contra **H. G. Wells**) turn out to be glorious creatures of fathomless dignity, no matter what their shape. A related theme is the notion that there are whole stories in the universe that are not (as yet) part of Our Story, but that **God** is writing for some purpose.

Thomas Howard

Also See: Modernity, Science

Bibliography
Lewis, C. S. "Cross-Examination"; "Religion and Rocketry"

Space Trilogy

See entries on *Out of the Silent Planet*, *Perelandra*, and *That Hideous Strength*

"Spartan Nactus"

Punch. 227 (December 1, 1954): 685 (under the pseudonym Nat Whilk). Revised and retitled "A Confession" and reprinted in *Poems* and *Collected Poems*.

"*Spartan Nactus*" (Latin for "Spartan Having Obtained") is Lewis's sharpest attack on modern **poetry**, especially that of **T. S. Eliot**. Lewis feigned being a dunce who could not understand the subtle nuances of contemporary poetic **metaphor** and **imagery**, condemned instead only to have stock responses to the figurative language of the past. While not a poetic manifesto, Lewis was clearly throwing down the gauntlet.

Don W. King
Montreat College

Spelling Reform (Letter)

The Times Educational Supplement (1 January 1960): 13.

In response to an ongoing debate raised by various articles and letters on the merits of spelling reform (beginning July 3, 1959, and extending until January 22, 1960), Lewis questioned the underlying assumption that it is necessary for everyone to spell alike. Since the English language is neither genuinely phonetic or genuinely etymological, he doubted that consistent spelling standards are "worth the trouble." Lewis recommended that emphasis be placed on an individual's logic and vocabulary instead.

Marjorie L. Mead
The Marion E. Wade Center

Edmund Spenser (c.1552–1599)

Born in London, Edmund Spenser attended the newly-founded Merchant Taylors School, where besides being grounded in Hebrew, Greek, and Latin, he met the **Renaissance** ideal of the perfect courtier; he was later known for living it. Entering Pembroke Hall, **Cambridge** in 1569, he was fluent in both French and Italian, was an enthusiastic student of both **Plato** and **Aristotle**, and seems to have preferred Virgil to Ovid. He had the puritanical and somewhat pedantic scholar of Pembroke, Gabriel Harvey, as his "entire friend" and was helped by him in his career. He took his MA in 1576 and left Cambridge. By 1578 he had become involved in Irish affairs and had made a close friend of Sir Philip Sidney.

In 1579 Spenser published his first important poetic work, "The Shepheardes Calendar." He was on government service for Elizabeth in Ireland from 1580 to 1590 and, back in London, published "Complaints" (1591), "Astrophell" (1594), the "Amoretti" and "Epithalamion"—both of which were connected with his courtship of and marriage to Elizabeth Boyle in 1594. In 1597 Spenser was back in Ireland where he was caught up in the Tyrone rebellion and had his home, Castle Kilcolman, sacked. He and his family narrowly escaped with their lives and returned to Westminster in December 1598, where he died a month later. He was buried, near Chaucer, in Westminster Abbey.

Spenser's greatest work was *The Faerie Queene*, begun probably by 1579 and remaining unfinished at his death. He completed six books of his "continued **allegory** or darke conceit" and had begun the seventh of the projected twelve books, each of which was to be dedicated to one of "the twelve moral vertues of Aristotle," when he died. It was written mostly in Ireland, where Spenser (an exile) loved the countryside and the desolation of the mountains, lived through political and military alarms and excursions, encountered heroes and villains, met the woman he loved, enjoyed friends, and combined the realism of those experiences with an idealism of fashioning "a gentleman or noble person in vertuous or gentle discipline." The first three books of "The Faerie Queene" were published in 1590, and the second three in 1596.

Spenser envisaged a vast heroic poem that would emulate and even overshadow the "Orlando Furioso" of Ariosto (1474–1533), then at the height of its fame. It had, however, to be an English national poem, based on English legend and in the national poetic tradition of Chaucer ("the well of English undefiled"). Thus, the work honors Queen Elizabeth (to whom it is dedicated) and those of her courtiers most powerful in the governance of the country. The plot is intricate and intertwined, involving chivalry and adventure described in a highly imaginative and misty style, but it is, ultimately, a moral allegory.

Lewis first became acquainted with Spenser in 1916 when he read *The Faerie Queene*—not "at one sitting," but mostly on weekends from October 1915 to March 1916, during his days with **W. T. Kirkpatrick**. Lewis regretted that the work was not longer. It remained a great favorite as can be seen by his discussion in ***English Literature in the Sixteenth Century***, (pp. 350–93) and in *Spenser's Images of Life*. It was primarily due to Lewis that Spenser recovered his position as one of the foremost English poets—sharing the honors with Chaucer, **Shakespeare**, and **Milton**.

John Bremer

Bibliography

Eastman, Jackie F. "C. S. Lewis's Indebtedness to Edmund Spenser." *Proceedings of the Thirteenth Annual Conference of the Children's Literature Association.* Susan R. Gannon and Ruth Anne Thompson (eds). West Lafayette, IN: Education Department Purdue University, 1988.

Gardner, Katherine. "C. S. Lewis as a Reader of Edmund Spenser." *CSL: The Bulletin of the New York C. S. Lewis Society.* 16 (September 1985): 1–10.

Hannay, Margaret P. "Provocative Generalizations: *The Allegory of Love* in Retrospect." *Seven.* 7 (1986): 41–60.

"Spenser's Cruel Cupid"

First published posthumously in *Studies in Medieval and Renaissance Literature.*

This essay is an analysis of Cupid and his arrows as portrayed in III, xi, 48 of *The Faerie Queene*. Lewis began with a discussion of the general disappointment of modern readers with **Edmund Spenser**. His verse is regular, his images appear banal, his language lacks "tensions and ambiguities." The only puzzle, said Lewis, is that Spenser appears to pity the dragon, and "[o]ne does not expect a writer of chivalrous romance to pity dragons." Lewis observed that there is not room for the "minute verbal explication in which the most vigorous modern criticism excels," but there is room for another kind of explication. This Cupid "is blind except to the pleasures of cruelty." The dragon, guardian of Chastity, is blind to all. For Spenser, Chastity means True **Love**, and so True Love is blinded by Cupid. In Spenser, as in Sidney, the arrows of Cupid are not just bodily desire, but the fruition of both lawful and unlawful love.

In his discussion, Lewis referred to the work Ovid, Homer, Lecretius, Plutarch, Boticelli, Alciati, **Plato**, Jonson, Milton, and Sidney, and mentions Greek **myths**, *Beowulf*, and the Volsung story—an extensive list for so short an essay.

Anne Gardner

Also See: Cupid and Psyche

Bibliography

Gardner, Katherine. "C. S. Lewis as a Reader of Edmund Spenser." *CSL: The Bulletin of the New York C. S. Lewis Society.* 16 (September 1985): 1–10.

Spenser's Images of Life

Fowler, Alastair (ed). Cambridge: Cambridge University Press, 1967.

In the late 1950s, Lewis gave lectures at **Cambridge** on **Spenser**'s *The Faerie Queene*. He intended to use his lecture notes as the basis for a book, but he died before the book could be written. A former student and later colleague, Alastair Fowler, took the notes and amplified them into a readable and coherent account, as close to Lewis's own views as was possible. This book was the result.

Lewis first read *The Faerie Queene* while under the tutorship of **W. T. Kirkpatrick** between September

1915 and March 7, 1916, as part of his own private reading program. At the conclusion, he wrote: "I have at last come to the end of the Faerie Queene: and though I say 'at last,' I almost wish he had lived to write six books more as he hoped to do—so much have I enjoyed it." Lewis read it again, many times, throughout his life, and never ceased to enjoy it, claiming that one of the first critical facts about the poem is that, once gained, it never loses a reader.

Brief though it is, *Spenser's Images of Life* shows us how to read *The Faerie Queene,* which Lewis regarded as perhaps "the most difficult poem in English." Lewis thought that the poem demanded from readers a "double response" of both simplicity and sophistication. But what Lewis meant by simplicity and sophistication was rather different from what one might expect.

According to Lewis, to read *The Faerie Queene* with simplicity is to read it as a good story; and as long as **Romanticism** lasted, this was possible for us. Today, however, both the poem's length and its use of multiple story lines seems to prevent it from being considered simple. Moreover, the unfinished state of the poem—it being about half of its projected length—obscures the way in which the interweaving of stories might finally be made clear and resolved.

Nevertheless, there is a way in which *The Faerie Queene* can be considered simple even today. "St. George defeats error, falls into pride, is dominated by despair, purged by penance, and raised by contemplation, and finally defeats the devil. . . . We are unaccustomed to respond to a content so simple."

To read *The Faerie Queene* with sophistication, meanwhile, requires us to enter into the way of thinking of the Elizabethans, to enter into their Model of the Universe (as we are invited by Lewis to consider in his book, *The Discarded Image*) and to understand their commitment to and use of Pageant. By Pageant, Lewis meant "a procession or group of symbolical figures in symbolical costume, often in symbolical surroundings." Much of Spenser's poem is the verbalization of Pageant; that is, it is not wholly narrative and dramatic, but it also invites us to look and to see the shows and the displays it presents. The poem presents meaning iconographi-

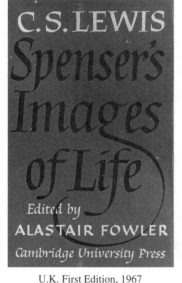

U.K. First Edition, 1967

cally, a way to convey meaning common to other forms of art.

The material from which Spenser could draw was extensive and various, including pageants proper, tournament pageantry, masques, traditional images of Gods, hieroglyphs and emblems, and philosophical iconography. These constituted a complex of iconographical traditions, a specialized and learned branch of knowledge, whose findings were available to all artists in whatever medium. Fifteenth-century Italian painter Botticelli's art, as art, is original, according to Lewis, but he accepts "traditional images, he loads them with wisdom from the philosophers and disposes them in divine compositions. And so, in my opinion, does Spenser."

While iconography was a learned art, it was also essentially a public one. "We often talk of the Elizabethan stage projecting out into the audience and involving them, so that real life merged into its portrayal in the performance. And with all iconography it was much the same." Iconography was not a comment on or criticism of life, but rather an accompaniment to it, a continual statement of it.

That Spenser mixed Christian and pagan icons is to be expected, for in this tradition **poetry**, but especially ancient poetry, was seen as a veiled form of **theology**. "Divine Wisdom spoke not only on the Mount of Olives, but also on Parnassus." Nowhere is this more true than in Spenser's use of "veiled Nature," which must be regarded as a symbol of **God**.

The view Lewis propounded inverts the usual understanding of historical **allegory**, according to which the purpose of interpretation is to find out the historical personages, events, and meanings hidden behind the allegory. According to Lewis, the proper interpretative movement is from the real, historical people into the work of art: "We should not say 'To appreciate Belphoebe we must think about Elizabeth I'; but rather 'To understand the ritual compliment Spenser is paying Elizabeth, we must study Belphoebe.'" For the reader of *The Faerie Queene*, the historical is nothing more than a point of departure.

Lewis, at the end of this book, took great pains to point out that Spenser's introductory Letter to Sir Walter Raleigh, which claims to expound Spenser's "whole intention in the course of this worke," gives a most misleading account of the poem. The differences demand an explanation, and Lewis suggested that Spenser's poetry was born out of deep brooding on his own experience and on the wisdom of the philosophers and iconographers, and he was completely obedient to the images that arose out of that brooding. But when forced into the academic or literary world he accepted any account of his work that was offered—but it never affected what he wrote. The unity of *The Faerie Queene* comes from Spenser's faithfulness to the images, in allowing them to be what they are, with no conscious, intellectual intent.

In Lewis's view, then, the account offered Raleigh was untrue, for the poem is not a story, an **epic**, but a pageant of the universe—of **Nature**—as Spenser saw it. This pageant, this vision is not mystical although it is certainly religious, based on the poet's worship of "the glad Creator," and it is a grand celebration of "fertility, spontaneity, and jocundity"—in short, of Life.

This way of reading *The Faerie Queene* caused a revolution in Spenserian studies and helped restore Spenser himself to the first rank of English poets, ranking with Chaucer, **Shakespeare**, and **Milton**.

John Bremer

Bibliography

Hannay, Margaret P. "Provocative Generalizations: *The Allegory of Love* in Retrospect." *Seven.* 7 (1986): 41–60.
Gardner, Katherine. "C. S. Lewis as a Reader of Edmund Spenser." *CSL: The Bulletin of the New York C. S. Lewis Society.* 16 (September 1985): 1–10.

Spenser's Irish Experiences and *The Faerie Queene* (Letter)

The Review of English Studies. VII (January 1931): 83–85.

Response to M. M. Gray's article (*Review*, October 1930) in which Gray maintained that Malory and his predecessors were the principle source of **Edmund Spenser**'s episodes of knight errantry in *The Faerie Queene*; Lewis disagreed, believing that Boiardo and Ariosto were the primarily influences on Spenser in those encounters in which knights were attacked by a rabble of robbers.

Marjorie L. Mead
The Marion E. Wade Center

Spirits in Bondage: A Cycle of Lyrics [Clive Hamilton, pseud.].

Originally published under the pseudonym of Clive Hamilton. London: Heinemann, 1919. Reprint as by C. S. Lewis, with an introduction by Walter Hooper. New York: Harcourt Brace Jovanovich, 1984. Also reprinted in *Collected Poems*.

This was Lewis's first published book and the most complete description of its genesis can be found in **Walter Hooper**'s introduction to the 1984 edition. In brief, most of the poems were written between 1915–1918, primarily when Lewis was sixteen or seventeen. Some were undoubtedly written while he was studying under **W. T. Kirkpatrick**, while others were written during vacations at **Little Lea**, after his matriculation and during military training at University College, **Oxford**, and still others during his time of service in the trenches of France. The book was initially turned down by Macmillan; less than a month later Lewis sent it to Heinemann where it was eventually accepted for publication.

According to Lewis the theme of *Spirits in Bondage* is that nature is malevolent and that any **God** that exists is outside the cosmic system. In a letter to **Arthur Greeves** he said that he did not believe in God, "least of all in one that would punish me for the 'lusts of the flesh'." But he did think that he had a spirit, and "since all good & joyful things are spiritual & non-material, I must be careful not to let matter (=**nature = Satan**, remember) get too great a hold on me, & dull the one spark I have" (June 3, 1918, *They Stand Together*). In a later letter he added: "[My book] is going to be called 'Spirits in Prison' by Clive Staples & is mainly strung round the idea that I mentioned to you before—that nature is wholly diabolical & malevolent and that God, if he exists, is outside of and in opposition to the cosmic arrangements" (September 12, 1918). It may have been for such ideas that **Warren Lewis** found the book distasteful; he wrote his father that although there was an "excellence" to "part" of his brother's book, "it would have been better if it had never been published. . . . Jack's **Atheism** is I am sure purely academic, but, even so, no useful purpose is served by endeavouring to advertise oneself as an Atheist. Setting aside the higher problems involved, it is obvious that a profession of a Christian belief is as necessary a part of a man's mental make-up as a belief in the King, the Regular Army, and the Public Schools" (January 28, 1919, *The Lewis Family Papers*). To mollify his father, Lewis responded and wrote: "You know who the God I blaspheme is and that it is not the God that you or I worship, or any other Christian."

In spite of these reassurances, the tone of the poems in *Spirits in Bondage* reflects an angry adolescent, shaking his fist at a God he denies, rejects, hates, fears, and yet admits to, longs for, seeks, and respects. Thematically, though Lewis provided a structure through his notion of a cycle, the poems fall roughly into two groups. In the first grouping, the overall tone is pessimistic. Life, often as a result of **war**, is seen as demeaning, futile, and empty; also, there is a contrast between the **beauty** of nature and the past versus the horror of war and the present. "French Nocturne," almost certainly a battlefield poem, reviews the stark tragedy of wartime. Other poems reflecting this include "Victory" (7), "Apology" (12), "In Prison" (19), "In Praise of Solid People" (42), "Oxford" (57), "Tu Ne Quaesieris" (68), and "Death in Battle" (74). Still other poems in this section comment upon a God who is hateful, cruel, and "red." He "kills us for His sport." The most shocking example of this is found in "De Profundis" (21). Additional poems reflecting this are "Satan Speaks I" (3), "Ode for New Year's Day" (13), "Satan Speaks XIII" (22), and "Alexandrines" (41).

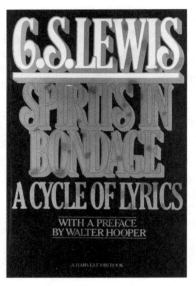

G.S. LEWIS
SPIRITS IN BONDAGE
A CYCLE OF LYRICS
WITH A PREFACE BY WALTER HOOPER
A HARVEST HBJ BOOK

Contrasting such pessimism, the second grouping of poems is more hopeful. Within this group, for instance, Lewis included poems suggesting that nature is beautiful and benevolent in the lyrical and romantic tradition of **Wordsworth**, Shelley, **Keats**, and **Yeats**. In "Noon" this lyricism is best expressed:

> And the honey-bee
> Hums his drowsy melody
> And wanders in his course a-straying
> Through the sweet and tangled glade
> With his golden mead o'erladen,
> Where beneath the pleasant shade
> Of the darkling boughs a maiden
> —Milky limbs and fiery tress,
> All at sweetest random laid—
> Slumbers, drunken with the excess
> Of the noontide's loveliness. (31)

Other poems reflecting this include "The Satyr" (5), "The Autumn Morning" (34), "The Ass" (51), "How He Saw Angus the God" (61), and "The Roads" (63). In still other poems beauty is the evidence that there is "something" beyond the material world as illustrated in "Dungeon Grates" (25). Other poems in this group are "The

Philosopher" (27), "**Milton** Read Again" (32), "L'Apprenti Sorcier" (39), "Song of the Pilgrims" (47), "Song" (50), "Hymn" (58), "Our Daily Bread" (60), and "World's Desire" (72).

Critical opinion on *Spirits in Bondage* has been scant; although it is Lewis's first published work, only twelve articles have been written focusing on these youthful poems. Chad Walsh's "The Almost Poet" from his *Literary Legacy of C. S. Lewis* was the first serious attempt to consider Lewis as poet. About *Spirits in Bondage* Walsh acknowledges Lewis's poetic inspirations as Housman, Hardy, Yeats, and Keats. Perhaps the most ambitious essay on *Spirits in Bondage* is Stephen Thorson's effort to follow its thematic pattern as a cycle of lyrics. While he adds little to Walsh's general observations, Thorson attempts to give a reading of the volume as a whole by tracing the poems, one by one, in light of the tripartite thematic structure provided by Lewis. Peter Schakel in his *Reason and Imagination in C. S. Lewis: A Study of Till We Have Faces* devotes a thoughtful chapter to Lewis's poetry in *Spirits in Bondage* and *Dymer*. Arguing the poetry demonstrates "a bifurcation and tension between the **rationalism** and the romantic" aspects of Lewis's personality (93), Schakel says, "its 'enlightened' rationalism on the one hand and deep sense of longing for a world of the spirit on the other, the collection provides an early and immature version of themes which would be treated much more satisfactorily in *Till We Have Faces*" (94).

Joe Christopher's 1994 essay, "Is 'D' for Despoina?" is fascinating speculation about whether Mrs. **Janie Moore** is the inspiration for the veiled Despoina in two poems from *Spirits in Bondage*, "Apology" and "Ode for New Year's Day." John Bremer's discussion of this same topic in his "From Despoina to Diotima: The Mistress of C. S. Lewis" is more thorough and perceptive, and in the end he disagrees with Christopher's identification of Janie Moore with Despoina. This fine essay ends with an intelligent discussion that posits possible references to "D" in the letters and diaries as Despoina (symbolically linked to the idea of "mistress" but not connected with the figure who is mentioned in *Spirits in*

Bondage), Demeter (the earth-mother), and Diotima (the introducer to **love** in Greek literature). Bremer's essay is must reading.

Don W. King
Montreat College

Bibliography

Bremer, John. "From Despoina to Diotima: The Mistress of C. S. Lewis." *The Lewis Legacy.* No. 61 (Summer 1994): 6–18.

Christopher, Joe. "C. S. Lewis Dances Among the Elves: A Dull and Scholarly Survey of *Spirits in Bondage* and 'The Queen of Drum.'" *Mythlore* 9 (Spring 1982): 11–17, 47.

_____. "Is 'D' for Despoina?" *The Canadian C. S. Lewis Journal: The Inklings, Their Friends, and Their Predecessors.* 85 (Spring 1994): 48–59.

Green, Rodger Lancelyn. "C. S. Lewis and Andrew Lang." *Notes and Queries.* 22 (May 1975): 208–9.

Kirkpatrick, John. "Fresh Views of Humankind in Lewis's Poems." *CSL: The Bulletin of the New York C. S. Lewis Society.* 10 (September 1979): 1–7.

Musacchio, George. "War Poet." *The Lamp-Post of the Southern California C. S. Lewis Society.* 2 no. 4 (October 1978): 7.

Sayer, George. *Jack: C. S. Lewis and His Times.* San Francisco: Harper and Row, 1988.

Schakel, Peter. *Reason and Imagination in C. S. Lewis: A Study of Till We Have Faces.* Grand Rapids, MI: Eerdmans, 1984.

Shaw, Luci. "Looking Back to Eden: The Poetry of C. S. Lewis." *CSL: The Bulletin of the New York C. S. Lewis Society.* 23 (February 1992): 1–7.

Thorson, Stephen. "Thematic Implications of C. S. Lewis' *Spirits in Bondage.*" *Mythlore.* 8 (Summer 1981): 26–30.

Walsh, Chad. *The Literary Legacy of C. S. Lewis.* New York: Harcourt Brace Jovanovich, 1979.

St. Mark's Church

C. S. Lewis attended St. Mark's Church in Dundela on a regular basis as a child. His maternal grandfather, Rev. Thomas Robert Hamilton, was the rector of the church. At St. Mark's Lewis was baptized (January 29, 1899) and confirmed (December 6, 1914). Additionally, his parents were married in the church on August 29, 1894. He remembered the rantings of his grandfather as "the dry husks of **Christianity**." He and his brother, **Warren Lewis**, disliked church services and formed a low opinion of Christianity.

Jeffrey D. Schultz

Bibliography

Lewis, C. S. *Surprised by Joy*

Sayer, George. *Jack: C. S. Lewis and His Times.* Wheaton, IL: Crossway, 1988.

Studies in Medieval and Renaissance Literature

Walter Hooper (ed). Cambridge: Cambridge University Press, 1966.

See separate essay entries on the following:

"Dante's Similes"
"Dante's Statius"
"*De Audiendis Poetis*"
"Edmund Spenser: 1552–99"
"The Genesis of a Medieval Book"
"Genius and Genius"
"Imagery in the Last Eleven Cantos of Dante's *Comedy*"
"Imagination and Thought in the Middle Ages"
"The *Morte D'Arthur*"
"Neoplatonism in the Poetry of Spenser"
"A Note on Camus"
"On Reading *The Faerie Queene*"
"Spenser's Cruel Cupid"
"Tasso"

U.K. First Edition,
Cambridge University Press, 1966

Studies in Words

Cambridge: Cambridge University Press. 1960.

Lewis would be somewhat taken aback by contemporary English departments, for a variety of reasons; one of those would be their emphasis on modern and contemporary literature. When he began teaching at **Oxford** in the 1920s, not only was there no tutoring in 20th-century literature, but even the Victorian period (which had ended some twenty-five years before) was considered too recent to be required on the English syllabus. (When the question came to a vote some time later, Lewis voted against adding Victorian literature.) To Lewis, and to most Oxford scholars who came to the university as undergraduates in the era of World War I, English meant the study of the language, and of literature that was old enough to need some sort of special training. Any educated person, it was believed, should be capable of reading and understanding modern literature.

This fact provides half the background for understanding the impetus behind *Studies in Words*; the other half comes from the fact that, at this time, every educated Englishman studied Latin. Doubtless many students in our time have wondered why 18th-century poetry has constant imitations of Horace and Juvenal. The answer, of course, is that 18th-century schoolboys constantly had to do English imitations of Horace and Juvenal in the classroom. In Lewis's time, schoolboys still had to study Latin before succeeding at universities; thus English dons were all conversant with that language, as well as their own.

Studies in Words is thus one of the least accessible of all Lewis's books. He assumes familiarity not only with English literature from Anglo-Saxon to the present (a given with Lewis), but with Latin and (in two chapters) with Greek as well. The following excerpt, from a typical chapter near the middle of the book, will provide its flavor: "You get what is called affectation (kakozelon) when ingenium lacks judicium." "It is a bad sign when a boy's judicium gets ahead of his ingenium." This contrasted pair will be familiar to all readers of neoclassical criticism. Harvey, in Cowley's Ode (stanza 13), has "so strong a wit as all things but his Judgment overcame." "Wit and Judgment often are at strife," says Pope. This example is from the chapter entitled "Wit," but not many readers will find it witty, or even find themselves illuminated about wit, for that matter. It is indeed for scholars only (and not many of those).

All this is about the book; but what actually is it? *Studies in Words* provides a linguistic tour of seven

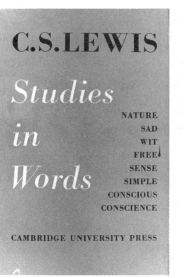

U.K. First Edition
Cambridge University Press, 1960

words: **"nature,"** "sad," "wit," "free," "sense," "simple," and "conscience/conscious." For each word, Lewis considered its Latin basis (and in two cases Greek basis as well) and studies how branches of meanings have extended from the main trunk of its earliest form. A chief reason for his doing so is to warn readers against falling into the trap of reading **Medieval** and **Renaissance** words as though they primarily carried the same meaning of today. The chief danger, Lewis thought, will not occur when a word's meaning has obviously changed; no one is going to read the King James **Bible** "Suffer the little children to come unto me" as saying anything about causing pain to children. In those instances, readers will either know the Renaissance meaning or, at the very least, will realize the current meaning doesn't fit.

The more serious problem occurs when the contemporary meaning is close enough to fit, more or less, misleading the reader into an understanding of an older passage. In the "Nature" chapter, Lewis cited a line from the second stanza of **George Herbert**'s "Love" (III) as an example: "I, the unkind, the ungrateful?" (The adjectives refer to the speaker's relationship with **God**.) Contemporary students no doubt regularly read "unkind" as meaning "not nice," when Herbert's real meaning, according to Lewis, is "unnatural." Lewis termed this misreading "disastrous." Most teachers of this poem, if their students thought "unkind" meant "not nice," would hardly consider the meaning of the line killed, or even seriously wounded.

Better for readers of literature are the useful tidbits constantly dropped along the way. Lewis noted, for instance, that in Medieval literature "sad" means not only "serious" (as readers of **Shakespeare** are familiar with seeing, as in "Say you this with a sad brow?"), but it means "solid" as well. Only someone thoroughly familiar with older forms of the language would be aware of this. As an example, Lewis cited Wycliffe's comment on Exodus 38:7 that the altar was "not sad but hollow."

In addition to these nuggets on specific works, Lewis also, in his usual casual way, mentioned what are commonplaces to him but new information to most readers.

In the "Sense" chapter, for instance, he noted that common sense is one of the traditional ten wits or senses attributed to humanity by ancient psychologists. The five outer wits, Lewis observed, are what today we would call the five senses; the five inner wits are memory, estimation (judgment), fancy, **imagination**, and common sense. Many readers of *Studies in Words,* perhaps most, will find these tidbits more interesting and more valuable than the main line of the work.

For the general literary reader, the most useful and interesting chapter will be the last one, "At the Fringe of Language." Here Lewis talked about language in general: what it does, how it describes, how it wounds. He commented upon the purpose of poetry and about what happens to the emotional content of words as they undergo linguistic shifts.

The final few pages of the book Lewis termed a "coda"; he said they would be a digression if the book were not so nearly done that there is nothing to return to. This coda is a discussion of the difficulty of adverse **literary criticism**. Lewis astutely noted that for many critics, with a book they really dislike, readers learn more about the prejudices and dislikes of the critic than they do about the book.

The other major problem with negative criticism is that "badness" is often hard to define. Here the examples are excellent. Lewis noted that a critic (he cites I. A. Richards) may be inclined to define bad poetry as that which appeals to stock responses. But Thomas Gray's "Elegy Written in a Country Churchyard" is nothing but appeals to stock responses, and it has been almost universally considered great for two hundred years. Moreover, the appeal to stock responses is part of what creates its greatness.

A critic might be tempted to say that a novel is bad because it's a "compensatory fantasy projected by a poor, plain woman, erotically starving." So, Lewis noted, is *Jane Eyre*. Similar examples he cites involves *Tristram Shandy* as an instance of a successful amorphous book and the works of **Jane Austen** as successful self-contained (oblivious to the outside world) books.

Studies in Words has the sophistication of Lewis's other books on language and literature, but for the most part, it lacks their charm. Its other main difficulty, in the contemporary U.S., is that there are few readers able to appreciate it; in today's English departments, Anglo-Saxon and Latin are not growth stocks. (The copy of *Studies in Words* used for this article had been checked out of its library, at a major university of 16,000 stu-

dents, only twice in the past decade.) To put it bluntly, if this book were not by C. S. Lewis, its readership among Americans would be just about at an end.

Marvin Hinten
Bowling Green State University

Also See: Education, Language/Rhetoric, Tutor

Supernatural

In an early 1940s essay Lewis called himself a "Christian . . . committed to supernaturalism in its full rigour" (**"Christian Reflections"**). But it was not always so. Throughout his teens and most of his twenties, Lewis cultivated a rationalistic and naturalistic mind that believed the physical universe is all there is: a mind completely alien to supernaturalism and **Christianity**. He remained an atheist until he was almost thirty. The story of how he came to believe in the supernatural, then **immortality** (a year later), then a personal **God**, then **Christ**, is chronicled in his spiritual autobiography, *Surprised by Joy*, and in his letters, especially those to his lifelong friend **Arthur Greeves**.

The implications of Lewis's belief in the supernatural are scattered throughout his work. In *Mere Christianity* and *Miracles,* he made supernaturalism and naturalism (**materialism**) the two elemental choices or presuppositions underlying all worldviews. All "real" religions, Lewis asserted, are supernaturalist. The supernaturalist believes in a reality beyond the material world; Lewis agreed that personhood, **reason**, and thought are supernatural, beyond mere chemistry. Lewis insisted in many places that God, though not absent from his creation, made time and space and exists apart from them. The supernatural or spiritual is more powerful than the natural because it subsumes the natural and brought it into being. If the whole universe were to disappear, God would be undiminished and could make it all over again (in *The Great Divorce*, for example).

Lewis came to see that a **philosophy** or **religion** beginning with a belief in the supernatural solves more problems and explains reality more fully than a belief system with a starting point of mere **nature**, which leads ultimately to despair and meaninglessness. The naturalist is forced to confront the death of the universe as its fuel is used up (the second law of thermodynamics). It follows that all civilizations, governments, human works, and life itself are temporary. And more importantly, without the supernatural, we can find no acceptable basis for morality. In *Mere Christianity* and *The Abolition of Man*, Lewis showed that the moral law depends upon the existence of the supernatural. A grasp of the supernatural even transforms our understanding and valuing of the natural: aim for earth, miss heaven; aim for heaven, get earth "thrown in" (*Mere Christianity*).

Other examples of the supernatural in Lewis's work are his concept of **joy** (the longing for **heaven**); the character of Aslan (one of many Christ figures); the archetypal struggle between **good and evil** in his fiction; and, as one of many evidences for the supernatural, the experience of the numinous in the opening of *The Problem of Pain* (nonfiction) and in the opening of *Perelandra* (fiction).

Lewis insisted that Christianity is supernaturalistic from start to finish: Christians believe that God created the world from nothing (*ex nihilo*), that God intervened miraculously in human history at many crucial times, that Jesus' deity is authenticated in part by his **miracles**, and that the key elements of Jesus' life are supernatural from his virgin birth to his atoning death on the cross to his resurrection and second coming. To this add the belief so central to Christianity and Lewis the evangelist that the new birth or salvation of every true Christian is a supernatural work, not mere intellectual assent. As with the **Bible** itself, take out supernaturalism in Lewis's life and work, and you alter their character beyond recognition.

Wayne Martindale
Wheaton College

Surprised by Joy: The Shape of My Early Life

London: Geoffrey Bles, 1956. First US edition, New York: Harcourt, Brace & World, 1956.

In the opening sentence of this volume, Lewis stated his purpose: "This book is written partly in answer to requests that I would tell how I passed from **Atheism** to **Christianity** and partly to correct one or two false notions that seem to have got about."

Lewis was very careful to confine himself "strictly to business," and to "omit everything (however important by ordinary biographical standards) which seems . . . irrelevant." This has not satisfied those who wanted an autobiography; even when it was first published, his physician and friend Dr. **Humphrey Havard** said that the book should have been given the title of "Suppressed by Jack."

Despite the detractors, the book is engagingly written and it is honest—not that other interpretations might not, on occasions, be truer, but Lewis plainly told what he thought in a simple and straightforward manner. It may be easy for others to observe that Lewis did not

understand his own early life or that he was too disingenuous to report it, but Lewis actually experienced his own life and the critics did not; and even when there might be disagreement about an interpretation or judgment, it is hard not to respect Lewis's frankness.

One aspect of Lewis's life that many people wanted to know more about was the relationship that Lewis had with **Janie Moore** from 1917 to her death in 1951, but they were disappointed. Her name did not even appear in the book. "I must warn the reader that one huge and complex episode will be omitted. I have no choice about this reticence. All I can or need say is that my earlier hostility to the emotions was very fully and variously avenged. But even were I free to tell the story, I doubt if it has much to do with the subject of the book." Loyalty and respect for Janie Moore prevented Lewis from discussing the matter—it would invade her privacy—but the real significance is that she had little, if anything, to do with his conversion.

One of the false notions that "seem to have got about" was that Lewis learned Puritanism in Protestant Ulster in his own home. Lewis denied this and reports that his father, **Albert Lewis**, was rather "high" church by current standards.

The book should be read for the light it throws on the nature of **joy** and the role that joy, in turn, played in Lewis's conversion and in human life.

The stages of Lewis's conversion can be simply stated and dated. In childhood and adolescence, he attended **church**, was unmoved spiritually, and had his prayers unanswered at the last illness of his mother and in his struggle with his sexuality. Disillusioned, he became, he thought, an atheist. This lasted until his early days at **Oxford** in the 1920s. Then came his intellectual grappling with Hegel and the Absolute, with subjective idealism, and his final grasping of "Spirit." But this was still insufficient, and the next step, to belief in **God**— in theism—was taken in May 1929. But theism is not Christianity, and initially there was no place for the Incarnation, which Lewis finally accepted on the famous ride to Whipsnade Zoo on September 28, 1931.

The text of *Surprised by Joy* gives (in round figures) 20 pages to preschool childhood; 110 pages to four totally unsuitable schools; nearly 20 pages to the Great Knock, **W. T. Kirkpatrick**; 30 pages to **Arthur Greeves**; and almost 60 pages to Oxford, the War, and Oxford again. In other words, about 75 per cent is devoted to Lewis's first eighteen years; the remaining 25 per cent of the text is given over to the next thirteen years. Lewis was well aware of this—it was deliberate—and he excused it by saying, "I never read an auto-biography in which the parts devoted to the earlier years were not by far the most interesting." His early years were, in Lewis's mind, the most formative and the most important, and he wanted the reader to see what kind of person he was as his conversion came closer.

Lewis stated that, between the ages of six and eight, he was living "almost entirely in my **imagination**," but he distinguished three levels of "imagination." The first was daydreaming and wish-fulfillment, which gave Lewis the occasion to magnify himself, to cut "a fine figure." The second level was Lewis's prosaic inven-tion, Animal-Land; he was a creator, but there was no romance or **poetry**. The third level—the highest level of imagination—came out of three episodes in Lewis's early life: the memory of his brother's toy garden, the "Idea of Autumn" from **Beatrix Potter**'s *Squirrel Nutkin*, and the lines from Tegner's Drapa that "Balder the beautiful is dead. . . ."

These three episodes had some-thing in common; each was an unsat-isfied desire "which is more desirable than any other satisfac-tion." This Lewis called joy—for him, a technical term, different from **Happiness** and Pleasure, with which it shares only one thing: anyone who has experienced it will want to expe-rience it again. The satisfaction of joy might even be a kind of unhappiness or grief, but we still want it.

In the ensuing years there were "stabs" of joy, but by his second year at **Cherbourg School** (1911) it had vanished from his life. Then, at a moment in time, Lewis at age thir-teen saw a headline in a literary peri-odical—"Siegfried and the Twilight of the Gods"—and immediately felt pure "Northernness," which reminded him of what he had lacked for so long, joy itself. From that time onwards, he knew that the supreme and only important object of desire was joy—to have it again.

Lewis explained that joy had in it an inconsolable longing—the German word *Sehnsucht*—and **Wagner**, first his stories and later his music, produced in him "trouble, ecstasy, astonishment, 'a conflict of sensations without name'." From Wagner, Lewis passed on to everything he could find about Norse mythology, and from these tales he again "received the stab of joy."

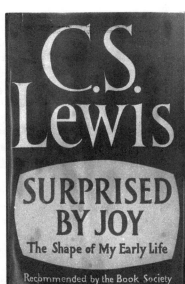

A consequence of this was that Lewis led two dis-tinct lives—one, a secret, imaginative life, connected with joy and of the utmost importance; and the other, his public, almost trivial outer life. There seems to have been no influence of one on the other. Lewis studied Norse and Celtic mythology academically and suddenly discovered that although his knowledge had increased, the joy had vanished again. He determined to recover it, without realizing that "the very nature of joy makes nonsense of our common distinction between having and wanting." He *wanted* to possess it.

Lewis observed that there is a resemblance between the Christian and the merely imaginative experience, in that all things reflect heavenly truth, not least the imag-ination. But at that time, he thought that he could repro-duce the "thrill" of joy—that he had the power to do it. He learned that he was wrong.

By 1915, his two lives were still distinct. "Nearly all that I loved I believed to be imaginary; nearly all that I believed to be real I thought grim and meaningless." Lewis then tried to weld together the imagina-tive longing that was joy with the ravenous desire for the Occult (derived in part from the early **Yeats** and Maeterlinck), but the known nature of joy protected him. And yet he wanted **Materialism** to be true— partly to get rid of childhood fears that persisted and partly to defend himself against the Occultism that he had rejected. At that point, in March 1916, he picked up **George Mac-Donald**'s *Phantastes, a Faerie Romance* on a railway station book-stall. The book contained the famil-iar things, but they were all different; they had a new quality, for they were bathed in Holi-ness. The common things were "drawn into a bright shadow," Lewis reported. "That night, my imagination was, in a certain sense, baptized; the rest of me, not unnaturally, took a little longer."

Lewis added that at Oxford in 1919–20 he tried to adopt a "New Look" intellectually; no more pessimism, self-pity, flirting with the supernatural, no romantic delusions. To avoid the dangers of occultism, he valued the ordinary and humdrum, and sought it out. The new **Psychology** required him to distinguish Imagination and Fancy from fantasies. Philosophically, Lewis was influenced by Bergson and accepted the necessity of existence of the universe and adopted a kind of "Stoical Monism." Joy became merely an "aesthetic experience," and it came seldom and did not amount to much.

In 1922–23, partly under the influence of friends—like **Owen Barfield**, **Neville Coghill** and **J. R. R. Tolkien**—the New Look was severely shaken, according to Lewis. Realism had been abandoned and **"chronological snobbery"** was itself outmoded. Lewis recorded that he had lost the initiative and that his "Adversary began to make His final moves." The first move was a chorus in Euripides' *Hippolytus,* which took him back into the land of longing; the second move was reading **Samuel Alexander**'s *Space, Time and Deity,* which gave him a distinction between enjoyment and contemplation that he applied to his joy. This led him to the discovery that he had not desired joy (as an event in his own mind) but that of which joy was the desiring. The third move was a linking of his new understanding of joy with his (now) idealistic **philosophy**. The fourth and final move was to progress from idealism to theism—Lewis admitted that "God was God" in the Trinity Term of 1929.

Before that event, "before God closed in" on him, Lewis had recognized that he had a free choice: "Necessity may not be the opposite of freedom, and perhaps a man is most free when, instead of producing motives, he could only say, 'I am what I do'."

The final stage of Lewis's conversion from theism to Christianity came about in a journey to Whipsnade Zoo on a sunny morning in September 1931. "When we set out I did not believe that Jesus **Christ** is the Son of God, and when we reached the zoo I did." He believed in the Incarnation.

Lewis, on his final page, reported that joy "has lost nearly all interest" for him, since he became a Christian. He still experienced the "old stab" just as often and as sharply as at any time of his life, but he now realized that joy was valuable only as a pointer. What it pointed to was what was valuable, and when he found that, joy became less important.

The title is taken from a Wordsworth poem:

Surprized by joy—impatient as the Wind
I wished to share the transport—Oh! with whom
But Thee, long buried in the silent Tomb,
That spot which no vicissitude can find?

Lewis was the one who was surprised by joy, even though for most of his life he had wanted it. What was

surprising was that his wanting had little or nothing to do with its coming, and that what it pointed to—Christ—was totally unexpected.

The whole poem must have been in Lewis's mind when he chose the title, and it is tempting to think that he transposed the meaning into religious terms. He needed a sharer, or, rather, the supreme sharer, Christ, whom he had kept buried in the tomb until his conversion. Christ had reappeared in Lewis's life and, for him, that was his resurrection.

This was not what Wordsworth had meant—he had his dead daughter in mind—and Lewis gave only the first line as the epigraph to his book.

John Bremer

Bibliography

Sayer, George. *Jack*. Wheaton, IL: Crossways, 1988.

Jonathan Swift (1667–1745)

It is not surprising that throughout his life Lewis felt affinity for the brilliant 18th-century writer Jonathan Swift, who, like himself, was born in Ireland, was deeply affected by loss of a parent, tried initially to be a poet, and experienced unusual relationships with **women**. Lewis mentioned in *Surprised by Joy* that one of his favorite books between ages six and eight was an unexpurgated and lavishly illustrated edition of *Gulliver's Travels*, and numerous allusions to Swift and the *Travels* appear throughout Lewis's literary and critical works.

His fullest discussion of Swift occurred in the essay **"Addison."** There he appreciated depths in Swift regarding **religion** that Addison never reached. But he disparaged Swift, along with Alexander Pope, as imprisoned by the humanist tradition, lacking the curiosity and openness to possibility Addison always exhibited. Swift had a more brilliant wit than Addison, and at his height has far more strength and splendor, but he also slipped into depths of hatred, bigotry, and even silliness.

The most notable example of a direct Swiftian influence on Lewis occurs in *Out of the Silent Planet*, for which *Gulliver's Travels* (1726) served as a primary model. Lewis followed Swift in using an imaginary voyage as a means of social criticism. Each takes his main character out of usual surroundings and plunges him into a place with new and unfamiliar customs, thus imposing on the character, and on the reader, a fresh perspective on his old world. As Swift had the Brobdingnagian King ask Gulliver probing questions about the English political and social system, so Lewis had the *hrossa* and *sorns* question Ransom and provide an outsider's assessment of our world. As Gulliver in the land of the Houyhnhnms suddenly realized that the disagreeable Yahoos were (or appeared to be) human, so Ransom suddenly recognized that the odd-shaped, unattractive creatures approaching him were humans, Weston and Devine. And as Gulliver in Houyhnhnmland had difficulty finding words to describe human attitudes and activities, so Ransom struggled to translate Weston's unreasonable, inhumane philosophy into Old Solar. The simplifications and reductions both writers employed in explaining human affairs to nonhumans become a key part of the **satire** against human folly and evil.

Peter J. Schakel

Also See: Good and Evil, Human Nature

Bibliography

Flieger, Verlyn. "The Sound of Silence: Language and Experience in *Out of the Silent Planet*." *Word and Story in C. S. Lewis*. Peter J. Schakel and Charles A. Huttar (eds). Columbia: University of Missouri Press, 1991: 42–57.

Keefer, Sarah Larratt. "Houyhnhnms on Malacandra: C. S. Lewis and Jonathan Swift." *ANQ: A Quarterly Journal of Short Articles, Notes, and Reviews*. 7 (1994): 210–15.

Lobdell, Jared C. "C. S. Lewis's Ransom Stories and Their Eighteenth-Century Ancestry." *Word and Story in C. S. Lewis*. Peter J. Schakel and Charles A. Huttar (eds). Columbia: University of Missouri Press, 1991: 213–31.

Lutton, Jeannette Hume. "The Feast of Reason: *Out of the Silent Planet* as the Book of Hnau." *Mythlore*. 47 (Autumn 1986): 37–41, 50.

Schakel, Peter J. "The Satiric Imagination of C. S. Lewis." *Studies in the Literary Imagination*. 22 (Fall 1989): 129–48.

Symbols and Symbolism

While **allegory** is not popular in our day, symbolism is found in almost all worthwhile literature. It is virtually a truism that any author who wants to say something significant will include some symbolism. It may not go very deep, but when it does, it often gives depth and meaning to the work.

In *The Lion, the Witch and the Wardrobe*, Aslan is clearly a symbol for **Christ**, the Witch is definitely satanic, and the children are like pilgrims in search of meaning. The wardrobe, meanwhile, is the symbol of entry into another world.

There are several symbols in Lewis's *The Great Divorce*. The Grey Town symbolizes **hell** and the beautiful outskirts of the mountains (to which the bus from Grey Town travels) are **heaven**, or the outskirts of heaven. The Red Lizard represents lust. And **George MacDonald** is the ideal teacher and guide. In Lewis's space trilogy, the Oyarsa of Malacandra represents an archangel and idealized masculinity (at the end of *Perelandra*) and Weston, who becomes the Un-Man, is clearly an agent of **Satan.** The Oyarsa of Perelandra symbolizes an archangel and femininity, and the Green Lady represents unfallen humanity. Ransom is a savior figure in all three novels.

In *That Hideous Strength* there are several echoes of Scripture that function like symbols. There is an echo of Pentecost when the gods descend on St. Anne's, especially on Ransom and Merlin. There is an echo of the Tower of Babel in the confusion of speech (which is somewhat humorous) at the N.I.C.E. banquet. There is an allusion to the battle of Armegeddon as the animals attack the N.I.C.E. There is an echo of Christ's ascension in Ransom's ascension to Perelandra to be healed of his wound (at the end of *That Hideous Strength*).

The human tendency to desire symbols and to find satisfaction in creating and discovering them shows how great is our desire for meaning. Human beings can bear anything if only they see some meaning in what they are undergoing.

Symbols help us to grasp the meaning of death, suffering, doubt, uncertainty, and so on. Human beings are the only creatures who can recognize and use symbols. Symbol-making is one of the highest human activities. They are wonderful because they greatly expand what can be said. One who is attuned to symbols learns much about life, **truth,** and goodness.

Corbin Scott Carnell
University of Florida

Also See: Imagery, Imagination, Redemption

Bibliography

Filmer, Kath. "The Polemic Image: The Role of Metaphor and Symbol in the Fiction of C. S. Lewis." *Seven*. 7 (1986): 61–76

T

Taliessin Through Logres

See entry on *Arthurian Torso* (Commentary)

Taliessin Through Logres (Book Review)

"A Sacred Poem." *Theology.* XXXVIII (April 1939): 268–76.

This review provided background to **Charles Williams**' poem by drawing on Williams' essay "He Came Down From Heaven." There was also a discussion of **allegory** and **symbolism**, and the distinction between them. Although Lewis had difficulty with some of the language and a weakness in "The Coming of Galahad," he said that the poem combined "jagged weight with soaring movement" and praised "its ability to narrate while remaining lyric, and (above all) its prevailing quality of glory—its blaze."

Anne Gardner

Bibliography

Williams, Charles. *Taliessin Through Logres.*

Taliessin Through Logres (Book Review II)

The Oxford Magazine. IXIV (14 March 1946): 248–50.

This review discussed the quality of **Charles Williams**' poem first in terms of his techniques. These are his reliance on irregular disposition of internal and half rhymes, and his use of "clashing stresses." Lewis then provided four reasons for the quality of the poem other than technique: the poem is unique and contains a world that is not ours; "the poem, once read, lays its images permanently on the mind"; the total effect is greater than one would assume from its parts; and the poem is irreplaceable in the sense of being unlike anything else.

Anne Gardner

Bibliography

Williams, Charles. *Taliessin Through Logres.*

"Talking about Bicycles"

Resistance. (October 1946): 10–13. Reprinted in *Present Concerns.*

Written in 1946, this article reported a supposed conversation between Lewis and his friend about the "four ages" his friend had passed through in his relationship with bicycles. The ages can be labeled as The Unenchanted Age, The Enchanted Age, The Disenchanted Age, and The Re-enchanted Age. The dialogue of the essay points out that these ages can be applied to nearly everything, not just bicycles. Obvious examples are **love** and **marriage** and **war**. According to the essay, it is most important to distinguish Enchantment from Re-enchantment and Unenchantment from Disenchantment; for example, among the poets, Homer is Re-enchantment while Macaulay is Enchantment; but reading an author "in whom love is treated as lust and all war as murder" it must be determined whether he is Disenchanted or Unenchanted. If he is Unenchanted, then "into the fire with his book," for he does not understand his subject.

There are political applications of this framework too, for example, in Aristocracy. Only Enchantment could allow us to suppose that humans trusted with power would not exploit it or that their ideals of honor and so forth would not degenerate; then follows Disenchantment, the age of Revolution. Our problem now is whether we can go into Re-enchantment, to realize that "the thing of which Aristocracy was a mirage is a vital necessity; if you like, that Aristocracy was right: it was only the Aristocrats who were wrong. Or, putting it the other way, that a society which becomes democratic in *ethos* as well as in constitution is doomed. And not much loss either."

John Bremer

Also See: Democracy, Hierarchy, Joy, Politics

Tao

A disastrous misprint in the published American version of Lewis's great 1943 essay **"The Poison of Subjectivism"** (*Christian Reflections*) may be Screwtape's revenge against the moralist who has done more to illuminate and promote **Natural Law** thinking than anyone else in the 20th century. Succinctly developing the argument that would emerge in greater detail later that same year in *The Abolition of Man*, Lewis attacked cultural relativists who assert that ethnocentric cultural and moral differences are so great that they explode the idea that there ever was or is a universal moral law. After an eloquent reassertion—later documented in the "Appendix: Illustrations of the Tao" in *The Abolition of Man*—of "massive unanimity of the practical [i.e., moral] **reason** in man," across space and time, Lewis identified it as "the Law of Nature." Lewis then went on to concede that "there are, of course, differences. There are even blindnesses in particular cultures—just as there are savages who cannot count up to twenty." The next, and crucial, sentence contains a catastrophic misprint (pp. 77–78 in the 1967 W. B. Eerdmans edition) that for its diabolical effect on the argument would have earned Screwtape credit with his superiors. In its published form the sentence reads: "But the pretense that we are presented with a mere chaos—*though* [emphasis added] no outline of universally accepted value shows through—is simply false and should be contradicted in season and out of season wherever it is met." The concessive subordinate clause beginning with "though" precisely destroys the coherence of Lewis's argument; the concession surrenders the very point at issue, the universality of value.

But in fact Lewis almost certainly did not write "though"; he wrote "that," which is precisely what the logic of his argument requires. The Collins Fount paperback edition of *Christian Reflections*, first issued in 1981 but reprinting the Geoffrey Bles edition of 1967, has the word "that" (p. 104) where the American edition has "though" (p. 77). It is precisely the case that Lewis wished to argue that a disinterested study of world cultures across time and space *does* reveal that an "outline of universally accepted value shows through." It is Lewis's contention here and in *The Abolition of Man* that "good is something objective and reason the organ whereby it is apprehended."

Lewis in these works developed and gave precise and powerful formulation to the Christian Natural Law tradition. Richard Hooker, **Jonathan Swift**, **Samuel Johnson**, and Edmond Burke had preceded him in doing so; the first three were decisive influences on his beliefs, character, and style. And though Anglican, the views of all five—Hooker, Swift, Johnson, Burke, and Lewis—are in continuity and conformity with their Catholic predecessors and contemporaries. As Anthony Quinton has recently noted, "Hooker argued for a more or less Thomist account of Natural Law, distinguishing it, as the Puritans did not, from God's law as given to men, not through reason, but by way of Biblical revelation" (*Oxford Illustrated History of Western Philosophy* [1994]). Four hundred years later, in a Fisher lecture at Cambridge University in the 1980s, Cardinal Ratzinger praised the insight and orthodoxy of *The Abolition of Man*.

By using the Chinese conception of the "Tao" as an equivalent for Natural Law, Lewis wished to overcome the ethnocentrism that suggests that Western civilization was uniquely or exclusively privileged in its ethical insight and heritage, and that others were "lesser breeds without the law" (see **Rudyard Kipling**). The great Chinese Christian jurist Dr. John C. H. Wu translated the initial line of Saint John's gospel into Chinese as: "In the beginning was the Tao, and the Tao was with God, and the Tao was **God.**" Lewis would have been delighted.

M. D. Aeschliman

Also See: Thomas Aquinas, Ethics, Morality, Natural Law

Bibliography

Aeschliman, M. D. "The Good Man Speaking Well." *National Review* (January 4, 1985): 49–52.
_____. *The Restitution of Man: C. S. Lewis and the Case Against Scientism.* Grand Rapids, MI: Eerdmans, 1998.
Stanlis, Peter J. *Edmund Burke and the Natural Law.* Ann Arbor: University of Michigan Press, 1958.
Yearly, Lee H. *The Ideas of Newman; Christianity and Human Religiosity.* University Park: Pennsylvania State University Press, 1978.

"Tasso"

First published posthumously in *Studies in Medieval and Renaissance Literature*.

This essay is for those extremely knowledgeable about world literature. Lewis tossed off incredibly erudite comments such as, "In 1634 Sir William Alexander in his *Anacrisis* quotes with approval from Sperone Speroni." To most readers these will be little more than odd-sounding (though mellifluous) names.

Lewis's main goal was to examine the influence of Italian Poet Torquato Tasso (1544–1595) on English literature to determine why it has been so slight. He tediously examined for three pages the comments of critics from about 1580 to 1720, then decided to pick up the pace a bit, letting the views of one critic serve for the next two hundred or so years of commentary. The two primary places Lewis found a Tassovian influence are **Edmund Spenser**'s *The Faerie Queene* and **John Milton**'s *Paradise Lost*.

Yet even here, in one of Lewis's least accessible works, nuggets of style and insight appear. Regarding some of **John Dryden**'s "miscarriages" (a fine word), Lewis noted that "we are too apt to assume that what a writer likes and what he can do coincide"—a pithy and apt observation. And one would hate to have missed Rymer's criticism that Tasso's *Jerusalem Delivered* contains "some superfluity of Fish." Unfortunately, those splendid moments come too rarely in this essay.

Marvin D. Hinten
Bowling Green State University

Technology

The systematic application of scientific knowledge to the affairs of life is what we call technology, and historians of **science** (such as Stanley L. Jaki) have shown that the scientific revolution reached the "critical mass" necessary to bear fruit in practical inventions by the beginning of the 18th century. In *"Descriptione Temporum"* (1954) Lewis concurred with the general consensus of cultural historians when he identified a great philosophical or ideological change as taking place "towards the end of the seventeenth century, with the general acceptance of Copernicanism, the dominance of Descartes, and (in England) the foundation of the Royal Society." It was at this time, in the quarrel of the "Ancients" and the "Moderns" in both France and England, that the modern idea of the inevitable collective progress of humanity by means of science and technology was first widely promoted by the "Moderns," although it had been adumbrated by Francis Bacon earlier in the 17th century.

Having seen technological firepower at work in World War I, in which he fought and was badly wounded, Lewis was aware of the dark possibilities of technology that early advocates of it such as Bacon had not seriously considered. His own views of it were precisely those of **Swift**—another Aristotelian Christian and partisan of the "Ancients"—as depicted in *Gulliver's Travels* (1726), a major inspiration for Lewis's own **space trilogy**. The Lilliputian king wishes to use the giant Gulliver as an offensive weapon against Blefuscu to further his own *libido dominandi* (lust for power). Later, the pygmy Gulliver, in a moral reversal of roles, tries to tempt the virtuous Brobdingnagian king with gunpowder to serve his *libido dominandi* and is morally censured by him in an unforgettable passage. The experimenters in the Grand Academy of Lagado engage in "Research and Development" that is either silly, counterintuitive, or destructive, or all three. The virtuous Houyhnhnms live lives of stoical dignity in a technologically primitive but morally advanced world. The belief in **Natural Law** and Christian charity suffuses Swift's book.

The course of 20th-century history seemed to Lewis to prove what is already obvious to Swift—that the increase in man's (or some men's) power over **nature**

did not necessarily bring or cause moral improvement. "Science without conscience," as Rabelais put it, "is nothing but the death of the soul," and frequently of bodies too. Thirteen million men were killed in World War I—60,000 of them in three days in July 1916 on the Somme. This was a world Lewis experienced.

The Abolition of Man and ***That Hideous Strength*** contain Lewis's most sustained analysis and depiction, respectively, of the philosophical and moral problems of technology, though several of his essays do too (see entry on **"Will We Lose God?"**). In *"De Descriptione Temporum"* (1954) Lewis argued that "Between Jane Austen and us . . . comes the birth of the machines. . . . It alters man's place in nature. . . . I conclude that it really is the greatest change in the history of Western man."

M. D. Aeschliman

Also See: Evolution, Materialism, H. G. Wells

Bibliography

Aeschliman, M. D. *The Restitution of Man: C. S. Lewis and the Case Against Scientism.* Grand Rapids, MI: Eerdmans, 1998.
Ellul, Jacques. *The Technological Society.* Grand Rapids, MI: Eerdmans, 1990.

Text Corruptions (Letter)

The Times Literary Supplement. (3 March 1950): 137.

Lewis targeted an inadvertent corruption of the text in J. Dover Wilson's edition of *Two Gentlemen* at the point where Wilson, himself, is illustrating just such a corruption in **Shakespeare**'s *Two Gentlemen of Verona*. Wilson responded appreciatively to Lewis's "entertaining" letter (*TLS*, 10 March 1950, 153) but sought to insure that there was no implication that Shakespeare was unable to distinguish between prose and verse.

Marjorie L. Mead
The Marion E. Wade Center

That Hideous Strength

London: The Bodley Head, 1945. First US edition, New York: Macmillan, 1946. An abridged version prepared by Lewis was published under the title *The Tortured Planet.*

That Hideous Strength (1945) is the third installment of Lewis's space trilogy begun in ***Out of the Silent Planet*** and ***Perelandra***. In it, Lewis reversed a technique that he brought into play in his other fiction. In the **Chronicles of Narnia**, we are taken *away* from his ordinary world into a region that cannot be located either on our maps or our calendars. Similarly, in *Out of the Silent Planet* and *Perelandra* we are whisked off to other planets. In ***Till We Have Faces***, we find ourselves in your classic "once-upon-a-time" locale, remote even from the records of ancient history with which we are familiar. In ***The Great Divorce*** we visit **hell** (or as it may be, Purgatory) and **heaven**.

In each of these cases, **Reality** hails the protagonists (not to mention the readers) with particular force and clarity because of its very remoteness and strangeness. We are off our own turf, and hence off balance and vulnerable. The shield of the familiar, which commonly assists us in keeping up the illusion of safety, has vanished.

In *That Hideous Strength* the direction is reversed. Reality (or Ultimacy, or the Unconditioned, or even the gods) breaks through the very flimsy scrim that hangs between our ordinariness and the princedom, dominations, and spiritual wickedness in high places of which Saint Paul speaks, and which we routinely tuck into a "religious" pigeonhole, thus neutralizing (we fondly suppose) its threat.

The narrative starts off unobtrusively enough. Bracton College is discussing the sale of a piece of college property. Nothing could be more routine or civilized: gentlemen and scholars in democratic debate. But it presently becomes clear that there is a Good Side and a Bad Side. (For Lewis, the notion that all parties to a discussion have equally valid points and equally blameless motives is a lie.) The "Progressive Element" in the faculty has an agenda that is nothing less than the redrawing of the moral map of the universe—nay, the virtual re-creation of the terms of human life. (This was written fifty years ago: Lewis had not heard of various contemporary lobbies whose agendas are identical.) No technique of cynicism, of back-stabbing, and of juggling with **truth** is ruled out in their tactics. Against this party stands the somewhat motley array of good people who seem able to do little but watch in horror as the Progressive Element progresses on its hell-bent way.

Presently the two groups separate into two communities. The Progressive Element takes up residence in a large mansion called Belbury, and we very quickly dis-

cover that, like hell, Belbury is nothing but a ghastly travesty of the Good. "We are a **family**," they claim loftily, but we are appalled at the denizens there: Lord Feverstone the raucous cynic; Straik the apostate priest; Filostrato who hates trees and leaves and loam and eggs and fur, and would replace all this riotous fruitfulness with metallic substitutes (he is a Gnostic); Fairy Hardcastle, the very archetype of femininity gone awry; Frost, with his opaque pince-nez and little, clipped white beard, reminiscent of **Freud**; and, worst of all, Wither, the Deputy Director, who turns out, really, to be a wraith. Wither has prostituted all his elegant articulateness to the service of non-meaning, and the lie that he worships has almost finished its work of leaching away whatever good solidity there might have been in him. He is Lewis's supreme image of the damned soul.

On the other hand, the Good people find their way, one by one, to St. Anne's. (It will be recalled that St. Anne, according to ancient Christian **tradition**, is the mother of the Mother of **God**. This community turns out to be the spiritual mother to one Jane Studdock, who, in her turn, becomes the mother of grace to her deeply misled husband, Mark, who has thrown in his lot with Belbury.) The household at St. Anne's is the one fragment left in England of Logres, the Arthurian kingdom where Charity was to be law. The miscellaneous denizens of St. Anne's include a Cockney charwoman; a Scottish skeptic; a bear named Mr. Bultitude; Dr. Dimble and his wife who is childless (the latter clearly an archetypal "mother: to all whom she meets"); and Grace Ironwood, a spinster in black who first lets Jane Studdock enter St. Anne's through a strait gate and narrow way—a small back gate in the garden wall (we shall recall that while Grace often seems austere to us, the instrument of grace, the Cross, is hailed in the liturgy of Good Friday as "sweetest wood and sweetest iron"). These denizens exhibit the reality of "family" of which Belbury is a hollow mockery. The head of the household is our friend Ransom, hero of *Out of the Silent*

Planet and *Perelandra*, who has inherited the mantle of Uther Pendragon and **King Arthur**.

Belbury busily sets about establishing a Gestapo-like state in Edgestowe, the little college town, headed up by Fairy Hardcastle in her jackboots, police uniform, and cigar. Their program also entails bulldozing into a muddy ruin all the quaint and domestic natural beauties that we treasure in an English village. But the great tension stretching the narrative tight is the race to see which household will gain the services of Merlin, Magician to the Court of Arthur, who is prophesied to put in one last appearance in this situation. He is innocent, and hence vulnerable to the blandishments of Belbury. It is critical that St. Anne's get hold of him first (which they do).

The narrative, at bottom, presents the ever-recurring fight between gnosticism, which hates the Creation, and sacramentalism (or Incarnationalism), which revels and exults in sheer life. We eventually discover that at the center of Belbury they have preserved a Head, kept alive with all sorts of tubes and attachments, the point being that the future Man will be sheer intellect, the body with all of its embarrassing viscera having been eliminated. The grim irony is that all of the intellectuals at Belbury worship this dribbling Head who can only moan out drivel and nonsense. The fatuity of hubris had reached its apotheosis here, and we find Wither, Frost, and the rest bowing in worship to non-meaning.

The very core of the drama, however, is the fight to save Mark, who begins the story as a selfish, callow, caddish young husband, deeply susceptible to all the specious attractions of Belbury. Jane, who also starts out in the grip of intellectual hauteur (I am an *intellectual*, thank you very much) climbs down the ladder of humility at St. Anne's and becomes capable of "saving" Mark by becoming what she was created to be: spouse and (we anticipate) mother.

That the gods are very much a part of the battle unfurls itself in the scene where Mercury, Mars, Venus, Zeus, and Saturn descend upon St. Anne's, and we find ourselves contemplating in almost paralyzed awe, not to say terror, the sheer, thunderous qualities of Reality, as each one descends.

The book has been criticized for what might seem to be its rather rickety structure. Too many elements. Not a tight enough narrative skein. (In America, Lewis published an abbreviated version of the novel under the title *The Tortured Planet*.) The structure may not be altogether misbegotten. Nonetheless, and paradoxically, the book may be Lewis's most powerful and prophetic story.

Thomas Howard

Also See: Imagination, Modernity, Politics, Science, Technology, H. G. Wells, Charles Williams.

Theme and Form

Lewis is one of the most versatile stylists ever to write in English. In each of his novels the style is unique. There is an almost naive charm in the way he described the unfallen planet, Malacandra, in *Out of the Silent Planet*. There is an almost Miltonic, poetic richness in *Perelandra*. (It is significant that Lewis was writing his book on **Milton** while he was writing *Perelandra*.) In *That Hideous Strength* there is a much more down-to-earth quality. The style in *Till We Have Faces* is at times primitive and penetrating. In the seven **Chronicles of Narnia** Lewis adopted a manner that is simple and straightforward yet full of **fantasy** and **imagination**. The style in *The Dark Tower* (which some do not regard as Lewis's work) is colorless—if Lewis wrote it, he was far from his usual ability.

Lewis's themes are many and various. He was frankly Romantic and wrote extremely good fantasy. He believed ardently in **reason** and as a Christian would argue that reason leads to **faith**. He exalted the Christian **virtues** of faith, **hope**, and charity, especially in *The Great Divorce* and in the Narnia stories.

Lewis was a supreme teacher in all his writings, his fiction, scholarly works, even his **poetry**. And he was didactic in a most appealing and memorable way. He taught his readers to love goodness, to obey **God**, to revere **beauty** as the creation of God, and to live harmoniously and unselfishly with others. He created real characters with whom his readers can identify: Ransom in the space trilogy, Lucy in the Narnia stories, Orual in *Till We Have Faces* (one of his most real and compelling characters), and others.

His early **allegory**, *The Pilgrim's Regress,* is subtitled *An Allegorical Apology for* **Romanticism, Reason,** *and* **Christianity**. Nearly everything Lewis ever wrote serves as **apologetics** for these three things. At a time when it was fashionable to be Counter-Romantic, he was unabashedly Romantic. He is notable for his preoccupation with *Sehnsucht*, the nameless, mysterious longing that is pleasurable and painful at the same time and which the language of discourse can hardly deal with. It requires music or poetry to express it.

Lewis's themes are many, varied, and sometimes complex. They include the need to find beauty, the necessity of hope, faith, and charity, the dangers of a secular social scientism, the deceitfulness of the self, the tendency to manipulate others, and the absolute necessity of believing in reason.

Corbin Scott Carnell
University of Florida

Also See: Evolution, Joy

Theology

C. S. Lewis was not a professional theologian, nor was he a "lay theologian," as some have claimed. He wrote no books of theology nor has he left us a system of theological thought. His religious works such as *The Problem of Pain*, *Miracles*, and *Mere Christianity* were intended to evangelize and to instruct in the basics of the common **faith** (orthodoxy) held by all Christians. When Lewis wrote on various theological or doctrinal subjects, he wrote as "one amateur to another" and often mentioned that his views were speculation or "guesses," not "final answers." Lewis called himself a "mere Christian" who was a defender of the faith and often submitted his religious manuscripts to theologians and ecclesiastics for correction and reproof. As an example, he submitted the manuscript of *Mere Christianity* to four ministers of different traditions (Methodist, Anglican, Presbyterian, Roman Catholic); all of these agreed with the basic tenets of his ideas with only a few exceptions.

Nevertheless, any person who wrote as much as Lewis did about matters of faith and doctrinal themes has definite theological presuppositions, and what Lewis wrote about theology was interesting and well worth remembering. In his essay **"Is Theology Poetry?"** (*The Weight of Glory and Other Addresses*, revised edition), Lewis defined theology as "the systematic statements about **God** and Man's relation to Him which the believers of a **religion** make." In *Mere Christianity* he said that theology is "experimental knowledge" that is initiated in people by God, and that it is "the science of God" that is practical and "like a map" that leads one to anywhere one wants to go. He further maintained that theology is the attempt to explain evil (*Letters of C. S. Lewis*); and that the true test of one's own theology is if it can be explained in common, everyday **language** or the vernacular (**"Christian Apologetics"**).

Lewis read widely in what might be called "classical" or "historic" theology—the church fathers, **Augustine**, **Aquinas** (especially his *Summa Theologica*), and the Reformers. His theology and knowledge of Christian doctrine were broadly based in the great creeds of orthodox **Christianity**, with its bedrock in the Augustinian and Platonic traditions. Before he became a Chris-

tian, Lewis had read authors like **Dante**, **Spenser**, **Milton**, Herbert, and Bunyan; these and other writers from classical literature such as **Plato**, **Aristotle**, and Boethius (*The Consolation of Philosophy*) gave him foundations for his theological and philosophical thinking. He praised Aristotle's doctrine of God in *The Problem of Pain*, and in **Reflections on the Psalms** called Plato "an overwhelming theological genius." After he became interested in Christianity, and during the time of his long conversion from **atheism** to theism to committed Christian belief, Lewis read the theological works of Saint Augustine (*Confessions, The City of God*), Thomas Traherne (*Centuries of Meditation*), Martin Luther (*Theologica Germanica*), William Law (*Serious Call to a Devout and Holy Life*), Thomas à Kempis (*Imitation of Christ*), and others. Lewis often acknowledged his debt to these writers for their clearness in presenting "basic" theological and doctrinal beliefs, and he reread their works for the rest of his life.

Lewis believed that in studying the older theologians he was best able to understand the true nature of the Christian faith. In an essay titled **"On the Reading of Old Books"** (*God in the Dock*) he wrote that only when a man "steps out of his own century" can he learn the many and varied meanings of Christianity. Corbin Scott Carnell has written (*Bright Shadow of Reality: C. S. Lewis and the Feeling Intellect*) that this was both an advantage and a disadvantage to Lewis in communicating Christian doctrine. His own theological works aimed at the clearness and conciseness of Augustine and Traherne and others, but he also had less to say to some people who were caught up in the ambiguities and complexities of modern theological movements such as Existentialism, Process Theology, and Neo-Orthodoxy.

Because of the tendency of some of today's Lewis scholars to label him strictly as "evangelical" or "conservative," many Lewis readers have come to believe that he distrusted all modern theology and theologians. This is inaccurate. Lewis disagreed with much of the extreme liberal theology of his day, especially that which denied the miraculous, and particularly the work of such theologians as Teilhard de Chardin, Paul Tillich, Rudolf Bultmann, and John A. T. Robinson (especially *Honest to God*), but he did read and agree with some modern theology. Although he read little of Kierkegaard, he recommended the Danish existentialist to others, saying "some find him useful" (*Letters of C. S. Lewis*). He was deeply influenced by Rudolf Otto's *The Idea of the Holy*, and there is an implicit reference to Otto's theme of the "numinous" in *Perelandra*. Later Lewis mentioned the book as one of the ten most important in his life.

Lewis also enjoyed and profited from works like Anders Nygren's *Agape and Eros*, and in *Letters to Malcolm* he praised Martin Buber (*I and Thou*): "how good Buber is!" And it is well known that **G. K. Chesterton**'s *The Everlasting Man* was very influential in Lewis's conversion, and in *Surprised by Joy* he wrote that this work outlined for him a very understandable Christian overview of history based on the incarnation of Christ. From his great friend **Charles Williams** Lewis learned that one's theology did not have to be informed by **reason** and dogma alone; it could also encompass paradox, openness to other religions and faiths, and the mystical. And from his lifelong friend **Owen Barfield** Lewis saw the value of using precise **language** in his theological thinking, along with an appreciation for the spiritual and the **imagination** for expressing one's deepest theological ideas.

Perhaps the most important influence on Lewis's thinking about theology was the work of **George Mac-Donald**. Lewis wrote that MacDonald "baptized his imagination" (*Phantastes*), and in his preface to *George MacDonald—An Anthology* Lewis wrote that Mac-Donald was his master and that he had never written a book in which he did not quote from him. Although he did not agree with MacDonald's belief in universal salvation, Lewis deeply admired the Scottish minister and novelist's devotion to God, his illuminating ethical insights, and his use of the religious **imagination**—all expressed in crystal clear language.

Because of these multifaceted strands in his thought, Lewis is difficult to classify theologically and cannot be called specifically "conservative" or "liberal" or "evangelical." On "basic" doctrinal issues he believed and wrote about what the majority of Christians believe— the incarnation of Christ, the truth of the **miracles** in the New Testament, the physical **resurrection** and second coming of Jesus, a balanced view of a God of **love** and judgment, a transcendent and immanent God, the three personalities of the Trinity, and the realities of **heaven** and **hell**. On the other hand he cared little for denominational distinctives, church polity, or atonement theories; nor was he a biblical inerrantist. He was open to truth in other religions and was very Anglo-Catholic in his views about purgatory, prayers for the dead, and regular confessions to a spiritual director. He took the Bible largely at face value and understood the word "Christian" in its original sense (based on Acts 11:26), as a person who accepted and followed the teachings of the apostles. His "mere Christianity" can perhaps be best summed up in a statement he made in an unpublished letter to his friend **Dom Bede Griffiths** (quoted in the preface to *Christian Reflections*): "When all is said (and truly said) about the divisions of Christendom, there remains, by God's mercy, an enormous common ground."

Perry C. Bramlett
C. S. Lewis for the Local Church

Also See: Anglicanism, Apologetics, the Bible, Books of Influence, Church, Conservatism, Holy Spirit, Language/Rhetoric, Metaphysics, Philosophy, Prayer, Revelation, Roman Catholicism

Bibliography

Carnell, Corbin Scott. *Bright Shadow of Reality: C. S. Lewis and the Feeling Intellect*. Grand Rapids, MI: Eerdmans, 1974.

Cunningham, Richard B. *C. S. Lewis: Defender of the Faith*. Philadelphia: Westminster Press, 1967.

Freshwater, Mark E. *C. S. Lewis and the Truth of Myth*. Lanham, MD: University Press of America, 1988.

Hartt, Walter F. "Godly Influences: The Theology of J. R. R. Tolkien and C. S. Lewis." *Studies in the Literary Imagination*. 14 no. 2 (Fall 1981): 21–29.

Holmer, Paul L. *C. S. Lewis: The Shape of His Faith and Thought*. New York: Harper & Row, 1976.

Lewis, C. S. *Christian Reflections*; *God in the Dock: Essays on Theology and Ethics*.

Lindskoog, Kathryn. *The Lion of Judah in Never-Never Land*. Grand Rapids, MI: Eerdmans, 1973.

_____. *C. S. Lewis: Mere Christian*. Wheaton, IL: Shaw, 1987.

Meilaender, Gilbert. "Theology in Stories: C. S. Lewis and the Narrative Quality of Experience." *Word & World*. 1 no. 3 (Summer 1981): 222–29.

Purtill, Richard L. *C. S. Lewis's Case for the Christian Faith*. San Francisco: Harper & Row, 1981.

Root, Jerry. "Following That Bright Blur." *Christian History*. IV no. 3 (1985): 27–35.

Willis, John R. *Pleasures Forevermore: The Theology of C. S. Lewis*. Chicago: Loyola University Press, 1983.

They Asked for a Paper: Papers and Addresses

London: Geoffrey Bles, 1962.

See separate essay entries on the following:

"De Descriptione Temporum"
"Hamlet: The Prince or the Poem?"
"The Inner Ring"
"Is Theology Poetry?"
"Kipling's World"
"Lilies that Fester"
"The Literary Impact of the Authorized Version"

"On Obstinacy in Belief"
"Psycho-analysis and Literary Criticism"
"Sir Walter Scott"
"Transposition"
"The Weight of Glory"

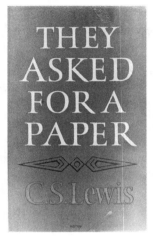

***They Stand Together: The Letters of C. S. Lewis
to Arthur Greeves (1914–1963)***

Hooper, Walter (ed). London: Collins, 1979. First US edition,
New York: Macmillan, 1979.

The letters C. S. Lewis wrote to **Arthur Greeves**
(1895–1966) document Lewis's life from his first meeting of Greeves in 1914 to a few months before Lewis
died in 1963. All the major characters in Lewis's life
story appear, including his brother **Warren Lewis**, his
father **Albert Lewis**, his self-chosen mother Mrs. **Janie
Moore**, most of the **Inklings**, a few of his students, the
long list of authors (more than two hundred) whose
books he read, and—in the most unguarded portrait he
ever achieved—himself.

The correspondence can be divided into three periods. The letters in the first period (1914–22) touch upon
Lewis's **Oxford** education, his service in the trenches
of France, his return and progress through several military hospitals, and the household (kept secret from his
father) that Lewis set up with Mrs. Moore near Oxford
as he completed his education. The correspondence was
then all but interrupted during an interval documented
by Lewis's diary, published as ***All My Road Before Me:
The Diary of C. S. Lewis 1922–27***. The second period
of letters (1927–47) began with Lewis's fellowship at
Magdalen College, Oxford, and is marked by chatty,

affectionate letters that show Lewis's development as a
major **scholar** and reveal his religious conversion. The
third period (1947–63) contain letters that are brief but
intensely moving, recording Lewis's years at **Cambridge**, his **marriage**, widowerhood, and final illness.

The letters of the early years began shortly after
Lewis met Arthur Greeves in **Belfast**, in April 1914,
where each discovered that the other shared his deepest
thoughts. Lewis wrote to Greeves in June 1914, while
in his last term at **Malvern** College. By September 26,
1914, he was at Great Bookham, Surrey, preparing for
Oxford. He had become the sort of adolescent who
loftily explained that the Hebrew name of Jesus was
Yeshua, and that **Christianity** was one of many
mythologies. During this period, lasting through 1917,
Lewis occasionally confided his sexual fantasies to
Greeves. Once ensconced at Oxford, he found himself
digging trenches as a cadet. Writing from Plymouth on
October 28, 1917, Lewis first mentioned Mrs. Janie
Moore, though not yet by name.

On December 14, 1917, he wrote from France, referring prophetically to Arthur Greeves and Mrs. Moore as
the two people who mattered most to him; he was to live
with this woman for virtually the rest of her life and to
write to Greeves for the rest of his own. He wrote nothing about trench warfare but on February 12, 1918,
described a French village with its crucifixes, granary,
dovecotes (which he sketched), and orchards, rejoicing
that he had nothing to do but read. A long silence followed as he returned to the Western Front and was
wounded. On May 23, 1918, he wrote again, mostly on
literary matters. This letter marked a major change in his
thought; his brush with **pain** and death had moved him
from **atheism** to gnosticism (dualism), and he told Arthur
that Matter equaled **Nature**, and Nature equaled **Satan**.
This, along with an enclosed poem, heralded the theme
of his first published book, *Spirits in Bondage* (1919).
He spoke only once about the trenches, on August 31,
1918, describing terror, filth, and exhaustion.

Happily returning to Oxford in 1919, Lewis wrote
during the first eight months of the year from his college
residence, while Mrs. Moore and her daughter Maureen
lived nearby. In February 1920, he announced plans to
move into her household, and on June 19, 1920, he wrote
lyrically of walking home to her past flowering hawthorn
trees. During the seven years that followed, he sent a single letter only for 1921,1922, 1923, and 1926.

The letters of the middle years began sporadically on
June 26, 1927, when Lewis described his meetings with
the Coalbiters, a group where he met **J. R. R. Tolkien**

and studied Old Icelandic. On September 25, 1929, Albert Lewis died. After his father's death, C. S. Lewis wrote to Greeves more regularly and at length. As before, landscape continued to be a frequent subject, along with his reading. But a new element was about to appear; on January 5, 1930, Lewis described a long country walk and discussed Jacob Boehme, who, he said, had shaken him up as no one had since **George MacDonald**'s *Phantastes*.

Mellow, mature, and leisurely, these letters to Greeves suggest a man with his grief behind him and a long career ahead. He now spoke of **Christ** and the Gospels in familiar terms. On January 30, 1930, he wrote in detail about the experience he later called "**Joy**," a sudden excess of numinous wonder. He described on April 29, 1930, his last visit to his late father's Belfast home, **Little Lea**, recalling Greeves to shared memories of an Ireland with dew-covered hills and misty woods, Lewis's lifelong image of goodness. This passage makes clear what the two men shared, why their **friendship** lasted, and what it meant to Lewis.

December 24, 1930, many letters later, found Lewis cutting firewood for his new household at **the Kilns**, where he spent the rest of his home life; he lamented that he believed in Christianity but could not feel its **reality**. On January 10, 1931, he described his first **walking tour** with his brother Warren; they visited Tintern Abbey, where he found the grass growing within the roofless building to be the holiest sight he had ever seen. Then, on September 22, 1931, he recounted a long night's conversation with **Hugo Dyson** and J. R. R. Tolkien, the trigger to his full conversion. In perhaps the most important letter of his life, October 18, 1931, he explained to Arthur how the death of Jesus could offer salvation to people of all eras and affirmed Christ's story as a **myth** that is literally true, having actually happened in the physical world. Although these letters are limpid and crisp in style, he had something to learn from Arthur Greeves, who, according to Lewis's reply of December 17, 1931, found *The Pilgrim's Regress* overfull of quotations and lacking in simplicity, two errors Lewis never repeated.

Between 1937 and 1947 the letters gradually became infrequent, though they continued to provide a clear record of his reading and his many publications; Mrs. Moore had begun her decline into illness and old age. Writing to Greeves on January 5, 1947, he meditated on their own advancing age, remarking ironically upon how adult his students had become in comparison to himself, since they only read modern books.

During the final years, beginning in 1947, Lewis's brief letters touched upon his occasional visits to Greeves in Ireland and Mrs. Moore's removal to a nursing home and subsequent death. The name of **Joy Davidman**, who was to become Lewis's wife, appeared on March 25, 1954, and on December 4, 1954, he wrote of his appointment to **Magdalene College**, **Cambridge** University. In a remarkable testimony to their continuing closeness, Lewis asked Greeves on May 13, 1956, to proofread *Till We Have Faces*, his final novel.

The two friends last met in June 1961, when Greeves visited the Kilns, heralded by a flurry of notes giving him directions. On June 30, 1962, Lewis mentioned a prostate problem, and on November 19, 1962, he lamented Arthur's weakening heart. A few months before he died, Lewis reported on September 11, 1963, that he had resigned from Cambridge and observed that he and Arthur would never see one another again while they lived. Their friendship had endured from adolescence to the brink of the grave.

Nancy-Lou Patterson

Bibliography

Barfield, Owen. "The Sound of Friendship." *CSL: The Bulletin of the New York C. S. Lewis Society*. 10 (May 1979): 5–6.

Hooper, Walter. "Speech Before the Portland C. S. Lewis Society." *Chronicle of the Portland C. S. Lewis Society*. 8 no. 2 (April-June 1979): 9–19.

Lewis, C. S. *All My Road Before Me*; *The Pilgrim's Regress*; *Spirits in Bondage*; *Till We Have Faces*

This Ever Diverse Pair (Book Review)

"Life Partners." *Time and Tide*. XXXI (25 March 1950): 286.

This book written by **Owen Barfield** under the pseudonym G. A. L. Burgeon deals with the rift between the private person and the public persona. Lewis described it as "a comic book with a nagging undertone of melancholy. It is high and sharp philosophic comedy."

Anne Gardner

Bibliography

Burgeon, G. A. L. *This Ever Diverse Pair*.

"Thoughts of a Cambridge Don"

The Lion (St. Mark's Dundela, Belfast). (January 1963): 11–21. Retitled in an enlarged form as "A Slip of the Tongue" and reprinted in *Screwtape Proposes a Toast* and *Weight of Glory*.

This short sermon preached by Lewis in 1956 is now most easily found in *The Weight of Glory*. It begins with Lewis noting that, in trying to say during a **prayer** that he wanted to pass through temporal things to get to eternal things, he had actually reversed the order. This seemed significant, Lewis noted, for he felt it expressed the real desire of his heart—not to have his normal life interfered with very much. This attitude, he observed, goes against the yielding to **God** that spiritual directors have repeatedly said is necessary for spiritual health. Lewis closed by saying that, while God's **grace** is what enables one to submit spiritually, that grace is generally granted to people who have made efforts to submit, over and over, as much as they can.

This sermon is more accessible than much of Lewis's nonfiction writing; he referred to only one work of literature and five figures from church history, and he used only one Latin phrase, immediately translated. The purpose of his sermon, Lewis said, is not so much to instruct as to compare notes, although as is usual with him the notes are instructive.

Marvin D. Hinten
Bowling Green State University

Also See: Destiny, Preacher, Reality, Spirituality

Bibliography

Morrison, John. "Oops." *CSL: The Bulletin of the New York C. S. Lewis Society.* 19 (May 1988): 1–8.

The Three Estates in Medieval and Renaissance Literature (Book Review)

Medium Aevum. III (February 1934): 68–70.

According to Lewis, the thesis of this book by Ruth Mohl is that "'the verse or prose catalogues of the classes of society and their 'defections' were regarded . . . as a distinct literary form" in Medieval times. The author "lacks certain qualifications for a sympathetic reconstruction of the past," although she writes agreeably and is able to incorporate abstracts of text "without extreme dullness." Lewis observed that Mohl's procedure was questionable and her thesis unproven, although there were incidental facts which may prove valuable.

Anne Gardner

Also See: Medieval World, Renaissance

Bibliography

Mohl, Ruth. *The Three Estates in Medieval and Renaissance Literature.*

"Three Kinds of Men"

The Sunday Times. 6258 (21 March 1943): 2. Reprinted in *Present Concerns.*

In this 1943 essay, Lewis claimed that "begging is our only wisdom," especially since want makes it easier. Yet "even on those terms the **Mercy** will receive us." The "beggars" constitute one kind of man. Another kind is made up of those who live for themselves, acknowledging no other claim upon them. The remaining and largest kind is made up of those who do acknowledge some claim upon them, and try to limit their pursuit of their own interests in accordance with that claim. This threefold division of people makes it disastrous to divide people by the two terms of good and bad. The largest group of people is "always and necessarily unhappy," for it can never do enough. "The Christian doctrine that there is no 'salvation' by works done according to the moral law is a fact of daily experience." We cannot go on by our own moral efforts; we must want **Christ**.

John Bremer

Also See: Faith, The Fall, Grace, Human Nature

Till We Have Faces: A Myth Retold

London: Geoffrey Bles, 1956. First US edition, New York: Harcourt, Brace & World, 1957.

Till We Have Faces was Lewis's last work of fiction and the one he considered his best. It was not well received initially, probably because of its difficulty and its differences from his earlier fiction, and it remains the least popular of his fictional works, though the most highly praised by literary critics. In retelling the **myth** on which the novel is based, Lewis creates a new myth, one that develops more completely and in a more satisfactory way meanings that earlier narrators of the myth were unable to grasp. But the result makes demands beyond those of Lewis's other works, demands many readers have found puzzling and daunting.

This story is different from the others in part because it was written with the help of **Joy Davidman Gresham**. Lewis found himself, in the mid 1950s, unable for the first time in his life to come up with an idea for a book. One evening, as he and Joy sat together, they began talking about the myth of **Cupid and Psyche**, which had haunted Lewis all his life, and bounced ideas back and forth. The next day Lewis wrote the first chapter of *Till We Have Faces.* Joy read it and made suggestions and Lewis rewrote it and went on to the next chapter, a process which continued for the rest of the book.

The book retells the myth from the viewpoint of one of Psyche's sisters, whom Lewis names Orual. One key difference from Lewis's other stories is his use of a first-person, unreliable narrator. This probably was suggested by Joy and may have been the key that allowed Lewis finally to deal successfully with the tale. All of Lewis's other stories are third-person accounts, with the narrator providing a reliable point of view to orient the reader. *Till We Have Faces* is written by Orual as a self-defense, an accusation that she has been treated unfairly by the gods and a defense of her own actions. Orual writes what she believes to be an accurate, truthful account of her life. It is up to the reader to recognize her faults and self-deceptions, without a reliable narrator's help.

Lewis's version of the story is set in an imaginary country, Glome, on the outskirts of the Hellenistic world, a century or two before the birth of **Christ**. It begins with the death of Orual's mother, after which Orual's father, the King of Glome, marries a new wife, who dies in giving birth to a baby who was named Psyche. The ugly Orual loves the beautiful Psyche devotedly and acts as mother to her, meanwhile ignoring her other sister, Redival. As Psyche becomes a young woman, she is so beautiful that people begin to worship her, instead of worshipping the local nature goddess, Ungit (their embodiment of Venus). After a plague and in the midst of a drought and famine, the Priest of Ungit tells the King that relief will come only if Psyche is sacrificed to Ungit's son, the "brute," by being exposed on a mountain, bound to a holy tree. The King complies.

When Orual goes, some time later, to bury Psyche's bones, she instead finds Psyche, in a valley, across a river, vibrantly alive and clothed in rags. Psyche invites Orual

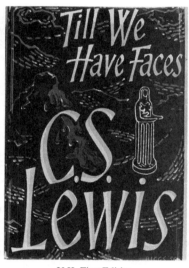

U.K. First Edition

into her palace, but Orual cannot see the palace or the magnificent robes Psyche says she is wearing, and Psyche admits she has never seen the husband who gave her the clothes, in whose palace she lives, and who sleeps with her at night. When Orual visits Psyche again, she forces Psyche, by threatening suicide, to light a lamp at night and look at her husband. Orual convinces herself that it is for Psyche's own good, though the reader must recognize that she is intensely jealous at having her place in Psyche's life taken by another and at being excluded from an area of Psyche's existence.

When Psyche looks at her husband, her relationship is destroyed and she is sent into exile. As Psyche goes,

Orual sees Psyche's husband in all his **beauty** and hears him tell her that she too will be Psyche and that she must die before she dies. Upon her return to Glome, Orual does not tell the Fox, her tutor and friend, what happened on the mountain and begins to wear a veil to hide her face and feelings from others. Soon after her return, the King dies and Orual succeeds him. She pours herself into official activities and becomes more and more the Queen (a masculine-like monarch), less and less Orual (a woman and a person), and time goes by swiftly.

Many years later she hears a priest in a neighboring country tell a sacred story about Psyche, and she recognizes it as her own story—but she says the teller got the story wrong, because he says both sisters visited Psyche, and they could see the palace and became jealous of it. So Orual decides to write her own version of the story, to get the facts right and to show how unjust the gods have been to her. She writes the account we have been reading. But in the writing process, she discovers how self-deceived she has been and how she has devoured people, especially Psyche, the Fox, and Bardia, the soldier who has served loyally as her advisor for many years. In a series of visions she shares the impossible tasks that Ungit assigned to Psyche. Through them she learns to think of others, instead of just herself, thus dying to self, as the god's words said she must, and in the process of learning unselfish love, *agape*, she becomes beautiful like Psyche and gains salvation.

A central theme of the book is **love**. The story shows how all of Orual's loves turn possessive and destructive (her motherly affection for Psyche, her **friendship** with the Fox, her sublimated but nonetheless real desire for Bardia). The story illustrates the theme of *The Four Loves*, that the natural loves can remain themselves, can remain loves, only if they are infused with, or transformed by, divine love, or *agape*.

Another key theme is the tension between rationalism and the divine. The Fox is a Stoic, attempting to rely wholly on **reason** (he is representative of the spirit of the Greeks and of the **Enlightenment**). Opposed to him are the Priest of Ungit, on the one hand, with his appreciation of a dark, mysterious holiness, and Psyche on the other, with her natural, intuitive response to the divine.

Orual, as the Fox's student, attempted to follow him and to reject the gods. She must learn that only through the numinous, through that which is beyond reason, can the divine be fully known.

In that context, sacrifice becomes a central motif in the novel. The motif appears first in the bloody sacrifices on the altar in the temple of Ungit, which the Fox teaches Orual to reject. It appears next in Psyche's self-sacrificial attitude, as she risks her own health to bring healing during the plague, and then as she accepts death on the mountain to end the drought and her people's suffering. Lewis said that one motif of the book was the way Psyche's love and sacrificial attitude display a naturally Christlike spirit. This motif also extends to Orual, who unconsciously lives a life of sacrifice, dies to self, first by devoting herself to her people and her country and then by performing Psyche's tasks for Psyche (substitution), and thus attains a Christlike spirit herself.

Still another major theme involves identity. Orual's lack of self-knowledge, her self-deception, is embodied in the veil she wears much of her life. The veil gives her an identity as the Queen, but allows her to bury her personal self and establishes a barrier between herself and others, and herself and the divine. She has no face, no identity, and thus has no way to relate to the divine. Only when she removes the veil, confronts her true self, and gains a "face" can she encounter **God** face-to-face, without defenses, excuses, or pretenses. Only then can she attain an authentic relationship with God, with others, and with herself.

Charles A. Huttar
Hope College

Bibliography

Christopher, Joe R. "Archetypal Patterns in *Till We Have Faces*." *The Longing for a Form: Essays on the Fiction of C. S. Lewis*. Peter J. Schakel (ed). Kent, OH: Kent State University Press, 1977: 193–212.

Donaldson, Mara E. *Holy Places Are Dark Places: C. S. Lewis and Paul Ricoeur on Narrative Transformation*. Lanham, MD: University Press of America, 1988.

Gibson, Evan K. *C. S. Lewis, Spinner of Tales: A Guide to His Fiction*. Washington, DC: Christian University Press, 1980.

Glover, Donald E. *C. S. Lewis: The Art of Enchantment*. Athens: Ohio University Press, 1981.

Holyer, Robert. "The Epistemology of C. S. Lewis's *Till We Have Faces*." *Anglican Theological Review*. 70 (1988): 233–55.

Howard, Thomas. *The Achievement of C. S. Lewis: A Reading of His Fiction*. Wheaton, IL: Shaw, 1980.

Kilby, Clyde S. "*Till We Have Faces*: An Interpretation." *The Longing for a Form: Essays on the Fiction of C. S. Lewis*.

Peter J. Schakel (ed). Kent, OH: Kent State University Press, 1977: 171–81.

Manlove, C. N. *C. S. Lewis: His Literary Achievement*. New York: St. Martin's Press, 1987.

Reddy, Albert F. "*Till We Have Faces*: 'An Epistle to the Greeks.'" *Mosaic* 13 (1980): 153–64.

Schakel, Peter J. *Reason and Imagination in C. S. Lewis: A Study of Till We Have Faces*. Grand Rapids, MI: Eerdmans, 1984.

Starr, Nathan Comfort. *C. S. Lewis's "Till We Have Faces": Introduction and Commentary*. New York: Seabury Press, 1968.

Ulreich, John C. "Prophets, Priests, and Poets: Toward a Definition of Religious Fiction." *Cithara*. 22 no. 2 (May 1983): 3–31.

Urang, Gunnar. *Shadows of Heaven: Religion and Fantasy in the Writing of C. S. Lewis, Charles Williams, and J. R. R. Tolkien*. Philadelphia: Pilgrim Press, 1971.

Van Der Weele, Steve J. "From Mt. Olympus to Glome: C. S. Lewis's Dislocation of Apuleius's 'Cupid and Psyche' in *Till We Have Faces*." *The Longing for a Form: Essays on the Fiction of C. S. Lewis*. Peter J. Schakel (ed). Kent, OH: Kent State University Press, 1977: 182–92.

Timeless at Heart: Essays on Theology

Hooper, Walter (ed). London: Collins, 1987.

See separate entries on the following:

"Answers to Questions on Christianity"
Canonization (Letter)
Capital Punishment (Letter)
"Christian Apologetics"
The Church's Liturgy I (Letter)
The Church's Liturgy II (Letter)
The Conditions for a Just War (Letter)
The Conflict in Anglican Theology (Letter)
Correspondence with an Anglican who Dislikes Hymns (Letter)
Death Penalty (Letter)
"The Founding of the Oxford Socratic Club"
The Holy Name (Letter)
Invocation (Letter)
Invocation of Saints (Letter)
"Is Theism Important?"
Mere Christians (Letter)
Miracles (Letter)
Mr. C. S. Lewis on Christianity (Letter)
"The Pains of Animals"
Pittenger-Lewis (Letter)
"Rejoinder to Dr. Pittenger"
"Religion Without Dogma"
Version Vernacular (Letter)

A Village Experience (Letter)
"Why I Am Not a Pacifist"
"Willing Slaves of the Welfare State"

"To a Friend"

See entry on "To G. M."

"To Charles Williams"

See entry on "On the Death of Charles Williams"

"To G. M."

The Spectator. 169 (October 9, 1942): 335. Revised and retitled as "To a Friend" and reprinted in *Poems* and *Collected Poems*.

This poem compares the impact the lives of two different men might have after death. The speaker's friend will have a positive one, fertile and inspiring to others. In contrast, the speaker sees his own impact after death as caustic, barren, and sterile.

Don W. King
Montreat College

J[ohn] R[onald] R[euel] Tolkien (1892–1973)

J. R. R. Tolkien was a valued friend of C. S. Lewis, a charter member of the **Inklings**, and world-famous as the author of the fantasy classics *The Hobbit, The Lord of the Rings*, and *The Silmarillion*. He first met Lewis in May 1926 at a meeting of the English Faculty at Merton College, **Oxford**, where he was professor of Anglo-Saxon. Lewis had just been appointed as **tutor** in the English department of **Magdalen College**, and although his initial response to Tolkien was not favorable, the two soon found common ground in their love of good talk and a shared admiration for "Northernness" or Norse mythology. In his autobiography, *Surprised By Joy*, Lewis wrote that his **friendship** with Tolkien had demolished two of his old Ulster prejudices and added: "I had been (implicitly) warned never to trust a Papist, and at my coming into the English Faculty (explicitly) never to trust a philologist. Tolkien was both."

When Lewis met and started to become friends with Tolkien, he was at the point in his spiritual pilgrimage where it was apparent to him that he had to accept or reject **God**. In Tolkien he found not only an inspired storyteller and comparable **scholar** but also a friend who was a man of personal integrity and a committed (Roman Catholic) Christian. After his conversion, Lewis called Tolkien one of "the immediate human causes" behind his decision to become a Christian. Tolkien had helped Lewis understand the true meaning of the Christian story as revealed in the gospels, and that the

accounts of **Christ**'s life and teachings ("true myths") had really happened and were grounded securely in historical fact.

After Lewis's conversion, his friendship with Tolkien deepened, and the two men continued to see much of each other through the years, both in Inklings meetings and in private talks and visits. Working together in revising the English syllabus at Oxford, they emphasized the study of medieval and Old English literature as a foundation for the study of modern literature. Lewis was lavish in his praise for *The Hobbit* (first shown to him in manuscript by Tolkien in 1933) and later called *The Lord of the Rings* "almost unequaled in the whole range of narrative art." Lewis's trilogy of space novels was at least partly written because of a "literary bargain" between Lewis and Tolkien to compose popular stories that had a "mythopoeic" intent. Tolkien enjoyed the space books, especially *Perelandra*, but was not happy with Lewis's later Narnian stories. He thought that Lewis had written them too quickly, that they were inconsistent in detail, and that they were unconvincing in their picture of a "secondary world."

Although Tolkien always treated Lewis personally with respect and affection, their friendship cooled and they saw each other less after the publication of the first volume of *The Lord of the Rings* in 1954. This was partly due to the discontinuing of the Thursday Inklings meetings in Lewis's rooms at Magdalen College, Lewis's friendship with **Charles Williams**, and Lewis's marriage to Joy Gresham. Nevertheless, Tolkien saw his friendship with Lewis as one of the great "compensations" of his life, and when Lewis died in 1963, Tolkien wrote: "We owed each a great debt to the other, and that tie with the deep affection . . . remains. He was a great man of whom the cold-blooded obituaries only scraped the surface."

Perry C. Bramlett
C. S. Lewis for the Local Church

Also See: Joy Davidman Lewis, Roman Catholicism

Bibliography

Carpenter, Humphrey. *Tolkien: A Biography*. Boston: Houghton Mifflin, 1977.
_____. *The Inklings*. Boston: Houghton Mifflin, 1979.
_____ (ed.). *The Letters of J. R. R. Tolkien*. Boston: Houghton Mifflin, 1981
Green, Roger Lancelyn and Walter Hooper. *C. S. Lewis: A Biography*. New York: Harcourt Brace, 1974
Sayer, George. *Jack: C. S. Lewis and His Times*. San Francisco: Harper & Row, 1988.
Tolkien, J. R. R. *The Hobbit, or, There and Back Again*. London: Allen & Unwin, 1937.

_____. *Farmer Giles of Ham*. London: George Allen & Unwin, 1949.

_____. *The Fellowship of the Ring: Being the First Part of The Lord of the Rings*. London: Allen & Unwin, 1954.

_____. *The Two Towers: Being the Second Part of The Lord of the Rings*. London: Allen & Unwin, 1954.

_____. *The Return of the King: Being the Third Part of The Lord of the Rings*. London: Allen & Unwin, 1955.

_____. *Tree and Leaf*. London: Unwin, 1964.

_____. *Smith of Wootton Major*. London: Allen & Unwin, 1967.

_____. *The Father Christmas Letters*. Ed. Baillie Tolkien. London: Allen & Unwin, 1976.

_____. *The Silmarillion*. Ed. Christopher Tolkien. London: Allen & Unwin, 1977.

_____. *Poems and Stories*. London: Allen & Unwin, 1980.

_____. *Letters of J.R.R. Tolkien: A Selection*. Ed. Humphrey Carpenter, with Christopher Tolkien. London: Allen & Unwin, 1981.

_____. *The Book of Lost Tales. Part I*. Ed. Christopher Tolkien. London: Allen & Unwin, 1983.

_____. *The Monsters and the Critics and Other Essays*. Ed. Christopher Tolkien. London: Allen & Unwin,

_____. *The Book of Lost Tales. Part II*. Ed. Christopher Tolkien. London: Allen & Unwin, 1984.

"Tolkien's *The Lord of the Rings*"

See entries on *The Fellowship of the Ring* (Book Review) and *The Two Towers* (Book Review)

"To Mr. Kingsley Amis on His Late Verses"

Essays in Criticism. 4 (April 1954): 190. cf. Kingsley Amis, "Beowulf." (January 1954): 85.

Amis's poem complained the hero of *Beowulf* was not human because we only see him engaged in fighting dragons and related activities. Never do we see him, for instance, lay with women. Lewis's response was a wry, epigrammatic criticism of Amis's deprecation of Beowulf's sexual discretion.

Don W. King
Montreat College

"To Mr. Roy Campbell"

The Cherwell. 56 (May 6, 1939): 35 (under the pseudonym Nat Whilk). Revised and retitled as "The Author of *Flowering Rifle*" and reprinted in *Poems* and *Collected Poems*.

An attack on the **politics** though not the **poetry** of South African poet Ignatius Roy Dunnachie Campbell (1901–1957). "Rifles may flower and terrapins may flame," the first line, alludes to Campbell's first long poem, *The Flaming Terrapin* (1924) and his later *Flowering Reeds* (1933). Stylistically, Lewis found in Campbell a kindred spirit since both were at odds with the modern style represented by **T. S. Eliot** and **W. H. Auden**; politically, however, Campbell's service on the side of the Nationalists in Spain offended Lewis. Interestingly, on November 28, 1946, Warren Lewis wrote: "A pretty full meeting of the **Inklings** to meet Roy Campbell . . . whom I was very glad to see again; he is fatter and tamer than he used to be I think" (*Brothers and Friends: The Diaries of Major Warren Hamilton Lewis*. Clyde Kilby and Marjorie Lamp Mead [eds]. San Francisco: Harper and Row, 1982.).

Don W. King
Montreat College

The Tortured Planet

See entry on *That Hideous Strength*

Tradition

One of Lewis's most notable characteristics as a critic, theologian, and novelist was his appreciation of tradition. It could almost be called veneration. Lewis did write and enjoy **science fiction**, a relatively modern genre. But at any given point in his career, if asked whether he preferred the present way of doing things or the way it had been done forty years ago, he would probably have preferred the past—whether the choices involved transportation (he didn't drive), communication (he didn't type), or **poetry** (he didn't write free verse). Alexander Pope said, "Be not the first by whom the new is tried / Nor yet the last to lay the old aside." Lewis was never in any danger of the former of those choices, but he often disobeyed Pope's latter warning.

His views in almost every area of life were old-fashioned: **politics**, **religion**, relationships. For instance, early in his career he fought vigorously against allowing **women** to take course work at **Oxford**, where he was teaching; including more women would weaken the curriculum, he felt. In a letter of July 9, 1927, to his brother, he indicated the best thing that had happened that term was a resolution limiting the number of "wimmen" (Lewis's spelling) at Oxford, thus enabling the school to avoid the "appalling danger of our degenerating into a woman's university." Fortunately, Lewis's views toward female education seemed to soften somewhat in later years, but as this makes clear, his natural reaction was old-fashioned.

This attitude carried over into his novels, where more often than not Lewis followed the method generally favored by authors until the start of this century: to tell stories that had already been told. To many contemporary readers, this desire to build on someone else's foundation seems less praiseworthy than erecting a building from scratch. But to most **Medieval** and **Renaissance** writers "originality" was less important than the quality of the final product. Surely the odds were better of finding a good story among the old "auctores" than of being able to create one independently. Isaac Newton's famous comment about being able to see further because he stood on the shoulders of giants was seen as true not only of **science**, where the building process was evident, but of literature as well. We can see the desire to retell old stories operating continually in the fiction of Lewis. *Pilgrim's Regress* is, of course, a version of *Pilgrim's Progress*. *Till We Have Faces* is a retelling of the **Cupid and Psyche** myth. *Perelandra* is **the Fall** of humanity; *The Magician's Nephew* is the **creation**; *The Lion, the Witch and the Wardrobe* is the death and **resurrection** of **Christ**. Even when an entire work is not based on a famous story, elements from the past repeatedly appear. *That Hideous Strength* includes Merlin; *The Voyage of the "Dawn Treader"* includes a sea serpent and the legendary one-footed men of Renaissance travel books that Lewis calls "Dufflepuds."

C. S. Lewis was perhaps more a product of Medieval and Renaissance thinking than any other 20th-century writer; it is noteworthy that his final academic position was chair of Medieval and Renaissance poetry at **Cambridge**. Like the writers on whom he lectured, Lewis respected traditional associations. A good example from the **Chronicles of Narnia** appears in the sixth chapter of *The Lion, the Witch and the Wardrobe*, where the children are being led to an unknown destination by a robin. Edmund suggests the robin may be an evildoer, luring them into a trap. Peter reflects on the possibility, then significantly remarks, "Still—a robin you know. They're good birds in all the stories I've ever read. I'm sure a robin wouldn't be on the wrong side." Lewis's allegiance to established **symbolism** comes from his archetypal view that most symbols become established because they resonate certain **values**. As he pointed out in his "personal heresy" controversy with E. M. W. Tillyard, *Romance of the Rose* could not be simply rewritten as *Romance of the Onion*.

Not only were Lewis's academic and fictional writings filled with tradition, but his conversations and personal writings were as well. One of the most common Lewisian literary characteristics is the use of allusion. We can take, from among a multitude of examples, the thank-you letter Lewis wrote to his father on May 26, 1925. Lewis had at long last (twenty-six years old) gotten a permanent job, an English literature position at **Magdalen College** in Oxford, and he wanted to thank

his father for having supported him for so many years. While composing the letter, Lewis casually throws in three obscure lines from plays of **Shakespeare**. In telling, near the end, of his efforts to break up a fight between a cat and a dog, Lewis describes himself as coming "between the fell incensed points of mighty opposites," a line from the fifth act of *Hamlet*. Not many writers so repeatedly blend the phrases of the past into their own writing under private circumstances, and not many writers have the blind confidence Lewis did in his correspondents' ability to recognize and appreciate many of the references he was using.

It is interesting to observe that the old-fashioned, traditional Lewis has lasted for several decades; more trendy British writers of the 1940s and 1950s are now forgotten.

Marvin D. Hinten
Bowling Green State University

Bibliography

Edwards, Bruce. *A Rhetoric of Reading*. Provo, UT: Center for the Study of Christian Values in Literature, 1986.

Howard, Thomas. *C. S. Lewis: Man of Letters*. San Francisco: Ignatius Press, 1987.

Keefe, Carolyn. *C. S. Lewis: Speaker and Teacher*. Grand Rapids, MI: Zondervan, 1971.

Walsh, Chad. *The Literary Legacy of C. S. Lewis*. New York: Harcourt Brace Jovanovich, 1979.

"Tragic Ends"

See entry on *The Death of Tragedy* (Book Review)

Transposition

Transposition was an important theological/philosophical idea for C. S. Lewis, one that he developed fully in his sermon by the same title (May 8, 1944). Lewis defined transposition as an "adaption from a richer (higher) to a poorer (lower) medium," such as representing the real world by a drawing. This concept was based on the Incarnation and Lewis used it to show the connection between the spiritual and material worlds. In the sermon **"Transposition,"** he used the example of speaking in tongues. Viewed by some as "low" (unintelligible and useless), the gift of miraculously speaking in another language can be viewed "from above" according to Lewis as evidence of the **Holy Spirit**'s activity. In *Miracles*, Lewis utilized the miracle of the feeding of the five thousand to explain transposition, and in *Reflections on the Psalms* he wrote that the **Bible** itself exemplifies transposition by proceeding "not by conversion of God's word into literature but by taking up of a literature to be the vehicle of God's word." Lewis also followed the principle of transposition in much of his understanding of the arts and often used it as interpretive tool for literary criticism.

Perry C. Bramlett
C. S. Lewis for the Local Church
Also See: Preacher, Theology

Gruenler, Royce Gordon. "C. S. Lewis and Imaginative Theology: In Memoriam." *Ohio Journal of Religious Studies.* 2 (November 1974): 99–104.

Payne, Leanne. *Real Presence: The Christian Worldview of C. S. Lewis as Incarnational Reality.* Wheaton, Illinois: Crossway, 1988.

Vincent, Paul. "C. S. Lewis As Amateur Philosopher." *CSL: The New York C. S. Lewis Society Bulletin.* 9 (24 April 1970): 1–3.

Yancey, Philip. "Hearing the World in a Higher Key." *Christianity Today.* 32 (October 21, 1988): 24–28.

Transposition and Other Addresses

London: Geoffrey Bles, 1949. First US edition titled *The Weight of Glory and Other Addresses.* New York: Macmillan, 1949. Revised and expanded edition as *The Weight of Glory and Other Addresses.* Walter Hooper (ed). New York: Macmillan, 1980.

See separate essay entries on the following for the original edition:

"Inner Ring"
"Learning in War-Time"
"Membership"
"Transposition"
"The Weight of Glory"
For the expanded edition see also:
"Is Theology Poetry?"
"On Forgiveness"
"A Slip of the Tongue"
"Why I Am Not a Pacifist"

"Transposition"

First published in *Transposition* and *The Weight of Glory*. Reprinted in the revised and expanded version of *The Weight of Glory* and *Screwtape Proposes a Toast*.

"Transposition" was a 1944 Pentecost sermon. Lewis began by discussing speaking in tongues, noting that it often can seemingly be produced by emotional

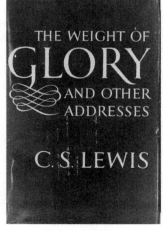

U.K. First Edition

effort, and thus we feel uncomfortable with it as a spiritual phenomenon. He observed that many things in life seem producible in more than one way, and that to a person familiar only with the lower variety the higher would seem unreal. To a person who has always lived in a dungeon, pictures drawn on paper would only seem to be lines. If you told this person the real world had no lines in it, he could not see any way for the pictures to exist. Some similar **transposition** may explain the **resurrection** of the body; we think in some equivalent of "lines," but the reality supersedes lines.

Though many might disagree, I do not think that "Transposition" can be called one of Lewis's more successful sermons. The idea is intellectually complicated, and more importantly, when explained, it does not seem to be as significant as the ideas Lewis usually presents. Several pages before the end Lewis noted that his "case is complete." He then rather clumsily added several points that were not particularly interesting or important.

Marvin D. Hinten
Bowling Green State University

Also See: Christ, Preacher, Reality, Spirituality

Bibliography

Gruenler, Royce Gordon. "C. S. Lewis and Imaginative Theology: In Memoriam." *Ohio Journal of Religious Studies.* 2 (November 1974): 99–104.

Yancey, Philip. "Hearing the World in a Higher Key." *Christianity Today.* 32 (October 21, 1988): 24–28.

"A Tribute to E. R. Eddison"

See entry on Letter to the publisher on dust cover of E. R. Eddison, *The Mezentian Gate* (Letter)

The Trinity

For C. S. Lewis, the doctrine of the Trinity was the best way to introduce **theology** to the Christian community. As one who strongly believed that theology should be based on the knowledge of **God** within the **church**, Lewis followed traditional Trinitarian thought (based on the creeds) in seeing our historical experience of God as revealed in the God of the Hebrews, **Christ** as the Incarnate Lord, and the **Holy Spirit** working within and through the Christian church.

Lewis knew that this doctrine was hard to understand, especially for laypeople. In *Letters to An American Lady* (April 17, 1953) he wrote that "even adult and educated Christians" have problems with the correct interpretation of the Trinity. At least partly because of this, and because he wrote most of his religious works for the layperson, Lewis used simple and easy to understand analogies and illustrations to explain the Trinity. In *Miracles* ("Christianity and 'Religion'") and *Mere Christianity* (**"The Three-Personal God"**), he defined God as "three Persons while remaining one being (God), just as a cube is six squares while remaining one cube (solid body)." Later he showed God as very personal in the Trinity while relating him to one's **prayer** life—he wrote that while we are praying to God, the God beside us (Christ) helps us to pray, and God (the Spirit) prompts or encourages us to pray.

In *The Screwtape Letters*, to show that God's love is the chief enemy of evil, Lewis had Screwtape write to Wormwood: "This impossibility He ['The Enemy," God] calls *love*, and this ... can be detected under all He does and even all He is—or claims to be.... He claims to be three as well as one, in order that this nonsense about Love may find a foothold in His own nature." The nature of God as love was very important to Lewis in his understanding of the Trinity. Richard Purtill has pointed out (*C. S. Lewis's Case for the Christian Faith*) that the idea of God as love as shown in the Trinity allows us to begin to see the full force of God's love. For Lewis, the God of love as revealed in three persons mattered more than anything else in the world. He compared this to a drama or dance and called for humans to take their place in it and "play out" that love in active love for God, our fellow humans, and God's created universe. According to Lewis, this "active understanding" of the Trinity would bring us joy, peace, power, and eternal life.

It should be noted that Lewis also mentioned the Trinity in his Narnian stories. One author has written (**Walter Hooper**, *C. S. Lewis: A Companion and Guide*) that if the tales have a theological weakness, "it is possibly that the Trinity ... is not properly represented." However, all three persons of the Trinity are represented specifically in *The Horse and His Boy*. A fearful Prince Shasta's question "Who *are* you?" to the Thing (or person) walking beside him is answered in three ways and with three different tones of voice that suggest the power of God, the eternal Word (Christ), and the subtle activity of the Spirit. This transforms Shasta, and he is no longer afraid but filled with awe and delight and wonder for the rest of his days.

Rev. Perry C. Bramlett
C. S. Lewis for the Local Church

Bibliography

Cunningham, Richard B. *C. S. Lewis: Defender of the Faith.* Philadelphia: Westminster, 1967.

Ford, Paul F. *Companion to Narnia.* San Francisco: HarperCollins, 1994.

Hooper, Walter. *C. S. Lewis: A Companion and Guide.* San Francisco: HarperCollins, 1996.

Lindskoog, Kathryn. *C. S. Lewis: Mere Christian.* Wheaton, IL: Shaw, 1987.

Purtill, Richard L. *C. S. Lewis's Case for the Christian Faith.* San Francisco: Harper & Row, 1981.

"The Trouble With 'X' ..."

Bristol Diocesan Gazette. XXVII (August 1948): 3–6. Reprinted in *God in the Dock* and *Undeceptions.*

In this article, Lewis addressed the familiar problem of how we deal with those people in our lives who are difficult. Usually, he hoped, these problems are not discussed with outsiders, but when they are we often are asked why we don't tell the offending party. To this query, there is no single answer. Most often we do tell, but we are not heard. Even if everything else is right, real **happiness** depends "on the character of the people you have to live with—and you can't alter their characters."

In some ways, according to Lewis, this is a glimpse of what **God** is up against. He has given us everything, and yet in every one of us is the persistent fatal flaw. God could change us, but he has made "a rule for Himself that He won't alter people's characters by force." He will change us, but only if and when we will let Him.

However great we see our faults, they are invariably greater than our perception suggests. Others see our fatal flaw as clearly as we see others'. Lewis's advice was that our job is to be as much like God as we can, willing to encourage change when it is wanted by others, and unscrupulous in our perception and evaluation of our own flaws. We must be ready and willing to change, because "[i]t's not a question of God 'sending' us to **Hell**. In each of us there is something growing up which will of itself *be Hell* unless it is nipped in the bud."

Anne Gardner

Also See: Ethics and Morality, Forgiveness, Sin, Values

"The True Nature of Gnomes"

Punch. 211 (October 16, 1946): 310 (under the pseudonym Nat Whilk). Reprinted in *Poems* and *Collected Poems.*

A speculative piece on how subterranean gnomes (dwarves) travel easily through the hardest stone and earth, only to be thwarted by the open air of caves or mines.

Don W. King
Montreat College

Truth

Against the postmodern assertion that truth is relative, Lewis championed the idea of objective truth, especially in the area of **ethics and morality**. Citing Paul's letter to the Romans, Lewis maintained that our minds have not fallen as far as our ability to keep moral law has, and he argued that humans have a natural capacity to apprehend moral truth through their **reason**.

This is not to say, however, that all religions or ethical systems are the same or that they are equally valid according to Lewis. He understood that reason permitted a certain access to moral truth, but he believed that such access was less than the fullness of truth offered by and through Christian **revelation**. To put this in later Christian language, "**Grace** perfects **nature**" and revelation perfects the earlier understanding. For example, there is an improvement and development from the Confucian "silver rule" (don't do to others what you do not wish them to do to you) to the Christian "golden rule" (do unto others as you would have them do unto you).

Despite such moral refinements offered by **Christianity**, Lewis cautioned us against ignoring the substantial similarities between pre-Christian thinkers searching for the nature of **happiness** and the Good, and Christians seeking to understand and live out the full implications of "the Word made flesh." After all, **Aristotle,** no less than Christian moralists, knew that one "must study virtue above all things [and] the student of politics ... must study the soul" (*Nicomachean Ethics,* 1102a5–1103b2). In *"De Desriptione Temporum,"* Lewis concluded that "Christians and pagans had much more in common with each other than either has with a post-Christian. The gap between those who worship different gods is not so wide as that between those who worship and those who do not."

Lewis believed that **philosophy** and **theology** were intimately connected in the quest for truth. He rejected the contemporary separation of philosophy from theology. Theology that is not rooted, in part, in a human ability to perceive the Divine would amount to gnosticism just as a love of wisdom without an open mind to the "numinous" (holy) would end up being a futile search for wisdom. For Lewis, as for Saint Damian, "philosophy is the handmaiden of theology." This understanding is more obvious by evaluating Lewis's method than by what he actually said.

Lewis began *Mere Christianity* with a chapter on the nature of an objective moral order: it is "right" and "wrong" (the inbuilt sense all people have or ought to have) that is a "clue to the meaning of the Universe." Lewis laid this foundation before moving on to address the question of God. His approach to truth is analogous to that of Saint Paul in addressing the "unknown god" preliminary to speaking of Christ in Athens (Acts 17:16–34).

As with his friend **J. R. R. Tolkien**, Lewis did not believe that truth was necessarily revealed in a "progressive" fashion and dismissed the idea that old-fashioned ideas are necessarily less true than something newer. Borrowing from **Barfield**, he referred to this notion as **"chronological snobbery."**

Lewis saw that certain tendencies in modern thought over past centuries (and he would agree that this has affected many Christians as well as non-Christians) have led to what he termed an inflation of the subject and a deflation of the object ("Preface" to *The Hierarchy of Heaven and Earth*). In this deflated world of the subjective self, "values" have replaced objective truths, principles, or norms, and it is maintained that these "values" are personal and that there is no basis upon which any may be deemed better than any others. Lewis, like Alasdair MacIntyre in our day (in his discussion of "emotivism" in *After Virtue*) understood that only a belief in a moral order—some version of "the Good" that is shared and pursued in common—could preserve society and individual souls from a world dominated only by power.

Without the "crude and nursery-like belief" in objective goods, Lewis believed that both **democracy** and freedom would be impossible. The task of knowledge was, for the wise of old, "how to conform the soul to reality" and the solution was "knowledge, self-discipline and virtue." The new idea is that reality must be subordinated to our wishes and that this may be accomplished by technical means. Lewis prophesied that **science** and **technology** freed from the controls of the objective moral order would be ready to do things "hitherto regarded as disgusting or impious."

Lewis's essays **"The Poison of Subjectivism," "Bulverism,"** and **"On Ethics,"** as well as his short work *The Abolition of Man*, provide his key works on this topic. *The Abolition of Man*, which appeared in the same year as his essay "The Poison of Subjectivism" (1943), marks some of Lewis's clearest writing about the nature of subjectivism and the corrosive effects that this view has for seeking truth. Since Lewis's day, the language of "values" has come to dominate much moral discourse, and it is fair to say that his own work was occasionally infected with it. Yet this language is antagonistic to the notion of shared goods that Lewis believed to underlie any meaningful notion of truth.

If "values" are merely personal (there being no meaning to objective goods beyond your or my personal choice) then on what basis can we speak of, say, "Christian values," "women's values," "American values," etc.? To paraphrase Lewis, if values are merely personal then why do we so often insist that they are shared? And if they are "shared" then how are they "values" in the subjectivist (and most common) use of this language today? In Lewis's words, "[n]ew moralities can only be contractions or expansions of something already given. And all the specifically modern attempts at new moralities are contractions" ("On Ethics"). Again, "philosophy which does not accept value as eternal and objective can lead us only to ruin.... the very idea of freedom presupposes some objective moral law which overarches rulers and ruled alike. Subjectivism about values is eternally incompatible with democracy" ("The Poison of Subjectivism").

Those seeking to follow Lewis's tradition and develop it will need to be careful to ensure that "values" do not come to further usurp the rich, and largely lost, tradition of the **virtues** (as principles, norms, truths, or goods) as an aspect of the fullness of truth to which Lewis dedicated his life.

Iain T. Benson

Bibliography

MacIntyre, Alasdair. *After Virtue*. Notre Dame: University of Notre Dame Press, 1984.

Purtill, Richard. "Did C. S. Lewis Lose His Faith?" *A Christian for All Christians*. A. Walker and J. Patrick (eds). London: Hodder, 1990.

"The Turn of the Tide"

Punch: Almanac. 215 (November 1, 1948) (under the pseudonym Nat Whilk). Revised and reprinted in *Poems* and *Collected Poems*.

"The Turn of the Tide" is a different kind of Christmas poem because Lewis focused upon the very moment of **Christ**'s birth and how it marks a universal turn of the tide: from the certitude of death to the promise of new life. He used a number of classical figures and images to suggest this return of life culminating the reigniting of the Phoenix.

Don W. King
Montreat College

Tutor

University College at **Oxford** offered Lewis a post as a replacement tutor in 1924, following his First in the English Literature examination. In 1925, Lewis was elected fellow at Oxford's **Magdalen College**, and he began his career as a tutor in earnest. During his three decades at Magdalen, Lewis was a conscientious tutor able to strike a balance among the demands of friendliness, intellectual rigor, challenge, and adequate preparation for his students' examinations. Tutoring is one unique aspect of an Oxford **education**; a special relationship develops between tutor and pupil because the setting is formally academic yet intimate and personal. Each week, the student may pour out his or her heart in written essays of three-thousand words that need to be logically defended. Depending on the nature of the **friendship** that develops, the Oxford tutor and student may sit on comfortable furniture in front of a blazing hearth and sip tea.

The oldest institution of higher learning in England, Oxford University consists of thirty-five colleges and various private halls established by religious groups. Each college is a corporate body distinct from the university and governed by its own Head and fellows. Each college manages its own faculty, curriculum, and admits undergraduates; however, the colleges do not award degrees. Most fellows are college instructors called "tutors." Each student at Oxford is assigned to a tutor who supervises the students' studies through tutorials. Tutorials are weekly meetings of one or two students with their tutor. Students may attend other tutors for specialized instruction and attend lectures given by university teachers. Students choose which lectures to attend on the basis of their own interests and the advice of their tutors.

Lewis's Oxford duties were threefold: university lecturer, responsible for lectures once a week; fellow, involved in administration of the College; and college tutor, responsible for all male students at Magdalen reading English. Lewis needed to instruct his charges in Old English, Middle English, and Modern English literature up through the Victorians. This instruction included history of the language and philology. Some instruction took place in classes, but most of the contact with students took place in tutorials, all individually conducted. Lewis spent an enormous amount of time giving tutorials and still was highly productive as a scholar and author. One of Lewis's first pupils at Oxford was **John Betjeman** (later poet-laureate of England), who did not immediately impress Lewis with his talents.

Lewis's first lectures at Oxford were inauspicious; eventually, however, following the fame of his publishing career and radio broadcasts during the war, Lewis became one of Oxford's most popular lecturers. In the 1940s, his lectures were so crowded that sometimes there was standing room only in the largest hall available.

In a letter written to **Warren Lewis** in 1931, Lewis described his "typical" day as an Oxford tutor: at 7:15 A.M., he was awakened with tea. After a bath and a shave, a brief walk followed. Lewis then went to dean's prayers at 8:00 A.M. in the college chapel, which lasted fifteen minutes. Breakfast was eaten in the Common Room; then Lewis left about 8:25 A.M. and went back to his rooms and answered letters until 9:00 A.M. From 9:00 A.M. until 1:00 P.M., he gave his tutorial sessions to pupils. At 1:00 P.M., Lewis was driven to Mrs. **Janie Moore**'s for lunch. Returning to the college in the afternoon, from 5:00 to 7 :00 P.M. Lewis had to lecture or receive students, followed by dinner at 7:15. On Tuesdays, pupils came to read *Beowulf* with Lewis from 8:30 until 11:00 P.M., when he retired to his college bedroom.

Lewis's career as a tutor ended in 1954 when he was elected a professor at Magdalene College, **Cambridge University**. Lewis accepted the new position in part to divest himself of the burdens of tutoring.

Jonathon L. Thorndike
Lakeland College

Bibliography

Como, James (ed). *C. S. Lewis at the Breakfast Table*. New York: Harcourt Brace Jovanovich, 1992.

Lewis, C. S. *The Letters of C. S. Lewis*.

Mountford, Sir J. *British Universities*. London: Oxford University Press, 1966.

"Two Kinds of Memory"

Time and Tide. 28 (August 7, 1947): 859. Revised and reprinted in *Poems* and *Collected Poems*. Also reprinted in part (last stanza omitted) in McGovern, E. "C. S. Lewis." *Dictionary of Literary Biography*. Volume 15 of British Novelists 1930–59. Detroit: Gale Publishers, 1983: 304.

A serious poem contrasting memories that delight with those that torment. Lewis used Persephone and Hades, kind mistress and grim master of the classical underworld, as apt personifications of these conflicting notions.

Don W. King
Montreat College

"Two Lectures"

See entry on "Who was Right—Dream Lecturer or Real Lecturer"

The Two Towers and The Return of the King (Book Review)

"The Dethronement of Power." *Time and Tide*. XXXVI (22 October 1955): 1373–74. Reprinted with *The Fellowship of the Ring* (Book Review) as "Tolkien's *The Lord of the Rings*" in *Of This and Other Worlds* and *On Stories*.

This review combines commentary on the second and third parts of **J. R. R. Tolkien**'s *Lord of the Rings*. Lewis began by countering the critics who complained that Tolkien painted everything in either black or white, noting the mixed motives of several key characters in the story. Lewis also refuted the idea that Tolkien wrote his **epic** as a warning against Russia and the hydrogen bomb. The moral of the story, said Lewis, if there must be one, is "a recall from facile optimism and wailing pessimism alike, to that hard, yet not quite desperate, insight into Man's unchanging predicament by which heroic ages have lived."

Anne Gardner

Bibliography

Tolkien, J. R. R. *The Two Towers; The Return of the King*

"Two Ways with the Self"

The Guardian. (3 May 1940): 215. Reprinted in *God in the Dock, Undeceptions,* and *Christian Reunion*.

In this article Lewis began by saying that "[s]elf-renunciation is thought to be, and indeed is, very near the core of Christian ethics." The issue of self-love, which is much discussed, is no easier. We are to **love** ourselves and not love ourselves, as we are to hate ourselves and not hate ourselves. According to Lewis, the issue here is not one of degree but of kind. The self can be regarded in two ways. On the one hand, the self is a creature of **God** to be rejoiced in. On the other, the condition of God's creature is now hateful because preference of "me" over my neighbor is wrong. According to Lewis, it is the job of the Christian to "wage endless war against the clamor of the ego as ego." The Christian must love "with charity instead of partiality." As final advice, Lewis said that "[w]e must die daily: but it is better to love the self than to love nothing, and to pity the self than to pity no one."

Anne Gardner

Also See: Ethics and Morality, Virtue

U

Undeceptions

See entry on *God in the Dock: Essays on Theology and Ethics*

"Undergraduate Criticism"

Broadsheet (Cambridge University). VIII no. 17 (9 March 1960).

In this article written in 1960, Lewis listed four faults of **literary criticism**. First, its tone of personal resentment; second, its ready acceptance of radical reinterpretations; third, its lack of knowledge of **Bible** and classics; and fourth, its approaching literature with the wrong kind of seriousness. But in these critical vices, according to Lewis, undergraduates only imitate their less excusable elders.

John Bremer

"Under Sentence"

The Spectator. 175 (September 7, 1945): 219. Revised and retitled as "The Condemned" and reprinted in *Poems* and *Collected Poems*.

Written from the perspective of the wild animals of England, this poem reflected Lewis's distrust of progress particularly as it involves the destruction of the landscape and its creatures.

Don W. King
Montreat College

University College, Oxford University

Lewis entered University College, Oxford, in April 1917 after having won a scholarship the previous December. He did not begin studies because of the outbreak of World War I. Instead, he moved to Keble College (where his roommate was **Paddy Moore**) for OTC. After the **war** he returned to University College in January 1919 taking his degree in 1922. In 1924, Lewis taught philosophy at the college.

"Unreal Estates"

See entry on "'The establishment must die and rot'"

Utopia

Throughout history, writers have debated the possibility of creating an ideal society. Lewis believed that **human nature** was so tainted with **sin** that no such society would be possible. In a speech on **"Learning in War-Time"** delivered just after the start of the Second World War, he even credited the **war** with ending "foolish, un-Christian hopes about human **culture**."

Two of his **science fiction** novels—*Out of the Silent Planet* and *Perelandra*—dealt with planets whose innocence was threatened by fallen humanity and the third, *That Hideous Strength*, with the danger to freedom from utopian engineering. Elsewhere, the diabolic Screwtape writes of keeping man so "hag-ridden by the Future" and a vision of an earthly paradise that he breaks God's commands.

Lewis's most sustained attack on utopianism came in a 1958 newspaper article, **"Is Progress Possible?"** There he warned that the scientifically run welfare state offered security at the expense of freedom and that the possibility of a "world Welfare State" was "the extreme peril of humanity at present."

Mike W. Perry

Bibliography

Fisher, Judith L. "Trouble in Paradise: The Twentieth-Century Utopian Ideal." *Extrapolation* 24 no. 4 (Winter 1983): 329–39.

Lewis, C. S. "Is Progress Possible?"; "Learning in Wartime"; *The Screwtape Letters;* "We Have No Right to Happiness"

V

Sheldon Vanauken (1914–1996)

Sheldon Vanauken was a close friend of C. S. Lewis, a professor of English and history at Lynchburg College in Virginia, and the poetry editor for *The New Oxford Review*. He was the author of a novel (*Gateway to Heaven*, 1980), a book about the Civil War *(The Glittering Illusion*, 1986), and a collection of poetry (*Mercies*, 1988). His last book, a collection of journal and newspaper articles, was published as *The Little Lost Marion and Other Mercies* (1996). However, Vanauken's best-known work was the autobiographical *A Severe Mercy* (1977), which was followed by a sequel, *Under the Mercy* (1985).

A Severe Mercy met with extraordinary critical and popular success, winning seven major awards ranging from *The National Religious Book Award* to *The American Book Award*. Translated into several languages, it was chosen "book of the year" by *Eternity* magazine and sold millions of copies in both paperback and hardcover.

The book is the story of the growth of love between Vanauken ("Van") and his wife Jean ("Davy"), their **marriage**, their conversion to **Christianity** while at **Oxford**, and her death in 1955. A large part of the story tells of becoming friends with C. S. Lewis and his spiritual influence on them. *A Severe Mercy* is the single longest known account of the impact of Lewis on the conversion and lives of specific individuals and contains eighteen letters from him to Vanauken. The title of the book was a term Lewis used in a letter to Vanauken (May 8, 1955) describing the often incomprehensible nature of God's **love** and actions for his creatures, and was also used by **Augustine** in his *Confessions*. The term "under the mercy" came from **Charles Williams'** novel *Descent Into Hell* and was used as a signature line by Vanauken in personal letters.

A Severe Mercy is an important book not only because it tells a poignant and (often) heartbreaking love story but also because it sheds much light on the apologetic and evangelistic methods of C. S. Lewis and shows how he dealt with people he knew personally over a long period of time.

Perry C. Bramlett
C. S. Lewis for the Local Church

Also See: Apologetics, Friendship, Mercy, Pain

Bibliography

Pfeiffer, Brian J. "A Psychodynamic/Family Systems Analysis of the Vanauken's Relationship as Described in *A Severe Mercy*." *The Lamp-Post of the Southern California C. S. Lewis Society*. 15 no. 3 (September 1991): 20–28.

Ramshaw, Walter. "Sheldon Vanauken's *A Severe Mercy*." *CSL: The Bulletin of the New York C. S. Lewis Society*. 10 no. 9 (July 1979): 1–6.

Vanauken, Sheldon. *A Severe Mercy*. San Francisco: Harper & Row, 1977.

———. *Under the Mercy*. Nashville: Thomas Nelson, 1985.

"Variation in Shakespeare and Others"

First published in *Rehabilitations*. Reprinted in *Selected Literary Essays*.

In this pre-World War II essay, Lewis contrasted the Elizabethan dramatists with writers from other periods, showing that one of the distinguishing characteristics of the Elizabethans was their tendency to pile up images, to use simile after simile to convey an impression. This metaphorical brilliance is mostly decorative in Marlowe and early **Shakespeare**; but in the hands of the great 17th-century dramatists, it combines **beauty** and illumination.

Lewis asserted that what sets Shakespeare apart from all other writers is his ability to combine lyrical brilliance (à la Aeschylus and **Keats**) with realistic character presentation (as in Austen and George Eliot). The rippling images serve both to beautify and to convey the idea of characters searching for words, trying repeatedly under stress to find some workable way to express themselves.

By the 1640s, Lewis remarked, this ability to multiply images had degenerated into fixation with images at the expense of dramatic development, until playwrights finally "turned round and round on the same spot like a dog that cannot make up its mind to lie down." This is a solid literary essay of a type rare today—explaining how authors achieve their effects.

Marvin D. Hinten
Bowling Green State University

Version Vernacular (Letter)

The Christian Century. LXXV (31 December 1958): 1515. Reprinted in *Timeless at Heart*.

A letter to the editor following up on a discussion between Lewis and Dr. Norman Pittenger in *The Christian Century* (Pittenger, "Pittenger-Lewis," 24 December, pp. 1485–86, and Lewis, **"Rejoinder to Dr. Pittenger,"** November 26). Lewis explained that he was not suited to write an article on translation for Americans since the vernacular would be different, if only in small ways, from the colloquial expression which Lewis would use as an Englishman. Lewis believed that understanding these subtle differences was so important that he recommended having both American and English ordination exams contain a passage from a theological work that requires translation into the vernacular of the particular country. If the candidates failed in this aspect, then Lewis felt they should fail the entire exam, for genuine belief and understanding of one's faith requires the ability to express it in the vernacular—and not simply in "learned" language.

Marjorie L. Mead
The Marion E. Wade Center

A Village Experience (Letter)

The Guardian. (31 August 1945): 335. Reprinted in *God in the Dock, Undeceptions,* and *Timeless at Heart.*

Lewis quoted from one of his correspondents, an invalid lady who has observed her elderly village parson growing so entrenched in his position to the extent that he no longer welcomes children in the church without an adult. The lady was appalled and commented that as a result of this as well as the priest's general neglect of parish duties (such as not visiting the sick) the village has "gone pagan." Since the *Guardian* was a weekly Anglican newspaper, Lewis thought this situation worthy of reflection by the *Guardian*'s readers.

Marjorie L. Mead
The Marion E. Wade Center

Virtues

At least as far back as **Plato** there has been an emphasis on the four "cardinal" virtues of prudence, **justice**, fortitude, and temperance. Lewis consistently endorsed this "doctrine of virtue" as an important discovery in human self-understanding. Lewis stressed (in *Mere Christianity, The Abolition of Man, Christian Reflections*, and elsewhere) that these "cardinal virtues" are not uniquely Christian. However, this fact does not make them any less important or any less Christian. They are both an integral part of the best of **philosophy** and an integral part of the Christian **faith**.

Prudence was defended by Lewis as "practical common sense," as when one takes the time to think through what one is "doing, and what is likely to come of it." Prudence is the "mold and mother" of the other cardinal virtues. None but the prudent can be just, brave, and temperate, and the good person is good only insofar as he is prudent. *Justice* is the notion that each person is to be given what is his or her due. The thread of this idea can be traced through **Plato**, **Aristotle**, Roman Law, **Augustine**, **Aquinas**, and **Kant**. Lewis built upon the great insights of the past when he identified three basic forms of justice: (1) the relations of individuals to one another; (2) the relations of the social whole to individuals; and (3) the relations of individuals to the purpose of human life as a whole. *Fortitude* includes the kind of courage that faces danger as well as the kind that sticks to the task at hand even if one does not feel like it. Lewis portrayed this great virtue in numerous ways. For example, in *The Lion, the Witch and the Wardrobe* Lewis wrote that Peter did not feel very brave just before his first successful battle; in fact, he felt like he was going to be sick. Still, he did what he had to do—and that was the mark of true fortitude. *Temperance* according to Lewis is "going the right length" and refers to much more than the question of drink. One can be just as intemperate about many other things.

In addition to his defense of the above mentioned "cardinal" virtues, Lewis defended the three "theological" virtues of orthodox **Christianity**: faith, hope, and **love**. *Faith* is the ability to affirm what one's **reason** has accepted as true in spite of changing moods. Faith must be trained. Neither Christianity nor any other view of the world will automatically remain alive in our minds. Daily churchgoing, Bible study, **prayer**, and acting in obedience to **God**'s commands are significant parts of the training. *Hope* is the desire or longing for **heaven** that is a part of all of us, even though we do not always recognize it.

Love is a state, not of the feelings, but of the will. It is a state of the will that one has naturally about oneself and that one is commanded to have about others. Love is the central meaning of our universe. It is the greatest of all the virtues. Our primary task is to know this love and to offer it to those around us.

According to Lewis (**"The Weight of Glory"**) if you asked twenty good men today what they considered the highest of the virtues to be, nineteen of them would reply, "Unselfishness." However, if you asked almost any of the great Christians of old, he would have replied, "Love." Our desires today are not too strong; they are too weak. We are foolishly preoccupied with the trifles of alcohol and **sex** and ambition when infinite **happiness** has been offered to us.

How does one become a virtuous person? Lewis's answer is practice. Just as practice plays a key role in making a person a good musician, a good sculptor, a good student, it would seem also to play a crucial part in making a good person. As Lewis wisely noted in *The Screwtape Letters* mortals tend to turn into the kind of beings they pretend to be. Thus, humans should not spend an inordinate amount of time reflecting on whether they have enough of the virtues; they should simply act as if they do and continuously apply the virtues to daily living.

Michael H. Macdonald
Seattle Pacific University

Also See: Alcohol/Tobacco, the Bible, Free Will, Good and Evil, Heroes, Modernity

Bibliography

Aristotle. *Nicomachean Ethics*
Plato. *Republic*
Pieper, Josef. *The Four Cardinal Virtues*. South Bend, IN: University of Notre Dame Press, 1966.

"The Vision of John Bunyan"

The Listener. LXVIII (13 December 1962): 1006–8. Reprinted in *Selected Literary Essays*.

Lewis began this essay by saying people "read with delight" *De Rerum Natura* by Lucretius, *The Anatomy of Melancholy* by Robert Burton, and *Pilgrim's Progress* by John Bunyan even when they disagree with the teaching of those books. It is hard to believe this was true even in the England of the 1960s when he gave this talk (now found in *Selected Literary Essays*).

Possible misperceptions aside, Lewis obviously loved *Pilgrim's Progress* (he calls it "enthralling"), and here he was able to explain why. Lewis admired the plot and found the dialogue compelling and realistic. He believed people tend to read it too fervently for the allegory and didn't pay sufficient attention to the story. The style, Lewis noted, is unlike that of its 17th-century contemporary, the King James Bible. To prove his point, Lewis drew attention to some fine battle **imagery** used by Bunyan.

The essay closed by considering why some people may dislike *Pilgrim's Progress*. It is, Lewis observed, unpleasantly sectarian. Some people dislike the sense of terror in the book, but Lewis indicates that, aside from **truth** or falsehood, it adds a literary edge. This article, like so many of Lewis's, will probably cause some read-ers to take a second look at a work they didn't think they liked.

Marvin D. Hinten
Bowling Green State University

Also See: Allegory

Visionary Christian: One Hundred Thirty-One Readings from C. S. Lewis

Walsh, Chad (ed.). New York: Macmillan, 1981.

A collection of Lewis readings.

The Visionary Company: A Reading of English Romantic Poetry (Book Review)

"Poetry and Exegesis." *Encounter*. XX (June 1963): 74–76.

Lewis found this "one of the most difficult books [he has] ever read." He was not certain that he understood Bloom's meaning, and apparently was not certain that Bloom did either. Bloom provided a study of Blake that was extensive and then discussed the **poetry** of other Romantics in the light of Blake. Lewis found Bloom's exegesis of Blake, if correct, clarifying, and the exegesis of others obfuscating.

Anne Gardner

Bibliography

Bloom, Harold. *The Visionary Company: A Reading of English Romantic Poetry*.

"Vitrea Circe"

Punch. 214 (June 23, 1948): 543 (under the pseudonym Nat Whilk). Revised and reprinted in *Poems* and *Collected Poems*.

In this poem, Lewis attempted to defend the witch Circe who in the *Odyssey* transforms Ulysses' men into swine. He suggested she did not lure the men, but instead reacted to protect herself from their lewd advances. However, when she saw the handsome and manly Ulysses, her brittle demeanor shattered like glass.

Don W. King
Montreat College

"Vivisection"

Boston: New England Anti-Vivisection Society, 1947. Reprinted London: National Anti-Vivisection Society, 1948. Also Reprinted in *God in the Dock, Undeceptions,* and *First and Second Things*.

In this essay, Lewis remarked that the discussion of vivisection has been marked by a lack of rational discussion. In order to begin a rational discussion, it is necessary to decide if **pain** is or is not an evil. If it is not an evil, then there is no argument against vivisection, nor for that matter, one for it. Proponents defend it on the grounds that it alleviates human suffering—thus arguing that pain is evil. The question remains then whether or not "one species should suffer in order that another species should be happier?"

According to Lewis, the traditional argument is apt to include the statement that animals have no souls. For a Christian, the only rational defense of vivisection is that man is superior to beasts (as guaranteed by **Revelation**), while for nonbelievers, "soullessness" justifies the act. However, if we justify the preference for man with a sentiment, argued Lewis, could we not also justify a sentiment for a white man against a black, or "civilized" people over "savages," or our class against others? Into what cruelty does this argument lead us? According to Lewis, "the victory of vivisection marks a great advance in the triumph of ruthless, nonmoral utilitarianism over the old world of ethical law." To those who say that remarkably little cruelty occurs, Lewis said "we must first decide what should be allowed: after that it is for the police to discover what is already being done."

Anne Gardner

"Vowels and Sirens"

The Times Literary Supplement, Special Autumn Issue (August 29, 1954): xiv. Revised and reprinted in *Poems* and *Collected Poems*.

"Vowels and Sirens" is a poem on the power of words. Lewis recounted the episode in the *Odyssey* when Ulysses has his men lash him to the mast of the ship, stuff wax in their ears, and sail within sound of the sirens. While their words are powerful and beautiful, they are lies—torturing him with unrequited longing for impossible desire.

Don W. King
Montreat College

Voyage to Venus
See entry on *Perelandra*

The Voyage of the "Dawn Treader"

London: Geoffrey Bles, 1952. First US edition, New York: Macmillan, 1952.

An absorbing adventure story, *The Voyage of the "Dawn Treader"* is the third Chronicle of Narnia Lewis completed. The book seems to have flowed from his pen more easily than all the other Chronicles, and it reveals Lewis in the white heat of storytelling of the mythopoeic

rather than the didactic kind. In a letter to Anne of March 5, 1961, Lewis said that *The Voyage of the "Dawn Treader"* is about the "the spiritual life (especially in Reepicheep)." Given the overall intent of the **Chronicles of Narnia**—the liberation of true feeling by the appeal to the **imagination**, the "organ of meaning"—this book is about what it feels like to be a member of the church (fellow adventurers) and what our Christian **values** call us to be and to do.

After writing **The Lion, the Witch and the Wardrobe** and failing in his attempt to write **The Magician's Nephew**, Lewis seems to have "seen" many of the mental pictures that inspired what later became the "The Caspian Triad": ***Prince Caspian***, *Voyage of the "Dawn Treader,"* and **The Silver Chair**: There is a record of Lewis's plot points for the triad that include human tyranny in Narnia, its history told by a dwarf, a voyage by ship, and "[v]arious islands (of Odyssey and Saint Brendan) can be thrown in. Beauty of the ship the initial spell. To be a very green and pearly story," children captured by enemies, a magic picture, and one of the Narnians admitted into our world. Once Lewis sorted these ideas out, he was able to complete *Prince Caspian* in something over six months and *"Dawn Treader"* in fewer than three.

Lewis finished *"Dawn Treader"* in the winter of 1950. He later made significant changes in the ending of the American edition of chapter 12 because his American publisher seems to have raised the issue of the Dark Island being too frightening for children. In an address he delivered in April 1952 to the British Library Association, he spoke to the objection that fairy tales are too violent for children: "I suffered too much from night-fears myself in childhood to undervalue this objection. I would not wish to heat the fires of the private hell for any child" (**"On Three Ways of Writing for Children"**). Lewis devised a new ending which took more seriously the fears of the human crew of the *Dawn Treader* but also said that Aslan liberates us from such fears, usually gradually. A year after the book was published, Lewis wrote a child: "By the way, do you think the Dark Island is too frightening for small children? Did it give your brother the horrors? I was nervous about that, but I left it in because I thought one can never be sure about what will or will not frighten people" (**C. S. Lewis: Letters to Children**). The latest editions drop the American ending in favor of the British, leading to the loss of one of Lewis's loveliest similes: "And just as there are moments when simply to lie in bed and see the daylight pouring through your window and to hear the cheerful voice of an early postman or milkman down below and to realise that it was only a dream: it wasn't real, is so heavenly that it was very nearly worth having the nightmare in order to have the joy of waking; so they all felt when they came out of the dark."

The story of the book begins with Edmund (age twelve) and Lucy (age ten) being forced by circumstances to spend the summer holidays with their unpleasant, nine-year-old cousin Eustace, the product of progressive parenting and schools. While mocking the painting of a fine Viking-type ship hung in Lucy's bedroom, Eustace and the two Pevensie children are drawn into the picture and the sea. King Caspian, now sixteen, jumps in to rescue them. Safe on board the ship (named the *Dawn Treader*), Caspian explains that he is on a mission to search for his late father's friends (the Lords Bern, Octesian, Restimar, Revilian, Argoz, Mavramorn, and Rhoop), whom the usurper Miraz (*Prince Caspian*, chapter 5) had sent to explore the lands beyond Narnia's Eastern Ocean. Reepicheep explains that he is fulfilling a lifelong quest to find the Utter East. No sailor even after a taste of Lucy's cordial, Eustace takes an instant dislike to the whole adventure, especially to the brave mouse whom he antagonizes to his own pain. On the Lone Islands Caspian, the English children, and Reepicheep are captured

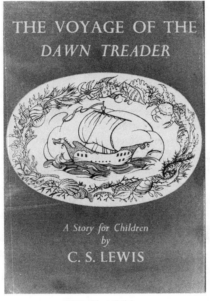

U.K. First Edition

by slave traders. Caspian is sold to Lord Bern, the others are rescued, and the Lone Islands are put under new management. The adventurers setting out again, their ship encounters a disabling storm, which causes them to put in at the island where Eustace becomes the outward reflection of his inward, dragonish self. Experiencing for the first time both the pain of loneliness and the pleasure of being liked and liking, Eustace is transformed into a boy by Aslan and restored to fellowship. They next escape a stupid sea serpent through the bravery of Eustace and Reepicheep and the temptation to greed on Deathwater Island through a warning apparition of Aslan. On the Island of the Voices Lucy overhears the voices of the invisible Duffers and offers to set them free by reciting the spell against invisibility in the Magician's Book upstairs in his magnificent home. There she experiences the temptations to become the most beautiful woman in the world (her inadequacy compared to her sister Susan) and to know her friends' thoughts (the temptation to which she gives in). She is restored by a story-spell and then recites the spell that reveals Aslan as one of the invisibles. He consoles her by promising to tell her the refreshing story (in point of fact, the gospel story) for the rest of her life. The adventurers next encounter a daunting, total darkness; but the human crew is embarrassed by Reepicheep ("a foot-and-a-half of courage") to enter it. By doing so they rescue Lord Rhoop and are rescued by Aslan in the form of an albatross. At the final island they encounter the last missing lords asleep at a mysterious banquet which is laid each sunset for travelers and removed each sunrise by birds that fly to and from the sun. A beautiful woman (Caspian's future wife) and her star-father explain that the lords will awake only if someone sails to the world's end and goes into the Utter East, never to return (Reepicheep's quest). The final part of the voyage takes them over sweet waters which taste like drinkable light and enable them to look at the sun. Reaching the Silver Sea of Lilies, Caspian decides to abdicate in order to join Reepicheep and will not listen to any argument until Aslan appears to remind him of his vocation. Aslan tells him that the three earth children are to go with Reepicheep. Reepicheep goes ahead in his little round boat into the east and the children beach their boat where a lamb invites them to breakfast. The lamb becomes the lion who explains that they had been brought to Narnia so that they might know him better on earth by the name he has there.

"Dawn Treader" was meant to end the series—at least until Lewis got inspired to write **The Horse and His Boy** and then was inspired by *The Horse and His Boy* to write the last three Chronicles: *The Silver Chair*, *The Magician's Nephew*, and *The Last Battle*. In *"Dawn Treader,"* the final four chapters' feeling of just controlled

ecstasy reminds one of the near rapture of the sermon **"The Weight of Glory"** and the Pentecost sermon **"Transposition"** during the preaching of which Lewis lost his composure as he strained to describe the ineffable. Through Reepicheep and Lucy Lewis finds images which give new meaning to the deepest Christian truths.

Paul F. Ford
St. John's Seminary

Bibliography

Ford, Paul F. *Companion to Narnia*. San Francisco: Harper-SanFrancisco, 1994.

Myers, Doris. "The Compleat Anglican: Spiritual Style in the Chronicles of Narnia, Anglican." *Theological Review.* LXVI (April 1984): 148–60.

Schakel, Peter. *Reading with the Heart: The Way into Narnia*. Grand Rapids, MI: Eerdmans, 1979.

Yandell, Steven. "The Trans-cosmic Journeys in the Chronicles of Narnia." *Mythlore*. 43 (August 1985): 9–23.

W

The Marion E. Wade Center

The Wade Center of Wheaton College is a research library and archive for seven British authors: **Owen Barfield**, **G. K. Chesterton**, C. S. Lewis, **George MacDonald**, **Dorothy L. Sayers**, **J. R. R. Tolkien**, and **Charles Williams**. Although originally named the C. S. Lewis Collection, the works of all seven authors were envisioned as part of the anticipated holdings from the beginning. The collection was established in 1965 by Dr. **Clyde S. Kilby**, professor of English Literature at Wheaton College. Kilby began the collection with fifteen letters from Lewis to himself and a handful of Lewis's books. By the time of his retirement in 1981 it had grown into an internationally recognized archive and study center. Today the Center houses over 12,000 volumes including first editions and critical works, more than 25,000 letters (approximately 22,000 are original), 1,066 manuscripts, over 12,000 articles (by and about the seven authors), 381 doctoral dissertations, 70 oral history interviews, in addition to current and discontinued periodicals and an audio/video library of over 800 items.

Lewis holdings include more than 2,300 letters, 11 typescript volumes of the **Lewis Family Papers** compiled by **Warren H. Lewis** (containing diaries, letters, and other family materials from 1850–1930), 21 volumes of Warren Lewis's diaries, family portraits, and photographs, many of the **Boxen** stories, 140 additional manuscripts (44 of which are original), 2,363 volumes from Lewis's own library, 179 doctoral dissertations written on various aspects of Lewis's work, 44 oral history interviews pertaining to Lewis, and 217 foreign translations. An arrangement with the **Bodleian Library** to exchange photocopies of portions of their Lewis manuscripts has greatly enhanced the holdings in both places.

In 1974, friends and family of Mr. Marion E. Wade, founder of ServiceMaster Corporation and C. S. Lewis enthusiast, established a fund to provide a yearly grant for the operation of the collection, and in his honor the name was changed to the Marion E. Wade Center. The Kilby Research Grant, established in 1982, is annually awarded to a scholar engaged in a publishable research project related to one or more of the seven authors who has worked on the project at the Wade Center. The Center also publishes the annual review *Seven: An Anglo-American Literary Review*. It was founded in 1980 under the inspiration of Dr. Barbara Reynolds, Dr. Beatrice Batson, and Dr. Kilby as a forum for informed discussion and assessment of the seven authors and is intended for both the general and specialized reader. The Center is open to the public. For information write to the Marion E. Wade Center, Wheaton College, Wheaton, IL 60187.

Christopher W. Mitchell
The Marion E. Wade Center

Bibliography

Klein, JoAnne. "An Open Treasure." *Wheaton Alumni*. (Summer 1994).

Mitchell, Christopher W. "30th Anniversary of the Marion E. Wade Center." *Seven: An Anglo-American Literary Review*. 12 (1995).

"Wade History Archive." Wheaton, IL: The Marion E. Wade Center, Wheaton College.

Richard Wagner (1813–1883)

Richard Wagner, born in Leipzig, struggled in the first half of his life as conductor and composer, but wrote, among other successful operatic works, *Rienzi, Der Fliegende Holländer, Tannhäuser,* and *Lohengrin.* Around 1850 he began work on *Der Ring des Nibelungen,* the poem cycle or libretto being finished in 1852. The music for *Das Rheingold* was begun in 1853, and that for *Die Walküre* in 1856 and the first two acts of *Siegfried* in 1857. Between 1857 and 1859, Wagner composed *Tristan und Isolde,* performed at Munich in 1865, and finished *Die Meistersinger* in 1868, before returning to complete the *Ring* by 1874. The complete *Ring* had its first performance in August 1876. Wagner's version of the Nibelungen legend is drawn from Medieval literature recording the stories and **myths** of the Teutonic peoples. These sources included *The Poetic Edda,* the *Saga of the Volsungs,* and the *Song of the Nibelungens.* Wagner's final opera was *Parsifal* (1882). Wagner transformed the very structure of opera and also became, with Liszt, the leader of one large segment of Romantic music.

Lewis met Wagner's work by chance while a student at **Cherbourg** in 1911. He came across a periodical in the schoolroom containing a review of the recent translation of *Siegfried and the Twilight of the Gods* by Margaret Armour; the review included illustrations by **Arthur Rackham.** One of them, accompanying Act III of *Siegfried,* shows the startled, awestruck Siegfried, gazing in wonder at the bare-breasted Brunhild whose long sleep he is about to terminate with a kiss. She is the first woman he has ever seen. Jack did not know who Siegfried was, but the picture gave him a sense of "northernness" and a rediscovery of **Joy.** Later, he was able to buy, with **Warren Lewis**'s help, the complete volume by Armour with all the illustrations, and also to collect recordings of parts of the *Ring,* beginning with *The Ride of the Valkyrie.* The love of Wagner and all things "northern" continued throughout his life.

Jack wrote of Rackham's artwork, "His pictures, which seemed to me then the very music made visible, plunged me a few fathoms deeper into my delight. I have seldom coveted anything as I coveted that book." He later found a synopsis of the *Ring* cycle, learned who Siegfried was, and then began his own poetic account.

John Bremer

Bibliography

Fritzpatrick, John. "Lewis and Wagner." *CSL: The Bulletin of the New York C. S. Lewis Society.* 12 (October 1981): 1–9.

Wagner, Richard. *Siegfried and the Twilight of the Gods.* Margaret Armour (trans). New York: Doubleday, 1911.

John Wain (1925–1994)

After World War II, John Wain attended **Magdalen College, Oxford,** and studied English with Lewis. In his work *Sprightly Running: Part of an Autobiography* (1962), Wain recounted his tutorials as well as meetings of the **Inklings** and the **Oxford Socratic Club.** Lewis was critical of some of Wain's account (see **Wain's Oxford [Letter]**). After serving as a lecturer at the University of Reading, Wain resigned in 1955 and began a successful career as a writer and critic.

Bibliography

Gerard, David. *John Wain: A Bibliography.* Westport, CT: Meckler Publishing, 1988.

Wain, John. *Hurry on Down* (1953). London: Secker & Warburg, 1966.

_____. *The Contenders.* London: Macmillan, 1958.

_____. *A Travelling Woman.* London: Macmillan, 1959.

_____. *Nuncle and Other Stories* (1960). New York: St. Martin's, 1961.

_____. *Weep Before God* (1961). New York: St. Martin's, 1972.

_____. *The Smaller Sky.* New York: Penguin, 1967.

_____. *A Winter in the Hills.* New York: Viking, 1979.

_____. *Samuel Johnson: A Biography* (1974). New York: Viking, 1975.

_____. *Where Rivers Meet.* London: Hutchinson, 1988.

_____. *Comedies.* London: Hutchinson, 1988.

_____. *Hungry Generations.* London: Hutchinson, 1994.

Wain's Oxford (Letter)

Encounter. XX (January 1963): 81.

Lewis corrected a number of factual errors and misunderstandings in **John Wain**'s *Sprightly Running* concerning his group of literary friends known as the **Inklings.** In particular, he clarified the relationship between himself and **Dorothy L. Sayers, Roger Lancelyn Green,** and Roy Campbell. Lewis also explained that in looking at the composition of the Inklings, Wain has confused personal relationships with intentional "alliances." In the same issue of *Encounter* (81–82), Wain responded that he sees his differences with Lewis as more a matter of emphasis and selection. He regretted any annoyance he might have inadvertently inflicted on his former **tutor** but reiterated his belief that Lewis's friends did at times serve as supporters (even as "allies"). In spite of this, however, Wain made it clear that he does not think that these relationships were arranged for "other considerations than the purely personal."

Marjorie L. Mead
The Marion E. Wade Center

Walking Tours

In the mid-1920s Lewis began to go on extended walks with **Cecil Harwood** and **Owen Barfield**. These walks lasted several days with the participants spending the evenings in a village pub or hotel. **Warren Lewis** joined in on the tours and his diary *Brothers and Friends* recounts eight tours that he took with Lewis and others between 1931 and 1939.

Chad Walsh (1914–1991)

Chad Walsh led a distinguished academic career as a professor of English at Beloit College in Wisconsin. In addition to his many intellectual interests, he published extensively on Lewis. His first encounter with Lewis was in 1945 when he read *Perelandra*. A year later after several letters to and from Lewis, he published an article in *The Atlantic Monthly* entitled "C. S. Lewis, Apostle to the Skeptics." Later this article was expanded to become the first book ever written about Lewis (*C. S. Lewis: Apostle to the Skeptics*, 1948). A reader of this work, **Joy Davidman Gresham** began a correspondence with Walsh. The correspondence continued after Joy's **marriage** to Lewis until her death. Lewis dedicated *The Four Loves* to Walsh because he had been partly responsible for bringing Joy and himself together.

Jeffrey D. Schultz

Bibliography

Walsh, Chad. *C. S. Lewis: Apostle to the Skeptics*. New York: Macmillan, 1948.

_____. "The Man and the Mystery." *Shadows of Imagination*. Mark R. Hillegas (ed). Carbondale, IL: Southern Illinois University Press, 1969

_____. "The Re-education of the Fearful Pilgrim." *The Longing for a Form*. Peter J. Schakel (ed). Kent, OH: Kent State University Press, 1977

_____. *The Literary Legacy of C. S. Lewis*. New York: Harcourt Brace Jovanovich, 1979.

_____. "C. S. Lewis: Critic, Creator and Cult Figure." *Seven*. 2 (March 1981): 66–80.

_____. *Behold the Glory*. New York: Harper & Row, 1956.

_____. *The Psalm of Christ*. Wheaton, IL: Shaw, 1982.

_____. *The End of Nature*. Chicago: Swallow Press, 1969.

_____. *The Unknown Dance*. New York: Abelard-Schuman, 1964.

_____. *Hang Me Up My Begging Bowl*. Chicago: Swallow Press, 1981.

War

C. S. Lewis was no stranger to war. An entire chapter in his autobiography *Surprised by Joy* was devoted to his experiences in the First World War. Like most young men in his generation, he lost friends in the war and was himself wounded by an artillery shell in April 1918.

None of those experiences led him into pacifism. In May of 1939, as Europe slid toward the Second World War, Lewis wrote a public letter criticizing a previously published article giving **"The Conditions for a Just War."** He believed that only confusion would result if average citizens tried to sort out complex issues such as whether there was a "considerable probability of winning." Instead, he suggested that believers focus on their responsibility to disobey unjust orders including those to "murder prisoners or bomb civilians."

During the first year of the war, Lewis spoke and wrote on war several times. **"Learning in War-Time"** was a speech given to **Oxford** students who questioned the importance of studying in the midst of war and was later published as a wartime tract. **"Why I Am Not a Pacifist"** was given to a group of pacifists at Oxford but not published during the war. Even those who, while not opposing the war, were stressing Britain's share of guilt for its start drew his fire in a newspaper article entitled **"The Dangers of National Repentance."**

Lewis believed that the British cause was "as human causes go, very righteous." But he also tried to put war into its place, pointing out that life is always lived on "the edge of a precipice" that tempts us away from our spiritual and cultural lives. In "Why I Am Not a Pacifist," he began slowly but eventually became blunt, telling his audience that because only free societies tolerate pacifism, if it succeeded it would be "taking the straight road to a world in which there will be no pacifists." He also pointed out that calling war useless because it did not end social problems made no more sense than criticizing a man who had just defended himself from a tiger because he was still troubled with rheumatism.

Mike Perry

Bibliography

Lewis, C. S. "The Conditions for a Just War"; "The Dangers of National Repentance"; "Learning in War-Time"; *Screwtape Letters* (chapters 5, 7, and 15); *Surprised by Joy* (chapter 12 especially); "Why I Am Not a Pacifist"

"We Have No 'Right to Happiness'"

The Saturday Evening Post. CCXXXVI (December 21–28, 1963): 10, 12. Reprinted in *God in the Dock* and *Undeceptions*.

According to **Walter Hooper**, this essay was the last thing C. S. Lewis wrote for publication before his death in 1963. In the article, Lewis began with the story of two people who are in **love** with each other but married to someone else. Clare defends them by saying that "[we] have a right to **happiness**." By this, Lewis understood Clare to mean a **natural law** that entitled her and her lover to happiness.

Lewis disagreed that Clare had such a sexual right. He argued that the right Clare claimed was merely an excuse for behavior that otherwise would be intolerable. Lewis acknowledged that we are indeed entitled to happiness but that it must occur within the confines of the natural law and of society's laws. Lewis concluded with the warning that if we perceive sexuality as superseding all other behaviors, we are ultimately destined to destruction.

Anne Gardner

Also See: Ethics and Morality, Immorality, Modernity, Psychology, Sex, Sin

"The Weight of Glory"

First published in *Transposition* and *The Weight of Glory*. Reprinted in *Screwtape Proposes a Toast* and the expanded version of *The Weight of Glory*.

"The Weight of Glory" was preached as a sermon in 1941 and is the first essay in the collection essays of that name. Lewis began by indicating that most people today would consider unselfishness the highest **virtue**, but Christians in the past would have given **love** that place. Thus today self-denial (i.e., the suppression of our desires) is seen as a virtue in itself. In **reality**, Lewis asserted, our desires are not strong enough; in particular, we do not seem to have the longing for "glory" that we should have. This glory is partly the approval of **God** and partly our entry into splendor itself. Lewis concluded that each "mere mortal" is actually an immortal, destined for glory or horror, and we should treat one another with the significance that implies.

This is Lewis's most famous sermon and justly so. A summary cannot do justice to the emotional, intellectual, and spiritual impact of the thoughts contained here. Lewis virtually always enlightens and usually edifies, but this is one of the rare occasions when a nonfiction essay of his primarily inspires. And in the conclusion, where he tells us our real relationship to one another, he shows how to react to these inspired feelings in ordinary life. A masterpiece.

Marvin D. Hinten
Bowling Green State University

Also See: Christianity, Destiny, Modernity, Redemption

Bibliography
Lewis, C. S. *The Great Divorce*

The Weight of Glory and Other Addresses
See entry on *Transposition and Other Addresses*

H[erbert] G[eorge] Wells (1866–1946)

Born in England seven years after Charles Darwin published his theory of **evolution** and dying a year after two atomic bombs ended World War II, H. G. Wells had a life that spanned the scientific revolution whose potential for good and ill was described so vividly in his **science fiction**. A century later, many of those novels continue to provide the basic themes for movies about time travel and invasion from outer space.

In *Surprised by Joy*, C. S. Lewis described his literary debt to Wells, noting that as a boy "The idea of other planets exercised upon me then a fascination quite different from any other of my literary interests.... This was something coarser and stronger. The interest, when the fit was upon me, was ravenous, like a lust." Lewis called his own planetary romances an "exorcism" intended to transform those coarse feelings into a "more elusive, and genuinely imaginative impulse."

Wells was pessimistic about man's future. He knew that evolution cared no more for human survival than for that of the dinosaurs. In his 1901 *Anticipations*, he described how humanity could take over its own evolution. He predicted that around the year 2000 a world state would begin to form. Ruled by a scientific elite, only "efficient" races and classes would be allowed to reproduce.

Excited by those ideas, Sidney and Beatrice Webb persuaded Wells to join the Fabian Society. The Fabians were British socialism's "inner circle." They believed socialism would result from a gradual growth in the power of scientifically trained bureaucrats. Like the members of N.I.C.E., the evil organization in Lewis's *That Hideous Strength*, the Fabians wanted to appear scientific and unpolitical. The goal Lewis attributed to that N.I.C.E.—"Man has got to take charge of Man. That means, remember, that some men have got to take charge of the rest"—was that of Wells and the Fabians. Lewis even gave Wells a role in the novel as Jules Horace, a short Cockney who popularized the ideas of N.I.C.E. much as Wells and George Bernard Shaw did with the Fabians.

Mike Perry

Bibliography

Bailey, K. V. "H. G. Wells and C. S. Lewis: Two Sides of a Visionary Coin." *H. G. Wells Under Revision.* Patrick Parrinder and Christopher Rolfe (eds). Cranbury, NJ: Susquehanna University Press, 1990: 226–36.

Coren, Michael. *The Invisible Man.* New York: Macmillan, 1993.

Downing, David C. *Planets in Peril.* Amherst: University of Massachusetts Press, 1992.

Lewis, C. S. "Is Progress Possible?"

"West Germanic to Primitive Old English"

"Preface." *Selected Literary Essays.* Walter Hooper (ed). Cambridge: Cambridge University Press, 1969: xv.

Academic and scholastic, this fragment (fifteen lines of a mnemonic poem) is still fun as Lewis playfully showed how various vowel sounds may have changed over the years.

Don W. King
Montreat College

"What Are We to Make of Jesus Christ?"

Asking Them Questions. Ronald Selby Wright (ed). London: Oxford University Press, 1950: 48–53. Reprinted in *God in the Dock* and *Undeceptions.*

Lewis began this article by pointing out the comic element in this question. According to Lewis, it is **Christ** who makes something of us, not the other way around. During his time on earth, Christ made statements that make sense only if they are the remarks of a madman or if they are true. There is no halfway, and no parallel in other religions.

Christ produced hatred, terror, or adoration in those around him. He was not legendary. Reports of him are not legends—they do not display the artistry of anything but **truth**. The authors say what they saw because they saw it, not to create an illusion or an invention. Lewis charged us "to accept or reject the story." For Lewis, it is only through Christ that we come to know truth, and so he is Absolute, Real, the I Am. That is what Jesus Christ is, independent of what we make him. Lewis asked us if we were prepared to accept his making of us.

Anne Gardner

Also See: Christianity, Myth, Reality

"What Christmas Means to Me"

Twentieth Century. CLXII (December 1957): 517–18. Reprinted in *God in the Dock, Undeceptions,* and *Christian Reunion.*

Lewis condemned the commercialism of Christmas in this brief essay, presenting four reasons why the annual frenzy of gift-giving and sending cards should be deplored. First, it wears everyone out, on balance causing "more pain than pleasure." Second, it is compelled. People are forced to give a gift to anyone who sends them one. Third, most presents people give are "rubbish." Fourth, the whole affair is one great "nuisance." Lewis concluded that the commercial frenzy at Christmas was a symptom of a crazy consumer society in which everyone survived by "persuading everyone else to buy things." Lewis made a similar point about the commercialism of Christmas three years earlier in his satire, **"Xmas and Christmas: a Lost Chapter from Herodotus."**

John G. West, Jr.

Bibliography

Lindskoog, Kathryn. "C. S. Lewis on Christmas." *Christianity Today.* December 16, 1983.

"What Chaucer Really Did to *Il Filostrato*"

Essays and Studies by Members of the English Association. XVII (1932): 56–75. Reprinted in *Selected Literary Essays.*

This critical essay by Lewis argued that Chaucer's *Troilus and Criseyde* is not a "modernist" updating of his original source, Italian poet Boccaccio's *Il Filostrato,* but rather reflects the English poet's deliberate "medievalization" of the tale. This early essay of Lewis's was profoundly influential and provided the foundation for the more elaborate and even more influential work on **allegory** and courtly **love** published as *The Allegory of Love* (1936).

In the essay, Lewis courteously but firmly rejected the established critical viewpoint of his day by demonstrating that Chaucer had no intention of "obeying the aesthetics of the twentieth century" in his adaptation of *Il Filostrato.* Lewis identified a fourfold process at work in Chaucer: (1) Chaucer wrote with his Medieval audience in mind, who expected and preferred **poetry** that had the "feel" of being a history; (2) Chaucer employed the varied tropes of **Medieval** rhetoric; (3) Chaucer wrote in a self-consciously didactic manner; (4) Chaucer imbued his work with the conventions and ideals of courtly love.

The essay demonstrates two qualities that resonate throughout Lewis's critical oeuvre: an uncompromising platform of historical research and painstaking linguistic analysis that helped him contextualize a text within its **culture**; and a bold fearlessness in taking on the generalizations of *status quo* with provocative generalizations and discoveries of his own.

Bruce L. Edwards
Bowling Green State University

Also See: Literary Criticism

Bibliography

Boenig, Robert. "Critical and Fictional Pairing in C. S. Lewis." *The Taste of the Pineapple: Essays on C. S. Lewis as Reader, Critic, and Imaginative Writer.* Bruce L. Edwards (ed). Bowling Green, OH: Popular Press, 1988.

Hannay, Margaret. *C. S. Lewis.* New York: Ungar, 1981.

Lewis, C. S. "The Anthropological Approach"; "De Audiendis Poetis"

Myers, Doris T. *C. S. Lewis in Context.* Kent, OH: Kent State University Press, 1994.

"What the Bird Said Early in the Year"

See entry on *"Chanson D'Aventure"*

"'Who gaf me Drink?'"

See entry on *Romanticism Comes of Age* (Book Review)

"Who Goes Home? or The Grand Divorce"

See entry on *The Great Divorce*

"Who was Right—Dream Lecturer or Real Lecturer?"

The Coventry Evening Telegraph. (21 February 1945): 4. Retitled "Two Lectures" and reprinted in *God in the Dock, Undeceptions,* and *First and Second Things.*

This essay begins with the conclusion of a lecture on **evolution** as "the very formula of the whole universe." It was, the narrator tells us, an impressive lecture by an impressive man. That night, the narrator has a dream in which the lecture continues but says all the wrong things—or at least backwards things. The Dream Lecturer says that all things descend. "The rude and imperfect thing always springs from something perfect and developed." In his argument, the Dream Lecturer points out that "[t]he embryo with which the life of each one of us began did not originate from something even more embryonic." The small beginnings of things come from mature things. Where does this process begin? From each greatness comes a smallness that develops into a greatness that gives the smallness, but where did this all begin? "[I]n the present, and in the *historical past,* we see imperfect life coming from perfect just as much as *vice versa.*" The Real Lecturer at least provided a starting point. The Dream Lecturer did not. Since life is

sequential, the process established and visible of the great and the small, its initiation must have come from outside the sequence itself. The progression described by the Real Lecturer is disproved by as many examples as support it. The endless succession described by the Dream Lecturer must be accurate, but its beginning must lie above and beyond the sequence. We must "look outside **Nature** for the real Originator of the natural order."

Anne Gardner

Also See: Bernard Ackworth, Corruption of Nature, Creation, The Fall, Human Nature, Reality

"The Whole Purpose of the Christian"

The Listener. XXXI (9 March 1944): 272. Retitled "Good Infection" and reprinted in *Beyond Personality* and *Mere Christianity.*

This was the original title of the third talk in Lewis's fourth series of radio talks. First printed in the BBC magazine *The Listener,* the revised chapter entitled "Good Infection" appeared in **Beyond Personality** and **Mere Christianity.** The early part of the chapter consists of a very good exposition at the popular level of the doctrine of the **Trinity.** Then Lewis asked, "What does it all matter?" His reply emphasized the role of the three-person **God** in a person's life. He asserted that "there is no other way to the **happiness** for which we were made." He continued that "if you want **joy,** power, peace, eternal life, you must get close to or even into the thing that has them."

Lewis pointed out that to get into this life of God, we must replace natural life *Bios* with God's life *Zoe.* **Christianity** offers us a way of making this exchange. "Every Christian is to become a little **Christ.** The whole purpose of becoming a Christian is simply nothing else."

Richard Purtill
Western Washington University

Also See: Holy Spirit, Immortality

"Why I Am Not a Pacifist"

First published posthumously in the expanded version of *The Weight of Glory.* Reprinted in *Timeless at Heart.*

This talk was given to an Oxford pacifist society (at its request) in 1940. Lewis began by discussing decision-making at length—how it involves facts, intuitions, and reasoning. Everyone agrees **war** is bad, Lewis noted. He then commented that we have more **reason** to support some people than others because of a closer connectedness—**family** members, neighbors, and so on. Next, Lewis appealed to authority and indicated that virtually all writers in history have supported participation in war, including religious leaders. As a closing, Lewis noted that pacifism is simply easier to pursue than being in the military; this should make pacifists suspicious of their motives.

In my view, Lewis did not display his finest reasoning in this article. His argument that pacifists contend "wars always do more harm than good" applies to only a minority of pacifists. The real question is simply whether Christians are allowed to kill in wars. And the religious writers Lewis quoted supporting war are all Catholic and Anglican, which permitted him a façade of unanimity; had he mentioned writers before 350 (Origen, Tertullian, etc.) or writers from peace churches (Woolman, Fox, Simons, etc.), the deck would not have been so neatly stacked.

Marvin D. Hinten
Bowling Green State University

Also See: Anglicanism, Christianity, Rationality, Roman Catholicism, War

Bibliography

Lewis, C. S. "Learning in War-Time"

"William Morris"

First published in *Rehabilitations*. Reprinted in *Selected Literary Essays*.

In this essay, Lewis offered a thorough analysis of the thematic concerns and narrative style of 19th-century British fantasist, **William Morris**. Lewis wrote this essay with a twofold purpose: to defend Morris's work against certain recurrent criticisms (for example, that his works were virulently escapist); and, to commend Morris as a gifted writer whose vision of "the ravishing sweetness and the heart-breaking melancholy of our experience" is poignant and relevant to the world-weariness endured by both believer and unbeliever.

Lewis praised William Morris as a modern "Pagan poet" who offers something invaluable to the "Christian reader," namely, the depiction of "a true skepticism," a "chemically pure" statement of pagan experience without "a bias to the negative." As such, in Lewis's estimation, Morris was "one of the greatest Pagan witnesses," a prophet as reliable as "Balaam's ass" to speak the **truth** about what life without **God** sadly must entail. Lewis regarded Morris as a salutary influence on his own fiction, and it is easy to trace in Morris's fantasies the Lewisian concept of *Sehnsucht,* that bittersweet longing for the transcendent in a temporal world

that points one either in hope to the **reality** of eternity or in despair to the emptiness of **materialism**. For Lewis, no author the caliber of Morris, who imbues his characters with such a futile "thirst for immortality," could fail to be instructive to the Christian.

Bruce L. Edwards
Bowling Green State University

Also See: Joy, Paganism

Bibliography

Edwards, Bruce L. *A Rhetoric of Reading: C. S. Lewis's Defense of Western Literacy*. Provo, UT: Brigham Young University Press, 1985.

Hannay, Margaret. *C. S. Lewis*. New York: Ungar, 1981.

Lindskoog, Kay. *Finding the Landlord: A Guidebook to C. S. Lewis's Pilgrim's Regress*. Chicago: Cornerstone Press, 1996.

Charles Walter Stansby Williams (1886–1945)

Charles Williams exchanged letters with Lewis in 1936. Encouraged by **Nevill Coghill**'s report, Lewis had read *The Place of the Lion* (1931) and wrote Williams with praise of his novel on March 11, 1936; at the time, Williams, who worked in the London office of the Oxford University Press, was proofing Lewis's book that was to be published as *The Allegory of Love*—indeed, according to **Walter Hooper**, Williams gave it that title. Williams responded, and the two became friends. Williams spent a weekend at Oxford with Lewis in 1938, and during the same year the two also met in London on July 4. Lewis, in the preface to the *Festschrift* published after Williams' death, *Essays Presented to Charles Williams* (1947), recalled the London meeting as "a certain immortal lunch" followed by an "almost Platonic discussion . . . for about two hours in St. Paul's churchyard."

These occasional meetings were followed by closer fellowship when Oxford University Press moved to Oxford in 1939 at the start of World War II. Williams became a member of the **Inklings** and attended the related Tuesday meetings at the **Eagle and Child** pub; Lewis spoke of him as giving a "liveliness and cohesion" to the meetings, and as being surprisingly learned in British literature from Malory on and in **theology** and history—and better than Lewis was at quotations. Lewis arranged for Williams to become a lecturer on literature at **Oxford,** and soon he became involved in tutoring at St. Hilda's College and giving various series of lectures. The lecture that Lewis praised in a letter to his brother was Williams' celebration of the virtue of chastity in

Milton's *Comus* (technically, *A Mask Presented at Ludlow Castle*), given on February 5, 1940. In 1942, Williams dedicated *The Forgiveness of Sins* to the Inklings, and Lewis dedicated *A Preface to Paradise Lost* to Williams. Other works were read aloud to the Inklings by Williams, and Lewis mentioned Williams' reading the first two chapters of "The Figure of Arthur" to him and **J. R. R. Tolkien.**

After Williams' death in 1945, Lewis gave a series of lectures on his Arthurian poetry, based in part on notes Williams had given him; this was combined with the unfinished "Figure of Arthur" into **Arthurian Torso** (1948). Even before this, the cross influences (or simply cross interests) between Williams and Lewis were extensive. Lewis wrote **That Hideous Strength** (1945), which has been described as a Charles Williams novel by C. S. Lewis (both in its Gothic and its Arthurian materials and in some details of its presentation of Ransom), and **The Great Divorce** (1946, dated 1945), a Dantean imitation. Williams wrote *The Figure of Beatrice* (1943), his study of **Dante**, and *All Hallows' Eve* (1945), his last novel—like *The Great Divorce* it presents afterlife experiences and it involves, among others, a painter. When Williams died suddenly on May 15, 1945, Lewis wrote, "No event has so corroborated my faith in the next world as Williams did simply by dying. When the idea of death and the idea of Williams thus met in my mind, it was the idea of death that was changed."

After Williams' death, Lewis wrote a poem **"On the Death of Charles Williams"** (reprinted in **Poems** and **Complete Poems** as "To Charles Williams"), suggesting a reorientation in seeing the world. He also wrote an obituary **"Charles Walter Stansby Williams (1886–1945)"** for *The Oxford Magazine* (unreprinted). Lewis reviewed *Williams' Taliessin Through Logres* (1938) twice; Williams reviewed Lewis's **The Problem of Pain** (1940), **The Screwtape Letters** (1942) twice (once with an imitation demonic letter), and *Beyond Personality* (1944) once.

Joe R. Christopher

Bibliography

Carpenter, Humphrey. *The Inklings: C. S. Lewis, J. R. R. Tolkien, Charles Williams, and their friends.* London: George Allen and Unwin, 1978.

Fitzgerald, Dorothy H. "C. S. Lewis and Charles Williams: Differences and Similarities in the Shape of their Thought." *CSL: The Bulletin of the New York C. S. Lewis Society.* 11 (March 1980): 1–11.

Hadfield, Alice Mary. *Charles Williams: An Exploration of His Life and Work.* New York: Oxford University Press, 1983.

_____. *An Introduction to Charles Williams.* London: Robert Hale, 1959.

Williams, Charles. *Windows of Night.* London: Oxford University Press, 1924.

_____. *Poetry at Present.* Oxford: Clarendon Press, 1930.

_____. *War in Heaven* (1930). New York: Pellegrini & Cudahy, 1949.

_____. *Many Dimensions* (1931). Grand Rapids, MI: Eerdmans, 1965.

_____. *The Place of the Lion* (1931). New York: Pellegrini and Cudahy, 1951.

_____. *The Greater Trumps.* London: Gollancz, 1932

_____. *The English Poetic Mind.* Oxford: Clarendon Press, 1932.

_____. *Reason and Beauty in the Poetic Mind.* Oxford: Clarendon Press, 1933.

_____. *Shadows of Ecstasy.* London: Gollancz, 1933.

_____. *Descent into Hell* (1937). New York: Pellegrini & Cudahy, 1949.

_____. *The Descent of the Dove: A Short History of the Holy Spirit in the Church.* London, New York: Longman's, Green, 1939.

_____. *The Figure of Beatrice: a Study in Dante.* London: Faber and Faber, 1943.

_____. *The House of the Octopus.* London: Edinburgh House, 1945.

_____. *All Hallows' Eve* (1945). Grand Rapids, MI: Eerdmans, 1981.

_____. *Arthurian Torso (Containing the Posthumous Fragment of the Figure of Arthur, by Charles Williams and a Commentary on the Arthurian Poems of Charles Williams by C. S. Lewis).* London, New York: Oxford University Press, 1948.

_____. *Collected Plays.* London, New York: Oxford University Press, 1963.

Charles Williams (Letter)

The Oxford Magazine. LVXI (29 April 1948): 380.

Lewis attempted to correct the attribution of a statement in an earlier review of **Essays Presented to Charles Williams** in which the reviewer had summarized: "What [Williams] *thought* was at constant issue with what he *believed*." Lewis points out that the sentence was not derived from anything he had said on **Charles Williams**. The reviewer, "J. M. T.," then responded, "But it is," and went on to quote several sentences from Lewis's foreword that J. M. T. believed confirmed his interpretation of Lewis's statements on Williams.

Marjorie L. Mead
The Marion E. Wade Center

Charles Williams (Letter—with Sayers)

The Times. (14 May 1955): 9.

A letter, co-authored with **Dorothy L. Sayers**, marking the tenth anniversary of **Charles Williams'** death. Lewis and Sayers suggested the appropriateness of remembering Williams' significant contribution to both the world of literature and religious thought. They note that public meetings are planned to commemorate Williams and his work in London, Oxford, and Cambridge.

Marjorie L. Mead
The Marion E. Wade Center

"Willing Slaves of the Welfare State"

The Observer. (July 20, 1958): 6. Reprinted in *God in the Dock, Undeceptions,* and *Timeless at Heart.*

In 1958, the British publication *The Observer* asked five writers to answer the questions, "Is man progressing today?" and "Is progress even possible?" The first essay in the series, "Man in Society," was penned by English novelist C. P. Snow and appeared on July 13, 1958. "Willing Slaves of the Welfare State" by C. S. Lewis appeared a week later. In this article, Lewis launched a withering attack on the modern state and its unelected bureaucrats.

One of Lewis's most avowedly political essays, "Willing Slaves of the Welfare State" lamented the omnipresent nature of the modern state. According to Lewis, the modern state offers to save society from its problems through scientific planning. In the process, however, the state deprives citizens of their economic and intellectual independence by regulating every sphere of their lives. The potential for tyranny in this situation is enormous according to Lewis, and he attacked the notion that bureaucrats should be given free reign to dictate government policies simply because they have superior knowledge. Lewis pointed out that political questions are preeminently moral questions about "what things are worth having at what price," and on these kinds of questions bureaucrats have no more right to dictate government policies than ordinary citizens.

In an era dominated even more by government bureaucracies seeking to regulate all aspects of human life, Lewis's essay seems eerily current. A more fully developed version of Lewis's thoughts on this subject can be found in *That Hideous Strength* and *The Abolition of Man.*

John G. West, Jr.

Also See: Politics, Science, Technology

Bibliography

Aeschliman, Michael D. *The Restitution of Man: C. S. Lewis and the Case Against Scientism.* Grand Rapids, MI: Eerdmans, 1983.

West, John G., Jr. "Finding the Permanent in the Political: C. S. Lewis as a Political Thinker." *Permanent Things.* Andrew Tadie and Michael Macdonald (eds). Grand Rapids, MI: Eerdmans, 1996.

_____. "Politics from the Shadowlands: C. S. Lewis on Earthly Government." *Policy Review.* (Spring 1994): 68–70.

"Will We Lose God in Outer Space?"

Christian Herald. LXXXI (April 1958): 19, 74–76. Retitled as *Shall We Lose God in Outer Space?* and reprinted London: SPCK, 1959. Retitled "Religion and Rocketry" and reprinted in *The World's Last Night.*

"Will We Lose God in Outer Space?" is a discussion of the potential theological and moral implications of space travel and especially of the discovery of forms of life on other planets. As such it has clear connections to issues raised and problems depicted in the first two volumes of Lewis's space trilogy, *Out of the Silent Planet* (1938) and *Perelandra* (1943).

The essay shows Lewis at the height of his powers as a speculative thinker and moralist, and suggests the freedom and insight made available to him by his firm grasp of the structure of Christian orthodoxy.

One inspiration for Lewis's science fiction writing and essays such as this one came from the great early novels of **H. G. Wells**, written before Wells "sold his birthright for a pot of message." The setting, plot, and atmosphere of the space trilogy owe a great debt to Wells, but the moral underpinnings owe nothing to him and a great deal to **Swift**. Like Swift, Lewis was a Christian Aristotelian whose mind and thought were pervaded by **Natural Law** as an ultimate presupposition and framework of evaluation.

Considering the possibility of animals existing on other planets, Lewis distinguishes, in this essay, between "spiritual animals" and animals "capable of pursuing or enjoying only natural ends." The former would have "rational souls" and "not merely the faculty to abstract and calculate," but the apprehension of values, the power to mean "good" something more than "good for me" or even "good for my species." Whatever their appearance or form, these rational-spiritual beings would have ultimate value in the same sense that a human person does or should.

Truly anti-imperialist and anti-anthropocentric, the essay contains passages reminiscent of the great peroration of Swift's Brobdingnagian King (at the end of Book II of *Gulliver's Travels*) and Swift's "Modest Proposal" and "An Argument Against the Abolishing of Christianity".

M. D. Aeschliman

Bibliography

Aeschliman, M. D. "The Decline and Fall of H. G. Wells," *The World and I*. (November 1993): 306–11.

_____. "Swift Agonistes," *National Review*. (October 24, 1986): 53–54.

Women

C. S. Lewis has often been accused of misogyny, but the truth is that his attitude toward women was generally enlightened. His book *A Grief Observed* is a heartbreaking account of his love for his wife. His personal favorite of all his fiction, *Till We Have Faces*, is an extraordinarily profound story about a woman. The most appealing human in his popular Narnian Chronicles is a girl named Lucy. His personal life and professional life included many women, and many of his correspondents were women.

In his autobiography *Surprised by Joy* Lewis fondly recalled the nursemaid Lucy Endicott who enriched his early years. The most important woman in his childhood, of course, was his mother, **Florence Augusta Hamilton Lewis**. In contrast to Lewis's father, who was overly emotional and illogical, Flora had a sunny, stable, sensible personality (as well as a degree in mathematics). She served as anchor to her husband, **Albert Lewis,** and as tutor and companion to her sons. Her sudden death from cancer in 1908, when Lewis was nine, destroyed forever the balance and happiness of the family. Lewis had some friendly female relatives, but there was no one at all to take Flora's place.

In an interview with Stephen Schofield (see *In Search of C. S. Lewis*) Malcolm Muggeridge spoke insightfully of an unsolved C. S. Lewis mystery: "Something hasn't come out. I think it has to do with his attitude toward women and sex, some evasion he is hiding from us. I think he was a very deeply sensual man; and he fought to put it away from him." The answer to Muggeridge's mystery turns out to be **Janie Askins Moore**. In the summer of 1917 Lewis was fond of a delightful nurse named Cherry Robbins, but then he met Mrs. Moore. Although she was still legally married and more than old enough to be his mother, by October they were evidently lovers.

When he returned from the war they moved in together, and she ruthlessly drained him of time and energy until her death over thirty years later. At first he kept his life with Mrs. Moore a secret from friends and relatives, and later referred to her as his foster mother. She provided no intellectual companionship and bitterly resented his eventual commitment to **Christianity**. A close reading of his surviving letters and published writings shows that for at least twenty years Lewis penitentially denied himself any sexual release at all. He would never explain his odd relationship with Mrs. Moore to his brother **Warren Lewis** or anyone else. He never dedicated a book to her and never mentioned her in his autobiography except to refer to a disastrous secret episode he deeply regretted.

During at least half of Lewis's career at **Oxford University** the atmosphere was chauvinistic. Even so, according to Norman Bradshaw, who studied under Lewis in the mid–1930s, it was a standing joke at **Magdalen** that whenever Lewis saw a woman enter the College he would run as fast as he could and lock himself in his rooms. And according to Patricia Thomson Berry, who studied very happily under Lewis in the early 1940s, he was thought to be a misogynist. She suspected that he had suffered some kind of shattered romance as a young man.

The misogyny rumor was so widespread that when **Clyde S. Kilby** went to meet Lewis in 1955 he left Martha Kilby outside in the car. When Kathryn Stillwell Lindskoog had tea with Lewis in 1956 she led off with the fact that she had been warned he was a woman hater who didn't associate with females. He boomed with laughter and was delighted with the absurdity of the rumor.

Lewis said privately that he would have married his friend **Ruth Pitter** (a major poet who hoped to marry him) if he had been one to get married. She, of course, knew nothing about his extraordinary sense of obligation to Mrs. Moore. Unfortunately for Miss Pitter, shortly after Mrs. Moore died in 1951, Lewis became involved with Joy Gresham and eventually married her. He exclaimed that he finally had the marital joy he had missed in his youth.

In spite of his warm regard for women, Lewis was a traditionalist when it came to gender in language and women in the priesthood. On November 8, 1945, he said he used boys to include boys and girls, and schoolmasters to include schoolmistresses. "There is lots to be said for political or economic equality of the sexes: but the claim for grammatical equality of genders is an unmitigated nuisance which should be resisted wherever it is met."

On July 13, 1948, Lewis urged his friend Dorothy Sayers (author of *Are Women Human?*) to publicly oppose female ordination in the Anglican Church.

Although she was opposed to it on practical grounds, she disagreed with Lewis's theological rationale and firmly declined. As a result, on August 14, 1948, he published his essay **"Priestesses in the Church."**

Kathryn Lindskoog

Also See: Helen Joy Davidman Lewis, Marriage, Sex, Sister Penelope

Bibliography

Bremer, John. "From Despoina to Diotima: The Mistress of C. S. Lewis." *The Lewis Legacy* 61 (Summer 1994).

Hannay, Margaret P. "Surprised by Joy: C. S. Lewis' Changing Attitude toward Women." *Mythlore.* 4 (September 1976): 15–20.

McGovern, Eugene. "A Reply to Margaret Hannay." *Mythlore.* 4 (March 1977): 27–28.

Muggeridge, Malcolm. "The Mystery." *Canadian C. S. Lewis Journal.* 26 (February 1981): 1–4.

Schofield, Stephen. "Girls, Music and Lewis." *Canadian C. S. Lewis Journal.* 58 (Spring 1987): 1–15.

William Wordsworth (1770–1850)

With publication of the *Lyrical Ballads*, Wordsworth and Coleridge launched the Romantic Movement in **poetry**. In this genre, the power of the **imagination** is stressed and poems are viewed as external expressions of the poet's internal thoughts. Romantic themes range from the ordinary and mundane to the **supernatural**, apocalyptic, and mysterious. In Romantic poetry, landscapes are endowed with human life, passion, and expressiveness. Wordsworth is known as a "lover of **nature**," for his poetry is filled with this expression of the grandeur and glory of nature. *The Prelude,* Wordsworth's intellectual and spiritual autobiography, was noted by Lewis for its portrayal of awe and fear in the midst of nature. Although Lewis mentioned Wordsworth's art and imagination fondly, he critiques Wordsworth in *The Pilgrim's Regress* for the extreme value he gives to the love of nature—making one believe "the picture [of Nature] itself was the thing you wanted." The title for Lewis' autobiography, *Surprised by Joy,* came from a Wordsworth sonnet of the same name.

Kristine Ottaway

Also See: Beauty, Romanticism

Bibliography

Noyes, Russell. *William Wordsworth.* New York: Twayne, 1991.

"Work and Prayer"

The Coventry Evening Telegraph. (28 May 1945): 4. Reprinted in *God in the Dock, Undeceptions,* and *First and Second Things.*

In this essay, Lewis presented an argument phrased as though it was his although it was clearly not. He admitted that answers to prayers are theoretically possible, but he still considered it infinitely improbable. **God** is all-knowing, and therefore he knows what is best and guides us accordingly. Lewis went on to say that this is the argument that has "intimidated thousands of people." The most common answer to this argument is that there are two orders of **prayer**, and this applies to the lower order. In that type of prayer, we might ask for particular needs or favors, rather than prayer that offers no advice but is simply "communion" with him.

According to Lewis, Pascal argued that prayer was granted to allow us "the dignity of causality." But Lewis said there are two ways in which we produce events. The one is through prayer, through which we affect that which happens, and the other is through work. In one sense, weeding and praying for an absence of weeds are comparable. Lewis quoted the old maxim, *laborare est orare* (work is prayer).

Anne Gardner

The Works of Morris and of Yeats in Relation to Early Saga Literature (Book Review)

"The Sagas and Modern Life: Morris, Mr. Yeats, and the Originals." *The Times Literary Supplement.* (29 May 1937): 409 (unsigned).

"The most interesting characteristic of [this] book . . . is the discrepancy between [Hoare's] actual literary experience and her implicit **literary theory**," said Lewis. Hoare claimed that the Medieval works are better than their corresponding pieces by **William Morris** and **W. B. Yeats**, and is on the whole appreciative and sympathetic to both the works and the translators. Lewis doubted that the works owe "as much to nature and as little to art" as Hoare suggested, and yet he found value in her work.

Anne Gardner

Bibliography

Hoare, Dorothy M. *The Works of Morris and of Yeats in Relation to Early Saga Literature.*

"A World for Children"

See entry on *The Hobbit: or There and Back Again* (Book Review)

"The World is Round"

Fear No More: *A Book of Poems for the Present Time by Living English Poets*. Cambridge: Cambridge University Press, 1940: 85. Revised and retitled as "Poem for Psychoanalysis and/or Theologians" and reprinted in *Poems* and *Collected Poems*.

This poem was originally published anonymously. However, six copies of *Fear No More* contained an additional leaf identifying the authors. One of these copies is in the **Bodleian Library**, Oxford. This lyric poem by Lewis recalls the nature **poetry** of **William Wordsworth**. The speaker appears relatively passive, intent on remembering the rich odors and brilliant **images** of a garden perhaps as an alternative to the dull, weary journey he is currently experiencing.

Don W. King
Montreat College

"The World's Last Night"

See entry on "Christian Hope—Its Meaning for Today"

World's Last Night and Other Essays

New York: Harcourt Brace & World, 1960.

See separate entries on the following:

"The Efficacy of Prayer"
"Good Work and Good Works"
"Lilies that Fester"
"On Obstinacy in Belief"
"Religion and Rocketry"
"Screwtape Proposes a Toast"
"The World's Last Night"

U.S. First Edition

Wynyard School

A month after the Lewis family moved into **Little Lea** (May 1905), **Warren Lewis** was sent to one of the worst schools in England, Wynyard School (also referred to as the concentration camp, or Belsen). After the death of Lewis's mother, **Florence Lewis**, his father sent Jack to Wynyard in September 1908 so that he could be with his brother. **Albert Lewis** believed that his sons would benefit from a boarding school education and go onto a public school and university. He based his decision on sending the boys to Wynyard on a prospectus and the fact that it charged only seventy pounds. His former headmaster from Lurgan College, **W. T. Kirkpatrick,** had recommended a school in Rhyl, Wales, but Albert rejected the advice because of its ninety-pound annual fee.

Wynyard was terrible. It was headed by a sixty-year-old clergyman, **Robert Capron,** who was brutal and insane. Little, if any, educational work went on there. The boys wrote home complaining about the school and pleading to come home. Albert finally sent his sister-in-law to investigate. While things improved for a short time, the boys once again wrote asking if they could be sent to **Campbell College** near home. In September 1909 Warren was sent to **Malvern College** and Jack returned to Wynyard for two more terms. The school closed at the end of the 1909–10 school year.

Jeffrey D. Schultz

Bibliography

Lewis, C. S. *Surprised by Joy*
Sayer, George. *Jack: C. S. Lewis and His Times*. Wheaton, IL: Crossway, 1988.

X

"Xmas and Christmas: A Lost Chapter from Herodotus"

Time and Tide. XXXV (4 December 1954): 1607. Reprinted in *God in the Dock, Undeceptions,* and *First and Second Things.*

This "Lost Chapter" concerns the island of Niatirb (Britain spelled backward) and the customs of its inhabitants in preparation for and during the celebration of "Exmas." The preparation lasts fifty days and is marked by sending squares of hard paper to friends and relations. The natives refuse to say what the purpose of the images on the paper is, perhaps hiding some mystery. When they receive cards, they throw them away. The process with gifts is much the same. The recipient must guess the value of the gift so he may send one of equal value. "And they buy as gifts for one another such things as no man ever bought for himself." Everyone becomes pale and weary, and the poorest dress in red robes and false beards. On the day of celebration they rest till noon, then eat five times as much as usual. A few of the Niatirbians have a separate festival called Crissmas, dur-ing which they do the opposite of those celebrating Exmas. They go to temples and partake of a sacred feast. They set out images of a Child, who is adored by a fair woman, shepherds, and animals. Upon inquiring of a priest why Crissmas should happen at the same time as Exmas, the author is told that it is not lawful to change the date of the festival, but it would be convenient if Exmas was held at some other time or canceled altogether. It is not credible that Exmas and Crissmas are the same, as Hecataeus says. "[I]t is not likely that men, even being barbarians, should suffer so many and great things in honor of a god they do not believe in."

Anne Gardner

Bibliography
Lewis, C. S. "What Christmas Means to Me."
Lindskoog, Kathryn. "C. S. Lewis on Christmas." *Christianity Today.* 27 (December 16, 1983): 24–26.
Lindberg, Lottie. "Lewis and 'Xmas.'" *CSL: The Bulletin of the New York C. S. Lewis Society.* 18 (December 1986): 1–2.

Y

William Butler Yeats (1865–1939)

This Irish poet and Nobel Prize winner is one of the greatest 20th-century poets of the English language. Throughout his life, Yeats was a religious skeptic who searched for an esoteric thought that could compensate for lost **religion**. His **poetry** and esotericism combined to create an elaborate symbolic system that was influenced by mysticism, realism, and the Pre-Raphaelite, Nietzschean, and Metaphysical traditions. His prose continually emphasized paradox and contradictions. Lewis mentioned Yeats's practice of **magic** and occultism in several works. But Yeats's effect on Lewis is most apparent in *Surprised by Joy*. There Lewis noted that in reading Yeats's prose (such as *Rosa Alchemica* and *Per Amica Silentia Lunae*), he came to see that it was possible for a "learned, responsible" writer to reject Materialist **philosophy**—for it is obvious from these works that Yeats "believed seriously in magic." As a result of pondering Yeats's uncommon beliefs, Lewis says "a drop of disturbing doubt fell into my **Materialism**."

Kristine Ottaway

Also See: Metaphysics, Myth, Friedrich Nietzsche, Reality

Bibliography

Christopher, Joe R. "From the Master's Lips: W. B. Yeats as C. S. Lewis Saw Him." *CSL: The Bulletin of the New York C. S. Lewis Society.* 6 (November 1974): 14–19.

"Young King Cole"

See entry on "Dangerous Oversight"

"You rest upon me all my days"

Preface to the manuscript "Half Hours with Hamilton" quoted in R. L. Green and Walter Hooper, *C. S. Lewis: A Biography*. London: Collins, 1974: 112. This is an earlier version of a poem from *The Pilgrim's Regress* (Book VIII, chapter 6) and is reprinted as "Caught" in *Poems* and *Collected Poems*.

This poem is an honest look at the difficulty of **faith**. In the poem, the speaker struggles to come to grips with a fierce omnipotence. He feels like a person trapped in a burning desert bathed by suffocating light and heat. **God**, like the sun, is an unyielding, unrelenting, uncompromising force.

Don W. King
Montreat College

433

Appendix A: C. S. Lewis Resources
Compiled by Mike W. Perry

Benison Books

Iain & Eleanor Benson
Tel: 604–947–2847
Fax: 604–947–2664
Email: iain_benson@mindlink.bc.ca
1223 Miller's Landing Road
Bowen Island, BC
Canada V0N 1G0

Speaks on the Inklings and sells books by all the Inklings plus Chesterton, Mac-Donald and kindred spirits. Information on hard to find books and secondary sources. The shop on a picturesque Island near Vancouver can be visited by appointment.

Bodleian Library

Tel: 01865 277175
Fax: 01865–277187
Email: jap@bodley.ox.ac.uk
Western Manuscripts
Oxford University
Broad Street
Oxford OX1 3BG England

Has an extensive collection of original Lewis manuscripts along with photocopies of most (though not all) of those at the Marion E. Wade Center. Access available to readers of postgraduate status or equivalent with a current Bodleian Library ticket. Contact the library for details.

C. S. Lewis and Public Life Project

Dr. John West, Discovery Institute
Tel: 206–292–0401, ext. 110
Email: jwest@spu.edu
http://www.discovery.org/lewis/cslewis.html
1402 Third Avenue, Suite 400
Seattle, WA 98101 USA

Holds conferences and publishes study group material examining how the writings of Lewis can guide Christians in their approach to politics.

C. S. Lewis Centenary Group

Mr. James O'Fee, Chairman
Tel: 01247 473124
11,
Raglan Road,
Bangor, County Down,
BT20 3TL Northern Ireland

Inspired by a Franciscan priest, Fr. Finbarr Flanagan, and meeting since 1995, the group will celebrate the centenary of Lewis's birth in the city of his birth, including a "C. S. Lewis Trail" around the sites of his boyhood. Future plans include a permanent group and center.

C. S. Lewis Center

Raymond Tripp
St. Mark's Parish
1405 South Vine Street
Denver, CO 80210 USA

C. S. Lewis for the Local Church

Interstate Ministries
Rev. Perry C. Bramlett
Tel: 502–897–7457
Email: cslewis@pbramlett.win.net
123 Bonner Avenue
Louisville KY 40207 USA

A full-time ministry offering seminars and book studies at your church or church retreat including Narnia for children.

C. S. Lewis Foundation

Dr. J. Stanley Mattson
Tel: 909–793–0949
Fax: 909–335–3501
Email: cslewisfoundation@juno.org
http://www.cslewis.org
PO Box 8998
Redlands, CA 92375 USA

Founded in 1986, the foundation holds a triennial C. S. Lewis Summer Institute at Oxford and Cambridge. It also owns the Kilns, Lewis's Oxford home, for use as a residence and study center for Christian scholars at Oxford.

C. S. Lewis Institute

Dr. Art Lindsley
4208 Evergreen Lane, Suite 222
Annandale, VA 22003 USA

C. S. Lewis Institute

Prof. Michael Macdonald, European Studies
Tel: 206–281–2209
Email: mmacdona@paul.spu.edu
Seattle Pacific University
3307 Third Avenue West
Seattle, WA 98119–1997 USA

Held every year since 1977, the Institute offers courses and public lectures with occasional major conferences (two published as books), films, banquets and study tours. Conferences held in partnership with Seattle University (Andrew Tadie, English Dept.), the Intercollegiate Studies Institute, and Discovery Institute in Seattle (John West). Contact Prof. Macdonald for details.

C. S. Lewis Reading Group

Neil Gussman
Tel: 717–392–1077
Email: neil@godfrey.com
115 S. President Ave.
Lancaster, PA 17603 USA

Meets bimonthly to discuss the writings of Lewis and kindred spirits. Occasional papers published.

C. S. Lewis Society of Lynchburg Virginia

Ed Hopkins
1500 Rivermont Avenue
Lynchburg, VA 24503 USA

Canadian C. S. Lewis Journal

Roger Stronstad
Western Pentecostal Bible College
PO Box 1700
Abbotsford, BC V2S 7E7 Canada

Began in 1979 and now published twice a year, the journal provides delightful reading for fans of Lewis, the Inklings and almost-Inklings such as G. K. Chesterton. Subscription: $12 US, $15 Canada, £6 Britain.

Colorado C. S. Lewis Society

Patrick T. Dolan, English Dept.
Email: pdolan@arapahoe.edu
Arapahoe Community College
Littleton, CO 80160 USA

Lewis books are read, chapter by chapter, and the meetings are quick and penetrating discussions of their significance for today. Attendees range from college age up and from all religious backgrounds.

Curtis Brown Ltd.

Haymarket House
28/29 Haymarket
London SW1 4SP England

Agents for Lewis's literary estate.

Cynthia Hathaway Donnelly

Tel: 540–236–9081
Email: cynthia@ls.net
205 Lafayette Street
Galax, VA 24333 USA

Teaches a four to six hour series for churches and other groups. Topics include: Lewis's life (particularly his conversion and time at Oxford), his Christian writings, and his fiction (with an emphasis on the Gospel message in Narnia).

Inklings Bookshop

Tel: 804–845–2665
Email: RIGHTBKS@INTERLOC.COM
1206 Main St.
Lynchburg, VA 24504 USA

A good source for out-of-print and hard-to-find book by Lewis and other Inklings.

Inklings–Gesellschaft

c/o Frau Irene Oberdšfer
Fax: (49) 5542 72357
Wilhelm-Tel-Strasse 3
D–40291
Dusseldorf, Germany

Founded in 1983, this international society publishes a book-length annual in German and English (*Inklings-Jahrbuch*) along with a newsletter (*Inklings-Rundbrief*). It also maintains a collection of books on the Inklings, Chesterton and MacDonald open to researchers.

Internet: C. S. Lewis Foundation

http://www.cslewis.org

Internet: C. S. Lewis Quote of the Week

http://www.infi.net/~oflare/Lewis.html

Internet: Cair Paravel

http://www.netten.net/~dpickett/narnia.html

Dedicated to Narnia.

Internet: C. S. Lewis and the Inklings

Dr. Bruce L. Edwards
http://www.bgsu.edu/~edwards/lewis.html

Internet: Harvest Books and Cyber Cafe

http://www.webcom.com/jzarra/books/harvest.html

An online Christian book store featuring Lewis.

Internet: Into the Wardrobe

John Visser
http://www.cache.net/~john/cslewis/

Internet: Jack!

Douglas Shieh
http://www.mit.edu:8001/people/douglas/lewis.html

Internet: Joseph Flynn Books

http://www.mac4hire.com/biz/jjf/

Specializing in MacDonald and the Inklings.

Internet: Lewis Legacy

http://www.discovery.org/lewis/cslewis.html

Back issues of Lewis Legacy available online.

Internet: Memphis C. S. Lewis Society

http://www.cslewis.home.ml.org

Internet: "Mere Lewis"

An active email discussion group dedicated to Lewis open to anyone with an Internet email address. To subscribe, send the command: subscribe merelewis FirstName LastName in the body of email to LISTSERV@LISTSERV.AOL.COM (Example: subscribe merelewis Jane Doe). For more information, contact dwalheim@aol.com (Debra Walheim).

Internet: Study Guide for Mere Christianity

Robert Wooldridge
Email: s980370@jinx.umsl.edu
http://www.anet-stl.com/~mcsg/

An online source of review questions for each chapter.

Internet: The C. S. Lewis Page

Loren Johnson
http://paul.spu.edu:80/~loren/lewis/

Irish Christian Society

Dr. John Gillespe
Languages and Literature
Ulster University
Coleraine, Northern Ireland

Holds a C. S. Lewis Memorial Lecture each year in Belfast.

Japanese C. S. Lewis Society

Tel: 0423–76–8211
Fax: 0423–76–8219
c/o Prof. Kazuo Takeno
Keisen Jogakuen College
2–10–1, Minamino
Tama-shi, Tokyo 206, Japan

Some 30 of Lewis's books have been translated into Japanese and in 1985, a society was begun by those interested in his writings. The society holds workshops and publishes an annual bulletin and books in Japanese including *A Reader's Guide to C. S. Lewis's The Chronicles of Narnia*.

Tom Key

1287 Lanier Blvd
Atlanta, GA 30306

Performs one-man shows of Lewis and Screwtape.

Lewis Legacy

Kathryn Lindskoog, Editor
Tel: 714–532–5376
Email: lindskoog@compuserve.com
http://www.discovery.org/lewis/cslewis.html
1344 E. Mayfair Avenue
Orange, CA 92667 USA

A quarterly newsletter published since 1988 with news, scholarship and recent discoveries on Lewis. Special attention to the debate over the authenticity of manuscripts published after his death. Back issues are available from the editor and the website. $10/year.

Marion E. Wade Center

Tel: 630–752–5908
Fax: 630–752–5855
Email: wade@wheaton.edu
Wheaton College
Wheaton, IL 60187 USA

Founded in 1965 by Clyde Kilby, it manages an extensive collection of original Lewis manuscripts including photocopies of most (though not all) of those at Bodleian Library. Publishes a journal, *Seven: An Anglo-American Literary Review.*

Memphis C. S. Lewis Society

Dennis Beets
Tel: 901–682–0129
Email: *WA4MFF@AOL.COM*
http://www.cslewis.home.ml.org

Meets monthly to enjoy good food along with readings, discussions and papers about C. S. Lewis. Publishes a quarterly newsletter.

Mythopoeic Literature Society

Dr. Kath Filmer-Davies
Department of English
University of Queensland
Brisbane 4072, Australia

Mythopoeic Society

PO Box 6707
Altadena CA 91703 USA

Founded in 1967, the society holds annual conferences and specializes in the imaginative writing of Inklings and other fantasy or mythic writers. Membership $5. Lewis-related publications are *Mythlore* (literary criticism, $15 for four issues) and *Mythprint* (book reviews and membership news, $7.50 for 12 issues). For reprints including the earlier Mythcon Proceedings and Narnia Conference Proceedings contact: Joan Marie Verba, Email: verba001@maroon.tc.umn.edu or PO Box 1363, Minnetonka MN 55345.

New York C. S. Lewis Society

Clara Sarrocco
84–23 77th Avenue
Glendale, NY 11385–7706 USA

Since 1969, the society has met each month in New York City. Its monthly bulletin, *CSL*, goes to subscribers around the world (write for a sample). Located in the publishing capital of the U. S., the society has excellent access to talented speakers and writers. All back issues are available at various prices; new members get a complete index. Subscriptions: $10 U. S., $15 foreign.

Oxford University C. S. Lewis Society

Michael Ward
c/o Pusey House, St. Giles
Oxford OX1 3L2 England

Portland C. S. Lewis Society

Tim Nelson
Tel: 503–321–6952
Email: tnelson@standard.com
PO Box 1324
Portland, OR 97207 USA

Meets monthly to discuss a book by Lewis or by someone who influenced his thinking.

Rathvinden Ministries

Doug & Merrie Gresham
Email: dhg@iol.ie
Rathvinden House
Leighlinbridge
County Carlow, Ireland

Lewis's younger stepson has a busy and varied Christian ministry. As a part of the Lewis estate, he works tirelessly to maintain its spiritual aspects. In addition, he and his wife have a large Irish country home that hosts training for the International Institute of Pregnancy Loss and Child Abuse Research and Recovery, an organization that, among other things, helps men and women cope with Post-Abortion Syndrome. They also welcome as guests Christian workers who need a restful vacation but have limited financial resources.

Salinas Valley Lewisian

M. J. Logsdon
Email: mjl@ix.netcom.com
2294 N. Main St., #48
Salinas, CA 93906 USA

No longer published but all 13 back issues of *Salinas Valley Lewisian* are available (U. S. $10, payable to M. J. Logsdon). They include a lengthy and unedited debate between Kathryn Lindskoog of *Lewis Legacy* and Logsdon over the Lewis estate and the authorship of some texts.

Southern California C. S. Lewis Society

Carl Swift
Tel: 818–355–9129
PO Box 533
Pasadena, CA 91102 USA

Founded in 1974 with a journal (*The Lamp-Post*) since 1977, the society meets each month at Fuller Theological Seminary. Back issues are $3 each. Subscriptions: $12 in USA, $15 US outside USA.

Toronto C. S Lewis Society

George & Margaret McLaughlin
Tel: 416–769–4444
Email: loretto@pathcom.com
103 Gothic Avenue
Toronto, Ontario, Canada
M6P 2V8

Formally begun in 1992 to explore Lewis's life and work, the society meets five times a year (September to May) and publishes a bulletin, *Pilgrimage*, three times a year.

Tulsa Area C. S. Lewis Society

Dr. Doreen Anderson Wood
705 North Lincoln
Sand Springs, OK 74063 USA

Understanding C. S. Lewis Workshops

Dr. Bruce L. Edwards
Tel: 419–372–7541
Email: edwards@bgnet.bgsu.edu
http://www.bgsu.edu/~edwards/lewis.html
English Department

Bowling Green State University
Bowling Green, OH 43403 USA

Offers an annual three day seminar on Lewis's life and work on the BGSU campus during the summer, and is available for on-site workshops on a wide variety of Lewis-related topics especially adapted for audiences such as teachers, church members, pastors, writers and Lewis admirers in general. Dr. Edwards also welcomes inquiries from those interested in doing graduate work on Lewis and the Inklings.

Western North Carolina C. S. Lewis Society

Don King
Email: dking@montreat.edu
Montreat College
Box 1267
Montreat, NC 28757 USA

Appendix B: A C. S. Lewis Timeline

May 18, 1862	Florence "Flora" Augusta Lewis (nee Hamilton) is born
Aug. 23, 1863	Albert James Lewis is born
Mar. 28, 1872	Janie Moore (nee King) is born
Aug. 29, 1894	Albert and Flora are married in St. Mark's, Belfast
June 16, 1895	Warren "Warnie" Hamilton Lewis is born
Aug. 27, 1895	Arthur Greeves born in Belfast
Nov. 9, 1898	Owen Barfield born
Nov. 29, 1898	Clive Staples "Jack" Lewis is born
Jan. 29, 1899	Jack is baptized in St. Mark's, Belfast
Apr. 21, 1905	Lewis family moves to Little Lea from Dundela Villas
May 10, 1905	Warren is enrolled by Flora at Wynyard School, Watford England
Aug. 19, 1906	Maureen Moore, daughter of Janie Moore and Courtney Edward Moore is born
Feb. 15, 1908	Flora undergoes major cancer surgery
Apr. 2, 1908	Richard Lewis, father of Albert, dies
Aug. 23, 1908	Flora dies on Albert's 45th birthday
Sep. 3, 1908	Joseph Lewis, Albert's brother, dies
Sep. 18, 1908	Jack is sent to Wynyard School which he refers to as Belson in Surprised by Joy
Sep., 1909	Warren becomes a student at Malvern College
July 12, 1910	Jack's last day as a student at Wynyard
Sep., 1910	Jack enrolled at Campbell College, Belfast
Jan., 1911	Jack is sent to Cherbourg Preparatory School in Malvern
Jan., 1912	Warren Begins to keep a diary
Mar., 1912	Warren is confirmed at Malvern College
Dec., 1912	Warren asks Albert for permission to smoke (his diary records that he and Jack were "confirmed smokers" in the Spring of 1911
May 24, 1913	Warren decides on the Royal Army Service Corps as a career
July, 1913	Warren completes his education at Malvern
Sep. 18, 1913	Jack is enrolled at Malvern College with scholarship
Sep., 1913	Warren begins private studies with Albert's former teacher, William T. Kirkpatrick in Great Bookham, Surrey
Nov., 1913	Warren takes army entrance examination for the Royal Military Academy at Sandhurst
Dec., 1913	Warren finishes his studies with Kirkpatrick and visits Jack at Malvern. The two return home together for Christmas
Jan. 3, 1914	Warren Enters Sandhurst
Jan., 1914	Warren places 21st out of 201 and is awarded a prize cadetship to Sandhurst
June, 1914	Jack and Arthur Greeves begin corresponding. Letters collected as They Stand Together
Sep. 19, 1914	Jack begins his studies with Kirkpatrick
Sep. 30, 1914	Warren is commissioned a 2nd lieutenant after shortened course of study because of the war

Nov. 4, 1914	Warren is sent to France
Nov. 28, 1914	Jack returns to Belfast
Dec. 6, 1914	Jack is confirmed at St. Mark's, Dundela
Feb. 9, 1915	Jack returns to Great Bookham
Feb., 1915	Warren is home on leave and Jack returns home for a visit
Apr. 18, 1915	Joy Davidman is born in New York City
Jan. 20, 1916	Jack sees a matinee performance of Carmen in London
May 19–25, 1916	Warren on leave in Belfast
Sep. 24, 1916	Warren promoted to lieutenant
Oct. 1, 1916	Warren promoted to temporary captain
Dec. 5–9, 1916	Jack sits for scholarship exam at Oxford
Dec. 13, 1916	Jack receives a scholarship to University College, Oxford
Dec., 1916	Jack begins a prose *Dymer*
Jan. 27, 1917	Jack returns to Great Bookham to prepare for Responsions
Mar. 20, 1917	Jack to Oxford for exams. Fails algebra.
Apr. 26, 1917	Jack arrives at Oxford to begin his studies
May, 1917	Jack joins OTC and is in cadet battalion in Keble College, Oxford. His roommate, assigned alphabetically is E. F. C. "Paddy" Moore
June 8, 1917	Jack meets Janie Moore
Sep. 18, 1917	Jack on leave. Spends first 3 weeks with Janie Moore in Bristol and last week with Albert in Belfast
Sep., 1917	Jack given temporary commission as 2nd Lieutenant
Nov. 7, 1917	Jack is sent to France
Nov. 9, 1917	Warren promoted to full captain
Dec. 23, 1917	Warren is sent to Mechanical Transport School in France
Feb. 1–28, 1918	Jack is in the hospital with trench fever at Le Treport
Mar. 4, 1918	Warren graduates first in class
Mar. 24, 1918	Paddy Moore reported missing
Apr. 15, 1918	Jack is wounded by a British shell on Mount Bernenchon during the battle of Arras
Apr. 24, 1918	Warren visits Jack in the hospital in Etaples France
May 25, 1918	Jack is transferred to Endsleigh Palace Hospital, London
June 14, 1918	Jack attends Wagner's *The Valkyrie* conducted by Sir Thomas Beecham at Drury Lane
June 16, 1918	Jack visits Kirkpatrick at Great Bookham
June 21, 1918	Jack attends Puccini's La Tosca
July 16, 1918	Warren learns to type
July, 1918	Jack is transferred to Ashton Court Hospital, Bristol
Sep., 1918	Paddy Moore officially declared dead
Nov. 11, 1918	Armistice is signed
Dec. 27, 1918	Jack returns to Belfast on demobilization leave
Jan. 13, 1919	Jack is demobilized and returns to Oxford
Jan., 1919	Janie and Maureen Moore move to 28 Warneford Road, Oxford
Feb., 1919	Jack joins the Martlet Society
Mar. 20, 1919	Spirits in bondage is published by Heinemann under the pseudonym of Clive Hamilton
Aug. 6, 1919	Jack and Albert have a serious quarrel
Aug. 22, 1919	Jack and Warren go to Dublin
Aug. 24, 1919	Jack returns to Oxford. The Moores move to 76 Windmill Road
Nov. 19, 1919	Warren is reassigned to service in England
Feb. 1920	Moores move to 58 Windmill Road

Mar. 31, 1920	Jack takes first in Classical Honour Moderations
Mar., 1920	Warren purchases motorcycle with sidecar
Jan., 1921	Arthur Greeves enters Slade School of Fine Arts, London
Mar. 14, 1921	Jack visits W. B. Yeats
Mar. 21, 1921	Jack again visits Yeats
Mar. 22, 1921	Kirkpatrick dies
May 24, 1921	Jack wins Chancellor's English Essay Prize on the subject of Optimism
June, 1921	After completing residency requirement, Jack moves into the home of Janie Moore
July 24, 1921	Albert visits Jack in Oxford, but is unaware of Jack's living arrangements
Apr. 7, 1922	Warren returns from Sierra Leone
June 29, 1922	Jack meets Alfred Cecil Harwood
June, 1922	Jack takes schools
July 7, 1922	Jack meets Owen Barfield
Aug. 1, 1922	Jack and the Moores move to Hillsboro, Western Road
Aug. 4, 1922	Jack gets First in Greats
Aug. 5, 1922	Warren meets the Moores for the first time
Oct. 4, 1922	Warren is assigned to RASC Colchester, Essex
Apr. 5, 1923	Dr. John Askins, Doc—Janie's brother, dies in Oxford
June 16, 1923	Jack gets First in English
June, 1923	Jack takes schools in English Literature
Dec., 1923	Arthur Greeves leaves Slade
May, 1924	Jack offered one year temporary post at University College in philosophy
Oct. 14, 1924	Jack gives his first lecture on "The Good, its position among values"
May 20, 1925	Jack elected fellow of Magdalen College, Oxford for five years from June 25, 1925
Jan. 23, 1926	Jack gives his first lecture on "Some Eighteenth-Century Precursors of the Romantic Movement"
Jan., 1926	Warren posted to RASC, Woolwich
May 11, 1926	Jack meets J. R. R. Tolkien
Sep. 20, 1926	*Dymer* is published by Dent under the pseudonym of Clive Hamilton
Sep. 26, 1926	*Dymer* published under the pseudonym Clive Hamilton
Oct. 4, 1926	Warren begins six-month economics course at the University of London
Dec. 21, 1926	Jack, Warren, and Albert spend their last holiday together
Apr. 11, 1927	Warren sails for Kowloon, China
May 2, 1928	Albert retires as Belfast Corporation County Solicitor, a post he held since 1889
July 25, 1929	Albert has x-rays taken
Aug. 6, 1929	Additional x-rays are taken of Albert
Aug. 8–10, 1929	Jack examining in Cambridge
Aug. 13, 1929	Jack returns to Belfast because of Albert's illness
Aug. 25, 1929	Jack writes Warren about Albert's illness
Sep. 22, 1929	Jack returns to Oxford
Sep. 25, 1929	Albert dies
Sep. 26, 1929	Jack arrives in Belfast too late to see his father
Sep. 27, 1929	Jack telegrams Warren about their father's death
Dec. 8, 1929	Jack and Janie Moore in Belfast until December 20
Dec. 26, 1929	Jack goes to Barfields for a stay in Long Crendon
Jan. 27, 1930	Jack reads paper, Some Problems of Metaphor, to Oxford Junior Linguistic Society
Feb. 24, 1930	Warren sails from Shanghai, visiting the USA on the way home
Apr. 4–8, 1930	First walking tour with Barfield, Harwood, and Walter Field

Apr. 22–24, 1930	Jack and Warren visit Little Lea
May 10, 1930	Warren decides (with Jack's approval) to arrange and edit the *Lewis Family Papers*.
May 15, 1930	Warren posted to Bulford
May 25, 1930	Warren accepts Jack and Janie Moore's offer to live with them upon his retirement
June, 1930	Warren visits Little Lea for the last time
July 7, 1930	Jack, Warren, Janie and Maureen inspect the Kilns
July 16, 1930	Their offer to purchase the Kilns is accepted
Oct. 10–11, 1930	Jack and the Moores with Warren's assistance move from Hillsboro to the Kilns
Jan. 1–4, 1931	Jack and Warren take their first walking tour together in Wye Valley
May 9, 1931	Warren returns to a belief in Christianity
Sep. 19, 1931	Jack has an important late night conversation with Tolkien and Hugo Dyson about myth, truth, and Christianity
Sep. 28, 1931	Jack returns to a belief in Christianity while riding to Whipsnade Zoo in the sidecar of Warren motorcycle
Oct. 1, 1931	Jack writes to Arthur Greeves that he believes in Christ and Christianity
Oct. 9, 1931	Warren sails for China
Nov., 1931	Warren commanding officer RASC Shanghai
Jan. 19, 1932	Warren receives letter from Jack telling him that they both share a belief in Christianity
July, 1932	Warren applies for retirement
Aug. 15, 1932	Jack goes to Ireland as a guest of Arthur Greeves until August 29
Dec. 14, 1932	Warren arrives in Liverpool from Shanghai
Dec. 21, 1932	Warren officially retires from RASC after 18 years and moves to the Kilns
Jan. 3–6, 1933	Warren and Jack take their second walking tour in the Wye Valley
Apr., 1933	Jack, Warren, Janie and Maureen vacation together for two weeks at Hambleden in the Chilterns
May 2, 1933	Jack and Barfield see Das Rheingold at Dovent Garden
May 25, 1933	*The Pilgrim's Regress* is published by Dent
June 1, 1933	First volume of *Lewis Papers* returned from the binders. The work is entitled *Memoirs of the Lewis Family: 1850–1930*
Aug. 3–15, 1933	Jack and Warren visit relatives in Scotland and then sail from Glasgow to London
Jan. 1–6, 1934	Jack and Warren take their third walking tour together
Jan. 3–5, 1935	Jack and Warren take their fourth walking tour in Chilterns
Jan. 13–16, 1936	Jack and Warren take their fifth walking tour in Derbyshire. Warren has a motorboat built for use on canals and rivers
May 21, 1936	*Allegory of Love* published by Oxford University Press
May 21, 1936	*Allegory of Love* is published by Clarendon Press
Jan. 5–9, 1937	Jack and Warren take their sixth walking tour in Somerset
Sep. 21, 1937	Tolkien's *Hobbitt* is published
Jan. 10–14, 1938	Jack and Warren take their seventh walking tour together in Witshire
Sep. 23, 1938	*Out of the Silent Planet* is published by Bodley Head
Apr. 27, 1939	*The Personal Heresy* is published by Oxford
Sep. 3, 1939	England declares war
Sep. 4, 1939	Warren recalled to active duty, posted to Catterick
Sep. 7, 1939	Charles Williams moves along with Oxford University Press from London to Oxford

Sep., 1939	Evacuee girls from London move into the Kilns
Oct., 1939	Warren assigned to Le Havre, France
Jan. 27, 1940	Warren promoted to the temporary rank of Major
Apr., 1940	First weekly Thursday evening meeting of the Inklings
May, 1940	Warren evacuated from Dunkirk
Aug. 16, 1940	Warren transferred to Reserve of Officers
Aug. 27, 1940	Maureen marries Leonard J. Blake, Director of Music at Workshop College
Oct. 18, 1940	*The Problem of Pain* is published by Centenary Press
Apr. 15, 1941	Belfast bombed
Apr., 1941	Jack gives first RAF talk
May 2, 1941	First of 31 *Screwtape Letters* appear in weekly installments in *The Guardian*
Aug. 6, 1941	First of Jack's BBC radio Broadcasts entitled "Right and Wrong"
Nov. 28, 1941	Last of the 31 Screwtape Letters appears in *The Guardian*
Jan. 11, 1942	Jack delivers second series of BBC radio broadcasts entitled "What Christians Believe"
Jan. 26, 1942	First meeting of the Oxford University Socratic Club
Feb. 9, 1942	*The Screwtape Letters* is published by Geoffrey Bles
July 13, 1942	*Broadcast Talks* is published by Geoffrey Bles
Sep. 20, 1942	First of Jack's "Christian Behaviour" talks delivered over the BBC
Oct. 8, 1942	*A Preface to Paradise Lost* is published by Oxford
Jan. 6, 1943	*The Abolition of Man* is published by Oxford
Feb. 22–26, 1943	Jack gives the Riddell Memorial Lectures in Durham (later published as *Abolition of Man*)
Apr. 19, 1943	*Christian Behaviour* is published by Geoffrey Bles
Apr. 20, 1943	*Perelandra* is published by Bodley Head
Feb. 22, 1944	First of seven talks on "Beyond Personality" delivered over the BBC
Mar. 27, 1944	David Lindsey Gresham born in New York City
Oct. 9, 1944	*Beyond Personality* is published by Geoffrey Bles
Jan. 8, 1945	Richard Francis Blake born to Maureen and Leonard Blake
May 9, 1945	World War II ends
May 15, 1945	Charles Williams dies
Aug. 16, 1945	*That Hideous Strength* is published by Bodley Head
Nov. 10, 1945	Douglas Howard Gresham born in New York City
Dec. 11–14, 1945	Victory Inkling holiday at the Bull, Fairford
Dec. 24, 1945	Augustus Hamilton, Flora's brother, dies
Jan. 14, 1946	*The Great Divorce* is published by Geoffrey Bles
Jan. 16, 1946	William Lewis, Albert's brother, dies
Mar. 18–22, 1946	Jack receives an honorary Doctorate of Divinity from St. Andrew's University
July 17, 1946	Jack meets poet Ruth Pitter
Mar. 29, 1947	Warren retires from the Officer's Reserve
Apr. 4–17, 1947	Jack and Warren holiday at Malvern
May 12, 1947	*Miracles* is published by Geoffrey Bles
June 20, 1947	Warren seriously ill from alcoholism while on vacation at Drogheda
Aug. 4–18, 1947	Jack, Warren, and Tolkien vacation in Malvern
Sep. 8, 1947	Jack appears on the cover of Time magazine
Feb. 2, 1948	G. E. M. Anscombe delivers "A Reply to Mr. C. S. Lewis's Argument That 'Naturalism' is Self-refuting" to the Oxford Socratic Club
1948	Joy and William Gresham convert to Christianity

July, 1949	Warren admitted to Warneford Hospital, an asylum
Oct. 20, 1949	Last recorded Thursday night meeting of the Inklings. Tuesday mornings at the Bird and Baby continue
Jan. 10, 1950	Jack receives a letter from Joy Davidman Gresham
Apr. 29, 1950	Janie Moore admitted to Restholme, a nursing home
Oct. 16, 1950	*The Lion, the Witch and the Wardrobe* published by Geoffrey Bles
Jan. 12, 1951	Janie King Moore dies at the age of 78
Oct. 15, 1951	Prince Caspian published by Geoffrey Bles
June, 1952	Jack and Warren vacation in Ireland
July 7, 1952	*Mere Christianity* published by Geoffrey Bles
Sep. 15, 1952	*The Voyage of the "Dawn Treader"* published by Geoffrey Bles
Sep. 24, 1952	Jack meets Joy Gresham for lunch at the Eastgate Hotel
Sep., 1952	Jack meets Joy Davidman Gresham
Jan., 1953	Joy Gresham returns to the US
Sep. 7, 1953	*The Silver Chair* published by Geoffrey Bles
Dec. 18–21, 1953	Joy Gresham returns to England with her two boys, David and Douglas. They visit the Kilns for four days
1953	Collins purchases Geoffrey Bles and becomes the publisher of many Lewis works
June 4, 1954	Jack accepts chair of Medieval and Renaissance English at Cambridge
Aug. 5, 1954	Joy divorces William Gresham
Sep. 6, 1954	*The Horse and His Boy* published by Geoffrey Bles
Sep. 16, 1954	*English Literature in the Sixteenth Century Excluding Drama* is published by Oxford
Nov. 29, 1954	Jack delivers inaugural lecture "De Descriptione Temporum"
Dec. 3, 1954	Jack completes his last tutorial at Magdalen College, Oxford after accepting chair at Cambridge
May 2, 1955	*The Magician's Nephew* is published by Bodley Head
Aug., 1955	Joy, David, and Douglas Gresham rent 10 Old High Street, one mile from the Kilns
Sep. 19, 1955	*Surprised by Joy* is published by Geoffrey Bles
Mar. 19, 1956	*The Last Battle* is published by Bodley head
Apr. 23, 1956	Jack and Joy are married at the Oxford Registry Office
Sep. 10, 1956	*Till We Have Faces* is published by Geoffrey Bles
Oct. 19, 1956	Joy admitted to Wingfield-Morris Hospital diagnosed with cancer
Nov. 14, 1956	Joy is seriously ill. Jack is determined to have an ecclesiastical marriage ceremony
Dec. 24, 1956	Jack and Joy's marriage announced in *The Times*
Mar. 21, 1957	Jack and Joy are married by the Rev. Peter Bide in her hospital room at Churchill Hospital, Oxford
Dec. 10, 1957	Joy is walking
Dec. 17, 1957	Dorothy L. Sayers dies
June, 1958	Joy's cancer in remission
July, 1958	Jack and Joy honeymoon in Ireland
Sep. 8, 1958	*Reflections on the Psalms* is published by Geoffrey Bles
Mar. 26, 1959	Jack elected honorary fellow at University College, Oxford
Oct., 1959	X-rays show the return of Joy's cancer
1959	Jack serves with T. S. Eliot and others on the Archbishops' Commission to Revise the Psalter
Mar. 28, 1960	*The Four Loves* is published by Geoffrey Bles

Apr. 3–14, 1960	Jack and Joy visit Greece with Roger Lancelyn Green and his wife
May 20, 1960	Joy undergoes surgery
June, 1960	Joy returns to the Kilns
July 13, 1960	Joy dies
Sep. 9, 1960	*Studies in Words* is published by Cambridge
June 20–21, 1961	Arthur Greeves visits Jack for the last time at the Kilns
June 24, 1961	Jack diagnosed with enlarged prostate; doctors decide it is too dangerous to operate
Sep. 29, 1961	*A Grief Observed* is published by Faber and Faber under the pseudonym N. W. Clerk
Oct. 13, 1961	A*n Experiment in Criticism* is published by Cambridge
June 15, 1963	Jack admitted to Acland nursing Home following a heart attack
Aug., 1963	Jack returns to the Kilns
Sep., 1963	Hooper returns to the US
Sep., 1963	Warren returns from Ireland
Nov. 22, 1963	Jack dies at the Kilns
Jan. 27, 1964	*Letters to Malcolm* published by Geoffrey Bles
May 7, 1964	*The Discarded Image* published by Cambridge
May 19, 1964	Warren moves from Kilns to 51 Ringwood Road, Oxford
Oct. 26, 1964	*Poems* edited by Hooper is published by Geoffrey Bles
Apr. 18, 1966	*Letters of C. S. Lewis* edited by Warren Lewis is published by Collins
Aug. 29, 1966	Arthur Greeves dies
Apr. 18, 1967	Warren moves back to the Kilns with Len and Mollie Miller
1967	*Letters to an American Lady* edited by Kilby is published by Eerdmans
Oct. 27, 1969	*Narrative Poems* edited by Hooper is publishe by Geoffrey Bles
Aug. 8, 1970	Warren told by doctors that he can no longer go on walks because of poor circulation
Jan. 2, 1972	Tolkien celebrates 80th birthday at Merton College
Apr. 9, 1973	Warren dies at the Kilns
Feb. 28, 1977	*The Dark Tower* edited by Hooper is published by Collins. The title piece's authenticity is questioned
Apr. 19, 1979	*They Stand Together* edited by Hooper is published by Collins
Apr. 11, 1985	*C. S. Lewis' Letters to Children* edited by Dorsett and Mead is published by Macmillan
Oct. 10, 1985	*Boxen* edited by Hooper is published by Collins
Jan., 1989	*Letters of C. S. Lewis and Don Giovanni Calabria* edited by Moynihan is published by Collins
Apr. 18, 1991	*All My Road Before Me* edited by Hooper is published by HarperCollins
May 30, 1994	*The Collected Poems of C. S. Lewis* edited by Hooper is published by Harper-Collins
Feb. 17, 1997	Lady Dunbar of Hempriggs—Maureen Moore—dies

Entry Guides

Concepts, Places, People, and Themes

List of Contributors

M. D. Aeschliman has written for journals on both sides of the Atlantic and has taught at Columbia, the University of Virginia, and two Swiss universities. He is currently *Docente* in English at the University of Italian Switzerland in Lugano and Associate Professor of Education at Boston University. His book *The Restitution of Man: C. S. Lewis and the Case Against Scientism* is being republished in a second edition by Eerdmans in 1998.

Iain T. Benson, studied in Canada, Scotland and England and holds degrees from several universities including Queen's and Cambridge. He is the Senior Research Fellow for the Centre for Renewal in Public Policy (Ottawa), a "think-tank" devoted to the relations between morality, culture, religious discourse, and public policy.

Rev. Perry C. Bramlett of Louisville, Kentucky is the founder of C. S. Lewis for the Local Church Interstate Ministries, a teaching ministry on the life, works, and influence of Lewis. He is the author of *C. S. Lewis: Life at the Center* (1996), and the only person in America who teaches Lewis to churches and groups as a full-time vocation.

John Bremer was born in England, and has degrees from the University of Cambridge, the University of Leicester, and St. John's College. He is Director, Institute of Philosophy, PO Box 518, Ludlow, VT 05149.

Corbin S. Carnell teaches 20th century British literature, world literature and film at the University of Florida. He has authored five books and more than three dozen scholarly articles.

Joe R. Christopher is a Professor of English at Tarleton State University, where he teaches advanced courses in Medieval and Renaissance British literature and the history of the English language. His writings on C. S. Lewis include his doctoral dissertation, *The Romances of Clive Staples Lewis*; his collaboration with Joan K. Ostling, *C. S. Lewis: An Annotated Checklist of Writings about Him and His Works*; and his volume in Twayne's English Authors Series, *C. S. Lewis*.

Alice H. Cook is a freelance writer and editor whose work has focused on 20th Century Christian writers and Southern Writers. She is a contributor to Beacham's *Encyclopedia of Popular Fiction* and resides in Bowling Green, Ohio.

Alzina Stone Dale is an independent writer/scholar with an MA in theology and literature from the University of Chicago Divinity School. She has published three biographies and many articles on the Oxford Christians and those who influenced them.

Mark DeForrest is a free-lance writer as well as an attorney in Washington State.

Bruce Edwards is Associate Dean of Arts and Sciences and Professor of English at Bowling Green State University. He is the author of two books on C. S. Lewis and regularly conducts a summer workshops on the life and works of C. S. Lewis at the BGSU campus.

Robert O. Evans, Professor Emeritus at the University of Kentucky and the University of New Mexico, has taught at a number of colleges and universities including the University of Wisconsin, the American College in Paris and the University of Saarbrucken in Germany. He is author of eleven books and more than fifty articles.

Paul F. Ford is a Professor of Theology and Liturgy at St. John's Seminary, Camarillo, CA. He is the author of *Companion to Narnia* (fourth edition: HarperCollins, 1994) and founder of the Southern California C. S. Lewis Society.

Anne Gardner is a free-lance writer and educator.

Diana Pavlac Glyer is Associate Professor of English at Azusa Pacific University. Her scholarship focuses on the mutual influence of the Inklings. She is active in the Mythopoeic Society and chair of their 1998 C. S. Lewis Centenary Conference. She and her husband Michael live in Sierra Madre, California.

Katherine Harper is a doctoral student in English at Bowling Green State University. Though she is not ordinarily a science fiction fan, she thinks that *Perelandra* is Lewis' masterwork.

Susan Henthorne is Vice President for Academic Affairs at White Pines College in Chester, New Hampshire.

Richard A. (Rick) Hill is an Associate Professor of English and directs the creative writing major at Taylor University. He has taught Lewis seminars at two colleges and is presently co-writing a book on teaching Lewis.

Marvin D. Hinten of Bowling Green State University wrote a dissertation on *The Chronicles of Narnia* to earn his Ph.D. He has published four books and hundreds of articles, with his latest book, *Church Challenge: A Fun and Fascinating Trivia Tour of Church History*, scheduled to appear in the fall of 1998.

Thomas T. Howard is Chairman of the Department of English at St. John's Seminary College in Boston. He is author of *Evangelical Is Not Enough*, *C. S. Lewis*, *Man of Letters*, and *On Being Catholic*.

Robert J. Hubbard is an Assistant Professor of Communication Arts and Sciences at Calvin College. He teaches courses in performance studies, theater and oral rhetoric, and directs productions in the Calvin theater season.

Charles A. Huttar is Professor of English at Hope College in Holland, Michigan. He has written and lectures extensively on C. S. Lewis. His works include *Word and Story in C. S. Lewis* which he co-edited with Peter J. Schakel.

Richard V. James was educated at the University of Virginia and at the Lexington Theological Seminary. He is currently pastoring the Burkesville Christian Church in Burkesville, Kentucky where he lives with his wife Mary and their three children: David, Laura, and Stephen.

Carolyn Keefe is Professor Emerita of Communications Studies at West Chester University, the editor of *C. S. Lewis: Speaker & Teacher* and a frequent speaker on Lewis. In 1990 the Council for the Advancement and Support of Education named her as the Pennsylvania Professor of the Year.

Don King currently serves as Vice President and Dean of Academics at Montreat College and holds the rank of Associate Professor of English. He has written articles on Lewis that have appeared in *Studies in the Literary Imagination*, *Mythlore*, and *SEVEN*, and he is finishing a book on Lewis's poetry that is due out in 1999.

Kathryn Lindskoog is a California author and college instructor who has been a C. S. Lewis expert since 1955; seven of her 18 books are about him. She met Lewis in 1956, and after he read her thesis in 1957 he wrote "You are in the center of the target everywhere. For one thing, you know my work better than anyone else I've met . . ."

Michael Macdonald is Professor of European Studies and Director of the C. S. Lewis Institute at Seattle Pacific University. He has edited (with Andrew Tadie) *C. S. Lewis and G.K. Chesterton: The Riddle of Joy* (1989), *Permanent Things* (1995), and written *Europe: A Tantalizing Romance* (1996).

Wayne Martindale, Associate Professor of English at Wheaton College, Illinois, is co-editor of *The Quotable Lewis*, editor of *Journey to the Celestial City: Glimpses of Heaven from Great Literary Classics*, and author of many articles on C. S. Lewis.

Marjorie Lamp Mead is Associate Director of the Marion E. Wade Center, Wheaton College, Illinois, and Production Editor for *Seven: An Anglo-American Literary Review*. Her publications include *Brothers and Friends: The Diaries of Major Warren Hamilton Lewis* (co-edited with Clyde S. Kilby), and *C. S. Lewis: Letters to Children* (co-edited with Lyle W. Dorsett).

Gilbert Meilaender has taught religious ethics at the University of Virginia and at Oberlin College and currently holds the Board of Directors Chair in Christian Ethics at Valparaiso University. He has written extensively on Lewis including *The Taste for the Other: The Social and Ethical Thought of C. S. Lewis.*

Christopher W. Mitchell is the Director of the Marion E. Wade Center, a lecturer in Theological Studies at Wheaton College, and the Book Review Editor for *Seven: An Anglo-American Literary Review.*

Kristine Ottaway graduated from Seattle Pacific University in 1996 with a BA in English and Political Science. She is currently pursuing her JD at the University of Virginia School of Law.

Nancy-Lou Patterson, Distinguished Professor Emerita, University of Waterloo, is Reviews Editor of *Mythlore*. An internationally recognized scholar, author and liturgical artist, she publishes frequently on C. S. Lewis.

Mike Perry is a professional writer with a special interest in the interaction between Christianity and the history of ideas.

James Prothero is the Senior Editor of the *Lamp-Post* of the Southern California C. S. Lewis Society, and is reading for a Ph.D. at University of Wales, Lampeter. He is also a novelist, poet, teacher of English, and a third order Benedictine.

Richard Purtill is Professor of Philosophy at Western Washington University. A recognized authority on Lewis's theological works, he has lectured and published widely on the topic.

Jerry Root is an Assistant Professor of Christian Education at Wheaton College. He is the co-editor of *The Quotable C. S. Lewis.*

Peter J. Schakel is Peter C. and Emajean Cook Professor of English and chair of the department at Hope College, Holland, Michigan. In addition to publications on Jonathan Swift and eighteenth-century satire, he is author of *Reading with the Heart: The Way into Narnia* and *Reason and Imagination in C. S. Lewis*, editor of The *Longing for a Form: Essays on the Fiction of C. S. Lewis*, and co-editor with Charles A. Huttar of *Word and Story in C. S. Lewis.*

Lyle H. Smith Jr. has taught at Biola University, La Mirada, CA since 1978. He is the author of articles on C. S. Lewis's theory and uses of metaphor, and is at present collaborating with Bruce Edwards of Bowling Green State University and Rick Hill of Taylor University on a book dealing with Lewis's complete published works.

Lynn Summer is a doctoral candidate in English Literature at Georgia State University. Her areas of interest include the Renaissance and Reformation, Christianity and literature, and, of course, C. S. Lewis.

Thomas Talbott is a Professor of philosophy at Willamette University in Salem, Oregon. He received his M.Div. from Fuller Theological Seminary and his Ph.D. from the University of California at Santa Barbara, and he is author of "C. S. Lewis and the Problem of Evil," *Christian Scholar's Review XVII* (September, 1987).

Jonathan L. Thorndike teaches British literature, composition and interdisciplinary humanities courses at Lakeland College in Sheboygan, Wisconsin. He recently published a book on the US Supreme Court case *Epperson v. Arkansas*, the first case in which the Court ruled on the teaching of creationism and evolution in public schools.

John G. West Jr. is an Assistant Professor of Political Science at Seattle Pacific University and a Senior Fellow at the Seattle-based Discovery Institute, where he directs the program on religion, liberty, and civic life. His previous books include *The Politics of Revelation and Reason: Religion and Civic Life in the New Nation.*

Charles Wrong studied briefly under Lewis at Oxford. Now Professor Emeritus, he had taught at a number of colleges in the United States including Brown University and the University of Florida.